GORE VIDAL

GORE VIDAL

A BIOGRAPHY

FRED KAPLAN

BLOOMSBURY

First published in Great Britain in 1999

Published by arrangement with Doubleday,
a division of Bantam Doubleday Dell

Copyright © 1999 by Fred Kaplan

The moral right of the author has been asserted

Bloomsbury Publishing Plc, 38 Soho Square, London, W1V 5DF

A CIP catalogue record for this book
is available from the British Library

ISBN 0 7475 4671 1

10 9 8 7 6 5 4 3 2 1

Printed in Great Britain by Clays Ltd, St Ives Plc

To

RHODA,

and to the memory of

JEROME BADANCES

Contents

P RELUDE

ROCK CREEK PARK Cemetery, Washington, D.C., November 1994. I prefer my subjects dead, I had told him. He responded that he perfectly understood but declined to do anything special to accommodate my preference. Now we are experiencing a different aspect of the subject. A few hundred yards away, the sculpture of a veiled, androgynous figure famously signifies the grave site of Henry Adams and his wife. The land slopes aslant the grassy November stubble to the comparatively obscure burial marker of a Marine killed at Iwo Jima fifty years ago. My subject and I are standing amid the dead. We are both very much alive. The object of the visit to Rock Creek Park Cemetery is to certify visually that the site he has requested for his burial is in fact what he had triangulated in his mind, what he had negotiated from afar with the Rock Creek Park Cemetery business office, and to sign the covenants and authorizations. He wants the site roughly equidistant from the famous Adams and the obscure Jimmie Trimble.

One can always be buried, someplace. But to be buried at a particular place for particular reasons takes planning and sometimes luck. The director of the cemetery, partial lord of all he surveys, thinks the site an excellent one. He is both businesslike and officious. Probably it gives him pleasure to anticipate a celebrity burial, the newspaper stories perhaps not far beyond the year 2000 that will identify the cemetery in which the famous writer has just been buried. The cemetery director is a relatively young man, certainly not a day over fifty. If the obituaries have any wit, they will remark that Gore Vidal at last owns property in Washington, D.C. "How do Mr. Vidal and Mr. Austen envision the monument?" Howard Austen has been Gore Vidal's companion for almost fifty years. There is some matter-of-fact discussion. My opinion is solicited. Since, if I survive my subject, I will someday describe in print the glint of medium-dark marble, the angle at which the two flat stones have been placed, the simplicity of the inscriptions, why not add to the day's solemn amusement the irony of the biographer being consulted about the burial circumstances? It is one of the rewards for having forgone my preference that my subject be dead.

We chat a little at the grave-site-to-be. With my shoe I prod up some soil and scuff it forward an inch or two across the fields of the republic. It is a bright, mild day that transcends funereal locations. Gore (mostly) and Howard seem satisfied. In the end they will both be here. That is, what remains of them. They have been almost everywhere on this planet, and they have had a few favorite places. The last decades have been spent mostly on a Roman Street and in a Ravello villa. But, about America, Vidal has written, *"Love it or loathe it, you can never leave it or lose it."* For the satirist there is no difference between loving and loathing. They are the same pleasure, the same pain. To be buried in Rock Creek Park Cemetery is to be buried as close to home as possible, a final statement about the pleasure and the pain of our American home. Before leaving the cemetery we stop at a small stone Gothic building, the business office. Here the *real* business is done. Gore signs various documents. Howard signs. I also sign. The biographer as observer, participant, witness.

CHAPTER ONE

Origins

1776–1925

GORE VIDAL'S last name is his father's family name, his first his mother's.
Born October 3, 1925, at West Point, New York, he was named, and thirteen
years later baptized by the canon of Washington's Episcopalian National
Cathedral Church, Eugene Luther Gore Vidal, Jr. His father, who had a
poor memory for such things, could not remember for certain whether his
own name was Eugene Louis or Eugene Luther. He mistakenly put Louis
rather than Luther on his son's birth certificate. His exasperated son remarked, years later, that since his father was then an instructor at West
Point, "He might have asked the head of his department what his name was.
'You know, I've forgotten my name. Could you tell me?'" At his baptism
the Luther was restored. He also added, as another middle name, his
mother's maiden name. His maternal grandfather, Thomas Pryor Gore, the
young boy's highest model of worldly achievement, was a United States
senator. Then, at the age of sixteen, Eugene Luther Gore Vidal, Jr., decided
that a partial act of self-naming would anoint him with the best of both
traditions. He wanted a sharp, distinctive name, appropriate for an aspiring
author or national political leader. "I wasn't going to write as Gene since

there was already one. I didn't want to use the Jr." He dropped his first two names and the Jr. Thenceforth he was, so to speak, just Gore Vidal.

———————

The Gore family saga is aggressively American, mostly Southern and Southwestern. When, in the early seventeenth century, the first Gores arrived in America from their Protestant Anglo-Irish origins, one brother went to New England, the other to Maryland, apparently never to meet again. The brothers probably came from Ireland, where the English Gores (of whom there were many) had been awarded land for service to the crown. They settled in Donegal, resolutely Anglo-Irish and anti-Catholic. Where they originally came from in England is unclear; so too is the nature of their service to the crown, though it probably had something to do with putting down the Irish. In Maryland, James Gore flourished, the patronymic father of seemingly innumerable farmers, ministers, lawyers, doctors, teachers, soldiers, politicians—three hundred years of ambitious, stubbornly assertive individualists. English and Irish origins faded into family legend and historical mist. They later associated themselves with the category Scots-Irish, which proved useful to those who wanted to make clear that though they were from Ireland, they were not Catholics. From generation to generation American Gores were to have names like James, Thomas, Manning, Austen, Albert, Notley, Elias, Ellis, Ezekiel.

The immigrant James and his immediate descendents leased and owned substantial tracts of land in what is now part of central Washington and in the Georgetown–Rock Creek Park area. They fought in the French and Indian and then in the Revolutionary War, by the time of the latter apparently staunchly anti-British. They were fruitful and multiplied. As each died, land had to be divided or sold or both. Each needed a property, a stake, an opportunity. Fortunately, there was always land to the west. Toward the end of the French and Indian War, one of the immigrant James's grandsons, Thomas, was granted or bought land in South Carolina. Selling extensive property in Maryland, part of the large family moved, before the Revolution began, southward and westward, to Chester County, near Spartanburg, in northwestern South Carolina. Thomas Tindal Gore, perhaps Thomas Gore's nephew, the son of his brother Manning, was born in South Carolina in the celebratory year 1776, and became the patriarch of the next generation. With his wife, by whom he had eight sons and five daughters, he raised cotton along the fertile banks of the Sandy River. In 1817, in wagons, Thomas Tindal moved his family south and westward, probably looking for better land, more land, more autonomy, some release for a combination of restlessness and ambition. His willful individualism traveled with the word of his Methodist God and the assumption that the Gores were a chosen people. Once more there was someplace better to the west. White American settlers and their government in Washington had from the beginning conspired to buy or conquer (whichever was more practical) the lands between the Atlantic Ocean and the Mississippi River.

First the Thomas Tindal Gores went to Alabama, on the northwestern border of Alabama with Mississippi, where whites were rapidly replacing Indians. Apparently Thomas Gore kept an inn and ran a livery barn in Pickens County. In 1830 he was elected a county commissioner and then ran for the Alabama state senate. In 1840 the patriarch took part of his family directly westward into north-central Mississippi to Choctaw County, which had once been the heartland of the Choctaw Indian nation. Some Choctaws remained behind, never to be assimilated, but most were forced farther west, by economic and military pressure, across the river to what was later to be part of Oklahoma. With other white settlers, the Gores seized the opportunity. Thomas Tindal Gore purchased from a Choctaw Indian for two hundred dollars a large property along the Yalobusha River in what is now Calhoun City, then a hardscrabble frontier town in a county in which the land was tough, resistant, and hilly, and no one wealthy. As the Gores moved westward, they farmed whatever was the best local crop of the region. They preached the Word. They healed the sick. They were quick-tongued, sharp-witted, smart. They talked and argued and argued and talked, sometimes for sport, always with passion. Thomas Tindal Gore's descendants were soon to fight (and some to die) in the Civil War, regional patriots, small slaveowners, hill-country farmers, Methodist ministers, noticeably idealistic, argumentative, hot-tempered, and clannishly loyal. "If a snake should bite one Gore, the entire family would swell from it." They were mostly unionists who found themselves trapped by local patriotism and pressure into fighting an enemy with whose underlying principle of national union they agreed. When the war came, they did their duty. They cared little about freeing slaves; they themselves had few or none. Plantation life and rule from Richmond were as alien as Northern factories and rule from Washington. But local autonomy was a rallying principle. Fighting for home rule, numbers of Gores were killed in battle.

Thomas Tindal's thousands of Calhoun County acres had to be divided among a large number of heirs, the most memorable of whom was Ezekiel Fletcher Gore, Gore Vidal's great-great-grandfather, an evangelist at the distant end of the Second Great Awakening, nicknamed "Rock," a Methodist minister of stubborn rectitude. With his Georgia-born wife, Mary Green, he populated this new world with twelve children. He was an indefatigable circuit rider with a flair for the dramatic. On one occasion he was summoned by the organizing committee of a revival to breathe new life into a passionless series of meetings. They did not know if he would come. "The next day the eleven o'clock hour was approaching, the congregation had assembled, and no word from 'Rock' Gore. As several men . . . stood outside looking in the direction from which he would arrive, they saw him rounding a curve in the road with his horse at full gallop. He rode up, tossed the bridle reins to someone nearby, took his Bible and went into the Church singing one of the great old revival hymns."

The next generation brought Ezekiel Gore's strong-principled religious assertiveness into the tumultuous post–Civil War politics of northern Mississippi. His numerous children were always politicians, and imbued their politics with the same passionate rhetoric that their grandfather had brought to his religion. The Civil War had impoverished a never particularly prosperous county. Postwar recovery was slow, cash scarce, crops poor. Reconstruction seemed to most Southern whites an abomination, though Choctaw County had relatively few blacks to enfranchise. And with the end of military rule in 1869, the Democratic Party that had dominated the county before the war gradually regained control, though not before the 1874 Reconstructionist Mississippi state legislature divided the county and named the northern part Sumner, after the Massachusetts abolitionist.

Republicans began to disappear from Mississippi. In 1882 the leaders of Sumner County succeeded in having its name changed to the less offensive Webster. Daniel had some of the mitigating afterglow of a belated Founding Father. Reconstruction had been beaten back, and demographics made white power secure; only 25 percent of the county's ten thousand residents were black. The pervasive problem was agricultural depression. People lived spartan lives, close to the proverbial bone. Material sophistication hardly rose above the level of their pioneer grandparents', though Ezekiel's sons were slightly better off than the average. Children of the Book, they were bookish enough to pursue professions as well as farm. To some extent they all became caught up in the tumultuous political events that dominated Webster County in the 1880s.

Born in Alabama in 1837, Thomas Madison Gore, Ezekiel's eldest child, Gore Vidal's great-grandfather, came to Mississippi as an infant in his grandfather and father's entourage. His education was rural. Law and politics fascinated him. As a young man he resented the idea of the Confederacy. He sat all day, hesitating, on the steps of the Choctaw County courthouse. Finally, he bit the bullet and enlisted as a private. The bullet bit back. He was wounded at the battle of Chickamauga. Later, he joked that "as far as he knew he was the only corporal in the entire Confederate army as everyone else that he met in later years was at least a colonel." He earned his living first as a schoolteacher, then at the intersection between politics and law. On the last day of December 1865 he married Carrie Wingo, two years his junior, a strikingly beautiful South Carolina–born Mississippian. In 1868 Carrie gave birth to their first child, a daughter, Mary, then in 1870 a son, Thomas Pryor, to be followed by two more sons, Ellis in 1874 and Richard (nicknamed Dixie) in 1883. In 1876 Thomas Madison Gore was nominated as the Democratic Party candidate for chancery clerk in Webster County. The nomination automatically meant election. That autumn the Thomas Madison Gore family moved to Walthall, the newly named county seat, where he took up his official duties. In a scarcity economy, political office was a valuable economic asset. Thomas Madison was reelected chancery clerk four times. But Democratic politics, simmering, soon boiled over. In Mississippi, dissident Democrats objected to what seemed the indifference of large agricultural and business interests, whose powerful political network controlled the state, to the interests of the small farmer. Proudly independent farmers lost their land. Sharecropping became a widespread humiliation. It seemed as if the state was being run by monopolies and banks.

The dissidents gathered force through the 1880s. In Webster County, farmers joined "The Great Agricultural Relief," which became "The Farmer's Alliance," part of the fabric of the emerging national populist movement that advocated political and monetary policies to help the farmer through hard times. Passions were high. Articulate, principled, and ambitious, Thomas Madison Gore gave his heart to the People's Party. As a dissident Democrat, he lost his party's chancery-clerk nomination in 1887. In 1890 the entrenched political powers organized a state constitutional convention. Outraged by the Democratic Party's support of even more restrictive suffrage (the final guarantee that Reconstruction had been defeated), appointed rather than elected judges (who would do the will of their masters), and tax breaks for corporations, Webster County populists rebelled. The powerful and rich were conspiring to keep them poor. They did not favor blacks having the right to vote, but they would be damned if they would allow their own franchise to be restricted in order to keep blacks disenfranchised. At a mass meeting at Walthall in July 1890 they resolved "That in order to preserve our Constitutional liberties, we oppose any amendment . . . that would lessen, impair or increase the vote of any legal voter." The new, more restrictive constitution was approved anyway. In Webster County the Democratic Party soon insisted that members sign pledges of support for its candidates. In July, at Walthall, the dissidents legally created the Webster County Populist Party, whose platform advocated "equal rights to all and special privileges to none, public control of communications and transportation, and election of United States senators by direct vote of the people." Thomas Madison's fate was sealed: he was never elected to public office again.

----·----

Born in December 1870, Thomas Pryor Gore, Gore Vidal's grandfather, was soon anointed "Guv" by his ambitious father, in anticipation of what the family felt sure would be his destiny. Young Tom remembered the garden where they lived in Walthall, overflowing with trees and flowers. "Somebody who loved the beautiful had lived at that place." Later he remembered vividly the colors and the shapes of the garden. As a six-year-old, in the same year he started school and learned to read, he heard his first political speech. When his grandmother, Rock Gore's pious wife, died in 1878, he went to the funeral. He never forgot that the gruel that she had once made for him was "the best stuff" he had ever tasted. At his father's knee he learned Webster County politics. At nine he suffered what seemed a minor injury to his left eye when a stick he and a playmate were throwing hit his lower lid. He could still see through it, but with diminished sight. Though his right eye was fine, premonitions of blindness began to haunt him. At school he became obsessed with rereading a story "about a blind swan and another about a boy who had lost both eyes accidentally at different times." In 1881 he got his first job, as a printer's "devil," setting type for a local Walthall newspaper. Later that year he was thrilled to be appointed a page in the state senate in Jackson. Within three days he learned all the senators' names.

But a sense of doom accompanied him. In Jackson he practiced being almost blind, holding a hand over his right eye, getting around as best he could with only his diminished left. When he visited the Institute for the Blind, he told a boy there that he did not know how long it would be before he himself would be a resident. He had a nightmare: "I dreamed I was blind and in the rotunda—the second story—where the capital met and . . . some of the boys had kinder hung me over that place for fun." Two days later he was demonstrating, for the children of the state senator at whose home he boarded, a crossbow that he had bought as a present to send home to his brother. It was a fragile contraption, dependent on worn rubber bands. When the children asked him to shoot it, he said he "did not want to as it was not shooting well. They insisted. I had it standing there on the floor. I dropped the arrow down the barrel. . . . I glanced down into the barrel to see if it was right, and while I was looking at it, it went off. It shot me in the right eye, blinding me on the instant." His father took him to New Orleans for medical treatment. Whatever sight he had in his left eye and the flickers of sight briefly restored in his right "gradually faded out."

Despite his blindness, his determination to become educated and a leader never weakened. In fact, blindness now became a force of concentration, almost itself a special power. Blindness was awful but also eerie and awesome, connecting him with Tiresias, Samson, and Milton. It was also a darkness against which his accomplishments would only shine the brighter, an unavoidable identification that would make him distinctive. He still hoped to rise to high political office. As a page in the state senate he had refused to sign a petition circulated by the other pages to have their one-dollar-a-day salary supplemented by a twenty-five-dollar bonus each session. He then wrote a bill, increasing salaries from one to two dollars a day. Introduced by a friendly senator, it passed. Back in Walthall, he attended school, with the help of relatives and friends who read to him. The school year was short, the facilities rudimentary. But he soon developed a prodigious memory. He also developed a soft spot for pets—a heifer and a pony, then chickens and roosters—which led to a lifelong slightly guilty passion for cockfighting. At sixteen he had his "first love affair" with a girl with whom he exchanged Valentine's Day cards every year of his life. For him blindness was not a disability. He would allow no one to make excuses for him. In high school, he helped organize a debating club, soon converted into a moot United States Senate, in which he was the leading speaker. It was exercise. It was sport. It was training for the real thing. When in 1887 a teacher from Kentucky organized the Walthall Normal College, "Guv" began his most intensive three years of formal schooling. Attending political meetings with his father, his uncles, his friends, he learned about politics in the passionate crucible of family, county, state. When he found a copy of the *Congressional Record*, he memorized the name of every United States senator. From then on, the thing he wanted most was to be one.

At his graduation from Walthall Normal School in June 1890, he gave such a highly regarded commencement speech on race relations that numbers of people suggested he be sent as a delegate to the state constitutional convention in Jackson. Since he was too young to qualify, the voters instead chose his uncle. Tom Gore became, for the summer months, an assistant to his sister, teaching at Embry, within sight of the house in which he had been born. That October he spent six weeks at the Institute for the Blind in Jackson, learning how to be as self-sufficient as possible, mastering the New York point-reading system for the blind. One of the very few books available contained the Declaration of Independence and the Constitution. He spent "a good many evenings reading that volume. I learned the Declaration of Independence by heart." In Jackson he haunted the convention debates. He soon taught in another town at a time of such pervasive statewide poverty that rural schools generally had one two-month session a year or, at most, two. His meager salary was paid in warrants. A fiery populist orator, he was now a leader of the opposition in Webster County. At a large meeting in July 1891 he was nominated for the state legislature. But the new state constitution had added an age qualification. Since he would not be twenty-one until early December, he had to withdraw. In September he sold at discount the warrants he had received for teaching (his sister contributed hers) and left Mississippi for Lebanon, Tennessee, not far from Nashville, to attend Cumberland University Law School. Since there were no law books available for the blind, his roommate read everything aloud to him. When

Guv's money ran out, his father sold a small tract of land to keep him there. In 1892 he returned to Walthall as a law-school graduate. He had twenty-five cents in his pocket. He still hoped to have the brilliant future in Mississippi that people predicted for him. The state convention of the People's Party made him a presidential elector. He campaigned widely for the ticket. Reading law throughout the year, he helped to try, successfully, two prominent criminal cases. But realistic opportunities for elective office in Mississippi seemed few and far between; the Democratic Party was still formidably entrenched, and many people above him on the slippery pole. The next year, twenty-three-year-old Tom Gore began to cast his ambitions westward.

One night that autumn his uncle, John Ellis, stayed with the Thomas Madison family. By chance he had with him a copy of a Texas newspaper in which Guv found the name and address of the secretary of the State Executive Committee of the Texas People's Party. He wrote immediately, asking what might be a good place in Texas for a young lawyer to settle. The answer, with two names to contact, came back: Corsicana, in Navarro County. The name struck a responsive chord. The previous Christmas a friend who had spent a year in Texas had been reading to him from a book that listed names of Texas counties and towns. Corsicana had stuck in his memory. Accepting an invitation from a populist leader to address the Navarro County convention, he left for Texas in May 1894 with a few dollars for expenses and barely enough for a return ticket. At the convention in Waco he spoke dramatically for William Jennings Bryan: suddenly Tom Gore was in demand as an orator throughout Texas. He spoke and debated until late October, then returned to Mississippi. In Navarro County, the populists won; they did not in Webster. Accompanied by his brother Dixie, Tom returned to Texas at the beginning of the new year. Helped by the Texas-Mississippi network, Dixie became deputy to the Navarro County district clerk. Guv, though, decided to give Mississippi one last chance. Populist sentiment was at its height. It was now or never. Returning to Walthall, he ran for the state legislature in the election of 1895. The Democrats, administering the death blow, accused Gore and the other populists of being "nigger lovers." Campaigning brilliantly, he still almost won. When the final count was in, he had lost by thirty-two votes. On the last day of the year he left for Texas again. He vowed never to return "until and unless" he had been elected to the United States Senate.

On the train chugging westward he read John Stuart Mill's *On Liberty*. The Declaration of Independence, *On Liberty,* and the Lone Star State seemed the right fit. Texas politics and opportunities glittered in the near distance. Perhaps there would not be as many people above him on the greasy pole as in Mississippi. First, though, he had to make a living. At the end of 1896, he and Dixie opened a law office; they soon had many cases but few fees. The nationwide depression of 1893 still pinched the pocketbooks of millions of people. Also, compared to oratory and politics, the law was dull, and he soon felt depressed. With his romantic dreams of high office on indefinite hold, he began to repeat to himself Cardinal Wolsey's lament, "Farewell, a long farewell to all my greatness." Handsome, smart, and articulate, he was intriguingly attractive and attracted to women. In 1895 a blind girl in Corsicana accused him of having made her pregnant. Gore tried to get her to abort with medicines. They finally succeeded with a blunt instrument. For whatever his reasons, he would not marry her. Perhaps the thought of a blind man being married to a blind woman seemed devastating to the aspiring politician. Apparently hopeful that a jury would not convict a blind man for seduction and abortion, he defied her threat to take him to court. At the last minute he begged her not to testify against him. It would ruin his life. Perhaps he promised compensation. When she relented, the case was dismissed. As part of the arrangement, his parents, who had followed their sons to Texas, took the girl in for a short while. In August 1896 he turned down an invitation to give a series of speeches in the main town, Palestine, in nearby Anderson County, because it conflicted with a speaking engagement elsewhere, but his brother Dixie forgot to send the telegram of regret. On his way to the station he received a second telegram, reminding him of the invitation, and he wired to Anderson County that he would come for a week. In Palestine, driven past the large ranch of John Thomas Kay, a white-bearded fifty-four-year-old East Texas pioneer, he asked his host to describe Mr. Kay and his daughter, and a few days later, at a county picnic, he met the dark-haired, dark-eyed, trimly petite, engagingly lovely Nina Belle Kay. "I fell in love with her the moment we met and made up my mind that day to marry her one day if I could." A serious circumstance conspired against the marriage: Nina's family did not want her to marry a blind man.

Probably of Scots origin, the Kay family had come to Texas from Anderson County, South Carolina. Born about 1842, the seventh child of James Warren Kay and his second wife, John Thomas Kay had fought at Bull Run. He had survived a long war. Like many, he eventually preferred the hard but independent life of a Texas pioneer to poverty at home. About 1875, after selling his interest in his family land to one of his brothers for fifty dollars, John, with wife (in late 1868 he had married Marcella Mc-Laughlin, a beautiful Mississipian of Creole origin), three children, and livestock, traveled by covered wagon to Palo Pinto County in North-Central Texas. The fifty dollars was all the money he had in the world. Along the route the grass was lush, water and firewood plentiful. But West Texas was harsh. The first winter they burrowed into a sod dugout and cooked on buffalo chips. More at home in farming than grazing country, they soon resettled in East Texas, near Palestine, in Anderson County, which had been named after Kay's home county in South Carolina. The land was rich, the hills rolling and wooded. In 1877, while still in Palo Pinto, Marcella gave birth to twin daughters, one of whom died. The surviving twin was Nina Belle Kay. When she met Thomas Pryor Gore in the summer of 1896, Nina Belle was the attractive daughter of a now moderately prosperous East Texas farmer. Her mother had died the previous year. Her father and four brothers "told her that if you marry that blind boy you're going to end up on a street corner with a tin cup. Just begging. She went ahead and did it anyway," her grandson later commented, "and never regretted it." They married on December 27, 1900. Her family's opposition was overcome only at the death of Nina Belle's father in the summer of 1899.

Between 1896 and the beginning of the new century T. P. Gore worked hard at law and politics. At first things looked promising. While Dixie minded the office, Tom worked the political hustings. The brilliant blind orator was much in demand. But, as in Mississippi, the leaders of the Democratic Party did not favor divisive populists undermining them from the left. When, in 1898, he ran for the House of Representatives as the Populist Party candidate, he lost decisively. Texas soon began to seem another dead end, as did his allegiance to the Populist Party. Early in the new century he shed both. With his bride, he decided on a new start, this time not to the west but a short distance to the north. Oklahoma was still a territory, actually two, one of them reserved for Indians, including those who had been driven from the Mississippi lands on which the Gores had settled. Politics and opportunity were more fluid there. Land could be staked. Everyone knew that the territories would eventually become a state. State political offices as well as land would be up for grabs. There would not be as greasy a pole to climb. With his bride beside him, Gore moved to the Oklahoma Territory. After settling in the new town of Lawton, about a hundred miles south of Oklahoma City, where he staked land and opened a law office with Dixie, he immersed himself in territorial politics and soon mastered its complications. Within a few years he became the best-known political orator in the area and a popular guest speaker in nearby states. The decision to shed his Populist Party affiliation came at the cost of his father's bitter criticism: when T.P. joined the Democratic Party, an angry Thomas Madison Gore denounced him at a public political meeting. "Guv" was still, though, against and for all the same things he had always been. But now he had a chance for political office, for the beginning of a real public career. Soon he was one of the most powerful political leaders in the territories, instrumental in the flourishing drive for statehood. In 1905 Thomas Madison died. In November 1907 the legislature of the newly created state of Oklahoma chose thirty-seven-year-old Thomas Pryor Gore as one of its two United States senators.

———•———

The Vidal family saga is quintessentially European. The name itself began to appear widely in Spain, France, and Italy about the twelfth century, either a corruption of the Latin *vitalis* or a translation of the Hebrew word for life. By the late Middle Ages some of the many Vidal families throughout the Mediterranean world were Catholic in origin, others Hebrew. Originally the latter may have been Jews living in the Roman Empire or Jews who had journeyed to and then stayed in the empire after its fall. Some Jewish Vidals became converts to Catholicism, often for convenience or safety. Many settled in France as well as Italy. After the expulsion from Spain in 1492, large numbers of Spanish Jews also settled in France, Italy, and Greece. Like the Jews who already resided in the Roman world, some retained their Hebraic identity, others converted to Catholicism. After a time both the original and the new conversos often lost awareness of their family's origins. They usually became merchants, tradesmen, and manufacturers. Some became priests. There was no better place to hide their origins than in the Church itself.

Eugen Felix Vidal, Gore Vidal's great-grandfather, who in 1849 emigrated from Feldkirch in German-speaking Austria to the American Midwest, was a Catholic whose ancestors for five hundred years were apothecaries and merchants. Some had married women whose names suggest they were from once Jewish families. Not unexpectedly, converso families often intermarried, and the pattern continued long after Hebraic origins had become only a rumor or been forgotten. Local oral memory kept alive the rumor that Eugen Felix Vidal's Catholic family was of Jewish origin. That the Vidals who emerged in the late eighteenth century in Feldkirch were apothecaries and merchants makes it likely that they descended from the Renaissance Vidals who were apothecaries, a profession that had orginally been largely in the hands of Jews. Eugen Felix Vidal's family in America inherited a sixteenth-century stained-glass medallion, about six inches in diameter, that shows a bearded man, wearing a hat, standing behind a counter, surrounded by jars, drugs, and other apothecary paraphernalia. His name is boldly printed: Casper Vidall. The date is 1589. This Casper Vidall had prospered as a pharmacist in Feldkirch in the late sixteenth century, the scion of a line of drug-manufacturing and -dispensing Vidals. The name then disappears from Feldkirch records, to reappear at the beginning of the nineteenth century when Johann Vidal, from nearby Forni Avoltri, reestablished the family name in Feldkirch. At first he was a successful grocer; then he bought the local pharmacy, first working with a partner who was an apothecary, then by himself. Most likely he hoped that one of his sons would become a doctor or a pharmacist and eventually run the business. After marrying a daughter of the former mayor, he bought a large, centrally located building, soon renamed Vidalhaus, for home and business. When his first wife died, he married Elizabeth Herzog, a German-speaking Catholic from the Tyrol. Their first child was born almost exactly nine months later, in October 1821. Twelve years later Johann Vidal died, leaving a widow who struggled to keep the business going and to support eight children. Around 1848 Elizabeth declared the pharmacy bankrupt and sold Vidalhaus.

In August 1849, a year of political turmoil in Europe, Johann Vidal's oldest son, twenty-eight-year-old Eugen Felix Vidal, a student at the University of Lausanne on Lake Geneva, married the Swiss-born Emma Traxler von Hartman and began to look westward for better opportunities. What Eugen was studying at the university is not clear, though perhaps it was medicine, a speculation that surfaced years later among the American Vidals. That would have been especially plausible for the son of a pharmacist. Emma came from a Swiss family of some interest. Her grandfather, Josef Traxler, was a member of Louis XVI's Swiss guard at Versailles, who escaped the democratic slaughter and fled to Madrid, where he served Charles IV, the Spanish king. When Napoleon invaded Spain in 1808, Josef Traxler raised a regiment at his own expense to fight for King Charles and was killed in battle, leaving behind a widow, Isabel, and daughter, Caroline. Either before or after his death, the Traxlers claimed reimbursement from the Spanish crown for the cost of the regiment the lieutenant colonel had raised. Payment was not forthcoming, the Spanish treasury empty. Isabel returned to Lucerne, where she struggled with heavy debt and little income. In Switzerland, the young Caroline also became an Army bride. Eventually, she suffered the same misfortune as her mother. Having married one of her father's Swiss Army comrades, Colonel Ludwig von Hartman, she found herself, after some years, the Widow Hartman. She had three daughters to raise. If Spain, though, would repay Josef Traxler's heirs, all would be well. The Traxlers and their descendents never stopped hoping. In the meantime, Caroline Traxler Hartman's daughter Emma, born in Switzerland in 1828, met Eugen Felix Vidal. When, in 1849, they married in Feldkirch, the only money they had was the elusive Spanish repayment. They soon decided that America was a better bet. Having determined that the prospect of opening a cheese factory in Wisconsin appealed to him more than remaining in the land of his ancestors, he and his bride and his mother-in-law, with a subsidy from the city of Feldkirch, emigrated to the American Midwest.

Little is known about Eugen Vidal for the twenty years between his arrival in America and 1870. Like many other German-speaking Catholic immigrants, the Vidals apparently went directly to the Midwest, to South-Central Wisconsin, first to Monroe, then Sauk City and Bangor (where Eugen paid taxes from 1866 to 1870), and then to La Crosse, in western Wisconsin, across the Mississippi River from Minnesota. The family surfaces in the 1870 census, which gives the forty-nine-year-old Eugen's occupation as chemist (his family's old-world trade) and real estate. Three children were born, Hermania (Fanny) in 1858, Felix in 1862, and Mary in

1864. Caroline Hartman most likely lived nearby or even in her daughter's home. And one day, around the year 1870, Eugen simply picked himself up, left his family, and wandered away. Some years after his disappearance, he returned to Wisconsin, for he was sustained for a short time before his death in 1892 in a nursing home run by the Milwaukee Catholic Sisters of the Poor. One of his children must have attended to his remains, since his gravestone has "Father" engraved on it.

"Father," but not provider. Emma struggled desperately, the New World even more difficult than the old. The 1880 census lists her as a drapemaker, a seamstress of sorts. Family legend says she worked as a translator "for foreign [-language] magazines and journals," translating from English into German, French, and Italian. Even if so, it would have been erratic, poorly paid work. The Spanish inheritance must have glittered like even brighter fool's gold. Eugen and Emma's children struggled also. None of them received an education. In the 1880s Hermania worked as a clerk and later married respectably. Family legend says that Mary, who married young, went to Chicago, where she became at best a kept woman, at worst a prostitute. "This was the great family secret. Pure Dreiser," Gore Vidal recalled. At the age of eighteen the patronymic heir was a laborer. Five years later, in 1885, still living with his mother in La Crosse, Felix Vidal became a machinist, the year after that a fireman for the Chicago, Milwaukee, and St. Paul Railway. Living at a boardinghouse in La Crosse, he presumably now stoked coal on trains in the upper Midwest. Caroline Traxler von Hartman died in 1883, as many years old as the century. Her daughter, sixty-three-year-old Emma, died eight years later in Hokah, Minnesota, across the river from La Crosse, where she had moved to live with her daughter Hermania.

The attending physician at Emma's death was Dr. Luther Lazarus Rewalt, Gore Vidal's great-grandfather. A capable doctor and a man of verve and talent, Rewalt had been born in Pennsylvania in 1838, one of three children of William Rewalt and Catherine McKinley. The Rewalts were of Dutch origin, probably Catholics. Luther had attended the University of Pennsylvania medical school and served four years as an assistant surgeon in the Civil War. In 1862 he married a fellow Pennsylvanian, Mary Jane McGee. The twenty-five-year-old Irish-Catholic girl had decided to become a nun, but the handsome doctor, three years younger, persuaded her to become *his* bride. Later, they became Methodists and then Episcopalians. In

1863 Mary Jane became locally famous as the "Heroine of the Susque-hanna." When a fire set by retreating Union troops spread, Confederate soldiers worked with the townspeople to save Wrightsville from destruction. In appreciation, Mary Jane Rewalt, who had labored valiantly during the crisis, hosted a dinner for the Confederate general and his staff. So gracious was she that they suspected she might be a Confederate sympathizer. A strong Union partisan, she explained that even enemies should show appre-ciation for humanitarian deeds. The Confederate soldiers left that same day for Gettysburg.

Sometime after 1872 the Rewalts moved to the northwest-frontier state of Minnesota, but why they left Pennsylvania is unclear. At least four of their five children were born in Wrightsville, including their third child, a daughter named Margaret Ann, born in 1870, who brought with her to Minnesota as a small child no memory of her Pennsylvania birthplace. Like all but one of her siblings, she became a Midwesterner. And why the Rewalts settled in Fulda, Minnesota, about two hundred and fifty miles due west of La Crosse, a little north of the Iowa border and only about fifty miles from South Dakota, is a mystery. The nearest city was Sioux Falls, South Dakota. What did Dr. Luther Lazarus Rewalt, a man of some sophis-tication and medical skill, who enjoyed eating and drinking well, who had a strong sense of personal style, *do* in Fulda, a town with fewer than a thousand people and great distances from any place he might have enjoyed visiting? Like many nineteenth-century rural doctors, he also owned a drugstore. Perhaps his work was enough to sustain his spirit as well as his pocketbook. In 1891 he was in Hokah, Minnesota, near La Crosse, where he attended the dying Emma Hartman. One of his granddaughters believes that her father and mother "became acquainted through [his] treating my grand-mother." At any rate, Dr. Rewalt's daughter, Margaret Ann, soon married Emma's son, Felix Vidal. By the early 1890s Felix, now in his thirties, had settled with his wife in the small city of Madison in eastern South Dakota, about fifty miles northwest of Sioux Falls and about a hundred miles from Fulda. They were to live there the rest of their lives.

———

Cold in the winter, hot in the summer, the weather in eastern South Dakota was more bracing than the culture. But the culture was real, specific, estimable in the Midwestern American sense. As with the weather, there were few modulations, little nuance. The Vidal household was part of the landscape. It quietly belonged. Anchoring a corner lot of about an acre, the house the young couple bought was an efficient three-story box, its plain lines relieved by a porch, with four bedrooms upstairs and the usual rooms below. Heated by ineffective air ducts, it felt cold in the winter, warm in the summer. Outside was often either bone-chilling or torrid. In the growing season a small garden flourished, devoted to vegetables, except for corn, which the vast fields of this farming world provided in such abundance that it made growing your own pointless. The Vidals walked the less than a mile downtown all the years that Gene, their eldest son, born in April 1895 and baptized Eugene Luther Vidal, was a child. The grade school and the high school were about four blocks from the house, with an athletic field on which, soon after the turn of the century, the eldest son began to play. When he showed medical evidence of an enlarged heart, euphemistically called an "athlete's heart," or perhaps tuberculosis, his father put up exercise bars in the backyard. Gene soon had an athlete's body and a heart for competition. Football, basketball, track, baseball—by his teenage years he was the premier all-around athlete at Madison High School.

Corn and wheat fields dominated the landscape. Most of Madison's approximately five thousand residents made their living as farmers or serving the farming community. Whether he was still a fireman or now an engineer running a train or had graduated to the administrative-clerical job he held in later years, Felix Vidal and the Chicago, Milwaukee, and St. Paul helped make the Midwest work. They transported what farmers grew and what farmers needed. The railroad brought Sioux Falls nearer: Minnesota, Wisconsin, and Illinois were part of the larger network. When on duty, Felix was away every second night. At home, Margaret ran the house and bore children. Two years before Gene, the first Vidal child, Lurene, had been born, then Amy in 1903, a new Margaret in 1910, a new Felix (nicknamed Pick) in 1912, when Margaret Ann was forty-two, a late pregnancy that shocked family and friends. They did not suspect that some of the long silences between husband and wife were being filled, at that late date, by lovemaking. The household finances were modest but stable. Unlike his father, Felix kept his nose to the grindstone. As far as his eldest son could tell, he had no ambition to accomplish anything more than to work obscurely as a minion of the railroad empire. As the World War approached, he concealed, outside of the household, his German sympathies. Though he put up exercise bars for his son, he had no interest in athletics. As Gene got older, Felix rarely attended his son's games. If he had any passion at all, it was politics: deeply moralistic and conservative, he was remembered for abhorring dishonesty in politicians and always voting for the Republican candidates whom he read about in the newspapers to which he subscribed, the *Sioux Falls Argus Leader* and the *Madison Leader*. Capitalism appealed to him. Religion did not. A nominal Episcopalian, he rarely went to church. Thin, taciturn, with icy blue eyes and a temper that sometimes burst into household dramatics, he was not a man who gave or showed love readily. From early on there seems to have been a chill between the father and his oldest son.

As a young mother, Margaret was attractive, full-figured, and broad-faced. Unlike her saturnine husband, she contributed constant good cheer to the household, the proverbial sunny disposition. Her own mother had died the year after Gene's birth. Felix's parents were already long gone. Gene never saw the paternal grandfather to whom he was indebted for his first name. Later, in old age, Luther Rewalt, for whom Gene had been given his middle name, came to live with his daughter and son-in-law in Madison. He died there in 1925, a dapper old man who liked to drink, who loved going to the movie theater downtown in a spiffy white suit, carrying an inflatable rubber cushion into which he blew air before ostentatiously sitting down, and who had invented Rewalt's Elixir, an all-purpose heavily alcoholic patent medicine that he and his favorite daughter manufactured in vats in the kitchen, bottled for sale from the porch, and packaged for the Brown Drug Company in Sioux Falls. In Gene's years in Madison, though, it was a house without grandparents. Some family lived nearby: Margaret's sister and her husband and, almost within reach, her brother Frank in Minnesota. A sociable rather than a religious woman, Margaret attended the Episcopal church every Sunday and participated in innumerable church activities. When Chattauqua made its regular visits to Madison, the Vidals attended all the lectures. Margaret, who belonged to a women's reading group, kept sets of books in the house, The Wonder Book and The Book of Knowledge. If her politics were her husband's, she had one separate plank: she strongly favored the vote for women. She marched in a suffragette parade in Madison and had herself photographed, dressed in semimasculine clothes, banner in hand, her principles clearly visible. But, as the keeper of the domestic keys, she did not manage economically enough for her husband. She had none of the German thrift he admired. She might well have wished that the Spanish debt (in family legend now worth millions) would allow her never to have to count pennies again. "By the time they told and retold that story," her grandson later remarked, "we were the Perhapsburgs waiting for our throne to be returned to us." She also had a disastrous tendency to gain weight: the pretty young bride allowed herself to become transformed into a matronly massiveness that her husband disliked and that later made her children uncomfortable.

In his mother's eyes, Gene could do no wrong. She beamed in his presence and, later, at the mention of his name. If his father took pride in him, he apparently never told his son. When the time came for the son to make judgments, the case was clear-cut. Eventually he seems to have disapproved of his father, perhaps for his temper, his emotional stinginess, his treatment of his wife. " 'I don't know why he was such a stinker,' " Gene later said to his own son. "That's the word he used," Gore Vidal recalled. "I think a lot of it had to do with his devotion to his mother. He felt that his father was rude to his mother and unpleasant. They apparently quarreled quite a lot, and Gene took his mother's side." Later, as he and his sister Lurene rose in the world, their mother's obesity became an embarrassment. But though they preferred to keep her out of sight, they undoubtedly loved her. As Gene did Lurene. Two years older, smart, willfully decisive (nicknamed "The Sergeant" by her critics in the family), and a great gossip, Lurene became the sibling to whom he was closest. They shared a childhood and its memories. When he went from grade school to Madison High, which had about three hundred students, his handsomeness made him popular with the girls, his athletic achievements and good temper with the boys. Early in the 1910 football season the starting quarterback broke his nose, Gene took over, and the quarterback never got his position back. Soon Gene had an attractive girlfriend on his arm, Leila Love, later a physical-education teacher in Madison. The boys did the usual behind-the-house and locker-room things, small talk, cigarettes, fantasies, bonding, perhaps some sex.

Like his mother's, Gene's temperament was placid, unargumentative, though somewhat impersonal. He charmed and impressed people, a combination of striking good looks and intelligence with shyness and dreaminess. He liked to tinker, to invent. Self-sufficient, self-absorbed, he gave more importance to activities than to people. Only on the athletic field was he noticeably competitive, a dynamic athlete who enjoyed being special, being admired, winning. Dark-complexioned, thin but wiry, almost six feet, with striking blue eyes, sharply angled face lines, high cheekbones, with excellent coordination and the desire to win, he seemed a natural athlete. He was not as aggressive, though, as his coaches would have liked. His manner implied that playing elegantly was almost enough. Early on he developed an ironic style, a sense of proportion that sometimes seemed amused indifference. He had no doubt, though, that athletic prominence was a way out of Madison. As the premier high-school athlete of eastern South Dakota, when he graduated in 1912 the University of South Dakota at Vermillion encouraged him to come. For many, Vermillion was the first step out of the relative emptiness of places like Madison. Since the family could provide little money, at first he worked at a local business as a janitor, learning his lifelong habit of watching his pennies. Fortunately, college cost next to nothing. Subsistence was cheap. Enrolled in the engineering program, with modest effort he began to get good grades, mostly B's and some A's. His interest was in designing things, inventing things, making them work. The College of Engineering caught the spirit of a heroicizing time, when the country believed that American character, epitomized by its engineers, would transform the world. The engineer's "college course should be loaded with the same risks and desperate chances that he will afterwards find in life, which is mainly an unbending effort to do the apparently impossible in which failure is worse than death. The engineer is the man to accept life in all its strenuous seriousness and the last man to expect the illusory advantages of special privilege." From the beginning, Vidal's athletic prowess and physical grace attracted notice. Soon he was setting records, helping the Coyote teams win in basketball, football, track, and baseball. An excellent punter, place-, and dropkicker, his evasively clever open-field running transformed him from quarterback to halfback, where he was still noteworthy for throwing and now for receiving also. In his junior and senior years he starred as the basketball team's high-scoring center in the days when a six-foot basketball player seemed tall, or at least tall enough, and then in his senior year captained the team to the state championship. At track and field he regularly won the university indoor and outdoor meets with an all-around competence at the various jumps, shot puts, hurdles, and pole vaults, including setting the state high-jump record. Even in baseball, the sport he focused on least, he pitched well enough to win his fourth "letter," the only athlete in

South Dakota's history, with one exception, to have done so: "the best all round athlete the Dakotas ever turned out," the local sports experts agreed.

Fame came partly from the innumerable South Dakota newspaper headlines that proclaimed the accomplishments of the Vermillion teams and their stars, especially Gene Vidal. His good looks and amiable intelligence made him eminently salable, a Midwestern, soon an all-American, role model. America loved its games and its playing-field heroes. In those distant times, before the triumph of commercialism, athletes were idealized for their manliness and their American virtues. Madison swelled with pride: "Local boy great star at state university." When Gene came home for holidays, he now had about him an aura. His siblings and their friends were in awe. In June 1916 he completed his engineering course. At home in Madison he deliberated whether to apply to the naval academy at Annapolis or to West Point, where he could continue his engineering studies and his athletic career. Someone of influence, eager to have him play football there, made "a vigorous plea that Vidal be sent to West Point." Congressman Royal S. Johnson used South Dakota's one appointment. At Minneapolis he passed the entrance examination with high grades. By late summer 1916 this "demon on the gridiron" was marching and practicing on the fields above the Hudson, at first kept under wraps by the Army coach the better to surprise opponents. For the next three years he set West Point records in football and track, and was soon to be known to a generation of Army enthusiasts as the best all-around athlete West Point had ever produced. As the starting halfback for a nationally famous Army team that beat all its major rivals, the South Dakota boy was now a national hero. He played before huge audiences around the country. At the Polo Gounds the "largest crowd that ever attended a sporting event" in New York City watched Army beat Navy. Film of the Army victory in the 1916 game, starring "Gene Vidal," shown along with *The Law Decides*, "A Powerful Gripping Drama in Seven Parts," could be seen for ten cents on the movie screens springing up across America. When he visited home, resplendent in his cadet uniform, "the whole town was watching him." Not everything, though, went smoothly in his cadet years at the academy. A debilitating war was devastating Europe. When the military and political brass cheered at the Army-Navy game, they also had other, more brutal games on their minds. So too did some of the cadets. As always, there was a glut of officers in the promotions pipeline.

Advancement came excruciatingly slowly in the peacetime Army. Cadets were more concerned about the lack of opportunity for promotion than about physical danger. After the 1916 academic year, Gene considered leaving for "some technical school. . . . At the present rate of promotion," Vidal and other cadets "see themselves second lieutenants on small pay," reported a worried sports reporter, "until they are old men with little chance of retiring at a higher rank than captain." Gene stayed. Soon, in response to America's entry into the war, graduation was accelerated. The class of 1920 graduated two years early.

At graduation Vidal had just come from a year of athletic triumphs in football that equaled his achievements of 1916 and were his best ever in track and field. And he had led his class in mathematics. Now he was a second lieutenant in the Corps of Engineers in what soon, in November 1918, became a peacetime Army again. Athletics, though, was still a ticket to prominence. The Army always delighted in showcasing itself. Soon Gene was playing basketball and football for the Army command centers to which he was assigned, first at Fort Humphreys in Virginia, near Washington, whose basketball team he captained, and then at Fort Howard, where he led the Army team through its football schedule. In June 1920, having won the decathlon at the Army championship games, he was chosen by the Army as its track-and-field representative to the Seventh Olympic Games to be held in Antwerp, Belgium. That summer, in Pershing Stadium in France, he won second place in the pentathlon. There were banner headlines in America. In late summer he returned home, first to New York, then to Fort Humphreys. Margaret Vidal came by herself to New York to see her triumphant son. At a football game to which he took her, the public-address system announced to the huge audience the presence of the newly returned Olympic star. The crowd applauded enthusiastically. When the basketball season began, he and his Army teammates went to play a game at Langley Field, Virginia. For fun, the Army pilots took them all up for a spin. Immediately sold on flying, he and his roommate asked for transfers to the Army Air Service and were sent to Carlston Field, Arcadia, Florida, for training. He had found his second passion. There he trained in World War I "Jennys" and, as always, starred in interservice games. The next year he had his wings. On a visit to New York, the handsome twenty-six-year old Army pilot and athlete met the attractive, flirtatious eighteen-year-old Nina Gore, the daughter of the senator from Oklahoma. In December 1921 the Washington newspapers announced the engagement. They were to be married early in the new year.

————•••————

The Gore and the Vidal family names were united on a cold day in January 1922, at Washington's St. Margaret's Episcopal Church, perfumed by pink roses and illuminated with soft candles. Nina, "attended by four bridesmaids, wore a gown of soft duchess satin trimmed with rose point lace." The groom and five of his ushers were in uniform. Newspaper accounts, which celebrated this Washington occasion, did not fail to mention that the ceremony took place "before a distinguished company representative of diplomatic, senatorial, congressional and residential society." At the last moment the bride's mother arrived, accompanied by the family doctor, apparently also a family friend. The senator was not there. Newspaper accounts stated that "Mr. Gore and Thomas Gore, Jr. were prevented from attending the ceremony by their attending physician."

What they were ill of or whether they were ill at all is not clear. Perhaps the senator was kept away by the "severe bruises" he had received in an automobile accident the week before in, of all places, Sioux Falls, South Dakota, where he had gone to give a speech. Perhaps flu, a life-threatening illness then, prevented the senator from attending. Perhaps he simply did not want to be at the wedding, since he did not think his daughter ready for marriage. A miscarriage kept away the only Vidal invited, Gene's sister Lurene. The groom apparently made sure his provincial father and obese mother did not come. Certainly the Democratic Gores and the Republican Vidals would not have been readily compatible. At the Congressional Club, friends of Mrs. Gore, who went home immediately after the ceremony, received the guests. That evening the bride and groom left for Fort Sill, Oklahoma, "where Lieut. Vidal is stationed." The handsome young officer had the pleasure of bringing "home" with him his young and beautiful bride. At last liberated from parental oversight and thrilled by the adventure of it all, the virginal Nina probably felt she was now starting her real life. Later, her son recalled, she told the story that "on her wedding night . . . when she lost her virginity she wet the bed which she always felt cast a pall over the marriage. . . . She was virginal, so she always maintained, and my father never said a word to the contrary."

Born in Lawton, Oklahoma, in July 1903, Nina (pronounced NÉYE-na) was a beautiful, lively child, the first of the two Gore children. That the Gores had any children at all was a surprise to the Senator and an annoyance to Nina Belle, who already had her hands full looking after a blind husband. She later told her grandson that rats had gnawed at her douche bag. To start her on the road to a useful life, her parents sent Nina to the Georgetown Convent School, in Washington, then to Holton Arms School. Nina had more interest in playing than studying. From childhood on, she was unconventionally beautiful, a slim, attractive figure, slightly bulging dark eyes, sharply defined full lips, and a decisive nose. Her hair was dark, usually cut short, flapper style. Less than medium height, she was appealingly petite. Her beauty was, nevertheless, aggressive. She let you know she was there. A member of the Junior League, she appeared regularly at all the places glamorous young Washingtonians should. A good athlete, with excellent hand-eye coordination, at school she had a heavy crush on an older girl, a star athlete with whom she exchanged vows of eternal friendship. Later she resented that her parents had not educated her for high society. She had not been "exposed," she complained. After Holton Arms, which she left without graduating, she refused even to consider going to college. Books were not her thing. She loved partying. Two centuries of Gore-family pioneers, farmers, lawyers, doctors—hardworking avatars of the republic's obsession with being serious—had unexpectedly produced a Jazz Age playgirl. The sober Senator, who had come to Washington "direct," so to speak, from the hardworking frontier territories, had a daughter whose highest devotion was to having a good time.

As to a profession, marriage would take care of that. For a moment, after her marriage, she fantasized about an acting career, like Tallulah Bankhead's, whose friend she was to become, or Joan Crawford's, almost her exact contemporary. She had one week on the stage in a road-show production of *The Sign of the Leopard,* at Washington's National Theater, chosen from among attractive young Washingtonians by a well-known actor-producer of the day who always cast a local girl in a bit part to increase attendance on tour. For Nina, it led neither to further roles nor to a screen test. Her bemused father remarked, "She wants to be a movie star without going to acting school. She doesn't feel she needs preparation for anything." Apparently the beautiful daughter of a powerful senator need not worry about taking care of herself. She would be taken care of. And she could handle herself. She constantly fought with her mother, in rebellion against limitations and rules. She idolized her father, his strength, his determination, his influence. That she was the daughter of such a man was one of the strongest elements in her self-definition. She loved him with an intensity that partly determined her relationships with men in her adult life. The Senator, in her eyes, could do no wrong. Her mother was mostly a bothersome rival and a nagging enforcer of rules for ordinary people.

At Fort Sill, Nina discovered that being an Army bride was not as glamorous as she had expected. Of course, Gene's Army buddies were fun. So too the drinking parties, though she was no doubt unhappily surprised to learn that in the Army's gender-segregated society the men had rituals from which Army wives were excluded. To her delight, she had a sleek black convertible roadster that, with her excellent coordination and love of speed, she drove with brilliant abandon. When she posed for photographs, her dark, explosive beauty and the car's sleek darkness seemed a perfect fit. How ironic, though, to be back in the dust bowl of her birth, from which her family had escaped. Gene's interest was less in parties than in flying. More than anything, his work absorbed him. By temperament he was elegantly serious. If he was glamorous, he was rarely self-conscious or purposeful about it. Late hours did not appeal to him. The ascent to high rank would undoubtedly be slow, even for the talented and well connected. From Fort Sill they happily went to West Point, where Gene had been appointed the first instructor of aeronautics, an assistant football coach, and coach of track and field. West Point was delighted to have him back. No one minded that his teaching assignment mostly provided cover for his contribution to the athletic program. His fame had made him a West Point legend: heads turned at the mention of his name. With his flying wings, his engineering degree, and his amiable camaraderie, he seemed a natural choice for the position. He even looked the role. As much as he enjoyed flying itself, he had no special desire to set records. Perhaps he felt he had already set, as an athlete, his fair share. His focus was on the engineering challenges of flight, on how aviation might change the world. But for the time being he thought mostly about athletics. Soon track and field at the academy were revivified. By spring 1923 he had convinced the West Point authorities that his athletes deserved the opportunity to compete in the tryouts for the 1924 Olympic Games in Paris. For the first time, at Yankee Stadium in September, Army track and field athletes competed away from home. In March 1924 the

Olympic Committee asked him to coach the American decathlon and pentathlon teams.

Nina also was delighted to be at West Point. It was much nearer
Washington and New York than Fort Sill. Still, life even at the Point was not
as fast or as glamorous as she would have liked. She had married, she
believed, a man on the rise, a famous athlete whom she would accompany in
his ascension into higher spheres. But that would not happen at West Point,
and an Army paycheck did not go far, especially toward the cost of a New
York or Washington social life. Whether or not marital trouble was already
brewing in paradise is unclear. She had married a quiet man of Midwestern
equanimity. Excessive temperament and explosive temper seemed to him
anathema. It would drain the life out of home, work, and play. Nina, on the
contrary, thrived on attitude, on emotional and verbal vividness, on exaggerated gestures of temperament and language. Argument was her mode.
Fighting gave her a charge. It was often the necessary prelude to sex. Gene
could not have found this readily assimilable to his temperament and to his
view of what a satisfactory marriage should be. He certainly did not want to
play his mother to Nina's version of his father. West Point Army society
would have found Nina a handful, not that its hard-drinking crowd of
officers and their wives did not often enjoy her company. Prohibition made
liquor even more pleasurably racy and exciting. She soon discovered she had
a taste for it. Though a little went a long way, she gradually increased her
tolerance. Gene hardly drank, partly by temperament; also, it was not
compatible with his devotion to athletics and coaching. To him, late nights
and hard drinking seemed mostly a bore. As the daughter of a famous
senator, Nina treated West Point as an extension of Washington. Influence
counted. She regularly parked her roadster in the superintendent's restricted
parking space. At first with noblesse oblige and then with exasperation,
Douglas MacArthur explained to her that the parking space was his. Army
regulations required that the superintendent *had* to park in his own parking
spot. Apparently Nina paid no attention.

When she became pregnant in early 1925, the decision to leave the
fortress on the Hudson was an easy one. They had been there almost three
years. Bored as an Army wife, Nina must have anticipated she would be
even more bored (and burdened) as the mother of an Army brat. And they
needed more than Army pay. Also, Gene's enthusiasm was turning to
commercial aviation, a new industry that would require its dreamers, plan-

ners, administrators, heroes, some of whom would become rich and famous. That Gene actually wanted to be a father is doubtful. For his career and his pocketbook, the timing was inconvenient. Probably the news came as a surprise. Nina, who may have seen her pregnancy as a ticket back to civilization, gave birth to an eight-pound boy at the Cadet Hospital at 11 A.M., Saturday, October 3, 1925. Major Howard Snyder, later to become the White House physician to President Eisenhower, was the first to hold the healthy child. A month later, with their one-month-old infant, Nina and Gene moved from West Point to the nation's capital. They were to stay temporarily with her parents at the Gores' newly built house in Rock Creek Park. The baby's cradle there was a chest of drawers. Gene had resigned from the Army. Nina was thrilled to be back in town.

CHAPTER two

A Washington Childhood

1925–1939

"IF RECURRENT DREAMS can be relied on," Gore Vidal recalled, "I . . . have a memory of being born. I am in a narrow tunnel. I cannot move forward or backward. I wake up in a sweat. Nina's pelvis was narrow and I was delivered clumsily, with forceps, by a doctor not used to deliveries: he was officer of the day in the Cadet Hospital." In *The Season of Comfort,* an autobiographical novel of his early adulthood, he dramatized his mother's pain and the child's birth struggle. "The child was partly born; it seemed reluctant to leave the darkness of the womb. But she would scream now. She would scream until she had thrown this thing out of her, until she had dragged her child into the light the living saw." His earliest vivid memory is of having his head stuck between the slats of a playpen in his bedroom at his grandparents' house, the beginning of his lifelong claustrophobia. His grandmother, who came in response to his screams, immediately freed him. He later remembered it as if the playpen were a prison and his much-loved grandmother his liberator. His mother was, as usual, someplace else, an emotional as well as a physical location. Though she later boasted she had breast-fed him to the age of one, she also thought it great fun to tell people that she never stopped smoking while the baby nursed. "She could draw a funny picture of her dutifully breast-feeding me while talking to people with ash like Vesuvius on my head," Gore Vidal recalled. She did not mind people seeing her body. She would hold court even on the toilet seat, with the bathroom door open. Hers was never a household in which the body was private. Partly it was because she had imbibed child-raising theories that advocated naturalness, parents and children seeing one another naked. She was, though, proud of her body and challenged her parents and the general puritan world with her amused indifference to their inhibitions. She was never indifferent to herself, to her claims to attention, admiration, and privilege.

For Gore, childhood was imprisonment, victimization. Later he was to see its drama as his attempt to leave it behind as quickly as possible. At best, parents and children spoke a different language, had different assumptions. Their interests usually diverged. At worst, they were enemies. Dependency, he was to conclude later, inevitably meant abuse. Parents, families, schools were like the slats of the playpen, the prison-house of the world, the incarcerating narrow pelvis twisting and forcing the child to take on the contours imposed by circumstances. The most unavoidable victimization was mortality itself. Not unexpectedly, his baby pictures show a seemingly happy, well-fed boy, with an inquisitive look and the possibility if not the fact of a smile. This was a resilient child. The bureau drawer at his grandfather's house was probably a cozy place to be. His mother breast-fed him successfully, though one year seemed enough. Easily bored, keenly concerned about keeping her figure, she quickly resumed her social life, turning him over to the bottle and nannies. Gene, who soon took the family westward to the University of Oregon, where he briefly served as head football coach, had on his mind the challenge of life and career after the Army. Still in demand as an athlete, he played professional football that year. But one football season at Eugene, Oregon, was enough. He was soon looking at other possibilities, particularly commercial aviation. It too would keep him on the move. Father and son were Big Gene and Little Gene. Big Gene had no hesitation leaving wife and child at the home of his in-laws, who, despite wondering how all this was going to turn out, found their son-in-law charming and likable. He was easy to have around. So too was Little Gene, whom his grandmother immediately adored. Nina Belle Gore, though, could have readily done without her daughter. When she was at home, there was never peace in the house. The boy himself was a pleasure, and his grandfather, when it became clear that Little Gene might be parked with them for long periods, began to make plans for him.

The Senator was in that worst of all places for a professional politician, out of office. Stubbornly independent, he had come to Washington in 1907 at the age of thirty-seven. Over the years he had never stopped learning things that interested him, especially monetary policy, trade, agriculture, and oil. He had become wise and sometimes cynical about the ways of Washington. About the damned human race he had begun to say that if there were any other, he would join it. In his heart and in some of his politics, he was still a grassroots populist and a fiercely aggressive individualist. At the Democratic convention of 1908, in Denver, he had made a brief but brilliant speech, though he had not been on the program and had been called on to speak extemporaneously during a lull. His speech had turned the convention to William Jennings Bryan. The Senator knew whom he favored and what he himself stood for. He believed in basic truths about money, work, nature, and human nature. Any nation or politician who denied them would, in the end, be decisively corrected. When root issues were at stake, he never varied, a combination of principle and stubbornness that verged on but never quite became arrogance. " 'After I nominated [Bryan] at Denver,' " he later remarked to his grandson, " 'we rode back to the hotel in the same carriage and he turned to me and said, "You know, I base my political success on just three things." ' The old man paused for dramatic effect. 'What were they?' " his grandson asked. " 'I've completely forgotten,' he said. 'But I do remember wondering why he thought he was a success.' " After a truncated initial term, having drawn the short straw when Oklahoma entered the Union, he was reelected for a full term and, in 1914, elected again. Even in the faction-ridden, backstabbing politics of Oklahoma, he had proved a success. Like his state, he held conservative views on economics and civil rights. He supported both small farmers and the emerging oil industry, and became the key figure in the creation of soil-conservation legislation and the oil-depletion allowance. Known for his integrity, he was both a flinty campaigner and an unbribable politician who lived exclusively on his salary. To some his blindness seemed an affliction that had raised him above ordinary limitations, a sign of integrity.

In 1913–14 he had a close call. It occurred in a Washington Hotel room, where an attractive Oklahoma lady, who had a constituent's petition, accused him of sexually accosting her. He might or might not have put his arm around her. A lapse in judgment or some attraction to excitement resulted in his allowing himself to be alone with her. Why he went to her hotel rather than have her come to his office is unclear. Her confederates, who had entrapped him, burst into the bedroom, which he later claimed he had been told was a parlor. Perhaps they knew about the blind girl he had impregnated two decades earlier. The conspirators were all Oklahomans interested in patronage and money. The plot had been masterminded and financed by a vengeful Oklahoma lawyer, whose claim for $3 million in fees for legal services to Oklahoma Indians the Senator had squashed. The other participants were enemies who saw an opportunity. Senator Gore responded with varying combinations of defiance and conciliation. He declined to pay them off, partly because he did not have the money, mostly because he knew the people to whom he would make the payoff would then publicly reveal it as evidence of his guilt. When his accusers attempted to sue him in Washington, he succeeded in thwarting them. Less successful in Oklahoma, where he was sued for $50,000 damages "for an alleged attack upon Mrs. Minnie E. Bond," he denied the charges. The trial, in Oklahoma City in February 1914, was a sensational melodrama with potentially serious consequences, a Victorian sex and power scandal whetted by the public's interest, whether he were guilty or not, in knowing how a blind man manages sexual escapades. Fortunately, the judge ruled inadmissible anything about Gore's life previous to this incident. Public opinion was mostly on his side in what the newspapers called "The Foul Plot Against Gore." The jury stayed out for less than three minutes. "Senator Gore and his wife stood immediately in front of the jury box," where they had been sitting throughout the hearing. When the foreman stated that the judgment was for the defendant, the courtroom erupted into cheers, "bedlam broke loose among the crowd." Mrs. Gore cried.

He had an even higher price to pay in 1920. He was defeated for reelection mostly because he had opposed America entering World War I. In 1912, with the election of a Democratic President, his star had shone brightly. He had campaigned vigorously for Woodrow Wilson. With the Senate mostly dominated by powerful Republicans, Wilson needed the support of the Senator from Oklahoma with a strong populist base who was widely admired for his legislative abilities. Gore saw the possibility for higher office, maybe ultimately the presidency. Though they were not essentially a compatible couple, Wilson and Gore danced together for a while. In 1914 Gore opposed American involvement in the war in Europe. So too did Wilson, publicly pledged to neutrality. In the closely contested election of 1916, Gore, whose hope to be nominated as Wilson's running mate had been disappointed, at first hardly campaigned; the relationship had cooled considerably. But Wilson soon seemed a likely loser, and in response to a desperate call from the White House, Gore agreed to go to California, where his populism and his South/Southwestern background made him a congenial figure. He campaigned vigorously and had good reason to believe that without his help the President would have lost California and consequently the White House. Naturally, their relationship worsened thereafter: Wilson was not pleased to be indebted to Gore. In fact, the President and his Anglophile supporters, who increasingly favored American intervention in Europe, soon came to hate the Oklahoma senator. From the depths of his personality, his principles, and his populist roots, Gore violently opposed the shedding of American blood on behalf of what he believed were corrupt, undemocratic European regimes. His voice was constantly heard in the Senate and throughout the land. A severe, almost mortal, bout of influenza diminished his energy but not his antiwar persistence.

When, in 1917, America entered the conflict, Gore voted for every bill in support of American armed forces while denouncing America's participation in the war itself. Principle overcame expediency. A man who did not easily make friends now made many enemies. Wilson denounced *him*. When war fever swept the country, some of his supporters and all of his enemies in Oklahoma could not or would not distinguish between his support of American armed forces and opposition to the war. Aware he was in trouble, he did not realize how seriously until, during his 1920 primary reelection campaign, his opponents made the eagle scream. Gore was unpatriotic. Gore had supported the enemy. Gore had betrayed his country. Gore was a traitor. He neither retreated nor apologized. He believed he had been both honorable and right. But it soon became clear that when the new term began he would be out of office. "He wrote himself out of the main script all his career," his grandson later remarked, "taking unpopular stands, telling people to go fuck themselves if they didn't like what he was doing. . . . The

Chamber of Commerce [in Oklahoma] sent him a telegram saying if he didn't support a declaration of war they'd see to it that he'd be defeated in the next election. He wired back, 'How many members of the Chamber of Commerce are of draft age?' He was a coalition of one. It was really his enchantment of the people, which was very powerful, that kept him in office. He was their voice. But if you go against a sudden tidal wave of feeling . . ." At the last session of the old Senate he hid in his desk a note stating when he believed he would return—in six or at the most twelve years—as authentication of his belief that he would be back, determined he would again become an active member of that exclusive club. In the meantime he settled for and settled down to the comparatively dull Washington life of a temporary ex-senator and a brilliant orator. He needed to earn a living. Oratory and the law had always been his bread and butter. His expertise in monetary policy and in oil depletion brought him clients for whom he felt he could lobby honorably. For the first time in his life he started to make money beyond his necessary expenses, much of which he used to purchase three acres of land in Rock Creek Park, at 1500 Broad Branch Road, on which he built a handsome house of gray-yellow Baltimore stone. He was the first Gore since the seventeenth century to own property in Washington. Secluded, almost rural, enveloped in woods and sunlight, the house was only a short drive to the Capitol whose dome could be seen from nearby heights.

Whatever his reservations in January 1922 about his daughter's marriage, at least she had been taken off his hands. Whether or not Gene Vidal was the right husband for her or, more to the point, she the right wife for anyone, he certainly hoped for the best. The news in late 1925 that Gene had resigned from the Army made the ex-Senator and Mrs. Gore anxious. Now Nina was back in Washington, more or less, and with a husband and baby. It was not exactly what the Gores had planned. It would cost money, and it would alter the household's life. They had not expected again to have at home their hot-tempered, strong-willed, fun-loving daughter, who had always been fire to Mrs. Gore's oil. And how much of the responsibility for the young boy would be theirs? At the beginning of 1926 the blind ex-Senator looked down, so to speak, at his first grandchild. He began plotting how the boy could be useful to him. If in five years he was still there, he could become his eyes. The light of reading needed to be kept lit.

On a hot night in summer 1929 the bright lights of downtown St. Louis, viewed from a hotel window, seemed icy white to the eyes of three-year-old Eugene Luther Vidal, Jr. In the days before colored neon, even commercial signs were white. He was aware of travel, of flight, of his mother and father, of the excitement of flying in an airplane for the first time, of a strange city far from his grandparents' Rock Creek Park home. After more than two years of occasional work, Gene Vidal had become a technical adviser and now assistant to the general manager of the first major American airline, Transcontinental Air Transport, which wanted to carry passengers coast to coast. Maddux Airlines had already been flying passengers throughout California and the West. Commercial aviation was becoming an industry. With Lindbergh's successful flight to Paris in 1927, with reckless but courageous fliers performing stunts and delivering mail, aviation was taking over the American imagination, a new frontier being explored and tamed. Amelia Earhart had just become the first woman to fly the Atlantic, and C. M. Keys, the founder of TAT, set her up in his New York office to help publicize the new era. She and Gene, now co-workers, were soon friends.

Famous as an athlete, knowledgeable as a flier and aeronautics expert, a former West Point hero, Gene Vidal could be invaluable to the new industry. In St. Louis he helped map and publicize the first transcontinental air route, which took its passengers by train from New York to Columbus, Ohio, then by air to Oklahoma, by train to New Mexico, and by air again to Burbank, California, all in forty-eight hours. The passenger terminals were "built right alongside the railroads. Apparently those in authority never thought passengers would ever be flown at night because these facilities were of permanent construction." In New York, in early July 1929, Earhart christened the inaugural plane *The City of New York* while the movie star Mary Pickford, across the continent, christened the plane flying in the other direction *The City of Los Angeles*. They still did not dare fly passengers over mountains or at night. Landing-field lights did not exist. Innumerable technical challenges needed to be met, and Gene Vidal was in St. Louis to help meet them. Nina was with him, eager to participate in the glamour and excitement. Earhart and Charles Lindbergh, who also worked for TAT, were either close by or crossing the continent, always in touch with St.

Louis. As all this swirled around him, what Little Gene remembered most vividly was going to his first movie. Talking pictures were a half step ahead of commercial aviation. As he toddled down the aisle with his parents, he heard an actress on the screen asking a question of another character in the movie. Little Gene himself, "in a very loud voice," answered.

There were two other soundtracks playing, those of his father's career and his parents' marriage. Both, at first, were distantly in the background. There were no questions for him to answer yet, no dialogue in which to participate. He had already begun to sense, and soon to be aware, that his father was a busy actor in the world of airplanes. It meant little more, though, than that Big Gene was an important man, away much of the time, which Little Gene accepted as a given. Actually, it provided opportunities that few children had. Later that year he himself flew the transcontinental TAT rail-air route, the first child ever to fly cross-country, probably because Gene thought it a great publicity idea to demonstrate that commercial aviation was safe and comfortable even for children. Actually, by modern standards it was neither, no matter how deluxe the airline tried to make the passenger accommodations. The three-year-old boy remembered "the lurid flames from the exhaust through the window." As the plane descended into Los Angeles, one of his eardrums burst and bled.

TAT was soon in financial trouble, partly because of the difficulty of obtaining government mail contracts in a corrupt political environment, partly because, a few months after Little Gene's visit to St. Louis, the stock market crashed. With losses of over $3 million due to high start-up costs and few passengers, TAT merged with Maddux Airlines. After additional mergers it became TWA. At Christmas 1929 the St. Louis executives, including Gene Vidal, were called to New York headquarters. All were fired. Angry at TAT for publicizing his release in order to placate disappointed stockholders, Gene soon helped convince two wealthy Philadelphia businessmen, the brothers Nicholas and Charles Townshend Ludington, to create a new airline that would fly every hour between Washington, Philadelphia, and New York, an early version of air-shuttle service. It would compete with Eastern Air Transport, a subsidiary of TAT's owners. Success would be a form of revenge. With his friend, the well-known aviator Paul Collins, Gene immediately became a vice president, to be joined the next year by Earhart, the three of them soon to be a pioneering triumvirate in setting up routes throughout the Northeast. They themselves had little or no money to invest. But they had expertise, brains, and vision.

Whether or not the boy heard his parents' raised voices behind their bedroom door, he soon became aware of differences not only in their personalities but in their fighting modes. Apparently they fought from the beginning. Later their arguments became so frequent, her anger so volatile, that Little Gene dreaded ever having to be there when they were together. Just as Nina was sarcastic and argumentative with her mother, she was, from the start, combative with her husband. An idolized athlete, a man of business and the world, Gene had little need for self-assertion. On the contrary, he effectively cultivated his natural penchant for understatement. Nina, though, had to keep repeating, loudly, her claim to attention. Her assumption of superiority, of sophistication, of importance far in excess of any reality often seemed abrasively irritating. Great fun with her friends, she was hell on those who lived with her. Whereas her mother thought her rude and selfish, Gene found her tediously devitalizing. One either fought back or quietly tolerated her addiction to scenes, histrionics. Her emotive pattern became unhappily predictable. With a cigarette between her fingers or lips, a beautiful woman whom one found either exciting or exhausting, she swaggered, she challenged, both verbally and physically. Initially, for Gene, the excitement dominated. Each was physically attractive to the other. Gene found his young bride's youth a turn-on. Later, she was to say that she had been infatuated, not ever really in love, with Gene Vidal, happy to have the opportunity to get out from under her critical mother, eager for marital adventure and freedom. Their erotic pleasure in one another soon seemed outbalanced, at least for Gene, by their emotional incompatibility. Mostly, he refused to fight, even to raise his voice. Patiently, he would wait out her tirades or leave the room, often dodging whatever was thrown at him: always words, sometimes any handy object. His rarely raising his voice provoked her even more.

By the nature of his work, he was often away. At home, during the work week, he had little desire to socialize at night, especially at the late parties Nina had longed for as an adolescent, become used to during their Army years, and now embraced as the climax of mostly uneventful days. Gene had pleasure in work, Nina had no work to do. Mothering was not a sustaining activity. Also, it often proved incompatible with her social life. Mrs. Gore soon became a surrogate mother, unhappy with her daughter, delighted with the child. Whatever her talents, Nina had no education to speak of, no vision of herself she could translate into vocation. After her one week on the stage, she regularly referred to "the brilliant stage career" she had given up because of her duties as wife and mother. Discipline, perseverance, follow-up were not her metier. She had already become very good at accusing others of the flaws she herself had: her husband, she claimed, was not ambitious enough, disciplined enough, persevering enough. In her son's later fictionalized account, her "one wish as a child had been to grow up and escape from her mother but, though she was grown now, she still had not escaped. If only Stephen [Gene] could find us a house in Washington. We have almost enough money now and Father is paying for the baby." She reproached him "for being incapable of making a home, of making money, of getting ahead." She soon became as disappointed with (and critical of) his slow progress toward wealth as she would have been of her own insufficiences if she had allowed herself to be self-critical. Later she blamed all on her parents. She had been neglected, perhaps abused. Her mother had spanked her. She had also had, from the beginning, painful menstrual periods, which seemed to her relevant to an explanation of her emotional fireworks. She preferred, always, blaming others, sometimes loudly. Little Gene, apparently, heard her angry voice from earliest infancy.

His own words soon found voice. An early talker, by his second year he babbled a great deal, thereafter incessantly. At the beginning he had difficulty with some consonants. D and B came easily, frequently. So Mommy became "Bommy"; Grandpa "Dah"; his grandmother, whose nickname was Tot, "Dot"; his own name not Gene but "Deenie." The mispronunciations delighted everyone so much, they became the intimate family nicknames. But he did not want other children to use this against him, to tease him in the playground and the school yard. To others he was Little Gene, but to the immediate family, when "I was a baby and young, it was Deenie," an act of self-naming, the transformation of a transient speech defect into a creation that anticipated his later fascination with language as self-creation. His verbal skills were precocious, his physical coordination good. He walked at about the usual age, and soon rode his first tricycle around the terrace of the house at Rock Creek Park. From early on, he posed amiably for photos, full-figured, blond-haired, inquisitive-eyed, with a slightly round face, in the usual short pants and wool sweaters of the day. But by the age of four he not only spoke back to voices on the movie screen:

he was an unstoppable conversationalist, "particularly in the kitchen with various black cooks. I dominated conversation with them. . . . Gertrude, one of the family cooks, used to lock me in the closet when she felt that I was being bad," a punishment greater than she knew, since he had claustrophobic anxiety attacks when confined in small places. Finally, "about the third time I began to sing 'Am I Blue?' which I knew all the lyrics of from the radio, from *Amos 'n Andy,* . . . that broke her up and that was the end of the closet." Soon he was the bard of the kitchen, making up stories to entertain himself and the cook.

Outside in the back the Senator kept chickens, perhaps in deference to his rural origins or to impress his visiting constituents. Deenie fed them, played with them. One night at dinner his grandmother urged him to eat his food. Suddenly the connection between what he was chewing and the animals outside dawned on him. He spat out the mouthful immediately. To his grandmother it became a challenge to get him to eat chicken. She disguised it, mixing it with potato or spinach. "Is this chicken?" he would ask. "No," she said. "It's gazeboo." "The gazeboo went straight into her face." It became a family story Dot loved to tell. If Nina, more corrective than commending, spent much of her time pursuing her social life, Tot loved him, supported him, praised him. If Big Gene was matter-of-fact about his son and preoccupied with business, Dah and Tot were there every day. Once, boasting his son had perfect balance, Gene had him demonstrate, successfully, on a tightrope. To impress his grandmother, Deenie piled up chairs one on top of another. Climbing to the top, he raised himself up straight while Tot kept saying, "Don't do that! Don't do that!" He responded, "I have perfect balance!" Suddenly the whole thing crashed down, "and I said, 'Goddamn it!' She had never heard a child swear before. She thought it was extremely funny." Each morning he joined the blind Senator "in the bathroom while Dah assembled himself for the day. It was a complicated ritual, because not only did he have to put in upper and lower plates of teeth but one of his eyes was glass, and I took exquisite and never-failing pleasure in handing it to him as the high moment of his toilette, the last part of the transformation from frowsy-haired old man . . . 'to mellifluous statesman.' " Disappointed in their own children, the Gores were delighted to have an amusing, intelligent, and well-behaved grandchild, despite the cost and occasional inconvenience. " 'Never have children, only grandchildren,' " the Senator would later say.

From early on, his grandmother read to him. These sessions soon turned into reading lessons as well as entertainment. "Central to her method was a tale of unnatural love called 'The Duck and the Kangaroo.' " When, just after his sixth birthday, he began first grade at the Potomac School on California Street near Connecticut Avenue, he could read somewhat, mostly because of his grandmother, partly because his grandfather had, during the previous year, already pounced. Every possible reader had for years been pressed into service for the eight hours or so each day that the Senator "read." " 'Milton's daughters,' he would say with a sweet smile . . . 'went blind reading to *their* father.' " When his own two children had proved abysmal readers, Mrs. Gore continued as she had for thirty years. So too did the Senator's longtime secretary. Mrs. Gore had developed the skill of reading to her husband while her mind was totally someplace else, but she longed for relief. To those who read to him, he was "a gentle and amusing tyrant . . . hard going, if you did not." At last, the blind man decided, he could start to reap the benefit of having an intelligent grandson. Little Gene could start fulfilling the role his grandfather had had in mind for him from the moment he had been cradled in a bureau drawer at Rock Creek Park. Actually, Nina and Gene now, finally, had an apartment of their own, on Bancroft Place above Dupont Circle, close to the Potomac School. But Deenie still spent much of his time at Broad Branch Road, looked after by his grandmother. Falteringly, he had begun to read out loud to his grandfather, applying the rudimentary skills his grandmother had taught him. The Senator slowly, patiently, nurtured his oral reading and his enthusiasm for books. In a house filled with bookshelves, the Senator knew the location of each volume. He would ask the boy to go to a particular shelf and get such-and-such a book down. Then he would tell him where to turn to in the book. Then the command was, "Read!"

Little Gene did his best, sounding out long or difficult words syllable by syllable. Gradually he improved his facility and speed. The boy had the advantage of the Senator having to teach him phonetically. When he stumbled, his grandfather would sound out the syllables. "I can still remember pronouncing long words, syllable by syllable. Not until I had got the sense would we move on." As a reward for what was initially, at five, hard and sometimes boring work (he could understand only part of what he read), the Senator would tell him stories, which he had started doing long before the boy could read at all. "Baby Gene," said a Washington newspaper feature article about the Senator, "runs among the stacks of books. . . . 'Tell me a story, Dad,' begs little Gene, bored with playthings. The Senator, eyes tightly closed, says nothing. 'Dad,' insists the boy, shaking him. 'Oh, Dad! Please tell me a story!' Silence. Baby Gene regards his grandfather with interest, observes naïvely: 'Why do you keep your eyes closed? You can't see anyway.' Sen. Gore, amused, opens his blind eyes, begins sententiously: 'Once upon a time. . . .'" And the Senator would invent stories, "just to take the curse off some of the stuff I had to read . . . about boys who lived up a tree in Mississippi and how they lived in the woods. He would interject these amidst bimetallism, to hold my interest with it." The Senator loved fact, information, analysis, the *Congressional Record*. He also, paradoxically, was a "passionate sight-seer. . . . One of my first memories is driving with him to a slum in southeast Washington. 'All this,' he said, pointing at the dilapidated redbrick buildings, 'was once our land.' Since I saw only shabby buildings and could not imagine the land beneath, I was not impressed."

Potomac School was mostly, in his memory, a blur. His fictional alter ego had been "sick to his stomach the first day, and all his memories after that were a confusion: noise, paste, paper, sandboxes." Later he recalled that "as we came downstairs, one of the teachers belted out *'Celeste Aïda'* on the piano. As a result, it is the only Verdi opera I don't care for." Even first-grade classes in those distant days were highly structured. For some reason, his best grades were in citizenship, mathematics, and music, his lowest in composition, reading, and spelling, as if this were some alternative Eugene Luther Vidal, later to be exchanged for the real one. His handwriting was already dreadful. His mother suddenly became concerned about him, particularly his grades. Why wasn't he making more of an effort? If he didn't do better, he would be punished. She decided a change of school was called for. Abruptly, for the next year, he was enrolled in the second grade at The Landon School for Boys, though the record is as much a blur and a blank as his memory. His home address was now again 1500 Broad Branch Road, Rock Creek Park. For third grade, Nina moved him again, this time to the larger Sidwell Friends School, where he was to stay for grades three through five. He had occasional conversations with Mr. Sidwell himself, "an ancient Quaker whose elephantine ears were filled with hair while numerous liver spots made piebald his kindly bald head." At all three schools reading was taught phonetically. Early on, at Potomac or Landon, he was taught by the Calvert method. "With Calvert you cut out pictures of Greek gods and you glued them into books," he recalled, "a form of teaching which doesn't exist anymore. They tried to make it interesting and visual, but you also had to know about syllables, that a sentence was made up of words which were made up of little syllables, like a train." During his first two years at Sidwell Friends the real Eugene Luther Vidal materialized, with A's in reading, history, and spelling and respectable grades throughout, except for the constant dismal D's for penmanship. On the playing fields he was noticeably uninterested, his marks low. In fifth grade all his marks plunged. Though forced to be there in body, he had withdrawn his mind. At home, at Rock Creek Park, he read to his grandfather and now, also, for long hours to himself. He soon began to write, bits of prose stories and poems. He had decided to do at school only what he was forced to. What he wanted was to read. The Senator had no objections. On the contrary: reading had become a strong bond between them. Nina, though, was appalled. She did not want a son who shut himself up with books, who did not "mix," one of her favorite words. Since she read little to nothing, a son who read a great deal worried her. He could not be up to any good or fit into her world. Irritated, she constantly urged him to play outdoors. She wanted him to get better grades, to be popular in ways that fit her values. School was the training ground, the entranceway to success, power, and glamour. Little Gene was simply not trying hard enough to do the right thing. Frustrated, disappointed, with an explosive temper, more volatile because of alcohol, she felt compelled to exhort, then criticize, then hit. His fictional surrogate in *The Season of Comfort* is beaten at least once a month, at one time with a switch from a dogwood tree "until blood came, until his bare legs bled. . . . The light of her cigarette burned red in the dark . . . and when he tried to hold the stick she burned one of his hands."

Sometimes indifferent, at other times bossy, Nina was frighteningly unpredictable. Occasionally she was companionable, chatty in a way the boy liked, especially as he got older and more curious about the adult world. "My mother didn't play with me. But she talked. She was very interesting. I knew all about being a kid. I wanted to know about being an adult. She gave a crash course. . . ." His father was as smooth, as soft-spoken, as ever. Consequently, Nina sometimes was furious at both of them, and by the early

1930s Gene and Nina found it increasingly desirable to spend time apart, much more than business and different social schedules dictated. When Gene did not act decisively enough to meet Nina's demands, her nervous system always required that she do something, such as change Deenie's school or come up with some slogan or strategy. What she hotly favored one day she often seemed to have forgotten the next. One thing her son could count on, though: she would be neither approving nor dependable. The action or word that on one occasion would produce no response on another would result in what he began to identify as a Nina-like scene. He could see it coming: a carping, self-aggrandizing tone, an abruptness of gesture, a twist of her cigarette. At the Bancroft Place apartment the mahogany coffee table had two deep burns from Nina's cigarettes. It seemed best to stay away from her as much as possible. He had an attractive alternative. At Rock Creek Park he could play in the woods and walk down the steep lawn to the stream filled with salamanders, water moccasins, crayfish, frogs. It was rock-littered, iron brown. At the edge of the woods stood a dilapidated slave cabin, somehow connected to a war from long ago that the boy soon began to romanticize, unlike his grandfather, who detested the war from whose aftermath his entire generation had suffered. His grandmother thought that the Confederate boys had reaped well-deserved disaster, the result of their love of fighting, gambling, whoring, and shiftlessness. In the center of the woods a spring bubbled up from the gray sand out of which "I used to build elaborate sand cities, usually in the style of those I read about in . . . *Arabian Nights,* a book I never ceased to read and reread." He liked to sculpt in sand and soon to paint. Near the house, which had a circular drive in front and a small fountain, stood a sweet-smelling rose garden. Toward the border of the woods a small vineyard of purple grapes glowed, clusters of which he would cut for his grandfather and himself to eat. Inside, in the entrance hall, smells from the kitchen met the other odors of the house: the perfume of cut irises in a bowl, newly applied floor wax, the musty mysteriousness of thousands of dusty books.

He began to read voraciously, in good weather by the stream, otherwise in an attic alcove window from which he had a view of the grounds. Newspapers covered almost every inch of the attic floor, old clippings, the *Congressional Record.* Undusted shelves lining the room were heavy with books that the Senator incessantly collected. When "campaigning, the first thing he would do is get a telephone book and locate the used bookstores," with the help of his secretary, his last assistant, Roy Thompson, recalled. "If there was one close by, we went to that. Many times he knew the bookstore and the proprietor. He'd say, 'What have you got?' Meaning what have you got in the fields that I want, history, government, and so on. Finally, he'd have six or eight books. The Senator would pile them up and say, 'Now, how much for the lot?' Then he'd pay, have them wrapped up and have them sent home to him—to his house, not his office. . . . These books, usually still in their original packages, would be at home in Washington. He'd say to me, 'Do you know where the books are that we got in Cleveland?' 'No.' 'Well, Tot will know. There's a book in there I want.' We'd open the package, and there would be the book. He always remembered what books he had." Soon the boy could find them as readily as his grandfather. Upstairs or outside he would read to himself, downstairs in the drawing room, by the fireplace, to the Senator. It seemed a touch of paradise. In a short story of his young adulthood he returns to the house in Rock Creek Park and meets his youthful self, as if that part of him were still there in what he came to remember as the place in which he had spent his childhood. He hears, from the top of the hill, his grandmother's voice calling him to dinner.

Observing his grandfather impressed him deeply. There was his massive appearance: elderly, dignified, a stentorian voice, pithy, colloquial, with the touch of a Southern accent, which became more pronounced when constituents visited. Suddenly he transformed himself into a folksy Southwesterner from the Bible Belt. A rather "subdued household" became lively with homey good cheer. The atheistic Senator, one of whose favorite jokes was that "the one thing that an all-powerful God can't do is make a year-old heifer in a minute," suddenly seemed a good-natured believer. His wife was also a nonbeliever. "They saw the worst of religion in the Bible Belt. And he never let on that he was not with them," his grandson recalled. "My mother would complain as a child that she couldn't read the funny papers on Sunday. A lot of things were forbidden on the sabbath. They were trying to conform for fear that the neighbors would find out if they didn't. A lot of snooping going on. If you were doing the forbidden things on the sabbath, you were in trouble in Oklahoma. I think there were only two or three times that I went with him to church. A Methodist church. It was only because he knew the preacher." As soon as the constituents left, quietness returned. The accent became more Washington than Southwestern. His performance

might have been different for the various Oklahoma Indian chiefs who
visited and whose interests Gore represented. Four Indian headdresses, gifts
from grateful constituents, impressed the young boy. Later they were given
to the Smithsonian. Then there was his grandfather's blindness. It was both
familiar and fascinating, the mesmerizing glass eye, the Senator's early-
morning magical transformation into a dignified politician. His secretary
recalled shopping with him in New York. "This store had thousands of glass
eyes, different shapes, different colors. He'd put this one in and ask me,
'Does it match?' One eye was gone. There was just a socket. The other one
was there, but he couldn't see with it." With his cane held in front of him,
"he had a sense of the presence of things. I can remember only one time
when he came in with a bump on his head. Someone had left a door open,
and he ran into it." His sense of smell and touch were keen. He humorously
remarked that since he "could touch a piece of furniture and estimate its age
. . . that if he ever ran out of a job he could make a living working for an
antique dealer." The mother of a classmate of young Gene's "would take
him around the house and he'd touch things and say, 'Oh, no, this is a new
remake of an old design.' He could tell," Wilson Hurley recalled, "by the
flattening of the grain of wood in the furniture how long the furniture had
been in use."

Most impressive of all, there was his grandfather as politician, a man of
power to whom the people and the halls of power were an extension of the
home in which he lived. The telephone frequently rang with calls from
famous Washingtonians. In November 1930 political power became palpable
for the five-year-old boy: Oklahoma reelected the ex-Senator. Early in the
new year, he returned to the Senate chamber to reclaim, triumphantly, the
piece of paper he had secreted in his desk ten years before. He was also
happy to reclaim his salary of $15,000, having the previous year lost most of
his money in the stock-market crash. Little Gene went to the opening
session of the new Senate. Later he created a semifictional account of
watching his grandfather on the day of his celebratory return to that large
gray-green room of "white skylights and green carpets." From the balcony,
as his grandmother held him on her knees, he could see "rows of desks and
grown men [who] sat at them or else wandered about the room talking to
one another." The newly elected senators ceremoniously entered, none of
them more distinctive than his grandfather. Soon Little Gene regularly
accompanied him to his Senate office and onto the Senate floor. Occasion-

ally he would see him ascend, as senators did in rotation, to the chair of the Vice President, the presiding officer. One hot summer day Little Gene walked down the Senate aisle without shoes and wearing only short pants, to be stopped short by the usually inebriated Vice President, who remonstrated to Gene's grandfather, "Senator, this boy is nekkid!"

One of the advantages of his grandfather having been reelected was that Little Gene could get books from the Library of Congress in his grandfather's name. The attic at Rock Creek Park overflowed with historical works. But since the practical, puritanical Senator had little to no use for fairy tales and fiction, it was thin in the kinds of stories most vividly represented in the child's imagination by *The Arabian Nights*. To the surprise of the Library of Congress, requests began to come from Senator Gore for the novels of L. Frank Baum. Little Gene read them one after another. He invented additional characters, one of them "a nymph who lived in Rock Creek and ate only watercress. . . . At seven or eight I asked my father if there was any possibility that Oz existed. He said no. Oz was just a fiction, a dream. He tried to console me by saying that science was just as interesting and exciting as the world of magic. But I saw through that one." The same year his grandfather reentered the Senate, Little Gene wrote a "novel," which he read aloud to the family, "closely based on a mystery movie" he had seen. "The character based on my grandmother kept interrupting everybody because 'she had not been listening.' " The family found it hilarious. He also bought books with the occasional silver dollar his grandfather gave him for his services as reader. Soon he had a small library of his own. It included adventure bestsellers of the day like the Tarzan series, popular classics like *Prince Valiant,* and cartoon books in a series called "Big Little Books." The *Washington News* contained comic strips, "Popeye" and "Dick Tracy," which he did not like, and "Maggie and Jeeves" and "Li'l Abner," which he enjoyed. From the radio, which the blind Senator Gore often found companionable, came *The Shadow* and *Amos 'n Andy,* two of the most popular, unforgettable programs of the day. "The whole house was built around the evening hour when my grandfather would have his one drink of the day . . . and listen to *Amos 'n Andy.*" He also discovered movies. Beginning the year his grandfather returned to the Senate, Little Gene became obsessed with the silver screen. The past walked and talked in the darkness of a movie theater, in films which he was to see between 1932 and 1935 like *The Last Days of Pompeii, Roman Scandals, The Mummy, The*

Crusades, A Midsummer Night's Dream, A Tale of Two Cities, The Scarlet Pimpernel, Marie Antoinette. It was the beginning of one of his most intense periods of movie-watching.

In the spring of 1932 present history came distressingly alive. When he heard that thousands of protesting "Boners" who had assembled were encamped around the city, he thought they were "white skeletons like those jointed cardboard ones displayed at Halloween. Bony figures filled my nightmares until it was explained to me that these were not from slaughterhouses but from poorhouses." Impoverished World War I veterans who demanded a bonus were rumored to have attacked the Capitol and to be looting stores. He imagined skeletons on the march. When the Senate met to vote on the Bonus Bill, he drove to the Capitol with his grandfather, who opposed the legislation. Senator Gore also opposed the Social Security Bill. A blind man who had risen from poverty on his own initiative, he believed it morally wrong to give people money. It would destroy character. As the Senator's car got close to the Capitol, Little Gene saw shabby-looking men holding up signs. "Before we could pass through the line, Gore was recognized. There were shouts; then a stone came through the window . . . and landed with a crash on the floor between us. My grandfather's memorable words were: 'Shut the window,' which I did." General MacArthur's soldiers, on horseback, dispersed the Boners and cleared Washington of the threat. They did not, however, immediately clear away the refuse left behind. The next Sunday, Big Gene took his son for an airplane flight over what had been the Boners' encampment. "There were still smoking fires where the shanties had been. The place looked like a garbage dump, which in a sense it had been, a human one."

The value of money was a prominent theme in the Gore household. The young boy heard speeches on it regularly. For the Senator, personal and public finances needed to fulfill the same basic accounting principles. The government held the people's money in trust. A balanced budget and a sound currency, backed by gold, was the government's sacred responsibility. Any deviation should be opposed as a matter of unalterable principle. A child of economic catastrophes, from the Civil War in the South to the depression of the 1890s, the Senator had experience with economic hardship. He had learned to watch his pennies, to spend assets sparingly, to live in expectation of more hard times just around the corner. The Great Depression of the 1930s did not come as a surprise to Senator Gore. His underlying adage, for himself and for government, was "Neither a borrower nor a lender be," unless absolutely necessary. Little Gene heard that message repeatedly, not only from the Senator but also, in a different voice and tone, from his father, who had made his way in the world largely indifferent to money but always with so little that he too needed to restrict his expenses. He was not eager to spend money on his son, partly because he did not have it, partly by temperament. Both Senator Gore and Gene Vidal kept their purses closely guarded. Small gifts were forthcoming, coins and birthday presents. His grandmother was more generous. Not unexpectedly, his impulsive mother was sometimes handsomely generous. But her gifts came with the characteristic barb, with touches of exaggeration and hysteria. In 1933 "the Depression was on every tongue. Even I knew what it was. You could see it in the streets. People selling apples and so on. My mother gave me for my eighth birthday a painting set, watercolors, with a solemn speech that this would probably be the last present I would ever get, as the Depression was upon us and everyone was broke and there was no money in the land. Her refrain from that moment on was that I just didn't know the value of money, I was indifferent to the price of things. . . . Those speeches came out of her sense of drama. She no more understood the Depression than I did."

March 1933. The excited crowd in front of the Willard Hotel on Pennsylvania Avenue, opposite the Commerce Department, had gathered to view the inaugural parade, the newly elected President about to deliver his speech in front of the Capitol. A loudspeaker system, which had been installed along Pennsylvania Avenue so the waiting crowd could hear the speech, suddenly came on. The high-pitched, patrician, mid-Hudson voice of Franklin Roosevelt crackled through the air. "We could actually hear his voice, all that distance, because of these speakers. They were hung on the streetlamps. It was a public-address system. And it was out of synch. So he would say, 'WE HAVE NOTHING—we have nothing—WE HAVE NOTHING—we have nothing—BUT FEAR—but fear.' It was doing this funny blip-blip." From a voice that was to speak familiarly to Americans over the next decade, they heard his soon-to-be-famous words twice. As Gene and Nina went up, with Little Gene and a group of their friends, to watch the parade from a rented room in the Willard, Gene Vidal was hoping that he would serve in the new administration. From the hotel window they had a perfect view not only of the parade but of the classically columned Department of Commerce building on whose second floor Gene might have his new office. It was a moment of high excitement.

Vidal got the prestigious job of director of aeronautics by route of both competence and politics. Both were necessary. The competition had been stiff. Able to demonstrate, with the first frequency-per-mile analysis, that profits in the airline industry would increase to a satisfactory level with an increased number of flights, Collins and Vidal had made the Ludington Line a success. When after a year of operation the airline showed a net profit of over $8,000, the Ludingtons were ecstatic. Despite a November 1931 accident that killed two pilots and three passengers, the airline had established an industry standard for efficiency, low costs, and safety. "That whole period was one of the most glamorous in American history," Gore Vidal recalled. "And very dramatic, since everybody was getting killed all the time. Until I was twenty I thought half my father's friends wore neck braces for ornament; they always landed on their heads, those that weren't killed." Fear of flying, understandably, kept passenger numbers low. Those who had flown one way often would, if the weather looked bad, cancel return reservations and take the train. Gene devised the policy of selling only round-trip tickets. The first Ludington Line flight of the day was flown by one of their best pilots, who was to report immediately, when he landed, on the weather along the route. "If he reported the weather to be all right," Gene recalled, "then we sent out the later scheduled departures; if not, they stayed on the ground." For "carrying a load of passengers in those days of no radio or other contact with the ground gave you gray hair. . . . When one of our airplanes was en route we never knew where it was until we saw it approaching the airport. When a plane was late, with a load of passengers on board, we really sweated it out. We operators stayed right at the airport until all planes were in or accounted for, regardless of the hour." Some passengers would "build up their courage by imbibing heavily" before the flight. "Sometimes they would carry a bottle of liquor on board." Since the plane windows could be opened, they often flung the empty bottles out. The bottle would hit the propeller, which bounced the pieces back against the fuselage, putting holes through it. Finally the windows were fixed in place permanently.

Equally dangerous to the Ludington Line were rival companies, piranhas eager to dominate routes and profits, especially the Curtis-Key group, for whom Vidal had worked at TAT. Its subsidiary, Eastern Air Transport, competed for government mail contracts, without which Ludington could not survive. Passenger income alone failed to cover costs, and political clout and corruption concerning the mail routes shaped the emerging industry. To help strengthen Ludington in its competition with Eastern, Vidal and Collins offered a revision of their initial contract that would decrease their now runaway salaries and options. Based on performance, partly measured in cost per flight mile, their bonuses would transfer most of the company's assets to them. They revised the formula downward. The Ludingtons happily agreed. But the real threat to viability was from Curtis-Key's political clout. Though Vidal demonstrated in memo after memo the strikingly lower cost at which Ludington could transport mail, Herbert Hoover's postmaster general preferred to award the mail routes to Eastern Air, without competitive bidding, at rates two to three times what Ludington offered. Without mail contracts, the Ludingtons saw the handwriting on the wall. Still, they had high hopes for a while longer. Wanting a more direct role in decision-making, they were eager to consolidate their executive headquarters in Philadelphia rather than Washington, the site of the operational facilities. When they insisted that Vidal move to New Jersey, Gene refused. He "didn't want to be away from operations." Disappointed in his decision, Nicholas Ludington brought in as president a TWA executive whose main innovation was to spend large sums on what Vidal and Collins thought extravagant frills. Gene was not happy. The idea for the airline had been his. His efficient planning had resulted in profits. Though he would have been pleased to have been elevated to the top position, he had not been offered the title. Also, since Vidal's and Collins's incomes were based on an incentive cost-efficiency formula and since costs per mile increased under the new president, their incomes declined sharply. The Ludingtons' profits disappeared entirely. In about three months, a no-frills had been transformed into a no-profit airline. At the end of September 1932 Gene resigned. Eastern Air Transport soon made an offer to the unhappy owners. The Ludington Line disappeared forever.

Gene's imminent appointment as assistant director for air regulation, then director of aeronautics, was the result of his relationship with Amelia Earhart, whose influence with the First Lady and with the President had paved the way. Earhart's boyish good looks, her combination of willfulness and feminine charm, her eagerness to advance women into new roles and to champion their equality, her courage as a pioneering aviator eager to publicize the new industry and women's rights, even her few early years as a social worker, struck an admiring chord in the older woman. But, whereas Eleanor may have been enchanted with Amelia, Amelia was in love with Gene. They had met in 1929 when both worked for TAT. When they became lovers is unclear, as is the kind and extent of their lovemaking, though Gene apparently controlled the affair and kept it as nondisruptive as possible. By the late 1920s, Nina and Gene had gone their separate sexual ways, though perhaps still occasionally getting together. How much Gene knew or cared to know is unclear. Nina's affairs were casual, spontaneous pleasures, sometimes helped by or even dependent on alcohol, an extension of an afternoon's boredom or a late-night party. Working and traveling for work, handsome, always elegantly dressed, prominently in the national news, Gene Vidal had innumerable opportunities. Affairs were commonplace, divorces a nuisance. When, in February 1931, Earhart married George Palmer Putnam, it was, for her, mostly a marriage of convenience. She insisted on the right to sleep with whomever she wanted, partly a statement of her attempt to redefine marriage, partly an expression of lack of erotic feeling for Putnam.

For Earhart, who expressed her romantic side in poetry and in adventuresome flight, her career came first. For Vidal, whose taste was for younger women, feminine in their figures and attitudes, Earhart appealed more as pal than lover. About aviation matters, they rarely made a move without consulting. Between 1929 and 1931 they saw one another regularly on their travels to air shows and publicity events around the country as well as in New York and Washington. In the comfortable Westchester County, New York, home that Earhart and Putnam established, Gene was, weekend after weekend, a frequent visitor who Putnam unhappily knew was a special friend of his wife's. When Gene came up from Washington, Amelia would drive the long distance to the airport or the train station to pick him up and take him back. When Amelia's cousin fell in love with Gene, she soon realized that when Gene and Amelia were together, they had no interest in anyone else. As late as 1935 Amelia kept a silver hairbrush with her monogram in the bathroom of Gene's apartment in Washington, "her hairbrush with her little red hairs in it, an antique sterling silver hairbrush with a little oval in the center with her initials in old English lettering and around it embossed roses and daisies. I always figured," Gene's sister-in-law recalled, "they were more than business partners. . . . When I saw that hairbrush, it was as if she had just been at Gene's apartment. I'm sure she stayed overnight."

With a large number of candidates for the position of director, Roosevelt, urged by Earhart and others, appointed Gene Vidal assistant director for air regulation, pending the reorganization of the aeronautics division. Roosevelt expected William Roper, his Secretary of Commerce, to run the department cheaply, effectively, and politically. There were two key issues in the aeronautics division: (1) how to create as many patronage jobs as possible without undercutting the division's technical mission and (2) how to create on a minuscule budget (40 percent less than the division had had previously) the large number of safety changes needed to create public confidence in air travel. Any new director of aeronautics would have his hands full. Franklin Roosevelt, Jr., the President's son, without much clout of his own, had pushed Gene's credentials for the directorship. They had recently become friends. Rumor circulated that Senator Gore was lobbying for his son-in-law. Years later Nina claimed that she and her father were responsible for Gene's appointment. Gore had campaigned for Roosevelt. But Roosevelt hardly owed Gore a favor and probably sensed that the senator from Oklahoma would be more foe than friend to the New Deal. In late 1932 Gene's connection to Senator Gore may have been in his favor but, if a factor at all, it was insignificant: Amelia Earhart and Eleanor Roosevelt were his champions and, later, defenders. He was shortly in need of defense. In fact, his tenure as director of aeronautics became embroiled in controversies that had little to do with him. When he was promoted to director in September 1933, the political die had already been cast.

As director, constantly in the field, often flying himself around the country, Gene Vidal made news, much of it serious, some of it controversial. In December 1933 *Time* magazine, in the process of becoming the journalistic voice of American nationalism, had highlighted his success with the Ludington Line by devoting its cover to his handsome face. To the general public he became known as an advocate of a two-passenger personal airplane he hoped would be as widely used as the automobile, a kind of Model T Ford of aviation. Despite widespread media coverage, the idea did not take off, mostly because it proved to be more expensive, impractical, and complicated than he had anticipated. At a time of stringent budgets it seemed to many that the director should not be diverting money from issues of air safety to what appeared an impractical project. Congress was constantly fighting about aviation policy and implementation. Caught between a political assistant secretary of commerce and a scheming assistant to the director, Vidal was soon on the hot seat. When Roosevelt, in February 1934, for political reasons, without taking proper advice, abruptly canceled all commercial airmail contracts and instead required the Army Air Corps to deliver the mail, eleven Army fliers were killed in crashes and expensive equipment destroyed. There was an attempt to blame Vidal. When Vidal declined to do the bidding of the most powerful man in commercial aviation, Juan Trippe, who had taken him and others on a TWA South American junket, Trippe and his Hearst newspaper allies became vituperative enemies. When another series of crashes shocked the American public, congressional hearings tried to blame the director of aeronautics. A well-known senator had been killed in one of the mishaps. The hearings exonerated Vidal; none of the other charges stuck to him. What was clear was that in the face of an insufficient budget Vidal had done everything possible to improve air safety, to regularize the industry, to encourage technical innovation, and to gain support for aviation as an essential part of the current and future American infrastructure.

When, in 1936, it seemed Vidal would be forced to resign, Earhart made it clear in a telegram to the First Lady that she could not fulfill her commitment to campaign for the President's reelection if Vidal were dismissed. When the waves were smoothed, Amelia and Gene arranged that Vidal write to the vice chairman of the Democratic National Committee to tell her that Earhart would, after all, campaign for the President. "We are all very grateful to you for . . . getting Miss Earhart interested in working for President Roosevelt," she wrote back to him. The director of aeronautics did his share also. As technical adviser to the Democratic National Campaign Committee's air fleet, displaying pro-Roosevelt banners across the country, his thank-you was to be jokingly commissioned "Flight Commander of Roosevelt Aerial Caravans." No one, though, could last very long in such a high-risk position. There were too many masters to serve and too little money with which to serve. Not a politician by profession or temperament, Vidal was good neither at bureaucratic infighting nor at administering subordinates. Office work bored him. He preferred tinkering, inventing, dreaming, publicizing. Many of his ideas, inevitably, were overtaken by technical progress, especially faster, safer, more cost-efficient large airplanes and airports that made air travel economical and instilled public confidence in its safety. Always the good soldier, Vidal had placed his resignation in Secretary Roper's hands numbers of times. He had agreed to stay on at the Secretary's pleasure in order to prevent the impression that Roper had capitulated to the Senate committee investigating the crashes. But Gene was relieved when, in March 1937, he was at last out of government service.

Some months before the country had a new President and a New Deal, Little Gene had a new school. His three years at Sidwell Friends, from 1933 to 1936, now went by in a blur, focused mostly by his enthusiasm for organizing a gang of classmates. His games were mostly imaginary, invented characters or toy soldiers. He played organized team sports only when forced. On the field, as the game progressed, he relieved the tedium by thinking of other things. "One reason I didn't like football was the boredom of putting on and taking off all that gear. Even so, at an early school, I made what I thought was an unusually brilliant touchdown against what proved to be, on closer analysis, my own school." Tall, thin, alert, well coordinated, he seemed to others a likely athlete. His father's athletic fame prompted the assumption that he would follow in his footsteps even if he could not fill his shoes. From an early age he did everything short of insubordination to disabuse people of this notion. His father took it with his usual good grace. His mother was deeply disappointed, even angry, as if it were purposeful defiance. She wanted her boy to be like other boys, even more so. Though now in their arguments she made fun of her husband's athletic achievements, she wanted Little Gene to put down his books and take up his playthings. She could not stand that he preferred to be solitary. "She was always on about that, my not getting good grades and not being a good mixer, not being a well-rounded person, not being athletic. I'd have to turn over a new leaf, she'd say." When one day he reported to Nina that Tommy Hopkins had been bullying him, she gave him a dog leash and told him to smash Tommy with it. Nina knew how to fight. She believed in all-out war. Her son learned to fight, especially how to counterpunch. Going back to the playground, he smashed Tommy above the eye with the dog leash. Thereafter, Tommy and he played together without incident. Another local boy,

Jim Tuck, accompanied by his governess, became a target at the Bancroft Street playground. "Gene was always clever enough to lure mademoiselle into chasing him. Then Tommy would pounce on me, rip off my hat, and push me into the sandbox," Tuck recalled. At Sidwell Friends, Gene created a gang, imposing a game of his own on others. At one end of the playground there was "a tremendous pile of lumber" formed from "the collapsed frame" of an old building where both gravity and the boys created rooms and tunnels, a clubhouse from which girls were excluded. Gene asserted himself as "king of the lumber pile. . . . We had all been warned not to go inside the ruin, a haphazard pile . . . with many intricate passageways and dead ends—a maze of delight where we would hide out, preparing for war with other gangs." Though not physically aggressive, he learned to be verbally and, when necessary, physically preemptive or retaliatory, to dominate by force of personality, by verbal skill, by cunning. He had decided that he would rather be victimizer than victim.

With Gene's appointment in September 1933 as director of aeronautics, the Vidals moved back to Rock Creek Park. Contentedly casual about it, Vidal wrote to friends that "the Gores, Nina, and myself have joined in opening up our former home in Rock Creek Park. . . . Come out. . . . It's just like a visit to the country." Given the businesslike frugality of both the Senator and Director, Gene probably paid a share of the costs. At a salary of $8,500, when one could rent handsome quarters in fashionable areas for less than $200 a month, the Vidals could have afforded their own apartment. Nina probably was unhappy to be living again with her parents. Her relations with her mother were no better than ever. But Gene's busy schedule from airport to airport around the country made Rock Creek Park seem sensible. It also had the attraction to Nina of Mrs. Gore being available to look after Little Gene. Nina sustained a formidable social schedule, with all the advantages she believed were the sacred entitlement of someone whom the newspapers had taken to calling, usually with an illustrative photograph, "one of Washington's most attractive young matrons." That autumn a *Washington Post* article, "Capital's Beauty Experts Give Advice on Best Coiffures, Gowns, Jewels and Cosmetics for Each Type," headlined Nina as "The Dynamic Type. The constant play of emotions across the expressive and beautiful face of Nina Vidal, her enormous brown eyes and flexible, generous mouth, place her first on the list of Washington's dynamic beauties."

In spring 1934 young Gene was sent to camp, though Mrs. Gore would have been happy to have him summers also. A friend of Gene's recommended William Lawrence Camp in Tuftonboro, New Hampshire, named after the Episcopal Bishop of Massachusetts and run through the Boston Episcopal diocese. A camp for poor and middle-class boys, it had no social or economic cachet: it was not where the children of the famous and/or the wealthy went. Impressed by his friend's enthusiasm, perhaps also by the low fees (fifteen dollars a week), Gene deputized her to pass along to the Director some of his questions, particularly about the quality of the counselors. Frank Lincoln responded, "We have not had a moral problem in the eight years of the camp and Mr. Vidal can rest assured that as the father of two young boys, eight and four years of age, I am on the look-out at all times for just such situations. . . . I hope we will have the pleasure of having Mr. Vidal's son in camp." Gene soon wrote that they had decided to send "our boy, age 8, for the full camp period." Quite used to being relocated by fiat, and now to an unlikely place, Little Gene accepted that he was, so to speak, on the move again, another turn in the merry-go-round of semihomelessness.

———————

From its high points distant Mount Washington shimmered. With New Hampshire's immense Lake Winnepesaukee nearby and the White Mountains just beyond, William Lawrence Camp provided deep vistas, dark woods, and cold water. It was a lovely summer world of blues and greens, on its fine days brilliant, on rainy days damp and moldy, smelling of the water that seeped into everything. The seventy-five boys, from seven to fifteen years old, and the counselors, all college students, slept in wooden cabins. Each held eight boys and two counselors, though some increased their capacity with double-decker bunks. Each morning, dressed in navy-blue pants and blue sleeveless underwearlike shirts emblazoned with the camp monogram, the boys aired their blankets over juniper bushes. Meals were at a large nineteenth-century structure with sloping floors called The Farm House, everything bent with the dampness of decades. A covered porch, where boys could eat whatever the weather, extended from one side. Counselors' assistants served meals. The boys peeled potatoes. "The Army was nothing but *déjà vu,*" Vidal recalled. "When I went in as a private, I felt, Jesus, I've already done this once." There was a huge barn for theatricals. The usual sports: woodcraft, woodlore, hikes, camp trips, campfires, camp songs, ghost stories, silly practical jokes, and, in those more innocent days, a totemic Indian mystique that organized the older boys into an exclusive group called the Braves.

In a highly regularized routine of daily camp activities, each punctuated by bugle calls, he went through the paces indifferently, sometimes evasively. There were no bullies to deal with. The counselors were serious, responsible, or at least not harmful, all from the Episcopalian world, some from as far away as North Carolina. One of them, who looked like Billy Graham and was going to be a minister, escorted Little Gene home by train at the end of summer. With another, in his fictionalized version of the experience, he had discussions about the soul, unable to understand why the counselor thought "spiritual things cause an inner peace which is more important than worldly affairs." Another was "a very nice-looking boy. . . . From Princeton. I see him very clearly now. Ginger-haired with freckles. . . . He was a Communist, perfectly open about it. It was fashionable in the thirties. We had discussions. I was fascinated by it." Sex was not part of the atmosphere, though bed-wetting was. "About four in the morning everybody would be waked up to catch the bed-wetters. As I was not one of them, I resented being got out of bed just because they were trying to catch them. They had some psychological theory that if you could catch the boy before he was wetting the bed he wouldn't wet the bed. He'd go and do it outside."

Everything seemed routinized, boring. The elite Braves, dressed up like Indians at secret campfire meetings, were a club he did not wish to join. Every moment he could manage not to be missed he went back to the cabin or found some quiet outdoor place in which to read. Wisely, the camp authorities left him alone. One day Bob Bingham, later to be a friend at Exeter, who "especially remembered the required cold plunges into the lake in the early morning," and with whom he had been teamed at the swimming pond in the safety-conscious buddy system, could not find him in or near the water. The alarm was sounded. Was he perhaps at the bottom of the lake? The rumor spread that he had drowned. Desperately searching the camp, they found him back at his cabin, reading. It was a lapse in thoughtfulness he regretted. But the books he got from the camp library sustained him, some P. G. Wodehouse and, particularly, the complete set (about a hundred) of the Horatio Alger series, with whose hero he strongly identified.

Part of their appeal for his fictional surrogate in *The Season of Comfort* is "that all these marvelous boys became successful. . . . He made up his mind to make something of himself . . . to be like Horatio Alger," in the face of his mother's constant prediction that he would amount to nothing because he was lazy, spoiled, spendthrift. "Then, his mind made up . . . he made an effort, usually a futile one, to be a good mixer." Already interested in politics, part of the childhood air he breathed in his Washington family, he preferred to talk with the counselors. The Sunday Episcopal service seemed to him to consist of boring irrelevancies. Myths were to be analyzed, not believed in. The most pleasurable ritual was Sunday dinner, when the cooks were off, "the best meal of the week. We had these pitchers of milk made out of dented pewter set on large trestle tables; then we each had a bowl and a big spoon and there was box after box of square crackers and a big thing of peanut butter and a big thing of grape jelly. And you would break up the crackers, pour the milk over them, and add the peanut butter and jelly until you had this purple slime. It was the most delicious thing I've ever had in my life. We lived for Sunday-night mush."

The blue lake, the hilly vistas, the long hikes and camp trips to the mountains he also enjoyed. "We'd go over to Chocorua," to the area of John Hay's summer home in the last years of his life, Henry James's friend and Theodore Roosevelt's Secretary of State whom years later Vidal was to transform from history into fiction. "I remember that as a very beautiful spot. And the White Mountains. The hiking and the woods were wonderful." Somewhere close by, he later realized, William James had had his summer home. One of the long trips in the camp truck took the boys to northern New Hampshire, on the Vermont border, where the Lost River, cutting a narrow gorge, had carried two huge rocks so close together that they and the slight opening between them were called the "Lemon Squeezer." "You thought that once your head was through you could never get your body through, and then it was very hard to get your head through." Suddenly he felt trapped, imprisoned, gripped by a claustrophobic anxiety attack. His legs going out from under him, he pulled himself through the dark, tight space. The walls gripped him on both sides. They seemed to go on forever. At last he was out, only to learn that camp tradition required that each boy go through three times. "Many years later I was discussing this with a friendly psychiatrist . . . and I was curious about prenatal memories, as I still am. . . . And I had totally forgotten the

Lemon Squeezer, but I certainly remembered always having been claustro-phobic. This was exactly like being born: you put your head through this thing and you see a glint of light and can you get the hell through or not? And he said, 'Well, that could qualify as a prenatal memory, if indeed there are such things,' and he said, 'Ask your mother.' So I asked her, and she said yes, she had a very narrow pelvis and that it was a near thing whether there'd be a cesarean and it was a very difficult birth and the back of my head was indented by her narrow pelvis."

At the end of summer 1934 he returned to Washington, to the second of the three years at Sidwell Friends School, now not only the grandson of a well-known senator but the son of a glamorous, newsmaking public official. In October 1934 the grandmother who had seen him only once, Margaret Vidal, died at the age of sixty-four in Madison, North Dakota. When he was still two, in 1928, his Vidal grandparents had seen their grandson briefly in a Chicago hotel when Gene and Nina were passing through by train. In early 1935 Felix Vidal died, at the age of seventy-three. "He had been exceedingly low since the death of my mother," Gene wrote to a relative. "Father was quite lonely and completely through with life." Gene had managed to keep both his parents away. There is no indication that Nina had met them other than the one occasion in Chicago. Margaret and Felix were not averse to travel: they had numbers of times visited their eldest daughter, Lurene, Gene's favorite sister. She had married Lloyd Jones, a successful stockbro-ker, and moved to Jackson, Michigan, not far from Detroit. On his own frequent travels, Gene occasionally visited his family in Madison and more often Lurene in Jackson, but he chose to provide Little Gene with no memories of Margaret and Felix. For the young boy, the Vidal grandparents were other people's images. Lurene soon came into focus as his formidable aunt. Gene's youngest sibling, named after his father but nicknamed Pick, had come into sight during the 1931 and 1932 football seasons, when the young cadet became the second Vidal to set records for West Point. Just twenty years old, Pick, working as a lifeguard, spent one summer with the Vidals in Washington, where he found Nina attractive.

Young Gene found his mother both attractive and difficult. Senator Gore's new secretary, the young Oklahoman Roy Thompson, who often came to the house to read to the Senator and each Sunday brought the newspaper, was shocked to walk by an open door through which he saw Nina naked from the waist up. Ten-year-old Deenie was in the room.

Suddenly catching Thompson's eye, she looked at him unflinchingly. "That was ordinary and normal for Nina," her son recollected. So too was her drinking, which had become frequent, sometimes heavy. After parties she hosted, when the guests had left, she finished the liquor that had been left in glasses. So too were her sexual adventures, often extensions of partying or titillation to relieve boredom. A servant reported some years later that Nina had spent an hour in her bedroom, one hot Washington afternoon, with her black taxi driver. The enchantment had long gone out of the marriage. Nina "was frivolous and always wanted to party, and Gene was worn out from working all day," Gene's sister-in-law remembered. She complained that she would be a better wife if Gene were a more available husband. When Deenie returned from camp in the late summer of 1934, he could not help but know his family life would soon change radically. There was occasional discussion of his future, including sending him to boarding school. That might speak effectively to Gene's travel schedule, to Nina's social whirl, to the unstable home life other than the stability the Gores provided. In April 1934 James Henderson, former coach of the University of South Dakota football team, now chaplain and math teacher at St. Albans School in Washington, had urged Gene "to consider St. Albans as a future school for your young son. We've got a fine school here and if you are at all interested come out and let us show you the works." Henderson also ran a summer camp to which he asked his old friend to consider sending his son. Gene was interested in St. Albans. "I believe it would be a good idea if we brought him out . . . one of these days, probably on Sunday, and talk with you about sending him to your school. We have been discussing the possibilities of sending him to a boys' school next year." But nothing came of it for the time being.

Sometime early in the 1930s Nina began an affair with the wealthy John Hay Whitney. It was slightly complicated (perhaps enriched) by Gene having an affair with Whitney's wife, Elizabeth. Which pair had started first did not seem to be an issue. By the fall of 1934 Nina was dreaming about marrying "Jock," whose influential family had made a fortune in newspaper publishing. Liz, in love with Gene, apparently would have been delighted to marry him or at least have him entirely to herself. Full-figured, athletic, she was stunningly attractive. "She wore her dark hair parted in the center, pulled back very tightly into a bun. She was funny, amusing, very beautiful. Her features were chiseled, a gorgeous nose, very wealthy and uneducated."

Ten years younger than Gene, she came from an old-line Philadelphia family. Her passion was horse breeding, horse racing, and beautiful dogs. To Little Gene, the exotic, animal-loving, regal-looking Liz seemed a desirable alternative to his mother. "She always had certain little dirt marks in the wrinkles around her neck. She was out there in the stables all day, and sometimes she didn't get around to bathing very carefully. But she was so beautiful, with her worn-down Indian moccasins; looked like an Indian princess. Black flashing eyes. . . . She was breathtaking. She looked like she should be on a stamp."

Jock Whitney's looks were not an issue. Accomplished, wealthy, powerful in the world of finance, media, and government, Whitney was someone Nina was eager to have. When Liz met Gene, "she liked him right away, and Nina said to Liz, 'You try and do something with him.' So Liz did," Gene's sister-in-law recalled. "She took him over. While Nina and Gene were still married." One evening Nina ran into Liz and Gene at a cocktail party at which she did not expect her husband. Caught off guard, "she went over and slapped Gene in the face." That may have had mostly to do with her mood that day. Nina was sleeping with Jock, among others. The "among others" finally led to the inevitable end of a tired marriage between incompatible people. "There was a guy called Doggy Waggerman, ugly but suave. He sold yachts to the rich. And when my father would not go out to parties and she wanted to go to bed," Gore was later told, "Doggy Waggerman would escort my mother. One night [in late winter or early spring 1935] my father was asleep and my mother came home. He found her in the bathroom douching herself. And he said, 'Well, Doggy Waggerman, of all people.' And she said, 'So what?' And that was the end of that." In that same year Eugene Luther Vidal, Jr., going on ten years of age, sat reading in an alcove in his grandfather's attic, deeply absorbed in a novel that seemed then and later to be almost preternaturally about himself. *The Spartan,* published originally under the title *Coward of Thermopylae,* by the now forgotten Caroline Dale Snedeker, is an example of a Victorian literary genre that retold classical legend, myth, and history as exemplary moral tales for Anglo-American adolescents. It is the story of Aristodemos, son of Lykos of Athens, whose Spartan mother, Makaria, takes Aristodemos back to her native Sparta after her husband's death. An Athenian of birth, valor, and high character, whose closest friend is the poet Pindar, Lykos has been killed in an athletic accident. Aristodemos is ten years old at the time, the same age at which, with total identification, Little Gene read *The Spartan,* whose title he unconsciously changed in his memory and always remembered as *The Athenian.* It is a tale of the triumph of individual courage and self-fashioning in the face of a mother's unloving rejection and a society's hostile narrow-mindedness.

———

As the express train left Union Station for Chicago in May 1935, Deenie played in the aisle with a toy silver train much like the Super Chief, which he had been given as a present. "I can remember playing with it, running up and down, wondering why I was doing that. Ordinarily I would be reading." Nina and he were on their way to Reno. Change and dislocation were becoming familiar to him. Later he was to develop a talent for self-consciously creating attractive places in which to live. Used to traveling from an early age, he was in the future to make certain that he had a home from which to leave and one to which to return. As the train pulled out of the station, Nina broke down and cried. Though she had long fallen out of love with Gene Vidal, she was off into the unknown, leaving one marriage behind, not certain what was next. She could, as always, fall back on her parents. But she (as well as they) would prefer that she manage on her own. She had in mind marrying someone rich. As he saw her tears falling, her son tried to be comforting. He got a nasty look. "That was the last time I made that error." As the train gathered speed, her spirits quickly improved. They were booked for a six-week stay at a Nevada dude ranch that accommodated ladies who desired to stay the time required to establish Nevada residency. Nina looked forward to having a splendid time in the divorce capital of the world.

The Washington agreement provided her with 40 percent of Gene's income for "her own use and benefit and the support, maintenance and education of Eugene L. Vidal, Junior, minor son of the parties." But 40 percent of $8,500 was a small sum on which to maintain her standard of living. Aware of this, she knew that without remarriage her current life was unsustainable. She had no career. She was not about to become a salesgirl to eke out a few dollars to provide a slightly better life for her son. John Hay Whitney was her target, though another eligible man had just appeared on the scene: Hugh D. Auchincloss, a wealthy Washington stockbroker. Of Scots origin, the large, disparate Auchincloss family's American originator had established himself at the beginning of the nineteenth century in New York City as a dry-goods merchant. An excellent businessman, he soon became rich. Over the next century and a half his descendants prospered in business and/or in economically advantageous marriages. Hugh Auchincloss's branch had become wealthy through his father's marriage to Emma Burr Jennings, the daughter of one of John D. Rockefeller's partners in Standard Oil. An unassuming man, attracted to aggressively high-spirited women, Auchincloss was taken with Nina, with her liveliness, her assertiveness, her sense of entitlement, her wide web of Washington political and social connections. To "Hughdie," as he was known to his friends, she was an exciting lady. With a son by his first wife, he was now eager to remarry the right woman. Nina at first did not reciprocate. He seemed to her a gray, blank man, hardly there when there. Though rich, he was neither handsome nor glamorous. Her eye, of course, was on Whitney, who had Auchincloss's main attraction and many others as well. Vidal, of course, needed Nina to remarry someone, the richer the better: 60 percent of $8,500 would not go very far even for an economical bachelor. Her remarriage would reduce his obligation to 20 percent, exclusively for his son's support. If he himself were to marry Liz, she would make her new husband and son comfortable with the piles of money she would get from Jock. If Nina were to marry Whitney, his money would make life easier for Gene and luxurious for her.

At the TH Ranch near Pyramid Lake north of Reno, they lived in comfortable cabins and dined in the Big House. Nina complained about the food. Gene saw nothing wrong with it except that there was a definite connection between the calves regularly slaughtered, skinned, and dissected in full sight of the paying guests and the tough steak on the table. In this small, fertile valley, surrounded by desert, trees and flowers flourished, horses were cosseted, cattle grazed. At Nina's insistence Gene had riding lessons. She required that he ride bareback. "She had been told by someone that that was the only way to become a good rider." His fictional counterpart in *The Season of Comfort* often goes riding with the niece of the ranch owner, to whom he tells stories about his Washington life. In return she guides him through the desert and shows him where to find gray river clay, which he uses to sculpt. The paint set his mother had given him for his eighth birthday had been put to good use. He had also discovered that he had a talent for making clay heads and figures, an activity that gave him much pleasure throughout his adolescence. The Oz books were on his mind, particularly the magical incantations whose spells and powers he used to imagine himself invisible or others frozen in place. With another divorcée-to-be, whom he remembered simply as Rosemary, he had long conversations. Lonely, good-natured, perhaps missing children of her own, she apparently found the young boy companionable. "My mother hated her, so there were scenes over my talking to Rosemary." Meanwhile, Nina was busy, enjoying the cowboys, some of whom considered the ladies-in-residence a fringe benefit.

As usual, "Nina was popular at the ranch," or such is the way Gore Vidal later depicted her in his fictional version. She loved playing cowgirl. "Every evening she went into Reno or to another ranch for parties. He didn't see her very much. When he did, she criticized his riding. If he complained about anything, the food, for instance, in imitation of her, she would tell him to stop his 'beefing'; she used many Western phrases now and she swore a great deal." One of her favorite phrases, "Let's face it," usually followed by some amazing realization about herself or others, such as "Let's face it, I'm just too self-sacrificing," began to ring in his ears. Suddenly Hugh Auchincloss appeared. In pursuit of Nina he had made the long train trip from Washington. Nina met him at the station in Reno. "Looking out of place in his banker's suit," pale against the deep tan of Nina and son, he probably had already proposed marriage. "Would he like him for a stepfather?" Nina privately asked Little Gene. "I said no, largely on aesthetic grounds." There was nothing dislikable about Auchincloss. But in comparison to his graceful father, Hugh, with his business suit, his owlish glasses, and his stammer seemed dull and cumbersome. Gene much preferred Jock Whitney. So too did Nina.

After the divorce was granted in Reno on July 3, they immediately returned to Washington, from which young Gene was shipped up to William Lawrence Camp again, for his second summer, much like the first. He would have preferred to stay with his grandparents at Rock Creek Park. Gene and Nina had each taken apartments, Nina at the well-known Wardman Park Hotel. Gene was busy at the Commerce Department and around the country, Liz Whitney much on his arm at social events. They were also *in* one another's arms. Many expected the couple switch to take place, the marriage partners to be exchanged. Soon Liz was to start divorce proceedings. But the negotiations were to be difficult, the lawyers' bills immense. Whitney's attorneys took a hard line. "So Liz, thinking of the best way of fighting back, just went over to the White House one day to see Franklin Roosevelt," Gore Vidal later remarked. "Just like that. No appointment. In fact, she used to go over about once a month and ask for all the news so that she didn't have to read the newspapers. And the President would gladly give her a general rundown on what was going on in the country. And this time she went in and said, 'Look, Jock and I have come to the end,' and here is Roosevelt sitting with the whole world falling to pieces about him: 'I've got to get a good divorce lawyer.' 'Well,' he said, 'I was never a divorce lawyer, but my partner, Miles Hern, is very good at trusts.' 'I took Franklin's word for it,' she later said, 'and I got cheated. By Jock's people anyway.' " Fortunately, neither Liz nor Gene was under extreme financial pressure. Liz was wealthy. Gene had enough on which to manage. Nina, though, was in trouble. In response to Hugh's proposal, Nina had said, "Oh, nonsense!" But in early July the Associated Press story on the divorce had reported that "Mrs. Vidal was recently reported to be planning a second marriage to Hugh D. Auchincloss, Washington broker, but her attorney . . . said he was 'personally satisfied' she had no such intention, at least for the present."

Back from summer camp, now in fifth grade at Friends, on the evening of his tenth birthday Gene was delighted to welcome his father's visit to his mother's apartment. His parents appeared more relaxed with one another than ever before, which he attributed to the divorce. On the subject of Deenie, Nina was expansively self-congratulatory. What an excellent job she had done as a single parent! Actually, she had been a single parent for only two months, and he had been at home with her only since the beginning of September. "Gene politely agreed with her. Then they discussed money, an urgent subject, always, with her, and one of no interest to him or me. I fell asleep," Gore Vidal wrote in his memoir. "I gather now what they had really discussed was the necessity of her marriage to Hugh D." Whitney had disappointed her. That marriage was not going to happen; it was time for the fallback position. While Auchincloss was on vacation in Europe, Nina had reached the glum conclusion that, with limited means and no Whitney, she was going to marry "the last person on earth she wanted to marry." Hughdie had apparently given Nina a marital blank check. He awaited her signature. Excited by Nina's attractions, he was eager for marriage to one of Washington's most glamorous ladies. In anticipation, he purchased a fifty-acre estate on the south bank of the Potomac in McLean,

Virginia, where he was building a huge neo-Georgian brick house called Merrywood, reminiscent of Mount Vernon in design but not scale. Nina made a condition of her consent that Hughdie not insist on their having sexual relations, "an informal prenuptial agreement" that "theirs would be a *mariage blanc,*" partly because she found him unattractive. She also believed, so she told her son, Hughdie was partly or mostly impotent. Though enchanted by his bride-to-be, he was still lucid enough to require a prenuptial agreement that granted Nina in the event of divorce only a fixed income of $1,000 a month for life. It was a substantial sum at a time when a United States senator's salary was $15,000 a year. But there was no provision for inflation. Why Nina allowed herself to be excluded from all claim against Hughdie's wealth beyond this amount is not clear. Apparently, though flexible on much else, he (or his lawyers and friends) were unalterable on this point. Hughdie assumed that Nina would be alterable on her condition about their sexual life. At least that was an "informal agreement."

Soon after his tenth birthday, sitting in class, young Gene was called out by his teacher. There had been a telephone call. Would he please come to the office? His mother was about to be married, and he was wanted at the wedding. "The announcement comes as a surprise," Washington was to learn in the next day's newspaper, "to members of Capital society, as no previous announcement had been made, although rumors had predicted the event since Mrs. Vidal returned from Reno several months ago." In a ceremony performed by a Presbyterian minister as the mid-October twilight darkened, Nina changed her name from Vidal to Auchincloss. She was now married to one of the wealthiest men in Washington. Little seemed to faze her, including that she did not in the least love him. For the second time her father was not at her wedding. Both her parents were in distant Oklahoma, the Senator preparing for his primary campaign the next spring. Relations between Nina and her parents were no better than they had ever been. This time "the bride wore a frock of dark gray velveteen fashioned with long sleeves and an ankle-length skirt." She looked beautiful, though noticeably less youthfully innocent than in her first wedding pictures thirteen years before. When the wedding story appeared the next day in the *Washington Post* under the heading "An Attractive Autumn Bride," Nina and young Gene were already in their new home.

CHAPTER three

First Flight

1935–1939

THE DESCENT down the hazardous rocky decline from the lawn at Merrywood to the banks of the Potomac he found both exhilarating and frightening. The river ran swiftly, especially in bad weather, white water breaking around small snags and islands. Warned never to swim in it, he was attracted to the river then and later in lifelong dreams that had a touch of nightmare to them, the descent "to the swift mud-brown, swirling river—going faster and faster, ecstatically unable to stop until the dream's end." The river was excitement, escape. Standing grandly on the high bluff, Merrywood was dull, problematic, philistine. The morning of his first night there, in mid-October 1935, he found his mother, wrapped in a dark-gray silk dressing gown, sitting on a step of the main staircase below the bedrooms. Probably, as always, she was smoking. This time she was flicking the ashes of dissatisfaction. During her nuptial night she had seen the abyss. Her complacency and self-confidence had been shaken. Sex with Hugh Auchincloss was a disaster. Could she face a lifetime of that? "Would you like us both to leave here and go back to live with your father?" she asked. Stunned, he mumbled that they had just arrived. Nina, according to her son, soon raised with Gene

Vidal the possibility of a reconciliation. He politely declined. She later widely reported that he had asked her to return to him, an offer *she* had declined because young Gene had stated that he preferred the advantages of life at Merrywood. She may have meant that she herself preferred them. Soon she learned to cope with Hugh's inadequacies as a lover. Eager for satisfaction, she found it in other places. Yusha, Hugh's son by his first marriage, tactfully remarked that Nina "did some things which hurt my father a great deal, and I was very close to my father and I resented that." Even young Gene came to sympathize with Hugh. Merrywood's only practical disadvantage was that it kept him away from what he thought his true home, at Rock Creek Park. Like Aristodemos, he felt in exile from Athens.

At Merrywood, Nina had no need of her mother to take care of Gene. "We were brought up by servants. It was the servants you played games with," servants such as Marguerite, Yusha's French governess. "I had a black nurse called Annie, and there were the servants of the house like Maria, my mother's maid. They kept us company." It was far from all bad. Maria "was a wonderful Bavarian woman, a great deal of fun. She spoke with a heavy accent. . . . We used to have seltzer fights in the pantry, the two of us. She seemed a hundred to me. But she was about fifty." Yusha's governess, whom Gene adored, also found him grown-up enough to play games with, his sexual initiation, though Gore Vidal declines to say exactly what they did. Jealous, protective, sensing something erotic between Marguerite and Gene, Nina fired her. She also gradually cleaned out the servants inherited from Hugh's first wife, including the Russian cook whose aromatic dishes Gene had found one of the most attractive aspects of Merrywood when he had first arrived. Also, she immediately began to have much of the house redecorated, her particular obsession a stunningly distinctive black-and-white art-deco recasting of her bathroom and bedroom. With Yusha, Gene battled for space and dominance. As at school, Gene wanted to be in charge. Yusha fought back. He had been there first. Gene was "a bully and invading my territory. . . . One day I got annoyed at him and punched him in the nose. Since that moment he became more respectful and we got along much better."

With Nina, Gene began to assert himself. Tall, thin, strong for his age, "he couldn't really be pushed around physically anymore." Nina stopped slapping him. But she was still mercilessly critical. Why was she always making sacrifices, she wanted to know, for him and for others, all of whom were ungrateful? Why was he so selfish and inconsiderate? Why didn't he mix more? Of what use was his reading, especially when he should be doing homework? Her complaints about everyone who did not measure up to her high standard of self-sacrifice were a regular part of life at Merrywood, including her good-humored comment every evening that Hugh's huge stuffed-marlin trophy above the dining-room fireplace took away her appetite. Why couldn't they get rid of that? When Liz Whitney gave Gene a toy Scottie, Nina claimed that the dog was a present for her. At Rock Creek Park there had been dogs, particularly a dalmatian given to Gene as a gift, but they could not get comfortable with one another: the dog scratched him badly. Also, any dog had to be kept out of the way of his blind grandfather. He immediately adored the toy Scottie, whom he named Wiggles. Nina, though, insisted that Wiggles was hers. To make the point, she brought him into her room at night. When he whined and scratched at the door, eager to be out, she became angry at the dog and at Gene. Soon she insisted that Wiggles be kept in a small pen behind the house. He was never allowed inside again. To Gene it seemed that Wiggles was being imprisoned, a victim of some of the same forces by which he himself was threatened.

By nature generous, amiable, fair, Hugh was a quiet man. He treated Gene well, especially with expensive presents. The first Christmas at Merrywood had a luxurious plenitude. The magnificent tree everyone helped decorate, the parties, the dinners, the mountain of gifts—all sharply contrasted with the modest Christmases at Rock Creek Park. The Great Depression's widespread economic misery hardly touched even the consciousness, let alone the actuality, of Merrywood. It was a world in which capital was king, in which Roosevelt was the devil who would destroy their civilization, in which Jews were evil socialists, the Irish ignorant papists fit only to be servants, and blacks essentially unchangeable primitives one step above the jungle. It was a network of powerful people whose wealth and social prestige defined itself partly by its high sense of entitlement. What was most important was to protect wealth and property. Nina gladly shared Hugh's high-Wasp life, and she brought to it, to her husband's delight, her own family and connections. Merrywood became a social center, briefly. Though Hugh was "a quiet but sincere anti-Semite," a few well-known Jews were invited, such as Walter Lippmann. Unmarried couples, like the journalist Arthur Krock and his lady, could come as long as they slept in separate rooms, though they were well known to be lovers. Appearances mattered. Senator Gore and his wife visited. Hugh was eager to have them: the Senator's anti-Roosevelt, anti–New Deal populist conservatism had much in common with the right-wing politics of Merrywood.

In Nina's hard-drinking world not to consume punishingly heavy amounts of alcohol would have been unusual. The son of one of Nina's friends, Patrick Hurley, Hoover's Secretary of War, remembered her drinking and her beauty. "In my society—northern Virginia, 1930s—a gentleman would consume in a day eight ounces of neat whiskey. You'd have highballs before supper, then drinking with dinner, and then drinks after dinner. These guys weren't lushes, and the whole society accepted this. To see someone take two or four drinks was not exceptionable, and what was frowned upon was he who took so many drinks that he lost control of himself and got into contentious arguments or fights, or women who got emotional and stormed out of the house . . . that we would look upon as so-and-so drinks too much." Even the more temperate Gores drank. The Senator enjoyed his two glasses of whiskey each evening. Mrs. Gore, more often than the Senator liked, drank too much at dinner and slurred her speech. The Senator's two brothers, successful lawyers, were heavy drinkers. Nina had already mastered the trick of keeping her disposition sweet in public, though she had consumed prodigious amounts of alcohol, then showing the pernicious effects afterward, privately, with her family. Probably her adjustment to her sexually unsatisfying marriage included increasing her drinking. It soon became talked of as excessive. Mostly family and servants, though, were in the line of fire. Years later one of her close friends remarked to Nina's son, "the thing I never could understand is that we would go to a party together and we would drink along with everybody else. I never saw her drunk at a party. Then I talked to her the next morning and she would say, 'I've got a terrible hangover—call me later.' . . . It was then I figured out that she got through the party without behaving disgracefully, then went home and drank a bottle. And started telephoning and denouncing everybody that she had a grudge against, a great trait of alcoholics."

As the liquor flowed downstairs, Gene usually stayed in his attic bedroom with his toy soldiers. Over time Hugh added large numbers of them to a collection that eventually reached more than three thousand. To the usual Christmas presents of tennis rackets, baseball gloves, and guns he was indifferent. He mostly wanted books. The toy soldiers, which became a pleasurable, imaginative preoccupation, he would deploy "by the hour" in reenactments of historical and literary battles of the sort he read about in Sir Walter Scott or saw in movies, "inventing stories for them, mostly nonmartial." In his mind now he could be an author himself, a writer like Scott, a creator of movie scripts like *The Crusaders*, imaginative extensions of what he read and saw, "an endless series of dramas." The family dramas he desired to escape. Those of the imagination, endlessly triggered by the toy soldiers, he embraced. There were, occasionally, contiguous public dramas. In December 1936 the family gathered around the radio in Nina's art deco bedroom to listen to the soon-to-be–Duke of Windsor's abdication speech. Tears flowed. Soon they were happily listening to the radio account of George VI's coronation. In the movie theaters, Pathé News provided memorable images of both occasions, grand spectacles of the sort Gene experienced in his attic theater with his own cast of thousands. Later he was to remark that though the Duke of Windsor, whom he knew in the ex-monarch's old age, "was of a stupidity more suitable to the pen of Wodehouse than of Shakespeare, he was to me forever glamorous because he had been artfully screened for me all my life, as had his family." Leaving the Translux Theater with his father, he was riveted by a display in the lobby of a miniature version of the coronation coach and horses. He desperately wanted it. By necessity and temperament always careful with money, his father "made an insufficient offer to the manager of the theater. Later I acquired the coach through my stepfather." It was a brilliant addition to his stage sets. Real and imaginative history merged.

The Pathé News of the Week movie camera turns. A blond ten-year-old and his father are standing beside a small, odd-looking airplane at Bolling Field, Washington. The boy wears short pants and a white polo shirt. The man is handsomely dressed, comfortable with the camera, a movie-star face. The boy's nervousness shows, his full face and turned-up nose, his youthful complexion glowing in the camera's black-and-white tones. The voice-over announces that the director of aeronautics has high hopes this prototype Hammond flivver will be the airplane of the future that everyone will own. Even a child can fly it. The dialogue begins. "We want to find out whether a ten-year-old youngster can handle it. What do you think?" Eagerly: "Sure, I'll try it!" His back to the camera, the bare-legged boy climbs, crawls in, takes the pilot's seat. His father follows. The camera closes on young Gene's hands demonstrating the controls, his father beside him. Gene Vidal gets out. If he stays, everyone will think he has piloted the plane. It slowly glides down the runway. The camera moves in. The boy is at the wheel. As the plane lifts off the ground, the boy-pilot is visible, behind him the larger silhouette of another figure. The plane makes a turn, disappears from the camera's eye, reappears, then descends, hitting the ground with a bump, then another, until it comes to a stop. The camera and his father greet the boy as he steps out. More dialogue. "What was it like?" "Easy." Boy grins for a second at camera, more like an aborted smile. Cut. Camera stops. The next week in the movie houses of the nation audiences watched the Pathé News brief feature in the usual snippet of news-as-entertainment. "Ten Year Old Boy Flies Airplane." Will Gene Vidal's dream of everyman in the air come true? If everyone can afford a car, won't everyone be able to afford a plane? Is a new era in flying about to dawn? The child watches himself on the screen at the Belasco Theatre.

On a warm Saturday afternoon in early May 1936 his father had picked him up at Friends School. As they drove off in Gene's signature nondescript Plymouth, the streets smelled of melting asphalt, the landscape was bright with the lush greens of late spring. He was hardly surprised when they pulled up at Bolling Field; he had been there many times for flights in Gene's small Commerce Department Stinson monoplane. On weekend days they would take pleasure trips around the Washington area, over the Maryland and Virginia countryside, regularly exhanging roles, one as navigator, the other pilot. They flew only in good weather, navigating done partly with gasoline-station road maps, mostly by sighting landmarks, following roads and railroad tracks. To the young boy it was now old hat, flying no longer a thrill. But this was to be different, not for them but for the camera. Suddenly he was excited, thrilled. The obsessive movie-watcher now realized he was about to have the chance to be in the movies. Imagining himself another Mickey Rooney, recently circumnavigating the globe as Puck in Max Reinhardt's version of *A Midsummer Night's Dream*, he too was about to fly into fame, so he allowed himself to fantasize. " 'Well, you want to be a movie actor,' " Gene said, " 'so here's your chance. All you have to do is remember to take off into the wind.' " As they parked, his father explained what he wanted him to do: take off, circle once, land, then answer a few questions. When asked what it was like to fly the Hammond flivver, he must stick to the script: "It was just like riding a bicycle." At the field, the plane waited. So too the camera and movie crew directed by Pathé News' premier cameraman, who had already filmed Gene Vidal many times. Gene's assistant hovered solicitously. Soon the camera rolled, father and son speaking their semirehearsed lines. Young Gene could not keep his eyes off the lens.

As they stepped up to the airplane, he felt the excitement of his acting premiere. He was not, though, to have the distinction of flying solo. Though more newsworthy, the news would not have been all favorable. It would have set a record for youngest person ever to fly alone. It would also have broken the law. That had been and would be done by others for the sake of the record. As director of aeronautics Gene Vidal was in no position to allow the law to be broken on camera. To be legal, the boy needed to be accompanied. They decide that Gene's assistant, who himself could not fly, would crouch in the small back seat, the size of a suitcase, as much out of sight as possible. Young Gene's father does the on-camera talking, joking deadpan about his age and whether he's sure he can fly the thing. With Gene beside him in the cockpit, young Gene demonstrates the landing gear. Then he is sitting alone, except for the man partly hidden behind him. Calmly, he starts the engine. He begins to feel anxious, not about the flight but about the camera. Will he perform well enough to be the new Mickey Rooney? He is experiencing the beginning of stage fright. Fastening his seat belt, he taxies downfield, starts the run. Soon the plane rises, the field falls below. Frightened, Gene's assistant keeps repeating superfluous advice about not flying into the wind. As he takes the plane on its circle above the field, he has no trouble keeping it stable. Then he circles again, which is not in the script, and brings the plane down. It hits the field hard, bounces, bumps, slows to its landing. Everyone is relieved. Young Gene's mind is now entirely, self-consciously, on the camera. How will he look? Will he be a success? When he steps out, the cameraman asks, for the world's ears, what it was like to fly the plane. Terrified, young Gene begins to lose his voice. He forgets his lines. "I said, 'Oh, it wasn't much' . . . and I stammered incoherently." Gene fills in. He turns to his son and gives him the cue again. "I remember the answer that he wants me to make: it was as easy as riding a bicycle. But, I had argued, it was a lot more complicated than riding a bicycle. Anyway, I am trapped in the wrong script. I say the line. Then I make a face to show my disapproval. . . . Finally I gave what I thought was a puckish, Rooneyesque grin." As he watched it in the Belasco Theatre, he "shuddered in horror at that demented leer which had cost me stardom." He had wanted to be a movie star, not a "newsreel personage."

The next month, in June 1936, also recorded by newsreels, the sixty-six-year-old Senator Gore crashed politically. After a primary campaign in which he emphasized his populist themes, he was decisively rejected by the Oklahoma Democratic Party. State politics and the temper of the times had turned against him. He seemed old-fashioned, inflexible. Also, having done legitimate legal work for one of the convicted principals in the Harding administration Teapot Dome scandal, in which valuable oil reserves set aside for the Navy had been sold without competitive bidding, his opponents accused him of having been involved in criminality. "This is the last relief check you'll ever get if Gore is reelected," they had told the voters. Most important, so did the incumbent President, who despised the retrograde, anti–New Deal, harshly outspoken Senator, who had deeply offended him by telling him to his face that he would be stealing money from the people if he took the country off the gold standard. Like those on the far right, Senator Gore was "convinced that FDR . . . was our republic's Caesar while his wife . . . was a revolutionary." Two retainers, one from the American Petroleum Institute, the other from the Chase National Bank, provided most of his income thereafter, about the same amount as his Senate salary had been. "He didn't take any money that wasn't rightfully his. And he did think up the oil-depletion allowance, which he thought was good for the state. And never got a penny," other than the income he earned, out of office, "as my grandmother bitterly would say, since all the senators and congressmen from Oklahoma were on the take and they all died rich. . . . Oil fields do get depleted," his grandson later remarked. "But so does the brain. I said I'd like a depletion allowance for writers, for our brains." The former Senator soon became active and successful as a pro bono lawyer for the land claims of Oklahoma Indian tribes. His pioneer ancestors would have been amused at the irony. For his grandson, who worshipped him, there was much to admire, nothing to criticize. In the attic at Rock Creek Park, young Gene put together a scrapbook of campaign newspaper clippings, partly an act of homage to his grandfather, mostly an expression of anger at those who had rejected him.

The Senator's bitter summer of 1936 was Gene's first in his new Auchincloss world. To his surprise, he was once more sent off to William

Lawrence Camp, though for August only. The rest of the summer was spent at Newport with his mother and stepfather, whose aged mother ruled over Hammersmith Farm, one of the grand nouveau-riche mansions built by the post–Civil War Newport robber barons, the gilded-age vulgarians whom Henry James so much despised when he visited the Newport of his youth. At Hammersmith Farm "the old lady still presided over two liveried foot-men as well as a conservatory that produced out-of-season grapes, more beautiful than a Vermeer painting, and about as tasteless." While Hughdie patiently waited for her to die, they stayed at a nearby house, at Hazard's Bay, with its own pond, the beach and sea in front. The next three summers Gene spent part of his time at Newport, building sand castles at Bailey's Beach, where he won a first-prize silver cup for a larger-than-life bust of Lincoln, and sailing, swimming, seeing movies, reading a great deal. Next door were Jim Tuck, from the Bancroft playground days, and his sister, whose mother had married Snowden Fahnstock, who owned the "cottage" next to Hammersmith Farm. They played "the usual kid games." Yusha was often around, though they still did not get along. Each Sunday they had lunch with old Mrs. Auchincloss. The first summer Nina was pregnant with the first of two children born during her marriage to Hughdie. One summer they took Gene to Watch Hill, Rhode Island. At Newport, he remembers, he was "a royal pain in the ass," boastful of his fame as a "newsreel personage," filled with a sense of his intellectual superiority and of his talents as a sculptor and painter (he always took his watercolor set with him), "the repository of a myriad of mediocre talents." Quick-witted, he was now himself sometimes sharp-tongued, ironic, even sarcastic. Preoccu-pied with Lincoln, he wrote in his notebook, under the preparatory draw-ings that he made for his sand sculpture, "Now he belongs to the ages." One hot summer afternoon, reclining on the lawn, watching the sailboats, he half overheard his stepfather talking about a family portrait of a lady named Theodosia, who had been Aaron Burr's daughter. Hugh was distantly re-lated on his mother's side to the nation's third Vice President, who had killed Alexander Hamilton in a duel. Thomas Jefferson's name came up. Just as the mention of Lincoln always brought to mind the memorial in Washing-ton, Jefferson meant to young Gene, partly, the memorial now in the process of being created. During that summer of 1936 he also tried, unsuc-cessfully, to read a biography of George Washington. It seemed to him unbearably dull. He never finished it. But the whispers of American history that blew around him on the summer breeze were already part of his consciousness. He would remember Burr.

———•—•———

The boring biography of "The Father of Our Country" had been assigned as preparatory reading for his entry, in September 1936, to a new school. When Gene and Nina decided in spring 1934 to send him to William Lawrence Camp, they had politely turned down Reverend Henderson's request that he attend Henderson's camp. They had responded, though, with interest to his eagerness to have Little Gene at St. Albans. Henderson had tried again in April 1935, urging them to "drop out here and look us over." Since they had been discussing sending him to a boarding school, "as soon as he returns from camp," Gene responded, "we will drop over some afternoon and visit with you as to enrolling him in your school." Both parents favored the change. Gene liked the low cost of tuition and board. Since St. Albans was both a day and a boarding school, Nina could deposit him there whenever it suited her. Life at Merrywood would be more comfortable with him around only on weekends. She would be happy to be rid of the daily presence of her book-obsessed, sharp-tongued son, who increasingly fought back, who more and more seemed an inhibiting depressant on her freedom to do as she pleased. Situated on the high rise from which the unfinished National Cathedral looked toward Washington, within an easy half-hour run from Merrywood, the school would be far enough for separation, close enough for supervision.

Originally the National Cathedral School for Boys, St. Albans, opened in 1909, had its conception in a bequest from President James Buchanan's niece to the Protestant Episcopal Cathedral Foundation of the District of Columbia. As the unfinished cathedral conducted what it considered God's business, the school presided over the mostly secular education of what was still, by 1936, only about a hundred boys divided between the lower and upper schools, grades five through twelve. The main school buildings were vaguely neo-Gothic, in imitation of the cathedral. Chapel was compulsory. Reverend Henderson, senior master of the Upper School, taught Sacred Studies and mathematics. In the Lower School the assistant headmaster, Alfred True, soft-spoken, responsive, thoughtful, was a secular angel of attentiveness who greeted his boys each morning in the entranceway. Headmaster Reverend Albert Hawley Lucas presided, an ex-marine who combined decisiveness, authority, and benevolence in the amounts that produced the successful headmaster of that era. He was both master and cheerleader. Lucas and True, working together with a dedicated, well-qualified faculty, gradually overcame the main problems: to make the Lower School attractive enough so that it would be a happy place for young boys and to make the Upper School sufficiently prominent and respected so that enough elite Washington families would send their high-school-age sons there rather than to the traditional New England academies. Lucas stressed discipline, athletics, and college-entrance preparation; True emphasized community, sensitivity, individual attention. To his faculty he was the best administrator they had ever seen, someone "who let people down very gently." Most of the students, like young Gene, who were in awe of Mr. Lucas, loved Mr. True. And Gene did not at all mind being a boarder, though he could not have known that True had strongly recommended that no Lower School boys board. They were too young, he believed, to be separated from their families. For Gene that was the attraction. Life at Merrywood was hardly domestic bliss. He was eager to get away.

In late August 1936 a counselor from William Lawrence Camp, on his way south, brought Gene home to Merrywood, empty except for the servants. The Auchinclosses were still on holiday. In mid-September, with twenty-one other boys divided into two sections, Gene began Form A, the equivalent of sixth grade. Initially he was a day student, though soon Nina arranged to have him stay at the dormitory for short spells and then to board entirely, which had been her original intention. As usual, his grades were mediocre, ranging from the usual high in spelling, for which he had a natural feel, to the low in penmanship, a lifelong nearly indecipherable scribble. For his entire three years at St. Albans his English grades remained poor. The system demanded memorization, with little to no emphasis on intellectual content. With a sonorous voice, he loved reading poetry aloud. When, as often required, he did so in class, his nuanced, actorly readings attracted attention and praise. But he refused to memorize poems. Demerits followed. Student essays were mainly parsed for formal grammatical correctness; beyond that, there was little analysis. Grades in English depended on memorization of grammatical categories, with examples. More than indifferent, he was hostile to rote learning. St. Albans gave him the gift of an inability to learn the language of grammar. Neither the system nor the student would adapt. On the athletic field he expressed his usual indifference, though he did his best with tennis, which he liked, and soon fencing. He now wore glasses, as little as possible to avoid both the stigma and the disfigurement. Subtle depth perception seemed the problem, an astigmatism that glasses did not completely correct. As the ball came close, it went slightly out of focus. Fortunately, none of his classmates ragged him about his incessant reading, his disinterest in athletics. It was a benign environment of what he remembered as very decent young people, among them George Goodrich, Barrett Prettyman, and Hamilton Fish. Two of the boys, Jim Birney and Dick McConnell, became friends, Birney a soft-spoken, outgoing, rather innocent son of a well-known Episcopalian abolitionist family, McConnell a more aggressive boy who was both rival and friend. "The only boys I ever really liked were at St. Albans," he recalled. "I can't say I was wild about any of them, but I mean I liked them as people."

Gene was not unhappy at St. Albans. Merrywood stood at most thirty minutes distant, unequivocal demonstration of his mother's desire for separateness. But Gene had begun to see the advantages of separation: it suited mother *and* son. One day, Nina, tired of complaining to Gene about his grades, came to see Mr. True. Gene's "grades must improve 'because,' she said, 'he is living in the lap of luxury now, but he's never going to inherit anything! And he doesn't understand the *value of money.*' " "Well, if you could just get him to do his homework," True said. "She confessed defeat: 'He locks himself in his room,' she said sadly, 'and *writes.*' " Gene declined to explain or reform. Frustrated, Nina kept demanding proof he was not slothful, a spendthrift, a disgrace to her social status and ambition, an improvidential ward of the family whom they would have to support forever. Sensibly, True realized that Gene cared little about grades, though even at that low level of motivation he performed adequately. Best to let him alone, since he spent most of his time reading, a constructive alternative to what boys were expected to do and, mostly, did. True understood boys; Nina did not. Quick to pursue her view of dysfunction, she became suspicious of Gene's imaginative games, one of which was role-playing and performance. She hated his constant reading. That he already knew a great deal of history and literature seemed to her irksome. What good could it possibly be? If pernicious, she was nevertheless sincere, eager to fix what she perceived as wrong, though her eagerness rarely produced sustained attention to the problem. When she decided his teeth needed straightening, she had her dentist install braces. "I had absolutely straight teeth, except for one incisor which was slightly off. So I had to have braces put on my teeth by a lousy dentist" because the children of everyone she knew had them. Then she forgot about them. "They stayed on much too long. They were never looked after again, and five years later my teeth were rotting away under these things." Eventually he was to lose all his upper molars.

When given, probably for his tenth birthday, a theatrical makeup kit designed to allow a child to dress up as historical and literary characters, he delighted in combining his fascination with history and role-playing, his second chance to be Mickey Rooney. The kit contained the basic materials and instructions for a wide group of characters, from Cardinal Richelieu to Mephistopheles to the prince of *The Prince and the Pauper*. The latter he had seen enacted in a recent film in which twins had played the lead roles. The notion of an alternative self, of being himself a twin, fascinated him. With the help of a white towel, which he had become adept at twisting into a turban, he used the makeup kit to play an Egyptian pharaoh, based on his favorite move, *The Mummy*. A black wig, a gift from Liz Whitney, enabled him to play Cleopatra, though mostly he impersonated male figures. Popular Hollywood movies were dressing up the world, especially its glamorous past, its famous historical figures and events. Downtown, at the Keith, the Palace, the Belasco, the Translux, the Metropolitan, and the Capitol; at the Blue Hen in Rehoboth Beach, Delaware, where he was taken sometimes for brief summer visits; in the movie house in Newport—each with its own particular aroma and atmosphere—he saw every new movie, accompanied, at the main Washington theaters, by an elaborate stage show. At the Capitol Theater "there were the Living Statues. Well-known historic tableaux were enacted by actors and actresses in white leotards." Gene's reading and moviegoing were part of a vast costume drama that he personalized. At first Nina took all this as another example of his self-involvement, like reading. At Newport a family friend, Sherwood Davis, set off alarm bells when he told Nina that Gene's love of theatricality was a danger sign that might indicate homosexual tendencies. "So Sherry Davis says he likes putting on makeup, he likes dressing up—watch out: that's what fags do. Sherry Davis was himself a fag and a bisexual. And she took that to heart, my mother. . . . I seem to remember that I was sent to a doctor. I don't know if it was a psychiatrist or a psychologist, probably the latter, who asked me sex questions and so on. I gave perfectly polite answers. And that was the end of it. She then loses interest. Never again does the subject come up."

As the leaves changed colors in autumn 1936, young Gene and his father, while Gene Vidal was still director of aeronautics, traveled northward by railroad through the Hudson River Valley to West Point, the military city high on the Palisades where Vidal had had many of his greatest triumphs. In 1925, when he left, he had been an assistant football coach, the track and field coach, and the instructor of aeronautics. He returned as a man of Washington and of the world, bringing along his eleven-year-old son, who had just started at a new school. Gene also brought with him one of his closest friends, Amelia Earhart, whose fame had risen to a dimension beyond Gene's athletic or professional achievement. She had become a national icon. Together the three of them sat in the stadium watching Army play Navy. As much as Gene was a familiar figure to the cadet corps, Earhart would have created the stir, her willowy figure, her blond-white eyebrows, her elegant clothes, the mystique of her courage, her fame for being famous. On their way back to New York, as Earhart's fans peered into the train compartment to get a look at their idol, she told the fascinated young Gene about her plans to fly around the world from east to west, to circumnavigate the earth, like Puck circling the globe. In her own way an actress of sorts, Amelia glittered in his eyes. Playing the grown-up, he asked what part of the flight she most worried about. Africa, she responded. She did not want to be forced down in the jungle. What about the Pacific? he asked. "Oh, there are always islands," she said. As they approached Grand Central Station, he asked if she would give him a souvenir. "Shortly before she left on the flight around the world, she sent me the blue-and-white checked leather belt that she often wore. She gave my father her old watch."

They had also given one another much of their company, both personal and professional, during the last six years. Gene rarely made an important decision without consulting her. Together, with Paul Collins, they had become in 1936 the founding organizers and major stockholders of an airline in New England, at first in conjunction with the Boston-Maine Railroad, later to be reorganized as Northeast Airlines. City-hopping together in a small plane, at least once with young Gene along, they laid out the routes along the railroad tracks. If it seemed an odd thing for a government official to be doing, apparently no one thought it remarkable. She regularly confided in him, and especially about her aeronautical plans. He was to be one of her closest consultants in her preparation for her ill-fated round-the-world flight the next year. Her marriage to George Palmer Putnam remained the open one she had insisted on from the beginning. Whether she had other lovers, male or female, she certainly had Gene Vidal in her heart. With young Gene she was playful, warm, glamorous, another one of his father's women whom he would have preferred to the mother he had. It was a daydream he allowed himself. Amelia Earhart and Liz Whitney were the prototypes of the older women with whom as an adult he was to have strong friendships, mother and grandmother figures not necessarily themselves very motherly but reminders of the mother he would have wanted or of the much-loved Nina Kay Gore. An occasional visitor at the Earhart-Putnam home in Rye, young Gene loved Amelia's company, her house, her aura, the maps spread out on the living-room floor, the jungle-animal-decorated wall-paper in the guest room. Walking with her on the boardwalk at Atlantic City, he noticed how many people stared at his famous companion. Another time, when he had been ill in Washington and she had visited him, he sculpted her head out of clay, a creation they both admired. Her beautiful voice, like his grandmother's, stayed in his memory. And now that he was writing a great deal of poetry, she read his and he hers, sometimes out loud to one another. As poets they were both expressive, though Earhart more personal, and equally untalented. For young Gene there was a glow to the relationship.

Apparently Nina did not feel especially threatened by Gene's friendship with Amelia, at least not to an extent that prevented her having lunch with Earhart at a Washington hotel the year before the divorce. Gene had hovered nervously in the background, afraid there might be a scene, especially if Nina had too many drinks. Perhaps Amelia's boyish looks disarmed or even attracted her. Shrewd and intuitive, she may have sized up the relationship as unthreatening. The Whitneys were then the targets anyway. But by autumn 1936 Nina had been married to Hugh Auchincloss for a full year. Since she had lost Jock, she was no longer in a mood to be happy if Gene married Liz. Whatever her many dissatisfactions, money was not among them, except insofar as she occasionally worried about her son's economic future, especially since he did not excel in school or mix with people. He was happy to mix at Langollen, Liz Whitney's horse farm in Upperville, Virginia, fifty miles from Washington, where Gene took him for visits and where Liz taught him to ride. With his father and his father's friends he felt comfortable. The glamorous ones, like Liz and Amelia, were very attractive. From a bachelor apartment at the Wardman Park, where he played tennis with Henry Wallace, Gene Vidal had moved to another apartment, on Connecticut Avenue. His son visited regularly. Liz was often there during 1936–37. Liz and Gene traveled together, at least once to Los Angeles, where Liz presented herself as a candidate in the international competition for the role of Scarlett O'Hara in *Gone With the Wind*, the movie based on the bestselling novel of the Civil War. Its male star was soon to appear in a film called *Test Pilot*, on whose set Nina was to meet Clark Gable and have an affair with him and also with her third-husband-to-be, an Air Force officer who served as technical consultant. Unfortunately for Liz, her estranged husband, the primary financial backer of *Gone With the Wind*, made it clear to the producer she was not even to be considered for the role. While Liz tried Hollywood, Gene busily attended the National Air Show in Inglewood. What is now the Los Angeles Airport was still a cornfield. They drove together cross-country, back to Washington, with a detour to visit Gene's brother Pick, now a young Air Force pilot, at Barkesdale Field, in Shreveport, Louisiana. Pick and his wife, Sally, insisted Liz sleep in the guest bedroom and Gene in the den. "We were very old-fashioned," Sally explained. A month later Liz was still not divorced. The endless legal-financial wrangling went on and on.

———

From the window seat of his St. Albans dormitory cubicle he could see the Washington Monument in the distance. The biography of "The Father of Our Country" which he had never finished epitomized the boredom of historical studies (and most of his classes). Now, deeply absorbed, he was reading *Gone With the Wind*. Through the Gores, he thought of himself as Southern, living in what was, prior to World War II, essentially a Southern city whose only industry was government. Southerners like his grandfather dominated the Congress, which despite Roosevelt's power still insisted it was the premier branch. Issues of honor, justice, seniority, home rule, and graft preoccupied the political rulers, whether they were of the Ashley Wilkes or the Snopes kind. Having been brought up in the home of a practical politician, Gene knew that the romanticism of Ashley Wilkes was nonsense. His grandmother's dismissal of gambling, whoring Southern boys getting their comeuppance was another antidote to idealization. Still, while he had no doubt that *Gone With the Wind* distorted history and human nature, he found the book deeply absorbing, a dramatization of the sort that made history come alive. The novel and film brought together his own growing interest in the American past and numbers of vivid self-reflexive moments, one of which was his self-awareness as he sat in that window embrasure, gazing out into the Washington distance, often looking down at the pages that were alive in his hands. It produced in his mind an unforgettable image of himself, there and then, becoming himself. Such visual images increasingly filled the storehouse of his mind, always there, readily available, instantly alive.

Life in the antiseptic Lower School dormitory was best lived imaginatively, "a long room with a linoleum floor, freshly waxed and lined on both sides with doorless cubicles," small, bare spaces with bed, chair, desk. Each day began with services in the Little Sanctuary, presided over by the headmaster, who had a sermon or homily for the school. An imposing figure, he was authority itself, speaking familiarly about honor, duty, country, about God, morality, and "character." He also had a sense of humor and a sharp eye for the personalities of his teachers and pupils. An avid athletic partisan, "The Chief" cheered as loud as the loudest at school football games. Though some parents found it unseemly, the Reverend Albert Hawley Lucas knew what he stood for and was not to be repressed. Among other things, he stood for winning football games and building character. He presided, for the boarders, over breakfast and dinner, each of the resident masters at the head of a table, where the food was competent, the atmosphere mostly pleasant. For the sixth- and seventh-grade boys, the homeroom teacher dominated the long teaching day. For Gene, Herve Gordon ("Papa") Chasseaud's much-loved "boudoir," the school library under the stairs in the Activities Building, was a primal location. Chasseaud himself had gathered most of the growing collection. A bibliophilic French teacher with attractively eccentric habits, he had a literary aura. In the Lower Form office, the school secretary and mother-confessor to many, Virginia Martin, sold cookies and milk during recess. One day a student ran in, exclaiming, "Miss Martin, there's a fire in the boys' room!" "First," she replied, "put on your tie."

The one master he did love was Stanley Sofield, his seventh-grade homeroom teacher, an eccentrically brilliant pedagogue whose personal charisma made him a powerful presence in the daily lives of his students and a

St. Albans legend. The only teacher Gene later came back to see and had a friendship with, Sofield had "magic with boys," partly based on an intuitive understanding of and a genuine affection for the species. "He had that magic quality of treating them as equals," Alfred True recollected. "They felt he was the man in charge, but he never condescended to them. No boy was ever a mystery to him." A Columbia University graduate, in his thirties when Gene was at St. Albans, Sofield was physically unprepossessing, a rather gawky pixie, "a plump young man with thick brown hair, glasses, a tapir's nose and small chin." Unmarried, his sexual interests unclear, he was strongly attached to a sister in New Jersey whom he helped economically and spoke with on the telephone every evening. Rumored among the masters to be homosexual, Sofield never made that a part of his St. Albans life. The boys knew him only as a brilliant teacher and a memorable character. With a sharp wit and a loud, demanding voice, he made the classroom his theater. The students he good-humoredly addressed as "gentlemen." Totally unathletic himself, he apparently enjoyed coaching baseball and cheering boisterously at school games. Flamboyant, "he knew how to control the boys and teach them also," to make the class interesting by investing it with personality and ideas. Passionate about the musical theater, each year Sofield directed the school Christmas musical, which he composed, frequently banging away at the piano. Afraid of performing in public, Gene would have nothing to do with the musicals, though Sofield, who had nicknames for most of the boys, would regularly sing to him, "Gene-y with the light brown hair." It made him writhe with embarrassment. Actually he was still blond, as his classmate John Hanes recalled, with straight hair darkening to brown, "good-looking although not pretty. Just a good-looking boy. Tall for his age." With another St. Albans master, Sofield directed a summer camp in the Adirondacks, where musicals were featured. He hoped Gene would attend. A regular if not heavy drinker who loved martinis, some mornings Sofield, bleary-eyed, would with a soft voice, a "gentle, grave manner, and a slightly pained squint," alert the students to his mood, which often produced histrionic demands for silence. Other times books or erasers would fly, unerringly, across the room toward offendingly loud or silly or unresponsive boys. Sofield's famous scream echoed throughout the Lower Form, part of its special character. His storms were unpredictable, though everyone expected them, and most enjoyed them. Usually he taught in a tone of "gentle expository reason." To Gene he seemed like "a benign

Nina"—the vitality, the histrionics, even the drinking, but without the destructive irresponsibility, the self-glorification, the cruelty. With everyone else Gene was reserved, mostly unresponsive. But he responded to Sofield's magic, part pedagogic calculation, part spontaneous expressiveness, a feel for boys and for schoolroom life that made him predictably unpredictable in the classroom.

At night, in the dormitory and study hall, there was homework, there were smells and noises and games, some very personal, others companionable, all the world-shaking dramas of companionship, ambition, rivalry, affection, health, illness, high spirits, love—the varied activities of a few dozen disparate boys between the ages of ten and fourteen who when the dormitory master, sometimes benign, other times a hated figure, shut off the lights, fell into the sleep of dreams and sometimes nightmares. In the dark one boy sometimes went into another's bed, for comfort, for sexual games. Others, awake, could hear the distinctive noises. Wet dreams, which Gene began to have, were whispered about. In the shower the boys visually measured one another, made note of who had pubic hair and who not: whoever boarded in the Lower School dorm was part of the community's self-scrutiny. One of Gene's school friends, who confided in him, worried about masturbating. He was trying desperately not to. Succumbing to temptation, he thought, was going to destroy his life. It was, Gene told him, his impression "that it probably did no harm at all. . . . He then said that 'everywhere you look there's something that sets me off.' 'Well, like what?' 'Well,' he said, 'the funny papers.' I said, 'I don't see anything sexy about them.' 'Oh,' he said, 'I do.' " At home, with his mother's casual nudity, with parents who had affairs, with his own erotic responses and erections, Gene was becoming aware of sexual feeling, though he still had a long way to go in getting right the facts about how babies were made. But he was unselfconscious about most of his personalized responses, which seemed to him perfectly ordinary, natural, acceptable. Unlike some of his friends, he had no religious scruples or anxieties to bring to bear.

At some level, Gene was determined not to be a good student and willing to take the consequences. Flashes of eidetic memory kept his mind alive with images that he gradually sought to embody in language, in the poetry he was writing, in prose essays, and especially in the made-up stories he had started putting down on paper years before. Also, his grandfather's carefully crafted combination of independence and political shrewdness seeped into his attitude, his consciousness. He wanted to be shrewd, power-ful, successful, President of the United States or at least a senator like his grandfather. He also wanted to be a great writer. But he did not necessarily want good grades or see any connection between them and his aspirations. He certainly did not want to spend his time studying things that did not interest him rather than reading what did. And he did not want to work to please people. The cost in self-respect and self-reliance would be too great. Also, he knew from experience with his mother that the more one tries to please some people, the more cruelty they inflict. His grades, in fact, did get significantly better in his second year at St. Albans than the low B average he had achieved the first, good enough for him to tie for fifth in a class of nineteen. In his third year he slipped back, probably for reasons as irrelevant to effort as the reasons he had risen before. In a pre-grade-inflation world, a middle B might have satisfied the school and his mother if it had been the result of disciplined application rather than natural intelligence. His mother accused him of sloth. The school mostly let him alone.

At St. Albans, church and state flourished in miniature. It was a microcosmic simulacrum of the world immediately outside. Many students were children of the government, sons of ambassadors, congressmen, civil servants, bureaucrats, military families. In the Lower School dormitory, power was important. Gene had no intention of allowing himself to be anyplace but at the top of the hierarchy of his boys' world. As at Friends, he took great interest in being in charge, at least to the extent of fighting back if attacked and organizing a group to assert himself and his values. When the boy he most palled around with, Dick McConnell, tried to turn on him in fall 1938, his response was aggressive. "In the dormitories they had these lockers which were about eight feet high, two feet wide, and two feet deep, with locks on them, where you hung your clothes. And it was McConnell's trick to get together two or three other boys and stampede somebody and lock them in one. I feared this more than anything in the world. I was a claustrophobe, and I avoided it by overthrowing McConnell, a preemptory strike so that it wouldn't happen to me. So I would not be shut up. In fact, I'd be running the show." Playing on McConnell's reputation as a bully, he got sixteen boys to sign a "Declaration of Independence" that he drew up. It had four articles. "I. We declare ourselves free of the tyrannical rule of Richard McConnell and Ashe-Mead Fuller. II. Every month we will vote for our president. The president will be the symbol of unity. He can not

command anyone to do anything that he does not want to do. III. Unless
everyone in the Dormitory agrees, there can be no organization in which R.
McConnell is involved. IV. We all agree to this." After his own signature
appears the word "President."

––––––––

At St. Albans, in the winter of 1937, Gene fell in love, both in the
unself-conscious schoolboy sense of natural physical attraction to another
and in the emotional (and long-lasting) preoccupation with an alter ego, a
twin who would be the playmate of his soul, a completion of the incomplete,
the perfect fit that makes two comrades into one friendship. It was a love
that had no need for loving words. Romantic jargon was out of the question
for these two very masculine young men. Neither of the boys would have
known how to talk that way or seen a reason for it. For both it was
prelapsarian, a combination of adolescent sex and friendship, an unspoken
enactment of what came naturally and gave pleasure. The boy, Jimmie
Trimble, was a young Washingtonian, almost precisely his age. Also tall,
with a lanky build and blond curly hair, one of St. Albans's premier athletes,
Jimmie excelled at every sport, especially baseball. The only books he read
voluntarily were about sports, to his mother's tolerant despair. From a
cultured home, he loved music, especially jazz and musicals, and played the
saxophone. Probably he participated in Sofield's Christmas musicals. Like
most of the boys, he worshipped his Form I teacher. Easygoing, amiable, he
was blessed with social intelligence and with a love of the athletic games his
talents could transform into popularity, success, even fame. At ease with
almost everyone, he made friends readily, attractive to and admired by both
sexes, a kind of normal, intelligent, uninteresting student athlete, in his own
and in his friends' eyes a future all-American and professional star.

A boy of the Washington suburbs, Jimmie attended first the Rosemary
Street School, then Leland Junior High in Chevy Chase. His mother, worried about poor instruction, soon enrolled him in St. Albans. Already a
locally famous student athlete, he had been tutored by his father and his
uncle, both enthusiastic baseball players and fans. Before St. Albans he had
been taken under the wing of a well-known local coach who had taught him
to become a sophisticated schoolboy pitcher. Ruth Trimble, who had divorced Jimmie's father and then remarried, was now in the process of
separating from her second husband, Jimmie's stepfather, who may have

taken liberties with the boy and who certainly had alienated Ruth. His stepfather was "creating trouble at home," she later said. With a well-to-do maternal grandmother footing the bill, Jimmie enrolled at St. Albans in September 1937. In fall 1937 Jimmie, like Gene, was in Stanley Sofield's homeroom class. The next year, in November 1938, eager to have him away from the tensions of her dissolving marriage, Ruth put him into the Lower School dormitory, if only for the one term. Gene and he were already friends, the result of an overture from Jimmie, who had come up to him and remarked on how much Gene seemed to read. The friendship intensified. In the dormitorywide shower ritual of inspection for new boys, Jimmie clearly was identified as belonging to Gene's elite group, boys with pubic hair. Naturally, identity and identification for the adolescents was partly sexual. When Gene, fumbling on the game-room floor at Merrywood, had a sexual experience with a female, he had his mind throughout mostly on telling Jimmie all about it. Jimmie had not yet been initiated. Jimmie was important. The girl on the floor was not. What he told Jimmie, other than that it was confusing and anatomically problematic, is unclear. The simple mechanics for uninitiated adolescent boys were usually formidable. But the fact that he had had such sex was an achievement to boast of. Twelve-year-old boys talked to one another about the heterosexual sex they had or might have. The other sex they just did, mostly without discussion, as Jimmie and Gene did one day on the white-tiled bathroom floor at Merrywood. Quietly, to avoid being heard by the butler, they rubbed their stomachs and genitals against one another into what Gene remembered as an explosion of perfectly blissful orgasm. Neither felt they had broken a sacred taboo. Neither, apparently, felt any guilt, though they both tacitly understood that this was a private affair. It was something they would talk about neither to others nor even, for that matter, between themselves.

Eager to have her son invite home schoolboy guests, Nina welcomed Jimmie, a sign to her that her solitary son was mixing, that he actually had friends. From the house they went often to the swimming pool, the poolroom, the squash court, the farm, the woods. One day they roller-skated on the squash court, ruining the expensive wooden floor. In the enclosure next to the garage they played with the dogs. Jimmie could not believe that Gene could not take Wiggles into the house. Most of all there was the river, where in the warm weather they swam, unafraid of the rapids and unconcerned about snakes. They sunbathed on the warm rocks. On one bright afternoon in 1938 they made love "in the woods above the roaring river," then swam against the dangerous current to a large glacial rock, where they lay next to one another. They had lots to talk about, mainly themselves, though not what they had done sexually and not often about girls either, but mostly about all the rest of their schoolboy world and their adolescent interests. Gene wanted either to be a writer or a politician, like his grandfather, with whom he had had many discussions about how to begin his political career, especially where he might reside so that he could have standing as a resident in order to run for office. Jimmie wanted to be a professional baseball player, and if not, or after, he would be a saxophone player or a teacher. But the present was pleasurably vivid. There seemed no reason not to think, or at least to daydream, that it would go on forever.

As the *Île de France* left New York harbor in June 1939, thirteen-year-old Gene was at last fulfilling his dream of sailing eastward to Europe, especially to Italy, where his mind and imagination had already been long resident. The ship's port of destination was Le Havre. It was to be the *Île de France*'s last voyage as a passenger ship. From the new Washington, with its vast neo-Roman buildings, the imperial city that Roosevelt had been creating, Gene happily began his voyage to the old Rome, the imperial city of ancient history. The books he had read, from *Plutarch's Lives* to *Stories from Livy*, the movies he had seen, from *Roman Scandals* to *The Last Days of Pompeii*, provided images and expectations. Before Rome, there would be France and England, both of which had been relentlessly filmed and both of which stood on the brink of another great military adventure. Like most Americans, young Gene opposed the United States fighting in a European war. Like his grandfather, he did not want one drop of American blood shed on foreign soil. In Washington everyone knew that war was coming but not precisely when. More than anything Gene wanted to see Paris, London, Rome before it became too late. As he stood on the deck, the *Île de France* sailing down the Hudson, through the harbor and into the open sea, he felt for the first time that the world lay all before him. He would now have a chance to see in actuality what he had read about and seen on the screen, to provide himself with images of himself as an actor in the film of his mind about the great events of the world. He would remember this first visit to Europe as the "pleasantest" time in all his school days.

In February 1939 at Merrywood, Reverend Lucas had baptized Gene into the Episcopalian flock. Sponsored by Nina and Hugh, he now also had his mother's family name as his own, Eugene Luther Gore Vidal. It was a baptism of form, not faith, with social rather than religious significance. Herself without concern for substance, always eager to observe the forms, Nina thought it a good idea. But the social event that Nina and Hugh most crowed about came in early June. All Washington was thrilled. "Their Brittanic Majesties," King George VI and Queen Mary, had come to America on a state visit to rally support for their country. American goodwill (and ships) would be necessary for Britain's survival. Mr. and Mrs. Hugh D. Auchincloss were the happy recipients of an invitation "to a Garden Party at the Embassy on Thursday, the 8th June 1939," the most sought-after invitation in town. In explaining the guest list, the British ambassador remarked, " 'It's rather like the kingdom of heaven. Some are chosen and some are not.' " As the royal family made their way along Massachusetts Avenue to the White House, Gene and Jimmie, in the hot June weather, watched the procession from in front of Hugh Auchincloss's town house, a yellow Italianate mansion. With State Department clearance, Auchincloss was about to sell it to the Japanese government, which wanted to make it the embassy of their puppet regime in occupied Mongolia. The State Department approved the sale but not the embassy. Later that same day, standing in a large crowd in front of the Treasury Building, Gene cheered the King and the President as they drove by in an open car, "the red-faced President Roosevelt" towering "over the small, brown-faced King of England beside him. Sweating crowds were waving American and British flags." It was as near as he got to the royal personage, but he was now eagerly about to get closer to the place from which he had come. On June 13 his first passport was issued. Still growing, he was five foot eight, with blond hair, brown eyes, a chickenpox scar between his eyebrows one of his "distinguishing marks."

Nina had already disappointed his transatlantic hopes at least twice. She "would announce trips to Europe and then cancel them. So my hopes would be high and then they would be dashed. In 1938 the *Gripsholm*, a Swedish boat, had scheduled a tour of Scandinavia. We were all set to go on that. But her exciting life always intervened so that was canceled." Then, in spring 1939, two St. Albans schoolmasters, Stanley Sofield and his friend and camp partner, Thomas Jefferson Barlow, eager themselves to see Europe again before borders closed and only military ships sailed, organized a student trip. The ostensible aim was to study French, the larger plan to see as much of Europe as possible. Even at modest cost to the students, it would allow them (and Barlow's wife) to travel free, perhaps even to profit. Sofield invited "Gene-y with the light brown hair." Nina said yes, perhaps among other reasons because she had decided against his wishes to remove him from St. Albans School. Dissatisfied with his mediocre grades, constantly arguing with him, unhappy with his bookish tendencies, she thought it best to move him again, this time far away. Why not allow him this European trip? It would provide a break and a distraction, a way of compensating for the impending dislocation, of making a point of her generosity and reasonableness. It would also clear the field for her infidelities. She preferred not to have Gene around to take notice of them. In her eyes, he was spying on her. Hughdie was less of a problem. "As her character was stronger than his," Gore Vidal later remarked, "she got away with almost anything and could have to the end," which was not far off. The war, though, was imminent. Since his father would pay the small cost, as the divorce agreement required, everything was easily settled. Sofield and Barlow were delighted to have him, along with about sixteen other boys, most but not all from St. Albans, who would at first spend four weeks "perfecting their French," as the phrase of the day had it, at Jouy-en-Josas, near Versailles, a short distance from Paris. From Jouy they would take frequent field trips and then, done with France and French lessons, they would go to Italy. Though Gene may have been brooding about the consequences of his impending exile from Washington in the fall, he put it mostly out of mind. Bad as it was, he would still see Jimmie, who was to continue at St. Albans, during school holidays. That the coming war might change all that never occurred to him. Whatever his remonstrances, and they were vigorous, he had no thought of a serious rebellion. What good would it do anyway? Only time would provide him with independence. Efficiently and enthusiastically, he focused on the grand European adventure.

Life at the École de Jouy-en-Josas, a few buildings and a small campus vacant of its usual people, was both familiar and exotic. Each morning there were classes in history and French, the afternoons free or booked for excursions. Dormitory routine, as familiar as at home except for there being only one unreliable toilet for everyone, had four boys to a room in a manor house with a domed ceiling. Classes, taught in French, were also held there in the smaller of two buildings, the larger occupied by female counterparts from a

New England school. One of his roommates was Hammy Fish from St. Albans. In their private room Tom Barlow and his wife, Lee, had a busman's honeymoon, having married the previous year. On a schoolmaster's salary any trips, let alone European honeymoons, were hard to come by. The study-abroad trip had been Barlow's conception. Tall, ramrod straight, a dignified Kentuckyan with "an aquiline Greek nose and dark eyes," Barlow was amiable but disciplined. Sofield was short, round, bespectacled, more indulgent. They made a good team. Oliver Hodge, a bilingual French teacher from Chattanooga, a close friend of theirs, provided language expertise. Each boy had a bicycle for local transportation, particularly regular visits to Versailles, though Gene often also walked the short distance to the pastry shops and the local sights. With a sharp sweet tooth, he found the pastry as memorable as anything else in the royal city. Moist baba au rhum melted in his mouth, disappeared almost immediately. "Very thin, tall, a good-looking boy," he could afford to indulge.

They went frequently to Paris by train. Recognized for his self-reliance, Gene was allowed to go off on his own, which he did enthusiastically. On Bastille Day he stood on the steps of the Grand Palais, watching French military might parade by, awed by its glory, thrilled to recognize in the flesh the French Foreign Legion he had already seen and loved in a movie called *Under Two Flags*. All Paris seemed like a movie anyway, until he "saw an open car containing a bald man in a business suit. I could spot a politician anywhere in any country. This one was the prime minister of France," Daladier, an unprepossessing figure who soon had the honor of turning France over to the Germans. The American visitor had a sense that this was a man who made deals, that the next year's Bastille Day parade would have a very different cast of characters. In his Paris wanderings he went to the Palais Royal, buying quite cheaply, as a favor for Nina, two eighteenth-century silver snuffboxes to add to her collection. To Gene, with European history in mind, they were reminders of the French Revolution, of the guillotine, of aristocratic privilege and political change. To Nina they were just snuffboxes.

Longer excursions by crowded bus filled with more young Americans, girls from the other school group at Jouy, took them in all directions, south to Orléans, to Touraine, to Blois, to Chartres, out to the Rhine to see the famous Maginot Line, filled with French troops that would stop any invasion from the west; north and east to Arras Cathedral and the battlefield cemeteries of the First World War. Poppies were in bloom. At Chartres they had the shock of seeing an elderly Frenchwoman, squatting, raise her skirts and relieve herself. It was as memorable as the cathedral. On the bus to the Rhine Gene sat next to Zeva Fish, Hammy's sister, with whom he instantly fell in love. "I thought she was wonderful. I was reading her my poetry, and *she* thought it was wonderful. She was an older woman, about sixteen or seventeen." The oldest woman on the bus was twenty-nine-year-old Lee Barlow, whom he thought very pretty. She also wrote poetry. On the bus they had at least two long chats on versification, about which she thought Gene needed to know more if he were going to be a *real* poet. A college-educated formalist, she decided she needed to teach him the language of prosody and metrics.

By late July war signals alerted Sofield and Barlow to the likelihood that they might not be able to have the entire summer in Europe. Accelerating their schedule, at the end of the month they went by train to Italy. They anticipated Rome eagerly, the part of the trip to which Gene most looked forward actually about to happen. Almost as if he feared Rome's splendor would be too much for him, he protected himself as the train went southward by keeping his eyes as much on the fascinating book he was reading as on the vista outside. It was an exotic adventure novel by Frederic Prokosch, *The Seven Who Fled*, about a journey across an imaginary Asian landscape. In Rome for the next two weeks Gene's eyes blazed, partly with the splendor of the ancient city, partly with the landscape of the novel, as if he were in two places at once, an increasingly characteristic trope of doubleness. Rome itself dazzled him. A passionate pilgrim, like Henry James, he feverishly exalted in the Roman monuments, the Roman streets, his mind filled with the literature he had read, the history he knew, his first taste of a city he was to visit many times. Eventually it would become one of his homes; now it was a dream realized, a young man's fascination with the material presence of what before had been only words, thoughts, imagined vistas.

In the Forum, with pieces of broken marble everywhere, he had his own Jamesian vastation, an epiphanic moment in which his eyes superimposed on the glittering debris the living reality of what had been, as if it were all alive again, as if the informed imagination could make visually real what had been dead for centuries. Walking through the Forum excavation, not yet sequestered from visitors, he picked up a small Roman head. He quickly hid it under his jacket. Ever alert, Sofield made him put it back.

From the Roman to the American Senate seemed to him an obvious continuity. He could see his grandfather there. He imagined himself, the supreme orator, in both Roman and American chambers. From the Forum to the Colosseum to the Pantheon, from one shining structure to another, he traversed ancient Rome. The simple storybook accounts of the Roman imperium from his Victorian edition of *Stories from Livy* provided adequate narratives for his imagination to people Rome visible with Rome past. Great marble statues of emperors and orators seemed almost to accompany him as he walked to them, by them, around them. With his schoolboy Latin he could read the obvious inscriptions. Standing on the rostrum where Mark Antony had spoken of the dead Julius Caesar, he felt the thrill of identification. He haunted the Forum and the Palatine. The Holy City's Christian churches and priestly presences he hardly noticed. Classical Rome possessed him.

So too did the dramatic history transpiring in the modern city. It was as if he were living in a newsreel. Everywhere there were Blackshirts. The garlic-smelling August air breathed war. Triumphant Italian nationalism, still drunk on Ethiopian victories, paraded in the streets, flexed its muscles and guns. Pathé News and The March of Time had given Hitler's and Mussolini's faces worldwide currency. So too had their politics and armies. If Americans were frightened, they were also fascinated, especially those who lived with and studied political power. In May, as if in preparation for his European trip, Gene had written for his St. Albans English class an essay called "A Comparison Between a Dynastic Ruler and a Totalitarian Ruler," a strikingly objective analysis of the Emperor Franz Joseph and of Adolf Hitler. He had read Hitler's *Mein Kampf,* a biography of Franz Joseph, and four encyclopedia articles, an ambitious undertaking for a usually indifferent schoolboy. He had also seen the film *Mayerling*. The subject fascinated him. For the first time his teachers took notice of substance as well as grammar, partly because the timely subject was compelling. Though brief, the essay is divided into three chapters, accompanied by his own competent pencil drawing of Hitler, with enough factual detail to be textured and creditable. The analysis is surprisingly sophisticated, the prose economically effective, occasionally graceful. A report rather than a condemnation, it leaves history to judge whether Hitler is "a madman or a genius."

As the train that had taken them from France to Italy made its first Italian stop, "fascist guards gave the fascist salute just as they had done in all those newsreels where Hitler and Mussolini were perpetual Gog and Magog to our days." One night at the Baths of Caracalla, part of a large audience to see an outdoor performance of *Turandot,* they suddenly saw in a railed-off box next to theirs Mussolini himself. Resplendent in a white uniform, he seemed almost part of the performance, as if Italian history and Italian opera were indistinguishable. To Gene he looked "almost as worried as Daladier. . . . At the first interval he rose and saluted the soprano. Audience cheered. Then he left the box. . . . As he passed within a yard of me, I got a powerful whiff of cologne, which struck me as degenerate. A moment later Mussolini was on the stage, taking a bow with the diva. The crowd shouted 'Duce' . . . he saluted the audience—Fascist arm outstretched. Then he was gone." Despite the cologne, the young boy thought Mussolini splendid, as spectacle, as politician. "That jaw, that splendid emptiness. After all, I had been brought up with politicians. He was an exotic variation on something quite familiar to me." The next year Mussolini was to be the dark but white-uniformed inspiration for his first "really ambitious novel," never to be completed, "about a dictator in Rome, filled with intrigue and passion and Machiavellian *combinazione.*"

Summer 1939 was closing around them, the days shorter, European politics dangerous. As they were well-connected Washington children, the American ambassador received them at the embassy, particularly since Ham Fish's father was chairman of the House Foreign Affairs Committee. Even in distant, domestic-minded Washington, foreign affairs were now on everybody's mind. Whether or not Sofield and Barlow read Italian newspapers or tuned in to other immediately available currents, they had reason to be nervous. Rumors of imminent war came from authoritative sources. If war were to be declared, the border between Italy and France would be closed. Mrs. Hamilton Fish, whose husband had close relations with the State Department, got a message to them, probably through the embassy, urging them "to get out of there quick," so Lee Barlow remembers. Perhaps Nina was the source of the urgent request that they leave Europe as soon as possible. "She fixed it up through our embassy somehow," her son remembers. "She would have gone straight to the State Department, to Sumner Welles or someone. All these people were coming to Merrywood. Probably one of them came to Merrywood, the undersecretary of something or even Cordell Hull, and said there's trouble coming. Try to get them out." Late in

August they made one of the last trains out of Italy. The border closed behind them.

From Saint-Malo they crossed the Channel. In London they found a gloomy, disappointed Britain preparing for war. From an ancient Bloomsbury bed and breakfast on Russell Square, with a "fascinating primitive bathroom," all soon to be turned into rubble, Gene quickly saw as much of London as he could. He had little time. The city was mostly shut down. When Germany invaded Poland on September 1, he stood in front of 10 Downing Street watching Neville Chamberlain, the Prime Minister whom he had often dressed up as and imitated, leave en route to Parliament to tell his nation that war was inevitable. "Thin little man. A wing collar, huge Adam's apple, uncommonly small head. No cheers, no jeers. The crowd simply sighs, in unison, on exhalation. Terrible, mournful sound. Chamberlain tries to smile; winces instead. Is driven off." Sofield and the Barlows rushed to the American embassy to get tickets for Lee and the boys to depart immediately. The two men, who needed to arrange for the bicycles and other luggage to be sent separately, would take a later ship. At Liverpool on September 3, the day Britain and France declared war, the boys were on a British vessel, the *Antonia*, sailing out into the Irish Sea. Wartime exigencies applied on the crowded boat. Nazi submarines prowled the North Atlantic. Soon they witnessed the almost incomprehensible: the *Antonia*'s sister ship, the *Athenia*, had been torpedoed on the final day of its eastward voyage from New York to Liverpool. "Longboats carrying passengers to the dull, misty green Irish shore. Consternation about our ship." They saw the *Athenia* turn up and then slip beneath the water. The sky and the smooth sea were gray. Some passengers on the *Antonia* urged that they turn back. The captain decided to go on. Soon they were sailing a zigzagging evasive pattern that added days to the voyage. Since the protocols and strategies for crossing the Atlantic in wartime had not yet been worked out, no one knew what to expect. But there were no further sightings or incidents.

Life settled down to the usual shipboard routine except that, to Gene's annoyance, the canteen ran out of chocolate, a major disappointment. To him it seemed mostly an adventure, not true history since he was not reading about it in a book, where real history exists. After a few days the adventure seemed ordinary, even boring, certainly not as scary as the countless scary movies he had seen. At night they sailed without lights. He and

Lee Barlow walked the deck in the darkness. She tried, again, to teach him versification. When she insisted on absolute metrical regularity, he cited a Keats sonnet as evidence that great poets sometimes write irregular lines. And why did he need to know the name of a metrical pattern in order to write poetry in that pattern? They were at a standstill. As they kept walking the deck in the darkness, the *Antonia* zigzagged westward. Soon the passengers discovered they were heading for Montreal, not New York. The eight-day trip took two weeks. From Montreal they took the train to Washington, where one of the first things Nina required was that Gene get his hair washed and cut at the Mayflower Hotel. As he looked down into the washbasin at the dirty water, his dark hair turning blond again, he realized, happily, that he had not washed his hair in three months. It had been a blissfully successful first European visit. His only problem was that he had been booked, involuntarily, for a further westward voyage. It was to, of all places, Los Alamos, New Mexico.

CHAPTER four

Brave New World

1939–1941

ON A HIGH MESA in the wilderness of New Mexico, thirty-five miles from Santa Fe, the eight-hundred-acre Los Alamos Ranch School was a quintessential American institution. Founded in 1917 by Ashley Pond, an educated Midwesterner from Detroit, it was now in the hands of an ex-Marine, ex–forest ranger named Albert James Connell, who, like Pond, proclaimed to the effete Eastern world that a rough outdoor life would turn sickly boys into healthy men. Muscle tone was everything. Deep breathing expanded the soul. Boys needed a rigorous schedule, tough conditions, exposure to the elements, survival skills, the transforming beauty and isolation of the Western wilderness. The smiling ghost of Teddy Roosevelt provided guidance and gave his blessing. What they needed also was distance from the effeminizing influence of women. Having served in Roosevelt's "Rough Riders," Pond believed that "boys became men more easily when separated from oversolicitous mothers." If America was being feminized, the Los Alamos Ranch School would save some of its sons. At night, with lights out, there would be only darkness and bright stars, swirling snows in winter, high pastures in spring, muddy dirt roads and clouds of dust as the seasons changed, a happy community of no more than forty-four boys whose parents would gladly pay the highest fee of any preparatory school in the United States to allow their children to breathe freely, their wayward sons to become straight arrows. The magic mesa, jutting out from the main range of the Jemez Mountains, surrounded by the Santa Fe National Forest, was partly a magic mountain, in some cases a sanatorium for the body, but in most, as the school grew, a place where "character" would be developed. Indeed, most of the boys were healthy enough when they arrived. By the 1930s "a lot of the people sent there were kids who were having trouble elsewhere, almost like remittance men from privileged families," one of the students recalled. What they needed to learn was discipline, toughness, manliness.

For Pond, books were an abomination. Nature and hard work provided lessons enough. An avid enthusiast of the Boy Scout movement, Connell had the brilliant idea to organize the school as an active troop, the only mounted troop in the country. Everyone would dress, including the teachers, in the same khaki uniform: short pants and shirt, with wide-brimmed Stetson hat, bandanna on the weekends, black tie on school days. The only concession to winter was woolen underwear. In warm weather the Scouts would be encouraged to go shirtless. Each boy would have a horse. Saddles needed to be polished. Salubrious packing trips into the valleys and mountains demanded perfection, outdoor spit and polish. The ranch, with its own water, electric, and sanitation systems, with "complete machinery for harvesting crops, hauling fuel and supplies, and building, maintaining, and clearing roads," needed to be worked. The boys would play their part. Schooling was at first barely relevant, then secondary. This was not to be a dude ranch but an authentic experience. When Connell took over the school from Pond, the ex-Marine realized that to be successful a ranch needed experienced hands and that to attract boys from well-to-do families who could afford the necessarily high tuition he also had to provide college preparation. These boys, who were not going to grow up to be ranch hands, needed to qualify for the prestigious universities of the country, to take their place in the national hierarchy as befitted their backgrounds. Eager to make a success of the school, he transformed Pond's vision of a ranch in which the boys did all the work into a school in which employees ran the ranch, occasionally helped by the boys. By the mid-1920s Connell had assembled a capable staff, under the headmastership of a smart Latin teacher from Yale,

Lawrence Hitchcock. Connell took care of recruitment, business, discipline, outdoor chores, and expeditions; Hitchcock guided the academic program. Soon the schedule was in place: half a day devoted to studies, half to becoming a self-reliant American male.

As an isolated school run by idealistic male romantics, the ranch on the high mesa had the feel of a muscular monastery, the kind of semiclosed male society in which Connell flourished. Married teachers were not encouraged, though one traditional family, Pond's daughter Peggy and her husband, the science teacher Fermor Church, raised three children there. Connell's compelling interest was in boys, their growth and maturation, their moral and physical well-being. A strict disciplinarian, imperious and mercurial, he enjoyed dominating them, teaching them what he thought of as manly things, particularly the skills of outdoor life and the high principles of Scouting, in both of which he had a mystical belief. When the boys cooked over an outdoor fire on their Saturday full-day trips or their overnight excursions to the high valleys, they did it, as they did everything else, A. J. Connell's way. Any boy who dared cook over an open fire rather than smoldering coals or whose skillet was the least bit dirtied by fire would know Connell's wrath. Verbally sharp, he made sure that everyone knew he did not believe in accidents. If something went wrong, it was always someone's fault, usually yours. He regularly proclaimed that "I know what's best for boys." Having named them "gibbons," he made regular efforts to catch them at what he assumed all gibbons do, bursting into a suspected boy's room to surprise the masturbating offender. "I've caught 'em at it," he would say. He also had his soft side, his gentle aspect, expressed in his fondness for colorful fabrics for his apartment, for hypnotic music like Ravel's "Bolero," for campfire songs and stories. He admired muscles, his own and the boys'. He had an eye for masculine attractions. The boys were subject to weekly physical inspections in the nurse's office by two of the masters. Connell, though, was usually there—to make certain proper procedures were used, to check out the boys' muscle tone, to ascertain just how much each had grown since the last examination. Some of his colleagues found it bothersome. Oscar Steege, the history master, thought "there was an erotic element in Connell's touching the boys," though he restricted his touch to arms, chests, and backsides, "and perhaps some of the boys felt this. . . . It didn't seem right. It didn't seem necessary. . . . That he had a sexual interest in the boys was generally recognized by us at the school.

And there was some unhappiness about this. Not that there were any overt incidents at all. That never happened. But he loved to touch them. I saw that."

―――――・――――

When, in mid-September 1939, Gene Vidal, almost fourteen years old, was driven, in a station wagon full of boys, across the arroyo, up the razor turns of the spectacular road cut out of the sold tufa wall of the canyon, onto the high Los Alamos mesa, he could have had little idea what to expect. He had been sent into exile, expelled from his Washington world and whatever semblance of a home he had, by a mother who applied the Los Alamos doctrine of separating boys from mothers with a vengeance. It was not that Nina did not want him to cling to her apron strings. She did not want him around at all. His Western destination had been determined the previous spring when Connell, on his annual recruiting swing through the Midwest and Northeast, had visited Merrywood, probably introduced to Nina by her good friend Patrick Hurley. Hurley's son was already a student at the Ranch School. The tall, gangly Wilson Hurley wanted to be an artist. His exacting, militaristic father, a powerful Washington political reactionary from Oklahoma who greatly admired Senator Gore, had been Secretary of War in the Hoover administration. "The General," as he was known even to his family, was not about to allow his son to become an effete aesthete. Wilson, who needed to be straightened out, had been sent west the year before Gene. At Merrywood, Connell, a handsome man of middle height, a strong, compact build, and close-cropped, thin gray hair, exerted his twinkling blue-eyed Irish charm. With the help of photos of the school and landscape, he soon had Nina convinced that New Mexico was just what Gene needed. The $2,400-a-year tuition at a time when the Depression-deflated Eastern schools were half that did not shock her: Gene's father was legally obliged to pay. The bills were to be sent directly to him. "I hated going to Los Alamos. I didn't have any choice. I was shipped off. If there had been sufficient coordination between my father and me, I could have headed it off, because he didn't want to pay that tuition. He didn't give a damn whether I liked the school, but it was the most expensive school in America. Nina was such a liar. She would have gone to him and said, 'Oh, he's dying to go out there! It means everything to him!' I can just hear her voice. She was never more rapturous than when she was lying."

By mid-September Gene was on the train to Chicago, with hardly a chance to say good-bye to Jimmie or anyone else. In Chicago he joined other Los Alamos boys for the descent to New Mexico. On the train they wore jackets, ties, some of them even hats, all from privileged families that subscribed to the sartorial decorum that bespoke their world. At Lamy, New Mexico, they were met by the school station wagon which provided a bumpy, slow passage on dirt roads through a starkly beautiful landscape the likes of which he had seen before only in Western movies. A month before, he had been among the glories of Rome, Paris, London. Suddenly he was on a high, immense Southwestern mesa called the Pajarito, the "little bird," whose occasional cottonwood trees gave Los Alamos its name. "The desert suddenly gave birth to a large wooden building with a high roof and a verandah, supported by round smooth wooden columns," he wrote in *The Smithsonian Institution,* evoking his first sight of Los Alamos Ranch School. Sunset on the distant Sangre de Cristo Mountains seemed brilliantly red with the blood the Spanish padres had imagined there centuries before. The thin, sharp air made its breathtaking demands. "As they approached the top of the mesa, the road became narrow and rocky. Tall juniper bushes on every side and the air sage-scented."

New Mexico had its glories too, and Gene was not immune to them, though it hardly attracted him to be at what seemed a glorified summer camp, a combination of a macho Boy Scout troop and an Outward Bound challenge to resourcefulness. With his usual good grace about matters he could not control, he made no fuss. "Going to Los Alamos was my fate. I had no control over anywhere that I went. I didn't like the idea of it, and I didn't like it when I got there." He began scheming immediately about how to get away. As always, he determined to be impersonally congenial. He knew how to be good company for those who liked that kind of company: conversational, verbally playful, amiably careful about boundaries, arrogant but generous. It was clear to him, though, from the moment he boarded the Pullman car in Chicago, that the school encouraged, even demanded, total immersion, constant daily engagement, full exposure to the communal experience. There would be little privacy here. The life of the body demanded shared sweat rather than solitary reading. Horseback was hardly a high cultural position. Since he was stuck, he would make the best of what he was stuck with, away from St. Albans, from Jimmie, from his father in New York, from movie theaters, museums, even farther from the Europe he had just visited. As he walked into Fuller Lodge for his first meal, he could see both the best and worst of what he would have to deal with. *There* were the forty-odd other boys, now, like himself, dressed in their Boy Scout khaki shorts and shirts. *There* were the masters—Hitchcock, Church, Whelen, Steege, Wirth, and a few others—a blur of unfamiliar adults in similar uniforms, and *there* was the only recognizable face, the center of authority, A. J. Connell, whom everyone knew was "The Boss," a kind of Twainian figure, like Hank Morgan in *A Connecticut Yankee in King Arthur's Court*, a man of great arbitrary energy who knew how to make the things of his world work and who believed with deep certainty that the practices and values of his school made boys into men.

Soon Gene was immersed in the daily routine. There would be no living here without that. Like the other boys, he was weighed and inspected for assignment to one of the four patrols—Piñon, Juniper, Fir, and Spruce—the assignment determined by size and physical maturity. Minds were not at issue. Assigned to Juniper, he learned that his sleeping quarters were one of the three verandahs of the Big House, the dormitory and classroom building where all but the Spruce Patrol (the oldest boys) were quartered, a three-story pine-log building surrounded on the upper floor by unheated roofless porches on which the boys slept year round. In severe storms removable awnings were dropped to keep out rain or snow, the night air cool in summer, freezing in winter. Bathroom facilities were sparse, always overworked. At night the boys had to come in to use the one toilet on each floor. Showering in the morning in the stalls on the third or on the first floor was a challenge. An unmarried master, who could retreat to a private room, usually slept on each of the three porches. Classes were held downstairs. Hitchcock and Connell had comfortable apartments on the second floor of Fuller Lodge, where a number of masters without dormitory duties also had rooms. Decorated with colorful Indian rugs, it contained the large dining hall, one end of which served as a stage for theatricals. At Fuller Lodge Gene soon discovered that the food at the Ranch School was good. Fresh vegetables came from the gardens, hearty cooking from the well-run kitchen. Upstairs Hitchcock kept his eye on the school's academic performance. Like Connell, he sometimes had boys to his apartment for soda and cookies, to listen to musical records, for social recreation. On rare instances the tables in the dining hall were cleared away to create a dance floor where

Los Alamos boys could host the girls from Santa Fe's Brownmoor School for Girls.

Surrounding the two main buildings were small huts, storage sheds, a huge barn, workshops, a guesthouse, a trading post for extras from candy to clothes, and the corrals that contained the sixty riding and ten workhorses. Every boy had one immediately assigned to him. Horses at Los Alamos were next to godliness. You did not, though, get to name yours. Those who had come before you had already done that. Gene's came with the name "Two-bits," a horse apparently low enough in the equine hierarchy to be assigned to a new boy who might not deserve or even be interested in a better specimen. Later, in *The Smithsonian Institution,* Gene's fictional surrogate was to gallop on Two-bits through the Los Alamos landscape. Jimmie Trimble, in historical reality now beginning the upper school at St. Albans, is in the novel the character "T.," a prodigy physicist in a world in which some of the usual laws of nature have been expanded:

> T. recognized his friend from the dormitory; the boy's family
> had been threatening to send him west. Now here he was,
> riding up to the window and then *through* the window.
> "Watch out!" T. yelled. Father Lamy was soothing. "We
> aren't really here. For them, that is! They're going to ride
> straight through us." So they did. T.'s friend, a blond youth,
> looked straight into his eyes and then said, to his horse,
> "Come on, Two-bits." Then Two-bits and his rider passed
> straight through T. and out the other side of the mission
> church.

Vidal's brief stay at Los Alamos was to take on the timelessness that combines personal and historical significance. To have been there soon before the bomb was to make the losses of World War II and the deathly explosion even more brightly searing for him.

———·•·———

There was no riding through or away for Gene, at least for that year. Day began each school morning at 6:30 A.M. By 6:45, regardless of the weather, the boys did calisthenics outside. If it had snowed, Connell made sure the exercise field had been shoveled. At seven o'clock, breakfast. The sleeping quarters would be straightened and cleaned to the required standards. Classes ran from 7:40 to 1 P.M. Class assignments and work schedules were determined by Hitchcock on an individual basis, the forty-four boys moving through a small number of classrooms mostly devoted to various levels of English, history, math, chemistry, French, and Latin. The main meal of the day was lunch, followed by a half-hour rest. Monday afternoons everyone did community service, usually physical labor on the grounds. On the other weekday afternoons athletics and recreation dominated, particularly horseback riding, which Gene quite liked. From 5 P.M. on, there would be study hall, dinner, study hall again, then gradually to bed on the open porches. Each Saturday there was the mandatory all-day horseback excursion for the entire school, intensified occasionally by overnight camping trips at Camp May, near the Jemez crest: a caravan of men on horseback and muleloads of supplies wending their way up to the beautiful high valleys for the ultimate, idealized Western experience. At night, around the blazing campfire, Connell would lead them in songs and cheers. As at Sidwell Friends and St. Albans, Gene found classroom routines insufferable. Unusual questions were discouraged, unconventional thinking mostly unwelcome. As usual, his grades were poor. Nina fulminated. His grandfather cajoled. "I am proposing," he wrote to him, "that you and I enter into a CONSPIRACY, not a deep, dark conspiracy, but just a deep one. . . . Let's conspire to give [your mother] the surprise of her life. The best way I can think of to do that is for us to resolve to make your grades for the last month the best that you have scored for the entire session!!! . . . That would surprise as well as please her. . . . My surprise, knowing you, is that you do not lead your classes each and every month." Gene's fantasy was to be free from all this as soon as possible, to be a writer, to be a senator, to rise to blessed adulthood where no one, or at least fewer people, would be able to tell him what to do.

There were also formal musical occasions at Los Alamos. One was the annual Gilbert and Sullivan operetta, that year *The Gondoliers*. Gene was a talented listener. So too was the older boy standing to the right, Alan Meyer. They did themselves and the production a favor by mouthing the words. From a modestly well-to-do Houston Jewish family, Alan had had a poem published in the *New Mexico Magazine,* perhaps the only other boy at Los Alamos with whom Gene shared a literary interest. The two poets became friends, which had nothing to do with Alan Meyer having already made it clear to everyone that his sexual interest was in males. Connell "knew about my sexual life at Los Alamos. In the year or two before Gene came to that school, I had made adolescent advances to some of the other kids in a rather tenuous and distant way, not doing any of the things that the books say that homosexual boys do to one another. . . . I was called in and told that if I didn't cut that stuff out I'd be expelled, so I cut it out. Mr. Connell certainly knew that if a pretty boy or a pretty girl passed through the room, my eyes would most likely follow the boy. I knew about Mr. Connell, but in detail no. I would have told on him? No!" Connell himself was perceived to be a threat. Sexual rumors circulated among the boys about masturbation—the arch sin of 1930s mid-puritan America—about two boys supposed to be actively sweet on one another, about Connell's proclivities. Rumors circulated that Connell had a special crush on a boy whom he "was teaching to have intercourse with a pillow." Some claimed he made advances to boys on the overnight trips, particularly the swimming parties to the hot springs and pools in the area or to the nearby Rio Grande. "He would go on tours," Gore Vidal remembered, "picking the better-looking boys to go with him. I would be on some of these trips. He'd always make overtures. I kept out of reach." One of the boys reported "rather grimly" on his experience. "During an overnight trip somewhere—perhaps Santa Fe—they shared a bed. I don't think even Connell would dare go any further than masturbation together. But even so. . . ." Gene's friend David Osborne, a talkative young man of great energy, confiding that he had resisted such an advance, made it clear he would protest publicly if Connell didn't stop. "It was a small place, and David told everybody. He told him not to harass him sexually, and then Connell stopped." "He did love boys," Alan Meyer remembered, "but I don't think he did anything to them other than fondle them." Even at the physical examinations "he never made a pass at anyone." Connell "would not have had any of his boys do anything to him, nor would he have penetrated any of them. I don't think there would have been anything Greek or French coming or going. I don't think so. That would have got around. We knew about such things, but on a very distant basis."

Happy to have Alan Meyer's company, essentially at ease with the other boys, Gene responded to Connell with neither outrage nor withdrawal. He simply wanted to get out of there as soon as possible. Private reading became his main sustenance, particularly a multivolume history of the world and books that came regularly from The Book-of-the-Month Club—which he had joined—a memoir by the last British ambassador in Berlin, Thomas Mann's entire *Joseph* tetralogy. "Practically nobody could read those books but me. I liked history. I made no difference in my head then between history and the historical novel. I came to know the difference, and in my old age I find that they are the same again. I've come full circle. There's no difference between the two in the light of eternity." Fascinated, he read Sholem Asch's *The Nazarene,* narrated from the point of view of Judas Iscariot, which he later concluded "was a great influence on me, and you might argue the case that both *Julian* and *Burr* come out of it." He "devoured every book that came." And then Shakespeare. "I've never read one of his plays," he wrote to his grandmother, "so I'm starting now." In a few months he eagerly read through the ornament of the Ranch School library, a complete Yale Shakespeare, one play a volume. It strengthened his language, sharpened his perceptions, provided alternative worlds. Words flowed from his pen into poems with the adolescent ease of a boy facile with language and ambitious to be a great writer himself. He enjoyed being witty, sarcastic, verbally aggressive. Entertaining the other boys with clever paraphrases, he especially impressed the impressionable Wilson Hurley with his take-offs on popular song titles. " 'It seems to me I've heard that song before.' He would come up with the title, 'It seems to me I've listened to that ditty previously.' 'Beat me daddy eight to the bar' was 'chastise me father an octave to the measure.' . . . We tried to excell each other in expression and vocabulary and make it humorous at the same time. . . . I remember Gore's favorite entry. He would walk in and with all solemnity say, 'I represent the papacy, and this is no bull!' He got so proud of that joke that we had to shut him off." As his contribution to a discussion of obscenity, Gene remarked about one of the noticeably narcissistic boys that "the most obscene thing I've ever seen is John Curtis putting suntan oil on himself."

Life at Los Alamos was not all isolation, tedium, resentment. A skillful painter, Gene did the stage sets for an abbreviated version of *The Comedy of Errors.* "A charming little kid," so he seemed to the older Alan Meyer, "full of bounce and smiles, and if he hated it, Lord, it didn't show, it didn't show at all. Walking over from some meeting at the Big House on the way to the lodge for lunch, I would fall in with him as with various other people for that little walk, and we did that, people did that. I remember him as a happy person." So did Wilson Hurley. "A bright, pleasant, bouncy little fellow, a happy young fellow," handsome, blond, slim but well built, he rode his horse competently, skied well, and did his chores with no more than the ordinary amount of complaint. That he had at least his fair share of physical courage was much in his favor." Indian culture interested him. Santa Fe was a growing white settlement surrounded by the remnants of ancient civilizations. Bright sun. Vivid blue juniper berries. "Intense blue sky. Desert. Clusters of silver-barked trees wherever there was a stream or a well." Mud-colored adobe huts where white people lived, "set back from the rutted dirt road. Indian villages were built against—or into—the sides of abrupt hills whose tops were flat." A half dozen local tribes still hovered between ancient customs and modern diminishment. The Los Alamos Ranch School had fascinating neighbors, though it did little, reflecting its times, to connect the school to that aspect of the history of New Mexico. But invited to the ranch, Indians from San Isidro, dressed in their totemic eagle costumes, performed their traditional dances, distant cousins of the Oklahoma Indian chiefs whose headdresses Gene had seen at Rock Creek Park.

More interested in their past than their present, he suddenly realized that just as he could seach for marble shards in the Roman Forum, here he could dig for Indian artifacts. There were Indian ruins all around, including immediately in front of Fuller Lodge, where in an area of packed mud the ridge of an old wall extruded four or five inches above the ground. Soon he got permission to dig. Playing archaeologist was more exciting than most of the other Los Alamos Ranch activities. The desire to dig, to uncover, to find out all he could about the past, to connect the past to the present had now a living tactile immediacy. Some years later he was to write a poem, "Walking," about the experience of finding an arrowhead in a dry arroyo as the sun turned red with evening, thinking of "the dead Indians," of the water flowing through the canyon as an image of historical time. Digging by himself, four or five hours a day, he began to discover pots and other shards. As he cleared away earth down to three feet, the outlines of long-hidden rooms became evident. Finally, after days, two rooms were excavated, to the annoyance of those who found it an unsightly inconvenience or a folly. But Hitchcock and others were impressed. At the school's request an expert came from Santa Fe. "It was an eight-hundred-year-old Pueblo Indian ruin." Though Gene was able to secrete away some small pieces of pottery for himself, most of it he was forced to give up to the experts. When the school authorities decided that the excavation would have to be filled in, he had a tantrum that produced a compromise. "They half filled it in, up to the adobe brick wall, the top two rooms." "Oh, my days," he later happily recalled, "as an archaeologist at Los Alamos!"

Soon he had the bright idea that Connell himself might be his ticket out. Whatever sex was going on between boys or between Connell and boys at Los Alamos, Gene had not participated in. He had steered away from "The Boss" as much as possible. "I was very pure then. It all seemed like a great mess to me, and my lust was not aroused by anybody there." But he disliked Connell, partly for taking advantage of the health examinations and some of the boys privately, mostly because he was the daily authoritarian embodiment of the power that had sent him into exile. Perhaps if he blew the whistle on Connell back in Washington, Nina would allow him to return to St. Albans or at least go to what he thought would be a more appropriate school. Since there was no way of avoiding the director, he might as well put him to use. At Christmas 1939 the two Washington boys, Wilson Hurley and Gene Vidal, traveled home together, the same train route they had taken westward in September. At Merrywood, Nina now had two children under her erratic guidance, Nini, two years old, and Tommy, recently born. Christmas festivities were gathering their usual momentum, the huge tree handsomely decorated, stacks of presents waiting to be opened. Visitors came and went, including Wilson's parents, who lived nearby at Leesburg and were part of the same extended circle of prominent Washingtonians who enjoyed the company of their peers. Gene quickly found the opportunity to tell Nina that Connell was "a sexual degenerate." Shocked, Nina thought that, if true, this was a danger to Gene. From her perspective he was already odd enough. She remembered Sherry Davis's analysis of Gene's fascination with costumes and role-playing and immediately took the bait. Gene must have felt secure enough or desperate enough to use an issue that might cut back at him. But at Los Alamos itself there had been no hint that he was implicated in Connell's activities. Nina immediately rolled up her sleeves and went to work, which suited Gene's purposes. At the first opportunity, drink in hand at a late-night party, she cornered Patrick Hurley. Inimitably direct, the "let's tell it as it is" Nina wanted to know whether or not what her son had told her was true. Was the director of the school a pansy? Horrified, in the small hours of the night, as soon as he got home, Hurley awakened his son. " 'I hear your headmaster's a queer,' " he said, and demanded that Wilson either confirm or deny what Gene had told his mother. Wilson had already been at Los Alamos for almost two years. His father, a supporter and advocate of Connell's regime, had visited the school. What the hell was going on? "Wilson played dumb or was dumb." The grilling was precise, harsh, military. " 'Well, he may be, but he's never mentioned or demonstrated it to me. I have never seen it in action, and so I can't depose on that subject.' So then he said, 'Well, has anybody ever laid a hand on you that way?' And I said, 'No.' " That satisfied "The General," who would have been eager to be satisfied. "Pat Hurley reported to my mother who said—a line I've always loved—'Why, it just shows that that boy of yours is a greenhorn!' " But the greenhorn had pulled off a clever maneuver.

Wilson and Gene took the train back early in the new year. When, traveling westward, they discussed the subject, Wilson still maintained that nothing of that sort had gone on as far as he knew except ordinary adolescent things, the same line that had gotten him off the hook with his father. As they ascended to the wintry high mesa, Gene had good reason to hope that this would be his last and only winter there. He had begun raising his voice on the matter, to his mother, his father, his grandparents. Usually tractable, he had insisted he would not return for another year. Soon Hurley telephoned Connell and asked him if he knew about the rumor that was going far enough around to have reached him in Washington. The director provided denials and assurances. Apparently Connell either knew or guessed the source of Hurley's information. Soon Connell let Nina and Big Gene know that their son would not be invited to return the next year. The reasons were of the most general kind, including that it would be in the young man's best interest to go to a school with a larger program. Since Gene had already made it clear he did not want to return, his quiet expulsion seemed easy enough for all to go along with. To Nina the only annoyance was that she would now have to find a new school for him. Gene Vidal was pleased to be relieved of the high tuition. The boy himself was delighted.

The school also would soon be moving on, out of material existence and into the pages of history. Those who had been students there were shortly to have Los Alamos seared into their memories beyond the ordinary memorable images of schoolboy life. On a spring morning in 1942, two years after Gene's departure, the students and staff at the Ranch School gazed up at the strange sight of a small airplane circling and circling. Connell guessed something significant was up. Such an expenditure of airplane fuel in wartime was likely to be consequential. Soon two authoritative strangers came to visit, General Leslie Groves and Dr. J. Robert Oppenheimer, plans and vision in hand. In a short time guards were posted around the perimeter of Los Alamos. In December an abrupt, bureaucratic notice from the Secretary of War arrived: land and buildings were to be expropriated for military use. Some compensation. Period. Connell, crushed, did his patriotic duty uncomplainingly. The Los Alamos Ranch School disappeared forever. So did the director, who died two years later, a man whose boys and whose mission had been taken from him late in life when a new beginning was impossible. The literal place name of the school on the mesa soon became awesomely famous, associated not with living boys but with devastated cities, not with the romantic American optimism and naïveté of Pond's vision but with the nuclear age and the Cold War.

———————

While home from Los Alamos for the Christmas 1939 holidays, Gene had the mixed blessing of seeing his recently remarried father. His own juniorship seemed vexatiously ironic: his father had just married a woman only six years older than his son. Young Gene already had one mother. What would be the point in having another, especially one almost his contemporary? Slim, dark-haired, bright-eyed, with classical features, twenty-year-old Katherine Roberts had come into his father's life like a breath of spring. "She was just so fresh," he told his sister-in-law. "She was fresh and new." He had fallen in love with youth, perhaps partly a statement of how much he disliked his own aging, how frightening the prospect of losing his athlete's fine body. Owen Roberts, Kit's multimillionaire father, with a seat on the stock exchange and a valuable art collection, provided his wife, from whom he had separated, and daughter with only a small court-mandated allowance. Kit had been working for the last five years as a Powers model, and she and her mother, from a well-established Southern family, had spent a great deal of time living in palatial splendor in Peking. "With what they would have paid for living on Central Park West, they lived in a palace with twenty servants." She had also attended finishing school in Connecticut and studied in Paris. The impending marriage came as a surprise to many. Skeptical, Kit's mother, who liked Gene, soon came around. Gene's sister Lurene inquired disbelievingly about the rumor. No, she had misheard, Gene teased. This was actually a poor young girl he was going to adopt, not marry. Liz Whitney was furious. She had not expected Gene to slip away. Apparently "she tried everything from threats of murder to suicide to blackmail, everything. My father said that to his last day he never figured out how she found out where Kit and he were spending their honeymoon. . . . But on their wedding night Liz started ringing about ten o'clock in the evening. Then he said, 'If Miss Whitney calls, don't take the call.' So then 'Miss Smith' would call, and it would be Liz again, denouncing my father for what he had done, for the terrible mistake he made throwing away his life and her life . . . Finally, he said, he had to take the phone off the hook because Liz wouldn't stop. Then the next day she wrote a slightly apologetic letter and sent him a wedding present, the most beautiful beige silk pajamas I've ever seen in my life. I know because he gave them to me. . . . He never wore them. It was the one color he couldn't wear, and she knew it. It made him look green. . . . I wore those pajamas for years."

The marriage took place mid-December 1939, in the bride's mother's Manhattan apartment. The New York and Washington papers noticed it prominently, the *New York Herald Tribune* previewing it on the morning of the wedding day: "Aeronautic Consultant and New York Girl, Recently of China, Plan Bridal." There had been no public engagement announcement. Gene's divorce prevented their marrying at the Episcopalian Church of the Heavenly Rest. Of Gene's family, only Sally and Pick attended, Pick the best man. Stationed in nearby Mitchell Field, he had seen a good deal of Gene since his move to New York. Why the wedding date had not been arranged so that young Gene could be there is unclear. On that same day he departed from Los Alamos for Christmas at Merrywood, where he was to bring Connell's predilections to his mother's attention. Perhaps preoccupied and, as usual, absentminded about arrangements, Gene may not have thought to align his schedule with his son's. Although always happy to have his father's company, the boy never *expected* to have it. It was not exclusion but misalignment, of a sort he had grown used to. Not that it did not sometimes disappoint him, as it did when, coming up from Washington by train, he regularly arrived at the entrance to the upper–Park Avenue building where Gene had a small apartment only to find that he had to wait endlessly, though they had made precise arrangements in advance. "I can

remember waiting for him six and seven hours outside his apartment building because he had forgotten I'd come up. And it wasn't any feeling against
me: he forgot everything. He was naturally vague. I can remember waiting,
waiting, waiting for him in the vestibule. . . . I took it for granted that
that was the way it was. I didn't like it. But I didn't dislike it. He always
charmed me. He was very apologetic. He didn't remember anything. . . .
His best friend of ten years earlier could be talking to him and he still
couldn't figure out who he was. Not good with names or faces. One of his
jokes: 'There are three things I can't remember: one is names, another faces,
and the third I can't remember.' He couldn't remember that he had an
appointment with me. Who knows what the hell he was doing! He wasn't
that rabid about business. . . . He refused to keep appointments and refused to have an office if he could help it. He liked puttering. He liked
inventing things. He was more apt to be working in a shed inventing molded
plywood or something. That was what interested him. Or fucking. Many
ladies."

Gene's failings were of a sort that never produced the level of pain that
Nina's did. Neither patriarchal nor nurturing, he had a talent for companionable good times. Lurene, puzzled, remarked that father and son behaved
more like brothers than father and son, " 'off in corners giggling at the rest
of us.' She didn't approve. Each had his role, and we weren't playing them."
Gene never gave advice. But he also never took credit for his son's achievements. "Friends of his would ask . . . what had he done that made me so
successful? 'Well,' he'd say, 'I think it's the fact that I never gave him any
advice and if I had he would not have taken it. And,' he said, 'we had a
perfect relationship.' " In warm weather they would take drives into the
country, particularly from his Manhattan apartment to Amagansett, Long
Island, to stay with his friend McClellan Barkeley. A successful portrait and
fashion painter, Barkeley had a way with beautiful young models, both in
paint and in the flesh. With Pick, Sally, and Gene, "Mac" attended a football
game at West Point. Broad-shouldered, mustached, with thinning hair,
about forty years old, he "wore sort of a gangster snap-brim hat and a tan
polo coat and a yellow wool scarf. He just looked so beautiful walking
around the stands trying to find our seats," Sally recalled. With an attractive
beach house, Barkeley was an amorous bachelor who had a love life perhaps
even more active than Vidal's. In summer 1939 he had introduced Gene to

Kit Roberts, who was posing for one of his *Saturday Evening Post* cover illustrations and whom he wanted for himself. She responded to Gene's advances, not Mac's. Still, he had attractive alternatives, whom he regularly hosted at his beachfront cottage. Each of the two rooms had four beds, one room for the young models, the other for the men on hand. In the summers of 1937 and 1938 Gene and young Gene visited numbers of times. "It was a house . . . filled with beautiful girls. I loved it. That would be great fun, sort of living on the beach." Young Gene enjoyed flirting with some of the girls, all of whom were indeed closer to his age than to their host's. Like his father, though in a different way, he was now noticeably charming. By 1939 "he was getting taller," his then twenty-five-year-old Aunt Sally noticed, "and he was always so skinny. He had on some sort of cute Western pants, with a Western cut." At the beach, in swim trunks, blond, pale-complexioned, hazel-eyed, with an inquisitive bright smile, usually in high spirits, he was a delight to have around. He soon had a ferocious crush on one of the young ladies, who was not at all unhappy about his being smitten. Nothing came of it, but it was fun and memorable.

Sexy, attractive, resembling the young Katharine Hepburn, madly in love with her husband, Kit had no desire to be a mother of any kind to his almost grown-up son. She knew intuitively that it would be a mistake. She had heard enough about Nina to stay out of the firing line. But young Gene felt the awkwardness, the tenseness, of having a stepmother. "My relationship with her was edgy at the beginning. Trying to get rid of one mother— just the word 'mother' was enough to start me climbing the wall—and here's a stepmother. Also, she was very sexy and just about my age." A consultant for the Bendix Corporation and a director of Eastern Airlines, Gene nevertheless had a modest income, and the bills from Los Alamos were huge. At Camden, New Jersey, he soon set up a small factory where he invented and tested variations on molded plywood parts for fuselages and wingtips, still preoccupied with making airplanes for individuals economically feasible. The process was patented as Vidal Weldwood. But there were start-up costs, few contracts, and little profit for his Aeronautics Research Corporation. Despite Kit's father's wealth, there was no family money available for her. When she took on some modeling jobs, Gene's resistance to having a working wife soon put an end to that. The news that young Gene would not be returning to Los Alamos came as a relief.

From the small apartment on East Sixty-fifth Street the couple occupied after marrying, they soon moved into a two-bedroom flat in the Wardman Park in Washington, familiar to Gene Vidal and the obvious place for a short-term residence. Probably he thought he might do better selling his innovative product if he were nearer the source of government contracts. In Washington he took Kit to tea at Rock Creek Park to meet Senator and Mrs. Gore. "Gene was never not friendly with them," Kit recollected. "He liked them very much. They were his family at that point. They still seemed like family to him. And they weren't all that crazy about Nina all the time either. . . . I think Gene was more of a son than she was a daughter."

When young Gene came home briefly to Merrywood during the Easter vacation and the summer of 1940, he stayed a few days with Kit and Gene at their apartment. Gradually the relationship between stepmother and son became calmer, more rational. In conversation he remarked to her that some of his friends had made comments about his father marrying such a young woman. She too, of course, had heard similar remarks. Since it was clear Kit had no intention of being in the least bit motherly, Gene soon felt more at ease with her and the marriage. Blissfully happy, having married "the love of her life," Kit did not care what people said. At Merrywood the Auchincloss menage had its complications. Yusha, frequently off at boarding school, was disenchanted with Nina as he observed the deterioration of the marriage. At Rock Creek Park the Gores watched their daughter's progress with quiet horror. Both Yusha and Hugh, to whom they were sympathetic, seemed like victims. The Gores "were in a class by themselves," Yusha recalled. "Both my father and I liked them very much. I think because they were Nina's parents I was always hoping that their daughter would come up to their standards. My father and I never understood how these charming, gentle people could produce a daughter like that." Still, when she was not drunk or angry, Nina could be enchanting, and Hugh had no desire to divorce her. The stammering husband did his best to keep domestic things going, though they rarely went well. In late spring 1940 he came up with a bright idea. Since Gene would not be returning to Los Alamos, why not send him to Hugh's own alma mater, Phillips Exeter Academy? That one of his business partners was a trustee might help. Gene Vidal had no reservations about that suggestion. The cost of a year at Exeter was less than half that of Los Alamos.

An elite school with high standards, Exeter expected even bright boys to get low grades. These were expected, though, to come *at* Exeter, not before. Gene's sponsors were estimable, his grades poor but not terrible. Some claim may have been made that he had special talents, in writing and painting. Certainly Auchincloss's name and his partner-trustee's would have been invoked. His father's and grandfather's also, which would have carried the weight of their careers in public life. It may have been a close call for the admissions office, which allowed Gene admission for September 1940 with a proviso: that he attend the five-week summer school to make up deficiences in his record. Before he knew it, he was grinding away at three onerous courses, two of them subjects he despised. Ironically, English was even more painfully offensive to him than Latin and math. Eager to be creative, to show his skills as a writer, he quickly found that his English teacher, Hamilton Bissell, was having none of it. "I'll allow you to write the way you want to, but first you must show me that you *can* write the way I want you to." Either Gene would grammatically parse standard English sentences and write dry, formal, correct prose, with the business letter as model, or he was in trouble. He was. Bissell ripped into his compositions. He responded resentfully, defensively. For the four themes he wrote each week he got C's and D's. When a boy sitting next to him strained to look at his paper during an exam, he ironically pushed it toward him. Bissell, who saw only part of what had happened, thought he was cheating, which further soured him on an arrogant student who resisted doing things the Exeter way. Bissell did what the rules required: he reported the offender to the acting principal of the summer school, Darcey Curwen. Expulsion should have been automatic. For some reason Curwen allowed him to stay. The grinding five weeks finally came to an end. Gene had failed Latin. He had gotten a D in math. He had passed English with a C, a very respectable grade at Exeter in the days before grade inflation. But all in all it was a dismal performance. He was happy to have the summer session done with.

Amid the banners, cheers, and hoopla stood the newly famous Mr. Wendell Willkie, the Indiana-born Wall Street lawyer about to receive the 1940 Republican presidential nomination. He would challenge the demon himself, Franklin Roosevelt. Caesar-like, by running for a third term, Roosevelt was about to turn the republic into an empire, all good Republicans and many conservative Democrats feared. Whomever they were for separately, they hated "that man in the White House" and worried he was about to deliver them up to the conflagration that had begun in Europe the previous September when young Gene and his classmates had sailed homeward from Liverpool. In the late-July weather, uncomfortable Philadelphia steamed. What better place, though, than the cradle of liberty from which to launch the campaign to save the republic! Crowds, heat, colorful banners, hot rhetoric, Liberty Bells, America First! Not a breeze was to be had except from ceiling and hand fans of the sort right-wing California Senator Vandenberg's supporters handed out by the thousands. "Fan with Van," they said, a message sufficiently ambiguous to lend itself to anti-Vandenberg jokes. An internationalist lawyer who had long ago left the Midwest, Willkie charmed Middle America with his Hoosier accent, promising little, implying much. He would keep America out of war, a sentiment that Senator Gore had heard from Woodrow Wilson in 1916, not long before Wilson decided that America too must fight. Blind, portly, white-haired, cane extended before him, immediately identifiable, Senator Gore was among ideological soulmates. Always obsessed with his favorite American spectator sport, he had taken his fifteen-year-old grandson to one of America's quadrennial spectaculars, a national political convention.

Earlier, at Willkie's hotel suite, on the reception line with his grandfather, Gene shook the soon-to-be-nominated, soon-to-be-defeated candidate's soft, sweaty hand. Now, from his seat high up in the bleachers, he could see at the press table far below, huge cigar in mouth, big round eyeglasses, stubby, wide-faced, acerbically satirical H. L. Mencken, a hero of American journalism whom Gene did not yet recognize but later identified from a newspaper photo. Politicians, favor seekers, power brokers—American history buzzed all around him at the hotel, at the convention, in the streets. Pink-faced from the heat, the normally gray-looking former President Herbert Hoover addressed the convention competently. Halfway through Hoover's speech, Gene's grandfather muttered, "He's the only person in this hall who doesn't know that he will never be President again." When Hughdie arrived, the three went to lunch at the Philadelphia Raquet Club. Youthful Senator Henry Cabot Lodge, handsome in a naval uniform, the center of attention, joined them. An enthusiastic Willkie supporter and a major contributor, Hughdie had had visions of the Italian ambassadorship dangled before his eyes. Lodge's father and Gene's grandfather had changed world history: together they had killed the League of Nations. At lunch they talked politics and war, the past, the future. "I remember thinking how extraordinary that this young handsome man is already a senator. Even at that age he seemed more in my age range than I had thought he would be. There was a slight stirring of ambition in me."

⸻

In mid-September 1940 an Auchincloss limousine took Gene from Newport to New Hampshire. The venerable redbrick preparatory school, for the next three years another one of his homeless homes, soon came into sight. For some reason his summer-school grades had not excluded him from matriculation as a Lower Middler (sophomore), though they were to be an accurate indicator of his later marks. That he was a celebrity boy who had flown a plane at ten years of age, grandson of a former senator, son of a former Roosevelt cabinet member, stepson of a wealthy alumnus whose partner was an Exeter trustee undoubtedly helped. That he was just plain smart, whatever his classroom performance, some of the Exeter people recognized. As he may have himself anticipated as he was driven into town in late summer, he was to be, in his own way, a distinctive student. The limousine moved up Main Street to the collegelike campus. He asked the chauffeur to stop. With the chauffeur's help, Gene's luggage was placed on the sidewalk. He did not want to be seen as a rich boy who had been driven to school in a limousine. As the car pulled away, he carried his bags across the street and up the hill to the academy building.

Having already spent the summer session there, Gene was not unfamiliar with the Exeter campus, but the sheer size of the student body and faculty—about seven hundred and fifty boys and more than seventy teachers for the autumn term—struck him as noticeably different from any school he had been to before. It did not seem in the least frightening; in fact, the larger the school, the less school- and prisonlike it felt to him. Still, it was a startling change. He had with some degree of suddenness gone from an experimental ranch school in the New Mexican wilderness to an elite New England preparatory school almost as old as the republic itself. Founded in 1781, its first famous graduate Daniel Webster, Exeter dominated, with half a dozen or so other such schools, the American Protestant establishment's educational system at the secondary level. A gatekeeping school, it sent huge numbers of its students to Harvard, Yale, and Princeton. From there the best went on to Wall Street law firms, high business positions, Ivy League professorships, government service, state and national political office. Some few struck out for the movie industry, for the arts, for wander years and wander lives. Occasionally some dropped out, to be referred to in the reunion classbook directories as "missing" or "unknown." "Exeter Fair, O mother stern yet tender," as the school song put it, trained national leaders. Just as there was correct "Exeter English," there was a correct Exeter ideology. A rigorous curriculum was based on the belief that mental is the highest exercise, playing fields are essential as adjuncts to the classroom, privilege demands civic responsibility, intellectual challenge sharpens the mind and character, competition makes men. Those who could not keep up would be eliminated. Those who did not catch on that the Exeter maxim, "There are no rules until you break one," meant that a first or at best a second infraction resulted in expulsion soon found themselves expelled. The emphasis was on stern rather than tender. Exeter prided itself on building "character."

A major gift from Edward S. Harkness had resulted in an educational innovation in 1931 that typified Exeter's dedication to intellectual excellence. The Harkness plan required and paid for low teacher-student ratios and a large number of small classrooms. Every class, composed of no more than twelve students, was to be taught at an oval seminar table, often in a room with a small subject-focused library. Relevant books and reference works were immediately available. Academic standards were high, the work ethic intense. Determined to match intellect to privilege and responsibility, Exeter created, with some of the Harkness money, a scholarship program, sending representatives around the country to identify and recruit the brightest, hardest-working boys. From the large academy building, on its rise above the campus, the lawns sloped toward residence and dining halls in two directions, additional classroom buildings, the chapel close by (daily attendance compulsory). Across Main Street stood the library, the student center, more residence halls, various administrative buildings, some faculty housing, the playing fields in the distance to the east. To the northeast, abutting the campus, was the old New England town through which ran the narrow, swift-flowing Exeter River, then marshes and a lake, with more Exeter property, then countryside. The school itself was mostly a self-contained world, sufficient unto itself, a total community. Town was there. But only gown counted. Whereas Los Alamos Ranch School had created unity by isolation, Exeter created it by intensity, by critical mass, by privilege, competition, and challenge.

Gene's venue was the debating hall and the library. At the academy building he had been handed his program for the year, the same subjects he had always hated—math, Latin, and the only slightly less distasteful French. English with Mr. Crosbie was genial, gentlemanly, dull, another exemplification of correct Exeter prose. Crosbie, a fellow student in the class remarked, "looks 80, stresses spelling and punctuation, and simple, straight sentences with an absolute fixed order of things." That Gene wrote poetry was fine, even good, but that was not what this was about. After starting with decent grades in Latin, he quickly descended to a D. "We pull Caesar apart," Otis Pease recorded, "noun from noun, verb from verb, and explain why and why not. You must 'know your grammar or get out.' " Gene barely ever rose above an E in math. In French he oscillated between a C and D the first term, mostly D's thereafter. Once he saw that the only way to do better in English was to give Mr. Crosbie what he wanted, he produced enough to rise to a C, though he did not conceal that this was a concession. Quick, alert, sometimes condescending in class, he made it all too easy for teachers to recognize that they had someone bright on their hands. Only fulfilling the required work tasks, though, earned good grades. That he read frequently, avidly, made no difference. Mostly he was reading the wrong books, especially histories and novels rather than required assignments. Even his English-class compositions usually fell short, especially during his first two years. But he sensed, quite rightly, they would not expel him, except for something egregious, an infraction that related to the character issue, to mother Exeter, "stern but tender." Short of that, he could neglect the classroom and still scrape by academically, though there would inevitably be tensions between himself and the faculty, between himself and his nightmares. "If you missed two chapels, you were out. You couldn't cut chapel. I still have nightmares about that. . . . I've done all that I have done. I am who I am now but I'm still at Exeter. . . . I have a list of the classes I should go to, and I haven't been to any of them. And we're doing the final exams. What should I do? And I wake up in a sweat." One teacher wrote on his department report that Gene might well become a credit to the school if they could stand him for another two years.

His best public performances were in the Daniel Webster Debating Hall, at the top of Phillips Hall, where the venerable Golden Branch and G. L. Soule debating societies and the Phillips Exeter Academy Senate met regularly. The competitive intensity rose to the intellectual and rhetorical equivalent of the controlled battles on the athletic fields. Any student could join either of the two societies. Members in the Academy Senate were elected. Debating was both a participatory and a spectator sport. At each debate four to six students got to speak. The rest served as audience, extended by other students and faculty who were attracted to the topic or the speakers. Boys who imagined themselves one day arguing important cases before the highest judges of the land or of reaching nationally re-nowned oratorical heights in the highest legislative arenas flocked to the debating hall, where the spiritual presence of one of the great original Exonians might inspire them. Accounts of the debates appeared prominently in the student newspaper, published twice a week, headlined with bold print as large and as well placed as any other campus event, other than football games. In autumn 1940, when Gene made his first appearance on the plat-form, debating had taken on a new urgency. Membership in the societies had increased. Whereas before debates had covered a wide range of topics, now the war in Europe, the prospect of America's entry, the policies of the Roosevelt administration, and the heated Roosevelt-Willkie election cam-paign dominated the interest and the passions of many. And war was on the horizon: Exeter boys knew that on graduation day they might indeed move from a debating society to a combat zone. Suddenly almost all the debates touched, directly or indirectly, on this subject. The national debate between those who wanted to avoid American involvement in this foreign war and those who had embraced the internationalist ideal of America as the arsenal of democracy had its microcosmic representation in this schoolboy world. Anger, anxiety, desperation were as much in the air as idealism, patriotism, and youthful courage.

Like his grandfather, Gene too wanted to be a senator, an elevation he easily achieved at the recently established Academy Senate. A mock legisla-tive body, it was large, unwieldy, given to committees, cabals, and postur-ing, an excellent place to gain and sharpen political skills. Within two weeks

of his arrival, he received notification that he had "been elected to membership in the P.E.A. Senate. If possible, attend the next meeting, Sunday, Oct.
9, 1940, in the Debating Room of Phillips Hall." He soon became one of the
senators from Virginia. "I don't remember what my first debate topic was.
. . . I remember the room was spinning around. I do know that I could
never speak without full notes. . . . I prepared carefully. . . . It took
time and effort to prepare for each debate. Then I learned the trick of
reading without appearing to read."

After dark the town of Exeter fell silent, even more so once cold
weather set in. On campus, night life was restricted to club activities, study
hall, the dormitory, the radio, private bull sessions, public debates. Each
Sunday evening the senators met in raucous session. On Wednesday night
the Golden Branch Debating Society assembled. Gene soon became a member, accomplished simply by attendance and then a maiden speech. With
notes in hand he appeared, fully formed it seemed, an electrically eager,
epithet-extending debater to be reckoned with, sharp and acerbic in his
spontaneous comments. He prepared for debates, not classes. On Friday
night the G. L. Soule Debating Society convened. At the beginning of
October the Golden Branch debated "Why Willkie Should be President."
The affirmative won. At the end of the month, as the election approached,
Willkie won the student poll, 438 to Roosevelt's 146, the faculty poll 20 to
18. Republicans' hopes, on and off campus, were high. In November many
boys stayed up late to hear the election results on the radio. Like the
majority of Exonians, Gene was disappointed. But at the same time as
Exonians favored Willkie, they also favored, by a smaller margin, that
America enter into a military alliance with Great Britain. Passionately sharing his grandfather's politics, the senator from Virginia took the conservative side in most debates: he was a happy, if not gleeful, warrior, like the
Roosevelt whose political skills he admired, whose views he opposed. He
increasingly perfected his Roosevelt imitation: "I *hate* wa*aaa*r! Eleanor *hates*
wa*aaa*r." Soon he organized an "America First" chapter. His more numerous, powerful opponents, led by the smart, articulate Tom Lamont, a grandson of J. P. Morgan's partner, had created "Bundles for Britain." London
was being bombed. German troops marched into Romania. Lend-Lease
ships sailed the North Atlantic to Britain. Gene and Lamont became instant
political enemies.

By spring his favorite faculty member, whom he never had for a class, was the anti-Exonian, ex-Princetonian Tom Riggs, who had recently come to Exeter. He was not there for long. Sharply intelligent, ironic, dissident, the outspoken Riggs, who taught English, attracted the disapproval of the largely mainstream Exonians. "He seemed fonder of the kids than of the faculty," one of his colleagues remarked, "whom he thought of as fuddy-duddy establishment people. Riggs had no anchors down—he was a free spirit who didn't care about gaining the respect of the Exeter people, and it was clear to everyone that he was there only temporarily. He rejected the discipline of the environment." When obliged to take his turn presiding at morning chapel, the scrawny, balding, sharp-nosed, jug-eared Riggs "would pull his clothes on over pink-and-white striped pajamas, plainly visible at wrist and ankle," Gore Vidal recalled, "and read the lesson and announcements in a voice like W. C. Fields." The principal, Bliss Perry, who had been leading Exeter since 1914, found Riggs a major nuisance. Gene thought him fascinating, totally admirable. Since Riggs encouraged him to talk about literature and politics on terms that did not include Exonian condescension or punitive put-downs, Gene felt conversationally at ease with him, someone he could express himself to and learn from. Acutely political, Riggs was the son of a former governor of Alaska. At Princeton, with other undergraduates, he had helped create in spring 1936 a national stir with the satiric "The Veterans of Future Wars." Its main platform was that all potential veterans should immediately receive a bonus of $1,000 so that they might get the full benefit of compensation *before* they were killed or maimed. "Soldiers of America, Unite. You have nothing to lose." The national press, partly bemused, publicized the new organization. Congress investigated. One humorless congressman called them "Communists because they welcome Pacifists and Fascists with open arms." They were beneath notice, he concluded, but should be investigated. Partly joke, partly angry satire, lightly serious, the witty Princetonians made their point effectively. Since the Veterans of Foreign Wars sold poppies to commemorate the dead, the Veterans of Future Wars sold poppy *seeds*. As opposed to American involvement in foreign wars as Senator Gore, Riggs came at it from the radical left. A Marxist, he seemed both brilliantly talented and sensibly antiwar. It was an eye-opener for the Senator's grandson. When Gene showed Riggs some of the Senator's speeches, Riggs ironically commented, "He knows how to make the eagle scream." At Exeter, T. P. Gore received scant respect. The Willkie Republicans, mostly internationalists, thought him a reactionary rabble-rouser who, fortunately, no longer served in the Senate. Roosevelt Democrats despised him. The radical left agreed with his antiwar views but nothing else. For the first time Gene had to take seriously criticism of his grandfather's political positions.

If he had no friends yet at Exeter, he had people with whom he was friendly. Both reserved and aggressive, he did not make friends easily. To some his aggressiveness seemed un-Exonian self-promotion, a personal projection that seemed out of place among New Englanders and their ethos. He was used to boasting about his grandfather and father and announcing that he himself expected to accomplish great things. Some he irritated. Others found his elegant abrasiveness interesting. One could never predict what he would say. Or if one were to predict with a likelihood of accuracy, the guess had to be he would say something outrageous or controversial or extravagantly self-regarding by Exonian standards. With a reputation for quips in conversation and barbs in debate, he made some of his classmates anxious. There would be a price to pay if one tangled with him. Used to being conversationally combative, he assumed that everyone would understand he meant nothing personal, that he intended to entertain, persuade, assert himself rather than put others down. Not everyone did. But his skills, his talents, and particularly his devotion to reading and writing made him stand out, attractively even if ambivalently, to some of his talented classmates. With two of them—A. K. Lewis, familiarly known as "A.K." or "Hacker," slim, dark-haired, with rimless glasses and cleft chin, the son of a well-known Harvard philosopher, and Robert Bingham, a tall, beefy, pink-complexioned New Englander with blue eyes, light-brown curly hair, a heart-shaped face, and invariably a bow tie—he soon became warmly friendly. Lewis and Bingham spent much time together. Bingham, Lewis recalled, "was very charismatic, with a wonderful sense of humor. I think he had more humor than anybody else I have ever met, humor as opposed to wit; he was a wonderful person and very generous."

———

At home for the Christmas 1940 holiday, Gene began a serious romantic whirl with a young Washingtonian beauty. He had known Rosalind Rust for years, one of the girls at Mrs. Shippen's mandatory dancing parties, where young people of a certain class began their amatory socialization, one of their first barely articulated negotiations into the marriage market that all were expected eventually to deal in. Prepubescent and pubescent Washingtonians of both sexes learned how to dance and proper dancing etiquette: how to hold one another, at the proper distance, with the right results. Hardly interested in dancing at all, Gene, like many boys, had reluctantly over the years done his required service at dancing school. At the usual round of parties for students home from school for the holidays, he suddenly found himself paying tender attention to a former dancing partner. A student at The Madeira School near Washington, two months older than he, more interested in parties than in books, Rosalind was a talented artist who drew and painted beautifully. Less worldly, more of a teenager, happy at parties and excited about Washington social life, she was the only child of Frances Rust, a well-known socialite long divorced from her now-deceased husband, who had lived a carefree, unproductive life as the favorite son of Washington real-estate magnate H. L. Rust. Having attended Madeira and graduated from Vassar, Frances was "definitely quite a lady," her grandson recalled, with "a great sense of humor," both genteel and down to earth. Estranged from her husband's family, she received nothing from them. Though there was a small trust fund for Rosalind, Frances maintained her social position on very little, just enough for household servants, dinner parties, good clothes, and modest comforts.

Sixteen-year-old Roz, her wide face accented by strong cheekbones, framed by rust-bronze short hair, had a light complexion, bright eyes, a low sexy voice, and elegantly straight posture. "She had a beautiful face and a beautiful body, with long legs and no breasts," a friend of her later life recalled. "She'd often wear bangs to accentuate the Slavic look," her Washington friend, Tish Baldrige, remembered. She was just two inches shorter than the almost six-foot-tall Gene; they were, that Christmas, a striking couple. Attracted to her sexually, he loved her bearing, her beauty, her touch of glamour. Like her mother, she was meticulously groomed, beautifully dressed. Eager to be his own man, to be as independent as possible, being in love with Rosalind seemed a step on the way. When he returned to Exeter at the beginning of January, Roz wrote in her diary, "I am crazy about Dini. I think of him all the time and the wonderful times we had at Christmas." She found him handsome and enchanting, "very sophisticated looking. He is tall, about 5 ft 11 ½ inches, with rather blond hair, large grey-green eyes, an aristocratic nose and a nice rather mocking mouth. . . . His eye brows are like this x x x very arched. He can raise his eyebrows one after the other, and wiggle his ears. . . . Dini is so divine looking."

Her attractions absorbed him during much of the Christmas holiday. As soon as he had confided to her his intimate childhood name, it became an expression of their possessive intimacy, though she soon recognized he was not an easy person to possess, that there was more adult calculation and coolness in his temperament than in hers. "He was so *very, very* sweet to me during vacation," she remembered, as she impatiently waited for a letter from him. Back at school she read *Jane Eyre*, which she found fascinating, in love herself with a man at a distance. When she did not hear from him throughout January, her daydreams intensified, her hopes trembled. She made excuses for him. Eventually letters came. She was more loving than loved, more emotionally eager and expressive than he, partly because she was less self-protective. Though he had no doubt that Roz would never turn into his mother, his distaste for and his distress at his mother's abusive behavior had left him wary. It had created the possibility that any potential wife might eventually be a real Nina, that any marriage might turn into the nastiness of his parents' relationship. But having a beautiful girlfriend had attractions. The experience with Jimmie had seemed perfectly natural. The affair now with Rosalind seemed equally natural. His view was that sex was simply bodily pleasure. Have it with whomever you wanted, with whomever it happened. Others or yourself. Male or female. It soon happened with Rosalind, probably that next summer, most likely at East Hampton, where she came to stay with him at his father's vacation cottage, as she did again the next summer. Kit was not impressed. "She wasn't my type. I just didn't take to her particularly. . . . I don't remember exactly why. I know I wouldn't have chosen her for a daughter." Kit may have preferred to be the only beauty around. At Exeter, where Roz came to dances numbers of times, she attracted admiring attention. She was a girlfriend easy to have. Apparently they had one another with pleasure. Rosalind later told a friend that Gore had been "my first beau and the best man I ever had. . . . The best man I ever had in bed."

After the Christmas holiday he returned to debating and to the library. He borrowed so many books that the librarians grumbled. Of course he returned to classes also, but with even worse results than before, except in art class, his only elective. Like Rosalind, though less talented, he had a facility for painting. Occasionally he daydreamed about becoming a famous artist. Sculpting had become even a greater pleasure than it had been when he had sculpted Lincoln's head in sand at Bailey's Beach. With clay and plaster of paris, he spent hours at the art studio in the basement of a classroom building, happy to do the class assignments and more. The result was his only A at Exeter. He was again regularly on and off probation and extra study halls. But when the most feared man on campus, the all-powerful dean of faculty, Edwin Silas Wells Kerr, who had put him on scholastic probation, called him in for what he felt would be a final reckoning that would have him on the next train to Boston, Kerr decided to keep him on the hook rather than expel him. At his room in Langdell Hall Gene now had a typewriter, one of the few boys to have one, not for his class assignments but for his own writing sessions. His first publication at Exeter was not in the literary magazine but in the newspaper at the beginning of March 1941, a long letter to the editors in response to an *Exonian* editorial by Tom Lamont, the leader behind whom "Give 'em guns, Gunnar" and other prowar boys rallied their impressive forces. With a gift for irony and invective, Gene confessed, after tongue-in-cheek praise for Lamont's fair-mindedness and restraint, that "there are, however, one or two places where I disagree with Mr. Lamont. First he states that 'we have lost another battle.' This evidently refers to the fall of Greece. The one word in that rather beautiful phrase which I do not understand is 'we.' Exactly what does that 'we' refer to: *The Exonian*? The regal house of Morgan? Or to England and the Allies? If that is the case then we must recognize Mr. Lamont as a British subject." That the fifteen-year-old could write with elegance and precision was clear. Lamont had a sharp tongue, a lively pen. But Gene's counterattack was strong stuff that alerted his schoolmates he was a formidable person to tangle with.

Despite his success as a debater, Gene still had as much in mind becoming a successful writer as he did pursuing a political career. Serious as politics were, much as he thought he might one day become a real senator and perhaps—why not?—President of the country, politics demanded elements of manipulation that literature did not. True, politics was the family trade, so to speak, his grandfather the model. Issues engaged him. Competition excited him. The weaknesses and strengths of people interested him. On the debating platform he was sometimes a fiery dynamo, other times a cool satirist, quicker with quips and rebuttals, with dismissive witticisms or self-serving evasions, than his competitors. But after all was said and all pleasure elicited, he still preferred the privacy of reading, the excitement and fulfillment of writing, the thrill of seeing his name in print, the dream of being a great artist like Thomas Mann, whose novels he had been devouring. Though there was nothing prohibitively incompatible between the two, there was, so to speak, already a small flag of caution, of muted warning, of likely distance between the inevitable dishonesty of political performance, of saying what they wanted to hear, and the assumption that literary art was dedicated to the private voice, to personal honesty, to a kind of truth-telling incompatible with political life. To do both would be a difficult balancing act.

Already in the spring of 1941 he had a public and a private voice. At his desk he wrote short stories, the first of dozens written at Exeter, and continued to consider himself a poet, though most of the few hundred poems he was to write had already been written. He added some to his pile, but at a much slower rate than before. As a poet he mastered a clear line and a vague lyricism, though his verse, even at its most lyrical, had a flatness of diction and metaphor that might have raised the question of whether he would not be better off writing prose altogether. Some of the flatness was purposeful, calculated restraint and understatement. But it did not work. Poetic structure escaped him as well. The shorter poems kept their form, but coherence generally came at a heavy price. Many of them, emotionally and philosophically abstract, dramatized heavy seriousness without human particularity. The poems drifted, floated, or fell heavily. The insufficiency of their language and vision betrayed them. They were competent without being real. Self-doubt about the poems crept into his consciousness, though not to the extent that he no longer thought himself a poet. But though he could not put his finger on the faults of his poetry, he began to rethink his literary career. He continued to show his poems and to seek their publication for the next half dozen years, but he began even during his first year at Exeter to give more attention to writing short stories and brief essays, having in mind that he might publish them in the campus literary magazine and beyond, in commercial magazines that actually paid money. And why not a novel? He was still fascinated with Napoleon, and the Mussolini he had seen that summer night in 1939 at the open-air opera in Rome came to mind as a likely model for a pseudohistorical novel. "So I invented a dictator in a southern country like Italy, a Mediterranean country. It was one of half a dozen novels that I started and never came near to finishing. . . . I did about twenty thousand words."

Some of his new friends were part of the Exeter literary circle. Bingham, an avid, ambitious writer, who had staked out for himself the generally accepted expectation that one day he would be famous, wrote for the newspaper and *The Phillips Exeter Review*. He served on both editorial boards. Another new friend, Lew Sibley, slight, bespectacled, handsome, an aesthetic-looking young man from nearby Newport, New Hampshire, whom he met through A. K. Lewis, had the reputation of being a brilliant poet. "An unassuming New Englander, he had a rather effeminate manner," Lewis recalled, "but Lew did not present himself as a homosexual or a homosexual target, and he clearly was not. . . . But he was utterly gentle in appearance, even fragile." Lewis himself had a gift for comic prose, for humorous essays and stories. They were already, as Lower Middlers who entered as freshmen in 1939, active on the newspaper staff and the literary magazine. Both excellent students, they soon were made editors of the *Review*. It made sense for Gene to join them there. By the end of the spring term, Bingham, who was assistant managing editor, had helped get him on *The Exonian* staff, though only, as a start, onto the business board. That Tom Lamont was president of the *Review* board may have kept him off the literary staff, though not entirely out of its pages. The next fall he was to have a poem published there. Bingham, one of the *Review* editors with Sibley and Lewis, may have felt sufficiently competitive with his friend to have conspired with Lamont, even if tacitly, to keep him off. Gene was to publish only three short stories there during his entire Exeter career, though he submitted dozens, all better than most of those published. When, the next year, Bingham replaced Lamont as president, he made certain that his ambitious friend published there only occasionally.

———•———

A hot, humid early-August night at Merrywood. Summer 1941. Nina, amid packing cases and luggage, smoked and paced and drank. She had asked for a divorce. She was leaving Auchincloss. Old Mrs. Auchincloss, in Florida, had offered her money, security, to stay. Another divorce for her son did not sit well with the wealthy matriarch. Nor with the Gores, who thought their daughter should leave well enough alone. There were children, two and four years old, but she was adamant. Just a week before, a

separation and trust agreement had been signed, including a small fund for
Gene, which Nina was to control, that would generate about $100 a month.
For once, she said, she was going to do something for herself. Her life had
been one long series of sacrifices for other people, especially for Deenie. She
had married Auchincloss only for his sake, to give him a good, secure home.
Anyway, she was madly in love with someone else.

A car pulled up to the mansion on the Potomac Palisades. Gene Vidal,
returning with his son from a vacation trip to Quebec, dropped off young
Gene at Merrywood. Quebec had been pleasurable, its European resonances
fascinating. Kit had had the good sense to allow father and son to go off
together. Hot, irritable, perhaps concerned that the trust agreement was not
as generous as she would like, Nina was delighted to have her ex-husband
there to fight with, to rake up old coals, to assert her fortitude in the face of
the injustices of decades. As usual, Gene declined to fight. Nina zeroed in on
an insurance savings policy. Gene Vidal had been paying the premiums, the
accumulation of which was to go toward their son's expenses for college or
career. Nina, though, wanted the policy signed over to her. As she talked,
glass of Queen Anne scotch in hand, she continued packing silver and linen.
She needed the money. It rightly should be hers anyway, she argued. Soon
Gene left. In a rage, Nina turned on her son. When words proved insufficient, she threw her liquor glass at him once again. Though she could no
longer actually hit him, she could still inflict pain. Furious, hurt, he picked
up his unpacked suitcases and strode out of the house. With luggage in
hand, at night, with no money, he walked along a country lane to the River
Road, then, sweating heavily, the three miles to the Chain Bridge across the
Potomac. A taxi appeared. He explained as much as needed to the driver,
who accepted his signet ring, his tenth-birthday present from his father, as
guarantee of the fare. Fortunately, Gene remembered the name of the hotel
at which his father was staying. When the taxi pulled up, his father paid the
driver. Young Gene got back the signet ring. Exhausted, he slept that night
on the sofa.

In the morning his father drove him to Rock Creek Park, where his
grandparents once again picked up the wreckage of their daughter's unstable
life. It was only a matter of another month before his return to Exeter.
There was much he could do at Rock Creek Park, including read to the
Senator. Gene Vidal's decision, though, was less easy than the Gores', not
because he did not have full confidence in them but because the situation

confronted him with the opportunity to define himself more sharply as a father. Why not simply take young Gene back with him to East Hampton, to a month on the tennis courts and the beach? He decided, though, to repeat the familiar pattern of leaving him with his grandparents, long understood as the surrogate parents with whom the boy stayed. His parents he visited. At East Hampton Gene had a small rented place and a young wife. At Rock Creek Park the boy could once again be restored to the familiarity of his most stable childhood home. Gene drove on to East Hampton, a decision this most nonintrospective of men was always to regret. Dot was delighted to have Deenie back. Soon Nina drove up. "Go on upstairs. I'll handle this," Mrs. Gore told her grandson. From the upstairs room above the front door he watched his mother confront *her* mother. Nina would be damned if she was going to give up that insurance policy that was hers "by right, and how could I, with any conscience, take *her* money when she was the guy who had got Hughdie to create a twenty-five-thousand-dollar trust fund for me as part of the prenuptial agreement? . . . Now you must throw him out." "He is our grandson," Mrs. Gore responded. "He stays here." "*I* am the mother, under the law I'm his guardian. . . ." "Under the law, this is my house, not yours. Now, *you* go away." Nina, stunned, rallied. " 'I'm coming in . . .' 'Oh no you're not!' . . . Dot . . . slipped inside the house and slammed the door so hard that the house shook." Nina got back in the car and drove off.

The month at Rock Creek Park was happy, productive, though Gene still felt trapped by his dependency. When not reading to his grandfather, a sort of singing for his supper, he frequently walked from Broadlands Road to the Library of Congress, where he read and wrote for hours at one of the long desks. Keenly aware that he did not have a penny of his own, he knew that even the small amount the trust fund would produce would not be his until adulthood, even if his mother could be prevented from appropriating it permanently. Generous in many ways, the Gores were not generous with money. Anyway, they had only a modest amount. His father could be counted on for little, his Exeter tuition and some pocket money at best. The Aeronautics Research Corporation was far from a smashing success, not to speak of the possibility that, with a young wife, Gene might soon have additional parental responsibilities. There would be no family inheritance, no Auchincloss money: if Gene followed the educational straight and narrow, his minimal expenses would be covered. Otherwise, and beyond that, nothing. The return to Exeter, then, he knew, was inevitable. The idea of college seemed anathema. His only hope was to cash in on his fascination with writing in a way that might get him out of this prisonlike enclosure. "I thought, Well, maybe if I write a book I can write my way out of this. The trap I was in. Because I was penniless. . . . So I had this blue notebook. Indeed, I'd go to the library reading room and started to write a novel, sort of a mystery story. The main character was called Smyth," the title *Mr. Smyth's Murder*. "That's all I remember about it. I must have written about thirty thousand words." Some years later Nina, who found it among a batch of his old papers, threw it away.

CHAPTER *five*

_____

Proudly Unfurled

1941–1943

WHEN EUGENE LUTHER GORE Vidal, Jr., returned to Exeter in mid-September 1941, Rosalind and he were a couple, covering the distance between The Madeira School and Exeter by letter and seeing one another during holidays. With Jimmie, who was at St. Albans Upper School, he had no contact. Much as Jimmie had made a deep impression on him, they went their separate ways with no need to be in touch with one another, busy with innumerable schoolboy things and with no indication of romantic longing. In the autobiographical novel *The Season of Comfort,* the character Jimmie, unmistakably based on Trimble, with whom the main character, based on Gene, has had sex at a place like Merrywood, also enrolls at Exeter. But there the two boys, with vastly different interests, drift apart uneventfully, just as Gene and Jimmie did from 1940 to 1942. At Exeter itself there was no sex for Gene. As far as he knew, for no one else either, though later reports from classmates indicate that some boys were having sex sessions with one another and that there might have been substance to the occasional rumor that some master was too close with a favorite boy. There were a few histrionic queens around. Some of the boys were quick to use the word "fairy" about others. Once a well-developed athlete rubbed his leg against Gene's in class. But he was not to be tempted, let alone seduced. If there was to be sex, he preferred to do the seducing. But in the competitive Exeter environment he rightly sensed that to be either seducer or seduced would make him dangerously vulnerable. With his reputation for cutting competitiveness, for arrogance and ambition in general, the notion of sex at Exeter seemed folly.

With Bob Bingham he double-dated Wellesley girls a few times. One night he and Bingham slept on a golf course near the Wellesley campus. A few times he went with other boys for sexual romps with Exeter town girls who made it a regular thing to be available at a nearby public park. To one of his roommates "Gore talked about his sexual life, but it was with women. He was rumored to have had some sort of liaison with a town girl, down at Swasey Park. He may have been boasting about how precocious he was." The formal school dances brought "classy" girls to the campus, including Rosalind. Most Exeter boys panted and groped, usually at arm's length, as their desires struggled with the mores of their class and time. To the extent that Gene was in love with Rosalind, he was neither frustrated nor distressed. She was a safe, rewarding place to be. Much of his energy went into reading, writing, debating. During the Exeter years he seems to have experienced neither romantic longing nor sexual angst. But he continued to experience classroom distress; brilliant as he seemed to some of his schoolmates, his preoccupation with reading and debating kept him in academic trouble. No amount of intelligence and cleverness could compensate for total unpreparedness. It was only a matter of time before he would be called before the dean again. During the fall semester he failed Latin, math, and English, and got a D− in French, the worst record of his six semesters at Exeter. His grandfather's encouragement, his mother's threats, fell on unresponsive ears. But he had a grand time in the debating hall. Within a month of the start of the fall 1941 semester he had been, he told his grandfather, in three "debates . . . and have made about ten speeches in the Senate. From the general look of things I think I may be President in the spring elections. My speaking has picked up considerably. One Senator said that I was the best orator Exeter has had since Daniel Webster—another said I was the damndest fool they have had since Robert Benchley. It is hard to know which to believe. I think the remark about Benchley hits the mark though."

At the school lecture series he heard the liberal columnist Max Lerner, a dazzling speaker "regardless of everything else . . . lecturing about how to jump blithely into the war in one lesson." Two of his poems were published in the fall *Exeter Review,* one of them a dark lament for some generalized "we" who "are lost to hope and God" titled "To R.K.B.'s Lost Generation," a lyric presentation of a comment by Bob Bingham about the post–World War I writers. A comfortable atheist, Gene himself had no reason to lament the loss. The poem appeared on the same page with a prowar sonnet by Tom Lamont whose final couplet concludes, "Thus eager youth forever quits debate,/And fighting with brave certainty meets fate." At a later Senate debate he was to dub one of Lamont's allies "The Senator from England." On December 7 the Japanese attacked Pearl Harbor. Gathered with other boys in the common room, ears glued to the radio, Gene heard the President's speech requesting a declaration of war. Tom Lamont, catching his eye, triumphantly sneered.

The boys now lived in an even more stygian darkness than the ordinary New England winter. All lights visible from outside were shut off at dusk. Air-raid wardens patrolled. Shortages of everything appeared. Rationing became a way of life. To help the war effort, some volunteered to do manual labor nearby, including digging out snow-covered railroad tracks. Exeter abruptly terminated the century-and-a-half-old practice of maids straightening dormitory rooms, and each boy now became responsible for his own. Some boys cleaned, some nagged, some dropped their clothes wherever they fell. In the dining hall the always boring food became even more marginal, less various. But everyone adjusted. Debates took on a more determinative force, though they had been quite hot before. Every boy knew that a military uniform was in his not-too-distant future. Like his grandfather, Gene continued to oppose Roosevelt but not the war. In Webster Hall he usually took the conservative side, with a touch of populism. In the Senate, where each senator represented his own views, he opposed New Deal legislation in general. On many issues his positions, indistinguishable from ex-Senator Gore's, seemed to some in the charged atmosphere laggard if not unpatriotic. "Exeter commences to be very war-like," he wrote to his grandfather, "and war lord Perry is girding up his loins. Restrictions are being foisted on us right and left; it is said that they may close down the Senate because of recent comments made by the worthy members in strident disapproval of faculty measures. As usual I was loudest; the faculty, like an elephant, remembers." One evening he trekked across campus to the football field with A. K. Lewis and Nat Davis, both also active debaters. At Gene's suggestion they climbed to the highest part of the stadium seats. Like Demosthenes orating with pebbles in his mouth to improve his speaking, they were each to improvise and cast their voices as far out as they could. In sequence each voice rolled across the open air and disappeared gradually into the northern darkness. Davis remembered that Gore's speech had been the best, his voice strongest. As a debater, his younger classmate John Knowles recalled, "Gore was very crisp and very good and very sharp. . . . What struck me about him was his fierce determination." He began now regularly to sign his name "Gore Vidal."

Home for Christmas 1941, he had a new temporary home to go to, his mother's attractive Georgetown house, into which she had moved from Merrywood. Nina was in love with a handsome Air Force brigadier general, Robert Olds, who had achieved fame as a Flying Fortress pilot and now had the responsibility of creating and running a vast air-transportation network called the Ferry Command. Its first job was to deliver bombers to England. Nonstop goodwill flights to South America had earned him the Distinguished Flying Cross. Many thought the forty-four-year-old General Olds, who had been General Billy Mitchell's aide, would soon command the entire Army Air Corps. Previously married, with four grown sons, always attracted to and attractive to ladies, Olds looked forward to marrying the vivacious Nina Gore as soon as legal niceties permitted. Her affair with Olds had precipitated her decision to divorce Auchincloss. Of her three husbands, she later told her son Tommy, "Olds was the one she loved the best. She had a crush on Vidal. I think my father was more of a pragmatic situation, kind of with their both falling into it. . . . And of course the bucks were there, so there was a financial reason, since my mother didn't have any resources. She loved Olds very much," though she had "more passionate sex" in extramarital affairs than with any of her husbands.

At Christmas her house was lively with guests, particularly Olds and his West Point friends. One night Gore sat with a group of them who were "denouncing that Jew Franklin D. Rosenfeld who had got us into the war on the wrong side. We ought to be fighting the Commies not Hitler. But then FDR was not only a kike, he was sick in the head—and not from polio but from syphilis. Anyway, everything could be straightened out—with just one infantry brigade they would surround the White House, the Capitol, remove the Jews." It was an odd though not unusual expression of Christmas

goodwill, stronger stuff than Gore had ever heard before. Hugh Auchincloss's soft anti-Semitism had not had the benefit of a military uniform or a
sharp mind. A consummate bore to his stepson even when being anti-
Semitic, Auchincloss later became the model for the tedious general in *Visit
to a Small Planet*. "His stories were never altered. He knew the original
Jewish name of every movie star who ever changed his name. That list runs
quite long. How he learned them I don't know. He didn't go to the movies.
I shouldn't think he read *Silver Screen*. But he had collected some thirty
names, and he always started with Kirk Douglas. This was about how the
Jews were everywhere. It couldn't be simpler. I wouldn't have said that he
would have cut the ribbon at Auschwitz, but at the same time, as a purist, he
would suggest some names that others might not know of people who had
passed. I can see him writing out a dossier to the authorities at Auschwitz,
'You may not know, but Kirk Douglas's real name is. . . .' "

Later that spring Gore confided to a new friend at Exeter that he had
had "a dream showing his mother standing with a submachine gun pointing
at her three husbands," perhaps an anticipation of his conviction that Olds,
whom he found charming but pompous, would suffer the same fate as his
father and Auchincloss. At home for the spring vacation, he had overheard,
from the next room, Henry Luce, one of Auchincloss's oldest friends,
propose to Nina. After they both had graduated from Yale, Hugh had
treated Luce to a trip to Europe and provided seed money for Luce's
fledgling magazine, *Time*. Clare Boothe Luce, his wife, Luce complained to
Nina, did not understand him. Nina turned him down. In June 1942 Nina
and Bob Olds married. Gore was not invited to the wedding.

At Exeter Gore had had a difficult term. He had started the new year
with his usual plunge into debating. His expectation that he would be
president of the Golden Branch proved unwarranted. When his grade reports in February indicated only marginal improvement, he was forced by
Dean Kerr "to stop all outside activity. . . . Am working," he assured his
grandfather, "an experience that is not untinged with novelty." Instead of
three failures and a D−, he now got four D's, the lowest passing grade. Still,
he got his nose up from the grindstone very soon, shrugging off his grades
as a modest practical inconvenience. His poetry was still on his mind,
including two new ones about his "reactions in France before the war."
Though he told his grandfather, "with the 'blithe spirit' of the young, I
think they are wonderful," he could not totally misunderstand the ironic

undertones of the preface Nat Davis wrote, at his request, to a small manuscript volume he had assembled. "These poems . . . are outstanding not only because of their own merit, but also because of the extreme youth of their author. . . . Perhaps the greatest gift Vidal makes use of here is his brilliant imagination, which, although it may, like Macbeth's 'vaulting ambition, overshoot its mark,' lends a color and vividness to the verse. . . . with his genius expressed haltingly and very dimly at times. . . . With this genius I can but say that [this] young poet will sometime hang the great and vacant night of American literature with stars." A new, more credulous friend, Wilcomb Washburn, noted in his diary that Gene boasted that "Putnam would probably publish a volume of his verse. . . . He has connections and I see no reason why it shouldn't go thru. His poems are good. He wants to win the Pulitzer Prize."

If there were an institutional Exeter poet, it was Robert Frost, who frequently spoke and read at chapel and special Sunday-night occasions. From nearby Vermont Frost made the trip to Exeter for the sake of both an audience and his slim pocketbook. To the young Exonian literati Frost had little cachet and no authority, a prophet without honor among the young of his own country. On a Sunday night early in May he talked "to a packed and sweltering chapel." Bingham and Vidal had been reading Frost, a book a day, feeling quite superior to a poet whom Lionel Trilling and others had taught them was "an old bucolic cornball," a boring bit of pastoral Americana. "Oh, God, yes, how we hated Frost the personage," Vidal remembered. "We all had to go listen to him. It was all right at chapel, since we had to be there anyway. He would come on other occasions. I don't know how they got us all in there. He was a great performer, but once you've seen him a dozen times. . . . In fact, Bingham wrote a very funny little parody: 'I see the birches bending row on row/Against the line of straighter darker trees./I like to think Robert Frost's been swinging there.' We were T. S. Eliot men." At one of his visits, Vidal recalled, Frost shocked one of the masters, a great admirer, when he "went out to piss in the woods beyond the baseball field. Then Frost leaned over and began to lick the bark of the tree. 'I can taste the sea salt,' he said."

When, the week after Frost, Ruth Draper, a superb actress and dramatic monologuist, performed, the chapel was again packed. Washburn, a little bored, was happy to be there with his friend. To Gore, Wid was both a comfort and a convenience. From an academic New England family, he had all the schoolboy discipline that Gore lacked. Constantly insecure, always serious, he had determined never to let lack of hard work prevent his success. Dark-haired, rugged, with a plain, almost handsome face, he excelled on the playing field as well as in the classroom. A "powerful-looking young man, quite big and strong," Hamilton Bissell recalled, "he was an outstanding varsity football player." Eager to be rewarded by the Exeter authorities, with not a hint of intellectual or moral rebellion, he found himself fascinated by the attraction of his opposite. An embodiment of the understatement that proper Exonians lauded, Washburn found Gore's mixture of compulsive overstatement and unembarrassed self-projection somewhat confusing. A literalist, Wid could rarely comprehend irony. But regardless of whether some of Gore's claims were put-ons, Wid had no doubt that his new friend was a genius with an original mind. Washburn believed that genius made its own rules. Eager to be accepted, to be praised, he allowed himself to be teased, occasionally to be mistreated. Foreshadowing the anthropologist he was to become, Washburn decided to record and study the practices of this exotic creature. Notebook in hand, he followed the schoolboy great man around. "My wonder that he should show an interest in me came to a head when he said I seemed very suspicious of him. I told [him] I wondered if he wasn't play[ing] with me as a cat does with a mouse for mere pleasure or some other object. It can hardly be a genuine interest unless he sees more in me than I think he does. Certain I am that he has his eye on the Presidency of the United States, and, if he doesn't try to become *too* clever, I am not so sure that he won't reach that goal."

Late in May, as the term came to an end, they went to the Senate banquet together. "I went over to his room before going . . . because he said 'he wanted [to] be late so they would notice him more.' We did get there late. He was seated at the left end of the main table and was ignored by all of the speakers. Therefore he lit a cigar, and drew laughter and much attention to him[self]. He looked exactly like a politician up there." At the end of the month the phenomenon was still under the microscope. "Instead of studying much, he reads about a book a day. He has gotten E and A in every one of his subjects for a month's mark. He tells me he has a library of 7,000 books, his mother 300,000 and his grandfather 500,000. . . . He gave me my first lesson in speaking today. I read his Litany for Living—a remarkable belief on religion." Before the term was over, Gore led the Golden Branch debating team to victory on the subject of paying overtime wages while the nation was at war. "Vidal stood out," the other diary keeper, Otis Pease, recorded. At end-of-term Prize Chapel, Wid "picked up $25 in history prizes," Gore a $10 debating prize. "Incidentally, he doesn't care to marry (he has no use for women) but he says he probably will—a political marriage with [the] Governor of Virginia's daughter to get his support for Senatorship." Actually, he and Rosalind had begun to discuss becoming engaged.

----·•·----

While working in July 1942 on the assembly line at his father's factory in Camden, New Jersey, Gore was called to the telephone. Kit was on the line with shocking, numbing news. Gene had had a massive heart attack, a coronary thrombosis. An ambulance had rushed him to St. Luke's; it was not clear he would survive. The train to New York seemed to move excruciatingly slowly. When Gore arrived, his father looked "nearly dead," his eyes "glazed yellow-gray from drugs," the hair on his chest now suddenly as white as the hair on his head. Just weeks before, they had played tennis together, his father as usual tutoring him casually in the strokes and strategies of a game that the middle-aged man, who found golf too slow, loved. To Kit "the heart attack was totally unexpected." Coronary pain had once before constricted Gene's chest, but he had kept the episode to himself, hoping that it would not happen again. Now "he had a huge hole in the main aorta. Had he not been an athlete he would have been dead. . . . That saved him." While his father's life was at issue, Gore went regularly to the hospital. Semiconscious, his father, who had recognized him when he first arrived, had tried to speak to him. "Haltingly, he told me to work hard. Neither of us had the right script for this scene." Death seemed unspeakable, a subject they both hated. Though controlled, almost stoical, Kit had bouts of despair. Fortunately, by the end of the week, it was clear that Gene would live. For Kit, who just four months before had become the mother of a boy, the relief was immense, the burden heavy. In addition to being a wife and mother, she was now likely to be a nurse of sorts for some time. The prescription was for a month in the hospital, then a year of recuperative inactivity. Heart patients were thought to benefit from absolute rest. Shocked by his father's brush with death, Gore felt his own mortality touched.

With his Exeter friend A. K. Lewis, he had come to New Jersey to sample what they both hoped would be the kind of experience young writers romantically idealize. Eager to have summer work, excited by the notion of contributing to the war effort, A.K. and Gore joined an assembly line "making wingtips for what was designed as a secret glide-bomber." They earned forty cents an hour. This would be the real world. The work of course proved tediously dull. Only one worker, a mad Englishman, seemed well suited for the job: he was "busy inventing a molded plywood tire. With each awful failure, his confidence grew." Early in the summer Gore had visited his father and Kit at East Hampton, probably with Rosalind. Gene Vidal was mainly preoccupied, for a second summer, with attempting to outplay the local tennis pro, a young man less than half his age. A heavy smoker since his late twenties, with a history of poor blood circulation, Gene had neither the breath nor the endurance. "What he was fighting was not the boy but age, which he couldn't face. He had never failed at any athletic task he had set himself. He was taking on the boy tennis pro at East Hampton . . . and he was out to beat him. The kid was a very good player. My father was forty-five or whatever and moderately sedentary and smoking in those days, and this triggered the heart attack. He'd play until his lips would get blue. . . . We'd all try to stop him. He had an obsession with beating this kid. . . . We all thought he was making trouble for himself."

In New Jersey, A.K. and Gore, sharing a room in a boardinghouse, walked a mile to have their meals. For recreation they mostly read and talked. In Manhattan, while Kit remained at the hospital with her husband, Gore stayed at his father's large apartment, a handsome rental at the corner of Fifth Avenue and Ninety-second Street, into which they had moved on their recent return from Washington. With views of Central Park and the reservoir, with four bedrooms and three maids' rooms, it occupied the entire fifth floor of an elegant fourteen-story building built in 1925 for the wealthy Barbara Hutton, who occupied an elaborate fifty-four-room apartment with a private entrance on the Ninety-second Street side. By the end of July, bored, restless, his father out of danger, Gore had had enough of wing tips and assembly lines. Leaving A.K., who stuck it out a little longer, he was off to Spokane. His new stepfather, the commanding general at Wright Air Force Base, provided the transportation. At Fort George Wright there was some advantage in being the visiting stepson of the general. Staying at the commanding general's house, reading Daphne du Maurier's novels, he soon found he did not care for his new stepfather nor, he thought, did his stepfather care for him. Nina was in good form, drinking less, perhaps constrained by the responsibility of her position. As always, she lived either in the past of grievances or in the spontaneity of the present. Eager to have him visit, the bitter argument of the previous summer gone from her mind, she had urged "Dearest Deenie," as soon as he had enough of factory work, to join them at the base. "The country is really lovely around here. I thought when you come out I might take a cottage . . . On the lake. . . . Much love—xxx Bommy." His own situation was much on his mind. If he could manage to accumulate enough credits, he hoped he would graduate the next June. Then, undoubtedly, the Army. But in what capacity? If he failed to graduate, the most dangerous infantry assignment would most likely be his fate. With all the military brass in his family, should he not be an officer, perhaps through one of the programs the Army was establishing for bright young men with officer potential? And what about Rosalind? Could they live on Army pay? One day, on the bus from the base into Spokane, with a clarity that thrilled him with its comprehensiveness, he sketched out in his own mind the literary career he hoped to have. "I put the political career on a shelf in my head. If it would turn out, it would turn out. . . . It was curious how accurate I was. I would try certain kinds of novels and write essays."

At Exeter for the fall term Gore was now, in his idiosyncratic way, somewhat of a campus celebrity. "I've been doing a great deal of orating and writing," he wrote to his father, thanking him for a small birthday check. "I've made four speeches before various crowds up to 500. They seem to like my speaking for though it is more or less the unpopular view point they always stage a very flattering demonstration when I get up to speak. Every day I learn something more about speaking. One of the strangest things is when some one gets up and makes a beautiful factual address and yet is accepted unfavorably by the audience, whereas somebody like me will deliver the most hackneyed overworked speech and they like it. It really is a fascinating study." Some of the students found him riveting entertainment. When one senator said, "I never liked that isolation pose of yours," he responded, to applause, "That was no pose; that was my wife." At a particularly loud moment in debate, he conceded, "I give the honorable speaker the benefit of the shout." To his grandfather he boasted of his mastery of generational rhetoric: "Gave a speech the other day on the post war world (hollow mockery that it is) but I received the biggest ovation that

I have yet received; they, it seems, liked my ending which was: 'this is our world, which we shall in a few years guide to our liking. Wars and leadership are not for the old, but for the young who have spirit if not the wisdom of the old. And this world tempered by the fires of war shall be ours, for you and me, and all of us together, *we are history.*' It is nice to tell people what they want to believe." Watching his performances with a worshipful yet critical fascination, Washburn noted in his diary, "Vidal more bombastic than usual in the Senate." Gore managed to get reelected senator from Virginia, but his hope of being elected president of the Senate was balked. "Isn't it amazing how the biggest man in the Senate is relegated to third place? I can never fathom the minds of idiots." With A.K. he made an arrangement that resulted in Lewis's being elected president of Golden Branch in the fall, with the understanding that Lewis would support Gore as president for the spring.

On issues he was both radical and conservative. "There never would be peace until the world had a common language, a common currency, and a common government," he told Washburn, who thought it worth putting in his diary. On the issue of a bill to form a federal board to govern labor, Vidal rose in the Senate "to lead the opposition," *The Exonian* reported.

> He compared Senator Murphy's speeches to the flow of hot lava, in that the further they go, the colder they get. He declared that although he was deeply dissatisfied with the present direction and state of the labor movement, he had by no means worked himself up into a hatred of all labor, as Senator Murphy apparently had. Labor, he cried, has built on this continent a nation of steel: we cannot turn and destroy it now. He contended that Washington bureaus are inefficient, ineffective, corrupt, and addicted to red tape, and denounced them for exemplifying the totalitarianism we are fighting against. President Roosevelt, he accused, is trying to use the war to make himself a dictator.

Smaller government, the division of the country into four self-governing sections, local rule but at the same time "one world," freedom for labor as well as capital, maximum democracy—the only problem was that the democratic electoral process favored mediocrity. He teased the literal-minded

Washburn, "At heart I'm a dictator." Washburn may have seen that the knife cut two ways, both a criticism of democracy and an ironic self-exposure that was also self-criticism.

During the November 1942 national elections he had a brush with campaigning in the real world. One of his favorite teachers, Henry Phillips, a handsome classicist with a Ph.D. from Harvard, encouraged Gore to join him in actively supporting the local Democratic candidate for Congress, Chester E. Merrill. Phillips managed the congressman's winning campaign. Eager to pillory the enemy, Gore wrote a satirical article for local newspapers. The New Hampshire Republican senator, Styles Bridges, he thought "a congenital idiot. Am I right?" he asked his grandfather. "He does more steady double talking than any man I've ever seen. If I couldn't make a better speech than he I'd never think of another election again. I asked him a great many embarrassing questions before the Republican rally. He squirmed, and not too artfully. . . . When I start running I am going to call spades spades, fools fools, new dealers jack assess, and I shall be beaten by a comfortable majority. How much truth can the people stand without choking?" Phillips—who played excellent jazz piano, knew the Manhattan jazz clubs well, coached the school rowing team, and had an understated sense of humor—found the seventeen-year-old an engaging challenge of the sort that made Exeter attractive. Sardonic, witty, reticent, Phillips was also a shrewd analyst of people and communal politics. When Gore challenged his claim that he knew how to make himself popular with his colleagues, Phillips quietly campaigned for an Exeter position for himself, primarily by hosting a clambake. His election confirmed the validity of his object lesson. Gore was impressed. Politics was as much cunning, persuasion, personal amiability as fiery speeches, sharp intellectual insights, dramatic assertions. In Phillips, Gore found a teacher who responded to him with a generous seriousness even when corrective. "Vidal has long talk with Dr. Phillips," Washburn wrote in his diary. "Latter says he's a materialist and should change. V says Phillips should go out in world and do something." Actually, in his way, Phillips did. Gore wanted a larger, more worldly audience.

Eager to know what his English teachers thought of him, Gore joined Bingham and Lewis in December 1942 in an escapade that apparently Bingham conceived. They broke into the English Department office. Rummaging among the files, they located comments that teachers made for the future reference of interested faculty members only. "A master complained that I seldom did the required reading but would often be found reading irrelevant books on history or novels not on the syllabus, like Mann's *The Magic Mountain*. Another wrote that as a writer and a speaker I was 'a soapbox orator.' Some people still think so." Exeter teachers adhered to the values of Exeter. They did not make exceptions. The exceptionalist got on their nerves. Later Vidal recalled, "There were certain English teachers whom I liked, but I only got one of them in class." Fortunately, since it would have meant instant expulsion, the culprits were not caught, but Gore had his mind on removing himself anyway, of liberating himself from Exeter, possibly at the end of that very term. The thought of starting either the University of Oklahoma or the University of Virginia in spring 1943 had occurred to him. Harvard was also a possibility. He took the college-board examinations but, he confided to his father, "the best thing is to wend my way as comfortably as possible through the war, and come back to Oklahoma, or some place where I have begun to know some people. This living in Washington is like living in a fascinating vacuum, and gypsying around is worse." Since he would not have a high-school diploma, Virginia was an impossibility. But his grandfather's prominence in Oklahoma made Oklahoma feasible. At his grandson's urging, the Senator wrote the university president, who immediately replied that they would be honored to have his grandson there. The technical impediments could be overcome.

For Gore the impulse was directed toward establishing a home in a state in which he could run for political office. The idea seemed to him a good one. But his wiser grandfather made the argument that at best he could have a year or a year and a half at the university before being drafted. The result would be that he would have completed neither Exeter nor Oklahoma. Incompletion had the scent of failure. It certainly would leave him empty-handed. Why not finish Exeter? The Army would inevitably follow. After that there would be the opportunity to make more rational decisions about his future if, given the military mortality rate, there was to be any future at all. The ex-Senator from Oklahoma was himself "somewhat bitter. He had been defeated in 1936. He also realized that I was an Easterner and would have great difficulty in conning the Jesus Christers which he had spent his life conning. . . . It wouldn't be much fun to represent them. I was officially headed there. But privately he was discouraging." What he probably did not tell the Senator is that it would take a large favor or a small miracle for him to graduate at the end of the year. Not only did he need better grades but he needed one more credit than a normal program for the term would allow. By the time he went to Washington during the Christmas holiday, he still had not decided if he would return to Exeter for his final semester, and before leaving for the holiday he had anguished through the contested Golden Branch election for officers. Suddenly a new party had entered its own slate. "Vidal tremendously worried all afternoon," Washburn, who "went out and got information and several promises to vote for Vidal," reported to his diary. "He wanted it as culmination to his career at Exeter. He complained about his best friends giving him bad news. . . . Our members took [our opponents' signs] from the givers in handfuls and tore them up." In his anger, Gore wrongly accused Lewis of going back on their agreement. But "the boys were effectively on Vidals side. . . . It was a rout. 40 for Vidal 18 for his three opponents combined. (Sibley voted thrice but. . . .) Watching Vidal's face was most enlightening. Taut, anxious, falsely relaxed, forced smiles; later, when he knew he had been elected, keen smile, sang hymn with gusto." Gore celebrated by not studying for the next day's French test. With that victory in hand, he pursued his holiday happily, putting out of mind, as best he could, his graduation problem. Perhaps something would work out. Perhaps he would pass math. The same D he had gotten for the fall term would suffice. In fact, his grades had just been the best he had ever gotten at Exeter, including a D in French, a C− in history, and a stunning B+ in English from a new teacher, Leonard Stevens. Even so, he still needed one additional credit.

On the train ride to Washington he contemplated Rosalind. Arm in arm, they soon dropped in on Mrs. Rust, who had just finished dining with friends at the Statler Hotel. Excited, the two seventeen-year-olds announced they had decided to get married. Handsome, precocious, a glamorous couple, with Army service in his near future, why not marry right after graduation in June (he did not say *if* he were to graduate)? Why not take this step into adulthood, liberation, self-possession? Delighted, Mrs. Rust assumed that Gore's well-known, high-powered Washington family would support the couple until the groom came into the money she assumed he would inherit. "Mrs. Rust was concerned about money," Rosalind's friend Tish Baldrige recalled. "Gore's family had the semblance of money, though, and anybody in those days who had good family breeding . . . was considered to be rich. They were rich in many ways, not in monetary ways but in respect and recognition." At Rock Creek Park, where he stayed with his grandparents, the announcement was met at first with deafening silence, then frosty disapproval. Was their grandson going to indenture himself to an early, moneyless marriage? There would not be a penny from the Gores. "Be *not* fruitful, do *not* multiply" became the Senator's maxim. His own disappointing children had married prematurely. Nina strongly expressed her opposition. She had heard, she said, with unself-conscious irony, that there was alcoholism in the Rust family. "She hated Rosalind, who I must say quite openly hated her . . . and said Rosalind's mother was an alcoholic, which wasn't true. My mother had that one mixed up. Rosalind's father was an alcoholic and had died early. I suppose she was thinking she wouldn't want two alcoholics' children to marry in case at a drop of a match, we'd both blow up. . . . I think she talked directly to Rosalind. Rosalind was a match for her. She wasn't afraid of anything and had much better manners than my mother. She could be very cool, very attentive and non-committal. My mother would end up battling Rosalind and get only a sphinxlike smile out of her. Rosalind handled her very well."

With Rosalind on his arm, Gore went to a Christmas-season dance at the fashionable Sulgrave Club. Jimmie was there. They had not seen one another since May 1939 at Merrywood. When he told him of his engagement, Jimmie immediately responded, "You're crazy!" It was the response of a sensible friend, himself pursued by and pursuing many attractive girls, who also expected to be in the Army within the next year or so. "We went downstairs to the men's room," Gore recalled years later, "with its tall marble urinals and large cubicles. I wondered what, if anything, he felt. . . . Fortunately, our bodies still fitted perfectly together, as we promptly discovered inside one of the cubicles, standing up, belly to belly, talking of girls and marriage and coming simultaneously." The position became a favorite one. "He always told me," a friend remarked, "when we used to speak about sex in bygone days long ago, he used to say that what he really enjoyed was belly-rubbing. It's what we all did at school and didn't know why it was so pleasant. One person gets on top of another and usually inserts his penis between the legs of the other or just lets it ride up and down on the tummy and eventually the friction is so pleasant you get a little come and that's even more exciting for that gives you more *raison.*" From Washington, Gore flew to Spokane, the ride arranged by the powerful general of the Ferry Command. To his delight, the Christmas-season festivities had, as USO entertainment, a number of Hollywood stars, particularly the beautiful

Joan Leslie and the sophisticated Adolphe Menjou. As the son of the general's wife, Gore sat with the honored guests. Joan Leslie he immediately fell in love with. A letter from the Senator, who had recently celebrated his seventy-second birthday, reached him in Spokane. The war was on the Senator's mind, including his own ancestors, some wounded, others killed, who had fought for or against the republic. "I cannot choose but wonder what your eyes will witness before you reach your 72d milestone—as I hope you will. I cannot repress the wish that you may not have to go to the wars. If you do I certainly hope that you come back hale and unharmed, and with your shield. If you should have to go I am sure you will behave as becomes your breed—with a record that every member of your Command would be proud to claim as his own." From Spokane, Gore went directly back to Exeter for the momentous spring term.

With Washburn the platonic love-hate relationship had intensified during these last months. In fall 1942 they had become roommates, sharing a large three-room suite at the top of Langdell Hall, usually reserved for a master but available because of the war, with another young man, a new student, Tom McFarland, from Birmingham. Bright, assiduously studious, a scholarship boy like Washburn, later to become a renowned Coleridge scholar, McFarland was insecure, talkative, arrogantly competitive, and attracted to his own sex. As with most Exeter boys, self-repression and the discipline of the environment kept that dampened as well as, in McFarland's case, an innocence about himself and the world. Fascinated by literature, a compulsive scholar, McFarland, whose room was down the suite hallway, noticed Vidal constantly pecking away at his typewriter, with piles of manuscript beside him, or frequently on the move, from one activity to the next. At first "I thought his name was Veedol, the name of a gasoline company of that time. I wrote my mother. No, my mother said, it's Eugene Luther Vidal. She had read an article in a magazine (I think *The Saturday Evening Post*) about Gore's father. My first impression was that he was supercilious." But he was impressed with Vidal's collection of books and classical records. "One of the reasons I didn't know him better was because he was too busy. He was a tornado. One of the reasons I could play the records and read the books was because he wasn't there—'I'm not here much,' he said. He had . . . lots of Modern Library books. Modern Library Giants. And some

records and an old-fashioned phonograph machine. . . . I remember
Strauss waltzes particularly. He was very generous. I could listen to the
records anytime I wanted to and I could borrow any of the books I wanted
to. . . . He looked very intense when he was writing." McFarland recognized the impressive bizarreness of this unpublished schoolboy already
thinking of himself as an important writer. Everyone, including McFarland,
noticed Wid's worship of Gore. "With Wid, Gore controlled everything.
Wid sort of just put his paws up. It was real hero worship. Anything Gore
said was a pearl of wisdom. Gore just totally dominated that relationship. It
was in the manner. He treated Wid very superciliously. And Wid always
took that."

Actually, it was not all worship on Washburn's part. Deeply conflicted
about his friend, from early on he hated as much as adored him, aware that
this experience was an opportunity for self-exploration, for some evaluation
of his own emotional and intellectual complexity. The attraction was not
sexual. Wid wanted to know what made someone like Gore, so different
from himself, tick. His worship was always made uneasy by mistrust. While
he tended, usually, to accept at face value Gore's exaggerated, even outrageous, statements about his family's prominence and power, he often saw
through the offhand schoolboy claims. When Gore's exaggerations were
meant to be funny put-ons, Wid usually missed the humor. One Sunday at
compulsory church services Gore read both their palms. "Vidal has a little X
on his upper palm which he says shows a person desiring power; he is going
to have two children; he says that a palmist once told him that he would go
mad. It will be very interesting to check the above with the facts." When the
roommates were required to be in by 7 P.M. as punishment for untidiness,
Gore apparently blamed McFarland but took it out on Wid. "Vidal said that
either MacFarland [sic] goes or he is going. . . . I sat there dumbfounded.
I realized more than I ever realized just how low he considers me. I remembered back to first of year when all was roses and he hinted of introducing
me to important personages etc at home and took me downtown to eat. I
also remembered that the only reason I came back here was because of him.
I sighed. Such is Vidal!" The room was inevitably a mess, as were all the
rooms of Gore's life except those—and they were soon all—that someone else cleaned. "Instead of cleaning up room or sweeping it out Vidal
brushes his peanuts under the rug, moves a few chairs around in the living
room, and then goes. He never touches the broom, he leaves broken Pepsi-

Cola bottles in bathroom, never cleans up latter altho he uses it six times as much as anyone else. And yet he has gall to say that he does more than I etc."

Apparently, as one way to communicate with Gore, Wid purposely left his diary available for him to read. In late April 1943, Wid wrote, "It's funny how my opinion on Vidal has changed. 1st practically worship. Second practically hatred. And now I almost think he's pathetic. He even asked me to type another of his stories (for which I waste a lot of time and get nothing). In the middle of it, he said 'You'll be able to write an essay on Vidal's style some day.' What colossal conceit. And acting as if I were a very lucky guy to be able to type out one of his rather poor stories. I was generating hatred all the time I was writing it." At the end of this paragraph, at the bottom of the page, Gore responded, "You poor unhappy person." When commenting on friends, Gore told him that he had had only five friends in his life, the rest "either admirers, satellites, etc." A friend had to be an intellectual equal. When he named the five, Wid was not on the list. "I wonder if I could ever hate him so much that I would not rest until he had been overthrown? I wonder; something in me says that hate is too petty a thing but then another says it is the determinant of getting things done. Willpower." For Wid the advantage was in the model, though he paid a price for his lessons. McFarland kept his distance, emotionally quirky enough himself to be unhappily self-sufficient. Bingham marveled sympathetically at Wid's ability to live with Gore. Bingham and Lewis, though, operated as his equals. One afternoon Bingham came into the Langdell fourth-floor suite and found Gore in bed, reading. "What are you doing in bed?" "Well, I get so tired standing around." Wid recorded Gore's witticisms: "Celibacy is an all-consuming canker." "Attractive women are never beautiful, and beautiful women are never attractive." "After a very cultured speaker: 'His voice brings starch to my shirt.' " "Definition of Intellectuals: People who hide trivialities in banalities." "Two minds with a single lack of thought." "The destruction of conscience is the beginning of happiness." Oscar Wilde had become one of his models.

––––––––

As he assiduously wrote dozens of short stories, some of them dashed off in hours, he knew that his efforts could not be fully separated from his rivalry with Bingham. His closest friend was his most prominent competitor and the *Exeter Review* gatekeeper. "One would think that with so much in common, the relationship would have been easy; instead, it was edgy," Vidal recalled. "So competitive was the atmosphere that he and I were soon in a struggle over which of us was going to be *The* Writer." Bingham, who had the final say on submissions, exercised his authority vigorously, sometimes self-servingly. With the support of Lewis and Sibley, Gore, who had been appointed an associate editor of the *Review* for 1942–43, finally had a story accepted, "Mostly About Geoffrey," a slight comic variant on the werewolf legend written in an expressive but compact prose, with a narrative frame both sophisticated and silly at the same time. The story worked, the elements well modulated and balanced. When the *Review* turned down one of his other submissions, accompanied by a long, critical, self-justifying harangue from Bingham, Gore submitted a story anonymously. Bingham thought it superb. When Gore revealed that the story was his, embarrassed, with some bluster, Bingham backed off. The winter 1943 issue contained two of Vidal's short stories. The lead story, called "New Year's Eve," was an effective depiction of a discomfiting flirtation between an older married woman and a young man in the presence of her Army-colonel husband. The other, "The Bride Wore a Business Suit," was surrealistically comic, about an absurdly innocent Exeter student who finds himself pressured by her gun-toting father into marrying a domineering young woman he has supposedly compromised. The *Review* faculty adviser, George Bennett, who encouraged Gore's writing, liked "New Year's Eve" and compared it to Katherine Mansfield's stories. Since Gore had not read anything by Mansfield, he took the compliment under advisement. The satiric tone of "The Bride Wore a Business Suit" is light but sharp, a jab at middle-class courtship, marital conventions, and marriage mores. The bridegroom's main preoccupation is whether or not he will pass Latin, a comic refraction of Gore's own academic anxiety. Also, he himself had just become inappropriately engaged. The rivalry with Bingham continued. Early in the spring term accusations surfaced at a heated Golden Branch meeting that Bingham had been appointed to the Exeter intercampus debating team in return for Vidal having been made an editor of the *Review*. If so, the tenuous alliance did not hold beyond the winter issue. Two of Bingham's stories appeared in the spring 1943 *Review,* none of Vidal's.

During the Easter break Gene Vidal, sufficiently recovered from his heart attack to come down to Washington, had a pointed conversation with

his son about his engagement. Though usually inattentive, almost indifferent, to other people's personal lives, including his son's, Gore's father
suddenly had an important point to make. Washburn, in fact, noticed that
there were "apparently strained relations between father-son," probably
about the engagement. How in the world could Gore, his father wanted to
know, support two seventeen-year-olds on an Army private's salary or on
any civilian salary he could expect to make? The discouragement was
couched entirely in financial terms. Gore could expect help from neither side
of his family. Resistant, he defended his commitment. Rosalind would remain with her mother while he was away. His pay would help cover some
expenses. If he were an officer, his salary would be higher. After the war he
fully expected to earn, though he did not quite know how, the approximately $500 a month they agreed would be sufficient. In love with Rosalind,
he did not want to give her up. To Gore, eager for independence, the
engagement represented a movement toward adulthood. He did have some
unexpressed hesitations, though his impulse was always to affirm what his
parents opposed, oppose what they affirmed. He carefully explained to his
father exactly how he would work out the financial challenge. But that
neither Rosalind nor her mother thought it a problem already troubled him.
Rosalind's "fascination with making it go ahead" and her mother's enthusiasm "gave me a certain pause. She saw me as a rich boy. I sure as hell
wasn't. Needless to say, between my father and the Senator the poverty of
our family was brought home to me."

Working long, almost inspired hours at his writing table at Exeter, he
felt increasingly certain what he wanted most in this world, other than to be
President, was to be a writer, to have the writing life, and if unlike Henry
James he could never imagine himself "just literary," nevertheless that
vision of himself that he had synthesized on the bus trip into Spokane the
previous Christmas dominated his consciousness. The kinds of experiences,
the freedom to travel, the disregard for anything but sustenance income that
might advance his career as a writer would be less sustainable if he were
married. As to sex, he believed he could have its pleasures as well with
Rosalind as with Jimmie, or with some version of both, as he desired. He did
not think himself caught between one or the other. Either or both were
suitable. But his struggle to become a successful writer would be against a
resistant, nonsupportive world. His family might be right to discourage his
taking on a responsibility that would limit him. No doubt the Senator and

even Gene Vidal "both intended to live a long time and they would give me nothing in between. It was very clear I was on my own. One can fight the world better than two."

With some displaced but compulsive self-focus, he read and reread that winter-spring of 1943 a controversial popular novel, Robert Newman's *Fling Out the Banner*. It "had an enormous influence on me . . . I remember being very shaken by it." Set at Exeter, the novel dramatizes four interlocking subplots: the disintegrating love affair between the main character, Paul, whose consciousness is the focus of the narrative—an aspiring writer, an avid student of literature, an excellent amateur boxer—and a tall, slim, beautiful town girl, Liz, who has lovely legs and brilliant posture; the relationship between Paul and his football-playing roommate, Boss McKenzie, who commits suicide after a series of rebellious acts, the last of which is a sexual encounter with one of his male teachers; the attempt of the homosexual teacher, Protius, to seduce Billings, an innocent young student; and Paul's attempt to work through his need to liberate himself from Exeter, from Liz, and from his adolescence in order to become both an independent adult and a successful writer. After a troubled reconciliation Liz and Paul break up at Paul's insistence: he is not ready for a commitment to her and he is troubled by inner conflict, some of which may be sexual. It may have to do with his feelings for Boss, it may not. Paul remembers Boss's earlier statement that we all have something of that in us. In one of the two dramatic final scenes of the novel, Boss drives off alone, fatally cracking up Protius's car and himself. He dies in the Exeter hospital. When Billings, in tears, tells Paul that Protius has raped him, Paul and other seniors punish Protius for this infraction of the code of conduct. They lure him to Paul's room, tie, gag, and beat him, shaving his eyebrows and a part down the center of his hair, a visible disgrace they think will make it impossible for Protius to stay at Exeter. In the final chapter, which takes place in the Exeter chapel, Paul calculates the hundreds of hours he has perforce spent there. "The eight o'clock bell began to ring and he started for his first class. It was math. And, on the way, he remembered that he was unprepared." In the end Paul punishes Protius for raping the young boy; life and society punish Boss for his instability, his rebellion, his self-punishing sexual involvement with Protius. Narrated in a plain, flat style, with echoes of Hemingway in the prose, *Fling Out the Banner* seemed to some a roman à clef, with potentially identifiable Exeter models. To many it was a realistic introduction into mainstream fiction of the forbidden topic of sex between men.

As Gore brooded over *Fling Out the Banner,* the identification he made between himself and Paul and between Roz and Liz was painfully strong. How he actually communicated his decision to end the engagement has been repressed—"blanked out." Neither the documents of the time nor Vidal's recollection permits an account. He may indeed have allowed Rosalind to become aware of the disengagement by the absence of reaffirmation, by his silences and his physical distance. Perhaps there was a direct communication, even a scene, between them, though the latter is unlikely. By the end of the Easter 1943 school break he knew he would not go ahead with the relationship, that he was in fact committed to their separation. It was not a question of postponement, of the possibility of resumption later. Once having made the decision, he made it forever. For him it was totally over, a termination that, as with all such transitions, he would make as abruptly as possible, with both eyes on the future. He preferred to be emotionally efficient, even if that efficiency appeared ruthless. As Washburn had remarked about him, if the end were literary greatness, then the means required creative efficiency.

Sex between men had a more direct presence that spring of 1943 in his fascination with Somerset Maugham. He had been brought, once removed, into Maugham's presence through his mother's bridge-playing partner, Michael Arlen, a Bulgarian-born British novelist of Armenian descent. Arlen's 1924 bestselling *The Green Hat* was his most successful in a series of romantic, bittersweet novels about fashionable London life. Arlen and Maugham were friends. Eventually settling in Washington and New York, a stellar figure in what was soon to be called café society, Arlen (and later Maugham) shared with Nina her passion for cards and society. Through his mother Gore had met Arlen at The Homestead, a resort in Hot Springs, Virginia, during a summer holiday in 1939. He found Arlen's conversation delightful, his literary glamour and popular success enviable. An even more successful novelist than Arlen, Maugham outshone and outsold him. Maugham played bridge with Nina at the Washington and Southampton homes of one of her wealthy friends, and years later Gore was to meet him twice. By his last year at Exeter he had read all Maugham's novels and most of his short stories. He shared the general high opinion of the autobiographical *Of Human Bondage.*

Two of Maugham's novels struck an especially responsive chord—*Cakes and Ale* for its suave depiction of writers and literary society and of an attractive blowsy female with a sexual heart of gold and *The Narrow Corner* for the homoerotic tension of its dramatization of repressed love between men. Nina and her bridge-playing friends knew from Arlen and others that Maugham's sexual preference was for hired men. In their suite at the top of Langdell Hall, Gore told the curious but disbelieving Tom McFarland, who had been looking at Gore's collection of Maugham novels, that Maugham was a homosexual. "I was dubious," McFarland recalled. "I learned later [that he was right]. Gore was always good with gossip about the famous. He was connected in a way that he would know things. Especially since these things weren't written about then. I think he used the word 'homosexual.' I think I realized that this was an interest of Gore's. I made the connection immediately. I think Maugham was interesting to Gore in that way. . . . Gore told me that Somerset Maugham would pay men to have sex. I got the distinct feeling that he was talking about a role model. Not in any sexual way. Somebody who had been able to get through life in difficult circumstances."

Encouraged by the *Review* faculty adviser, a Maugham enthusiast, and by his senior-year English teacher, Leonard Stevens, Gore wrote an essay on Maugham for English. It did not touch on Maugham's sexuality. That would have courted trouble. Finally, in his last year at Exeter, he had in Stevens a teacher eminently suited to his intellectual and creative needs. In order to graduate in June Gore had to pass math, but he also needed one additional credit. Assigned to Stevens's English 4 for the academic year, he soon discovered that if he could be moved for the spring into English 5, "a special high-powered honors class" that carried one additional credit, he would have that problem solved. For the four fall-term grading periods in English 4, Stevens had given him a C+, then two B's, and finally a B+. Bingham, Sibley, and Lewis, whose grades were always high, had already been assigned to the honors literature class. Keen to join them there, both to authenticate his claim that he was their equal and to make his June graduation possible, Gore was delighted when Stevens moved him into the elite course. He boasted, prematurely, to his father that now he "will definitely graduate in June (they moved me up to English 5 which corresponds to third year college English)," though, he confessed, his marks were "hitting their mid winter slump: it has happened every year of my school life. I suppose I shall have to begin struggling again." English 5 was more pleasure than struggle, the readings diverse and challenging, from Plato's *Republic* to Conrad's *Lord Jim*. Formerly a successful graduate student at Harvard, assistant to the famous scholar of American literature, F. O. Matthiessen, Stevens had given up on getting a Ph.D. partly because of bad eyesight and a young family, mostly because he discovered he loved reading but hated research. He had just that year come to Exeter from teaching at Yale. "Slow-moving, soft-spoken, broadly tolerant and understanding, a bulky man of about 5'10", he had a large, squarish head and wore thick glasses for his weak eyes," Hamilton Bissell recalled. "Not handsome but . . . arresting, with a quick smile, not a grin, with a soft voice and a loud wife," whose vivacity Gore liked. Stevens "had an infallible judgment about people, especially the students. He could never be conned. . . . He knew the essence of the Harkness table, which was to think and get other people to think by asking questions. He had a great deal of patience and prudence, but was also strong and would take no nonsense. His notion of respect was that we take the subject seriously, we respect the subject. Gore, of course, came in with a swagger, and Leonard was the perfect teacher for him."

Stevens took Gore and his literary efforts seriously, including his essay on Maugham, which began with a sentence characteristic of Vidal's later style: "I have become increasingly tired of being told that Somerset Maugham is at best a competent writer of words and at worst a cynical master of the cliché." A judicious overall evaluation of Maugham's career up to that point, the schoolboy elements are easily outweighed by the intelligence of some of the comments and by the combination of seriousness, personal responsiveness, and syntactical clarity that transforms simplicity into sophistication. The style is more mature than the judgments. Both, though, are impressive. What he did not show Stevens was the novel inspired by Maugham's *Cakes and Ale* he began writing that spring. Though he was never to bring it to completion, he was to work on it sporadically for the next two years. In the end he had an approximately 52,000-word manuscript of some thematic and linguistic sophistication, in a cool, direct, witty style, with aspirations to a worldliness that the author's inexperience could not sustain. "There's no way of burning it, is there, the Maugham novel?" he was to ask fifty years later.

In its fourth section, where the novel breaks off, the Maugham-like main character departs for the South Pacific. The young Vidal's imagination has carried his character as far as he can go. The South Pacific is not only beyond his experience but beyond his imagination. Not able to write himself onto that map, he let the character and the novel go, but not before he had created an effective structure in which the third-person narrative is divided into three sections, each told from the point of view of a friend of the main character, the recently deceased world-famous writer James Morrison. The doctor, the sculptor, and the publisher have known him from the start of his career. All are attending his funeral. Some minor touches drawn from Vidal's life appear—an autumnal scene set in Rock Creek Park, descriptions of Paris that draw on the author's recollections of his visit in 1939. But the two major elements of the unfinished novel have sustained autobiographical intensity. Modeling the main character on his reading of Maugham's most successful novel and his personal awareness of Maugham's life, what Vidal "was trying to write," he later claimed, "was really *Cakes and Ale* all over again, with Maugham instead of Hardy, Arlen instead of Hugh Walpole, and myself as Maugham writing it." In Maugham's novel the narrator is a version of Maugham himself. Of the three main characters, two are novelists, supposedly modeled on Thomas Hardy and Hugh Walpole, though the fit is loose; the third the sensually liberated wife of the Hardy-like character with whom the narrator has had an affair many years before. For Vidal, aspiring to be a successful worldly writer himself, what more clever though derivative way to begin than to model his novel on a successful novel, to identify himself with Maugham? The resemblances are vague, though. Vidal's narrator is a Maugham-like narrator but not a character, let alone a novelist-character, in his narrative. No equivalent of Hugh Walpole exists. James Morrison's wife, a minor character, has no resemblance to Maugham's Rosie. The novel is entirely about James Morrison, and the energy of the depiction is less with the development of his career than with Morrison's and his friends' efforts to deal with his homosexuality. Morrison is both the public Maugham and the private Maugham, loosely disguised but sympathetically if somewhat clinically defined. The issues are dramatized, or at least discussed: are homosexuals born or made thereafter? What is the appropriate relationship between one's private sexuality and one's public career? To what degree does a writer who is a homosexual include (or exclude) that from his public writings? It is more than the seventeen-year-old Vidal can handle, though he does not always fail by much. Vidal clearly enjoys the combination of the fact and the pose of worldly sophistication, of being beyond Romanticism, that the Maughamian example provides. It is more explicit, less tortured, more wittily worldly on the homosexual theme than *Fling Out the Banner*. Gore's interest in the subject as early as the spring of 1943 suggests it may have played some role, even if a less than fully conscious one, in his decision to end the engagement to Rosalind.

⸺ ⸱ ⸺

Unlucky with husbands, Nina Gore Olds found herself suddenly, after less than a year of marriage, husbandless again, though this time not through her own doing. In late April, Bob Olds died of complications from pneumonia after a heart attack at the Tucson, Arizona, Desert Sanatorium. At the end, in great pain, unable to breathe, he had died in an oxygen tent. Nina had stayed with him throughout. Actually Olds had been in ill health for some time, and Nina may have become aware of his condition as early as the previous Christmas. In February 1943, when he was relieved of his command so that he might undergo treatment in Tucson, she had wired her son at Exeter to tell him where she now was and why. That the distinguished Air Force general had succumbed to illness at the age of forty-six was not what Nina had contracted for. Her son had remarked to Washburn that "he pitied the fact that his mother did not marry Luce (*Life, Time, Fortune*) because then he would be all set." But the remark was more solipsistic than cruel. He had no reason to dislike the rather likable Olds, two of whose sons, cadets at West Point with whom Gore remained friendly for some years, had just managed to reach Tucson in time to see their father alive. Uncharacteristically, Washburn used the occasion to retaliate. "Because he's just another step-father, and because I couldn't honestly say I gave a damn, I expressed no condolences; merely confining myself to remarking when it would come out in *Time*. . . . I knew beforehand that such things weren't the things to be said, but some strange force made me say them." Gore himself memorialized his second stepfather in a poem, a valorization of the warrior who does not die in battle, the pilot who dies on the ground: "They say that even eagles die./Some die in flight, but oftener I/Am told they'll die on a stone-sharp cliff/Alone, where those who've watched them fly/Can't see them earth-trapped, and remember,/And remember."

That he himself might face death in battle was an anxiety shared with his Exeter classmates caught between duty and fear, courage and cowardice.

His own view of where he might fit into the military was governed partly by self-interest. Service was unavoidable, even desirable, especially since he understood that any chance for a political career after the war would be damaged if he could not say that he had fought on behalf of his country. With a father and uncle West Point graduates, he had an inescapable family tradition. Short of incapacity, one did one's duty, and duty had the functional attraction of taking one out of adolescent bondage into adult self-sufficiency. As infantilizing as the Army might be in its control of the daily routines of life, it supplied a salary and sometimes provided adventure, experience, growth, if one did not have to pay too high a price. The price he did not want to pay was to be cannon fodder. Or at least, if he were to be cannon fodder, he preferred to be on the front lines as an officer. To be that, he would have to graduate from Exeter in June and then attend one of the officer-training programs the armed services had initiated. Most were for college students, especially graduates, but with the prestige of Phillips Exeter Academy and the influence, if necessary, of his father and uncle, he might be admitted to one of the programs. The immediate challenge was to graduate from Exeter. English 5 gave him the extra credit he needed, but he still had to pass his other courses. It looked almost certain, though, that he would fail mathematics again. That would be disastrous. At worst he would be drafted into the infantry, destined for the European or Pacific front lines. At best he would have to take some sort of summer makeup program. For the month of April he had gotten an E in math and an E+ in French. History, English, and art seemed secure. Assigned to study hall again, unusual for a senior, he cut back on everything but classes. The French he restored to its usual D status, but it soon became clear there was no likelihood he could pass math. Like Paul in *Fling Out the Banner,* Gore had been unprepared for so long that no amount of preparation, even if he were capable, could help now. He confessed his miserable situation to the math teacher. With bombs falling and bullets flying, the math teacher took an un-Exonian liberty with the "stern mother's" usual standards. "All right," he said. "I agree, you'll never pass this subject, not in a million years. So I'll do something unheard of. I'll pass you with a D in this course. But you must promise me two things. One, you'll never breathe a word of this to anyone. Two, you'll never never take another math course again!"

Now on a clear path to graduation, Gore again had time for other things. At the final meeting of the Senate verbal fireworks had flared. The topic was a bill against lynching. "Those attending the meeting might well have thought they had instead wandered into a meeting of the Society for the Preservation of American Wit," *The Exonian* reported. Vidal took the contrarian states'-rights side against the bill. It passed handsomely. With Bingham, who had again severely criticized one of his stories, he had a "terrific feud," the climax of which was a single-spaced two-page letter of counterattack by Gore to Bingham, partly humorous, mostly sarcastic. Soon they were amiable again, working together on the class yearbook, *The Paean*. Their arguments about art he thought so good he used them in a discussion with McFarland. Washburn listened. "On the surface and to the casual observer, he would seem to know a great deal about art. Distortions of Greek statues he said were looked upon with horror but we've gotten used to them as we have with Rembrandt's shadow technique. He thinks that distortion today will in time be accepted by the people who will get used to it. He doesn't seem to differentiate between slight distortion for more beauty of former painters and the great distortion for god-knows-what ('design' Vidal calls it)."

Graduation Gore anticipated as celebration and liberation. As to academic prizes, he had no doubt he would not win one, perhaps with the exception of the English 5 composition award which, to his surprise, Bingham and Lewis won. In the informal senior-class ballot for comico-serious designations, his classmates pronounced him class "politician" and class "hypocrite." For the latter honor Bingham came in third. Somewhat tongue-in-cheek, it also embodied the reality of perception and attitude. A. K. Lewis was named "wittiest," Bingham was third in that category and second in most likely to succeed. Washburn had priority as class "grind," the positive side of which was his being named valedictorian. Running for class orator, Gore came in second to one of his debate opponents, the "interventionist" Irving Murphy, who also beat him out in the informal election for "best speaker." It was a disappointment. Lewis was elected class historian, Bingham class poet. Along with Washburn, they would have the positions of prominence on class day and at the graduation ceremony.

On a hot mid-June weekend, Exeter green and bright, hordes of parents began arriving. Gene and Kit came up from New York. Nina, waiting out the war on the West Coast, did not attend. On Saturday afternoon, sunny but with a cooling breeze, with eight hundred people watching, Gore marched into the gymnasium in cap and gown for Class Day activities.

As class poet, Bingham read "very effectively," Otis Pease thought. The gist of it was that the dream of the "perfect school" comes true at Exeter. As class historian, Lewis, deadpan, read a humorous account of the qualities of the graduating class; including their aggregate weight and height. Washburn gave a brief valedictory farewell to liberal education for the duration of the war. More long-winded, Irving Murphy insisted on inflating his class oration to match his inflated opinion of how much its members would contribute to American politics and government in the future. He neglected to make any reference to how many of them might make their greatest contribution by being killed. Ten of Gore's classmates were soon to die in the war, including Lew Sibley.

In the late afternoon Bliss Perry and some faculty wives entertained the visitors with punch and cookies on the lawn. That night almost everyone dined at the crowded Exeter Inn, then went to the graduation ball, attended by celebratory boys and lovely girls. For this occasion Gore had a replacement for Rosalind. Kit came as his date. Uninterested in schoolboy dances, Gene Vidal, happy to accommodate his son, stayed at the inn. Seventeen-year-old Gore Vidal had on his arm the most beautiful woman at the dance. Everyone soon knew she was a professional model from New York. People were bowled over. He did not say, as some later invented, "I want you to meet my mother!" The fun and glory were in Kit being his date. "Gore suggested it," Kit recalled, "and Gene encouraged me. I think he wanted the glamour of taking a model to his dance and telling all his friends." Graduation on Sunday was "stifling hot, humid." There was a thunderstorm late in the day. In the morning, at the last Exeter church service Gore was ever to attend, Perry bade farewell to the class. His subject was "faith" in the future. At the ceremony that afternoon he made another speech. Each graduate rose as his name was read, placed cap on head, tassel on left. They then formed a circle on the lawn, where each received his diploma from the hand of the principal. The imminent thunderstorm came as a relief. At dinnertime the rain poured down.

———————

From Union Station in Washington Gore departed, once more by train, for the Army Special Training Program (ASTP) in Lexington, Virginia, set up for educationally advantaged enlistees under the age of eighteen who were too young for regular Army programs. He had enlisted in New

York City on July 29, 1943, his home address his father's 1107 Fifth Avenue apartment. There was one stepsibling there, Vance, another well on its way. The large fifth-floor apartment, with views of Central Park, had a room for Gore, converted from a maid's to a family bedroom. His father's East Hampton summer hospitality was in easy reach.

Most of July, though, he stayed, for the last time, with his grandparents at the large stone house overlooking Rock Creek Park, the happiest home of his childhood. Dot and the Senator were delighted to have him there. With heating oil rationed, it had become difficult to heat the house for the winter. Having thought they had sold it, when the deal fell through they reoccupied the house that summer. Soon it was to be out of their hands forever. Some part of the long summer days Gore spent reading and writing. Late afternoons he went to his grandfather's downtown office to escort him home.

Nina, who with Tommy and Nini, her two children by Auchincloss, had gone from Tucson to Los Angeles, was living now in a bungalow at the Beverly Hills Hotel. With $1,000 a month from Auchincloss, some additional money for child support, her pension as the widow of a major-general, and complete Army medical care, she could afford a comfortable life in wartime California. She had Hollywood friends, some through Olds, who had consulted on numbers of films, including Clark Gable's *Test Pilot*. She had also met Doris Stein, now her closest friend, the beautiful wife of one of the reigning Hollywood talent entrepreneurs, Jules Stein, later a major player in the making of movies. Having slept with Gable, Nina hoped he might propose to her. They had become intimate drinking buddies. When she played bridge and gin rummy with Michael Arlen, she told him Gore was "working on a jealous inspiration inspired by him," actually his Somerset Maugham novel. Arlen won $400. "I'm the unluckiest gambler in the world," Nina complained. "I don't know why I do it." Warmed by the Los Angeles sunshine, she settled in for the duration.

In the company of a hundred other seventeen-year-old Washington boys, Gore marched into Union Station early in August "and onto an ancient train that let us off in or near Lexington, Virginia." Having escaped Exeter, he found himself on August 7 a student of sorts at, of all places, the venerable Virginia Military Institute. The campus was redbrick, traditional, lovely, the air and landscape late-summer green. Everywhere strapping cadets marched, shoulders square, to the beat of a military and scientific drum. The ASTP students wore Army uniforms without a corps designation. His blond hair now brown, his eyes hazel, his complexion ruddy, his height 5 feet 11¹/₄ inches, a private in the "Enlisted Reserve Corps," Gore immediately discovered to his shock that this three-month intensive program trained not general officers but engineers. Someone who had sworn an oath never to take another math course, who had little to no background in the sciences, was suddenly plunged into a hastily devised college-level preengineering program intended to teach bright high-school graduates enough physics and math to qualify for the Army engineering corp. They would be expected to assist senior Army engineers in building and/or blowing up bridges around the world. "I am now a goddamned engineer," he told his father. "First of all we are in regular army uniform all the time. Second we are in the regular army. Third this place trains only engineers. I can't get in the Amgots [American Military Government in Occupied Territories] or foreign language group because they require a BA. Nor in psychology or personnel because they require an MA. Nor in pre-med because they require two years of college." Could his father help him get a commission or at least a transfer to a situation more appropriate to his abilities?

Classes each day until 3 P.M., then exercise and drill till dinner: physics, trigonometry, military science, engineering, chemistry. At least history and geography had some connection with his interests. The staff came from the regular Virginia Military Institute faculty. One day an elderly colonel accosted him on campus. Why didn't he play football like his father? Two of the faculty were congenial, especially a young English Department teacher, Carrington Tutwiler, a Philadelphian with a doctorate from Princeton, who encouraged his writing. A nephew of the novelist Ellen Glasgow, he was himself literary enough to be interested in a young man who wanted to be a writer. Though Gore worked some evenings on the Maugham novel, a bit of which Tutwiler read, he showed him mainly poetry, which he continued to turn out, much of it increasingly dark in abstractly unfocused ways. Still, it was competent, and impressed Tutwiler. The schedule, however, permitted little time for writing. "I compose sonnets in the latrine," he told his father. In his English class the group of twenty-five students studied Supreme Court decisions for structure and style as well as content, Tutwiler recalled. Actually Gore enjoyed the toughness of the regimen, particularly the physical training. On the first day he took satisfaction in being able to do twenty-five push-ups. By the end of August he had been made a platoon leader, promoted to corporal. "I'm having a fine time yelling 'Thirsqawthirplu-tuneawpresencountedfor,' " he wrote to his father. The food was surprisingly good, with meat plentiful. On weekends he and two roommates spent hours in noisy roadside bars where men in uniform and local ladies flirted, nostalgic wartime popular songs mixing with thick cigarette smoke. "There was a wonderful roadhouse near by which we would get to, with a jukebox and the hot-eyed girls from the neighborhood. It was very erotic, and they were always playing 'Paper Moon' and 'Don't Get Around Much Any More.' There was a pleasant air of doom about it." Weekend passes were easy to get. He caught a mild case of flu. "I always seem to catch something when things get a little rigorous. . . . I am getting high marks in everything but physics. Maybe I'll pass maybe I won't but I'm too damned tired most of the time to care. I really enjoy this business altho I'd like to sit still sometime and think." Later he had some nostalgic good feeling for the crazily dislocating combination of activities. After Exeter, VMI seemed grown-up, purposeful, even if bizarre.

A sharp pain in his stomach soon proved to be appendicitis. Operated on by an Army doctor, Gore found the aftermath "very unpleasant. I was flat on my back for a week then the Dr. bade me rise and walk, which I did." When he returned to classes, his physics marks plummeted. The ten days or so he had missed contributed to the decline. Most likely it would have happened anyway. "I dread the outcome. There's a story here that an AST student dropped a pencil in class, and while he was leaning over to pick it up he missed a term." Not that he was uninterested in physics, an interest that would express itself almost a lifetime later in his manipulation of modern theories as part of the plot of *The Smithsonian Institution*. The physics instructor, Colonel Willard, whose name he was to make use of in *The City and the Pillar*, let them in on a military secret: the atom had been smashed. That it had occurred at the site of what had once been the Los Alamos Ranch School was still top secret. Gore's other grades were still good. He was even elected class president, 85 votes to 22. Despite the appendectomy, he felt physically fine, partly because during the recovery period he was relieved of physical training and marching. "Maybe I should have tried for West Point earlier in life—or played football—there is a certain parallel," he joked to his father. He had a two-week furlough coming up at the end of August. If he could hang on scholastically, he might make it through. "Privates have happy if short lives." But, as he feared from the beginning, he could not sustain adequate grades in subjects he had no aptitude for or interest in. The second half of the intensive physics course was a disaster. So too math. Suddenly, by mid-October, it was all over. As it became evident he would fail these courses, he was quite understandably expelled. This was hardly a blow to his ego, and, as he often did in such situations, he had anticipated the inevitable and made alternative plans. He had been regularly in touch with his father and Uncle Pick. The practical problem was immediate. Assigned to Fort Meade, near Washington, as an expendable infantry private he might spend the rest of the war there or he might suddenly find himself on a troopship to the European front.

At Fort Meade the Army found appropriate jobs for him. At first he was assigned twenty-four-hour KP duty. The only advantage was an endless supply of delicious pork chops with which he stoked his lanky frame. Working through the day and night, he slept most of the morning in a noisy barracks. After six hours' sleep, back to work. Then he was assigned to the night shift in a small, dark furnace room in a barracks building. Soot made the darkness heavy. Wooden bins contained endless mounds of coal. There was no time to read, little to sleep, between firing and stoking. He slept on the concrete floor. When the floor got cold, he awakened and knew it was time to feed the furnace. In the red-glowing darkness, muscles tired, sweating heavily, shoveling coal into a fiery furnace, he found little consolation in observing that they too serve who only stand and shovel. It would be a hell of a place to spend the war.

CHAPTER SIX

A Border Lord

1943–1946

THANKSGIVING 1943. Peterson Field, Colorado Springs. A cold, invigo-
rating wind blew constantly. Liberated from the coal furnaces of Fort
Meade, Private Gore Vidal went directly to the command headquarters of
the 268th Army Air Force Unit to thank Uncle Pick. "Don't announce me.
Just let me go in," he said to the startled corporal guarding the entrance to
the base commander's office. "I don't know why the enlisted man went
along with that, but he did," Sally Vidal remembered. "Gore threw his hat
into the office, and then he popped in and said, 'Daddy,' or some crazy thing
like that. We just had a ball with him. He was so funny and so weird." Uncle
Pick "almost fell thru the floor," Gore wrote to his father. "He's still not
quite sure whether I'm supposed to be here or not."

When furnace duty in Maryland had begun to feel endless, Gore had
made his urgent request to the informal West Point Protective Association.
West Point people looked after their own. His father and uncle were both
high-ranking members, former football greats, Pick now commander of the
newly formed Fighter Wing—the largest in the country—designated to
provide support for the Second Air Force. Gore's request was simple: "Get

me out of here!" In Beverly Hills, Nina was disappointed that he had left the relative safety of the Army Special Training Program. "I couldn't be more upset over your plans not to go through with the schooling. I'm in hopes your Dad's plans will turn out a pipe dream—for I think it a great mistake not to go through with this course even though you don't like it. This other way there is no telling what may happen to you. . . . I don't like at all the Pick set up. . . . There is no point in your going to a combat zone." Events had already overtaken Nina's reservations. Gene Vidal talked to a classmate in charge of personnel in the War Department. Pick requested his nephew be transferred to the Army Air Corps for service at Peterson Field, his operational headquarters, one of more than a dozen bases under his command. The Air Force still part of the Army, the transfer was easily effected. Suddenly relieved of duty at Fort Meade, Gore was ordered to report, after a brief furlough, for abbreviated basic training at Fort Dix, New Jersey, a transfer point for reassignment and travel. Relieved, exhausted, waiting, he spent a few weeks with his grandparents at their new Washington residence, an apartment on Crescent Place. Having just turned eighteen, he happily enjoyed the attractions of the bustling wartime city. Downtown Washington adventures appealed to him; the streets, the movie theaters, the parks were filled with men on the loose, particularly energetic soldiers and sailors. It was a cool, erotic change from the fiery furnace at Fort Meade. With his grandfather he had his first adult conversations. Dot was as loving as ever, happy to have him home, pleased to have Nina on the other side of the continent. With new orders in hand, Gore once more left from Union Station, the train crowded with servicemen, wartime security tight. At Fort Dix the transfer and new orders caught up with him. From Fort Dix to Denver, then Colorado Springs.

Soon he began to feel "human again." Assigned to Quonset-hut barracks, he had no complaint about his quarters. Autumn weather was bracing, the late-November sky clear, snow-covered mountains to the west. At night soldiers took turns feeding the black iron coal-burning stove in the middle of the barracks room. During the day, assigned to A-2 as a clerk-typist, Gore was put to the comparatively light work of writing for the base newspaper. Since his uncle, Sally Vidal recalled, had no doubt that " 'That's the smartest enlisted man I've ever had,' he gave Gore the job of base historian. Somebody's got to write this all up." There were no physics tests, no furnaces to stoke around the clock. He had time to read and write. From the small base library he borrowed books, mostly novels, soon aware that one useful thing the Army did was provide books for those few soldiers who wanted to read, including a series of special armed-forces paperback editions. With the unfinished Somerset Maugham novel on hold, he began working on a new idea he had for a novel, to be called *The Deserter*. As happy as he was to be at Peterson Field rather than Fort Meade, clearly he still would have preferred to be someplace other than the Army. The new novel did not get very far. Both his imagination and confidence in the venture deserted him when he found he could not effectively describe Mexico, to which he had never been but to which the main character flees. Early in the new year he returned to the Maugham novel, soon to break off again, finally, and wrote more poems, ambitiously enlisting his father to forward a book-length poetry manuscript to a New York literary agent, Gertrude Algase, who had taken some interest in his work. She hoped to sell some of his fiction, including the opening chapter of *The Deserter*. The poems must have seemed to her dauntingly nonsalable. Literary in a nonliterary world, Gore impressed one of the professors at the college in Colorado Springs. Amanda Ellis "encouraged my poetry. . . . She was an English professor, a fat, enthusiastic spinster who knew Ted [Edward] Weeks of the *Atlantic Monthly*. So I was soon sending stuff off to Weeks and so on, to no avail. But I saw a good bit of Amanda while I was there." She felt "confident that he will like it," he told his father, "and if he likes it will publish it with Little, Brown, without strings. So all progresses well, perhaps." In Colorado Springs she introduced him to local celebrities, particularly the elderly painter, illustrator, and cartoonist, Boardman Robinson, a far-left political satirist who directed the Colorado Springs Fine Arts Center. On a self-description, probably to accompany a manuscript Algase circulated to publishers, Gore indulged in the career-building, cute-toned exaggerations from which young writers get pleasure: "Has been published in numerous magazines and first book *RECREATION PERIOD* (collected poetry) scheduled to be published in late spring. Spent much of life travelling Europe, U.S., etc. . . . Now writing a novel that is unique: a) it is not autobiographical b) it is not the great American novel."

However comfortable his life had become at Peterson Field, the notion of going to Officer Candidate School, preferably in Miami, appealed to him. He filed an application. "I'm really going," he partly joked to his father, "because I discovered that if I get thru it I'll be the youngest officer in the

history of the army! We have to keep that exceptional Vidal theory alive."
When Pick would get his promotion to general was a subject of enthusiastic
amusement. In response to his father's comment that Pick did not seem
ambitious enough, Gore expressed his daydream that his uncle, who had an
interest in political office, return, after the war, to South Dakota to run for
the Senate and himself for the House. "That would be colorful and unique.
Castle in the air." Regardless of poor eyesight, Gore was optimistic that he
would be leaving soon for OCS. In the meantime, life at Colorado Springs
had its attractions. Ellis invited him to talk to her senior class and lecture to
a group of high-school English teachers. Probably he read his poems. The
USO had a poetry prize contest, which he soon won with his elegy to
General Olds. Unlike other enlisted men, he was often Pick and Sally's
guest, especially on weekends, at the luxurious Broadmoor Hotel five miles
from Colorado Springs, which the Army had taken over for officers' quarters. It had a well-trained international staff and "displaced Japanese from
California, who worked as gardeners." The eighteen-year-old private frequently had his dinner at a table filled with the commander's guests, mostly
visiting brass. Christmas he celebrated with his aunt and uncle, their small
daughter, Victoria, and Nina, who flew in from Los Angeles to spend the
holiday with her son. Wrapped in her luxurious fur coat, with matching fur
hat, her bright rubies gleaming, attractively suntanned, she swept into the
Broadmoor, the ex-sister-in-law of the commander of the base and the
widow of the former head of the Second Air Force. When Victoria lost her
toy battleship on the lake, she came in crying. Gore consoled her, slightly.
" 'My,' he said, 'she takes adversity hard. But wait till she's lost her first,
second, and third husbands.' " He had been looking forward to his mother's
visit. Fortunately, it went well, neither of them in a fighting mood. Nina's
heavy drinking apparently did not erupt into dramatics or disablement until
New Year's eve, when she got drunk. Most officers and their wives were in
no condition to notice. With everyone expecting to be imminently off to
Europe or the Pacific, alcohol and cigarettes were the drugs of choice.
Mostly, though, Nina's visit was a success. She departed with the expectation that Gore would visit her soon in Los Angeles. Air Corps flights were
readily available on military planes. As long as there was room, enlisted men
could fly home on furloughs.

   To Gore's discomfort and perplexity, he had been getting phone calls
from Rosalind, now a student at Vassar. He discouraged her. There was a

handsome, red-haired Southern boy in the barracks who could neither read nor write. "When I was CQ, he'd often stay in the hut rather than go to Colorado Springs, and I'd tell him stories, like a child. I even tried Shakespeare on him. Romeo and Juliet. He loved the plot. . . . The verse, what I could recall, moved him, and he would play idly with what he called his 'fuck-pole,' but in no provocative way. . . . There was a great deal of [same-sex] sex going on. In the States it was dangerous on post. But in nearby Colorado Springs there were many men eager to know us, and once, as I was blown by an old man of, perhaps, thirty—my absolute cutoff age— he offered me ten dollars, which I took." With raging hormones, after the comparative asceticism of Exeter and the exhausting regimen at VMI, he now had the energy and opportunity for sexual encounters. "Having discreet sex with strangers didn't begin until I was in the Army. . . . But the great promiscuity began in Colorado Springs." The excitement was in anonymity, transgression, the almost infinite opportunity for pleasure without the tedium of establishing a relationship or the danger of entanglements. There were few or no queens in sight. Most of those in uniform sexually active with other men looked and spoke like men who were sexually active with women only. Gore, eighteen, lanky, almost six feet tall, with a deep baritone voice, actually had only two sexual escapades in Colorado Springs, one at the Broadmoor, one in town. They seemed to him just as natural as his relationship with Rosalind had been. If the world chose to see it differently, it was the world that was at fault.

Soon after the New Year he hitched a ride eastward with Pick, who piloted a B-24, with Gore in the gunner's turret, to frigid Sioux Falls, South Dakota, from which they drove the short distance to Madison. For the first time he saw his father's boyhood home. "It was a wonderful trip and we met just about everyone in Madison. Stayed with Amy," Gene's youngest sister, "and saw the house you were born in and all the landmarks. . . . I liked Madison a lot. . . . It's one of the few places where they pronounce Vidal right." Many of the Madisonians he met were hoping Gene would build a Vidal Weldwood factory there. From Sioux Falls they flew to the East Coast. At first Gore felt certain he would be going to Officer Candidate School in March. Then what had seemed probable in late 1943, now, in early 1944, appeared "a bit far off, though I think it will swing through in time." His myopia was one impediment: he needed glasses for accurate vision. As OCS seemed less likely, he raised the possibility of West Point. But "if your eyes aren't good they won't even give you an exam. I looked into . . . every avenue possible to become an officer." When he learned that the Army had closed the ASTP program and sent all its enlisted men to the front lines, he realized what a close escape he had had. If he were going into a battle theater, he wanted to go as an officer. Another scheme came to his and Pick's minds. If he could get a "direct commission," he could skip Officer Candidate School entirely. His eyesight would not be an issue. If one of his father's high-ranking friends in the Pacific would request him through the War Department, then General MacArthur could instantly make him an officer in the field. "After I get commissioned out there Pick (when he's a Gen.) can ask for me as his aide and I'd come gaily back. . . . I'd get a nice trip thru the south seas; see Australia and be an officer." That scheme never got off the ground. For the time being he had to settle for promotion to corporal clerk-typist stationed at Peterson Field.

With a five-day pass he flew from wintry Colorado to sun-happy Los Angeles. Nina, at her Beverly Hills Hotel bungalow with Nini, Tommy, and a maid, greeted him warmly. He was eager to meet Nina's famous Hollywood friends. Actually, since Nina never went to movies, she usually did not recognize the luminaries. But at the fashionable hotel and parties, many hosted by her friend Doris Stein, who had also just had her fortieth birthday, Nina met them simply as attractive people, most of whom were impressed by her East Coast upper-class social standing and her partying good spirits. Still a social backwater, Hollywood found the daughter of Senator Gore, the ex-wife of Hugh Auchincloss, and the widow of General Bob Olds an attractive asset. She seemed high-class Eastern nobility. One evening Gore noticed Nina, drunk, spending a long time in her bedroom with a handsome hotel employee who had carried her in from a chauffeured car after a late party. At the Beverly Hills Hotel pool, Clark Gable, on leave from the Army, put Tommy on his back and gave him a swimming lesson. When Tommy urinated, Gable threw him off. Both heavy drinkers, Gable and Nina "would be drinking through the golden hours of the day." One evening Nina took Gore, in uniform, to a crowded party. "All of the Hollywood people were in a terrible state of shame that they weren't in the war. I remember Sinatra coming over to me—he couldn't have been nicer— feeling terribly guilty. He was getting an awful lot of bad publicity because he'd stayed out of the war. . . . I was the only soldier there." When Gore was introduced to Leslie Charteris, who wrote the "Saint" stories, it occurred to him that since someone had to be lucratively paid to write movie scripts, he should keep that in mind for the future. He met Doris and Jules Stein, both soon to become friends and supporters. To his father he wrote, "met everybody in Hollywood from Jack Warner to D. Lamour who isn't so much."

Life at Peterson Field continued with tedious repetition, most of it benign, some of it, like his visits to Colorado Springs, enjoyable. Like many, he waited. March, April, May, June. Pick himself, who had at last received his general's stars, longed for his orders to go overseas. Suddenly, in July, uncle and nephew had good news. Pick took a fighter squadron to Italy, Sally and the children soon to leave the Broadmoor for her family's Texas home. Gore, promoted to sergeant, was assigned to the Second Air Force Rescue Boat Squadron, a unit for which he had volunteered. Shortly he was on his way to Louisiana for training missions on Lake Pontchartrain, near New Orleans, though stationed in Baton Rouge. It was not Officer Candidate School, but at least he was on the move. So too were the Second Air Force pilots. While flying training maneuvers over the lake, they sometimes found themselves ditching planes or parachuting into the water. Rescue Squadron "crash boats" completed the training rescues, which were both real rescues for the downed pilots and real saves for the crash-boat crews. Everyone assumed that soon they would be doing this under fire or at least in a war zone. Vidal was occasionally out on the water, a deckhand whose job required him to do everything, from participating in the rescue to maintaining the boat. His qualification for seaworthiness consisted simply of his attesting to having had small-craft experience as a recreational sailor at Newport. Perhaps he exaggerated the frequency of his sailing activities. Probably nobody cared. It was, unfortunately, not a sufficiently challenging change from the uneventful routines at Peterson Field. Since there was little crash-boat work, he was also assigned to the newspaper staff, where he did the same kind of in-house reporting/editing he had done in Colorado, "writing most of the newspaper," whose main substance was the usual Army tedium. The slack rescue-boat training allowed frequent visits to New Orleans. Dinners at Antoine's, seafood in streetside cafés, lively bars where he could nurse a beer through the evening—New Orleans fascinated, beguiled, enchanted him. In Baton Rouge, with the encouragement of one of the crash-boat captains, he took an examination for warrant officer, to serve as first mate on an Army transport ship. In effect, the Army ran a huge navy, the transport wing of which mainly moved supplies. One could become an Army warrant officer without going to Officer Candidate School. Since warrant officers were in short supply, all he need do was pass an examination in the principles and practices of navigation. Strongly motivated, he memorized the navigation textbook without understanding much of it, let alone knowing its practical application.

Shocked, he learned that he had passed. Confused in its endless paperwork as to whether Gore E. Vidal was a corporal or a sergeant, the Army resolved the problem in late October. Effective November 8 he was discharged formally from military service as a sergeant in the Army of the United States and appointed, under the category "maritime technical specialist," a United States Army temporary "Warrant Officer, Junior Grade," serial number W2139622. Soon he was on his "way west on a train with the windows down, sleeping on the floor . . . headed for Seattle. First we stopped at Marysville near Sacramento." Nina came up from Beverly Hills to see her son before he was to ship out for a combat zone. After "two or three nights at Marysville . . . we were again on the train, with the curtains down, and ended up in Fort Lewis, Washington, from where we embarked for the Aleutian Islands." He was going to, of all places, Alaska. The orders read, "Permanent station outside the continental limits of the United States, arctic climate." The night before departure, in the Snakepit Bar of the Olympic Hotel in downtown Seattle, he picked up a merchant marine. Despite his wedding ring, the older man of about twenty-five seemed delighted to be propositioned by a handsome young warrant officer. "Smoky, raw-wood paneled dive, powerful smell of beer, cheap Ivory soap, fog-damp woolens . . . bodies that smelled." They could not get a bedroom in the crowded hotel. In a samples room where salesmen showed their wares he got more than he had bargained for. On a cot at the far end of the room, with no plan of procedure, he paused. "Suddenly, he was on my back. I tried to push him off. He used an expert half nelson in order to shove partway in. I bucked like a horse from the pain, and threw us both off the bed. We rolled across the floor, slugging at each other. Then, exhausted, we separated. He cursed; dressed; left. That was my first and last experience of being nearly fucked."

Three days after Christmas, having sailed up through the inland channel route on the troop-crowded United States Army Transport *Chirikof,* he
was in Anchorage, "in sunny Alaska," he wrote to his father. As the soldiers
had marched onto the boat in Seattle, an Army band had played Judy
Garland's "Trolley Song" from *Meet Me in St. Louis.* The trip was long,
dull, uncomfortable, the scenery beautiful, the weather delightful. In
Anchorage, "a frontier town, pretty much like a horse-opera town with
saloons," the days were short and dark, the landscape white. To his surprise
it seemed less cold than New York in the winter, not even "as cold as
Exeter." On New Year's Eve, unused to handling liquor, he got drunk and
was officially reprimanded. There was little to do at Fort Richardson but
wait out the weeks before orders came for relocation to the Aleutians. He
thought he would have six months of Army tedium in which to finish
writing a new novel on which he had made the first tentative beginnings in
the last week; then perhaps one of his father's West Point friends would still
be able to arrange a direct commission in the field.

Two weeks later, still in Anchorage, he had reason to believe he would
soon be on his way, "either (a) in command of a power-barge (crew of 15)
or (b) first mate aboard an FS [Freight Transport] boat—crew of 30—I'm
looking forward to this great new experience with mingled feelings. . . . I
think 6 months of this will be very stimulating." Many soldiers in
Anchorage, he noticed, seemed to enjoy life there. "In fact many of them
wouldn't go back if they could—and they certainly wouldn't go to a more
active theatre—this army gets more and more depressing; everybody just
coasting along." But being a warrant officer gave him "deep satisfaction."
At Fort Richardson he had the job of putting soldiers through drill at the
port; his mind, though, was mostly on his publication prospects, particularly
whether or not his agent had been able to place his poems. "Am getting to
work on a piece of prose about this part of the world—sent a story to
Esquire which they felt because of its military nature they'd rather not print
now but might after the war—it was really a flattering letter which they
don't usually do—still I'd like to *sell* something." Nina flew in from Los
Angeles for a quick visit, and "we had a pleasant time." Late in January
orders came at last. Shipped to Chernowski Bay, Umnak Island, almost at

the far end of the one-thousand-mile-long Aleutian Island chain, a thousand miles west of Anchorage, he was now the first mate on a freight-supply ship, with a crew of thirty, making the run between Chernowski Bay and Dutch Harbor, a hundred miles to the east. He stepped off the boat for the first time onto Umnak Island, "which is remote, desolate, sad . . . in the midst of a roaring blizzard," so an observer remembered. "He caught my attention at once by his self-possession. . . . What I remember is that he was very young, and that he kept looking about, taking everything in, while the other soldiers, mostly older, were grumbling and cursing and pulling their fur parkas about their faces. I watched him as he stamped his boots in the snow and turned his head this way and that." In port the crew slept on the boat, the bay as calm as a lake. Soon the weather was surprisingly warm, almost springlike, the volcanic landscape eerily barren, without any vegetation at all. The two towns were rugged, provincial, dominated by the Army, still tiny even with their swollen populations, mostly basic facilities and tawdry recreation for the soldiers: bars, prostitutes, the usual meager Army library, supply depots, occasional movies, bored men.

The library and the movies kept him sufficiently entertained. To his pleasant surprise many of Frederic Prokosch's novels were there, most of which he read for the first time. Having so much enjoyed *The Seven Who Fled* on the train to Rome in 1939, he wanted to read them all. Most of the movies he viewed for the second or third time, one a night in a big wooden shed. Later he remarked that of the eleven million men in the service, "maybe one million saw any action. The other ten million of us sat and saw movies. That's all we did on the Army posts. So I saw every movie made in the '40s." At one of the educational lectures "we soldiers were briefed on the difference between a life-size cardboard cut-out of a nude Chinese youth and one of a Japanese youth. The briefing officer noted such differences as the bandy-legs of the 'Jap,' so unlike the straight, smooth limbs of the 'Chinaman.' But the principal difference, he said, pointing his pointer, 'Is that the Japs have a lot more pubic hair than the Chinks.' Needless to say, mine was the only voice raised at the briefing. How, I asked, does one persuade a possible enemy to reveal the difference?" In fact, while in the Army he was never to see *any* yellow-skinned person at all. At sea, life on FS-135 was routinized, under the command of an able captain, "a fine fellow, 25 yrs old, [who] has spent several years in these waters. I'm in for a very interesting time, I can see. Can't say much more about my job or anything else for that matter, but the food is good and I have a cabin to myself." He intended to begin writing again soon. "I think perhaps I'll be a seaman for the rest of my life," he joked to his father. "You know, the salt water runs through my veins—ah the sea! I can just hear the tide coming in. It seems as if it's only a few feet away from me. As a matter of fact it is only a few feet away."

Not only was it close but often high. The rough winter waters were a challenge, sometimes a threat. Fortunately, the experienced captain did not need to rely on his poorly trained, inexperienced first mate. "It was so foggy that no one ever discovered that I couldn't set a course. We relied on point to point navigation." In early February the weather changed, the wind stronger, the seas higher. The barometer quickly fell precipitously. Suddenly a huge storm, known locally as a "williwaw," an Eskimo word, roared down from the Bering Sea with gale-force wind and blinding snow. The rough sea imperiled any ship caught in the open. Luckily, FS-135 was in port when the storm hit. From within the protected bay Gore had the luxury of being able to say that "it has been extremely unpleasant." The williwaw passed but stayed strongly in his mind, both the distinctive peculiarity of the word and as a possible setting for the dramatic action of the novel he had begun at Fort Richardson. *The Deserter* had been mostly deserted. A short novel set at sea, in which men deal with some basic force of nature and elemental emotional conflict, with a distant nod to Conrad and a closer debt to Stephen Crane, would be the best challenge. Soon he was making the first halting efforts at writing a new novel. It went slowly, almost begrudgingly, as if the elements themselves did not want him to write about the elements. But he was resolute. By late February, "in the hours waiting to go on watch," he had written about ten thousand words and soon found himself doing about a thousand a day. Within a month he had completed the first chapter and the two first parts of the second. "When the weather is good here it is perfect. I am at present *both* thinking and writing—also reading a great deal."

News of the Russian entry into the war against the Japanese marked by a battle in the Bering Sea reminded him that he was both in and also missing the war. It seemed unlikely that any fighting would ever come his way. "In fact—now that the weather's clear—this is a good place to spend the war, though it's hard not to feel a little guilty. Still something might happen here—it's hard to tell." On shipboard, as if to compensate for inaction, "an epidemic of Hearts" broke out, "which is murderous. The 2nd mate no longer speaks to me, and everyone is quite disagreeable. It certainly is one hell of a game," he told his father. So too was the Army in general. Still, he decided again to put "in for OCS fairly soon. I think it would be a good idea to hold a regular reserve commission in anticipation of the next war." On the one hand he was happy not to have to fight. On the other, life in the Aleutians was beginning to become tiresomely dull, and he resented not having full officer status. He made one last try. His rating as first mate was excellent, his probationary period completed. "I continue to discharge my duties as 1st mate in absolute silence. It's amazing how good they think you are when you make no sound." Captain John Weiler, First Lieutenant William Kasper, and Lieutenant Colonel Clarence Johnson did the paper-work, checking off pages of rating scores, testifying to their belief that he would be an excellent officer. It still seemed possible. "When I went in as a private," he later commented, "I felt, Jesus, I've already done this once at camp. Now I've got to do it again. And I still have recurring nightmares that I am my age today and I am who I am and I am back in the Army. I've been called back in as a warrant officer and I haven't got my complete uniform and nobody believes that I'm actually a warrant officer. So they think I'm a private. And I say no. And they say, 'Where's your rank? Where's your serial number?' I don't have them. It's like the old dream of being back at school when you're fully grown up. I have that with the military."

He also resented the news that Kit and Gene had made him a half-brother again, this time to a girl they named Valerie. Discreetly, good-humoredly, he registered his concern that a man who had almost died two years ago and whose income had been severely curtailed partly because of health was not being self-protective enough. "It's good to hear your last traces of thrombosis are going." But he saw indeed that his now prematurely white-haired father would never be the same again. The heart attack had taken from him his edge of energy and ambition. Now Gene Vidal, never an enthusiastic parent, had become a father again at the age of almost fifty. Gore blamed Kit. But he realized that this was the likely result of Gene having married a woman half his age who may have thought of this second child as reasonable compensation for having to look after an ailing husband. And it may have been possible that Gene, as a life-affirming statement of his own, had participated fully in the decision, if decision it were. Since Gore, of course, could do nothing about any of this, he congratulated the parents and wished only happy things for the child. Also he expressed some of his resentment. "Give [Kit] my best and I hope she'll be up and around soon. I understand the 2nd is a snap. Now [all] she has to do is get small pox and you have a thrombosis . . . and it will be just like old times." Not that his own interests were threatened in any material way. He counted on his father for help only to the extent of the bonds that had been put aside for his college costs. Each month since he had enlisted, he had saved most of his $150 salary. Now the additional overseas pay allowed him to bank his entire base pay. It was adding up. So too was his manuscript. "In another 2 months" he expected something to send to a publisher or a new agent. "Read and eat a lot, though I've lost weight. This tricky weather is apt to keep you nervous on a run."

On deck one day a sudden squall in below-freezing weather drenched him with numbing coldness. He immediately began to shiver. Wrapped in blankets, he thawed out in his cabin. One day it was calm, placid, another rough and stormy. When the wind blew from the south, a ghostly white mist enveloped their arctic world. Stepping lively at the bow of the ship as it pulled into Dutch Harbor a few days later, the first mate shifted his weight to initiate his jump to the dock. Suddenly he could not propel himself forward, his right knee locked in place. He could not unbend his leg. As Freight Supply Ship 135 came close to the wharf, Gore realized that he could not make the jump. "As first mate it was my job to jump off the bow onto the wharf and to see that the spring line was secure, and I couldn't make the jump because I didn't think I was going to make it, and my leg had locked on me, and I thought Jesus I'm going to fall between the wharf and the ship." Quickly he had a deckhand take over his duties. Driven first to a doctor, who took X rays, then to the base hospital, he remembered the arctic drenching of a few days before. Since then his joints had ached, but he had assumed it was superficial, temporary. Everyone stationed on the frigid Bering Sea more often than not ached from the arctic cold. Now for two days he could not walk at all. A week later, at the end of March 1945, still hospitalized, he was relieved of all duties. The diagnosis was acute rheumatoid arthritis. He immediately knew that he would never go to Officer Candidate School. Soon on his way to Anchorage for medical observation, he realized also that he probably would never see the Aleutian Islands again. "In fact, I'm apt to be washed up in the army. . . . I'm feeling rather desolate about the whole thing," he wrote to his father. "It, the arthritis, is not really painful, but one feels weak and aching and every now and then my left shoulder aches like all hell. Finger joints are swollen so I can't write much. Am waiting now for a plane." At Anchorage he was taken directly to the hospital at Fort Richardson. "They've been testing several gallons of my blood and I have a feeling I may be here a long time. Have no idea what they've found wrong or what they'll do. If the climate is to blame (and I think that's what they'll find) I shall go back to the States. That's about the best news I've heard." Medical observation reconfirmed the earlier diagnosis. The prescription was rest and rehabilitation, preferably in a warm, dry climate.

Listening to the radio at the Fort Richardson hospital, he was startled by astounding news: FDR had died. The next day, April 13, the newspapers confirmed the story. For Gore and his grandfather the news had personal resonance. The President who had occupied the White House all Gore's conscious life, whom he had imitated to the amusement of friends and enemies, whose policies he had opposed as a debater at Exeter, who had become his and his grandfather's nemesis, had passed from the stage of what even his enemies admitted were his brilliant performances. He had been an act impossible to compete with or ignore. "I was relieved. We were done with him. He had been around so long. I was so tired of him. And my imitation of him was by now so good I was eager to imitate somebody else." But he was stunned that someone who had seemed eternal was gone. "It seemed impossible that this larger than life King Kong of a newsreel politician was dead. I was delighted, of course. He had got us into the war; he had established a dictatorship; he had defeated my grandfather in the election of 1936." Both his grandson and the Senator took satisfaction that the latter had outlived his enemy, that the man who had thought himself "indispensable" had been dispensed with. "I thought your comment on the tragedy was classic," the Senator wrote to his grandson. "If it had got to the lips of the newspapermen it would have gone the rounds . . . I mean your epigram, 'The king is dead—long live the president.' "

He was glad to be on the move, flying southward to Los Angeles, this time to stay for a much longer period than his previous brief visits from Colorado. The Army doctors had recommended a few months of hospitalization for further observation, therapy, and reassignment. With the Army's preference for placing patients near their families, Gore had in mind the perfect place. "Although I did not want to be near my mother, I wanted to be near Hollywood. I was hooked on movies." The Army soon assigned him to Birmingham General Hospital in Van Nuys, just a short distance from Beverly Hills. With him he had about thirty thousand words of his novel-in-progress, his depiction of life on a boat like his own FS-135, focused on two competitive crewmen whose antagonism leads to the death of one in the freezing arctic waters as the other (who has thrown a hammer with the intent to hurt but not kill) decides, in a split second, as the seas are still high from a brutal williwaw that almost destroys the ship, not to call for help. The tone is bleak, the Army tedious, the men ranging from competent to self-serving, the mission of the freight ship to carry a party of officers to their destination. Despite the likelihood of severe weather, the ranking officer in transit has insisted on departure because he vaingloriously wants to demonstrate to his superiors that he will get where he believes his report is required, even against obstacles. The captain of the freight ship, though he has the right to say no, gives in. They find shelter during a lull in the storm. The captain then makes his second error of judgment: he decides to resume the open-sea voyage in the hope the worst of the williwaw is over. It is not. When they finally make it to their destination, he has two unhappy situations to deal with: one of the crew has fallen overboard in unexplained circumstances, and he himself is blamed for bad judgment in having agreed to undertake the trip by the very self-serving officer who had urged him to sail. With about one quarter of the book in hand, unsure how to develop his initial conception, Gore brought the gray "Accounts" ledger with him on the flight to Burbank. His other manuscripts he had shipped. He feared, though, that just as he had not been able to finish the Maugham novel, so too he would not be able to finish this one. With his right hand swollen from rheumatoid arthritis, writing was physically difficult. But he was also emotionally blocked. For a while he "abandoned the book. I could never finish anything, I decided. I was full of self-contempt."

Still, there would be time to work on it, at least for as long as the Army supported him during his convalescence and thereafter, if his duties were light. For the moment, having completed one more chapter, he put the manuscript aside. With the war coming to an end, what he would do next and how he would earn his living were much on his mind. Whether it were to be literature or politics (or both), for the time being he found Hollywood riveting. From the hospital he could easily hitch to Beverly Hills and stay with Nina whenever he could be away more than the day. The Steins found him clever, witty, adorable. "Jules went on and on for years that he was the first to see my talent. Doris had a job at the Stage Door Canteen," Gore recalled. "Jules drove—can you imagine in those days tycoons actually drove themselves—he drove Doris and my mother and me to the canteen. I sat up front with Jules, the girls sat in the back. We had a long talk about politics and so on. From then on, for the next half century, Doris said, 'Well, it was Jules who said that the young man is going places. He is so intelligent.' And probably meaning so unlike his drunken mother, whom Jules couldn't stand. Jules was the biggest agent in the business. He didn't become a power mogul until he got Universal. He'd handled everybody. It was through him that I met Bette Davis, who was in the first movie I wrote a dozen years later. He was wildly in love with her. Jules got me passes for all the studios." After years of watching movies on theater screens, Gore now could watch them being made on the famous sound stages and back lots of Hollywood. "We were watching . . . *Marriage Is a Private Affair* by Tennessee Williams. . . . Lana Turner was in that. . . . I'd sleep at the hospital. Sometimes on weekends I'd be allowed to stay at my mother's bungalow in town. By then my mother was generally pretty drunk every night, so I'd be on my own at night. I'd cruise around, get picked up, and then slip out the side door before any action occurred." On one occasion Hollywood came to the hospital. "Charles Laughton, unannounced, arrived at the library to read to a dozen of us who were interested—he started with Whitman then proceeded on to Brecht's *Galileo*, which B was writing for him in the Hollywood Hills."

Gore tried, with little success, to work on his novel. And something else was amiss, actually astray. The footlocker containing the manuscripts he had written in Colorado and Alaska, which he had had shipped to Van Nuys, was missing. It contained short stories, poems, fragments of novels. As the days went by, as comforting as was the California sunshine, as fascinating as his insider's view of the film industry, he felt a void, an absence, a potential loss that soon developed into realized disaster. There was no sign of the footlocker. It never turned up. Characteristically, he took the disaster with a mixture of stoicism and anger, and soon maximized the attractions of the present. Since he was not making much progress with the novel, he began to go almost daily to the sound stages. Jules Stein's passes

opened every door. At the Beverly Hills Hotel the composer Vincent You-
mans, ill and lonely, asked the young writer to create some lyrics for him to
set to music. He did. But nothing came of it. On weekends life with Nina
had a flashy impersonality. She took her handsome son, resplendently patriotic in his military uniform, to the parties Doris and others constantly
hosted, at which he more readily recognized Hollywood stars than she did.
Drinks. Cigarettes. Handsome men. Beautiful women. Nina stunningly
dresssed. There was no mirror in which she did not see her attractive self.
Guiltless, she slept with whomever she wanted. The Steins' eleven-year-old
daughter, Jean, noticed, as did Gore, how unnoticed they both were by Nina
and Doris. "We didn't really have mothers. They were so busy. They were
very narcissistic women . . . who didn't really have interest in their children. They were mainly interested in themselves." Nina was "incredibly
beautiful, very striking, very strong, very willful."

One afternoon, as he sat by the hotel pool, about to start on a visit to
some of the studios, he began to overhear a conversation about a film. A few
feet away two fat men in bathing suits were discussing a script they were
writing for a movie called *Siren of Atlantis*, starring Maria Montez. If they
had been dressed, they would have been wearing berets, he imagined. If
they had been smoking, they would have been smoking cigars. They were
working out the plot. "It was so hilarious I couldn't tear myself away. I
think the title must have come up and stuck in my head, and of course Maria
Montez was a great favorite of people who loved bad movies, as I did."
Maria Montez and the title of the film remained in his mind. Decades later
they contributed to the creation of *Myra Breckinridge*.

At the hospital he began to emerge into reasonable health and some
restlessness. His swollen right knee and finger joints returned to normal,
though he still had some immobility and dull aches. Eager to visit his father,
whom he had last seen the previous fall, he solicited a leave from Van Nuys
long enough to allow him to hitch a ride to New York in early June 1945.
Sally had joined Pick, recently returned from Italy, at Mitchell Field. At Kit
and Gene's Fifth Avenue apartment Gore was also reunited with his poetry
manuscript. His father, for whom publishing, let alone poetry, was mostly
an unknown, had given it to Gertrude Algase, who had been unable to find a
publisher for it. But unexpectedly the beneficent long reach of Amelia
Earhart blessed him once again. While Gore was in New York, a struggling
Earhart biographer, Janet Mabie, came to 1107 Fifth Avenue to interview

Gene, who was eager to help a project that valorized his dead friend and the pioneering days of the airline industry. Gene said to her, in Gore's presence, as they were chatting away, " 'Oh, Gore's written a book!' 'Oh!' she said." Mabie proposed a meeting between Gore and her editor at Dutton. The Dutton editorial director, Nicholas Wreden, hoped that Gene Vidal could be persuaded to write a memoir. Accounts of the glamour and celebrities of the early aviation industry appealed to a wide reading public. With no intention of writing anything, Gene put Wreden on tantalizing hold. Meanwhile he pushed Gore, whom Wreden met and immediately liked. Wreden passed along Gore's book of poems to Dutton's poetry editor, an accomplished poet, Louise Townsend Nicholl, who liked it. She told him she would make the recommendation to publish the poems at the next editorial meeting, in a month or so.

Wreden had his own proposal for the Dutton proprietors and for Gore. Since Dutton was eager to have new young voices, why not bring onto the staff an energetic young writer who could alert the house to people and projects that would give Dutton a leg up on the postwar world of returning soldiers and the eager anticipation of a new postwar literature? Though it had never occurred to him that he might earn his living as an editor, Gore immediately accepted. The totally unexpected had happened: his book of poems had been accepted for publication, and he had been offered a job. He could join Dutton when he was discharged from the service. In early July, after two months' rehabilitation at Van Nuys, he was called to appear before an examination board of three senior medical officers. He still had occasional aches, pain, and stiffness from swollen joints. The mysteries of rheumatoid arthritis left doctors perplexed, in disagreement about diagnosis and treatment. Fortunately, the Army doctors did him no harm. The board reviewed the records, questioned him. Clearly he would not be sent overseas again, regardless of how long the war lasted. Since there was no cure, he would be entitled, at discharge, to a small disability pension if he would agree to stay in the Army for approximately another two years. If he would forgo the pension, he would be discharged in approximately one year. In any case he would be assigned for six months to "temporary limited service" in a warm, dry climate, "duty not involving excessive physical exertion." He did not hesitate a moment. "I said, 'Let me out! I don't want the pension.' I wanted to get out, I wanted to get into the world. Going into the Army at seventeen was a relief. I'd gone into another prison, but it was a much bigger prison than any school." The assignment was, inexplicably, to a training center, Camp Gordon Johnston, at Carabelle on the west coast of Florida. With orders to report in mid-August via Fort Dix to the redistribution center in Asheville, North Carolina, for transport to Florida by August 19, Gore said good-bye to Nina, to the Steins, to Hollywood glamour. He had another cross-country train trip ahead of him. Since the eastward route required connections through Chicago, he decided to stop in Jackson, Michigan, to visit his favorite aunt, the sharp-talking Lurene and her husband, Merle. A welcome visitor, he enjoyed the assertion of Vidal family identity, the voluble pride of Lurene in his father and now in him also. Handsome, young, happy to be alive, slim in his brown Army uniform, the world all before him, his war was coming to an end.

As he stood in his aunt's garden, bright with flowers on a sunny July day, someone he vaguely knew from one of the many Washington schools he had been to, though he could not remember which, now a neighbor or visiting a neighbor of Lurene's, joined him. "Oh," Carter Sparks said, as the conversation went on, "did you know that Jimmie Trimble's dead?" Shock. Silence. Resistance. Numbness. What did that mean? He held the "stark announcement" at a distance, temporarily. The immediate facts were blunt, brief, though it would take much of a lifetime to assemble them more fully. He vaguely knew that Jimmie, whom he had last seen during Christmas 1942 in Washington, had gone from St. Albans to Duke University. Since Jimmie was underage, his mother would not give him permission to enlist. Six months later, at eighteen, he had joined the Marines. With numbers of opportunities to use his baseball skills to stay out of combat, he had insisted that he take the same chances as most others. In August 1944 he became a scout-observer in the South Pacific. From October 1944 to February 1945 he was stationed on Guam, from where he soon wrote to his mother that "I'll never forgive myself for refusing to follow your advice to stay in college. After the war we won't receive any credit for having been out here." At the end of February, while Gore was in the Aleutians, Jimmie landed on Iwo Jima. On March 1 he was killed in heavy action with the enemy. What Gore knew now was the bare fact of his death in action, casually mentioned in an idle conversation by someone who had no idea what their relationship had been, even that they had been friends. How to absorb this? How to deal with it?

Stunned into feeling and thinking as little as possible, he left Jackson for New York. Gene and Kit, with three-year-old Vance and the infant Valerie, were at East Hampton, where Gore joined them, at some basic level eager to affirm by the very presence of his body in Long Island summer sunshine that he himself at least was alive and well. He had come through the war. He had a life and a future, a book of poems to be published, the offer of an editorial job in New York. The impact of Jimmie's death he put on emotional hold. In the warm evenings at East Hampton the popular John Drew Summer Playhouse provided theatrical entertainment and theater people, both of which he enjoyed. Someone pointed out Thornton Wilder. And he met a brilliant lyricist named John Latouche, famous for his wit and high spirits, a magnetic figure in New York social and artistic nightlife.

In the restorative sunshine, on the beach, a happy accident occurred. With no advance warning, suddenly he was introduced to a man with dark hair and black eyes, "who looked more like a pirate than a writer," named Frederic Prokosch, the novelist whose narratives he had obsessively read without any notion that the "two fascinating words" that made up his name had attached to it a living being with whom one day he might shake hands. Handsome, athletic, proud of his movie-star good looks and his excellent tennis, Prokosch had recently returned from Europe, where he had served during the war as cultural attaché in Stockholm. He had been well known if not famous since the publication of *The Asiatics* in 1935, *The Seven Who Fled* in 1937. Born in 1908 in Madison, Wisconsin, the son of a brilliant but repressive linguist of Czech origin who, for their own good, never praised his children, the thirty-seven-year-old Prokosch was literary, successful, magnetic. "I found him a very erotic writer, and there he was sitting on the beach. He had rented a cottage on the beach with a Swedish boy, and I got to know him." Before the war Prokosch had graduated from Yale, earned a doctorate in medieval English, then studied at King's College, Cambridge, where he had been great friends with two other literary Americans from Yale, Robert Giroux and John Kelly, both of whom Gore would soon get to know in New York. Like Kelly and Giroux, Prokosch's main sexual interest was in men. Eager to get away from the Manhattan heat, he had come to East Hampton to enjoy the cool breezes. By temperament a poetic lyricist of solitude and personal voyaging, Prokosch had an immense capacity to be impersonally charming. Gore found him, as he was, "amiable but distant." An inveterate traveler who delighted in the exotic, a restless man who loved his own loneliness, who struck many as cold and aloof, his highest interest was in reading and in literary culture. When Gore told him how profoundly his "early adolescent self" had been affected by his novels, "he found this amusing: 'How *sensitive* you must have been!' And the pirate laugh would roar." The meeting was preface to a long, intermittent friendship. With Gore's own book-in-progress substantially under way but not completely done, the accidental meeting on the beach at East Hampton with a writer whose novels he read and admired gave a small additional affirmation to his own sense of himself as a novelist. It was welcome if for no other reason than that he was having difficulty finishing *Williwaw*. He did not want it to be another in what seemed to him already an all-too-long list of novels never completed.

———

Summer 1945. Manhattan. East Hampton. Suddenly, in August, earth-shattering explosions. New sights for a new world. The war was about to be over. Years of scarcity and sacrifice were at an end, an age of prosperity to begin. For millions of servicemen it was now time to come home. Many already had. But first, a grand cosmic light show. Los Alamos suddenly became a household name. On August 6 the world learned that Hiroshima had been destroyed by a powerful new bomb. The world of TNT had been transformed into the atomic age. On August 9 Nagasaki mostly disappeared. For most Americans it seemed the right thing to have done. The war in the Pacific would not be prolonged by a contested invasion of the Japanese homeland. The mushroom cloud immediately became the talismanic sign of the new age. With his father, who was fascinated by the new technology and informed about the progress of the bomb, Gore had long conversations. News reports touted a golden age of cheap electricity through nuclear power; radioactive fallout was a secret not to become part of public discussion for a year or so. In New York, where he spent part of July and August, Gore had his father's apartment to himself. Central Park foliage was green, lush, the city filled with servicemen. Raunchy bars and clubs overflowed with men on leave. In the fashionable Astor Hotel one side of the elegantly erotic art deco black bar was for male-male encounters, the other for male-female. The excitement was riveting. In the city he regularly walked from Ninety-second Street through the park or along Fifth Avenue to the glittering, crowded euphoria of a midtown about to celebrate the war's end. August 14. Japan surrendered. V-J Day. The American party began. Millions filled Times Square. Joining the huge crowd, Gore both watched and participated in the celebration, New York on an all-day all-night binge of revelry, parties in the street, fireworks in the sky, strangers embracing, a grand sense of relief inseparable from pleasure. We had come through. The war was over. The next morning he woke up in bed with a stranger. He had forgotten how they had met.

Convalescence in East Hampton alternated with Manhattan adventures. For the first time he went to the Everard Baths, the object of a long-tired witticism that called it the "Ever Hard," the famous emporium of grime, steam, and flesh on West Twenty-eighth between Broadway and Sixth, which since its opening in 1888 had descended from elegance to seediness. Its attractions, though, had made it an internationally renowned center of sex for men interested in men. During the war, with hotel rooms costly or simply unavailable, the baths, open all night, were more popular than ever, their clientele even more various. Soldiers with conventional domestic lives found the baths a convenient place for sleep, showers, and sex. The general habitués were a mix of every sort of interest and background. In the showers, the steam rooms, the small pool, in the long corridors and tiny cubicles, valuables checked securely, safely casual and anonymous, wrapped only in white robes, uptown and downtown people, tourists and soldiers, businessmen and show-business stars, workingmen and society nobs met in what had become institutionalized single or multiple encounters. After a night on the town, soldiers and sailors and all the usual clients would end up at the baths, sometimes a tired, often a bacchanalian mix. It "was sex at its rawest and most exciting, and a revelation to me," Gore recalled. "I felt the way the Reverend Jerry Falwell must feel when he visits the Holy Land."

Sometimes the encounter would originate someplace else, at a club or a movie theater, on the street or at the Astor Bar, which became one of Gore's regular early-evening stops, at times so crowded with uniformed men on the prowl that few civilians dared enter the sacred precinct. One evening at the Astor a small voice from a short, moon-faced, bespectacled man, "a little brown pot, big glasses, unprepossessing," not in uniform, said, "And so to bed!" Kimon Friar, a Turkish-born, Greek-speaking American poet, translator, and teacher, ten years older than Gore, had noticed under the young man's arm a copy of Samuel Pepys's salaciously frank eighteenth-century diary, whose characteristic refrain "And so to bed!" is its signature phrase. Pepys, bed, and Gore's good looks were incentive for Friar, who immediately in one unstoppable breath told him who he was and what he did, including that he was now an instructor of literature at Amherst College. His best student and close friend, at whose parents' apartment in New York he usually stayed, was a talented young poet, James Merrill. Friar had "already mastered the art of not listening to others with an air of attention," Gore later remarked. When Friar proposed they go someplace quiet to talk, Gore invited him home to 1107 Fifth Avenue. Friar, who seemed likable and intellectually attractive, was amazed to learn that a book of Gore's poems had been accepted for publication. Happy to talk about poetry and art, Gore immediately made it clear that bed together was not in their imminent futures. There was to be no sex. At the apartment Friar looked around at the sweep of rooms, the views of Central Park. His own immigrant background and hand-to-mouth economic life found it all very upper-class. Still, he had a trump card. James Merrill's father, one of the founders of a famous Wall Street firm, he said, putting it all in perspective, "is a lot richer than yours."

By mid-August Gore was on his way to Camp Gordon Johnston, via a rest and transfer stop in Asheville, North Carolina. As the crowded train rose into the foothills where the Blue Ridge and the great Smoky Mountains meet, he thought the countryside beautiful: pine-covered slopes, the sudden deep green of high valleys, endless curves and mountain vistas. The only thing he knew about Asheville was that the writer Thomas Wolfe had grown up there. *Look Homeward, Angel* had been not only one of the popular literary novels of his Exeter years but so well thought of that it had been assigned as required reading in English classes. On the one hand he disliked Wolfe's elaborately lyrical prose, and Exeter classmates had teasingly called to his attention the name of Wolfe's central character, Eugene Gant. "I think the hero of Tom Wolfe's *Look Homeward, Angel,*" Wid Washburn remarked, "was someone whom Gore didn't want to share a name with." That may have reinforced his own name change to "Gore." While at Exeter he jotted down in a notebook the phrase "Look Downward Angel," perhaps the title of an unwritten parodic short story. On the other hand, Wolfe and Vidal shared a birth date, exactly twenty-five years apart. There seemed something fateful about that. In Asheville he searched vainly for Wolfe's childhood home. The "vast resort hotel for damaged officers"

where he shared a bedroom with five other men was near George Vanderbilt's massive Biltmore, at which Henry James had stayed, uncomfortably, in
February 1905. From Asheville he went, finally, in the heat of late August,
to Camp Gordon Johnston, on Florida's Gulf Coast, between Panama City
and Tallahassee, near Apalachicola Bay and its resplendent beach. Assigned
as officer in charge of the mess hall, his light work left him with time and
energy to return to the manuscript in the gray accounts ledger he had taken
with him. He wanted to finish *Williwaw*.

But he could not move it that last short distance to its end. The beach
was one compensation. Though he had been to Hobe Sound on Florida's
east coast, where the Auchinclosses had a home, this was his first experience
of the gulf. Always a happy swimmer, he loved the water and the sun.
Another compensation was the invitations from solicitous matrons, eager to
provide a social life and possible matches, to visit the sorority houses at
Florida State University in nearby Tallahassee. With most college-age boys
in the service, it was an advantage to have Camp Gordon Johnston close by.
The ladies were always "on the lookout for gallant young officers." Hospitality was welcoming, congenial. With other officers he went to dances and
took long walks with flirtatious belles happy to have male companionship.
"Spanish moss hung in the middle distance." The manners and rules were
quaintly post–Civil War, picturesquely Victorian. One of his fellow officers,
Wade Hampton, who joined him on the Tallahassee visits, had been at
Exeter with him. A descendant of a Civil War general and South Carolina
politician, he also fantasized about high political office, especially the presidency. For Gore it was a taste of the social attractions of college life without
having to be a college student. At the moment, though, his most focused
ambition was to finish the novel. During the day his mess-hall duties took
some time and little attention. At night there were movies, a seemingly
endless supply of Hollywood films shown and reshown at every Army base
around the world, the one ready source of entertainment for millions of
bored soldiers. One evening he saw *Isle of the Dead* with Boris Karloff, an
actor whose performance in *The Mummy* had settled deeply into his memory
as a young boy in Washington and had haunted his imagination since. There
was something magical, evocative, energizing for him about the performance and the film. "So Boris Karloff, as a Greek officer on an island at a
time of plague, broke, as it were, the ice," he recalled. Suddenly he was able

to write again, almost instantaneously, with automatic but determined perseverance. He had "no idea what it was in the movie that did the trick." Having been assigned as officer of the day to night duty in a room empty but for typewriters, he sat down at a machine, the gray ledger beside him, listening each evening to weather reports. Suddenly "a hurricane was on its way up the Gulf, heading towards us." Some combination of *Isle of the Dead*, the room filled with typewriters, and the threatening storm energized his creativity. "I zoomed right through the book there." Within a few weeks he had finished *Williwaw*. He felt immense relief and satisfaction. He had actually completed a novel, at last. And it seemed to him cogent, taut, readable, mature. "With the finishing of this book, my life as a writer began."

Thin, a little under six feet, with a crew cut, still in uniform, Gore found himself less than two months later, soon after his twentieth birthday, sitting at his own desk in the Fourth Avenue offices of the venerable New York publisher E. P. Dutton. With Pick again stationed at Mitchell Field and his father's Fifth Avenue address available as his home, he had had no difficulty arranging a transfer back into the Army Air Corps to serve once again under his uncle's command. Since he had served as base historian at Fort Peterson, what more suitable light-duty assignment than base historical officer in the Public Relations Office at Mitchell Field? By early August his new home was a barracks on Long Island, his half-time duties mostly routine paperwork. Like innumerable servicemen, he waited to be mustered out as the Army bureaucracy slowly processed millions into the civilian population. With ample free time, he went regularly into Manhattan, staying overnight or on weekend leave in the back bedroom at 1107 Fifth Avenue, sometimes at the Everard Baths or in a hotel. "Gore would come when he wanted to see his publishers or his friends," Kit recalled, "but he didn't stay very long usually." At first, though, he had no publisher for the novel. Having hand-copied the portion of *Williwaw* from his notebook and added to it the new typewritten pages, he gave what he thought a clear copy to Robert Linscott, a senior editor at Random House who had been recommended to him. "So Linscott called me in. He couldn't have been nicer, this old man, and said it is customary in publishing to submit a manuscript that has been typewritten. I thought he lacked dedication and perhaps should find another field of work. So I withdrew haughtily from Random House." But he soon had it fully typed.

With Gene he had lunch at a midtown restaurant with his Dutton mentor, Nicholas Wreden, and a senior editor, John Tebbel. Neither was aware that Gore had written a novel; their professional eyes focused exclusively on signing Gene Vidal to write his memoir. "Gore was still in uniform. Nick sat next to the old man, and I sat next to Gore," Tebbel remembered. "Those two got into a conversation, and Gore and I were talking. He said to me, 'While I was in Alaska, I wrote a book. Would you read it and tell me what you think of it?' I said, 'Sure, I'd love to.' And so he brought it down to the office the next day and I read it that night, and when I came in in the morning I said to Nick, 'We've got to have this book. You've got to read it.' So Nick did read it, and he agreed with me. The editorial board read it, and we bought it right away." Tebbel suggested minor changes. On October 19, working with his usual dispatch, Gore told Kimon Friar that revisions "should be finished this week, much to my relief." Everything went smoothly. By late November 1945 he had in hand a contract, with the usual royalty starting at a rate of 10 percent for the first 5,000 copies and an advance against royalties of $250, to be paid on the signing of the agreement. *Williwaw* was scheduled for late-spring publication. That lunch meeting also gave focus to the understanding that he would come to work for Dutton as an associate editor. A venerable firm, it still had some of its mechanics and much of its frame of mind in the world of quill pens and handwritten ledgers. In attitude the firm was conservative, its proprietors, the brothers Eliot and John Macrae, a mixture of eccentricity and competence. A spiritualist who had casual conversations with ghosts and had created Dutton's list of books on the occult, Eliot Macrae ran the firm with a successful specialty in true-adventure stories for adults; the occasional bestselling lowbrow novel, such as Mickey Spillane's crime-sex stories; the ongoing sale through innumerable editions of a perennial occult bestseller called *Cosmic Consciousness*; the popularity of Albert Terhune's dog books; and John Roy Carlson's World War II book, *Undercover,* which Tebbel had recently procured and which had already sold over a million copies. The most valuable Dutton property was *Winnie-the-Pooh*. Gore soon proposed to Wreden and Tebbel that he edit and Dutton publish an anthology of war verse. They liked the idea. *Williwaw* was scheduled for June 1946 publication, his volume of poems for summer 1947. Gore suggested to Kimon Friar that they collaborate as co-editors of the anthology. "I envision a collection of the better poetry written in the times of war since the *Iliad*. Less Kipling and more Spender, more of your metaphysical people. On the other hand as this would not come out until 1947 at the earliest the subject of War might be anathema. Therefore one might think of a collection of poetry from this last war by people one has never heard of; in other words a portrait of the recent war in poetry written by the people who fought in that war or suffered in it."

Suddenly he was not only being published, he was publishing others. Every Thursday he came into Dutton from Mitchell Field or from his father's apartment for editorial-board meetings. Regular office routine would not begin until his discharge. At the end of each week he collected his $35 weekly salary, paid in cash in a sealed envelope, perhaps an expression of the firm's old-fashioned attitude, as if the world even of paychecks seemed insufficiently Victorian, too modern for a business whose ideas as well as origins predated the Civil War. Both unreconstructed Virginians, the Macraes felt that publishing was a profession for gentlemen. A short trim man with a straightforward manner, Eliot kept Confederate battle flags in his "very literary looking" book-lined office. The Macraes preferred manly books. On the surface *Williwaw* was just that, though its jaundiced view of the Army and of human character might have distressed them if they had read beyond the surface. Excellent readers, Wreden and Tebbel knew it indeed was not a gentleman's book in the old-fashioned sense, but they were keen on bringing into Dutton new voices. Gore could help identify them. Both had come to Dutton within the last two years. Tebbel, unlike Wreden, soon left publishing for a career as a freelance writer and teacher of journalism. Originally from Michigan, he had worked at a half dozen major newspapers, most recently at the *New York Times*, and had been managing editor of *The American Mercury*, H. L. Mencken's distinguished satirical magazine. Thirteen years older than Gore, anticipating a great career for the young writer, Tebbel liked him immediately. They were soon friendly, almost exclusively at or after work, when they would sometimes finish the day after one of Gore's office visits with drinks at the Gramercy Park Hotel and dinner at a local restaurant. Gore's lively conversation amused Tebbel, though he seemed "rather shy and sometimes even tentative, even about his own work. Obviously he believed in it very much, but he did not have the kind of personality he has now. I don't know when it changed. Probably he changed slowly. In those days he was a little tentative. He believed in himself, but he didn't push himself and he was not really, at least publicly, egotistical. He was good company."

As editorial director and by personality, Wreden dominated the literary operations of Dutton. He had been brought in recently from Charles Scribner's Sons, where he had been a director, to run the literary side of the firm. To bolster his authority he was elected vice president and a member of the Dutton board of directors. Together he and Eliot Macrae made all publication decisions of consequence. When Tebbel left late in 1946, Wreden became Gore's editor, a relationship of mutual respect and affection that lasted for over fifteen years. An expansive man who ate, drank, and smoked enthusiastically, bearlike in size and energy, Wreden was a presence in the publishing world. Articulate and persuasive, often dressed in sports jacket and slacks, he was fair-complexioned, "tall and large, heavy, over six feet," Tebbel recalled, with "a fascinating voice, a rumble with a very slight accent," a small dark mustache anchored by a bold nose, sparkling light-blue eyes, thick brows, and unruly curly hair. A White Russian émigré born in St. Petersburg in 1902, he had fled to America as a young man. His father had been surgeon general of the Imperial Russian Army and private physician to the royal family. So too had his grandfather and great-grandfather. After education at a German preparatory school and the Russian naval academy, he had come into active service as a young cadet and then lieutenant in time to fight against the Turks, the Austrians, and the Germans in the Baltic Sea. When the Russians were defeated in 1916, he fought with other royalist cadets against the insurrectionists in St. Petersburg and then gave his loyalty in 1917 to the democratic Kerensky government. When the Bolsheviks took power, he joined the White Russian forces, fighting until 1920. His family lands had been confiscated; his future in the Soviet Socialist Republics was the firing squad. In June 1920, as a mess hand, he landed in New York harbor, where eighteen years before his grandfather had disembarked from a luxury liner as the Russian delegate to the conference of the International Red Cross. Soon he was a longshoreman, then an accountant, then a lumber dealer in North Carolina, where he married and had three children. For a short while he worked for the Civil Works Administration in Texas and began a memoir of his experiences in the Russian Revolution, which he published in 1935. He became a traveler representing publishers, a bookstore manager in Detroit, manager of the well-known Scribner's bookstore in New York, and then, finally, a Scribner's director.

Despite bad teeth, half of which had fallen out because of his terror of the dentist, Wreden was quick to laugh, an avid conversationalist, and an occasional monologuist. "He was a two-fisted drinker, and he liked people and people liked him, so he had a big social life with authors." He was, Vidal recollected, "a big jolly fat man and rather sly, rather sharp." A happy member of The Players Club, he loved entertaining and conviviality. His old and new Russian friends, all hostile to the revolution from which they had fled, found a convivial welcome and great quantities of vodka at his Park Avenue apartment, where he lived with his second wife and their three children. Publishing suited him perfectly. So too did Gore. The respect and affection were mutual. Wreden treated Gore with avuncular attachment and commitment, as an important acquisition, a sharp young man who could write powerfully and maybe, as his career developed, brilliantly. In addition, he genuinely liked this handsome, somewhat vulnerable, increasingly well defended young man less than half his age, who had a fine sense of humor, who had read a great deal, who came from an interesting background, and who had great promise. Like Tebbel, Wreden believed that authors of fiction might benefit from suggestions but never from commands; that the editor's responsibility was to guide, never to lead; that when a writer wrote well, the editor should not get between him and his audience. It was a world of laissez-faire publishing. Editors selected works and writers. If they themselves believed in a writer, they assumed there would be an audience for him. The financial investment for new authors was small: advances against royalties did not involve trips to the bank for either party. If a book earned little, that was acceptable, especially if the book had appreciative reviews, if there were an audience for it, even if small. The first, most important audience was the editor and the publisher. Wreden was enthusiastically on Vidal's side.

Ambitious, encouraged, Vidal began to write a second novel, with the working title *The Myriad Faces*. With ample energy and time, he had no reason to discount his assumption that what writers do is write as productively as they can. Immensely facile once under way, he felt an access of energy partly derived from having at last finished a full-length novel. He had proved to himself that he could do it. Though years later he was comfortable admitting he had failed to complete any of the novels he had started before *Williwaw*, that winter he went so far as to tell Carrington Tutwiler, with whom he had resumed contact, that he had actually finished the Somerset Maugham novel. A vivid anecdotalist and storyteller who occasionally exaggerated to make his point or for self-promotion, he was a dedicated non-liar who rarely lapsed. Partly he wanted to distinguish himself from Nina, whose lies tormented his childhood. Mostly, telling the truth was a way of making the world more reliable, of feeling reasonably confident he could proceed on the basis of what he had been told and what he had told others. It was also self-assertion—he was not afraid of the truth, about himself and others. His interest was in knowing it rather than distorting or evading it. His lie to Tutwiler suggests the high level of anxiety his inability to finish any novel before *Williwaw* had created. Even with *Williwaw* scheduled for publication in June 1946, he still needed to soothe that wound by telling Tutwiler he had finished the Maugham novel and voluntarily discarded it, presumably because it was not up to his own high standards. The new novel was well under way before the end of the year, its initial premise the depiction of "myriad faces," the multiple daily roles of a war veteran who embraces the nondramatic anonymity of middle-class life as a Wall Street broker. "It's an idea that has always intrigued me: the different faces that one person assumes during a day, the different reactions that people have to him." He was hoping to follow the anticipated success of *Williwaw* in June with an even greater success soon afterward. He was eager for acceptance, critical acclaim, the presence and reputation that comes from having a list of books already published, the financial reward that would enable him to live on royalties and devote himself exclusively to writing. He wanted not a single book but a career in the larger sense, like Somerset Maugham, though more literary, an American Thomas Mann who would write both contemporary and historical novels. In Washington, still in uniform, he visited his grandparents. "I sit with Dah in the living room of his flat in Crescent Place. . . . Dah rocks in his Mission chair. Discusses my political career and what he calls 'the New Mexico option,' because 'Oklahoma is too volatile.' He always winced at the thought of his Bible-loving constituency. 'Of course, you were born in New York. Why not take advantage of that? Why not get yourself a district in the city? You pay Tammany Hall your first year's salary and, except for city matters, they leave you alone.' I thought this a dead end." His mind was not on politics or a political life but on being, for now, "just literary."

New York City life flowered around him, the city, alive with returning servicemen, now about to become its early postwar self. Rationing was over. Military victory was also economic triumph. Soon there would be the first new cars, houses, home appliances in over five years. Factories would begin to turn out civilian clothes. No other industrial country had survived the war with its productive capacity intact, let alone immensely increased. No other country had the atomic bomb. If there were foreign enemies, they were powerless against America. If there were problems at home, like labor unions beginning to insist on a greater share for the workingman in America's prosperity, they would have to be dealt with. For the moment, in the first flush of the war's ending, national tensions were in temporary harmony. In a few years the United Nations Headquarters Tower would dominate the view from midtown to the East River. New York's economic power and international fame made it America's magnet city. Theater, ballet, art, music, literature, publishing, fashion—young people from every section of the country came to have their chance at the arts and at modern life. New York's energy gave it an electric excitement.

More quickly than most, Gore now had a job in an industry thought of as glamorous and a beginning as a soon-to-be-published writer. With his father's spacious Fifth Avenue apartment available to him, he had suitable housing. Handsome, articulate, with a slightly aggressive but still amiable social manner, he felt at ease with a variety of people with different backgrounds. At the baths, at one-night pickups brought to inexpensive Times Square hotels, he had all the sex even his expansive, virile desires could accommodate. That part of life, sex but not love with strangers, was easy, quick, mechanical, pleasurable in the most uncomplicated way. At Dutton he had his Thursday editorial meetings, his reports on manuscripts, his camaraderie with Wreden, Tebbel, and Louise Nicholl. Still in uniform, he had to spend part of his time at Mitchell Field, but his New York social life was expanding. He was meeting people of interest, some of them writers. With evenings at clubs like the Blue Angel, where John Latouche knew everyone, he was soon getting to know and be known to everyone. To help increase circulation in his right leg, still inhibited by the remnants of rheumatoid arthritis, he enrolled for ballet lessons, paid for by the G.I. Bill, at the George Chafee Studio on Fifty-sixth Street. There he met a tough young

Irish boy from New Jersey with whom, among others, he regularly had sex
for a while. The lessons were his entrée into the ballet world. For Gore, as
for many others, the 1944 ballet *Fancy Free*, soon transformed into the
Broadway musical *On the Town*, became the New York anthem, heralding
an American Golden Age.

By Christmas there were two new attractive women in his life. Cornelia Phelps Claiborne he had known vaguely in his Washington childhood,
partly as a friend of Rosalind Rust, mostly as someone trained in the same
dancing-school and party rounds as he. She was the daughter of Cornelia
Enson, an intellectually accomplished Washingtonian who had gotten a
doctorate in economics from Columbia and made a considerable amount of
money investing. Her daughter's paternal roots anchored her in the Virginia
Claibornes, whose history and social prestige originated in the eighteenth
century. Thomas Jefferson's friend William Charles Claiborne had been
appointed governor of the Mississippi Territory, then been elected governor
of and senator from Louisiana. With residences in New York (where she
lived on East Sixtieth Street over the Copacabana nightclub) and Washington, the driving, ambitious Cornelia Enson had become Mrs. William A.
Moncure by the time Gore renewed his relationship with her daughter. Two
years younger than Gore, Cornelia had attended the demanding St. Timothy's School in Maryland, where "the girls had to confess and were punished
for thinking things they weren't supposed to think" and where the long-
standing rule that girls had to wear shifts even when privately bathing
remained in effect until her second year. Relentlessly literary, Cornelia
benefited from rigorous classes in English literature. In 1943 she went to
Vassar, along with her St. Timothy's classmate and friend Betty Pollock,
who remembers Gore visiting in uniform sometime in late 1945. With Betty
Pollock, Cornelia and Gore's former girlfriend Rosalind had formed a
Vassar trio in 1943–44, "so bright and full of energy and full of life." The
three of them, Pollock recalled, "were born mutinous and rebellious and
bred to be successful." Dark-haired, clear-complexioned, quite beautiful,
Cornelia had a luminous smile and shining gray-green eyes. Tall, with a fine
figure, she limped slightly, probably the result of a childhood illness. She
also had high literary ideals and ambitions. Serious, witty, charming, she
expected to be a famous poet. By late 1945 she had had enough of Vassar.
The glamour of her mother's New York social life and the cultural excitement of Manhattan were irresistible.

In New York she and Gore at first made a social, then an amorous couple. With her well-connected mother, distinguished name, and high social standing, Cornelia was invited everywhere in the 1945–46 social season. Suddenly New York ballrooms were again illuminated. Corsages, fancy dresses, society orchestras, bright glittering eyes—the marriage market bustled once more. Resplendent in his youth and his Army uniform, Gore was an attractive escort. The handsome couple danced at the Cotillion Room and sipped drinks at the Café Pierre. Society-page montage photos in New York newspapers showed them at nightlife play in sequences that included the likes of Mrs. Anthony D. Duke and John Jacob Astor. Photographed at the Wedgwood Room at the Waldorf-Astoria, Cornelia was described as "one of this season's most popular debutantes." Gore escorted her in December to the Liberty Ball at the main ballroom of the Waldorf-Astoria, the delayed coming-out dance for about fifty "young ladies of society. The two of you walked out on the stage," he recalled, "and she does her curtsy to society and that's the debut. I think I walked out on the stage with her." Gore seemed eligible, attractive, someone even to fall in love with. To Cornelia he also had the distinction of being a young writer about to publish his first novel and an editor at a major publishing house. More aggressively literary than he, she had greater interest in Dostoyevsky than in society dances. She talked irrepressibly about literature, sometimes excessively, as her less literary friends, even including Gore, remarked. Soon they both were entranced, particularly Cornelia who for a short time imagined that Gore and she might marry. Adept at keeping different kinds of friends apart, he kept her mostly unaware of his other lives, including another, even more magnetically attractive woman he had met the previous month and who, in December, he was seeing a great deal of.

Anaïs Nin came into Gore's life through the agency of Kimon Friar one Sunday afternoon in mid-November 1945. Accepting Friar's invitation to hear him lecture at the 92nd Street YMHA on the depiction of love in Plato's *Symposium,* Gore found himself, in his warrant officer's uniform, seated next to the one unoccupied chair at the end of a long seminar table. At the head, Friar waited to begin his performance. Behind him assorted people sat in haphazard rows of folding chairs. Suddenly a slim, medium-tall, dark-haired, doe-eyed woman, dressed in a close-fitting black dress, slid into the empty seat next to his. She wore a distinctive heart-shaped, white-veiled hat modeled after the headdress most associated with the executed

Scots Queen, Mary Stuart. With tight-drawn, porcelainlike skin, silver-polished nails, penciled arched eyebrows, she was beautiful enough to seem, in a certain light, ageless. If he knew that she was the already legendary, mostly unpublished writer, Anaïs Nin, whom Kimon probably had mentioned to him, he did not let on. He could not know that her husband, Hugh Guiler, was sitting on one of the folding chairs behind them, his characteristic position in relation to his wife.

Anaïs's side of the twenty-year-old marriage had gone through a stellar list of serious lovers, including the writer Henry Miller, the analyst Otto Rank, and most recently the critic Edmund Wilson, and a longer list of transient sexual encounters. The most devastating affair had been with her father, a professional concert pianist who, after deserting his young children, had engaged with his grown daughter in a mutual seduction. Seeking revenge for his mistreatment of her as a child, Anaïs used the affair to inflict as much pain on her father as she could. Born of mixed Spanish-Cuban origin in Paris in 1903, she had been brought up mostly in New York by her mother, who supported the family giving music lessons and borrowing from relatives. As a young bride Anaïs began with her banker husband, whose family opposed the marriage, a long residence in Paris, where she used his salary to support Henry Miller, among others. When war broke out, she and Hugh returned to America to live in the newly revived bohemian world of Greenwich Village. At her studio she had a secondhand printing press on which she set type for her own diary and thinly disguised fiction. Depressed by the difficulty of finding an audience for her work, she lived on hope, despair, and, occasionally, the injections of Dr. Max Jacobson, a reckless New York doctor who had become well known for dispensing energizing drugs to many of New York's creative dynamos. They had little money now, mostly because Anaïs supported some of those she slept with. Sexually driven both for pleasure and self-assertion, she idealized all-absorbing romantic love and attempted to anchor what she believed her literary genius in her ongoing diary, in which she wrote her feelings in a romantically lush prose style. Her fiction reworked her diary entries, many of which she changed to make more flattering to herself. She hoped to publish, if not all, then at least long sections. The diary would, she felt certain, convince the world of her genius.

When the handsome young man sitting next to her asked if she were French, she answered seductively in her small-girl, breathy voice, immediately drawn to his attractiveness. He had overheard her speak to her friend, the experimental moviemaker, Maya Deren, who sat a few chairs away. Deren, Nin later wrote in her diary, had said to her, "You look dramatic." She had responded, "I feel like Mary Stuart, who will soon be beheaded." Then Vidal had leaned over and asked his question. Vidal remembers that "I said to her, 'You look like Mary Stuart.' She said—soft voice, French accent, 'Does that mean you will cut my head off?' " Whether or not he introduced himself as "a descendant of Troubadour Vidal," Nin would have liked it if he had, though so one-toned herself she would not have been able to know whether he was being humorous or ironic. To her he was immediately a romanticized figure, a young man she desired. "He is luminous and manly," she wrote in her diary. "He is not nebulous, but clear and bright. . . . He talks. He is active, alert, poised. He is tall, slender, cool eyes and sensual mouth." Apparently, during the brief intermission, he told her much about himself, his mother, his family, his work. A seductively engrossing listener, Anaïs encouraged him to tell all. He told her more than the guarded young man usually told anyone, let alone a stranger. Anaïs, who specialized in seduction by mutually expressive instant rapport, emphasized that they had both been deserted as young children. That should be a bond between them. They were not and could never be strangers. They agreed to continue talking at her apartment.

CHAPTER SEVEN

Two Eagles

1946–1947

AS HE ASCENDED the stairs that evening in November 1945 to Nin's Greenwich Village apartment, Gore felt the attraction of her erotic glamour. She appeared bewitchingly female, a European woman of allure and accomplishment. They talked for hours, or Gore mostly talked, continuing from where they had left off that afternoon. Hugh stayed away, as he did by arrangement on such occasions. The small apartment had only a single room, with "an alcove in which she had a stove where she cooked. It had a glass sort of ceiling," Gore remembered. "She had painted all of the glass with designs . . . like a skylight. . . . There were a couple of mattresses up on top of each other which were used as a sofa until she went to bed." As much preyed-upon as preying, as much dovelike as vulturine, Anaïs wanted nothing more than a perfect love, a total passion. Now forty-three years old, she still thought such perfection possible. When depressed, she confided her despair to her diary. When one love failed her, she searched for the next. When she could not find a publisher for her diary, she kept writing, plotting, trying to compel the world to agree to be her audience. Looking into her various mirrors, she worried about her looks. Masterful at disguising her age, she sustained the illusion, as best she could, that her beauty would last forever, an avatar of her sex, a pure representation of some mysterious female essence. To Gore there seemed something eternal about her.

By the beginning of winter they were intimate friends. "Since our last meeting have been seeing much of Anaïs Nin," he told Friar. They were not lovers, though, except by companionship and rhetoric. Anaïs hoped to change that. His resistance puzzled her. In the interim he had other uses, particularly to help her get her diarylike fiction published. As an editor whose first novel Dutton had scheduled for spring publication, Gore had influence there. But resistance to Anaïs was strong. Neither Wreden nor the Macraes liked her work. Wreden thought it puffy, inflated, insufficiently concrete. The Macraes thought it unreadable, probably immoral. By looks and reputation Anaïs seemed someone they should not be publishing. That they would make little to no money doing it was a certainty. Gore, though, pushed her aggressively. "I think that Dutton will publish her," he wrote to Friar, "but I am confident that they'll do her as she is. The point that I've put across, and to which they are most amenable, is that she is a prestige and not a commercial author and therefore she must stand as she is. To my mind she is one of the most exciting authors now at work." Wreden finally agreed to publish *Ladders to Fire*, entirely out of support for Gore. The Macraes went along. Ecstatic finally to have a trade publisher, she was by midwinter passionately in love with her benefactor. His own fascination with her was certainly a sort of love as well, though whereas she had no ambivalence about consummating the relationship, he had deep hesitations. Whatever he felt sexually about her, he did not feel it compellingly. Initially she found his evasion of a sexual commitment baffling. Confident of her attractiveness, she assumed that his resistance could be overcome. At first she thought it the result of inexperience. Then shyness. Then fear. As she learned more about him, she applied her psychoanalytical wiles. Having herself been analyzed, she felt qualified to analyze others. She believed she could save him from the supermasculine hard shell with which he had self-protectively surrounded his "true" inner self. When she read *Williwaw*, she found it a representation in style and attitude of all she hated in modern American writing, from Hemingway to James T. Farrell, a tough-as-nails "this is the way the world is" realism. "He has great assurance in the world, talks easily, is a public figure, shines. He can do clever take-offs, imitate public figures. He walks in easily, he is no dream-laden adolescent. His eyes are hazel, clear, open,

mocking." The fault was in his infancy and childhood, his mother's dominating embrace of social power and material values, his deforming early
exposure to corrupt adults at a time of great vulnerability. It had robbed him
of his childhood, had deprived him of the normal stages of emotional
growth. In Anaïs's analysis he had been traumatized at an early age. And it
was there he was still stuck, a victim of his childhood attempt to defend
himself. His ambivalence about his family expressed the war within him
between his mother's values and his poetic inner self. Convinced he had one,
she believed she was the person to help him discover and assert it. In her
eyes his hidden life, if allowed to flower, would bloom with a warmth of
romantic expression that would make his the masculine equivalent of hers.
She desired the diarist within him to bloom. She wanted him as lover to be
her perfect other self. The villain in the melodrama was Nina.

Soon Anaïs had reconsidered why he would not go to bed with her.
Actually her wiles, her charms, her attractions had been partly successful.
She had no doubt he was in love with her. To that extent she had succeeded.
Though he could not fully satisfy her need for more emotional intimacy, he
talked to her more openly than to anyone else. "I do not want to be
involved, ever," he told her. "I live detached from my present life. At home
our relationships are casual. . . . I like casual relationships. When you are
involved, you get hurt." But he was involved. With gesture, with facial
expression, with an intuitive feel for one another, they interacted as if they
were lovers. Among their friends it was assumed they were. To Kit, Anaïs,
whom Gore brought to the Fifth Avenue apartment and to whom Gene took
a liking, was Gore's "girlfriend." At Dutton everyone, from Wreden to the
secretaries whose hearts fluttered each time he appeared at the office, assumed they slept together. In Gore and Anaïs's Greenwich Village world it
was simply a given that they were madly fucking. When Judith Jones, a
young Dutton publicist and friend of Gore's, saw the mattress in Anaïs's
apartment, she could not help visualizing Gore, whom she found attractive,
and Anaïs "tossing together." Intensely preoccupied with one another,
spending a great deal of time together in December 1945 and from January
to May 1946, they tried to find some way to work through the obstacles.
Finally, under the pressure of her constant effort to bring him to bed, he
decided to tell her about his sexual preferences. He wanted to propose that
she make an accommodation, that she accept he would continue to have sex
with young men while having an intimate relationship with her.

The news did not shock her. She herself had had sex over the years with numbers of women. She had been obsessed with Henry Miller's wife and perhaps, once or twice, in love with other women. In fact, she cared less about his orgasms with transient men than about his failure to give enough of himself emotionally to her. The depth of his involvement, greater than with anyone else heretofore, was not enough. She wanted his soul, for his sake, she believed, more than for her own. And now, she felt, she had another key to his personality, another insight into his deep childhood traumas. Again the villain was Nina. His moodiness, his occasional coldness, the hardness of his prose, what she saw as "his desperate need to assert himself," his self-protective embrace of rational analysis, his seeming rejection of romantic love had another explanatory component—his preference for homoerotic sex. And she believed she knew the source of that. He would not go to bed with her because of his mother. Because of her he hated all women. There was always, she generalized, "some traumatic event which caused fear of woman," even hatred. "It is totality the homosexual fears. He separates love and sexuality." She had, in her last assertion, a point he later recognized and recommended as a sensible policy. But in 1945 he was struggling with the distinction, partly because he desired to escape what he considered society's limiting sexual classifications, mostly because he was genuinely enamored. He feared labeling that might be used against him. "Queens" and "fairies" dominated society's vocabulary about men who had sex with men. He had no desire to complicate his life with public announcements about private matters. With his penchant for compartmentalization and separation, very few people knew, as Anaïs soon did, about his hours at the Everard Baths or his nights in Times Square hotels or his cruising at the Astor Bar. Those who more or less knew were mainly a small group of homosexual and bisexual men he was beginning to meet in the ballet and theater world but whom, early in 1946, he had just begun to associate with. It would take Cornelia Claiborne a year or two to wonder why Gore was not interested in her in quite the same way as other men. So too Judith Jones, who assumed that Gore was a potential lover "because of the relationship with Anaïs and because he was very flirty—he liked women, you can tell that he was responsive. . . . We went to a French restaurant one night together . . . and I was dying to have Gore at least take my hand, to do something physical. That's when I began to suspect that he really wasn't . . ."

Anaïs now thought it her mission to save him. "What I see in the homosexual is different from what others see. I never see perversion, but rather a childlike quality, a pause in childhood or adolescence when one hesitates to enter the adult world. The relationship based on identification, on twinship, or the 'doubles,' on narcissism, is a choice more facile . . . than that between men and women. It is almost incestuous, like a family kinship. . . . Whenever I came close to a homosexual, what I found was childishness . . . and always some traumatic event which caused fear of woman, hence the hatred of her." Unaware of Jimmie Trimble and of Gore's fascination with twinship, Anaïs complicated her self-serving etiology with occasional insight. It was as if she sensed Jimmie Trimble in the background. In the foreground, though, was Nina, exactly the same age as Anaïs. Anaïs began to pressure him to give it up, to grow up, to get it up with *her*. Apparently she induced him to try, probably on the mattress at her Greenwich Village apartment. It was not satisfying to either. She resented that her mission of total conversion had hardly been advanced. He resented being pressured. But the experience did not drive them apart. The bond, through the spring of 1945, remained strong. They were like two eagles who had embraced in flight. Their talons were dug deeply into one another. They could not fly on together this way. But they could not find a way to let go.

—————

Early in January 1946 he told Carrington Tutwiler, "I have been busy writing, going to the theatre, having odd pains in my stomach, falling in love, and being a soldier on alternate Wednesdays." Anaïs took satisfaction in noting that whereas *Williwaw* had been dedicated to Nina, a play he wrote in a twenty-four-hour period just before Christmas, called *Time of Darkness*, he had dedicated to her. "It's based on the legend of the werewolf brought up to date and made a symbol of the shadow and the surface sides of the man etc etc. I've been threatening for such a long time to write a play that it's a relief to get one done. I'll send you a carbon if it gets to that stage." Fortunately, it did not. The play went into his drawer of unfinished or unsatisfactory manuscripts. The concern with the theme of division, of the clash and choice between alternative selves, that had been central to the play he now moved into the novel he had been working on since late autumn. "I am very happy with parts of it. I have an occasional hot flash when I think that I am forgetting how to write but a little flattery, well a lot of flattery, does me no end of good and I attack my typewriter like Tarquin doing whatever it was he did. . . ." But midway through, the emphasis changed from *The Myriad Faces* to *In a Yellow Wood*, a title taken from Robert Frost's poem about diverging choices, the new emphasis the result of his awareness that his affair with Anaïs represented a choice between her bohemian antisocial underworld and the social-political empowerment represented by his father and grandfather. She asked him to walk with her down dark romantic paths, and literally envisioned him as a Romantic poet. "Coming down the road thoughtfully the other day," she wrote to him that summer, "you looked like Keats."

By mid-January he could at last take off his Army uniform. Before Christmas he had visited his grandparents at their Washington apartment, where he and the Senator had talked about his political future. The New Mexico option seemed a possibility, at least to Senator Gore, who outlined a plan that would have his grandson become a presidential elector there in 1948. It would position him to run for Congress. Just out of uniform, billed as the young Army veteran with a famous political name, supported by the Senator's friends, he could start his political career. When he returned to New York, that political road must have seemed less concrete, less alluring, than it had in his grandfather's living room. As *The Myriad Faces* was transformed into *In a Yellow Wood*, to be dedicated to Anaïs and two-thirds finished by late February, it changed into an expression of his awareness that he had another choice to make between a different set of divergent roads. One led to a political, the other to a literary career. Sometimes both seemed possible. But in sober moments the unlikelihood of combining public-political self-creation, an image acceptable to the electorate, and writing honestly at a high literary level seemed formidable. For months he had appeared each Thursday at Dutton; his residence still remained Mitchell Field. His visits to Nin's apartment were mostly on Sundays, before returning to Long Island. On January 7 the official memo, "Separation of Surplus Officers," stated that "Gore E. Vidal . . . has declared his desire to be relieved from active duty with the Armed Forces." He celebrated his release in mid-February by dining at the Charles Restaurant with Anaïs. "My terminal leave terminated itself in mad mad revelry on the 15 Feb," he wrote to Tutwiler, "and Vidal was led by the hand into the wicked maelstrom of modern publishing so faithfully but ineptly described by Bunny Wilson." Nin wrote in her diary that "he was in civilian clothes, looking more slender, more youthful, and more vulnerable." The subject of Nina soon came up. "He told me his mother said to him: 'No one will ever love you as I do.' He had wanted his mother to die." Anaïs certainly did. Despite her absence, Nina was very much a presence. When Gore took off his uniform, he had no civilian clothes to wear. Nina, when she had moved to California, had gotten rid of all his things, "which was really very bothersome. I was stuck with nothing but Army clothes, which I wore for about a year. She didn't think I was coming back, I suppose, or if I did I'd be totally changed. I got a sort of blue tweed suit, a hideous-looking thing, but I thought it looked fine. I had one suit. I wore it most of the time."

No one, least of all he, minded the monotony of his wardrobe. He did, though, mind the tedium of his daily office stint. At first it had seemed bearable. Soon his reworking of *Myriad Faces* began to reflect, in the main character's resistance to his stockbrokerage office routine, Gore's increasing dissatisfaction with traveling each morning (often by taxi) from his father's apartment, where he slept and wrote in the back bedroom, to Fourth Avenue and Gramercy Park, where he spent the day reading manuscripts, writing reports, and participating in editorial meetings. Later in the day he returned uptown, sometimes via Anaïs's apartment or the Everard Baths, the Astor Hotel Bar, the Times Square hotels. "Being an editor is dull but not tiring and I have other relaxations," he told Tutwiler. The better part of life, he soon realized, was not spent at the office, though office life was not initially unbearable or unpleasant, especially his conversations with Wreden and Tebbel. The Dutton staff welcomed him. His attractions were appreciated, a handsome, congenial, often funny young Army veteran with a crew cut who brought to the staid publishing house new blood. With Eliot and John Macrae his relations were congenial. Both of them eccentrics in their different ways, he mostly avoided them, except that John had the habit of waylaying office-hall wanderers for long, nonintelligible sessions in his office, where he would say avuncular things such as "Publishing is like a river." When in the spring Gore tried to persuade Eliot Macrae to publish an early version of James Baldwin's *Go Tell It on the Mountain* titled *Cry Holy,* Eliot defined himself by responding, "No, I'm from Virginia!" Baldwin, whom Gore had met at a party at Anaïs's, "was a vivid creature . . . full of energy, with a personality that oscillated between Martin Luther King,

Jr.'s . . . and Bette Davis's." He had to return to the author "the neatly typed manuscript in two torn cardboard boxes."

With Wreden's approval Vidal soon was coming into the office less regularly, mostly to pick up mail and manuscripts and for meetings. He still received $35 a week. At his father's apartment his housing was free. Having saved much of his Army pay, he projected that with decent sales of *Willi-waw* he might have as much as $10,000 by late in the year. Also his father had purchased $20,000 worth of railroad bonds to cover the costs of the college education he increasingly determined not to have, despite Bingham's blandishments from Harvard. If redeemed that year, the bonds would be worth about $14,000. If he could persuade his father to turn that money over to him, he could easily afford not to continue at Dutton. Except for the confusion about Anaïs, the world lay all before him. "Everything is contingent on the war. The war saved my life. The war kills Jimmie and saves me. It gets me out of the family. It gets me on my own. I come out of it with $10,000, which was a lot of money in those days, and a published book. I certainly couldn't have done that if I'd gone from St. Albans to Harvard." Within months of his arrival at Dutton he was plotting his escape from there too. Most of all he wanted to go to Europe, to see Rome again, to renew the excitement of his 1939 visit, which stayed in his mind as the most pleasurable experience of his life.

By mid-spring Gore turned in *In a Yellow Wood* to Tebbel, who found it boringly flat, not nearly as taut, as focused, as compelling, as the first novel. "Well," Tebbel thought, "it's okay and he'll do better things." Wreden did not much care for it either. But their faith in the young writer was not in the least shaken. Putting on a good face, they diplomatically told him they looked forward to bringing it out sometime early in 1947. Tebbel thought Gore "a marvelous talker and conversationalist," an especially good storyteller. He spoke much about his family, particularly his grandfather. One day after work, Tebbel recalls, he and Gore "were having a drink in the Gramercy Park . . . and he began talking about homosexuality, though not in terms of himself but about his feelings about gay people and what not. I said to him, 'Have you ever written about this?' He said, 'No, I've thought of doing it.' I said, 'You really ought to think about writing about this, since you feel this way about it. It's something maybe you want to write about.' " Precisely what he had already thought about doing is unclear. Stylistically, he told Tutwiler, his next book would experiment with elements of high modernism. "My third book which won't be started for another year is going to be something wonderful if I can do it at all no chapters no commas except where they are needed for meaning and perhaps no quotation marks: the idea being that a story should be simple and easy to read and not cluttered up with archaic rules . . . and other things that irritate the eye." He seems to have had in mind a public flouting of the Exeter rules for good writing, a small bit of revenge against the Hamilton Bissells of the world. Since Joyce and Stein had already paved that road, there would be little danger in taking it himself, other than the possibility of artistic failure. Most likely, though, what he had in mind in his conversation with Tebbel was more dangerous, more fraught with the risks of self-exposure. To mainstream publishers and most reviewers, the subject of homosexuality was anathema.

Like everyone else at Dutton, Tebbel had no inkling of Vidal's sexual preferences. Given Vidal's demeanor and the widely shared stereotypes about homosexuals, Tebbel assumed that his interest in the subject was impersonal, sociological, literary. Probably, Vidal recalls, he talked about and described to Tebbel homosexuals he had met or heard about in Los Angeles in spring 1945. Through Anaïs he had recently been introduced to two social and artistic centers in which homosexuals were explicitly central, some of them queens of the sort he found irksome. At Leo Lerman's Upper East Side town house the Russian-born eccentric embodiment of artistic camp and *Harper's Bazaar* high fashion held court to a huge circle of partying friends and acquaintances from the art, fashion, theater, dance, and literary worlds. The party hardly paused, particularly on Sunday nights. Usually in bed in robe and Turkish fez, Lerman received hordes of guests who wandered through the four-story house, famous people such as Martha Graham, Nora Kaye, Marlene Dietrich, Maria Callas, William Faulkner, Evelyn Waugh, Cecil Beaton, and Diana Vreeland. Rising New York artistic stars like the lyricist John Latouche found Lerman's hospitality congenial. So too did young writers like the twenty-one-year-old Alabama-born short-story writer Truman Capote, whom Gore met that spring at a party at Anaïs's apartment, at which he mostly noticed the strikingly beautiful writer Jean Garrigue, a lesbian Anaïs found attractive. The prancing, handsomely compact Capote, who seemed to Gore excessively and self-promotingly effeminate, an extravagant queen eager to use his mannerisms to make sure

e Vidal's paternal grandmother,
. Felix Vidal, c. 1930.
rtesy of Margaret Sutton)

mas Pryor Gore as a young lawyer
orsicana, Texas, c. 1900.
:onsin Center for Film and Theater Research,
Vidal Collection)

(Clockwise from top) Nina Kay Gore,
Nina Gore, Thomas Notley Gore, and
Senator Thomas P. Gore, c. 1916.
(Courtesy of Gore Vidal)

ht) Senator Thomas Pryor Gore at
Washington office, c. 1912, dictating
is secretary, Roy Thompson.
rtesy of J. Roy Thompson, Jr.)

Senator Thomas P. Gore and
Nina Kay Gore at Rock Creek Park, c. 1940.
(Courtesy of Tom Auchincloss)

Lieutenant Eugene Luther Vidal,
c. 1920. (Courtesy of Margaret Sutton)

Nina Gore at the
wheel, probably Fort
Sill, Oklahoma, 1922.
(American Heritage Center,
University of Wyoming)

The wedding of Nina Gore and Eugene Luther (Gene) Vidal, Washington, January 1922.
(Courtesy of Gore Vidal)

(Left) Gene Vidal and son at Rock Creek Park, where they lived with
the Senator, c. 1927. *(Right)* Nina Gore and son at Rock Creek Park, c. 1927.
(Both photos: Wisconsin Center for Film and Theater Research, Gore Vidal Collection)

Eugene Luther Vidal, Jr. (Gore Vidal),
at Rehoboth Beach, Delaware, c. 1927.
(Courtesy of Gore Vidal)

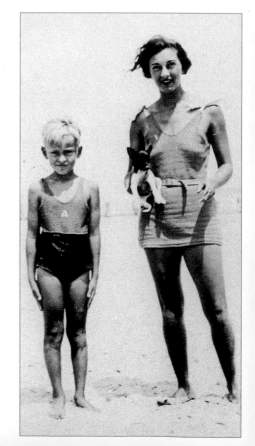

(Right) Gore Vidal with Nina Vidal
at Rehoboth Beach, c. 1930.
(Courtesy of Gore Vidal)

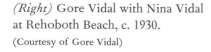

(Above) Gore Vidal, c. 1936.
(Wisconsin Center for Film and Theater
Research, Gore Vidal Collection)

(Left) Gore Vidal, with his father,
about to pilot a plane at the age of
ten, Washington, May 1936.
(Courtesy of Gore Vidal)

(Below) Amelia Earhart
and Gene Vidal, early 1930s.
(American Heritage Center,
University of Wyoming)

Merrywood in the late 1930s. (Courtesy of Gore Vidal)

Gore Vidal (left) and Jimmie
Trimble at St. Albans School,
c. 1937.

(Courtesy of Gore Vidal)

Gore Vidal and his half-sister Nina (Nini)
at Merrywood, c. 1938.

(Courtesy of Nina Auchincloss Straight)

Gore Vidal's passport
photograph, 1939.
(Wisconsin Center for Film and Theater
Research, Gore Vidal Collection)

Gore Vidal and Nina Auchincloss at
Merrywood, c. 1938.
(Wisconsin Center for Film and Theater
Research, Gore Vidal Collection)

Gore Vidal, with his trophy for a sand sculpture
of Lincoln's head at Bailey's Beach, Newport,
with Hugh D. Auchincloss III (Yusha), c. 1938.
(Courtesy of Gore Vidal)

Gore Vidal (seated, second from left) with his Boy Scout Troop
at Los Alamos Ranch School, c. 1941.

(Los Alamos Historical Museum)

people remembered him, immediately saw the author of *Williwaw,* which was about to come out, as a rival for literary celebrity. Gore had no doubt they would be competing for the same glittering prizes. His first book of short stories about to appear, Capote asked Gore, as they paused for a moment to talk, the self-reflexive question, " 'How does it feel to be an *onn-font-tarribull?*' "

In February *Harper's Bazaar* had paid Gore $25 for one of his poems, "Walking," which it published that October, an evocation of historical layering set in a New Mexican landscape reminiscent of Los Alamos. It gave him great pleasure finally to have a poem appear in print, especially in such a widely read magazine, though his sights were now mostly set on fiction, the novels and short stories for which, it must have occurred to him, *Harper's Bazaar* would be the perfect venue. Lerman, one of the literary editors of *Harper's Bazaar* with Mary Louise Aswell, under the leadership of George Davis, had made the magazine into the premier marketplace for quality short fiction. Gore, though, had not written any stories since Exeter. Or at least there were no later ones extant, since most of what he had written in the Army, other than *Williwaw,* had disappeared with the loss of his trunk. But it was not out of the question that *Harper's* might publish a portion of a novel or that he might write new short stories soon. As part of his work for Dutton he helped Harold Vinal, the editor of the poetry magazine *Voices,* find young poets to freshen its stale lineup. Five of his own poems appeared in the summer 1946 issue, the last poems he was ever to try to publish. Soon he became even better friends with Louise Townsend Nicholl, Dutton's poetry editor. A plump, graying woman of fifty-five, Nicholl was a distinguished minor poet who had published widely in prestigious magazines, had brought out three volumes of poems that Dutton had published, was active in the Poetry Society of America, and became the first woman to win an Academy of American Poets fellowship. More traditional than Wallace Stevens or Marianne Moore, she had a fine ear and a spare precision of language that expressed feeling by understatement. Her imagination never soared. But its closeness to the concrete and the natural anchored its metaphysical resonances in the things of this world. Her clear syntax and sharp particularity made her eminently readable, both sophisticated and accessible. Gore admired her poems and liked her. "We were great buddies . . . friends for years." Tebbel liked her also. "A very gentle, pleasant woman, with a sweet voice; she of course knew many poets. She handled all the poets that we had, and it's through her that we got poets we never would have had otherwise. Dutton and poetry were her life." Gore recalled that every day "she took the train from someplace in New Jersey to Dutton and back again. I don't think she went anyplace else in her life. Unmarried, she was satisfied with the Grand Central Station Stauffer's, where she'd buy pumpkin pies and take them back to New Jersey. I said the least you can do, living in your mother's big old house in New Jersey, is make your pumpkin pies." But, like most editors, "she had too much to read." More like his grandmother than the other women in his life, she made a happy contrast with Nina and Anaïs.

The other artistic salon at which he found himself had been created in a more elegant East Side Beekman Place brownstone than Lerman's by the formidable Peggy Guggenheim, who actually had more shrewdness than money. Her wealthy father had descended with the *Titanic*. She and her sister somehow had been left very little. With a sharp eye for personalities and value, she had been collecting modern paintings as well as talented people. Ultimately the paintings were to make her fortune. Having married, among others, Max Ernst, she specialized in surrealist art. When she returned from Europe to American safety during the war years, she opened an art gallery devoted to "Art of This Century." She had Jackson Pollock paint large murals in the foyer of her residence so that visitors would not be bored while waiting for the elevator to take them up to the salon. To the young Vidal "she looked like W. C. Fields, with a huge nose. She tried to have a nose job before cosmetic surgery had become superb, and it was botched. It was worse than what she had started with. What she started with was perfectly alright but she wanted perfection." Full-figured, passionate about her two miniature dogs, with what Anaïs called her "clown face," Peggy was obsessed with modern art and its makers. Well known in the New York artistic world as "the queen of foreigners," she particularly attracted Europeans to her parties, painters like Léger and Duchamp and surrealist poets like André Breton. Soon herself to establish permanent residence in Venice, she amused herself in New York's dynamic art culture until France and Italy once again became viable.

With Anaïs, who introduced him to her, Gore found Peggy Guggenheim's foreign-inflected salon alluring. At one party he met Parker Tyler, "pastry-pale, beady-eyed, thin-lipped," the author in 1947 of *Magic and Myth of the Movies*, with whom he shared a preoccupation with film, and whom he would one day transform into a fictional character of sorts in *Myra Breckinridge*. James Agee, the *Time* film critic who had published, under the title *Let Us Now Praise Famous Men*, his article on Alabama sharecroppers, with photographs by Walker Evans, seemed "sadly amiable." Gore noticed that his eyes were bloodshot. In Agee's presence the poet, editor, and novelist Charles Henri Ford, a close friend of Tyler's, leeringly remarked to Gore, "You can't be a good writer because you have such lovely legs," then danced off. Gore said to Agee, " 'I'd like to break Charles's legs.' Agee was soothing; then he said, most thoughtfully, 'These fairies can be surprisingly tough.' "

Years later in Venice, Peggy, remembering spring 1946, remarked to Gore, " 'Oh, you were with Anaïs. I always wondered about that. She was very stupid, wasn't she?' That was Peggy's conversational style. I said, 'Yes, I suppose all in all I have to say yes. She was fairly stupid.' 'I suspected that. You must not have liked that, did you?' And I said, 'Well, I didn't notice it for a while.' 'Well, yes,' she said, 'I know.' She was thinking of all the dumdums she had put up with, like Jackson Pollock. Her biggest affair was Beckett. 'I was in love with him for six months,' she said. 'That's longer than I've ever been in love with anybody in my life. I suddenly realized that he didn't want me, he wanted a boy.' I said, 'That's not unreasonable, Peggy.' 'Well, I didn't say it was unreasonable. I was just slow to understand. Anyway, I was in love for six months. That's the maximum in my life.' "

Through Anaïs he had met Maya Deren, a beautiful surrealist filmmaker of Russian-Jewish background influenced by Cocteau. Fascinated by film and psychological imagery, herself a surrealist of sorts, Anaïs fantasized she might be elevated into fame and fortune by the transforming magic of Maya's camera lens. Deren's films had the potential to provide the best cinematic representation of her own subjectively imagistic fiction. She hoped that one of her novels or pages from her diary might provide the script for a Maya Deren movie. She imagined herself in the starring role. At Friar's lecture in November 1945 she had introduced Gore to the filmmaker. At Maya's Greenwich Village studio she had the opportunity to share with him her admiration for Deren's aggressive promotion of her own artistic career, a lesson to them all, Anaïs concluded. Fascinated himself by movies, though of a different sort, Gore happily accepted Deren's invitation to perform with Anaïs and others in one of her films. Without dialogue, usually running between fifteen and thirty minutes, they embodied the director's general instructions to the performers, most of them friends, to respond to a situation, some small portion of which she would film. Film stock was expensive. She had little to waste. In March, Gore found himself milling around with Anaïs under hot lights at a large party scene with thirty or so of Maya's friends. "Gore and I decided to act pretty well as we do when we are together, a mixture of playfulness, key words, seriousness, and connections with what we are writing," Anaïs wrote in her diary. Interested in the spontaneous, insistent but always vague, the energetic Deren kept them at it for twelve hours. Finally she filmed a segment, part of a film she called *Ritual in Transfigured Time*. Later Gore noticed, disappointingly, he was on-screen for only a few seconds. When initially asked to appear in the film, starring Maya and a black woman, Gore remarked, " 'If only my grandmother could see me now.' The Gores were Reconstruction Southerners. . . . They did not believe in equality. In response to my teasing on the subject, Dot said, 'If any of my descendants ever mixes our blood with theirs, I'll come back and haunt him.' I said, 'Well, you've got a lot of haunting to do right now since half the mulattoes in Mississippi are related to us.' She changed the subject." Gore's Greenwich Village world, especially its surrealist component, would have seemed even more bizarre to Dot, though she would have readily understood its politics. When Anaïs at last saw the finished film, she was furious. Maya's magic camera had been less than flattering to her friends, especially Anaïs.

With days at Dutton, occasional evenings with Cornelia, filmmaking with Maya, parties with Anaïs, at her apartment, at restaurants, at Peggy Guggenheim's, at Leo Lerman's, at the lively Blue Angel nightclub, where he saw John Latouche and met the stage designer Oliver Smith and probably Smith's cousin, the composer and writer Paul Bowles, New York kept Gore busily engaged. When he became friendly with Stanley Haggard and his boyfriend, Woody Parrish-Martin, who designed the dust jacket for *Williwaw* and *In a Yellow Wood*, he floated the idea of the three of them getting a brownstone which, with Anaïs, they would share. He knew about such an arrangement in Brooklyn Heights. The idea never took off. Work at Dutton made him restless, impatient for more time for writing. Tebbel's suggestion that he write about sex between men began to loom larger, to point in a dangerous direction.

Except for his relationship with Anaïs, he did not want to complicate friendship with sex. The division seemed sensible, a way of maximizing his opportunities and rewards through efficient separation and distribution. Romance was not out of the question. But it was generally undesirable, and he had enough of something of that sort with Anaïs. For companionship, though, he had almost unlimited energy. When Dutton published in spring 1946 a popular bestseller called *The Manatee*, he met the author's stepdaughter, Constance Darby, a close friend of Judith Jones. He found her vivacious gaiety compelling. Connie "hated her stepmother and I hated *The Manatee*, so we had a lot in common," he recalled. When they introduced him to their other closest companion, Sarah Moore, also recently graduated from Bennington, he had three new friends. "Judy was a great beauty. And Connie was kind of rowdy, charming." Sarah, the daughter of the composer and Columbia music professor Douglas Moore, was "a mater dolorosa, a lady of the sorrows." Gore was "sort of fascinated by her," Jones remembered. "She had a very quirky mind, very intellectual, very critical. She sometimes looked like a Charles Addams woman, long dark hair, slightly—well, not quite sinister—but as if she didn't quite belong to the world, and that sort of fascinated Gore. . . . There was something wonderfully outrageous about her. She dared to be a maverick." Connie, seriously literary, worked as an editor for Lippincott. He found her "the most fun of the three. She had great energy and she was very funny." With a capacity for drink and wit, "she was always able to spar with him in a lively way, and to get him sometimes, and he liked it," Jones recalled. "He really admired her. . . . She wasn't naturally a pretty girl. . . . But she radiated such personality and she seemed very feminine. She was very blond. Fair-skinned. She tended towards plumpness. She kind of bustled. . . . Nothing bothered Connie." Like Gore, the three graces were also just turning twenty-one.

That summer at Douglas Moore's Riverside Drive apartment, which the young women occupied while the Moores were away, they regularly hosted dinners and parties. Publishing people and writers came. Judy did the cooking. "I was always the cook. I liked to cook. I just was very adventuresome as a cook. Nothing fazed me, I don't know why." A great deal of liquor and ice disappeared. People enjoyed getting drunk. At the piano Connie played beautifully and sang Cole Porter's "Night and Day." The only song she knew, she played it at every party. No one minded. It became a signature melody for those warm evenings. Below the high west windows the Hudson picked up the last of the sunlight, the rising moonlight. Palisades Park glittered in the darkness of the Jersey shore. A ferry visibly made its way across to the amusement park. "They were great parties," Gore remembered. Judy, whom he adored, fascinated by the camellia-white luster of her skin, had been having an affair with the poet Theodore Roethke, her former Bennington teacher. He was a fellow guest one of Gore's evenings there. Judy watched closely. "I wouldn't say they took to each other. It was always Gore goading what he thought of as the sort of square heterosexual male. . . . Roethke was about fourteen years older than I was. I remember an atmosphere. There was strain, apprehension between them." Both playful and competitive, Gore enjoyed, as he often did, ratcheting up the verbal interplay to what others thought a contentious level. Apparently Roethke did not like being called "our senior poet." The inaccuracy of the description had a mocking edge. "I think [Gore] loved to sort of shock people, their complacency. I think he thought he was good for all of us, shaking us up."

"Roethke and I didn't take to each other at first," he remembered, "but then we did. She was having a big affair with him. Yes, I was teasing him. I didn't know he was insane, nor did Judy." Perhaps he resented Roethke's influence over the three young women. "And the great day [came the next year, 1947] when we went to the Gotham Book Mart, he and I, to kiss the ass of Cyril Connelly in order to get into *Horizon*. So we went with Judy and all of literary New York was there and everybody thought this odd little man was a fag. So there were Theodore Roethke and I turning on the charm like nobody's business, me armed with my short stories, Ted with his poems, and Connelly was very polite to us. Then, before we knew it, Cyril had gone off with Judy, leaving a stunned Roethke, poems in hand."

———

With advance copies of *Williwaw* available in April, he eagerly awaited the mid-June official publication date. Coming downtown to the Dutton offices one afternoon, he saw through the taxi window a highly publicized young candidate for Congress in Massachusetts walking along Park Avenue, in front of the Raquet Club near Grand Central Station. He recognized him from newspaper photographs, and years later, in his memoir, put his recollection in the present tense: "In the left-over-from-the-war khakis that we all wore, skinny, yellow-faced Jack Kennedy is wandering down the west side of the avenue. In a blaze of publicity, he is now running for Congress.

Our fathers are friends, but we've never met. As I watch him, I wonder, have I made a mistake. . . . Shouldn't I have followed my grandfather Senator Gore's plan and set out for Congress instead?"

Fortunately, the early word on *Williwaw* was encouraging. Dutton had scheduled advertisements for the week of publication, two in the daily *New York Times,* two in the daily *Herald Tribune.* If reviews and sales were good, other ads would follow. Much depended on what happened in the first weeks after publication. Eager to see copies in bookstores, to have reviews in hand, the young author felt the usual anxieties, though he had reason to be hopeful. So far the in-house response was good, the word-of-mouth positive. Also, he had not only finished his second novel but had begun to think seriously about his third. Both compulsive and excited by his own facility, he had at this moment only the vaguest sense that he himself ought to put up a yellow light, that he might damage his market by making too frequent demands on it. *In a Yellow Wood* was scheduled for the beginning of the next year. If he began soon to write the novel that he and Tebbel had talked about and finished it quickly, there would be a backlog. But what was most on his mind at the moment was the reception of *Williwaw.* In late April, advance copies were sent to distinguished people, from Henry Miller to Eleanor Roosevelt. Though she did not usually review fiction, Mrs. Roosevelt may have remembered the author's connection with her husband's director of air commerce and with Amelia Earhart. She soon praised *Williwaw* in her *New York World-Telegram* column as "vividly engrossing" by an author who "has promise of doing interesting work in the future." Despite her disappointment with her young lover and her fear that *Williwaw*'s arctic ice had frozen his heart, Anaïs wrote a testimonial letter of strong praise for a book she quietly disliked. "I feel that, as a novelist and poet, he is strikingly close to that source of emotional power from which comes all great art. *Williwaw,* a story of conflict and the sea, is written with the simplicity of a legend."

A rush of reviews from around the country praised the book. Only a few disliked it, though many noticed, in passing and mainly forgivingly, its slightness and underdevelopment. The influential Orville Prescott in the daily *New York Times* thought it "continually interesting . . . a good novel" with "sound craftsmanship. . . . a good start toward more substantial accomplishments. He is a canny observer of his fellow-man. He can write. With such a good beginning there is no reason why he should not go far ahead." Reflecting its own environment, the *Los Angeles Times* thought it "clever, hard-boiled, full of punch," recasting it as if it were *film noir,* a novel scripted by Raymond Chandler or Dashiell Hammett. *Williwaw* "stamps Vidal," the *Boston Globe* claimed "as one of the most promising and enterprising young authors to capitalize on his war experience." The First World War had produced Hemingway and Fitzgerald. Who would the novelists of this next generation be? Few reviewers commented on *Williwaw*'s nihilistic tone, its bleak view of human nature, almost as if, having won the war, peacetime America could not even recognize a dark account of the war experience. Norman Rockwell sentimentality dominated the national optimism. But there was some room for *Williwaw*'s amoral realism, especially since it dramatized individual character and psychology rather than national pride. When the reviewer for the influential *Saturday Review of Literature* emphasized that "it is a novel of great promise by a young man whose skill as a craftsman is more important than his service as a soldier," Dutton placed more ads in the daily *Times* and *Tribune,* new ads in the Sunday book reviews, and a large spread in the *Saturday Review.* That the author was twenty years old was noted prominently. His photo on the book jacket impressed people with his striking good looks. Having hoped that *Williwaw* would get them off and running in the race for new voices, Dutton was exuberant. The morning after Prescott's review appeared, Gore came into the Dutton office. He was surrounded by congratulations. " 'Did you read your review in the *Times*?' I said no. And they said, 'It's Orville Prescott and it's very good.' I said, 'Who is Orville Prescott?' I didn't even know that the daily *Times* had a book review. I had never heard of Orville Prescott, and they thought I was putting this on. . . . Here I am associate editor, in title at least, at a publishing house, and I didn't know the name of the most important and powerful book reviewer and he'd given me a rave review that morning. Not only did I not read the *Times*, I didn't know his name." With a batch of reviews that the publicist had collected, he went into an empty office where a little later Tebbel found him "almost in tears. I was mystified. . . . But he had found the inevitable bad ones and couldn't stand it."

———·✦·———

Mild June weather. *Williwaw* was in the bookstores. From Washington, Cornelia, who had taken a job with the State Department, reported,

"My Love, To say that you have *fait sensation* in Washington is also to say nothing, the moppets are rushing in droves to Brentano's, they discuss your book instead of the weather, it's really remarkable." He had recently been to Washington to visit his grandparents. Nina was back in town, about to resume her East Coast life. Soon she was searching for a house in Washington. Though he had dedicated *Williwaw* to her, he was convinced she had not read it and never would. That did not prevent her boasting to people about her son's success. Probably she shared Gore's view that he owed her for the Hollywood advantages she had made possible for him in 1944–45. At a party at her Washington apartment, Cornelia still felt chemistry between the two of them. "Mother thinks you write like Shakespeare," she wrote him afterward. "I think that's quite a nice touch, considering the source, don't you? You do at that as a matter of fact. Shakespeare, but a fairly dyspeptic Shakespeare. I wish I understood you." With good-humored irony she signed herself "undyingly passionate." In New York he found waiting a letter from Henry Miller thanking him for a copy of *Williwaw*. "Amazing what you have experienced, by the age of twenty. Don't die there at Dutton's! A writer needs life, not the aura or ambiance of the literary world."

Bob Bingham wrote from Harvard, where he thought Gore should enroll and join him in his Shakespeare course with Matthiesson, a Proust, Joyce, and Mann course with Harry Levin, and a novel-writing course with Delmore Schwartz, a rising young critic, poet, and playwright, as Bingham described him, even as, Bingham acknowledged, Gore was. Vidal, though with no intention of ever becoming a student again, attended one of Levin's lectures and had a glimpse of Matthiesson in the hallway. He himself was no genius, Bingham wrote to Gore and, though he hated to admit it, he recognized that Gore was a sort of genius whose energy and vitality did away with the need for basic training. But he still urged him to enroll at Harvard. Gore's energy and vitality could accomplish so much more if they were fed and nourished a bit more before turning them loose on the world. When Gore reported to their former Exeter teacher Henry Phillips that he found Bingham and Lewis working hard at their studies, Phillips remarked, "It is too bad, for had they been industrious here, they could have been imaginative at Harvard, where it is more to the point to be so. As it is, they must now reverse the normal roles." Though Bingham urged him to reconsider his decision not to become a student, Gore's visit reconfirmed his determination to take a different road. Why, he thought, should the author

of a critically acclaimed first novel, with a second finished, a third almost
under way, a participant in major New York salons and on speaking terms
with world-famous figures, sit at the feet of tedious academics? Gene Vidal
reluctantly agreed to give him the railroad bonds he had designated for his
college costs. "I then, with my usual flair, thanked him very much and
cashed them in." With the Army money he had saved, with $665.88 in
royalties on a sale of 2,811 copies of *Williwaw* and more to come (at 10
percent on a book that sold for $2.50 his accumulation even from good sales
could never be huge), and with $14,000 from the railroad bonds, he had a
nest egg. In a worst-case scenario he had enough to support himself for at
least three years while devoting himself to writing. In the best alternative he
would earn enough in royalties so that he would have to spend only a little
of what he had. Determined to support himself by writing, he soon resigned
from Dutton.

Feeling that New York's distractions undermined his concentration on
work, he fantasized about some retreat, a place away from the wear and tear
of New York City life, protected, by distance, from time-consuming literary
people and politics. Europe still gleamed in his mind's eye. He wanted to
travel there at length and settle for a while in Paris or Rome. Much of
Europe, though, was still in ruins. Early postwar recovery was barely on its
way. Guided tourism, let alone free travel, was discouraged and partly
prohibited by military authorities. Europe, then, was out of the question.
Perhaps he would try New Orleans or even Mexico, the setting for the novel
that he had started in 1944 but abandoned because he could not concretely
enough imagine a country he had never visited. As a leitmotif undermining
these expectations of travel was the problem of Anaïs. He had resigned from
Dutton. Cornelia now recognized he was not likely husband material. But he
was still entangled with Anaïs. On the one hand, having been shocked to
discover she was more than twice his age (she had shown him a copy of a
book that contained her date of birth), he had suddenly a heightened sense
of their unsuitability. Her beauty now seemed less powerful, her voice less
enchanting. Her lushly subjective romanticism began to get on his nerves.
On the other hand, he still felt entangled. Her commitment to him had a
totality and generosity he could not readily forgo. She saw and responded to
a side of him much of the world knew little about. Like others, she thought
him sometimes arrogant, mocking, insecure, assertively ambitious, but she
had also seen him moody, gloomy, depressed, worried about his career. He

had confided his anxieties to her in ways he had to no one else, partly because he trusted her, mostly because he felt strongly the genuinely intimate rapport between them. No doubt she still had much to give him of which he still had need. Though he had been unable to agree to her initial terms, her accommodation to his desire that they each carry on separate sexual lives made that less an issue than it had been. He soon sounded her out on whether she wanted to travel with him or join him wherever he came to rest. The former seemed impractical, the latter possible, though much would depend on where. If Europe had been available, she might indeed have agreed to go with or join him, the possibility of returning to France much on her mind. But their discussions now, and their letters once he left, had the resonance of eagles disengaging even when reunion was the topic.

To escape the New York summer weather he went, soon after his return from Washington, to East Hampton, where he stayed, as usual, with Gene and Kit. Probably he saw Nina, who was visiting friends in nearby Southampton. *Williwaw* was a boasting point. His own attraction to sun and sand soon had him tanned, relaxed. His father's membership gave him the advantages of the exclusive Maidstone Club. The John Drew summer theater had its usual entertainments, part of a lively summer scene that included theater and ballet people from New York. Anaïs came to spend a week in a rented room "in a picturesque cottage." She recorded in her diary that Gore "suggested I spend a week out there." His version is different. "It was her idea, not mine, for her to come. We go together to the public beach by back roads. I am terrified I'll be seen with her—an older woman, who was less than radiant in the full sunlight. I cringe at my snobbism." A *folie à deux*, each should have known better. Anaïs disliked East Hampton. It seemed pretentious, arrogant, monotonous, the people "zombies of civilization in elegant dress with dead eyes." Anxious, out of place, unrenewed, she needed sleeping pills. When she rode through town to the beach on a rented bicycle, she guessed, correctly, that he felt ashamed of her, that he thought her cycling inappropriate, because either she seemed too old for cycling or it was socially embarrassing, or both. "A group of us would gather at the beach. Gore would walk down from his chic beach club and join us." Mostly he left her alone, to her chagrin, her pain. At the club, on the beach, he had handsome young male companions, a friendly, athletic type from Michigan, William Beaumer, and "a beautiful-looking man," the same age as Gore,

Andres Devendorf, whose wealthy father owned a luxurious East Hampton home. Gore's ready practical tolerance for privilege appalled Anaïs. Whereas upper-class privilege affronted her romantic idealization of feeling, of spirit, of soul, to Gore it was a cultural and social given he could readily tolerate, even enjoy. Having lived at Merrywood, spent summers in Newport, Maidstone seemed to him just another upper-class Wasp watering hole. It was not so much that Anaïs was out of place in East Hampton but that they were, as a couple, mostly slipping away.

By late August, as he made travel plans, neither of them really desired that they include her. Late in the summer he was on his way to New Orleans. He and Anaïs were still intimate friends, still allies. In anticipation of hostile reviews of her new novel, he had left with her a long letter in its defense, to be sent to newspapers if necessary, that made clear, even if it exaggerated, his admiration for her as a writer, as a literary personality, and as a modern woman. "New Orleans," he soon wrote her, "is quite lovely and the food marvelous and I am relaxing mightily. . . . I am at peace and contented by motion. I think of you as you know for you have no competition. Like a true Celt I draw closer when I am alone." Yucatán had been in his mind as an exotic place he would like to visit. His plane from New Orleans took him to Mérida, his first visit to Mexico. Soon he was in "a Palace in an ancient city surrounded by a jungle. I expect to be here 2 weeks. For 3 dollars I have a most royal suite with ceiling so high there is an echo. The town is pretty and old. I am beginning to work again. . . . I think of you often," he wrote to Anaïs, "and, strangely, so newly arrived, look forward to getting back. The sun is marvelous. I have no pain. Write, Cherie, all my love, Gore." To some extent he wrote what he knew she wanted to hear. It was partly a role he played. But he played it with no one else. The special relationship was attenuated but still extant. Having brought with him a small batch of novels, he immersed himself in D. H. Lawrence, whom he was to keep reading for the next few months. *The Plumed Serpent* seemed particularly appropriate, and Lawrence provided a fictional version of the bisexual current that had been part of his tension with Anaïs, who herself had, years before, written a book about Lawrence. Though she genuinely missed him, she had no illusions about their future together. "I was afraid to say how much I missed you that you might interpret it as calling you back— But I am not calling you back, just following you in your wanderings . . . steeling myself for the truth, the future. You know, you must not, out of your deep gentleness and tenderness, sustain this illusion that I have no competition."

In Yucatán he found the ruins of Mayan civilization architecturally and historically interesting. But his curiosity about them was not compelling. His model for such things was, as always, Rome. He liked the warmth, the visual beauty, but Mérida was not, for him, a livable city. Within a few weeks he was in flight again, farther south, this time to Guatemala City. To his pleasure he found that the largest city between Mexico City and Lima, Peru, was wonderfully attractive, with an "old city" that had survived disastrous earthquakes and gleaming new buildings that were beginning to dominate the skyline. "This place is growing more on me every day," he told his father. "You have never seen any place so clean and in spots ultramodern. The food is good. The pastry in one shop better than anything I've ever eaten. There are book stores, movie houses, modern hospitals etc." Guatemalan politics, though, were primitive, brutal, a hissing snakepit. Behind the scenes the United Fruit Company, with huge banana plantations and its own railroads, controlled the country. Governed by the liberal administration of President Juan José Arévalo, Guatemala was still economically a feudal regime. The closely allied military and the old colonial families who owned the coffee plantations had a tight grip on power. Indian labor, on which the plantations depended, was poorly paid and sometimes coerced. The strong reform groups to the left, including the partly legitimized Communist Party, were pushing for expropriation of unused land, for a more even distribution of wealth, for greater democracy. When Gore arrived in Guatemala City in mid-September 1946, the Arévalo government and the old oligarchy were in the early stages of a struggle. Within five years it would explode into revolution, repression, and death. In the bright sunshine, the dark night of Guatemala was soon to begin.

―――――――

In a short time Gore had a comfortable room in a boardinghouse run by a Guatemalan businessman, Carlos Urruella. The city was exotic yet civilized, urbane yet comfortable, everything inexpensive. "Labor is cheap: a cook for ten a month. Prices on everything else have gone up but are still way below NYC etc standards," he wrote to his father. He could almost live, if he were prepared to be economical, on the hundred dollars a month the Auchincloss trust fund provided. Now that he was of age, at his insis-

tence Nina had begrudgingly turned it over to him. Ironically, some of the
fund was invested in United Fruit. Celebrating his twenty-first birthday in
Guatemala City, he quickly established his usual schedule, writing part of
the day, then walking, touring, stopping at bars, restaurants, sampling the
nightlife. What did not grow on him was bullfighting, which seemed to him
animal torture. When he attended his first, he walked out.

With his easy, attractive manner, he began to meet interesting people,
some fellow boarders, others in the general run of city life. Distinctively a
handsome, formally dressed American, carrying himself as if he were worth
knowing, he was soon introduced to Guatemalans from prominent families,
particularly to the Vasquez Bruni family members of his own age. A wealthy
clan, their Guatemala City town property occupied a full square block.
"The family patriarch was of Colombian origin, and he held what seemed to
be the lifetime hereditary rank of minister from Colombia to Guatemala."
Mention of his grandfather, of his father's service in the Roosevelt administration, of the Auchinclosses, would have opened any resistant doors.
"There's a delightful ruling class here which I've been running with lately,"
he wrote to Gene Vidal. "They own Guatemala, have great plantations etc. I
meet the President next week. The nice thing about such a small country is
the fact that everyone knows everyone else. There's a good size foreign
colony of diplomats and writers and painters." In the Vasquez Bruni family
"there were three sons—one a true wit named Ricardo," and a beautiful
daughter, Olga, nicknamed "Cookie," with whom he soon became friendly.
The Vasquez Brunis comprised, he thought, "an enchanted world."
Cookie's closest friend, Felicia Montealegre, an Argentinean, said "with a
heavy accent that she was going to go to New York and marry the most
famous man there. She went and married Leonard Bernstein." Another
Guatemalan, Mario Monteforte Toledo, was less wealthy but more intellectually interesting. It immediately became clear to Monteforte, though less
clear to Gore, that the young American knew nothing about Central American politics. To Monteforte, about ten years older than Gore, his American
friend seemed naïve about such things even in his own country. A handsome, energetic essayist and poet, Monteforte was a liberal socialist. President of the Guatemalan Congress, widely regarded as a likely future
president of the country, he tempered his hope for social reform with a keen
sense of the power of the alliance between Guatemalan social conservatives
and foreign economic interests.

At the boardinghouse Gore met a casually companionable young man, Pat Crocker. A blond Californian expatriate and alcoholic in his late twenties, "short and pink and dumpy," Pat had come to Guatemala to paint, which he did with more irregularity than talent. Competent enough, he had the virtue of high spirits, reasonable reliability, and an enthusiasm for the country. Gore was soon fondly addressing him as "Dear Blubber." With only a slightly extravagant touch and tone, his campy humor delightful, Pat was not queen enough to get on Gore's nerves. His mother, Penny, who had joined him in Guatemala and who looked "just like him," was as amusingly pleasant and eccentric as her son. They both had found Guatemala blissful, especially its low cost of living. When Gore arrived, Pat already knew the country well. He had a large circle of hard-drinking American expatriates, to whom he introduced his new friend. With excellent Spanish, he was a valuable companion on excursions into the country or when anything came up that needed more Spanish than Gore's few phrases. In Guatemala City, English mostly sufficed, but not in the country, except in the nearby city of Antigua, the sixteenth-century capital, a town of ten thousand, less than an hour's drive away. It had become a museum of colonial architectural history. Partly destroyed over the centuries by earthquakes, it had, with its distinguished ruins, magnificent views, and superb climate, become an attraction for wealthy Guatemalans, as well as for European and American expatriates, who found the capital too large and crowded. Five thousand feet above sea level, framed on three sides by huge volcanic mountains, with its romantic ruins, its grid of picturesque streets, its indigenous population of dark-skinned Indians whose lives appeared hardly changed from what they had been a thousand years before, Antigua seemed a small paradise. When Gore arrived with Pat Crocker for his first visit within a month of coming to Guatemala, the city took his breath away. He thought he had never seen a place quite so beautiful.

———

At his writing table in his room in Guatemala City, through September and October 1946, Gore worked on his new novel, as usual writing on yellow legal-size pads when available or in notebooks with lined pages. That seemed to him appropriate for fiction. What had emboldened him to commit himself to write this novel about love between men may not have been clear even to him, though Tebbel's encouragement probably played a role. He had cast himself as a mainstream novelist writing about issues the American literary world at large could accept as appropriate for a general readership. He still desired that venue, that view of himself as a writer. But something indefinable had happened, the result of which was his new willingness to take the chance, which he thought manageable, of allowing readers to associate him with the subject. Normally cautious, calculating, shrewd about risks, he thought this now a risk worth taking, partly because he underestimated or did not foresee some of the consequences. Also, as counterpoint to his caution, he had a selective reckless streak, whose operative constituents included anger, arrogance, and courage. It may have been, partly, his experience with Anaïs that propelled him forward: the novel taking shape had as much to do with his view that romantic idealization of love in a sexual relationship was deadly as with homoerotic sex per se. He had seen, he believed, nothing but difficult if not disastrous marriages. Senator and Mrs. Gore had managed a companionable longevity, but that weighed less heavily in the consideration than his parents' nightmare. If it were better to marry than burn, it would be better not to marry at all, since in American society burning was more likely to occur within than outside marriage. Romantic self-destructiveness, he had good reason to believe, did not distinguish between heterosexual and homosexual, married and unmarried.

As the novel took shape, he sought to create a homoerotic bildungsroman, a traditional narrative cast against an idyllic background of first love in which two young men, Jim Willard and Bob Ford, with echoes of Jim and Huck in *Huckleberry Finn,* are separated and take different roads of education and growth, one into a romantic idealization of that early homoerotic experience and a series of homosexual relationships; the other, for whom the early experience is almost forgotten, into the heterosexual world. When they meet again years later, Jim, rejected, deeply disappointed, and in a violent rage, semiaccidentally kills Bob. It is a devastatingly bleak conclusion. The protagonists, at the end, are not defined by their sexual practices; the issue is not sexual orientation but human nature. Nina and Gene, Anaïs and Gore, the two couples most relevant to Gore's experience, have as much if not more impact on the novel than the experience with Jimmie Trimble. In the natural course of events Jimmie and Gore had separated. Neither had fought the separation. If Jimmie had lived, Gore had no doubt they would have gone their different sexual ways. The novel begins as an imaginative projection of what might have happened to two young men who had had an early experience similar to theirs. It soon transforms their particular sexualities into a universal theme that applies to every possible combination in which romantic love dominates: what begins idyllically ends tragically.

By early November the novel was "almost complete and I am retitling it *The City and the Pillar,*" he wrote Anaïs, whom he had seen in New York during a hectic week in late October. He had returned to attend the book parties honoring the publication of her *Ladders to Fire*. "I am more pleased with this than anything I've done." He prefaced it with a quotation from Genesis, "But his wife looked back from behind him and she became a pillar of salt," partly an allusion to Sodom and Gomorrah, mostly an emphasis on the inherently destructive romantic obsession with the past. "In two weeks I'll have finished my new novel," he wrote his father. That "puts me way ahead of schedule. I think I might write a children's book afterwards." With a first draft of *The City and the Pillar* in hand, he already had two more novels in mind, the "children's book" a sophisticated anticipation of magical realism in a novel about King Richard's troubadour, to be called *A Search for the King*. Nina was also very much under consideration. "My next novel will be about mothers," he told Gene Vidal. "Lurene and Nina should be interested. I have a theory that parents get as much understanding from children as they give. It is wonderful to me how a woman can live 43 years and learn so little about people and herself . . . and have such pretensions." He already had a tentative title, *The Womb*, a disguised autobiographical narrative about his own struggle to navigate through that narrow passage.

In a Yellow Wood, which was scheduled for publication in early 1947, now seemed to him unsatisfactory. Some of its flaws he blamed on its having been written in New York City, which he thought uncongenial, actually damaging, as a place for him to write, though he recognized that *In a Yellow Wood* also suffered from the limits of its initial conception and the structural confusion of his having changed halfway through, under the influence of his relationship with Anaïs, the situation of the main character. By contrast *Williwaw*, written before he had come to New York, and now *City*, written almost entirely in Guatemala, seemed to him vastly superior. Still, with *In a Yellow Wood* scheduled for publication in March, Dutton undoubtedly would not want to bring out *The City and the Pillar* until the next year. And if he began *The Womb*, as he felt himself almost compelled to do, he would have that finished much before *City* was published. "I can't seem to stop

writing books," he told his father. To constantly have a backlog was unsettling, the long gap between completion and publication discomforting. And
in the case of *The City and the Pillar*, what if another writer were to publish
a novel on the same controversial subject? Would it not steal his thunder?
Actually, Wreden and Dutton welcomed the delay, nervous that *The City
and the Pillar* might damage their young author's career. "I took my time to
reread [it]," Wreden wrote to him. "You are excellent about cutting and
polishing your own stuff. Few people can do it as well as you can. The book
is more compact and better for it. I shall not bring up the question again, but
do let me know whether you want *The City and the Pillar* scheduled for
January and whether you might, at the last minute, send in your new novel
and substitute it for *The City and the Pillar*."

With Pat, Gore returned to Antigua, whose beauty this time he found
so compelling he immediately began to consider using some of his money to
buy a house there. "Pat said there's this wonderful part of a church for sale.
We went out and looked at it and I said, 'Well, I would love to own it.' I was
feeling very high over *The City and the Pillar* and thought of it as a place to
get away to, so I said I'll buy it if you'll live there and help me to fix it up."
Now twenty-one years old, he had never lived in a home in which he had
felt secure. From his earliest childhood each of his parents' homes, from
Bancroft Place to Rock Creek Park to Merrywood, had been severely
compromised. Either it had been a site of fierce marital battles or someone
else's home in which he was a long-term guest or a residence provided by
his mother's marital adventures or his father's bachelorhood and remarriage.
In her own way Nina found transience attractive, domesticity incompatible
with her impatience and volatility. His most settled, congenial home had
been his grandparents' in Rock Creek Park. Thereafter it had been expulsion into institutional dormitories, first St. Albans, then Los Alamos, Exeter,
the Army. In New York, welcome as he was at his father's apartment, he
was still a guest. He had grown used to hotels, a habitual traveler occupying
rented spaces whose impersonality was part of the price of travel.

But the notion of having a home of his own spoke to a substantial need
for domesticity, for a piece of the earth that had on it his stamp of choice
and taste. Why not Antigua? Attractive, distinctive homes were cheap.
"There are large palaces for sale for next to nothing," he wrote to his father.

During the winter the weather was superb, "dry and warm, rather cool in the evenings. . . . For swimming there's Lake Atitlán which is the most beautiful lake in the world." From New York or wherever else he spent the rest of the year he could fly to Guatemala. "It'd be perfect to work here in the winter and rent it in the summer." In fact, it might even be profitable, he told his father, who had queried him about opportunities for a Vidal Weldwood factory in Guatemala City. "The place is getting ready for a deluge of Americans leaving America; might not be a bad idea to be first." In fact, after the church he had first seen proved impractical, he had found through Pat Crocker the house that "I'm tempted to buy if I can get it," a small building, 4 de la 3a Avenida Norte. It had once served as a convent, attached to the beautiful ruined colonial church of Our Lady of El Carmen in the center of Antigua, a short walk from everything, including the town square. "It's 300 years old with three rooms and a large walled garden in back; it's in good repair and I'm told it could be had for less than a thousand dollars. I've made friends with some of the wealthier families in Antigua and they are keeping an eye on me to see that I don't get gypped. I have a feeling however that the owner doesn't want to sell. I'd like however to live down here . . . if I had a house." Unfurnished, some of it dilapidated, without a sufficient kitchen and with no bathroom, it would need major repairs. Pat would be the perfect overseer, with his good Spanish, his ample free time, his permanent residence. In return for living at the house he would take on this and other things, a kind of majordomo whose residence was his payment. If Gore could get the house at a low enough price, the cost of the renovations would be manageable. The price turned out to be $2,500, not including improvements. It still seemed reasonable, "with a beautiful tropical patio and a 16th century chapel and bell tower—the remains of a ruined cathedral."

With a draft of *The City and the Pillar* finished in late November, he focused on completing the purchase. "Everyone compliments me on how cheaply I got the place," he reported to his father. "It seems that the rush for Antigua land is begun and prices are beginning to go up. I plan to spend another 2500 on putting in a bathroom, etc. I have my own water. It's all one story." A guest the next summer recalled that "there was an atrium, and the whole convent was built around this atrium. During the earthquake a pillar had fallen across the atrium, the whole open part, and it stayed there. It was like part of it then. It just became automatic that you'd step over this fallen pillar that had been there for a hundred and fifty years." Gore's enthusiasm may have made it seem less the odd commitment that it was for a young man of twenty-one who had been in Guatemala for less than three months. The need to have a place of his own compelled him into an engaging recklessness. He sent drawings of the floor plan to Anaïs as well as Gene. Though much of the fire had gone out of the relationship with Anaïs, there were still warm coals or at least warm rhetoric. "My plans," he told her, "are to return to NYC next month back here in March (with you I hope) after the book and then around May to France. This is a beautiful place and were it not for you I should never return to New York and that ghastly world." But before he could live comfortably in the house, the renovations had to be completed, especially the installation of a bathroom, a functional kitchen, and an additional room to serve as his study. "There was a garden right next to a big chapel that went with the house. There was a sliver of garden behind it, an oblong in which I had put one big room with the little garden leading up to it, and that's where I worked. The other rooms were on the street." Pat was put to work almost immediately. Monteforte, who frequently came to Antigua to see his Indian mistress, stopped by, the first of many visits. As had become usual, they argued about politics. Sitting in the patio, bounded by the high wall of a ruined church, or "under a pepper tree, near an ugly square fountain like a horse trough," they had happily contentious discussions in which Gore took his grandparents' anti-Communist, anti-Rooseveltian high line that emphasized economic self-reliance. Monteforte argued for a socialistic reorganization of economic inequities and teased him about his friendship with the wealthy Vasquez Bruni family who, of course, opposed land reform. Why don't you tax, Gore responded, the United Fruit Company? Who would prevent you? " 'Your government,' Monteforte explained. They had kept the former dictator in power. 'Now they're getting ready to replace us.' . . . 'Why should we care what happens in a small country like this?' Mario gave me a compassionate look—compassion for my stupidity. 'Businessmen. Like the owners of United Fruit. They care. They used to pay for our politicians. They still pay for yours.' "

Work on the house, as usual with such things, went more slowly than had been anticipated. The cost increased beyond the estimates. From Washington, Dot provided her usual loving voice and "a small check" to buy something for the Antigua house. It "sounds *so intriguing*. I feel that I have to go right down there." She also provided home news: the Senator, who had been very ill, would never be his old self again; Nina was in New York "trying to get something [more] out of Hugh for the children," a persistent activity. Gore's mind, though, was mostly on the attractions of Guatemalan life, on the satisfaction of having finished *The City and the Pillar,* and on bringing to some sort of new equilibrium his relationship with Anaïs. He had no regrets about buying the house. "There are warm springs and pools within a short walk. . . . The *most* beautiful lake in the world is 3 hours by bus. You have never seen such beauty—deep blue surrounded by smoking volcanos." At Lake Atitlán, he met the Danish writer Karl Eskelund, author of *My Chinese Wife.* "He's getting me published in Scandinavia and you too," he wrote to Anaïs, "when he sees you." Gore himself planned to see her soon. He needed to return to New York to have *The City and the Pillar* typed. He had raised the thought that she might return with him to Antigua. But, sensibly, she did not want to. In December in New York Connie Darby had expressed to Anaïs her puzzlement at Gore's buying a house in Guatemala. Like many, Connie still assumed that Gore and Anaïs were lovers. "Just had a disturbing talk with Connie," Anaïs wrote to him, "who . . . was filled with compassion for you and I being separated, thinks something has gone wrong, was shocked at your buying a house so far from me—so I guess I may have to explain the truth—for I can't bear this misunderstanding anymore—or Connie's pity. You are quite happy, at peace and working without me—and I don't like long distance relationships—please tell her the truth—or do you want me to?" Throughout the autumn his letters to Anaïs had continued to represent his commitment to her in terms far stronger than the reality warranted. Though she still desired that he commit himself to her, she had not the slightest hope he would. What had happened in East Hampton had "left quite a scar— Like a nightmare, in which my desire to be near you, my willingness to relinquish everyone, everything, was answered by complete frustration." She had determined to change the terms and rhetoric of her passion for him. "My intuition tells me you are romancing—don't be afraid to tell me—I can take it now. . . . Passion . . . purifies everything. . . . One is only good and chaste after passion. . . . I feel *now* like a saint—and not when I live like a nun. . . . America is the most impure country in the world, because it is ashamed of passion, of nature. . . . Tell me how you are—I won't be jealous—! I *know*—I love you deeply, cheri, my mystical sex follows you in your long voyage."

Actually *his* description of his mostly ascetic life in Guatemala was of more relevance to him than her. "I've been a monk, a saint here," he wrote back, "but you have every reason to be surprised for I am too. This is the first time in my life. It was something of a test. Now I feel more at peace than ever before." In fact, what was becoming clear to him was that, whatever Guatemala's attractions, sexual opportunities there were limited. Commercial sex between men was difficult to come by. Venereal diseases, not held in check by the rudimentary public-health practices, rampaged. In Antigua "there are a number of homosexuals . . . artists and so on. I enjoy their company but that's all. They will amuse you I think." The quick, anonymous encounters he preferred were not readily available. "I was having no sex at all in Guatemala," he later remarked. "It was driving me crazy, not having sex. Who would I do it with? The natives were too primitive. To a foreigner they were pretty ghastly, and I had never had much traffic with queens in my life, so what was there? And I could end up with clap, or what I thought was clap. Venereal disease was all over. Penicillin wasn't down there." In Guatemala City "there was one girl I was quite interested in but nothing ever happened." With a great deal of sexual energy, he had very few practical outlets for it. "The irony of it all," Anaïs remarked, "you go to Guatemala and you live like a saint." But she had no illusions about why or about the future of their relationship. "Now I know that no sooner will I arrive you will turn towards someone, because, cheri, no matter how *real* your love for me is, you are motivated by compulsions deeper than any love for me, compulsions which have nothing to do with me, of which I am merely a symbolical victim." She urged him not "to come to NY for me—I'm happier when you are happy and well."

In fact, despite his rhetoric, including his reference to their going to France together that next spring, he returned to New York in late December 1946 only secondarily to see Anaïs, primarily to get *The City and the Pillar* typed. As soon as he arrived, he went to spend Christmas with Nina, who had been spending so much time in New York in order to pressure Hugh for more child support that she had taken a small apartment on Eighty-fifth Street. She had also recently broken her ankle. He had arranged his travel schedule to be with her on the holiday. "She was drunk when I walked in, and she immediately picked a quarrel. She was hobbling around on crutches, and I just slammed the door and left." Furious, he vowed never to speak to her again. His best revenge, he decided, for a lifetime of such damaging behavior, would be to write *The Womb*. He had already resolved to return to Guatemala in late February or early March, determined to be away from New York when *In a Yellow Wood* would be published. Still supportive of his career, hoping for the change that would affirm her view of the kind of novelist he ought to be, Anaïs looked forward to reading the manuscript of *The City and the Pillar*, which Dutton had scheduled for January 1948. "Are you coming back with your book all finished?" she had asked. "The evolution between Book I and II, and the one within Book II [*In a Yellow Wood*] itself is so quick and so rich—that I await this one with a sense of anticipatory delight." She approved of his D. H. Lawrence reading. Probably she hoped that the homoerotic element in *The City and the Pillar* would have the resonant mystery of the magical relationship between the two main male characters in *The Rainbow*. "I have no doubt about your writing," she claimed untruthfully, "but I would like to see you happier in your life— Is a mountain a lake and a book enough?" She again urged that he try psychoanalysis. He predicted a new consanguinity between them. With the publication of *City* "we'll both be outcasts. . . . The deep-rutted critics will be as frightened of me as of you."

When he suggested she return with him to Guatemala in March and they leave from there for France, she glamorized the invitation into a proposal of marriage that in itself was no proposal at all, neither in her terms nor his. Gore, she wrote in her diary, wants to marry me and lock me up in Guatemala. In fact, waveringly and sometimes inconsistently, both were moving to bring the rhetoric of the relationship to as full a close as they had brought the relationship itself. Her intuition told her it was over. That he wanted to imprison her in marriage and in Guatemala was her way of expressing what was impossible for both of them. He had no desire to do either. His rhetoric expressed his desire to keep her still within his power, to test his strength, and also to let them both go their separate ways. The good things they could do for one another had already been done. There was little more possible. In New York in early March he telephoned her with his last bit of good news. "He fought for me at Dutton," she wrote in her diary. "And won. They wanted to wait two years to publish *Children of the Albatross*. They will publish *Children of the Albatross* now!" The reunion was at first happy but hesitant. Both had accepted the narrower parameters. Gore gave her at last a copy of the manuscript of *The City and the Pillar* to read. The homosexual relationship seemed to her depressingly grim, the main characters adolescent. But what most upset her was that one of the female characters seemed at least partly based on herself. The character has lines around the eyes, makes vain attempts to disguise her age. To Anaïs it seemed an aggressively hostile parody, a brutal caricature. "No woman wants to read that about herself," she complained. At the Ritz Bar on Madison Avenue she told him unequivocally and at length that he had betrayed her, that, whatever their differences, this caricature was a deeply painful personal attack that she would never forgive. But she soon partly did. Within a short time she had made enough of an adjustment, encouraged by his protestations and blandishments, by his desire not to let her get fully away just yet, by her own unwillingness to give up on something she had not yet fully given up on, to allow a reconciliation that would permit them still to share something special. When he left to return to Guatemala, he renewed his invitation to her to visit. Partly it was loyalty, affection. Partly it was bravado.

The reception of *In a Yellow Wood* in March 1947 was only slightly disappointing, primarily because author and publisher expected so little. Dutton, which had had strong doubts from the beginning, was not surprised that sales were dismal. Vidal's confidence in the book had diminished at some late stage in the writing or revision. All in all, the reviews were tolerable, a few strikingly good, especially those in the *New York Herald Tribune* and *Chicago Sunday Tribune*. Enough were temperately phrased, cordial, if not to the book then to the author, so that little damage was done. A number of reviewers thought it a success within its narrow canvas, its "controlled naturalism," though others could not disguise their conviction that the author had weakened it by insisting that an unfocused main character somehow could convey interestingly the boredom of his own life. Some sensed that a deep structural flaw in the novel resulted from a failure of initial conception or a change in focus in the writing of the book. Why Vidal should be writing about "a strange, oblique sort of war casualty" the reviewers had little to no grounds on which to speculate. His own hopes for a major success, for greater fame and financial rewards, were now centered on the new book, *The City and the Pillar*, which he believed a vastly better novel.

Before returning to Guatemala, he accepted Bingham's invitation to visit him and A. K. Lewis at Harvard. Bingham urged him to bring a car in which they could drive to Exeter for a day or two. The much-admired Tom Riggs, who had been visiting at Lewis and Bingham, had read a few pages of *In a Yellow Wood* in an advance copy Gore had sent Bingham, who passed along Riggs's complimentary comments. Generously, Bingham himself had nice things to say, but, in order not to keep saying only nice things, criticized what he thought an excessive amount of flat description in the first part. Though he recognized that it was part of a stylistic strategy, it seemed to him tedious overkill. They soon drove up together to Exeter, where Gore had the pleasure of showing off a copy to his valued Exeter teachers, George Bennett, Leonard Stevens, and Henry Phillips. Later, when his uneasiness about the defects of the novel became self-critical defensiveness, he remonstrated to Stevens, " 'Sir, if you had read this [in manuscript], you would never have let me publish it.' " Stevens responded, " 'Well, Gore, you've got to study much more about writing. I suggest that you do a lot of reading of Henry James.' " About a year and a half later, Stevens's widow recalled, "Gore wrote him an eight-page letter . . . in the manner of Henry James on eating a breakfast—eggs and so on."

Back in Antigua by the publication date, he was happy to see that the house renovations had been progressing well under Pat's supervision. Each morning, still in his bathrobe, he would write in the room most distant from the street or in the small cobblestone patio, which Pat had planted with grass and small local plants. "I must construe this home as a symbol," Gore wrote to Anaïs. Occasionally he reverted to his self-dramatizing, melancholy rhetoric: "But there is no heart to it, of course. These days I am a solo dancer, dancing magnificently with no audience. My attachment to you continues, it grows more poignant, more vast, more hopeless with each day. . . . It is there, it hurts. I have sometimes the feeling that too much of me was left in the womb . . . what . . . was not born at all. . . . I feel a stranger passing through, the books are only shadows I cast before the sun." This had little to do anymore, if it ever had, with his relationship with Anaïs. *The Womb* began to take shape rapidly, hardly a shadow at all, this time a transparently autobiographical bildungsroman, powerfully conceived and brilliantly executed, in which Nina and he have the starring roles, with slightly disguised versions of his father, of the Gores, of Hugh Auchincloss, of Rosalind, even of Liz Whitney in the secondary parts. The portrait of Nina is both powerful and relentlessly devastating, a narcissistically destructive mother from whom her vulnerable son, depicted from birth to his Army service, struggles successfully, though with great pain, to liberate himself. His anger at Nina, his bitterness at what she had not given him, his sense of her lacerating destructiveness, and his ambivalent but deep love for her attained a charged focus. Their innumerable arguments and reconciliations found their novelistic equivalent. Of course, much from the life is eliminated and effectively heightened. Experimenting with stream of consciousness, with indirect monologue, with non-narrated transitions of time and place, the novel has a high modern feel, now much beyond the influence of Maugham, with Joyce, Lawrence, and Mann as part of the palette. Jimmie Trimble is renamed Jimmy Wesson. The relationship of William Giraud and Jimmy Wesson parallels Gore's and Jimmie Trimble's, though the novel makes them classmates at Exeter also. Rock Creek Park, St. Albans, Reno, Newport, Merrywood, Exeter, East Hampton are the settings. In a self-exposing monologue, Nina (Charlotte Giraud), fueled by alcohol, excoriates her former husband and her ungrateful child for their failure to appreciate her, to acknowledge her sacrifices, to love her as she deserves. Soon totally alienated from his heavy-drinking mother, William "remember that [her] affectionate moments were as intense, as consuming, as her angry ones. But generally he could only remember the times of anger and destruction." In the final scene, wounded on a European battlefield, he learns about Jimmy's death in the Pacific. "Spring, like all other seasons, was bitter."

Writing through the late winter and spring of 1946, a little after midsummer he had finished. Along the way he changed the title from *The Womb* to *The Season of Comfort*, taking the bitter irony from Rimbaud's *A Season in Hell*. "My bitterness toward my mother," he wrote to Anaïs, "is almost gone; it is in the book now and I am pleased with the work. She wants to come here in August and I shall let her." The intense rhetoric in his letters to Anaïs became slightly less heightened, less self-reflexive, though he repeated numbers of times his invitation to visit him that summer, undoubtedly sometime other than when Nina would be there. There was, in fact, a reasonable amount of social life in Guatemala City and Antigua, with the Vasquez Brunis and Monteforte, and a large community of Americans. He soon started a friendship with Dan Wickenden, a slim, dark-haired, bespectacled American writer of thirty-two whom he had met in a hotel lobby in Guatemala City the previous November. Wickenden was staying on, at least until the spring, working on a novel and enjoying the Guatemalan landscape, which he hoped to make the setting of his next one. A little edgily competitive with one another, they still found much to talk about, particularly literature and their different views about the novel as an art form. Wickenden's first novel, *The Running of the Deer*, published in 1937, had been a bestseller, his third, *The Wayfarers*, in 1945 had been picked by Orville Prescott as the best novel of the year. When in November 1946 Vidal gave Wickenden the manuscript of the unrevised *The City and the Pillar* to read, Wickenden criticized it on artistic grounds. For a practitioner of and believer in the novel as large, sprawling, epic, with grand characters, *City* seemed too minimalist, propagandistic. But he admired Gore's courage in taking on the subject and thought highly of his talent.

Through Pat, Gore also met the painter Bob Hooton, another American expatriate, as well as, in Antigua and at Panajachel on Lake Atitlán where Pat had a house, a varied group of American writers, painters, tourists, residents—a supportive, gossipy, heavy-drinking community that saw one another at parties, in the marketplaces, and at restaurants. Though more Pat's friends than Gore's, they were an active part of his quiet but still necessary social world. Not that he would have liked it noisier, but he was all too soon becoming uncomfortably aware of the limitations of Antigua. Full of intellectual energy, he found few people he could talk with about subjects that interested him. Local gossip and conversation with boozy expatriates only went so far. "There are some intelligent people: an elderly witty de Charlus French Count, a Socialist President of Congress etc etc but nothing more meaningful than good company." Work preoccupied him, obsessed him. But he still wanted more stimulating company and activities than Antigua provided. Movies, theaters, concerts—there was almost none of that. Landscape and weather were proving not to be theater enough.

Restless, he flew to New York in early April. Staying at his father's apartment, he had in hand now most of the reviews of *In a Yellow Wood*, a batch of which he sent down to the Gores in Washington, who impatiently awaited his visit. The Senator had become preoccupied with the practical details of his grandson establishing a political career in New Mexico, a subject that Gore had evaded by his flight to Guatemala and which seemed even less likely now with the imminent publication of *City*. The Senator, who knew little about the potentially disqualifying novel, spun his clever political webs, sketching out the strategy that would have Gore a presidential elector in 1948, then a congressman or senator, then (though never explicitly stated) President. By the end of the month Gore was on his way back to Antigua via New Orleans, where he paused for a brief visit. Anaïs suddenly appeared, on her way to California on a two-month-long car trip with her newest lover, a handsome twenty-eight-year-old recently divorced Californian, Rupert Poole, who desired to put Anaïs more in touch with the mystical earth, "a better balance between body and spirit." Neither artistic nor intellectual, Poole lacked a profession, even an avocation. In a 1941 Model A Ford roadster they chugged into New Orleans. Anaïs introduced the two men, who got along quite casually and comfortably. Gore took them to meet a painter friend of his, Olive Leonhardt, who had done a surrealistic portrait of Anaïs, though they had never met. After hesitations and reservations, Nin was eventually to commit herself to a bigamous marriage to Poole, whom she loved. At the same time she remained married to Hugh Guiler, maintaining, at great cost, separate East and West Coast lives. When she soon wrote to Gore in terms that indicated her genuine passion for Rupert, he urged her to seize the opportunity for the fulfillment she had always been pursuing.

Completing the revisions of *Season* in Antigua in May 1947, Gore looked forward to a summer of work and relaxation. Dot and the Senator, eager to visit their favorite grandson, made plans to travel to Guatemala by boat from New Orleans at the beginning of September. July and August they expected to spend in Florida (where they would visit the Senator's brother, Dixie), Oklahoma, Texas, and New Mexico, and return to Santa Fe in late September or early October, perhaps with Gore. The Senator still hoped his grandson would follow his advice and establish himself in New Mexico. The Gores never got to Guatemala, their grandson never got to New Mexico. In Oklahoma, Mrs. Gore, widely recognized in her circle as perhaps the worst driver in the United States, slammed into the back of a truck, hurting them both seriously, but especially the Senator, who spent months in St. Anthony's Hospital in Oklahoma City. The event eerily replicated an automobile accident, after which they had been reported to have been killed, when Gore was at St. Albans. Soon after his return to Antigua, his father wrote to him about a visit to Washington, where he had had dinner with his former in-laws and seen Nina. "The Gores seemed well but Nina seemed at her worst. I barely know her anymore. I hope that the change is due to a hangover." It hardly made her son feel regretful about his depiction of her in *Season*. But he had other reasons for discomfort, an uneasiness, an anxiety, a depression that seemed to have settled on him and which he could not readily shake. "Remember," his father wrote to him, "the more unusual the person the more serious ups and downs he has. You were about due for a temporary one." His savings-account balance was being depleted faster than he had anticipated, mostly because of the cost of the house. When Gore morosely complained about his dwindling money, Gene characterized his son's letter as "rather sad" but sharply asserted that "it is difficult for me . . . to feel sorry for anyone under forty years of age who is healthy." Eager to do a little complaining of his own, he responded to Gore's comment that his "house [in Guatemala] was handsome, living was cheap and the weather serene," "we have a lousy but comfortable house [in East Hampton], living is shockingly expensive, and the weather has been the worst in many years."

The response had no effect in taking Gore's mind off his own dissatisfactions, among them the scheduled publication of *City* in January 1948. It was not an unmixed blessing. He resented that two other novels on the same topic were appearing, to some extent stealing his thunder, as he had worried might happen. He also feared adverse responses. Some might connect the topic and the life of the author. He had done his best to make the novel as objective, even as clinical, as possible. It would be unreasonable, though, not to expect the connection to be made. That he would not have the stage entirely to himself seemed Dutton's fault. He blamed them for the delay. In early June he was the beneficiary of another mixed blessing. *Life* magazine ran a visually impressive photo article titled "Young U.S. Writers: A Refreshing Group of Newcomers on the Literary Scene Is Ready to Tackle Almost Anything." Three quarters of the first page consisted of an attractive photograph of the youthful Truman Capote, elegantly dressed, cigarette in hand, seated casually but dramatically in an artfully arranged portion of a prebellum Southern living room. Then followed two pages with modest-size photos of Jean Stafford, Thomas Heggen, Calder Willingham, and Elizabeth Fenwick, then two pages of mostly text on the second of which appeared three small photographs, one of them an awkward depiction of "Gore Vidal, 21, [who] writes poetry and Hemingwayesque fiction. He was in the Aleutians, now lives in Guatemala." In the text the smaller half of a paragraph said some obvious and uninteresting things about him. Since the article was mostly its visuals, anyone with no special interest in the other writers would be likely to remember only the very large eye-catching photo of the "onn-font-tarribul" who, for reasons Gore could only imagine and perhaps fulminate obsessively about, had been given undivided star billing. It would have been even worse if he had not been included at all, but "how absurd to feature Capote—instead of you," Anaïs loyally wrote to him.

In a short while he began to feel ill, a low-grade feverish discomfort with assorted aches and some listlessness. His stomach bothered him. Perhaps, he thought, he had a spastic colon. Having finished *The Season of Comfort,* he speculated with a kind of bilious good humor, that so much imaginative exposure to Nina had made him feel sick. Working in the garden or in the back room, he began to fiddle in a desultory way with some early jottings for the book on King Richard's troubadour. In a while he felt better but still not quite right. Anaïs, who had already crossed the country twice since they had last seen one another in New Orleans, was now in Acapulco, close to the Guatemalan border, a short plane trip or a day's bus ride from Guatemala City. Still unresolved about whether she would stay with Rupert in California or Hugh in New York or neither, she accepted, in July, Gore's long-standing invitation to visit him in Antigua. Though they were still closely intertwined, there was now a distance between them others could sense, an almost antierotic aura. But the emotional alliance was strong. When Anaïs, broke, had become pregnant in June, probably by Poole, Gore sent her $1,000 to pay for an abortion, insisting she keep the leftover money for travel expenses to Guatemala. "I should like it if you can come down here and spend July or earlier whenever you've recovered." On the one hand, she liked the idea. "Maybe when I come down you'll get a little second hand car and I will drive you around everywhere. It gives such freedom." On the other, on the assumption he was happy in Guatemala, she stressed that "the less we are together the better for both of us . . . for it will help you find THE relationship—someday." She then decided to go to France instead, which seemed a good idea to him. "We will always have each other, and continuity in our bond." Anaïs insisted, "but at the present moment I could not stay at peace anywhere, and would not make you happy. I have only a short time to find a permanent passion—and my quest must continue. As you know, sex is not just sex for me, but the sun, moon, earth, sea, and salt of life, the impetus to creation—the only form of life for me. . . . Our bond has no need of the physical presence except now and then." Bored with Antigua, somewhat ill, he flirted with the idea of going with her. When her European plans fell through because of money, she decided to go to Mexico. "Perhaps if you're tired of Guatemala you might like to meet me there," she wrote to him. "If you still feel lonely and need me or don't sell the house and don't want novelty I will fly to Guatemala for a few days. . . . Cheri, I love to be with you, you know that, but under ideal conditions for both of us, which means Romance [with others]." She had another idea. "We could meet in Mexico City for excitement, and . . . I can present you with a blond boy 20. . . . We don't like each other physically (we tried!) but he wants to drive me around devotedly and he is h.s. and I'm sure would love you."

Anaïs loved the Antigua house, the marketplace, the town itself, the magnificent scenery. With her usual flair, she dressed attractively in colorful combinations of Greenwich Village and Guatemalan styles. She wore open sandals, braided her hair with "pink and green and orange yarn." In the eyes of one American visitor, she was still in love with Gore. They managed in the house quite nicely, with Pat, with two servants, with meals of delicious shrimp paella and dinners at the homes of Gore's Antigua friends. In the hot summer weather they swam in his neighbors' pools. He took her on excursions to the top of one of the nearby volcanoes and to Lake Atitlán. One day, walking alone along one of Guatemala City's main streets, he turned in response to a voice that said, "Gore!" It was Andres Devendorf, his East Hampton friend, accompanied by a friend of his, Dominick Dunne. Between their junior and senior years at college they had come to Guatemala City ostensibly to study Spanish, mostly to get away from home and have an adventure. Gore immediately invited them to visit him in Antigua. Though he was not at his best with the visitors, Anaïs was, delighted to have companions. Devendorf and Dunne immediately quit their Spanish classes and came regularly to Antigua. Much of the day Gore kept to his study, trying to make progress with *A Search for the King*. But he still did not feel well. He had a recollection of having eaten something weeks before that seemed viscerally related to his sense of being ill, though he could not make any direct connection. Nonetheless he managed to be hospitable to both young men, whom he liked. A short, bright-eyed, somewhat innocent youth of twenty-two from a well-to-do Connecticut family, Dunne had served admirably in the Army and been awarded the Bronze Star for bravery in the Battle of the Bulge, what he later remembered as one of the proudest achievements of his life. "I was this shy, sissy, stuttering, hopeless kid, in my family hopeless, in the Army hopeless." But he had saved some fellow soldiers' lives. Eager for the company of talented, successful people, he had the immediate sense that Anaïs was a famous person simply by her bearing, her attitude. Gore, he knew, was already famous. An avid reader, Dunne admired *Williwaw*, envied the publicity surrounding its publication, wondered what he might do to become famous also. In Antigua, Dunne had his "first view of people I always knew I was going to be with, artistic, bohemian, rich people. They weren't only society people going to parties. They were people who seemed to be writing books or painting pictures or doing something artistic also. But they all seemed to be comfortably incomed. One way or another I was going to be a part of that world." He liked Pat, who was funny. "He was hilarious, in fact, and he was kind of campy in wit."

Gore graciously included the visitors in his social activities. Dunne noticed that here was someone of his own age who owned a beautiful house, ran it with servants in an orderly, grown-up way, knew everyone of interest around, and had a manner that seemed totally self-possessed. "He'd already finished *The City and the Pillar*, and I had inside knowledge of it and bragged about it later. I was aware of it and of the topic of it and Anaïs had read it. . . . She talked about it. We were there to have fun. We were just kids. On top of which, Gore had attitude. . . . That's what gives famous people this thing so that when they walk into a room you look." Not everyone always found the attitude attractive, but that was not the point. It was a phenomenon, a projection of energy, of self-regard, of presence. One had it or one did not. Mesmerized by Anaïs, who found it pleasurable to hypnotize him, Dunne had long talks with her, enchanted by her exotic sophistication, her foreign beauty, her glamorous stories. "I didn't even know who Henry Miller was, and she was talking about Henry Miller. She seemed to know everyone. I was just riveted by her. It's like she knew every moment that the camera was on her. If she caught you—and she knew she had got me—she played the part." Flattered that she seemed to prefer him to the handsomer Andres, Dunne was infatuated. Busy in his studio, slightly ill, Gore took no notice. On a hot night they "took a plunge in somebody's swimming pool. . . . We didn't have clothes on, but there was nothing improper about it," Dunne recalled. "I swam over her. She was doing the backstroke and I was doing the breaststroke. And it was sort of sexy." As usual, Anaïs had found "romance." When she left to return to Acapulco, Nick and Andres followed. "Things clearly had gone sour between her and Gore . . . and she left and I went with her. And Andres went with us. I wanted to go with her. Not that this was some great romance. We had a little fuckette for nine days or so, and then she left me for a kid younger than me," a Mexican beachboy.

Still feeling unwell, Gore nevertheless joined Anaïs in Acapulco, unaware that Nick, who had left to return to Williams, had even been there. Anaïs had urged him to come to the seashore, where they both thought he might recover from whatever had been making him sick. On his way he stopped in Guatemala City to say good-bye to Olga Vasquez Bruni, who noticed how unwell he looked. When he arrived in Acapulco in the late-summer heat, his face was yellow from jaundice. That night at dinner he ate "oily chicken served in half a coconut full of nauseous yellow cream." As he collapsed with fever and nausea, he wretched from his memory that about six weeks before he had eaten something equally dangerous from a large cauldron in the Antigua marketplace. It now seemed inseparable from the indefinable ill feeling he had been having for so long. Unable to do anything but stay in bed, he read the only book he had with him, a volume of Blake's poems. Thereafter he always associated Blake with insufferable heat and "longed-for death." He had never before felt so physically miserable. "A Swiss doctor fed me charcoal and corn flakes. The diagnosis was hepatitis A. . . . They didn't know what to do in those days." Between her visits to the beach Anaïs nursed him, though for a short while she (and the doctor) thought that nothing would save him. Within two weeks he lost thirty pounds. Gradually, with medical attention and rest, he began to get better. When well enough to travel, he and Anaïs went to Mexico City, partly because it was on his route back to the United States, partly to consult with a specialist who told him his blood tests showed that he had had hepatitis for some time, that he had been suffering from it through much of the summer in Antigua, and that he had had an acute attack when he had arrived in Acapulco. He was lucky to be alive.

CHAPTER EIGHT

The Golden Age

1947–1948

SUDDENLY HIS LIFE took an unexpected leap into passion. In late summer 1947 he was recuperating at East Hampton. The hepatitis had gradually disappeared. As his appetite returned, he began to reclaim some of the lost thirty pounds. Morose and unfocused, he was happy to have Anaïs at a distance. Over the last year, in Guatemala and New York, he had complained that his life lacked a grand romance, while at the same time he had strong reservations about the value in general of any kind of "romance" at all. Whether he wanted or felt capable of an affair with anyone was a consideration. "Have you the temperament to secure and hold a lover?" a friend had asked him the previous winter. The answer had been the same as it had been to Anaïs. But he now gave a different response to twenty-two-year-old Harold Lang, the California-born ballet and musical-comedy dancer, famous for his pirouettes on- and offstage. "We met," Vidal wrote in an unpublished 1947 short story, in "a wood-walled bar in the beach town, the bar where the people in the summer theater gathered." Lang was performing in *Look, Ma, I'm Dancing,* one of his many musical-comedy roles, as he alternated between the Ballet Theatre (later renamed the American Ballet Theatre) and Broadway musicals, a lead dancer in the movement that narrowed the gap between classical ballet and American popular-theatrical dance. "Harold was a magnificent dancer," a balletomane recalled. "He wasn't a perfect dancer. But he was witty, and vivid, and so intelligent onstage. He didn't have a beautiful body, but a handsome one." With a throaty, effective singing voice, Lang reached musical-comedy stardom in *Kiss Me, Kate* in 1948 and in the long-running 1952 revival of *Pal Joey*. His first great success had been in Jerome Robbins and Leonard Bernstein's *Fancy Free* in 1944, the ballet soon transformed into the musical *On the Town*. At East Hampton that summer Lang was having sex with the male author *and* the female lead of *Look, Ma*. His friend Joe O'Donohue, a high-society habituée of Manhattan nightlife and later a friend of Gore's, recalled that "Harold and I used to go off on the town. I took him to nightclubs and especially to Harlem. Harold and I had sex together, but it was a casual thing. Harold was very easy about that sort of thing." Sometimes mooningly romantic, often promiscuously unstable, Lang ranged from carefree to compulsive. Notoriously randy and random, he had affairs, usually brief, with both sexes. As much a sexual athlete as a ballet dancer, to the young Gore Vidal he "was just extraordinary to be with. . . . It was really the sexual life force. I've never seen anything like it and never saw anything like it again. . . . It was 'the greatest ass in history,' as Bernstein said, and Lenny was a true authority."

After their first flirtation in the bar, Gore went to watch Harold at rehearsal. Dark-haired, a few inches shorter than Gore, with whitish-blue eyes, a trimly muscular body, lithe strong thighs, a boyish face, and roguishly attractive smile, Harold had wonderful elevation as a dancer and riveting stage presence. Gore himself had become a minor balletomane the previous winter and spring. At the Chafee Dance Studio he had enjoyed his own restricted athleticism, therapy for his rheumatoid arthritis. Hanging around Manhattan bars frequented by dance people, he met numbers of young dancers, began to attend performances, particularly of the Ballet Theatre, and met its director of public relations, Sam Lurie. After a few more nights at the same East Hampton bar, they left together and cycled to the dancer's boardinghouse. Lang invited Gore up to see his room. "It began then." That first night Lang was the pursuer, Gore emotionally reserved, hesitant. The next day they argued. "I wasn't capable of an affair, he thought. . . . I seemed so much like so many other people he knew. I couldn't answer him. If he couldn't see how different I was. . . . Then, as suddenly as before, just when I was about to leave, he said, 'Let's go to bed'; that was the way the loving started." As Gore's fictional surrogate confessed, "I had never known anything like this and in the dark he whispered to me, don't louse me up; and then I loved him and, since he was afraid of me, I removed all my armor to show that I was the one vulnerable, that he was safe. I knew that night of something he needed that I couldn't give, and that gave me anxiety. . . . But now I was loving for the first time and everything was new." For the first time he was actually making love with the intent to give as well as get pleasure. It was a new experience. Unfortunately, it was soon less than idyllic. Lang was moody, erratic. After that first week at East Hampton, he put Gore off with the story that he had an ex-lover staying with him, from whom he was in the process of trying to extricate himself. Each day at the beach, Harold mostly absent, Gore diverted himself with Ethel Merman, the Broadway star with the stentorian singing voice "who was quite intrigued with the idea of her voice resounding in a monastery. She has," he wrote to Pat Crocker, "very likely, the worst figure of any woman in the world but she is amusing and loves to discuss things in terms of male genitalia. We got on quite well and she can't wait to read the C and P. 'Don't read much but love books about homos,' " she said.

Eager for a holiday and a retreat, Harold suggested they take a trip together, preferably out of the country, when Look, Ma, I'm Dancing closed. Soon after Labor Day they flew to Bermuda. All was well again. They lounged together in the sun, enjoying the stillness, listening to the waves, swimming in the reef-protected bay. Lang decorated their attractive four-room cottage, inexpensive in the off-season, with large pink hibiscus flowers. At night they gazed at a star-white sky. On bicycles they enjoyed pedaling up and down hills to the nearby village, where they watched ships coming into the harbor, enjoyed the sunsets, and went to the movies. To help pay for the trip Gore wrote a brief, perfunctory travel article about Bermuda, which he hoped Town & Country would take, though the editor soon responded that it is "a bit dry and stereotyped for us." Lang, who sometimes drank too much, kept away from the bars for the first week. "We stayed at home and read, played cards, made love, and tried to talk to one another, but he thought I was bored, and I knew he didn't understand what I said to him." Great gossips, they talked about the few people they both knew. Beyond that there were vast gaps. Tension developed. Insecure even as an entertainer, Lang felt disappointed in himself and in his insufficiently responsive one-person audience. "One night he decided he was going to drink. . . . After that, every evening, there was a tug-of-war; should we go into town and go to a bar or not. I never wanted to. . . . And then one day everything went wrong: he decided he didn't want any more sex for a while; I didn't satisfy him. He didn't want to talk about this; he didn't want to talk about anything, only to repeat the jokes, the chatter of the theater world. . . . The nights were more terrible for I slept beside him and could not have him. I knew he hated making someone else happy, and I could understand this since I was the same way but not with him. . . . Finally, one morning, I took him against his will and he was angry and hurt. We fought and I was ready to fly back. . . . He asked me to get him an analyst when we got back, he felt that he would go to pieces soon. He'd never believed in analysis but now he'd try anything."

In New York they lived together for the next month at the Chelsea Hotel. For a moment Gore enjoyed the hope they might go to Europe together in the late winter. Bursting with enthusiasm, he came into Judith Jones's office at Doubleday. Having left Dutton for what she thought a more literary house, she hoped to lure Gore to their list for his next novel. "Though I shared the office, I was alone in the small room. And he said, 'I've fallen in love.' I thought it was with a girl. 'And I'm going to Italy with *him.*' I said, *'Yes?'* It was someone in the ballet. He was just— I mean I've never seen him that way. Just dancing in seventh heaven, like a guy in love." "My life is completely governed these days by my grande affaire," he wrote to Pat Crocker, "and the grande affaire opens on Broadway [in *Kiss Me, Kate*] in Jan. I've gotten so sick of theatre people that I could shriek and that might be a good excuse to come back to Guatemala." The history of the affair could be reduced to a few sentences. At East Hampton "I fell madly in love with an unfortunately too famous and too desirable dancer and musical comedy star; we dashed off to Bermuda together for September, came back, went through some mutual scenes of hysteria a la Max and, at the moment, are living uneasily together in the Chelsea Hotel while he rehearses and I work on my fifth book and, believe it or not, take four hours of ballet training a day. What will happen to me if I fall in love with a doctor I don't know: eight years of medicine I guess."

Harold went twice a week to a midtown therapist, "Jules Nydes, M.A.,

Consulting Psychologist." Always hesitant about psychiatry for himself, Gore had reluctantly gone the previous year to Anaïs's analyst for a few sessions, an unhappy experience. He worried that analysis would undermine his creativity. Bored with her psychological jargon and her faith in its powers, he had gone mostly to placate her, partly because he recognized his moodiness, felt his depressions, knew indeed that he harbored immense anger against Nina. When the analyst had asked him probing questions, Gore had responded, "Don't be impertinent!" After a few tense sessions they had parted, the analyst's final riposte, "You think your shit is better than other people's shit." Nina herself, sneeringly hostile when drunk, had off and on urged him to get professional help. Years before, prompted by her friend Sherry Davis, she had had young Gene examined by a psychologist who had concluded that there were no grounds for concern. With the publication of *City*, Nina was forced to see things in a different light. But whatever her mood of the moment about Gore's sex life and his male friends, she shared the widespread conviction that homosexuals were sick creatures. If only Gore would shape up, would set his mind to it, he could be perfectly normal. Homosexuality was curable by psychotherapy, so the 1952 *Diagnostic and Statistical Manual of Mental Disorders* claimed, and large numbers of young men with doubts about their sexuality sat in analysts' waiting rooms. A devotee of Freud, Anaïs also believed that Gore needed professional help: homosexuality was arrested development. From his point of view, whatever his problems, they had nothing to do with sexual inclinations and practices. Sometimes with cold logic, other times with angry rhetoric, he signaled how sensitive he was to the subject. He especially resented that what he did not feel as a problem others condemned as either vice or illness. In Harold's case he urged and arranged therapy not because of Harold's sexuality but because his irrational behavior threatened their relationship. Desperate, for the moment he was willing to try it himself.

In early October Harold suddenly disappeared from the Chelsea Hotel and, apparently, from New York. He left no message, no note of explanation, no forwarding address. Angry, hurt, Gore tried to find him. Making an appointment with Lang's therapist, he sat through an awkward session, hoping he could get Nydes to tell him Harold's whereabouts. Having guessed why Gore was there, Nydes told him nothing. He returned for one more session. Soon, though, he located someone who reported that the dancer had gone to San Francisco to visit his mother. What to do? He decided to write to him there. "My dear Harold-—I suppose that you're with your mother since someone said you'd gone to California. I hope you plan to continue the analysis; I haven't talked to your analyst since that's unethical but I gather . . . that all was going fairly well. As I told you in my letter I'm going to another [therapist] . . . and I seem to be getting a grip on myself; as you might have guessed I was quite upset over not having heard from you even though I understood why you were scurrying about. Analysis is quite a frightening experience. I think we've both reached a similar impasse when our careers don't give the same satisfaction, the same forget-fulness as they once did; it's not a pleasant thing to see oneself but it must be faced sometimes. I think this is the right moment for you; I know it is for me. I hope you go on with it." The letter was never sent. When Harold returned from California, he focused on rehearsals for the January opening of *Kiss Me, Kate* and resumed a sex life he had hardly repressed during his six weeks or so with Gore. "He was a star on Broadway in *Pal Joey*, and at least three times he was arrested in men's rooms on his way to the matinee," Gore remarked. "They had to hold the curtain while the police let him go, and if the police didn't let him go, his understudy would go on. Now, that's madness. And I'm aware of all this, that he's so compulsive, so crazed. He was wrecking his career. I don't think I was being entirely self-centered. What I was saying to Harold is that knowing what I know about you, it's a very good idea that you go through analysis or something, because some-thing terrible is going to happen within three or four years. It did." Gore's own halting experiment with analysis abruptly ended. So too had his grand passion, though not quite as abruptly. While hoping that Lang might return to him, he began writing a play that reflected his feelings of loss. "But I find the theme of elusiveness a little too personal and poignant at the moment to write about. I must wait until I'm settled; until I've heard from you. My feelings about you are unchanged; from now on it's up to you to preserve this: if you want it. . . . I wish you'd write me."

There was a reconciliation, though it did not last long. "I seem sub-merged in the dance world," Gore wrote to Pat Crocker. He had met two more ballet dancers, Leon Danielian and Johnny Kriza, well-known young performers both of whom soon became his friends: Danielian a premiere member of the Ballet Russe de Monte Carlo, Kriza best known for his title performance in the Ballet Theatre's production of Aaron Copland's *Billy the Kid*. By the beginning of the new year "the dancer affair" had come "to a painful end and I now have a new lover," probably Johnny Kriza, "very pleasant, very cozy." Convenient, companionable sex, it had none of the romantic intensity of his affair with Lang. *The City and the Pillar* was about to be published, scheduled for January 9. Europe, as always, was much on his mind, though no longer with Harold as his sailing companion. In the late fall Prokosch, from Capri, urged Gore to come to Italy. At first he thought he would go to Guatemala about the middle of February. Since his house in Antigua had been rented, he proposed to Crocker that he stay with him for a month at his house on the lake "on the usual sharing basis: this includes marimba workers etc." But the idea of Guatemala again soon seemed less and less appealing. By mid-January 1948 he had made up his mind to go to Rome.

Almost one year before, while Gore was still in Antigua, Prokosch, having decided to live permanently in Europe, had written him that "I very much want you to meet John Kelly, who is an old Yale and Cambridge and Istanbul friend of mine. . . . Write to me . . . and tell me all the dirt about Guatemala—more sex details, less architectural." In spring 1947 Gore went to Cismont, near Charlottesville, Virginia, to visit Kelly, whom he had recently met in New York, the first of numbers of visits and the start of a friendship to last until Kelly's death in 1966. In his mid-thirties, pudgy, dark-haired, an alcoholic who passionately loved the opera and ballet, Kelly had offered numbers of times that spring to help Gore give "romance" a try. Through Kelly, Vidal met Bob Giroux, Kelly's friend and his editor at Harcourt, Brace, which was about to publish Kelly's novel, *All Soul's Night*. At Cambridge, Kelly, who had been born in New Jersey in 1913, had studied economics with John Maynard Keynes. A well-read, cultured, witty man with a passion for music and for Times Square sex, Kelly, who was "wildly funny," Gore later recalled, and had "sad, velvety eyes," alternated his New York activities with his life as a Virginia country squire. "John was a romantic, a male Anaïs Nin," Gore recalled, "without being as dumb as she was. A romantic Irish tenor who knew everything in the world about music and a rather good writer, very literary. And very good company till he would try to be romantic. He was easily held off." Kelly was married to Betty Wagner, a wealthy woman from Staten Island, whose family was the source of his money. Their mansion, Cross Meadows, and the land in

Cismont came from Betty's mother, who had moved there. Kelly had met Betty in Virginia and married her at her mother's home, which later became his. Actually there were no horses or livestock at the Kellys'. They were, though, in the midst of genteel, high-toned horse country and good friends with many of the local squires. Life at Cismont had English country rhythms: horse training and hunting clubs dominated. When Giroux visited, Kelly would insist he go to the club with him. " 'But I don't hunt!' It didn't matter. They'd all go and, like everyone else, drink so much they couldn't get on a horse anyway."

Admiring and affectionate, Gore found Kelly companionable. His visits to Cismont were restful, even when Kelly made advances, as he did periodically. Gore would say no, and Kelly would drink more and then usually pass out on the floor, where he would sleep for hours. At Cismont he played Wagner and Verdi incessantly. In New York, in a tuxedo, with Giroux or others, he would appear for almost every performance at the Metropolitan Opera House. That his propositions were bumbling, his soul romantic, his epistolary style engaging, added to his charm. "Having spent, it appears, a lifetime with you, the separation is becoming acute," he wrote after Gore's first visit. "Will you come for a week-end?" He was also a master of romantic melancholy. "You make me sad, because I want to be with you and I am not. Such feelings alarm me. I cannot bear to think that I am anywhere other than according to my desire." Thoroughly in love, he nominated himself, through much of 1947, to satisfy Gore's often-expressed thought that he needed a lover. His comments on Gore's complaints were often humorous. "What do you mean by 'intermittent sex'? Do you mean that you have sexual intercourse at irregular intervals, or that the intercourse itself is subject to interruptions? If you find it impossible to communicate on this subject, send me a picture. . . . I hear my wife coming up the drive, which means lunch, so I shall close in the midst of deep thoughts about you, dear Gore, and in the hope that I shall hear immediately. . . . You do not always say 'no.' I remember that you sometimes write something that looks like, Yes." The "yes" was to confidences, not intimacies.

So too with Dan Wickenden and Cornelia Claiborne. Gore had continued his friendships with both when he returned from Guatemala in late summer 1947. At home in Westport, Connecticut, assiduously at work on his latest novel, Wickenden saw Gore only a few times in New York. But they continued the correspondence about themselves as novelists that they had begun when Wickenden had left Guatemala. Genially but aggressively, Wickenden attacked his friendly rival. Mostly Gore defended his work, particularly *In a Yellow Wood* and *The City and the Pillar,* both of which Wickenden thought enervated. Wickenden set out at length what he thought were the weaknesses of Vidal's novels and Vidal's view of the novel as a literary form, in constant unfavorable contrast to himself and his own vision of the novel as bourgeois upbeat epic on the level of entertainment in which fullness, vigor, raw life were everything. His own novels were stabs in that direction, with the merit of energy rather than art. When he began a chapter, he rarely knew where it would end. Vidal's novels seemed to him too controlled, too intellectually programmatic, too unlike his own. Rising to the challenge, Vidal defended himself, though not at as great length as Wickenden attacked. His counterattacks, equally self-defensive, did not fully conceal an underlying disquiet, not about his bleak themes but about his flat tightness of tone and language. At work on *A Search for the King,* he hoped for more resonance. The imminent publication of *City* was much on his mind. Wickenden did not in the least disapprove of its subject matter. In fact, he admired that aspect of the novel and anticipated that it might be a great success.

By this time Cornelia, whether she had read *City* in manuscript or not, had fully realized that Gore's sexual inclinations would keep them, at best, friends and social companions. "I don't need to write to you of my heart because you are always there, but you never answer," she told him in fall 1947. Aware of his involvement with Anaïs, she felt baffled about the nature of the attraction and assumed it had to be sexual. But she could not quite see what Gore saw in Anaïs, or so she told him. Actually, by the time she was aware of it as a relationship, it was already mostly over. Gore himself, though, kept Cornelia's attention. His combination of self-involvement and talent impressed and baffled her. "You have a Christ complex, an Oedipus complex, a Hitler complex, and a complex complex. There really isn't anything wrong with you at all if you could forget about all these complexes." But she had become quite certain she was not "capable of making [him] stop being wretched . . . so there isn't really much point in trying." But she believed in his powers, his talents. "You can be a great writer and a great man. It's so unbelievable that anyone is capable of doing both [literature and politics] that you really should try it. . . . It would encourage humanity a great deal." Busy as managing editor of *The Hudson Review,*

Cornelia herself continued to be intensely literary—editing, writing poetry, wondering where her situation and talents would take her.

Still optimistic that the subject of *City* would not be held against him, in autumn 1947 Gore applied for a Guggenheim Fellowship for 1948. The project was his novel in progress, *A Search for the King*. The success of *Williwaw* and *In a Yellow Wood* might make him an attractive candidate. Whom to ask for recommendations? Since Orville Prescott had reviewed *Williwaw* favorably in the *New York Times*, Gore thought it reasonable to ask him. Prescott said yes, though apparently Gore did not read sharply enough between the lines of his assent. "I would be glad to serve as a literary reference to you in your application for a Guggenheim Fellowship, providing that my having read your first book qualifies me. Unfortunately, I did not get around to *In a Yellow Wood*. . . . By the way, could it be possible that you are writing too quickly? It seems to me that your rate of output is amazing. But then, everyone has to perform his own job of work in his own way." Gore soon learned that Capote had also applied. Whatever his own chances, he was happy not to be dependent on any support other than his savings and his writing. He hoped that his royalties would make viable his determination to devote himself fully to writing. By early December 1947, before the recommendations were due, advance copies of *City* became available. Prescott, who a few months later felt such moral outrage that he declined to review it, may have known enough about it from word-of-mouth or his own reading for it to have influenced his letter of recommendation. Wreden wrote a smashingly laudatory letter. So too did Nathan Rothman, who had praised *In a Yellow Wood* in *The Saturday Review of Literature*, and Bob Giroux, who recommended Gore "in the highest terms." But Prescott damned him with less-than-faint praise. "I do not know enough about Mr. Vidal to feel justified in urging his project upon you. An historical novel about Richard I and Blondel seems to me so conventional and even popular a literary project that it might well take its chances with others of its type. So, I can only say that I know Mr. Vidal to be a gifted young man and to suggest that his need for a scholarship and your own opinion of the merit of his work in progress should be the deciding factor." It was a killing letter, against the ethical grain of the widely accepted understanding that if one cannot write a good recommendation one should decline to write at all. Gore did not get the fellowship. Neither did Capote. "Shocked, we compared notes. Studied the list of those who had received grants. 'Will you just look,' moaned Truman, 'at those *ahh*-full pee-pull they keep giving *muh*-nee to!' " A promising young writer, E. Howard Hunt, to become infamous decades later in the Watergate investigations, received a Guggenheim Fellowship that year.

———•———

Once he had decided to sail for Europe in mid-February, Gore's spirits lightened. New York sparkled a bit more brightly in his restless eye. Johnny Kriza provided pleasure, the usual erotic release. Nina, intermittently, got on his nerves. The previous summer she had dried out at Silver Hill, in Connecticut, an expensive retreat for alcoholics, her mind partly on elaborate schemes for becoming a leading figure in creating support systems for alcoholics, partly on legal procedures to get additional money from Auchincloss. Anaïs pulled strings to arrange lectures at college campuses, the most prominent at Harvard at the beginning of January. Soon she was off to California. Parties were still a staple of Gore's New York activities. He went to one "for Cecil Beaton and found him dull. Had dinner with Glenway Wescott who is charming." Eager to meet the much-admired novelist Christopher Isherwood, who he hoped would like *The City and the Pillar,* he was disappointed to learn he had been out of town when Isherwood had passed through. "He is now touring South America with his love, a boy photographer." He sent Isherwood, as he sent others, including Thomas Mann, advance copies, with handwritten notes and inscriptions. Worried its reception might not be entirely positive, he tried to get endorsements that could be used as blurbs or in follow-up advertisements to help counter negative reviews.

In January 1948, at the home of the writer Glenway Wescott's sister, Gore met John Horne Burns, whose successful war novel, *The Gallery,* he admired a great deal more than he did the thirty-one-year-old Burns himself, "a difficult man who drank too much, loved music, detested all other writers, and wanted to be great." He seemed monstrous, envious, bitchy, drunk. With "a receding hairline above a face striking in its asymmetry, one ear flat against the head, the other stuck out," Burns was "certain that to be a good writer it was necessary to be homosexual. When I disagreed he named a half dozen celebrated contemporaries, 'A pleiad,' he roared delightedly, 'of pederasts!' But what about Faulkner, I asked, and Hemingway. He was disdainful. Who said *they* were any good? And besides, hadn't I heard how Hemingway once. . . ." A harbinger of Italian delights, Burns extolled the attractions of Italian boys, whom he called *topolini*. Gore thereafter referred to them as "mice." The word itself seemed to bring Italian pleasures closer.

Hollywood, another exotic landscape, had been on his mind during much of 1947, and still had importance to him even as he prepared for his departure for Europe. Numbers of talented writers, including Isherwood, had found sustenance writing screenplays for the movies. It had occurred to Gore early on that he might supplement his novel-writing income or even if necessary earn his living in Los Angeles. The occasion when he had overheard two scriptwriters working beside the pool at the Beverly Hills Hotel stuck in his memory. That his mother was good friends with Doris and Jules Stein could be a help. Before leaving for New Orleans in late summer 1946, he had sent some of the good reviews of *Williwaw* to Felix Ferry, Nina's Beverly Hills friend, an agent with Famous Artists Corporation, whom he had met the previous spring. Perhaps a studio might be interested in optioning *Williwaw* and/or contracting with its author to write scripts. A year later, from Antigua, he had assured the desperate Anaïs that "if I get a Hollywood job then there will be a great deal of money. Think about this for I am serious." He hoped something could be arranged through a contact at Columbia Studios. Toward the end of 1947 Ferry encouraged the neophyte to provide a story idea that Ferry might try to sell. "A short to the point story with a not too extensive background is one of the most welcome commodities in Hollywood today. Have you any in mind which might do? If so, please put it on four or five pages which would be quite enough to sell the idea, especially when it is as beautifully written as your works are. Then there would be a chance to see you with it and have you come out here to enjoy a little of this season's sunshine."

———————

The beginning of the new year in New York had its own brightness. Finally, on January 9, 1948, Dutton published *The City and the Pillar*. All at Dutton held their breath, having moved into what seemed perilous, uncharted waters by publishing a book that made an argument for the legitimization of sex between men. The Macraes were uncomfortable. Advance orders of 5,000 copies, though, were good enough for Wreden to hope it might be a bestseller. Word-of-mouth provided news of the novel's controversial subject. Vidal's reputation, as the author of *Williwaw* and as a well-publicized *"enfant terrible,"* helped stimulate bookstore interest. He had already pocketed his largest advance against royalties, $2,000, the final $1,000 on the day of publication, replenishing his bank account with enough to pay for much of his European trip. The well-known English publisher and editor John Lehmann, whom Gore was soon to meet, had contracted with Dutton for British rights. A number of foreign-language editions seemed likely. Wreden, though, still worried that his prize author would be damaged by the book's enemies. Fortunately, readers, despite mixed reviews and occasional sharp attacks, found the subject absorbing. Amanda Ellis, who had befriended Gore in Colorado Springs, came by for a visit, enthusiastic about her former protégé's success. From Lima, Peru, Christopher Isherwood responded to Vidal's letter with enthusiastic encouragement and permission to use his praise in advertisements, though he disapproved of *City*'s ending: it would encourage the widespread prejudice that homosexual relationships always ended miserably, a self-defensive comment echoed by a large number of homosexuals happy to see their sexuality taken seriously in fiction but distressed that society's impression that homosexuals all come to a bad end would be reinforced by Jim's murdering Bob Ford. Isherwood, it seemed to Vidal, preferred propaganda to artistic integrity. It was, though, the start of a friendship. "Thank you for what you say about my writing," Isherwood wrote to him. "That makes me very happy. . . . It's nice to be a stimulus—and especially to another writer. . . . And do please write. I love getting letters, and most of my friends seem to regard me as temporarily dead."

From his Pacific Palisades exile Thomas Mann thanked the young writer for his gift copy "with your personal inscription. Your novel, which has afforded me a noble entertainment, is a valuable addition to my English library. The interesting book has my most sincere wishes for the success it deserves." In his private diary Mann remarked on how much it had stirred the banked fires of his own past, how powerfully and personally he identified with the novel's subject. From California, Anaïs, to whom Gore had written announcing his bestsellerdom and offering her money, wrote back with congratulatory kindness, especially since she did not like the book and believed it contained a mean caricature of her. "Already I'd heard that you were *the* best seller! I'm happy because money *can* be magical when well used—I think it was sweet offering me some—I like your saying it even if I won't take advantage of it. . . . Cheri, I feel as exactly close to you as you to me and of the most durable quality. . . . You have won all your battles, you know— You have more power to love richly than any young man I know—you have physical beauty *and* charm *and* a heart *and* a gifted nature—I should know, who know you deeper— So be happy. . . . Our only enemy is doubt, lack of confidence— Have faith, have faith." From Rome, Prokosch, who passed his copy around among eager friends, urged Gore not to worry "in the *least* about the sex angle—it is obviously treated very cleanly and manfully." Come to Europe, he urged, delighted to learn at the end of the month that Gore was almost on his way.

First, though, the newspaper reviews, crucial to the book's sales, had to be absorbed, confronted, evaluated. It was not an easy and hardly a pleasant experience. Gore had worried about what the reaction might be, what effect it might have on his future. He had thought he had realistically assessed the risks, the parameters of response and their impact. Somewhat naïvely he had assumed that whatever the range of response, its effect would be brief, limited, and manageable. He had hoped for fame and fortune. Now all he could be sure of for the moment was notoriety. As the reviews came in, the Dutton publicity department created its usual excerpts for trade distribution and advertisements. The controversy was a publicist's delight. "Some rave about it," a Dutton advertisement heralded in bold print, quoting one word from the laudatory review in *The Atlantic Monthly:* "Brilliant"; "Some are shocked," quoting one word from the hostile review in the *Chicago Tribune,* "Disgusting—but it became a best seller." By mid-January *City* was "a bestseller in New York at the rate of 1,500 a week and should show on the bestseller lists in three weeks, thank God." Before publication Dutton had increased the first printing from 5,000 to 10,000 copies and the advertising budget, for a book that sold for $3.50, to $5,000, approximately the equivalent of $50,000 today. "The fan mail," Gore wrote to Pat Crocker, whose copy was avidly passed from hand to hand in their Guatemala circle, "has been amazing, but no enclosed pictures so far." On February 8 it was number fourteen on a national list of sixteen; by February 22 it had risen to number seven (Capote's *Other Voices, Other Rooms,* he noted, was number eleven on the same list). "The book sells merrily; it's now the #14 bestseller in the country. #2 in New York; #3 in Los Angeles;

#1 in San Francisco. . . . Tell Wickenden," who had returned to Guatemala, "that *The Atlantic Monthly* gave me a wonderful review. The rest have been quite awful."

To celebrate the ratings Wreden hosted at his Park Avenue apartment a dinner party for a number of his bestselling authors, including Cleveland Amory, whose *The Proper Bostonians* was on the nonfiction bestseller list. Kit and Gene walked over with Gore from the Vidals' apartment on Fifth Avenue. Gene queried Wreden about how the book business worked. "You know, it astonishes me in a country the size of the United States how few copies you can sell of anything," Gene remarked. "Of anything! I could make a celluloid napkin clip and sell more copies of it in the country tomorrow than you can sell of a book, and you have more means of publicity with a book than I would have with my celluloid napkin clip. But I would know how to sell it." Gore was lively, amusingly conversational. Mostly, though, the talk was about success, not about how small even bestseller sales were, and not about reviews.

The bad ones, though, were difficult to shake off. He did his best, writing to Pat Crocker that they were "flatteringly violent," essentially of two kinds, both more unrelentingly hostile than he had anticipated: the homophobic Middle American outrage—epitomized by review headlines such as "A Sordid Picture of the Male Species," "Tragedy of Perversion," and "Abnormal Doom"—and the attacks on the novel's artistry, most of which had an ummistakable moral underpinning, but a few of which, notably Leslie Fiedler's in *The Hudson Review*, found *City*'s failures to be entirely aesthetic. With great praise for the novel's honest embrace of "drabness" and for its effective dramatization of "seedy torment," Fiedler gave it the respect of serious literary criticism: "the book cannot even hold rigidly to the impersonality it proposes, the scarcely more than animal awareness of its athletic protagonist; there are, on the one hand, long artificial speeches diagnosing homosexuality and proposing Utopias for its free play, and there is, on the other hand, the suggested symbolism of the novel's name—an illegitimate device, proposing to supply with the five words of a title a dimension of symbolism that the book otherwise ignores." In brief, Fiedler argued, the novel's admirable sincerity had expressed itself in a flat naturalism that fell short of effective dramatic and symbolic representation. The problem was in the young writer's artistry, not his subject. It was a conclusion to which the author himself would give serious even if self-defensive attention. Gore, though, insisted on blaming Cornelia, as managing editor of *The Hudson Review*, for Fiedler's harsh review, an expression of his increasing anger at what he had begun to feel, after the publication of *City*, was a homophobic cabal to wound him by attacks or eliminate him by silence.

Some of the hostile reviews combined moral outrage with aesthetic criticism, the most damaging of these by C. V. Terry in the *New York Times Sunday Book Review*, so brief that it signaled contempt, so clever that it allowed its moral disapproval to be carried simply by indirection, misrepresentation, and code words: "Presented as the case history of a standard homosexual, his novel adds little that is new to a groaning shelf. Mr. Vidal's approach is coldly clinical . . . this time he has produced a novel as sterile as its protagonists." Like character like author, every reader was meant to assume. When Gore wrote a sharp letter of protest to the *New York Times*, the *Review* declined to print it. The daily *New York Times* expressed its disapproval by silence. No review at all. The *Times* management had a commitment to their version of "All the News That's Fit to Print." An admirer with close contacts at the newspaper's executive level reported that the decision had been made by the owner himself, Julius Ochs Adler, who had decided that the *Times* would accept ads for *The City and the Pillar* but not review it. Good reviews were few and far between, mostly notably in the *Brooklyn Daily Eagle*, *The Saturday Review*, and *Atlantic Monthly*, which called it "a brilliant exposé of subterranean life among New York and Hollywood expatriates from normal sex . . . an attempt to clarify the inner neuroses of our time, of which the increase in homosexuality and divorce are symptoms." Like other thoughtful readers, the *Saturday Review* commentator called attention to the culturally revealing coincidence that Alfred Kinsey's groundbreaking statistical study, *Sexual Behavior in the Human Male*, had been published within a month of *City*. If Kinsey's statistics were correct, Vidal's dramatization spoke to a sexual activity so much more widely practiced than had heretofore been believed that the society would be better served by open, enlightened discussion than by medieval repression. The *New York Times*, self-consciously and self-righteously inconsistent, decided it would review but *not accept ads* for Kinsey's scientific study.

Gore soon came to value the Kinsey connection. In spring 1949 he was to talk at length to the avid scientist in the mezzanine of the Astor Hotel.

Clipboard in hand, the tired-looking "gray-faced man" with a crew cut, wearing a polka-dot bow tie, was interviewing homosexual artists for a book on the relationship between sexuality and creativity. He was eager to talk to Vidal, to whom he had written, complimenting him on *City*, which he had read carefully, expressing his hope that "we will have a chance to meet someday." Kinsey "told me that I was not 'homosexual'—doubtless because I never sucked cock or got fucked. Even so, I was setting world records for encounters with anonymous youths. . . . I tried to tell Kinsey about Jimmie. But I had not yet read Plato; I had no theory. Kinsey gave me a copy of *Sexual Behavior in the Human Male*, with an inscription complimenting me on my 'work in the field.' " Gore gave Kinsey an autographed copy of *The Season of Comfort*. In the long interview at the Astor, he may indeed have told him much about the novel's heroine. Nina knew all she wanted to know about *City* and *The Season of Comfort* from what others told her. Gene said almost nothing to his son about *City*, other than that it was "interesting," his nonconfrontational way of saying he had nothing happy to say about his son's sexuality. His wife, Kit, assumed that he was deeply disappointed, among other reasons because he had hoped that Gore would marry and make his own father a grandfather. "Yes, you had to assume that the author of *The City and the Pillar* was either homosexual or very observant," Kit remarked. "Gene wasn't enthusiastic." He feared that the book would damage Gore's career. In Washington his grandparents passed over *City* and its reviews in silence.

As he sailed out of New York harbor in mid-February 1948, bound for Naples, the twenty-two-year-old author leaned against the railing, salt spray rising from waves breaking against the *Neue Helena*. He happily posed for a photograph. With a black tie against his white shirt, plaid-patterned sport jacket, a look of anticipation and certitude in his eyes, he felt every bit the well-brought-up young American artistic entrepreneur off again to see the world. *The City and the Pillar* had risen to number five on the *Times* bestseller list. His intention was to go to Rome. Naples was an accidental destination. At last he was on his way again, this time to the place to which he had frequently dreamed of returning, the Europe of his childhood reading, of his fascination with ancient history, of the happiest experience of his school days, his summer 1939 visit to France and Italy. Had Europe been available in 1946, he never would have gone to Guatemala at all; now he was back on course. He had with him in his cabin the manuscript of his novel-in-progress, *A Search for the King*, which he would work on during the two-week voyage, and a diary he had started to keep at the beginning of the year to record his ascension to bestsellerdom and his triumphal progress, including this grand European tour. Probably he had Byron in mind. The entries for the first six weeks of the year, so Vidal recalls, had less to do with triumph than with anguish, a linguistic grinding of his teeth in response to *City*'s stormy reviews. The diary for 1948 is the one document that Vidal declined to make available to his biographer.

After a placid two-week-long winter crossing the port of Naples came into sight on the first of March. Wind and sea spray brought him for the first time to southern Italy. From a distance, sunlight and steel-gray sky made monochromatically bright the high outcropping of Capri to the south, Ischia to the north. The curve of the Bay of Naples seemed graciously cupped. Vesuvius's flat volcanic peak, slouching dramatically in the background, highlighted the city's low silhouette, its pre-highrise skyline. As the ship came into the harbor, the still-unreconstructed devastation of the port provided the prelude to a mostly bombed-out city, people living and working in partial ruins. "The whole waterfront had been smashed up, bombarded." Impoverished Italy had barely begun reconstruction. At the Excelsior Hotel, where he stayed for the night, extensive repairs were under way, the bathroom half paved with marble, the rest raw cement. With a group of fellow passengers from the *Neue Helena,* he went to a live sex exhibition, a specialty performance at the local whorehouse for hard-currency tourists.

From Naples he went the next day to Rome. As the train entered the city from the south, he saw once again the landmarks he had kept vividly in memory since 1939. The sharp winter light made their uniqueness even more distinctively pristine. No sooner had he put his bags down at the Swiss-run Eden Hotel, near the Via Veneto, than he was off to feel Rome beneath his feet. He immediately walked across the city to the Colosseum. The nighttime quiet seemed preternatural, so unlike the rush of traffic he had experienced before the war. "Very, very dark. No lights. No cars in the streets. A very strange time," he later recalled. "A wartime feeling still." But it was recognizably Rome, even in the darkness. The Colosseum cast its silhouette against the night sky. In the circular amphitheater the silence felt ancient. The Forum seemed much the same as it had in 1939, still accessible, without barriers or guards. Back at the hotel he found food scarce, the meat at dinner likely to be something strange and stringy, probably goat. There were vegetables and oranges, as the season permitted, but imports were few, manufactured goods hardly available, luxuries nonexistent. The black market flourished for those with foreign currency, especially dollars. With fuel oil unavailable at any price, people were cold even in the mild Roman winter. The sun, when it shone, was a cherished blessing. From Paris another American writer, Tennessee Williams, who was soon also to come to Rome, wrote, "I am writing this lying up in bed because it is too cold to get up or out. . . . I have been moving from hotel to hotel trying to find one that is heated."

Early in March, as Gore awakened to his first morning in Rome, there were signs of spring. "First impressions: Acid-yellow forsythia in the Janiculum. Purple wisteria in the Forum. Chunks of goat on a plate in a trattoria." Suddenly he was high with the whirl of visual pleasures, revisiting with happy eyes the monuments, the remains of pagan and Christian civilizations, combining the pleasure of new experience with an overlay of vivid memory. Just as years later he encountered in his visual memory, as he walked in Rome, a presence as real as any other of the passersby: the Gore Vidal of this visit now; so too he now encountered his thirteen-year-old self, the schoolboy rapturously reeling from one long-anticipated site to another. "In Rome whenever I turn down the street which goes past the Hotel Eden," he wrote years later, "where I lived when I first came to Europe after the war, I can sometimes see myself coming up the street, a ghost not knowing he's being watched by me, by a stranger old enough to be his father, and yet the instant we pass one another and I see the same face I look at every day—but as it was then, unlined, pale, intense—time overlaps for an instant and I am he. I know what he is thinking, where he is going." Rome began to become inseparable from a personal palimpsest, as if he were writing himself onto the city and the city onto him, his experience over the years taking as its visual and verbal model the overlayered archaeological levels of Roman history. At a table in his cold hotel room he worked in longhand on *The Search for the King*. The first line he wrote, once settled, was particularly expressive of his strong sense that he had as an ultimate goal some personal version of the power of the Eternal City: "Toward some further mystery time moved, and the days, the moments of light and dark passed, and he moved, like time, toward a mystery he could not name, a place beyond illusion, larger than the moment, enlarged by death." For him the movement toward mystery, "beyond illusion," interfaced with consciousness in the passion he felt for the past, in the energy he felt in his writing.

Aware that there were other American writers and artists in Rome, all part of the Grand Tour of 1948, he balanced his quiet hours of work on *Search* with an active Roman street and café life. Eager to meet everyone, he expected that everyone in the American community would know his name, particularly the artists and intellectuals. Also, those with a special interest in the subject of *City* would almost certainly know of its existence, if only for its association with scandal, one of the advantages of having published a controversial bestseller. Public discussion of the subject was still mostly muzzled. As to the act itself, that was another matter, especially in impoverished Rome, where he was delighted to discover that John Horne Burns's "topolini" were indeed widely available. Burns responded to Gore's letter of confirmation, "I'm happy to know that you're picking up mice in Italy. Italian mice are most agreeable." Used to the restrictions and conventions of cruising in New York, newly arrived Americans found postwar Rome and Paris refreshing. "Honey, you would love Rome! Not Paris, but Rome," Tennessee Williams, who had arrived from Paris while Gore was at sea on the *Neue Helena,* wrote to a friend. "I have not been to bed with Michelangelo's David but with any number of his more delicate creations, in fact the abundance and accessibility is downright embarrassing. You can't walk a block without being accosted by someone you would spend a whole evening trying vainly to make in the New York bars. Of course it usually cost you a thousand lire but that is only two bucks (less if you patronize the black market) and there is never any unpleasantness about it even though one does not know a word they are saying." Fritz Prokosch greeted Gore with a touch of coolness, happy to have his company though unable fully to contain his annoyance at *City*'s success. With Prokosch he immediately toured the usual spots, from the Pincio, a favorite pickup place for sexual partners, to Doney's, a popular café on the Via Veneto, an informal headquarters for coffee, drinks, and conversation. Mornings he walked the few streets from his hotel to Doney's to have breakfast with Prokosch. At a nearby table Orson Welles usually sat alone, reading. Around the corner from his hotel, on the Via Aurora just below the Borghese Gardens, the newly famous thirty-six-year-old Tennessee Williams had a few weeks before rented a sunlit apartment he was in the process of decorating. One of its ornaments was a young Italian. Romantically self-indulgent and at the same time serially promiscuous, he had immediately found one to his liking.

Four months earlier the spectacular Broadway success of *A Streetcar Named Desire*, in the first of its over-three-year run, had made Williams an American celebrity. Short, well built, with a tendency to be stocky and puffy, with a small dark mustache, brownish complexion, and an intelligent, laughing glitter in his light-blue eyes, Williams was tasting the first fruits of fame and freedom. He had enough money now to live as he pleased. With a wickedly delicious sense of humor, his broad Missouri drawl deepened by his long residences in New Orleans, he loved being funny, outrageous, spontaneous. An eager drinker, he had a great thirst for parties and fun, for sociability and titillating emotional drama, especially the histrionics of his own life. With a talent for moodiness, capriciousness, and unexpected emotional tropes, he enjoyed big scenes both on- and offstage. Hypochondriacal, he told everyone in Rome he had been hospitalized in Paris for fatal pancreatic cancer. It actually had been for tapeworm. During the next few months he and Gore played the European stage together.

The two met on a shining early-March day, introduced at a party for visiting Americans in a baroque apartment at the nearby American Academy, high on the Janiculum. The view from the sun-filled windows held the palpable tone of the quiet city. Prokosch was there. The host was the American composer Samuel Barber, who, Gore noticed, spoke Italian fluently, unlike the other newly arrived Americans, who at best spoke adequate French. Williams looked unmistakably, unforgettably, familiar. "I had actually seen but not met him the previous year," Gore remembered. "He was following me up Fifth Avenue while I, in turn, was stalking yet another quarry. I recognized him. He wore a blue bow tie with white polka dots. In no mood for literary encounters, I gave him a scowl and he abandoned the chase just north of Rockefeller Center." Since they *both* liked young men, they were not meant to be sexual partners. As the introductions were made, the conversation immediately turned to New York City, though not directly to that first encounter. " 'I particularly like New York,' " Williams said, " 'on hot summer nights when all the . . . uh, superfluous people are off the streets.' " Then "the foggy blue eyes blinked, and a nervous chuckle filled the moment's silence." The differences of personality were already clearly established in the difference in artistic self-definition—the emotional dramatist and the intellectual novelist; the romantic, theatrical hysteric and the witty, coolly observant man of ideas. Yet there was an immediate affinity, a sense of mutual responsiveness. To Gore, the playwright, fifteen years older, looked ancient, clearly a member of the next-older generation. "Williams is not at all what you might expect the most successful playwright since Shakespeare—well, O'Neill—would be like. He has a funny laugh, heh-heh-heh, and a habit of biting his knuckles to make them crack," he later wrote. To Tennessee, Gore was handsome, sexy, funny, talented, ambitious. Each responded to the other's gift for language, to the satiric voice, the elaborate put-on, the practical joke, the self-defensive, sometimes aggressive vulnerability. Despite differences, they immediately liked one another. They soon knew each other's quips and cues; they could read one another's body language and facial expressions; they knew when the barbed wit was about to strike or the clownish joke about to be performed. "Tennessee," Gore later recollected, "was the greatest company on earth. We laughed. He had a wild sense of humor, grotesque, much like mine, and we just spent a lot of time parodying the world, mocking and burlesquing everything and everybody. He wasn't a terribly good mimic . . . but he could do numbers. He could do a dying heroine for you. Or he could do an addle-headed piece of trade for you. He could do these characters, much the way he wrote them."

In a newly purchased Army-surplus jeep, with a canvas roof neither could figure out how to put up, they were soon off on a trip down to Naples, where Gore had first disembarked, then south along the Amalfi coast to Positano and Amalfi. It had taken Williams an entire afternoon, he told "Dear Blood and Gore," to do the "transfer of jeep-ownership red tape." In Rome in 1948 it was easiest to communicate leaving a note with a concierge. "We're definitely going to Amalfi Sunday morning," Tennessee assured him. In the meantime, at dawn, Williams, drunk, drove the jeep, which had a defective muffler, up and down the Via Veneto and then to St. Peter's, where he raced through the wind-blown fountains to cool his head. He loved the roaring engine, the sense of freedom. An amazingly bad driver with terrible eyesight, almost blind in one eye, he seemed indifferent or oblivious to how easily he could have been killed or killed others. Apparently the roar from the muffler and the absence of other vehicles prevented mayhem. Positano and Amalfi, set in the steep hills above the sea, remained vivid in their memories, each to return later to what seemed one of the unspoiled natural paradises. The coast from Naples to Sicily combined visual splendor, medieval life, and rich classical associations. But "our drive down was through nothing but ruined cities that had been bombarded either by our fleet or by retreating Germans. Everything was a mess." In Amalfi they stayed at the Luna Hotel on the coast highway. There were no other guests. As in Rome, they could live and dine handsomely on an extraordinarily favorable exchange rate in an impoverished Italy. A thousand feet above them, obscured by the high cliffs, was the town of Ravello, which they did not visit, where La Rondinaia, a villa that decades later Vidal was to buy, served as a convalescent home for injured British officers.

As they toured, each time they got out of the jeep, even for brief stops, they had to remove all their possessions. There was no way to protect anything from theft. Even when they stopped for lunch, everything had to come out, including Gore's manuscript of *A Search for the King*, which he had taken with him and which he worked on in hotels. He put it inside his shirt for safekeeping. "I wasn't going to leave it in the car and have it stolen. Stolen and then tossed away. Every time I got out of the jeep, I made sure I had the manuscript with me. We didn't know how to put up the canvas top of the jeep. Anybody could have got in." Williams, who was working on *Summer and Smoke*, probably had that manuscript with him. They had a photo taken of the two of them, Gore leaning against the hood, one foot on the bumper, Tennessee sitting on the hood, his arm around Gore, which they had made into a postcard. Gore proudly sent it to friends and family. "That happy picture of you and your friend nesting lazily on that Jeep was too much for me," Judith Jones responded. "I've decided to take your suggestion—I shall be sailing on the Vulcania on the 18th of May." To Anaïs he wrote lovingly, "Write me in care of American Embassy Rome. I think of you cherie; you are still closer to me than anyone else. I want so much to see you. I think about you constantly; glad you're happy with RP." In response to a letter from Nina that had reached him at American Express in Rome, he wrote on the back of the postcard, "Tennessee Williams *(Streetcar Named Desire)* and me—we're touring Italy in his jeep. Lousy weather, dangerous politics, working well. . . . Life is luxurious and cheap." "I have never laughed more with anyone," he remembered.

Life was great fun, both on the road and in Rome, though there were the usual anxieties and complaints, most focusing on the reception of *City*. It had made him an uneasy celebrity and a ready target, even among friends.

When Williams and Prokosch were sitting in Doney's, Vidal came by, so Bill Fricks remembered. Vidal stopped and asked Prokosch if he had gotten the copy of *City* he had recently dropped off at Prokosch's hotel. A few polite remarks were exchanged, and Vidal left. Then Prokosch said to Williams and Fricks that Vidal was "a terrible writer, the book is bad, and we'll never hear from Vidal again—he'll probably never write anything more and nothing worth reading." Years later, when Fricks conveyed the story to Vidal, Gore responded, "I always knew that Fritz hated the sale of my books." Rarely an enthusiastic reader of anything, Williams "got through *The City and the Pillar*. He disliked the ending. He said, 'I don't think you realize, Gore, what a good book you've written.' He thought I'd just put on a hokey ending for commercial reasons." Williams mistakenly assumed that Jim Willard's father was modeled on Gore's and "said of the family scenes, 'Our fathers were very much alike.'" Toward the end of March, celebrating his thirty-seventh birthday (he claimed it was his thirty-fourth), Williams threw a large party at his Via Aurora apartment. In the crowded rooms everyone spoke English and some French, except for occasional Italians, mostly attractive young men, including Williams's latest passion. The wealthy British-born art connoisseur Harold Acton, a longtime Italian resident, had come down from his Florentine villa, La Pietra, to inspect the invasion of American artists. He seemed to float "like some large pale fish through the crowded room; from time to time he would make a sudden lunge at this or that promising piece of bait." Acton later criticized the young Americans for being more interested in sex than in Italian culture. Condescendingly haughty to seemingly provincial Americans who hardly knew a word of Italian, Acton politely deplored "our barbarous presence in *his* Europe."

A greater barbarity threatened. The strength of the national Communist parties among the working classes in Europe was epitomized by the possibility that the party would actually win the Italian election in April. In America, the Communist threat in Europe seemed almost to bring the red tide to American shores. The Bolshevik scare dominated American headlines, the Marshall Plan and McCarthyism opposite sides of the same exaggerated anxiety. Americans in Italy "were told the communists were going to win and that there'd be a bloodbath," Gore later wrote. The Gores, in Washington, now very conservative, were eager for their grandson's views. "This country is all wrought up about Europe, Asia, and the whole world.

There is a great deal of war talk in the air," the Senator wrote to him, urging him to "remain in Italy until after the election . . . unless you think that it is too dangerous?!?!?" From New York, Gene Vidal, who gave him the bitter news that *City,* sinking fast, was number ten in the *Herald Tribune* and last in the *New York Times Book Review* bestseller rankings, also had the dreaded Communists in mind. "You must be wading in Communists according to the most recent war scare via our DC Administration. The elections in Italy are supposed to be something." When Gore mentioned he might leave because of the threat of postelection violence, Tennessee was baffled. The Russians "are not a predatory people," he announced. " 'I don't know why there is all this fuss about international communism.' I disagreed. 'They've always been imperialists, just like us.' 'That's not true. Just name one country Russia has tried to take over? I mean recently.' 'Latvia, Lithuania and Estonia,' I began . . . 'And what,' asked Tennessee, 'are they?' "

In late March, as another manifestation of his desire to meet the famous, gently teased by Prokosch, who gave him "the impression that this sort of busyness was somehow vulgar," Gore visited George Santayana. The eighty-five-year-old Spanish-born American writer, philosopher, and Harvard professor put the likely Communist takeover into larger perspective. A hard-headed, rational Catholic whose religious faith did not require that he believe in miracles, Santayana had retired to spend his last years at the Convent of the Blue Nuns on the Celian Hill, having discreetly left the Bristol Hotel soon after the Germans occupied Rome. When Gore expressed his residual "America First" horror at the possibility that Italy might go Communist, "Santayana looked positively gleeful. 'Oh, let them! Let them try it! They've tried everything else, so why not communism? After all, who knows what new loyalties will emerge as they become part of a—wolf pack.' " What seemed his cynicism revolted the American innocent who had been brought up in an environment in which the only political leader worse than Roosevelt was Lenin, a difference of degree, not kind. Santayana seemed to Vidal to look exactly like his grandmother, except bald. "He wore a dressing gown; Lord Byron collar open at the withered neck; faded mauve waistcoat. He was genial; made a virtue of his deafness. '*I* will talk. You will listen,' " he always made clear to his American visitors among whom were Edmund Wilson, who seemed to Santayana very self-important, and the poet Robert Lowell, his "new friend" who would have a difficult life as a

Catholic in Boston. "The black eyes shone with a lovely malice." On Gore's first visit one of the Irish nuns, "a small figure, glided toward" him, asked him his business, and brought him to Santayana, who after a few questions was interested or bored enough to invite him back to his cell. It had an iron bed with a screen around it. There were few books other than his own. He was reading Arnold Toynbee's *A Study of History*, which he separated from its binding, tearing away each page so that he could hold one at a time. Another day Gore brought with him Barber, Prokosch, and Williams, the playwright a reluctant visitor. Williams stared "at the old man with great interest." Neither had any idea who the other was. Afterward Williams remarked, " 'Did you notice how he said 'in the days when I had secretaries, *young men?*' " Santayana probably had no idea what *The City and the Pillar* was about. Gore, though he had read *The Last Puritan* as an adolescent, had not understood or sensed its homoerotic element. Another time they talked about Henry James, whom Santayana had known. "He gave a sort of imitation of Henry's periphrastic style; then sighed. 'Oh, the James brothers!' He sounded as if he were invoking the outlaws." Reminiscing about his youth, Santayana told him, Vidal later wrote, that there had been "an opening at Harvard in philosophy and not in architecture, which is what he really wanted to do. Since he was very well read and a thoughtful man and a poet, with secondary but real gifts, he said, 'Oh, well,' and became a philosopher. To the horror of William James," with whom he never got along. Serious, innocent, fatuous, the young Gore Vidal, thinking of his own ambition, complained, "In America literary reputations come and go so swiftly." The response was immediate. " 'It would be insufferable if they did *not.*' " At the third, final visit, in the beginning of April, as Gore rose to go, Santayana said, " 'I shall give you a book,' " and took a copy of his autobiographical *The Middle Span* from the bookcase. " 'What is your name?' " he asked. " 'I shall write for you. I rarely do this.' . . . 'For Gore Vidal, George Santayana, April 1, 1948.' 'It is your April Fool's present.' "

<hr />

Taking seriously the threat of postelection chaos, Gore had decided to leave Italy, even if only temporarily. Perhaps he would return after the election or go to Paris or London instead. Election-scare warnings from the American embassy seemed good enough reason to do what he had it in mind to do all along: visit Egypt. Greece was out of the question because of the violent political situation there. In his youthful imagination Egypt glowed with the excitement of Hollywood movies like *The Mummy*, with the alluring power of its imperial political and cultural role in the history of the ancient world, from Shakespeare's *Anthony and Cleopatra* to Shaw's *Caesar and Cleopatra*. Since he wanted to see everything, why not the magnificent pyramids, the mysterious temples? Cairo was a short plane ride from Rome. With the manuscript of *A Search for the King*, he flew into Egypt on April 2, thrilled at the contrast between late-Victorian Cairo and the ancient ruins that surrounded it, a Middle Eastern version of Rome. Still ruled by a remnant of the Ottoman Empire, Egypt unstably combined Turkish and European colonialism, Arab nationalism, tribal customs, and excruciating poverty.

From his room at the moderately priced El Mint Hotel, near one of the great pyramids, he had a Westerner's-eye-view of modern Egyptian misery and ancient Egyptian glory. At a club one evening he saw the white-suited, obese King Farouk, the monarch of nightclubs, with the usual European blonde on his arm. "Like a Mafia don, with dark glasses, he was surrounded by plainclothesmen, also in dark glasses." At the old Shepheard's Hotel, the historic gathering place for Anglo-Americans, Gore observed with interest the colorful eccentricities of a late-colonial world, partly English, mostly French. Cairo was "like a French provincial village in those days," he later remarked. Taken up by Mehmed Abib, "a strange little man who was chasing me around . . . the grandson of the last Ottoman Emperor or Sultan who was married to the sister of Zog of Albania," he got a fascinating glimpse of Ottoman-Albanian high society, which included "two beautiful Romanov princesses . . . in exile. A rather exotic foreign enclave with much intrigue." Abib wooed him "sadly and hopelessly beside the pool at Mena House. He looked like a sensitive dentist. He was the only person I ever met who sighed the way that characters are supposed to sigh in novels." The pudgy, ineffectual Abib was easy to keep at arm's distance. After a week in Egypt, Gore wrote to Williams that he feared disease more than he felt tempted by Egyptian opportunities. Perhaps he had Flaubert's example in mind. "I am glad you did not have carnal associations in Cairo," Tennessee wrote back, "not only because it would have interfered with the glorious work but because I kept thinking, if Gore is not careful he will catch one of those things from the dirty Egyptians."

In Cairo he spent part of each day writing, working at his hotel or in one of the public rooms at Shepheard's. Finishing *A Search for the King* on April 8, he quickly wrote a play, a variant on *The City and the Pillar* and *The Season of Comfort*, with a bitchy Nina-like mother and a homosexual son, whose father had been homosexual, torn between his relationship with his mother and his love for another young man, named Jimmy. It seemed to him a "powerful play," though later he was happy to forget most of what it was about. Oddly enough, he wrote to Nina about it, though probably without giving her any details. She knew little to nothing about *The Season of Comfort*, which was not to be published until the next January. Anticipating a *Streetcar Named Desire*–like Broadway success, Nina was "thrilled over the play. Air mail me with whom it is," she wrote to him, "for I am going to N.Y. and want to read it, unless you can send me a copy. I can hardly wait!" She imagined herself its producer or at least an instrumental money-raiser among her theater and society contacts. "I think I am sure of money for it," she wrote to him. If another one of her financial negotiations with Auchincloss worked out, she hoped "to catch a boat in May." Fortunately, he did not send her the play. "Bright eyes!" Tennessee wrote him from Rome. "This is glorious news about the play," though he cautioned that "glorious plays are not usually written in such a short time." Usually there were innumerable tedious revisions. "Still, by all means send it to me. When a thing goes that quickly it is a good sign, for it means that the impulse was vital and the vision was clear." The good news was that Helen Hayes was going to star in London in *The Glass Menagerie*, Williams's first play, which had initially fizzled on Broadway. The jeep was still his maniacal pleasure. Always warmly attracted to Gore more than either of them found practical, "I close now with an affectionate and mildly libidinous kiss on your soft under lip which I never kissed."

Street life in Cairo was exotic, hot, dirty, the April sky relentlessly bright. At first the nights were cold. Then the heat intensified and, without air-conditioning, even the nights were warm. Gore tramped through Cairo, "a ferocious sight-seer," fascinated by the mixture of old and new, of Arab and European. "I did nothing but sight-see, and then I moved on," along the Nile to the ancient sites of Karnak and Luxor and the Valley of the Kings, where he was "overwhelmed by a sense of the past, and the knowledge that there is no mystery at all about our estate despite the beautiful progression of the Book of the Dead. . . . We come and we go and the time between is all that we have." He was to write later in a pseudonymous fiction that "as the train moved through the outskirts of Cairo," it was "a strange spectacle by moonlight: thousands of mud hovels, each with the yellow flickering light of a lantern in the window. Dark shapes moved quickly in the shadows; other shapes huddled around tiny fires in front of the huts. The modern city was now only a blur of electric lights in the distance, hidden by this sweep of slums, which were as old as the Bible, unchanged since the days of the Pharaohs." In his mind, at Luxor, he heard a first-person fictional voice resonating with the possibility of a novel, at least partly set in Egypt, about last things, our end in our beginning, the first stirring of *Messiah*. He kept in mind for future use the image of the ancient desert landscape. Cairo and environs, especially the atmosphere of seedy intrigue, decadence, and poverty, seemed both exotic and familiar enough to become part of his reservoir of usable experiences. Still, despite its attractions, two to three weeks of Egypt were enough. The heat had become constantly oppressive. It was difficult to sleep, even in otherwise comfortable hotels.

Back in Cairo he had enough energy to book a flight to Paris, where after a brief stint at the Pont Royal Hotel in whose downstairs bar Jean-Paul Sartre and Simone de Beauvoir frequently sat, he soon set himself up at the Hôtel de l'Université, a small boardinghouse-hotel on the Left Bank, run by a good cook. Tennessee, up from Rome, joined him there. "There were a bunch of English and Americans . . . and then the academics or academics-to-be and then Tennessee and me." They shared the second floor. Gore usually wrote in the back. The more social and alcoholic Tennessee drank with visitors in the front. There were "two rooms and a bath for him on the street side and one room and a bath for me in the back, with the stairwell between." One of the raffish hotel's attractions, Williams remarked, was that " 'it suited Gore and me perfectly as there was no objection to young callers.' " Busy traffic pounded the stairs. "The Bird and I did like the same type, and we would pass boys back and forth. Once, after an unsuccessful evening's prowl of Saint-Germain, we returned to the hotel, and the Bird said, 'Well, that just leaves us,' to which he says I said, 'Don't be macabre.' " Apparently, though, Gore had little difficulty making up for his Egyptian abstemiousness. In a short while he had all the usual one-incident pickups, most of them French trade, and at least one affair in which the affections if not the heart were touched. Still open to or at least occasionally brooding about the possibility of romance, he attracted some who invested romantic feeling in him.

———·•·———

Almost as quiet as Rome, in spring 1948 the streets of Paris were uncrowded, the city experiencing the predawn of its postwar awakening. For visiting Americans the favorable exchange rate, French eagerness to be in the cultural-tourism business again, the enthusiasm of once more renewing the historical Franco-American handshake—all this gave Paris a roseate early-morning glow. Suddenly transatlantic ships were coming into Le Havre, planes landing at Orly, ferries crossing the Channel. American artists and writers, having been excluded by a brutally long war, wanted to be in Paris again.

Having finished a draft of *The Search for the King,* Gore began to rework the manuscript. When he gave the play he had written in Cairo to Tennessee to read, the latter "pronounced it the worst play he'd read in some time, and I solemnly abandoned playwriting for good, after first pointing out to him that a literary form which depended on the combined excellence of others for its execution could hardly be worth the attention of a serious writer, adding with deliberate cruelty that I did not envy him being stagestruck and his life taken up with such frivolous people as actors and directors." It was not a renunciation Vidal was able to sustain. What sustained him most in Paris was the pleasure of simply being there at a golden time. The chestnut trees were in bloom, the food wonderful. Elegantly shabby, Paris looked lovely. "We lived as if it would be forever summer."

His long-hoped-for meeting with Christopher Isherwood happened accidentally, in late April, at the Deux Magots café, where Isherwood and Bill Caskey, an American ex–merchant marine and professional photographer, were sitting. As Gore walked by, he recognized from photographs the well-known forty-four-year-old Isherwood, just one year younger than Nina, author of successful novels and the celebrated *Goodbye to Berlin.* The British-Hollywood expatriate had already entered literary mythology as the third in the Auden-Spender triumverate. Well read in a way that none of Vidal's American writer friends were, Isherwood, with his humor, his delight in word games, parodies, spoofs, and class-conscious ironies, delighted Gore. " 'I am American literature,' " Gore announced one day. " 'I feared as much,' " Isherwood said. "Although the voice was controlled, I saw the mounting terror in his eyes as we deconstructed American literature not only past but yet to come, making, as we did, spacious room for ourselves among the ruins." At that first meeting Vidal seemed to Isherwood "a big husky boy with fair wavy hair and a funny, rather attractive face—sometimes he reminds me of a teddy bear, sometimes of a duck." His talk about sex seemed youthful, cute, silly, with phrases like "peeing machines," "mice," and "we looked at each other and our tails started to wag," and his disbelief in romantic love and certainty (if it existed) about its tragic, doomed nature, left Isherwood skeptical. He himself, who had no difficulty reconceptualizing marital romance into a homosexual variant whose model combined romantic devotion and domestic harmony, lived with the rough, irritable Caskey, who thought Gore the typical product of an American prep school. Gore thought Caskey suffered from a case of "terminal jealousy." What Isherwood respected immediately, though, was Gore's courage. "I do think he has that—though it is mingled, as in many much greater heroes, with a desire for self-advertisement," he wrote in his diary. With youthful self-enthusiasm and bestseller narcissism, Gore asked for advice on " 'how to manage my career.' "

They had dinner together the next two nights. Eager to talk about other writers and about Isherwood's Hollywood life, Gore learned that Isherwood and Gore's English publisher, John Lehmann, were great friends. The next afternoon they went out to Versailles, where Gore had last been in summer 1939. Isherwood found it disappointing, too "big and barracklike." "I don't know when I've met anyone I liked so much in such a short time," Gore wrote to Lehmann. When Isherwood left for England, he took with him a copy of Gore's play, the *idea* of which, he soon responded, was "very interesting and even potentially great." But "the basic weakness seems to me to be in the character of the mother. . . . She simply isn't interesting; too bitchy. She should be a genuinely tragic figure. . . . I even think there should be a big scene between her and Jimmy. . . . I don't mean that you should be more shocking, more outspoken, but I want you to be more human." Isherwood read it as a play-in-progress. So too, and much more so, was the relationship. "I am so glad," he wrote from London, "we met in Paris, and I hope we'll see more of each other from now on. I don't feel like I've really talked to you yet." They both looked forward to Vidal coming to London in June.

In Gore's conversations with Isherwood, Truman Capote's name had come up. Vidal was irresistibly drawn to the slightly sore subject of his competitor, among other reasons because Capote was about to arrive in Paris. Somewhat disingenuously, Vidal had written to Lehmann in London, "If you see Truman Capote before he comes over here give him my number. I look forward to seeing him." It could only have been on the principle that it is best to have your enemy in sight and in front of you, though they were not in any manifest way enemies yet. They were slightly friendly catty rivals, each of whom, traveling in some of the same literary circles, accepted the necessity of occasionally running into one another. When Capote, who was having lunch at the Deux Magots with his friend Johnny Nicholson—who later that year opened Café Nicholson in New York—introduced him to Gore, Nicholson immediately saw that "they weren't friends." Gore was "very handsome, very distinguished-looking, very proper. No way was he bohemian-looking." But "Truman had written his book. So we had two rivals. That I knew. They were two personalities," though "at that time they were very proper with one another." They were also each looking over his shoulder at the other's progress. Eager to combine histrionic charm with sharp intelligence, Capote treated every situation as a stage performance whose message was the assertion of his desirability and brilliance. Like Vidal, he believed in advertising himself. Unlike Vidal, he had a mystical faith in his ability to make reality conform to his desires. A performance personality, he frequently improvised, sometimes recklessly, often cleverly, softly blurring the boundary between convincing others and convincing himself. If he could do one, he could do the other. Soon after arriving in Paris, Capote was in high form, entrancing Vidal and Williams "with mischievous fantasies about the great." He flashed a brilliant amethyst ring. " 'From André Gide,' he sighed." Soon after Truman and Gore met Camus at a publisher's party, Truman began telling everyone that Camus had fallen madly in love with him. "Apparently the very sight of him was enough to cause lifelong heterosexual men to tumble out of unsuspected closets," Vidal later wrote. "The instant lie was Truman's art form, small but, paradoxically, authentic. One could watch the process. A famous name would be mentioned. The round pale fetus face would suddenly register a sort of tic, as if a switch had been thrown. 'Eleanor Roosevelt. Oh, I know her *intimately!*' "

His lies infuriated Vidal, who, though he thought he had amiable relations with Capote, soon discovered that his rival was bad-mouthing him everywhere and at every opportunity. "All the writers are here," Gore wrote to a new correspondent, the critic John Aldridge, "and the atmosphere is heavy with competitiveness. Someone might one day remark in print that American writers are the most highly competitive and mutually antagonistic in the world." Though some found Capote charmingly entertaining, Vidal was not alone in thinking him offensive. The novelist Calder Willingham, with whom Gore had become casually friendly in 1947–48 in New York, found Capote as untenable as did Vidal. He is "insincere, extremely mannered . . . snobbish," Willingham wrote to Vidal. Though attractive, clever, and "an excellent talker," he "tries too hard to be charming . . . busy all the time at the job of getting ahead. . . . Also, he uses his homosexuality in this; he uses it as comedy, and plays the role of the effeminate buffoon, thus making people laugh at him. It gets attention." One of the dangers to Vidal was his own potential overreaction. Sometimes quick to anger, his counterattacks occasionally strained other people's credulity: Capote could not be as bad as all that. To some, such as Sandy Campbell, Tennessee Williams's friend, Gore seemed "obsessed with Truman and his success." He "talked about Truman continually, putting him down, insisting that Truman had never met Gide, Cocteau, etc." But, later, "I realized from Truman's demeanor, his sudden quietness, his failure to make any claim of friendship or acquaintance [with Gide when they ran into him in Taormina in 1950], that they had never met before. What I had taken to be one of Vidal's jealous libels was true." As to Capote's claim of an affair with Gide, Gore himself shortly had a chance to put it to the test.

John Lehmann came from London to Paris, among other reasons to discuss with his newest American acquisition his hope that he would revise the ending of *The City and the Pillar* for the British edition. Like Isherwood, he thought the violent ending both off-putting and bad publicity for homosexuals. Early in the year Lehmann had received happily the news "that you and Tennessee are moving in our direction across the globe." Vidal, though he resented Lehmann's pressure on him to alter the ending, was pliable or ambivalent enough so that from early on he committed himself to make changes. "I don't think I need tell you that your book will be a bit of a problem child in London," Lehmann told him at the beginning of May, "and there are one or two points I am anxious to take up with you in connection with this." When Gore seemed almost to volunteer changes,

Lehmann was pleased. "I'm very much interested to hear that you are thinking of revising the end of *The City and the Pillar*. I would welcome this, and feel sure that we could easily come to an agreement about when the next text should be ready." In London, Gore was a subject of friendly gossip. "Christopher came to stay here," Lehmann wrote to him, and "we talked a lot about you." From the first, though, Vidal did not trust John Lehmann. "After Isherwood went to America [in 1941]," Lehmann "regularly said that Isherwood had never written anything good since," Vidal recalled. "Lehmann was a great gossip, and he had implacable malice. He just wasn't likable. He had some charm and some wit. He was a very handsome man. Extremely. . . . But there was something off-putting about him. I didn't like him dictating to me what to do with my book," though by mid-May Vidal had explicitly expressed himself as "not very happy with [*City*] as it stands" and preparing "to rewrite [its] ending." To some extent his accommodation was strategic and deferential. "Would it be possible, if the *City* is a success, to bring out the first two books? I know nothing of English publishing conditions: perhaps this would not be practical." Having had Dutton send Lehmann galleys of *The Season of Comfort*, Gore was eager to have Lehmann commit himself to publish all his novels in England. Lehmann was clear in his own mind that he would make a commitment only to *City*.

A tall, handsome, pale-complexioned, peremptory man with receding blond hair and icy blue eyes, the forty-one-year-old Lehmann came from two Victorian publishing and literary families, one of Scottish, the other of German-Jewish origin. His grandparents had been intimates of Dickens, Browning, and Wilkie Collins, among other great figures of nineteenth-century British literary culture. His sisters were the actress Beatrix Lehmann and the novelist Rosamond Lehmann. At Eton and Cambridge, Lehmann had expanded his inheritance into more current circles, including Bloomsbury. He had begun working in 1931 for Virginia and Leonard Woolf's Hogarth Press, which published his poetry, and become a partner in 1938. His greatest success came as editor of the groundbreaking semiannual journal *New Writing* and *Penguin New Writing*, and, later, of *London Magazine*. Well known in the tight-knit British literary world for his interest in homosexual books, he ran his small publishing house from a vantage point of great prestige but from a weak financial-business position. With the end of the war he had begun to give great emphasis to taking on up-and-coming American authors, including Vidal. He had already made up his mind "to capture as many of the new postwar generation of American writers as possible." Having just returned from a successful book-buying trip to New York, he happily embraced Isherwood, who had been staying at Lehmann's house at Egerton Crescent in Kensington, and was reunited with his companion Alex Racine, a distinguished Polish-born ballet dancer. Late in May he took the boat-train to Paris, where among other things he signed Tennessee Williams to a publication contract and took Vidal to meet André Gide, who just the year before had won the Nobel Prize. Disappointed that Gide had not read *The City and the Pillar,* a copy of which he had received from a friend, Gore took pleasure in meeting the acerbic writer. At seventy-nine, Gide was still alert enough to express his formidable personality and mind in the cleverness of his language and the keenness of his satiric eye. Gide's defense of Communism and his championing of homosexuality had made him controversial, a writer who was both widely hated and deeply admired. He was *cher maître* to those who admired his courage, a Bolshevik fag to those who detested his politics. To the young American, Gide had fought and had suffered from the French version of the same enemies who so viciously attacked *City.* As they rang the doorbell in the rue Vaneau, Lehmann noticed Vidal's excitement. Gide was the first prominent writer he was to meet who combined a literary career and an intense interest in politics and the first who dared, defying convention, publicly to defend same-sex relationships as natural.

In the sunny apartment, in his book-lined two-level library, Gide, "short-legged, deep-chested, with a large egglike bald head on which was perched a *vie de bohème* velvet beret," wearing "a dark green velvet jacket" and large eyeglasses, greeted them. He appeared to have big peasant hands. When Vidal congratulated him on the Nobel Prize, Gide, beaming, responded, " '*Premier le Kinsey Report, après ça le Prix Nobel.*' " The open championing of homosexuality was no longer summarily disqualifying, a message Gore was happy to hear. Though limited by his Exeter schoolboy French and Gide's preference not to speak English (apparently Lehmann did not attempt to act as intermediary), they talked briefly about Oscar Wilde and Henry James, whose popularity among Anglo-Saxons puzzled Gide. He had met the other *cher maître* at a dinner on New Year's Eve 1912. Gide, an admirer of Conrad, wrote English well enough for him to have translated Conrad into French. Suddenly the telephone rang. Rather slyly, Gide held the phone so that his visitors could hear the voice, whispering "Henri de

Montherlant," a writer Vidal especially admired. Open on Gide's desk was a "pornographic novel by an Anglican priest recently retired to the English countryside. The pages were beautifully hand-printed, and there were a number of drawings of boys being debauched. With a grin Gide said he had received the manuscript sometime ago but had not yet decided how to answer its priestly author." When Vidal asked him, "How did you find Truman Capote?" Gide responded, "Who?" Finally he understood whom Gore was asking about. " 'No,' he said, 'I haven't met him, but several people have sent me this.' From his desk he held up the photograph of Truman from *Life*. He grinned. 'Is he in Paris?' " Before Gore left, Gide asked if he would like a book as a gift. *Corydon*, Gore replied, Gide's best-known explicit defense of homosexuality. Surprised at the request, "I never give that book," he said, perhaps meaning it was never asked for. He inscribed a copy *"avec sympathie."* As they walked down, he said, in English, "Mind the step!"

American accents dominated the linguistic cacophony of Paris. A half century earlier Henry James had called it "the bark of Chicago in the streets of Venice." Everywhere Americans heard American voices, especially in restaurants, bars, museums. Sometimes one ran into overly familiar voices, unhappily. A red-faced, drunken American, who had had enough, shouted out in a restaurant as Capote was telling stories at a table in the back, "For Christ's sake! Wherever I go I hear that American faggoty pansy voice! Can't I ever get away from you guys?" On his way to New York from Morocco, the composer and writer Paul Bowles, fifteen years older than Gore, came by to see Tennessee. Bowles, who had just finished his first novel, *The Sheltering Sky*, had agreed to write incidental music for *Summer and Smoke*, scheduled to premiere in New York in the fall. Vidal and Bowles had met in passing in New York the previous year. Elegantly dressed as always, the thin, blond, rather delicate Bowles and his new friend took a walk "down an empty street off Saint-Germain. Suddenly, a radio is turned on behind a shuttered window and the street is filled with the music of Bizet. Paul complains that composers now think of him as a writer and writers as a composer and that, as a result, he is nowhere." Bowles had just met Saul Bellow, whose *Dangling Man* Gore admired. James Baldwin was soon to be in Paris, as was Norman Mailer, whose recently published *The Naked and the Dead* Vidal thought "a clever, talented, admirably executed fake," part jealousy, part accurate analysis. Soon Irwin Shaw was to produce "another one of those monsters called 'great war novels.' They're all so phony, so dull that I wonder that anyone takes them seriously; I suppose," Gore wrote to Lehmann, "it's all a part of our manifest destiny, artificial plumes on the eagle's wings." The newly arrived Judy Jones ran into her New York friend on a Paris street. "He had a very young man with him," whom he said he had picked up the night before, "a little disreputable-looking. He could have been a sailor. Gore came and sat with us in the cafe and kept him sort of at another table. I remember his making the kinds of remarks he makes today about young men being just for sex and there's no love involved. Here was sort of this scruffy-looking character at the next table."

At a large, shabby, heavily curtained apartment in the rue du Bac, Vidal was introduced by John Lehmann to Denham Fouts, a semilegendary, cadaverous opium addict from Jacksonville, Florida, who had spent much of his life as the consort of numbers of wealthy older men. His own preference was for young boys. From his glory days with British lords and King Paul of Greece, he had fallen on hard times. During much of the war he had lived with Isherwood in Los Angeles, the basis for the character Paul in *Down There on a Visit*. Irregularly supported by his longtime friend and companion, Peter Watson, the wealthy backer of *Horizon* who had recently set him up in his Paris apartment with an impressive Tchelitchew painting hanging over his bed and a large fluffy white dog, Fouts stayed in bed during the day, took brief walks at night, his "nocturnal Proustian life," as Isherwood called it, and smoked as much opium as he could afford. On his table was the *Life* magazine photograph of the ubiquitous Capote. Bright light hurt his eyes; he blinked a great deal. Solemnly he passed the pipe around to Gore, who with Lehmann sat on the edge of the bed. "It made me deathly ill, and I never tried it again," Vidal recalled. Fouts was to appear as the central character in his short story "Pages from an Abandoned Journal." Later that year he died in Rome.

There were, for Vidal and other American writers, French voices, but they were often voices with a purpose, particularly because American money and American art were a formidable presence in war-impoverished France. When the flamboyant surrealist novelist, moviemaker, and dramatist Jean Cocteau wanted to obtain the French rights for *A Streetcar Named Desire* for Jean Marais, he invited Tennessee Williams to a splendid lunch. Tennessee, who brought Gore along to translate, was so ignorant of French that he could not tell how limited Gore's was. "Marais looked beautiful but sleepy. Cocteau was characteristically brilliant. He spoke no English but since he could manage an occasional 'the' sound as well as the final 'g,' he often gave the impression that he was speaking English. Tennessee had no clear idea who Cocteau was, while Cocteau knew nothing about Tennessee except that he had written a popular American play with a splendid part in it for his lover. . . . No one made any sense at all except Marais who broke his long silence to ask, apropos the character Stanley Kowalski, 'Will I have to use a Polish accent?' " However, if there were no practical incentives, the French, especially the literary establishment, preferred to keep their distance. American voices were barely tolerable. When Tennessee threw a large party at the Hôtel de l'Université, hordes of French actors came, hoping to get a part in Cocteau's version of *Streetcar*. Through a French intermediary or, so he claimed, by telegram, Williams had invited the one person he most wanted to meet, the novelist and philosopher Jean-Paul Sartre, who with his companion Simone de Beauvoir and his rival Albert Camus dominated early post–World War II French culture. When Sartre did not appear at Williams's party, "one of the guests went to fetch him." He "refused to come. Very French. Williams was highly pissed off." He surmised, probably correctly, that Sartre "regarded me as too bourgeois or American or God knows what." In general, Vidal later commented, "the French gods kept their distance from all of us."

With hot weather in Paris, sharing colds and stomach problems with everyone he knew, Gore was relieved to visit London in mid-June. For the time being he was not writing anyway. Nina, traveling with friends, had shown up in Paris for a couple of days. In London he stayed with Racine ("a very ladylike man and a marvelous Blue Beard and a much admired dancer") and the less likable Lehmann at 31 Egerton Crescent, near Harrods. Low on cash, he was happy to save. What he had in the bank in New York was not readily available, and he preferred to live off new income, if possible. Nothing more was forthcoming in royalties from Dutton until October. Lehmann, though, had a small amount of sterling for him, part of his advance for the British edition of *City*, handled through his recently obtained British agent, Curtis Brown, which acted as Dutton's representative in England. With prices low, a little sterling went a long way. The young man the agency assigned to handle his account, Graham Watson, twelve years older than Gore, found him a challenge and a pleasure to work with, though there was little work at the moment. He also thought him "enormously handsome." Lehmann's office, "a small operation" at 8 Henrietta Street, was on the ground floor of the Curtis Brown building. To Watson, "Lehmann was a charmer. I liked him very much. He had very sort of blue eyes, very, very blue eyes. Somehow one felt, 'Watch it!' He was Okay. Very much, of course, in literary London at the time." As soon as Gore arrived, Lehmann was quick to take possession of the ration book he had been given at the border. Food was scarce. "To an American eye, English life was of a terrible rationed drabness." In exchange he got "a mess of fish with one egg clotted over it at breakfast. I ate the rationed egg and left the fish." Watson first met Gore at the Hyde Park Corner apartment of the aristocratic Edward Montague, who had gone to prison for eighteen months for an affair with a young boy, which became a "notorious court case. . . . I think it was Montague who asked me to meet Gore, and there was this bit of rough trade there. . . . I don't know whether it was Gore's rough trade or Montague's rough trade." It was part of normal activity for both of them. About those who had homosexual affairs or romances, the same ongoing curiosity and gossip occurred as about heterosexual relationships. And Gore, who sometimes could gossip as avidly as Lehmann, immediately found himself the youthful student in a long-established, stratified, but unified London literary society. Enmities were long-standing. Friendships durable. School ties binding. Privileged families and aristocratic names had special social prerogatives. The ruling powers exacted their tributes. A quick learner, Gore was soon getting the hang of it.

Literary London assembled at Egerton Crescent, partly to meet Vidal and Williams, mostly to see one another. Williams, in London to attend *The Glass Menagerie* rehearsals, was co-guest of honor at a party Lehmann threw for his two American authors. Isherwood, who had come down from his family home in Cheshire, greeted Gore affectionately. They had exchanged a number of letters since Isherwood had left Paris, particularly about Gore's play. "Why not come over," Isherwood had urged. "London is well worth seeing, if Truman and Caskey haven't wrecked it by then!" Isherwood himself had not seen London since his departure with Auden for America in 1939, an expatriation that had seemed wartime desertion to some of his countrymen. Graham Greene, V. S. Pritchett, and William Plomer came to Lehmann's party. "V. S. Pritchett was amiable," Gore recalled. "The novel.

Yes. Yes! The novel. 'Ought to have a lot of sex in it,' I proclaimed. 'Oh, quite. Yes, yes a lot,' " Pritchett responded. The author of *Brighton Rock* seemed as "gray-green as his name." E. M. Forster's arrival caused a stir. He was less than warm to Isherwood, who had recently sent Forster at his King's College, Cambridge, residence a copy of his latest novel. From across the room "Christopher asked, 'Morgan, did you get the copy of *Prater Violet* I sent you?' . . . Forster went on chatting to William Plomer and seemed not to have heard. Christopher swallowed more gin. 'Morgan!' . . . 'Yes, Christopher.' Morgan's twinkle never ceased. 'I got it.' Then he turned back and continued his conversation with Plomer, leaving Christopher garroted in plain view." It was an explicit lesson in literature as blood sport. "Forster had developed . . . an unremitting censoriousness. He was always in court, seated on the high bench, passing judgments, a black cloth on his head. Christopher was hanged not so much for *Prater Violet* but for having left England before the war." Later that night Isherwood, drunk, beat up Caskey. The next morning he told Caskey that Gore had done it.

Forster, who had read *Streetcar,* was "very excited at meeting Tennessee," Gore later wrote in his memoir, "which I considered unfair since I had read and admired all his books while Tennessee, I fear, thought he was in the presence of the [creator] of Captain Horatio Hornblower. . . . Forster, looking like an old river rat, zeroed in on Tennessee and said how much he admired *Streetcar*. Tennessee gave him a beady look. Forster invited us to King's for lunch. Tennessee rolled his eyes and looked at me. 'Yes, I said quickly.' " It turned out a sour disappointment. Gore, who admired Forster's novels, already disliked Forster. His malicious humiliation of Isherwood the night before had been off-putting. Still, eager to know a writer he admired, to have a sense of personal relationship that suited his own hope for achievement and importance, he accepted the invitation for a reluctant Williams and for himself, aware that Forster's interest was in Williams. The next morning he dragged the always-late Tennessee to the railroad station. They had missed the first train. Relieved, Williams refused to wait. " 'But we *have* to go,' I said. . . . 'Your fan is a very old man, sitting on a stone lion and waiting for you, not me, to come to lunch.' . . . Tennessee was not moved by the poignant tableau. 'I can't,' he said, gulping and clutching his heart. . . . 'Besides,' said Tennessee primly, wandering off in the wrong direction for the exit, 'I cannot abide old men with urine stains on the trousers.' " Faced with unattractive alternatives, Vidal went by himself.

"Forster's look of disappointment was disheartening." After a bad boiled lunch they went to Forster's rooms, where he showed the young novelist a copy of the manuscript of his unpublished homoerotic novel, *Maurice,* which, he said, he had declined to publish while his mother was alive. When, as Forster took him dutifully around Cambridge, Gore used the Americanism "pretty" in a positive sense, he had the distinct impression that to the censorious Forster he had doomed himself forever to nonexistence.

Literary royalty and glamour, however, did half bow, mostly silently, in Gore's direction: remnants of the Bloomsbury world such as Harold Nicholson, whom he ran into numbers of times, and Duff and Lady Diana Cooper, with whom he later became friendly, the ghosts of Virginia and Leonard Woolf and Vita Sackville-West. Lehmann had known them all. A member of the Auden generation, he introduced Gore to Stephen Spender, whose friend, the poet C. Day-Lewis, was the object of Rosamond Lehmann's passion. The new monarchs of British literary society, the exotic Sitwells, were constantly evoked in party conversations, their angular aristocratic presences notable even though Gore did not meet them until later in the year. Such were their powers, particularly Edith's, that they could make strong literary men quake.

At another London party he was invited by the wealthy Sir Henry Channon, enthusiastic about the author of *The City and the Pillar,* to a country weekend late in June at Kelveden, near Plymouth. An American by birth, "Chips" Channon, who had married an heir to the Guinness fortune, had written a successful book on Ludwig of Bavaria and kept an elaborate diary he hoped would one day make him the Saint-Simon of modern Britain. He found Gore's Nordic-looking crew cut and blond good looks a turn-on. A member of the prewar Cliveden set, Channon had been pro-German. It apparently was not held against him now. Charming, immensely sociable, he gave entertaining, well-attended parties and moved in the highest social circles. "Everyone mocked Chips, but he more than sang for his supper; in fact, he himself provided the supper in his great silver and crystal dining room copied from one of Ludwig's castles." Somewhat self-defensively, Gore managed to have Tennessee invited, both of them driven down in the car Channon sent for them. At Kelveden, Gore's first experience of a British country weekend, they were introduced to Channon's companion, Peter Coates, though Channon spent much of the time talking about his passion for the playwright Terence Rattigan. "Sexually, he [Channon] preferred men to women and royalty to either," Vidal later observed. At lunch the talk was of royalty and writers. When Tennessee wanted to know what the royals talked about, their host responded, "Each other." Channon said that he had gotten many long letters from Proust, none of which he had kept. "How was I to know he was a genius?" In the afternoon Gore and another guest, Field Marshall Sir Claude Auchinlech, prompted by Channon and Coates, who teasingly encouraged a winter-spring romance, strolled together through the gardens. Later Gore did his best to entertain with dinnertime stories of Cocteau and the French literary world. Bored, Tennessee retreated to his room and insisted on their leaving before lunch the next day. As Channon escorted them to the car taking his guests back to London, he rushed to greet a newly arrived guest and then returned to say good-bye to Gore and Tennessee. "That is the queen of Spain," he said.

Inadvertently Gore became indirectly connected to real royalty through a new friend, Judy Montagu, an intimate friend of Princess Margaret, who eventually was to become his friend as well. In the kitchen of Auburon Herbert's flat, near Victoria Station, on a sun-bright afternoon, he met the daughter of Edwin Montagu, who had been in Prime Minister Asquith's cabinet, and Lady Venetia Stanley, from a distinguished aristocratic family. Asquith himself had been in love with Venetia, though Judy's actual father was probably the Earl of Dudley. Three years older than Gore, she was a tall, plain, handsome woman, with a long equine face and large, square figure, mouse-brown hair, blue eyes. She was a different kind of beauty, with great personal presence. "Very glamorous. She made the weather. A great wit." Gore and she immediately liked one another. Judy asked Auburon about his sister, who had, they all thought, the misfortune to be married to the difficult Evelyn Waugh. Interested herself in some sort of matrimonial alliance, since her career clearly had to do with existence rather than achievement, Judy told Gore she was going to marry the American journalist Joseph Alsop, whom she had met during his London visits and whom Gore knew from his parents' Washington world. Alsop had sometimes watched Gore and Jimmie Trimble play tennis at Merrywood. Somewhat impulsively, Gore told her that Alsop's only romantic attachment, as far as he knew, was to a handsome ex-sailor from Brooklyn named Frankie Merlo. Gore's precipitate words probably made little to no difference to a marriage proposal unlikely to have been realized anyway. Joe Alsop was to become one of Gore's Washington friends and, years later, Judy and Gore were to have a friendship in Rome, prefigured by this meeting in summer 1948.

Through Tennessee he met the actor John Gielgud, ineptly directing *The Glass Menagerie*, and Helen Hayes, the "first lady of the American theater," starring as Amanda Wingfield in the British production, still in rehearsals. In late July it was to have its opening in Brighton and then London. The rehearsals were going badly. Everyone sensed that they were about to have a failure on their hands, partly because neither Gielgud nor the British theater public had much feel for the American particularities of the play or for Williams's romantic/gothic sensibility. In addition, Williams had no enthusiasm for Helen Hayes, though Gore rather liked her. With grim imperial omniscience, the actress told the playwright, the director, and the cast that the play would be a failure. She was right. The only pleasure the British theatrical world provided Williams was his meeting with an almost twenty-seven-year-old Russian-born British actress of minor talent and small roles, Maria Britneva. They had probably first met at a party given by Binkie Beaumont, a well-known London theatrical agent. Within days the three were great friends—Tennessee, Maria, and Gore walking the Strand together, eating toffee candy that pulled out one of Gore's false teeth, laughing, joking, finding themselves immediate comrades in carefree silliness. Petite, slim-waisted, dark-haired, flaming-eyed, with full but sharp lips and a slightly irregular nose, Maria was simultaneously peremptory and responsive. A quick, passionate talker, she was voraciously expansive, enough to have people whom she valued disappear in her embrace. Maria found Tennessee magnetic, sexy, needy. She soon cast herself in the role of devoted sister-caretaker, though she would have liked lover, certainly wife, if Tennessee had been so inclined. Gore liked her free spirits, her ambition, her rashness, her sense of humor. He hoped to see her in London whenever he returned, or, even better, in New York. Williams fled to Paris in mid-July and purposely did not attend the London opening.

Having had enough of London, Gore himself returned in early July to the Hôtel de l'Université for what he decided would be his last month in Europe. Paris seemed the better place to spend the final weeks. On July afternoons he prowled "the streets, empty of traffic in those days." Having heard from Jean Cocteau of a male brothel that Proust had frequented, he located the Hôtel Saumon, near the Place de l'Humanité, allegedly "lugubriously furnished with Mother Proust's furniture." He went numbers of times, partly for the boys, mostly to question the ancient proprietor, an Algerian. " 'Oh, he [Proust] would just look. That's all. There were holes—you know, in the walls.' " Through a crack in a door, customers could view and select from the half dozen or so working-class boys who lounged in the sitting room. One day, crossing the Pont Neuf, Gore recognized one of the boys he liked, walking with a baby carriage and a pretty, pregnant wife. The two men smiled at one another and walked on. For the French young man, a student, it was simply a way to earn money. The next year a new, more moralistic government closed the Paris brothels.

From Paris, Gore complained to Lehmann that Lehmann had cast him in an unfavorable light by widely quoting his having said about someone that " 'I used him.' . . . I don't think it was wise of you to repeat that since, for one thing, you completely misunderstood what I meant. . . . American is not English even though it has a familiar ring; then, too, I freely admit to having no romantic notions about trade. But I don't think you meant it maliciously since I like you and feel, naively perhaps, that people I like won't make bitchy remarks." Lehmann blamed mischief-makers. "Now I think you must surely realize by now that I'm fond of you, and believe in you." It was not to prove a creditable claim.

Restless, eager to be home, Gore canceled his boat ticket and bought plane passage. He had had enough of living out of a suitcase, even of traveling, though he had proposed to the London editors of *Vogue* an article for them on Ischia and Capri, which the New York editors had declined to commission. Now he wanted to work on revising *A Search for the King,* and he had some short stories in mind. The best place to do that would be at home, wherever that was or might be—New York, Washington, East Hampton. He had every reason to feel that his European trip had been successful, the first of many reaffirmations of the vision of himself he had cherished since he had first learned to read and which his 1939 voyage had made a vivid part of his consciousness. At the beginning of August he flew westward. "A note to tell you," he soon wrote to Lehmann, "I am back amongst my people ready to lead them to the new Sodom, out of this pillar-marked wilderness."

CHAPTER nINE

Byron Without Greece

1948–1950

AS GLASSES TINKLED at a Georgetown party in December 1948, John Galliher, a friend of Nina's, introduced Gore to a slim, dark-haired, small-voiced woman with whom, Galliher immediately reminded him, Gore had something in common. They shared a stepfather, Hugh Auchincloss. Nineteen-year-old Jackie Bouvier had heard much about her slightly older, enviably successful quasi-relative who had already published three novels. Her mother was Nina's successor. Gore had indeed heard something about the family that had moved into Merrywood soon after his departure. In the back of Miss Bouvier's mind was the hope he might be helpful to her getting started in a career, perhaps journalism or photography, something to do with the arts, most likely in New York. After a few pleasant words about Merrywood, still her official residence, they may indeed have identified their shared inheritance—fractured families, difficult mothers, problematic childhoods. Nina was not at the party. But Galliher, Gore remembers, said to him years later, "Gore, I've gone to bed with your mother, and I'd like to go to bed with you." "It doesn't sound like me," Galliher remarked, meaning only the wit. But the fact and the desire were real. "Nina and I were

friends," he recalled, "and it was like having another lovely glass of champagne. It wasn't a very serious performance. . . . It was always a possibility with me or another man. It was just a pleasant occasion. She was an
interesting lady. And Gore was also very attractive then, a very handsome
man and great fun to be with." A wealthy Washingtonian, somewhat
younger than Nina, Galliher had become her devoted friend. They shared a
life of parties. "She was so beautiful, a very handsome woman. . . . She
played cards and backgammon and she was a good dancer. All those things.
A social woman. . . . She went everywhere. . . . She was very smart,
fun to be with, ready to play and have fun and to have an interesting social
life. And she was a very earthy, sexual woman too. . . . Nina didn't talk
much about Gore to criticize him. I remember only something about her
talking about Gore and a ballet dancer. She said that was really too much.
We never went into details. 'A ballet dancer. Really! This is too much! What
now! Really!' she said. You know, like that."

After the party, planning to spend Christmas and the first few months
of 1949 in Antigua, Gore took a cab to Union Station to catch the overnight
train to New Orleans. With *The Season of Comfort* about to appear, he was
eager to be away. Perhaps he feared Nina's likely reaction, especially since
things had been going comparatively well between them. That summer she
had been eager for him to return home, mostly because of their shared
anxiety about the Senator's health, partly because she genuinely missed him.
When the Gores had gone to Florida that past June, she had been afraid
"Dad will never get back alive." Crippled, aged, the Senator was a painfully
unhappy sight to his grandson on his visits to Washington between his
return from Europe in August 1948 and his departure for Guatemala in late
December. As Nina went off to Yale for her reformative course on alcoholism, she wanted to know when Gore would be "heading home—I have a
yen to see you." Volatile, unpredictable, still drinking heavily, she had given
him good reason to think the relationship would soon explode again, as it
regularly had over the years, particularly with the publication of *Season*.
Certainly he wanted to be out of New York when the book appeared.

At first he had thought of going to Europe, this time with Tennessee
Williams and Paul Bowles, who had urged him to join them on a winter
transatlantic crossing that would take them to North Africa, and then Williams to Italy. Nina had written Gore a damaging letter urging him to attend
to his "mental health." She meant his sexual proclivities, which, as a believer

in psychoanalysis, she considered an illness that needed to be cured. With the publication of *The City and the Pillar* he had, so to speak, come out. She had not previously been aware, at least consciously, that he was not "a regular guy." Now, to her mind, his troubled personality was the source of their mother-son difficulties.

> *I think it would be a good idea if you put off Europe as long as you can and take advantage of perhaps becoming* comfortable *with yourself—Europe will still be there! We come from pretty tough stock, and you will, with luck, have fifty years more of living with* you—*and those* providence puts in your circle. Sweetie *you have too much ability to permit letting the ropes to be fouled. It is awfully tough, though, on super sensitive folks like us. I've always wanted the moon—and it is usually cheese. You are young enough to orient. Do! There is a man that has done a great deal of good for several friends of mine, Lawrence Kubie, an analyst, top flight—in tele. book—on my cuff talk to him too—you know there is nothing like getting confidence and a feeling of security—* don't overlook anything that might help—*and you know as feeble as it may be darling, when you put your hand out and mine can be there it will be—* Love—Bommy.

Kubie, Gore knew, had advised Tennessee Williams to give up writing and boys.

At first Gore enthusiastically accepted Williams's and Bowles's invitation. Then he changed his mind, partly because he had it in mind to write a new novel, this one set in Guatemala. It made more sense to spend the winter there than traveling in Europe. Perhaps Nina's advice gave him pause. Certainly it would be cheaper to live in his own house in Antigua, the rent from which produced very little profit and which he had again been giving serious thought to selling. On the train to New Orleans he began to write *Dark Green, Bright Red*.

The late summer and fall of 1948, after the return from Europe, had been mostly uneventful but pleasurable, except for his increasing frustration with Lehmann's resistance to publishing any of his novels other than *City*.

With *City*, Lehmann was cautious on moral grounds, but, "considering that [John Horne Burns's] *The Gallery* doesn't appear to have made a single moral ripple, I think with care we ought to be all right." Vidal had hoped Lehmann would bring out *The Season of Comfort*, a copy of which Gore had had Nick Wreden send him in October. The verdict on that was still out. For a short time he was "in the midst of my I AM A FAILURE mood, a chronic disease with me." All his *real* illnesses, he told Lehmann, "have been related back to my revolting liver," the result of the hepatitis attacks of summer 1947, "and that is currently being treated." Lehmann was not having his complaints either. "Good God, if I'd managed to get three books out by the time I was 23, and had the fun with one and the success or scandal you've had with another, I should not have been depressed but almost unbearably conceited. I feel sure it must be a purely physical reaction, simply coming from doing too much and living too scandalously." By October, Gore was busy "getting the two books ready and fooling with a hopeless play. I've written two short stories; the only new work since spring. One gets very well-paid for such things and I'm planning more when I really learn how to write them." One, called "The Robin," partly about the horror of death, dramatizes the decision of two boys to put a wounded bird out of its misery, their emotions hovering between compassion and cruelty, shame and pleasure. "Not much news," he wrote Pat Crocker in the late fall, "many parties, much intrigue and little work." In fact, if the latest potential buyer for the Antigua house was serious, why not sell it? "Since I am embarked on my annual response (a peculiar Freudian slip) I mean to say romance, I shall undoubtedly be in New York forever."

In late summer he had spent time at East Hampton, staying at his father's rented place and visiting Nina in Washington and Southampton. With two young stepsiblings at the Fifth Avenue apartment, he stayed for a while at the Chelsea Hotel, then for a brief time in Tennessee's apartment while Williams was away, then in a sublease on East Fifty-second Street, downstairs from the ballerina Nora Kaye, who had been married to one of the literary heroes of his adolescence, James T. Farrell, everything of whose he had read at Exeter. One night her bathtub overflowed, flooding his apartment, leaving them both discomfited but even friendlier. Anxious, as always, about his career, still angry about *City*'s hostile reviews, perhaps what Nina thought his discomfort with himself was his ongoing preoccupation with his personal and professional pulse. Articulately egomaniacal, he was clever at both self-assertion and accommodation. Nina, a real and a necessary foil, unable to make peace with let alone lovingly accept his sexual preferences, inevitably fueled (sometimes with alcohol) the worst in her and in him. On the one hand she could boast publicly about the success of her son the bestselling author whose name frequently appeared in the newspapers. On the other, she could glower bitterly, in bars and cocktail lounges, about her son "the faggot," one of the undeserved blows fate had inflicted on a blameless mother.

With rivals Gore was both self-asserting and accommodating, even for a brief time with Truman Capote, whom he saw more of in New York during the fall of 1948 than ever before or again. "Truman is everywhere," Gore wrote to Lehmann, "giddy and mad and not working but rather charming I think (young writers who don't write always charm me)." He was still friendly toward Capote, though there was no real friendship. Frederick Buechner's *A Long Day's Dying*, about to be published by Knopf "with much fanfare," reminded him of "the way Truman would write *if* he had a prose style instead of that peculiar interior decorator's way he has of constructing a Saks Fifth Avenue window and calling it a novel," he wrote to Lehmann. The day after Gore's twenty-third birthday, Vidal and Capote concluded a night on the town by going together to the Everard Baths. "It was strictly voyeur time," Gore recalled. "Lights were dim. But each of us was sufficiently well known so that we did not particularly want to be recognized." Truman babbled on about how wonderful Tallulah Bankhead had been that evening in the premiere of a revival of Noel Coward's *Private Lives*. Wrapped in white towels, they went about their separate activities, probably literally, in the case, looking over one another's shoulders. As they slunk along the corridor, someone who knew them both, "the greatest gossip in town," rushed up and shouted, "Ah see you! Ah see you!" Gore occasionally declined to say harsh things about his competitor, perhaps influenced by the companionable atmosphere promoted by "parties and gatherings" at Tennessee's apartment and by the excitement of the Broadway premiere in October of *Summer and Smoke*. The barbs between Vidal and Capote were often mediated or amplified by third parties, though Williams had no favorite to play when he wrote to his own and Capote's good friend, the novelist Donald Windham, "I think you judge Truman a bit too charitably when you call him a child: he is more like a sweetly vicious old lady."

Gore had found amusing Capote's performance at Williams's apartment one August evening, soon after Truman and Tennessee had returned from Europe on the *Queen Mary*. Capote lived nearby with Johnny Nicholson, who had just opened his café on Fifty-eighth Street. Tennessee and Gore came back to Tennessee's flat with an actress, Jane Lawrence Smith, to find Truman and Carson McCullers's young cousin "in the apartment undergoing questioning by a detective." Earlier, after waiting for Capote, who was late, Williams had gone off. When Capote had finally turned up, frustrated at not finding Williams at home, he had climbed in through a ground-floor window. Two policemen, seeing him in the act, assumed they were about to catch a burglar. "By the time we arrived," Gore remembered, "Capote had matters well under control." The police "were listening bug-eyed to Capote, who was telling them *every*thing about the private lives of Mr. and Mrs. Charlie Chaplin." Truman, delighted when Walter Winchell reported the incident in his gossip column, had made sure Gore's name was not included in the report. Gore evened the score twice, the first simply a practical joke, as he told it to Paul Bowles. While working on the score for *Summer and Smoke* for which he was writing incidental music, and anticipating spring publication of *The Sheltering Sky*, Bowles was staying in grand comfort at the Sixty-first Street town house of his friend, the torch singer Libby Holman, to whom he and Latouche introduced Gore. With his usual marvelous mimicry, Gore called Williams on the telephone, pretending he was Capote, and induced Tennessee to make "uncomplimentary remarks about Gore's writing." When, a few days later, Gore next saw Tennessee, he made "oblique but unmistakable allusions" to comments Tennessee had made to the person he thought Capote. "To Tennessee it seemed quite obvious," Bowles wrote in his memoir, "that Truman had run to Gore and maliciously repeated the telephone conversation. As a result he was angry with Truman, which had been the object of the ploy." In November, *Life*, on the occasion of a New York visit by Edith and Osbert Sitwell, had invited a group of America's most famous poets to appear in a celebrity photograph to be taken at the Gotham Book Mart, New York's best-known high-literary bookstore. Its energetic owner, Frances Stelloff, frequently held book parties and hosted literary people. Both Sitwells, Gore wrote to Lehmann, "have taken their social success with the ease and the calm of Plantagenets among colonial gentry." Surrounding the royal couple were W. H. Auden, Stephen Spender, Randall Jarrell, Delmore Schwartz, Marianne Moore, Elizabeth Bishop, Horace Gregory, Charles Henri Ford, among others, and

Tennessee Williams. While the group was not strictly limited to poets, Williams was poet enough. Gore had managed to get himself included somehow, though even less a poet than Williams. Capote was furious. "You're not a poet at all!" he said to Gore. "What right do you have to be there?" More to the point, he was furious that he had not been included in the august company.

———————

At ease with and attractive to members of his mother's generation, that fall Gore had met three extraordinary people with whom he was to remain friends until their deaths. Eddie Bismarck—handsome, slim, clear-eyed, fair-haired, a grandson of the nineteenth-century German chancellor—came from two families of aristocratic distinction in the Austro-Hungarian and German empires. By 1948 he had for a decade been closely associated with Mona and Harrison Williams. From Kentucky, Mona Strader had risen to the pinnacle of international society through beauty, charm, good taste, and three useful marriages, the last to the wealthy Harrison Williams, twenty-three years her senior. By the early 1930s, New York, London, Palm Beach, and Riviera society celebrated her, as did the prestige fashion magazines, as the best-dressed woman in the world. Her glamorous parties and personal splendor expressed "perhaps the first private life to be shaped and pitched for public consumption." An attractive homosexual, Eddie Bismarck shared with Mona Williams, starting in the late thirties, a life of good taste and fine society. As companion, secretary, and adviser, he was perfectly acceptable to Harrison Williams. An outspoken anti-Nazi, the only member of his family to oppose the National Socialist regime, Bismarck had lived some golden years between the two world wars, a benign aristocrat supported by his wealthy brother Otto. A world traveler of exquisite taste, Eddie collected antiques and occasionally took on clients whose homes he redecorated. When he fled the Nazis, he found himself penniless. With the domination of Central Europe by Communist regimes, the capitals of his youth were again closed to him. A comfortable life with the Harrison Williamses in New York, Palm Beach, and Capri became his fate.

Bismarck invited Gore to one of the many grand dinners at the Williamses' thirty-room Georgian mansion on Fifth Avenue and Ninety-fourth Street, a few blocks from Gene Vidal's apartment. Though loved for himself alone, on this occasion Gore was loved also for his friendship with Tennessee Williams, now at the height of his fame. *Streetcar* had been running on Broadway for almost two years, arguably now the most famous American play by the best-known, most widely publicized living playwright, though his most recent play, *Summer and Smoke*, Gore wrote to Lehmann, had "received, for the most part, hostile and bitter notices." Through Gore, Eddie invited Tennessee to the dinner. Unconventionally, Mona sat the dramatist on her right, Gore on her left, surrounding her bejeweled elegance with two handsome young writers who, like everyone else, dressed formally for the occasion. Among the thirty or so guests was Eddie's cousin, Countess Cecilia Sternberg, a witty, unconventional aristocrat who had been brought up in Vienna. At seventeen she had married Count Leopold Sternberg, the heir to estates in Bohemian Czechloslovakia. Having lost everything to the Nazis before the war, he had had his property expropriated a second time, by the Communist government. Without resources, the Sternbergs had recently arrived in New York with their eleven-year-old daughter, Diana, exiles once again, reliant for the time being on their personal attractions, their distinguished names, and their large network of European connections, which included, through Eddie, "Aunt Mona," as Diana called her.

Wandering out of one of the maid's rooms upstairs where she had been put to bed, Diana, on the balcony above the marble staircase, heard voices, laughter, a voice singing Russian songs. In his dressing gown, Harrison Williams, who had declined to attend the party, joined her. The singer was one of the guests, the actor Yul Brynner. In the salon they all enjoyed his handsome good looks, his striking visage, his deep romantic voice. Prince Serge Obolensky, a New York society celebrity of White Russian origin who was divorced from the wealthy Alice Astor but ran the St. Regis hotel for Alice's brother Vincent, sat near Mona and chatted with Cecilia, who soon turned to Tennessee. At first she assumed he must be a relative of Harrison Williams. She had never heard of *Streetcar*. Within a few minutes of conversation she was convinced that he disliked her and had turned away. "You'll like Gore Vidal much better," Eddie assured her. "He's brilliant, but in a way more like us. Suffered as much from family tradition as we did in our youth." "Is he by any chance the boy who looks like an archaic Apollo?" Introduced to Gore, she thought him "charming and amusing," his eyes "alive with humor, and so was the smiling mouth." Gore thought her exotic, beautiful, fearlessly herself, an embodiment of an aristocratic world that had its own rules, its own freedom, liberated from the constraints of middle-class life, distinctly its own thing, possessed of a certain laissez-faire wisdom about life. With Mona, Eddie, and Cecilia, in New York and then in London and Capri, he was to become a good and caring friend. Later, eleven-year-old Diana was to become a close friend.

He was more likely to be found, though, at the equally festive but less elegant parties of ballet and theater people, at gatherings of editors and writers, with Sarah Moore and Connie Darby, with whom he continued to have good times, at various popular bars that artistic people frequented, and especially at the Astor Bar, which he still visited often. He went regularly to the well-known Blue Angel on Fifty-fifth street off First Avenue, the most popular club for classy entertainment, for high spirits, for adventuresome socialites, rubbing shoulders with those of accomplishment and celebrity. At the Astor he met the Columbia University Shakespeare scholar Andrew Chiappe, also there to pick up trade, accompanied by his good friends Bob Giroux and John Kelly. Kelly introduced Gore to the impressive Chiappe, who knew most of Shakespeare by heart and had "a rather penetrating very beautiful voice, a Shakespearean actor's voice." With a sharp critical mind, Chiappe could not only recite but interpret Shakespeare with a brilliance that immediately impressed Gore. "He looked Dickensian," Jason Epstein, later to be Gore's editor, recalled, "a set of spheres, a big round head and round body. He walked like a ballet dancer and was very fastidious." Gore found him striking. It was the start of a friendship. Sam Lurie, the publicist for the Ballet Theatre, whom he already knew, he now got to know better. "Dorothy Parker, when she needed a joke," Gore recalled, "would go to him. She thought he was the wittiest man in New York." One day a group that included Sam and Gore were trying to remember where the phrase "always be kind to strangers . . . for they may be angels in disguise" appears. "We were talking about trade, I suppose. Well, Sam says it's in the Bible, and somebody said, 'Yeah, it's in the Book of Hebrews.' And this guy goes over to a Bible and riffles the pages and says, 'There's no book of Hebrews here.' And Sam says, 'That's the Racquet Club edition.'" At the exclusive Blue Angel a sailor somehow got in. "Sam went over and sat beside him and tried to open a conversation with him. The sailor was surly. Sam rolled off the stool and onto the floor, where he lay on his back like a turtle. As waiters moved in, Sam, from the floor, said to the sailor, very quietly, 'You don't seem to realize that I could ruin you socially!'"

During the autumn of 1948 the ballet world engaged Gore even more than it had in spring 1946, partly because some of its major figures were his friends, from his upstairs neighbor Nora Kaye to Antony Tudor, the choreographer for the Ballet Theatre; to Leon Danielian, a lead dancer first at Ballet Theatre and then at the Ballet Russe de Monte Carlo; to his former lover Harold Lang; his occasional companion Johnny Kriza; and the witty Sam Lurie. Like others in that golden period when ballet flourished and three or four companies circulated from one city to another in Europe and America, Gore attended the ballet regularly, sometimes numbers of times a week, occasionally with John Kelly, who was madly in love with Leon Danielian, to whom he had created a small shrine in his bedroom at Cismont. Dressing rooms were open to Gore, ballet-world parties embraced him. Tudor, whose ballets he admired, lived nearby on Fifty-second Street with his companion, Hugh Laing. Though no longer sleeping together, Gore and Harold remained friends, though Gore worried about Harold's increasingly dangerous sexual escapades, which began to threaten his career. Gore and Johnny Kriza had become good friends. "Gore liked Johnny," Sam Lurie, one of Kriza's close friends, recalled, "but I don't think he was passionate about him the way he was for a while about Harold." A character dancer with a flair for acting, the short, dark-haired, craggily handsome Kriza, son of working-class Czech immigrants from Chicago, had been the protégé and lover of Ballet Theatre dancer Anton Dolin, who in 1941 had danced the first *Bluebeard* with Alicia Markova, Antony Tudor, and Nora Kaye. With Lang and Robbins, Kriza became famous as one of the three sailors in *Fancy Free* and performed brilliantly in *Billy the Kid*, a role with which Gore strongly identified. "Copland's music certainly flowed through that strong body, particularly the percussion." In that role Kriza may have seemed to Gore an alter ego. "He was absolutely fun to be with," Lurie remarked, "terribly bright, humorous. . . . He and Gore may have had sex, and I would say if it was important to Gore they would have. . . . Promiscuity was Johnny's middle name. . . . Johnny was very attractive as a personality. Not beautiful as some people are, but he was an extremely personable, attractive, bright, humorous companion, a beautiful body. . . . Great charisma. . . . By today's standard he certainly was not a great dancer. And his success as a star should be attributed to the war, because many of the best dancers were in the service and he was not. I think because of the homosexual thing. . . . Because the company toured a great deal, he had friends all over the country. No matter what city you went to, if you mentioned John Kriza among the ballet crowd, they not only knew him but they adored him. Even the people who didn't think that he danced that well. He was so likable and endearing."

So too was John Latouche, known to everyone as "Touche." By fall 1948 he was becoming one of Gore's regular companions, partly because of his wickedly funny, widely talented irrepressibility, also because in the postwar decade he had become a pervasive presence in New York artistic circles. Latouche immediately liked Gore. They made plans to collaborate. Why not write a play together, a comedy or a drama, particularly a screen-play, where there was money to be made quickly? Everyone knew and many loved Latouche, if not for himself alone, then for his talent and his high-spirited zaniness. Immensely but idiosyncratically social, he was everyplace, at artistic-social dinners, at the ballet and theater, in Virgil Thomson's high-art musical circle, at Leo Lerman's and Peggy Guggenheim's salons, in the nightclub world of the Blue Angel and Libby Holman, with New York society and artistic celebrities like Joe O'Donohue and the novelist-photog-rapher Carl Van Vechten, with Greenwich Village friends like the novelist Dawn Powell. Sleeplessly, from dusk to dawn, at openings, parties, dinners, bars, clubs, he was part of a New York nightlife that dressed for dinner, partied in tuxedos in Harlem, embraced high musical culture and the latest jazz, and for a while seemed to have revivified its own version of the high-kicking spirit of the 1920s. That Latouche was usually broke made no difference. Constantly abuzz with schemes for musical comedies and dra-mas, enamored of the Broadway musical theater, he had had a number of fame-creating successes as a lyricist, from *Flair Flair the Idol of Paree* as an undergraduate at Columbia to the patriotic cantata *Ballad for Americans*, which Paul Robeson made famous in 1939, to the Broadway musical drama *Cabin in the Sky*. If as an artist he was, as the composer Ned Rorem remarked, "a sort of preface to Sondheim," someone who "mingled with the upper crust but catered to the middlebrow," he was a preface with a distinc-tively unforgettable personality, "the most irresistibly quick man in the world," witty, funny, perceptive, generous.

A heavy drinker and, by the late 1940s, regularly dependent on a pharmacopoeia of pills and injections in the Max Jacobson age, Latouche had been born in 1919 in Richmond, Virginia, to a fractured family with an absent father and a strong mother, to whom he remained devoted. He had won a scholarship to Columbia, embraced a *New Masses*—Communist phase, discovered poetry, musical lyrics, and sex with men, married in 1940 and quickly divorced the daughter of a former United States ambassador to Spain, spent fourteen months in the Congo ostensibly to make a documentary film but producing a book instead, served in the Navy in the Pacific, and ultimately returned to New York to pursue art, good company, infinite fun, and high fame. He knew how to amuse himself and other people, though not everyone was amused. He "thought he was a Communist," Joe O'Donohue recalled. "He'd go to dinner parties in a black shirt rather than in evening dress. He was attractive to hosts at these fancy parties as an oddity. He was a short man, tending to pudginess. Not good-looking at all. He'd try to dominate conversation." To Johnny Nicholson, an admirer, "he looked like a frog. A great friend of his was named Spivey. She was an entertainer. She worked in Tony's East Side. She opened her own club called Spivey's Roof. She was just called Madame Spivey. If you met her, you would know you had met somebody. She and John Latouche were very good friends. He wrote songs for her. One night after the club we all went up to Harlem to have spareribs. It was about four or five o'clock in the morning, and he was talking about his hometown and how the dogs used to bark in the morning. Before you knew it, he was on his hands and knees like a dog, howling, showing us. It was enchanting." Like most everyone else, Gore was enchanted.

Though he had six months earlier declined Bowles's and Williams's invitation to go to Europe with them at the end of 1948, Gore still had it in mind to go to Europe, probably in spring 1949. He hoped to be in London for the publication of Lehmann's edition of *The City and the Pillar*, scheduled for May. Not that he was happy with Lehmann. Indeed, he was simmeringly furious. Soon after his arrival in Antigua, he had written him a friendly letter. "Serene and working for the first time since last May. Started a book on a revolution in a country like Guatemala and a rather humorous story, a bit anti-revolutionary in tone but unpolitical, absolutely unpolitical—to be called, I think, *Dark Green, Bright Red*—the jungle and blood; any number of other symbols can be safely maintained. I'll send you *Search for the King* (how is that title?) around March when I make it ready for press—turned out fairly good they tell me, be out next January. Did you get

S of C, and what do you think of it?" On January 3, 1949, Dutton published *Season* in New York. Within a few weeks Gore wrote Lehmann twice more, tactfully but with an anxious subtext. Are you going to publish *Season?* Vidal's next letter crossed Lehmann's in the mail. "I have such a high regard for your gifts," Lehmann wrote in the middle of January, "that I cannot conceal my disappointment, which Rosamond shares. . . . It strikes me as a tired book." Though not entirely wrong about some of *Season*'s weaknesses, Lehmann had no eye for its strengths. To Gore, Lehmann was for the moment a hateful semi-enemy. What was the point of having a publisher who disliked one's work? Isherwood advised him not to "break with John yet. At any rate, not until *The City and the Pillar* has been published. I think changing publishers is always a pity, anyhow. One suffers for it. . . . It has to be weighed carefully, like a divorce." Gore took Isherwood's advice. Lehmann, who published *Dark Green, Bright Red* in 1951, was to be out of business as a publisher soon, essentially because he was undercapitalized and overextended. "Bad management," Graham Watson remarked. "Lehmann went bust because he was an intellectual nonbusinessman and he had a taste for certain types of books, fairly eclectic and fairly intellectual." To Gore the rejection was both painful and infuriating. Rather than respond to Lehmann, he kept silent for months. In April he wrote to him, "as to *The Season of Comfort:* I've made no attempt to get another [British] publisher for it; on the other hand I'm not anxious, at the moment, to let you see any new work. We both have plenty of time to think all this over." He had been uneasy about Lehmann from the beginning, but he had had high hopes that as author and publisher they would flourish.

After two months in Guatemala, Gore returned to New York at the end of February 1949, anxious about reviews of *Season* and about his health. "Did I tell you I arrived in NYC," he wrote to Pat Crocker, "with a nasty case of clap contracted from one of the bels of Panajachel?" On Latouche's recommendation he went to see the omnipresent Dr. Max Jacobson, whom he had first learned about from Anaïs. He was "a friend of the stars. If you went out with Tennessee, suddenly Jacobson would be at the end of the room." Having chatted with him at numbers of parties, Gore thought him charming. Anyway, he was "the only doctor I knew. . . . I go over and he's delighted to see me. . . . There I was, at twenty-three, ready to become an addict of Max Jacobson, and since I had a long life ahead of me, he'd have a lot of revenue. So he was twinkling. And I said, 'I've got this problem.' And I whipped out my cock and I said, 'You know, I've got this clap.' He turned white. 'For God's sake, go to a doctor. I mean, I mean . . . go to a urologist.' Not interested at all in what would have been a real illness. . . . It turned out not to be venereal disease. Something to do with strain, as they call it. But it looked like clap and it seemed like clap." Pat found his evasion worth teasing. "Your disease is a direct result," he wrote to him, "of your filthy bed habits, your complete lack of taste etc. Body juices indeed. That was pus you were sliding in on." Having sex with strangers entailed risks. Within limits, they seemed worth taking, especially when the worst consequence was a venereal disease. Sulphur and the newly emerging antibiotics made the threat bearable, the diseases, if treated, manageable. "The mice and pussycats are as rewarding as ever. True love hides but croons from afar," though this "afar" in spring 1949 seems to have been Houston, where he went on a book-signing and lecturing tour in early April. The Houston "true love" eventually faded entirely out of memory. At parties, at bars, in New York or wherever he traveled, there was the expectation of erotic excitement, of one-night or even fifteen-minute pickups, none likely to have any emotional content. As he had told John Lehmann, "I freely admit to having no romantic notions about trade."

On the morning of March 16, 1949, seventy-eight-year-old Senator Gore, at home in his ground-floor apartment on Crescent Place and Wisconsin Avenue, while teasing his wife at breakfast, suffered a fatal stroke. The long-articulate life fell into silence. The day before, his assistant, Roy Thompson, had brought him his income-tax forms to sign, his signature the last official act of his life. On the morning of St. Patrick's Day the Senator's ex-son-in-law and his grandson came down together by train from New York. Gene Vidal had known and liked Senator Gore since the early 1920s. To his grandson he had been the most formative positive influence of his early life. Dot "wept quietly, but talked coherently." Visitors came to pay their respects to the widow, many of them ancient Washingtonians whose hands also had once held the reins of power. The Oklahoma Senate and House delegations paid a call. Always the consummate politician's wife, Dot "greeted each by name. Never got a name wrong. Remembered to repeat

Mr. Gore's good opinion of the visitor." There was no body to view. When Gene and Gore arrived, the remains were en route to Oklahoma for a ceremonial funeral.

Much remained, however, for Gore of his grandfather's legacy, including the all-too-ready availability of self-assertion through lineage, a calling card that if left too often at too many doors might indeed not serve him well. At Exeter his frequent reference to his family had impressed some but offended many. It was a temptation difficult for a young man to resist. Later that calling card was to be used more selectively, and indeed transformed into a playing card in a self-conscious literary and political strategy, Senator Gore as both a point of reference through which to make his own political positions more rhetorically effective and Senator Gore (and his Washington world) transformed into fiction and memoir. The imprint was deep, perhaps the best of it the influence of T. P. Gore's love of argument, his attachment to fact and rational analysis, his deep engagement with history and books, his sensitivity to language, particularly to irony, and his satiric humor. "If there were any other race but the damned human race, I'd go join it," the Senator had said, a disenchantment with human nature as deep as Jonathan Swift's and Mark Twain's. Years later, in Chicago, Saul Bellow asked the visiting Gore Vidal if Bellow could bring his young son with him to the hotel to say hello: "I want him to meet someone *really cynical!*" Gore responded with a gentle but firm corrective: *"Realistic!"* Unlike cynicism, realism had comic potential, perhaps most happily illustrated by one of T. P. Gore's campaign-trail stories about "the hitchhiker [in the 1930s] who was hitching a ride out on the highway in Oklahoma, and a big, long Cadillac with a chauffeur stopped, and the man in the back said, 'Do you want a ride?' The hitchhiker said, 'Oh, yes, that would be great.' He said, 'Well, I'll tell you. It's campaign now, and I'm a Republican. I've got a Republican badge on here, and I don't allow anyone to ride in my car unless they wear a Republican badge. Would you mind?' 'Oh, no, no.' He got in. They went several miles down the rode, and the hitchhiker said, 'Oh, stop the car!' 'Why?' 'See that peach orchard out there? The peaches are just becoming ripe, and I want to get some.' The man said, 'Do you own this place?' He says, 'No, I don't, but I've been a Republican for ten minutes, and I'm just dying to steal something.' "

In early April, Senator Gore's friends and family gathered to take him the last solemn mile. Dot was her usual brave, composed self. Gore was not there. If Dot had known that he was only four hundred and fifty miles away, in Houston, she might have found his absence even more difficult to understand. At the end of March, having been invited to sign books and lecture, he spent ten days or so on the road, first in New Orleans, then mostly in Houston and Dallas. None of this was especially memorable except for the few days in Houston, which "was a crazy town, fascinating, very Trimalchian. I had quite a good time there," mostly partying, enjoying his status as a visiting literary celebrity. Sylvia and Ted Brown, former New Yorkers with whom he stayed, hosted a reading, a book-signing, and a well-attended cocktail party at their bookstore, the main intellectual-social center for Houston writers and readers. One of the ballet companies was in town. So too was a beautiful, wealthy Houstonian who was in love with Leon Danielian and hoped he would marry her. Leon was on tour in Canada. Gore happily had her on his arm at numbers of parties, especially the late-night revelry the ballet company enjoyed and at which Gore was welcome. In Oklahoma City, the Senator was being buried. In Houston, Gore partied, to the "chagrin" of his grandmother, to his own as well, he later said. Partly he wanted to avoid seeing his mother: mostly he combined resolute stubbornness with an overwhelming fear of death, the power of which he first felt fully at this time and which for the rest of his life kept him away from almost every funeral he could reasonably have been expected to attend. Confinement in a narrow coffin surrounded by earthy darkness was an imaginative claustrophobe's worst nightmare. "I didn't want to go. My thanatophobia took over. I always was afraid of death and funerals. Going back to my first knowledge that there was such a thing. Why do anything about it?" But his grandmother may have felt equally strongly that his place was with her in Oklahoma City. His fear may have been incapacitating. It also may have had in it some combination of defiance and denial.

He would have liked also to defy the critics, many of whom did not find *Season* convincing. Some could not understand why a book focusing on a mother-son relationship was stubbornly antipsychological, especially the abrupt ending. Others found the novel excessively psychological. Amid substantial praise there was a backwash of reservation from those who felt its stylistic modernisms forced and awkward, its psychological insights routine, its energy level low. His Houston friends may not have celebrated his visit any the less fulsomely because the headline editor for the *Houston Post* had called it, in bold print, "An Error for Gore Vidal, A Mother, A Son and a Debacle." The reviewer had concluded that "the entire book is so fuzzy, so uncertain as to be unworthy of a review of this length." Vidal himself, the *Houston Post* insisted, as did many of the negative reviews, "is important as one of the nation's most promising writers." Undoubtedly "a writer of genius," claimed the dyspeptic *New York Post* reviewer, who found himself "disliking intensely every character in Gore Vidal's novels." There was also widespread praise for *Season,* laudatory reviews in the *Herald Tribune* and *Saturday Review,* among others. Even among the harsh critics, including those who urged him to return to the realism of *Williwaw,* a general consensus existed that a major novelist had emerged with the promise of a substantial oeuvre. Eager savants tried to predict and influence its direction. On one side was the alliance of John Aldridge, soon to publish his influential *After the Lost Generation,* and the Orville Prescotts of the newspaper reviewing world. On the other, those who placed primary emphasis on the novel as an aesthetic entity, to be judged not by moral content but on artistic merit. Aldridge believed that the worthiness of a novel importantly resided in its value structure, the degree to which it represented some culturally desirable and sanctioned moral stance. Prescott insisted that the values had to be those of his conservative middle-class constituency. With Aldridge, Gore did a tentative dance for a while, beginning with the critics's favorable comments in *Harper's,* which had occasioned the beginning of their relationship. Gore had some residual hope that despite his emphasis on values—often a code word for ideological litmus tests, including homophobia—Aldridge would be an ally, someone with whom he could have constructive dialogue about his work and the novel as a literary form. From Paris the previous year he had been both friendly and frank when he had written to Aldridge, "I'd like to talk to you about writing. I seem to have no very firm convictions only a kind of luminous tenuous attitude." Over the next three years they were to see one another occasionally in New England and New York, to correspond at some length about their different views of art and, inevitably, to end as enemies.

After *The City and the Pillar,* though Gore had a supporter at the *New York Times*—the poet and editor Harvey Breit, who soon managed to get the *Times* to publish his feature profile of the young novelist—he began to hate the *Times* in general. Prescott refused to review anything of Vidal's. Even Breit's effort fell short of satisfaction. When the interview-article came out early in February 1950, Vidal felt that each of his "bejeweled epigrams was ruined by Mr Breit's poor memory; each time he very nearly got the point, he came close enough to make me look a trifle more foolish than usual. *I* think the whole interview makes me look marvelously clever, brilliant and pretentious." Like most writers, he needed the *New York Times*'s support, the visibility and sales its favorable reviews generated. Like many, he came to hate its conservatism, its hostility, and, worst of all, its neglect. Not to be reviewed, or not to be reviewed prominently enough, was a form of erasure. Somewhat battered but still standing, he had enough vulnerability to be hurt, enough resoluteness not only to keep going but to recast the moment into an overview of the longer perspective. "Thus do I," despite the onslaught, "most ancient and revered of young authors, speak, dedicated as I am to longevity and performance and hopelessly jaundiced," he wrote to his lukewarm British publisher. He feared that having exposed himself with *The City and the Pillar* to a homophobic culture, he would be forever anathema to the champions of Middle American normalcy. He would be living for a long time, as he had not fully enough anticipated, though he had been warned, with the backlash against his third novel. He tried to keep his sense of humor. "The critics still regard me," he wrote to Pat Croker, "as a variety of poison oak and the girls are waiting for me to lead them like a Priapic Piper into the new Sodom, with milk and honey blest." He could neither mollify the critics nor satisfy the girls. At least Dutton and Nick Wreden stood strongly behind him, though sales of *Season* were modest compared to those of *City* and *Williwaw*. *A Search for the King* was scheduled for January 1950 publication. Except for minor revisions, he had finished *Dark Green, Bright Red*. Before leaving for Guatemala the previous December, he had met with Wreden at The Players to complain about Dutton's sales efforts and the long delay between his completion of a novel and its publication. Wreden had been sympathetic, conciliatory, constructive. But Dutton, in essence, had done and was doing its best. Though Gore had flirted with switching from Dutton to Doubleday, he was realistic enough to realize that the change probably would do him little to no good. There seemed no pressing enough reason to fly from one evil to another. He did his best to publicize himself, something for which he had a natural talent, refined by his publicity-conscious political family and childhood. Since he had been proclaimed by numerous commentators as an important literary voice of the new generation and since "New Writers" was a topic that caught people's attention, he worked up a lecture, a version of which a

Dallas newspaper published in coordination with his visit, on "The Young Writer in America." It was his first literary essay as a professional writer.

The previous fall, at the invitation of a young instructor, he had given an early version of it, called "Writers of the 40s," at City College of New York. In Houston he gave the lecture at the University of Houston and in Dallas at the Cokesbury Auditorium. In New York late in the month he went up to New Haven to lecture at Yale's Dwight Hall, sponsored by the Graduate School, where his friendly professorial audience gave him high praise. "I liked [your lecture]," one wrote to him, "because it was fearlessly presented, uninhibited by academics, fresh and youthful, assailable in only a few spots. I would advise a slower reading of it next time. It is too full of vitamins to be digested at the rate you deliver it." Washburn, Bingham, and Lewis were being lectured *at* by professors at Harvard. Here Gore was lecturing *to* the Yale equivalent of those lecturing to his former Exeter colleagues. The observation gave him pleasure. So too did a late-night telephone call from a distant but familiar voice. "So that's what you thought of me!" After all these years, a friendly Liz Whitney was on the other end of the line. She had recognized herself as one of the minor characters in *The Season of Comfort*.

As the weather turned warmer, Gore looked forward to his mid-May departure for Europe, first to London for Lehmann's publication of *City*, then to Paris, probably to Rome, perhaps Spain, and Morocco to see Paul Bowles. When Leon Danielian, "very chatty, very sociable," also planning a European trip, suggested they sail together on the *New Amsterdam*, he was delighted to have Leon's company. Even with Capote he could be amiable enough, as he was at a lunch hosted at a midtown restaurant in early April by another young Southern writer, Speed Lamkin. Short, porcine, effeminate, Speed seemed to Gore one more of the apparently endless train of new writers about to burst, so each thought, into glory and wealth, "new comets about to flash from darkness to darkness." Actually he did not think Lamkin formidable competition. Lamkin had invited Vidal, Capote, and Alice Astor, the glamorous, understated, beautiful mother of Ivan Obolensky, one of Speed's good friends from Harvard. Lamkin "had me and Truman Capote to lunch," Gore recalled, "and he told everybody he had both of us because we weren't speaking. 'I just couldn't figure out which one I wanted for lunch, so I had both of them.' That was his glamorous week." Suddenly Gore and Alice Astor caught one another's eye and began to talk. Slim, medium-tall, dark-haired, with deep brown eyes and a touch of mysterious exoticism, she seemed to Gore compellingly attractive in a way that touched his feelings and his curiosity. Like Anaïs, at certain angles, in a certain light, she was beautiful, both abstractly distant and absorbingly receptive, intensely there and someplace else. Her low-toned, English-accented voice charmed with its distinctive sensuality. Remarkably young-looking for her age, she was forty-six, the same age as Anaïs and Nina. Wealthy, a lover of the arts, three times divorced and about to be divorced from her current husband, highly placed in the New York and London social worlds, she apparently found Gore as absorbing as he found her. He wanted to know her better. Since he was sailing in mid-May, it was obvious that they had only the opportunity of this one meeting now. But he had intimations of a friendship to come.

This time Gore sailed not to Naples but to Le Havre, where he and Danielian took the ferry and train to London. Lehmann and he put a good face on their relationship, Lehmann the aristocratically self-confident publisher high on the totem pole of an elite, self-assured London literary culture; Vidal the young author determined not to be put down by anyone, but also unwilling to give up entirely on Lehmann. Before the *New Amsterdam* sailed from New York, he received a telegram: "Suggest you both stay with me first three days no time for letter now All news then Love—John" to which he responded, "BOTH ARRIVING EGERTON AFTERNOON TWENTYFOUR [May] = GORE." London in May 1949 was more of what he had experienced the previous summer: a round of parties attended by Lehmann's literary friends, ostensibly to celebrate the London publication of *The City and the Pillar,* and many of the same people, particularly Judy Montagu, from the London social world. Since Isherwood could not come down from his family home in Essex, they missed one another. Gore hoped he might see him in Paris. The British press on the whole had mostly good things to say about *City,* a reception Gore found happily different from the American, the start of what thereafter always seemed to him a better public response to his works in Britain than at home. The self-congratulatory Lehmann boastfully admired his own courage in bringing it out.

Gore soon crossed to Paris. Some of the previous year's cast had reassembled, particularly Tennessee, who came up for a brief visit from

Rome, where he had been since midwinter, and Capote, who had sailed for a long stay in Europe soon after the April lunch with Gore and Alice in New York. Maria Britneva was close by. She had spent much of the fall and winter of 1948 in New York, looking for stage work, enrolling at the newly formed Actors Studio, getting to know Marlon Brando and other New York theater people, strengthening and expanding her relationship with Williams and his friends, including Gore. In New York they had gone to Coney Island together, where she and Gore had had their heads photographed next to one another on comic cardboard bodies. Since she could not be Williams's lover, she could be loving, useful, and supportive. In spring 1949 she returned to her London home, hoping for theater work there, and welcomed Tennessee in April when he came for the English production of *Streetcar*. Williams felt sorry for her. "She detests London and has fallen out completely with the Beaumont office so she has no prospect of work here. . . . Seems to have no interesting friends here, nobody she likes much and her family is quite poor, except for an aunt who treats her rather coolly. Poor child. I think she may go over to Paris with us for a couple of weeks, but when we return to Rome I don't know what her plans will be. London is just as amazingly dull as ever! And to live here, Oh Jesus!" Capote, with his now signature Bronzini scarf, longer than his body was tall, twirled around him and flowing flamboyantly, pranced happily about Paris. His friends worried that his scarf would catch and choke him to death. His enemies hoped so. When Gore, just arrived and staying, as was Danielian, at the Pont Royal Hotel, made the mistake of showing Capote a draft of his short story, "The Robin," Capote read it and said, happily, " 'It doesn't work!' " One evening, with a large group, they found themselves at a well-known dance hall where men danced together. The band played that season's popular hit, "Bongo, Bongo, Bongo, I Don't Want to Leave the Congo." An enthusiastic dancer, Capote pulled Gore onto the dance floor. Gore, though he did not mind being admired, did not, unlike Truman, use his body or his movements exhibitionistically. Anyway, he had little talent or interest in dancing, which he had disliked since his Washington dancing-school days. Immediately he turned and left the dance floor. For Capote, who thought himself irresistible, there may have been attraction as well as competition, a hope of conquest as well as an act of payback. Each knew how to get on the other's nerves.

When Gore had arrived in Paris, Paul Bowles was there, having come from London, where Lehmann was arranging for late-summer publication of the British edition of *The Sheltering Sky*. He and Gore took long strolls together. In the bar of the Pont Royal they amused themselves "examining the literary habitués of the place." Sartre walked by their table "and bowed as he mumbled: 'Bonjour.' " Both were too startled to say anything. They had assumed he would not recognize them. Eager to return to Morocco, Bowles soon left, repeating his invitation to Gore to visit him in Tangier, where he and his wife Jane had created North African lives and domiciles. Both were deeply attracted to the exotic Arabic world, what seemed to them its power and centricity, a place of primal origins from which Europe and America could be observed at a distance. Morocco provided for Bowles an attractive balance of alienation and familiarity. "I have absolutely no desire to go to any part of Europe, so un-European do I feel these days," he had written to Gore. A handsome, graceful man, an inveterate traveler whose bags were often packed, he now found Morocco the home to which he always returned, its Anglo-American expatriate colony his social world, its Arabic young men his lovers, its mysterious desert the place where he felt closest to vital life. "I must admit," he wrote to Gore, "I didn't think you'd ever show up in Morocco." Apparently, when Gore had decided not to sail with Williams and Bowles in December, he had hinted he might show up later in Tangier. "Morocco isn't at all . . . monstrous," Bowles wrote to him, "but you doubtless wouldn't like it—you're not that depraved yet. But wait." In Paris, Bowles repeated the invitation. Gore again said he might come.

There were some Paris conquests. One day he strolled near Saint-Germain-des-Prés with a talented young American composer on his arm, Chuck Turner, later to become Samuel Barber's companion. Bowles's friend Ned Rorem, a young Francophile composer who had met Gore in New York and admired him, thought them an odd couple. "But then, opposites attract—not that Chuck and Gore were opposites, at least in their physical urges." For Gore opposites did attract, particularly men on a lower educational and social level than his own. For companionship and intellectual stimulation he had friends like Bowles. Whatever contributed to the decision, he soon left Paris, this time alone. Perhaps Paris life had grown dull; he would certainly have been happy to leave Capote behind. He did not mind in the least traveling alone. Sometimes intensely social, he also liked solitude, his own company. By train he headed south across the Pyrenees for his first visit to Spain, to see the places that had cachet and resonance in his imagination, that he had read about in literature and history, including the evocations of the Alhambra from his childhood reading of Washington Irving. Modern Spanish culture did not especially interest him. Having been disgusted by the cruelty of the bullfight he had seen in Guatemala City, he found the blood-and-sand spectacle viciously primitive, an aspect of Spain connected to the fanaticism of its Catholic heritage that exemplified the kind of religion he especially disliked. From Granada he wrote to John Kelly, complaining that his writing and feelings were "frozen." "That is nothing to worry about," Kelly assured him. "It will not hurt you to relax for a while. And if you feel tired of sex, you may be ready for something better in that and other lines." At Córdoba and Seville he found the great mosques breathtaking, extraordinary architectural structures magnificently decorated. Moorish Spain came alive in his imagination. Why not, he thought, write a novel in the manner of *A Search for the King,* about Boabdil, the last Moorish ruler of Spain? The topic lingered for a while in his head, though he was never to write it. "A lovely journey into the heart of Spain," he wrote to Latouche. "It beateth. I feel as if I were on Mars. The only 'foreign country' in the world. . . . A crown of *twigs,* dear heart, and an easy birth." From Seville he took the train to Algeciras on the Mediterranean, Gibraltar "the first big rock to the right." North African lights glittered across the strait.

As he had planned, he soon crossed to Africa. Bowles, surprised that the visit was actually occurring, welcomed him to the Moroccan landscape and the Anglo-American expatriate world. A newly fashionable gathering place for what Gore thought of as traveling queens, Tangier had its early post–World War II cast of colorful characters, some always on the move, some in comfortable houses, attracted by the weather, the beaches, the cheap cost of living, the easy availability of drugs, the Arabic ethos that permitted every sort of sex under terms totally independent of European puritanism. Sir David Herbert, the son of the Earl of Pembroke, Tangier's "unofficial social arbiter," and the visiting Cecil Beaton, widely admired for his scenery and costume designs, his photographs and wit, anchored the British social presence; the Bowleses and their traveling compatriots and guests, the American. Paul and Jane both had their homosexual lives, often with long-term companions. Both regularly smoked a North African version of mari-juana. Bowles, who was working on a new novel, a short story, and an opera for Libby Holman, was also supervising the renovation of the large house he lived in, high on a steep cliff outside town, with "a sort of lighthouse on the top, with quite the best view here." A fine but now nonproductive writer, Jane Auer Bowles, eight years older than Gore, born to a Jewish family in New York, had a mysterious Arabic lover who dominated her somewhat unstable life and mind. Hostile to Gore, whom she suspected of having an affair with Paul that threatened their idiosyncratic relationship, the small, dark, unpredictable Jane gave him the creeps. For Paul, Gore had great affection and respect.

Immediately on Gore's arrival in Tangier in the last week in June, they made plans for visits to Casablanca and Fez and perhaps a trip into the desert, for which Paul had a mystic feeling and had written powerfully about in *The Sheltering Sky,* a novel Gore soon read and liked considerably. The July weather was magnificent, unending days of cloudless skies. He thought Casablanca at best interesting. The long-discussed Sahara voyage, though, never occurred, and Tangier, all in all, despite the high-partying British and American social life, felt like a disadvantaged backwater. His small rented house in town was a hovel. Scorpions seemed unattractive companions. Tangier's dirt and poverty, its crumbling seediness, its absence of rational organization and intellectual culture seemed considerable liabilities, its exoticism, repellent. Unlike Bowles, Gore felt European. As in his visit to Egypt the previous year, he did not find modern Arabic sensibility or culture interesting, let alone alluring. Why should one isolate oneself in Morocco, he felt, if you could be in Paris or Rome or even New York? The handsome local boys were not sufficient compensation, and he did not enjoy smoking kif, Bowles's favorite drug. Much as he enjoyed Paul's company, he had little desire to stay for any length of time. A cablegram from Capote to Bowles announced Truman's imminent arrival, to Gore's surprise, with his companion, Jack Dunphy. Capote had no idea that Vidal was there. Gore insisted that he and Bowles go down to the dock; in the distance they saw Capote at the prow of the ship, ready for his entrance, looking eagerly toward the shore, Bronzini scarf floating about his neck. From the dock Capote's small body allowed his shoulders and face to be just visible over the ship's railing. As soon as he was in range, Vidal and Bowles began waving their arms wildly. Capote saw the two figures, began waving his scarf. When he recognized Gore standing beside Bowles, "he did a little comic-strip routine," Bowles recalled. "His face fell like a soufflé placed in the ice-compartment, and he disappeared entirely below the level of the railing for several seconds. When he had assumed a standing position again, he was no longer grinning or waving." Soon recovering his equilibrium, Capote stayed in Morocco for most of the rest of the summer, finding Jane's company delightful, spending more time with her than with Paul, and enjoying a frenetic whirl of parties and exotic experiences with Cecil Beaton, whom he idolized. Gore left late in the first week in July. Two weeks had been enough. In August, back in New York, he received a letter from Bowles, whose wry report reminded him why he had left Tangier. "Truman gave a mad party . . . at the cave of Hercules, with a large Arab orchestra, much champagne, and hurricane lamps fainting in the gale. Themistocles passed out on hashish, after drinking several bottles of champagne. Cecil said: 'How heavenly!' The Arab orchestra, plus porters and pussycats (Vidalese) had cases of Coca Cola. The sand sifted in and Truman found a huge centipide at his feet, nearly dying of horror. Well, actually it was a night of horror; everything went wrong." Gore was glad he had stayed only two weeks.

On a Florida Beach, Gore and Johnny Kriza enjoyed the late-August sunshine. It had been a glorious ride down from New York in Johnny's big car—which he had named "Floristan"—for a two-week holiday. They stopped at beaches along the eastern coast of Florida, in good-humored high spirits, visiting friends from the ballet world, "receiving the homage of the balletomanes in their beachside houses." When they had sex together, it was, as they both preferred, casually thoughtless. It had no emotive content, no consequences. "I was, during that time, devoted only to health and beauty," Gore wrote to Lehmann. Fond of one another, they had fun together, in a time and place where all that mattered was the attraction of well-favored bodies, exercised and tanned in the bright sun. Any obvious shadows seemed to come only from palm trees. The moment was so charged with the present that he and Johnny could find it possible, at a stretch, to think the present might go on forever. Actually, Johnny was not used to doing any thinking at all. For Gore, it would have been unusual, perhaps impossible, for there not to be an elegiac shading to the happy sky.

In New York through late summer and autumn 1949, staying some-times at his father's apartment, mostly in hotels, he proofread galleys of *A Search for the King* and finished the revisions of *Dark Green, Bright Red* for

which Lehmann had pushed. "I agree, of course," Gore wrote to him, "with
what you have to say that one should not create characters that are lifeless
and dull merely because the originals might appear that way; on the other
hand I think creation of character in a novel is very much a business of
chance; either the magic happens or it doesn't. I'm not sure that a 'real
character' can be created by some correct or logical process, Aristotelian or
not. Peter can't be remade as a character, certainly, but I think what you
mean is not that personality should change or grow but that it should be
revealed; in that case, I can do something about him. I'm not sure what just
yet." He had not given up hope that Lehmann would publish other of his
novels. In early November he sent him the revised *Dark Green, Bright Red*.
"A great deal of work has gone into it and I am pretty well pleased now.
I've made some cuts and a few additions; most of your objections have been
taken care of and Peter is less shadowy, I think." He soon sent him one of
the first printed copies of *Search*, which Lehmann chose not to publish,
though why he selected the less successful *Dark Green, Bright Red* is unclear,
especially since the subject of *Search* made it a likely read for an English
audience. *Williwaw* had made Vidal well known. *The City and the Pillar* had
made him famous. He himself shared the general lack of enthusiuasm about
In a Yellow Wood. *Dark Green, Bright Red* had mostly its narrative drive to
recommend it. That the artistically interesting *The Season of Comfort* was
vastly underrated resulted from the inevitable focus on its psychological
mother-son drama. In addition, for a writer so young to have written so
much so quickly made many uncomfortable, some resentful. Haste was
sometimes evident. Often it made no difference. Partly he was driven by the
desire for prominence, and by a seemingly inexhaustible energy, but he also
needed to support himself. "Contrary to legend, I had no money. Since I
lived on publishers' advances, it was fairly urgent that I keep on publishing
every year. But of course I *wanted* to publish every year. I felt no strain,
though looking back over the books," he remarked decades later, "I can
detect a strain in the writing of them. Much of the thinness of those early
novels is simply the pressure that I was under. Anyway, I've gone back and
rewritten several of them. They are still less than marvelous but better than
they were."

Even with publishing six novels in five years, he had still earned only
modest sums. Though he did well with *City*, none of the others sold enough

to make the bestseller list, let alone provide him with much more than the average $2,000 advances he got for the last three. The nearly 30,000-copy total sale of *City* netted him approximately $9,000 over a three-year period. The trust fund that Nina had gotten Auchincloss to provide and which she had relinquished when he became twenty-one provided a small sum, varying in relation to the securities markets, usually around a thousand dollars a year. To the extent that he stayed at his father's apartment, he had a partial rent subsidy, though he preferred to stay there as little as possible. Most of the money he had saved in the Army and from the railroad bonds set aside for college costs had been absorbed by his living expenses. He was economical, but he was not thrifty. Bohemian self-sacrifice and ascetic sparseness did not appeal to him. Though he had no need for luxuries, for first-class travel or deluxe hotels, he still needed money to cover his ordinary expenses. With the exception of a smash bestseller of the sort that stayed at the top for a long time, a novel was not a paying proposition. Publishers had not yet developed the tendency to give highly thought-of "literary" novelists huge advances. Even successful novelists had to scramble for money: some scrambled into university jobs, others into writing for the popular culture. As Gore looked around him in mid-1949 for additional ways to earn money, he took notice of television, a new phenomenon. "All my literary friends," he wrote to Pat Crocker, whom he urged to find a buyer for his Antigua house, "from Jean Stafford to Truman Capote are writing or trying to write television." He himself began to make inquiries. Perhaps television, perhaps the movies. "They feel about me, generally, that there is nothing I cannot do (this is said by irritable admirers) or that there is nothing I *will* not do (more the majority opinion, I think) . . . the truth is I don't want to go to work in an office. On such soft negatives are airy empires built." One of the things he *would* do, he decided, is write a pulp novel. An idea had come to him in mid-March while on the train to attend the bereaved Mrs. Gore. Before leaving for Europe in May, he had put into Dutton's hands a commercial fiction of about 55,000 words, dicated into a Dictaphone machine in about a week, called *A Star's Progress*, to be published under a pseudonym, the surname taken from the much-frequented Everard Baths. The conspiracy appealed even to the staid Dutton proprietors, who early in July drew up a contract, with an advance of $1,000, for the pseudonymous Katherine Everard. "Very intrigued with new novel, but why assume another name?" Anaïs wrote to him from California. "Why not add to *your* legend? . . .

I'm flattered that you haven't proposed to anyone but me—I'm happy too. . . . I wish I had known of your trip to Spain."

The galleys were ready in September, publication scheduled for February 1950, one month after *A Search for the King*. No one other than the author and a few people at Dutton were to know that *both* had been written by him. Critics had already found his productivity suspect. If he associated his name with *A Star's Progress*, his credentials as a serious literary writer would be weakened. His critics would complain that not only did he write too much too quickly but that he also had written a steamy potboiler. The Orville Prescotts of the world would feel vindicated, probably maliciously vindictive. Dutton's production manager, who sent Katherine Everard the galley proofs at a Ridgewood, New Jersey, address, had no idea that "Dear Miss Everard" was anyone other than she appeared to be. Enjoying the conspiracy, John Macrae, soon after publication, happily told Gore, "I have to sneak around and write to you about Miss Kitty's book. Here is the review in the *Times*. Not too bad. When you mention her in your letters just use the work K. I mean the letter K. I keep worrying for fear someone will find out." No one did. The complacent *Times* reviewer, who thought the book okay of its kind, was readily taken in. The governing board of The Pen and Brush, a Manhattan club of female "professional writers and artists," wanted, "in recognition of [her] work," to have Miss Everard "as a regular member."

Despite Vidal's efforts to write down, *A Star's Progress* is a classy piece of pulp fiction. The author's hand is evident throughout. Set mainly in Monterrey, New Orleans, and Los Angeles, it is a partly original, partly formulaic female bildungsroman in which a beautiful, graceful, gifted Mexican-born dancer, perhaps modeled on Rita Hayworth, eager to escape her family's poverty, rises, with the help of numbers of men, to Hollywood stardom, though not to happiness. Despite her talent, she is a victim of forces she can at best accommodate to, at worst be damaged by. Her talent and willpower can take her only so far, though they do take her to fame and notoriety. At the age of thirteen she dances in a raunchy New Orleans nightclub. One year later she becomes the mistress of a wealthy man more than four times her age, who takes her to Los Angeles. With the help of powerful Hollywood supporters, she soon becomes a film star. When she falls in love with her handsome bisexual co-star, she is stunned to learn he prefers his own sex to hers, that he is in love with a man. Escaping her misery, she has a sensationalized affair with a European prince. In the end she returns to New Orleans, where she carefully, deliberately, kills herself. Like that of *The City and the Pillar,* the narrative is framed by an opening and closing set in a bar in the novel's present. The narrative pace is artfully varied, mostly brisk and focused. Drawing on his 1945 stay in Hollywood and his frequent visits to New Orleans, Vidal sharply evokes the two cities with a casual but concrete indirectness that makes them more than scenery and less than performers. When Graziella Serrano (as the movie star Grace Carter) goes to Nevada for a divorce, she stays at a dude ranch very much like the one Nina stayed at in 1935. Grace's bisexual lover, Eric, a name that Vidal was to use again in *Two Sisters,* "sooner or later . . . always managed to prove that every man in the world was like himself" sexually, a Vidalian position of some later prominence. "The name Duluth," where her mother was born, "had always intrigued" Grace, as it did her creator, who was to use it as the title for one of his most compelling fictions. As in *Williwaw,* elegant directness of style is everything. The prose is spare, precise, sometimes luminous in its exactness, interesting in its rhythms, sophisticated in its elaborations. Throughout, alas, convention and public morality press hard on the narrative. Grace Carter cannot escape the punishing hand that demands she pay for her transgressions with death, though her bisexual co-star remains happily unscathed. But for Grace punishment is inescapable, such did the genre, the publisher, and the public demand. A strong character, she is not strong enough; she is a weak link between, looking backward, Moll Flanders and, looking forward, Myra Breckinridge.

Financially the experiment was a limited success. Sales were modest. For one week's work Gore earned $1,000 and an additional small amount for the paperback, which Pyramid Books published under the title *Cry Shame!* Though he had nothing to be ashamed of, anonymity made sense. The money helped, but he had hoped for much more. He and Dutton kept the secret. Apparently he did not tell even his closest friends, like Williams, who had gone to Hollywood for some script work, or the restless Bowles, who had begun to plan a trip to Ceylon hoping Gore would join him there, or his new friend, Alice Astor, whom he had now begun to see frequently. In the country Alice stayed at a fine, square, gray-fieldstone Queen Anne–style house on the Hudson in Dutchess County, simply called Rhinebeck, for the local town. The land had been a wedding present to her and her first husband from her usually stingy older brother, Vincent. He had inherited much of the family fortune, including a huge tract of Rhinebeck land called Ferncliff, a small portion of which, about one hundred acres, he gave to Alice and Serge Obolensky. In New York she stayed in great comfort with her teenage daughters at the Gladstone Hotel, which she made a center for visitors from England, artistic and otherwise, and where she occupied one half of the eighth floor, naïvely thinking how economical she was by forgoing the expense of running a town house with servants. To go to Rhinebeck she got her doorman to hail a taxi, Gore recalled. " 'Do you mind taking me to Rhinebeck?' 'Where the hell is that?' 'I'll show you the way.' Mr. DiNapoli drove her back and forth for the next three or four years. 'He's so wonderful, and it's so simple. You just ring him and he takes you there.' Of course he was charging her on the meter, and she could have bought the cab by the time she finished with him."

Alice and Vincent had inherited great wealth, in Alice's case a $5-million trust fund, when their father, John Jacob Astor IV, divorced from Alice's difficult mother, had gone down with the *Titanic*. Originally German-Jewish merchants, the primal Astors had made a fortune in the early-nineteenth-century fur trade in America and in New York City real estate. The family divided into American and British branches. Alice's early years were spent in both places. When her beautiful, imperious mother, whom Alice always feared, married an English aristocrat, Lord Ribblesdale, she settled permanently in London. Credible rumor and her non-Astor-like dark hair and features had persuaded Alice and others that John Jacob had probably not been her father. At twenty-one she married, in defiance of her mother, a divorced, impoverished Russian prince, Serge Obolensky, a handsome cavalry officer with whom she had fallen in love. After six years of marriage and a son, she fell in love again, divorced, and remarried the attractive Raimund von Hofmannsthal, the son of the world-renowned Austrian playwright, with whom she had two daughters. As she was prone, Alice fell in love again, as did Raimund. Soon they were each very much off on their separate affairs, Alice's life divided between London, Austrian holidays, and Americans winters. In the mid-1930s she fell in love with the celebrated dancer and choreographer of the Sadler's Wells Ballet Theatre, Frederick Ashton, whose main interest was in men. "Freddie was quite able to leap into bed with her, which he wasn't with many, whatever he says," one of Alice's daughters recalled. Always interested in the arts, Alice immersed herself in Ashton's ballet world. Ashton found Alice attractive and useful. To the extent that her attentions were comfortable, he enjoyed the advantages of her wealth and social entrée. She hoped they would marry. By the early 1940s she had for some time known that nothing more would come of her love for Ashton. When the war started, she married Philip Harding, a writer for *The Financial Times*, a close friend of the poet John Betjeman, and a homosexual. One war and one daughter later, she divorced him and moved back to America. With her characteristic passion for unsuitable men, she married a British architect, David Playdell-Bouverie, also homosexual, who was happy to be made wealthy. Each new marital start seemed to her a hopeful beginning, a love that could not fail. Within three years Alice was in the process of divorcing him. By the late 1940s, with the divorce from Bouverie imminent, she allowed herself to hope for a short while that Freddie Ashton and she might take up again. In 1949 she persuaded the skeptical impresario Sol Hurok to bring to New York Ashton's Sadler's Wells Ballet, which in October opened a triumphant season that combined the best in British and American post–World War II ballet.

———

Having resumed her conversation with the young writer she had met in the spring, Alice invited him to Rhinebeck for a midautumn weekend with her friends from the ballet world. During the last days of October, Gore went up to Rhinebeck by train. To his left the wide Hudson flowed downstream. Westward, across the river, his birthplace held its stone prominence high on the palisade. The train stopped briefly at Hyde Park, then Poughkeepsie, then Rhinecliff, the Rhinebeck-area station. It was a route associated with his father, with Amelia Earhart, with "that man in the White House," with some of the origins of his life. From the window, eastward up sloping lawns, across spacious autumn vistas, he could occasionally glimpse the mansions of the Dutchess County gentry, families like the Roosevelts and the Astors, who beginning in the late eighteenth century had settled into huge riverside estates. At Rhinebeck, Gore immediately saw that Alice was "wildly in love" with Ashton, "his talent, his charm, and the difficult time that he gave her. She loved having a difficult time. It was always the case that Alice was more in love with someone than he was with her." In New

York, where he sat next to Ashton at the Sadler's Wells performance of one
of Ashton's ballets, and at Rhinebeck that weekend, Ashton flirted with
Gore. A compulsive parlor entertainer, Ashton amused them all with imper-
sonations and mimicry. "I spent a weekend with Freddie A. at Alice
Bouverie's in the country," Gore wrote to John Lehmann early in November. "The rest is silence." Lehmann of course knew what the "silence"
meant, though it did not mean anything between Gore and Ashton other
than that Ashton was, as usual, pursuing young men and, as often, being
turned down. It was Alice whom Gore did not turn down.

From the beginning they had a mutually acknowledged platonic rapport, a friendship that he valued immensely, that had something to do, at
least at first, with who Alice was, but also and always was essentially a
personal spark between two people who warmly liked one another in a
deeply intuitive way. "I was sort of aware of Gore's homosexuality," Alice's
daughter Romana recalled, "but I was also aware of my mother's penchant
for having love affairs with homosexuals. She was the sort of woman that if
Gore was going to have an affair, she would have one with him." If Alice
was in love with Gore, as Romana came to believe, her attentions had
something of the familial to them, a sororal or even motherly engagement
that immediately attracted to Gore the hostility of her son, Ivan, Speed
Lamkin's friend, who fancied himself a novelist also and who had gone into
publishing. More than anything, "she was trying to make everyone aware
what a young genius Gore was. She was very admiring of his work. How
talented he was," Romana recalled. "She thought he was underappreciated
and badly reviewed. Though she was right about him, I think my mother
would get involved with a man's career and with a particular interest only
when she was in love with him." Whether in love or not, Alice desired to
have him closer. Later that month Gore spent another weekend at Rhinebeck, enjoying his hostess and her guests, the comfortable, spacious house,
the late-night entertainments, the notables from the ballet world, the luxury
of servants, including a marvelous Russian chef whom Alice had kept as her
divorce settlement from Obolensky. His specialty was a superb mushroom
soup and an irresistible chocolate cake. These culinary delectations must
have reminded Gore of some of the better aspects of Merrywood. On a
weekend night, after a heavy Slavonic meal, he dreamed a scenario that the
next morning he turned into a short story, "The Ladies in the Library,"

which he dedicated to Alice. Most of the guests that weekend were English, including Judy Montagu.

One damp late-November afternoon Alice took her guests for a drive northward along the River Road. Gore drove with Alice in her small car; the others were chauffeured separately. The Hudson glimmered to the left. Fog rose along the river, the woods white with mist. Their destination was a deserted early nineteenth-century Federal Greek Revival house, called Edgewater, in Barrytown, little more than a railroad station and a post office not far from the town of Red Hook, about ten miles above Rhinebeck. Alice told him, as they drove, that the house, on three acres, built in 1820 for a branch of the wealthy Livingston family, had been acquired a century before by her Chanler relatives, one of whom, the eccentric Chapman Chanler, lived nearby. In the late nineteenth century the essayist John Jay Chapman, who had married a Chanler, had lived there while building his own house. It was one of Alice's favorites. As they pulled into the driveway, immediately to the west, very close to the road, Gore saw the brick profile of the house, especially an octagonal addition on the north side. The New York Central tracks ran a few yards to the east, parallel to the driveway, which ran along the house's north-south length. With Alice in the lead, "we walked along between the railroad track and the back of the house, which is how I think of it, but it was actually the old front door, and Alice knew it as that. Then she wanted, as usual, to see if it was open. She was a magician with keys and locks. But it wasn't open, so we then walked around the south end, and I saw this big block of a house." In front of them, to the west, as they came around the back, across a sloping field of grass that rose to their waists, was the wide river. Weeping willows marked the boundary between land and water. Beyond: a railroad bridge, a small island, the western shore, the low rise of "the delicately irregular line of the pale-blue Catskills . . . like the flourish beneath Washington Irving's signature." As they walked through the high grass toward the river, he turned and saw behind him, facing the river, the Greek Revival colonnade: six white-painted columns rising three stories high. They all looked back, somewhat dazzled, at the true front of Edgewater. He had never seen anything so beautiful. Classically proportioned, it seemed magical. As he saw the colonnade, he knew that he wanted this house.

Actually, to his surprise and delight, the obstacles to acquisition were not as formidable as he had feared. The house had gone from the Chanler to the Chapman family, and in 1946 it had been purchased by Laura Taylor, who had had it on the market for some time. When, with Alice's help, he learned that the asking price was $16,000, he was heartened. In fact, he immediately became a believer. He had no doubt he could somehow raise that amount. He would need the down payment and a mortgage. Perhaps Pat Crocker would succeed in selling the Antigua house and that money would be forthcoming. He soon found out why the asking price was noticeably low: the interior was in disrepair and the New York Central Railroad ran on the track that came within ten yards of the house. Most of the grand Hudson River houses were high up on a bluff, a distance from the track, which ran mostly along the river. At Edgewater the railroad ran on the landward side. For most, the proximity of the train made the house undesirable, though by 1950 changes in transportation that soon made the railroad comparatively unimportant had reduced the number of trains on the route and made their passage less frequent. Years later, in one of his novels, Vidal evoked what the experience must have been like in the nineteenth century. "We looked and saw just back of the house one of Commodore Vanderbilt's monsters: some thirty freight cars jerked and rattled past as smoke and burning cinders erupted from the locomotive, making a huge cloud that obscured half the sky. During this visitation even the natives did not speak. We stood mute, motionless, as ashes fell about us like a dark rain. . . . 'It's all the fault of my husband's father. He said, 'Oh, how marvellous!' when they wanted to put the railroad through. 'It'll stop and pick us up whenever we want!' Well!" Surprisingly, the idea of the railroad hardly bothered Gore. As guests over the years were to remark, it seemed, though the house shook whenever the train passed, that he hardly noticed. Whereas most people saw heavy expenses for repairs, he immediately saw an opportunity to get a house he passionately wanted at a cost he could manage. The repairs could be done later, slowly, over time. As much as he had wanted anything, he wanted this house. He did not want to live in New York or any city. Edgewater had proximity without subservience. It was close enough but separate. He felt the same impulse that, four years before, had got him to buy the Antigua house. Except for his grandparents' Rock Creek Park home, he had been a transient in his formative years. He did not belong at any one of the houses his mother had him at or sent him away from. At boarding school he had been a traveler with no home to come back to. No one but he himself had or ever would provide him with one. He wanted a home of his own, and he had an instinct and an eye, despite obstacles, for houses and locations that fulfilled that sense of himself, that embraced beauty, distinctiveness, grandeur.

————•——

While he and Alice made inquiries and he began gradually during the winter and spring to see the shape of his likely purchase take form, he also had a busy season with writing, friends, and travel. Having written "The Ladies in the Library" at Rhinebeck, he decided to write more short stories, in hope of magazine publication and perhaps a book of stories. Wisely, he made no attempt to revive those he had written at Exeter or to publish "The Dancer," though he had enough confidence in "The Robin," his most successful effort, to publish it, albeit not in a prominent place. The short-story form did not intrigue him, but it interested him enough so that his desire to do something successful within it and his hope that he might earn some money to help with expenses encouraged him to write a group of them during the winter-spring of 1949–50. They brought, however, only modest sums, mostly because homoeroticism, their prevailing subject, made them unsuitable for the high-paying-mass circulation magazines such as *Mademoiselle* or *The Saturday Evening Post*. They turned out to be almost entirely an artistic venture. Neither as separately published stories nor when published as a collection did they attract the attention *The City and the Pillar* had. More subtle, more artistically nuanced, the best of them, "Pages from an Abandoned Journal," "Three Stratagems," and the allusive "The Ladies in the Library," have an indirectness, a delicacy, and an artistic integrity that give their underlying subject a viability it had never before had in American literature. Most of the stories were written in Key West and New Orleans. Always restless, Gore had vaguely expected, when leaving Morocco in July, to spend January 1950 with Bowles in North Africa. As he told Lehmann, "I think Paul Bowles and I will cross the Sahara; I should like to do a journal of that trip, for my amusement anyway. I've become awfully fond of journal keeping." The latter was an exaggeration. Except for the journal he had kept during the first four months or so of 1948, he had at best kept a sporadic record. The Sahara trip dropped from both their agendas, especially because by October Bowles had become strongly attracted to the idea of visting Ceylon. "I still have a mad desire to see that part of the world, even briefly," he wrote, encouraging Gore to join him.

In fact, Gore had had no desire to visit Morocco again, and Bowles's invitation in early December to join him en route to or in Ceylon suddenly seemed just the right thing. Restless, eager not to be in New York for the winter, perhaps with touches of Somerset Maugham in his imagination, he decided to go. Bowles, on his way by slow boat, wrote from Antwerp, suggesting he consider flying directly to Ceylon or alternatively to Naples, where he could meet Bowles's boat and sail the rest of the way with him. Bowles had half expected to see him in Antwerp or in Naples "on the dock waving." But he thought it more likely that Gore would "take the high road," since, unlike Bowles, he did not mind flying, "and be in Ceylon before me." Gore, though, booked boat passage from New York, with a stopover in Rome and Cairo, on an American President liner to depart on January 9. "I may also do a travel book about Ceylon," he wrote to Lehmann, "full of pussycat episodes most excitingly handled. Paul's book [*The Sheltering Sky*] has been alternately praised and attacked here. Some thought it Kafka; others . . . Elinor Glyn. I shall be gone thank God when *Search,*" scheduled for January 10 publication, "appears to the ravenous public." He spent the evening before departure with John Latouche and the actor Burgess Meredith, who amused them about his recent divorce from Paulette Goddard. "She even wants my donkey, which she hates." On the morning of departure Gore posted a letter to Bowles telling him he was on his way. When, soon after, with his baggage, he went to the busy pier, he had a rude shock. Somehow he had miscalculated, whether out of some underlying hesitation about going at all or plain fuzzy-mindedness about dates. The boat had departed *as scheduled* the previous day. He did not look into alternatives. Instead he went to Key West and then New Orleans.

For six weeks Bowles anticipated Vidal's arrival in Ceylon. In the middle of January, the departure-day letter in hand, Bowles finally wrote to him, "Is it true that you will actually arrive here? I hope you'll let me know the disembarkation date well in advance so that I can meet you at the boat. . . . You must be staying a while in Egypt en route. But you hate it there. So perhaps not. . . . It will be wonderful to see you here." In late February, furious, the usually placid Bowles expressed his disappointment. "What nonsense! Missed the boat, indeed! How was I to know that? I was literally expecting you from one day to the next, put off trips in order to make them with you when you came. I wrote you in Rome. Perhaps the American Embassy knows enough to forward it to New Orleans." "He was quite rightly pissed off," Gore later remarked. By the end of the letter, though, his anger had cooled. "You never would have done any work if you'd come, so perhaps it's just as well," though there may have been something of a taunt in his observation that "one is at a premium here among the collegians, and can pick and choose. The only trouble is that one chooses everyone. So, as I say, perhaps it's just as well for your own peace of soul that you stayed in God's country."

In fact, there was enough to pick and choose from in Key West and New Orleans, though Gore was still passionate enough about his Houston friend to have told Lehmann in early November, exhausted from revising *Dark Green, Bright Red,* that "in a few days I retire to Houston for love and a rest from work." He does not appear to have gone to Houston then. With his bags packed in January, the boat to Ceylon having left without him, he went by bus to Key West, eager for the warm sunshine and Tennessee Williams's company. To Williams's surprise, "after writing me only three days previously that he was catching a boat for Ceylon, close on the fugitive heels of Paul Bowles, Gore Vidal suddenly startled me out of my wits and my power of speech when he stalked into the living room a few days ago without ringing or knocking and immediately began to browse through my manuscript which I was checking over. He said he had missed the boat." In Key West, Gore regaled himself "among the husks of mermaids," enjoying what were mostly fair to good reviews of *Season* that Dutton forwarded. "I now think that perhaps *Search* is a good though slight book," he told Lehmann, to whom he had sent a copy in the hope he might publish it. "It was certainly wonderful fun to write and my fears about it came, I think, from a sense of having cheated, having avoided a major theme in favor of something less demanding, less painful." Once Williams got over the shock of Gore's sudden appearance, they had a good time together at the beach and at bars. "In those days there was nobody in the town. The streets were empty," Gore recalled. "You could park anywhere. South Beach was where we went." Both were brown from the sun, slim and muscled from swimming. Williams's rented house on unfashionable Duncan Street became a daily stop for conversation, for drinks, for quick-witted camaraderie.

At Key West, while Williams worked on *The Rose Tattoo,* Gore began the short stories he eventually published under the title *A Thirsty Evil.* "I am working slowly, quietly," he told Lehmann, "with greater concentration than I used to in the mad gaudy days of the early books. I've just done a very fine short story," probably "Three Stratagems," "in a way the best thing I've written: Tenn agrees too. I am brooding about what to do next. I have a hundred plans." They did not include staying in Key West, which he left at the end of January, mostly because New Orleans, especially during Mardi Gras, offered more opportunities for adventure and entertainment. Also, Williams was soon to go to New York, which Gore had no intention of returning to until spring. "Vidal has departed," Williams wrote to Donald Windham. "The queens took a dim view of him, which doesn't matter. . . . I miss him, for it is comforting to know somebody who gets along worse with people than I do, and I still believe that he has a heart of gold." As always, "New Orleans was wonderful." Vidal was soon comfortable enough in a nondescript furnished apartment in a roominghouse at 812 Dauphine Street, in the midst of the French Quarter attractions. "I had half of one floor overlooking the street. Very comfortable," he recalled. "You went out to eat. Very cheap." Soon after arriving, he wrote to Lehmann that "the Endless Quest for the Beloved has brought me to this city where, contrary to popular opinion, no men of letters save myself decorate the streets and boites, although, at Mardi Gras, I believe Glorious Williams will be among us here." At least he was closer to Houston. "Haven't seen the Beloved yet. The B. is in Houston. Lad of Houston ere we part give me back oh give me back. . . ." For the time being he stayed in New Orleans, where he had numbers of friends, especially Bob Tallant, the novelist, and Olive Leonhardt, the painter he had met in Guatemala and to whom he had introduced Anaïs in 1947. Much of the local camaraderie was at bars, where he observed his New Orleans friends drink at a volume so great that he could not keep up with them. "All alcoholics and all dead long, long before their time."

One night on Bourbon Street he noticed in a tight pair of Levi's an acquaintance from Exeter, J. Winter Thorington, an Alabamian from Birmingham. Stepping out of the shadows and startling Thorington, Gore said, half jokingly, "I'd never have taken you for a hustler." Thorington responded, "Well, I'm not trying to be a hustler." As for Gore, it was Thorington's first Mardi Gras, one that stuck in his memory as the wildest of the many he was to attend. "I remember the weather at Mardi Gras 1950 was just perfect," another friend of Gore's recalled, "absolutely perfect." They went together to bars and parties and ate, Thorington recalled, "at some of the great restaurants and went to several spots around town and I really thoroughly enjoyed it." Lafitte's Blacksmith Shop was a favorite. "Yes, he did like to pay for sex, and he told me the reason why. He said that he liked it that way because then nobody owed anything to anybody. . . . I remember on one occasion when there was a hustler involved. We did go back to that place at 812 Dauphine Street. I was a little surprised, to be honest about it, as to his being a bit cool toward the guy after everything was all over and we were walking back up toward Canal Street. . . . He didn't seem interested in carrying on a conversation, so I just did it myself. . . . He probably figured that everything was even steven at that stage of the game and he didn't owe him any conversation or any money or anything else." When Thorington needed to interrupt his stay by driving back to Montgomery, Gore went for part of the ride. He had never seen the eighty-mile stretch between New Orleans and Gulfport. "I was curious because we were in Gore country. The Gores are from the northern part of Mississippi, but we have relatives all over the Delta, and I'd never seen the Delta. That was my real reason for the trip." From Gulfport he took the bus back to New Orleans, from which at the end of February he went by bus to Houston, presumably to pursue the now totally unremembered romantic object. Apparently his Texas affair did not prove satisfactory, the experience disappointing and still unresolved. "Houston is all very strange and sad and baffling," he told Lehmann. "I am in one of those curious situations when I don't at all know what is happening. Are there schools where one can learn to be ruthless? Well, all this will pass. . . . What will one be like at eighty? with the Nobel and a secretary?"

Working on the short stories in the morning, he had time on his hands the rest of the day, part of which he spent socializing, much of which he spent reading. He went regularly to the public library, reading fiction widely, from Dickens's *Hard Times* to Calder Willingham's new novel, which, to his disappointment, he thought "a piece of total trash; I haven't the nerve to write him what I think, and he awaits with some interest, I think, my comments." For the first time he was also studying Plato, especially the *Symposium*, which excited him a great deal, particularly because its depiction of human sexuality encouraged his own similar consideration of the subject. Heretofore he had lived his bisexuality, from Jimmy to Rosalind to Anaïs to Harold to his Houston romance, with modest to nonexistent defensiveness, but recently, and especially now while reading the *Symposium*, his ideas on the subject began to become self-consciously coherent.

Inevitably they were self-justifying, but now had reference to a body of literature and to a set of historical examples that provided a cultural and intellectual framework. He began to think seriously about human sexuality, the relationship between the body's natural responsiveness and cultural conditioning, about sex, gender, and society. His enthusiasm for his view of the subject had its aggressive side, which new friends in New Orleans—long-term British visitors Geoffrey and Penelope Moore—sometimes found tedious but hardly alienating, mainly because they did not take seriously his argument that "all the great literary people in the world have been homosexual." Both the handsome, pipe-smoking Geoffrey, five years older than Gore, who taught at Tulane and ran a literary radio-interview program for the university, and Penelope, a talented journalist, enjoyed his argumentativeness. They both had been successful debaters at Cambridge. It seemed excessive to them when Gore, a formidable debater also, argued that heterosexuality was "a bad thing." But it was a legitimate debater's point, especially when the argument was almost always the other way around. The mysteries of homosexual cruising, though, were much beyond Moore's romantic puritanism. "My idea of homosexuality was derived from obvious queens, which we used to call them at Cambridge, and there was Gore coming from the YMCA, all muscular, and he used to say, 'Oh, you are so cozy about this kind of thing. Look, there's a boxer there, there's a football player,' and so he educated us." When the three went out together, Gore would say, " 'You don't believe me, do you? You don't believe me. Look at that chap over there, that guy over there. I'll get him before the night is through. I'll get him.' And there was this great brawny thing. I took it all as a joke, you see. But he was dead, dead, deadly serious. . . . Probably the act of penetration was pretty repellent to me, and so he said, 'Oh, we don't do that! We don't do that!' 'What the hell do you do?' And he used a curious expression: 'Belly rubbing,' which apparently meant kind of masturbating against each other without using hands. I had never heard of that."

Having discovered that the well-known young novelist was in town, Moore, who wanted him for his radio broadcasts, had telephoned. Gore came over to the small patio apartment on Ursulines Avenue in the slave quarter. They all took to one another right away. "He was just mad about her," Gore recalled. "She was a lean brown woman, rather sort of athletic, with a sexy look in her eye, not beautiful but handsome and well made . . . and a bit passive." Gore often came to their place for dinner and drinks, or they went to restaurants. "He kept dropping in. We'd just look up, and there was Gore. We never made any appointments. He was just there. He was very welcome, anytime." Moore, late in March, had Gore on his radio program, *Looking at Books*, to discuss the state of the novel, a version of his talk on novelists of the 1940s. Both young, attractive, articulate—one with a crisp British accent, the other a deep-toned American voice—they dazzled the local audience and enjoyed being written up handsomely in the two local newspapers. New Orleans seemed marvelous to both of them, pristine, unspoiled. "We used to see the cat girl and hear the old musicians play 'When the Saints Go Marching In' in the Quarter. Those were grand old days," Moore recalled. "You never had to bother then about being mugged or anything like that, or at least we never bothered, and we never were. It was a great life." For Gore also, who planned to stay in New Orleans until the warm weather in April. Afterward, he told Lehmann, "I may do a short Hollywood stint this spring for cash; plans are uncertain, at the moment, depending on Houston . . . among other things."

The short stories were going well. When he sent "Three Stratagems" to James Laughlin, Laughlin liked it and accepted it for fall publication in New Directions' *New World Writing #12,* an annual anthology. "It's one of the few serious short stories I've ever written," he told Laughlin, "and I'd not like to see it die somewhere among the lingerie of *Mademoiselle* or on the front shelves of the Lady of the Gotham Book Mart." Sales of *Search* seemed likely to be about 10,000, less than he had wanted but about what his novels since *City* had averaged. He had in mind two new ideas, one a novel about the Roman emperor Julian, still quite vague in conception, the other about a charismatic, apocalyptic religious figure in modern America, per-haps a new messiah whose views would turn Christianity on its head. The latter would be, he partly joked, his masterwork, "the monster which I've been sniffing around for five years, the story of the second coming. Pray for me. . . . Soon I shall begin work on *The First and the Last;* it may very well be the last novel for, if I do it right, I shall have nothing else to say for many years to come. Not, as Mr Maugham has remarked, that *that* is any reason to stop." With Lehmann there had been something of a rapproche-ment, with a touch of personal affection, as if now it were an old friendship that transcended serious annoyances, though Lehmann, soon to be out of business anyway, still declined to publish anything since or before *City* except *Dark Green, Bright Red*. Vidal himself was beginning to develop some perspective about his novels, including *City*, whose message he considered on target but whose aesthetic success he thought modest. "You know," he wrote to Lehmann, "I've had to learn how to write since *Williwaw* and it's not been easy. Most people seem to be born knowing their way through literature, the young lions at least, like Truman. I have had to fuss and groan no end, these last four years especially, and, at last, a natural manner seems to have been shaped, both literate and true. But then who can tell? . . . I am as usual in one of my melancholic reveries in which I feel like going off to a war. How awful to be Byron without Greece!"

Back in New York at the beginning of April 1950, he became preoccupied with writing an essay, provoked mostly by his reading of Plato and his discussions with the Moores but also by a piece called "New Innocents Abroad" by William Barrett in the *Partisan Review*. Vidal had no disagreement with Barrett's slighting reference to the "scandalous" conduct of American queens in Europe, but Barrett's general homophobic miscomprehension of the variety and prevalence of homosexual behavior among American men appalled and angered him. "It is *their* attitude and *their* influence on society which is of importance, not that of the poor parodied queens who are to the homosexual world what the musical comedy minstrels are to the Negros, the *yentas* to the Jews." The statistics from the Kinsey Report needed to be taken into account; practices in other cultures, especially in ancient Greece, needed to become part of the descriptive and definitional discussion. He undoubtedly had in his memory Anaïs's and Nina's semi-Freudian simplifications about arrested development and the desirability of psychoanalytic treatment. He had no doubt that his love for Jimmie, whose lost presence and image stayed sharply in mind, had been honorable and natural. And was there anything significantly different between consensual commercial sex with men and the widespread commercial sex between men and women? "I am designing," he wrote to Lehmann at the middle of April, "a set of Dialogues" as well as an essay "on homosexuality, from a Platonistic and affirmative point of view, suggesting that perhaps Jewish-Christian morality is at fault and not the human race." They would be grounded in, among other things, the intensive reading he had been doing. "I have been studying hard these last four months all of Plato, all of Vergil (translated since I have forgotten my Latin). Boethius *(Consola-*

tions) and so on. It has been revelatory and I am still somewhat stunned by it all; to me, in school, the classics consisted of those dreary battles of Caesar recorded in War Office prose."

For the first time he set out his argument that for many men homosexual acts are normal (natural) expressions of their sexuality, just as are heterosexual acts, and that cultural and social conditions usually determine whether men have sex exclusively with men, with women, or with both. Men who had sex with men did not need to be cured. They were not ill. Queens were another matter. "As a matter of fact, the queen world frightens and depresses me and in its hysteria I see all the horror of the world brought into focus and, when I am particularly tired and despairing, I find myself almost prepared to accept the doctrine of original sin, no longer a Pelagian heretic or a classicist but, like my Italian ancestors, a good Roman Catholic." But "pederasty among the non-neurotics is by no means a negative act. It is not the result of a delayed emotional development nor is it a substitute for heterosexual relationships; a man is a pederast not out of hatred or a fear of women but out of a natural love for men which is traditional, affirmative and, in the best sense, respectable." Plato was a more authoritative witness than Barrett. So too was Kinsey. The argument, alas, was put into print only metaphorically, typed rather than published, and though he had had in mind submitting it to *Partisan Review*, he thought better of it. Probably he remembered the hostile reaction *The City and the Pillar* had provoked. Perhaps best to wait for another day in which to engage publicly with that issue again. The essay went into his collection of unfinished and/or unpublished manuscripts, a trunkful of which he had arranged with Pat Crocker to send back from Antigua, partly because he expected soon to have ample storage room of his own, mostly because he urged Pat to intensify his search for a buyer for the Antigua house. He needed a sale as soon as possible. "I am now in the throes of buying a place up the Hudson and so must sell, if possible, my Antigua seat." New York City seemed unattractive even in the spring. "This city depresses me more and more," he told Laughlin, "and every year there seem to be fewer and fewer people I want to see. The fault is no doubt with me since I have never much subscribed to the egalitarian dogmas: I am one of God's little misanthropists."

By May the prospects for buying Edgewater were bright. By June he could "hardly think of anything else," he told Carl Van Vechten. "My usual hobbyhorses [are] unridden and gathering dust." With the moral support of

Alice, with whom he spent some May and June weekends in Rhinebeck, he moved closer to a purchase. The owner was delighted to have a buyer. The buyer did not think to haggle about the price, since it was so low anyway and no one seemed to think bargaining part of the ambience of the transaction. He visited his mother and grandmother in Washington. They seemed eager that he have Edgewater, which they both thought would be a fine place at which to visit him, perhaps even for substantial portions of the summer, which made them even more willing than they might otherwise have been to lend him $3,000 each. With that $6,000, he applied to the Rhinebeck Savings Bank for a mortgage of $10,000, at the going interest rate of 3 percent, for a semiannual mortgage payment of $300 for the life of the loan. The bank agreed to lend him the money. A little more than two months before his twenty-fifth birthday, the legal papers were signed. Edgewater was his.

CHAPTER *ten*

A Room of His Own

1950–1955

FROM THE AIR, Edgewater was grandly impressive. Its white colonnade in front of the Parthenon-like façade glittered in the August sunshine. The night before, Miles White—the award-winning theatrical costume designer for *Oklahoma!* and *Carousel,* who had met Gore in the late 1940s and shared with him a circle of New York artistic friends—had been at a Manhattan party. A heavy drinker, he had awakened too late to take the only morning train that would get him to Edgewater in time for lunch, the start of a weekend in the country house Gore had bought just a month before. Worried that there would be other guests waiting, embarrassed at the thought that he would disappoint his host, Miles flung himself out of bed. At the Thirty-second Street East River airport he hired a small seaplane to fly him up. The plane held steady to the eastward side of the river, past Hyde Park, Poughkeepsie, Rhinebeck, the river houses impressive in their wooded settings. Suddenly Miles recognized the railroad bridge and island landmarks. "That's it!" he shouted. There was the shape of the land and the distinctive building his host had described. As the pilot taxied toward the dock, Gore came out of the house, down the steps by the colonnade. He quickly walked toward the river. Miles got out. As the seaplane taxied off, gaining speed, ascending, the two friends walked up the slope. The waist-high grass still had not been cut.

Soon after he moved into Edgewater in late July 1950, Gore sat down in the large octagonal room at the north end on the first floor and wrote, "She wore her trauma like a plume." He had not been able to resist that sentence. Just as he had a new house to live in, he had a new novel to write, though he had not intended to write another just then. But they seemed to go together, as if the move had energized his imagination. He had, finally, a house of his own, one he really wanted, a place that had all the advantages and possibilities for anchoring him to a local habitation and a name. Antigua had been too distant, too limited. Though it spoke to his impulse to establish his own domestic space, it did not fulfill that desire. Edgewater he knew from the beginning would be different, would be successful. It did not matter that the grass demanded cutting, the interior was in disrepair, the building needed painting, the New York Central trains shook the building, the front door was blocked by a foot-high mound of compacted soot that made the kitchen the only usable entranceway on the front side of the house. Confident that in due time all this would be taken care of, he was less certain about where he would get the money. Television was a possibility, and he soon adapted two Somerset Maugham stories. "Some network asked me. . . . I was quite thrilled to be asked to write two of them." At first he thought they would be used. "I thought they were quite good. But I didn't do them in the ordinary TV form, and the people couldn't understand the plays because they weren't in standard format. I never made that mistake again. But I got paid something." Even when they fell through, he still had high hopes. "One of those shows," he wrote to Lehmann, "(and they do good things: Conrad, Hawthorne, James) a month and I shall be able to live in style up here, composing slowly and elegantly my first major (it must be everything now, everything!) novel." He soon wrote another short story, "Erlinda and Mr. Coffin," "rather long, nonhomosexual, faintly ghostly and legendary in tone." But "there are no places here that publish longer pieces, aside from the quarterlies which I always regard as a last resort since I feel in need of money rather than prestige these days." Hollywood was a possibility. For the time being, though, his overtures got nowhere, and he was disappointed that Isherwood made no effort to help him. It did matter, however, that the house was not sufficiently winter-livable. Since he had to put $3,000 into repairs that needed to be done right away, he took the money from his depleted savings. "I've bought an 1820 Georgian house on the banks of the Hudson," he happily complained to John Lehmann. "It is very handsome and fine with an octagonal library and vast white columns, six of them, supporting a Parthenesque facade. I shall die of starvation before many moons have passed but the death will be serene I am sure, with a view of the river and my own seven acres of woods and unkempt lawn." In the meantime he found himself totally absorbed in and entranced by his new novel, for which he had a title, *The Judgment of Paris*. Perhaps it would bring in some money beyond the usual modest advance, though his expectations were qualified by the worry that his "Meredithean comedy" was "destined . . . to be read as little as that great man's works are." More important, he felt himself on the verge of a major change in writing style and novelistic vision.

At Edgewater he was delighted to have guests and to be a guest, mainly at Alice Astor's. With her help he soon had furniture, delivered by truck from the warehouse where she kept large numbers of things she had been collecting, particularly because she had a mania for buying furniture and had in mind furnishing a grand London house to which she would someday retire. "A sofa and some beds were delivered, all on loan. Like a set director, she did all the rooms and then from time to time she'd come over and take the furniture away." One of the beds went upstairs to the third floor, into a bedroom assigned to John Latouche. He was expected so frequently that he was to have his own designated room. Actually, he stayed more often at Alice's nearby and was a frequent visitor at her suite at the Gladstone Hotel. They had become lovers sometime earlier that year. It seemed clear that Alice, as usual, was the pursuer, Latouche the pursued. That his two best friends were for the time being best friends was a great convenience for Gore, who regularly had dinners and lunches with them at Rhinebeck and had them over to Edgewater, where he finally, sweating heavily, cut the waist-high grass himself. Day visitors from the city came and now, with the extra beds, overnight guests, though the small, inconvenient kitchen and his rudimentary skills as a cook made most meals semi- (or even non-) events. "Life in the mansion is serene," he told Pat Crocker. "Numerous visitors and a ruinous series of repairs, however, are reducing me to a wreck and I can't wait until I make some more money, to finish the house up. *Vogue* is doing a piece on it which should be very chic, so chic

that I will then have to pay double for everything from the local cretins."
Vogue never published the piece, and, despite the expense, he was still eager
to have visitors. "My dear Carlo," he wrote to Carl Van Vechten, as he did
to numbers of friends, "if you are mobile some day in the week, or over a
weekend, come up here and sit between the columns and contemplate the
river. The directions are simple: get on the Taconic Parkway and follow it
until it ends at Red Hook, then drive through Red Hook toward Barrytown
(clearly marked at various intersections). Go to the railroad station, cross
the tracks, turn left and there I am, the only house on the river at that point.
Do come."

When there were no visitors, he embraced the solitude that Edgewater
provided, the opportunity for long periods of reading and writing, particularly the former. The autodidactic impulse, from childhood on, was strong.
This time, though, the reading, connected to the new novel, had a purpose,
part of an effort to recast himself as a novelist. He had begun to feel
frustratingly disappointed with what he called "the national style," the flat,
spare, unpoetic, naturalistic prose associated at its best with Hemingway,
which had come to dominate American literature in the 1930s and 1940s.
Within it he had written two bestsellers, but he had a low opinion of the
artistic merit of *The City and the Pillar*, he thought *In a Yellow Wood* a
dismal failure, he still deceived himself into thinking *Dark Green, Bright Red*
a success, and he himself missed the desirable differentness and perhaps new
opportunity represented by *A Search for the King*. What he did see clearly,
he told Lehmann, is that "I am not a naturalistic writer. . . . and it took
me some time to discover that I was never going to master that method, that
my own gifts, such as they are, are of quite a different sort than I had first
suspected. The enormous aesthetic failure of *City* finally convinced me of
this." Whatever reputation *Williwaw* had earned him had been "swept away
by the scandalous success of a naive and hastily written book which, though
eminently true philosophically, was not well done, and, in consequence, I
was regarded as a most barbarous sort of young naturalist, a pale Dreiser
and a queer one at that. It has been a very humiliating experience for me,
these last two years, to endure the reputation of that book and to realize,
worst of all, that it is now considered worthy and rather dull, well-meaning.
. . . Read with a friendly eye, dear John, my nervous apologies; I am not
frank often and, in letters at least, never coherent for I write them late at
night, groggy with fatigue, rage and pleasure."

A great admirer of Mann, he now also began reading everything by George Meredith—"the Milton of novelists"—Flaubert, Smollett, Scott, and Henry James, the last having been recommended to him rather slyly by his Exeter teacher Leonard Stevens, with whom he still corresponded. On one of his trips to Southampton he bought the complete New York Edition "for $125. I had $300 in the bank. That's all I had." He now read James through from beginning to end and added, to his exposure to the seriousness of Jamesian high comedy, a careful reading of the bawdy intellectual comedy of a group of Latin authors, particularly Petronious and Apuleius. They seemed models for some synthesis of his own that would capture in modern terms the tradition in fiction that brought together humor, satire, and high intellectual seriousness about society, culture, and the human condition. He had no doubt about his own narrative skills; he knew how to tell a story. With a gift for language, for the sharply witty phrase, the turn of words that captured an intellectual or a social reality, he realized now that he had been sacrificing this talent on the altar of somber naturalism. As a poet he had expressed linguistic and tonal rhythms gracefully. Why could he not create a more supple, expressive prose that would bring into his fiction the virtues of his talents as a poet? In conversation he had a gift for being both funny and truthful at the same time. Why could he not write fiction that would embody that aspect of himself, completely suppressed in the naturalistic mode, that expressed the seriousness of sharp wit and high comedy? As he began writing *The Judgment of Paris*, sitting in the quiet beauty of the octagonal room, looking out at the early-autumn Hudson River landscape, he knew he was making a decisive change in his artistic self-definition. "My place is incredibly beautiful," he wrote to Lehmann; "the leaves are turning and I composing, slowly, *The Judgment of Paris*."

On Labor Day, 1950, a month after his occupying Edgewater, a significant piece of the puzzle of Gore's life began to fall into place. Walking down a corridor in the Everard Baths, wrapped in the usual towels, his eyes met those of a twenty-one-year-old New Yorker, Howard Auster. "I saw Gore coming down the corridor, and he was really something. Good-looking. Somehow our eyes struck. In the corridor. Towels here and a schmatte there. Then we started talking and ended up in bed. And it was just a total disaster." But in a larger sense it quickly became a great success. "There was an enormous attraction, but it wasn't physical. But it didn't matter, you know. It was a kind of relief. I felt like I had met a soul mate. . . . At the end—and you never exchange names—I couldn't resist, and I said, as I was putting my clothes back on, 'Now, listen, tell me who you are?' And he said he was a student at the University of Virginia. On the chair was a copy of *The New Yorker* and a book and maybe a copy of another prestigious magazine. I said, 'Ya know, you're full of shit!' He said, 'What do you mean?' I said, 'No one who's a student at the University of Virginia reads *The New Yorker* magazine.' I thought he might say, 'Well, fuck you. Who are you to know?' Instead he was delighted. He said, 'You wanna have lunch tomorrow?' I said, 'Yeah,' and I gave him the number of the Lever Brothers mailroom, where I was working, and he called the next day at twelve o'clock precisely. He said, 'Come on over to the Plaza.' 'Okay.' 'One o'clock or whatever.' So I went over. He started the control-freak business right at lunch. An artichoke with hollandaise. The most gentile of vegetables."

Born into a working-class Jewish family, commuting daily from his parents' Bronx apartment to his job in Manhattan, Howard Auster was barely a third-generation American. His maternal grandparents had come from the Polish Pale, his paternal from Marienbad, impoverished Yiddish-speaking Jewish immigrants whose family histories in America embodied the usual pattern of immigration, return, desertion, remarriage, ghettoization, and gentile-phobia in the first generation, slow assimilation in the second and third. His maternal stepgrandfather worked a rented farm in the northeastern Bronx, then gradually sold off pieces of property he had bought or claimed he owned as the urban population expanded northward. The extended-family life at the isolated farm was Howard's most attractive childhood memory, a brief period of stability. For his mother, Hannah Olswang, born in 1908, the farm provided a refuge from her marital miseries during the first six years of Howard's life. Eager to be free of her parents' heavy-handed constraints, without education or vocation, at eighteen she had married Harry Auster, a compulsive gambler who earned his living as a taxi driver. Two years later she bore their only son. Having assimilated Hollywood images of glamour, Hannah, using the name Ann and changing Auster to Austen, worked as a hatcheck and cigarette girl at a nightclub, the first step, she hoped, toward a show-business career. A pretty young woman, she could dance and sing well enough to make the dream but not its realization possible.

Howard's father, born in 1905, left fatherless at the age of about five and working for his living by the time he was twelve, embraced his working-class ethos and his gambler's compulsion. His own father, who had immigrated from Austria, had started a small business in New York. When he went to Europe for a visit, he never returned, leaving his wife and five children to fend for themselves. As if his first family never existed, he remarried. Without education or vocational skills, his deserted wife sent her children to work as soon as possible. A rigidly Orthodox Jew, she pronounced anathema on whoever did not follow the rules, including her eldest daughter, who later became the mainstay of the fragmented family, the only aunt Howard remembered with any fondness. His grandmother "didn't know what Judaism meant. She just followed the forms. She also never learned English." Uninterested in religion except insofar as not wanting to offend the neighbors, Ann and Harry Auster struggled financially, fought bitterly, separated, reconciled, loved one another after their fashion, and set themselves up in the shadowland between working-class and lower-middle-class venues, mostly in the Pelham Parkway area of the Bronx. For Harry, life was mostly sporadic work, heavy gambling, the daily sports pages, and the poolroom. For Ann the hair tint of the day, the newspaper gossip columns, her work at nightclubs on the lowest rung of showbiz life were all major preoccupations. Though money was always short, each summer they went to the Jewish Catskills for a holiday, the high point of their year. At Public School 105, Howard, without much assistance from his parents, performed adequately. "I don't think my father ever read a book in his life. He did, though, help me in my early years in school. I remember I was having trouble learning the alphabet. He took pieces of cardboard and wrote out the letters and taught them to me by rote. That was it. I suppose the main part of it was my fault: He wanted me to be interested in baseball and sports, which he never played. He liked pool and he liked gambling, and I felt that I disappointed him."

At about five or six Howard "discovered masturbation. But not with my hand. It was rubbing against something. I didn't know what it was. And I was doing it on my bed one day in this terrible one-room apartment we lived in then on Stratford Avenue, and they came in. I didn't stop. I was

happily humping away. Well, my father didn't do anything. My mother hit
me. I don't know what consequences this later had on my life. Of course, it
made sex all the more interesting." Initially Ann Auster seemed glamorous
to her young son. "My mother getting dressed up and beating up every
eyelash to go out at night. She was a bit of a flapper." And at first his father
had appeared strong, exciting, someone to look up to. Soon, however, both
parents seemed dull, hostile, rejecting. Like his mother, perhaps in imitation
of her, he discovered early on that he had a good voice and loved singing
popular and Broadway-musical songs. But "my mother was totally discouraging, except that I do remember, which shows you the extent of their
religiosity, that when it came time for my bar mitzvah—'Well, what'ya
wanta do? I'll give you singing lessons or a bar mitzvah!' That's how deeply
religious they were. I would have loved singing lessons. But I said, to please
her—I'll have a bar mitzvah. I'll go to six weeks of Hebrew school.' Of
course she loved giving the party. They showed off. I was aware that I liked
singing, and I wasn't as diffident then. Earlier there was this kid's hour on
radio. I got her to take me for an audition. I was so sure I would pass it. And
I guess I didn't at all. And coming home on the train I remember that my
mother would not talk to me. To this day I don't know why I didn't pass the
audition. I remember being nervous beyond belief." For some years thereafter "that rejection inhibited me from singing. It was like a little secret of
mine. The fear of criticism, and of course when my sexual thing came along,
this was another way of just exposing myself." As he went from grade
school to Christopher Columbus High School, he felt that his parents disapproved of him, that their world was small and boring. At about ten he had
discovered that he liked sex, especially with boys and men, the secretive,
transgressive element a great thrill, partly connected in his mind to his
mother's having hit him when she found him masturbating. "I did it once, I
think, with the super's son—that was enjoyment. I did get blown in the
park, I must have been eleven, by a twenty- or twenty-one-year-old guy.
But I really did the seducing. . . . I was really very aggressive about it as
a child. Far more then than I would ever dream of being now. And that kind
of sex was so exciting. I continued that in high school."

More than anything, he wanted to get away from his parents, to get
away from the dullness of his working-class and lower-middle-class Jewish
Bronx world. Always told that money was short and that his parents were
making sacrifices for him, he was eager to be independent. Like his father,

he started working at twelve, mostly after school, weekends, and summers, as a soda jerk in local candy stores. "One of my reasons for working was so that I could get away from my parents and my neighborhood and I could meet people to have sex with. And then it became a total addiction that I adored." College was his passage out of that world. He applied to and was admitted in 1946 to New York University at Washington Square. With his own savings and earnings, he could just barely pay the tuition. To his parents, college was a foreign world. They did not want him to know more than they did, to rise above them. When, later, he confided to his father his worry that he might not be able to continue at school, his father responded, " 'Good! You can drive a taxi! You can get a job as a trucker!' " Instead he worked long hours at the soda fountain in a Walgreen's drugstore near the Paramount movie theater, a job he liked. The customers were interesting, amusing, varied, the neon-lit show-business Times Square atmosphere attractively glamorous. He loved the glitter, and it paid almost all his school bills. Living at home, he had no rent. His parents put pressure on him to live with them (not that he could have afforded to live anywhere else), partly because they benefited from his baby-sitting for his only sibling, a sister twelve years his junior, also because they considered it shameful for a son to live outside the house until he married or moved away. Perhaps because he felt guilty living in the home of people he increasingly disliked, he succumbed one summer to his parents' wish that he work as a waiter in their beloved Catskills near the resort they stayed at. When business turned bad, the owner fired almost all the waiters. Without any summer earnings, he had to withdraw from college. Soon he had his Walgreen's job back. Resuming college the next semester, he was back at his old Manhattan haunts—the Village, Times Square, the Everard Baths as soon as he turned eighteen, the Upper West Side. "Anonymous sex, in parks. That sort of thing. . . . Being on display at the Paramount Theater and at Walgreen's, I was picked up so many times, and then on Seventy-second Street and Broadway. Just young male flesh. My first really serious encounter was with a woman who must have been a prostitute; she must have been about eighteen or twenty at the most. She really came on strong. She invited me to a place—it wasn't an apartment. I had never had that kind of experience before in my life. I was willing to try it. But I was so terrified. I couldn't get a hard-on. First of all, she was older. I was seventeen. She might have been twenty-one or -two. I didn't find her that attractive. So that was a disaster. What I immediately did to reassure myself was to go to Seventy-second Street and get picked up and get blown by a guy."

Cute, with red-brown hair and freckles, about medium height with a trim, nicely proportioned build, refreshingly straightforward and innocently unsophisticated, Howard was both street-smart and charmingly young. When they met at the Everard Baths on Labor Day, 1950, Howard, who had graduated from NYU in June, appealed to Gore not because of any particular sexual chemistry between them but because he was refreshingly different, youthful, and roughly charming. That he was a relatively uneducated boy from the Bronx was in his favor. Intellectuals and well-educated Wasps were the proverbial dime a dozen in the world in which Gore had been brought up. Howard's Jewishness, to the extent that Gore thought about it at all, was transgressive in a minor key, something that might have appealed to his self-assertiveness, his rejection of the prejudices of the Auchincloss and Gore worlds. So too Howard's working-class background. Gore had had considerable sexual experience with boys from the working-class world. But now here was one for whom he had an immediate strong feeling of protectiveness, companionability, seniority, whom he could jokingly refer to as his "child." Both were eager for friendship, for family on their own terms. Both recognized some potential for creating a relationship that might substitute for what they had been denied or had rejected. If they were, from that first encounter, an odd couple, they were an odd couple that made sense. That distinctive familial chemistry was there from the beginning. Howard was immediately in awe, entranced. They were soon having dinner together every night. When Howard could not afford to pay his half of the expensive restaurant bills and asked if they couldn't go to cheaper places, Gore responded, " 'Why should I suffer because you don't have any money? I'll pay for the dinner, and you give me what you can.' I couldn't argue with that."

A week or two after Labor Day, Gore said, " 'Come up to the country this weekend.' " Not " 'would you like to or'— Just: 'Come to the country this weekend!' 'Well, I'm busy, I don't know if I can make it.' 'Well, if you can't make it, then good-bye!' I didn't know if that meant forever. And besides, I really did want to go up. I had nothing else to do. So I said, 'Okay.' So I came up for that weekend. There was no sex, no sexual tension. There might have been jealousy early on. He told me—don't expect sex. I would have gone on doing it. I didn't care. I would have gone on willingly.

But it wasn't sexual, physical love. I kind of moved—not moved in—I was never sure, that's why I never took it very seriously. If it ended, it ended. Which took a lot of the tension out of it. I suppose I ended up being a permanent playmate, Greek chorus, and Jewish mother. Who could ask for anything more? I got the company of Gore. Beyond anything I really ever dreamed of. . . . I know people are puzzled by how it works between me and Gore. I've been plagued by that all my life. What do you say? 'Hi, I'm Howard Austen, I'm associated with Gore Vidal, but we don't sleep together?' You assume when two men are living together that. . . . It was a corner that they put me into that I just had to accept. Even today. There's no defense. If it were true, I would not be ashamed of it. People have done a lot worse than Gore Vidal, even though he's fat. The truth is the truth."

———

To celebrate Gore's twenty-fifth birthday and the publication of *Dark Green, Bright Red*, Nina decided to make a grand birthday party for her son. Though most of their lives they had fought bitterly, at the moment they were in a quiet passage in their ongoing pattern of separation and temporary reconciliation. Nina's $3,000 loan toward the purchase of Edgewater had given her a proprietary interest in the house. At the Volney, where she took an apartment for her extended New York City visits, she played cards with her alcoholic neighbor, Dorothy Parker. Boiling pot after pot of coffee, Nina tried to stay on the wagon. Regularly she fell off. Most of the time she dressed glamorously, elegantly. In public she was usually vivacious, a dominating presence. In September she came up to Edgewater for her first visit, delighted to have lunch with Alice Astor, whom she soon began to refer to as "my friend Alice Astor." In fact, Joe O'Donohue recalled, "she would refer to 'our friend' and even 'my friend' Alice Astor, which would make Gore furious." When she noticed Howard, she thought him cute and inconsequential and began various small efforts of noblesse oblige, including trying to teach him proper Wasp table manners. "The first time I met Gore's mother was at the party at the Café Nicholson in October 1950. She seemed wonderful to me. I loved glamorous people, party girls. She was a star. Even Gore would agree on that. I don't know whether she accepted me reluctantly or whether she was convinced that I was going to be a permanent part of Gore's life. She had her own gay world. She knew how these affairs began and ended with the speed of light."

In New York, dragging eleven-year-old Tommy around with her, Nina arranged to have Gore's birthday party at Café Nicholson on Monday night, October 2, when the restaurant would otherwise be closed. Food from the party would come from a caterer Nina would obtain. Gore, through Johnny, would supply the room and the lovely back garden. He also, of course, would supply most of the guests, from a list of his famous friends whom Nina was eager to meet and have a high time with. For Nina it was somewhat down-class. But it gave her the chance to be managerial, to show the world her interest in and her closeness to her son, to rub shoulders with what to her was a glamorous though less refined world than her own. As usual, she intended to be splendid. Among other things, she had had a large cake made with bright green-and-red lettering in the shape of the book she had not read. Soon after the party began, she swept in, dressed in glittering silver lamé, "a fabulous figure," Nicholson remembered, "a very handsome woman," glamorously, superciliously, and probably happily out of place. Since Anaïs was there with Hugh Guiler, they must have met, the only encounter between them, though in the noisy excitement of the party they probably at most eyed one another in passing. Anaïs would have been more interested, though disdainfully, in Nina than Nina in her. Gene Vidal was there, with Kit. When Gene sat next to Anaïs, she startled him with her frank conversational references to Gore having been her lover. Gore introduced his mother, as he did his father, to Tennessee Williams, John Latouche, and Carl Van Vechten. Oliver Smith, the prominent New York set designer, was there, Nick Wreden and Louise Nicholl from Dutton, Harvey Breit from the *Times*, Alice Astor, Connie Darby, Sarah Moore, the actress Ella Raines—related to Gore and Nina through her marriage to one of Bob Olds's sons—and about seventy-five of Gore's old and new New York friends, including editors from *Vogue* and *Mademoiselle*. When Miles White entered, he noticed a shy-looking young man standing alone near the entranceway. Shy himself, he kept Howard company. So too, a little later, did Johnny Nicholson, who was frightened of Nina. Toward the end of the party Gore "made a gracious little speech about what an occasion it was etc., etc., 'particularly when I can,' I said as I cut the cake, 'eat my own words.' "

Through the fall of 1950 the domestic rhythms of Edgewater took shape. Before driving to the Rhinecliff station to welcome his new friend to Edgewater for his first visit, Gore had put a pork roast in the oven. When they returned, "the roast was dried out and terrible. And that was it—the whole dinner. Well, perhaps he had some vegetables or something." Gore seemed to think that he had prepared an excellent meal. "So I said, 'Maybe I'll try the cooking.' I was *hungry*." Howard cooked thereafter, making pleasurable use of "fresh ripe Dutchess County tomatoes in July and August from the roadside stands. And the corn," which Gore always remembered as the best he had ever eaten. At least one weekened meal, usually Saturday night, was at Alice's, where her Russian chef kept guests happy. On Sunday they often ate at a nearby lobster restaurant. The driving was done by Gore. In the Aleutians he had occasionally driven a jeep over the roadless tundra. He knew how to start and stop. That, though, was the extent of his driving skill. Howard did not drive at all. For local driving (Gore initially took the bus or train into Manhattan) he needed a car. "I went into Rhinebeck and bought a Model A Ford, a couple of hundred dollars," Gore recalled. "In those days nobody asked you for a driver's license. I lived there. I said, 'Will you tell me how this thing starts?' And they started it and showed me the throttle. I remember that. 'This is in case it doesn't start. You do that.' 'Where's the brake?' I knew about the brake. 'How do you stop it, etc.?' 'The pedal.' I got into the car," without a license, "and I drove it from Rhinebeck to Edgewater." Howard, who stayed from Friday through Sunday, found that social life revolved around guests, at Edgewater and at Alice's. Gore went regularly into Manhattan once or twice a week, often staying overnight, enjoying New York literary society, particularly, for example, Edith Sitwell who was over for a lecture tour in November and the New York opening of Williams's *The Rose Tattoo* in early February 1951. Gore paid all the bills, though often he worried about where the money for major expenses would come from. During the week Howard still lived with his parents. Then, late in the year, an ex-cab-driver friend of his father, who had gone to college, showed up with his fifth wife. Howard's mother had told him about her son's glamorous new friends. "He was the only person in that milieu to whom those names would mean anything." Soon Ann Auster was laying down the law. Howard would have "to give up all these friends because Sam . . . had done some research and found out my new friends were homosexual. I took a bag—I don't know why we even had a bag—and packed my clothes. I didn't say a word. 'You're moving out?' That's when she called me a degenerate." In late autumn he moved into the Manhattan YMCA, then early the next year into a shared, subleased, $75-a-month furnished apartment on the top floor of an abandoned synagogue on East Seventy-second Street.

For Christmas, Gore and Howard took the train down to Washington, where Howard had never been, to visit Nina and Dot. Gore's temporary truce with Nina now provided a painful example of its fragility and Howard his first experience with Nina drunk. They arrived in good Christmas cheer at her large four-story row house, 3226 N Street, one floor of which she occupied, the others of which she rented, except for a guest apartment Dot sometimes stayed in. Probably she was there now, though not Gore's thirteen-year-old half-sister Nini, who, with a temper of her own and after a fight with her mother, had gone to live with her father. She preferred an Auchincloss Christmas. Eleven-year-old Tommy, home from boarding school for the holiday, showed Howard the Edgar Rice Burroughs Tarzan and Mars books that had once been Gore's and that Tommy had saved when they had left the Woodland Avenue house. Few of Gore's other childhood books remained, and all his papers had been discarded. Fascinated by the Tarzan books, Howard sat with Tommy, leafing through one of them. Tommy then went to bed, early. He was suddenly shocked into awakeness by Nina. "God, it was an awful thing. She came in, and she was naked, and she hit me a couple of times," Tommy recalled. He had never seen his mother that way before. "She woke me up. I must have said something that set her off into a drunken rage. Something like kids do. She may have spent too much money on me, and I wasn't appreciative enough or something. Then she got sick and vomited on me. Gore was there, but he was in another apartment." The next day Gore explained to Tommy "that 'your mother's not well.' I guess she felt badly about it. Afterwards she never remembered what she had done. I didn't go near her for two years after that. . . . I was in boarding school anyway." Frightened, he also moved to his father's. Janet Auchincloss's rages were slightly less intolerable, and at least she was not his mother. When he left, Nina got rid of "all the toys and all the clothes and all the books" Tommy had, including those of Gore's that Tommy had salvaged. For Gore the scene was familiar, one of many he had experienced, some of them when he was as vulnerable as Tommy. Nina's friend Joe Ryle remembered what for him was the sadness of Nina's self-destructive behavior, particularly how, when Nini and Tommy were coming home from school for holidays, Nina would be "so marvelous and be on the wagon for two or three weeks before they came home, totally. Not a drink. The minute those children would arrive, she'd go falling-down drunk. She just couldn't cope with— I don't know what it was she couldn't cope with. It was just so sad." Sometimes she could stay on the wagon for months. AA helped. At times in the mid-1950s "she was quite self-analytical, but she was also always excusing herself," Gore recalled, "and trying to find excuses for what she knew was incredibly bad behavior, even as drunks go. She blamed her bad behavior on having been neglected as a child and so on and so forth. But she knew that didn't play with me, because I knew too much about her parents, so she then said that she had agonizing menstrual periods. 'I had the longest menopause in history. It went on for years. It was agony. All the night sweats and nerves.' I said, 'I guess a lot of it was DTs too.' "

Though he felt sorry for Tommy, the Christmas nightmare did not ruffle Gore's good spirits. Except for his concern about money, things were going well, and he had hopes that either television or pulp fiction would provide him with additional funds. There was the possibility of reprints of his novels, a backlist that he hoped the new paperback industry would make available. Victor Weybright, who had originated New American Library with Signet and Mentor paperbacks, was successfully pushing mass-market fiction. Gore had just met Weybright, a stolid, dark-haired man, elegantly dressed in hand-tailored British suits, his ever-present pipe accenting his jowls. "Weybright looked like Evelyn Waugh," Jason Epstein recalled, "and tried to act like him, to look elegant. He was a very good businessman." From an agricultural family long settled in rural Maryland. Weybright had gone from the Wharton School to editing an important Washington social-science research magazine to four enjoyable wartime years in London as the American liaison with British scientific and cultural organizations. Before leaving England he had made an arrangement with Alan Lane, the pioneering creator of Penguin Books, to buy out Penguin's fledgling American operation. Weybright hoped to do for paperbacks in America what Lane was doing in Britain. There was some possibility that Weybright would arrange with Dutton a new paperback edition of *The City and the Pillar*. Also, he had in mind a paperback anthology of quality literature, to be published a few times a year. By spring 1951 both projects were in the air. Weybright, who had been having great success publishing mass-market originals of Mickey Spillane's subliterary detective fiction, may have suggested to Gore he might earn much-needed money by writing an upscale version of Spillane, sophisticated murder-mystery thrillers to appeal to the high end of the paperback market. Vidal remembers that the suggestion came from Weybright, partly compensation for his resistance to publishing Gore's out-of-print novels with the excuse that literary novels did not sell in paperback, though he boasted he had been the first to sell Faulkner widely when he put a steamy cover on his edition of *Sanctuary*. More likely he feared the taint of a novel and a novelist associated with homosexuality. The chronology and the record suggest that in the spring of 1951 Gore himself thought of what were soon to become the pseudonymous Edgar Box mystery novels. As a reader of Agathie Christie and S. S. Van Dine, he felt he knew the genre. That summer at Edgewater, experimenting for the first time with a Dictaphone, he dictated in about a week *Death in the Fifth Position*, the first in the Edgar Box trio.

At ease in the octagonal study, the house still somewhat haggard and underfurnished, he had worked through the winter and spring completing *Judgment* and trying to get various moneymaking projects off the ground. Through Harvey Breit he had done a review in February for the *New York Times Book Review*, another for *The Saturday Review*. It soon seemed evident that he would make very little from *Judgment*. In late June 1951 he had finished the novel. At best, he anticipated, it would sell his usual 10,000 copies. In October 1950 he had arranged to be paid by Dutton $450 a month from November 1, 1950, to October 1, 1951, mostly advances against royalties for *Judgment* and for the next novel he had in mind, tentatively titled *The King James Book*. That money would stop soon. At the same time as he finished *Judgment*, Gene Vidal, consulting with his son, leased a small factory in Poughkeepsie with a contract to make a thousand plastic bread trays a week for the General Baking Company. He previously owned a similar factory in New Rochelle, which had recently burned. Probably the plastics were dangerously flammable. Gore, from nearby Barrytown, was to be director of personnel. Perhaps there would be profits for both father and son. "He was actually running his father's factory," Tommy Auchincloss recalled, "or at least that was the impression he gave me. His father would come down and visit. Gore was basically the one who was going over there and checking things." A disastrous fire two years later was also to close the Poughkeepsie factory, with little or no benefit to either. But beginning in the summer of 1951, it was something that Gore kept one eye on. Gene, who regularly inspected the factory, stopped at Edgewater for brief visits.

That same summer Gore had long-term visitors, though they did not distract him from work. Dot, who came to see the house, did not stay long. Nina, who had Tommy for the summer, initially intended to stay much of July and August, the 1950 Christmas fiasco long out of her mind. She would help decorate Edgewater. The octagonal room, like much of the house, needed painting. As always, to pass time during the evenings, they played gin rummy. "Nina wouldn't take my beating her at gin rummy terribly well, and she never paid me what she owed me. Oh, we played just for pennies. And even that was more than she would pay." Soon Nina was happily aflutter at an invitation to be a celebrity bridge-playing guest on the maiden voyage of the transatlantic liner the *United States*. Why could she not leave twelve-year-old Tommy with Gore at Edgewater and she herself sail off on this glamorous adventure? Amiably, Gore agreed. While he worked on *Death in the Fifth Position* and answered, as Tommy noticed, stacks of letters, Howard entertained Gore's half-brother. In addition to the press of work, Gore felt he was "not very good with children. I can manage babies. They're like cats. But much older children, I don't know what to do with them. Tommy was the wrong age. If he were an adolescent, I'd have been able to talk to him." Gore would talk to him, Tommy recalled, about his work, his friends—one of them a famous ballet dancer who could jump four feet in the air. He would not play with him, though. The highlight of Tommy's summer was when Howard, his ubiquitous Lucky Strike cigarette in his mouth, took him to Coney Island. "We went to a burlesque show," Tommy recalled. "I probably talked Howard into it. I had a prurient interest in that kind of thing, and I never had any sense that he didn't." After a few weeks Gore and Dot arranged for Tommy to spend the rest of the summer in Newport with the Auchinclosses. When, after a month, Nina returned, clearly something had gone wrong on her trip, perhaps some aborted romance or imagined insult. She did not seem, though, "in such bad spirits. But she was raging at Hughdie for having taken the son that she had left there, and then she decided to kill herself. She took a lot of pills, and my grandmother knew she wasn't up and heard this terrible snoring from her room where she had passed out." The local doctor saved her.

———

At Alice's grand hostelry and at Ferncliff, Vincent's larger estate nearby, Gore had the advantage of both friendship and entertainment on a high scale. Alice, who split her time between the Gladstone Hotel and Rhinebeck, was delighted to have her artistic-intellectual young friend nearby, especially during the fall and winter weekends when most of her Dutchess County society was away. Though Gore, who disliked Edgewater's winter cold, soon began regular Key West visits for at least one winter month, he stayed during part of the off-season. Oblivious to seasons or class distinctions, Alice had little interest in warm-weather winters. Howard was regularly, kindly welcomed at Rhinebeck. Alice "looked like a Byzantine princess. Very dark, with brooding eyes, Byzantine-Etruscan. She never wore much makeup, but of course she didn't have to. I see her constantly playing with her earring. Not with great speed, but as if her hands were always busy with worry beads. She smoked constantly." Her young teenage daughters, Emily and Romana, were around. So too her eldest, Ivan, who detested Gore, probably suspecting, as he did of many of his mother's friends, that he was getting money from her and perhaps had designs on Ivan's inheritance. He was right to the extent that Alice invested $2,500 in June 1950 in a Latouche-Vidal "literary idea" called "The Devil May Care," one of a number of ideas and outlines they created together, the most substantial a screenplay called *Love Is a Horse Named Gladys*. Actually, Latouche got the entire $2,500. It was a device to funnel money to him. Always broke, he lived from hand to mouth, sometimes desperately morose, often charmingly inventive. One day when Gore was visiting him at his lower–Park Avenue apartment, some men came to seize his furniture for indebtedness. "They asked him if he were John Latouche. 'No,' he said, 'I'm Louis Latouche, his brother!' In a short while he had charmed the men not only into believing this but into going away without the furniture." Except for the loan of some sofas and beds, most of it returned by the mid-1950s, Gore himself took nothing from Alice.

A fountain of humorous anecdotes and witty comebacks, Latouche often lived up to his reputation of being the best talker around. Gore, who had begun to hear some of Latouche's favorite stories too many times, especially about his adventures in Africa, set him up amusingly one night at Edgewater. With his eye on his watch, making sure to get the timing right, Gore interrupted the flow of conversation, suddenly saying to Latouche in an amiably insistent voice, "Why don't you tell everyone your African story?" Latouche launched into it. Just as he came to the climax, the New York Central Railroad roared by, shaking the house, drowning him out.

Like Latouche, Alice loved the night, whether partying in New York or staying up until the small hours of the morning, playing cards and Chinese checkers, chatting, gossiping, telling stories, always sleeping late. When guests came for lunch, she quickly dressed, dashed out of her bedroom, went out the back door into her car, and had the chauffeur drive her around to the front, as if she had just arrived from a morning out.

Soon after moving into Edgewater, Gore was delighted to discover he had some interesting neighbors in addition to Alice. In Barrytown and nearby Red Hook lived a number of accomplished people, one of whom, Alan Porter, he became friendly with. Another, Joe O'Donohue, whom he already knew from the New York ballet world, became a good friend. A small, humorous man who always laughed at his own jokes, Porter, the first curator of photography at the Museum of Modern Art (despite being totally color-blind), came up regularly from New York. His friend Greta Garbo sometimes came to stay with him at the old Lutheran church he had converted into a residence. There he headed what he and his friends, particularly Paul Kent, Billy Baldwin, and Jack Frear, called "the sewing circle" and what the locals called the "Boys from Barrytown." Jack Frear and Jimmy Whitfield "had a house called Dovecote, and they were known as the Doves of Dovecote. And Whitfield was a cousin of Calder Willingham. I saw him occasionally," Gore recalled. "The only ones I saw were Alan Porter, who lived next to Don Wilson and Paul Kent." Old-fashioned, with an odd rustic accent, Porter was an amusing eccentric. "If someone had gone to bed with someone," O'Donohue recalled, "Alan described it in one sort of little Revolutionary-time dialect, 'He put the boots to him.' He was a very strange little guy. A perfectly nice man, who laughed all the time." Another, more eccentric neighbor was the son of the essayist John Jay Chapman, the heavy-drinking Chanler Chapman who ran a highly personalized local newspaper. For whatever his reasons, including perhaps that John Jay Chapman had once lived in Edgewater, Chapman felt free to come over and make himself at home anytime, which Gore resented and soon put a stop to. O'Donohue, however, was always welcome. A handsome, slim man, elegantly dressed and fastidiously outrageous in manner and conversation, he had lost the inherited fortune that had allowed him to live a cultured, high-society Manhattan life during the 1930s and '40s, a friend of Carl Van Vechten, Cole Porter, and Clifton Webb, a premier member of café society from Harlem to Park Avenue. "Very handsome in an elegant, aristocratic way," Sam Lurie recalled. "A snobbish type, I suppose you'd say today. Tall, thin. Very good-looking then. Great charm. Well mannered." A society columnist named Maury Paul, who wrote under the name Cholly Knickerbocker in the Hearst papers, called him "The last of the Perhapsburgs." Having recently bought, with the help of Alice, who found it for him, a small house in Red Hook, he stayed much of the winter.

Many of Alice's literary guests were treated to the luxuries of her brother Vincent's estate. Tennessee Williams enjoyed swimming in the indoor pool, wearing a bathing cap, as Romana noticed with some astonishment, and the Sitwells, particularly Edith, came. Alice would bring them over to Ferncliff for the hospitality of Vincent and his wife, the former Minnie Cushing, one of whose sisters had married Jock Whitney—in Nina's mind still the man who had "got away"—after his divorce from Liz. The aristocratic Sitwells, for whom the Gladstone was not posh enough, stayed free at the St. Regis Hotel, which Vincent owned. "We're in some little hotel. Osbert, what's the name of it again?" Edith would say. "Oh, the St. Regis. Yes. Perfectly nice." Gore, who had met Edith and Osbert in New York in autumn 1949, found the Sitwells' eccentricities—their odd, elongated, skeletal frames and especially Edith's witty flamboyance—compelling. When after a lunch together Gore, Paul Bowles, and the very tall Osbert, whom Bowles had been eager to meet, walked on Fifth Avenue toward the St. Regis, the two younger men found that Osbert, who had lost some control of his limbs because of Parkinson's disease, began to take longer and longer strides. They could barely keep up. "I raced beside him, trying to hold him back—and down to earth like a balloon—while Paul, who is short and slight, had now left the pavement and was flying through the air, clinging to Osbert's arm for support." At the height of her reputation as a poet, over six feet tall, wittily wicked, Edith in her sheer entertaining bizarreness appealed to Gore's sense of humor as well as to his sense of history, as if some medieval Plantagenet had come alive again. When he complained to her about a foolish British review of *The City and the Pillar* in the *Times Literary Supplement*, she said, "But they do books on Icelandic runes very well." In preparation for her sitting next to the conversationless Vincent at her first lunch at Ferncliff, Edith took counsel with her fellow guests. " 'What am I going to talk to Vincent Astor about? I've heard he's very difficult.' They said. 'Look, what he really loves is facts.' 'Ah!' She was put next to Uncle Vincent at lunch," Romana remembered, "on his right.

People were wondering how this was going to go. Uncle Vincent was amazed when she turned to him and said, 'So glad to meet you. Tell me something—you're probably the only person who can tell me—how many girders does the Eiffel Tower have?' She kept my uncle talking about the Eiffel Tower for the whole of lunch."

Close to Edgewater, though worlds away from Ferncliff, Bard College provided entertainment of a different sort and, during the first half of the 1950s, a few local friends, particularly the poet Ted Weiss. A small, arty, serious school, with a special emphasis on literature and the humanities, Bard, years before cast off from Columbia University without an endowment, frequently teetered on the verge of bankruptcy, its faculty underpaid and overworked in a demanding tutorial system. Students got much individual attention. Faculty rarely had time for anything else. Still, in the 1940s and '50s, when academic jobs were especially scarce and widely underpaid, Bard attracted distinguished people who came as visitors or stayed for a few years, writers like Mary McCarthy and Saul Bellow. Three years after moving into Edgewater, Gore had not met the peripatetic Bellow, to Ted Weiss's surprise, and "since I plan to shut the house in a week or so we are not apt to meet: there is a rumor he may not be long up here, that the open road, more grand appointments await him. I have not read his book [*The Adventures of Augie March*] but it sounds most energetic and respectable." A young poet of distinction and an enthusiastic teacher of literature, Weiss and his wife Renée, a violinist, had been publishing their influential small magazine, *Quarterly Review of Literature,* since 1943. They regularly organized poetry readings and conferences at the attractive riverside campus that over the next decade brought to Bard most of the best-known poets of the period. Unenthusiastic about academia, having narrowly escaped Harvard, Gore was enthusiastic about the Weisses and accepted some invitations to readings at the nearby campus, one to hear Jean Garrigue, whom he had met through Anaïs years before in New York and to whom he had introduced the Weisses, another to hear Wallace Stevens. Gore recalled, "Here was this fat solemn businessman in a three-piece suit, a typical insurance salesman from Hartford. 'Well, it's a remarkable time in the arts,' he said. 'I'm supposed to be talking about modern poetry today. I think that's the subject I was given, and I don't know what to say in a period that has something no other period has even had, a Museum of Modern Art.' Well, I fell apart. Nobody else could see the joke. I thought it hysterically funny. I read him then. I used to read a lot of poetry. . . . I went into the war with Auden's anthology, which I carried all through the war, two or three volumes. . . . I got through the war with him." On another occasion at Bard there were "three British poets," Gore reported to Lehmann, "very dreary . . . D. Gascoygne ('nearer my God to thee'), Graham (hearty, solid, regular feller) and a Miss Raine ('I loathe Jane Austen') . . . for a literary jamboree . . . being strange to these shores they were unaware that anyone took poetry seriously enough to want to discuss it in PUBLIC, so one had the feeling that their most central modesty was hopelessly violated by the tough young New Yorkers who put to them long technical questions. The session broke up with one sharp youth remarking from the floor that, among other things, the supernatural was an abstraction . . . to which Mr D. G. gulped with pain and said in a strident choked voice, 'The Supernatural is Not an Abstraction!' ending the symposium." Some of the Bard poets came for parties at Edgewater, especially the much-liked Weisses. One afternoon, at the time of the publication of *Judgment*, as they were chatting about things literary, Gore, defiantly and defensively, told Ted, "Well, my best novel is at least as good as the worst of Henry James."

His outward gaze was mostly turned toward New York, his inward focused on intense reading. Still, the Weisses were fun and nice, and Gore's larger New York City literary life, soon to be extended to television and then the movies, seemed exotic to them. When Ted asked him to satisfy one of his students' curiosity about Tennessee Williams, Gore graciously responded,

> As for Tennessee, you may pass on to the young man the information that he reads a great deal of verse, almost no prose of any kind, that the greatest single literary influence on him was Hart Crane (he set out to be a poet, not a playwright) and a later but less influential mentor has been Rilke, in translation. He admires Sartre's plays, despite a fierce snub we both received from that busy little Caesar (I *don't* share Tenn's admiration) one afternoon in Paris. Among contemporaries T.W. personally likes Carson McCullers, Windham and myself . . . putting up with those works of ours he cannot bring himself to read with good humor and right feeling. He does not like novels though he will read short stories with

some pleasure. He has had little personal contact with other
theatre writers. He once wrote O'Neill a fan letter after *The
Iceman Cometh*, getting a long response, shakily written. I read
it but can't remember what it said. So much for my talents as
a recollector of the great.

Down the road from Edgewater, near the entrance to the Bard campus,
Gore and Howard found a better use for Bard than its academic resources.
At Adolph's, a small tavern and student hangout, Howard met some of the
more adventuresome members of a faculty and student body that had its fair
share of men interested in men. Some he occasionally brought back to
Edgewater.

Though he never spoke at Bard, Gore had begun to supplement his
income and cultivate his audience by lecturing. "My life has been desperately busy these last few months," he told Lehmann. "Every other week I
go out to lecture to Ladies' clubs: the Midwest, New England, the South, all
over. I do it all in a sort of daze, for the money. I have also had my father
move one of his small factories within two miles of my house, to provide me
with a sinecure, which it will do very nicely as soon as the troubles stop but
after six months they still persist." Late in 1951, on his way to Philadelphia
to lecture, as he drove through Manhattan under the elevated subway tracks,
he banged his car into a steel post. Miraculously the car was intact and no
one else hurt. His ribs, though, were badly bruised. He simply drove on.
Fortunately, if the police had been involved (apparently they were not), at
least he now had a driver's license. A fast driver who frequently exceeded
the speed limit, he had recently been stopped for speeding on his way to Joe
O'Donohue's in Red Hook. "The state trooper called me over and said.
'You're speeding. I have to give you a ticket. Where is your license?' And I
said, 'Well, I don't have one.' He thought I was either joking or I didn't
have it with me. He chose to interpret it that I didn't have it with me. I had
the registration. 'Okay," he said, 'the magistrate is over there. You go and
pay your fine for speeding.' So I went to the justice of the peace with this
thing and I said I've been speeding. And he said, 'Well, where's your
driver's license?' I said, 'Well, I don't have one.' He said, 'You mean you
don't have it with you.' 'No, I never got one.' 'You never got one!' and he
became extremely interested in the case. . . . 'Well, why didn't you get a
driver's license?' 'It just never occurred to me.' " With aching ribs, he drove

on to Philadelphia and gave his lecture. Isherwood, who had just been at Edgewater for a visit, was there with John Van Druten to attend an out-of-town performance of Van Druten's adaptation of *Goodbye to Berlin*, *I Am a Camera*. To Gore, who joined Isherwood at the theater, it seemed more Van Druten than Isherwood. Still aching, he drove back to Edgewater, where the doctor diagnosed and taped up four broken ribs. "I am in physical discomfort most of the time with these ribs but," he told Lehmann stoically, "that sort of thing is not eternal."

At Williams College, where he went to lecture in mid-May 1951, the bookstore manager, Raymond Washburn, a Vidal enthusiast, eagerly greeted him. He had been to Edgewater for a visit, where Gore had introduced him to his grandmother, whom he found "characteristically fascinating." They had all gone over to Alice's for lunch. Latouche's "conversational ability" impressed Washburn. "I'm not sure," he wrote to Gore, "I could survive a long siege of it, for either my mental capacities would shrivel away (what few there are) being blanched in the reflective glory of his verbal acumen, or the constant assaults upon my ears would soon leave me deaf and dumb." From Barrytown, Gore took the train to Williamstown, where Washburn and others had arranged a meeting with students eager to talk to him about the ongoing public discussions he had been conducting with John Aldridge on the future of the novel. That evening he gave a talk on literary reputations, mostly to faculty, one of whom, Richard Poirier, who had just come to Williams and was the same age as Gore, persistently took him to task for his undervaluation of Faulkner. Faulkner had been the subject of Poirier's recent Ph.D. dissertation. He "didn't really care much for Faulkner," Gore later remarked. "I had been brought up by a family from that area. He was so startling and exotic to Northerners but was too down-home for my taste." In the argument that developed, Gore challenged Poirier to name one writer not sanctioned by academia that he liked. Had he read Meredith? Poirier had not. "Your view on every writer is exactly that of every English teacher." Poirier kept pushing. "How do you explain the lack of acceptance and popularity of Faulkner in this country? He has greater fame in France.' Gore wouldn't have any of this," Poirier later said. " 'But Faulkner has been accepted here,' he said. 'He's a revered figure.' Then, as he went on, I began to see that what he was really saying is that Faulkner's reputation was quite adequate to the attainment. And this was the beginning of my friendship with him and my deep reverence for his sweetness. . . . He was immaculate-looking, stately-looking, princely. He looked like a young prince. He had a wonderful voice and inflection, and above all he was always very, very gracious and charming, as I've always thought him to be." In New York, in fall 1951, when they ran into one another at one of Poirier's hangouts, the popular Blue Parrot, they joked pleasantly together, the start of a friendship.

Inviting her to visit in late-summer 1951, Gore wrote to Anaïs, who was spending much of her time in California, that Edgewater is "a perfect summer house, airy and full of green light." It was a happy refuge, especially from discussions about values, a perfect place for work. Though there was still a distance to go, the house was shaping up. Basic repainting had been done, repairs made, sufficient furniture was in place. Howard, with Alice's help and Nina's suggestions, began to redecorate. "My mother, her twelve-year-old son, a colored cook and *her* twelve year old daughter are all in the house for the summer," he told Anaïs, "and I rather like the activity: I feel quite patriarchal. Not easy to work but soon, when the library floor is painted and the new shelves are put up, I will lock myself away and begin my Messiah novel." But money was very tight. The $1,000 advance for *Death in the Fifth Position* helped. So too did Dutton's willingness to advance money on a monthly basis. The small amounts from the Auchincloss trust took care of the very low mortgage payments, but austerity was still necessary. Howard paid his own bills in New York. Eager to get out of the mailroom at Lever Brothers, when he was turned down for every job he applied for in advertising, on Gore's recommendation he changed his name on his résumé from the identifiably Jewish Auster to Austen. Whether that change made the difference or not, he got the next two jobs for which he applied, first as a sales and display assistant at Helena Rubenstein, then as an advertising-agency account assistant at Batten, Barton, Durstine and Osborne. Whenever there were joint activities, Gore paid, as he did for everything at Edgewater. He had a strong sense of possession, a country squire comfortable in a house that increasingly reflected his vision of himself.

At Columbia University one evening in February 1952 Gore joined Malcolm Cowley, the literary and cultural critic born in 1898, who had analyzed the post–World War I generation in *Exile's Return,* and the much younger John Aldridge for a forum discussion of the state of the novel. The relationship with Aldridge had grown more complicated than simply critic-pseudo-novelist and novelist-occasional-critic jockeying for position and prominence. Initially Vidal had thought Aldridge might do something important for him and other writers of his generation. If Aldridge was to be the preeminent critic of his time, the new Edmund Wilson, then his imprimatur would be valuable. By 1952 Vidal was beginning to see that Aldridge would not rise to Wilson's level. He later began to think of him as another version of Orville Prescott; it was becoming clear that Aldridge might become an enemy, certainly not a supporter. After their correspondence in 1948, they had met in New York in fall 1949, having lunch and spending part of an afternoon wandering around the midtown bookstores, at each of which Gore looked for his own books. "Maybe he thought it would be impressive," Aldridge later remarked, "if the stores had his books. I think he wanted my support, and for a long time I think he thought he had it. I reviewed about three of his books in the *Times,* always somewhat mixed. But he seemed to think that that was just fine." Aldridge's review of *The Judgment of Paris* was not unfriendly, but it was condescending and had in it distant homophobic touches. As always, his main thrust was "values," the absence of moral values in contemporary fiction, equating a novel's value quotient with its literary merit. Latent in Aldridge's emphasis was the likelihood that writers who were homosexual, such as Williams, Isherwood, and Vidal, would fall damnably short as artists simply on that basis. At Columbia each of the participants had given a brief talk about the novel and then squared off in an amiably contentious performance, Gore much the best public performer of the three. "On the strength of that," Aldridge recalled, "we were invited to Princeton to do the same thing again. Cowley said we were 'the happiness boys.' We were anything but spreading happiness; we were talking about the contemporary novel."

That spring, at Princeton, the critic R. P. Blackmur, who had arranged the rematch, introduced them for another semistaged literary slugfest. They were joined by the young novelist William Styron, who had recently published *Lie Down in Darkness* and whom Gore rather liked. As the well-attended discussion turned hot, Gore said to Styron, " 'Do you notice that there's basically no interest in you and me and only in the two critics?' A college audience took them seriously and Styron and me as people of no consequence. Producers of raw material, which they in turn shaped. Values, Values, Values. Then Aldridge said that there weren't many values anymore in a modern society like the United States because there was no class system, except there were pockets like the Army where there was hierarchy and a class system and you could write about class. And Cowley got up and said, 'Values, Values, Values.' He had kind of a funny lisp on V so it sounded like a W. 'There are plenty of values. Everywhere you look there's a value of some kind.' And I got up and said, 'Mr. Aldrich was born in Sauk City, Iowa, or some such place, and was a brief time in the East and then he came back and taught in some Middle Western place. Since he's never knowingly encountered the class system, he doesn't think it exists.' I said, 'Anyway, I'm glad he's here at Princeton, where there are so many members of a class higher than he, and all eager to condescend to him.' " Afterward they went to the Nassau Tavern. Blackmur, with whom Gore would have liked to have talked about Henry James, had left immediately after introducing the speakers. He was stuck again with Cowley and Aldridge, among others. The principals kept hammering at the putative gap between values and literary merit. "I had to leave early," Aldridge recalled. "But he and I were going at it strongly. I was talking about my old theme of values. 'Oh, God,' he said, 'you need values to get out of bed in the morning.' "

In summer 1952 Gore went up to Putney, Vermont, to participate in the Windham College Writers Conference, which Aldridge directed, where he met and rather liked Aldridge's new wife. The novelist Vance Bourjaily, whose *The End of My Life* had established him as one of the writers who, along with Vidal and Norman Mailer, Aldridge had written about in *After the Lost Generation* and whom Gore had recently gotten to know in New York, was there. "I went to Vermont to lecture under Aldridge's auspices," he wrote to Anaïs, "a cold brilliant lecture which was completely hated, to my surprise since I made a number of what, I thought, were illuminating remarks on the literary art . . . but then of course illumination is the last state of being tolerable to our countrymen, especially writers and would-be writers, my audience." When, that same summer, John Bowen—a young English writer who had just graduated from Oxford and had favorably reviewed *The City and the Pillar* under the title "Kiss Me, Hotlips, I'm Asbestos"—came up for a weekend visit on his way to take up a graduate fellowship at Ohio State University, Gore and he swam out to the small island in the river. "There was a middle-aged Swede . . . there at the same time," Bowen recalled. "I only remember an open fire. The middle-aged Swede I think had the vague idea that I'd been invited to go to bed with him, but I was prudish then, perhaps even more so than now. And so I disappointed him." He and Gore liked one another immediately, and when they began to correspond, Bowen regularly addressed him, though they were about the same age, as "uncle" and Gore addressed Bowen as "nephew." He "was standing to me in an avuncular relationship because I knew nothing about the United States. So it became a joke between us that he was acting as my uncle, standing in loco parentis, being my American uncle." With Bowen the relationship was clearly noncompetitive. With some of his American contemporaries, many of whom Gore was seeing at literary gatherings in New York, the story was more complicated.

———

Encouraged by Vidal and the challenge of bringing new writers to the attention of the large audience for paperbacks, Victor Weybright in late 1951 decided to see if he could get a paperback literary serial, *New World Writing*, off the ground. Edited out of the Signet-Mentor offices, it would appear four times a year in book form with original material by a mix of new names and the best-known writers of the day. At the same time Ian Ballantine's Pocket Books decided to sponsor, with John Aldridge and Vance Bourjaily as editors, a similar paperback anthology, *discovery*. Suddenly both were competing for material. Authors were being pursued for contributions. Publisher-sponsored parties at which liquor and conversation flowed brought potential contributors together. *New World Writing* had the advantage of Weybright's experience and Gore's contacts, which he immediately put to the service of the new venture, excited by its prospects, by its potential impact on the literary scene, and by the satisfactions of his own central role. Weybright, who now had the first of Gore's Edgar Box novels in hand, consulted frequently with him about the new project, usually at lunch in Manhattan. Gore thought of himself as the unofficial editor, though it had been agreed that there would be no formal editor. Arabel Porter, Weybright's assistant, an intelligent, hardworking cross between a secretary and an editor in charge of reprints at Mentor, would be the coordinator. Soon busy writing letters to friends and acquaintances, Gore helped obtain contributions for the first volume, with additional material for volumes to follow, from Isherwood, Williams, Auden, Kimon Friar, and Carson McCullers, among others, then poems by Ted Weiss and Louise Nicholl, even a story by Bob Bingham, who was in New York working as an editor for *The Reporter*. "Material is being collected now," Gore wrote to Lehmann. "Chris (who is most enthusiastic) will let some of the fabled diary be done. Tennes-

see's Lawrence play will be done in toto. There's an essay on Carson by
Oliver Evans, an essay on architecture by Philip Johnson . . . and stories
by Gore Vidal et al." "Erlinda and Mr. Coffin" appeared in the first issue,
"The Ladies in the Library" later. *discovery* had the attraction of Vance and
Tina Bourjaily, who at their Greenwich Village apartment hosted ebullient
parties, the venue for a great deal of heavy-drinking literary sociability. It
also had the disadvantage of the two editors' not seeing eye to eye on much.
At one of the Bourjailys' parties Gore met a young lawyer, Louis Auchincloss, a talented short-story writer just about to publish *Sybil*, his second
novel, to whom Gore was related by his mother's marriage to Hugh. Gore
pulled him in as a contributor.

Eager to help Weybright assemble the best writing of the period, Vidal
knocked himself out in a venture that seemed worth the effort. "I am going
out of my mind," he had written to Lehmann late in 1951, "New World
Writing, lecturing, manufacturing, as well as battling with the last proofs of
Judgment." But it was not a complaint. "The great project of the moment
has to do with Signet," he explained. "Due to MY exertions for the past
year, Victor Weybright (whom you met in London recently) is going to put
out four collections a year of *New World Writing*, an American child, in
spirit, of *New Writing* and *Horizon.* . . . I shall be, if it succeeds (first issue
in April), a permanent sort of reader. . . . You are of course vital to the
undertaking so do be receptive. I think well of it. . . . There has never
been anything like this in America since the great days of the *Atlantic
Monthly* in the last century: a national showcase for the best writers." To
Arabel Porter he wrote regularly, recommending writers, evaluating material, making suggestions, "an editor without portfolio," as he put it to
Aldridge, from whom he diplomatically solicited a contribution. As the
April 1952 publication of the first issue became imminent, he concluded that
"New World Writing is triumphant, in advance at least." Though they had
agreed there would be no single editor, he felt he had edited the volume and
that that should be acknowledged somehow. He also believed that
Weybright had explicitly agreed that if the first issue were successful, Gore
would formally be appointed editor of future issues. When the first issue
came to hand, he was shocked to see Porter prominently proclaimed editor.
At the back, in small print, he was thanked, with two others, for helping
make the volume possible. It felt like a betrayal. At a party Weybright
hosted, attended by most of the contributors, the publisher made a gracious

speech thanking them. "Auden stood around sullenly and occasionally muttered, 'How much are we going to be paid?' " Weybright cheerfully ignored
Auden. Angry, Gore reproached Weybright. But, the publisher explained,
Porter *had* to be the editor. "But I *did* edit it," Vidal remonstrated. "I asked
him afterward, 'Why have you left me out?' 'Well, Gore,' he said, 'I can't
make this any single writer's anthology.' 'You mean you can't make it mine,'
I said. And he stammered around and then said, 'Well, you are thanked in
the first issue.' . . . I knew that I'd been fucked yet again." Still, he hung
in with Weybright, whom he otherwise liked. Soon Weybright agreed to
publish under the Signet label a number of Vidal's novels, including *The
Judgment of Paris*, and eventually *City*. Gore continued during the next two
years to do his best for *New World Writing*. The idea still seemed to him a
good one.

From Edgewater he made frequent trips into Manhattan. Having
skipped Key West that winter, he was happy to see, in May 1952, the
countryside around the river come alive. "I have been busy," he wrote to
Aldridge, "weeding gardens, composing the journal, studying the daffodils
(the first one opened yesterday . . . awfully odd-looking, too, a kind of
hybrid), communing with Weybright on the November issue of *N.W.W.*
and preparing, God help me, a reading at a theater in the Village called *The
Circle in the Square*, booked right after a Welsh road-show named Dylan
Thomas." The combination of country life and city adventures agreed with
him. When he came to town, he struck friends and acquaintances as beam-
ingly healthy and attractively young. To Tina Bourjaily, a pretty, amiable
woman with striking blue eyes, whose parties he often attended, he seemed
"much healthier than anybody else. . . . There was a great deal of body
abuse going on. We didn't exercise, we drank a lot, we sat around and
smoked. He always came in like a fresh breath from the country. Apparently
he did a lot of work around Edgewater. He appeared youthful to me. Very
youthful and very handsome." Unlike the *discovery* and *New World Writing*
crowd, he hardly drank and did not smoke. The Bourjailys had been evicted
from their first Manhattan apartment when the young novelist James Jones,
who had published *From Here to Eternity* in 1951, drunk, threw up in the
stairwell. Downtown, in their Greenwich Village flat and at other literary
parties, floating from apartment to apartment, literary friends had long
nights of drinking and conversation that Gore sometimes joined for the
company. "What people wanted to do when they got together was to have a

drink," Tina recalled. "We gave parties for almost any reason. A party could be three or four people who just happened to be there. Or calling up others. You could have a few drinks and then flow into the subway and up to somebody's apartment." William Styron, Norman Mailer, Herbert Gold—who had just begun his writing career with *Birth of a Hero*—and even Ralph Ellison were part of the *discovery* group, the emphasis tilted toward what Gore thought a somewhat too heavy-handed naturalism. Aldridge came in frequently from Vermont, tall, blond, always combing his hair, an eager lady's man hoping for conquests, including Anaïs Nin, and Tina Bourjaily remembered that he "never went anywhere without a toothbrush and brushed his teeth furiously as if it were his conscience." Calder Willingham, from Georgia, often visited, his hair red, his neck almost red, with a thin face and curved nose, a clever, amiable man with a great deal of talent as novelist, playwright, and screenwriter. Late in the year Gore co-hosted a party at the Bourjailys' apartment, competing with them to see who could produce the most famous literary names. Gore's trump card was Tennessee Williams. "Katherine Anne Porter said she didn't like to go out, even though he invited her. She was another important guest. We were trying to one-up one another," Tina recalled. "Tennessee Williams and Calder Willingham. . . . Our apartment was this long flat, a long, long hallway, and then you had the option of going this way laterally to the kitchen or bathroom or bedroom and then two doors came into the living room and dining room. Williams somehow got into the bedroom. There was Tennessee Williams standing alone. I took him out and said to this assembled group full of themselves, 'This is Tennessee Williams!' Dead silence. First the poor man got lost in the bedroom, then he came into a room that went absolutely dead when I made the announcement. He was that big a celebrity."

The Bourjailys themselves Gore became quite fond of, especially Tina, an easy-tempered Midwesterner via California from a strong-willed Scandinavian farming family. She seemed to all of them a beneficent presence. She "looked like a very pretty Zelda Fitzgerald," Gore recalled. "Tina was slender, vivacious, quick, very droll. Vance was quite slow, and she was very quick. So she was the one." Vance, who struggled during these years to write his own fiction and who began to look to television to earn a living, functioned effectively as one of the editors of *discovery*. Gore found him pleasant, amiable. Olive-skinned, Syrian-looking in background, Vance was the son of journalists: his mother had been a popular novelist and then owned a small rural newspaper. He and Tina had married in 1946, in their early twenties, gone to Bowdoin College, then in 1950 moved to New York, where Vance, who had published a first novel based on his war experiences, was to take his turn at the literary wheel of fame and fortune. Tina was to support them, which she did with a job at *Woman's Day* magazine. By late 1952 Gore and the Bourjailys were good friends.

Louis Auchincloss came to the revels; soon the two semi-cousins were companionable both in New York and at Edgewater. Tall, dark-haired, craggy-featured but handsome, always well dressed, with a high-pitched voice whose accent was a mixture of Groton and Upper Manhattan, Auchincloss had decided to combine a legal with a literary career. The upper-class legal and social world was his subject. Gore soon began to use him as his lawyer. If you could not trust Cousin Louis, whom could you trust? Like Vidal, Auchincloss was a great admirer of Henry James and Edith Wharton. Gore immediately thought he was a good writer, an excellent human being. They both enjoyed occasionally gossiping about their shared world. Always ready to argue that every male was potentially homosexual, Gore would teasingly call Louis "Louise." Their main subjects together were literature, history, and their own careers. Auchincloss was the conduit in the Bourjaily world to the Upper East Side, to occasional dinners and parties that he hosted and introductions that he made. For Auchincloss the Bourjailys were the conduit to Manhattan life below Fourteenth Street, to the less refined but dynamically talented circle of mostly Greenwich Village people, one of whom was Norman Mailer, a swaggering, heavy-drinking young man from a Brooklyn-Jewish background. Handsomely rugged, short, somewhat thickly stolid, pugnaciously physical, with electrically bright blue eyes, Mailer had just published his second novel, the much-reviled, highly political *Barbary Shore*. He had hoped to duplicate the bestselling success of *The Naked and the Dead*, which he had published in 1948. Mailer, who seemed both by personality and conviction even more radical than he actually was, had the impression that Vidal was an elitist conservative. "In those days," Mailer recalled, "before he became a liberal, Vidal was an archconservative, virtually a loyalist. He was well known for that." Aggressively masculine, Mailer had no sympathy for homosexuals, and *The City and the Pillar*, as well as Vidal's obvious attitudes in the public part of his private world, had made his interests well known to his friends and to New York literary society. Mailer flourished in a world in which conquests were everything, women and booze the drugs of choice. For those who were married, "every-body was switching partners," Tina Bourjaily recalled. "That was the name of the game." Actually, both Mailer and Vidal were sexual marauders, with only certain minor differences in taste to distinguish them. When they first met, in 1952, at a party at the lower–Fourth Avenue apartment of the actress Milly Brower, they were aware they had much in common, especially an extraordinarily high energy level, an ambitious competitiveness as writers, and the will to dominate circumstances and people. Both were fascinated by power, including their own. "He was a very good-looking young man," Mailer recalled. "He came over and said, 'Well, at last we meet!' He had the same voice then that he has today. . . . He said, 'Well, now, Mailer'—mind you, we're the same age—'How long did your grandparents live?' 'Well, they both died when they were sixty-nine.' 'Aha, I've got you then. My grandparents lived to a very ripe age. You know what that means?' I said, 'No, I don't.' 'I'm going to outlive you. And because I'm going to outlive you I'm going to have the final say on both our careers.' It was the same Gore even then."

Eager to get away from the cold Edgewater winter, Gore went to Key West in early January 1953 for almost three months, as he was to do for a shorter period in 1954, stopping in Washington to pick up his grandmother, who drove down with him. In South Carolina they stopped to visit some of Dot's cousins. When she told him, "You mustn't stir up more snakes than you can kill," he asked her "if this was an old South Carolina saying. She said, 'No, I think I just made it up.'" In Key West the sunny warmth pleased both of them. Since Dot did not care for Gore's favorite, the Southernmost, they stayed at a place more attractive to her, almost as close to the beach, dining at the Tradewinds. "I am in the throes of losing weight on the beach at Key West," he wrote to Arabel Porter, "small lumps of lard upon the sand to extend the image wilfully." The topic and the theme were beginning to become a recurrent one, the natural tendency of his body to thicken around the middle, much as his grandfather Gore's had, now regu-larly asserting itself against his thin frame. Only severe dieting helped. "I hope in a few weeks to be a slim golden youth again or at least a faintly decrepit facsimile. Let me know what goes on in New York." He was at work on a new novel, to be called *Messiah*, and was planning the second of his Edgar Box mysteries. The tentative title was *Kill Him in the Shell*, to be set in East Hampton. He was also preparing an essay on the contemporary novel for *New World Writing*, a longer, more subtle version of the lecture he had honed over the years, to appear under the pseudonym Libra. He had no difficulty writing in his motel in the morning, enjoying the beach and good company for the rest of the day. Tennessee, recently returned from Rome, frequently met them at South Beach. "We made our way through sailors on the sand to a terraced restaurant where the Bird sat back in a chair, put his bare feet up on a railing, looked out at the bright blue sea, and, as he drank his first and only martini of the midday, said, with a great smile, 'I like my life.' " While the early-retiring Dot slept, Gore, with Tennessee, Frankie, and other friends, enjoyed lively nights at the Key West bars.

Generally there was no emotional price to pay for his sexual adventures. One of his Key West encounters, though, which took place in 1953 or 1954, was costly. Some months after leaving Florida, he was told by a woman he had known in Key West that he was the father of the child she was bearing. She asked him to pay for an abortion. The claim was credible enough for him to accept the likelihood that it was so. Worried, he confided in Tina Bourjaily. The woman, he told her, was a waitress whom "he'd had an affair with. . . . 'We humped for two weeks . . . and Gore's going to be a daddy.' . . . It was a worry. He wasn't being boastful at all. I thought he was anxious about what was going to happen. It wasn't something that should happen. This was a real problem. Here he was having a heterosexual relationship, and it went bad." In New York, anxious and distressed by what might happen, he asked Louis Auchincloss's advice. "I was feeling a bit of strain and a bit lost about how you go about these things. I didn't know what the repercussions were going to be." Louis advised that he send an untraceable money order for the $780 for which he had been asked. He did. A local Key West doctor apparently performed the abortion, at least so Gore was told. With brutal animus, some Key West enemy made sure later that year that he heard a nasty ad hominem story. "It's about the sickest story that I've ever heard. A faggot doctor-abortionist had a Christmas tree, and on it was a fetus and he said that's Gore Vidal's child." There is no certainty there was any child at all. He may have been the victim of an extortion scheme. Or of a cruel practical joke or a combination of both. Whatever the reality, it was a painful experience that reinforced some long-standing attitudes. He had no doubt that he did not want to be a father. He had seen too much of bad parenting in his own life to take the risk of repeating what he had experienced with a child of his own. Also, the domestic arrangements required by the effort to be a responsible parent were inconsistent with the flexibility to travel for work and pleasure as he desired. He preferred to be mentor rather than parent, and when he sometimes referred to Howard as his child, it was in that sense—someone to whom he was teaching the manners and mores of the sophisticated world. The issue of metaphoric parenthood, however, became a concern and gradually a preoccupation, partly related to his role as a novelist-creator, later to be a central theme in *Two Sisters* and *Burr*.

Through the Bourjailys, Gore met Francis Markoe, an elderly Yale-educated Francophile with a passion for Racine, amateur theatricals based on sixteenth-century masques, and young men. Markoe had an attractive house and guest cottage with a Chinese garden at Water Mill, near Southampton. He was "really a great old-fashioned queen," Gore recalled, "very exuberant, an old-school Edwardian sort of style; he would go on about the king's guardsmen." The Bourjailys were Markoe's guests for much of the summer. Gore, who had had lunch there in summer 1952, had invited Markoe to Edgewater, which he visited the next summer, driving up from Water Mill in his chauffeured car with his own guests, the Bourjailys and their infant daughter. Howard was there and some of Gore's ballet friends. The Bourjailys recalled that Gore was very kind to their little girl. Vance remembered Markoe "being very excited to learn that I knew Gore and very eager to meet him. . . . Mr. Markoe . . . by being on the state parole board—he'd gotten all the prisoners when they came out of prison—and he liked them—he would pick somebody that he'd met from this group and offer him a job as a chauffeur or a houseboy. He got men that way. He had some money growing up that he'd run out of; then he married a wealthy older woman."

One afternoon at Edgewater in 1953, Markoe and the Bourjailys were visiting for the weekend. As they played croquet on the lawn sloping down to the river, Gore knocked Tina Bourjaily's ball into a berry bush. "For a long time there was a thorn in my finger that never came out. He had forced my ball into the bush, and I had gone in after it. . . . He had no sympathy whatsoever for my ripped finger. I did get my ball back in play." The visitors noticed that Edgewater was underfurnished. "It was elegant, except that you were waddling around in an unfurnished palazzo." While they slept in the guest room in "a four-poster bed that belonged to Mrs. Astor," the Bourjailys had the characteristic Edgewater experience of being shocked awake by the noise from the New York Central. At night Vance and Gore swam out to the island in the river. Tina and Frank Markoe sat on the lawn, talking. "We thought it would be fun to light little balls of newspaper for them to see, and we lit them all along the columns so that it was dazzling flame. It was very theatrical. We hoped that they could see it from the water. You couldn't burn the place down. We were sitting there, and Mr. Markoe said to me, 'There's only one commandment I've never broken: I've always honored my mother and father.' I thought, 'Oh, my God, all those others!' " In a lighter key, Gore was working on his new Edgar Box mystery, with the revised title of *Death Likes It Hot*. Soon after Markoe's Edgewater visit, Gore drove down to Water Mill for a weekend. The gardens were lovely, the house charming, the entrance hall decorated with a mural depicting naked men. Markoe put on two plays on the lawn, in both of which he performed, one a Racine drama, the other something Vance had written based on an idea as old as H. G. Wells's *The War of the Worlds* that was again popular: visitors to earth from outer space. Gore complimented Markoe for his "startlingly excellent performance in Racine: I think it as good as the Comedie." In Vance's play "Mr. Markoe was a visitor from outer space wanting to blend into this strange little planet he'd landed in. He thought the appropriate dress for the part was a baseball umpire's; that was his costume. I can't remember what occurs in the play." The Bourjailys were delighted to see Gore again. Conservative communities, Southampton and East Hampton were still almost exclusively a combination of summer enclaves for wealthy old East Coast families and quiet year-round working-class villages. The first early wave of artistic people had just begun to flow in. The Bourjailys had been pleased to have Adele and Norman Mailer's company for some weeks at Markoe's earlier in the summer, though much of Markoe's high-social community had been scandalized. It seemed clear to Tina that Markoe "lusted after Gore like crazy, but I don't think he ever got him. He was almost seventy at the time. . . . One day, when Gore was there, I went over to the house by mistake. Mr. Markoe was walking around in a short smock. He climbed up on a ladder, to get some china, I think. He didn't have anything on under this short smock, so I said, 'Excuse me!' He was all visible. It was part of the show for Gore. . . . I think Gore was more amused than anything. It was kind of sweet and pathetic."

There was little sweetness to Vidal's encounter in 1953 with Jack Kerouac. At the San Remo, a Greenwich Village coffeehouse, on a stiflingly hot night late that August, Kerouac hailed him, somewhat high, probably a combination of alcohol and sexual anxiety, and introduced him to William Burroughs, who was eager to meet and talk to Vidal. Gore had met Kerouac some years before at the Metropolitan Opera House, at a ballet performance starring Leon Danielian. Gore had gone with Nina and John Kelly, who was still in love with Danielian. In the club circle they met Kelly's good friend, the publisher Robert Giroux, whose guest was a handsome, dark-haired young writer, three years older than Gore. According to Gore, Kelly had had sex with Kerouac, who half concealed behind a frenetically macho manner a nervous, uneasy attraction to men as well as to women. Gore thought him handsome, sexy. Often volubly confused and energetically self-hating, Kerouac had since that first meeting established close friendships with Allen Ginsberg, Neal Cassady, and the older William Burroughs. Though he had just written *On the Road*, he was still mostly unknown, the Beats not to coalesce into prominence as a movement until 1956 and the book not published until 1957. A fiercely competitive writer, Kerouac had read *The Judgment of Paris* with resentment, even contempt, an expression of the confused envy, oscillating between hero-worship and hostility, that he felt for Vidal's celebrity. He and Burroughs liked nothing about *Judgment* except its "satirical queer scenes" and the book-jacket photograph of its attractive author. With his own self-defining barbaric yawp, Kerouac detested the fascination with stylistic elegance and classical balances Vidal had begun to reveal in *Judgment*. Such novels seemed to Kerouac "sophomoric imitations of Henry James," an archenemy whom he felt needed to be erased as an influence on American literature. Novels like *The Ambassadors* he felt utterly worthless.

But the full range of their differences was not part of the encounter that evening at the San Remo, where Kerouac had "recognized him from the night I'd met him at the Met ballet when in New York in a tux I'd cut out with tuxed editor to see glitter nightworld New York of letters and wit." Gore had no idea of the ambivalence or depth of Kerouac's feelings toward him; his own antipathy to the Beats and his fear of the significance of their success were in the future. When they left the San Remo together to go barhopping, Burroughs soon became uncomfortable with, if not embarrassed by, Kerouac's behavior. Fawning and assertive, sincere and mocking, the drunk Kerouac kissed Gore's hand and said flattering things, which he later dramatized in his censored, parodic account of the evening in *The Subterraneans*. At that time neither Burroughs nor Vidal was aware they had both been students at Los Alamos Experimental Ranch School, that they had in common, among other things, A. J. Connell. Despite his manic years, his drug habit, his rebelliousness, his autobiographical first novel, *Junkie*, which had just been published, Burroughs dressed and acted publicly in a way that his St. Louis–Burroughs Adding Machine family would have found perfectly respectable. When Kerouac swung from a few lampposts, Burroughs said good night to both of them. Kerouac proposed to Vidal that they get "a room around here." They went to the familiar Chelsea Hotel on Twenty-third Street, signing their names in the register. Gore told the clerk that "this register would become famous." In Vidal's account they first showered together, then went to bed. A red neon light flickered with a rosy glow through the shadeless window. Kerouac blew him. Then they rubbed bellies for a while. Then Vidal flipped him over and attacked him from behind. Years later he still remembered that he "stared at me for a moment . . . forehead half covered with sweaty dark curls—then he sighed as his head dropped back on the pillow. . . . The rosy neon from the window gave the room a mildly infernal glow." In the gray morning, with hangovers, without much conversation, they prepared to leave. Kerouac, who had no money, needed subway fare. Vidal gave him a bill and said, "Now you owe me a dollar." In Vidal's account Kerouac was impotent. He slept on the bathroom floor, not in the bed. In his own account in *The Subterraneans* Kerouac left out the sexual details entirely so as not to offend his mother, Allen Ginsberg, whom Gore liked, later told Vidal. Apparently Kerouac boasted to friends later that day, "I blew Gore Vidal!"

———•——

How to make an adequate living in a depressed book market still perplexed Gore. He was neither Mickey Spillane nor Erskine Caldwell. Serious novelists were not doing well in general. One day on Fifth Avenue he ran into William Faulkner, to whom he had previously been introduced. Uncharacteristically chatty, Faulkner advised against Hollywood, his own gold-plated but still-sustaining egg. Faulkner's novels had earned next to nothing in hardcover. Only now were Weybright's paperback reprints, with their sensationalized covers, bringing in any money. For Gore there were

the Edgewater bills. The cost of a car. Ordinary living expenses. To Howard, who had moved out of his shared Seventy-second Street apartment to a
modest Lexington Avenue walk-up between Fifty-seventh and Fifty-eighth
streets, Gore now paid $20 a week as his secretary/assistant, soon raised to
$40. When Gore was in Manhattan, he often stayed with Howard rather
than at a hotel or his father's apartment. Strenuous efforts to write pulp
fiction for money were not sufficiently successful. In November 1949 he had
accepted a fee of $2,500 to revise a badly written adventure novel set in
Turkey, with the understanding that his name would not be associated with
the published book. The revision may have destroyed its pulp-fiction credibility. No publisher would take it. In June 1953 he had published *Thieves
Fall Out* under the name Cameron Kay—a Kay cousin's Christian name and
his grandmother's maiden surname—a Gold Medal mass-market original
for which he earned a little over $3,000. At a retail price of twenty-five cents
a copy, not even the sale of about 300,000 copies could produce much
income for the author. Not quite as revealing as *A Star's Progress*, it nevertheless had many effective Vidalian touches, the setting drawn from his
Egyptian experiences in 1948, a combination of hard-boiled suspense, a
strong love story, and a political/social drama that pits the individual
against a corrupt society. "You sneak!" the Gold Medal editor wrote to him.
"Why didn't you tell me you were that world-famous crescendo-making
writer, Gore Vidal, instead of pussyfooting around with a cardboard alias?"
In November 1953 he had signed a contract with Avon Publications for a
mass-market novel called *The Pursuit of Vice*, for which he received a $1,000
advance. Later, when it was clear that he no longer had an interest in writing
it, he reluctantly returned the money. The short stories published in *New
World Writing* earned only a few hundred dollars. In January 1954 he
delivered the second Box manuscript, in June the third, *Death Before Bed-
time*. The money was already spent, partly in the twelve $450 monthly
payments from the December 1952 agreement with Dutton, then in an
emergency $1,500 advance in August 1953, and another $1,750 advance in
December. Future earnings would probably at best pay off the advances.
There was no more to be gotten from Dutton for the time being. When with
sickening apprehension he saw realized his fear that *Judgment* and now
Messiah, dedicated to Tennessee Williams, the first inklings of which had
come to him in Egypt and which he published in early 1954, would at best

earn back a little more than their advances, he pushed harder to engage with the only other two sources of writing income, television and movies.

Actually, he had been trying the movies since 1946. Nothing had worked out, neither an adaptation of one of his novels for the screen nor a studio contract for his writing services. He had not given up. Through Tennessee he had gotten access to the best-known theatrical and movie agent of the time, Audrey Wood, who handled Tennessee's plays. That had started in 1948 when Henry Volkening, a New York literary agent who represented him for a short time, sent Wood *The Different Journey,* the play Gore had written in Egypt and, with Tennessee's help, revised in Paris. Volkening accurately anticipated Wood's response. They both thought the play awkward, amateurish, and censorable. Because of its homosexual theme, Volkening felt certain a producer would at least have to *"worry* about the New York police." Wood thought he needed "a good technician to work" with him. "Ideally you need that ugly word a 'dramatist collaborator.' " At the beginning of 1950 Gore had tried Wood again, though this time with an offer of his own writerly services. "I think," she had responded, "that rightly agented you could become a successful Hollywood writer and that this might well balance your budget in times of a depressed book market generally." It was a boulevard he had been trying to walk up since 1946, through Felix Ferry and other Hollywood studio people at Famous Artists, at Columbia Pictures, and in 1952 at Paramount. The Goldwyn office responded encouragingly to Wood's overtures. "Mrs. Goldwyn thought you were 'a very erudite young man' " and a possibility for the future. Nothing came of it. In November 1950 he had contracted with his semi-relative, the actress Ella Raines, to write a screen treatment, "a ski story," which would have a starring role for her. It fizzled out. When Latouche and Vidal teamed up to write screenplays, Wood had wished them a "happy honeymoon." In July 1950, in response to three ideas for screen treatments they had devised, she had admitted "I'm very fond of each of you but having read the three ideas for screen-originals you recently submitted to me, I don't think either of you are taking the picture business too seriously these days. . . . Each of these three ideas seems very trivial, seems very forced, seems very phony to me. . . . Do either of you two ever go to see a motion picture?" The next year they got no place with their screenplay, *Love Is a Horse Named Gladys*. They had also tried to write a

Broadway musical together. "I am trying to buy a house and write a musical comedy with La Touche, all at once," he had written in June 1950 to Robert Halsband, a young eighteenth-century scholar and book reviewer for *The Saturday Review*. Wood kept trying, without success, to sell screen rights to his novels, particularly *Death in the Fifth Position*. Her sources told her that "it is very difficult to sell a mystery melodrama, a light comedy, or an average triangle drama, primarily because the TV channels are so full of this kind of thing. . . . I don't think I am going to be able to help you on this" or anything else, she confessed. Wood's assistant in charge of radio and television tried, at Gore's request, to get him some television jobs. Nothing happened. "As you know," she told him, "the competition is very keen these days." Since he and the Liebling-Wood Agency were not getting anyplace, they parted company.

Whatever he had tried, no one particularly wanted his services. At best he had been able to scrape up a few television-writing assignments in 1951 and 1952. His Maugham adaptations had been an unsuccessful first effort. A quick learner, he had realized he needed to master the basic techniques of writing for television if he were going to have any chance of success. He hoped he could learn by practice and get paid at the same time. Luckily, in 1953 Ella Raines was starring in *Janet Dean, Registered Nurse*, "an eternal series. Mrs. Eric Ambler was in charge of this program," Gore recalled. "She's English and had been the right hand of Alfred Hitchcock. It was Ella who said, Why don't you do one of these? So I worked with Joan," who was "the producer of my first TV play, 'The Jinx Nurse.' " The work was almost anonymous, but he could present it as a credential on his oral résumé, proof that he knew how to do this kind of thing successfully. Since he needed an agent who could influence network producers to hire him, he had gone to the top, to Jules Stein, the head of MCA and the husband of his mother's best friend. Stein had been warmly avuncular over the years and, aware of his novels, thought him very talented. Ready to help, he sent Gore to John Forman and Tom Moser, two television agents at MCA in New York. For whatever their reasons, they declined to take him on. Stein "didn't think when he sent me to them that they wouldn't handle me, since he was the head of the firm. But that's the way big hierarchies work. If your connection's too high up, it's useless. You can only deal with somebody who's closer to where the work is. They thought he was so imperial and far away that he wouldn't know or notice."

Unwilling to give up, he went, late in 1953, to the head of drama in the television department at the William Morris Agency, MCA's prime competitor. Harold Franklin, a balding, graying, handsome man in his late forties, bespectacled and dressed immaculately, immediately decided that he might be able to help and that he probably liked this young, attractive, articulate novelist. True, Vidal's only experience was the unproduced Maugham adaptations and 'The Jinx Nurse' show. But Franklin, a shrewd and thoughtful man, an avid reader with a conservative, almost scholarly air, had both presence and intelligence. "He was vibrant," a younger colleague recalled. "When he walked into a room, you knew he was there. He was not an insecure agent who had to be on all the time. He seemed to have strength." Talent, Franklin thought, was more important than experience, especially in a young industry. He said to Gore, " 'just think of something, a one-paragraph idea.' I thought of *Dark Possession*." Franklin sent him to see Florence Britton, the story editor for CBS's *Studio One*, sponsored by Westinghouse, one of the premier weekly one-hour television drama anthologies. At lunch together, eager for scripts, she commissioned him to write it. The fee would be $750. A few days later he had it done. "The year is 1904," *Dark Possession* began, a story of schizophrenia or dual personality in which a woman, split into two people one of whom has murdered her husband, writes incriminating notes against herself. When, at the climax, her doctor tells her she has written the notes herself and that she is the murderer, she kills herself. Soon slotted into the insatiable weekly production schedule, revisions and rehearsals occurred quickly and mercilessly. Like all *Studio One* dramas, the script had to be exactly sixty minutes minus two commercial breaks. On February 15, 1954, *Dark Possession,* "written especially for Studio One by Gore Vidal," starring Geraldine Fitzgerald, with Barbara O'Neill and Leslie Nielsen, produced by Felix Jackson and directed by Franklin Schaffner, had its premiere. The broadcast went coast to coast. Suddenly twenty-eight-year-old Gore Vidal had a much larger audience than he had cumulatively for all the novels he had published.

CHAPTER ELEVEN

Intolerable Absences

1955–1957

IN MAY 1955, soon after the telecast of *Visit to a Small Planet*, flying overnight on the red-eye from New York to Los Angeles, Gore Vidal was a nationally known television dramatist. It had all happened in little more than a year. That he had published seven novels was fine and good, and there were many who waited for his next. But television success had begun to provide him with something that writing fiction had not, the glow of celebrity and the security of a good income. If he were a success in television, movies could not be far behind. One or the other or both would, he now had no doubt, provide him with the money to support Edgewater and himself. At least he would still earn his living as a writer, even if these collaborative media demanded craftsmanship more than art. As an art form, he still embraced the novel, and he felt certain that neither the networks nor the film studios would in the long run interfere with his commitment to writing fiction. It was clear to him that in his case at least he could separate the part of his brain devoted to craftsmanlike scripts and the part that created serious literature; he felt in no danger of cross-contamination. Good at compartmentalizing, it seemed to him better to earn his living, since it had come to this, writing for television or movies than working in advertising or teaching. At a minimum it was more interesting; the people more various, accomplished, and attractive; the stakes higher; the money better; the visibility greater.

Between his inaugural appearance with the production of *Dark Possession* in February 1954 and his departure for Los Angeles he had established a reputation and career in an industry that had already transformed American culture. With the end of the war, commercial television became a reality. By 1950 it had become a pervasive cultural presence. By 1953, 80 percent of American homes had television sets. Two national networks, CBS and NBC, with their affiliates, controlled the airwaves, distantly followed by ABC. In each major city there were numbers of unaffiliated local channels. Expansions, mergers, buyouts, new licenses, technical innovations—suddenly a highly profitable television marketplace existed. Power was being grasped and consolidated, fortunes made. Remunerative protocols between American business and the networks were being worked out. Business discovered that it had a powerful new tool for selling products. Together the networks and business decided that that was what television would be about. Since government, a willing collaborator, determined who could legitimately cash in on the fortunes to be made, many legislators became shareholders in new stations. Advertising agencies became powerful players, intermediaries between advertisers and the networks. Talent agencies representing writers, actors, directors, and producers saw a profitable opportunity to package programs. At first there had been only nighttime television. Now, with daytime and late-night, a huge amount of salable airtime needed to be filled.

For much of the 1950s the networks filled some of their most profitable hours with live television drama. At first the production facilities of the Hollywood movie studios were hardly involved, and movie libraries had not yet been sold to fill television airtime. In Manhattan empty warehouses were converted rapidly into production and broadcast facilities. For those early years television originated almost entirely in New York, from the earliest remedial newscasts to Edward R. Murrow to the comedy of *Your Show of Shows*, *The Jackie Gleason Show*, and Milton Berle's *Texaco Star Theater*, to the dozen or so dramatic anthologies, each of which presented weekly an original self-standing dramatic play: *Studio One*, *Philco Television Playhouse*, *Kraft Television Theatre*, *Goodyear Playhouse*, *Robert Montgomery Presents*, and *Playhouse 90*, among others. In 1954 four of the ten top-watched programs in the country were anthology dramas. Since technology had not yet made immediately editable tape available, the ten to forty million households a week that watched one or more prime-time television dramas saw the program simultaneous with its first and only creation. Legal restrictions and technical limitations resulted in kinescopic recordings becoming only archival records. Suddenly there was a new, demanding but exciting source of remunerative work for actors, producers, technicians, directors, and writers, particularly those who could create actable dialogue, construct dramatic stories, and adhere to the technical limitations of television broadcasting. "You have no idea," Gore wrote to Kimon Friar, "how many good things get done in that vast vulgar medium. The people who produce and direct are all young and clever. The actors of course are the best in the world . . . any great star or any good Broadway performer is available, such being the lure of money, steady occupation, and an audience of thirty millions."

Fortunately, he had no association with any left-wing political organizations that might have darkened his name, as Latouche's had been, by inclusion in *Red Channels, The Report of Communist Influence in Radio and Television* (1950) or on later lists. Latouche "was turned down by the Communist Party," Gore remarked. "He was so humiliated by this that he would never tell even the FBI, so he was blacklisted for years, even though he was not only not a party member but had been rejected by the party as too frivolous and a sexual degenerate." Such blacklists were now, with the dominance of Senator Joseph McCarthy's anti-Communist investigations and the start of the Korean War, blighting many careers. Latouche was unemployable in television. Though Gore had come some distance from his grandfather's anti-Roosevelt conservatism in domestic matters, his mind was only moderately on political considerations. In foreign affairs he still believed in the cautionary principle of America First. McCarthy he detested. Eisenhower seemed blandly empty-headed, a political front for big business. Suspicious of Truman's commitment of American troops to a Korean civil war, he had begun to think anti-Communism would at best be used as a weapon to suppress civil liberties at home and expand America's sphere of influence abroad. At worst it would be the trigger for a nuclear war. The arms race seemed inevitably catastrophic. To the extent that he had a political affiliation, it was with the Democrats; but mainly he was against the hawks who dominated both major parties.

"My own days are alternately serene and hectic," he told Kimon Friar.

"I write plays occasionally for television, a fascinating occupation but tiring," though he seemed tireless to most people. Hal Franklin had done well to take a chance on him. With the market's insatiable demand for scripts, opportunities came quickly. Within days after the success of *Dark Possession* he was at work on new assignments. For the one-hour program he had received $1,400. "The day after my debut in February of 1954," he wrote a few years later, "I was committed seriously to writing for the camera. I discovered that although the restrictions imposed by a popular medium are not always agreeable, they do at least make creative demands upon one's ingenuity." He had much to learn, among other reasons because he did not own a television set and had hardly watched television at all. His two attempts to write for the stage had produced untenable manuscripts. From Key West, in December 1953, while he worked on *Dark Possession,* he corresponded with Franklin about a number of television treatments he had proposed, one of them based on *Messiah*. Franklin found the central character unacceptably static. As Vidal proposed ideas, Franklin responded, providing suggestions for revision, determining which producer to send what to, whom to approach directly, whom indirectly, what might appeal to whom. "We were like two generals," Gore recalled, "going over a battlefield trying to figure out how to win it." Their first victory actually came not as an original drama but as a streamlining of the American colonial dramatist Royall Tyler's *The Contrast* for the Ford Foundation's *Omnibus* program, which he wrote during one weekend before leaving for Key West and whose telecast actually preceded *Dark Possession* by over a month.

Ideas came quickly. As soon he had a concept in mind, he had the language for presenting it as a story outline that agents and producers could grasp immediately. Some of the original ideas combined his own emotional and political preoccupations. In summer 1954, while working at Edgewater on another Edgar Box, he outlined in detail ideas for two resonant television stories, the first called *Sovereign State,* the second *Billy the Kid*. In *Sovereign State* the main character, an ambitious, pragmatic governor, accidentally gets into a conflict with the federal government. When he threatens secession, he becomes nationally famous. At the end, though he losses, he is "still smiling, more dangerous than ever having discovered the pleasures of power . . . our young governor is going to be heard from again, in a larger, more dangerous way. . . . The point to a study like this is, I think, important. A fact missed by the general public (and certainly by most of the intellectuals

who brood on political matters) is that these political climbers, these dictators in embryo are *not* Iagos, are *not* devoted to any set of diabolic principles, are, actually, nothing more than beguiling men who find it easy to set
aside all those tacit rules by which . . . no matter how reluctantly . . .
most lives are lived. I have known a good many political figures and a set of
more charming, more amoral men one could not encounter. To do a portrait
of one would, I think, be a public service . . . no horns, no halo. There
will be, I hasten to say in this fearful time, no McCarthy analogy possible
. . . because, properly done, neither his enemies nor his admirers will
recognize him in my governor although, in fact, he is humanly closer to my
protagonist than to their conflicting black and white." The other project,
Billy the Kid, was an extension of his obsession with Billy that had begun at
Los Alamos. "I have read book after book about him . . . I can't think
why." In a long letter to Harold Franklin's assistant he outlined a story that
was to continue to haunt him for much of his life, about an American outlaw
with whom he deeply identified, someone permanently young, undyingly
loyal to personal bonds, resolutely insistent on individual autonomy, and
defiantly critical of injustice, especially when state-sanctioned. Both ideas,
which had no takers for the time being, were put on the back burner.

In late February 1954 he signed a contract to do for CBS's *Suspense* a
half-hour adaptation of Faulkner's short story "Smoke." When Martin
Manulis, the charming, handsome, immensely capable CBS director, ten
years older than Gore, who had known John Latouche at Columbia and
Alice Astor in England during the war, heard that Vidal was interested in
doing the adaptation of "Smoke," he was enthusiastic. Manulis had come to
CBS in 1952. "I had never been in television, very rarely had seen one, and
didn't own a set even." Since coming out of the Navy, he had been directing
in the theater, where he had had a major success with a revival of Noël
Coward's *Private Lives,* starring Tallulah Bankhead. "I had known of Gore,
but I wasn't even up on the fact that he had done some television before
that. . . . I was under the impression that this was the first television show
that he ever did. I don't know how this came about, but someone told me
that he might be a possibility for that because especially as it was a Faulkner
story, it might be something that would appeal to him." The William Morris
Agency also represented Manulis. Probably Harold Franklin brought them
together. "It did appeal to him, and we had a nice success with it, and we
did the other one right after that," Manulis recalled. "The only surprise was

that he was interested in doing a television adaptation. He seemed awfully young to me . . . and very handsome. When I met him, I thought this guy could well be a leading man. He had the trimness of someone who had been in the Army. . . . He seemed eager to do the adaptation and very happy that we'd asked him to do it." They became friends almost immediately. "GET WRITING, PUSS," Manulis telegraphed him in March. "WE WANTED A GREAT SCRIPT YESTERDAY." Broadcast in early May, "Smoke" was so successful that *Suspense* hired him to adapt Faulkner's "Barn Burning" for an August production. In late May his adaptation of the novel *A Man And Two Gods* appeared on *Studio One*. Since he could do an adaptation over a weekend, an hour-long original play in a week or two, in the rest of 1954 he did about a half dozen more, his February 1955 one-year anniversary in television marked by the performance of two of his adaptations, Henry James's "The Turn of the Screw" for *Omnibus* and Stephen Crane's "The Blue Hotel" for *Danger*, and his hourlong original drama *A Sense of Justice*, for *Philco Television Playhouse*, with an excellent performance by E. G. Marshall, who had starred in the two Faulkner adaptations. Of course Franklin did not find buyers for all Gore's story ideas, the most ambitious of which was his proposal for a series called *Devil's Theater*, dramatizations of human frailties in which he proposed that "the role of the roguish Satan" be played by someone like the Hollywood actor Louis Jourdan. Another, *Traveller in Time*, sends a young physicist back in time to change history by preventing the assassination of Lincoln. For some scripts he wrote and which were produced he used a pseudonym. "I can't even remember what name I used. I did *The Tell-Tale Clue* twice. Awful stuff. Rod Serling and I alternated. We were getting fifteen hundred dollars for a half hour. Nobody had ever seen such money before."

After the telecast of "Barn Burning" in May, he hosted at Howard's Lexington Avenue apartment a party for everyone connected with the production and invited friends like the Bourjailys. Nina, living at the Volney, enjoying the reflected glory of Gore's television success, came. He was happy to celebrate the triumph of the performance and how far he had come in just six months. In April the script of "Smoke" had received, in advance of the actual telecast, the Edgar Allan Poe Award as the best mystery television play of 1954, the award presented on April 21 at a dinner at the Stork Club. His name was now on a short list of superior television dramatists, which included Rod Sterling, Reginald Rose, Horton Foote, and Paddy

Chayevsky, whose *Marty,* on *The Goodyear Playhouse* in May 1953, had made him arguably the best-known playwright in America. Gore's boast to John Aldridge that "Yes, I am television's king," was only a small exaggeration. His claim "that "television itself is a river of gold" was a greater one. Like his well-known colleagues, Vidal received a flat fee for his scripts. Since there were no multiple performances, a royalty schedule was irrelevant. For a half-hour script writers received between $500 and $1,200, for an hour script between $1,200 and $2,500. He had earned about $7,000 his first year writing for television. It was hardly a great deal of money, but it did make all the difference for the time being, since he had very little other income. In addition, he liked writing for television. The writing and production process were completed swiftly, intensely. Problems arose quickly and were disposed of immediately. It was also the first time he worked collaboratively. Some people he worked with he liked, especially his agent, Harold Franklin; the story editor for *Studio One,* Florence Britton; the low-keyed, flexible director Franklin Schaffner; performers like Leslie Nielsen, Geraldine Page, and E. G. Marshall; and the director for the Faulkner adaptations, Martin Manulis. For the first time he had the camaraderie of colleagues, the advantage of quick, full immersion, the reality of partial control over the process and the result. As the cast rehearsed, he often rewrote thoroughly. The principals lived intensely together for about two weeks. They watched, usually sympathetically, one another try, stumble, rise, sweat, even throw up, the camera relentless, the only direction forward once the telecast began. During rehearsals Gore made a point of absorbing the technical details to help himself write more craftsmanlike scripts. After the performances, at Downey's and other popular bars near the West Side studios, they drank, unwound, and did postmortems together.

For Gore it was a new experience, much of which he enjoyed and learned from, despite his resolute conviction that all this was craft, not art; that the total control of his artistic destiny that he preferred was still available to him only within the novel form. In late March 1955, when he thought he had essentially finished his adaptation of the George Kaufman/Edna Ferber Broadway hit *Stage Door* for the television series *The Best of Broadway,* to star Rhonda Fleming and Diana Lynn, he found that Felix Jackson, the producer, needed an immediate change. He had "an immense practical problem," he told Gore. Rhonda Fleming "signed without reading the play and was told that her part would be first-rate. In addition to that, she is getting first star billing over Diana Lynn. Don't ask me why and how. . . . You have done a great job. . . . You have done the right thing with this adaptation, but I must now ask you to do the wrong thing. If Miss Fleming reads this draft, she'll walk out on us, and I simply cannot risk that. Therefore, I must ask you to enlarge [her] part. . . . Gore, I imagine you'll hate me for this, but something on this order has to be done . . . and don't carry a gun when we meet." In fact, he apparently did not in the least hold it against the producer and did what had to be done. As a sweetener, he found Rhonda Fleming stunningly attractive, Diana Lynn compellingly interesting. "Do you realize," he wrote to Jack Aldridge, an eager pursuer of women, "tonight I have dinner with Rhonda Fleming? Say you envy me!"

He did, however, usually have more control over his original scripts, one of the best of which, *Summer Pavilion,* was in rehearsal for *Studio One* in late April for an early-May telecast. Influenced by Tennessee Williams in its evocation of Southern repression and hysteria, it had in it "a lot of my own family," Vidal recalled. Starring the eccentric, assertive stage veteran Miriam Hopkins; her sister in the play, Ruth White, "one of the great actresses of that period"; and the young Elizabeth Montgomery. The main character was partly based on Mrs. Gore. Dot "was never that vain or that closed to the world. But she did have a kind of run-on act, which was a sort of filibuster, especially with strangers to whom she didn't want to say anything personal about herself or the Senator. Each political wife has her own style. So I used hers." But, he conceded, "if my grandfather had had two eyes," he would have been the father-in-law in the play, "reading a book, paying no attention, occasionally checking into the conversation, often deliberately missing. That was very T. P. Gore, an allusive man in a literary way. . . . Elizabeth Montgomery was adorable." Montgomery, Vidal recalled, "was quite nervous, because Miriam was an overpowering star of the theater and movies who said to her, 'I just don't know what you're doing acting. You have no talent for it. You should be in college. We'll go on with the scene now, won't we?' Knocking the girl three ways to Sunday. But Elizabeth was very tough." Late in the winter he flew to Los Angeles to do an adaptation of John Marquand's novel *Sincerely, Willis Wayde,* for a CBS dramatic series. "The only sad aspect of being a hack is that one is called upon to adapt the work of more successful hacks," he wrote to Aldridge about adapting Marquand.

Hollywood itself was not uncongenial, especially when he considered the possibility of making much greater sums writing for movies than he could make in television. He had some discussions at Columbia Studios about the possibility of work for him there, and most likely also at MGM, at whose commissary he had lunch with Christopher Isherwood. Isherwood told Gore "that he had just written a film for Lana Turner. The subject? Diane de Poitiers. When I laughed, he shook his head. 'Lana can do it,' he said grimly. Later, as we walked about the lot and I told him that I hoped to get a job as a writer at the studio since I could no longer live on my royalties as a novelist (and would not teach), Christopher gave me as melancholy a look as those bright—even harsh—blue eyes can affect. 'Don't,' he said with great intensity, posing against the train beneath whose wheels Greta Garbo as Anna Karenina made her last dive, 'become a hack like me.' But we both knew this was playacting. . . . He had been able to write to order for movies while never ceasing to do his own work in his own way. Those whom Hollywood destroyed were never worth saving." Isherwood had been fighting with the Breen Office censors, who claimed that his script condoned adultery. "If they had their way," he wrote in his diary, "adultery would be punished by stoning, and homosexuality by being burned alive." Gore now met Leonard Spigelgass, the senior writer at MGM, who with his intelligent sharpness about all things Hollywood and record of successful films dominated the writers' table at the MGM commissary. To Gore, during his brief visit, Hollywood seemed desirable. In early March he went down to Philadelphia to see the out-of-town opening of Tennessee's *Cat on a Hot Tin Roof,* where he joined numbers of his friends from the Williams circle— Carson McCullers, James Laughlin, Maria Britneva, and Williams's good friend Paul Bigelow. Isherwood was there to see the play. Later that month Gore helped Tennessee celebrate its triumphant New York premiere.

That same spring Vidal had an idea for a television comedy with a political message. Visitors from outer space, usually hostile and frightening, had been one of the staples of the Western imagination for centuries. Orson Welles had terrified American radio audiences with *The War of the Worlds,* his dramatization of invaders from Mars, intended as radio fiction but initially taken by many as a news report. Hollywood had discovered that alien creatures sold tickets at the box office, epitomized by the successful 1951 film *The Day the Earth Stood Still.* At Water Mill in the summer of 1953 Vance Bourjaily's skit with visitors from outer space had comic overtones, though apparently no political agenda and none of the major satiric premises that struck Gore as a good idea for a one-hour television comedy to be called *Visit to a Small Planet.* The main character, from a distant world, comes to earth with the expectation that he will amuse himself with the spectacle of human beings at war, an amusement available only in primitive places like the earth. When Kreton falls to earth at the home of a TV-news commentator, he proceeds to use his special unearthly powers to foment a combination of comedy and terror, the perfect formula for a satirical attack on human small-mindedness and self-destructiveness. Eager to enjoy the grand nuclear fireworks spectacular, Kreton seems more fascinated with weapons as toys than even the American and Russian generals. Kreton (cretin) has his plans frustrated at the end by fellow otherworldlings who come in a flying saucer, in the equivalent of asylum white coats, to take him back to the institution for the demented from which he has escaped. Retarded, his is the mind of a child. The earth is saved, but not from itself, since of course the satirical thrust associates Kreton with military and political hawks. For the audience the nuclear-arms race and the Korean War are the context. The enemy is not in our (or other) stars but in ourselves. Delighted with the idea, whose comic realities were soon made especially sharp by the wit of so many of Kreton's lines, Gore wrote the one-hour teleplay with his usual speed and handed it over to Harold Franklin. "I am at heart," Gore confessed later in regard to *Visit,* "a propagandist, a tremendous hater, a tiresome nag, complacently positive that there is no human problem which could not be solved if people would simply do as I advise." Whatever Franklin's anticipation, *Visit to a Small Planet* was not an easy sell. Political subjects, no matter how distanced from the identifiably topical, were not welcome in television drama. Whereas some years before, advertisers simply bought time blindly, now they were in tight alliance with the television networks, determining what programs were viable vehicles for the sale of their products. After two of the major series turned down *Visit,* NBC's *Philco-Goodyear Playhouse,* broadcast on Sunday nights, agreed to do it. At CBS the decision had been made by the sponsor's advertising agency. " 'Too much social significance.' . . . It's a maddening business and I don't know why we put up with it," the producer of *Studio One* bitterly reported to Gore. Probably at NBC it slipped by their usual self-censoring, perhaps because so much of its surface was funny. In late April the telescript was in rehearsal, with the British comic actor Cyril Ritchard playing Kreton. On Sunday night, May 8, its performance, viewed by about thirty million people, had an electrifying impact. "With some anxiety we waited for the roof to fall in." It did not. The major reviews were superb. At a party at the Manulises', where he happily met John Steinbeck, Gore basked in his success. When he left for California, he was more readily and widely identified with television drama than he had ever been with fiction.

———•———

After arriving in Los Angeles in May 1955, that very day Gore and Manulis were at the television studio working on an adaptation of Hemingway's *A Farewell to Arms* for the dramatic series *Climax,* which was telecast on May 26. Now a top CBS television producer, Manulis was charged with improving the overall quality of *Climax*. The adaptation starred Guy Madison and Diana Lynn, the actress Gore had met during the rehearsals for *Stage Door* and with whom he got along wonderfully. Something sparkled between them. Enchanted, he looked at her with adoring eyes. The script, though, and the performances other than Lynn's were less than glittering, partly the difficulty of transforming Hemingway's novelistic speech into effective dialogue for actors. The best part of the rehearsals was the opportunity to spend time with the slender, blond, Los Angeles-born actress, who was between husbands and whose smart, flirtatious intensity became an addictive enjoyment. "She had this elegant sort of kittenlike manner with very sharp eyes," Gore recalled, a pert nose, and an attractively angled face. Her look radiated witty good humor and well-informed intelligence. As a child she had been a piano prodigy, her avenue into the movies and a long-term contract with Paramount, where in 1942 she debuted in a Billy Wilder comedy, *The Major and the Minor*. She then had almost ten years as a successful child and teenage actress. When her adult movie career as a leading lady faltered, she turned to television drama. Suddenly she was a great success again. During much of May and early June she and Gore had a good time together, socially as well as professionally, with a tactile engagement unusual for Gore. "Diana and Gore had a special friendship," recalled Dominick Dunne, who later, when he too was brought out to Hollywood by Manulis, became a close friend of Lynn's. "There was a deep, deep affection there. If he ever could have been in love with a woman, she's the one. . . . Gore was mad about her."

One evening at a Hollywood party, Gore recalled, as they made their way through a room with about ten couples, "she murmured to me, 'Do you realize I have been to bed with every man in this room?' " And she was by no means promiscuous in the civilian sense of the word. We were all in the business. She'd been a child star, so she'd been around for twenty years. One weekend Gore and Marty Manulis, "tourists from the East who had heard of Palm Springs," drove out to the desert, where they stayed at a pleasant motel, relaxing, swimming. At some of the larger towns they drove through, Manulis remembered, Gore said, " 'Let's find the library.' He was looking to see whether his books were taken out more or less frequently than Capote's or Tennessee Williams's. . . . I never saw anyone do that before." From Gore's point of view "every writer does that. I never introduced myself to the librarians. You sneak around and you find your books on the shelf and you see when was the last time it was stamped out. Then you look at Capote and Mailer."

While he worked on numbers of scripts for *Climax*, two other projects kept him busy and busily moving. The playwright George Axelrod, whose comedy *The Seven Year Itch* had been a Broadway success in 1953, approached Harold Franklin about Axelrod's producing a Broadway version of *Visit to a Small Planet*. Three years older than Gore, Axelrod had charm, good looks, self-confidence. *Will Success Spoil Rock Hunter?* had become his second Broadway hit, his screenplay for *The Seven Year Itch* about to become a successful movie with the cachet of Marilyn Monroe in one of the starring roles. An excellent technician, clever rather than deep, with a sharp eye for the main chance, Axelrod had decided that an expanded version of *Visit*, with the right star, would be a Broadway success. The plan was to have *Visit* on the Broadway stage at the beginning of 1956. With Gore's approval Franklin closed the deal at the beginning of June. Cyril Ritchard was signed to star *and* direct. In late May, Gore flew first to New York, then to Jamaica, where Ritchard had a vacation home and where they discussed Gore's expansion of *Visit* for stage production. "Dear Gorgeous" and "Dear Gold Dust," Ritchard teasingly addressed Gore over the next few months in their correspondence about the play. "I'm delighted to hear that *Visit* is too long . . . much better that way." Back at Edgewater for the rest of June and early July, Gore worked at the revision, with suggestions from Axelrod. "I have been studying this goddam play for two weeks,"

Axelrod wrote, "and I am now absolutely convinced that we have a complete natural. . . . As I said in New York, the only problem is the girl and the two boys—the rest of it marches like a little doll."

At Edgewater, as Gore worked on the revision of *Visit*, his thoughts returned to his stymied career as a novelist, particularly the reception of *Judgment* in early 1952 and of *Messiah*, which Dutton had published in March 1954. Heinemann, his new British publisher, had recently brought out *Messiah* in London. Neither novel had been reviewed in the daily *New York Times* or in *Time* magazine, probably the result of the ongoing influence of those, like Orville Prescott, who had hated *The City and the Pillar* on moral grounds. *The Judgment of Paris*, an intellectual and satirical fable embedded in a semirealistic narrative, recounts the adventures of an indeterminately talented young American in early-postwar Europe and Egypt as he is given the opportunity to choose, in the form of three different women, between power, knowledge, and love. A novel of ideas, it is also a novel about sexual identity, partly satirical, often comic in its depiction of human nature, particularly the hilarious Roman homosexual-bathhouse scene. Its secondary characters are both bizarre exaggerations and interesting ideas, the novel's energy directed toward an elegance of overview that has great success in its balanced structure, its sharpness of language, and its comically playful engagement with fundamental choices for intelligent people. In the end the main character surprisingly, perhaps unfortunately, chooses love. Unlike Vidal's previous novels, *Judgment* rejects some of the conventions of literary realism while still sustaining a coherent narrative. It has more in common with Fielding's *Tom Jones* than with the treasured and influential warhorses of nineteenth- and twentieth-century realism, especially turn-of-the-century models like Gissing, Galsworthy, and Hardy. As he wrote *Judgment*, Vidal felt that it represented a new beginning for him, a decisive turn away from hard-core realism toward Meredith and Henry James, toward comic elegance, poetic turns of language, tighter form, satirical deflation, an intellectual sweep that embraced the tradition of the novel of ideas without giving up accessible coherence, the pleasures of readability. To his disappointment, despite moderately good reviews, *Judgment* sold poorly. Nick Wreden tried hard to get him to redefine success. Given the depressed book market in general, especially for serious literary fiction, a sale of 10,000 copies should be applauded. To Gore it had not felt like applause. Partly he blamed what he insisted were poor sales on the refusal of the daily *New York Times* and

Time magazine to review it. In the *New York Times Sunday Book Review* John Aldridge had qualified his praise with reservations and summarized the author as heretofore a "relatively rare sort of young writer in whom precocious creative energy is largely unaccompanied by precocious creative brilliance." But Aldridge's praise was also strong. *"The Judgment of Paris* is the best and most ambitious of his novels, the richest in texture and the most carefully executed. . . . Vidal has found a way to a dramatic statement of his theme." For some reason, with *Judgment,* "values" did not carry the Aldridge day, though numbers of reviewers also expressed some moral censure, as did the *Miami Herald* reviewer, whose editor headlined his comments, "Vidal's Latest on Depravity Just So, So." Still, despite the disappointing sales, the critics, even when overall judgment was mixed, had found much to praise, especially the novel's stylistic brilliance.

Vastly more powerful, pointed, and ambitious, *Messiah*—later to become a cult novel, with touches of Swift, Orwell, and the satirical inversions of William Blake's *The Marriage of Heaven and Hell*—attacks Christian hypocrisy, organized religion, and the death cult behind Eisenhower's American sunshine. The main character, who in his old age narrates the events, is Eugene Luther, partly named after the author, amid other autobiographical touches, including a beautiful evocation of the Hudson Valley summer landscape at the novel's beginning. In his old age, hiding in Egypt, Eugene Luther fears he will be discovered by Cavites, followers of the dominant new religion of the world, named after John Cave, a hypnotic, charismatic exponent of a religion whose psychological and philosophical insight was that death was real, final, and stingless, and under appropriate conditions should be embraced. When Cave is assassinated by his disciple in charge of organization and dissemination, whose name is Paul, Cave's vision is turned into an organized, powerful, wealthy, and authoritarian religion. Eugene Luther's important contribution, even his name, is erased, except that the main anti-Cavite heresy is called Lutherism. Flawed from the beginning, Eugene Luther is sexually impotent or at least unarousable, but in the face of this and as part of his understanding of John Cave's original vision, he nevertheless affirms that life is potentially rich, desirable, and improvable. He embraces Cave's vision because he believes that Cave intends it to enrich life in the present, to rid human beings of the evasive, destructive emphasis on an afterlife, a mythical, controlling, exploitive heaven and hell of the dominant Christian sort.

As Gore, writing *Messiah,* looked around him, he had seen an America dedicated to Senator Joseph McCarthy, to superficial Christian piety, to suppression of individuality and free speech, to increasing authoritarian control through media and political pressure, to the use of nuclear terror if not nuclear war to intimidate dissent abroad and at home, and to the triumph of Henry Luce's vision that the mission of America was to bring to the entire world *Time* magazine's combination of Christian and capitalistic doctrine. America's business and America's God would rule the planet. In *Messiah* Vidal provides an alternative vision, or a vision in which Cavism recapitulates the history of Christianity and capitalism together and brings oppression to the world again. He had hoped that *Messiah*'s artistry would make the horror unmistakable to its readers. As with *Judgment,* the sales again had reached only 10,000. Though the daily *New York Times* and *Time* magazine, predictably, did not review it, the reviews across the country and in England had been generally good; some, like those in the *St. Louis Globe-Democrat,* the *Richmond News-Leader,* and the *Boston Globe,* superlative Most reviewers, more or less, understood the novel. "This quite serious satire is written in a rich, almost baroque style. It moves with power and conviction," wrote the critic for the *Norfolk Virginian-Pilot.* The more independent the newspaper, the less connected to corporate and national power structures, the better the reviews tended to be, though the *New York Mirror* and the *Chicago Sunday Tribune* thought it spellbinding and provocative. A new friend and admirer, Lucien Price, an Exeter graduate whose Boston high-culture credentials were impeccable and who headed the *Boston Globe* editorial staff, thought the book so powerful and important that he had made it the subject of a lead editorial. As Gore in the summer of 1955 gave thought to where he had been and where he now was, he had paused retrospectively. *Messiah,* he wrote to Kimon Friar modestly, "was a noble failure, though I think it has certain virtues." He had no illusion that great art was possible in television drama or even on the stage, at least as he experienced his own dramatic talents. "A gift for playwriting is only a form of cleverness," he later recalled, "like being adept at charades or double-crostics, while novel writing goes, at its best, beyond cleverness to that point where one's whole mind and experience and vision *are* the novel and the effort to translate this wholeness into prose *is* the life: a circle of creation." But at least now, writing for television, he was "doing something people really wanted. All my life I had been writing novels, and nobody wanted novels by me or by anybody else."

———————

In early July 1955 Howard, who had been spending weekends in Barrytown, easily enticed Gore home to Edgewater with a reminder that their enormous roses were in bloom, the house was sparkling, their dog Tinker, the black cocker spaniel whom they had gotten as a pup in 1951 (his name derived from "Tinker-Bell," Howard's nickname), missed Gore as much as Howard did. Howard's nickname for Gore, "Me Me," was both affectionate and realistic. Earlier in the summer Howard had enjoyed a weekend with Nina who the previous year had bought a large Victorian-style shingle house on Main Street in Southampton, where Howard had been her guest for a few pleasant weeks. Increasingly bored during the last two years at the advertising firm, resentful that he had not received an expected raise, Howard had recently resigned. A singing career was a still-unrealized hope. Doing something in the theater world appealed to him and seemed more possible with Gore's television and now Broadway work. With Gore away and with ample time, Howard began to take care of the bills at Edgewater, to handle the accounts, to attend to the details of domestic business, to deal with the accountant, Leonard Strauss, whom Gore now employed as a business manager handling his rapidly increasing cash flow. Howard's role in their domestic business arrangement began to be more clearly delineated. What had been a casual arrangement was formally verbalized, his salary as secretary doubled. Gore's television income gave them a latitude that they had not had before. Without the constraints of daily work in Manhattan, Howard could now travel with Gore, including to Los Angeles if Gore's stay should prove this time to be a long one. "Me Me's" working schedule and preferences in general would determine both their residences.

In July, Gore rewrote *Visit* and attended rehearsals in New York of his newest television drama, *The Death of Billy the Kid,* which was televised on *Philco Television Playhouse* on July 24th. He later described it as his favorite of all his television plays, "though by no means the most admired." Billy had of course been on his mind for years, and Harold Franklin had finally found a taker, Fred Coe, a senior NBC producer, for the presentation Gore had laid out the year before in his letter to Helen Harvey. Coe, in overall charge of the *Philco Television Playhouse*, chose Robert Mulligan to direct. How to dramatize Billy's ruthless life and well-deserved death was a challenge, the difficulty of balancing his and the frontier's cruelty with the meaningfulness of the other things Billy stood for—the independence, the romance, the defiant individuality of his code of loyalty and self-assertion. "My decision, finally, was to show not so much Billy himself as the people who created the myth of Billy the Kid," a myth that Gore desired to deepen and extend, among other reasons as a critical statement about corporate America in the self-satisfied 1950s. To play Billy, Coe had found the perfect young actor. Only James Dean or Marlon Brando might have done as well. Brando, the star of *A Streetcar Named Desire*, Gore had met in New York through Tennessee Williams. James Dean he soon met in Hollywood. They both had an electric edge of defiance. But Paul Newman, a young television and theater actor, turned out to be the perfect choice.

Soft-spoken, calm, and unprepossessing offstage except when on a drinking spree, onstage Newman dominated the camera with his bright-blue eyes, his small, lithe figure, his preternaturally delicate handsomeness, and the unspoken effect of great but barely restrained emotional power. He had the perfect combination of vulnerability and strength for the role. A matinee idol in the making, eight months older than Gore, part Jewish, part Hungarian-Catholic, a Yale graduate student from a Midwestern business family who had recently separated from his wife and their children to live with an aspiring young actress from Georgia, Newman hit it off immediately with Vidal. During rehearsals they began to get to know one another. Newman's tight schedule had him bleary-eyed. After the Sunday-night performance of whatever his current role, he regularly took the red-eye to California. At Warner Brothers he was making his first film, *The Silver Chalice*, one of the fruits of his Broadway success in William Inge's *Picnic*, in which he had starred (his ladyfriend, Joanne Woodward, as talented a performer as he but with less potential for Hollywood megastardom, had understudied). Gore and Howard had each separately met Woodward in New York, Gore through a mutual friend, Bill Gray, whom Woodward had known from Louisiana State University. A great admirer of Williams and Vidal, Gray had brought Woodward, a struggling actress, to a party in midtown Manhattan in 1952, where he had introduced her to Vidal. Gore had hardly any recollection of the meeting. She had thought him handsome, almost beautiful, and was deeply impressed with his accomplishments as a writer. Howard met her about the same time at a party at Johnny Nicholson's café, also through Bill Gray.

Immediately after the telecast of *Billy*, Newman flew to California to continue filming *The Silver Chalice*. Gore, who had more scripts to write for *Climax*, including an adaptation of *Dr. Jekyll and Mr. Hyde*, was in Los Angeles by the end of July. Soon the preliminary discussions with MGM began to bear fruit. Howard flew out to join him for what looked like an extended stay. Woodward joined Newman in Los Angeles, partly to be with him, also to continue her own television career there and for the possibility of a movie role. By August they were all in Los Angeles, staying at the same hotel, the Chateau Marmont, the favorite of New Yorkers from the theater and literary world.

From his room at the Chateau Marmont, Gore, looking out on Sunset Boulevard, saw a huge rotating statue of a woman holding a sombrero, an advertising billboard with a massive bosom. On mornings when he woke up with a hangover, it made him think that he "knew what death would be like." To his shock, he soon had the bad news of the real death of someone he had a loving regard for, his editor, Nick Wreden. Early in August 1955 the fifty-three-year-old life-loving Wreden had unexpectedly died of a heart attack in a Masachussetts hospital. The previous year he had left Dutton, "after much soul-searching," to become editor-in-chief at Little, Brown, in Boston, to which Gore had agreed to follow him. Wreden "was overweight, drank too much, talked too much, lived too much," one of his associates later remarked. He had been a mentor, a supporter, a friend. He would be missed.

Actually, independent of the hangover or the bad news about Wreden, Gore recognized that Sunset Boulevard's visual gigantism represented not only death but Hollywood's fascination with bigger everything, with special effects as a definition of cultural literacy. It was a reference he filed away mentally, to make use of later in *Myra Breckinridge*. Now, though, he had his own relationship with Hollywood. At the beginning it was on a small scale, in tune with the kind of tightly focused, low-budget dramatic plays that Hollywood turned to in imitation of television's success. Reeling from a precipitous fall in revenue that had begun with the advent of television, the film industry in general was desperately trying to keep a tighter control on costs, to make cheaper films, to search for new formulas. In March, when Gore met with Jerry Wald of Columbia Pictures, Wald had indicated a strong interest "in working out some future association with you." Nothing had developed. In early July, Dore Schary, the head of MGM, decided Gore would be perfect for a screen adaptation of Paddy Chayevsky's teleplay *The Catered Affair,* to which MGM had purchased the rights. Since all Vidal's work had been for television, why not have a successful television writer revise and expand a teleplay as the script for a full-length movie?

In fact, the assignment made perfect sense from Gore's and MGM's viewpoint. It was a version of what he already had experience doing. MGM's risk was modest. Whatever Chayevsky's feelings, he joined Gore and Isherwood for lunch in early August, after which, Isherwood wrote, "he described how he is haunted by a feeling of horror and unreality which he can only reduce by constantly smoking, and by eating chocolate cake." On July 11 Gore signed a standard "so-called week-to-week employment contract," at a salary of $2,000 per week, to adapt *The Catered Affair.* "Week-to-week" meant that either party could terminate the contract at will with one week's advance notice. For *Billy the Kid* NBC had paid him in total $2,250. As long as he turned in satisfactory pages on a regular basis, Metro-Goldwyn-Mayer would pay him almost that each week he was under contract. Suddenly he found himself in Culver City, sitting in a small office or having lunch with famous MGM contract writers, who immediately tried to break him of his practice of writing rapidly. He assumed he could, as usual, do his entire script in a few weeks. "So my friends at the writers' table . . . just said, 'Gore you've got to go along with us. This is how we do it here. We have our traditions. Three pages a day. Five days a week. . . . Write it in five hours, if you think you can . . . but give it to them at the rate of three a day, or we're all in trouble." In the next office, he wrote to John Bowen, "is Christopher Isherwood, now completing his second decade in the vineyard (a bad little wine but amiable)." Leonard Spigelgass, a trim, elegant New Yorker in his late forties, with thick dark glasses and "a sort of Noël Coward Englishy voice," dominated the MGM writers' table and reminded Gore of Sam Lurie. They liked each other immediately. Witty, realistic, and authoritative, Spigelgass had written more than a dozen successful movies, mostly light comedies. In a scaled-down, vulgarized version he was to be the model for "the wise hack," a semifictional character in Vidal's essays about Hollywood.

Vidal's pages were well received by the director Richard Brooks, still struggling to establish himself and in the process of having his first great success, *The Blackboard Jungle*, and by Sam Zimbalist, a veteran producer in his early fifties with whom Gore quickly developed a respectful working relationship, one of the few senior Hollywood figures for whom he felt personal affection. By mid-December, Dore Schary was thanking Gore "for the good script you've turned out. I know we'll get a wonderful movie." Having finished it quickly, Gore had cooperated with his fellow writers and turned it in over a few months. Pleased with his ongoing work on the script of *The Catered Affair*, MGM asked him to create an original screenplay based on the Dreyfus Affair, which Schary, an advocate of movies with a social message, had been persuaded would make an excellent film. In early October, Gore took the plunge from a week-to-week employment contract to a more complicated one that in effect gave MGM exclusive rights, at the studio's option, to his screenwriting services for an additional four-year period at $2,000 per week through 1956, $2,250 for 1957, $2,500 for 1958, and $2,750 for 1959. He would be expected to do one script a year, in residence, if called for, at the studio for about four months annually, and be free to do as he wanted with the rest of his time. It was a breathtaking increase in his income, though he soon discovered that it elevated him into the onerous 90-percent tax bracket prevailing throughout the 1950s. "I couldn't absorb the fact, I couldn't believe that all of the work that I had done in my life would be taken away by the government." If he saved enough, he might liberate himself to return to writing only what he wanted to write. There were dangers. The contract contained an important qualifying clause. If he refused to accept an assignment, he would be off salary and his contract obligation extended for a period equal to the length of his suspension. For the moment it was not a problem. He happily turned in his pages and began to see *The Catered Affair*, starring Bette Davis and Ernest Borgnine, take shape for March 1956 national release. His studio obligations, as he had anticipated, took only a small portion of his time. Away from the studio, he enjoyed Los Angeles life, sometimes writing at his studio office, other times at the hotel, as much engaged with his own larger ambitions as with his movie work, the first stirrings of a new novel in mind. "I have finished *The Catered Affair,* " he wrote to cousin Louis in September, "and I am being tempted at the moment with *Captain Dreyfus* which this studio wants me to write and, if I decide to do it, I shall probably stay on until December. I can see, three thousand miles away, the delicate, knowing smile which at this moment flickers, as we novelists say, across your lips. Is the great American legend about to claim another sacrificial victim? Has the hereditary taint of the American man-of-letters asserted itself so fatally again? No. Tell it not in Bourjaily's house nor publish it in Mailer's, but another Vidal novel burgeons slowly in the shade of Mammon. . . . *Washington, D.C.* "

Social life was also burgeoning. With Diana Lynn he went to movie-world dinners and parties. The relationship was also private, teasing, self-consciously provocative, both aware of its complexities. "One night after dinner we ended up in Diana's apartment," Howard recalled. "Gore and Diana were writhing on the floor, but they were drunk and dressed. I went to the john or something. One could say that she made advances, but Gore welcomed them. He had a special thing with her. They didn't do it that night because I came back into the room." To Louis Auchincloss, Gore humorously proposed an exchange. "I live a life here of marvelous glitter which I will tell you about at length only in exchange for all the latest [New York] gossip, literary or real-worldly." At the swimming pool at the Chateau, Howard and Gore found their New York acting acquaintances, Paul Newman and Joanne Woodward, whose relationship with California was also ambivalent. Like many theater and television New Yorkers still feeling out their attitude toward Hollywood, they too had taken refuge at the down-class, somewhat seedy Chateau Marmont, a huge, dark, rambling imitation of a French castle, with no lobby and irregular rooms and suites that kept out the intrusive sunshine. The darkness gave the hallways a Gothic tone that allowed Easterners to feel they had not yet succumbed to Californian values. "Life at the Chateau Marmont," Woodward recalled, "was dark and strange. And we were closeted in together because we were all from New York." There was no bar, no restaurant at which to preen or socialize. Room service came from a contingent of garage hands and young boys available to bring back take-out food from local restaurants. Pickups from the street, of whatever sex or age, regularly came up by elevator directly from the garage level to the hotel rooms without anyone's noticing their comings and goings. Separate, a thing of its own despite its Sunset Boulevard location, the

Chateau seemed both arty and bizarre, a place where reclusive people could hide and where it had also become fashionable for well-known theatrical people and writers from the East to stay. James Dean was sometimes there, as were Marlon Brando and Marilyn Monroe. On arrival, guests could look at the register to see who of their friends was in residence.

Paul and Gore, who enjoyed drinking and plotting together, began to plan, at Gore's urging, how they might get Paul's studio, Warner Brothers, to do a movie version of *Billy the Kid*, with Paul in the starring role. Gore would expand the teleplay into a feature-length script. "Paul was so beautiful," Joanne recalled," and he was a wonderful actor. I don't know what the attraction was for Gore. I don't know whether Gore thought Paul was so gorgeous and all of that. And Howard and I got along." Around the swimming pool the four chatted, began to become friends. Gore seemed handsome, brilliant, awesomely accomplished. Joanne immediately began to read his novels, "flattered that Gore would deign to pay attention to dumb me. . . . It was an odd grouping of people. It was interesting because we met people through Gore," including Nina. "I somehow have a strange image of Nina in a slip at the Chateau Marmont. . . . I didn't like her. . . . On the other hand, being the age she was at that time, how difficult it must have been for her for her gorgeous son to turn out to be someone she didn't expect. Also, he was so patently superior to her intellectually and in every other way. . . . I'm sure she was competitive. She never had that sort of admiration. . . . I just remember her in a slip, by that time the remains of a good-looking woman. She'd been beautiful. Gore really looks like his mother. She was a striking woman. As I recall, she was rather witty. She had a manner that was a bit overwhelming. She was very theatrical. But I didn't like her. Well, of course I knew that Gore didn't like her. I think maybe he loved her, and that was the tragedy."

At nearby Malibu, Gore and Howard visited regularly with Isherwood and his new companion, twenty-one-year-old American-born Don Bachardy, whom they had met in New York the previous year. Gore found the thin, blond, chicken-hawk-handsome Bachardy, an unformed neophyte who gradually discovered his passion for painting, much preferable to the contentious Caskey. At Isherwood's cliffside Malibu house, with a valley view and a glimpse of ocean, there were dinners and parties. They enjoyed one another's humor. They often laughed at the same things. Through Isherwood, Gore met Gerald Heard, Auden's friend, an Irish-born convert to Southern California, an ascetic through whom Isherwood had met Swami Prabhavananda to whose teachings he had become devoted. Gore did not in the least share Isherwood's obsession with Vedanta. Or with high romantic love. Isherwood simply assumed that Gore and Howard were lovers, engaged in the same drama of romantic angst as he and Bachardy. At the studio, walking around movie sets together, Isherwood noticed that Gore "looked at the books to see if any of them were by him." Depressed, irritable, drinking heavily, "feeling that life is really too much trouble," in his diary, where his dark side often dominated, Isherwood transformed a generally happy friend into a source of his own depression. "Being with Gore really depresses me, unless I'm feeling absolutely up to the mark, because Gore really exudes despair and cynical misery and a grudge against society which is really based on his own lack of talent and creative joy." The analysis was at least partly self-projection. In fact, Gore was in good spirits. The money from MGM was a blessing. He had a channel for his "grudge," the revision of the satirically powerful *Visit to a Small Planet,* an exemplification of his lifesaving ability to make art of his anger. If his mordant distrust of romantic love and family life seemed cynical to some, he thought it realistic. If his anger at those he felt had harmed, him, particularly his mother, seemed excessive, it was a measure of the degree to which he needed to defend himself against pain. If his satiric hostility to nuclear politics and conventional social mores sometimes had a Swiftian edge, he thought his response warranted by the provocations. He sometimes preferred to make a point more than spare a feeling. But his weapons of choice were wit, irony, and art.

Doing rewrites as *The Catered Affair* was filmed, working on the Dreyfus film, he and Howard stayed a while longer at the Chateau Marmont, then rented a house in Laurel Canyon, where they stayed until late December. Reading various books on Dreyfus, he found himself caught up in both the theme of injustice and the challenge of creating an effective script. "I am here doing, of all things, *The Dreyfus Case* for the screen," he wrote to Lehmann, "and there are moments when I believe this might be a good and useful production: each generation dearly needs to have Dreyfus re-interpreted." Hollywood cruising had its usual satisfactions. No one at the Chateau cared or even noticed whom you brought to your room. Isherwood, despite his somber diary entries, was a frequent host, often good-humored in Gore's company, his home a center for the more cultured movie-industry people, particularly writers. On New Year's Day 1956, CBS telecast *Portrait of a Ballerina,* which Gore had adapted earlier in the year from *Death in the Fifth Position.* There were, though, good reasons to return to New York. Gore and Howard missed Edgewater and New York friends. Also, Axelrod's intention to put the stage version of *Visit to a Small Planet* into production for a spring premiere was still in place, though he was having difficulty raising the required $75,000, mostly because investors doubted that an expanded version of *Visit* or any other television play could be produced successfully on Broadway.

Early in January, they were on their way to New Orleans, where they stayed at the Lafitte Guest House for a few weeks, then to New York, to which, despite the winter cold, they were happy to return. Gore was not happy, though, to learn that Axelrod and his associate, Clinton Wilder a cousin of the novelist Thornton Wilder, had decided to postpone *Visit* until early 1957. They had not been able to raise the necessary money. Though the delay was a disappointment, there were many other things to attend to. Themistocles Hoetis, whom he had met in Tangier, urged Gore to allow his Zero Press to publish Gore's short stories, to which he now added a seventh, "Pages from an Abandoned Journal," based on an episode in the life of Denham Fouts. Though Gore had reservations about Zero Press, he decided to give Hoetis the book. "I didn't want to do *A Thirsty Evil* with a conventional publisher. I've always liked the idea of doing small editions, not available to the general public." The book was dedicated to Howard. For Ballantine Books he put together an original paperback anthology of *Best Television Plays,* which included *Visit to a Small Planet,* and wrote a brief introduction, "Notes on Television," which he published also in *New World Writing.* In February, Howard began as assistant stage manager for Axelrod's *Will Success Spoil Rock Hunter?,* a foot in the Broadway entertainment door that he hoped might open wider. As a condition of Howard's getting the job, Gore agreed to reimburse Axelrod for his salary.

At the beginning of March 1956 *The Catered Affair* opened nationwide to great praise, particularly for Vidal's script, which the reviewers greeted as an original screen version, not a narrow adaptation of a teleplay. Even the somewhat carping, generally annoyed Chayevsky thought Vidal's approach desirable. "I think you were very right in making *The Catered Affair* into your own script instead of trying to mimic my approach. I am sure it will be a much better picture that way." Later there was to be some genuine warmth between them. Now it was muted respect, and anger on Chayevsky's part, especially at the change of name to *The Wedding Breakfast* for the British version. "Everywhere Chayevsky went, they only knew *Wedding Breakfast*. Nobody mentioned *The Catered Affair*. It was *Wedding Breakfast* with Bette Davis. And he kept trying to explain that, well, it wasn't his, it was mine. You can't get very far with that with the press, which never gets anything right. There was a lot of resentment. Then we became friends eventually." From Hollywood, Newman kept him up to date about his effort to persuade Warner Brothers to make a full-length film from Gore's *Billy the Kid* teleplay. Gore would expand it into a movie script. Newman would star. The same team, Robert Mulligan and Fred Coe, who had done it for *Philco* would direct and produce. Newman was doing his best, with the help of MCA and William Morris, their respective agents, to make it happen. Fortunately, they were making progress, he told Gore, and the only thing holding them up was Jack Warner attending Grace Kelly's wedding.

As Gore worked on the Dreyfus script, his salary from MGM continued. Since he could now afford it, he and Howard decided to give up Howard's small Lexington Avenue walk-up and get a larger apartment. In the fall Howard, with Nina's assistance, found a one-bedroom fifth-floor apartment they liked in an attractive prewar building at the corner of Fifty-fifth Street and First Avenue. They already knew 360 East Fifty-fifth Street through friends. Miles White had the apartment down the hall. In November 1956 Gore signed a two-year lease at a rent of $175.70 a month and, though he lived more at Edgewater than on East Fifty-fifth Street, it became his New York City residence, where he and Howard (who stayed there during the week) entertained and lived when not in the country. Nina and Howard decorated the apartment. Gore paid for the furnishings. It was at Edgewater, though, that he felt most at home and worked best. In January, Zimbalist, who soon went to London to produce a remake of *The Barretts of Wimpole Street*, reported that everyone concerned at MGM, including Dore Schary, liked the Dreyfus script. "They definitely want to go ahead with the picture." In March, Vidal proposed to Manulis that he do for CBS's *Playhouse 90* a project he had "been saving for many years . . . the story of my grandfather, Thomas Pryor Gore," focusing on the Senator's early life. The script would end with his election to the United States Senate, "the excitement of an underdog victory, his father and mother with him from Mississippi, astonished and delighted at their son's success when they had always, secretly, feared he would end his days in a home for the blind." Manulis loved the idea. "GO AHEAD WITH GRAND-DADDY," he telegraphed Vidal in London, where he had gone after a brief visit in Los Angeles to join Zimbalist to consult with him about the Dreyfus script and prepare it for filming.

His six weeks in London were mostly a delight. Claridge's, which he could not have afforded had MGM not been paying his expenses, was elegantly posh. Judy Montagu was around. Edith Sitwell invited him to her club, where her comic eccentricities amused everyone. He met his Heinneman editor, Dwye Evans, whom he asked to send copies of the British editions of *Messiah* and *Death Likes It Hot* to Mona Williams, now the Contessa Bismarck, living mostly at her villa on Capri. After Harrison's death it had seemed an intelligent convenience for Eddie and Mona to marry. At dinner at the 120 Mount Street apartment of Mike Canfield, the son of the eminent Harper & Row editor Cass Canfield, on leave from publishing to work as the American ambassador's social secretary, and his wife—Jackie Kennedy's sister Lee who had married Canfield in 1953—Gore met a vivacious, outspoken American actress and writer, Elaine Dundy, and her British husband, the well-known drama critic Kenneth Tynan. His own date was the actress Ella Raines, his quasi-relative, who was in London to do a play. Elaine and Ken, who lived immediately above the Canfields, had been invited down for drinks. Elaine was at work on a novel; Ken, the drama critic for *The Observer*, had recently become script director for Ealing Studios, newly purchased by MGM. Soon Gore and the Tynans were on a first-name basis. They had friends in common, and Elaine recalled that he had been pointed out to her in New York at the opening of Tennessee Williams's *Cat on a Hot Tin Roof*. "The next day we talked on the phone. Gore said, 'What are you doing? I just had a good bowel movement, and now I'm just lying here looking at the ceiling. What are you doing?' 'I'm reading the Sundays. What does the ceiling look like?' 'Tidy.' " It was the start of a friendship.

One day he went to Southwark Cathedral with another new friend whom he had met briefly before in New York, the British journalist and left-wing Labour Member of Parliament, Tom Driberg, twenty years older than Gore. Driberg, who had already had a controversial career advocating the legalization of drugs and homosexuality, was a flamboyantly expressive gay man in the London social-political world. Both great talkers, they delighted in endless banter and gossip about politics, people, art, sex. Driberg, a member of the Labour National Executive Committee who under the pseudonym William Hickey had for fifteen years written a column in the form of a diary for the *Daily Express,* knew everyone of consequence in British public life. Soon after sailing to New York in May, Gore, at Edgewater, read a volume of Driberg's columns. "I very much enjoyed your diary which I read on the return trip: I liked the war reporting and the king's funeral and I think you come through in those casual pages much better than you think . . . that does sound patronizing but it's not; none of us really has much admiration for himself and I think your remarkable duality which we discussed at the entrance to Southwark cathedral has put one part of yourself in flight from the other." American politics were on Driberg's and Vidal's minds as an election year approached its early summer. Eisenhower would be running again. Adlai Stevenson would again oppose him. "The political world here is looking up as the firm hand at the tiller seems to be faltering even in the eyes of Republican newspapers," Gore wrote to Driberg, "though they will doubtless run the great warrior dead or alive; Stevenson's chances are bright and if I can possibly find the time I will work on the campaign." He did not have the time and would not find it. He was still on assignment with *I Accuse,* "though the movie business is staggering again and I am told there is panic in Culver City: what fun to have worked in the movies just at the end . . . what a Byzantine time this is! The novel declining, the movies, at least phase one, stopping, and homosexuality, once our nation's pride and source of strength (oh, pioneers!), become unfashionable . . . well, let it come down."

Live television had not only come down but was coming to an end. Having agreed to do for Fred Coe, the producer of NBC's *Playwrights '56,* a new television play he thought might well be his last, during May 1956 Gore wrote *Honor,* a drama about a wealthy Southerner who faces a vital decision during the Civil War: whether to allow Yankee troops to occupy his mansion or destroy it by fire. Gore asked for and got what he believed the largest sum ever paid for an original television drama, $5,050. With Coe he had "amiable relations." Directed by Victor Donohue, with a cast led by Ralph Bellamy and Leo G. Carroll, *Honor* was telecast in mid-June, a powerful antiwar play that was as sophisticated and as emotionally compelling as anything yet produced on television. Some of its force came from the author's personal world, from the death of Jimmie Trimble, from the North-

South conflict and the importance of the Civil War in Gore family history, and especially from his preoccupation with the clash between social pressure and individual self-determination. With the television play about his grandfather on hold, he thought this might be his last appearance on the small screen for some time. That suited him well. The pay from MGM was substantial, and he hoped he might soon start preparing to write *Washington, D.C.* or turn to his long-standing desire to do a novel based on the life of the Roman Emperor Julian.

At Edgewater a full, delightful summer was ahead of him. With his new affluence, despite the heavy taxes, he and Howard had done enough fixing up so that the house looked lovely, though still sparsely furnished. "Wooden chairs. The kitchen had a table, and there was little or nothing in the dining room," Paul Newman recalled. "There was some soft stuff, but it was sparse. I liked going up there. It was a good way to get out of the city. Stayed overnight, long weekends." The roses were in bloom. Gore expected Paul and Joanne together and separately, especially Joanne, who had committed herself to doing *The Two Mrs. Carrolls* in July at the nearby Hyde Park Playhouse. Later in the summer, once rehearsals began, Joanne moved to Edgewater. Gore looked forward to a visit from his grandmother and soon had a brief visit from Sarah Moore, whose father was collaborating with Latouche on *The Ballad of Baby Doe,* to be premiered that summer in Central City, Colorado. Latouche, now at work on the lyrics for the Leonard Bernstein–Lillian Hellman musical, *Candide,* was his usual manic self, unstoppably talkative, always amusing, with a thousand ideas. There was soon good news that cheered both Gore and Alice Astor. The premiere of *The Ballad of Baby Doe* had gotten rave reviews. Alice and Latouche, though, had ceased to be lovers. She had taken up with a professional parapsychic researcher—partly scientific, mostly far-fetched—whose institute she handsomely supported, a relationship that her friends worried about. To Gore she seemed much the same, always happy to see him in New York, warmly welcoming at Rhinebeck, where he and Howard went regularly for lunch or dinner.

Dot soon came for one of her annual visits. When, at the same time, Joanne's mother visited New York, Gore invited her to join them at Edgewater. In preparation for the visit, he and Joanne agreed to suggest to the ladies that they were going to get married. "Somehow we decided that it would be a wonderful idea if my mother and Gore's grandmother thought we were engaged. It would make them very happy. I don't think I got to the point of telling my mother that we actually were. I kind of intimated. I don't know whether or not Gore told Mrs. Gore that we were engaged. I remember we had a delightful weekend. And the ladies really did like each other, being two Southern ladies." Actually, at a restaurant in New York they had a more serious discussion about marriage. For Gore the question had arisen before, most seriously with Rosalind. Occasionally rumors circulated that Gore, charming and flirtatious with women he was attracted to, was going to marry, usually, so the speculation went, to provide marital cover for a political career. Sometimes he himself raised the possibility, usually ironically or humorously, sometimes with a touch of sincerity. For Joanne, in despair at what seemed Paul's disheartening slowness in divorcing his wife, the thought was not implausible. "Why not marry Gore?" Then "we decided that there was no way we could ever go to bed together because we would laugh. So that was not possible. I was thinking, 'Oh, God, if I'm never going to marry Paul, I might as well marry Gore.' And I remember saying, 'What would we do about Howard?' That's when we decided that the answer to life was for Gore to run for President. He would win the election, and we would overrun the government and create a constitutional monarchy. I would go to the White House and be the First Lady. And once again we said, but what about Howard? I think if we had gotten to that point and Gore had said, 'Let's get married,' I might very well have done so. Because I was very fond of him. Many people have had that sort of marriage. I can't imagine how long it would have lasted. I would have driven Gore crazy, or he would have driven me crazy." Gore, in this case or in any other after Rosalind, never made the fatal proposal.

But it was a "hilarious couple of weeks," Joanne remembered. It seemed to her that Gore had a wonderful life at Edgewater, with work, friends, visits, family. Dot's presence was a beneficent one, the old lady plainly dressed, mostly in dark clothes, with her sharp tongue, her Southern accent, her wry sense of humor, her obvious delight in her grandson. "It was sort of a mutual admiration society," Joe O'Donohue recalled. O'Donohue thought her delightful and enjoyed her stories about the Gores' early days in Oklahoma. Gene and Kit, who had moved to Montevideo— the estate in Avon, Connecticut, Kit had inherited from her father—stopped by a few times. Dot and Gene chatted amiably on the front porch, old friends with much shared family history behind them, particularly a daughter and a wife. Pick and Sally, driving to West Point with their daughter and her friend, visited on a Sunday afternoon. They were introduced to Joanne and her mother. Gore, indicating Joanne, told them that Mrs. Gore had said, " 'That's a nice girl. Why don't you marry her?' " By mid-July the summer guests were gone, the house quiet. Gore, as always, was at work in the octagonal study, reading, answering correspondence, polishing *Visit*, thinking about strategies for *Julian* and *Washington, D.C.* One evening, soon after her birthday, he had dinner with Alice at Rhinebeck, the two of them alone, formally dressed and handsomely splendid.

Two mornings later, sleeping late, Gore and Howard were awakened by Alice's butler Stanley shouting up to them. In the warm air Stanley's voice rose with horrible news. Alice had been found dead that morning in her town house in New York. The shock was chilling. It seemed unbelievable that fifty-four-year-old Alice Astor, so quietly alive at dinner at Rhinebeck a few nights before, could suddenly be gone forever. "She couldn't stand the heat, Gore commented, "and she was worn out and had to pack to go to Lake Placid to be lady-in-waiting to Lady Ribblesdale, her mother, and she was grim at the thought of packing in all that. She was found dead in the bathroom. She had fainted and hit her skull on the toilet bowl. The medical examiner certified she had died of a heart attack." Latouche soon called from Central City, Colorado, which he was about to leave. Having heard the devastating news, he suggested they arrange a special memorial service. He would call again from his summer cottage in Vermont. The call never came. Horton Foote, the well-known television dramatist and Latouche's friend, telephoned early in the second week of August. The news was grim, the timing uncanny. On August 7, soon after his arrival in Vermont, Latouche had suffered a massive heart attack and died almost instantly. Rumors quickly circulated that each had been murdered. Then that Alice had committed suicide. "Some thugs appeared at my Uncle Vincent's apartment," Romana recalled, "saying that they would get it to the press that my mother committed suicide if Vincent didn't pay them off. He refused and had the butler throw them out of the apartment." Coroners' reports apparently produced nothing suspicious. Latouche's fatal occlusion may have been facilitated by his usual brandy and drugs. Fainting in the heat, perhaps medicated, Alice's fall split her skull. She may have had an exacerbating angry argument with someone earlier that evening. There was suspicion of foul play, apparently unfounded, and a police investigation. Some hint of mystery remained in both instances.

Latouche's death stunned his friends. "He never could sleep," the novelist Dawn Powell wrote, "lights on all night—so there were sleeping pills and for the grim collaborators demanding the real work, he must have Benzedrine, Miltown tranquilizers, Nembutal, dex. I'm sure this was a desperate, hysterical escape from Lillian Hellman and others waiting for his output to finish up *Candide*. Like George Gershwin—a natural gusher that grim syndicates tried to harness for the stock exchange. Ending up now an incorrigibly sweet, indestructible little ghost." For Gore, Latouche's death was a wrenching loss. Alice's, though, stunned him, then destabilized him, sent him into a heart-protecting numbness whose inverse, a few weeks later, was a sudden, dangerous rise in his blood pressure. His doctor preferred not to tell him how frighteningly high it was. His four grandparents had all had high blood pressure, his father had suffered a life-altering heart attack at a relatively early age. He was soon on Sepersil to keep his pressure down. He felt and looked distraught. "It was the first time that someone I was close to had died." When Alice's body was brought up to Rhinebeck for burial, Joanne came from New York to be with him during the funeral. "I remember walking away from the grave site with Gore and looking over at him, and there were tears running down his cheek. I couldn't say anything, so I took his arm. It must have been terrible, terrible for him." Within a short time there was another unexpected death. The New York Central demanded a blood price. Tinker, their exuberant black cocker spaniel who had become a happy member of the small Edgewater family, a daily presence for over five years, made a fatal error. A train slashed him badly, cutting him almost in two. There would be no more Goreish-Tinker babytalk. He and Howard were again devastated. After some weeks he began to get a grip on his pain. "I have lost, in order," he wrote to Edith Sitwell, "my publisher of ten years, Alice, Latouche and, introducing the maudlin Anglo-Saxon note, my dog was killed last week . . . all of which darkened the sun to say the least. Alice was worst of all and I know you must have felt it, too. Most friends when they die don't, I think, if one is entirely honest, too much upset one by their departure . . . after all, we shall follow too, but there are rare ones like Alice who are simply missed, whose presence was wanted, whose absence is intolerable."

However deep his sadness, he soon began to absorb it, to disguise it. If he could avoid going to a funeral, he always would, as he had his grandfather's. When friends died, he preferred to write his consolation letters from a distance. The measure of the impact of Alice's death was how little he resisted standing by her grave site. His tears for her were spontaneous, incalculable. But what he feared most he usually found ways to avoid. There was something irrepressible about his own evasive energy, the purposeful denial, the unwillingness to position himself close enough to death's work to concede his own vulnerability except as mordant humor, sharp wit. Since the Sepersil created a chemical depression and made it difficult to work, he stopped taking it. His blood pressure soon returned to normal. What he enjoyed and embraced most was personal energy, his capacity for cathartic work, his commitment to work for his own and the world's sake. In the face of obstacles, even deep grief, he would assert his desire, discipline his concentration, even the more intensely. To him that meant life, his own especially, the experience of his strong will to support the highest assertion of the value he placed on being alive. Each day at Edgewater reminded him of Alice. He would need to live with that. But it did not make the house any less dear to him, any less the place where he did what made him feel most alive. Perhaps indeed Alice's death entwined Edgewater even more deeply into his dreams. Comparatively immune to depression, he felt a sadness that did not sap his energy. His ability to work continued and sustained him through loss.

By late summer he was back at his desk, revising *The Judgment of Paris* for a new paperback edition. Hopeful about the *Billy the Kid* project, he worked on the script. Axelrod had at last raised enough money to schedule *Visit* for early 1957, part coming from an inebriated Marion Davies, William Randolph Hearst's mistress—whom a mutual friend, the screenwriter Charlie Lederer, had induced to sign a check for $10,000—and some coming from his Broadway friends, including Martin Gabel, the producer and actor, and his actress wife, Arlene Francis. Next year, whether the play succeeded or not, Gore hoped would mark his "uninvited return to the novel." Two new dogs, also cocker spaniels, named Billy (the Kid) and Blanche (DuBois), gifts from Joanne and Paul, began to become dear to him. Late in the fall Howard, with Joanne and Paul, had seen a "pups for sale" sign at a nearby farm. "When Gore saw them," Howard remembered, "he looked at them and turned around and walked away, and then he fell completely in love with them."

In New York he took his skinny, dark-eyed semi-relative, who in 1953 had married Senator John Kennedy, to a television studio, where he noticed Nick Dunne, an assistant director. The program in rehearsal probably was *Robert Montgomery Presents*. "The show started each week," Dunne recalled, "with me standing in the middle of Studio 8H at NBC, and Robert Montgomery would be in a balcony looking down on us, and I would say, 'One minute, Mr. Montgomery!' And he would say, 'Thank you, Nick, and good evening, ladies and gentlemen.'" Dunne's job was to place set markers on the floor with masking tape. "While I was down there on the floor, Gore came in with Jackie Kennedy, and he said to me, in a really snobbish way, 'What are you doing on the floor?' . . . like I'd fallen to a lower station. He was making a joke for her. It wasn't cruel. But it was just this side of cruel. Then we just started running into one another." Everyone who knew her called the unprepossessing, doe-voiced, shy Mrs. Kennedy "Jackie." Restless, vaguely ambitious, not yet ready to sacrifice herself entirely to her husband's career, she hoped to become an actress. Some years before, she had thought that Gore might help her get into journalism. Now, with his television and movie connections, she hoped he would introduce her to some opportunities in that world, despite her husband and his family's opposition. In late 1952 John Kennedy had become a senator. In 1956 he had made an unsuccessful run for the vice-presidential nomination. If he had won, he would have gone down to defeat on the Stevenson ticket. If Stevenson had won, Gore soon told him, his fate would have been worse. "He was amused when I suggested that he might feel more cheerful if every day he were to recite to himself while shaving the names of the Vice-Presidents of the United States, a curiously dim gallery of minor politicians." In Georgetown that fall, Gore, visiting the Kennedys, found Jack "in a bathrobe. Nothing under it. Face swollen. Impacted wisdom tooth. 'How can I speak tonight in Baltimore, looking like this?' 'Isn't he vain?' Jackie purrs." Gore's own repressed political ambitions rose to more than usual consciousness, the road not taken.

Preparations for *Visit* now began to move more quickly, relentlessly. At Edgewater, putting what he thought were final touches on the script, Gore braced himself, he wrote to Edith Sitwell, "for a February debut in the theatre. It is odd that of all the things I have wanted to be in my life (Byron, Thomas Jefferson, Huysmans, Henry James, Petronius and United States Senator) playwright is the role which least appealed to me. I was born unstagestruck and, as a result, have had my better successes, recently at least, in that world. I suppose glory like love comes most quickly (though not most meaningfully) when unsolicited." The money was at last in place. Reluctantly, Axelrod and Wilder had invested some of their own. Though Axelrod had great faith in *Visit*'s likely success, the rule was to invest only other people's money. A quiet, capable man, who preferred working behind the scenes, Wilder complemented Axelrod's gregarious flamboyance. Having had his eye on the Booth Theatre, Axelrod was delighted to get it beginning early in February. Out-of-town tryouts in Boston and New Haven were scheduled for late January, with Cyril Ritchard as star and director. In December, Gore attended auditions; in early January, intensive rehearsals where, sporty in an open shirt and sweater, serious in glasses, pencil in hand, he made changes in consultation with Cyril and George. Conrad Janis and Sarah Marshall had been chosen to play the young lovers; Philip Coolidge, Sarah Marshall's father; the comic actor Eddie Mayehoff, an expert at blustering pomposity, the Air Force general in charge of dealing with the alien visitor. The best and best-known ballet and Broadway designer, Oliver Smith, Bowles's cousin, whom Gore had known for years, a good friend of Sam Lurie and Miles White, did the sets. Inevitably, despite his hands-off directorial style, Ritchard found it difficult to act the major role *and* direct the play. "Cyril had a wonderful technique for directing," Conrad Janis recalled. "He had the most lines, so he put himself in the middle. Then the people with the next-most lines were on either side of him, and the people with the next-most lines were on either side of them, and finally Cyril would look up and say, 'Oh, we seem to have gotten ourselves into a line. Well, break it up, break it up!' And that was how he directed us. Anyway, Gore would sit out front and watch this." He could hardly believe his ears and eyes. "Cyril Ritchard was a sweet man," Gore later remarked. "He was also easily the stupidest man I've ever met." Soon, to everyone's relief, Axelrod in effect became co-director.

As Gore and others participated in the rehearsals, they realized that much was right about the play, especially the basic concept, the talented cast, the witty lines, the satiric edge. But there were obstacles as well. Gore soon worried that it would be an embarrassing disaster. No television play had ever been successfully redone for the Broadway theater. People in general simply did not believe it possible to do that. The cast was effective, except for Ritchard's inability to learn his lines, perhaps because as director he had too much on his mind, mostly because some constitutional quirk resulted in his being unable to recognize that when his memory failed him, he had substituted an entirely different word of the same number of syllables for the word he had forgotten. Usually the new word made absolutely no sense in the context. His laggard memory worried everyone. Eddie Mayehoff seemed perfect as the pompous Air Force general, his plastic face a constantly redesigned gallery of funny but appropriate expressions, and the chemistry between Ritchard and Mayehoff worked wonderfully well, though Mayehoff, a difficult man with prima-donna pretensions, got on everyone's nerves, the one discordant personal element in the company. Axelrod "sort of shoved Eddie Mayehoff down everybody's throat. Cyril hated him, which was wonderful. We were able to use that. Their mutual loathing was splendid. It gave us some conflict that perhaps our drama didn't already have." All this seemed manageable. But when rehearsals graduated to trial performances in New Haven and then Boston, everyone immediately realized there was a serious problem. In the middle of January, in New Haven, where Thornton Wilder came to the performance, a blizzard kept many people away. The audience seemed cold, unresponsive. The play seemed not comic but menacing.

For the Boston opening the house was sold out. People had come up from New York. Gene and Kit had driven from Avon. Howard was there. When the curtain descended, there was sinking uneasiness. There had been very little laughter. The audience had not seemed to like it. The critics enjoyed it even less. One Boston reviewer, who acerbically wrote that *Visit to a Small Planet* would have a short visit on Broadway, epitomized the general view. Word immediately got back to New York: the play was in trouble. Perhaps only Axelrod managed to be upbeat, telling funny stories to the cast, after the performance in Boston, about Jayne Mansfield's auditioning for her role in *The Seven Year Itch*. But "the out-of-town tryouts were a disaster," Sarah Marshall commented. Author, director, and producers pondered what to do. The problem seemed to be that the play was not comedic enough. The commercial theater required an imbalance, heavily titled toward humor, between comic entertainment and serious message. The funny lines, the witty situations, the comic paradoxes and entertaining tensions were being outbalanced by the serious satire, the scathing antimilitaristic indictment, and the discomfiting high stakes of the nuclear context. Sarah Marshall remembered "Gore saying at some point, 'I wanted to write an antiwar play, and the only way to write an antiwar play is to write a prowar play." Audiences were too uncomfortable, even too frightened, to laugh. The stakes were high. This was the commercial theater. Like the movies, it had its particular audience, its popular-culture necessities. Reluctantly, Gore saw the point. "Gore turned serious," Axelrod commented, "when the audience didn't want him to . . . and . . . he attempted to say something and, God forbid, you can't do that. So I sort of persuaded him to have a hit comedy instead of a serious flop. He went for it, reluctantly." More than anything, he feared failure. More than anything, he feared returning to California, which he had to do shortly after the opening, with the entire country knowing his play had been a failure. In fact, he most feared having to face the barbed wit of the writers' table at MGM. There would be sharp humor and false sympathy at his expense. It was too painful to contemplate. Immediately he began to make changes, outwardly resigned, inwardly seething. But he was resolutely, triumphantly practical. Two scenes were dropped, one radically changed. A mushroom-cloud background was eliminated from one of the sets. The play he left behind in the earlier versions, "though hardly earth-shaking, was far more interesting and true," he felt, than the one they were now performing. But "because it costs too much to put on a play, one works in a state of hysteria. Everything is geared to success. Yet art is mostly failure. It is only from a succession of daring, flawed works that the occasional masterwork comes. But in the Broadway theater to fail is death." From the tryout in New Haven until the New York premiere, "I was more dentist than writer, extracting the sharper (and not always carious) teeth."

On the train ride from Boston to New York, as author, director, and producers mulled over their situation, they were still uneasy, mostly frightened. The cast was anticipating a fiasco. Sitting separately, Sarah Marshall said to Conrad Janis (they soon were playing lovers in real life also) that she thought she had detected a flaw in Cyril Ritchard's performance the correction of which might make all the difference in the play's reception. It seemed to her that Gore had intended Kreton to be childishly unaware of exactly what a nuclear bomb was and what the consequences of nuclear war would be. The original text had designed the role to be played as a child amusing himself with firecrackers. Instead Ritchard had transformed Kreton into a mustache-twirling villain. Therefore "everything he says takes on an almost Hitlerian meaning." No wonder the audience was not laughing. Convinced she was right, Janis went immediately to the compartment where Gore and Axelrod were. "I said, 'George, can I speak to you for a minute?' " So George sat down. I was the one who said to him, even though it was Sarah's idea, 'You know Cyril is playing it all wrong.' This was absolutely an astounding thing for the juvenile to say to the producer and director. But George, who was no dope, sat there and said. 'What do you mean?' We proceeded to explain to him what it meant that the character understood what an atomic bomb was. If, conversely, he didn't and thought it was a giant firecracker that made a lot of noise, the audience could then say, 'Oh, well, he's mistaken, and he's not a bad person, and if he did know it was going to kill millions of people and pollute the air, he certainly wouldn't do it.' Which is exactly what happened. George told that to Cyril, who understood it immediately. We met the next day in the lobby of the Booth Theatre to rehearse the play in the men's room, actually the lounge downstairs, because the stage was being used, in front of the washrooms with chairs posted instead of props. Cyril had changed the character, and it became Noël Coward in his hands."

As *Visit* opened in New York on February 7, 1957, the cast and playwright were still pessimistic. Sarah Marshall heard one of "the Shubert guys say to Clinton Wilder, 'Do you want the moving-in bill put on the moving-out bill to save money?' " Most everyone concerned hoped, at best, to avoid embarrassment. If they had not laughed in New Haven or Boston, why should they laugh in New York? Before the performance Ritchard told the cast to go to Sardi's and have an extra glass of champagne to loosen up. When the lights went down, the Booth Theatre was filled with critics and theatrical notables, with friends of the cast and production, with the glamorous first-night audience that characterized Broadway premieres at a time when Broadway was American theater and theater culturally important. Still, for the rest of the seats "we had to drag people in, because we had no advance at all." As the first act progressed, the cast began to sense that this was different from New Haven and Boston. The audience *was* laughing. At the end of the first act Martin Gabel turned to his wife, Arlene Francis, and said, " 'Heh, you know this is pretty funny.' And at the end of the second act he turned to her and said, 'You know, I think this thing is going to be a hit.' And in the middle of the third act, he said, 'You know something, Jesus Christ, we have money in it!' "

Sardi's restaurant awaited, a cast party and the ritual of waiting for the early reviews, which would be out by the time people had finished their entrées. Nina was there with John Galliher. Gene and Kit had come in from Connecticut. Sally and Pick, stationed again at Mitchell Field, had attended the performance and came to the party. "The whole family was there," Sally recalled. "About fourteen of us. We were his family. He had gotten the tickets." Axelrod had been so desperate to get out word of mouth that *he* had arranged with a popular radio-talk-show host to read the reviews, even bad, over the air from Sardi's as they came in. "When the first one was this tone poem by Walter Kerr to Eddie Mayehoff, I had him read it and he burst into tears." Brooks Atkinson in the *New York Times* thought Ritchard's performance "a comic masterpiece." "The atmosphere was jubilant," John Galliher recalled "Nina was very proud." She seemed to Gene "to take full credit." Every reviewer praised the play and lauded the playwright. The premiere was the first of 388 performances. Unexpectedly, Gore had a Broadway hit. The next day, as he flew to Los Angeles, he felt the relief of knowing that when he appeared at the MGM writers' table, he would be on the receiving end of congratulations and jealousy.

With the satisfaction and money from a Broadway hit, the spring and summer of 1957, spent mostly working in California except for June at Edgewater, were seasons of relative triumph. Gore's grief at Alice's and Latouche's deaths subsided. He missed them both, especially Alice. But he had a healthy amount of the ordinary capacity for bearing loss. Perhaps the one loss he might not have borne, except at a cost almost beyond bearing, was the loss of Howard, who was becoming, gradually, the indispensable man. When there had been a brief scare in 1955 about a cancer on Howard's ear, Gore, Isherwood noticed, was deeply worried. Fortunately, it turned out to be inconsequential. When MGM assigned him to work on a script with the working title *Spectacular,* he quickly saw that nothing would come of it. Since he was still paid $2,000 a week, it hardly mattered. *I Accuse* had finally gone into production, delayed mostly because of a casting problem. Zimbalist, frustrated, had not been able to obtain a major star for the main role and eventually settled on the talented José Ferrer, who was eager to play the lead and direct. At least it was being made. The filming, at MGM's Ealing Studios near London, moved along fairly rapidly during late winter and early spring 1957.

The one fly in the professional ointment that demanded immediate attention, much of it distressing, was *Billy the Kid*. Warner Brothers, prodded by Newman, had finaly made a commitment to do it. Before immersing himself in the Broadway production of *Visit*, Gore had agreed with Newman that Fred Coe, with no movie experience but great television success, would produce it and Robert Mulligan would direct. They thought it reasonable to assume that the same team that had been successful with the television production would be successful with the movie version. Gore would use his television script as the basis for an expanded, full-length movie version. He had already given Coe a new script as the basis for his final draft. It would be his movie. When he arrived in Los Angeles in February, he learned that Coe had fired Mulligan and hired another director from television, Arthur Penn, whom Coe preferred. He had also brought in a journeyman scriptwriter, Leslie Stevens, to revise Gore's screen version, now to be called *The Left-Handed Gun*. In effect, Gore would have almost nothing to do with the film. Coe, he felt, had self-servingly betrayed him. "To be fair to him—I don't see why I should be—but to be fair to him, he was on his uppers. He was scared. There was no more of what he did, live television drama. Now he had to jump to the movies. He sees what he thinks is a stupid movie star in Paul Newman and a scatterbrained playwright who's all over the place in me, and he has an opening to get in and take it over and did." Penn, whom he thought Iago to Coe's Othello, he despised. Paul, he believed, had done nothing to prevent this happening, partly out of inexperience, mostly because of an unwillingness to offend powerful people at a time when his own movie career was still at its beginning. Gore, in New York, had assumed that Paul was looking capably after both their interests. Under the circumstances it was not a realistic assumption. "I wish," Newman remarked later, "Gore had written the screenplay. Maybe I should have pushed a little more for that to happen. But I didn't know much about the politics of Hollywood."

With Fred Coe, Vidal tried a combination of thin honey and forcefulness. By early April it was clear that Coe had the legal power to enforce his changes. Warner Brothers would support the producer. Since the William Morris office in Hollywood represented all the principals except Newman, it would not work against the interests of the majority of its clients, though it would do its best to provide equity for Vidal. "In principle," Vidal agreed with Coe, "there is certainly nothing wrong with your calling in another writer and probing with him the script, but I believe you should have done me the courtesy of telling me *before* you made this arrangement rather than after." He was, though, reduced to moral suasion. "I never thought I should ever have to remind you that it was I who wrote the television play, and interested Paul Newman in the picture, and got you involved as *our* choice of producer and that had I not been actively goading everyone concerned from July 1955 until last summer when you became operative, there would have been no production. . . . I realize that as time passes and you and Arthur work long together in warm communion, your own contributions to the script will loom larger and larger while my own will appear villainously small. Let me say you were, as always, sensitive and wise, cutting, directing, tightening, accenting, while Arthur gave us some fine visual settings. But to hammer the point home, the essential conception was mine and the narrative was mine. I now find myself in the odd position of having designed a house for myself only to find that the contractor has moved in and that I may or may not be invited to the house warming." His only meaningful weapon was the threat of withdrawal and an appeal to their common interest. "To get down to cases, this is the problem for me: a) I will not share billing with another writer; b) nor can I honestly take credit for another writer's work; c) I have no intention of withdrawing easily. I believe it unwise, for both our sakes, to have a complete falling out now, tempting though it might be. We have a common interest in this project." The changes Stevens, Coe, and Penn had made, he felt, had ruined the screenplay. When he gave them the opportunity to redo it, with his assistance, they declined. "I shall want to pull out altogether," he told Harold Franklin. "I shall be paid. I shall get back my screenplay." With the assistance of William Morris, happy to mollify him if they could do so without alienating the others, he regained control of his original script for the teleplay. He hoped to have the chance someday to make it his way. In the meantime, he refused to have anything to do with *The Left-Handed Gun* other than accept the money due him from the acknowledgment that it was based on a television play by Gore Vidal. It was an unhappy lesson in Hollywood politics.

In June, in Washington, there was a happy but complicated summer moment, the marriage of his half-sister, twenty-year-old Nini Auchincloss, to a Washington lawyer-businessman and aspiring politician, Newton Steers. Nini, who had hardly been a presence for Gore since Hughdie and twelve-year-old Gene had had one of their few talkative dinners alone while Nina was in the hospital giving birth to her only daughter, had recently reentered his life. Dark-haired, slim, flirtatious, eager to please, quick to anger, over-sensitive to slights, with more than a touch of her mother in her looks and her personality, Nini was a mixed blessing. On the one hand, she repre-sented the possibility of a sibling relationship, of meaningful family. On the other, she epitomized some of the unattractive burdens of family history. About two years earlier, Gore had taken Nini and their mother to the Blue Angel. "Nini began one of her hysterical tirades that she had known only two ladies in her life, one was Aunt Janet [Auchincloss], the other was Mrs. Gore. She said this in front of my mother, who, surprisingly, took it. Just didn't blow up. In fact, I nearly blew up. I thought all of this was terrifically rude, since it was my party. She was there only because my mother had brought her; even if she was my half-sister, I didn't know her. I just thought how awful she is." Her temper seemed to be as explosive as their mother's. Her sense of entitlement was as great. As a child, she and Nina had fought, almost violently. Without either Gore's strength or his talent, she had not succeeded in transforming Nina's tarnished gifts into personal gold. Feeling wounded from an early age, she made much of her wounds, as if she could construct a personality on her battle scars. With some mischief-making delight, she had, some months before, showing off to the dull Auchinclosses and carrying on her personal war with her stepmother, insisted on Janet's inviting her glamorously successful half-brother to a large lunch party at Merrywood. Nini's half-sister, Lee Bouvier—with her husband, Mike Can-field, whom Gore had seen in London earlier in the spring—was there, along with an assortment of Auchinclosses and their friends. When Gore, who had not been back to Merrywood for over fifteen years, arrived, Janet delayed lunch in order to have another table set, because, Oatsie Leiter recalled, "there were too many for the big table. So we all trooped in, and most of us sat down at the big table. In the corner, at the window," Janet had set up a small card table "for four people, at which sat Gore Vidal, little Jamie Auchincloss, little Janet Auchincloss, and Mary Victoria Leiter, my daughter. They were then eight to ten years old. . . . Of course Janet did this on purpose." After a short while "the roars of laughter that came from the table of four! I mean, the children were beside themselves, rolling on the floor, screeching and screaming with joy. What Gore was saying to them God alone knows. But I want to tell you that it killed every single bit of conversation at the big table. No one could utter a word, they were so dying to hear what Gore was saying." In the drawing room tart-tongued Janet said to Gore, "Nini always hated you until you became a success in the theater." "Why should she be any different from the rest of you?" Gore replied.

When Nini had walked out on Nina, she had exchanged her mother for the different but equally difficult Janet, whose two daughters had become active half-sisters, companions but also rivals who shared, and helped ratchet up, her view of the importance of wealth and of a money-producing marriage. "Janet was a little more punctilious than Nini's mother and of course was not an alcoholic," Gore later commented. "She was a born troublemaker. Jackie was very good to Nini and Lee not while the father was a perfect nullity." Life at Merrywood had its Gothic side, its coldness and unrelieved materialism. Nini, who had gone from Farmington to Bryn Mawr, thought she might go to law school or into journalism. Actually, her preference was to be a writer like her half-brother, though she had little sense of what being a writer entailed, especially the necessity for disciplined hard work. With a substantial trust fund from her paternal grandmother, money should not have been an issue. Indeed, it was not when she married Newton Steers, who had no special fortune of his own, an assiduous, intelligent, well-known Washington bachelor with barely sparkle enough to make him attractive to hard-pressed hostesses desperate to fill dinner-table seats. More than twice Nini's age, as Gene Vidal had been when he married Nini's mother, Steers had little idea of what marrying Nini Auchincloss was getting him into. Eager to liberate herself from her mother and stepmother, Nini thought that marrying Newton Steers made sense. Though they were to have four children, the marriage, predictably, was to have little equanimity and to end in recriminatory disaster, some touch of which Louis Auchincloss, who had gone to Yale with Steers, anticipated when Nini told him at a cocktail party she was going to marry him. "Newty! My Newty! My classmate! He's much too old for you. Get someone closer to your own age!"

On a mild June day at Washington's St. John's Church, distinguished as the church of the presidents, Nini, as she walked down the aisle, had on her the eyes of the Washington and Newport world that had defined her life—the Auchincloss family, her Bouvier stepsisters, Jackie's husband the senator, and other assorted congressmen, senators, and denizens of the

Washington social-political world, including senators-to-be John Warner and Ted Kennedy, even Nini's second-husband-to-be, Michael Whitney Straight. Nina, apparently sober, was there. Dressed for his formal role as one of the innumerable "groomsmen," Gore watched his sister embrace her bliss with a strong sense that marriages in general were likely to be bad things. "I shall be happy to serve you as an usher at the interesting event," he had responded to Newt's invitation. "Marriage of course is a disastrous step so you will need as many witnesses to your folly as possible." Nina, estranged from Auchincloss not only by divorce but by years of embittering effort to increase her settlement and get additional child support, had not been invited to attend the reception. Probably she would not have come anyhow. Howard had been invited to neither. As they sat next to one another in the limousine driving from the church to Merrywood, Jack Kennedy, whose humor and ruthless self-confidence Gore liked, said he thought Nini would have done better to marry his brother Teddy. At Merrywood, Jackie and Gore went up to the second-floor landing together to look at what had once been Gore's bedroom and then Jackie's. The room and the view from the window were eerily familiar. She reminisced that when she had gone riding soon after moving into Merrywood, she had worn some of his old shirts that she found there. As he looked down into the garden from the window, his memory revived scenes and people from his past. The opening scene of what would be his novel *Washington, D.C.* began to form in his mind. A little later in the garden, as toasts were being offered to the newlyweds, he stood next to Ted Kennedy, who "raised high his champagne glass and then poured its contents over his handsome youthful head." It was a shadow play of past, present, and to come.

CHAPTER twelve

Open and Shut

1957–1960

DOGS RUNNING ON the beach and barking in the sunlight. Sand. Water. Billy and Blanche running with the happy pack. On one side the Pacific Coast Highway. On the other, the beach, stretching southward to Santa Monica. To the east and south, the movie studios, Culver City, Hollywood, downtown Los Angeles. In late July 1957 the four of them had rented Shirley MacLaine's beach house, 38 Malibu Colony. Unmarried, Newman and Woodward feared adverse publicity. As part of a residential quartet, they had the advantage of less vulnerability and the companionship of friends. "The intention really was that we were acting as beards for Paul and Joanne, because Paul hadn't got his divorce. There were photographers hanging around everywhere," Gore recalled. "A house with four people in it seemed less sinister than one with two, of whom one was married." Gore and Howard loved being on the beach. Each morning Joanne went to United Artists, where she was filming *The Three Faces of Eve*. Paul drove off to Warner Brothers, making *The Left-Handed Gun,* which he called *The Left-Handed Jock-Strap*. Gore occasionally drove to his Culver City office at MGM, where he worked reluctantly on the script of *Spectacular,* had lunch at the writers' table, and heard regularly from Sam Zimbalist, again in London, who had his hands full finishing *I Accuse* and worrying about the unworkable script he had in hand for MGM's long-planned remake of *Ben-Hur*. *Spectacular* was an incubus. "I am bogged down in a movie," Gore complained, "and so unable to write anything of interest. Prose is still in abeyance."

Much of his income went for taxes and living expenses. Woodward was paid $500 a week; Newman, paying alimony and child support, not much more. Neither pair alone could have afforded the $1,500 rent for the Malibu house. Howard and Gore had separate rooms, Joanne and Paul shared another, with two small rooms in the back for guests, especially Newman's brother and mother and then Nini, who arrived noticeably without Newt, as if she needed a West Coast holiday after their honeymoon in Venezuela. Howard gave up his larger room to Nini and briefly doubled up with Gore. "Paul, Joanne and I are now living together in the house at Malibu, a combination to delight the readers of *Confidential*. Happily, the house is big and we keep out of one another's way," Gore wrote to Bill Gray, the mutual friend who had introduced him to Joanne. Newman remembered "a lot of linoleum floors and that Joanne would start mopping them at seven o'clock in the morning and finished mopping about eight o'clock at night. It was pretty carefree, a lot of outdoor cooking." For him, at least. Finally, exasperated, Woodward rebelled against being what she called "the mother of them all." "God, what a time! It was very funny," she recalled. "I was this virago who would storm around. There were white floors. Of course everybody was traipsing sand in. I did nothing but mop floors and wash underwear. For everybody."

There were regular parties, the grill smoking, the drinks flowing. Isherwood came with Don Bachardy. Other Hollywood writers, various friends and colleagues of the Newmans and of Gore, visited regularly. The French writer Romain Gary came for drinks. Anaïs, living in Los Angeles, still hoping that one of her novels would be made into a movie, came over at Gore's invitation and enjoyed being introduced to the Newmans. In her own mind she gave more value to what she considered her success in love than to Gore's success in work. Gore had, she assumed, what he wanted, which included a new friend, the actress Claire Bloom, who joined them frequently at the Malibu house, where she entertained them with her "extraordinarily funny" imitations of Queen Elizabeth II, as Isherwood noted. Gore had met

Claire in London in 1948, introduced backstage when he and Tennessee went to see John Gielgud, who was to direct *The Glass Menagerie*. Seventeen years old in 1948, dark-haired, slender, with rivetingly sweet brown eyes, Claire was performing with Richard Burton, with whom she soon fell in love, in *The Lady's Not for Burning*, a title that had an anticipatory irony in regard to the young actress's romances. A Londoner of Jewish background, classically trained in drama school and at Stratford-on-Avon, she projected an attractively empathetic vulnerability and a sturdy delicateness that in 1952 had contributed to her performance in Chaplin's *Limelight*, which made her a movie star. Numbers of films quickly followed, including her haunting rendition of Lady Anne in *Richard III* with Laurence Olivier. In New York, on New Year's Eve 1956, at the Plaza Hotel with a friend who was a friend of Howard's, she had joined the Newmans, Gore, and Howard for drinks. She had no recollection of their brief meeting in 1948. Interested in literature and art, with little in the way of pretension, somewhat reserved, perhaps even "demure," far from being "probably quite a bitch," as the irritable Isherwood surmised, she immediately enjoyed Gore's company. "I sat next to Gore, and we started to talk and kept talking," she recalled. "It was so nice to talk to someone so interesting." In California for the filming of *The Brothers Karamazov*, without a community of her own in Los Angeles, she was delighted to have Gore's company and to enjoy the Malibu camaraderie. "I had an apartment on Charlottesville Boulevard, a rather elegant apartment in which I was extremely lonely." Gore, to cheer them both, visited with caviar and champagne. He introduced her to all his friends. Responsive to her beauty and intelligence, he found her more than another friend. Suddenly they were intimately friendly. Without touching, they apparently touched one another, the start of an enduring friendship they both valued. From the beginning, she recalled, it was "very easy, very intimate and charming, fun, jokes. It's always the same, it's always been the same."

Unable to realize his desire to return to fiction, Gore was nevertheless about to appear again in bookstores. The prospect, as always, made him anxious. "I dread my return to the bookstores," he told his editor. "But those are not things to consider, if one did there would be no authorship." In June 1956 he had gone from Edgewater up to Boston to meet his new publishing team at Little, Brown; his editor, Ned Bradford; and the publisher, the formidable Arthur Thornhill, a small, spare New Englander who owned and ran the house with decisive Yankee efficiency. Nick Wreden, who had become Little, Brown editor-in-chief in June 1954, had written Gore a congratulatory note in May 1955, after viewing the telecast of *Visit to a Small Planet,* "probably the best TV play I have ever seen. You were really at your best and that, *as you well know,* is something!" When Wreden suddenly died in August 1955, Ned Bradford became his successor. Wreden and Vidal had already agreed that Little, Brown would publish a volume of Gore's television plays, featuring *Visit,* for which he had written a preface. Bradford turned out to be as intelligent, supportive, and engaging an editor as Wreden had been. In early 1956 Little, Brown published the book that marked Vidal's first appearance as a Little, Brown author, *Visit to a Small Planet and Other Television Plays.* Dedicated to Harold Franklin and Florence Britton, it contained eight plays—*Dark Possession, A Sense of Justice, Summer Pavilion, Visit to a Small Planet, The Death of Billy the Kid, Smoke, Barn Burning, The Turn of the Screw*—and a concise, gracefully written "Foreword," retitled, for separate publication in *New World Writing,* "Writing Plays for Television." Its optimism about the continuation of the Golden Age of television and about its author's imminent return to writing prose proved unwarranted.

In 1957 Little, Brown published as a separate volume the expanded stage version of *Visit.* For Thornhill, who hoped that Vidal would one day become a bestselling novelist again, it was an easy but shrewed investment. Actually, Vidal gave the book reluctantly to Little, Brown. "I should have preferred Random House to Little Brown," he had written in February to James Oliver Brown, his agent, "but of course we owe LB something and the book, of course, is theirs." A well-known literary agent, with an Ivy League manner, usually sporting tweeds and pipe, to whom he had been introduced by Louis Auchincloss, Brown had recently become Gore's representative, though he had little need for a literary agent, since he had only the plays to sell. William Morris handled his television and theater work, which Brown would have liked to have done. Brown managed only the book-publication arrangements with Little, Brown and, like the publisher, hoped Gore would have something more profitable to offer in the future. In Boston in June 1956 Gore was impressed both by Thornhill's obvious talent for maximizing profits, which he hoped would work in his favor, and his ability to drink four martinis without their having the slightest effect on his lucidity. In fact, though, Gore's mind was more on his frustrated desire that New American Library bring out paperback reprints of his novels, particularly

The City and the Pillar, which had been out of print for over a year, than on Little, Brown's publication of his television plays. If Jim Brown could do him any real good as an agent, it would be in getting Dutton to release the titles they still controlled and Weybright to make more of his backlist available. Dutton continued to decline to cooperate. "I would not get into a row with Dutton at the moment," Vidal advised Brown. "They will never relinquish their rights and you would just be involved in a long hassle." Weybright was happy to publish paperback reprints of the three Edgar Box mysteries. Indeed, he urged that he be allowed to provide the real name of their author in the expectation that that would make them even more profitable. For Gore, no matter what the sales, the profit would be small. He declined. "The Edgar Box thing is a problem. . . . I want to keep the separation distinct, as much as possible, between my hack writing, no matter how charming, and the serious novels, no matter how dull." To Jim Brown, who emphasized how troublesome these negotiations were, he admitted that he had "never been able to understand the curious jinx on these novels nor Weybright's reluctance to do them. When I lost the critics after *The City and the Pillar* and, generally, lost the public after *The Season of Comfort,* I might have survived if Victor had done as he was at one point obligated contractually to do: reprinting *Judgment.* . . . The argument that I am not commercial is, alas, rather hideously exploded by my Faustian success in television, movies, the mystery story and the stage. . . . I have done him a good deal of service both tactically and artistically and though the things I did for him I wanted to do, like *New World Writing,* I nevertheless find it mysterious that he did not reciprocate. Publishers do owe something to their writers. Good writing is not so common that it can be lightly passed over. . . . Barring a premature death, I shall be center stage for a good many years and, from time to time, I am quite sure that my publisher and reprinter will benefit materially. I think that now is the proper moment to convince Victor that my demands are just and my memory of neglect long." More than anything, the stage success of *Visit* prompted Weybright to begin putting more of Vidal's novels back into print over the next few years, though in 1957 his resistance was still strong.

To make more attractive Little, Brown's edition of the expanded stage version of *Visit,* Gore wrote a brief preface, which he disarmingly began with the confession that he was "not at heart a playwright. I am a novelist turned temporary adventurer." Though he lamented his absence from prose fiction, explaining that he had undertaken dramatic tragedy and satire as an expediency in a world that had made earning one's living as a novelist difficult, the preface itself was an excellent example of another genre, the prose essay that he had eased into as well. A number of brief reviews he had done had provided limited opportunities for literary analysis, though it was not literary analysis in any formal sense that especially interested him. When he looked at a literary work, his interest was in its nature, the relationship between its virtues and his capacities as reader, some combination of wit, lucidity, the conversational voice, and the integrity of the reading experience. "Writing Plays for Television," his foreword to the 1956 volume of television plays, caught some of the emerging essayistic tone. In the preface to the 1957 edition of *Visit*, the focus is on the process of creating a Broadway hit, the central self at issue is his own. It was this prose essay, brief as it is, in which he first found his voice as an essayist. When the *New York Times* declined to run it as a separate piece, he sent it to Bob Bingham at *The Reporter*, who had urged Gore to do reviews for him and who now had the bright idea of inviting him to be *The Reporter*'s regular theater critic. The essay appeared in July, the first of numbers of essay-reviews on drama he was to write for Bingham, whom he now saw occasionally in New York, a brief revival of a less intense version of the friendship they had had in their Exeter days. Married, a father, still hoping to establish himself as a novelist, Bingham had settled in as a hardworking, modestly paid editor at *The Reporter*, later at *The New Yorker*, resigned to behind-the-scenes anonymity in his daily work, ambivalent about Gore's success, bitter about his own failures, especially critical of what he considered Gore's self-promotion. To Gore, Bingham seemed to have lost the ambition he had had at Exeter, perhaps, Gore wondered, a casualty of Bingham's brutal war experiences, a victim of some existential burnout. He was "a very good writer, a good journalist, and he wrote a novel which wasn't very good but it wasn't bad either and when it got rejected he gave up. I said," Gore recalled, "that's not how you do it." Some failure of nerve, perhaps of self-esteem, seemed at issue. "We worried about his character, that anybody could be so broken in spirit as to work for Max Ascoli," the owner of *The Reporter*, "a real tyrant. Bob got on with him very well, which worried us, because nobody of mettle put up with him. . . . I remained fond of Bob. But I didn't see him much. A classic case of marriage parting old friends." But there was still affection between them, and some teasing good spirits.

When Bingham named his son Thomas Truman Bingham, the Thomas for Tom Riggs, one of their favorite teachers at Exeter, the Truman for Harry Truman, "I always accused him of using it for Truman Capote, as he knew that I disliked Truman. 'At least call him Tru-Gore Bingham,' I said."

With his weekly salary from MGM and his royalties from the continuing run of *Visit*, he was more concerned with finding ways to keep a larger portion of his income than with making more. When he had hesitated for some weeks about taking an unattractive script assignment, MGM had suspended him, and he worried about the fact that his contract required his weeks on suspension be added as additional weeks of contractual responsibility, extending its life beyond its original terminus in 1959. Often enough, a contract writer who unexpectedly had a Broadway success demanded to be released or that his studio contract be renegotiated. Hollywood executives generally still bowed before the prestige of the New York theater. When Gore had returned to MGM in February 1957, after *Visit*'s glowing reviews, Sam Zimbalist, with paternal pride, had taken him for the first time into the executive dining room, where he was greeted with congratulatory handshakes and backslaps. He had not thought, though, to try to change or break his contract. After a brief suspension he agreed to work on the script for *Spectacular*, but the length of his contract already was beginning to have some of the feel of a prison sentence, especially since he had to keep postponing work on *Washington, D.C.* and *Julian*. Deductible expenses against income helped fend off the worst depredations of the high income tax, but, still in the highest tax bracket, with the advice of his accountant, Leonard Strauss, he looked to two strategies to soften the annual blow: the first a retirement annuity that sent all his royalties for *Visit*, about $300,000, directly into an annuity account with Massachusetts Mutual; the second the purchase of rental property as an investment that would produce income against which there would be deductible management and maintenance expenses and possibly residence for himself in part of the building.

In late June he agreed to purchase for $90,000 416 East Fifty-eighth Street, a four-story brownstone with floor-through apartments. Paul Kent, one of his neighbors in Barrytown and a friend of Alan Porter, was happy to sell it to him. Short of immediate cash, Gore borrowed $9,500 from Nina, probably for the binder, and then went to contract in September, when he paid in cash a sizable portion of the purchase price, the rest partly a personal mortgage from Kent, partly a bank mortgage, a portion of the payments to be covered by the rental income. It was a sensible purchase. Unfortunately, there was some confusion with an inconsistent, sometimes incoherent Nina about whether he was supposed to repay her immediately or whether he was to repay over a period of time or whether she had actually intended to lend him the money at all. Apparently it had been a loan, to be repaid at mutual convenience. In October, in a panic, Nina claimed she should have been repaid long before. Suddenly, but not for the first time, she seemed to be irrationally lashing out at him. Their business communciations now went through Leonard Strauss. From Southampton, Nina wrote to Strauss, "I have told Gore, and I wish to tell you so that there will be no misunder-standing, that his first financial *must* is to pay off the 9500 dollars that I put into the fifty eighth street place. . . . I also think that Gore needs to learn a business lesson, one does not use other peoples money in any way without their consent. I would never have agreed to a loan, I do not have the cash to operate the way I wish, to be able to, when conditions are the way they are going to be, and have that much on loan." Gore had Strauss immediately send her a check for interest at 6 percent for three months, two weeks later a check for $3,500. The remainder followed shortly. Whether Nina in Octo-ber had forgotten the terms of late June, or whether she had misunderstood, or not been in a position to understand, what they had agreed to, she transformed what was at worst a misunderstanding into another painful experience for her son, who had to have felt the punitive nastiness of the claim that "Gore needs to learn a business lesson." After a period of some modest good feeling, it felt, for Gore, like old times again.

———•———

In spring 1957 Sam Zimbalist, appalled at the awful script he had for the remake of *Ben-Hur*, sounded out his young writing star about doing a thorough revision. Drastic changes were needed to make it filmable. The successful 1925 silent *Ben-Hur* had become one of MGM's signature films, a totemic invocation of the studio's glory days. With profits continuing to decline, MGM executives hoped that a remake of *Ben-Hur* would revivify if not the studio system then at least the financial bottom line. Karl Tunberg, a well-established, well-connected journeyman scriptwriter, had, implausibly, been given the assignment. His specialty was light comedy, his most suc-cessful movie *Rebecca of Sunnybrook Farm*. Zimbalist, with some anguish, immediately realized that Tunberg's unwieldy, undramatic script would have to be redone by someone who knew something about first-century Rome. It would be more than ordinary polishing. Well read, interested in history, with a practical pen for dramatic economy, planning to write a novel about the Emperor Julian, Gore seemed just the right person. The assignment, though, did not appeal to him. *Spectacular* was dud enough. *Ben-Hur* might be worse. If he had to earn his living writing movie scripts, then he preferred at least to write the script, even if an adaptation, from scratch. With no wish to offend his paternal supporter, he tactfully begged off the assignment, leaving Zimablist to find someone else to solve his problem. Gore suggested Isherwood. The three of them had lunch together. After some deliberation, Zimbalist backed away from hiring Isherwood. From Vidal's perspective, that was that. It was not his problem.

When the Malibu arrangement ended in late September, he was delighted to have some time at Edgewater. The Newmans, among others, came to visit, the river was attractive, the autumn weather lovely. As usual, by himself and with guests, as long as the warm weather lasted, he swam out to the island and back, eager for the exercise. Oscillating between slim firmness and noticeable expansion, he worried about his weight. He had bought an exercise machine, kept upstairs in his bedroom, to help him keep fit, which he soon declared a resounding failure.

From the bedroom window, from the octagonal study, from the perspective of the French doors that looked out on the lawn, from almost every angle and position, the river was there, the hazy blue Catskills in the distance. Friends came up by train from New York, for the day or overnight. Jean Stein, ten years younger than Gore, Doris and Jules's daughter, whom he had last seen as a young girl in Los Angeles, stayed overnight. Claire Bloom visited. She was astounded at how Gore seemed simply not to hear the train roar by. Sam Lurie, who had briefly been on retainer as Gore's press agent, came up with his companion and co-worker, Stanley Kaminsky, who recollected "being awakened at about two in the morning after having gone to bed and suddenly being . . . terrified. I thought it was an earthquake." In the octagonal study Gore labored on a new play, a development of his Civil War teleplay *Honor,* which he began to revise for full-length stage presentation, somehow preferring to do that than to work any further either on *Washington, D.C.,* or *Julian,* perhaps because he expected that

MGM, to whom he was still under contract, would soon give him a new assignment. The telescript about his grandfather that he had promised Manulis was still on hold.

In Manhattan, Howard and Nina had made the one-bedroom apartment at 360 East Fifty-fifth Street comfortable, a place where both men stayed and where they sometimes entertained. It was considered Howard's apartment. Miles White down the hall had windows facing their bedroom window across the courtyard. When Gore hosted a party, they often made room by putting the coats in Miles's apartment. Oliver Smith, with his tall, lithe, handsome figure, his blond—now white—hair, was regularly in sight with Sam Lurie and other ballet people. Paul Bowles still occasionally came to New York. One evening Gore and Howard went to a party hosted by Cecil Beaton at which naked, muscular young men had been hired to serve drinks and exhibit their bodies. Theater and movie friends were around, and Gore began now to be a regular at "The Party," the gatherings of the elite of the New York and Los Angeles entertainment worlds, a movable celebrity feast, the world that Latouche had introduced him to, the world to which his television plays, his Broadway success, and his Hollywood status now gave him full entrée. His youth, his handsomeness, his wit were welcome, the attraction of his being both an intellectual *and* a celebrity. The Party's shifting and simultaneous forms flowed to both sides of the continent, many of the people the same. Doris and Jules Stein in Los Angeles were one of the focal points. The actress Ruth Ford's apartment at the Dakota in Manhattan was another. In New York the partygoers always gathered for Noël Coward's regular visits from London. Gore was delighted to meet him. *Visit to a Small Planet* was still running. The expectation was that he would write another play, that he would compete with George Axelrod (and, at some remove, with Coward himself) for Broadway's crown. As a successful playwright, he now began to make television-talk-show appearances, mostly to push *Visit*, among them *Today* with David Garroway, Jack Paar's *Tonight Show*, and David Susskind's various talk programs.

The unavoidable assignment from MGM came late that fall. It had the advantage, unexpectedly, of requiring his presence in London, where his adaptation of the bestselling novelist Daphne Du Maurier's *The Scapegoat* would be filmed, under the aegis of the head of MGM's British production at their Ealing Studio, Sir Michael Balcon, the man who had given Hitchcock his start and also who had been responsible for what came to be known as the Ealing comedies. The well-known director of *Kind Hearts and Coronets*, Robert Hamer, would again have his friend Alec Guinness, who in *Kind Hearts* had proved himself the master of multiple roles, for the dual-character starring role; Bette Davis, whom Gore persuaded to take the part, and Irene Worth were set for the important female leads. MGM had wanted Cary Grant for the film. Du Maurier and Guinness, whom Du Maurier insisted on because she thought he resembled her father, had formed a limited partnership to do the film. Soon thinking better of doing it themselves, they persuaded MGM to back and release it. When a first screenplay proved unsatisfactory, MGM decided that Gore would be the right person for the task. Kenneth Tynan, whom Balcon had hired early in 1956 as his script director at Ealing Studios, had probably either raised Vidal's name or added his enthusiasm when MGM had queried Balcon about assigning Vidal to the script. It was a far better, more interesting, and prestigious assignment than anything he had been offered before, a sign of MGM's confidence that the thirty-two-year-old writer could hold his own in such company. In early November he sailed to England, first for consultations, then for work. On the *Queen Mary*, his first-class ticket paid for by MGM, he dined regularly in the Grill, undeterred by the stormy weather, on what seemed to him the best food he had ever eaten. Just before leaving, he had gotten a copy of the novel and read it for the first time.

As usual, as soon as he arrived in London, he quickly got to work creating a script, which he felt confident he could do successfully, though he soon discovered that Du Maurier had strong ideas about how it should be done. The author of *Rebecca*, a novel Gore had thought "ravishing" at thirteen and which had been made into a successful movie, Du Maurier exercised considerable influence on the filming and was "unconsciously condescending" to him. "I came to know what an experienced butler must feel in a stately home. I was, she would say to others, 'the hack from Hollywood,' which was not too far off the mark." On the side, Gore and Hamer made parodic fun of Du Maurier's prose. But he managed to create a workable screenplay that, when it opened the next spring in New York, was praised more for its successful moments than for its overall achievement. In the editing Bette Davis's role was gradually cut to an extended cameo appearance, for which she blamed Guinness. Guinness himself had his hands full with the domineering Du Maurier and with his gradual assumption of Hamer's responsibilities as the director's heavy drinking, which everyone on the set tried to cover for, eventually disabled him. With the droll, cynical Hamer, during one of his better weeks before the filming started, and with Maria Britneva, whom Gore had invited along, he went to France, searching for a filming location. They spent some icy, wintry days in Le Mans. Maria was her usual manic, effervescent company. They ate well, and Hamer drank, pulling a flask from his pocket as they drove, toasting the "winter wonderland." Though Gore was to leave before the actual filming began, he and others covered as best they could for Hamer, and when later Hamer made some changes in the script, Gore did not mind, partly because he had little enthusiasm for the script in general. "I would have been delighted if Robert got *all* the credit."

Staying in luxury again at Claridge's in late November and December, Gore and the Tynans resumed and increased the good fellowship that had begun the previous spring, though the strongest current of affection soon flowed between Gore and Elaine rather than Gore and Ken. As often, Gore's delight in attractive, witty, luminescent women, his combination of empathetic and principled support—especially in Elaine's case for her work as a writer—created a mutual enchantment. His hard, biting, often hilariously perceptive humor fascinated her. She admired his unsentimentally objective view of people and the world, so different from the self-pitying subjectivity of her husband and most of the men she knew. At the same time she felt Gore's capacity for friendship, for loyalty, for unhesitating supportiveness. At work on her first novel, *The Dud Avocado,* to be published the next year, she appreciated his encouragement, his helpful suggestions. The contrast with Ken was both liberating and additionally discomfiting, a signifier of the long-standing and increasing tension between husband and wife. When Ken discovered that his wife was writing a novel, he whined, "But when I married you, you weren't a writer." Both found Gore attractive, fascinating, accomplished. When Gore, who was picked up each day by car for the drive to Ealing, invited Tynan to ride with him to the studio, Ken, for whom early-morning hours were bleary-eyed, incoherent, and coffee-driven, reported to Elaine that the experience was totally unnerving. At that hour of the morning Gore spoke in clearly enunciated, fully formed sentences.

Four years older than Gore, the daughter of a well-to-do New York Polish-Jewish immigrant family, the beneficiary of a liberal education and increasingly liberated from the cultural and sexual restrictions of her parents' world, Elaine had moved to Paris in 1949. She was interested in acting and painting. Dark-haired, sensuously engaging, energetic and nervously talkative, she was a lively presence. In 1950, on a London visit, she met the tall, flamboyant, stuttering, self-dramatizing young theater critic. Two weeks later Tynan asked her to marry him. "I am the illegitimate son of the late Sir Peter Peacock. I have an income of X pounds per year. I'm 23, and I will either die or kill myself when I reach 30 because by then I will have said everything I have to say. Will you marry me?" Three months later she cabled her Park Avenue family, " 'Have married Englishman. Letter follows.' " Born in Birmingham, the illegitimate son of a bigamous father, Tynan was a volatile combination of brilliance and histrionic insecurity. A great success in the Oxford University theatrical world, always eager to hold court, which he did with wit and riveting sartorial flamboyance, Tynan was an Oscar Wilde of sorts, though without the talent and artistic discipline. His stutter seemed an almost emblematic flaw. Handsomely sensual, with a high-pitched attention-demanding voice, he had a touch of the theatrical queen. He wore bright clothes, odd color combinations, and a Mickey Mouse wristwatch before these had become a lifestyle statement. Always personally onstage, more than anything he wanted to be noticed. Everything about the theater interested him—acting, directing, producing, evaluating. But what most engaged his frenetic energy was being a celebrity, someone to be noticed and reckoned with in that most publicly defined of all artistic provinces, the theater. He had great skill with language, less with people. Alec Guinness readily admitted that Tynan's reviews were wonderful unless you happened to be the subject of them. Turned on sexually by light spanking of women, emotionally frivolous and irresponsible, by 1958, at the age of thirty-one, he had become Britain's premiere chastiser of theatrical performances, the widely read reviewer for *The Observer,* a witty critic well suited to the role but at odds with his own conflicting compulsion to be of the moment and at the same time to do something more enduring. He had essentially recognized, though, that he did best with short pieces. He was neither personally nor professionally suited for the long haul.

Days were spent at the Ealing Studios at Elstree, evenings at Claridge's and with London friends. The American ambassador, John Hay Whitney, with whom Gore had a tenuous connection through Nina and Whitney's former wife, invited him to an embassy function. He ran into a presence from the past, Cornelia Claiborne's mother, who was also staying at the hotel and en route to visiting her daughter, who had married an

Englishman. There were marital problems, for which she blamed her son-in-law. "She was going down to the country" to see them, Gore recalled, "and she was debating—she talked with a very tough Virginia accent—about the possibilities of smuggling a gun into the house and taking care of him, murdering her son-in-law." A movie deal was in the process of being made for *Visit to a Small Planet,* and Eric Burger, an American professor of German literature with extensive contacts in the German publishing and theater world, had been at work successfully since August arranging a Berlin production of the play, which had been in rehearsal since early December. For the premiere on December 23 at the Renaissance Theater, Gore flew to Berlin, his first visit to Germany, where he spoke at a fireside discussion on American literature for a group of fifteen German writers, the talk arranged by the Berlin Cultural Affairs branch of the United States Information Service. The movie negotiations had gotten under way before he had left New York. Abe Lastfogel at William Morris, whom Gore had met socially in New York and who had handled the deal, cabled him that they had been successful in holding out for $150,000. The film, for which Gore did not write the script and over which he had no control, would star Jerry Lewis and be a critical and commercial disaster, an exemplification of the ongoing problem of Hollywood for the novelist or playwright, which has resulted in the widespread wisdom that the best thing to happen is that Hollywood pay vast sums for rights, then *not* make the film.

A London theatrical run for *Visit* seemed likely, at least at first, both to Gore and to Hugh (Binkie) Beaumont, a top London theatrical producer. Gore was skeptical about Beaumont, who was enamored of star actors, thought little of writers and directors, and already had a long history of failed British productions of American plays, especially Tennessee Williams's. But most roads to a West End production went through Beaumont. Fortunately, the stellar British actor Robert Morley was interested in playing Kreton. But he insisted as a condition of his commitment that the American aspects of the play be transposed into their nearest British equivalents. While he was in London for *The Scapegoat,* Gore had numbers of discussions with Morley, which made clear that he would pay a heavy price for Morley's commitment: Morley demanded 50 percent of the royalties and that he himself Britishize the text. Gore loved Morley as an actor. He seemed right for the part. Offering to revise it himself, he quickly produced a version for the British stage. " 'This will never do,' Morley said. 'Let me do it, and it will be so much easier for you, and I know how the jokes should go.' A lot of American humor, though, was unknown to him, and I said, 'Do you mind if I mark the play where we get a laugh?' He thought this was outrageous. 'How do you know where you'll get a laugh?' I said, 'Well, it's been running a year or two. There are five or six companies out there playing it somewhere or other. Of course I know where the laughs are. It's a good idea, if you're going to play it, that you should know what's funny, since it may not occur to you what in the American style is funny." He soon sounded out Alec Guinness as an alternative. Guinness, though, did not think the role suitable for him. "I do agree that the tone of Kreton's dialogue is resolutely frivolous," Gore responded, "entirely Cyril, and hardly you. But there are many different ways of playing the part." Guinness firmly declined. Since without a well-known star there would be no production, it was Morley or no one. From New York, Clinton Wilder and George Axelrod urged Gore to be flexible, which he did his best to be. "As I am interested only in art," Axelrod joked, "and you are interested only in money (which means we have the same ends at heart), I must strongly urge you to give this serious consideration. Should you prove recalcitrant, I shall be obliged to recall you to the States for further brain-washing in the Green Room. . . . We can make a bundle in London and I am absolutely sure this is the way to do it." To their bitter disappointment, by late 1958, despite attempts to find common ground, Gore ended the negotiations. He could contemplate forgoing a portion of his royalties, but the notion of giving up control of his words to Morley's revisions he found unacceptable.

———————

Christmas 1957 in London unexpectedly turned into the dark side of Dickens's *A Christmas Carol.* Eager for family, Gore had invited Nina to join him there for the holiday season. Feeling a twinge of guilt at disliking his mother, he thought this might make up for it. He also invited Howard, who consulted with Nina. Their hope was that they could both book passage on the *United States* and come across together. Since they had been compatible often enough at Edgewater, there was no reason to think he could not have the company of both in London, especially since he planned to rent a large flat, the grandeur of which, with three servants, he thought Nina might enjoy. He and MGM anticipated there would be about two to three months more of work. It would be more comfortable than staying on at Claridge's, at least in regard to having guests, and since the studio would pay for either, he could thus have guests without incurring extra expense. There was the likelihood of a visit from Paul and Joanne. Paul's marital situation had sufficiently cleared so that finally they could marry, which they did on December 26, 1957. Having been busy in New York attending to the recently purchased building on Fifty-eighth Street, Howard felt the attraction of spending the Christmas season with Gore in London. It would be his first European trip. For some time Nina had been busy in Washington, attempting to rent two vacant apartments in the N Street building. For the last year or two there had been a truce between mother and son, though Nina's aggressive tongue and habits sometimes caused tension. She still constantly put him down "terribly," Howard recalled. "Even when she wasn't drunk. Not so much to his face, though there were arguments. . . . She always had to be right. And she would challenge him when she knew nothing about the subject. . . . *She* wanted the attention, she felt competitive. As Gore was with her. . . . When an argument began between them, I would quickly leave the room. I felt that I shouldn't be present. The arguments were always about how Gore didn't really live up to or face up to 'it'— what? everything! anything! money! She didn't make an issue of his sexuality head on, and if she did, I would have been out of the room long before. But she might have. She would go around to all the bars in New York and tell people, 'Oh, my son is a homosexual. Pity me.' Nina had her litany, 'I never had any luck.' " After the opening of *Visit,* after a night on the town she had unexpectedly appeared at Edgewater, banging on the kitchen door, with a young man she had picked up whose father was a well-known Pan Am pilot whom Nina knew. Drunk, first she fell in the mud at the door, then, as Howard and Gore lifted her up, said, "He's got the biggest cock I've ever seen." For a few days she disappeared with her young man into one of the guest bedrooms. Sandwiches were sent up.

After "trying like hell," she wrote to him, "to arrange getting over," she pulled strings finally to get passage on the solidly booked *United States.* When nothing was available for him, Howard arranged separate passage, sharing a cabin on another boat. Nina seemed in one of her capable periods, handling her Washington business, preparing for departure. Perhaps, since the episode at Edgewater in the spring, she had been making one of her periodic efforts to dry out, sometimes with the help of AA successful for as long as six months. Gore, anticipating visitors and eager to be out of the hotel, had rented for £50 a week a large triplex flat at 37 Chesham Place in Belgravia, a corner building in an early-nineteenth-century row of houses built around a small private park, near Cavendish Square, not far from Knightsbridge Road and Hyde Park Corner. He had gotten the flat through the son of its owner, who insisted on being paid in dollars to avoid taxes. Spacious, grand, with a huge drawing room on the first floor, uncomfortably furnished with Marie Antoinette furniture but excellent for large parties, with ample bedrooms and servants' rooms, the flat seemed perfect for his needs. When Nina arrived just before Christmas, it was not yet ready for occupancy; he put her up next to him at Claridge's. To his disappointment, from the moment of arrival she was drinking. Perhaps she had begun on the transatlantic voyage, where liquor, as usual, flowed freely and Nina, not a reader at all, would have had little to do other than socialize. After a period of relative abstinence she would have been ready, the temptation irresistible. She also may have been nervous in anticipation of her arrival. Visits with her son, let alone long ones, almost always resulted in tension. She also expected the London social world and the American embassy to welcome her, but whatever her expectations, she had to have sensed that it was not a sure thing. Her one prominent contact was her former lover, the ambassador, whose patronage could open doors to her. It would not have been unnatural for her to fantasize about a resumption of their affair of twenty-five years ago. "In her mad Blanche DuBois way," she had almost assumed it would happen, Howard recalled. Soon after arriving, she put in her call to Jock Whitney at the embassy. Whitney did not call back. Drinking steadily, announcing that she had a bad cold, she locked herself in her hotel suite. When Robert Morley came by to talk with Gore about *Visit*, impressed with Morley she stirred herself enough to listen through the door. When the servants tried to use their passkeys to get in to clean, she forced them to stay out. The hotel management was not happy. To Gore's relief, Chesham Place was finally ready. They moved in on December 28. In the meantime Howard had arrived.

Nina managed to pull herself together, enough at least to appear, as she often did, stunningly attractive, wearing a turban, in a satiny pastel-flowered hostess gown, "all blues and grays and pinks," at a small party for London friends that Gore hosted early in January. With sharp painterly acuity Don Bachardy sketched her in his mind as she talked with Isherwood, probably with no idea to whom she was talking. "She had very strong features, heavy-lidded eyes, strong, staring eyes. They pinned you. There wasn't anything else coming from them except their strength. And there wasn't any kindness in her eyes. . . . There was a very strong resemblance to Gore. She had a glass in her hand and was certainly drinking, and she was very voluble. She had a red mouth, a red-gold dark lipstick. . . . She was absolutely accessible, though. She was really outgoing." In company she had her distinctive combination of beauty and presence. Nervous about giving parties with Nina around, Gore felt constrained by her drinking. He did not feel it safe to include her in his own social rounds. In addition, he went almost every working day to Elstree, still regularly giving Ken Tynan a ride, for script consultations and revisions. Howard, who had more free time, was prepared to take up, as he had done at Southampton, the role of Nina's escort, especially on ordinary activities about town. But as she continued to drink and her call to Whitney went unreturned, her own worst nightmare materialized: the London social world had no interest in her. Being Senator Gore's daughter and the ex–Mrs. Auchincloss had no currency here. With no reason to dress and with a glass in hand, she spent hours sitting on the back stairs at Chesham Place, haranguing the servants, gradually but inevitably deciding that her London social opportunities had been destroyed by factors totally beyond her control. She announced herself a victim. She was not being invited out because everyone of course knew that Howard was a Jew and a fag. In her mind she had accepted Gore's allegedly frequent invitations that she spend Christmas with him in London as a favor to him and with no knowledge that Howard would be there. If she had known, she would not have come. "She would sit in an old wrapper, rather like her coeval Tallulah, body exposed, on the back stairs," Gore recalled, "talking to the servants about her son the fairy and his Jew boy." Howard was unhappy but not shocked. He did not for a moment believe Nina anti-Semitic. Nor that she disliked him. She had available to her a class-based vocabulary that, drunk or angry or hurt (or all three), she instinctively used, with neither irony nor awareness of how others might respond. An easy target against which to express her bitterness at the world and her anger at her son, Howard was conveniently there. She herself, she firmly believed, was in no way to blame for any of this. Nor was Howard, in any personal sense: it was simply that her son's being a fag and his companion not only a fag but a Jew had made a London social life impossible.

Simmering, furious, Gore began to find her presence intolerable. Her

Rosalind Rust, c. 1942.
(Courtesy of Edes F. Talman)

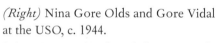

(Right) Nina Gore Olds and Gore Vidal
at the USO, c. 1944.
(Wisconsin Center for Film and Theater Research,
Gore Vidal Collection)

Nicholas Wreden, Vidal's editor
at Dutton, c. 1946.
(Courtesy of Peter Wreden)

Anaïs Nin and
Gore Vidal, New York,
c. 1946.
(Wisconsin Center for
Film and Theater Research,
Gore Vidal Collection)

Cornelia Claiborne and Gore Vidal
at the Café Pierre, New York, c. 1945.
(Courtesy of William Fitzgerald)

Gore Vidal (right) and Harold Lang,
probably in Bermuda, 1947.
(Wisconsin Center for Film and Theater Research,
Gore Vidal Collection)

Nina Gore Olds studying her father's favorite document, c. 1946.
(Courtesy of Tom Auchincloss)

Nina Gore Olds, c. 1946.
(Courtesy of Tom Auchincloss)

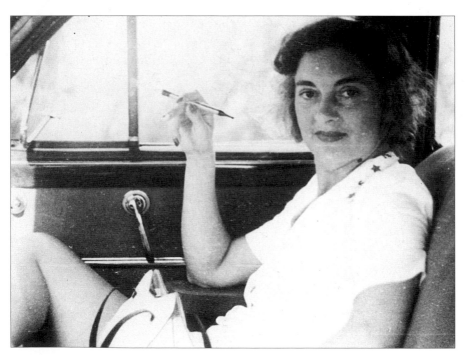

Tennessee Williams and Gore Vidal, Key West, c. 1950.

(Courtesy of Gore Vidal)

(Left) Tennessee Williams and
Gore Vidal, Rome, 1948.
(Wisconsin Center for Film and Theater
Research, Gore Vidal Collection)

(Below) Howard Austen at the age of
about fifteen, c. mid-1940s.
(Courtesy of Howard Austen and Gore Vidal)

(Center, left) Gore Vidal, Truman
Capote, and Tennessee Williams,
New York, 1948, at a party
celebrating the opening of Williams's
Summer and Smoke.
(Photo by Jo Healy. Courtesy of Erin Clermont)

(Left) John Latouche and Alice Astor
in the mid-1950s.
(From the John Latouche Papers, Rare Book and
Manuscript Library, Columbia University)

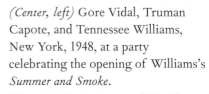

(Left) Gore Vidal playing with Blanche and Billy at Edgewater, c. 1957.
(Courtesy of Gore Vidal)

(Right) Howard Austen with Billy and Blanche at Edgewater, c. 1957.
(Courtesy of Howard Austen and Gore Vidal)

(Below, right) Cyril Ritchard and Gore Vidal reviewing the script of *Visit to a Small Planet*, 1957.
(Performing Arts Research Center, New York Public Library)

(Below) Gore Vidal as himself in *The Indestructible Mr. Gore*, 1959.
(Wisconsin Center for Film and Theater Research, Gore Vidal Collection)

Gore Vidal, unknown person, Marian Seldes, William Shatner, and E. G. Marshall, rehearsing for *The Indestructible Mr. Gore*, 1959.

(Performing Arts Research Center, New York Public Library)

(Right) Gore Vidal (right) and Christopher Fry, the two uncredited writers responsible for most of the script of *Ben-Hur*, Rome, 1958.

(Wisconsin Center for Film and Theater Research, Gore Vidal Collection)

(Below) Gore Vidal (right) and Sam Zimbalist in Rome, 1958.

(Wisconsin Center for Film and Theater Research, Gore Vidal Collection)

(*Above*) Kenneth Tynan and Elaine
Dundy, Marylebone Register,
London, January 25, 1951.
(Courtesy of Elaine Dundy)

(*Above, right*) Andy and Fred Dupee
at Edgewater, c. 1959.
(Courtesy of Andy Dupee)

(*Right*) Barbara and Jason Epstein,
c. 1960.
(Courtesy of Barbara Epstein)

Fred Dupee and Philip Rahv, c. 1960.
(Courtesy of Andy Dupee)

drunken behavior and hateful speech were rising to the level of a primal curse, a pollution that no act of his so far had or could alleviate for long, let along lift permanently. He felt nothing but rage. If this were Oedipal, it was startlingly reversed. His father was no problem at all. He would have liked to kill his mother. She kept drinking. She kept sitting on the stairs in the flat, making trouble. She told outsiders she had a horrible cold that indisposed her. She then demanded that Gore cash into pounds her dollar check for $10,000, the equivalent of £4,000. She had to have the money for some undisclosed reason. With stringent currency restrictions on the import and export of sums above £50, the demand created serious technical difficulties. "She went on and on, and she started giving orders to Gore as if he were a lackey," Howard recalled, "to tell him to go and cash this check in American dollars. Nobody at the bank knew her. It was irritating the hell out of Gore. She was endless about it." Busy each working day at Elstree, resistant to Nina's alcoholic bullying, Gore refused to take care of it for her. If she wanted it done, here were the directions about whom to see and what documents to bring. Used to giving orders and having them obeyed, Nina exploded into even more vehement statements of what she had been saying repeatedly for almost two weeks. Whitney would not call because of "this household!" She was living with two fags, one of whom was a Jew! Clearly she was not after Jews or fags. She was after her son. Hurt herself, she assumed she would feel better if she hurt him. She had been doing that since his childhood. She was treating him as she always had, exacerbated now by the pain of Whitney's rebuff and by what it stood for—a fifty-five-year-old, heavy-drinking, twice-divorced, once-widowed woman whose glory days of prominence and beauty were rapidly disappearing. It was no longer a pleasure to look in the mirror. She would never again see herself beautiful and beloved in someone else's eyes. Drunk, self-destructive, raging through the flat, aware that there would be consequences, she would not let up. Furious, his patience at an end, fantasizing about murder, Gore finally said, "I think it's time for you to leave," and put a return ticket in her hand. Stunned, she was soon on her way back to New York. She had not seen any necessary connection between her behavior and her son's response.

With Nina gone, their spirits lightened as if the plague had been lifted, the curse for the moment inactive. London pleasures resumed, the household now a temporary Dickensian domestic bower, including the dour English butler, Tattersall, whose stereotypical name, as if out of a Victorian novel, made up for his grimness. In late January the honeymooning Newmans arrived, Joanne four months pregnant. After a week at the luxurious Connaught, then a week in Paris and Switzerland, they moved into the Chesham Place flat. It "was very dark and, my God, was it cold," Joanne remembered. "There was no central heating, and we used to run from fireplace to fireplace, from room to room." As she woke up after her first night, she sensed someone's eyes on her. "I looked up, and there was this man looking like Uriah Heep, saying, 'And what can I . . . ?' He was terrifying." A Dickens enthusiast, she had recently been given a complete set of The Inimitable's works by Gore, who told her, admiringly, that she was "the only person he knew who read that kind of thing." Despite the chill, they had a convivial time, and Howard soon fired the butler. While the others were off someplace for the evening, "I was giving a dinner party on my own. I don't know why. And I fired him during dinner and then said, 'Oh, my God, what have I done? Gore and Paul and Joanne are going to come back, and there's no butler, no servant.' When he told them what had happened, all three "gave such a sigh of relief. These three strong characters: none of them had the strength to fire Tattersall, which they all wanted to do." For Joanne, with her interest in art and culture, experiencing London in Gore's company was pleasurably enriching. Eager to teach, especially his friends, as well as learn, he provided historical descriptions, a running commentary about things he thought would interest them. They took numbers of short London excursions together, including one to Hampton Court, where Paul, for whom this was a first European visit, kept saying, "I've never seen anything like this before!" It seemed "tender and sweet" to his companions. "It was the beginning of a thoughtful life, particularly for Paul," Howard remarked. "Joanne wanted always to dedicate her life to culture. It's not that Paul was against it. It was like this is sissy stuff. But at Hampton Court he was saying, this is grabbing me. I'm so impressed." For Newman, his relationship with Gore in general was, among other things, an exposure to ideas and activities he had not had an opportunity to experience before. "I was very much from the provinces, and Gore's familiarity with literature and other things set off a constant buzz in my head," Newman later remembered. "I think I realized what a great opportunity I had to get educated when I met Gore."

Soon after the Newmans arrived at Chesham Place, the bitter aftertaste of Nina's visit became foul. Though out of sight, she was not out of mind.

There was probably some discussion with the guests or at least offhand comment about Nina's visit. Gore was aware that "Joanne didn't like her mother, and Paul hated his mother, and Joanne hated Paul's mother, so we were in the bad-mother sweepstakes, all three of us. We used to argue competitively whose mother was the worst. I'm happy to say that I won hands down. They knew my mother, and I knew theirs." Whether or not they retold together their woes, the sad tale was intensified by a letter from Nina that came as they were planning a grand party, for February 20, to celebrate the Newmans' wedding and Joanne's birthday. At length, Nina presented her formal indictment of her son and his companion, her litany of woes and accusations that she had been preparing in fragmentary bursts throughout her visit. Her life had been ruined, she wrote, by her son and particularly his companion. "It was this venomous letter," Gore recalled. "She attacks Howard as the reason why Jock Whitney and her other grand friends couldn't come to the house, and her failure to connect with her grand friends she blamed on him, and on his presence." Something snapped shut in Gore, permanently. Nina's nasty words about Howard were the occasion, not the reason. She had said so many harsh things already, had for so long made so many exculpatory excuses that blamed him for much of what had gone wrong in her life, that blaming Howard now for her London disappointments seemed no more than another in a long list of self-justifications. Howard himself did not take her rantings personally. This was not about him. It was about Nina and Gore. Gore refused to show the letter to Howard; he showed it only to Joanne. Then he burned it. It was the only time in his life he destroyed a document. Then he wrote a letter to Nina. "I'll never see you again as long as you live." He kept his word.

———•+•———

The subdued lighting threw a warm glow across the elegant room. By 9 P.M. on February 20, 1958, the large eighteenth-century salon at Chesham Place embraced about a hundred guests. The party was in full blaze, in honor of the Newmans and also an informal farewell party for Gore, who planned to return to America early in March. American and London theater and movie people drank, ate, talked. When the Tynans arrived, Claire Bloom, whom Gore had asked to come early to help with preparations, looking radiantly beautiful, walked over to Ken and said, "You swine!" so Claire recalled. "Fuck you!" Joanne saw her lips pronounce. Tynan had written harshly about Claire's performance in her London play *Duel of Angels*. Though Gore's discussions with Morley about a British production of *Visit* were not going anyplace, Morley came, as did Ralph Richardson, Peter Hall, and John Gielgud. Gore's former publisher, John Lehmann, and Lehmann's formidable sister Rosamund were there, along with Edward Montague, whom Gore had also met in 1948. Now that Lehmann was no longer his publisher, whatever they had to talk about they discussed less tensely, and Gore had a chance to provide recompense for all the parties he had been invited to years before at Edgerton Crescent. The young John Bowen, pursuing a career as novelist and dramatist, whom Gore had not seen for some time until a recent dinner, happily moved, though at first paralyzed with shyness, among the famous faces. So too did Maria Britneva, who in 1956 had married a British minor aristocrat, Peter St. Just, and recently had given birth to a daughter. People Gore knew from the Ealing Studios came. Later in the evening, sitting drunk in the middle of the floor, the American actress Kim Stanley, celebrated for her prominence in "The Method" and idolized by Joanne Woodward, had an attack of what she called "the frankies" and told Robert Anderson what a terrible play *Tea and Sympathy* was. Stanley was in London to star in the first British production of Williams's *Cat on a Hot Tin Roof*. Anderson began to cry. Gore and Howard thought it a memorable party.

The script for *The Scapegoat* had been completed. Pleasurable as London had been, Gore missed Edgewater, and the longer he stayed on, the longer he perpetuated his absence from writing fiction, though the problem was less London than his contract with MGM. Despite high taxes, the stage and movie income from *Visit* and what he had saved from his MGM salary began to provide breathing room if not security. The final installment of his debt to Nina had been paid by his business agent in New York. The East Fifty-eighth Street building, where Gore and Howard still hoped to have an apartment for themselves, was sustained by the rents. Edgewater now cost much less to maintain in relation to the size of his income, and he felt increasingly confident that he could, if necessary or if he had the inclination, at any time replenish his bank account by freelance scriptwriting. But the MGM contract obligated him through 1959, perhaps longer, if one added on the weeks he had been on suspension plus any future suspensions if he chose not to accept an assignment. Walter Wanger had wanted him for *Cleopatra*. Fortunately, he had already been committed to *The Scapegoat*. The casting problems for *Ben-Hur* had been resolved, with Charlton Heston to play the lead role, though Sam Zimbalist and William Wyler, the director, had initially preferred Marlon Brando or Paul Newman, neither of whom was available. But the script problem remained.

Suddenly, as Gore and his houseguests were approaching the end of their London stay, they were jolted out of all other preoccupations by Joanne's suddenly becoming ill. She was in the process of miscarrying. Gore immediately got in a well-known London doctor. Joanne was quickly out of danger, grateful to her "wonderful" doctor, who had her moved to nearby St. George's Hospital. Committed to be in Los Angeles for the filming of *Cat on a Hot Tin Roof,* Paul left reluctantly. Gore and Howard flew back to New York early in March. "And there I was in London in the hospital," Joanne recalled. Claire Bloom, who thought her "very much alone, and, after all, it was my city," came to see her every day. "That very nice doctor then put me on a plane and sent me home. It was a terrible end to a lovely honeymoon."

At Edgewater, what to do next was much on Gore's mind, especially in light of the MGM contract and his expansion of *Honor* into a full-length play now called *March to the Sea.* So too was Nina, though with a willful finality that at least encouraged him to feel that that part of his life was behind him. In response to her hateful letter he had written, before leaving London, the last letter he was ever to write her, his own counterbrief to her accusations. "She carried it around with her for years. . . . She carried it with her everywhere. Showed it to my father. He said it was almost worn out. . . . It was falling apart. My letter made quite an impression on her, as it was intended to. And why shouldn't it? She was an Alibi Ike, as she used to call others. It was always the fault of other people. And now what better card to play than that her son has turned on her after she invented his career, saved his life, paid for his publicity, made him a star, and then he rejects her." Nina's lament he kept at a distance, though just as she retold repeatedly the story of his rejection of her, he repeated often enough, and savagely in his memoir, his version of her treatment of him. If one wins "the bad-mother sweepstakes," one never fully recovers. But this final turn simplified things for him. The essential damage had long been done and in place. This, now, was damage control. As a strategy it suited him well, among other reasons because of its efficiency. He saw no hope for recuperation, for redress, or even for cessation. As long as he associated with Nina, he would be subject to her damaging behavior. Better to put an end to it, forever. On the sidelines, careful not to say a word, Howard watched and wondered. As someone brought up to view the parent-child bond as unseverable, no matter what the provocation, he could not imagine a permanent break.

Before Gore could do more than catch his breath at Edgewater, the opportunity arose to terminate his MGM contract on favorable terms. On the outskirts of Rome, the Italian government's 148-acre Cinecittà Studios, with its nine sound stages, had been rented by MGM for the construction of huge sets representing ancient Rome and Jerusalem, including a hippodrome for *Ben-Hur*'s climactic chariot race. The cast, the director, the technical crew, the thousands of extras, the huge supply and logistics enterprise, all under Sam Zimbalist's control, were rapidly moving into place, budgeted at $15 million, then the most expensive film ever to have been made. With the studio system collapsing, the movie producers now prohibited by law from owning movie theaters, television eroding its audience, MGM hoped to save itself from bankruptcy with a blockbuster spectacular, the first of its kind, at a time before the hyperbolic vocabulary of blockbuster and special effects even existed. Suddenly the remake of *Ben-Hur* seemed like a last chance to regain the mass audience lost to television. This heavy responsibility was placed on Zimbalist's shoulders. An MGM loyalist, like everyone in the movie industry he believed, as he wrote to Gore, that television was "monstrous to give entertainment away for nothing, even if most of it is pure mediocrity." For five years the major obstacle to making *Ben-Hur* had been the script. Zimbalist thought Karl Tunberg's unshootable. Two well-known playwrights had been brought in, serially, as script doctors—Maxwell Anderson, the venerable but radical author of *What Price Glory?* and *Winterset*, and S. N. Behrman, a witty author of Broadway comedies and a long list of successful Hollywood films. Behrman had spent about a month attempting to "polish" it, the verb an all-purpose Hollywood euphemism that often meant salvaging through extensive revision. How much Behrman did is unclear. Anderson, who soon realized he was too ill to work, returned the script, terminating the assignment.

In spring 1957 Gore had declined Zimbalist's request that he help with the rewrite, though it meant temporary suspension. Now, in late March 1958, with the hammers pounding at Cinecittà, Zimbalist and William Wyler began to panic. The Tunberg-Behrman script still needed substantial revision. Its grasp of the ancient Roman world was modest to minimal. Much of the dialogue varied between flat Americanisms and stilted formality. The crucial relationship between Ben-Hur and Messala seemed senselessly formless, ineffectively motivated. Without a sharper, more cohesive script, producer and director feared a disaster, a nail in MGM's coffin rather than Lazarus brought back to life. Zimbalist, though, had great confidence in Vidal. As a scriptwriter, as Sam Spiegel remarked, "he's not half as good as he thinks he is, but he's twice as good as the others." If there was anyone at MGM to whom Gore owed a favor, it was Zimbalist, whom he had allowed himself to like, who had liked and treated him paternally. When Zimbalist now called, Gore said yes, with one condition. In exchange for agreeing to work on the *Ben-Hur* script, would MGM release him from the remainder of his contract? Zimbalist agreed to take the request to the MGM executives. It must have seemed like chutzpah to them. He was, after all, required by that very contract to work on *Ben-Hur,* his only leverage his willingness to go on suspension, which would have unhappy consequences for him. Zimbalist, eager to have him work on the script and motivated by personal affection, apparently did his best to make the case. MGM soon agreed. At the end of the third week of April, Gore flew to Rome, a destination resonant with his own previous visits and the special place it had held in his imagination since childhood; this unexpected confluence of events now brought him back to a city he had always cherished to work on a film set in ancient Rome. Work was to start on April 23. At the same time he was also writing, in the early, formative stages, a much-pondered novel, to be narrated in the first person, about the life of the fourth-century Roman Emperor Julian.

Still, the formidable challenge of revising the Tunberg-Behrman script was not any easier for its being met on a Roman site, and since Gore's last visit to Rome had been almost ten years before, he did not have any certain anticipation of how the city would strike him now. With Zimbalist and Wyler he flew overnight from a chilly, late-winterish New York into a Roman spring. On the plane Wyler, who had been a production assistant on the silent version of *Ben-Hur* almost thirty-five years before, read the latest version of the script. "As we drove together into Rome from the airport, Wyler looked gray and rather frightened. 'This is awful,' he said, indicating the huge script that I had placed between us on the backseat. 'I know,' I said. 'What are we going to do?' Wyler groaned. 'These Romans. . . . Do you know anything about them?' I said yes, I had done my reading. Wyler stared

at me. 'Well,' he said, 'when a Roman sits down and relaxes, what does he
unbuckle?' " As Gore caught his first sight in ten years of Rome, mostly
recovered from its wartime devastation, it seemed to them all that it might
take as long to repair the script as it had to repair the city. Rome, though,
appeared as lovely, as mysterious, as richly warm as it had each time he had
been there before. Walking the well-known streets to his favorite familiar
ancient and modern sites, he began to have "Roman fever" again, the
feeling that it was a place in which he could be happy.

At Cinecittà he joined Zimbalist and Wyler, both anxious about the
script and desperate to make it workable. Final touches were being put on
the expensive sets. Actors were rehearsing, hammers pounding, art and
design people sketching, costumes being stitched, hundreds of tons of camera equipment moving into place, everyone being paid. Wyler spent days
watching every Hollywood film set in ancient Rome that could quickly be
flown to him, probably by courier from New York or Los Angeles, as if he
could learn what he needed to know about ancient Rome from Hollywood's
prior versions. Between daily conferences with Zimbalist and Wyler, Gore
began to rewrite the script from the beginning. His expectation, part of his
agreement with Zimbalist, was that he would spend four to six weeks
working on the script. Zimbalist hoped he would stay and work, as needed,
throughout the entire filming. Always rapid, Gore felt that whatever good
he could do would be done in five weeks or so; anyway, he wanted to be
back in New York for what he hoped would be a deal for a Broadway
production of *March to the Sea*. With so much riding on improving the script
as quickly as possible, Zimbalist had hired the sophisticated British playwright Christopher Fry, though he had no movie experience, also to work
on the script, with the notion that Gore, since he was there first but would
not stay throughout, would start at the beginning and Fry would begin at
the end, so they could expeditiously meet in the middle. Somewhere about
the halfway point they would sink the golden spike.

In the meantime, with Gore each day providing pages for shooting,
the filming began, Heston in the title role, the British actor Stephen Boyd in
the other crucial part, Messala—Ben-Hur's Roman friend from childhood,
by now his enemy—much of the rest of the cast well-known movie veterans
like Sam Jaffe, Hugh Griffith, and Jack Hawkins. "When I was finished with
a scene," Gore later wrote, "I would give it to Zimbalist. We would go over
it. Then the scene would be passed on to Wyler. Normally, Wyler is slow

and deliberately indecisive; but first-century Jerusalem had been built at enormous expense; the first day of shooting was approaching; the studio was nervous. As a result, I did not often hear Wyler's famous cry, as he would hand you back your script, 'If I knew what was wrong with it, I'd fix it myself.' " The crucial problem that needed fixing was the absence of creditable motivation for Messala's punitive hatred of Ben-Hur. Political differences alone seemed insufficient. Gore suggested to his colleagues that he write into the script by indirection that Messala's fury is that of a lover scorned, that the Roman who has loved Ben-Hur since childhood turns against him because Ben-Hur declines to respond. For a Roman there would be nothing shameful about such feelings. For Ben-Hur, a Jew, they would be anathema. Wyler was shocked, frightened. That might make the problems they were confronting even worse. Gore reassured him. There would be no overt discussion, let alone depiction, of love between men. Messala's love for Ben-Hur would be presented indirectly, almost subliminally. Zimbalist hesitated. If it were done effectively, he realized, they might get away with it, and at least it would focus some of the emotional intensity between the men in a way that would make Messala's motivation credible without ever being explicit. Wyler reluctantly agreed to try it. They agreed not to say a word to Heston, whose cooperation had no relevance. Messala was the key. When they spoke to Boyd, he grasped the point immediately. His performance quickly embodied Gore's vision and revision. When they watched the daily rushes of the early scenes, all of which Gore wrote, they liked the results, including Heston, who viewed their power simply as the result of his and Boyd's fine acting of what in his mind was a straightforward political disagreement. Heston, smiling, in costume, with his friendly hand on Gore's shoulder, happily posed for a photograph with Gore, Wyler, and Christopher Fry.

With the filming going better than they had hoped, Gore worked each day with Zimbalist and Wyler, reconceiving important scenes and writing new dialogue. "I am doing a fast rewrite of a mammoth epic called *Ben-Hur*," he wrote to Paul Bowles. "I start at the beginning whilst my co-author, Christopher Fry, a nice little man who looks rather the way Shakespeare must've looked starts at the end and works toward me. It is predicted that we shall meet during the chariot race, though I rather hope to see him in Pilate's audience chamber. What fun art is!" The film's ancient world became more anchored in historical reality. The dramatic conception sharp-

ened. The dialogue had some rhythmic credibility. Though in the long run
no revision could make the film either intelligent or interesting, Vidal's and
Fry's work made the film believable for a mass audience, a Hollywood
spectacular in which the basic emotional and technical scaffolding was
strong enough to support its bombast, intellectual emptiness, and religious
sentimentality. It was a film for its time. It would offend nobody. It would
attract large audiences. It was good for MGM and Hollywood. And for
Wyler, Zimbalist, and everyone connected with making the film, including
Heston and Vidal, it was a triumph of sorts. For Gore it had, as he wrote
and worked with his colleagues, the satisfaction of a challenge well met. He
liked his colleagues and the experience. He was satisfying his last responsibility to his MGM contract. And it was a pleasure to be in Rome again,
where he kept working on the script from the beginning of the last week in
April to the end of the last week in May, a total of five weeks minus one day,
at a salary of $2,250 a week and all expenses. Occasionally he even found
himself contributing to the correction of little ludicrous things. "Luckily, I
was on the set at the begining of the shooting and so was able to persuade
the art director to remove tomatoes from Mrs. Ben-Hur Senior's kitchen.
Otherwise, [she] might have had Hannah prepare a tomato and bacon
sandwich for her daughter Mary." Zimbalist was delighted with Gore's
substantial contribution and on May 24, a few days before Gore's departure,
gave him a handsome briefcase as a personal token of appreciation. Zimbalist still wanted him to stay for the entire filming. Gore declined again. "This
is not a going-away present," Zimbalist wrote in the note that came with the
gift. "This is only to keep me from worrying over your losing more pages of
your goddam good play," *March to the Sea*, which Zimbalist had recently
read. "Thanks for helping out."

During the next weeks, as the filming proceeded, Gore's friends on the
set kept him abreast of progress. Morgan Hudgens, the MGM publicity
director for the film, sent him photos and a report on the last day of May.
"The horses began pounding around the Spina today—quite a sight," and
"the big cornpone," a derisive nickname for Heston, "really threw himself
into your 'first meeting' scene yesterday. You should have seen those boys
embrace! . . . We miss you." So too did Zimbalist, who early in June also
reported on "our first big day of the race. . . . Willy [Wyler] has not read
beyond the first 10–12 pages of the new script," overworked and exhausted
by the grinding daily schedule. "Again I want to thank you for helping out.

My only regret is you couldn't stay longer, which would have enabled you to work a bit more slowly. I think some of the scenes suffered because you had to rush to get them done before you left. Christopher has completed the ending. . . . It reads and feels very good. . . . Mary asked me to send her love. You also have mine." At the end of July, Zimbalist, who expressed his hope that Gore would find time to do the script for his next film, brought him up to date again. "The new opening you wrote worked out well." Gore's main contribution had stretched from the opening to the chariot scene, as he wrote less than a year later to William Morris when the question of how many and whom of those who had contributed to the script should get on-screen credit.

> I rewrote the script from the first page through the chariot race; P. 180. Christopher Fry wrote the rest. I kept the construction of the old script (with one important change) but I rewrote nearly all of the dialogue, as I have indicated. After I left, perhaps a third of my dialogue was in turn rewritten by Fry. In any case, I should say a third of the picture shot is my dialogue. As for construction, in the scene where Ben-Hur first meets Messala, in the old script they quarreled and fell out. In my version, P. 19 to P. 31, I broke the scene into two parts. First, at the Castle Antonio; second, at Ben-Hur's home. I also put in the business of the brooch for Tirzah, the horse for Messala, etc. From 12 to 31 the script filmed is all mine (I was there while it was rehearsed, while much of it was shot). The same goes for all dialogue in the chariot race sequence. Tiberius at Rome, and the other places indicated in the script. I was asked to stay on till the end of the picture but could not; we parted most amiably; and Willy Wyler will, I am sure, back me up as to authorship of the parts in question.

When the arbitration panel of the Screen Writers' Guild decided that Tunberg, one of its clubbable own, should have exclusive credit for the script, Wyler fiercely but unavailingly objected. Having become quite collegial with Fry, Wyler found it infuriating that Fry would get no credit for his work. Fry pressed Wyler to insist that Vidal be given credit for his substantial contribution. The Guild ruled that Fry had not contributed the minimum one third. Despite evidence to the contrary, they also concluded that Gore had not. Ironically, though later he was to fight numbers of times to have his name removed from association with a film, this was one instance in which he desired the credit he deserved. Unfortunately, Zimbalist was not there to make the case for Gore, though probably he also would not have been succcessful. At the last stages of filming, after Gore had returned to New York, Zimbalist unexpectedly died of a heart attack. "I was more upset than I thought I would be by Sam Z's death," Gore wrote to Isherwood that fall. "It almost doesn't do to get to like anybody if he is going to die on you."

Despite his efforts during the rest of 1958 to find a producer for *Fire to the Sea*, Gore had no success. There were too many things wrong with the play, including the general assumption that even a good Civil War play would have difficulty attracting a sufficient Broadway audience. Producers wanted another comedy from him, not a historical dramatic play. "My career as a dramatist has come to a grinding halt," he confessed to Isher-wood in the late fall. "No star will do the Civil War play." Before going to Rome in April, he had told Tom Driberg, "I should love a British visit, but I am deep in a play for the fall, and my novel about Julian." In April he had published in the *Nation*, the beginning of a long association, an essay on satire, "The Unrocked Boat: Satire in the 1950s," with some sharp analysis of American cultural and political distaste for satirical art, including the observation that "the Christian victory, though it did not bring peace on earth, did at least manage to put a severe leash on the satiric impulse. . . . If ever there was a people ripe for dictatorship it is the American people today. Should a home-grown Hitler appear, whose voice, amongst the pub-lic orders, would be raised against him in derision? Certainly no voice on television: 'Sorry, the guy has a lot of fans. Sure, we know he's bad news, but you can't hurt people's feelings. They buy soap, too.' " Even when he wrote on subjects ostensibly literary, his comment was now becoming in-creasingly political. Louis Auchincloss wrote to tell him he thought it his finest essay yet, a brilliant piece. Late in the spring he went out to Long Island for a week of brainstorming with librettist Howard Dietz and com-poser Arthur Schwartz at Dietz's home. They had proposed he write the book for a new satirical musical based on a recent popular novel, *The King*

from Ashtabula. Since the success of *Visit* he had had numerous such propos-
als, including from Cole Porter and Richard Rodgers. Each time his agent
Harold Franklin urged him to do it. Each time he responded, "I have never
read the press of any musical in which the book was ever praised. It's always
the weak point. You know, 'Had it not been for a banal book by Gore Vidal
this would have soared.' " Despite the attractive company of Lucinda Bal-
lard, a theatrical costume designer and Deitz's wife, the week did not prove
productive. Each time Gore proposed an idea as they walked in Dietz's
lovely garden, Dietz, full of energy though suffering from the onset of
Parkinson's disease, and Schwartz, "solemn, rabbinical, and rather humor-
less," would shoot it down.

At Edgewater through the summer and fall he returned to *Julian*,
trying to set up the opening chapters. "No more movies for some time," he
had promised himself and Paul Bowles, "and perhaps, if things work as they
ought, I shall be novel-writing next year. I find I miss prose. It has been four
years since I have written anything but clattering dialogue. I persist for the
money: in another year I shall be financially independent. Also, it is delightful to be patronized as a corrupted hack by the corrupt hacks. I have never
been quite so pleased with myself." Actually, the summer at Edgewater was
dreary and wet. "I still have occasional attacks of my Roman fever—a
spiritual fever, that is, and I could, I think, live there till the end. But I am
disloyal to the house and the river: neither is at fault that it is in America."
Anaïs, eager to have his help, wrote a bitter account of her own Hollywood
disappointments, to which he responded sympathetically, though he also
teased her about the credibility of her diary. "No one will believe your
diaries, you know, which will insure you an immortal niche amongst the
fabulists: oh, to have it all ways! . . . Yes, Europe was wonderful. I had
the best four weeks of my life in Rome, seeing people I'd not seen in ten
years, recapturing *that* time, less the pain. . . . And I suddenly find myself
longing to live in Rome . . . the first urge I have had in eight years to be
any place but home. You are right about California. I tend to go mad there:
eat too much, drink too much (I am now thin, abstemious and quite uncon-
querable in spirit.) I am out of the MGM contract at last and I have no plans
for another picture."

By late 1958, despite his promise to himself and his general disinclination, he was working on another film. When he received a request from Sam
Spiegel, an Austrian-born independent producer whom he already knew

from Los Angeles, to write a movie version of Tennessee Williams's *Garden District,* he could not resist. Spiegel's 1954 production of *On the Waterfront* had been a commercial and artistic success. Tennessee had declined to do the adaptation himself. Soon after Spiegel telephoned Williams to buy the film rights for *Suddenly, Last Summer,* the second of the two *Garden District* plays, Gore, in early autumn 1958, joined Tennessee and Spiegel in Miami. "Sam was on a boat. I went to stay at the Dupont Plaza Hotel, and Tennessee was also there," Gore recalled, "and it was just to have a chat about the script and so on. I was being auditioned, I guess. Tennessee had insisted on me." When he received the assurance that he would be the sole scriptwriter, he agreed, partly as a favor to Tennessee. *Julian* went on the back burner again, as did a production of *March to the Sea.* A brash, aggressive producer whom some thought vulgar and undiplomatic, Spiegel soon signed Montgomery Clift, Elizabeth Taylor, and Katharine Hepburn for the principal roles. Clift, a movie actor of great talent, with Oscar nominations for *A Place in the Sun* and *From Here to Eternity,* whose alcoholism and homosexuality had devastated his personal life, had an apartment on the Upper East Side and sometimes cruised in some of Howard and Gore's circle. "Montgomery Clift was in love with the actor Kevin McCarthy, Mary McCarthy's brother," Gore recalled. Kevin "was seriously married but very fond of Monty. He was also upset because he thought Monty was killing himself." Gore found Spiegel a fussy, domineering producer, "always destructive and generally pointless. He loved the power of ordering script after script. On *Night of the Generals* I wrote, at his demand, a thousand pages. On the other hand, Sam was very intelligent, somewhat unusual in films."

Tennessee he was happy to see. The friendship remained strong, based on affection and a shared sense of humor, refracted through their awareness that a decade ago they had been relatively young together, though they saw less of one another since Gore had stopped going regularly to Key West. When Williams had an opening and a party, Gore was likely to be there. In London, Maria Britneva was a bond between them. They shared a group of New York friends and acquaintances, mostly on the Upper East Side, at Café Nicholson and at the round of parties and happenstance meetings in the area of East Fifty-fifth and East Fifty-eighth streets. Frankie Merlo, Tennessee's lover and still Howard's and Johnny Nicholson's friend, and Tennessee continued their relationship, though occasionally with great difficulty and some separations. Probably America's most famous playwright, Williams was certainly its most notorious. The raw emotional power of his dramatizations and subject matter had risen to the level of a cultural incitement. Since the success of *Streetcar* Williams's ascendancy had had simultaneously a complicated downward drift, mostly due to the fact that he could never again replicate that triumph, partly because American mainstream culture found his themes offensive. A deeply flawed craftsman and aesthetician who repeatedly dramatized versions of the same hysteria, by the late 1950s Williams, an addictive personality, sustained his nerves on a well-stocked pharmacopoeia of Seconal and sleeping pills. Success and stability were slipping away. Hysterically, though not inaccurately, he believed that many critics, and society in general, were eager to bring him down. That Spiegel wanted to make a major movie of *Suddenly, Last Summer* was both daring and prescient. It dramatized both late-1950s cultural repression and the incipient countercurrents that would radically change sexual politics in the 1960s.

Before returning to New York to work on the script. Gore went to Palm Beach with Tennessee to visit the Kennedys, vacationing at Joseph Kennedy's Palm Beach estate. Jackie, who had heard that Gore and Tennessee were in Miami, eagerly invited them to lunch, excited about the opportunity to meet the famous playwright. The rather apolitical Tennessee, who had heard of neither of the Kennedys, took Gore at his word that Jack was likely one day to be President. "I hadn't realized how long it was from Miami, so I drove. We were an hour late for lunch. The Bird was restive, blaming it on my driving. I said, 'I'm certainly not going to let you drive.' So we did a lot of quibbling on the way. Then we had a great lunch." When they arrived, Jack was target-shooting on the lawn, apparently with results that indicated he was a poor shot. Tennessee asked for the rifle and immediately shot three bull's-eyes. Jackie flattered the famous playwright, saying she was jealous of her half-brother Tommy, whom she mistakenly believed Tennessee had taken to Coney Island in 1951. As if already running for higher office, Jack, still a senator, praised one of Tennessee's less successful plays, *Summer and Smoke*. In a good mood, Tennessee whispered to Gore as, going in for lunch, they walked behind Jack, "Look at that ass." "You can't cruise our next President," Gore sternly said. To Williams the young couple looked far too attractive ever to qualify for the White House. If Gore had told Tennessee about the stirring of his own dormant political aspirations, the playwright presumably would have told him the same thing.

In September 1958 Gore went to California, "to get a director and star for his . . . play," Isherwood remarked in his diary. "I do like him. He is handsome, sad, sardonic, plump—quite Byronic in a way. . . . Gore's favorite quotation 'I am the Duchess of Malfi still.' He sees himself as an ex-champ, out of condition and punchy who still has a fight in him." Some of his fight was with the Beats, particularly Kerouac, whose success he resented, partly because he thought Kerouac's prose flaccidly antiliterary, almost incoherent. Also, if the public wanted to read Kerouac, why would they want to read him? "Gore regards me," Isherwood observed, "also as a neglected writer of quality, so he feels a bond between us." Gore also felt a bond, though of a thinner sort, with Mailer, at least in their mutual detestation of the Beats. Mailer had been unable to repeat the success of *The Naked and the Dead*. Both his second novel, *Barbary Shore* in 1951, and his third, *The Deer Park* in 1955, had been poorly received. Mailer had begun to redefine himself as a political and cultural critic, his new authorial persona soon to have its 1959 debut in *Advertisements for Myself* in which, as Gore had started to do, Mailer first found his distinctive nonfictional voice as an essayist. When Mailer, having decided to try for a theatrical production of his own adaptation of *The Deer Park*, looked for a helpful private audience for a reading of the play, he invited Gore and Montgomery Clift to join him and his wife, Adele, at their apartment on Perry Street in the Village. Gore's opinion as successful playwright would carry some weight. When Gore asked if he could bring Elaine Dundy, Mailer said yes. The Tynans had moved to New York in September 1958, Gore delighted that Ken had accepted *The New Yorker*'s offer that he try a two-year stint as its theater critic. Soon after his return from England in March, Gore had queried Tom Driberg, "What news of Ken, et al? or did I dream these wraiths in a nodding winter?" Suddenly, six months later, the Tynans were part of the New York scene, Ken as flamboyantly distinctive as ever, Elaine as energetically explosive, now herself the author of a successful novel. Gore saw "a good deal of the Tynans," he wrote to Driberg. "He has raised the level of criticism or rather indicated how it might be raised in New York, a hick town which attracts the world's venality if not affection. But I don't see the effect of his work lasting; we don't like that sort of thing." Eager to introduce them to his New York friends, he hosted a party in their honor in November 1958, guests shoulder to shoulder at the small East Fifty-fifth Street apartment, many of them theater distingués like Moss Hart, Ruth

Ford, Zachary Scott, Adolph Green, and Betty Comden, eager to meet the West End's *enfant terrible* who now was to have some of the fate of Broadway in his hands. "I gave a party for the Tynans," Gore wrote to Tom Driberg, "and it all went well until Ken, goaded beyond endurance, took Norman Mailer apart at supper."

In late autumn, at Mailer's apartment, Norman, Gore, Adele, and Clift each read a part. Elaine was the audience. When Gore, sometime before the reading, had told Sam Spiegel, with whom he was working in New York on the script of *Suddenly, Last Summer,* that Monty was to be there, Spiegel asked him to report back on Clift's condition. With constant talk of Clift's heavy drinking, Spiegel worried about his reliability. "And I said I would, knowing that of course I would lie if I found him drunk, which I did," Gore recalled. "So I lied to Spiegel with great joy and said, 'He was wonderful.' Spiegel deserved everything he got in this way." At first the reading went well. "Gore was very nice," Mailer remembered. "He was generous that night, as one can be when talking to an aspirant. He kept saying, 'Well, this is good, this really ought to go somewhere, and so forth and so on.' . . . He was almost always on the generous side. He protects his generous side and doesn't want people to know too much about it, and of course I loved his arrogance because it came with style. That was part of his charm." As the reading progressed, Clift, drinking, began to slur his words. He soon passed out. At that point Gore, at his own suggestion, began to read Clift's part. The play, which he had read in manuscript, he thought not bad at all. Elaine, who did not like it, began to express her criticism to Mailer, who tactfully, even gently, deflected her remarks, reminding her that it was a rough draft of a work in progress. Elaine, Mailer recalled, "was dynamite. You'd get along with her sometimes. Sometimes you'd have a terrible fight. Sometimes you wouldn't speak for half a year. Sometimes you'd be great friends again. Elaine's ten kittens in one bag." She was an honest kitten that night. More in sorrow than anger, as Mailer was bringing the reading to a close, she said, "Norman, this is shit!"

———————

Roman fever had touched Gore in May 1958, but he still felt passionately about Edgewater, in love with the house and location. He had no reason to think, when he returned from London in March and then from Rome at the end of May, that he would not be able to resume his Dutchess

County life. The house had been a blessing to him, even when he could barely afford it. By springtime 1958 the garden and lawn were resplendent, the house handsomely comfortable, much of it Howard's doing. Though it was a particularly wet summer, Gore easily resumed his usual work schedule, making progress with his plans for *Julian*. In the fall, urged by Bob Bingham, he became *The Reporter*'s drama critic, which he was to do for two years, the best of his reviews collected later in his first book of essays. Sam Spiegel began to keep him busy with calls and conferences about *Suddenly, Last Summer*, a draft of which he had under way by late summer. The writing of *Julian* was still on hold again. Soon he had no doubt that he genuinely disliked Spiegel, resented his interference, and had little respect for his abilities. Such, however, was the price for augmenting his bank account so that he might in the near future be free to return to fiction. If he resented paying the price, he still paid it energetically, as if he had no choice other than to give to whatever project to which he had committed himself his full focus. Also, despite the demands of these secondary, moneymaking projects, he kept time free to continue and even intensify his reading about *Julian*. He bought and absorbed every book on the subject he could get his hands on, and he returned to the New York Edition of Henry James, rereading much that he had read before.

Now, to his delight, he had someone to discuss James with. Before leaving for London late the previous fall, he had met in New York, probably through Andrew Chiappe, Frederick Wilcox Dupee, Gore's Dutchess County neighbor, a former Bard professor, now a well-known literary critic and Columbia University professor since 1948. The Dupees had recently moved from their Red Hook farmhouse into the newly purchased Wildercliff, a large, lovely riverfront house built in 1798, about ten miles south of Edgewater, sufficiently distant from the railroad tracks so that they were not disturbed by the train. "They bought Wildercliff for $45,000," their friend, the editor Jason Epstein, recalled. "It was like buying the Taj Mahal. Fred must have had a little family money. But they never had enough to paint it or furnish it." Gore had followed up their meeting by having Dupee sent a copy of *Messiah*, which arrived when Gore was still in London. The perceptive, ironic Columbia professor had replied with the well-phrased literary response that Gore eagerly looked for from a distinguished critic, an effective mixture of encouragement and honesty. "I can't say . . . that [*Messiah*] appeals to me as much as your other books, especially *Judgment of*

Paris. Is *Messiah too* fantastic for a good working fantasy?" If Gore would like, Dupee would be "glad to deliver a short lecture" on several of his theories of fantasy, "if you will bring your notebooks. . . . Or just come for dinner when you're in Barrytown and we'll talk about something else." Or they could get together for drinks in New York, where Dupee taught three days a week. Eager for literary talk, Gore found Dupee enchanting, the most intellectually interesting company he had ever had, someone whose sensibility and mind were permeated with and totally defined by his commitment to literary high culture. He seemed to have read everything. A slow, readily distracted writer, he had published in 1951 an excellent short book on Henry James.

Twenty years older than Gore, from a prominent Joliet, Illinois, family originally from New England, where his mother's family had been since colonial times, Dupee had been eager from childhood to assimilate into the Eastern intellectual establishment. At Yale he had been delighted to be among the elite, soon becoming friends with other lively students like Dwight Macdonald, with whom, along with Philip Rahv, he was to be one of the co-founders of the *Partisan Review* in 1934. Without much interest in or regard for politics, he had briefly imagined himself a left-wing labor organizer, working for the Communist Party on the New York waterfront, and was for some years a *New Masses* stalwart. From Yale he had gone briefly to Bowdoin College, then to Bard for almost twenty years, where the charismatic teacher impressed students and colleagues with his rueful charm, his delicate irony, his literary sensibility, the teacher rather than the scholar, whose most engaging métier was the classroom, the social gathering, the short essay, the tutorial. As her tutor and the director of her senior thesis at Bard, he had met his wife, Barbara Hughes. Nineteen years younger than he, "Andy" was from a working-class Irish-Catholic New Jersey family, her mother an alcoholic, her maternal grandfather, William Hughes, a self-made man who had become both a socialist and a United States senator. She and her Bard friends "admired and adored" Professor Dupee, a "very attractive, faintly sad and handsome man. . . . His nervousness, his tenseness, his grace were irresistible," Andy recalled. Petite, blue-eyed, a lively conversationalist with more courage than wisdom, Andy thought that he might as well marry her as someone else. It seemed the right thing—exciting, bold, pleasurable, a kind of triumph. Fred, who liked the idea, was soon also in love. It would be easy for him to think the changes would be for the better.

By 1958, now with two young children, they had been married twelve years. "It was great marrying Fred," among other reasons, "because he had all these wonderful friends—Nancy and Dwight and Nathalie and Philip Rahv, for example." Andy liked and admired Dwight Macdonald, the radical political analyst and perceptive *New Yorker* essayist, though "they all drank a lot and Dwight later drank too much and went to pieces." Once they had dinner at the apartment of the poet Delmore Schwartz, whose 1938 volume *In Dreams Begin Responsibilities* had established him as one of America's best-known young poets and who had succeeded Rahv in 1943 as editor of *Partisan Review*. He and Dupee were old friends. "At dinner, Delmore said to Fred, 'I always thought of you as someone who suffered more than anyone.' " Fred responded, " 'Oh, I'm very happy.' "

Soon after they met in spring 1958, Gore invited the Dupees to Edgewater. Andy found him enchanting. After numbers of martinis, they drove over to Wildercliff, where they kept drinking. The evening was convivial, happy. Gore seemed to Andy "very imperial and Roman and grand," handsome and glamorous. They began to tell one another the stories of their lives. Fred, drunk and exhausted, soon went to bed. "Gore staggered out to drive home." Andy urged him to stay overnight in their guest bedroom upstairs. He refused. As he left, he kissed her passionately, or so she felt it. She fell in love with him "right there and then." For a while she could not get him out of her mind. Aware of his television and movie career, the Dupees were at first suspicious of his intellectual credentials. Both avid readers, they had not yet bought a television, partly out of principle, mostly out of intellectual snobbishness, and they had indeed vaguely heard of Gore before they met him as someone who wrote television dramas. They were not impressed with his media career, though Fred, always the starry-eyed idolator from a Midwestern small town when it came to the socially elite and to Hollywood stars, held this against Gore only to the degree that it kept him from writing serious literature. Eager to be the writer he defined himself as, temporarily enchained to the money-producing mill, Gore found Fred's company delightful and salutary. With a delicate mentoring touch Fred urged him to return to novels. They began seeing one another regularly. Dupee soon became one of his closest, most admired friends.

It was a friendship complicated, though more so for others, especially Andy, than for Gore, by Dupee's balance of contradictions, the inconsistencies of his life and his difficulty in sustaining its varied elements. Charming, good-looking, slim, somewhat delicate in appearance, with engaging eyes, Dupee had instinctively raised vulnerability to an art form, eager to be protected by others from whatever threatened his stability, his happiness. Two of the threats came from drink and sex. The former was an occupational and generational hazard. Drunk, Dupee could be unpleasant, aggressive, angry, less than charming. The latter had the hazardous discomfort of ambivalence; the difficulty of sustaining both loyalty to his wife and his other desires caused him occasional embarrassment and much distress. Constantly concerned that people would know about his furtive sexual life, he found the danger of exposure exciting enough, or punishing enough, so that he did the things that would ensure that many of his Hudson Valley friends and some of his New York colleagues knew. When, late in spring 1958, he came to dinner at Edgewater to meet Frederic Prokosch, who had come with Jack Bady for the day from New York, Dupee, Bady recalled, invited him outdoors to show him the stars and explain the constellations. The dinner had not gone well. The Bard guests had been condescendingly disdainful of Prokosch, holding against him his popular success and his expatriatism. When Fred and Jack Bady went outside together, Bady had the impression that Dupee was flirting with him. So too did Gore and Prokosch, who joked and bantered lightly about it afterward. Unlike Gore, Dupee was deeply vulnerable and somewhat romantic. Capable of sudden enthusiasms, he knew how to fall unhappily in love, usually with inappropriate people, none of whom threatened his marriage. Deeply divided, often guilty, never having come to some sort of reasonable détente with society's prohibitions, he felt the necessity to keep up appearances, to subject himself and his family to the strains of his divided personality, his life as only a partly successful balancing act. At home Andy, always forgiving, deeply in love and deeply loved, provided balance, comfort, a sustaining family life that Fred embraced. Lively, literary, and, unlike her husband, not only political but truly radical, the essential and attractive caretaker, she made the marriage and the family work. Not without flirtations and attractions of her own, Andy partied, laughed, argued at home and in the general Bard College and Hudson Valley society with an intensity and vivaciousness that made her presence a complement to her husband's. It was a world they shared. When Gore came into Fred's life, he came into hers as well.

For over half a decade Gore's life at Edgewater had revolved around Alice Astor, John Latouche, and visits from his grandmother, as well as the refurbishing of the house and its transformation into a comfortable small mansion whose location on the river made it memorable. Most of the major people of those Edgewater years were now dead, distant, or disabled. The Newmans had not become part of the mise-en-scène until 1955. There were still minor improvements to be made on the house, though the problem of the small kitchen was never solved, even though it and the house had been well run for the last two years by the Wheelers, two of Alice's servants whom Gore had employed after her death and whom Howard and Gore later fired when he found them more interested in adjusting the house to their own schedule than to that of its occupants. Starting in mid-1958 Gore's life at Edgewater entered a second stage. His expansive world substantially widened. There were still some Bard College friends, especially the Weisses, and Bard College visitors, such as Robert Lowell, who came over. People visited regularly from New York, some of those he worked with on films or had worked with on television, and literary friends, including Louis Auchincloss, whom he saw, however, more frequently in town. But there were now, he discovered, more people in the country to visit and have visit him.

By the end of the year Gore's Edgewater and Hudson Valley social life was in full flourish, as it was to continue, more or less, for almost five years, especially with the Dupees and Richard and Eleanor Rovere. With the Dupees he discussed mostly literature. Soon after the party for the Tynans, Dupee, "in his cups," said, "always repeats: we had Jim Farrell, you have Mailer . . . one every generation . . . nothing changes." With Rovere, a political analyst and investigative reporter of distinction, the Washington correspondent for *The New Yorker,* who lived and worked in a handsome, modest house in Rhinebeck between visits to Washington, Gore discussed mainly politics. Well connected, especially interested in Democratic Party affairs, essentially conservative, Rovere had a long friendship with Arthur Schlesinger, Jr., with whom he had collaborated on a book, *The General and the President,* about MacArthur and Truman. Gore met the Roveres in 1958 as they were all going through the wedding-reception line of the daughter of Bard College's president. Soon guests at Edgewater, the Roveres "found Gore fascinating and funny and very vain. He would often preen," Eleanor Rovere noticed, "and he couldn't pass a mirror without straightening his hair or combing it. But he was redeemingly self-conscious and ironic about his own vanity and was very, very funny about it." With the Dupees they often saw Gore on weekends at Wildercliff, in Rhinebeck, and at Edgewater, where the Roveres were delighted to meet other guests, often from the entertainment world, particularly Claire Bloom, who soon came up with her husband-to-be, the actor Rod Steiger, and the Newmans. It was heady, amusing, but also somewhat exotically suspect to intellectuals who were not used to celebrities. Often bored, even with guests of distinction, Gore would sometimes on Sunday mornings take them to meet the Dupees or the Roveres. One day he brought Isherwood to Wildercliff to meet Fred. When Isherwood, Andy recalls, saw that the Dupees wrote telephone numbers on the wall in a small alcove where the telephone was kept, he wrote his number on the wall. "It seemed both a shy and an engaging thing to do. 'Please call me, too,' it seemed to say."

When Gore had no weekend guests, he sometimes came alone on Sunday mornings to Wildercliff, where he and the Dupees sat for hours reading newspapers, talking, drinking. Guests at Wildercliff often became Gore's guests also, and some of them friends. The Dupees introduced him to the literary critic Lionel Trilling, one of Fred's colleagues at Columbia, and to Trilling's wife, Diana, who had begun to assert herself as a literary reviewer for *The Nation*. Lionel, Gore liked and respected. Diana he thought pretentious, ludicrously self-important. Philip Rahv, through whom he began an association with the *Partisan Review*, had Gore's immediate respect, and soon his affection. A Ukrainian-born Jewish literary and political dynamo who had come to America as a young man, and a longtime friend of Fred's, Rahv was an essayist of distinction, one of the founding editors of *Partisan Review*, the man Mary McCarthy had left when she married Edmund Wilson. Gore admired Rahv's pithy wit, his sharp one-liners, his political and literary intelligence, though he did not at all share his now-attenuated Marxist-Trotskyite politics. When Vidal referred to George Steiner's recent book, *The Death of Tragedy*, Rahv commented, "One of the get-rich-quick boys." Rahv invited Gore to contribute to and support *Partisan Review*, both of which he did, the former with an essay, "Love, Love, Love," the latter with a check for a thousand dollars. Gore found Saul Bellow, who shared a house in nearby Tivoli with Ralph Ellison, "standoffish with me. But couldn't tell whether it was anti-fag or commercial success or both." Bellow's intellect he admired and enjoyed, especially his sharp comments about books and people. *Dangling Man* and *The Victim*, Bellow's two early novels, he thought deserved their success, *The Adventures of Augie March*, which he admired, a little less so. The less explicitly

intellectual Ellison, whose *Invisible Man* had won the National Book Award
the year after *The Adventures of Augie March*, he found charming, his sense
of high propriety both engaging and amusing, except when he talked endlessly, boringly, about some subject that interested him. One day Ellison and
Paul de Man, the Yale University literary critic and deconstructionist, came
by. "Ellison was a very proper man," Andy Dupee recalled. "To get a rise
out of him, Gore teased him" about the contrast between Ellison's formal
manners and prejudiced white attitudes about black culture, "and then
danced with Ralph's wife, Fanny, in a very suggestive way. De Man and his
wife looked very proper, and probably tried not to notice." Gore especially
liked Ellison's wife. Whatever the provocation, Ellison never rose to the
bait.

At Edgewater in summer 1958 the Dupees introduced Gore to two of
their younger friends, a married couple, both in publishing, Barbara Zim-
merman and Jason Epstein, well-educated children of successful, assimilated
Ashkenazic Jewish families in the Boston area. Barbara had come to New
York in 1950 at the age of twenty-one from a literary education at Radcliffe.
In 1951 at Doubleday, where they both worked, she had met Jason Epstein,
a recent Columbia University graduate who was serving as a publishing
intern. At sixteen he had entered Columbia during one of its most expansively exciting times, when the combination of older students whose educa-
tions had been delayed by the war and an exemplary literary-intellectual
faculty created one of the golden moments of American higher education.
With Columbia his campus, New York City his world, Jason flourished. His
four years at Morningside Heights had been the most formative of his life,
exposing him to great minds and great books, filling him with enthusiasm
for the continuing education of the mind. "The best years of my life," he
recalled. "I never got over them." Publishing, in the still-old-fashioned
world of the fifties, seemed the perfect venue, a world in which literary and
intellectual values maintained their traditional prominence. Bestsellers supported but did not dominate editorial decisions. A bright intern could rise
quickly. "I thought I'd go to work for a week in publishing. I didn't want to
write a Ph.D. I didn't want to be a teacher." At Columbia his favorite
teacher, among figures like Lionel Trilling, Richard Chase, Mark Van
Doren, and Quentin Anderson, had been Andrew Chiappe, whom Barbara
thought "a slightly tragic, slightly comic figure and a nice man. . . . He
was hard to be fond of because he was a very isolated, lonely, needy guy.

Very dandyish, rather arch and very funny." Through Chiappe, the best man at the Epsteins' wedding in 1953, they met Fred Dupee, whom Jason found "enchanting, indescribable. One of the most intelligent people I've ever known." Soon Jason published Dupee's *Henry James* in the new Anchor-Doubleday paperback series which, with Chiappe as consultant, he initiated. "Fred was wonderfully attractive, very, very good-looking, and brilliant. The mind was wonderful. I wish he'd written more. What he wrote was wonderful, but he should have done more. That was the pity. The essays were so good. If he had had a little more edge to him, he could have been Orwell or someone like that. He had the right sensibility. Something held him back." By the mid-fifties the Epsteins and Dupees were warm friends, and both couples, intensely literary, had connections to people who were already part of Vidal's world. Gore, Barbara Epstein remembered, "had movie-star looks. . . . He had already published quite a number of books. We all fell in love with him. . . . We were all so young. I was twenty-eight, Gore thirty-three, Jason twenty-nine. We were all very adorable." With the Dupees they went regularly to Edgewater, usually in the afternoons, each couple with a young child whom Gore mostly ignored. "Jason and Gore liked one another and were very good friends. They had similar temperaments in the sense of being very anarchic and funny and smart."

———

Working on the script of *Suddenly, Last Summer* at Edgewater into the winter of 1958–59, Gore was happy to escape the cold weather for a Florida visit to consult with Tennessee and Sam Spiegel. Filming soon began in England, the outdoor scenes shot in Spain, the locations partly determined by Elizabeth Taylor's tax considerations. Gore kept away from both filming locations. He made some progress with *Julian*, whose completion, he realized, would take at least two, perhaps three years of concentrated writing. But his focus on the novel was partly undermined by his increasingly revived interest in doing something political, both in literature and in life, though soon the two could not be separated. With something political in mind, he soon revived discussions of a television drama based on episodes in the early life of his grandfather, which Manulis had encouraged years before. The possibility of a brief, in fact singular, revival of his career as a television dramatist he found appealing. He was soon at work on a script that he had ready for performance by late fall 1959. As a dramatist, script-writer, and novelist, he had opportunities to be in the public eye, some of which he regularly took, particularly appearances on radio and television talk shows. By late 1959 he had appeared numbers of times on the most widely viewed, Jack Paar's *Tonight Show*. At best, talk-show hosts thought him good for their ratings, at worst a class act mixed in with the talking chimpanzees, with one of which, the infamous J. Fred Muggs, he literally found himself paired early one morning on Dave Garroway's *Today*. Hand-some, articulate, distinctively himself, the camera liked Gore. Despite the occasional butterflies in his stomach, he enjoyed the opportunity to be famous, or at least notorious. Though he made such television appearances as an author-dramatist, his remarks, especially with the wide-ranging Paar, were often political. And he and Paar liked one another. With the young David Susskind, who courted controversy in a pioneering, issue-oriented talk show on local New York television, he was even more at home, wel-comed regularly for long discussions. Producers and talk-shows hosts liked his charm, his wit, his good looks, his ability to talk casually and interest-ingly about well-known people, and his talent for the acceptably irreverent, effectively expressed. If such entertaining talk was ultimately about very little or even nothing, that hardly mattered. It cost him little. He simply talked, with professional self-projection, his presence and ego expansive, gratified. A public figure of sorts, it made sense to stay in the public eye, if the price were small. Like a professional performer, he kept his nerves and nervousness behind the curtain.

That summer, in late August and September, he spent three weeks in Provincetown, on Cape Cod, which he had never visited before, thinking through a new play on a political subject. He had conceived the play in its basic outlines while strolling on an abysmally hot day in July on the lawn at Edgewater, having just reread Henry James's *The Tragic Muse*. He imagined the structure of the play as a Jamesian series of reversals and exposures. The main characters came fully to mind. Soon after his return from the Cape, he wrote the first draft of *The Best Man* with his usual swiftness. Hoping to have it on Broadway early in 1960, he began to push the wheels that would make it move into place, the first step getting the play into the hands of the producer Roger L. Stevens. When Stevens's young assistant, Lyn Austin, read it and immediately told her boss, "We must do it," the production assessments and process began, with the target an early-1960 Broadway premiere. Gore himself had in mind the possibility of being before the public not only in literature but in life. The visit with Tennessee in 1958 to the Kennedys at Palm Beach had begun to stir his dormant political ambitions. If Jack Kennedy could be a senator, why could he not be something equal or even better? Why should he not carry on his grandfather's legacy? By early 1959 it had become clear that Kennedy would be a formidable candidate for the Democratic presidential nomination in 1960. The television drama based on T. P. Gore, to be called *The Indestructible Mr. Gore,* and to appear as a live broadcast on the NBC *Sunday Showcase* in December 1959, with Gore himself as narrator, had originated in his mind three years earlier. But his decision to proceed with it now may have been inseparable from his burgeoning political preoccupations.

At Hyde Park he visited Eleanor Roosevelt, with whom he had a connection through his father and whom he now admired considerably more than he had ever admired her husband. When in spring 1959 he purchased for a modest sum the Hyde Park Playhouse, a summer theater, in an effort to save it from extinction, he got Mrs. Roosevelt's attention. Interested in local cultural affairs, she invited him to her home, where he quickly discovered he had a cool, perceptive, and amiably patronizing great lady with whom to discuss politics. Why not consider running for Congress from the 29th Congressional District? he mused in her presence. Heavily Republican, it had not elected a Democrat in fifty years. It might be worth a try. She did not at first encourage him, suspicious that his views might still be more T. P. Gore than FDR. She soon let him know that she would support his candidacy, which, as he thought about it, began to seem to him feasible. His face and name were familiar to many from TV. His political background and instincts were strong. He was an excellent public speaker. With his handsome house at Edgewater, he was very much a Dutchess County resident. With the Democratic Party so used to defeat, the power brokers might find him attractive enough to carry the banner, if not to victory then to an advantageous loss. Perhaps he could revive the political career he thought he had relinquished when he had published *The City and the Pillar.* If it was wishful thinking, it had some solid basis in the reality of the moment. If it was incompatible with his resumption of his career as a novelist and if it would certainly put on hold again the writing of *Julian,* this did not seem sufficient deterrent. If the question of how his sexual identity might affect his political opportunities and what such a change in career would mean to

Howard ever arose, the answers made no difference to his decision. After some discussion with the crucial people, particularly Joe Hawkins, the Democratic Party county chairman, it was clear to him that the nomination was his for the asking. During the late fall of 1959, when *The Best Man* went into rehearsal, Gore had a secret known only to a very few: he had decided to run for Congress.

CHAPTER thirteen

Something to Say

1960–1963

SUDDENLY ONLY TWO things were on his mind—politics and the theater. They were inseparable, though. *The Best Man* had been conceived as an expression of political ideas. If it were successful, it would provide him with all the advantages of a Broadway hit and a highly visible platform from which to pursue the Gore passion for practical politics. No matter how hard he had tried to be just literary, financial exigency had forced him to be literary in an extraliterary way. He had no intention of living in a garret. Life without a certain modest amount of freedom and comfort seemed unacceptable, and comfort was readily obtainable. His "hack" writing had provided that. Though there was only a middling equity in reserve, he had no special desire to be rich, his highest fantasy of wealth that he would never again have to worry about the cost of having his manuscripts typed. He was confident that if necessary he could always knock out a screenplay assignment. A Broadway hit, as *Visit* had been, would take care of some years of financial need and provide him security for the three years he needed for *Julian,* the first two chapters of which he had written at last in April 1959. Victor Weybright soon agreed to publish in a Signet paperback original, to be called *Three*, a reprint of *Williwaw*, *A Thirsty Evil*, and the first appearance of the *Julian* fragment, scheduled for spring 1962. When Gore showed the chapters to Louis Auchincloss, he got strong encouragement. "It is now your bounden duty to drop everything . . . and *get on with Julian*. It is just as good as your own outrageous conceited estimate of it."

But the political siren sang, the temptation to try to metamorphose into an actual officeholder suddenly more strongly felt than it had been since his discussions years before with his grandfather about the New Mexico option. His attempt to go to Washington to fight for justice had begun, at least as an idea, as early as 1956, during the Stevenson campaign against Eisenhower. Gore attempted to help Stevenson and the local Dutchess County Democrats by getting Kennedy, a contender for the vice-presidential nomination, to make an appearance in the district. "DEAR GORE," the Massachusetts senator had telegraphed, "AS I AM OBLIGED TO MAKE TRIP TO THE WEST AT REQUEST OF STEVENSON HEADQUARTERS IT WILL BE IMPOSSIBLE FOR ME TO COME TO POUGHKEEPSIE. I HOPE YOU WILL EXPRESS MY REGRETS TO THE PEOPLE THERE WITH BEST WISHES JACK KENNEDY." The Dutchess County Democratic leaders knew Vidal as an enthusiastic supporter with friends in the highest political places. He had sometime late in the fall confided to Jackie his plan to run for Congress. Jack thinks it's a marvelous idea, she wrote to him, urging him to consult with her husband. The two of them could decide when would be the best time for Jack to speak in his behalf, probably, she thought, nearer to the election than March or April. She had been Gore's guest for an evening in New York and gratefully appreciated his having taken her to a party at the Scotts' and introducing her to the Tynans. It had been a great thrill for which she thanked him effusively and signed with her usual XO (hugs and kisses) Jackie.

Though he had supported Stevenson in two previous elections, he admired Kennedy. He had no doubt that Kennedy would win the nomination and election, and saw himself running quite compatibly, both ideologically and temperamentally, on the same ticket. Also, familiarity bred a desire for power for himself. Perhaps his own turn was coming, at least his opportunity for some high office. Why should not the Exeter schoolboy who had been "the senator from Virginia" be the congressman from the 29th District? Of course there were obstacles. His private life might be used against him, and the district was heavily Republican. Both, he thought, could be managed, if not overcome. After a brief discussion with Kennedy about Jack's promiscuous sex life, Gore felt reassured. They don't dare, Kennedy told him. Otherwise you'll do the same to them. Gore himself saw that the best way to deal with voter-registration odds was to be famous or at least widely recognized. His television appearances on network talk shows helped. If he were to have another Broadway success, he would be in even greater demand. If the play dramatized contemporary American national politics, the propinquity between that subject and his own congressional campaign had to be noticed.

Besides, he now felt he had something to say. The message was slightly to the left of liberal, to be measured less in relation to the liberal wing of the Democratic Party than by the great distance he had come from his grandfather's conservatism. Though some radical ideas and impulses were simmering within him, his intent was to provide reasonable new ideas, a mixture of common sense and intellectual perception. Philosophically he was now closer to Franklin Roosevelt than to T. P. Gore, particularly on economic issues. If the government were going to take such great sums in taxes out of his pockets, he felt it should at least spend the money on reasonable programs that would benefit the public, the most important of which, he believed, should be federal funds for education. Except for its small Northeastern liberal establishment, the Republican Party still defined itself in opposition to the New Deal. Except for local porkbarreling, so too did T. P. Gore's heirs, the Southern Democratic oligarchy, whose major concern was to keep power in white hands. Civil rights was the enemy at home. Abroad, for the right and center of both parties, and for the Republican liberals, the enemy was international Communism. Vast portions of the government budget went with bipartisan support to military defense, to the great profit of the powerful defense industry. In Korea we had fought a war to an embarrassing stalemate to prevent Communist expansion. At home we had experienced Senator Joseph McCarthy's campaign to keep the Communist conspiracy from turning America red. Adlai Stevenson had lost the two most recent presidential elections to Dwight Eisenhower, a bland, hands-off President who kept the Republican right and left in perfect anti-Communist, pro-defense, cool-on-civil-rights balance. It was a winning formula John Kennedy admired for practical reasons. If he could add to it youth, "vigor"—a favorite Kennedy buzzword—and the assertion that it was time for a change, he might be able to defeat the likely Republican candidate, Vice President Richard Nixon.

Kennedy, who had few ideas, let alone new ones, looked to charisma and political organization. Vidal would have been happy to rely on charisma *and* political organization. He had some of the first but little of the second. He also was challenging a well-entrenched Republican incumbent, J. Ernest Wharton, a colorless, fifty-year-old, semiarticulate archconservative dentist and dairy famer from Columbia County, in an overwhelmingly Republican district. And, though he hoped to win, Gore had no doubt that, to whatever extent he was in the race for personal satisfaction, he was also there because he believed that ideas counted and that he had an invaluable opportunity to contribute to a public discourse in which the commitment of the Founding Fathers to open discussion would be realized in political debate. Unlike Jack Kennedy, he had a strong residual idealism, especially on issues of justice, partly an expression of his intellectual honesty and his determination never to falsify ideas. Intellect and ideas were sacred. So too were first principles. It was not a self-definition that even in the best of practical circumstances offered much hope for political success. Kennedy knew what had to be done to get votes, including manufacturing a nonexistent "missile gap." Vidal knew how to articulate with witty precision ideas and arguments he believed in. He was to put his strongest emphasis on advocating federal aid for education and American recognition of China. In broader terms he advocated dialogue with one's enemies, the movement toward eliminating nuclear weapons, a smaller defense budget, strong antipollution measures, and the abolition of capital punishment. If these were not necessarily winning views in the 29th Congressional District, they were certainly provocative ones. If they were not radical ideas, they were definitely to the left of much of the party that would nominate him. Whatever the reasons to be pessimistic about the electoral process, he was not. Something within him, perhaps beyond reason, had shaped him to believe that it was his moral responsibility to try to improve things, and that Americans, with better leadership, would respond to a call to justice and common sense.

When rehearsals for *The Best Man* began in January 1960, Gore had already known for some months that the New York State Democratic convention, when it met in April, would offer him, and he would accept, its congressional nomination for the 29th District. The statewide party bosses would approve whatever candidate the leaders of the 29th District, which included Dutchess and parts of four neighboring counties, agreed on. The district had been heavily gerrymandered to favor the Republicans. In the late fall of 1959 Vidal met with Joe Hawkins, a ruggedly handsome Poughkeepsie politician, a traditional mainstream Democrat with a keen sense of practical politics, who had been alerted by mutual friends to their eminent young neighbor's interest in the nomination. Probably the 29th District Democratic Party leaders knew that Vidal's skills as a playwright and screenwriter had enough of a political dimension for him to have been invited in 1957 to the White House—an invitation he had accepted—by Eisenhower's chief of staff to help prepare a draft of the President's response to Governor Orval Faubus when he threatened to defy legal orders to desegregate Arkansas schools. Hawkins, whom Patsy Walsh, one of his colleagues, recalled as "a typical Irish politician, down to earth and cigar-smoking," liked what he saw and heard. It was the beginning of a working friendship. Eight years older than Gore, with flashing bright-blue eyes, dark hair, and a cheerful sense of humor, a party loyalist who lived and breathed politics, Hawkins dominated the district's Democratic organization. One of his political co-conspirators, William Walsh, who had known Gore since 1950, when he had served as the bank's lawyer for the purchase of Edgewater, recalls that he brought Hawkins and Gore together for lunch at the Nelson House in Poughkeepsie in late fall 1959. Desperate for a creditable candidate to make a respectable run, Hawkins felt he had his man. Within a short time the arrangement was sealed. In return for the nomination Gore committed himself to do his honorable best. Hawkins had good reason to be impressed. The grandson of a famous senator, the young man looked impressively telegenic; he spoke vigorously and persuasively; and he knew, or knew people who knew, the elite of the Democratic Washington political world, from Eleanor Roosevelt to John Kennedy. Though knowledgeable on national issues, he would need to acquaint himself with the concerns of a district of dairy farmers, but that seemed easily within reach. If he had any liability, it was that he might not have or be able to simulate the common touch, to act on the wisdom that wit and intellect are counterproductive in American politics. Still, Hawkins had no doubt that Gore was the best that the 29th District Democrats could do, and Vidal in absolute terms had many attractions. Registration statistics, not the candidate, were the obstacle.

Like millions of others, Hawkins probably saw in mid-December on NBC's *Sunday Showcase* Vidal's *The Indestructible Mr. Gore,* one of the last television dramas broadcast live, with Gore himself as narrator. With the help of the producer, Robert Alan Arthur, whom Gore had worked with before and whom he respected, he had created a script that was stunningly effective in conveying the character of young T. P. Gore in a dramatic presentation representing both the personal life and political hopes of the Senator-to-be. The Senator's past and his grandson's present were inextricably mixed into the foreground of the teleplay. As narrator, Gore appeared regularly on camera, himself a character of sorts in the drama, an emotionally engaged voice-over, the intermediary between the story and its audience. As much there as the characters, played by William Shatner, E. G. Marshall, and Inger Stevens, the narrator by association inevitably projected his own political credentials. The performers themselves were anxious, aware that this was live television, without the security of videotape. When he took Inger Stevens's hands in his, he was surprised that they were dry. " 'Are you really calm?' And she said, 'I'm not,' and she was trembling." E. G. Marshall "kept trying to drive me crazy. It was live, and I had no cards. I was going to have a TelePrompTer, and it broke down. So there I had eight million people watching me, and I had no preparation because I hadn't learned the lines. . . . Marshall, who never knew his lines, would always be seated at a table, and his dialogue would be in front of him. When we got to that technical run-through, they had patched up something. Not quite the cues I'd expected but it wasn't too bad, only you could see me squinting, trying to read the lines from the thing. . . . Marshall said, 'Don't worry, Gore. It's only television.' When I got to my scene with him, E. G. went up on his lines. Very satisfactory."

In his teledrama Gore purposely exonerates his grandfather in the story of the blind girl's pregnancy. Vidal presents the claim as false and T. P. Gore's opposition to a shotgun wedding heroic and principled. Gore had multiple reasons for tampering with the truth. The most important was that his grandmother, increasingly ill, suffering from a debilitating case of Parkinson's disease, would be watching the program. Also, it would not serve his own image to have his grandfather so depicted. With one exception, the Senator's outraged brother Dixie, this was the official family version everyone wanted to hear and which Gore himself wished were true. Dixie let his nephew know he did not like the falsification. The program deserved and received superb reviews, in which Dot took great pleasure. In April 1960, during a short visit to Washington to publicize *The Best Man*,

Gore saw her briefly. "She had two or three strokes and got over each one till the last," he recalled. "She was shaky. She shook to death, literally. She couldn't stay still. They wouldn't give her enough drugs. So with the shaking, she had a heart attack. The doctor was the same one who used to give my mother morphine. Dot took some Demerol, but it wasn't enough, and she wanted more. She would cry out for the Demerol, and the doctor would say, 'Oh, no, it will be habit-forming.' I did my best to try and get some black-market Demerol, but I didn't know how. And she wanted to die." Nina, who had seen the telecast, wrote from Southampton, "I loved the way Dad finally came off, and I loved how soaringly happy it made Mother—you should be very pleased and proud."

Soon, with Joe Hawkins's encouragement, Gore had begun to accept invitations to speak at district events. Within four months he had made at least thirty appearances, mostly before business groups and fraternal organizations, especially when the word got out that the well-known playwright and television personality was available. The most frequent questions addressed to him were "What's Jack Paar really like?" and what kind of sexual pervert was Sebastian in *Suddenly, Last Summer,* which had been released in December 1959 to reviews mostly hostile on moral grounds but to great box-office success. Jack Paar, he would answer, is the same off-camera as he is on. About Sebastian he would be good-humoredly evasive, on the assumption that anyone who asked the question already knew he was homosexual. Anyway, discussions of political ideas needed to be avoided until he declared his candidacy, though his appearance late in the year before a group of Dutchess County judges allowed him to deliver a cleverly argued, powerfully phrased speech in a debate on capital punishment whose conclusion declared that it "is nothing but the blood vengeance society takes upon one of its members. Society's anger is often justified: there have been terrible crimes. But society's vengeance merely compounds the crime." The audience probably did not fully appreciate the self-reflexive humor of his example of how sorely most of us are tempted at one time or another to murder someone. "On the morning when I have had an unjustified bad notice in the newspapers (all my bad notices are unjustified), I have often drifted into a bloodthirsty reverie," he told them. "Suppose I got on the train at Darien with Mr. Orville Prescott of the *Times.* I sit next to him in the club car. He doesn't know what I look like despite his venomous attack. I engage him in conversation. We have a martini. I slip a tablet of deadly poison into his. He takes it. I get off at the next stop. He dies in horrible agony at home that night and no one suspects me because I was in New York. I have pulled off any number of brilliant crimes in my daydreams. But why don't I do them in life? Because I am stopped by my moral sense."

Fortunately, Orville Prescott was not the *New York Times* drama reviewer. *The Best Man* opened at the Morosco Theater on March 31, 1960, to unanimously positive reviews, especially from the *Times*'s estimable Brooks Atkinson. From the moment the cast had assembled for rehearsals at an untenanted New York theater, the participants, especially co-producer Lyn Austin, knew it would be a success. "We were all sitting in this space, on the stage actually," Austin recalled, "and we began the reading, and I had this sort of tingle. You could just tell that it was coming right off the page. You knew then." Before he'd even had script in hand, Gore had gone the previous summer to the most powerful New York theatrical producer, Roger Stevens, partly because Stevens, a Democratic partisan, had a strong interest in politics. An active Stevenson supporter, in 1956 he had been chairman of the candidate's finance committee. As a young man in the 1930s Stevens had made a fortune in real estate in Detroit and had become the leading sponsor of the Ann Arbor Drama Festival. From there, in 1949, he came to Broadway, where he co-produced a hit musical version of *Peter Pan,* the first of dozens of profitable hits during the next decade. In 1951 he became famous as the leader of a real-estate syndicate that bought the Empire State Building for $50 million, an astronomical sum then. Probably Gore had met Stevens in 1957, at the time of the Broadway success of *Visit to a Small Planet,* perhaps not until summer 1959. Usually Lyn Austin was the first reader of manuscripts under consideration by the Playwrights' Company. But Stevens, she recalled, "had already read it and had pretty much decided to do it. . . . I guess he read it first, because it was a pretty prestigious offering and he respected Gore." Actually, Gore and Stevens had had dinner at the Colony to discuss the idea of the play before a word of it had been written. A big, balding, soft-spoken, impressive man, Stevens immediately liked the idea. From Provincetown, in August, Gore sent him the first act. Stevens was enthusiastic. He felt the same way about the second and third acts. In New York in late summer there was an instant rapport between Stevens and Gore and between Lyn Austin and Gore. Excited about the play and its author, the producers were determined to do everything in their power to have the success they believed the play merited.

There were the two usual major concerns—casting and financing. Austin took charge of the former, Stevens the latter. An experienced, highly-regarded director, Joe Anthony, whom Stevens approached in October, agreed to direct. Having decided that Melvyn Douglas would be perfect for the leading role of William Russell, the Adlai Stevenson–like candidate, Lyn pursued him relentlessly, despite his reluctance to take on the demands of a Broadway play. Everyone had assured her that she would never get him. Gradually she wore down his resistance, appealing to his political values as a liberal Democrat, married as he was to Helen Gahagan Douglas, the former congresswoman from California who had been savaged by Nixon as "the Pink Lady." Finally, after a series of calls from her Swiss hotel that threatened to preempt her mountain holiday, Lyn persuaded him to sign on. With Douglas in place, Lee Tracy, a veteran Broadway and film actor who was to receive an Oscar nomination for his performance in the film version of *The Best Man,* agreed to play the Harry Truman–like character; Frank Lovejoy, the character loosely based on Richard Nixon; Leora Dana, the crucial role of William Russell's estranged wife. When the cast and author met for the first time, mutual respect was high, camaraderie warm, the expectation of success strong. It seemed to all the participants time for a sophisticated play about American presidential politics that treated politicians as complicated human beings with multiple agendas, all of which embodied their strengths and weaknesses as people. None of the principals, the performers immediately saw, were either all good or all bad. The read-through went well. The lines were crisp, witty, intelligent, the characterizations interesting, the structure of the play logically and emotionally driven both by external events and inner necessities. A Stevenson supporter, Douglas felt he could do an inspired job with his role.

If the underlying message was that American politics safeguarded the republic by excluding the worst candidates even if at the price of excluding the best, everyone recognized that the premise was plausible, perhaps even convincing. After reading the script, which Gore had sent him, Jack Kennedy said to Jackie, in regard to William Russell's womanizing, " 'Is Gore writing about me?' " She passed the gist of the conversation along to the playwright. Gore's depiction of Kennedy's two rivals appealed to the presidential hopeful. When Kennedy told Gore that "in a campaign, we don't have all that much time to talk about the meaning of it all," Gore agreed but said that "no audience would understand the shorthand that politicians talk

in." Neither Douglas nor Roger Stevens seemed especially bothered by
Adlai Stevenson's objections, communicated through Stevenson's good
friend Agnes Meyer, the widow of the former owner of the *Washington Post*.
Stevenson feared that audiences would identify him with William Russell,
the excessively high-minded candidate who has great difficulty making up
his mind about whether he should use damaging information about the
private life of his chief opponent. "I have always felt that one takes a moral
position about actions," Gore wrote to a correspondent some years later,
"but not about people since people are capable at any given moment of a
wide variety of responses both good and bad, and the more deeply one
examines a character the more difficult it is to give out marks to the whole. I
learned this with *The Best Man*. No one liked the play when they read it.
The good guy tended to be vacillating (not to mention promiscuous which is
supposed to be a bad thing), and the bad guy was decisive and a good
husband, full of love. It was all just too peculiar. As Adlai Stevenson wrote
unhappily to Roger Stevens, 'it is an ugly play.' " For Stevens the situation
was awkward. He was again one of Stevenson's chief fund-raisers. Still, he
could not be pressured on the matter, and its timeliness appealed to everyone connected to the play, especially the producer, who added that to the
other attractions he presented to potential investors. With his usual adroit-
ness, Stevens began to raise the $105,000 necessary to bring it to Broadway.
Vidal's share of this was an advance of $500. If the play were to succeed, he
would have 5 percent of the first $5,000 weekly gross and a larger percentage
thereafter. If not, he would receive nothing more than the $500. Joe An-
thony, who would also share in the profits, persuaded Gore to lighten the
ending considerably. In the original version, the Nixon-like candidate gets
the nomination. In revision, as the three men talked over the script through
the fall and early winter, a dark-horse candidate, eventually triumphant, was
introduced. Sharply critical remarks about Eisenhower and Stevenson were
eliminated. All references to which party's convention was being depicted
were removed. When Stevens made a deal with the Sheraton Hotel chain
that it pay for the sets, references to the Sheraton were substituted for "early
Conrad Hilton." At one of the rehearsals in January, to which Gore had
invited Louis Auchincloss, Gore agreed immediately to a change in the
dialogue prompted by the director, who thought a particularly witty remark
about the Republican matrons of the country would offend some of the
audience. Astounded, Louis, who did not know that Gore had decided to

run for Congress, protested that such a witty remark should not be cut. Gore repeated, "Cut it!"

In mid-March, after a week of fine-tuning in Wilmington, Delaware, the company of *The Best Man,* nervous but anticipating success, took the train to Boston, where Stevens put them all up at the luxurious Ritz. Despite Stevens's efforts, the play was not yet fully funded. Partly because of its political content, mostly because Stevens's usual investors had taken heavy losses in recent plays, investors had been slow to commit themselves. Fortunately, the Boston reviews were excellent, the word of mouth descending to New York favorable. Lucien Price wrote Gore a long letter of analysis and praise. "Never in my lifetime had I expected to see and hear American politics handled so without gloves." *Variety*'s critic wrote that "by the time *The Best Man* reaches Broadway, it should be ready for the hit class." Nervous, at dinner with Elaine and Ken Tynan one evening during the Boston run, Gore expressed his anxiety. Ken assured him, Elaine recalled, " 'I know it's going to be a hit. I can tell.' It was nothing about, 'Oh, it'll be a hit, and that's that.' Ken simply knew and wanted Gore to know that he knew." Stevens quickly disposed of the rest of the shares, including an investment by Howard of $1,575, or one unit, which represented three fourths of 1 percent of the value of the play. Two weeks later, on March 31, *The Best Man* premiered at the Morosco, the theater that Stevens thought perfect because of its reputation as the classiest house for serious drama. The first-night audience applauded warmly, the buzz in the theater cheerfully enthusiastic. Experienced theater hands, though, knew that the audience at a premiere often has special reasons to seem delighted. Gore and Lyn Austin, behind the railing in back of the orchestra at opposite sides of the theater, worried and paced. As usual, Roger Stevens did things in high style. Everyone went to Sardi's for a champagne dinner party, which the producer hosted. Kit and Gene were there. Howard's parents came. Gore's father, handsomely at ease in evening dress, "loved the success and the glamour," so it seemed to Howard. Nina, with whom Gore had not communicated for over two years, had not been invited. When rumors about the early reviews began to arrive, the response was ecstatic. The *Variety* reviewer called Stevens to tell him he planned to give the play a superlative notice. "The room began to buzz with a report that Walter Kerr of the *New York Herald Tribune* was calling the play 'a knockout.' Several minutes later, copies of the New York *Daily News* and the *New York Mirror* were available, with rave reviews. The *Herald Tribune* appeared at about twelve-thirty, and the rumor about Kerr proved to be correct. When Brooks Atkinson of the *Times* also pronounced *The Best Man* a hit, it very plainly was." Gore was euphoric. The play was to run for 520 Broadway performances.

———

In late October 1960, when a carping Robert Kennedy, two hours late, stepped out of the small plane that had just landed at Saugerties Landing in Ulster County and greeted the 29th District's Democratic candidate for Congress, Gore's intensive campaign had been in high gear for over four months. In early April the district's Democratic committee had formally offered him the nomination. So too did the tiny Liberal Party. Since then Joe Hawkins's good judgment had been confirmed. His main liability as a candidate, Gore told his two young campaign assistants, Janet Caro and Ruth Davis, as they drove to events around the five counties, was that if he told the voters what he really thought, they never would elect him. In four of the counties the registration was about four to one Republican, in Dutchess, influenced by Poughkeepsie, the odds only slightly against the Democrats, though even many of the Democratic voters were considerably more conservative than liberal. To many of them, federal funds for education and a national achievement test for schoolchildren in order to qualify for the funds seemed an unconstitutional, even Communist idea. Advocacy of the admission of Red China to the United Nations seemed unattractively radical. Before conservative groups Gore found it expeditious to emphasize family heritage, movie stars, and personal charm. To be elected he needed to swing twenty thousand Republican votes into his column, virtually an impossibility, as most political realists recognized, including friends like Dick Rovere and politicians like Joe Hawkins. From the start he had taken refuge in multiple motives for his candidacy, including the claims of civic responsibility, the fulfillment of family heritage, and the pleasure of high-level mischief-making. That he could not win he would never admit, though he remained throughout realistic about the odds. "The morning after the Boston opening" of *The Best Man* he "gave three speeches in Dutchess County and then flew back to Boston. It's remarkable how much energy one has when one's caught up," he wrote in "On Campaigning," an unpublished early-1960s essay.

When Robert Kennedy, who knew that the presidential election would be excruciatingly close, confronted him at Saugerties Landing and testily demanded to know why he was not doing more to push the national ticket, Gore could only answer frankly, "Because I want to win." The swing voters in the 29th District, to the extent that such a phenomenon existed in that Republican world, were suspicious of the Catholic Kennedys. While Gore admired Jack, he had little respect for Bobby, who seemed to him a relentlessly prejudiced Catholic ideologue who saw the world exclusively in terms of good and evil, all issues as black or white. At study sessions at his home in Virginia with invited intellectual guests, Robert Kennedy, Gore had heard from mutual friends, had revealed the intellectual flexibility of a rhinoceros. Anyway, there was no chance that the national ticket would carry the district. Rabidly partisan, as it made sense for the national campaign manager to be, Robert Kennedy believed that the Kennedy greater good would be and must be served by the self-sacrifice of all his supporters. Gore said no. Whatever chance he had of winning, he wanted his vote count to be as high as possible. From the start of the campaign, and as a condition that Joe Hawkins had agreed to, he had made himself as much an independent candidate as possible. He publicly supported Kennedy. But as he campaigned, his emphasis was entirely on other things. Apparently Jack, with his wry practicality, understood perfectly. Bobby never forgave him.

That it would cost money to run even a congressional campaign had not been much on Vidal's mind when he had encouraged Hawkins to arrange the nomination for him and when he had accepted. The 29th District Democratic committee had little to offer. Gore himself had no intention of spending any more than tiny sums of his own money. Wharton had the wealthy Republican machine behind him. He had become congressman, so rumor had it, when a powerful New York State Republican wagered with Governor Thomas Dewey that he could take "the most obscure person from the most obscure county and send him to Congress." Wharton had been his exemplary choice. Gore, Janet Caro, recalled, "was very harsh—funny— about his opponent," who had compiled an empty record as a legislator and who, except for one occasion, declined to appear on the same platform with Vidal. Wharton's was a winning strategy. By mid-August, Gore was advised that his harsh even if witty personal attacks were counterproductive. "Sell yourself, don't knock J. Ernest," Ruth Davis advised. "Much of what you say about him is taken as 'disrespect.' " And, Davis counseled, "This makes me sick! sick! sick!!—but be sincere! sincere!! sincere!!" The challenge was to disguise his feelings, sugarcoat his ideas, one of which at least was instantly attractive to voters of both parties and soon reached a larger constituency. Why not give idealistic youngsters when drafted into the military the opportunity to work as American goodwill ambassadors, bringing their technical skills to Third World countries where, under American supervision, they could help local people improve their living standard? When on one of his visits to Washington he mentioned the favorable reception the idea had been receiving, the Kennedys, separating the concept from military service, reconfigured it as the Peace Corps, which within weeks Kennedy formally advocated. Though its origin in Vidal's proposal was not acknowledged, he was delighted to have made that contribution.

That the 29th District Democratic Party had little to contribute to his campaign was not a serious problem. Large sums had never been spent on congressional elections there. The party battle lines were sharply drawn. Wharton felt no need to spend anything but paltry amounts. Gore raised about $2,000 in contributions, almost entirely from friends. Print ads in local newspapers were cheap. When the largely Republican papers attempted to decline his ads, a group of Poughkeepsie merchants, mostly Jewish, who supported his candidacy threatened to withdraw their advertising. The newspaper owners immediately relented. As a supporter of Israel and as a public political statement, Gore was later to buy a $1,000 Israeli bond. Radio interview programs were delighted to have him. Leaflets, handbills, and posters cost next to nothing. The Democratic Party network provided foot soldiers, particularly the inexperienced but energetic Caro and Davis, both of whom enjoyed Gore's entertaining company, and others, including Pat Walsh, Bill Walsh's wife, who also drove him to events. Don MacIsaacs, his competent campaign manager, arranged his schedule, taking care of a thousand and one technical details. There were endless daily coffees and evening meetings, especially with small groups, many of them women delighted to hear about Jack Paar and Paul Newman and occasionally something specifically political. That Vidal was the author of a controversial novel, *The City and the Pillar,* or of any novels at all, almost none of the voters had any notion of. His advisers wisely counseled that the candidate do everything possible to keep his novels and his personal life out of the campaign. Howard kept as much in the background as possible, though of those who knew him as Gore's secretary, some assumed he was also his personal companion, especially since he was regularly at Edgewater. With his own interests and somewhat puzzled about what Gore's election might mean to their life together, Howard preferred to have little to do with the campaign. "I really had *nothing* to do with that campaign," Howard recalled. "I didn't like the campaign, all those people. . . . I was running away from that kind of world, and Gore was running to get into it after he had left his aristocratic world. I couldn't understand it. I can't understand why anybody would want to be elected." When Wharton's supporters attempted to damage Gore by alluding in broad terms to his sexual preferences, they did not get far. It was to some extent a forbidden topic, and the use of it risked damage to those who used it. At most, an anonymous whispering campaign could be sustained. That one of the crucial plot ploys of *The Best Man* involved a false accusation of homosexual activity against the Nixon-like candidate was both ironic and too thin to be of any use to Gore's political enemies. Soon he was telling noticeably often the story of how he *almost* married Joanne Woodward. The issue mostly disappeared. The Democrats would automatically pull the lever for him, the Republicans for his opponent. In realistic terms, the only issue was how many of the small number of independents and soft Republicans he could attract.

To tempt these voters to give him a hearing, he had at least one effective weapon, some formidable friends, though their impact could cut both ways. To the extent that they were prominent Democrats, they solidified his Democratic support, but they were not likely to help with independents or Republicans. To the extent that they were celebrities, they did bring out people regardless of party affiliation, eager to see Joanne Woodward and Paul Newman, for example, both of whom came up at least twice to widely advertised rallies and both of whom, nervous, did their best to tout their good friend. Glamour helped. But with the stolid Republican mainstream it was an entertainment, not an influence. Eleanor Roosevelt, totally unglamorous in appearance, was both celebrity and prominent Democrat. From the beginning she liked and supported Vidal, though at first she had had reservations about his candidacy. She may have wondered whether he would actually take the campaign seriously. She also knew how formidable were the odds. Her husband had not carried the 29th District in any of his four presidential campaigns. From the moment in fall 1959 that Gore had arrived at Val-Kill, her Hyde Park home, and discovered her arranging gladioli in a toilet bowl to keep them fresh, there was a low-keyed rapport between them. As the campaign swung into high gear in August 1960, she happily allowed herself to be photographed at Hyde Park inaugurating a series of coffee meetings for the candidate. "My husband always said: one has to have the hide of a rhinoceros to survive in politics," she remarked to him at dinner one hot June night at Val-Kill a month before the Democratic convention in Los Angeles. The other guests were the labor leader Walter Reuther and Franklin Roosevelt, Jr. "Eleanor Roosevelt's curious small eyes turned, looked straight at me," Gore later wrote. "They are her most interesting feature, the whites very clear, the blue somewhat opaque; when she thinks you are not watching her, she watches you; to catch her staring at you makes her flush and sometimes she will giggle nervously and look away; the eyes are those of an interested girl." She told him, probably unconvinced by his claim that he was protected by bright armor, that people in Hyde Park who had known her husband all his life believed that he did not suffer from polio but " 'from something you get from not having lived the right sort of life,' " perhaps an allusion to Gore's also being vulnerable to the charge that he had not lived "the right sort of life." Reuther had traveled to Hyde Park to try to convince Mrs. Roosevelt to support John Kennedy. Franklin, Jr., had just come from campaigning for Kennedy in West Virginia. For some time now Gore had been in the Kennedy camp. Earlier in the year Dick Rovere had privately told Gore that Kennedy had Addison's disease, which would put him in an early grave, a fact Rovere intended to reveal in an article in *Esquire*. Jack, who had heard of Rovere's intention, called Gore from Washington and blandly, persuasively lied: "Tell your friend Rovere that I don't have Addison's disease." Mrs. Roosevelt—partly because she detested the Kennedy patriarch, Joe Kennedy, for his pro-Nazi, anti-Roosevelt sympathies at the start of World War II, partly because she distrusted Jack and Bobby for their friendship with Joseph McCarthy— remained loyal to Adlai Stevenson. Just before the evening at Val-Kill, at a small dinner party at Alice Dows's, Gore had heard Mrs. Roosevelt's detailed indictment of Joe Kennedy's cowardice and perfidy. Like Dick Rovere, with whom Gore wagered on the issue, Mrs. Roosevelt did not believe that Kennedy could win and did not want him as the candidate. Her dinner guests did not get her to change her mind.

———————

Smoke hovered over the convention hall in Los Angeles in July. The atmosphere seemed especially surreal to Gore as he stepped from the gallery "into that vast hall." There was a "terrible strange blue light over every-thing." He was feeling ghastly, suffering from ambulatory pneumonia, as a doctor soon told him, probably caught on the flight out, though except for some totally energyless, feverish hours in his hotel room he kept to his full schedule as an alternate delegate from New York. Throughout, however, he felt disoriented, and it seemed odd to him to be in Los Angeles not "as a reigning screenwriter but as a delegate." His request had been honored by the New York party bosses, a routine accommodation for a congressional candidate. That he was a friend of the Kennedys and the author of a currently running Broadway hit having special appeal to politicians would not have been irrelevant. Unlike most of the New York delegation, headed by Robert Wagner, New York City's mayor, Gore was at home in Los Angeles and both served himself and paid back small debts by hosting for his state's delegation a celebrity-studded Hollywood party at Romanoff's restaurant on July 12. It was one of the early synergistic mixtures of Holly-wood and politics, "easily the best attended and highest calibre affair given during Convention week," an acquaintance somewhat hyperbolically wrote to Gore. Norman Mailer, sitting at the bar, drinking heavily and glowering, said enviously, "I hate you. You're too successful," though Gore could not help wondering if what he himself felt was not illness but jealousy of Jack Kennedy. Movie stars like Gary Cooper, Bing Crosby, and Charlton Hes-ton, whom Gore knew from the filming of *Ben-Hur* and who at this time had no quarrel with Vidal's account of his contribution to the script, rubbed shoulders, among dozens of other stars, with all the important Democratic politicians, including Lyndon Johnson—with the exception of John Ken-nedy, whose night it was to be out philandering, Gore later observed. It was still a splendid party, confirmed by the fact that the *New York Times* picked up a story first published in a Poughkeepsie newspaper accusing the New York delegation of "neglecting its duty" by attending. This gave the *Times* the opportunity to headline, "Vidal Denies Democratic 'Malingering' by New York State Delegates at Los Angeles." The night after the nomination he was himself a guest at another Hollywood political bash, this one hosted by Tony Curtis and his wife Janet Leigh, surrogates for Frank Sinatra, who had been prevented from being the official host by the Kennedys' concern that his Mafia associations might damage Jack's chances for the nomination. "It was a dreadful evening," Gore recalled. "Curtis gave an all-star party for the victor, and Jack didn't come. There were a lot of round tables, about two or three hundred movie stars, and I was waiting there at the main round table where Janet Leigh presided with Frank Sinatra and some bimbo and me. They waited for Jack and they waited for Jack. Eunice went to the phone. Came back to report, 'He's gone to the movies!' Which meant that Jack was off fucking. I looked at Sinatra, and it was Attila the Hun. If he could have killed Jack and half the earth, he would have."

The evening before, in the convention hall, still feeling wobbly but determined to be there for the climactic moment, Gore ran into John Kenneth Galbraith, the six-and-a-half-foot-tall Harvard economist, an enthusiastic Kennedy stalwart, and the slim, small, bespectacled Harvard historian Arthur Schlesinger, Jr., with his characteristic bow tie, who had recently turned from Stevenson enthusiast into committed Kennedy partisan. Galbraith had made his popular reputation with his book *The Affluent Society,* an influential social and economic analysis of post–World War II American prosperity. Schlesinger had published the first volume of what was expected to be the definitive history of Franklin Roosevelt's presidency. After attending the Boston opening of *The Best Man,* Schlesinger, who predicted that "the play will be a great success," had written Gore an encouraging letter and invited him to a dinner party at his Cambridge home. "The Reinhold Niebuhrs and the Edmund Wilsons will be there and, I think, John Strachey." Gore, who had met Schlesinger through Rovere, had urged Rovere to tell Schlesinger to give up on Stevenson. When he did, Eleanor Roosevelt thought it a betrayal. Both intelligent liberals, Galbraith and Schlesinger had signed on to provide Kennedy with ideas and words. As the roll call of the states proceeded, there was an electric thrill in the blue light. When Wyoming's votes put the Kennedy candidacy over the top, the three men exploded simultaneously amid the general eruption of wild cheers and ecstatic applause. They all congratulated one another. They felt allied with destiny. The young political columnist, Murray Kempton, looking up at Gore from his typewriter, said, " 'Is this . . . *all* there is to it?' " Ted Sorenson, a member of Kennedy's inner circle and his chief speech coordinator, came up to them out of the crowd. Mutual congratulations again. The three of you "ought to get cracking now," he said. "We've got to get a good acceptance speech," a draft of which Gore, still feeling ill, quickly wrote and sent to the Kennedy suite at the Biltmore. Apparently it never got into Sorenson's hands. "Jack also asked me. At Hyde Park he said, 'You know, we have everything but words. I haven't got anything to say.' " The good-spirited trio, soon awash in rum, went off together to a popular Polynesian restaurant in Beverly Hills. Neither members of the Kennedy inner circle nor his recreational companions, they had not been invited to join the nominee's celebration. At dinner they debated which one of them "would tell Jack to stop saying 'between you and I.' " In the middle of dinner Gore suddenly thought of Eleanor Roosevelt's "last appeal to the convention. We were making a mistake, she had said, waving a long finger at us, if we did not nominate Stevenson. But no one had listened. Her passion for Stevenson was the source of many cruel jokes and her loathing of the Kennedys thought to be unfair: the father's sins ought not to pass to the next genera-tion. With a twinge of guilt, and some malice, I asked my companions, *'Have* we made a mistake?' Certainly not! They were euphoric." In front of the restaurant Galbraith tried to turn the restaurant's decorative ship's wheel, shouting " 'This is the ship of state!' " As it was immovable, several spokes broke off.

Returning to the daily grind of his campaign, the endless upbeat talks to every conceivable civic and political group in the face of formidable registration odds, Gore moved through the tedium of his July and August schedule. "Some days I do seven eight nine coffee hours with women with hats," he wrote to Isherwood, his words coated with ambivalence and irony. "You cover an entire township or ward that way. They get maybe fifty women with hats in a room and you pop in and chat shyly about the Major Issues and then cut out. In addition, I address farm bureaus, labor picnics, party rallies. . . . Then there is the TV where recently on CBS I was quizzed just like the President on my Views. My answers were a lot like the President's, too. I may not be very smart but I'm sincere and that's come through which I think is a lot more important than making jokes or talking over people's heads." His assessment was mildly optimistic. "Jack, Jackie are doing well," he told Elaine Dundy, "and he will win though the press has come out for Wm McKinley and will not back down, fearing the Democratic process's great waiting goose. I am in terrible danger of win-ning myself. I've never worked so hard at anything." His half-sister Nini came up to cover his labors for the Tennessee newspaper whose Washington correspondent she had become through the good offices of a well-known Washington journalist, a friend of the Kennedys. A conservative Republi-can, Nini "was reacting against her mother, a drunk, and her mother's promiscuity and reacting against Jackie and Lee being fast," Gore thought.

"She was going to be the bluestocking. She was going to be the intellectual. She was going to be the one who read books and wrote books, the great brain. . . . I think she wrote rather viciously" about the campaign. "She never showed me, and I never asked. She was so right-wing, and I was a friend of Mrs. Roosevelt, and I introduced her to her, and she described Mrs. Roosevelt as the devil. It goes back to her own right-wing instincts, which come out of a battered childhood, and a battered child generally ends up trying to batter other people." From Washington, Jackie, eager to provide practical help, sent Gore a copy of one of Jack's pamphlets from his first campaign for the Senate and a detailed letter about what should go into his publicity material. She'd be interested to read it, as she knew everybody would, she wrote to him. She urged him to mail it to as many people in his district as possible and wait till nearer election time.

In mid-August he finally succeeded, to the delight of local Democrats, in cashing in his most valuable celebrity chip. Kennedy came to Dutchess County. Newspaper photographs highlighted the two men standing together, identifying the congressional candidate as "a personal friend" of the presidential nominee. Joe Hawkins's eyes worshipfully glittered with Irish pride. Actually, Kennedy's determinative reason for coming to the 29th District was to mend fences with the still-unenthusiastic Eleanor Roosevelt. He knew he had little chance of carrying the area. But Mrs. Roosevelt's approval would have national circulation. He wanted Gore to be his intermediary, which Gore was happy to be. In June he had kept Kennedy informed about his own campaign and about the attempts of people like Walter Reuther and himself to persuade Mrs. Roosevelt to be less hostile to Kennedy's candidacy. "Needless to say," he reported, "these sessions are always most interesting for what is *not* said. I have a hunch she was depressed by Stevenson's waffling." As to helping with Kennedy's speeches, "I hardly have time to prepare my own . . . but if you want me to act as emissary to those liberal establishments to which I have a key (Ascoli, the *Nation, PR,* etc.), I'll be happy to. I think at one point, if you have time, you should meet the various contiguous worlds of Norman Mailer, Philip Rahv, Trilling, etc. They view you with suspicion but I have a hunch you could win them around. If you like, I'll set up something along those lines. Their influence is formidable." They were, though, not votes or minds that Kennedy, at this point in his campaign, was interested in. But he did query Gore about how best to approach Mrs. Roosevelt, on which Gore gave detailed suggestions, including the necessity to keep Joe Kennedy out of the conversation if at all possible. On a mid-August Sunday, after a moderately successful lunch with Mrs. Roosevelt, Kennedy shared the platform at Hyde Park with Dutchess County Democrats, especially his "relative by marriage," as the newspapers put it, at a celebration of the twenty-fifth anniversary of the signing of the Social Security Act. "Vidal has the will and the vigor and he understands the need for action in this changing world," Kennedy told the press. The *Hyde Park Independent* headlined, "Kennedy Stumps for Vidal." Because of a death in the family, Mrs. Roosevelt canceled her appearance at the rally. Kennedy praised her profusely. Later she issued a tepid endorsement.

Wharton, meanwhile, at a self-confident, semiconcealed snail's pace, kept to his sure-win, no-idea campaign. At their one appearance on the same platform, Wharton stolidly repeated his mantra, the solid true-red-white-and-blue American conservative versus the reckless-spending pinko-liberal. All Vidal had was personality, energy, and ideas, and sometimes a sharp tongue. Inevitably, both friends and enemies would stay in place. New York City newspapers, though, paid more attention to the 29th District than they ever before had to an upstate campaign. Gore could command press, a two-edged sword. When he excoriated the FCC for television's low standards, particularly the prevalence of violence, Harriet Van Horne in the *New York World Telegram* devoted a full column in praise of his views. "As proof of how dreadful TV is, the Dutchess County candidate cited '14 Westerns in a row and rampant sadism.' " But Van Horne clearly saw the problem. "It was refreshing," she concluded, "to meet Mr. Vidal, though his attitude toward the business of running for office seems to preclude his getting elected. You have to lust after the office, Mr. Vidal, act like Plain Folks, talk in platitudes, promise everything . . . and above all, pretend you're a great fan of Westerns." Wharton did not have to do any pretending. He was a natural. Gore was not capable of going far enough into pretense. Just before mid-September, the *New York Times* ran a sly but hostile feature article that capitalized on Gore's penchant for witty observations and added distortions of its own. If he had indeed been "sprawled barefooted in a gilded fauteuil of his luxurious octagonal Empire study" and let "his cocker spaniel lick the Château d'Yquem off his fingers" in the presence of the reporter, which Vidal denies, highlighting such details among other possible details could only have been antagonistic journalism. So too the coded homophobic paragraph lead: "A bachelor, he lives in lonely splendor in an 1820 Greek Revival mansion." Certainly he had made no pretense that he was just "Plain Folks," and not to have anticipated hostility and effectively controlled the interview was characteristic of his general trustingness. In an unguarded moment he told the *Times* reporter, assuming the comment off the record, "If this were not a Presidential year, I might have a chance. As it is, every four years, about 20,000 extra people crawl out of the Hudson Gothic woodwork up here to vote for William McKinley." The article's author, Ira Freeman, Gore recalled, "giggled a lot and said, 'I don't know anything about politics.' 'So why were you sent here?' He followed me around, polishing his misquotes. The usual *New York Times* ax job. Generally they didn't cover campaigns that far north, but they made an exception in my case. They even went so far when *The Best Man* opened—it did get a very good review from Brooks Atkinson, and the Sulzbergers loved the play—but Lester Markell, who was in charge of the Sunday Magazine section, canvassed six writers to get an all-out attack on me. Rovere was the one I learned this from. They all turned him down except Douglass Cater, who'd been at Exeter with me. So he wrote this piece called 'Advise and Dissent' on *The Best Man.*' Lester wanted to take care of the two fags— Allan Drury, who'd written a novel, and me. It was a fairly harmless piece, but the extent to which the *New York Times* will go to destroy people is to this day awe-inspiring. Look at their editorials on Clinton. But there comes a point at which you become so at home with your audience that there's not much they can do about you." Wharton and the Republicans widely publicized the insulting remark "about 20,000 extra people" crawling every fourth year "out of the Hudson Gothic woodwork up here to vote for William McKinley," quoted by Ira Freeman in the *Times*. Whatever small chance Vidal had to attract non-Democratic votes evaporated. His campaign people knew it. Probably he did too, though it did not prevent his finishing out the campaign with a number of energetic flourishes, one of which was a quick trip to Berlin in early October, as the guest of Mayor Willy Brandt, for the opening of the German version of *The Best Man* as the lead play of the Festival of Berlin. It enabled him to publicize through banner headlines his anti-Communist beliefs and his support for protecting freedom in the divided city, including sending more American troops, perhaps the only instance ever in which he supported an American military presence in a foreign country. The Berlin trip would help counter the accusation that he was a pinko-liberal and demonstrate that, in contrast to Wharton, he had some interest in and knowledge about foreign affairs. He liked Brandt, who treated him as an American dignitary, and *The Best Man*, the only American play chosen for the festival, was warmly received. While in Berlin, he saw a number of existential symbolic plays, by Ionesco and Beckett among others, which gave him pause about his career as a playwright. Well-made realistic plays like *The Best Man* might be going out of fashion. Soon after his return, Harry Truman, a prototype for one of *The Best Man*'s main characters, came to nearby Fishkill to rally Dutchess and Putnam County Democrats in the best "Give 'em hell, Harry" style. A huge crowd came to Racine Manor, a handsome resort, to see the former President. A yellow fountain poured martinis, a red one Manhattans. Patsy Walsh was thinking, "Who would want to be a Republican?" As the well-known creator of a fictional portrait of the former President and as the local candidate for Congress, Vidal had the privilege of introducing Truman, whose old-fashioned integrity he praised. Infuriated at Nixon's slurs against his patriotism, Truman attacked the Republican deficits and Nixon's failures. The crowd loved it. Truman then returned the praise, introducing Gore, whom he strongly endorsed as "The Best Man." "Hope I haven't harmed you," Truman said to Vidal at the end of the rally.

Neither "The Best Man" nor even a respectable dark horse was to win in the 29th District. On Election Day Vidal voted the straight Democratic ticket. On election night, November 8, he drove to Democratic headquarters at Joe Hawkins's office in Poughkeepsie with Elaine Dundy and his father, both of whom had come up to lend moral support. Still movie-star handsome, as always elegantly dressed and dignified, Gene drove. Howard sat with Elaine in the backseat. "When we got there and were just getting out of the car," Elaine recalled, "Gene turned to Gore and said, 'It's just like another opening night, isn't it?' And Gore said in a really steely way, 'With this exception, that it's a fork in my life.' " They joined Joe Hawkins for the election-night ritual. Gore had brought with him signed copies of some of his novels to give as gifts to his campaign workers. Janet Caro's copy of *Messiah* he had inscribed, "For Yallum—/Who plumbed the depths of human ingratitude and returned a finer person for her descent, in recognition of her organizational skill, her cunning on the telephone, her news-releases and her pluck—with the candidate's homage and gratitude and love." She had seen him at his articulate best and had felt the sting of his irritable worst.

As the first returns came in and Gore carried Poughkeepsie, Elaine thought he might win. The experienced politicians in the crowded room knew better. He had carried Poughkeepsie by a moderate margin and lost the larger Poughkeepsie area. "None of the returns were any good, from the beginning," Caro knew. "Poughkeepsie came in first, where he should have been doing well, and he wasn't doing well enough." Soon "the rural vote came in," Elaine recalls, "and the room seemed to thin out considerably." Though it would take a few days before the final vote was tallied, the results would not have been a surprise to anyone at Democratic election headquarters that night. He had done well, given the odds. With 43.3 percent of the vote, he had done better than any Democratic candidate in recent history and over 5 percent, or 20,000 votes, better than the Democratic national ticket. In the 29th District, Vidal was more popular than Kennedy. That he had failed to lure a large enough number of Republicans to vote for him surprised no one. Finally, "Gore said, 'It's over!' and conceded it. We got into the car," Elaine recalled, "came back to Edgewater. We all stayed up, except Gore, because the Kennedy thing was very, very close; we didn't hear about California until the next day." In his unhappy heart he was thinking, " 'Oh, no, not Jack also!' " Exhausted, he went to bed. "The next day he said—I heard him on the telephone—to his agent, 'I've lost the election. Get me a job.' "

—————

With flashbulbs popping so frequently as to rival the neon signs, President-Elect Kennedy, greeted at the door by the proud author, swept into the Morosco Theater on December 6 to see *The Best Man*. Kennedy had barely won the election, probably only because he had been the beneficiary of some tainted Chicago votes that had enabled him to carry Illinois. Within a week after the election, from Miami where he had gone for some sunshine, Gore told the President-Elect, "If you had not won, I would have emigrated. I'm only sorry I won't be in the House this January to help counter balance in some small way the powers of darkness gathering there. For the record, I did cut my Republican's plurality by 54,000 votes; from 77,000 in '56 to 23,000; I ran ahead of the ticket, carrying all the cities, losing all the countryside; a famous defeat, but still a defeat." In fact, he had not been contemplating emigration, regardless of the results of the election. He had three suggestions for the inaugural speech: that the new administration challenge young people through the still-unnamed Peace Corps, that the administration energize the American people with a realistic but imaginative program for space exploration, and that the President give serious weight to the widespread anxiety that massive homogenizing forces in the culture threatened individualism. "I think a President who will openly recognize this fear for what it is, who shows a sensitivity to the origin of that fear will go a long way toward winning the sympathy and allegiance of the many." As to himself, "If I can help you in any way, let me know. I am free as air. One request: my interest in elective office continues but I'm going to need some governmental experience to overcome the mysterious argument: what does a writer know about politics? If there is anything connected with education, foreign affairs and, God help us, culture (both Kultur and Kitsch) that I might do, in a general or specific way, remember me. Otherwise, I shall be branded forever as the candidate who wrote a movie for Elizabeth Taylor." In his private mind he was dubious about running for office again. But he had not ruled it out, and his comparatively good showing gave him reason to believe he might be a successful candidate under more favorable registration circumstances.

Jackie soon answered his letter to Jack. It was such a marvelous letter from you, she wrote to him, and she had been deeply touched. Most of all, she was sorry that he had not won, though he had been so brave to try, given what an incredibly unpromising district his had been. Don't worry, she assured him. She was confident he would win the next time. She herself was so exhausted she had collapsed, she confided to him, especially under the burden of taking care of all the details that followed the election. Hurry back from Europe, she urged him, and please call the White House after the inauguration. It would be a joy for both herself and Jack to have him there as a guest. And she had some special good news: Jack was going to see *The Best Man* on the next evening. With only one night in New York, he had chosen to see that play rather than *Camelot,* she remarked with an exclamation point—and she did not blame him in the least! In fact, Gore had decided that if Kennedy were to offer him some suitable position, he would seriously consider it, though his letter was also a pro forma bow to the new leader of the party and the country. "Kennedy used to joke," Vidal recalled,

" 'I think the ambassadorship to Mali is open.' He would come up with these grotesque ambassadorial assignments for me. It's not a serious request for a job. It's a polite acknowledgment that he's the head of the party." In the meantime, he found it amusing to observe the President watching *The Best Man*. At the moment when the dialogue alluded to the sexual promiscuity of the Kennedy-like character, the President laughed with what seemed a combination of pride and uneasy self-recognition. "He looked quite nervous. . . . He gave a lightning look at [his friend] Chuck Spalding and sat lower down in his chair."

Immediately after the election political friends and supporters urged Vidal to begin campaigning for the 1962 election, either for Congress or for the Senate, an office that had more appeal to him and which he now had more strongly in mind as a possibility than he could have had before the 1960 campaign. There would be both honor and pleasure in following his grandfather into the upper chamber. Still, he felt a deep-seated ambivalence, a fundamental hesitation. The campaign had been tediously all-consuming. Did he really want to do that again? And what would holding office be like? Except at the absolutely highest level, would it not demand a grind of legislative and constituent responsibilities that he had no special interest in, a life without serious ideas or intellectual content? Politics had been the family business. Politics was, so to speak, in his blood. But beyond that, why would he actually want to be elected? During the campaign, the skeptical Fred Dupee, who, Gore recalled, "was constantly sneering at my activism," had expressed his disapproval numbers of times. Gore's greatest talent was as a writer, Dupee believed. He should devote himself to that. At a party one evening at Edgewater the composer Virgil Thomson, an acerbic leader of the musical avant-garde who had collaborated with Gertrude Stein on the opera *Four Saints in Three Acts* and been for a decade the influential music critic of the *Herald Tribune,* and who had taken a liking to Gore who he hoped would write a libretto for him, rebuked Dupee. Novelists, he argued, needed to be involved in and know about the life of the world. On the morning after the laudatory reviews of *The Best Man*, Thomson had telegraphed his congratulations. "Call and come when you can. Would you maybe like a party? I have some good wine." For Thomson there seemed no necessary reason to choose between politics and literature. Dupee, who thought them incompatible, may have been more right than Thomson. It would have been difficult if not impossible for Gore to have performed responsibly as an elected official and at the same time carry on as a writer of fiction. Political and literary ideas were compatible. Political office and a literary careeer were not.

In Miami, Gore enjoyed the sunshine, apparently by himself, though by early December he and Howard had decided on a European trip, among other reasons to spend Christmas in Paris with Joanne and Paul, there for Paul's contribution to a movie, *Lady L,* co-starring Sophia Loren. Gore had accepted an invitation to be a judge at a television festival in Monte Carlo in mid-January. What to do next, in the larger sense, was on his mind. The director Frank Capra had approached him about making a movie based on *The Best Man.* "But if I do it," he told John Bowen, "most of the acid will be retained undiluted, or so I hope." CBS television had queried him about doing a series of four "Kultur television shows, acting as narrator, the Alistair Cooke kind of thing: I am big on television: 'his rapier wit, his clarity' (I have yet to say anything remotely intelligent on the small screen but the *style* suggests that I have greatness in reserve: I do smile quite a lot though, having had my two incisors capped with plastic)." The television idea appealed to him, at least to his sense of humor and his competitiveness. "All my life I wanted to beat Lennie [Bernstein] to his knees at his own game," he wrote to Elaine Dundy, "and I will, and you know what, I'm going to be the first gentile President after LENNIE." If he were to remain in politics, he could write essays and plays. But could he write fiction? "I fret about prose, torn between D.C. novel and *Julian,* " he wrote to Isherwood. "Nothing gets easier, does it? Not even for Mole's ancient friend Rat who once cut to the cheese with such directness. But this is just despair before focussing the camera. Can never estimate distances, light meter broken. Ah, well."

As the author of a successful Broadway hit, he was being encouraged by producers, including Roger Stevens, to write another, though his experience with *March to the Sea* at the Hyde Park Playhouse had not been satisfying. After one week of mid-August 1960 performances Gore had prevailed on David Samples, the producer and director, to rearrange the repertory schedule and do a second week. The reviews had been mixed to poor, though it had done well at the box office, mostly because of Gore's name. With Gore's financial help Samples had taken over the Hyde Park Playhouse in 1960 and happily agreed to put on *March to the Sea.* Gore hoped that a successful week or two there would allow him to reopen the possibility of a Broadway production. Unfortunately, attendance dropped considerably the second week. "I'd started a newspaper, called the *Hyde Park Townsman*," Gore recalled, "just because the Poughkeepsie paper was not covering me in the campaign. It was a weekly. Potentially it could do rather well. The critic on the paper didn't like what Samples was doing and so my own paper was attacking my own theater," especially *March to the Sea*, which the theater critic thought badly acted and ineffective. "I let everyone alone." Gore never expected to and in the end did not get back his $6,000. It was from the first a slightly self-interested benefaction, not an investment. Money was not a pressing issue. His profits from the ongoing run of *The Best Man* were substantial, even more than from *Visit*. Some of it went into an annuity, some scheduled as deferred payments over numbers of years, a portion into savings and investments, including soon the purchase of another brownstone building on East Fifty-eighth street, almost directly across from 416. Howard, who managed both buildings, was charged with the renovation of an apartment at 417 East Fifty-eighth into their living quarters. In the meantime they continued to stay at the rented East Fifty-fifth Street apartment.

Christmas and New Year's in Paris helped put the election even further behind him. "Paul was working with Sophia Loren on *Lady L*," Gore remembered. "Joanne and I were fascinated and would ask him what she's like. 'What's who like?' 'Sophia Loren. You've been working with her.' 'Oh.' 'What is she like?' We were dying to know. This was at the height of her beauty and sexiness. 'Well, she was late for work this morning.' 'Oh, what else? Is that it? What's she like?' 'She has this accent.' We never got more than that out of him. Joanne always suspected the worst." The Newmans had rented a dark, cold apartment in Montparnasse because Joanne had thought it romantic. Gore and Howard stayed comfortably at the Hotel Plaza-Athénée, and Gore made it a point not to return to Washington for the inaugural ball to which he had been invited. The actress Shelley Winters, making *Lolita* in London, reminded him that they had talked at the New York opening of Tennessee's *Sweet Bird of Youth* about going together. Over lunch in Paris he teamed up with Art Buchwald for one of Buchwald's funny columns, "Interview with a Gracious Loser." "I was very depressed," Gore told him, "until I started reading up on other great losers, and then I took heart. I think the greatest loser of our time—the one who has been an idol to all other losers—is Thomas E. Dewey. . . . Another inspiration to all losers is Harold E. Stassen. . . . He has given us all courage to go on. . . . I don't dare put myself in the same class as these men. Obscurity is something you don't lightly achieve." Lucien Price thought he heard echoes of Gore's prose in Kennedy's inaugural speech. But, though Gore anticipated social and even political contacts with the White House, his Kennedy connection seemed an attractive ornament, not the major engagement. Before the campaign had begun, he had published in *The Nation* a provocative essay, "The Twelve Caesars," whose graceful authoritativeness was witness to how far he had come as a Roman historian and as an essayist. Suetonius, he wrote, "in holding up a mirror to those Caesars of diverting legend, reflects not only them but ourselves: half-tamed creatures, whose great moral task it is to hold in balance the angel and the monster within—for we are both, and to ignore this duality is to invite disaster" Probably early in 1961 he wrote, though never finished, "On Campaigning." What to do next as a writer and general recuperation were of more concern than the inaugural celebration.

In February, soon after returning from Paris, he invited Norman Mailer and his wife and three-year-old daughter to Edgewater for a weekend, with Mickey Knox, a young actor and childhood friend of Mailer's. When Mailer had published *Advertisements for Myself* in 1959, Gore had written a cordial review in *The Nation*, "The Norman Mailer Syndrome," later reprinted as "Norman Mailer: The Angels Are White" and then as "Norman Mailer's Self-Advertisements." "I had written," Mailer recalls, "that thing about him that he had half liked and half didn't like, about his writing. I think it was called 'Quick and Expensive Comments on the Talent in the Room.' He had written fairly well about the book, and we stayed reasonably friendly but not close, never close." "The Talent in the Room" had given deep offense to two of Mailer's closest friends, James Jones and William Styron. Gore, who had not been as egregiously savaged, shrugged off Mailer's condescension as well within the bounds of their usual exchanges. In late November 1960, Mailer, destructively drunk, had made headlines greater than any of his books had or would. After a tense party at their New York apartment, he had stabbed his wife with a kitchen knife. Mailer fled. Fortunately, help came quickly. Adele's life was saved, and Knox and other friends soon persuaded Mailer to turn himself in. Adele declined to press charges. They moved back in together. During the Mailers' weekend at Edgewater, the Dupees came over; they talked about Gore's campaign and about literary things. Gore's Hudson River Valley friends were morally outraged. How could he have Mailer at his house? "It was a marvelous evening," Mailer recalls, and Gore was very entertaining. "Here's this couple—here's the fellow who's stabbed the woman, and now, my God, there they are in the house, something like that." For a short time Mailer had become a social pariah. "But Gore was generous, and it really meant something, you know, that we'd be invited out socially like nothing had happened. He was really fulfilling— Well, I certainly thought of him as a friend at that point. It was a supportive gesture." But even this occasion was not without the usual competitiveness. "At one point Gore said to me something to the effect of 'Until you've known an Arab boy, you don't begin to know what sexual pleasure's all about.' And I turned to him and said, 'I am married to an Arab boy.' Adele has a lot of Gypsy and Spanish blood and Indian blood and could pass for an Arab lady. Gore did not have a rejoinder to that."

———————

At his motel in Provincetown in late August 1961, Gore received a call from Jackie, who in July had written to invite him to the Kennedy compound at Hyannisport, preferably in August, as the weather was horrible at the moment. Gore had sent the Kennedys some of his books, which she looked forward to reading. The copy of *Messiah* they had both earmarked for Jack. Please promise, she insisted, to return to her what she felt was a ghastly picture of herself that she had given him. She was getting a better one taken in Paris shortly and, she assured him, when prints arrived she would send him a copy of the new picture to replace the old. Soon after returning from *his* Christmas trip to Paris, he had succumbed to the temptation to write another play. Roger Stevens had pressured him to capitalize on the success of *The Best Man*. But he had no compelling idea. Searching for something viable, he racked his brain and imagination. An admirer of the Swiss playwright Friedrich Dürrenmatt, he decided that an adaptation-expansion of *Romulus* for an American audience might allow him to create a viable dramatization that would bring together Roman history and contemporary politics. A comedic dramatization of the fall of the Roman Empire had possibilties. Dürrenmatt's *Romulus* had been a failure in Europe. Gore thought his English version might correct the faults of the original. Roger Stevens was enthusiastic, or at least committed enough to put the production in place. Joe Anthony again would direct. Cyril Ritchard, brilliant in *Visit*, agreed to play the title role. The play was scheduled for a late-December New York premiere. At the same time Gore's idea for a Washington novel resurfaced with some force, prompted by his recent political experiences and also by recurrent autobiographical musings. With two chapters of *Julian* in place, he also wanted to give thought to when and how to carry on with that novel-in-progress.

He had gone to Provincetown partly for a change from the steamy summer heat at Edgewater. But he also had gone to lose weight, one of his frequent flights into seclusion to cut himself off from the usual food temptations. Eating gave him great pleasure. It also rapidly swelled his face and figure. With his public image in mind, he found it practical to go on starving as well as eating binges. Excess came easily. So too did ascetic discipline. Soon after arriving, he had sent to nearby Hyannisport funny caricatures of the Kennedys drawn on cheap local souvenir plates. He had assumed that the Kennedys were in Washington, not to arrive until his stay in Provincetown was over. When the dinner invitation came, he drove his rented car to Hyannisport. As he approached the house, he was stopped at a number of guardhouses for security checks. It was a noticeable change from more relaxed earlier days. Over the next week he visited regularly with the Kennedys, the most sustained period he had ever spent with Jack. Jackie especially seemed eager for his company, so much so that on the last day of the month she drove to Provincetown, with Jack's friend Bill Walton, to have dinner and go to the theater with him. Though she loved her national celebrity, she had discovered that being the wife of the President had its drawbacks, especially the limits on her personal freedom. Eager to get away from Jack's family and Hyannisport stultification, that morning on the phone she had consulted Gore about what disguise she should wear. At his motel she bounced up and down on the bed in playful, semi-anonymous pleasure. With the Secret Service doing its best to keep up discreetly, they went to the Chrysler Museum, then to dinner and the playhouse to see Shaw's *Mrs. Warren's Profession*. Though the theater had no prior knowledge they were coming, everyone recognized her. Some may have recognized Gore. "The boy taking tickets was so overcome, he gave us all his programs." When they came out, the street was crowded. Word had spread. Afterward, at a raunchy nightclub they were asked for identification, and a drunken lout "recognized Jackie and said, 'So all the stories are true. Why don't you come on in?' " They fled to a more sedate place. "Upstairs was another bar, frequented by lesbians. Jackie was fascinated but dared not look in." The tense, long-standing difficulties of her marriage were evident. The tables had turned somewhat, Bill Walton told Gore. Before, Jack had regularly been "brutal to her in public." Now that she too was a star, he teasingly called her "the sex symbol" and actually, perhaps for the first time, desired her. She had begun to needle him mercilessly. But the President still wanted to hear any and all sex gossip from Gore and everyone else. " 'He's rather sad these days,' " Walton remarked. " 'Nothing happens except Jackie, maybe twice a week.' "

In April the British *Sunday Telegraph* had published Gore's portrait of Kennedy, and in June *Life* carried his interview-profile of Barry Goldwater. Kennedy had good reason to expect Goldwater to be his Republican opponent in 1964, though he and Gore also talked, as Kennedy regularly did, about Nelson Rockefeller, who he feared would be more formidable. He had no doubt he could defeat Goldwater, whom he liked. Gore's casually devastating "Barry Goldwater: A Chat" is as much about the art of politics and the desire for power as about the likable Arizonan. "To the artful dodger rather than the true believer goes the prize," Vidal had written. Insufficiently dodgeful, whatever his ideology, Goldwater was unlikely to defeat any artful politician. If the essay is condescending, its condescension is inseparable from its combination of the personal voice and the authoritative view. Goldwater, as he speaks for himself with laudable honesty, provides in his own words perfect examples for the essay's main point. In "John Kennedy: A Translation for the English," Vidal noted that Kennedy's "face is heavily lined for his age" and that his smile "is charming even when it is simulated for the public." The candid touches effectively strengthen an essay whose portrait of the pragmatic Kennedy translates into the archetype of the artful politician—sly, crafty, improvisational, aware of the conventions, intellectually "dogged rather than brilliant . . . icily objective in crisis," perceptive about what the moment will permit and what the moment requires. His youthful energy, Vidal surmised, might indeed provide our civilization with a second and last chance to stir itself out of its torpor. Written immediately before the Bay of Pigs, it is a cautious portrait. The prospects are there, but the verdict is still out. To what extent Kennedy would become a Cold War warrior Vidal did not fully anticipate. The Bay of Pigs episode itself was hardly decisive, and transcriptions would later make clear that Kennedy had chosen the least confrontational of the proposed responses to the Soviet threat.

In and out of the Kennedy house at Hyannisport for much of that week in August, Vidal had various casual conversations with the President, a shorthand record of which he made at the first opportunity, for him an unusual practice. Years later he made effective use of his notes in his memoir. Jack and he gossiped, dined, played backgammon, talked politics at length. Gore admired the President's pragmatic intelligence, his powers of cold analysis, his self-serving ruthlessness. And it was a change and a delight to have a President who actually read books, who was interested in being knowledgeable and well informed. Gore saw the promise, the possibility, of such talent being put to national service on behalf of desirable changes. What he had begun to fear, quite tentatively, was Kennedy as heir of the foreign policy of Truman and Eisenhower. Thoroughly anti-Communist himself, Vidal feared anti-Communism as the excuse for excessive militarism, for potentially self-destructive commitments abroad. Khrushchev and tension over Berlin were very much in the air. Reservists were being called up. Gore and Arthur Schlesinger, who had become a full-time presidential adviser and who was very worried about the Berlin crisis, compared notes about the President's mood. Bobby Kennedy came by numbers of times from his nearby house. Once the brothers went into a corner of the room, bending their heads together secretively over a letter from John McCloy about Russian-American tension. Less hawkish in private than in public, Jack seemed to agree with Jackie's comment, "Yes, it would be better to be red than dead, not maybe for oneself, but for the children." When the subject of his personal security came up, the President, who believed that a resolute assassin could always find his target and who had told Gore an ironic story of how a British prime minister had been electrocuted by a telephone after he thought he had been safeguarded against a threatened assassination attempt, expressed his resigned stoicism. To Gore's mind, Jack had already so often narrowly escaped death because of ill health that he had been conditioned to have no confidence in having a long life.

Fortunately, there were also lighter subjects to discuss. Hughdie and Janet were a favorite topic, the dreaded in-laws, one of whom bored, the other tongue-lashed you to death. When Gore told Jack that he had in mind to position the President as a conservative in an article he intended to write to counter an article called "The Future of Liberalism" by one of Gore's ambitious ultraconservative contemporaries, William F. Buckley, Jr., who had recently surfaced as a propagandist for the far right, Kennedy touchily objected. "Just talk to Eisenhower if you want to meet a real conservative," he said. The most Hollywood-involved of American Presidents until Ronald Reagan, Kennedy pumped Gore about movies, theaters, starlets. They discussed Fellini's *La Dolce Vita*. Kennedy liked Gore's view that Fellini's movie, exploiting Anglo-Saxon Puritanism, pretended that "this was decadence when it was only life as it is lived," and Jackie complained that her mother-in-law frequently reminded her that all the movies Jackie liked were on the Catholic Church's proscribed Index. Though the presidential couple took this all rather lightly, Bobby did not. Gore noticed that the conversation was always serious when the more puritanical, rigidly Catholic younger brother was present. Clearly, Bobby had not forgotten Gore's refusal to push harder for the national ticket during his congressional campaign. Unlike his brother, the Attorney General wore his grudges on his sleeve, and also unlike Jack, he had an uninflected sense of moral standards. Uncomfortable with those who were not straight arrows, he disapproved of Gore, whose sexual interests were beyond his comprehension or tolerance. Undoubtedly he believed that homosexuality was moral depravity, an illness of the soul that needed to be cured or damned. Salvation was at issue. When he walked into a room that contained Gore, one could feel his almost palpable antagonism. That he and Bobby did not like one another was of little consequence. They were publicly cordial. When Gore (with Eleanor Roosevelt) recommended Joe Hawkins for a position in the Justice Department, Bobby assured Gore "he will be given every consideration."

From the time of the inauguration through much of 1961, Gore was invited a few times to the White House. When Jackie returned from her Paris trip, she sent him an inscribed copy of the more flattering photograph: "For Gore, who makes it impossible to look this serious, with affection, Jackie Kennedy." With some pride, he displayed it in a place of honor at Edgewater. After all, he had known her before her husband had, and she had come to him for advice about a career when she was an unknown. Going upstairs to the family's private quarters at the White House for dinner one evening, what most struck him was the smell of frying onions, the quotidian even in high places. Not that he was not proud to be at the White House. On one occasion, he called Roy Thompson, T. P. Gore's last secretary, who had known him as a boy, simply to tell him where he was calling from, both a boastful and a nostalgic bow in the direction of his grandfather. The White House connection had its attractions, though he was feeling increasingly edgy about his own political career, leaning more and more to the notion that he ought to get out entirely and return full-time to writing. Yet he still kept open his options in the 29th District and even the possibility of the Senate. When he received an official letter in September requesting that he agree to be appointed to the President's Advisory Council on the Arts for the National Cultural Center, he perfunctorily accepted, partly because it seemed easier than explaining a declination, though he had no intention of attending the committee's meetings.

In early November 1961 he was busy in New York with rehearsals of *Romulus*. There seemed little reason to be optimistic that the play would be as successful as *The Best Man*, let alone a success at all. The first act was tediously troublesome. Cyril Ritchard's comic flair for the outrageously campy did not convey the Roman emperor's serious side and the play's significant historical elements, including the analogy between the Roman and the American empires. Lyn Austin, who had not had the same tingle as she had had with *The Best Man*, was happy to have another of Roger Stevens's associates, Robert Whitehead, be the hands-on producer. Though he had not yet faced it consciously, Gore sensed that his decision to adapt the Dürrenmatt play had been a mistake. Also, he would soon have to make up his mind whether to run for Congress again. Joe Hawkins pressed him for a decision, as ambivalent as Gore about whether it would be a good idea. The Senate seat came up again. For both, he had until late winter to decide. But the longer he waited, the less likely his chance of success. Maybe the best thing would be to chuck political life altogether. He had seen much during the first year of the Kennedy administration that had drawn home the disadvantages of political office. For the first time he admitted to himself that both holding political office and writing novels was untenable. At this point he received an invitation from the President and Mrs. Kennedy to attend a large dinner at the White House on November 11. As he went down to Washington for the grand dinner, he was not in the best of moods. Recently he had written for *Esquire*, for which he now did occasional political columns, about his outrage at the Justice Department's indifference to the FBI's disregard for civil liberties. Bobby Kennedy seemed either too much in sympathy with or too much under the thumb of the powerful FBI director, J. Edgar Hoover. Gore had written directly to Bobby at the Justice Department to complain about FBI coziness with the Ku Klux Klan. The Attorney General had responded with curt dismissiveness. Still, this was a celebratory evening. The Kennedy administration had come into power almost exactly one year before. It was the first major social dinner they were hosting, in honor of their glamorous Italian friends, the Agnellis, owners of Fiat, and, apparently, also in honor of the Radziwills, Jackie's sister Lee and her tenuously royal Polish businessman-husband. Franklin Roosevelt, Jr., whom Gore knew through Eleanor and who represented the Agnelli business interests in America, was being rewarded for his early support of Kennedy by a White House dinner for his clients.

Arriving by car with Schlesinger and his wife and John Kenneth Galbraith, Gore anticipated an evening of ostensible glamour and real boredom. About a hundred fashionable guests in tuxedos and evening dresses. Elaborate White House hospitality in spaces small for the event. Music. Dancing. Dinner. Flashes of crystal catching light. A hum from dozens of indistinguishable voices. In the Red Room he unexpectedly found himself face to face with the Auchinclosses. Marriage to Nina had brought Hughdie access to a senator. Marriage to Janet had brought him to the White House. With his usual good manners Gore attempted to maneuver the encounter onto high ground. With characteristic quarrelsomeness Janet responded rebukingly to an elaborate compliment from Gore about how well she had performed as a stepmother to Gore's sister Nini. Why are you attacking your mother? Taken aback, Gore answered that he thought he had been complimenting Janet. Extricating himself as quickly as possible, he moved into the adjacent Blue Room. There was barely standing space. Groups of chairs, mostly occupied, were scattered around. He was delighted to see Jackie, seated amid other occupied chairs. Never quarrelsome, she could be counted on for her usual purring pleasantries. Since the chairs around her were taken, he squatted next to hers, steadying himself by placing his hand across the back of her straight-backed chair, his arm brushing her back and shoulders. Jackie seemed happy to see him. They chatted amiably. As she turned her head to talk to someone on her other side, Gore felt his hand being removed from behind the back of her chair and shoulder. Looking around and up, he saw Robert Kennedy, who then immediately walked to the door separating the Blue from the Red Room. Unaware of what had happened, Jackie continued her other conversation. Gore went immediately to Kennedy. It had seemed to him a personal attack, as if the Attorney

General were some high-toned puritan butler policing the room. "Don't ever do that again!" he said to Kennedy. " 'Fuck off, buddy boy,' " Gore recalls Kennedy responding, "to which one of America's most distinguished men of letters responded, 'You fuck off, too.' " Since clearly he had the Attorney General's ear, Gore renewed the complaint he had outlined in his *Esquire* article about the FBI's acting in the South as an anti-civil-rights terrorist organization. Kennedy responded that it was none of his business. Gore said that as a writer he would make it his business. Kennedy answered that he was not much of a writer. Later, Gore heard that Kennedy claimed that Gore had said, "I'll get you!" No one had seen the encounter. No one else heard the dialogue.

Within minutes the two men separated. Gore fled into the Green Room, "not from Bobby but from a terrible bad karma in the air." Before he could move across the room to Lee Radziwill, who had waved to him, Lem Billings, a Kennedy friend, suddenly confronted him with his disregard of the Council on the Arts. He had not gone to one meeting. Why did you accept, Billings wanted to know, if you weren't going to attend? Vidal's explanation did not satisfy Billings. Gore, for whom a social event was not an appropriate occasion for ironing out business disagreements, felt attacked by someone inexplicably quarrelsome at a time when the occasion required social pleasantries. Leaving Billings, he found himself at a table with Ethel Kennedy, Robert Kennedy's wife, and two other equally dull people, a tediousness that flowing champagne helped make tolerable. Everyone drank handsomely. After midnight, eager to leave, Gore signaled Schlesinger about departure. Schlesinger had found the evening tense. After only one year of the new administration, "the mood . . . was different," Schlesinger wrote in his diary. "People were tired. . . . There was an undercurrent of edginess everywhere." John Kenneth Galbraith's table, at which he had been seated with Eunice Shriver, Tish Baldrige (Jackie's social secretary), "and some lady who is doing the White House furniture," had not been scintillating either. "A loud jazz band made a nerve-curdling but pleasant racket." Gore tried to negotiate a taxi. A crowd of Secret Service men, ushers, and guests blocked the exit. It seemed sensible to wait for Schlesinger. The President came by. " 'You know, I'd like to wring your brother's neck,' " Gore said to him. " 'That's the White House. Don't worry,' Jack said. So I just sort of sat around, and Jack was off in a corner with a beautiful girl, having a chat." Finally, hours after midnight, Schlesinger got Gore, Galbraith, and George Plimpton into his car. Plimpton, whose years at Exeter overlapped with Gore's and who, as editor of *The Paris Review,* had been establishing a literary-social career in New York, had been thrilled by his White House evening. In the car Gore may have told them something about his encounter with Bobby. If the champagne had at first calmed him down, more of it inflamed him. Galbraith remembered nothing about that part of the conversation. He had had "a great deal of champagne" and remembered "telling Gore Vidal on the way home that Shakespeare was almost certainly better than he. Gore was mortally insulted but took it well." The next morning Gore called Schlesinger to give his account of his confrontation with Bobby. Schlesinger recorded a version identical, except for some inconsequential phrasing, to what Gore told others then and afterward.

Unpleasant as the episode had been, there were no immediate consequences. "Actually," Gore wrote four years later to Louis Auchincloss, "we both behaved like children and neither can take much satisfaction from any version." No one at the White House took it seriously, even Robert Kennedy, for whom it may have seemed just another unpleasant encounter with someone he already disliked. Gossip, of course, quickly embellished it. But the President essentially dismissed it as the kind of thing his brother had a penchant for. Bobby had never been diplomatic, let alone tactful. It was not his strength. It was certainly not his job. Jackie did not in the least hold it against Gore. If what she heard about the interchange had importance for her, it was simply to try to remember to keep the two men apart, or at least avoid being together with both of them, something unlikely to happen anyway, unless it were at some other White House party. As always, such parties were a trial to Gore, and they intensified his ambivalence, his awareness that he was in the process of deciding to give up politics and New York/Washington social life altogether. But neither Jackie nor he saw this as any impediment to their cordiality. There were no further invitations to the White House that winter or spring 1962. Probably that would have been the case even if Gore and Bobby had been cordial. The White House had other social and political fish to fry, both at home and abroad, and there never had been an ongoing intimacy except with Jackie, who easily turned such friendships off as well as on. She did not turn it off with Gore regardless of what had been reported to her about the White House incident. When in early-summer 1962 he sent her a copy of *Three* and his first book of essays, *Rocking the Boat,* which contained the *Sunday Telegraph* article on the President, her response was friendly. She had just read his article on Jack and couldn't wait to get to the others in the volume. Since it was at last lovely summer, she would have leisure time to read, and she longed to know more about Julian the Apostate. She hoped that they would be seeing Gore soon and urged him to get in touch with her at Hyannis, where she would be for all of July.

Rocking the Boat formally introduced Gore to a wide public as a more-than-occasional essayist. It was favorably reviewed, though its political articles riled conservative critics, some balm to the ache caused by the failure of *Romulus,* which had opened at the Music Box theater on January 10. Oliver Smith had designed the sets. "After a disastrous run-through," Gore recalled, "he was sitting behind me in the theater—he leaned over and said—he called everybody cookie—'Well, cookie, it isn't Aeschylus.' " At Sardi's he waited with the Roveres and Dupees for the first reviews. They were mixed but far from damning. Most reviewers found the first act "flat and ponderous," some consolation for Gore, since the first act was Dürrenmatt, the second newly composed. "Let us be grateful for *Romulus,*" the *New York Times* reviewer concluded, "for a witty, slashing half-play assuredly is better than none." Roger Stevens soon spent $50,000 of his own money on advertising to keep the play alive. But audiences did not come. It ran for only sixty-nine performances. "I decided," Stevens wrote to Gore at the middle of March, that "the fight was hopeless. . . . I just had lunch with Cyril, who still can't understand why we closed the show, but, as you know, actors are very vague about financial details. . . . I hope . . . that by now you've finished at least two plays so that we can get back some money for our backers." For Gore the retrospective analysis was frank. "I liked the notion of *Romulus.* It had failed everywhere, in Germany and so on, and I thought I could fix it and I couldn't. It runs out of gas halfway through. Once you know the plot, it's repetition. I did my best with the ending to try to open it up and make it a little larger than it was. If I'd had a better actor— I picked Cyril Ritchard in a moment of madness. He was a good comic basically, and he was wonderful in *Visit.* But he was not made

for this. I should have waited: I could have gotten Paul Scofield, who might
have given us quite a different play. It didn't work. It's never worked in any
language. It was a mistake."

When *Romulus* closed, Gore was abroad. He had no intention, for the
time being, of providing Roger Stevens with another play. A Broadway
show had some of the same risks as a political campaign. Usually a great
deal of effort and money produced no return at all. At least with a book, the
book remained, a tangible embodiment of effort and imagination. Also, his
confidence in the well-made realistic play that commercial theater encouraged had been undermined by the impact of the expressionistic plays he had
seen in Berlin in 1960. Commercial theater seemed an untenable arena for
effective symbolic or intellectual drama. Theater itself had never, he had felt
from the start, been his most empathetic forum. He liked the glamour, the
wide exposure, the opportunity to make a great deal of money. Unlike
fiction, though, theater demanded excessive simplification of a sort his intellect and artistry did not readily embrace. He had done it for television, for
movie scripts, for Broadway. But the enterprise had all along had an explicit
Faustian element to it. He had not sold his soul, but he had sold his time and
his pen, and the commercial devil, so to speak, had kept his side of the
bargain. Large sums of money had been paid him, enough so that if he
invested wisely and lived reasonably he would not have to write exclusively
for money perhaps ever again, or at least for some time. And if he chose to
do so, he could do it selectively, bound by neither long-term contract nor
immediate necessity.

His campaign for Congress had had nothing Faustian about it at all.
He had immersed himself in politics partly because he had, so to speak, been
genetically programmed to do so, partly because ambition and circumstance
had come together to hand him the opportunity to run for office. It was to
remain an ongoing virus in the blood. But by early 1962 the virus had lost its
strength. That he would ever be elected to high political office seemed less
and less likely. Another campaign would probably be more a forum for
articulating his ideas than a practical avenue into political service. In the
ordinary run of things he was simply not electable. The extraordinary
sometimes did happen, as it might have if he had been willing to continue to
pay his 29th District political dues and make himself available for the
congressional nomination in 1962 and, if necessary, again in 1964. Still, to
run he would need some reasonable assurance that he had a respectable

chance to win. When Joe Hawkins urged him to try again for Congress in 1962, it was clear he had a better chance to win than in 1960. But the prospect of being a congressman had lost much of its attraction. During the spring and summer of 1962 he was given strong encouragement by the New York State Democratic establishment to run against the Republican incumbent for the Senate. He did some preliminary evaluations, including employing a professional analyst to evaluate the electoral situation, which reinforced his sense that Jacob Javits was virtually an unbeatable incumbent. Gore would have liked to serve in the Senate, but what was the point in spending time and money for an almost certain defeat? If he gave serious consideration to a long-term political plan, which would have encouraged him to accept losing in 1962 so as to position himself perhaps to win in 1966, he most likely found the thought of how he would have to spend his time during these years repellently chilling.

Eager to get away, he accepted an invitation from the Italian line, promoting its New York–Italy service, to sail as its guest to Rome and Athens early in 1962 on the *Leonardo da Vinci*. "It's not like a celebrity cruise as we envision it now," Joanne Woodward recalls, "where people go on the cruise to entertain. The celebrities then were not expected to do anything. They were just to be there." As a famous playwright, Gore seemed attractively compatible with other stars from the entertainment world. Gloria Swanson was on board, and his New York friends Ruth Ford and Zachary Scott. Howard would fly to Italy to join Gore there. Why don't you come on the cruise also? he had asked the Newmans. "I said, 'Oh, no, I can't do that! My babies! My babies are small. What if something terrible happens to them? I couldn't do that!' So we said we couldn't go. Paul in the meantime made me feel very guilty, saying, 'We never do anything! We don't go anywhere! Let's do something!' And I said, 'My babies! my babies! How can I go?' And then, finally, Okay. But we didn't tell Gore that we were going. There was a farewell party on board, and we went and we chatted. Of course we had taken our bags on and had them hidden away. We spent the time at the party with Gore. Finally the announcement came, 'All ashore that's going ashore.' We said, 'Well, Gore, have a wonderful trip. We'll see ya.' And we went downstairs, clutching martinis, as if we were going to leave. We waited until the ship sailed out of the harbor, and then we went back upstairs. Gore was still sitting there, clutching a martini, one of many, I'm sure by then, and he looked up and said, 'Wait, you're supposed to be off! You're supposed to be off!' It was great fun and a wonderful trip." Food was piled high, especially mounds of caviar. Liquor flowed. Gore read Isherwood's recently published *Down There on a Visit*, which he found powerful and funny, though he disagreed with Isherwood's emphasis on an aggressive division between hetero- and homosexual, as if the two had to be constantly at war. "You do make me laugh," he wrote to Isherwood. "That image of the poster: won't you please help? nearly got me from my bunk to the deck of the Leonardo." In the evenings the passengers were treated to movies in which the Newmans starred, including *Cat on a Hot Tin Roof* and *The Three Faces of Eve*. One of Gore's films was shown, *The Catered Affair*. One elderly lady developed a crush on him, another on Paul. Each, starry-eyed, followed her idol around the ship.

After a smooth Atlantic passage, the Mediterranean provided heavy seas, destabilizing storms. Howard joined the boat at Palermo. When they got to Athens in rough seas, the Newmans had had enough of the cruise. "No sooner had Howard got on," Woodward recalls, "than we had this terrible storm. There were suddenly ropes all over the boat. Howard said we had to get off instantly. So we got to Piraeus and jumped ship. Got all our bags off." Gore and Howard, soon joined by Elaine Dundy, who came from London, went on to Rhodes and other Aegean sites. Elaine's marriage had gone from frenetically embattled to bitterly divisive. She had been attempting, irresolutely, to divorce Ken, or at least to make a separation stick. During Tynan's two-year stint at *The New Yorker* she and Gore had become close friends, "inties" (short for intimate), a word she enjoyed using. Ken and Gore had continued as ordinary friends. On her visits to Edgewater, Gore had happily become her "dear Gauze," a familiarity that encompassed a mixture of infatuation and love. Both accepted it as simply their ongoing enjoyment of one another. It involved pleasure, fun, help, a substantial correspondence when apart. Gore gave her much good advice about a play she had been writing, soon to be produced in London. One night at Edgewater, both drunk, they had gone to bed together. Now, at a particularly tense time in her life, she was delighted to be invited to join Gore in Athens, especially since she could share with him his fascination with the ancient world. The voyage had turned into what had been Gore's underlying reason for the entire trip, an on-site survey both through the eyes of the present and through an educated imagination that evoked the past of the lands Julian had lived in. Athens, where they spent almost a month, astounded him. The

American literary critic Leslie Fiedler welcomed them to a circle of American, British, and Greek writers who had made Athens in the fifties and early sixties a well-fabled artistic and cultural center. Conversation, sunshine, sex, food, the low cost of living—for a moment Athens seemed golden again. "I have just come back from Athens (a first visit; I am Hellenophile)," he was soon to write to the Greek ambassador to America, who had written him a "good and constructive" letter about the two chapters of *Julian* that had been published in *Three,* "where I completed a long section on J. at the university (from Ennepius) and at Eleusis. . . . Do you know my new friend [the Greek poet, Niko] Gatsos? or my old friend Kimon Friar? I have never felt more completely, atavistically at home than in Athens; yet I am of Roman descent!"

From Athens he and Howard went on to Egypt, Jordan, Israel, Lebanon, Cyprus, Turkey, Athens again, and Rome. At Istanbul they explored the marketplace, examined the mosques. Julian the Apostate was on Gore's mind. Egypt seemed hardly different from when he had been there in 1948. From Jordan they attempted to cross into Israel at the Mandelbaum Bridge. Fortunately, the cooperative Jordanians manipulated their passports so that they could enter. At Tel Aviv they enjoyed the beaches. The handsome sabras compelled notice. He liked the lively, articulate, intellectual young Israelis. Jerusalem, for Gore the symbolic center of three restrictive, puritanical religions, did not appeal to him. Whatever impact his brief stay in Israel and Jordan had on him, his imagination was elsewhere. The Middle East's European and classical past riveted his attention, with special emphasis on the conflict between the classical and the Christian worlds that had been the dramatic center of Julian's life. The Arabness of the Middle East held no attraction. It was a world, so he wrote to Isherwood, where "there are no facts, no information." When he failed to locate a copy of *Down There on a Visit* to replace the one he had given the Newmans, he had a quick lesson in the unavailability in the Middle East of Anglo-American literary culture, especially books. When they arrived in Beirut, he was happy at last to be again in a heavily European-influenced city, Lebanon noticeably less impoverished than other countries they had been to, including Israel. And, at last, there was good food. In Turkey he viewed the sites associated with Julian's reign. Returning to Europe, his second visit to Athens followed quickly after his first. The Greek sun, the blue-green sea, Piraeus in the distance from the Athenian hills, the white millennia-old marble resonating under an absolutely clear winter sky everywhere he walked—suddenly Athens seemed a place he needed to return to, a place he could perhaps live in.

At Delphi he was deeply touched by the ancient mysteries, the prophetic voices, the omphalos representing the beginning and the end. On a moonless midnight in February 1962, with the sky filled with stars, Gore ascended by himself to the ruins of the Temple of Apollo. The clear light seemed illuminated silver against darkness. The Gulf of Corinth breathed in the descending distance. This was a place of classical and stoic sharpness. The temple had, millennia before, been dedicated to the sunlight Gore himself worshipped. But it was also the place of dark, sibylline mysteries. As he stood on the spot where Greek mythology said the world began and where the ancient oracle at Delphi had forecast the future, he felt more strongly than ever the inseparability of past and present, and he felt that the visionary connections he could make through his imagination and artistry were as thrillingly close as he or anyone could ever hope to come to bringing them together. Like the Eleusinian Mysteries, whose site near Athens he had recently visited, this too was an ancient mystery that spoke deeply to him about the powers of the pagan past. It seemed to connect him with his childhood reading, with the strange formative power that *The Spartan* and indeed everything about the classical world had exerted on him from the beginning of his conscious life. The moment was both exhilarating and frightening. Suddenly the dark side of his vision took form. In the starlight, as he walked through the ruins along the Sacred Way to the temple, he could see, as he was to write in *Drawing Room Comedy*, an unpublished play, "the golden eagles of Apollo, circling among the cliffs." There was a wind in the pine trees, and as he came to the altar, he turned— "and there . . . was the mountain. And I said, 'Look, at the strange shape the mountain makes. . . . See? It's like the wings of a great eagle.' " And then "the eagle seemed to rise higher and higher in the sky, covering all the stars, until at last the great wings shut . . . peacefully . . . gently . . . finally. The wings had now blacked out the sky."

In Rome he saw familiar places and people, including the Hollywood producer Walter Wanger, ill from his disastrous involvement with *Cleopatra*. "Takes lots of pills," Gore told Elaine. "Hands shake when he discusses Liz and Richard . . . wanted to hold his head which has tremors like Parkinson's, held it, did no good." Classical and literary Rome seemed as attractive as ever. As lively as Athens had been, Rome seemed the more livable, partly because Athens was relatively isolated. If he were to live in either while writing *Julian,* Rome had the advantage of an excellent library at the American Academy. From Rome they went to Capri, to visit Eddie and Mona Williams Bismarck at Mona's magnificent floral gardens and lovely Palazzo Fortina, high up on a cliff from which there was a splendid view of Ischia and the Bay of Naples. All the water for the garden had to be imported from the mainland through a special tunnel and pipeline she had built. Stylish, wealthy, but in her own way reclusive, Mona spent more and more time on Capri, where Gore renewed the friendship that had begun in New York in 1948. "Week in Capri with Bismarcks, beautiful, otherworldly." But "what's other world like? dull." Capri was a place to visit, not live in, so he thought. When he confided to Mona that he might enjoy a long stay in an apartment in Rome, she suggested someone who could help. By early March they were back at Edgewater, where he found himself happily energetic, for the first time in almost a decade focusing exclusively on fiction.

If having two novels in mind—one partly under way, the other in the planning stage—was a problem, it was neither so great nor so dividing that he could resist (or perhaps even wanted to resist) actually starting in May 1962 to write *Washington, D.C.* With politics mostly behind him or on indefinite hold, with no movie or theater commitments, almost everything literary seemed possible that summer. Probably he wrote the first chapter in May, the storm scene in which Peter Sanford sees in flashes of lightning his sister Enid and Clay Overbury making love, a scene whose coordinates had first come to his imagination when attending his half-sister Nini's wedding at Merrywood in 1957. "I am here for the summer," he wrote Isherwood, "immersing myself in the novel after nearly ten years' vacation in the theatre. I find planning it hard: it is a time novel; fifteen years, Washington DC, what has become of us, all that. I am using up everything on this one: I have a sense if I don't get to it now, the game is up and I shall have to go on being a rattling public man until some disaster due to one's own eccentricity puts out the light." He also sent Isherwood a copy of *Three,* which "contains the first third of a novel about the Apostate. It's nicely written, I think." So nicely written and so compelling that he kept at work at it also, and soon mostly put aside *Washington, D.C.,* for increasing immersion in *Julian.* Dutchess County friends and visitors kept the usual social-intellectual life bright. The Dupees and the Roveres were around, as well as Bard College people, and they all made the regular rounds for Sunday-morning newspapers and brunches and afternoon cocktails and evening parties. With Dupee, who urged him to devote himself full-time to writing, Gore discussed mostly literature and people. Dupee particularly urged Gore to develop and engage what everyone had now recognized was a great talent for the personal essay.

Jason and Barbara Epstein, who usually stayed with the Dupees, now regularly came over to Edgewater. Jason, who had become executive editor at Random House, where he was also in charge of Modern Library books, was eager to have him as a Random House author. The previous spring he had tried to induce Gore to write a book for him. "Take, say ten or a dozen of America's presumed leaders and really let yourself go as you did, for example, when you wrote about Mailer. . . . I don't think we have to ask the question: can this republic survive? In the long run, of course, it won't. Nothing does. But there are questions to be asked about the quality of life here and now and one way to answer them, approximately, is by examining our representative men. . . . These men can be approached and measured as representatives of a culture and a history in much the way that Proust or Tolstoy or for that matter Mailer can be." Gore did not take the bait.

> I see your point but I suggest that politicians cannot be
> written about in the same way as one writes about novelists.
> Why? Because to be a critic one must have at all times the
> sense of alternative. One says 'no' to this because one says
> 'yes' to that. In literature we call an alternative a touchstone. I
> do not like the novels of Marquand because I like the works of
> Proust. One is compared to the other and in the comparison
> the first is measured (and sometimes the second is illuminated). Or even in the context of the same man's work: I do
> not like *A Fable* and I do like *Light in August,* two things are
> compared: one we accept as excellent, the other proved faulty
> by comparison. By comparing Mailer to myself, to our contemporaries, to Tolstoy I was able to examine his work from a
> number of angles (alternatives) and I could give him within
> that frame a mark. Politicians in a society like ours are not so
> easily explicated. You feel it of little importance what bills
> they propose, what positions they take: but those actions are

their work . . . their novels. Motives are always fascinating
to speculate on but, finally, they are as irrelevant to the man's
effect as the motive of a novelist: it is not why you write it, it
is what you write that creates the Kingdom of Heaven. Political motives tend to be simple, in any case: the man wants to
prevail. Democratic politicians in this country are perhaps the
only true existentialists in the world.

As an essayist, Gore saw clearly that his deepest impulses were satirical, and
"like most satirists I am a reactionary: I like the old republic, repelled
though I am by many of its manifestations now. I see Caesarism as the
alternative, and I cannot make up my mind whether or not it is a good thing
(in my bones, I *know* it is bad). Yet under good Caesars we might enjoy a
Pax Americana without too much limiting of individual freedom. But under
bad Caesars . . . well, we know what to fear. As I told you when I saw
you, in my own divided state these days I would hesitate to engage in such a
project unless I was absolutely clear, for good or ill, as to an alternative.
Displeasure with what is, is not enough." And he was still committed to
Little, Brown.

In fact, "displeasure with what is" *could*, in certain literary circumstances, be enough, an alternative view he was to find increasingly tenable.
The great Roman and British satirists had created enduring literature with
an indignation, sometimes "savage," that had contained no remedial program, no proffer of reasonable alternatives. To see intensely what was
wrong was often, actually, more artistically viable than to propose what
might be right, or even simply better. The limitations of human nature and
the human situation were the raw material for art. But what Epstein proposed was not art; it was social science and intellectual analysis, something
that both author and editor knew that Gore sometimes could carry off
brilliantly. But except for the occasional essay, this was not what he wanted
to do now. He had freed himself from the need to write for money. Ideas
fascinated him. But he wanted ideas in the formal structures and with the
imaginative opportunities that only literature, particularly the novel, offered.
In August 1962, when John Aldridge commented in a *New York Times Book
Review* article, "What Became of Our Postwar Hopes?" that Vidal had told
him that he had given up on the novel as a currently viable literary form,
Gore reacted angrily. Aldridge had either misunderstood or purposely dis-

torted what he had said. On the contrary, he wrote to the *Book Review,* he was committed to writing novels. Two of them were under way. "Now, of course, I never abandoned the novel. In fact, I have just finished writing one," he exaggerated. "More to the point, I never made the announcement referred to, publicly or privately. I add the 'privately' because Aldridge always tended to rely too much on what someone said at a party." He never forgave Aldridge for what he felt was a recklessly damaging slur, especially at a time when he was trying to reestablish himself as a novelist. His response to Jason's proposal had been an indirect affirmation of this commitment. He wanted to put his energies into fiction. It was the form in which his literary ambition had started, and where he expected it to continue and eventually end. Through the summer of 1962 he worked with increasing intensity on *Julian.*

Suddenly in August, tired and overweight, he went to Key West, where he was, he told Alice Dows, "so bored—but then again never so healthy and *thin:* it is like being reborn. I need another ten days or so and then I should be able to face everything in the fall, even an election!" But he was not in the end to be tempted by the Democratic nomination for the Senate. The odds against winning were too great. By the end of the month he had said no to that. There were the usual invitations to appear on television, some of which he accepted, particularly Susskind's *Open End* and *The Tonight Show,* partly because he thought it good for his career, mostly because he often had something he wanted to say. Through the fall he worked as diligently as he could on *Julian.* But there were pesty interruptions, many simply the inevitable requirements of daily life at Edgewater or at the apartment in New York. One was the sad occasion of Eleanor Roosevelt's death. At Hyde Park, in the rain, he attended the funeral on November 10. This was one of the rare occasions on which he wanted to pay his last respects in the traditional way. The Roosevelt family had invited him to both the public and the private ceremonies. As he drove through the heavy traffic, the crowds were almost impenetrable. The rain kept falling. For him it was a dismal, funereal day filled with thoughts about the death of a great American who had been a friend both to his father and to him. He "stood alongside the thirty-third, the thirty-fourth, the thirty-fifth, and the thirty-sixth Presidents of the United States, not to mention all the remaining figures of the Roosevelt era who had assembled for her funeral. . . . She was like no one else in her usefulness. As the box containing her went by me, I thought, well, that's that. We're really on our own now."

Other interruptions arose from the temptations of ordinary social life. Some were business details, many of which Howard handled. But his temperament and his situation made Gore constantly available to calls, to requests for help, for participation in one thing or another, whether personal or social or political. Just before mid-November he went for five days to "The First *Show* Magazine Inter-American Symposium," at Paradise Island in the Bahamas, one of those irresistible invitations. Among the nineteen North American participants were Max Lerner, whom he had heard lecture at Exeter, the playwright Edward Albee, the composer Aaron Copland, and the dancer Katherine Dunham. Arthur Schlesinger and William Styron attended. So too did Norman Podhoretz, the young editor of the New York Jewish intellectual magazine *Commentary,* and Richard Goodwin, now a member of the Kennedy administration, who when he had come to Dutchess County in 1960 as a Kennedy advance man had stayed at Edgewater. Nini was delighted to accept his invitation that she join him there. (Later Gore discovered that the symposium had been sponsored by the CIA.) Though he had sufficient discipline to shut himself off for a certain number of hours each day, usually from morning into midafternoon, the discipline took its toll, the interruptions still came.

Since he could write anyplace, he began to think more and more about spending half of the next year abroad, in one of the places that had always gripped his imagination, where he could work on *Julian* free from the pressure of interruptions, some of them inevitably irresistible, that he had at home. Athens had appealed to him. Rome was always close to his heart, "Roman fever" a lifelong happy disease. He had no intention, though, of living abroad permanently. His thought was to spend part of the next year in Rome, with frequent pleasurable visits to Greece and other places. That seemed acceptable to Howard, who was not enthusiastic about even that schedule. Howard saw no reason, for himself, to leave Edgewater and New York. What would it mean to his own latent desire to have some sort of career, particularly to sing professionally, though he recognized that his difficulty with stage fright and his lack of training were formidable obstacles? Still, he had a full life at home. If he went abroad with Gore, that life would have to be re-created. They would be thrown back more on one another, Howard particularly on Gore. Was that a commitment he wanted to make, an experience he wanted to embrace? In the late fall, suddenly, Howard became ill. Potentially life-threatening cancer seemed likely. "At first Sloan-Kettering Memorial Hospital was so crowded they couldn't take him in," Gore recalled. In the three weeks that it took to get admitted, during which they worried that this might be cancer, Gore tried every conceivable contact that might help expedite admission. "We pulled all sorts of strings." Finally, in late November, he had this "big thing cut out of his throat, a benign growth but a huge one on the thyroid. . . . Frank Merlo," Tennessee Williams's longtime companion, "had just come to the hospital to die, so Tennessee and I would go there together. He'd visit Frank, and I'd visit Howard." During the surgery Gore paced the halls, the streets. Suddenly one of the foundations of his life was threatened, and though there were never explicit words to this effect between them, clearly the threat was to the one person in the world he cared most about. "I remember once," Joanne Woodward recalls, "when Howard had a cancer and there was the possibility . . . He was terrified. Oh, he loves Howard very much. I don't know that he would ever say that. . . . Sex is sex, right! But . . . Howard's the only person I know with whom he's had a long-term relationship. I'm sure it wasn't a sexual relationship. Gore found in Howard the perfect caretaker of the legend." The growth was removed, the surgery successful. By Christmas he was out of the hospital.

With a deep sigh of relief, they went ahead with Roman plans. Through a contact they had subleased for a year an apartment in Rome's old city. Howard, heavily bandaged, would stay on in New York for the rest of his recovery, perhaps a few weeks at most before he could fly, and to make the necessary business arrangements for Edgewater and the brownstones. Then he would join Gore in Rome. Before leaving New York, Gore received a telegram from Nina. "HEAR YOU'RE LEAVING FOR A YEAR. THINK WE BETTER GET TOGETHER AND MAKE UP OR HAVE A GOOD FIGHT. HAPPY NEW YEAR LOVE BOMMY." He did not respond. In late January 1963, after sailing to Naples and taking the train up to Rome, Gore took possession of a furnished apartment at 4 Via Giulia, between the Tiber and the Campo dei Fiore. One of his first meals was at a restaurant that was to become a favorite, La Carbonara, at the top of the Campo dei Fiore, facing the black statue of Giordano Bruno, who had been burned there as a heretic in 1600. The beneficent Roman winter sunshine warmed him happily. Howard soon came, with their dogs Billy and Blanche. The manuscript of *Julian,* written on yellow, lined legal-size paper, began to grow. Each morning he lived imaginatively in the fourth century. In the afternoons he walked across Rome to the American Academy, whose library had everything he needed. The streets of Rome delighted him. The balance between the ancient and the modern he felt within himself. Evenings he spent at trattorias, with friends and visitors. He had begun the most creatively fruitful decade of his life.

CHAPTER fourteen

Delphi

1963–1966

ON ONE LEVEL, the temporary move to Rome in January 1963 was an escape from a form of death. Gore had come to dislike Manhattan and New York City life. His dislike was later to rise to detestation. He felt that he could not flourish as a writer in New York, that he needed distance, not only from the city but from America as well. Even at relatively secluded Edgewater, daily distractions were unavoidable. The move to sun-filled Rome promised a long visit with classical culture and the opportunity to focus his mind and imagination fully on his work. And the Italian acceptance of the casual pleasures of daily life seemed as close to the pagan world as anyone in the modern world could come. Rome, especially for foreigners, was a happily anti-puritan place. And in Rome he could also leave behind the temptation to try for political office again, a form of death to the degree that it would always be a restriction on his imagination, his literary work, even his freedom to speak his mind. And leave as well the lure of television appearances. Taking an apartment on Via Giulia seemed likely to provide relief from their fatal attractions. More than anything he wanted to finish *Julian,* a novelistic canvas on which he could explore some of the coordinates of the vision he had had at Delphi. In February 1962 he had found Athens a congenial place in which to write his account of young Julian's initiation at Eleusis. Rome seemed the right venue for him now. And if politics, television, and New York City distractions were metaphoric depredations, there were also real deaths to deal with via an imagination that so embraced living energy that the fact of death brought him as close to panic as he ever came.

Gene Vidal's heart attack in 1942 had changed his own life. Less directly so, his son's. But the fear that he might suffer his father's fate was never far from Gore's mind. Coronary disease ran in the family on both sides. His father had never been the same again. As far as he had gone, he would go hardly any further. What seemed in retrospect to his son a golden beginning with the promise of high achievement and station had dissipated after 1942. Thereafter, his father seemed somewhat afraid of life. He had settled for much less than what he might have done and been. The heart attack seemed to Gore the turning point. As much as he deeply loved his father, he felt the disappointment. He himself feared that he might be cut off before he had his chance. With more than a touch of hypochondria, he metaphorically kept his hand on his own pulse. When it seemed possible, in late fall 1962, that Howard had thyroid cancer, their world tilted abruptly into fear. Both of them trembled for one another and for themselves. Gore's overpowering relief when Howard's tumor was benign steadied him. He had no doubt, though, that the strong stomach pains that he himself felt after settling at Via Giulia in January 1963 were the result of how anguished he had been during the past months. Soon after arriving in Rome, he was unhappy to learn that he had "(a) a duodenal ulcer, (b) a malfunctioning liver, (c) a spastic colon," he wrote to Alice Dows, "none of these things particularly fatal but all these together depressing. But I have a good doctor (just to check on *him* I use a second doctor and act upon the consensus!), and I live on rice and milk. . . . They expect the ulcer to be gone in another two weeks." Still, he felt like Prometheus being tortured, even if moderately. "The vulture has two heads," he told Fred Dupee, "one to the liver bent, the other to the duodenum; but the beaks are blunt; heads droop. We regain our health, slowly." Fortunately, "Howard is recovered." Fred wrote back, "I hope your liver is improved, dear Prometheus—just shoo that nasty eagle away." The dogs, though, were mimicking their masters. "Blanche nearly rode on ahead to the great shining kennel in the sky . . .

but is finally cured of nephritis by a local vet. . . . Billy has had two epileptic fits." Their maid at Via Giulia, who concluded that Billy was possessed of the devil, constantly made propitiatory signs to ward off the evil eye. Deep within the pagan sunlight, as Gore had always known, is the inescapable darkness, the evil eye of catastrophe, of death. He feared it for himself and for those he cared about. In life he always did his best to keep even the thought of it at a distance. In literature he engaged the darkness by dramatizing its marriage to light. Persephone and Pluto were in an eternal embrace. The Eleusinian Mysteries were life-enhancing. "Energy is eternal delight." All things change except the process of change. His stoic consolation was in that.

He could manage only a thin stoicism in the face of his grandmother's illness. When he had seen her in late fall 1962, the sight had struck despair into his heart. By mid-1962 she was too ill to be taken for drives in the car Gore had recently bought for her. She could no longer read or write. Theresa, her maid, took care of the household; a day nurse was always on duty. When Gore came with Nini to the Crescent Place apartment in late fall 1962, Dot did not recognize him. A moment after they left, she asked Theresa who that man was, and then sent her to catch him. She was too late. "I can not express my feeling," she told Gore, in a letter dictated to Theresa who imposed her informal grammar on Mrs. Gore's sentences, "when I found that I did not recognize who you was when you last visited me. You seemed to have been much more slender. You looked as you did when you and I went to Key West Fla. You was my first grandchild. That will remain with me as long as I shall live." For Christmas, he sent her two nightgowns, which she enjoyed wearing. Before leaving for Rome in mid-January, he visited again. There seemed reason to believe she would linger for months, if not years. But in late April she took a decisive turn toward death. Two strokes rendered her mostly speechless. Her kidneys began to fail. On May 8 she died. "Things were rather in a turmoil at the apartment what with Nina, Theresa, Dot's day nurse, Roy Thompson," and other people there. "She was holding Theresa's hand, as they were turning her over in bed, when she died. . . . I distinctly remember," Dot's son Tom explained to Gene Vidal three weeks later, "someone say that Gore had been notified of Dot's death, but in the intervening days, not having heard from either him or you, it raised some doubts in my mind that [either of] you were notified. A cousin of ours asked Nina a direct question on the matter in Oklahoma City, and she said that she had sent Gore a cable."

If so, Gore, in Rome, never received it. His first notice of Dot's death came weeks later in a letter from Roy Thompson, as lawyer for her estate, who wanted to know Gore's wishes about the disposition of the car registered in his name. "I know that you were distressed at not being able to be here at the last. The truth is that for quite some days before death your grandmother would not have known whether or not you were here. So be it!" Tom Gore meanwhile wrote to Gene, who forwarded the letter to Gore, "It is a blessing that she has departed the earth and is now where she longed to be for the last few years. I can honestly say that she is out of the misery she lived in." Gore had no argument with that or with Tom Gore's contrite apology for the failure to notify him. Tom Gore had assumed that his sister had indeed done what she claimed she had. Nini, Gore's half-sister, might have known not to make that assumption. But Nina did not herself notify either Gore or Gene, and she had no hesitation cabling Gore on other occasions when it suited her needs. Perhaps exhaustion and shock absorbed all their mental energies. Gore of course had written Nina out of his life. Perhaps her silence and then her probable lie to her brother may have had a touch of unconscious or even conscious revenge. Probably he would not have been able, even if he had been notified immediately, to attend the funeral, and perhaps he would have preferred to stay away, as he had when his grandfather had died, from such proximity to death. In accord with her wishes, Dot's body was taken immediately to Oklahoma City and quickly buried, with only the briefest of ceremonies, beside her husband's in the family plot. In Rome, unaware of what was happening in the land of his ancestors, Gore went about his daily business, working on *Julian* in the mornings, taking long walks in the afternoons. His grandmother had frequently, in better days, reminded him that eventually he too would be called home. " 'There's room for you, too,' Dot would say, enticingly. 'We can take four more.' "

From Rome he felt that broad aspects of American politics could be seen clearly, if not more clearly, than from up close. He had decided in 1962 not to run for office again, at least for the foreseeable future. But as a compulsive observer with keen political instincts, he had not and would never forswear writing about the American political scene. That, he felt, was not in the least incompatible with his career as a novelist. He had ample energy for both, and his fiction and political essays shared an interest in the disposition of political power. As he worked on *Julian,* he had vividly in mind his next novel, *Washington, D.C.,* a small part of which he had already written. And what was the Emperor Julian himself if not a masterful politician? Since the publication of his first essays in the early 1950s Vidal had, over the next decade, achieved some reputation in that form, and the publication in 1962 of *Rocking the Boat* had brought his essayistic skills to the appreciative attention of a wide audience. He had happily given up his post as *The Reporter*'s theater critic. Regular, forced playgoing bored him. But politics did not. With the encouragement of Harold Hayes, a tactful North Carolinian in his mid-thirties who in 1960 had become *Esquire* magazine's managing editor, he had been doing a short political and/or literary column regularly enough so that it appeared frequently. With the support of Arnold Gingrich, *Esquire*'s publisher, Hayes had begun his successful effort to change *Esquire* from a magazine for men, providing mainly sexual titillation and fashion advice, into a general-audience anthology of sophisticated fiction and cutting-edge journalism emphasizing the personal voice. Mailer's impressionistic account from the left of the 1960 Democratic convention had become the prototype of what was now being called the New Journalism, and *Esquire* attracted its most talented acolytes, like Tom Wolfe and Gay Talese, while it also published fiction by, among others, Truman Capote and James Baldwin. The far-right wing of the new personal journalism was represented by William F. Buckley, whose account of his worshipful fascination with Whittaker Chambers had appeared in the September 1962 issue. *Esquire* had suddenly become an important magazine. Hayes considered Vidal one of his premiere writers.

Under the title "The Best Man 1968," published in March 1963, Vidal provided Hayes with what was to be *Esquire*'s most widely discussed article of the year. "Was I getting revenge on Bobby for that night at the White House? Who knows? I do know it was all Harold Hayes's idea, that piece. I made clear that I disliked Bobby for President. I also disliked Nelson Rockefeller. So I was ecumenical about the two potential candidates." While working on *Julian,* Vidal took a few days soon after his arrival in Rome to cast into sharp prose his prognostications not about the upcoming 1964 but about the far-distant 1968 presidential election. Since Jack Kennedy seemed a shoo-in for 1964, the question to ask, the essay argued, is who will be the candidates for 1968? Both Vidal's picks were wrong, for unexpected reasons. Nelson Rockfeller's political career would not survive the Republican Party's 1964 Goldwaterite sharp turn to the right. Two assassinations were to prevent Robert Kennedy from inheriting his brother's crown. No one paid much attention to what Gore had to say about Rockefeller. But his depiction of Bobby as a mean, graceless, illiberal, and puritanical politician, unqualified by temperament or judgment to be President, became a widely disseminated story of its own. British and American newspapers ran accounts of the article. Some saw it as a harsh, unwarranted attack. Others found it plausible. That the author was distantly semi-related to the Kennedys made the story even more delicious, especially to those attracted to the human overtones of the frontal assault. In a devastating account of a Kennedy study group whose guest was the British philosopher A. J. Ayer, Gore highlighted Bobby's intellectual and verbal crudeness. When Ethel Kennedy asked, in response to Ayer's sophisticated philosophical presentation, "What about God?," "the result was splendid comedy." Ayer became somewhat flustered. "Bobby muttered, 'Can it, Ethel.' And it was canned until, at the end, Bobby asked, in perfect seriousness: 'But don't you believe in right and wrong?' Ayer capitulated. This was the sort of question usually put early on to a teacher by an adolescent. . . . Our most admired Presidents have not been zealots. They cannot afford to be without seriously deranging the balance of the State. . . . In temperament, John Kennedy is perfectly suited to the Presidency. His brother is not. He would be a dangerously authoritarian-minded President."

Vidal and Harold Hayes had anticipated broad publicity and squeals of outrage. Walter Cronkite, on the most-watched American television network news program, held up a copy of *Esquire*, whose cover featured Bobby sitting in his brother's White House rocking chair and the headline "When Bobby Kennedy Takes Over," to illustrate his brief comment on the subject. "Sorry to hear about the ulcer," Hayes wrote to Vidal. But "what do you have to worry about, for God's sake, sitting it out there on the Via Giulia. I'm the one Bobby can get his hands on, not you." But Hayes was delighted that the article was "raising quite a nice little stink." Every major magazine and wire service picked up the story. As Vidal had predicted, *Esquire*'s circulation for the March issue shot up "conceivably to the highest mark we've reached," Hayes reported, "in the past two or three years." The Kennedys, though, were furious. Vidal inevitably had to pay a price for such mischief-making. Fortunately, it was a price he had been prepared to pay, even if he had not anticipated how definitive a separation from the Kennedys would result from this offense. The 1961 altercation at the White House, unpleasant as it had been, had been a private matter. That the press had picked it up as high-level gossip could hardly be held against Gore. Jackie, in fact, had essentially ignored the incident. Jack had dismissed it as another example of the meaningless bickering people close to White House power were prone to. But this, now, was a direct public attack on a cherished member of the Kennedy clan. Whatever its personal dimension, the attack was political, as if Gore had taken it on himself to affect the family's presidential hopes for Bobby. But since it was an attack on his character, the only response available to the Kennedys was public silence and private fury. And Vidal's attack triggered others. "Did you read the piece on Bobby in *Newsweek*?" he wrote to Louis Auchincloss, himself a distant cousin of Jackie's through Hugh's marriage to Janet. "It is savage and infinitely more documented than my casual commentary." From New York, Auchincloss expressed his delight with the article, "which has stirred up a lot of comment. I must say that I loved it and that 'Can it, Ethel!' has become to me the symbol of the administration. I am tired of the Kennedys, or rather of Kennedyphilia, and I was happy to have you put the whole business on a frankly sinister basis." Vidal reported to Hayes in March that "a courier from the White House came through town, met on the sly: 'outrage' in the palace." The courier may have been Richard Goodwin, who "came to town and we had dinner. . . . He reports JFK's 'outrage' at the piece and so forth. Bobby told a friend of mine (not knowing he was) that he could not retaliate because the attack was 'frontal,' this means of course that it will be *next* year's taxes that send me to jail. I rather expect some funny business from him but I daresay I'll survive it." The situation was double-edged. As Gore recognized, some would use his attack on Bobby to condemn both himself *and* Bobby, and to undermine Jack. "The London papers and—of course—*Time* have been here to see me. I expect *Time* will be able to kill two birds with one stone, the Kennedys and me. I don't look forward to their axe-job but then all things pass." What had now passed conclusively, and perhaps without Gore's full anticipation, was not only his friendly relationship with the President but his friendship with Jackie. The family demanded total loyalty. Jackie, who understood these matters, had no hesitation about her Kennedy commitment. Later the President's wife was to develop her own special relationship with the President's brother. Gore and Jackie were never to talk to one another again.

When Walter Cronkite held up to his huge television audience the copy of *Esquire* that contained Vidal's article, he was responding not only to its newsworthiness but to the fact that the New York newspapers were on strike. That put a slight additional edge of responsibility on other media. With a print-news blackout in New York that lasted for more than three months in late winter and early spring 1963, the usual vehicles for disseminating information and ideas were sorely missed. Television took up some of the slack. But in a society still anchored to the written word, although the mooring was adrift, the absence of a daily print forum reminded New York's literary culture of just how much it depended on the book-review sections of the major newspapers, especially the *Sunday Times Book Review*. At best the *Book Review* was superficial and capricious, at worst narrow-minded and obtuse. Post–World War II American magazine culture had moved decisively toward the economics of mass circulation. *The Saturday Evening Post* typified Norman Rockwell popular culture. *Vogue* and the other fashion magazines were no longer or hardly publishing fiction. For literary short-story writers the market was bleak; for essayists it was dismal; for book reviewers, critiques mostly had to be of newspaper sound-bite length. *The Saturday Review of Literature* was the only weekly magazine devoted exclusively to reviewing books and highlighting literature and was, in fact, becoming increasingly unviable. In 1952 it had dropped "of Literature" from its title. By 1963 it was of minor influence and soon to disappear. By the early 1960s the two magazines dominating the shrinking market for serious literature and ideas were the venerable *New Yorker* and the brash *Esquire*. Both paid reasonably well. Vidal had been shut out of *The New Yorker* from the start of his career. His attempts in the late 1940s to publish fiction there had been rebuffed. Though he admired the magazine, it was clear from early on that his short stories did not meet the moral standards or fit the literary mold *The New Yorker* embodied. It "was a marvelous support group of middlebrow writers called John like Cheever and Updike," Vidal observed. "A great showcase, and it gave them money, prestige. After I had a hit play on Broadway and was writing essays for *The Reporter* and *Partisan Review*, Richard Rovere, my neighbor, the Washington correspondent for

The New Yorker, says you've got to write for *The New Yorker.* And I said, 'I don't see why I've got to. I've got other places. But certainly the money's better there.' And he said, 'I'll fix it up for you. Go see Shawn.' I go to *The New Yorker,* and Mr. Shawn is busy. A Miss Edith Oliver will receive me. She's been there forever. She used to do off-Broadway reviews. And she says, 'Oh, yes, Mr. Rovere said you might be coming in. Tell me, what have you done?' Here I've got a play on Broadway, seven novels, etc., etc. I said, 'Oh, that's too boring to go into. There's a copy of *Who's Who in America* behind you. Why don't you look me up?' Oliver was brisk. 'Well, why don't you, the next time you do a piece, if it's not too much trouble, mail it to me here at *The New Yorker?*' " Unlike *The New Yorker, Esquire* sought controversy and emblazoned on its provocative covers the names of writers as diverse but as dynamic and volatile as Mailer, Buckley, and Vidal.

Responding to the opportunity created by the newspaper strike, having for a long time felt the need for a publication that would provide space for full-length essay-reviews, Barbara and Jason Epstein, with their friend the essayist Elizabeth Hardwick, took their courage in their hands. Money was in more limited supply than courage, so the decision in midwinter 1962–63 was to put out one issue of what they had decided to call *The New York Review of Books.* "There had been a lot of talk," Barbara Epstein recalled, "about how lousy the *Times Book Review* was. Jason put it all together and said this is what we ought to do, and we can get publishers to advertise because they've got no place else to go. We put it all together. But none of us had any money. We first asked Norman Podhoretz to edit the magazine with me. Jason wouldn't do it because he felt it would be a conflict of interest since he was with Random House. Thank God Norman turned us down. Said he couldn't afford it." Podhoretz also worried that the review might compete for readers and contributors with *Commentary,* whose editor he had become in 1960. The *Partisan Review* editors also had their reservations. "*Partisan Review* stopped being what it used to be with the start of *The New York Review of Books,* " Richard Poirier recalled. "I remember [William] Phillips saying, rather querulously, 'Who needs *The New York Review of Books?*' . . . and what he meant was that they didn't need a rival for attracting New York and European talent." When Podhoretz declined, the Epsteins "asked Bob Silvers, who was an editor at *Harper's* and very smart. What we did was run around to publishers. Jason . . . got them to advertise. We called up all the people we knew and admired to contribute—including Gore. They didn't get paid. We didn't get paid. Everyone was so disgusted with the *Times* and eager for us to be a success. We were great friends with the Lowells, and to pay the printer, Cal Lowell [Elizabeth Hardwick's husband, the poet Robert Lowell], who was the only one who had any capital, put up $4,000 to guarantee the bill. He didn't have to pay it actually; it was a guarantee against the printer's bill in case we couldn't pay it. But we got enough advertising."

Much of the New York intellectual and literary world was enthusiastic. Through the Epsteins and Hardwick, the editors had a deep circle of friends, among them Mary McCarthy, Dwight Macdonald, Fred Dupee, and Gore Vidal, all of whom wrote essays for the first issue, which appeared in late February 1963. Vidal, who reviewed sharply a volume of John Hersey's essays, *Here to Stay: Studies in Human Tenacity*, was pessimistic about the *Review*'s future. "What did you do for the Jason-Silvers review?" he wrote from Rome to Dupee. "I did Hersey, but wrote Bob he was out of his mind if he thought American publishing would greet warmly Aunt Mary, Dwight, you, me, et al. They would pay, I think, for us to shut up." But when the end of the newspaper strike brought back the *Sunday Times Book Review*, the new *Review* still seemed viable. "So then we decided to do another issue," Barbara Epstein recalled. "We paid the contributors nothing for the first, then I think five cents a word for the second. Bob Silvers was working so hard he got sick. We raised real money over the summer of 1963 and started publication in September. . . . We raised only $115,000. You couldn't start a little shoeshine stand on that today. Then we got a publisher, Whitney Ellsworth, who came to do the business side. Then after two or three years we were in the black. It was all so cheap. Paper was cheap. We took next to nothing, But we paid the authors." From Rome, with the first issue in hand, Gore again wrote to Fred Dupee. "I like [your essay on *Black Beauty*] much the best of the pieces in the *Review*. I hear that Silvers is ill; I hope not seriously; he is needed. I hope they *don't* ally with *The New Rep*. The whole point is that here at last is a literary review, the only one on a national scale, and if it is to be an adjunct of a liberal paper, no matter how good-natured, it is promptly limited and who needs it? I can't see myself writing for *N.R.;* one always could and didn't because there wasn't . . . oh, to hell with it. The thing's bound to go wrong. The stars are wrong." But the stars were propitiously aligned. Within two years of its initial publication, *The New York Review* became the most widely read, most influential American literary-intellectual journal.

With Barbara Epstein as his editor, Vidal and *The New York Review of Books* were to become almost synonymous. Many of his best essays were to appear there. And though the relationship was to have its rough moments, it was to prove a reasonably smooth, substantially beneficial author-journal engagement. Soon after the editors decided in late spring 1963 to try for an ongoing permanence, Barbara suggested to Gore that he write a review essay of a new book of stories by John O'Hara, a writer whose work, he was to conclude, "cannot be taken seriously as literature, but as an unconscious record of the superstitions and assumptions of his time." This was to be the way in general in which his essay contributions originated. Barbara proposed that he might be interested in reviewing such and such a book or books. Constantly alert to appropriate topics for him, she then sent him, if he indicated interest, the appropriate volumes. Responsive to his sensibility and his strengths, she had the advantage of knowing him well, both personally and professionally. Though in 1963 Gore's friendship with Jason was the primary of the two, in later years that altered. Eventually it changed conclusively. As an editor Barbara had a sharp sense of structure and tightness but she also knew when to hold back, and Gore had no strong feeling early on that he was being edited in any substantial way. Since he conceived his literary essays as encompassing a general evaluation of the writer's career or a broad overview of the topic, the ample lead time the *Review* provided suited him perfectly. There would be a target date but never a deadline. Before writing, he would read the author's entire *oeuvre*. He would carefully conceive, write, and rewrite, with concentrated focus, in what Fred Dupee thought of as his brilliantly informal style. "He always praised my tone," Gore gratefully recalled, "and he said, 'You write like some great conversationalist lying relaxed in a hammock, talking whatever comes into your head, and it is perfect for its subject,' something like that. It was the ease of my voice he praised. He usually gave no compliments to anybody." Barbara agreed with Fred. She knew she wanted Gore to become an ongoing *New York Review of Books* writer, and she knew how to make it likely to happen. Publishing circumstances were in their favor. *Esquire* provided Vidal with a forum for political articles. So too did *The Nation*. Now he had a desirable home for his literary essays.

Though he complained in late winter 1963 that "I have an ulcer, don't drink, have a short temper and constant melancholy without the fine ups and desperate downs of the grape," his melancholy did not prevent him moving ahead briskly with *Julian* and having a busy Roman social life. Henry James was sometimes on his mind, including James's heavy London social schedule. "In a way I'm grateful for the ulcer: no drinking for months which will give me courage *not* to dine out 174 times (the Master's number) this season." He reminded himself that he had come to Rome for a "quiet time." Somewhat shy, sometimes reticent, qualities he managed often to obscure by overcompensation, he hoped for some happy balance between sociability and work. In his daily schedule, writing, reading, and exercise took priority. He walked everywhere. In the afternoon he went daily for workouts to a newly opened American-style gym run by an American named Ed Cheever. The weather felt to him like the Hudson River Valley in October, which he liked. But he also enjoyed visitors and visiting, though usually late in the day. There were ample opportunities for both. A solid three hours of writing in the morning usually exhausted his primary creativity; then there was correspondence and, with long calls to Britain and America ruinously expensive, almost all communication was by mail. Dinner was sometimes at the flat, where the maid Vitalia cooked, though Howard did the shopping and occasionally cooked also. Often, though, it was at a trattoria, particularly his favorite, La Carbonara, where, as in Rome in general, the dollar went a long way, and it was not expensive to indulge his usual desire to be host. Even the large Via Giulia apartment was reasonable, the equivalent of about $200 a month, though they had had to commit themselves to paying for a full year despite their intention to occupy it for only half that time. It "was sublet from an old English gentleman who had been married to an Italian," Howard recalled. "He worked for the British diplomatic corps. The William Morris office in Rome went to an agency and got it for us. It was on the ground floor, a garden floor, with a long big hall, with a staircase going up to another floor, where there were the two bedroom suites and, I guess, a servant's room in the back. To the left was the main salon and the dining room and the garden on two sides. The bedrooms were just above that. It was a strange-shaped apartment, but it was, for Rome, very elegant and with lots of space."

Soon after they settled in, the British novelist Angus Wilson stopped by for a visit. "He has gained weight," Gore wrote to Louis Auchincloss, "and looks rather like Margaret Rutherford" and "sounds like the Queen. . . . He is the most operative man-of-letters since Hugh Walpole, but flawed by intelligence. I do like to see and hear him; less to read his novels, but the stories were marvelous." Wilson was, he told Dupee, "in that euphoric state the British fall into the moment they get out of England, rather like the Institute" (Rovere's joking name for when Gore, Fred, and he would get together) "at the second martini on a summer's day. . . . Since he is the best of talkers and very quick, one forgives the busy-ness, which goes even beyond Mailer if only because Angus has a plan of battle for a war he means to win as opposed to Norman's doomed uprisings, invariably put down by govt. troops. With firm resolve, Angus has attended every writer's conference in every country, addressing each provincial literary parliament in its own language, including Danish." Terry Kilmartin, the influential editor of *The Observer* and translator of Proust, with whom Gore had become friendly in London and for whom he had begun to review, stopped by, eager to talk about literary things and people. A visit from Tom Driberg, regularly to drop in on Gore's Italian life, was imminent. The Anglo-Italian connection immediately became part of his Roman world. The centuries-long British presence still flourished. There were the famous ghosts from the past, the artistic and the aristocratic English who had intertwined their lives with the Italian world. Gore knew very well where Keats was buried, where Turner painted, where Byron flamed. But the current British presence in Rome was less literary than social, often on the highest levels, mainly centered around the estimable Judy Montagu, Gore's friend from his London visits in the late 1940s. Having moved to Rome in the 1950s, Montagu had taken up residence on the Isola Tiberina, a perfect combination of seclusion and accessibility not far from Via Giulia, in a charmingly complicated duplex apartment with medieval vaulted ceilings, whose ancient Roman foundations had probably been part of the Temple of Aesculapius. Attached to her island and to Roman history, married to the American painter and photographer Milton Gendel, who had lived in Rome since 1950, she anchored the British Anglo-Roman social world, partly by the force of her own intelligent graciousness but also by her friendships with and social command of distinguished visitors, the foremost of which was Princess Margaret. She and the princess "were best friends, and Judy was the mistress of the revels," Gore recalled. The Princess was a regular visitor at Isola Tiberina, with her husband Tony Armstrong-Jones. So too were other interesting English, from Diana Cooper to Evelyn Waugh to Iris Tree. The art historian John Pope Hennessy visited regularly. Italian aristocrats and artists were often in attendance. Peggy Guggenheim came from Venice. As jet travel promoted international connections, Montagu's American friends, including Arthur Schlesinger's wife, who had become the president of the Tiber Island Historical Museum Association, also made Isola Tiberina one of their destinations. Soon Gore and Judy were having amusing lunches together, often just the two of them. "She was quite unattractive," Howard, who rarely got to see her alone, recalled. "She had a horsey face, but thoroughly enchanting. . . . She was about five foot six, with a decent figure but nothing you would look at. She didn't dress badly, but she wasn't stylish. She and Gore were buddies. She had a very good sort of masculine sense of humor. A very upper-class lady. Gore adored her, and she adored Gore." Judy, Gore wrote to their mutual friend, Tom Driberg, "is splendid company, as always, an island of illuminating malice in a pasta-sea."

Though he missed American friends and Edgewater associations, many of them came regularly that spring and summer. Rome seemed on everyone's itinerary. Close friends stayed in the guest bedroom at Via Giulia. In June, Kit and Gene came for a brief stop on a monthlong European trip, father and son pleased to see one another, though Gene felt overtired from travel and depressed at having too little interesting professional work to do. Despite appointments to various military and aviation-industry committees, he felt put out to pasture. Late in the spring Fred Dupee, traveling with Andrew Chiappe, stopped by for a visit en route to an academic conference in Yugoslavia. Roman life appealed to Fred immensely. In the summer, when Gore and Howard were away, Andy Dupee and her daughter, having a European summer, stayed at the Via Giulia apartment, which they found comfortable enough except for the mess Blanche and Billy made each night in the kitchen. Elaine came from London, with her ten-year-old daughter, Tracy. Unfortunately, the enchanting Tracy had "a hacking cough which has nearly sent us all riding on ahead: the viruses of childhood are fatal to adults: King Herod's gesture was no doubt a sanitary one." Also, that week the heating system at Via Giulia failed, so "the last week has been hell." "Everyone seems to be visiting Rome and it is just like the country: I am an inn-keeper, which I mind only about half the time."

Mostly, the guests were welcome, including the always amusing Sam Lurie, with his companion and colleague Stanley Kaminsky. "We will arrive in Rome June 1 and will stay till the 4th, then on to Positano, etc. Will you be there? Would you like us to stay with you? . . . Why does Bobby Kennedy only stare when I mention your name?" "Dear Maureen O'Hara," Gore replied, "Yes, you . . . will be welcome. . . . You had better have a lot of gossip and better than your meagre letter suggests. Meanwhile I remain as always a Great American."

At a Roman dinner party early in June, Sam and Stan met a new friend of Gore's, the attractive Alice Boatwright, known as "Boaty," a Southern-born New York– and London-based movie publicist. Her extensive sociability and her familiarity with an ever-widening circle of well-known people had been elevated into a professional art. Boaty "was very amusing," Stanley recalled. "But a name-dropper, and even that's funny, unintentionally. . . . We all had dinner together at a restaurant in the ghetto area, in an old firehouse. Sam and I decided that we would try to stump her. While we were talking, with all these names flying around—we had a client for a short time named Mark Brandel, whom nobody really had ever heard of whom we knew. He was English. I said to Sam or Sam said to me, 'Oh, by the way, have you heard anything from Mark Brandel?' We expected Boaty either to say nothing or to say who was Mark Brandel or to react in some way. Boaty said, 'Do you know Mark Brandel? I talked to him not two weeks ago when I was in London. He's fine. You know his book is doing very well, etc., etc.' And on she went. She knew exactly who he was, which was rather remarkable. . . . Then later, in New York, at a party, she was there, and I said, 'Boaty and I know each other from Rome, where we met.' Before I could get another word out, Boaty said, 'Stanley and I met at Gore Vidal's the day Pope John died.' It was true. When we were there, Pope John died. And I thought, how wonderful! Even I couldn't put together in one sentence Pope John and Gore Vidal." Later in June, in a Rome crowded with participants in the papal conclave, Gore, at 3 A.M., with one hundred thousand other people, saw Pope John XXIII lying in state. With so many American newspaper people in town, it felt like home. There were also Americans who were in town permanently, or at least, like Gore and Howard, for long residences. One stellar friend, in the tradition of Gore's "old ladies" for whom Dot was the prototype, was the American popular novelist, Grace Zaring Stone, whom Gore had met in New York in the late fifties and who regularly spent part of the year at her Greenwich, Connecticut, home and three or so winter months happily in Rome, often accompanied by her daughter, Eleanor. Frank Capra had turned the best-known of her novels, *The Bitter Tea of General Yen* (1930), into a successful Hollywood movie. A witty, self-confident woman with a strong sense of presence and international sophistication, she found Gore an attractive companion whom she loved to have join her for tea or dinner, often at her hotel near the Parliament buildings. They shared a sense of humor, an enthusiasm for language and life. Both were perceptive analysts who turned gossip into wit and wisdom. She "was kind of divine in her own way," Howard thought. "Funny, funny, funny. She was so crazy about Gore then that she resented my presence, but I didn't mind. Gore and she had a wonderful relationship. . . . We'd take her to the opera, we'd take her to dinner. She was just wonderful company. First of all she was a writer and knew everything about writing. She and Gore would spend hours talking."

Two Americans on the scene when Gore arrived quickly became friends. Mickey Knox, the young actor and Norman Mailer's childhood friend, whom Gore and Howard had met in New York and who had been a guest at Edgewater, had recently moved to Rome. He had had difficulty getting jobs in America either because of an early Communist Party affiliation or because of an affair with a Hollywood movie executive's wife. Married to Mailer's ex-wife's sister, Knox had moved from Paris to Rome to do a movie. Short, handsome, he was a down-to-earth, fun-loving friend, frequently hustling for work, whose unmistakable New Yorkishness was part of his charm. As the center of a flourishing European movie industry, Rome attracted many Americans, including Clint Eastwood—whom Gore regularly saw at his daily workouts at Ed Cheever's—revivifying his dormant career in what came to be called "spaghetti Westerns." More important, Gore soon met George Armstrong, an American journalist from Little Rock who had gone to Harvard and had fallen in love with Italy in the summer of 1948. In 1950 he had enrolled at the University of Florence under the G.I. Bill. On his return to New York, Italy seemed the blessed place. When his landlord offered to buy him out of his $28-a-month subleased apartment, he used most of the money to purchase passage to Naples via Tangier. For a long time he did not, so to speak, look back. Life in Rome was cheap. Entertaining companions, good food, and nonpuritanical sex were readily available. A movie enthusiast, he enjoyed the interaction of Cinecittà and

Hollywood. Earning a living, though, was sometimes a struggle. He did a daily column for an American-run English-language daily, then "air-mailers" for American newspapers, and soon articles for the London papers, especially *The Guardian*, and also *The Economist*. In June 1963 a friend told him that Gore Vidal was staying in Rome. He soon stopped by the apartment. When Howard opened the door, Armstrong noticed piles of yellow legal-size papers stacked on a hallway table. "That looks like manuscript," he said. "Yes, Gore's new book." "I guess that'll be a lot of work for you." "Are you kidding—I don't do typing! Not on your life!" It was the start of a friendship, with Gore, not Howard. Later, George was to do some of the typing, for which Gore paid him. Over the next decades he was to be, among other things, a traveling companion, especially to the Italian cities they both were enchanted by. "He was all of what was left of my Exeter world," Gore remarked. "He was at Harvard when all of my Exeter class-mates were there, and he knew them all. He didn't hang out with them, but he knew them, and it was all the same generation. We knew many of the same people from the forties. He was a great fan of the movies. Had Roman fever too, as I had. So we had a confluence of interests." A thin, somewhat delicate-looking man of medium height, diplomatic in manner though an assertive conversationalist, alert to social nuances and interested both personally and professionally in political and cultural life, he was happy to match Gore's late hours drinking wine at outdoor cafés, a regular part of Gore's Roman life.

To his delight Gore soon discovered that Claire Bloom, with her husband Rod Steiger and their three-year-old daughter Anna, had taken an apartment in Rome, which they were to occupy for part of each of the next five years. Bloom and Steiger had married in 1959. Rome became their headquarters, to which they returned and from where they left in the usual traveling life of the actor. Movies were being made in Italy, England, Spain, and North Africa, as well as Hollywood. Rome was the perfect place to be. Gore and Claire quickly intensified their friendship, a combination of deep but mostly unspoken affection and mutual respect. In Rome over the next years Claire was a constant companion. "Those were great days," she recalled. "We did marvelous, wonderful things. Day trips. I remember going with him to some place associated with Coriolanus, and it was unbe-lievably hot. Gore insisted that we climb up to the top despite the heat. I almost got sunstroke. And he just goes on. I never wanted him to feel that he was with a woman and that it was boring. We wanted to keep up with him. . . . We were climbing up to see a Volscian ruin. . . . We had lots of Etruscan expeditions. Gore always said that my great excitement was to find the Cloaca Maxima. He's right. It was built by the Tarquins, a Tarquin king of Rome, the oldest kings of Rome. I found it very exciting. We had lots of wonderful expeditions." Steiger, trained at the Actors Studio in New York, where Mickey Knox had gotten to know him, and who in 1954 had received an Academy Award nomination for *On the Waterfront,* was busy doing a series of international films at Cinecittà. At dinners and parties, often with other movie people, Gore and Howard found Steiger's aggressive self-involvement tolerable but unattractive, "the kind of actor," Howard recalled, "who'd take out his wallet and show you his last review, which he actually did one night. . . . He was overwhelmingly egotistical." Mickey Knox also found Steiger difficult to like. "He was full of mannerisms, the actor. He'd get serious and heavy. He was no fun at all." In an unguarded moment Gore told Knox that he had been in love with Diana Lynn, whom he had seen less and less of in the late 1950s, though they remained on good terms, their pleasure in one another undiminished, though now mostly in recollection. Lynn had married Mortimer Hall, a wealthy New York newspaper heir, exchanging her acting career for a family and comfortable domesticity.

One of the attractions of Italian life was the availability of wonderful places to visit beyond Rome, both to the south and north, with even Greece relatively nearby. Though he had no special feeling for Egypt, when Harold Hayes proposed he write about Nasser and Soviet-American rivalries there, Gore was sufficiently tempted by the thought of again visiting the ancient sites to accept Hayes's offer. He flew from Rome to Cairo. April in Egypt shocked him. "This was the hottest spring in years," he discovered, "in the Valley of the Kings where the temperature [was] over a hundred and the blaze of sun on white limestone blinding." Egyptian politics seemed emblematic of the Arab mind, structured on coordinates totally out of the rational Western framework. The Suez Canal conflict of 1956 had even further embittered Arab-Israeli relations. When Vidal asked a prominent Arab if the Israelis did not have reason to feel threatened by the announced intention of the Arab countries to drive them into the sea, he got the usual unsatisfactory answer. What he did see clearly as his own view of the American-Soviet conflict was evolving into a strong conviction that America vastly overestimated the Soviet threat was that, with its technological level abysmally low, Russia had real reasons to feel threatened. With such friends as Russia, Egypt hardly needed enemies. Soon after returning to Rome he wrote "A Passage to Egypt: A Sophisticated Traveler's Adventures and Observations in a Most Curious Country," which *Esquire* published in October. He was much more interested, though, in seeing more of Italy than Egypt. Eager to view at leisure places he had visited only in haste or had been dreaming about since his first visit in 1939, he could hardly wait to get going, despite the bothersomeness of his ulcer, and despite his commitment to finishing *Julian*. With a hired car and driver, he took a six-day excursion to Naples, Cumae, Pompeii, Herculaneum, Amalfi, Paestum, Agropoli, Lecce, Brindisi, Foggia, Lucera, Troia, Caserta, and back to Rome. "This was to me the greatest joy of living in Italy, like driving to Cremona, a city that I didn't know, going to the best hotel, to a marvelous restaurant, getting to know Cremona for two or three days, and then we'd go home." In late April, with Rome unseasonably cold and his bones chilled, he took the train to Taormina with Howard and Maria Britneva, his first visit to Sicily, where he ran into Nan and Gay Talese, the former an enterprising young editor, the latter a rising journalist especially interested in cultural issues, both of whom he knew about but had not met before. Sicily, he wrote to Fred Dupee, "is splendid just now, very rich, green, wild flowers, and bunnies romping among the ruins of worse as well as better days." He toured the island in a rented car, *Blue Guide* in hand, then flew back to Rome, where, refreshed, he immediately returned to *Julian*. "All in all a quiet time though people keep coming, expecting to be amused and I am at that part of the book where I don't want to see anyone," he wrote to Alice Dows. In early June he was traveling again, this time to Spoleto, where he enjoyed Menotti's company and stayed with him overnight, then to Assisi, Perugia, and Orvieto, a short but pleasurable trip. A longer trip late in June gave him even more pleasure, but at a price. "Please come, *please come!!!*" Elaine Tynan had urged, signing her letter with hearts and cupid arrows. As another reclamatory effort in the late stages of their tumultuous marriage, the Tynans had planned an eating tour in France, to start from Paris, where Gore joined them on June 22 for "a pleasantly bloating" experience, which soon left him with pounds to work off at Cheever's gym. From Paris they went mostly to three-star restaurants in Lyons, Vienne, and Lac d'Annecy. "I did the driving," Gore recalled. "Ken couldn't drive. . . . He would sit with a map, and I would do the driving and he would direct." Ken and Elaine managed to do only a little sniping. The Tynans went on to Spain. Gore returned, via Switzerland, to Rome.

With Howard in late June he came back to Paris, where for $3,000 he bought from the actor Robert Wagner a jet-black 1961 Jaguar, the cost of which he asked his accountant in New York, the well-known Bernard Reiss, to deduct as a business expense. A self-important cultural entrepreneur very much involved in the arts, who had collected a fortune's worth of modern paintings, Reiss years later was to be involved as executor in the contentious disposition of Mark Rothko's estate. Since Gore's work was his pleasure, his pleasure his work, and he used the car to go places he might write about or to see people he had business with, it seemed a deductible expense. When Gore was audited, as Gene Vidal also was at about the same time, he suspected it had more to do with Robert Kennedy than with questionable deductions. The audits were almost always resolved in his favor, though a large part of his income still went to taxes, and his residence abroad did not entitle him to any special tax arrangements. As he worked on *Julian,* with one eye on his bank account, he suspected he might soon have to accept one of the lucrative screenwriting proposals he was regularly sounded out about. "I begin to think I shall never finish *Julian.* It has got very long but I hope another month will see it in shape," he told Alice Dows. For the time being, his answer was no to film offers. He kept writing *Julian,* and with Howard or with George Armstrong, occasionally with both, he went on excursions. In the fast, graceful Jaguar, they drove in mid-July first to Spoleto again, then to Florence and Siena, then up to Lugano and back to Rome, the pleasure of the adventure only partly marred by their different driving temperaments. Howard "couldn't stand Gore's driving." "And I was a good driver," Gore insisted. "That was your opinion." Howard admitted he was "very conservative. I didn't have the competitiveness on the road that Gore did." "Yes, but you also didn't have the accuracy." "Maybe not, but I wasn't as bad. . . ." "If the important turn was to the right, he doesn't really know right from left, so he'd make a left turn. I would be steaming. My blood pressure would be tripling. He would defend his position, no matter how incorrect. He'd say, 'Well, it said to go to the left.' I was not stoical about his driving. I generally drove. We drove all over Europe with me at the wheel." The black Jaguar performed well, though both drivers' blood pressures boiled. Passengers were often shocked at how intemperately they railed at one another, though the minute they arrived some place it was as if they had not been fighting at all. Soon, when Gore proposed motoring tours, Howard declined to go, for both their sakes.

With *Julian* written but not quite finished by early summer 1963, Gore did not in the least mind having to fly to New York and then Los Angeles at the beginning of August to put in two weeks on the preparation of *The Best Man* for filming. In mid-July, Fred Dupee came by on his way back to New York. "I doubt if he will ever be able to live in Rhinecliff again," Gore wrote to Alice Dows. "He is quite euphoric in Italy. I do a lot of sight-seeing, very little social life; and regular exercise (I have become mad on the subject: one feels so much better)." As much as he himself loved Rome, he missed Edgewater. While at Via Giulia, Dupee read much or all of the manuscript of *Julian*. "I listen to him (he was a great help on the first part)," Gore wrote to Ned Bradford, his editor at Little, Brown. He is "the only critic I *can* listen to with profit." With his flight home imminent, he confided to Dows that he did "miss the country but the vacation from the U.S. was needed," alerting her to his return to Edgewater and to American scenes in general, though only for the summer and early fall. Howard, with Blanche and Billy, would stay on at Via Giulia. Gore would rejoin him as soon as *The Best Man* filming permitted. Distressed at the awful Hollywood mess that had been made of *Visit to a Small Planet*, he wanted to make sure *The Best Man* film had some reasonable resemblance to the wit and vision of the play. Its critical and financial success had been gratifying. Even Howard's tiny investment had been rewarded tenfold; within three months of the opening, he had received a check for $15,750 to add to his annual $6,000 salary from Gore, an arrangement that had made the business part of their relationship explicit and provided a modest independence. Gore's profits had been put immediately into a Lehman Brothers Profit Sharing Plan. The income from the plan provided about $10,000 a year.

In early summer 1960 United Artists had bought the Playwright Company's share of the film rights for $300,000. Eager to keep as much control as possible, Gore agreed to "be a sort of producer as well as the writer of the screenplay." He would be paid $100,000. When United Artists engaged the famous Frank Capra to produce and direct, Gore became concerned. He was not an admirer of *Mr. Smith Goes to Washington* or *Meet John Doe*, an

Italian-American immigrant's utopian fantasies about how American politics ought to be. "Even at twelve, I knew too much about politics to be taken in by his corny Mr. Smith coming to my town." Capra's apple-pie American-ism seemed incompatible with *The Best Man*'s political realism. If Capra made the film, Gore feared it would be as disastrously different from his playscript as had been the films made from *Billy the Kid* and *Visit to a Small Planet*. Uneasy, he had gone to see Capra soon after United Artists bought the rights. "Suddenly, Capra was inspired. 'Let's open this up,' he said, small bright eyes like black olives. 'At the convention, on the first day, our good guy—we'll get Stewart or maybe Fonda—he goes out into the crowd, where all these little people are the—you know, delegates.' . . . What, I asked, masking my inner despair with a Mickey Rooney smile left over from Boy Airman days, 'does he *say* to them that's going to be so important?' Capra was radiant in his vision. 'He quotes Lincoln to them. . . . Now then, get this, *He dresses up as Abraham Lincoln.* Then he gives them the Gettysburg Address, or something.' I said that I thought that this was truly inspired. Then I went to United Artists and got Capra off the movie and put myself in control. Next I picked a pair of bright young producers to pro-duce, and we hired a director who had worked for me in television."

Apparently he met Stuart Millar first, before Millar and Larry Turman had become business partners. "I was lunching with Stuart at the Oak Room at the Plaza," Turman recalled, "and he had met Gore or something, and Gore came up, and Stuart said, 'Gore, this is my new partner, Larry Turman,' and Gore said, 'Stuart, I knew when you fell you'd fall hard.' " Millar, who had been an assistant to William Wyler, and Turman, from a lower-middle-class Los Angeles family, both about the same age as Vidal and partners since 1959, had had a small-budget/strong-profit success with *The Young Doctors*, whose entire production cost had been $1 million. United Artists had also grown nervous about Capra. They had in mind an expenditure of no more than $1 million in addition to the $400,000 purchase price. Capra, they had begun to suspect, would want to spend much more. Probably, then, both Vidal's concern that Capra would make the wrong kind of film and United Artists' about cost resulted in a new production team. Most likely, Harold Franklin at William Morris raised Millar's name. Young, energetic, sufficiently experienced and very cost-conscious, Millar and Turman seemed just right. Franklin Schaffner, a handsome, taciturn man with a reputation for being particularly good with male characters and relationships and who, before doing movies, had made his reputation in live television, where he had directed Vidal's first play, *Dark Possession*, seemed a sensible choice. Gore liked and thought well of him. Vidal soon had a screenplay ready. The script conferences went smoothly. Vidal found the producers capable and companionable. Millar and Turman thought Vidal charming, bright, sophisticated about most movie things, and pleasurably easy to work with, "the consummate professional," as Turman later remarked. At first the plan was to make the film in 1962, for 1963 release; then in 1963, for 1964 release, though there was disagreement about when in 1964 to release it. The producers thought it should open at the start of the summer political-convention season. United Artists thought that might be more damaging than helpful. By spring 1963 the cast was in place. To everyone's delight, in April Henry Fonda had unhesitatingly agreed to play William Russell. The producers cabled the good news to Vidal in Rome. Cliff Robertson, fresh from playing John Kennedy in *PT 109*, signed on for the Nixon-like candidate. Though Joanne Woodward turned down the role of his wife, Edie Adams immediately accepted the part. Lee Tracy, who had been splendid in the play, agreed to do the Harry Truman–like character again. Vidal suggested Ann Sothern for the meddling Democratic committeewoman. When Turman was away, Millar signed Margaret Leighton for William Russell's wife. When Shelley Berman screen-tested for the role of the informer, everyone thought him perfect for the part. Two excellent actors took important small roles: Gene Raymond and Kevin McCarthy, Mary McCarthy's brother, whom Gore knew from their overlapping New York worlds. With the budget and production schedules set, space was rented at Columbia Studios; the Los Angeles Sports Arena would serve as the convention hall, and the hotel scenes would be shot at the Ambassador. By early August, when Gore arrived at Edgewater, everything was ready. In California during mid-August they worked on the final shooting script, which they finished by the end of the month.

In Los Angeles, Gore enjoyed Isherwood's company, though most of his other friends were out of town. The relationship gave him great pleasure, and Isherwood's candid entries about Vidal in his private diary, often in the tone of a loving but analytical father about a complicated son, reveal Isherwood's affection for him. "I do like and admire him—absurd and serious simultaneously, and all the time," Isherwood wrote. Himself an incurable domestic romantic, Isherwood found Gore's sex life incomprehensible, just as he thought Gore's political enthusiasms incompatible with his artistic aspirations. When Gore had been in Los Angeles for the July 1960 Democratic convention, Isherwood found him enjoying "playing the role of the reckless young political gambler, rushing to fame or disaster. He enjoys playing with the idea that the Republicans will launch some terrific smear campaign against his private life. . . . He talked about 'the new Athens' which will arise when Kennedy is in power; but at the same time he described, rather admiringly, instances of Bob Kennedy's ruthless methods. Gore also admires Jack Kennedy's ruthless sex life. As for himself, he claims that he now feels no sentiment whatever—nothing but lust. He can't imagine kissing anyone. The way he has to have these sex dates set up is certainly compulsive." Whatever his personal practices, Gore was more concerned than Isherwood, and a great deal more practical, about the larger issue of the relationship between consensual sexual conduct and legal statutes. For that, among others reasons, politics was more important to him than to Isherwood, and among those of Isherwood's generation the person with whom Gore most shared a sensibility and a dialogue about such matters was his British friend, Tom Driberg. Before leaving Rome at the end of July, Gore had urged Driberg, as a member of Parliament and an important Labour Party leader, to help persuade Labour to support reform of the British legal statutes concerning homosexual practices, known as the Wolfenden Laws. "If your party would only support Wolfenden reform" in the upcoming election "it would make many well wishers breathe easier." The issue was to him inseparable from the overall health of a modern liberal society. "I am troubled by what seems to be a new puritanism rising in England, fully blessed by socialism which does like nothing better than to involve itself in private lives under the guise of 'morality' and the good life, not realizing that the 'morality' is Mosaic in origin and beautifully antipathetic to the good life." Unlike Isherwood, Gore looked to larger issues and particularly to long-term practical consequences. "This election is a most important one," he told Driberg, "and not just for your nice island. It means that the West is *consciously* moving toward the planned society and Americans will respond in kind, perhaps in '68. But if the planning is *au fond* neurotically based I see a perfect nightmare come to life: a controlled, illiberal, authoritarian society, drawing for its authority on all the evil, anti-life sources which so appeal to the northern peoples. I hate the word 'puritanism' with a passion, for it implies that (a) what is pure is a deducible abstraction and

(b) it invariably involves restraint, preferably imposed forcibly on others. I do feel quite nervous during this period: things can go awfully wrong."

On *The Best Man* sound stage, where these issues had a muted presence in the play's plot and themes, the important things went well. True to form, Schaffner got fine performances out of the male characters, though Cliff Robertson, who was used to acting leading-man roles, proved annoyingly persistent in his attempt to make clear to the world that this was for him a "character role." He had dyed his hair partly white in order to make himself appear older. Unfortunately, this made him look too old for the age of his character. Also, the directors, as a realistic touch, had at some cost created mock covers of *Time* magazine with a photo of Robertson as the Nixon-like character. They had been created before Robertson had dyed his hair. Despite persistent efforts to get him to have his hair revert back to its normal color, Robertson resisted, and two weeks of shooting time were lost. Schaffner had poor luck with two of the three female roles, at least in Gore's view. Since Ann Sothern had been his suggestion, he took the blame himself. "She was terrible. She wouldn't say a word [of the script]. She'd make up her own jokes, which she thought were really cute. She lost every laugh. Edie Adams was pretty good, and Margaret Leighton was having a nervous breakdown because Tony Quinn had dumped her. So she was having crying jags and complaining about being in an American script. I said, 'Well, why did you take the job?' Frank was a good director. But he couldn't direct women. All the women were bad. If he'd known how to talk to women, he might have been able to help them." Turman, who thought all the female performances good to excellent, had more trouble with Robertson than with anyone else, and in the end thought the film an artistic success. When he realized the script was too long, he was delighted to find Gore responsive. "We were already shooting when we decided to take six or eight pages out. . . . Gore rolled up his sleeves and we worked. He was never defensive about it."

When the rough cut was ready in December, Gore returned to Los Angeles. The producers had cabled him on November 11, "SHOOTING COMPLETED ON YOUR EPIC THIS AFTERNOON STOP ALL WENT WELL STOP HOPE TO HAVE ROUGH CUT MID DECEMBER CAN YOU PLAN ACCORDINGLY." Unaware, in Turman's view, that a rough cut was just that, Gore was appalled at the infelicities in the film, convinced that his blundering colleagues had produced what would be for him another movie disaster. Upset, he told

Millar and Turman that unless they made major improvements he would insist his name be disassociated from the movie. His colleagues tried to calm him. A superb film editor, Robert Swink, assisted by the young Hal Ashby, did his usual excellent job, as the producers had anticipated. Gore was delighted with the final cut. So too were the critics when the film opened in April 1964. The reviews were almost unanimously good, the film a critical success. Financially it at best broke even, further support for the common wisdom in Hollywood that political films do not do well at the box office. At the Cannes Film Festival in May 1964, where it was an unofficial entry, the French critics and audiences loved it. Gore joined Turman and Millar and their wives at Cannes. As he drove into town, to his annoyance he saw a sign trumpeting *"The Best Man,* a film by Franklin Schaffner." The *auteur* theory that overvalued the director's contribution stared him in the face.

At Edgewater for a month in early fall 1963, he enjoyed the rose garden and the company of Dutchess County friends. He was happy to see Alice Dows again. Rovere and Dupee were in good form, the former reconciled to the Kennedy presidency, the latter attempting to make his adjustment from his Roman freedom to Wildercliff domesticity. Andy and Fred were more than usually on edge with one another. Gore, who still adored them both, did not think their marital complexities were his concern, though Andy felt that Gore's influence in Rome was somewhat to blame for Fred's change in mood. "Andy's the real thing," Gore recalled. "Andy's Ishmael—she was there. She was the center of all our lives up there." An effervescent, attractive Canadian-born writer, Margaret Shafer—with her husband, Fritz, a professor of religion at Bard—had joined the Rovere-Dupee circle beginning in 1959 and was delighted to find herself part of Gore's summer world as well. She looked up to Rovere as a mentor, and she and Andy soon became good friends. One day Jason Epstein, the nervous neophyte owner of an expensive new motor yacht, puttered up to the dock at Edgewater. The Dupees, whom Jason and Barbara had picked up in Rhinebeck, were aboard. They were on their way northward to Lake Champlain. As they left Edgewater, Gore said to the Dupees' daughter, the Dupees and the Epsteins "will not be speaking to each other by the time they get back!" The trip was a disaster.

In Manhattan, Gore stayed at the Algonquin, where he had lunch with

Dawn Powell, whom he admired and liked. An Ohio-born New York writer of unsuccessful plays and brilliant but modest-selling satiric novels, Powell had been a good friend of John Latouche's and had thought Vidal "an extraordinary individual with a rich, articulate gift" from her first meeting with him in 1954. Louis Auchincloss was in town. What they referred to as Howard's apartment at 360 East Fifty-fifth Street had been sublet, though the tenant was not paying the rent. From Rome, "feeling slightly bored and depressed," Howard had been trying to get the tenant either to pay up or leave. "It's almost two months since I've seen you," he wrote to Gore, eager for his return. The two buildings on East Fifty-eighth Street bumbled along decently despite an occasional problem, though Howard's desire to have room made available at 416 for an apartment for them was still unfulfilled. With Harold Hayes, who had commissioned him to write a piece on the future of the Kennedy presidency, Gore had some contentious back-and-forth about a draft that Hayes did not think worked well enough. When he left for Rome in mid-October, the article for *Esquire* was still unsettled, though he was at work on two essays that were to appear in December: "Citizen Ken," a review of "The Wit and Wisdom of J. K. Galbraith" for *The New York Review of Books*, and "Tarzan Revisited" for *Esquire*. "James Bond, Mike Hammer, and Tarzan," he concluded, "are all dream selves, and the aim of each is to establish personal primacy in a world that, more and more, diminishes the individual. Among adults, the popularity of these lively fictions strikes me as a most significant and unbearably sad phenomenon." Barbara Epstein kept discreetly reminding him to write the O'Hara essay, which he soon did.

Happy to be back at Via Giulia, Gore began carefully to go over the 200,000-word draft of *Julian*, which he had had typed in New York, to be sent as soon as possible to Little, Brown in order for galleys to be set up. "I can't tell much yet how *good* the book is," Gore had written to Wreden's heir, Ned Bradford, when he had finished an earlier draft, "but I guarantee you a large scandal which I don't for once at all look forward to. But the thing took a certain line and I had to follow. Anyway I'm sure Boston is already too confining for your activities. You won't mind being driven out by the Irish." In October 1963, Bradford, about to read that draft himself, had cabled Gore, "JULIAN READ BY AN ASSOCIATE EDITOR WHILE I WAS IN CALIFORNIA AND HE SAYS QUOTE IT'S PROBABLY ONE OF THE MOST IMPORTANT BOOKS WE'VE PUBLISHED IN THE LAST TEN YEARS AND WILL REESTAB-

LISH VIDAL AS A MAJOR NOVELIST." Bradford had given the associate editor, Herman Gollob, instructions to find passages to cut from the long manuscript. On Bradford's return, when Gollob was asked what could be cut, he responded, "Not a word!" Bradford, who had nurtured the Little, Brown relationship with Gore through the unremunerative *The Best Man* and *Rocking the Boat,* provided unhesitatingly supportive enthusiasm. "A Midwesterner from an old New England family who had worked himself up from book salesman to editor in chief, Bradford had both literary and commercial good sense.

Late in October, Gore and Howard drove for a few days' refreshment to Florence and Siena, then in November by train to Bologna, where they rented a car for a visit to Ravenna and Ferrara. On November 22 Gore went to the beach at Ostia and that night to a movie house in Rome. During intermission there was a foreboding buzz, with the name Kennedy mentioned many times. Suddenly everyone in the theater knew what had happened. "I didn't believe it," Gore recalled. "There had been a mistake. That's not the right plot." Kennedy's serious joke about assassination had come true. The shock was as surrealistically dissociative for Gore as for the stunned American public. The literally unimaginable had happened. He was quickly on an airplane to Washington to attend the funeral. He had warmly liked John Kennedy, with whom he had felt a sympathetic identification. What many had seen as Kennedy's faults Gore had seen as virtues, and his promiscuous sexual life, which only a small number of people knew about then, had exemplified for Gore a desirable and admirable defiance of American puritanism. But his closest relationship in the Kennedy world had been with Jackie. It seemed the right occasion to have a reconciliation with her, which he had gotten an indication, probably through his half-sister Nini, she was willing to have. "I flew back for the funeral, but there was much 'confusion' over tickets ('the French foreign minister *must* be in the church') so one did not attend," he told Louis Auchincloss in January. "I suspect Bobby's hand, even at the edge of the grave. But one had made the gesture of solidarity. Jackie's mood, apparently, was one of rage more than grief: how dare they do this to us! But then Merrywood was always a bit like Colchis. Yes, Jack is a sad loss. He was adorable and one enjoyed his wit and pleasure in himself and the comedy which turned so unexpectedly black. If ever one doubted the wisdom of Greek tragedy, doubt no longer: nothing vast ever entered human life without a curse, as Sophocles more or less

wrote. So I watched it all from in front of the White House. As the coffin
came out of the White House and then went up to the Capitol, I did my best
to pay obeisance and then, when that was over, I went out to California"
where he saw, ironically, the unsatisfactory rough cut of *The Best Man*.

Soon after New Year's Day 1964, in Rome, he was finally done with
Julian. "I have finished the last galley . . . and sent it off to the publisher,"
he wrote to Louis Auchincloss. "I feel like Gibbon—in Geneva, wasn't it?
When he let the empire fall at last. I can't wait to know what you think of
the book. I'm not optimistic about its chances in the bazaars of the republic
but, all in all, I think the work is nearly what one wanted—well, *finished*
anyway." When Isherwood stopped by, exhausted, on his way back to Los
Angeles from a visit to India, Gore gave him the revised galleys to take back
to New York to deliver to Little, Brown. Having had an incident some years
before when some valuable manuscript was nearly lost because of mail and
customs complications, he was happy to have a personal courier. Auchincloss, who had loved the early chapters that had been published in 1962 and
to whom Little, Brown soon sent bound galleys, thought *Julian* superb.
"The book is a *delight*. So keen and funny and beautiful. And Julian comes
so remarkably alive—what I had thought would be almost impossible." As
useful testimony to his admiration, he sent off a superlative blurb for Little,
Brown to use in its advertising. In Boston the Little, Brown people were
gearing up for what they now believed was a likely bestseller, a historical
novel that would appeal to a variety of audiences, from popular to intellectual, from religious to worldly. The ghost of Nick Wreden would have been
pleased.

When the Little, Brown contract had been signed in December 1962,
Victor Weybright, who had encouraged the writing of the novel, partly
because he believed that religion was such a popular topic among American
book buyers that even Gore's take on early Christianity would sell, purchased paperback rights for New American Library. Arthur Thornhill's
negotiating magic produced an unusually large payment. For the Little,
Brown hardcover edition Gore had foregone any advances against royalties
in exchange for a straight 15 percent royalty. He did not want to be indebted
to his publisher and could afford to take his profits from earnings, not
advances. Whatever it would earn was to be paid to him in once-a-year
installments of $15,000. "B-of-M Club is still brooding over *Julian*," he told
Louis Auchincloss, "fat chance they'll ever take it. I can see already the

letters from Catholic ladies cancelling membership." He was happily surprised when the Book-of-the-Month Club reviewers selected it for prominence and Little, Brown's owner again worked his Yankee bargaining and
bookkeeping legerdemain. The Club paid $250,000 to make it its main
selection, an extraordinary amount in 1964. With his old detested nemesis in
mind, Gore suggested to Bradford that they pick a publication day in the
New York Times's rotation of daily reviewers on which Orville Prescott
would not be reviewing. "I'm so happy you like the book," he wrote to his
English editor, Dwye Evans at Heinemann. "It was written in blood. I've
never put so much into anything and I hope it turns out as well as Little
Brown believes. I feel almost safe about its British reception—but who
knows?" American publication was set for April. Though the signs from
America were good, he still felt, after ten years, so aggrieved and resentful
about the reception of his earlier novels, particularly the moral outrage at
The City and the Pillar and the poor sales of *Judgment* and *Messiah,* that he
prepared himself inwardly for the worst. Three months later, on a hot
summer day at Edgewater, as he stretched out on the grass, he had the
supreme delight of reading in The *New York Times* that *Julian* was number
one on the bestseller list. Exuberant, he took a victory swim out to his island
in the Hudson.

At Edgewater that summer he reveled in the satisfaction of being a
critical and commercial success again, though now at a level of sales and a
uniformity of praise that far exceeded anything he had written before. The
reviewers were almost unanimously enthusiastic. Here and there one carped
at the length of the novel or at the realistic, mostly critical depiction of
fourth-century Christianity. Some found tedious, as Gore feared they might,
the philosophical-intellectual dimension of Julian's mind. But the novel
touched both an interest and a nerve as the decade of the sixties began to set
its main cultural concerns into sharper visibility. Many read the novel for its
historical interest, its vividness of depiction of ancient cultures, its resonating evocation of daily life in Athens, Constantinople, and Antioch. The
clever narrative interweaving of three voices gave definition to each voice
and point of view. *Julian* dramatizes the life of the fourth-century Roman
Emperor Julian, known after his death by the Christianity he rejected as
"The Apostate." Born in A.D. 331, the nephew of the Emperor Constantine,

who had Julian's father murdered, Julian rose to supreme power in the
Roman Empire through a series of stunning military victories in Gaul, the
revolt of his troops against orders from Rome to send them to fight in
Persia, and the unexpected death of Constantine II. In Vidal's version Julian
is elevated by the insistence of his own troops that he take power, and
Julian's dying wife, Constantine's sister, advises him to accept the imperial
offer. To nip rivals in the bud, Constantine had had Julian's two children
killed. Eager for a scholar's life, initially educated in a combination of
Christian and neo-Platonic ideas, Julian privately had rejected Christianity,
which Constantine I had made lawful in 313 and which had since become the
dominant religion of the Roman Empire. As emperor, Julian publicly advocated a return to a new synthesis of pagan mystery cults and sun worship. A
reluctant ruler and a fastidious advocate of personal liberty and public
morality, Julian died in battle in 363, sixteen months after becoming emperor, probably killed by his pro-Christian Roman enemies in the ranks
behind him. A novel of ideas as well as of historical pageantry, *Julian* draws
on a variety of contemporary historical documents to provide an accurate
factual presentation of life and politics in the fourth-century Roman world.
For the narrative, Vidal creates his own imagined version of a memoir that
Julian may actually have written but no longer exists. In the novel that
memoir, written during his last campaign, has survived Julian's death. Seventeen years later, Priscus and Libanius, who had been in their youths
Julian's friends and teachers, conduct an exchange of letters about the
memoir. At Libanius's request, with which the novel begins, Priscus sends a
copy to Libanius who thinks of writing a sympathetic biography of Julian.
At the center of the novel is Julian's first-person account of his life; the
memoir is surrounded by and interrupted by Libanius's and Priscius's in-
tertextual and extratextual comments.

As a historical novel, *Julian* seemed a compellingly successful manifestation of the genre. At the same time, those readers with a feel for their own
world sensed as they read that a novel about a society fundamentally divided
in sensibility and in philosophical views, tearing itself apart about issues of
succession, belief, and performance, and desperately trying to hold itself
together as an empire, had enough in common with America approaching
the mid-1960s to make the reading experience eerily, if unself-consciously,
contemporary. America itself was about to split apart around the issue of the
Vietnam War and empire and simultaneously about whether the country was

to be an embodiment of Christian values in the most conventional sense. Both readerships substantially overlapped, as the novel indirectly framed issues and currents in the culture about which many felt uneasy or at least concerned. Beyond that, critics overwhelmingly praised the sharpness, the originality, the credibility of the language of the narrators, as if this English-language novel had so successfully located itself in the minds of people from distant cultures as to make their passions convincingly contemporaneous with its readers'.

Before departing for his American appearances for *Julian* and *The Best Man*, Gore and Howard, early in February, went to Greece. Gore returned to Delphi on a cold, rainy day. He was disappointed to see that the ruins had now been roped off to prevent the damage that came from visitors' treading on them. But the experience of Delphi still resonated. And the image of the Apollonian eagles with widening, sky-darkening wings stayed vividly in his imagination. In Athens, where he had aches and pains from the flu, he enjoyed Nikos Gatsos's company and that of his old friend Kimon Friar, who now lived there. "I have been possessed by a play [to be called *Drawing Room Comedy*], of all things," Gore told Louis Auchincloss. "Two acts. I am nearly finished with the second. Most ambitious and *horribly* funny. It will be perfectly unique *if* I can pull it off. So that's ahead of us for the fall. Fiction must wait for next winter and more Europe. Then the D.C. novel," which he had recently resumed working on, though quite tentatively. "So this is the year of the comeback when like some seedy star of an earlier era one lurches back onto the boards to a burst of nostalgia for the grand old trouper. I see it all. Then shut my eyes." At the end of *Drawing Room Comedy* the main character, whose eyes are shut by death, remembers a visit to Delphi and the closing wings of the Apollonian eagle that stand for the shutting-down of his life. He has had a massive heart attack at an ordinary dinner party in an Upper East Side Manhattan apartment. Most of the action takes place in the short time that exists between the coronary thrombosis and the exhaustion of his few remaining heartbeats. In the spaces between those last literary heartbeats, Gore must have recalled and felt his father's near-fatal attack of 1942. The unproduced and unpublished play, which almost reached the New York stage in late 1964, expresses a high artistic moment in Vidal's lifelong thanatophobia.

In mid-March, Gore was in New York and then in Washington, where as part of the publicity for *The Best Man* film there was a screening and large reception with many well-known political people. "A rather lousy film," he told Dick Poirier, probably before he had viewed the final cut, which he may have seen for the first time at the Washington screening. On the same day, as he soon learned, his old mentoring friend and admirer, Lucien Price, who had been so laudatory and companionably supportive when Gore's literary career in the 1950s had looked grim, had died in Boston of a ruptured aneurysm. Price had written several admiring pieces about Gore in the *Boston Globe*, where he was senior editorial-page editor and a columnist, "and in the dark days was a most bright companion." Gore was pleased that Lucien had been "able to read at least half of the novel, which would not have been written without his bright example and sly maneuverings." His schedule in the first half of April brought him once and sometimes twice to Washington, Boston, Chicago, Houston, and Los Angeles, both for *The Best Man* and for *Julian*, for newspaper, radio, and television interviews, including *The Tonight Show* and *What's My Line?*, as well as his usual appearances with David Susskind on *Open End*. With the 1964 party conventions imminent, he had his talk-show eye particularly on the Republican convention. Johnny Carson and he had discovered they admired and challenged one another. Serious books and interesting, controversial authors, especially if they had camera presence, still drew enough viewers so that ratings did not suffer. In fact, there was reason to believe that when Gore was on, Carson's ratings increased in the major cities, though they also decreased in rural America. When he arrived in Houston the day after a national television appearance with Hugh Downs on *Today*, where to prove a point about the power of television to sell books he had talked at more than usual length about *Julian*, the Little, Brown representative who greeted him at the airport told him that every copy in Houston had been sold. Would he please not appear on television again until they could restock the bookstores? Publishers were beginning to learn, though often slow to digest the lesson, about the force of television publicity. By early May, exhausted from over a month of appearances, Gore was happy to rest at Edgewater, though in June he went to Boston for two days of interviews. As *Julian* climbed the bestseller list, he felt that both it and he had earned its success.

So too had he earned his brief late-June and July rest at Edgewater, with the usual friends nearby, occasional visitors, and Howard at work making improvements in the Barrytown house and planning renovations at 416 East Fifty-eighth Street that would provide them at last with an apartment there. At 416, when a tenant left and the vacant parlor floor became their two-bedroom apartment, Howard gave up 360 East Fifty-fifth Street. They soon hosted a fortieth-birthday party for Paul Newman at the new apartment. "At last," Howard felt, "we had this place in New York City that we could call home," though Gore disliked it from the first moment they occupied it. The apartment seemed dark, closed in, and he did not like the idea of living in New York, though they were to make 416 their base whenever they were in Manhattan until 1970. He much preferred Edgewater. The next year he was to buy 417 East Fifty-eighth Street, another brown-stone, for $87,000 and invest $40,000 in improvements. One apartment there, a triplex that Howard thought they might use themselves, they rented to Franklin Roosevelt, Jr. In 1968 Gore could not resist an offer of $250,000 for 417 by developers anxious to use the lot as one of three on which to build an apartment building, though Howard thought selling it a financial mistake. When Fred Dupee had reported to Gore in January 1964 the rumor that Edgewater was for sale, he had responded emphatically, "Edgewater is not for sale; its master, yes!" Both, in fact, were at most occasionally for rent, and Howard was supervising the installation of a swimming pool on the lawn just south of the house in anticipation of cool pleasure during this and future summers. Though they missed Rome, Edgewater was still home for Gore, and Howard enjoyed New York City life considerably. The sublease on the Via Giulia apartment had expired, not to be renewed. For Roman visits Gore would have to stay at a hotel until they located a new apartment, which he had it in mind to do for January 1965. The summer of 1964 and the rest of the year would be mostly at Edgewater and traveling, starting with a mid-July visit to the Republican convention in San Francisco, which he was to cover for *The New York Review of Books*. He was also to appear there regularly as co-host with David Susskind on an interview and commentary program.

Having published a devastatingly lucid article about Goldwater in *Life* in 1961 and devoted the less notorious part of his article "The Best Man: 1968" to the political chances of New York's Governor Nelson Rockefeller, Vidal would be on the scene at the Cow Palace in San Francisco for Rockefeller's humiliation by the Republican right wing. Having believed and predicted in 1963 that Rockefeller would be the Republican presidential nominee in 1968, Gore was able to observe what was to him the chilling triumph of the revivified Republican conservative movement. Goldwater supporters dominated the convention. Well organized, with deep roots in the increasingly powerful Sunbelt; xenophobic; anti-immigrant; fearful of Communism abroad; eager to scale down big government, decrease taxes, and improve business profits at home; strongly beating the drums of battle for their fallen hero, Joseph McCarthy; most of all advocates of Christian morality and tight social control as the key to American prosperity—they hissed down Rockefeller, who represented to them Eastern liberal Republicanism and personal immorality. Rockefeller had recently divorced and remarried. That was disqualification enough. "Who present that famous day can ever forget those women with blue-rinsed hair and leathery faces and large costume jewelry and pastel-tinted dresses with tasteful matching accessories as they screamed 'Lover!' at Nelson? It was like a TV rerun of *The Bacchae*, with Nelson as Pentheus." As a well-known liberal television personality and political commentator associated with the Democratic Party who did occasional man-on-the-street interviews and appeared each night from a convention-hall studio, Vidal himself was no more popular than Rockefeller among those Republicans for whom the media people seemed mostly devilish enemies. The atmosphere was tense, confrontational, the majority of delegates committed to a Manichaean battle between the forces of good and evil. Goldwater's slim chance to win the election made no difference to his supporters. Only ideology mattered. They were there to make a point, and to capture and revivify the Republican Party for the conservative movement.

Susskind's program at the Cow Palace was, of course, a sideshow, though prominent political people eagerly appeared for the advantage of the exposure. Norman Mailer, writing about the convention, "wanted to be on with us every five minutes, and we were glad to have him," Vidal recalled. Mailer had become a pugnaciously outspoken television regular in New York, always eager to appear, often on Susskind's show. "One night—I think it was the night Goldwater was nominated—David and I were worn out. We hadn't had a proper dinner since we got there because we'd go from the convention to broadcasting to interviewing. So we didn't go on. Norman was upset: 'Gore, this is the most important night of our lives.' I said, 'David and I are tired. We've been on every night.' " Still friendly, their ordinary discourse was banter, competitive witticisms, and Mailer had met his third wife, a young English journalist named Jean Campbell, at a party Gore had given at the 360 East Fifty-fifth Street apartment in spring 1961.

"Oh, yes, she was very attractive, very bright," Vidal recalled. "Her grand-father was Max Beaverbrook, and her father's family were the Argyles. She was in her twenties, a working journalist. She was having an affair . . . with Henry Luce. And she didn't have much time for anybody else until she met Norman. She promptly broke up with Luce and married Norman." Gore, who thought Campbell striking and interesting, gave Mailer the im-pression that night at Gore's apartment that he himself was amorously interested. "I think Gore had had some idea of possibly having some sort of liaison with her. . . . But Jean and I really hit it off, and we just left the party together and started living together a few days later and eventually got married and were together for the couple of years we were together. And we saw a fair amount of Gore after that." When he left the party with Camp-bell, Mailer thought Gore looked startled. "I think he's always had sexual interest in women. I don't think it ever came to the point of critical interest. I don't think it ever reached critical mass, put it that way. A great many women have adored him and are very loyal to him. Elaine Dundy used to adore him. . . . A lot of women have liked him a great deal. My present wife likes him. Yes. He's charming with women." In 1964 Mailer and Campbell were still married. Later, when she was living in Rome, Gore asked her, " 'What on earth attracted you to him?' 'I had never gone to bed with a Jew before.' I told Philip Rahv this. 'She might have tried out a few of us before she went off with Norman. To give her a little wider range of choice.' "

Another assiduous pursuer of TV cameras, with whom Vidal had already begun an ongoing series of confrontational television entertain-ments, was also at the convention. An enthusiastic supporter of Goldwater's conservative agenda, eager to become the foremost young spokesman for what he termed "the radical right," William F. Buckley, Jr. had from an early age embraced political conservatism with the passion of a religious defender of the faith. The same age as Gore, he was born into a large Irish-American Catholic family whose patriarch had made and lost great sums in the oil business in the Southwest and in Mexico and had settled into insular self-sufficiency in Sharon, Connecticut. Ambitious both for the minds and souls of his progeny, Buckley, Sr., had sent them to study in France and England. The home atmosphere was relentlessly devout, the family's pious and pre–Vatican II Catholic faith its overriding loyalty, the faith and the church transcendent realities. The Buckleys had no doubt that God and the devil existed in tangible ways, that the dominating structure of life was a cosmic conflict between the forces of good and evil, and that eventually their Catholic God would be victorious. For the young William Buckley secular politics was religious warfare in another form. The only politicians and policies meriting support were those whose values cohered with the Buckleys' Catholic vision. Since the supreme enemy of the Church was godless Communism, the ideological and political conflict, in the light of which all else was secondary, was between Christian America, the bastion of the free world, and the atheistic Soviet Union, where freedom was enslaved.

A bright, sinewy, argumentative mind, a gifted, acerbic debater with a talent for and a love of language, Buckley discovered his lifelong mission as an undergraduate at Yale: to translate his religious beliefs into political philosophy and practical advocacy. The right wing of the Republican Party was his natural home, Senator Robert Taft of Ohio his ideal. His two combative heros soon became the rather simple Joseph McCarthy and the complicated Whittaker Chambers. The enemies (actually, the forces of evil) were Communism, liberalism, unionism, humanism, atheism, the Democratic Party, and any and all movements that did not give highest priority to the forces of law and order. Anarchy and chaos needed to be rigorously suppressed. Buckley did not himself desire to be elected to political office. His talent was for advocacy, not administration or legislation. His vocation was to influence others, to heighten awareness, to serve as a spokesman, to gather like-minded colleagues into an articulate solidarity. An instinctive propagandist, he knew that evasive simplicity works well in public discourse. A talented sophist, he had the ability to use language to simplify complex issues and to complicate simple issues, as he chose. Nuance and shading hardly interested him, though he mastered a variety of rhetorical devices to create the impression that as a debater he paid his dues to intellectual subtlety. When he graduated from Yale in 1946, his intellectual and religious views were strongly in place. So too was his determination to fight God's enemies as tenaciously as possible. In 1951 he published *God and Man at Yale*, a journalistic exposé of the degree to which Yale University had become a center of liberalism in literature and politics. In 1954, in *McCarthy and His Enemies*, he defended Senator McCarthy's anti-Communist crusade. In 1955 he founded the *National Review*, an expressive embodiment of its editor-owner's radical conservatism. A tireless lecturer, eager to persuade and propagandize, by the early 1960s he was on his way to becoming a national figure.

Vidal and Buckley met for the first time in New York in September 1962, on an *Open End* program in which Susskind pitted them against one another for the entire time. They were, from an even earlier date, natural enemies who gradually became aware of one another's existence. In his mid-twenties Buckley had read *The City and the Pillar* and disapproved of it on moral grounds. For Buckley, homosexual acts were sinful, those who performed them inevitably to be slightly if not harshly identified mainly by this deep perversion. When Gore and Buckley agreed in late 1961, at the request of the Associated Press, to debate in print the "liberal" versus the "conservative" position, their names were publicly juxtaposed for the first time. In preparation for his article Vidal got from a friend at *Life* information from its files on Buckley. In his column Buckley argued the conservative view that liberalism was an intellectually bankrupt political philosophy responsible for most of the ills of the twentieth century. Somehow liberalism was to be blamed for both Hitler and Stalin. Vidal argued that the real conflict was between conservatives, like John Kennedy, and reactionaries, like Barry Goldwater. The reactionaries, who had strong reservations about majority rule, feared democracy. To Buckley and his associates Vidal seemed a dishonest fanatic of the extreme Left and almost certainly a homosexual; they believed homosexuality to be an illness. In mid-January 1962, on one of his frequent appearances on the Jack Paar *Tonight* show, Vidal referred in passing to a recent *National Review* statement harshly critical of Pope John XXIII's liberal social positions. The *Review* had called the Pope's recent encyclical "a venture in triviality." The Pope supported aid to underdeveloped countries, which Buckley opposed. He also seemed insufficiently distressed about the Communist threat. To Buckley, the enemy was now within the gates. In a following issue Buckley reported to *National Review* readers that many American Catholics, disapproving of the encyclical, accepted the Church as "Mother," not "Teacher." Mainstream Catholics were incensed. From Vidal's point of view Buckley's attack on the Pope's views emblemized the extremism of radical conservatism. Paar agreed. Either Paar's office called Buckley and asked him if he would like to respond, as Buckley recalls, or Buckley called Paar and requested equal time, as Vidal recalls.

Buckley's first national television appearance the next week was a splendid success. Irregularly handsome, with a genius for distorting his facial features as if his skin were soft plastic and an ability to contort his figure into an infinite variety of slouches and stretches, he took to television with sly enthusiasm. The camera found him interesting if not fascinating. His face was often a highlight of the show. He knew intuitively that it was better to be a "character," visibly if not eccentrically distinctive in voice and appearance, than to be ordinarily handsome or conventionally photogenic. Outspoken, witty, clever, aggressively and self-expressively abrasive, with a sense of humor that tended toward ironic repartee, sometimes ponderous with a touch of pretension, Buckley entertainingly fenced for about fifteen minutes with Paar and his colleague, Hugh Downs. His voice and mannerisms were both riveting and engagingly self-parodic. A television star was born. As a liberal Republican, Paar engaged Buckley in an effort to define words like "liberal" and "conservative." Buckley defended McCarthy, advocated that America invade Cuba, and proposed that serious consideration be given to going to war with Communist China. In passing, Buckley accused President Truman of having called President Eisenhower anti-Semitic and anti-Catholic. To Paar, Buckley's positions were chillingly inhumane, as he soon told his audience. Harry Golden, the Southern Jewish humorist, who came on after Buckley had left, quipped that Buckley wanted to "repeal the twentieth century and also defeat Roosevelt for a second term." The problem with Buckley, Paar told his audience, was that he did not like people. He certainly did not like Gore Vidal. As with so many of Buckley's appearances in public debate, his appearance on the Paar show was prelude to more. Statements needed verification or amplification. Vidal returned to the Paar show to respond to Buckley. Buckley and Paar exchanged additional clarifications. Vidal bet Buckley, through Paar, that he could not prove his claim that Truman had called Eisenhower anti-Semitic and anti-Catholic. Buckley provided his "proof," a press report that Truman had referred to Eisenhower not being sensitive enough to Jewish and Catholic political concerns. In context it did not seem proof at all to Vidal or Paar. "Are you, on top of everything, a welcher?" Buckley responded. "I had assumed you would apologize for the distortions and untruths you spoke about my family and myself and the *National Review*. Very well, we'll let that go. You are not that kind of man."

By the time they appeared together in September 1962 on the Susskind show, the personal pot was boiling, at least from Buckley's point of view. He was especially ill at ease about Vidal's and other people's references to his dogmatically Catholic, ultraconservative family background, with hints of dark views and unattractive prejudices. Rumors had surfaced that his father was anti-Semitic. One family incident apparently pained and worried him. In May 1944 three of his sisters, with two other adolescent girls, had desecrated the Reverend Frances James Cotter's Epsicopalian church in Sharon. Apparently Buckley, Sr., had fulminated in his daughter's presence against the minister's wife, a real-estate agent, for selling a house in Sharon, a city known for its restrictive covenants, to a Jewish lawyer. The girls may have thought they were doing their father's bidding, though, according to William, Jr., his father and mother were in South Carolina at the time of the incident. With sexually suggestive cartoons from *The New Yorker* and centerfold Vargas girls from *Esquire,* they smeared and decorated some of the church pews and prayer books. The outraged Cotters and other parishioners reported the hate incident to the police, who soon, tipped off by a Buckley employee, had incontrovertible proof that the daughters had done the deed. William, Jr., himself was not involved. He was at the time at Fort Jackson, South Carolina. Humiliated, perhaps ashamed, even penitent, the young Buckley girls were lightly punished by the local court. Buckley, Sr., severely admonished his daughters for the shame they had brought on the family. Soon the court record was moved from Sharon to Hartford. Whatever Buckley, Sr.'s, view on Jews and his impact on his children, the family was eager to put the incident behind them. Later, William Buckley denied that the incident had anything to do with anti-Semitism at all. It "was utterly unrelated to any real estate transaction in which the rector's wife engaged." The record suggests otherwise. Also, having lived companionably for years with the nearby Episcopal church and the Cotter family, why would the young ladies suddenly have decided at this time that the church deserved to be desecrated? Devoted to his sisters, William Buckley, Jr., hoped, for their sake as well as his own, that the incident would receive as little publicity as possible in the future.

However, to his distress, he learned in March 1959 that the actress Jayne Meadows, the daughter of Reverend Frances James Meadows Cotter, who had been a witness to some of the events of 1944, had at a television studio "regaled" CBS reporter Mike Wallace with an account of the incident. Like her husband, Steve Allen, Jayne Meadows abhorred Buckley's radical conservatism. "Evidently the entire studio was your audience," a pained and angry Buckley wrote to her. "Is it your intention to publicize the episode indefinitely? Or is there a point, say on the twenty-fifth anniversary of its happening, when you will feel that the story of an evening's aberration by three of your childhood friends has earned retirement from an active role in your repertory? Do you, in recounting the story, remark the fact that my three sisters, all of whom you knew well, had distinguished careers in school and college, untouched by scandal of any sort; and that not a man or woman who has ever known them, then or now, has ever imputed to any of them a trace of malice or bias?" With a talent for taking other people's rhetorical simplifications and shorthand attacks with serious literalness, he was aggressively self-defensive about his family. Perhaps the Sharon incident had made him especially sensitive about what he considered personal attacks, and less than sharp in drawing the line between political and personal rhetoric. (When in September 1964, on a radio talk show, he allowed his audience to think he believed that American Jews were in general historically prone to be sympathetic to Communism, he gave those aware of the Sharon incident further reason to think him at a minimum insensitive to Jewish concerns and, worse, prone to making racial generalizations.) At the same time the *National Review* was becoming notorious for biting, brutal, often painfully insulting headlines and editorials many readers thought racist. Either there was a moral blind spot or a self-indulgent fascination with the language of exaggeration. Also, it had begun to be clear to those who disagreed with Buckley that he considered threats to sue for libel an appropriate extension of open debate. In October 1961 he had implied to the publisher of the *New York Times* that he might sue the newspaper for libel, a threat he made against numbers of opponents in the late fifties and now in the sixties as well, if the *Times* did not stop misrepresenting the *National Review*. "Your reporter wrote as though it were the organ of a Nazi-like movement which included Lincoln Rockwell and the California anti-semites; now you suggest it is the right-wing counterpart of Communism." Whether or not the *Times* reporter was in any way culpable, Buckley characteristically counterattacked aggressively. His own rhetorical simplifications he avidly defended as incontrovertibly true. As a television entertainer he was deadly serious, and potentially lethal.

Fortunately, Vidal's and Buckley's fireworks during two hours on the Susskind show focused on public issues, not personal matters. The TV critic for the *New York Herald Tribune*, Jack Iams, thought it "one of the most stimulating programs ever offered by *Open End* . . . an intellectual free-for-all that must have left both participants nursing their lumps together. Aside from the mental gymnastics . . . it was the suavity and polish of their respective performances that made the program a consistently fascinating one." It was Buckley, though, who was the surprise. Whereas the reviewer had expected Vidal to be excellent, the "virtuosity that Buckley brought to his role, however infuriating it may have been at times, was truly remarkable. The supercilious manner in which Buckley displayed his vast erudition, the flashes of wit and velvety insults that were sprinkled throughout his remarks, reminded me of Noël Coward acting in one of his own plays. Buckley even looked a little like Noël Coward when he delivered a line like, 'I wish you wouldn't sound so fatigued when confronted by historical facts.'" Whatever the innuendo of the Noël Coward comparison, which caught an aspect of Buckley's manner that further complicated the Vidal-Buckley relationship, the reviewer apparently intended it as a compliment. In San Francisco in July 1964 Vidal and Susskind took on Buckley again. The focus was on the Republican Party convention and its candidates. That Lyndon Johnson would be the Democratic nominee was a foregone conclusion. What to do about the Vietnam War was one of the dominant issues. Buckley, like Goldwater, favored harsh escalation. Both combatants kept the gloves of civility on. The reviewer for the *San Francisco Chronicle* had the feeling that Buckley, whose "facial expressions are unequalled by anyone in show business with the possible exception of Martha Raye," and Vidal "were acting—like professional wrestlers—according to a rehearsal plan." Another observer commented that it seemed "Susskind was a zookeeper trying to prevent two hissing adders from killing each other. But the hissing was always wreathed in benign smiles." When Vidal claimed that Buckley's efforts to provide Goldwater with an acceptance speech had been summarily turned down, Buckley's hiss intensified. He felt it was an unfactual attempt to humiliate him. "For the record," Vidal wrote to a Buckley supporter after the convention, Goldwater's press secretary "told Douglas Kiker, Norman Mailer and me that B. had telephoned him 'ten times' the day of the nomination and that he had 'picked up the phone once,' and that when B. 'had sent some stuff over I took it in to the Senator and he said 'I don't want to read this.' After the show, Buckley protested to Nellor [Goldwater's press secretary] who wrote him a letter, denying he had said what the people had heard him say. . . . In any event, for me to suggest that there might be a rift between Buckley and Goldwater is to help Goldwater tremendously. So loyal partisans should be pleased." Buckley, who disputed Vidal's account but never challenged his witnesses, was bitterly angry.

Amid a varied, busy schedule, politics partly preoccupied Gore for the rest of the year, though Lyndon Johnson's defeat of Goldwater in November diminished for the time being his concern that Buckley and his conservative cohorts were about to take over America. Before returning from the West Coast after the San Francisco convention, he spent some weeks in Hollywood, having responded to the pressure, especially increased by his tax liabilities, to do some well-paid hackwork for MGM. He had in fact over the past year been trying unsuccessfully to sell a movie script of his own, a political satire called *O Say Can You See*. British producer Tony Richardson liked the script but could not make a commitment. Back at Edgewater in September, Gore had his usual social rounds, while Howard ran the house and attended to the New York brownstone. Since Gore did not have the equivalent of Ed Cheever's gym available at Edgewater, he bought an expensive exercise machine that sent an electric current through the muscles and promised to reshape them more handsomely. Gore, Eleanor Rovere recalled, finally realized that it was hopeless and gave the machine to her. Ordinary exercise seemed more effective, and he did his best to establish a daily routine. "Gore was very vain," Eleanor thought, "and hated to get fat. He told Johnny Carson one night on television, 'As you can see, I've been on the Orson Welles diet.'" He had the blessing (and the occasional disadvantage) of seeming dazzlingly handsome, and often glamorous, an Apollonian figure to some, to others too attractive not to be suspected of something. Of what? Of being too talented. Of being too handsome. Of being too well born and at ease. Of being too ambitious. Of being a collection of qualities that had to have some character flaw at their hidden (or not too hidden) center, perhaps arrogance, or vanity, or some punishable vice.

Except for a two-week visit to London and Rome in early fall to push the British edition of *Julian* and perhaps to look into an apartment for January, Gore spent the rest of the year at Edgewater and in New York. In November, in New York, he voted for Lyndon Johnson, the last time he was ever to vote, though later he happily declined to attend the inaugural ball to which Vice-President–Elect Humphrey had invited him. Johnson had promised a New Society. Having gotten through Congress the Civil Rights legislation Kennedy had failed at, Johnson was infinitely preferable to Goldwater, who had threatened the use of nuclear weapons in Asia. At a minimum Goldwater would expand the Vietnam War. Johnson promised peace. Gore also voted for Kenneth Keating for the Senate from New York, the only time he had ever voted for a Republican. Gore strongly preferred the liberal Keating to Robert Kennedy, whose movement toward the left Gore thought calculatingly self-serving. His personal reservations about Kennedy would have precluded his supporting him under almost any circumstance. Perhaps he could distinguish between personal hostility and objective judgment. Perhaps not. In this case there was no need to, though the fact that he actively campaigned for Keating, something he had done for no political candidate other than himself, spearheading the "Democrats for Keating" committee, suggests the degree to which personal feeling and political disagreement coalesced. Robert Kennedy was nevertheless elected the junior senator from New York. Gore found the election result so distasteful that he said very little about it, though before the voting he had had his say in various forums, including numbers of television shows: Susskind's, as usual, and also the popular *Steve Allen Show*, where his remarks about Buckley prompted Buckley to write to Allen that Gore Vidal "lied last night on your program."

Since finishing *Julian*, Gore had done a few essays, the form increasingly congenial, his voice more noticeably elegant and conversational. One appeared in the *Herald Tribune Book Week*, on the television blacklist, the other in *The New York Review of Books*, about the magical children's-book author, Edith Nesbit. "As an adult writing of her own childhood, she noted, 'When I was a little child I used to pray fervently, fearfully, that when I should be grown up I might never forget what I felt and thought and suffered then.' With extraordinary perceptiveness she realized that each grown-up must kill the child he was before he himself can live." For Gore, the shadow of Nina lurked in those sentences. Actually, Nina had tried to materialize again as a presence in his life but he kept her at more than arm's length, dealing with her claim that he owed her money through his accountant, whom he instructed to give her something, as he was to do numbers of times over the years. He did not feel generous. He did not believe he owed her anything. And a condition of anything he would give would be that the contact be through an intermediary. His father he saw with reasonable and happy regularity, at Edgewater, in New York City, even a few times in Avon, Connecticut.

Gore still had reason to hope that the play he had worked on since its first conception at Delphi and recently completed, ironically called *Drawing Room Comedy*, would have a Broadway production. The powerful producer David Merrick had made a commitment to do it; preliminary discussions had reached the reading and casting stage. Then, suddenly, Merrick had canceled the plans. His justification was that the play was too depressing, that Broadway audiences would not flock to see the protracted depiction of a man dying of a coronary thrombosis. In London, in January, Gore sounded people out about a British production. "If you can come up with a production and a cast that might have a chance," he told the actor Jerome Kilty, who was interested, "then I see no reason for not trying it out in London." For a short time there was a Berlin opportunity at the Schiller Theater, perhaps with some of the same people who had done the successful German version of *The Best Man*. Neither London nor Berlin worked out. To Gore's disappointment, the play was never performed. Without a performance, he had no interest in pursuing publication. The manuscript went into his storage chest, which now had an additional drawer. He had recently been approached by the University of Wisconsin and the Wisconsin State Historical Society at Madison, which, in the process of building a television and movie archive, urged him to deposit his papers there. Ironically, his prominence as a television and movie dramatist had brought him to Wisconsin's attention. Though they were somewhat aware of his novels and essays, his achievement as a dramatist was foremost in their minds: that was what they were specializing in. To get that material they would have to ask for everything, which they assumed would be, in the future, predominantly movie scripts. No other library had asked for his papers. The tax laws provided that the fair market value of such material, as ascertained by an expert, was deductible against gross income, very much like a business expense or loss. It seemed sensible to Gore to accept the invitation. Soon Howard was sending, on an irregular basis and later quite regularly, cartons of manuscripts and personal papers to Madison. The library gradually realized that it was getting more than it had initially expected. Later, Gore realized he was locked into a relationship he had made without adequate consideration of other possibilities. Still, it was a practical advantage to have an archive for his papers, though the tax advantage would not last long, and it also had some of the feel of a date with posterity.

In the meantime, his datebook for 1965 quickly became filled, primarily with movies, four of which he worked on between the beginning of the year and his fortieth birthday in October. He was well under way with *Washington, D.C.*, as he told Louis Auchincloss, and by summer he had done about half the novel, though "I cannot tell yet what I am doing or how well I am doing it. The subject is slippery. And I have so many themes, having to do with those changes in time which affect us all humanly while affecting, quite as dramatically (but hardest to dramatize) the Republic which became reluctant empire, or was it so reluctant? Also I am having difficulty with the whole moral aspect of our lives, privately and publicly. What is a right action? What means may be used safely to achieve what ends, no matter how temporary?" The subject was more ostensibly autobiographical than any fiction he had written since *The Season of Comfort*. With his fortieth birthday on the horizon, family history was so much on his mind that, on one of his trips between Rome and Paris, he drove to Feldkirch, the Alpine home of his Vidal ancestors, from which he sent postcards and longer reports to his father about what he had seen and learned, the beginning of what became a lifelong interest in discovering just who the Vidals originally were. It was also on his mind that his father had just had his seventieth birthday. "It doesn't seem thirty years since your 40th birthday [April 13, 1935] which I recall almost as vividly as my tenth. I suppose the only thing worse than being 70 is *not* being 70, so there is something to be said for healthy survival. Apparently we are fairly long-lived." His father's seventieth birthday, among others things, had made Gore even more palpably anxious about the history of heart disease on both sides of the family. As a writer he was drawn to the subject of time's passage. Unlike his father, he searched for some anchor for his present consciousness in his connection not only with his personal past but with his family's, both the Gores' and the Vidals.' Feldkirch he found "charming but gray and rather gloomy, dominated by Jesuit schools. . . . I spent an hour with the priest of St Nicholas Church in Feldkirch, going through the records. He knew only German but I did figure out that your great grandfather Joseph Felix Vidal had a long life and at least 2 wives, though it is just possible that the 2nd mother of his second batch of children might not have been a wife. . . . I'm going to put someone on the records to find when he family came to Feldkirch from Venice." Apparently the last Vidal had left Feldkirch in 1947. Later, when Gore told Gene that there was some possibility, so local rumor and other considerations suggested, that the family had once been Jewish, Gene thought the speculation slightly amusing and mostly uninteresting. Gore found it fascinating.

In January, Gore and Howard moved back to Rome, this time to an adequate apartment dominated by red wallpaper, at 29 Via de S. Elena, a small street in the old city close to the cat-filled ruins of the Templi Republica and not far from the Bernini tortoise fountain near the Palazzo Mattei. The slanted street was protected on both sides from the busy traffic in the nearby Piazza Arenula and the frenetic Corso Vittorio Emanuele by small buffer streets. Like the apartment at Via Giulia, it was a sublease, a furnished convenience, a home base in Europe in the city they preferred to any other, though Gore soon left Rome for two weeks in Athens for discussions with the director Jules Dassin—an American filmmaker who had established himself in Europe after he had been blacklisted and whose recent *Never on Sunday* had been an international success—about a movie based on the life of Pericles that they had agreed to do together. *Washington, D.C.* he worked on steadily though not quickly, expecting to make a major leap forward in the summer. Roman life he found as restful, as congenial, as ever, and he resumed his usual Roman schedule, including the gym and evenings with friends. Howard made the adjustment rather easily, and so too Billy, though Blanche, not unexpectedly, died in February. The Roveres sent Billy their condolences. "He is now an only dog but incredibly brave," Gore responded. "I am so completely content on this side of the Atlantic," he told Fred Dupee, "the sight of the Campidoglio once a day is all I need to remain stable. The novel goes well, though I must go back to Washington soon and remind myself of what I am recalling and what inventing and what has gone right through the perfect sieve my memory is." In mid-February he flew to Washington to lecture to a large audience at the Library of Congress on "The Novel in the Age of Science." His half-sister Nini hosted a well-attended party for him. "It was Guermantes with enough Madame Verdurins to lend vivacity to the revels," he later wrote her. It was also material for his Washington novel. With a new Paris-based agent for movie assignments, Alain Bernheim, Gore had offers for more scripts than he could possibly do, and the four offers that he did accept he did partly because he could not resist keeping busy, partly for the money and his unwillingness to cut off future offers by creating the impression he was never available. *Pericles* helped keep him occupied during the first half of the year, as did rewriting the scripts of *Is Paris Burning?* and *Night of the Generals*, then late in the year *The Doctor and the Devils*, from a script by Dylan Thomas.

"I don't know whether or not this sort of caper is a sign of masochism," he wrote to Fred Dupee about movie rewriting, "but I do like the plunge into something difficult and different; also novels that flow too swiftly from the pen usually end up sounding like Mailer." Francis Ford Coppola was his assistant scriptwriter for the disastrously bad, multi-language *Is Paris Burning?*, which had innumerable problems, including the French-language part of the script. "I was stuck there five weeks trying to rewrite an unactable script. The guy directing didn't know any English. My dialogue was already written for the crucial stuff. It was cut, cut, cut." But the Paris weather was lovely, the food wonderful. Mary McCarthy was also in Paris. Although she and Gore had many friends in common, particularly the Dupees and Phillip Rahv, they were not friends, and McCarthy's usual contentiousness brought out his own. At dinner they argued mildly about something inconsequential, and it seemed to typify for Gore the unsatisfying busyness of his Paris schedule. "Paris was too much, too many people from Aunt Mary to the D. of Windsor. I told him what you *really* felt about him," he joked to Fred Dupee. "He said 'What?' That Hanoverian will always hit the NAIL on the head." The more intelligent of the Hanoverians he now met in Rome at Judy Montagu's, whose dinners for Lady Diana Cooper and the American newspaper publisher Kay Graham, he attended. In the summer "Princess Margaret arrives to stay with Judy and we are all alerted to amuse her. But will she amuse us? That is royalty's last function." He now spent two evenings with her and found her attractive. She "turned out to be quite splendid, droll, with at least 3 manners, all beguiling. One: gracious interested lady visiting the troops. Two: bitchy young matron with a cold eye for contemporaries. Three: a splendid Edith Evans delivery in which she plays at Q. Victoria with slow measured accents: 'We are not partial to heights,' she intoned gravely over a chicken wing, 'not partial at all.' That took care of Switzerland."

Pericles soon proved a total disappointment. In February, Gore expressed his perplexity about it to Rovere. *Pericles* is "a vast undertaking and whenever I get nervous at the thought of writing dialogue for Socrates, I think of Shakespeare who took on everything and didn't seem to mind—or know that most of the facts were wrong. The nightmare is introducing characters: 'Sophocles, I want you to meet Euripides, a promising young playwright.' Margin for error is luxurious." The well-known Dassin, Gore wrote to Dupee, who was always interested in movie people, "is a cheery man who has entirely forgotten why it was that he became a Communist. I suspect it was the result of a desire to conform. Already a small power struggle is beginning. He wants Melina [Mercouri, his wife] to play Aspasia. I suspect this casting could easily sink the project. Anyway, every film is a war and I hope to be back to the novel by summer." Gore liked his script. But Dassin was not satisfied. "It was too tough for him. After all, Pericles was a politician and Jules was a sentimental leftist. He wouldn't have been any good at making that film anyway. We were still going ahead with it with Melina Mercouri and then the colonels came and that was the end of the project." In February he returned to Delphi, a source of deeper things than movies, and in June, with Howard and Boaty Boatwright and a new friend, Sue Mengers—an ambitious, raunchy, blond New Yorker who had gotten her start as a William Morris mailroom clerk and had just begun her rise to Hollywood power as an agent—he took a ten-day cruise of the Greek islands and Turkish coast. "Boats . . . are hideously expensive, so Howard's friends had better kick through with their share," he had told Dupee in February. By the end of the trip they were all still speaking to one another, and Gore, though they were still Howard's friends more than his, had found the two entertainment-business ladies entertaining. After Paris and London in the late fall to work with Sam Spiegel on *Night of the Generals,* and even to Portofino for discussions on Siegel's yacht, Gore confessed to Dupee that so much moviemaking had been hard on his nerves. He had done "4 films in a year which was to have been spent on the novel, further aggravated by ratcheting about from London to Paris to Rome, eating and drinking too much and talking too much to Sam Spiegel." But it was the tick of the clock, the rustling of the turn of the calendar page that he heard involuntarily and tried in his art to turn to some sort of advantage. "Being 40 has not thrilled me—symbolist that I am—and various malfunctions of the body though not serious fray the edges," he wrote to Fred, as at Via de S. Elena he looked out through the terrace window in the November sunshine. But at least "today the sun is shining; there was rain last night; the terrace chairs are wet; I sit inside; do some pages of script; read Harold Acton's *Bourbons of Naples;* worry about my health; wonder why I drink so much wine (particularly last night); deplore the slackening of the waist-line despite the gymnasium; and see this page end, like all things."

CHAPTER *f*IFTEEN

Trapped in a Nightmare

1965–1968

FROM THE TERRACE of Gian Carlo Menotti's palazzo at Spoleto, Gore watched the cascading fireworks against the dark sky. "Rome in August has been perfect. Cool weather. Superfluous people gone," he told Louis Auchincloss. As he worked, during the summer of 1965, on *Washington, D.C.,* he was happier in Rome as a place to live than he had ever been anyplace else. It was a pleasure to escape New York's claustrophobic literary bickering. Since jet travel now rose almost to the level of commutation, he could be "home" quickly enough whenever he wanted or needed to be. Edgewater still drew him back, though selling it came to mind. He settled for ambivalence. In late February an old literary nemesis, Truman Capote, showed up in Rome, "wreathed in friendship which I almost take to be sincere." In the last decade they had seen one another infrequently, only in passing. Though Gore preferred distance and indifference, some of the old rancor still existed. "We had a pleasant drunken evening recalling who had said what about whom and I must say my blood pressure began to rise all over again, but then all ended well. He has apparently finished that book [*In Cold Blood*], though the last two times I saw him he had just finished the book on each of those occasions. I can't get over how his appearance has changed (I can hear him on the subject of me), but he is an interesting brickish color now, rather lined, with a jaw worthy of Somerset Maugham. For the first time in twenty years I suspect that he is intelligent."

Capote's friendliness worried him. "I found him positively affectionate, which is sinister," he told Nini. "What can he be up to? He even spoke disparagingly about the court-in-exile, about Jackie's continual 'vale of tears.' " Despite Gore's inclination to be trusting, he still feared Capote's instability. When in early 1966 Dupee published in *The New York Review* a long essay on Capote, Gore responded privately that "I thought you said all the right things most subtly and though the first impression was perhaps too admiring (from my icy point of view) it struck, doubtless, as you say, a proper balance. . . ." Gore had further refined his own hesitant view about Capote's intelligence. "What I find perennially discouraging in Truman's work: the same quality that I find always in him, a profound silliness at every level; he is mind-less in the purest sense; but an animal shrewdness has made him succeed in the jungle, like those silly lizards which can take on any shade and so avoid becoming dinner." It was a reminder of what life would be like in New York.

The guest of honor at Spoleto was Ezra Pound, attending a performance of his "Villon music and ballet," which Gore found dull. Pound himself was fascinating. If he wore on his deep-lined, craggy visage the bitter impressions of his years of incarceration at St. Elizabeth's, he exhibited his scars mostly in silence. "He seldom speaks; poses constantly, chin down, face sombre; wears a black velvet jacket, Lord Byron open shirt; looks spry for his age but old. At the end of the performance, a youth asked him in my hearing, 'Did you like it, sir?' A long pause then: 'mumble mumble technique, but horrible mumble mumble.' Which struck me as fair criticism." On the terrace, as the crowd watched the fireworks, the poet was "attended by his faithful old mistress and the usual contingent of Menotti's gentle young men and stern Principessas. Pound by fireworks was the best part of the festival. He gave us all the poses except hand to cheek. The eyes looked like an old wolf's mediating one last slaughter. 'Champagne, maestro?' Menotti kept repeating nervously but only silence from the old actor. Poets are perfect hell and it seems that the better they are the cornier the performance." He preferred Yeats to Pound, he wrote to Dupee.

The lovely summer had actually ended on a bleak, more sobering note than the posturing of poets, the unexpected death of Harold Franklin in New York. Franklin, who had earned Gore's respect and affection and whom he credited largely for the television career that had saved him from semi-penury in the early 1950s, had "died of a thrombosis three weeks before he was going to be married for the third time," Gore told his father. "Perhaps he was lucky. But one misses him." It took Gore a while to shake "the gloomy news." With Franklin's death he no longer had an agent for American television and movie work, though at least for the time being that did not seem a liability. Actually, the management of the William Morris Agency assumed that someone there would take over from Franklin, especially since their senior literary agent, Helen Strauss, had persuaded the reluctant author to allow her to do the three-book contract he had signed with Little, Brown in December 1962, the first of which had been *Julian*, the second to be *Washington, D.C.* The third was "a novel on a subject to be mutually agreed upon." An aggressive woman who noticeably enjoyed her power and the perquisites of her job—and whom Herman Gollob, who had worked for her at the William Morris Agency, described as "the Queen Elizabeth of agents"—Strauss, Gore felt, had used her harsh charm to badger him into accepting her offices. He had agreed mostly because it was the inattentive path of least resistance, partly to do her a favor. Since Little, Brown already was his publisher and Gore essentially dictated the financial terms, Strauss had to attend only to contractual paperwork.

Their residence in Paris in spring 1965 made clear to both Howard and Gore how much more they preferred Rome. Howard had found Paris life pleasant, but in Rome he had more friends and a settled domestic routine. Nightlife and cruising were easier, more casual there, and there were "the beautiful Italian boys," to one of whom Howard had the year before developed an attachment and helped get to England and America. When Dick Poirier visited at Via Giulia and Via de S. Elena, he especially enjoyed Howard's company, his slangy language and good humor. "Some of those idioms in Gore's more comic novels are ones that he could easily have learned from Howard. Howard exposes himself to young people of a certain class who use these sort of raunchy, funny, comic slang terms which Gore was exposed to, I believe, through Howard." In Rome, Poirier especially enjoyed cruising with him. "That's the way gay life was in Italy in those days. It was very seductive. It was sort of older to younger brother, and in the sixties it still wasn't that easy for a young Italian guy to sleep with a woman, a young girl. He may have wanted to get married but didn't have much money. This sex for money and favors was sort of a common thing to do. . . . And you'd meet very, very sweet boys. The other advantage of it was that you didn't need to cruise, that is, you knew where these guys were and you got to know them and they'd introduce you to others, so you'd have a whole social life. That was perfect for Gore, and he liked the types, the Italian boys who were available, as I did. In a sense, whenever we went out, we'd be looking at good-looking people. . . . In Rome it was the practice to take the boys back to the apartment. He'd pay them and give them clothes. They were very sweet. A few times I'd be sitting out in the front room with Howard. Gore would come in with someone and introduce him. One time he was passing through with someone I had met before and said to me, 'Say good-bye to Antonio.' "

Soon most of their Roman hellos and good-byes were taking place in a new, more glamorous flat. The Via Giulia duplex apartment had been attractive, but the flat at Via de S. Elena was only satisfactory, a two-bedroom, triangular-shaped, third-floor walk-up of no distinction though pleasantly decorated, on a street that seemed increasingly noisy, subleased for six months at a price for which Howard soon realized they could get an annual unfurnished rental. In May, while walking Billy on the far side of the Corso Victor Emanuele not far from Via de S. Elena, Howard turned down the Via Di Torre Argentina in the direction of the Pantheon. The landlady of the large corner building, number 21, was putting up a "for rent" sign. A seventeenth-century palazzo, its gray stone and dirty yellow-tinted plaster exterior, as with many Roman buildings, had been darkened by age, neglect, and pollution. Instead of continuing on his walk, Howard stopped to inquire about the apartment. "Gore says it was really the dog who found it, because he led me right there," Howard recalled, "which he did. He was tyrannical. I went up and looked at this apartment and couldn't believe my eyes. We were paying $350 a month for the three months on the sublease, and the apartment on the Via Di Torre Argentina was a hundred dollars a month, or something like that, for twelve months." Actually, the rent in lire turned out to be about $270 a month. Beyond the porter's station was a grand staircase and an archaic semi-open iron elevator shaft rising to the sixth-floor penthouse. "As soon as the dog walked into the apartment that first time, he lifted up his leg and pissed. 'This is my territory.' " When Howard saw the three large bedrooms, the small servant's room, the salon, the dining room, and the twelve-foot-wide and sixty-foot-long terrace on two sides, looking west and northeast, with magnificent views of Roman rooftops and church domes, he agreed with Billy. So too did Gore. Directly below, where Corso Victor Emanuele and Via Di Torre Argentina met, heavy traffic raced and swerved. The noise would be a problem, but it was a steady, distant hum, and they were high enough so that traffic fumes might not reach them. Across the Corso were the ruins of the Temple Republica. The horizon on two sides was bright with rooftop gardens, the higher sight line an extended sweep of the old city extending toward the Tiber and the hills beyond, "a fine if jumbled view of golden buildings, one twisted tower (Borromini's St. Ivo), the green Gianicolo and a dozen domes, the nearest Sant' Andrea della Valle (*Tosca*, Act One), the farthest St. Peter's like a gray-ridged skull." It was not to be resisted. By late May, Howard was busy furnishing the apartment with tables, mirrors, and chairs from Roman antique shops. "Howard is fixing it up and it should be splendid," Gore wrote to his half-sister, Nini. Soon the terrace was green and bright with potted plants. Gore built a trellis for vines. "The new place is already livable and with the plants on the terrace looks like a house in the country," he told his father, whom he urged to visit. "Furnishing a flat here is not unlike writing *Ben-Hur*, only less aesthetic." Howard had a fine time doing most of the work. A designer friend decorated the studio and living room. Since live-in help was cheap, they found a man to occupy the servant's bedroom in the darker back of the apartment, someone to look after things, especially to water plants when they would be gone. In June they moved in. Gore was pleased and excited. "We're in the new flat," he told Fred Dupee, "a penthouse on a crumbling palazzo facing Largo Argentina with two huge terraces and a total view of the city. . . . Life above the Largo is splendid; flowers blooming, bougain-villea splendid."

Unexpectedly, he had a Roman home. There had never been any intention on either of their parts to settle there permanently. It was simply a place to visit for extended periods, for as long as three to six months a year. Roman fever had possessed him for decades; living there was cheap, the food superb. Italian casualness about consensual sex made that pleasure comfortably available. They did not have to be looking nervously over their shoulders for the puritan gestapo. The loss of the election in 1960, the disaffiliation from the Kennedys in 1961 and 1963 made a holiday from America desirable. Gore still could keep his hand in American politics as a commentator from abroad, and his interest in as well as repulsion from America's mid-decade nightmare in Vietnam fueled both his sense of the advantage of being at a Roman distance and his compelling interest in being involved. As he worked on *Washington, D.C.*, he felt that his residence on a Roman street actually helped clarify his view of Washington. He had no intention, though, of being an expatriate. "Rome? Why Rome? That decision wasn't made," Howard felt, "and I'm never allowed to make those decisions except if I want to. Sometimes it's just easier to follow. I don't know why I went along. I guess I'm passive. As long as I had my New York life part of the year, I'd be happy to spend three months in Rome in my own apartment. It wasn't seen as a permanent move. As Gore pointed out, what's the difference between having a house in the Hamptons and having an apartment in Rome? It's just one flight. No, Gore didn't have in mind the possibility of permanent residence." But taking and furnishing the Via Di Torre Argentina apartment was significantly different from previous subleases. The material difference was that they could stay as long as they liked whenever they liked in a place whose furnishings were associated with choices they had made. For Gore the difference was not determinative, but it was unself-consciously compelling. He had distanced himself physically and emotionally from Edgewater. Though the attachment was still strong, the notion of selling it became less forbidding; he had established an alternative. For someone who had felt homeless through much of his earlier life, the drive to create a home for himself was always powerful. Suddenly now, in Rome, he was worrying about whether or not the plants on the terrace would be properly watered when he was gone.

————

Working through the summer of 1966 on *Washington, D.C.*, he slowly brought the book to a close. "Not since Tolstoi and *Anna Karenina* has a writer so much hated his book while doing it. Let us hope the issue is as happy for me as it was for him," he wrote to a young academic who had sent a list of questions in preparation for writing a book about him. In mid-September he "put the date on top with relief: the novel is finished or at least the last chapter is finally written and the rest of it is in fifth and penultimate draft. Four years since I started work, and I must say I would gladly have burned the whole thing a dozen times. Others can now do it for me." He felt less happy with the manuscript than he had with *Julian*. "I have never had such a difficult time," he confessed to Nini, "shuffling and re-shuffling, unable to say precisely what I mean yet unable to capture that tiresome ambivalence which keeps me from being one of those great vivid *definite* figures, like Norman or even Saul." He expected it would "be rather worse reviewed than usual. New Frontiers men will be upset; and of course it is 'clinical.' " He had meant *Washington, D.C.* as a meditation on the passage of time and the changes that had characterized post–World War II American public life. "I'm afraid," he told Nini, "that where I thought I would be at my best and most lucid I've simply bungled the job . . . that is, philosophically, the catching of the wheel as it turns in the night, the sense of a republic becoming an empire, the loss of the private conscience which so entirely informed a TPG or an Eleanor Roosevelt and does not, as far as I can see in these swinging times, obtain for anyone including myself except upon desperate occasions when one must be, if not right, good, and define the term. Not easy. But the book reads rather well; my dread narrative gift sweeps all, alas, before it. I think if I knew the subject less well I might have imagined it better. You'll be amused to find that the political tone is downright reactionary when not 'pragmatic' as they used to say at Camelot. But we are all prisoners to our age and the best of us never sees more than a bit of sky over the wall."

Its strong autobiographical base reverberated with his own feelings while he was conceiving and writing the novel. The elderly Senator Burden Day and the Blaise Sanford family (Blaise, his daughter Enid, and son Peter) are the most important characters in *Washington, D.C.* The setting is the capital of the country for the ten-year-or-so period that surrounds World War II. Franklin Roosevelt, Burden's political nemesis (as he was Senator Gore's), is a hovering, pervasive shadow as well as a real presence. Burden's story is one of personal and political defeat. His defeat is also, secondarily, at the hands of the new generation, represented by his assistant and then replacement, Clay Overbury, a John F. Kennedy figure. It is clear that Overbury will be not only senator but President. Blaise becomes Overbury's intimate ally and supporter; and not because Overbury has become his son-in-law, a marriage he initially opposes. Indeed, his willful, promiscuous, and explosive daughter, Enid, Overbury's wife, is institutionalized by Sanford and Overbury to advance Overbury's career. Blaise's son, Peter, Enid's sister, whose growth and education into manhood and political awareness comprise one of the important strands of the novel, cannot save her, though he can save himself by becoming independent of his father and molding his literary and moral sensibility into a post–World War II career that has at least the possibility of major accomplishment in the next generation. Nina, who was out of Gore's life, was not out of his thoughts. In the character of Enid, she is central to the novel. Senator Gore and Gore family history weave through the plot. Senator Day lives at a recognizable version of the Gores' Rock Creek Park house. Laurel House is clearly Merrywood. Elements of prominent Washington people and places appear, most of them modestly disguised, all subordinated to the novelist's imaginative overdrive as he makes fictional wholes out of real fragments. Historical figures appear directly or indirectly, a development of what he had first done in *Julian*, Vidal's own characteristic variations on the traditional genre of the historical novel taking shape. The influence of Thomas Mann is in the deep background; Henry Adams's Washington novel, *Democracy*, and Adams's view of America's political leaders pervade the foreground. Adams's anti-Semitism, still vigorously alive in 1930s Washington, *Washington, D.C.* exposes and condemns. In the favorable depiction of the Jewish character Irene Bloch, an ambitious hostess based on a well-known socialite of his Washington world, Vidal's detestation of prejudice and injustice has some of the force of personal experience, even if obtained through various substitutes, especially Howard. "My novel presents an accurate view of the anti-Semitism of that society and how Irene, as I call her, triumphs in the book," Vidal commented, "and how Gwen [Cafritz] is Irene in life, and Gwen loved it." The depiction of widespread Washington anti-Semitism would disturb some readers, especially reviewers who preferred to think that such sentiments did not exist in the nation's capital.

If the dark side of the Kennedys casts a shadow in the novel, it is in Vidal's concern that Robert Kennedy, waiting in the Senate, will capitalize on his brother's assassination and the turmoil of Vietnam to make himself a viable candidate for the presidency in 1968. Gore had come to detest Lyndon Johnson, the peace candidate of 1964 who had cravenly embraced a war America later learned even he did not believe in. But there was no reason to think he would not run for reelection. The only foreseeable opposition to Johnson within his own party was the Kennedy mystique. Senator Eugene McCarthy and the New Hampshire primary were a year in the future. In a cogent, sharply structured essay, "The Holy Family," written in fall 1966 and published in *Esquire* in April 1967, the legend-making power of the dead

JFK to make RFK a contender underlies Vidal's overriding concern with the question of "what sort of men ought we to be governed by in the coming years. . . . But if it is true that in a rough way nations deserve the leadership they get, then a frivolous and apathetic electorate combined with a vain and greedy intellectual establishment will most certainly restore to power the illusion-making Kennedys." The immediate issue was the Kennedy mystique, the more important concern the difficulty of a democracy's elevating appropriate people to positions of high leadership. "Holy family and bedazzled nation, in their faults at least, are well matched," he wrote. It was not a message everyone wanted to hear or be associated with, including the editors of *The New York Review*, which turned down the essay, the first of Vidal's that the *Review* declined. "The fierceness and relentlessness of tone," as if he were out to get Kennedy, Barbara Epstein explained early in October, had put the editors off. He agreed to do revisions. The editors had discussed and discussed the piece. Barbara, clearly upset, wrote to him in November about the revised version. She was afraid that they just could not publish it. She was sick about the whole thing, aware of how much work he had put into it originally, and how much anguish it had cost him to cut it. But there were no extra-editorial reasons for their decision, she claimed; the essay simply was not successful in its own terms. He did not believe her claim that it had been declined for aesthetic reasons.

By mid-November 1966, Little, Brown was printing galleys of *Washington, D.C.*, Thornhill and Bradford anticipating a bestseller. Robert Fetridge, the brilliant, heavy-drinking Little, Brown publicity director, began to plot his strategy, which included sending Roman coins to reviewers and bookstore managers. At the same time, Gore was in California with a strategy of his own, an extensive cross-country speaking tour, mostly at universities, that would put him before huge audiences of young people, partly in anticipation of the appearance of the novel but mostly to have a sense of what was going on in the country. "The thought of all those students across the country is beginning to alarm me," he had written to his father in June. "I'm not sure I have their range. Anyway it will be instructive, for me." The New York–based Harry Walker Agency, "Representing Distinguished Platform Personalities," handled the arrangements, initially to Gore's dissatisfaction. They quickly learned, though, what was wanted. Too often, he felt, his representatives coasted on the arrangements he had made and on the attraction of his name. At the beginning of October he had spent a week in Britain at interviews and receptions arranged by Heinemann to publicize the British edition of his second volume of essays, which Little, Brown had brought out as *Reflections Upon a Sinking Ship*. By mid-October, he was in New York for a two-week lecture tour of New York, New England, and Ohio; in early November, via the Midwest, to San Francisco, where he began a seventeen-campus series of California lectures, which returned him to New York in December, with an appearance en route in Little Rock. His topic throughout was mostly politics. Literature he wrote about. Politics and contemporary life seemed more appropriate for large audiences, among other reasons because he felt he had a significant message to deliver about the national abuse of power embodied in America as an imperial nation. The campus audiences were astoundingly large, irrepressibly enthusiastic, especially in California, where he realized to his delight that he was immensely popular with college students. The center had moved considerably to the left. The Vietnam War dominated what was a genuine but dangerously volatile national debate. Change seemed possible. Issues of domestic and international justice dominated the discussion. As he saw the audiences of thousands that attended his lectures, felt the touch of crowds of admirers eager for his presence, his words, and his autograph, his latent political ambitions again revived. Perhaps the Exonian senator from Virginia could become the Democratic senator from California, though the practical obstacles were substantial. For the time being, as the trip came to an end, the possibility lodged in a distant but still-active part of his mind. When he returned to New York, he had been on the road for over two months. Seemingly inexhaustible, he was now exhausted. But it had been exhilarating. The news in New York was excellent. *Washington, D.C.*, had been bought by the Literary Guild book club. In Washington, before Christmas, Nini and Little, Brown co-hosted a huge dinner party in Gore's honor, many of the guests well-known Washington people. Howard, who had spent much of the fall at Edgewater, closed the house, "amongst frozen pipes," and left for Rome. By early in the new year both had returned to Via Di Torre Argentina and Italian sunshine.

As is often the case with writers after a change of location, Gore began to feel strong creative urgings. The previous August he had told Ray White, doing the Vidal volume in the Twayne Modern Authors series, that he had three novels in mind. Since the last three "were written over a long period of time, I'd now like to sit down and write a book straight through to the end. One of the three has a title: *Academy of Drama and Modelling*, but I can't say much about it yet, other than I think it will be funny." Someone he knew in Miami, whom he thought a perfect fool, had had the notion to create a school of drama and modeling, an idea Gore thought wildly funny and "a wonderful idea for a novel." Aaron Burr was seeping through his unconscious mind into a consciously identified presence. Burr had come to his unfocused attention as early as the day at Newport in the late 1930s when the name, mentioned in conversation, had drifted up to him on the sea breeze. In late 1965, thinking about subjects for a play, Burr came to mind as a possibility, just shortly before Nini named her newborn son Burr. "Just when I contemplate a play about Aaron Burr you re-cast him or pro-create him. Now, hopefully, I won't have to write it."

Before he could commit himself, though, to write anything substantial, he had a duty to perform for himself and his publisher, a whirlwind ten-day publicity tour for the Little, Brown edition of *Washington, D.C.* Soon after its publication in early February it had appeared on the bestseller list. It was now climbing rapidly toward the top, which puzzled many reviewers, partly because they could not or did not want to believe that its realistic depiction of American political life was truthful. There was a respectable number of very good reviews, though most emphasized its commercial qualities, occasionally ambivalent about whether its riveting readability did not somehow need to be apologized for or at least put in the context of its insufficiencies, especially its exaggerated presentation of Washington sex and greed. From Gore's viewpoint exaggeration was impossible. Some, like John Kenneth Galbraith, defended John F. Kennedy's posthumous reputation from the imputation that *Washington, D.C.*'s Clay Overbury was based on the character of the assassinated President. Gore agreed, but for artistic, not moral reasons. "Clay is *not* JFK, not remotely," he responded to Louis Auchincloss, who felt that Kennedy had been maligned. "Nor is he—in his creator's eyes—a monster. The similarity to Jack is, simply, the way money is used to promote illusions and win elections. . . . The only deliberate likeness to Jack is the sexual promiscuity and I think I have got the point to each: sex as a means to power not over the woman so much as over the other men involved with her. In any case, no one can say that my explication of that aspect of life is *ever* pejorative." Though Auchincloss attempted to deny the realities of Kennedy's character, he embraced the artistic and thematic achievement of the novel. Gore was the best novelist writing in English about politics since Disraeli, he wrote in a widely read review. Of course, not many readers knew that Disraeli had been a novelist. Years later Auchincloss recounted meeting Robert McNamara in the cloakroom of the Century Club. "Didn't you know all about Jack's women in the White House? You were at the White House frequently." "Yes," McNamara said, "but we didn't know that there were that many!" The novel, though, was not about transient politics or judgments about sexual practices. Few reviewers had any sense of its elegiac nature. "My own impression of the book," Gore told Louis, "is that it is unexpectedly sad, and I can't think why. My contempt for the empire has always been, I thought, complete but cheerful. Instead I am as gloomy as Tacitus without ever being able for one moment to believe, as he did, that the Republic was much better. I did find it significant that none of the book-men in their chat-pieces seemed aware of the book's theme." Some were, but their voices were mostly lost in the sensationalistic chirping about Vidal as Suetonius taking salubrious delight in exposing the flaws of our leaders. He had wanted to be Tacitus.

In late April he flew to New York for the publicity tour; this was the time to strike. Having limited the tour to New York, Boston, and Washington, he made effective use of television appearances, especially *Today* and *The Merv Griffin Show*, where he talked less about *Washington, D.C.*, than about his disapproval of Lyndon Johnson and the Vietnam War, though the segue from one to the other was especially easy. When letters began arriving in response to his attack on the war, he was surprised and pleased that about half approved of what he had said. Certainly his Dutchess County friends did. Just before his departure for New York, Barbara Epstein had described to him a Peace March to Washington that she, the Dupees, and the MacDonalds had participated in and had remarked on the noticeable absence of people like Arthur Schlesinger and Ralph Ellison.

Literary and national politics, though, overlapped. Gore had certainly enjoyed Harold Hayes's account at the beginning of April of a conversation with Barbara Epstein and the publisher of *The New York Review of Books* at the George Polk Memorial Press awards luncheon. "Miss Epstein was going on," Hayes told him, "about how wonderful [*Esquire*'s] cover was and the illustrations inside." Hayes asked the publisher, referring to "The Holy Family," " 'Why'you-all hadn't taken that piece?' The publisher turned to Miss Epstein and asked, 'Why hadn't we all taken that piece?' She said, 'Our reasons are private.' A stunning *mot juste* and one I will try to remember for my own purposes." From Gore's perspective the editors had succumbed to a desire not to offend the Kennedys, particularly the powerful senator from New York, though an assumption that the author's tone would be held against the *Review* suggests a sensitivity that focused on larger concerns of influence and constituency. Certainly many of the *Review*'s liberal pro-Kennedy readers hoped that Robert Kennedy would become a rallying figure for opposition to the Vietnam War and would find a way to wrest the 1968 Democratic nomination away from Lyndon Johnson. His earlier career and character, they felt, could easily be disregarded. "You can't really separate the personal from the professional relationship," Barbara Epstein of course knew. "I was upset about it. . . . I hate not to publish anything by Gore. He's of great value to me as a contributor and as a friend." Actually, its publication in *Esquire* rather than in *The New York Review of Books* worked to Vidal's advantage. It gave the article more national presence and readers, almost as if it had found its true best home, for which it should have been intended originally. The same could not be said about another essay, "French Letters: The Theory of the Novel," that Barbara Epstein had urged him to write that late winter and early spring of 1967, which the *Review*, after initial enthusiasm, turned down. The change in reading tastes and the decline in readership associated with two oppositional phemonena—the increasing dominance of mindless television and the rise of a self-con-sciously arcane, theory-dominated approach to writing and discussing novels epitomized by "The French New Novel"—both worried and an-gered Vidal. Whatever merit could be discovered in writers like Robbe-Grillet, Nathalie Saurraute, and John Barth, they seemed intent on turning the novel into a specialty genre for an intellectual elite. To Vidal and others, their theorizing seemed "portentous." And television and other electronic communications seemed likely to put an end to literature as they had known it. "Our lovely vulgar and most human art is at an end, if not the end." As he wrote to Fred Dupee, "I struggled 2 months with the piece on the New French Novelists, a labor of hate and exhausting. The result is a bit dense but I think pretty good." At first Epstein found the article "very good, indeed," though a little long. Then the editors turned it down, perhaps because one or more found the subject itself boring. "That was a big mistake," Epstein later acknowledged, "because it was a very good article." Its most appropriate venue had somehow for the moment lost its sense of itself and its good judgment. *Encounter* published it in December 1967.

As soon as Gore returned to Rome in early May, he sat at his large writing table in the sunlight that came across the terrace from the long Roman skyline and began to write *Myra Breckinridge*. The most immediate specific stimulus was his response to a request from Ken Tynan to write an erotic sketch for a musical sex show, to be called *Oh! Calcutta!*, which Tynan hoped would be theatrically innovative and immensely profitable. Always short of money, Tynan, who had remarried, had recently borrowed £1,000 from Gore. Harold Pinter was "co-devising and co-directing," Tynan explained. "It's to be an erotic evening with no purpose except to titillate, arouse and provoke . . . the whole thing very elegant and per-verse, every heterosexual fetish fully catered for and no crap about art." By the late 1960s Broadway and even London West End censorship had loos-ened enough to make the production possible. Tynan invited a dozen writers to write a sketch that would dramatize the writer's favorite erotic interest. "A sketch on the organization of an orgy, for instance, might be attractive," he wrote to Gore. The sketches would be the basis of a revue that would represent the usual standardized erotic interests. "Generally, he wanted something far out for *Oh! Calcutta!*" Vidal recalled. "Myra'd do business for spanking. After all if she were just dildo wielding. . . ." But as soon as Vidal got going on the sketch, "it got more interesting and I certainly wasn't going to waste it on a review-sketch." Almost immediately he had left Tynan's request far behind. Into his conscious mind came a sentence, "I am Myra Breckinridge whom no man will ever possess," as if that were the talismanic combination of words in which was contained the entirety of a novel, few of the details of which he yet knew. Cool and analytical as he could be as a writer, he believed in and gave authority to his unconscious. "It's the conscious mind I don't believe in," he later seriously quipped. There were some things that were clear to him from the moment he began something not for Tynan but for himself and a larger audience. This would be a comic novel, satiric, parodic, fearless, he hoped, in its imaginative engagement with cultural tropes about gender, sex, politics, literature, and film. His recent reading of the French novelists, both the fiction and the theories, was much on his mind, stimulating within him a self-consciousness about the process of writing so strong that it would be part of the fictional narrative. *Myra,* he quickly decided, would be Myra's own journal, written for publication, and Myra would have some of her creator's awareness of recent trends in writing and theorizing about the novel. He would not be

bound by the conventions of realistic fiction. At certain points in the narrative Myra and her creator would overlap. He could flow into and out of her
as he thought desirable; as a character, she would be in the tradition of Moll
Flanders, Pamela, Becky Sharp, Isabel Archer, Kate Croy—the powerful
feminine figures of the literary past. In regard to the author-character relationship and the usual coordinates of the realistic novel, the model would be
Laurence Sterne and Tristram Shandy. *Myra Breckinridge* would be an "invention," and though what would come after was not in his mind at the
moment, he would later write a series of such novels, from *Myron,* a sequel
to *Myra,* to *The Smithsonian Institution,* all of which assumed the imaginative freedom to rearrange the usual coordinates of time, space, and cause
and effect. The tonal model would be Jonathan Swift, particularly "A
Modest Proposal," and also *Gulliver's Travels.* As wonderful as the world
might be, it was also a hateful world whose depredations could best be
evoked in literature with Swiftean "savage indignation," with no-holds-
barred satiric aggressiveness and parodic anger. Gore was himself angry,
and very disappointed in what human beings had done and were doing to
our planet. His own country was among the most powerfully predatory
destroyers. Its puritan tradition devoured people's natural instincts and
chances for happiness by rigid, self-serving moralism. Its expansive and self-
deluding greed was making dollar materialism more triumphant than ever.
In Vietnam we were destroying a semi-helpless people, wasting our own
substance, coarsening our national life, dividing America with an intensity
that threatened national chaos. And literature seemed to be fading away into
either an artifact from the past or the preserve of an elite few.

From the start, as Myra came to life in his imagination, she joined in
his mind with the idea for a novel about an academy of modeling and drama.
In 1952, in an early draft of *Judgment,* he had had what he had thought a
"wildly funny chapter" depicting "a perfect heterosexual marriage between
Myra and Myron and they constantly quarrel. . . . So Myra and Myron
entered my head at the time of *Judgment of Paris* and . . . it was excised
from it at Anaïs's request on my behalf, for my own good. Such a serious
book, any glint of humor she loathed." The conversation between scriptwriters that he had heard in 1945 by the Beverly Hills Hotel swimming pool
about *The Sirens of Atlantis* surfaced. Somehow it was to be part of the mix,
for the novel would be permeated by film culture and history, from Fay
Wray to Maria Montez. Parker Tyler, whom he had met decades before at

Peggy Guggenheim's New York salon, had written a now-out-of-print Freudian study, *The Magic and Myth of the Movies,* which he had on hand to bring in as a semi-parodic presentation of the high culture's intellectualization of Hollywood. Breckinridge itself was a name with two associations, one immediately available from his historical reading, the first and only Vice President of the Confederacy. Years later, when he was sent an obituary of John "Bunny" Breckinridge, who had died at the age of ninety-four, he was prompted to recall another overheard conversation. "I *do* remember—my mother's circle at the Beverly Hills Hotel, they loved talking about our feathered friends, referring to fairies—one might have been Bunny Breckinridge of San Francisco. I was then in the Army. So they could talk fearlessly in front of me since I was no longer a child. I don't remember the sex change at all. I don't think that was discussed. Bunny Breckinridge was a famous queen who had married and gone to prison in that order or, if not in that order, the other way around, and all the ladies had met him, including my mother, and that was all, and then I never thought of him again. I was halfway through *Myra Breckinridge* before I realized that Myra had been a man."

From new moon in April to new moon in May, he wrote the entire first draft of *Myra Breckinridge,* an imaginative riff more deeply absorbing and fulfilling than any single writing experience he had ever had before. As he wrote, he felt his expressive powers at their height. He was writing from deeper, more spontaneous sources than had readily been reachable in previous attempts. For the first time he was decisively and totally liberated from the narrow realism from which he had started. *Williwaw* was light-years away. The experience was liberating. The restraints he had felt before no longer restricted him. At forty-two, he now had an increased, more sharply formed, perhaps even more courageous commitment to self-expression that took chances both with artistic form and with self-revelation. The change in cultural climate that the sixties had brought had also contributed to making *Myra* possible. The erotic elements seemed appropriate, actually necessary, essential to the thematic challenge in which titillation became the lure with which to implicate readers and make them aware of the damage society had done to our natural selves. Myra (who had once been Myron) was more victim than victimizer. The sex-change operation embodied his/her capability for bisexual roles. But in her tormented expression of sexual and psychological instability, it also disembodied society's self-destructive rules about sex and gender. Deeply anti-Christian, the novel attacked a civilization that had forced many people to be at lifelong war with themselves. And the individual internal war mirrored the warlike predilections of the society in general, of which Vietnam was but the most recent, though one of the worst examples. So self-distressed and self-destructive was the polity that the best way to capture it in fiction was with this kind of extrarealistic, imaginative explosion into transgressive literary language and aesthetic form. And the appropriate tone that would effectively match the dark vision had to be comic: the comedy of despair, laughter that went beyond tears. The outrageous was aesthetically appropriate, from jokes to darkness.

After finishing the first draft of *Myra*, Gore, with Howard, Joanne, and Paul, sailed out of Piraeus on a hired yacht with four staterooms, for what they expected to be ten days of lovely Adriatic sunshine. The isles of Greece were before them, Rhodes their destination. The four of them had now been friends for over ten years. When she had finished *Judgment of Paris*, Joanne had telegraphed Gore, "AM AT YOUR FEET ARTISTWISE SUCH A BEAUTIFUL MIND BETWEEN THOSE FLAPPING EARS." She regularly remembered to send him birthday greetings. Howard usually sent celebratory greetings to Joanne and Paul, and Howard and Joanne had grown especially fond of one another. But the Edgewater and Los Angeles days of regular companionship were behind them. Inevitably they saw less of the Newmans. In general, their Dutchess County life seemed mostly over, though they still saw and wrote to their friends. "Edgewater," Fred Dupee wrote to him that July, "is pretty enough to break your heart—yes, even yours—with the willows still shimmering demurely despite all they have seen and heard over the years. I told them you had only gone away for a while and were on the best-seller list and would be back sometime and everything would be *all right*." But Edgewater seemed more and more in the past. Margaret Shafer and her husband had been spending the year on a sabbatical in Rome. For the first time they got to know her well and found her company lively, an attractive lady whose beauty they enjoyed and whose worship of Gore, Gore enjoyed. The Dupees they always saw on their visits, and Fred's Roman holidays were holidays for them as well, an opportunity for Gore and Fred to talk about books. Dupee still had no equal as a critic in Gore's mind. He rarely saw the Roveres now, though he was usually happy to see them. Clearly,

Gore's high valuation of his Roman life made it inevitable that he would have less frequent and less sustained time with his American friends. "I am getting sentimental in my dotage," Newman had written to Gore in 1965, that he longed to crack a bottle with him. It had been long, he joked, since he had seen him facedown in a urinal. Whatever direction they were facing, they were usually at a distance from one another.

When they sailed out of Piraeus, they looked forward to a happy holiday together. The external omens, though, were not good. Gore had done all the arranging. "That is not Gore's strong point," Joanne remarked. It turned out that the crew spoke no English or French. The captain seemed not to know quite what he was doing. Some of the worst storms of the decade, rarely seen in May, kept the seas high and rough. Despite the obstacles, some things went well, and both Paul and Joanne enjoyed Gore's accounts of the relevant mythology and literature, especially on Rhodes. As usual, he delighted in being charmingly tutorial. To the Newmans his knowledge seemed breathtakingly encyclopedic, and they blessed their good fortune in having such a superlative personal guide. But the weather was recalcitrant throughout. As soon as they sailed, Athenian sunshine turned dark over the rising seas. Soon they were sloshing around in wind and water. Gore and Paul played chess and read. Joanne embroidered and read. Howard nervously watched waves and crew. The captain, alas, seemed uncertain. "We got on ship and we took off . . . and ran right into another boat," Joanne recalled. "Instantly. This was the first thing we did. And then I discovered . . . that this was the first time that the skipper had ever skipped, as it were." But Gore felt he had reason to believe that the Greek captain was an old salt. To deal with the storm that first night the captain shut off the engine. It made matters worse. In the dark, he anchored in a bay off an island, probably afraid to bring the boat in. In the morning, hungry, they wanted to eat. Apparently, though, there was no food aboard. And "nothing on the boat worked," as Paul quickly noticed. "The motorboat wouldn't work. We went into the island in a three-man dinghy . . . looking for food, since the skipper wouldn't sail out because of the weather. We bought bread and cheese and vegetables and had all these groceries in bags. Howard stepped onto the outside gunnel as we were getting into the boat. We all went immediately overboard. By this time the word had spread on the island that some American movie stars were on board, so I surfaced to the polite applause of certain onlookers. The food was gone. Everything."

When the weather briefly became calm, they sailed on. After a number of island stops in just-bearable weather, they were detained by the Greek Navy. The skipper had sailed into a sensitive military area. There had recently been a military coup. Greece was under martial law. "The Greek Navy fired a cannon at us and stopped us. We had to follow the Navy ship out away from that island and to another island. I thought Gore was asleep. Once they started firing at us, I said to Joanne, 'Jesus, get downstairs! Lock yourself in the bathroom.' I thought it might be guys from the other end of the political spectrum who might want hostages or might want the boat." Gore came up on deck. He seemed perfectly calm about what was transpiring. "It never occurred to Gore," Joanne surmised, "that anything would happen to him, especially in that day and age. How dare it! We were so young. He was perfectly happy and went back downstairs and back to his book. Howard and I were sitting clutching each other, saying 'Oh, God!' " Soon a stocky captain came on board. Newman, who had been in the Navy during World War II, did not like the look of it. "The captain had some guys with machine guns with him. I like mature guys if they're holding machine guns. These were young kids who stood with their guns ready on each side of the rear gunnel. They demanded to see our passports. They looked at them and us very suspiciously. Perhaps they thought we were political activists looking to create an incident. The Navy captain, after looking at all the papers we had and reading them slowly, finally grabbed the document I had from the American embassy stating who I was. I had lost my passport. On the day we were leaving Athens, we ran to the American embassy, which issued a temporary visa saying, This is Paul Newman, the actor. The captain kept reading it over and over. Then he stopped abruptly, looked around, and saw me. He looked at me for what seemed a long time. He put the document down and seemed to think for a moment. Then he went to the two machine-gunners and said, 'Off!' We surmised that he realized that we were American movie stars and that he didn't want an international incident. That got us off the hook, just barely." Actually, Gore soon told Fred Dupee, "the only real diversion" on the entire trip "was when an idiot captain brought us too close to the island where 10,000 political prisoners are kept and we were fired upon and boarded by the Greek navy. Fortunately the face of the international film favorite saved us from arrest as potential Pimpernels." By this time Joanne had had enough. She was getting "grumpier and grumpier," especially when the steward didn't close a porthole and the rain soaked one of her favorite dresses. Feeling a little claustrophobic below, she decided to spend some time on deck, despite the weather. "As I was sitting on a trunk, a wave hit us broadside, the whole ship went that way, and the trunk with me on it came careening down and hit the side of the deck. I almost went overboard. At that point I was—Ahhhh! 'Get me out of here! I'm going to drown! My children are going to be orphans! Ay, ay, ay!' I was really getting hysterical. Paul said, 'Wait a minute, wait, wait! We'll get into someplace.' So we convinced the skipper that we had to go into the lee of some island nearby." But she had had enough. She was quietly emphatic in her most ladylike way: "Get me off this fucking boat!" When a ferry on its way to Piraeus came by, she jumped ship. Happy to be back in Athens, she had some delightful days there on her own and then flew to London. The three men finished their island tour. Howard and Gore returned to Rome, the Newmans, via Rome, to sunny California. "Greece was depressing," Gore wrote to his father, "bad weather, worse politics. The Newmans just left. Finishing a new novel and waiting for war. Not a pleasant time."

    As Vidal reworked his first draft at the beginning of June, war broke out in the Middle East. The British novelist Elizabeth Bowen stopped by at the Via Di Torre Argentina to visit. "She was writing *Eva Trout,* which proved to be her last novel, and I was working on *Myra,* and we were talking about the war. I remember sitting there, very friendly on the sofa, and I said, 'Well, this war could escalate and be nuclear and it could be the end of everything.' She said, 'Yes, I've considered that. I only hope they wait until I finish my new book. I'm so pleased with it.' I said, 'That's exactly my feeling. I don't care what they do after the war. I want to finish the book.'" With Rome blazing in the July sun, he finished *Myra* and mailed it to Little, Brown, where he expected that Arthur Thornhill, who had objected to the depiction in *Washington, D.C.,* of two boys masturbating, would find it offensive and that Ned Bradford would immediately see its value. He was not concerned, though, that Thornhill's inhibitions would influence his business judgment. He believed he had written a work of both literary distinction and commercial value, especially if its sales were not undermined by the usual narrow-minded, moralistic newspaper reviewers whose standard of "common decency" was one of the philistine mentalities that *Myra* existed to challenge. Still, he realized that *Myra* demanded an imaginative engagement and a suspension of middle-class prohibitions that might damage its sales. He had in mind suggesting to Little, Brown that they not send out review copies at all but have the book suddenly appear in bookstores with a publisher-created and -driven publicity campaign that would preempt any damage reviews might do. To Fred Dupee, for whom bestsellerdom was suspect, he wrote that "it is really very extraordinary and will save me from becoming a Mary [McCarthy] novelist bestseller-fate. I seem to have spent my life in getting into categories which, with some ingenuity, I get out of." Of course, both Little, Brown and *Myra*'s author preferred that it sell every bit as well as *Julian* and *Washington, D.C.* With Dupee he promoted a consanguinity of literary sensibilities. With Little, Brown he wanted a bestseller. "I think the book absolutely riotously funny," he wrote to Bradford. "But it will be a bit tough to sell to the middle aged ladies who buy novels. That's why I hope the store clerks are well bred and the price sufficiently low to appeal to the young who don't ordinarily buy hardcover books, and men who don't either. If the paperback people are not afraid of censorship, I think we can extract a pleasant fortune from them."

At the end of July he sent the revised manuscript to Christopher Isherwood, who immediately telegraphed back, "I AM HONORED AND DE-LIGHTED TO HAVE ANY BOOK OF YOURS DEDICATED TO ME." *Myra*, among other things, continued the discussion on sex and gender the two writers had begun in 1947. Isherwood was the appropriate dedicatee. Whatever their differences about the degree to which ideology and political action should influence aesthetic matters, it was a subject essentially embedded in both their sensibilities. In August, having read *Myra* twice, Isherwood expressed his total admiration. "In my opinion it's your very best satirical work. It's wildly funny and wildly sensible. Even when I was laughing most I was overcome by your wisdom and seriousness." As Vidal had reason to know, Isherwood rarely gave compliments. But he did share perceptions, one of which Vidal probably both by nature and by inclination (if nature ever succumbed) had nothing to say about, to himself or anyone else. And even the usually frank, self-confident Isherwood provided a hesitant, qualifying, perhaps even self-protective clause. "What makes the book so truly remark-able is that—I know I'm not going to be able to express this as well as I should like, especially in the haste of letter-writing—behind the apparently fantastic doings and behaviour of Myra-Myron there is an entirely realistic and very subtle psychological self-portrait. The doings and the behaviour are seen, by the time one has finished the book, to be a symbolic play or ballet." If it was a point the author preferred not to traffic with, it was an important key to the power of the novel that none of the reviewers, even those who had high praise, were to perceive. Beyond the fantasy, the realities the novel grapples with are brilliantly defined.

As soon as the manuscript was in the mail to Little, Brown, Gore and Howard drove northward to Milan, then through the Black Forest—which he had never seen before, though he had written about it in *Julian* (and gotten it wrong, he now realized)—"then by slow degrees to Paris, destroying the liver enroute," then across to London to participate in publicity, mainly television appearances, for the publication of the British edition of *Washington, D.C.* To his surprise, the British reviews were uniformly better than the American. It soon appeared on British bestseller lists, readers eager to have what appeared to be the inside story of Washington life and American politicians. "Still a good deal of, oh, people can't be that bad!," he reported to his father. "To which I respond that I regard my characters as, generally, more good than bad, pointing out that it was fate not I who created LBJ, a figure far more lurid than anything a novelist would be allowed to get away with on the page." Artistic license seemed impossible in what was now becoming, artistically and politically, a licenseless world. The escalation of the war in Vietnam and Johnson's obsession with a disastrous policy sickened Gore. The positive letters he had received in response to his television attacks on the President gave him hope that perhaps the American people had more sense than they were credited with. "I have never in my life had such a strange sensation of being trapped in a nightmare and knowing that there is nothing one can do but, in the dream of falling, wait for the crash. I suspect it is all biological; too many people—war and famine. We have the second; the first approaches." It was the front-page, real-life version of what *Myra-Myron* dramatized.

From London he returned to Rome, the depressing Aegean rains now almost evaporated from memory, for two memorable late-summer holiday excursions. Howard did not accompany him for either, which was often the case when Gore did high-social things of the sort he had begun to do regularly in Rome with the Crespis and Pecci-Blunts, Italian and Anglo-Italian aristocratic families who eagerly solicited him to have a "palace life."

Beginning in 1966 he had more invitations than he had time or desire to accept. They usually did not include Howard, which neither of them corrected or opposed. It was easier that way, and behind Howard's response was the thought that he might not or would not feel comfortable with such people anyway. If it was the path of least resistance, at least there was little tension about it between them. The early-August quietness in Rome had its self-generated counterpoint, as if no sooner had Gore finished one flurry of activity than he experienced a combination of emptiness and eagerness to be busy at something again. Success rarely bred self-imitation. By personality he desired variety, and boredom frequently seemed an evil to be fled from or worked out of at almost any cost. "I'm now happily in Rome," he told Nini, "heavily air-conditioned, writing some pieces to go into the next book of essays. If only some kind muse would say, stop, please. You don't need to write any more. Such relief." The alternative to writing, always available in his thoughts, was, of course, politics. It regularly came to mind, even if its focus had an impracticality evident even to him. As soon as he returned to Rome, he confessed to his father, whom he urged to visit them at the new apartment, "I am becoming restless, bored with being (as of last Sunday's *Times*) the #2 bestseller [with *Washington, D.C.*]. Perhaps I should go into the N.H. Primary! Life is so short, temptation so great, satiety so swiftly arrived at." His two late-summer holidays dramatized other people's satiety, or at least how they overfilled their own personal worlds. With Diana Phipps, whom he saw almost whenever he visited London, he went to Sardinia on a ten-day holiday with British royalty. Through Judy Montagu he had been readily accepted into Princess Margaret's Anglo-Italian circle, the London end of which Diana Phipps had become a part of. The young girl he had met with her parents at "Aunt Mona's" New York mansion just as she was entering adolescence had become an attractive, full-figured, dark-haired young widow with a daughter, who, despite working as an interior decorator to provide income, managed to live a glamorous life with no shortage of eager companions and ready entrée into London society. She entertained regularly with her mother, the Countess Sternberg, now widowed, who lived with her. She bore her own aristocratic background and her personal impressiveness with dignity and freedom. In London she was someone desired and desirable, "stunningly beautiful, dark haired, with a graceful figure, long arms," as her friend, the writer Antonia Fraser, recalled. Diana introduced Antonia to Gore, the start of another, though less intense, friendship. Ten years younger than Gore, Diana was one of the most attractive women he knew, and she soon became one of the four or five women in his life to whom he felt an attraction that rose to the level of a serious, even if mostly speculative, interest.

At first they had agreed to spend time together in August at a house in Salzburg that Diana planned to rent. When she made other travel plans, that fell through, but in late August, when she took a house for herself and her daughter on the Costa Esmeralda in Sardinia, next door to where Princess Margaret and her husband were staying, Gore joined her for ten days. Sardinia he thought a ghastly island, "a terrible place, made worse by the quarreling Snowdons. On the evening of the princess's thirty-seventh birthday she and Tony had a splendid row," he wrote to his father. "They're both nice separately but together hell." The four of them would go out to dinner every night. "Like so many good-looking women, Princess Margaret likes plain-looking women like Judy," he remarked years later. "Tony was flipping lighted cigarette butts [at Margaret] at a nightclub on her birthday. Then he got up to dance with Diana. Margaret said, 'Let's dance.' I said, 'I don't dance.' Finally, I paid the bill, and Diana . . . swept a curtsy such as you've never seen since Marie Antoinette and marched out without a word. The next day we went to lunch with Annie Fleming, a witty, rather nasty woman. Political hostess. Widow of Ian Fleming. Before that Lady Rothermere. At lunch was Princess Margaret. She was in good form. She said, 'I want to apologize to you for our behavior last night. It was intolerable, and I've been trying to write a letter of apology all day. Thank God we meet at lunch and I can say it.' She's well brought up." Diana herself he thought "in good form." But, shortly afterward, reading Saint-Simon, he thought that only the French master of social cynicism could have done the royal bickering justice.

In early September, in Venice for a short holiday, he attended a masked ball where he had a wittily acerbic exchange with one of America's peculiar variants on its own royalty, Clare Boothe Luce, who had been ambassador to Italy and whom Gore had known over the years through the Auchincloss connection with Henry Luce. The overheard conversation in 1942 in which Luce had proposed to Gore's mother had stayed in his mind, an ironic subtext to his awareness of Clare's successful careers as playwright, journalist, and diplomat, and the advantages of her husband's power. "I said," he wrote to his father, "I felt novels were finished. She said, 'Yes, but there's still a kind of fiction people love!' 'Yes,' I said, '*Time* magazine.' 'No,' she said, 'I meant fiction.' 'I know,' I said, 'I meant *Time.*' 'Don't be naughty,' she said, 'I meant detective stories.' Then she insisted we be photographed together in the room where Browning died." Venice itself, though, seemed perfect, a city that transcended human affectations. "So it goes," he wrote from both sides of the ironic divide to Fred Dupee, who, like Gore, would have felt the glamour and at the same time mocked himself for having felt it. "So it goes. A summer of Capri," where he had visited Eddie and Mona, who at seventy-six still seemed "extraordinarily beauti-ful. . . . Sardinia, Venice, the life of the beautiful people, almost as tiring as Red Hook–Rhinebeck."

While the perfections of Venice occupied his eyes, his mind was partly on *Myra*. To Fred he sent a postcard the illustration of which was Carpac-cio's painting of St. Jerome leading a lion into a monastery, the monks fleeing in terror. "Old Gore leading *Myra Breckinridge* into the literary arena." It seemed unlikely that many readers would flee in terror, and many might buy the novel anyway, though Little, Brown and he did anticipate moral disapproval from certain quarters and legal pressure from others. Censorship would not be an issue in the United States, where *Myra* seemed certain to meet the legal standard that judged a work in its entirety. Arthur Thornhill, encouraged by Ned Bradford, who thought *Myra* brilliant and funny, quickly overcame his squeamishness about associating Little, Brown with a novel some would define as pornographic. Brilliant at his business, he was soon to sell Little, Brown to Time Warner, which allowed Bradford, who had an interest in the sale, to write good-humoredly to Gore "from one millionaire to another." Britain was another matter entirely. Some of the monks did flee in terror. Gore's ongoing London publisher, Heinemann, declined to publish *Myra*, mostly because it feared that an association with the book would affect Heinemann's reputation in a way that would damage sales. A smaller but less timid publisher, Anthony Blond, stepped in, pro-vided that Gore would respond satisfactorily to pages of objections raised by its own lawyers, some of which had to do with obscenity, some with libel. Under pressure from an increasingly nervous Blond, Vidal made numerous changes to minimize the possibility of the government prosecuting publisher and author for obscenity. He resented the attempts at what he felt to be censorship, though he uneasily cooperated, to his lasting regret. The issue of libel was resolved quickly with Little, Brown via a request that Gore sign a statement holding the author entirely responsible if he and Little, Brown should be sued. Reasonably confident that America's libertarian libel laws, especially in regard to public figures, made a suit unlikely, Gore agreed. Britain's much narrower libel laws presented a different challenge. They regularly forced publishers into nervous self-censorship whenever manuscripts referred to living people. Blond feared that he would be sued. Undercapitalized, he might be driven into bankruptcy by legal fees even if he successfully defended himself. Blond's lawyer's objections, though, were comic. Would the publisher not be vulnerable to be sued for libel by Ava Gardner since Myra fantasizes having an affair with her? Apparently the lawyer did not know that Ava Gardner existed to be fantasized about. Otherwise, she and her Hollywood studios would soon be out of business. Most of the objections were of this sort. A few, though, had enough surface plausibility for Gore to agree to make some minor alterations that satisfied the publisher. Apparently the changes as a whole did not satisfy W. H. Smith, Britain's largest bookseller, which refused to sell *Myra* except on special order. Legal censorship still existed, though by 1968, the year also of John Updike's *Couples* and one year before Philip Roth's *Portnoy's Complaint*, larger changes were occurring. In distant Australia, *Myra* itself became the text of a court case resulting in a ruling that allowed Australian readers to determine what books they would read. Extralegal voluntary moral censorship, like W. H. Smith's, often in the form of economic pressure, increasingly became the major weapon of those who believed that elite ethical police should make decisions about what books could be available to the public.

With Little, Brown there was another issue: whether or not *Myra* should fulfill the "third book" clause of their 1962 contract. "I'm trying to make up my mind whether or not we should include *Myra Breckinridge* in the old contract (the third book I'd always planned to be essays)," he wrote to Bradford in the middle of July, as he sent off the manuscript to New York. Actually, Little, Brown had no problem with *Myra*'s being counted as the third book or as part of a new contract that would include *Myra* and future novels. Vidal, in fact, had multiple agendas, and his major target was William Morris, not Little, Brown. "It may well be," he told Bradford, "that if there is a large advance from paperback a separate contract should be drawn since I don't look forward to my heirs getting 15 Gs per annum for the rest of the century," the amount that Vidal and Little, Brown had agreed in the existing contract that Vidal would take each year under a tax provision allowing royalties to accrue and tax to be paid only on withdrawal of the funds. "Anyway, do give me figures so that I can brood." His Little, Brown account contained over $100,000, royalties from *Julian* and especially *Washington, D.C.* It was reasonable to assume that the profits from *Myra* would be substantial. Little, Brown itself was uneasy about holding large amounts of his for more than a brief time. What he really had in mind was cutting William Morris out from any share in the profits from *Myra*. Having become a William Morris client for his television work through Harold Franklin, he had drifted into becoming a literary client as well. In Gore's judgment the agency did little to nothing for its percentage of his royalties, and he increasingly disliked Helen Strauss, who constantly publicized the wonderful things she had done for him and at the same time paid no attention to his backlist, as if that were beneath her interest. Actually, the dislike was mutual, as Owen Laster, a young agent who had finally gotten his wish to move from William Morris's television to its literary department, noticed and as Strauss later confirmed in her memoir. "Helen was ugly but she had presence," Laster recalled. "She had a classy elegance to her and a touch of the tough lady. When she left William Morris, she was sixty-three years old and had been here for twenty-four years. She started the literary department. She was a powerful agent," among her clients James Michener and Robert Penn Warren. "She always wore labels. If she had a fur coat, it was from a fancy place. Gore didn't really respect her very much. . . . When he delivered *Myra* to Helen Strauss, she said to me, 'This is his pornographic book.' " His anger at Strauss never subsided. "She couldn't read a book," he remarked years later. "She never read a manuscript. I only took her on out of pity because of Harold Franklin, and, my God, never do anything out of pity on this earth. Every time that I have been seriously damaged professionally and sometimes personally, it's been because I was sorry for somebody. And now here I am being held up by what is essentially a non-agent. Then I read her memoir in which she dismisses me. I sold out to fame, she claimed, as if she knew anything about what I ever wrote. She had no idea."

To his delight, in 1967 Strauss was lured to Hollywood by a high-paying offer and California sunshine. Vidal's agency contract with William Morris, scheduled to expire on August 15, was up for renewal. This seemed the perfect opportunity for him to leave. Sue Mengers, on the rise at Creative Management Associates, was eager to have her friend as a movie and television client. That would take care of that aspect of his work, though he insisted, despite her pressure, that Alain Bernheim still negotiate his European movie deals. For the time being he would handle his literary rights himself, except in Britain, which Graham Watson at Curtis Brown very capably arranged. He did not brood long and soon notified William Morris that he would not sign a renewal. He then told both Little, Brown and the agency that *Myra* would not be the third book in his 1962 contract. That would be a volume of essays. He requested that Little, Brown draw up a separate contract for *Myra*. Consequently, he maintained, the agency would not be entitled to any commission from its sales. William Morris disagreed. So too did Little, Brown, though it had no material interest in the change. Its priority was to keep Vidal on its list. If indeed Vidal had all along intended the third be a volume of essays, his intention was contradicted by the words of the contract, which stated it was to be "a novel on a subject to be mutually agreed upon." Perhaps his anger blinded him to the contract's language. More likely he chose to base his campaign to cut out William Morris on a purposeful misreading that would force the agency either to sue him or to compromise. An actual suit was unlikely. He could force the "novel" to be a novel other than *Myra*, but he could not offer a book of essays rather than a novel. Thornhill and Bradford got out of the line of fire. Gore agreed in writing that if the dispute went to court, he would assume full responsibility should the publisher be cited as co-defendant. In New York he met with Nat Lefkowitz, William Morris's president, a tough defender of his agency's rights. Lefkowitz argued that *Myra* was the "novel" the contract referred to, and consequently the agency had all rights of literary representation. In addition, Lefkowitz maintained that William Morris, not CMA, had the right to negotiate the movie deal, which meant an additional percentage. At first neither party would budge. Vidal proposed that the third novel "to be mutually agreed upon" be a reprint of the now-out-of-print *Williwaw*. That seemed ludicrous to everyone except him. Finally, after some months, a compromise was effected. Vidal agreed to give the agency its percentage of the royalties on the sales of *Myra* and its subsidiary interest in the movie deal, in effect acknowledging that it was the third book of the 1962 contract. William Morris agreed to relinquish its claim to represent Vidal in the sale of the movie rights, hardly a significant concession, since the negotiation did not begin until after the expiration of his agency contract. Little, Brown substituted the volume of essays for the third novel and drew up a new, separate contract for *Myra,* though this made no material difference to either Little, Brown or Vidal. In February 1968 Little, Brown published *Myra Breckinridge.* Within weeks it was a nationwide bestseller.

While *Myra* soared, Gore's hope that he would have a new Broadway success plummeted. Soon after finishing *Myra* in midsummer 1967 he channeled his restlessness into a new play, *Weekend,* which opened for tryouts in New Haven in February, in Washington for two weeks at the National Theater on February 18, and then premiered at the Broadhurst Theatre in New York in mid-March. *The Best Man* team of Roger Stevens and Joe Anthony produced and directed. John Forsythe played the leading role. The title was as innocuously misleading as that of the still-unproduced *Drawing Room Comedy.* Like *The Best Man,* it was a satiric attack on political moral- ity, on ambition and prejudice, this time a dramatization of the Washington world of the mid-1960s, the realistic, sometimes harsh topical allusions to well-known figures, especially Lyndon Johnson, ummistakable. Washington reviewers and audiences responded enthusiastically, at least partly because of the notorious "inside the Beltway" syndrome. Here was a play about their favorite profession and their own recognizable world. At the Washing- ton premiere one of Lyndon Johnson's daughters, who with her husband had come as the guest of *Washington Post* theater critic Richard Coe, re- sponded to a harsh reference to her father by ostentatiously walking out of the theater. When the reviewer gave the play a mixed to poor review, Gore angrily drew attention to the fact that he had expressed his prejudice against the play even before seeing it by bringing Johnson's daughter with him as his guest. "At least begin by saying I came to the theater with Lynda Bird Johnson, who hated the play because it made fun of her father. She was raging as she went up the aisle. I was standing in the back and heard it all." The play's mode was realistic-ironic, the structure conventional, none of the characters especially riveting, the clash of ideas and prejudices effectively projected and recognizably part of the revolution in sex, race, and politics that by 1968 had become the visible wounds of a country in turmoil. The Vietnam War inflected national life. Bobby Kennedy and Johnson nervously confronted one another, one soon to be dead, the other to relinquish office, though the year's tragic events were still to come. Hardly influenced by professional newspaper critics, the Washington audience was enthralled by *Weekend*. The play was a capital event in a city in which there were few such cultural performances. Notable Washington figures rushed to see it. Nini and Gore hosted a huge celebratory party, and Nini soon had a crush on the handsome leading man. In New York and Washington, then in Canada and on the West Coast, Gore combined appearances for *Myra* with publicity for *Weekend*, at least to the extent that two such simultaneous achievements made the drum rolls even more triumphal. There seemed good reason to expect that *Weekend* would have a long Broadway run. When the play opened in New York, the critics were devastatingly hostile, some for aesthetic, some for political reasons, perhaps even at some level uninterested in the ostensible subject. It was attacked for its conventional form. Much of the irony was missed. After twenty-two performances, *Weekend* closed.

———•———

"My entire life is now devoted to appearing on television: a pleasant alternative to real life," Gore quipped to friends in March 1968 as he began to bring to a close his intensive schedule of appearances for *Myra*. When he returned to Rome in April, he expected to spend a quiet spring and summer in Italy. Underexercised and overfed, he resumed his daily exercise regimen at the gym. He even began "to look muscle-bound," he wrote to his father, "but one feels better—another week of the US and television and I could have reached the end." Suddenly a new television opportunity became available, something more intensive than anything he had done before. ABC Television News offered him the opportunity to appear on a fifteen-minute prime-time slot each night at the national party conventions in August, seven or eight evenings in all. He would represent the liberal left. William F. Buckley would represent the conservative right. The veteran television newscaster Howard K. Smith would moderate. Unlike its rival networks, ABC had decided not to televise the conventions' proceedings in full. Instead each night the network would provide an edited videotape selection of the days' events, live coverage of the most important nighttime activities, and adversarial commentary by two well-known political entertainers who were already notorious adversaries. ABC hoped for a victory in the ratings war; Buckley and Vidal each hoped triumphantly to represent their views and themselves. Neither ABC nor the participants could know that their own face-off would be a small-scale version of larger, more dramatic, and more image-powerful battles in the Democratic convention hall and in the Chicago streets.

When Gore accepted ABC's invitation, he was unaware that Buckley had been approached as early as spring 1967. Buckley was the only spokesperson for the right who was well known, photogenic, and entertaining; the network needed him in place. In the six years since his ascension to television regularity, he had become a distinctive performer whose turns and tics created photo-compelling high TV political drama, marked by the success of his talk program, *Firing Line,* on which he appeared with guests chosen for the likelihood that the interaction would produce semi-intellectual entertainment. *Firing Line* existed to provide a forum for Buckley and his views. It instantly became a rallying focus for conservative opinion. Unlike Vidal, Buckley had committed himself to television as a propaganda weapon in the political-cultural wars. His career had been narrowly focused, devoted to argumentative political discourse, including running for mayor of New York in 1965 on a platform guaranteed to make his views well known but to minimize his votes. His "self-appointed job, since graduating from college," he later said, had "been to defend publicly my position on political matters." *Firing Line* was an extension of the *National Review,* except that to attract a national audience it was necessary to structure the presentation as a clash between confrontational views. Supremely self-confident, Buckley generally gave the liberal devil his due. Formidable representatives of other viewpoints regularly appeared on the program. Vidal himself, though, had not been invited, partly because he had made it clear in public comments that he would not accept an invitation, mostly because he was the one person Buckley found so distasteful that he preferred to avoid the emotional provocation Vidal's presence aroused. In Buckley's view, as Louis Auchincloss surmised, Vidal *was* the devil, "Not the devil's emissary but the devil himself." Auchincloss had never seen Buckley lose his composure, ever. "Cool, bland, he rolls his blue eyes upward gracefully and calmly and dismissively in the face of provocation and attack. Always. Except with Gore." With Buckley committed, ABC asked him if there were anyone from the left whom he preferred not to be paired with. Vidal, he responded, suggesting a half dozen or so other names, among them Norman Mailer, Arthur Schlesinger, and John Kenneth Galbraith. Sensing the likelihood of television drama, ABC of course selected Vidal, though it claimed to have eliminated alternatives on the basis of informal soundings, even research. When informed that Vidal had been selected, Buckley neither strongly objected nor withdrew. He apparently preferred to appear on national convention television with Vidal than for Vidal to appear with someone other than Buckley.

By mid-July, Gore was in New York, eager to see friends, the private and the public air charged with anger and hapless foreboding. In anticipation, the conventions seemed both superfluous and signifiers of disaster, some of which had already devastatingly struck. There had been two years of sporadic but serious urban riots, most of them related to civil rights for blacks. The Tet Offensive in January 1968 had left Vietnam policy in bankrupt shambles, its leadership discredited. Public opinion was turning against the war. In April, Martin Luther King, Jr., had been assassinated in Memphis; in June, Robert Kennedy in Los Angeles. To Gore, King's assassination represented America's ineradicable racism. Kennedy's was an ironic tragedy, the unexpected exit of an enemy whose transformation into a supporter of the underprivileged and an opponent of the war Gore could not believe in. Both deaths seemed emblematic of the country's commitment to violence. Many feared that what had seemed the worst was only prelude to something even more horrible. Most commentators expected it to be a difficult summer. In late spring, antiwar protests at campuses, particularly Berkeley and Columbia, had provoked university authorities to elicit police intervention. Buildings were occupied, property damaged, students dragged off to jail. In May, Fred Dupee, uncharacteristically political again, had gotten his eye blackened and some teeth broken when he stood with the students. "I assume you are collaborating with the forces of freedom at Hamilton Hall," Gore wrote to him, tongue in cheek, from Rome. "So difficult in revolutionary times to know which side to join in order to betray. Best tend the garden, I suppose, though I'm catching the activist fever again. But what to do? There seems no solution to anything, and nothing worth suspending disbelief for. The Thirties were easier." By July the upcoming Vidal-Buckley television appearances had taken on a minor press life of their own, partly because commentators anticipated that their "debates" might capture and encapsulate some of the strongly held views that divided the country. Buckley supported the war, Vidal did not. Buckley advocated suppression of demonstrations for peace or civil rights. Vidal did not, or at least he favored giving the demonstrators their due.

Their mediated interchanges began in early August in Miami. Sometimes the mediation failed. Buckley's distaste for Vidal was immediately
apparent. Vidal was cooler, more urbane, his body language less expressive
and explicit. Actually, his manner of being above the personal effectively
conveyed his view that his opponent was, in his eyes, a nonperson. To
many, Buckley's voice seemed snide, Vidal's condescending. They alternated between attempts to discuss the issues and inevitable digressions, some
devoted to undercutting the other's credibility or viability. Each advanced
his own position primarily by attacking his opponent's, often in the form of
a correction of allegedly false or misleading assertions. Their interactions
verged on bickering rather than on sustained presentation of a response to a
substantive issue. Each tried to be witty. The strain showed. Inevitably the
reviews were mixed, often a reflection of the political affiliation of the
reviewer. No one had expected it to be sweetness, but it was also rarely
light. To some extent ABC had miscalculated. Some of the audience cheered
for Vidal, some for Buckley. But many found it too gladiatorial, the personal
too inappropriately dominant. At the same time, the ratings were good, at
least partly because ABC had correctly anticipated that whatever the other
networks were showing was likely to have less interest for the viewer than
Buckley-Vidal, even if there were strong reservations. From the participants'
point of view the engagement was not pleasurable. It was hard, dangerous,
and mostly unsatisfactory work. Both their egos were enormously at stake.
It was hand-to-hand battle, and each wanted the victory that neither had any
chance of unequivocally achieving. Their partisans were immovably in
place. Some were open-minded enough to do their best to keep score
objectively. Many were not. If there was any vast uncommitted audience, it
was more interested in *I Love Lucy* than in Vidal-Buckley, and to the extent
that the audience was political, its desire was for both conventions to make
some significant contribution to resolving the national nightmare. Nothing
that these commentators might say could contribute to that. In fact, partly
because of the format, mostly because of the nature of things, neither Vidal
nor Buckley had anything new, let alone impressive, to say about the
Republican process of choosing Richard Nixon as its standard-bearer. Both
made reasonable, sometimes shrewd comments about the cast of characters
of the moment, particularly Rockefeller on the left and Reagan on the right.
The personal invective was sharp but mostly under control. At the end of
the four days it was clear that Miami had been easy. The minor divisions

within the Republican Party were readily reparable. As the party out of power, it was not the focus of responsibility for the state of the nation. The streets of Miami were sunny and calm.

In New York for two weeks in August, Vidal, as did Buckley, took informal soundings among friends and acquaintances and sought the readily-forthcoming praise of partisans. Whatever Vidal's noticeable departures from Democratic Party orthodoxy, everyone to the left of Buckley who was not a partisan Republican agreed with Gore's attacks on the illiberal conservatism that Buckley represented. For Gore there was, as much as anything, the heady awareness of national fame that saturation television exposure provided, and some anticipatory anxiety about the Chicago convention. Senator Eugene McCarthy of Minnesota had emerged in the winter and spring as the only prominent Democrat willing to oppose Lyndon Johnson's Vietnam policy. In March he had made a strong enough showing in New Hampshire to embarrass Johnson and make his own candidacy viable. When in late March, Johnson announced he would not stand for reelection, Vice President Hubert Humphrey became heir apparent. A long-standing liberal with impressive credentials, as Vice President he had subordinated himself to Johnson, including giving his unqualified public support to the war. Robert Kennedy's death in June left the war's numerous opponents with no alternative but McCarthy, yet Humphrey would almost certainly be the nominee. If he accepted a war plank and continued to advocate Johnson's Vietnam policy, the party would be irreparably split. Governor George Wallace of Alabama, representing prosegregationist and redneck populism, seemed likely to draw more votes away from Democrats than Republicans. Humphrey would inherit a relatively worthless nomination. Both Buckley and Vidal knew Richard Nixon was likely to be the next President.

When he flew to Chicago late in August, the author of *The Best Man* knew that the best man would not win the nomination. He had, though, become an avid McCarthy supporter, despite the odds, hoping delegates would at least succumb sufficiently to pro-peace pressure not to write into the party platform a pro-war plank. Each night he appeared on the ABC news with Buckley. The exchanges immediately became directly confrontational. Between conventions, Buckley had read *Myra Breckinridge*. At the Republican convention he had considered attacking Vidal as a pornographer—but he had not then read *Myra*. Now he had no doubt that Vidal was a pornographer whose credibility as a commentator on political events should be emphatically destroyed by that fact. For Buckley all political questions were essentially moral issues. Immoral people should have no political credibility. How dare the author of *Myra Breckinridge* attack the Republican Party as immoral? Furious, Gore responded with a defense of his novel's seriousness and a counterattack on his attacker. As the evening went on, matters got worse in the studio. Each morning, with John Kenneth Galbraith, Gore went from delegation to delegation to try to get support for McCarthy. "Vidal was achieving much political celebrity," Galbraith later wrote in his memoir, "by flagrantly libelous exchanges on television with William F. Buckley," with whom Galbraith was cordial though in total disagreement on political issues. "In my introduction of him to the state delegations I would suggest that Vidal's congressional campaign a few years earlier . . . had established an all-time record for Democratic defeats. This Vidal would deny. 'A good solid defeat but not a record.' Then, unfailingly, would come the question: 'Mr. Vidal, where is your friend Mr. Buckley?' 'Mr. Buckley?' he would reply with a surprised look. 'Oh, Buckley. He's over at the Wallace headquarters stitching hoods.' " Unfortunately, neither television protagonist was any longer capable of humor when on camera together. Clearly, visibly, they were getting on one another's nerves, digging into one another's skin, as if sharing a stage had become a combination of tedious and unbearable. When Gore saw Norman Mailer chatting amiably with Buckley, he assumed that Mailer had gone over to the enemy.

For Vidal, when the convention approved a pro-war plank, the scene turned even darker. The Humphrey-Johnson victory was imminent, and the gentlemen in the studio were being upstaged by events in the streets and in the convention hall. The Chicago police could not accept that the antiwar demonstrators had the right to say whatever they wanted in any fashion that did not threaten lives or property. The Chicago Democratic establishment, controlled by Mayor Richard Daley, who supported the war plank and detested even peaceful demonstrations, instructed the police to use force if necessary to control the crowd. In effect, he ordered that the demonstrations be suppressed, which the police themselves were eager to do for temperamental and ideological reasons. Some of the demonstrators provoked repression. They assumed it would work to their favor. They taunted the police, mainly through obscenities. Suddenly, without any immediately flagrant act of provocation, the police attacked, severely clubbing many of the demonstrators in nearby Lincoln Park. The television cameras broadcast the carnage to the nation. It looked like a war scene, something Americans associated with repressive regimes, like Hitler's Germany and Stalin's Russia. The public, generally more sympathetic to the police than the demonstrators, found both appalling. In the convention hall the governor of Connecticut, Abraham Ribicoff, a longtime Kennedy stalwart who had served in his cabinet and now supported Senator George McGovern, looked down at Daley from the platform on which he was giving a nominating speech, not more than twenty feet away from the mayor, and said, as the networks broadcast his words, "With George McGovern we wouldn't have Gestapo tactics on the streets of Chicago!" Furious, purple with rage, Daley "shouted back with words that, while drowned out in the bedlam, were lip-read by many in the national television audience: 'Fuck you, you Jew son of a bitch, you lousy motherfucker, go home!' " While Buckley shared neither Daley's crudity nor his political affiliation, their cultural and temperamental predilections were similar, though they came to them from radically different backgrounds. Though Daley was a vulgar political operative and Buckley a sophisticated intellectual ideologue, their take on disorder had much in common. Under almost no circumstances should it be permitted. Like Daley, Buckley more than disapproved of obscenities. He found them emotionally inflammatory, hostile to cultural stability. To permit such language or conduct in public was to let the barbarians in at the gate. If discouragement was not effective, repression was in order. And while he did not condone police violence, he did not believe that the police deserved to be criticized for reacting violently to such provocation, or at least that much emphasis need be put on that reaction. The problem was not repression but revolution, not the misuse of power but the abuse of free speech.

When Buckley and Vidal joined Howard K. Smith in the ABC studio on Wednesday August 28 for the next to last of their live convention telecasts, both men had experienced their own versions of the nation's distress. They had separately trembled through the long night and horrible day of demonstrations, confrontations, and assaults, each deeply identifying with the national trauma. But they had experienced separate nightmares. For Buckley, vicious anarchy had its dirty hands around the neck of the republic. For Vidal, the police state and the American empire were murdering free speech. Both, in their different ways, as the circumstances warranted, were angry and frightened. For Buckley, there was victory in the horror. The forces of law were restoring order. A Nixon victory in November now seemed assured. The Democratic Party had wounded itself mortally. For Vidal, who abhorred the ameliorative acceptance of the status quo at a time when radical change seemed essential, there was an almost tragic sense of "I told you so." That night Howard K. Smith set the scene for their comments with selected clips of the street clubbings and beatings. The antagonisms of their previous appearances had an even darker, more somber cast. The context was now violence, not words. When Gore referred to the beatings in the streets as "police violence," Buckley defended the Chicago police. They had been, he argued, provoked beyond endurance. Only a small number of them had been violent. The entire police force should not be blamed. What about the fact that the demonstrators had raised a Vietcong flag? Howard K. Smith asked. Was that not an extreme provocation? Was that not equivalent to Americans' raising a Nazi flag during World War II? No, Vidal responded, America was not officially at war with the Vietcong, and consequently nonviolent expressions of opposition to the war were constitutionally protected.

The sharpness of the exchanges, the hostility in their voices intensified. Buckley was angry, defensive, and aggressive. Vidal was angry, aggressive, and defensive. For Buckley, the police needed to be defended, the demonstrators attacked; for Vidal, the reverse. Yes, Buckley responded to Smith, the demonstrators had behaved like provocateurs, just as George Lincoln Rockwell and the American Nazi Party had when they had marched recently in Skokie, Illinois. Repression was justified. Buckley may have had in the back of his mind Ribicoff's statement about Gestapo tactics on the streets of Chicago. Both Smith and Buckley had introduced the comparison into the telecast by reference to how American pro-Nazis were and should have been treated during World War II. "As far as I'm concerned, the only pro- or crypto-Nazi I can think of is yourself," Vidal replied. "I was trying to think of the word fascist," he later explained. "It had gone out of my head. The only word I could think of— I was stalling for time until I could remember. I knew I was going to end up saying . . . so I was stalling for time until I could remember. So I said 'the only pro-'—can't remember—'the only crypto-'—can't remember—'Nazi I can think of is you.' It was all because the word 'fascist' didn't come tripping off my tongue." Furious, his voice rising to a half shout, Buckley turned on Vidal. "Now, listen, you queer!

Stop calling me a crypto-Nazi or I'll sock you in your goddamn face and you'll stay plastered." "Gentlemen! Gentlemen! Let's not call names," Smith pleaded. "Let the author of *Myra Breckinridge* go back to his pornography and stop making allusions of Nazism," Buckley shouted with uncontrolled anger. Stunned, for the moment reduced to disputing Buckley's claim that he had served in the Marines, Vidal could hardly believe that Buckley had revealed both his homophobia and his temper on national television. It seemed almost a victory for him. "What about Sharon?" Vidal said. Howard K. Smith attempted as quickly as possible to bring the combatants under control, to turn away from invective to issues.

But ABC had achieved climactic drama. The network's choice of disputants had paid off, even if in an excessiveness that had its embarrassing side. The ten million people watching had heard a first, something almost unbelievable in those censored and sensitive days. Buckley had not only used the word "queer" but had used it as a censorious epithet. Whether the target was or was not homosexual made no difference. It simply was not done. He had used a homophobic epithet at a time when the general understanding was that such epithets were only for private use. The advocate of high public standards had broken not only the national prohibition but his own Christian and civic code. It was a deeply embarrassing, even shameful moment. When, in 1962, after he had clashed with Vidal on the Paar show for the first time, Buckley had composed a telegram to Paar: "PLEASE INFORM GORE VIDAL THAT NEITHER I NOR MY FAMILY IS DISPOSED TO RECEIVE LESSONS IN MORALITY FROM A PINK QUEER. IF HE WISHES TO CHALLENGE THAT DESIGNATION, INFORM HIM THAT I SHALL FIGHT BY THE LAWS OF THE MARQUESS OF QUEENSBURY." Wisely, he had not sent the telegram. Unwisely, he had now said much the same on national television.

As the fifteen minutes limped to a close, all three men, still stunned, could not have been more relieved for the camera no longer to be running. Gore, who was being interviewed by a reporter for *Life* magazine, stayed a few minutes longer in the studio. Buckley, accompanied by his son Christopher, went to his trailer, where he met Paul Newman, who had continued his nightly habit of going to Buckley's trailer to help himself from the ample supply of beer and then taking his can to Gore's nearby trailer, where the two friends would discuss the telecast. Newman, a delegate from Connecticut, had watched each night's telecast from the ABC control room. Just after he left Buckley's trailer, he met Buckley, still seething, and immediately said

words to the effect of "That was the most disgusting display I've ever seen."
"But Vidal called me a Nazi," Buckley responded. "That's political," Newman said. "What you called him is personal." Buckley declined to see the
difference, and of course Vidal had not called him a Nazi, though the
comparison was not clearly enough identified as metaphoric for it not to be
inflammatory. It would have been the rare person who would not have taken
it personally. But it also would have been the rare person who would not
have understood that Vidal meant that Buckley, by defending what Ribicoff
had called "Gestapo tactics" and by his long-standing advocacy of repression of inflammatory acts of free speech and aggressive first-strike action
against those with whom America had foreign-policy disagreements, had
certain Nazi-like views and values. It was a harsh way of stating what Vidal
and many others believed. If Vidal had said "fascist," as he had intended,
Buckley's response might have been different. If he had explained that the
intent of the prefixes "pro-" or "crypto-" was to emphasize that he did not
mean the designation to apply literally, as if Buckley belonged to a Nazi
Party, past or present, Buckley might not have felt quite as demeaned.
There seemed no reason to think, however, that any of the viewers missed
that it was a comparison, not an equivalence, something one would say in
the heat of debate as a vigorous way to condemn an opponent's views. As
such, Vidal thought it no worse than on the far edge of normative public
discourse. Buckley, though, was furious. The unforgivable had occurred. He
may have feared, or instinctively felt the possibility, that Vidal might bring
up the 1944 Sharon incident, which had been a stain on the family's honor. It
would be all too easy to make the connection between the accusations of
anti-Semitism against his sisters and the "pro-" or "crypto-Nazi" description of himself. As they left the studio, Gore said words to the effect of "We
put on a good show." Buckley turned away. The next night both appeared
subdued, drained, mostly going through the motions. Neither addressed the
other directly. When, in November, Buckley agreed to fulfill his ABC
commitment to appear with Vidal in New York on a postelection summa, he
insisted on arrangements that kept them not only physically apart but invisible to one another. They entered and exited the studio by separate doors.
They sat on opposite sides of a gray curtain drawn across the room. His
anger at Vidal was intense. But he was also deeply disappointed with himself
and angry at himself. He could not let go of his anguish. Vidal assumed that
the episode was over.

CHAPTER SIXTEEN

From Chicago to Ravello

1969–1972

IN FEBRUARY 1969 a telephone call to Rome from Harold Hayes, the editor of *Esquire*, alerted Vidal that the Buckley affair was not over. Except for some minor consideration, Vidal had given little thought in the intervening months to the mutual name-calling the previous August. He abhorred Buckley's politics, he thought little (and badly) of him personally. When his father had expressed concern that Buckley's condemnation of him as a "queer" before millions of listeners might harm his public image, Vidal played down its significance. "I said, 'Forget it, Buckley's considered a far greater creep than I am. This is the way the world goes.'" Reviewers had widely noted the inflammatory exchange. Most, forbidden from printing the homophobic epithet, concluded that Vidal had gone far but Buckley too far, that the association of Buckley with Nazi-like views, strained as the comparison might seem, had a basis in the widely held view among liberals of Buckley's political philosophy and consequently was not totally inappropriate in a polemical argument. Immediately after the telecast, ABC canceled the planned time-delayed West Coast broadcast of the segment. Static was used to cover the word "queer" in its archival tape. Clearly the network wanted to distance itself as much as possible from Buckley's epithet and the possibility of being named a co-defendant in a libel suit. Vidal's public attitude was flippant, dismissive, though with an edge of allusion to his own (and others') view that Buckley's manner had about it something of the queen, as if to call attention to the ironic implication of someone who considered it the height of condemnation to call someone a "queer" himself seeming somewhat suspect. "I've always tried to treat Buckley like the great lady that he is," Vidal told the *Chicago Sun-Times* in a morning-after interview. "He's given to neurotic tantrums and I feel sorry for him. He doesn't make much of a point. It's mostly rabid insults and very little substance." So the phone call from Harold Hayes came as a sharp surprise.

Buckley had had no intention of letting go. "I don't want to talk about him," he had told *Newsday* the day after the broadcast, referring to Vidal. "I'll write about him myself when I get around to it." He had been brooding on the event since its occurrence, and in November 1968 he called Hayes, with whom he had a personal as well as a professional friendship. " *'Mon vieux,'* " he began, Hayes later wrote, " 'I have something to ask of you. I want to write about that row I had with Vidal on television last summer. Would you be interested?' Sure, I said, but in light of the embarrassment to everyone concerned, including 10 million viewers—why?" Buckley responded, " 'I have been hounded at every turn about my part in it. I think if I were to try and write about it I might be able to work out why I said what I did. I will need some length, and I must be assured that your lawyers will allow me to call Vidal a homosexual in print. Otherwise there is no point in my undertaking it.' " That Buckley was interested in justifying himself and punishing Vidal must have been clear to Hayes. Otherwise, private opportunities "to work out why" would have sufficed. Hayes, who "preferred Buckley as an individual over Vidal and Vidal's politics over Buckley's," responded with cautious eagerness. As an editor he felt the attraction of famous names and lively controversy. *Esquire,* though, had two concerns: its professional responsibility to be fair to both disputants and its potential liability in case one or both should sue for libel. Two questions had to be addressed before Hayes could respond. Would Buckley accept that *Esquire* had to give Vidal the opportunity to respond? Yes, Buckley agreed, as long as it was not in the same issue. Hayes consented. And what would *Esquire*'s lawyer say about Buckley's insistence that he be allowed to call Vidal a homosexual? Would Vidal have the basis for a legal suit against the magazine? *Esquire*'s best protection, advised its attorney, Harold Medina, was to make certain that whatever it printed was "true in fact and fair in comment." Was Vidal, in fact, a homosexual? If so, *Esquire* could accept Buckley's condition. Hayes immediately set two staff researchers to search for corroborating information. Though the result indicated that Vidal had never himself admitted the applicability of the description, there seemed enough support for the claim to protect *Esquire* in the event Vidal should sue. Medina suggested that Buckley be encouraged to go forward, though the lawyer reserved final judgment pending his reading of the full article. "I told Buckley to proceed," Hayes wrote, "and then I called Vidal in Rome. 'Why are you giving space to that dimwit? He's mad. He exists in the mind of the public only because of his attacks against me. I won't dignify his dreck with a formal answer. But I'll tell you more when I see his manuscript. I might write my answers in the margins.' I told him Buckley's condition that he could not respond until the subsequent issue. 'In that case,' said Vidal, 'I'll wait and see what he writes.' "

When Buckley's article arrived at the *Esquire* office in late February, Hayes, after Buckley revised an unsatisfactory ending, sent a copy to Vidal in Rome, another to Medina. "He's pretty rough on you, but you would have expected that," Hayes wrote to Vidal. "In what form would you like to respond and can you meet the schedule we have in mind?" he asked, as if there were some certainty that the publication process would move forward. Actually, the editor, his publisher, his managing editor, and *Esquire*'s lawyer had serious reservations. If they published Buckley's article alone, Vidal might sue. But if Vidal chose to reply in print, *Esquire*, they decided, would proceed only if it could publish both articles after each author had seen and stated his objections to the other and only after *Esquire* had arbitrated "whatever differences remained." In Rome, Gore read Buckley's article. When Don Erickson, *Esquire*'s managing editor, called to get his response, Vidal said, "How does the word 'injunction' strike you?" He was coming immediately to New York for a consultation with his attorneys and for discussion with *Esquire*. This was now a serious matter about which he could no longer afford to be flippant. Buckley's article seemed not only inaccurate in fact but whiningly self-serving and viciously homophobic. It was a theodicy of sorts, a justification not of God but of Buckley, an egomaniacal self-projection so vast that it seemed satanic, the devil in the guise of infinite self-righteous rectitude. The only thing about his conduct for which Buckley felt he needed to apologize was that he had lost his temper. "Once at my office," Hayes reported, Vidal "argued at great length against our going forward under any circumstances. It was exactly what Buckley wanted, Vidal insisted; Buckley would be the only one to gain, all others would lose, for Buckley's only purpose was to call attention to himself. Moreover, *Esquire*'s risk was the greatest of all, for Vidal had never acknowledged— 'Never once,' he emphasized—that he was homosexual. It was a dirty business, he concluded, and we—*Esquire*—should have no part of it. I tried to counter each point he raised in the interest of clearing the air between both men once and for all and then, finally, I asked if he seriously wanted me to abandon the project altogether. To his great credit, he answered: 'I wish you would, but if you decide to go ahead I won't try to stop you. I'm not in the practice of censoring by any means. If you do go on, I will sue you only if you refuse to print my response.' " Hayes thought he could control the process and satisfy both authors. "And so we went on."

In Rome, as Gore reread Buckley's apologia, he saw there was a cosmic politics at work here larger and more important for Buckley than the usual polemics about left and right, liberals and conservatives, though that of course had its importance. On the personal side, Buckley thought it unforgivable that Vidal had attacked his family. The attacks consisted of the few remarks in 1962 about his reactionary father and the cryptic reference in the August 28 telecast to the 1944 incident at Sharon. That Vidal seemed to him regularly to distort his political views and to have engaged in a systematic campaign to deflate his reputation was barely this side of tolerable, as long as he had his chance to respond. Of all his political opponents, Vidal seemed most to get under his skin, partly because one of his strategies was to help an opponent to self-destruct. And Buckley had done just that on the convention broadcast. Dissatisfaction at his own public intemperance may have given special force to his need to justify himself. Apparently he had in mind some cathartic self-analysis. Political differences alone, Gore realized, could not satisfactorily account for Buckley's vehemence. Vidal's attacks on his family had been unpleasant but muted, though Buckley's sensitivity to the subject made it personally explosive, an issue of honor and empathy. In fact, one of the sisters who had participated in desecrating the church he saw almost every day in her capacity as managing editor of the *National Review*. Still, neither political differences nor the family references seemed to warrant another full-scale engagement with Vidal. The "pro- or crypto-Nazi" remark had been the only statement that it might be argued was personally defamatory. The Sharon incident had never been discussed in public. What Buckley seemed now to want was some version of public confessional, the point of which would be that not he but Gore Vidal was the real sinner, apparently even at the cost of a response that had the potential to spotlight what he wanted most to keep out of public discussion. His essay, both Hayes and Vidal immediately saw, was not self-analysis at all. It was not a defense of family honor. It was not especially a re-airing of their political differences. It was the avenging sword of religious rectitude striking down the heathen. For Buckley, the proper action was a full-scale attack on Vidal's character, epitomized by two unforgivable elements, one a sin, the other a sickness. Vidal, Buckley argued, was a money-grubbing pornographer whose immorality was purposeful, self-conscious, and self-serving. That was a sin. He was also a sexual deviant, and that was an illness. But unlike most sick people, he did not want to be cured. In fact, "the man who in his essays proclaims the normalcy of his affliction, and in his art the desirability of it, is not to be confused with the man who bears his sorrow quietly. The addict is to be pitied and even respected, not the pusher." By characterizing Vidal as a "pusher," like Socrates corrupting the youth of Athens, the logic of the argument was that the society would be better off if the pusher were somehow destroyed.

Within the month Vidal had drafted an essay in rebuttal. If Buckley felt free to attack his sexual life—which, though Buckley continued to make homophobic comments in private, had not been a part of their initial public discussions—Vidal would feel free to attack Buckley in similar ways, the first of which Buckley's essay gave him the opportunity to do. Buckley had begun the essay with a lengthy excursus on an accusation made by a journalist that Buckley frequently used "faggot logic," whatever that was. The journalist apparently meant that he had been bitchy in an ad hominem way. At some length Buckley referred to numbers of such references to him in the press and asked why it was acceptable to refer to his "faggot logic" and not acceptable for him to call Gore Vidal "a queer." Vidal had an opening he could not resist, part of which he used to clarify what he thought the obvious protocols in the use of prejudice-laden references and part of which to discuss the possibility that, in regard to Buckley's sexuality, where there was smoke there might be fire. Perhaps there was some reason he struck so many people as queenlike. Since Buckley had insisted he have the right to discuss Vidal's sexuality in his essay, why should Vidal not have the right to discuss Buckley's? And Buckley himself inevitably had to bring back to public attention, by quoting the exchange, the phrase he had found so offensive. He could hardly exculpate himself without reference to what had triggered his explosion. Since Vidal's reference to Buckley as a "pro- or crypto-Nazi" was part of a political argument, that seemed to Vidal to justify his making one of the organizing principles of his rebuttal essay the history of anti-Semitism in the Buckley family. The Sharon incident would help elucidate Buckley's prejudices and some of his politics. With the help of researchers, Vidal obtained the evidence about the participation of Buckley's sisters in the church desecration. Though she requested that her name be kept out, Jayne Meadows provided some of the details. Since Buckley was claiming the moral high ground, it seemed appropriate to reveal that some of it was below sea level.

Esquire's response to both essays was to try to protect itself against the possibility of either author's suing it for libel. Buckley's response was to attempt to force Esquire to force Vidal to eliminate the parts of his article that Buckley did not like. The issue was initially engaged on the level of fact. At Esquire's request, Buckley and Vidal were required to provide corroboration for claims of fact. Whatever they could corroborate, Hayes accepted as publishable. But much of the tension was about opinion, and there the lawyerlike phrase "fair in opinion" came in as the standard to be upheld. Inevitably, opinions about "fair in opinion" differed. Vidal made demands of Buckley's claims of fact. Buckley did the same of Vidal's. The adjudication process seemed to go on endlessly. Finally, after two months of attempting to serve as honest broker, Hayes was exhausted, almost ready to rue the day he had decided to proceed. Medina was regularly consulted. Buckley kept his lawyer busy. So too did Vidal keep his, William Fitelson, a successful entertainment lawyer who seemed from the start noticeably out of his usual waters. The antagonists received the customary cautionary lawyerly advice. Vidal removed certain provocations. Buckley removed some as well. More inclined to let Buckley have his say than Buckley to allow him his, Vidal mainly forced corroboration for claims of fact and defended his own, including getting additional evidence to support his account of the Sharon incident. With a low-threshold libel detector, including declaiming that he would sue if Vidal repeated what Buckley now regularly referred to as the libelous August claim that Buckley was a Nazi, Buckley pressured

Hayes and Vidal with threats. When Hayes pointed out that since Buckley himself had quoted it in his essay, Vidal could hardly be expected to respond without quoting it also, Buckley seemed to withdraw his objection. When Hayes argued that as long as Vidal had corroborative evidence for his claims of fact about the Sharon incident, it was not libelous for him to interpret the incident as anti-Semitic, he thought he had reason to think Buckley did not disagree or at least would not make his disagreement the basis of a libel suit. Vidal was not as convinced, aware that Buckley over the last decade had sued for libel in roughly analogous situations in which the suit seemed intended to stifle free speech, especially criticism of Buckley. In 1966 Buckley's lawyer, C. Dickerman Williams, a civil-liberties attorney who had defended numbers of freedom-of-speech cases, had successfully so defended Buckley in a libel suit brought by Linus C. Pauling, whom the *National Review* had described as a Communist fellow traveler. Williams was now carrying Buckley's repressive libel banner against Vidal's free-speech defense. In the Pauling case Williams had won dismissal on the grounds that Pauling was a public figure, one of Vidal's defenses against Buckley.

Gore now revised his article to meet what *Esquire*, prompted by Buckley and its own attorney, considered "true in fact and fair in comment." Hayes felt confident that Buckley would recognize that *Esquire* had acted in good faith, that it had followed the agreed-upon procedures, and that unpleasant interpretations of accurate facts were constitutionally protected speech acts. Finally, at the end of April, unwilling to protract the vetting process indefinitely, already months behind schedule, Hayes called a stop to the cross-commentary. Buckley had stated unequivocally that he would sue *Esquire* and Vidal if *Esquire* published the last draft that he had seen. "You understand, I hope," he told Hayes, "that I am driven to making this statement because I wish to prevent the publication of libels, rather than merely to punish the author of those libels." Hayes then went through Vidal's article again, making changes he believed eliminated or at least substantially decreased Buckley's grounds for complaint. On April 28 Buckley responded to Hayes's request that he now allow both articles to be published, "Dear Harold, You ask, would I, as a favor to *Esquire*, permit *Esquire* to publish about me things that aren't so? Yes, I will—assuming that Vidal's piece is otherwise corrected, and that I am satisfied that he will not attempt to publish his libels elsewhere." Hayes made further changes in response to Buckley's directions and to conform to *Esquire*'s lawyers *"mini-*

mum libel restrictions." At that point, as far as *Esquire* was concerned, it could now publish unless one or both authors withdrew his essay. Vidal detested Buckley's article. But he had no further objection to its being printed in the August issue. His own was slated for September. Buckley did not withdraw his essay. If he had, *Esquire* would not have published Vidal's. Apparently much of Buckley's strategy had been to pressure *Esquire* to publish his alone. Shortly after Hayes's decision to publish both, Buckley's lawyer informed Vidal that his client was suing Vidal for libel. The suit had already been initiated in United States District Court. The legal papers were in hand.

Hayes was stunned. Buckley's suit against Vidal seemed an unreasonable attempt to prevent his having his say in an essay that appeared to *Esquire* to meet reasonable standards of truth and fairness. Was this also a message to *Esquire*? Would *Esquire* also be sued if it printed Vidal's essay? Hayes had to begin to consider what had seemed to him inconceivable. Vidal also had threatened to sue *Esquire* if it published Buckley's article. But his intent was to condition the withdrawal of the threat on *Esquire*'s publishing his as well, since Buckley was pressuring the magazine to publish only Buckley's. When Vidal's revision met *Esquire*'s conditions, his threat to sue was moot. He said nothing more about it. Hayes had believed that Buckley's threat was also moot. In general, he had trusted in what he believed to be Buckley's sense of fairness, among other reasons because he genuinely liked and admired him. As a journalist-editor, Hayes had assumed that in the end Buckley shared his view that controversial articles that met his own profession's standards of interpretive fairness should not be prevented from being published by recourse to legal pressure. If both parties were to have their say, what better jury and judge than the court of public opinion? But a week before he learned that Buckley was suing Vidal, Hayes had had a preparatory jolt. The New York magazine world buzzed with gossipy tremors. On May 6 and 7 Buckley had sent telegrams to twenty magazine publishers: "LAST AUGUST I WAS DEFAMED ON NETWORK TELEVISION BY MR. GORE VIDAL. MR. VIDAL HAS NOT RETRACTED HIS LIBEL OR APOLOGIZED TO ME. ON THE CONTRARY, HE HAS SOUGHT TO GIVE RENEWED CURRENCY TO THAT LIBEL AND TO LAUNCH OTHERS, TO WHICH END HE SUBMITTED A MANU-SCRIPT TO ESQUIRE MAGAZINE WHICH ESQUIRE DECLINED TO PUBLISH BE-CAUSE IT WAS DEFAMATORY AND UNTRUE. MR. VIDAL'S ACTIVITIES HAVE LEFT ME WITH NO OTHER RECOURSE THAN TO A LAWSUIT, AND ACCORD-

INGLY I HAVE FILED SUIT AGAINST MR. VIDAL FOR FIVE HUNDRED THOUSAND DOLLARS IN DAMAGE. I ADVISE YOU OF THESE PROCEEDINGS BECAUSE I HAVE BEEN INFORMED THAT MR. VIDAL IS BENT UPON CIRCULATING CHARGES ABOUT ME WHICH ARE ABSOLUTELY UNTRUE. I WRITE TO REGISTER MY WILLINGNESS TO COOPERATE WITH YOU IN ANY WAY . . . SO AS TO GUARD AGAINST YOUR JOURNAL'S INADVERTENTLY CIRCULATING MR. VIDAL'S DEFAMATORY MATERIAL." In the telegram to *Playboy* he added, "I HAVE JUST BEEN INFORMED THAT IN THE JUNE PLAYBOY YOU PLAN TO PUBLISH STATEMENTS BY VIDAL WHICH I CAN PROVE TO BE DEFAMATORY. I REQUEST OPPORTUNITY TO PROVE TO YOU THAT SAID REMARKS ARE FALSE SO THAT YOU MAY ELIMINATE THEM FROM THE ISSUE." A general interview with Vidal that appeared in the June *Playboy*, one of a series of interviews with celebrities that the magazine published regularly, made some of the same points about Buckley that were in his rebuttal article for *Esquire*. *Playboy*'s editor-publisher, Hugh Hefner, was not intimidated by Buckley's telegram. "Speaking as one publisher to another, I must tell you that I do not regard Vidal's remarks as published in the June issue as actionable. They must be read in the context of the well publicized dispute between the two of you. Indeed a contemporary piece concerning either of you which did not in some measure reflect the views of the subject toward the other would have to be considered incomplete." In fact, *Esquire* had not declined to publish Vidal's article. It had simply said that it could not publish it without revision. The same had been said of Buckley's. By the time of Buckley's twenty telegrams, Vidal's revision had been approved by *Esquire*'s lawyer. But apparently, despite having given his conditional go-ahead to Hayes, Buckley still had not accepted that *Esquire* would publish it. When he incorrectly got it into his head that Vidal was trying to find an alternative publisher, he precipitously sent the telegrams, the result of which was to make twenty influential people curious about what it was he so desperately wanted to suppress.

Hayes soon learned, in fact, that Buckley still hoped that *Esquire* would publish his article but not Vidal's, or at least that *Esquire* was still susceptible to pressure from him. This worrisome scenario was dramatized in a semi-threatening letter in mid-June: "I am sure there is practically no chance at all that Fate will require me to sue *Esquire*, but I must remind myself that the last exchange I read between Williams and Medina had Williams contending that one version of Vidal's piece was libelous with

Medina disagreeing. And the further datum that I would not be shown V's piece as finally accepted, nor even advised as to whether a version has been accepted. Understand, I am quite certain that there will be a happy ending to all this. . . ." On July 17 the August issue of *Esquire,* with Buckley's article, appeared on the newsstands. In early August, with Gore's essay about to appear in the September issue, or perhaps with an advance copy in hand, Buckley asked John Kenneth Galbraith's advice. Galbraith had read Buckley's essay, perhaps Vidal's. "Your *Esquire* piece, as always, is lively . . . and in spite of the incredible length, it is very interesting," he wrote to Buckley. "But it lacks plausibility. . . . You are talking about a staged row between two highly experienced controversialists. . . . That was ABC's intention when they engaged you. And there is further and devastating weakness in your case when you concede that you first refused and then accepted Vidal. Obviously you accepted a risk of which you were aware. . . . As entertainment you perhaps could pursue this controversy. An an issue of justice you simply cannot. That holds especially for the courts. . . . Were you the literary cynosure of the SDS [Students for Democratic Society] my advice would not be different except as I might suppose your instinct for self-preservation to be less developed." On August 18 the September *Esquire,* with Vidal's article, "A Distasteful Encounter with William F. Buckley," appeared on newsstands. That same day Buckley's lawyer filed suit in United States District Court against the magazine. It demanded $1 million in compensation for emotional and financial damage done to the plaintiff. The charges were essentially the same as those against Vidal. Vidal had willfully defamed the defendant by charging that he was a Nazi, a homosexual, a war lover, and an anti-Semite. *Esquire* had conspired with Vidal by encouraging him to write the article, guiding him in its construction, and providing a forum for its publication.

———•———

For the next three years the lawyers flourished in a complicated legal dance. Vidal immediately instituted the obligatory countersuit, the purpose of which was to put pressure on Buckley to drop his. The charge was that Buckley had attempted to infringe his right of response. When Buckley's lawyer asked the court for summary judgment, the court dismissed Vidal's nuisance suit, which did not surprise any of the participants. As far as the law was concerned, Buckley had every legal right to pressure *Esquire* not to publish Vidal's rebuttal. Whatever *Esquire*'s and Vidal's view of Buckley's ethics, it was not a legal matter. Buckley's libel suits against *Esquire* and Vidal were the main show. Each was a separate suit, though it was clear that a decision in one would have relevance to the outcome of the other. Legal maneuvering, naturally, created long delays. Both Buckley and Vidal soon changed lawyers, each dissatisfied with his representation. C. Dickerman Williams was replaced in 1970 by Charles Rembar, a sophisticated attorney well known for his defense of a civil-liberties suit in which the free-speech issue had been paramount. An accomplished man, small, thin, handsome, one of the best-known civil-liberties lawyers in New York, he had written interestingly about his accomplishments. Rembar's cousin, Norman Mailer, had recommended him to Buckley, a reminder to Gore of how chummy Mailer and Buckley had been at the 1968 Democratic convention and corroboration of his view that Mailer had become an enemy. Vidal's own lawyer, William Fitelson, had proved as unsatisfactory as Dickerson had proved to Buckley. From the start Gore felt he was being represented erratically by an office attracted more to glamour than to legal legwork. In New York, in early February 1972, Vidal was subjected to a long session with Buckley's lawyer and a stenographer. Rembar was shrewdly, relentlessly effective, intelligent and well informed about literary and linguistic matters in ways that most lawyers are not. He grilled Vidal for hours, including a sustained attempt to get him to define the word "homosexual," during which Vidal provided self-protective answers, including a great deal of purposeful smoke screen in which he asserted that there was no such thing as a homosexual or a heterosexual, only homosexual acts and heterosexual acts. In the end Gore thought he had done well, though he was not happy with his representation by Fitelson's office. When Richard Poirier was subpoenaed to testify about *Myra Breckinridge*, Fitelson advised him to disregard the subpoena. Poirier saw that as a likely route to a jail sentence for contempt. In March 1972 Vidal replaced Fitelson with Edward Weisl of Simpson Thacher & Bartlett, recommended by Gore's half-sister Nini, who knew Weisl socially. The son of one of William Randolph Hearst's lawyers, an intelligent, shrewdly combative inquisitor, Weisl eagerly took on the case. In the view of Fitelson's successor, "the judge really was prejudiced against him very badly. I think Fitelson and his associates were very aggressive and came to court with a chip on their shoulders. They were real New York types, theatrical types, and the judge wasn't used to those kinds of people. They were great theatrical attorneys, one of the best. The judge was a Jew himself," though a conservative upstate Republican. "They were very aggressive. I've had negotiations with them on other matters. They hadn't, in my view, prepared themselves well for Gore's case, not because they were bad lawyers but because this was an area that was totally unfamiliar to them." By late winter 1972 it looked almost certain that the case would have to go to trial. Weisl did not think there were grounds for a libel conviction. "It was all in the heat of debate. What Gore said was intemperate but not libelous. Gore shouldn't have said that Bill was a 'crypto-Nazi.' It's an unpleasant thing to say. He should have apologized and Bill shouldn't have sued. Bill seemed to be in the habit in those days of suing people. I assume he was feeling litigious. I don't like using the libel laws unless there's real damage, real malice. . . . Homosexuality had nothing to do with their discussion. What they should have done is fought a duel. Instead they went and forced the taxpayers to pay a lot of money and enriched a bunch of lawyers who are rich enough already."

Depositions were required. Hayes and his research assistants were deposed. Exhibits were collected, including all drafts of both essays. Motions and countermotions were filed, affidavits sworn to. Search-and-reveal orders kept Vidal's lawyer, Buckley's lawyer, the *National Review* staff, and *Esquire*'s lawyers and staff busy providing documents, many of them trivial and barely relevant. In late March 1972, in a marathon four-day session, Weisl did a superlative job deposing Buckley. He grilled the plaintiff with merciless, perfunctory politeness. He had cleverly seen that if he could get Buckley to take responsibility not only for his signed articles in the *National Review* but for its editorials, he could then introduce into the record statements from the *Review* that supported Vidal's claim that Buckley had views that reasonable people could readily compare with those held by Nazis in Hitler's Germany; that Buckley was hostile to Jews, blacks, and immigrants; and that he advocated first strikes against foreign governments. As a matter of fact and pride, Buckley took responsibility for the editorial content of his magazine. Weisl found no shortage of editorials and articles that supported Vidal's claims. Item by item they were made a part of the record.

For *Esquire* the situation was complicated. Its lawyer, Harold Medina, later to become a prestigious judge, was held in the highest respect. His advice throughout had been cautious, thoughtful, sound. He could not be blamed for Buckley's monomaniacal pursuit of repression and vindication, and once in the grip of the legal process Medina was well aware that anything could happen. A mild man, Harold Hayes was angry and also afraid. The legal nightmare of libel accusations and court machinations seemed infinitely dark, an unjust imposition he had gone far to avoid and that he believed he did not deserve. *Esquire*'s publisher, Arnold Gingrich, saw his legal costs mounting. From the beginning it was clear that if Buckley persisted, a large part of *Esquire*'s resources, including the time of its editors and staff, would have to be expended on defending itself, whatever the outcome. It was not what a magazine was in business to do. Medina asked for a summary judgment of dismissal. So too did Weisl. In both cases, in separate rulings, the court did not grant it. Judge Richard H. Levet, after an examination of the documents, ruled that the defendants had not demonstrated the impossibility of the plaintiff's making his case. The judge ruled that Buckley *might have been* libeled or *might not have been* libeled; only a full examination of the actual facts during a trial could determine that. The plaintiff was entitled, then, to plead his case to a jury. The court would not throw out his case, as *Esquire* had requested. He could voluntarily withdraw it if he chose, or he could proceed with his suit. Buckley won nothing with this ruling except the right to go to trial to attempt to prove he had been libeled. In Buckley's case against Vidal, however, Levet gave Weisl a favorable ruling on which defenses he would permit and which he would disallow. "We have won, all things considered," Weisl told Vidal on July 11, "a substantial victory in the case. Judge Levet upheld what I believe to be the most important defense in our answer in part, that of fair comment which allows us to go into all of his political views and the 'heat of debate' defense which tends to excuse all remarks made. . . . At the same time, he denied the *Esquire* summary judgment motion on the grounds that malice and reckless disregard of the truth might be provable by Buckley, which I doubt." Judge Levet had also made part of his formal opinion an assertion Rembar and Buckley would have reason to find worrisome. After reviewing the *National Review* statements Weisl had provided in his brief, Levet concluded that "if a reasonable man could make reasonable inferences from plaintiff's statements that plaintiff Buckley could be categorized as a 'pro-crypto-Nazi,' 'anti-black,' 'anti-semitic' or a 'warmonger' and if these phrases meet the above-mentioned standards of fair comment, then paragraphs 5th through 31 should remain. . . . The court must conclude that Vidal's comments in these paragraphs meet the minimal standards of fair comment. The inferences made by Vidal from Buckley's statements cannot be said to be completely unreasonable." Weisl had good reason to feel optimistic.

After three years of expensive maneuvering, there were now reasons for the principals to bring the case to a close. Judge Levet's point was clear. If Buckley wanted to vindicate himself, he would have to go to trial, theoretically two separate trials. But he had been put on notice that his chances of winning against Vidal were slim, and a representative New York jury, Buckley and Rembar could be assured, would contain at least some blacks and Jews, though Levet had made it clear that whatever the composition of the jury, the permissible reasonable defenses favored Vidal. Buckley's chances of winning against *Esquire* may have been better, though still slim, depending on further rulings about *Esquire*'s permissible defenses. When Buckley "realized that we could embarrass him by recitation of all those articles from the *National Review,*" Weisl later commented, "and when the judge wrote his one- or two-sentence opinion saying that a modern jury would find a man holding such views to be sort of a pro- or crypto-Nazi, Buckley realized that he was in big trouble." Still, *Esquire* felt disappointed that Levet had not granted its motion for summary dismissal and, burdened by the costs Buckley's suit had already entailed, it seemed desirable to settle if some compromise that allowed *Esquire* to maintain its principles and its honor could be effected. Medina and Rembar quietly negotiated. When he learned that Rembar had asked Levet for a postponement because he was negotiating with Weisl, Weisl immediately informed the judge that this was not the case: the lawyers for Vidal and Buckley were not negotiating. In fact, "it was made perfectly clear to Mr. Rembar . . . that the settlement which he envisioned had no possibility of acceptance." He urged Levet to set a date for the trial. Clearly, Rembar had not made an offer Vidal could accept. But he had made an offer that *Esquire* could. In late August that negotiation had reached a result satisfactory to both parties. *Esquire* would publish in its pages the statement that the lawsuit was "honorably terminated" and that the magazine itself did not share Vidal's view of Buckley. "We published that article," Hayes later wrote in *Esquire*'s pages, "because we believed that Vidal had the right to assert *his* opinions, even though we did not share them." Throughout *Esquire* had "acted both with empathy and neutrality toward Buckley as well as Vidal." It also agreed to provide *National Review* advertising space in *Esquire* free of charge to a retail value of approximately

$10,000, which would in effect cost *Esquire* nothing. The magazine, however, would pay Buckley's legal fees, approximately $115,000. In return, Buckley would drop his suit against *Esquire,* absolve it of all liability, and agree not to pursue the matter again. In late August, Rembar informed the court that the plaintiff and *Esquire* had reached a settlement. Two weeks later Vidal learned that the suit against him was also being dropped. Since Vidal would not concede or compromise, Buckley decided simply to terminate his action.

The legal cacophony finally became silence. Hayes, with some quiet time to sort things out, concluded that he had made a mistake at the very outset. He had allowed Buckley to use the pages of *Esquire* to attack Vidal personally, to state that Vidal was homosexual and his political views were consequently not worth listening to. That had been a serious error, "which is why I now personally believe I, too, owe Gore Vidal an apology," he later wrote. Vidal had responded partly in kind, so Hayes concluded, but in every case in his rebuttal article in which he had attacked Buckley personally he had linked the attack to Buckley's politics. Buckley's attack, however, was relentlessly personal and existed in and for itself. Sadly, self-critically, Hayes wished that he had seen this as clearly at the beginning as he now did at the end. Though the legal war was over, there was one last skirmish in which Buckley had another lesson to teach Hayes, though Vidal and the historical record were his primary targets. The Buckley-*Esquire* suit had been settled in late August. There was, however, a delay in the official public announcement of its terms. *Esquire* assumed that a statement along the lines agreed on in a future issue of its own pages would be sufficient. Buckley was eager to hold a press conference as soon as the settlement had been reached, though at first it seemed difficult to understand why. *Esquire* had admitted no culpability, its only significant concession the agreement to pay his legal fees, an acceptable price to accept to avoid the cost of going to trial as long as the settlement made clear that the magazine had not behaved illegally or unprofessionally. It seemed sensible to Buckley to delay his press conference until the conclusion of discussions between Rembar and Weisl, during which, Weisl reported to Judge Levet, Rembar provided "a total misrepresentation of the settlement with *Esquire* (he stated it involved a $115,000 payment by *Esquire* to Buckley)," as if the money represented damages rather than legal fees. The public-relations battle still remained to be won. On September 25, one day before the notification of withdrawal of his suit against Vidal, the *National Review* held a press conference and issued a publicity release, composed and signed by Buckley. *Esquire* had not been given even the courtesy of notification. The major newspapers and wire services carried the story the next day. Hayes was shocked. Vidal and Weisl were not. Buckley's loudly trumpeted statement differed significantly from the facts and from what *Esquire* had agreed to. With what seemed to Hayes ruthless disregard for the truth, Buckley proclaimed that the court

> has now sustained my suit against *Esquire* and correlatively against Vidal, by ruling that notwithstanding recent Supreme Court decisions, Vidal's article was defamatory and the case would have to go to trial. Having lost its motion, *Esquire* has agreed to publish in its November issue a full statement totally disavowing the views of Vidal. And has agreed to compensate me for the legal expenses involved in bringing about a judicial determination satisfactory to me. One hundred and fifteen thousand dollars is the cash value of the settlement. Having disposed of Vidal's lawsuit, I am instructing my attorneys to take the necessary steps to discontinue my actions against him to avoid the time and expense of trial. In the long period between the publication of the libel and the disavowal of it by *Esquire*, I have learned that Vidal's opinions of me are of little concern to the public. A fortiori, they should be of little concern to me now that the publishers have disavowed them. Let his own unreimbursed legal expenses . . . teach him to observe the laws of libel. I hope it will not prove necessary to renew the discipline in future years. There are limits even to my charity.

Esquire of course had not agreed to and did not in November "disavow" Vidal's charges against Buckley. They simply said they did not share Vidal's opinion of Buckley, but since it was "fair in comment," they were perfectly within their rights to publish it. *Esquire*'s publisher wrote to *Newsweek*, which had taken Buckley's claim at face value, that *"Newsweek* quite incorrectly characterizes the statement in our November issue concerning the settlement of Buckley's suit against us as a 'disavowal' of Vidal's article. On the contrary, it clearly states that we published that article because we believed that Vidal had the right to assert *his* opinions, even though we did not share them." *Esquire* had not libeled Buckley, and neither had Vidal, as far as the court was concerned. The court had *not* sustained Buckley's case against *Esquire* and had *not* sustained his suit "correlatively against Vidal." These were falsehoods, apparently an attempt to manipulate public opinion and the historical record. The court had *not* ruled that Vidal's article was "defamatory." It had ruled that the case would have to go to trial *in order to determine as a matter of fact whether or not it was defamatory*. The cash value of the settlement with *Esquire* represented *only* Buckley's legal expenses, under the circumstances hardly a triumph for the plaintiff. Since Judge Levet's analysis of Vidal's alleged libelous statements about Buckley implied that Buckley might have an impossible time proving to a jury that they were technically libelous, Buckley's implication that of course he would win the suit, that he had in fact won it already, was casuistic at best. Even the simplistic headline of the *New York Times* account of Buckley's press conference was more truthful than Buckley's inaccurate press release: "Buckley Drops Vidal Suit, Settles with Esquire." Medina was furious. The press release was in direct "contravention" of his agreement with Rembar. When *Esquire* privately protested to Buckley, Buckley wrote to Hayes, "I do not propose to reopen the controversy. . . . I presume you are writing to appease Gore Vidal," certainly an accusation that Hayes did not at all deserve. As if endless repetition of a falsehood would somehow make it true, Buckley willfully repeated his claim, as he was to do ever afterward: "You are incorrect in saying that the court did not find Vidal's article defamatory." Perhaps Buckley had been able to convince himself that it had.

In the 1960s ultimate truths had been impinging on Gore's life with an irremediable finality that had begun with the death of his grandmother in 1964. Of all living people, other than his father, Dot had been his most dearly beloved. Lesser loved ones fell away. In late winter 1966, at the age of fifty-three, John Kelly died after surgery in New York, a victim of overweight, heavy drinking, and a weak heart. Kelly's death seemed best understood as a sacrifice to the gods of self-destructiveness. It had not been a life devoted to sustaining life. Andrew Chiappe, whom Gore had last seen when he had come to Rome with Fred Dupee in 1963, died of a heart attack in Paris in May 1967 at fifty-two. As with Kelly, Gore had seen less of the

reclusive Chiappe in the 1960s, though his resonant Shakespearean recita-
tions kept a place in Gore's memory and remained the first association that
came to mind when Shakespeare was mentioned. Both Kelly and Chiappe
had been mentors of sorts in the 1950s. Fred Dupee had been a mentor with
whom Gore had had both an intimacy and a regularity of helpful communication that he never had with Kelly or Chiappe. But by the end of the decade
the good friends had become alienated. Arguably Dupee had been Gore's
closest friend of the late Edgewater years, beginning in 1958 and continuing
for a full decade that the move to Rome in 1963 only partly attenuated. For
much of those years, with Andy and Howard, they had had a kind of family
life together. After 1963 they continued to see one another in Rome and
New York, and they corresponded regularly at a level of literary resonance
that kept their lives intellectually and emotionally connected. In 1963 Gore
and Howard had left their elaborate tropical-fish aquarium with the Dupees.
Andy worried about the fish; she kept them in the living room near the
fireplace because she worried they would die of the cold at Wildercliff
during the winter. The fish became a motif and a preoccupation. One night
Andy smelled smoke. Wildercliff, which had been built in 1798, was far
from fireproof. That night the house did catch fire, probably from under the
fireplace. But Andy saved the fish. One night she dreamed that she took the
fish to the zoo.

The fish had a simpler time of it than the people. By the end of the
decade, the Dupee/Vidal ménage had collapsed, shattered by tensions
largely generated by Dupee's difficulty in satisfying the conflicting demands
of his fragmented life. His 1963 Roman visit had infuriated Andy. It seemed
to bring out what, from her perspective, was the worst in Fred. She threatened divorce. The same thing happened in 1967, additionally complicated by
Andy's feeling that Gore and Howard encouraged Fred's Roman adventures. Dupee was always a welcome visitor in Rome, a valuable literary
confidant whose comments as an early reader of *Julian,* then of *Washington,
D.C.* were valuable for the revision process. Apparently Gore and Howard
enjoyed Fred's openly flamboyant sexual escapades abroad. His double life
in New York seemed to them burdened by clanking chains. When Fred read
Myra Breckinridge in manuscript in summer 1967, he thought it "a brilliant
tour de force; written with great energy and obvious pleasure; limited and
two-dimensional in its self-imposed caricature-style, but to my mind *much*
better than anything Nathanael West wrote! . . . The pornographic cli-

max is a brilliant success, of course, and the best (and most amusing) thing of that type I've read." When Andy read it, furious at both Fred and Gore, she threw her printed copy out the window. When, in 1968, Gore and Howard came for the first and last time for lunch at the Manhattan apartment on Morningside Heights into which the Dupees had just moved, the relations were strained, the atmosphere tense. Andy felt betrayed and bitter. Gore had no idea why or at least no sympathy with her resentments. At sixty-five, soon perforce to retire from Columbia, Fred was depressed, restless, emotionally exhausted, and deeply unhappy. Howard hardly noticed that the three principals were suffering. Soon the Dupees moved to California for a semiretirement in which Fred taught occasionally at Stanford and Berkeley, totally separating himself from his New York world. He wrote nothing more. After that unhappy lunch, Gore and Fred never saw one another again. When Fred died in California, a little more than ten years later, Gore wrote to Andy, "For the last few weeks I've been thinking about Fred. In fact, drove to Big Sur and spent the night Dec. 23 [1978]. I rang but got no answer. Went on to San Francisco and tried again. We thought we'd drive back down and make one more effort but took the plane, and that was that. I think the Roman death highly in character—and what a complicated, layered and counter-layered character it was. The last years didn't sound too splendid. . . . I have too many thoughts to come up with one, or even two. Sadness: that we'd not seen each other for so long. There aren't many people left to talk to. How fast it goes! An unoriginal truism that would have Fred speaking in *italics,* 'single quotes,' "double quotes"— *speaking*. Love, Gore." Andy resented the letter and did not respond.

The world Kelly, Chiappe, and Dupee had been a part of in the 1950s and '60s had been steadily fading away, and in the case of Edgewater itself Gore had now determined to cut the attenuated cord. In early 1969 he finally put it up for sale. There seemed no practical reason to keep the house. In New York they stayed at the East Fifty-fifth Street apartment or at 416 East Fifty-eighth Street, where they had moved some of the furniture from Edgewater, although Gore disliked the apartment. By the end of the year Edgewater had been sold to a wealthy New York businessman, William Jenrette, for $125,000, a handsome profit on Gore's initial purchase price of $16,000. Jenrette soon transformed it into an expensively restored historical showplace. In October, Howard arranged to ship Gore's books to Rome and organized a sale of the furniture. When Howard could not resist selling two chairs that had been set aside for Barbara Epstein at double the price they had agreed on, she was "shocked and furious with me—and I could kill myself for having been talked into it," Howard wrote to Gore. "I've apologized but I don't think she really accepts—I'm not going to take money for the other two things she wants and pay for shipping them." Dispossessing himself of Edgewater simplfied Gore's life desirably. It had begun to seem impossible to take care of the house from his European distance. But he knew, and afterward always felt with dreamlike resonance, that his Edgewater associations inextricably interwove the key experiences of his personal and professional life. It had been his residence during a golden time. Latouche and Alice Astor had been his friends and mentors then. The last, best years with his grandmother, the start of his relationship with Howard, the years of financial struggle when through television and movies he had triumphed economically, his partly successful political campaign in 1960, his return to writing fiction, and his victory swim in the river when *Julian* rose to the top of the bestseller lists—Edgewater had been for a decade and more an inextricable part of his life. It was never to stop being a part of him. But some of the anxieties that owning the house created and that contributed to his decision to sell it were always connected to darker, retrogressive fears about loss and death, about the difficulty of holding back inevitable, ultimate changes. The longer he lived in the house, the more it became clear to him that he would not live there for the rest of his life, or live anyplace forever. Change and dissolution were the laws of material reality. Nothing escapes, and both *Julian* and *Washington, D.C.* were strongly elegiac evocations of worlds past, present, and to come. There was no going back. "I still dream about Edgewater," he said in the late 1990s. "That I bought it back and have gone back to live but everything's falling apart. Time has undone Jenrette's work. The river has eaten away the lawn. No, I don't put any interpretation on that dream. No, I wouldn't like to own Edgewater again. Too much work. You can't live in those houses without servants, and there aren't servants. . . . I couldn't maintain it at a distance, and it constantly needed repairs. I finally sold it. I've never regretted selling it."

At the beginning of 1969 he rented, with the help of Alain Bernheim, a large apartment in Klosters, Switzerland, that had been occupied by Anatole Litvak, the director of *Sorry Wrong Number* and *The Snake Pit,* a good friend of the Bernheims, in a four-story chalet-style building called Casa Willi in the center of the small town. Klosters was the vacation home of artistic and literary people, including the novelist Irwin Shaw—whose *The Young Lions* was one of the best known and most commercially successful World War II novels—who lived there year-round, and movie people, among them Greta Garbo, who visited regularly. Shaw, whom Gore liked, had become the unofficial mayor of the Klosters international community. In a valley, surrounded by high mountains, Klosters was brisk in the winter, bright in the summer. From the balcony on one side of the apartment the views were spectacular. "It was a skiing place, and we went for the winter, for about two or three months," Howard recalled, though neither of them did downhill skiing. Still unspoiled enough in 1969 for artistic people to afford, from Christmas through February Klosters became a winter playground, though its period of high-fashionableness was still to come. Gore signed a five-year lease for the equivalent of $300 a month, with a payment of $7,000 to Litvak for his furniture. The flat, Gore recalled, "had formerly been Greta Garbo's, and she moved down the street. . . . Then up the street was Irwin Shaw, who sort of ran the town. The Jimmy Joneses and the Sam Spiegels were in and out of town. Much too Hollywood for my taste. Beautiful country and wonderful air and I loved cross-country skiing, and I did a lot of that. A very healthy period." Garbo, who came to Klosters every winter to visit a friend, usually stopped by in the mornings to join Gore and Billy for a walk. At the railroad station she bought every movie-gossip magazine. One night Gore entertained Garbo, Irwin Shaw, and the writer Martha Gellhorn, who had been married to Ernest Hemingway. Overwhelmed by Garbo's presence, Gellhorn could not stop talking. The next morning she apologized to Gore: "But what else do you do when you finally meet Helen of Troy?" Helen of Troy also enjoyed trying on Howard's clothes, which fit her. "She always wanted to dress up in my clothes or Howard's clothes," Gore recalled, "and be a boy with other boys. She took Howard's blazer and Nehru jacket and never brought them back." At the end of the winter season the town was quiet, semi-deserted. When they occasionally spent a few summer weeks at Klosters, the vistas were green and vast, the weather comfortable. They were to keep the apartment for five years, then to give (rather than sell) the lease to the Bernheims. "I don't know why we gave it up. Well, things got very cumbersome," Howard remarked. He had to look after the building and apartment in New York City, the flat in Rome, now Casa Willi.

Having given up Edgewater, Gore needed a replacement. The apartments in New York were for visits or rentals. The Via Di Torre Argentina apartment had become home for the time being. But having been brought up, even if peripatetically, in houses, his mental model of architectural domesticity had the separateness, the privacy, and the size of a freestanding house. As much as he felt at home in Rome, the attractive apartment seemed ancillary, or at least partial, to be completed by another residence, preferably not in a large city, not necessarily in Italy. He had already begun to pressure Howard to keep his eyes and ears open about the possibility of a country place, the European replacement for Edgewater.

The home-lust was further complicated by Vidal's political alienation because of America's Vietnam madness and his dissatisfaction with his high taxes, much of which went to support a war he detested. During their August 1968 appearances on television, Buckley had contemptuously referred to him as an expatriate. He did not feel like one, at least in the traditional sense embodied in Henry James's long English residence and assumption of British citizenship. He felt more like Mark Twain, who over a ten-year period had taken multi-year-long vacations from America, returning only for business visits. Distance clarified perspective, kept emotions under control. To the extent that he might obtain tax advantages if he resided abroad, Gore would be happy to have them, but his overriding motivation was to keep a healthy distance. European life appealed to him emotionally and culturally. Whatever price he would pay to live abroad, especially in regard to his career as an American writer, he was willing to pay, though probably he did not fully appreciate how alienating to many Americans his long-term foreign residence would seem and what consequences would result from forgoing on-site opportunities for career promotion. It would be seen as expatriation, which went against the national ethos. It was something an American writer would have to explain, and no explanation could ever completely suffice. Spurred by his disgust with the war, he considered making the ultimate statement beyond expatriation. In 1969, while establishing residence in Switzerland, he explored the possibility of becoming a Swiss national. It would have meant giving up his American citizenship. Residence was feasible. Nationality, though, was too technically complicated, Swiss regulations too restrictive to make it sensible to pursue. Even the tax advantages of Swiss residency soon proved illusory. He next tried Ireland, with whose prime minister his Hollywood friend John Huston put him in communication. "I confess that when I wrote threatening to change my nationality [because of the Vietnam War], I never dreamed my rhetoric would ever be translated into action," he explained to the prime minister. "Like most writers, I am prone to spur others to positions I myself never quite get around to taking. But this is the exception: last April I became a resident of Switzerland simply because one has to have an official residence somewhere and the United States was mine no longer. This month I sold my house in New York State and am now poised for permanent departure. . . . I'm aware that the honorable course for me would be to stay and fight. But I am now 44 with work to do and so think it time to leave the marching and fine speeches to those who are not only younger but more optimistic than I." Ireland offered a tax haven for artistic people who could demonstrate Irish descent. Gore could easily do that on both sides of the family. "I would indeed live in Ireland with pleasure and, come to think of it, symbolically it is perhaps the best gesture I could make at this time: to return after more than two centuries to the family's point of origin. Certainly this is a nice symmetry. The American experiment has gone wrong while the troubled country that could sustain us is now coming alive, and proves the better place to be."

From the Irish point of view he would not have to give up his American citizenship. In January 1970 and through the spring, after "a fascinating trip to Dublin," where "they may take me in," he wrote to Tom Driberg, his agent looked into available houses in Fitzwilliam Square, then on the Elgin Road, then in Merrion Square, none of which proved satisfactory, partly because of his ambivalence about living in the heart of Dublin. When he mentioned his interest in a country residence, his agent quickly found an attractive property in Knock, Lowertown, Schull, County Cork, at a price he was willing to pay, as well as the projected cost of extensive renovations over the next two years to make it attractively livable. To Howard, the thought of living in Ireland at all, let alone rural Ireland, seemed absolutely mad. "I refused to set foot in the house in Ireland. I thought it was madness. Klosters, Ireland, three apartments in New York, an apartment in Rome, and then La Rondinaia came along. It was just driving me insane. Probably Gore was looking for a home." Ireland, Gore explained, "was because I'd said, when I spoke out about the Vietnam War, that if the war went on I'd change nationalities. Besides that virtuous motive, the unvirtuous one was that you pay no tax. So I could have made a fortune had I shifted over to Irish nationality, protesting the war and saving

my money from the government at the same time. But my man, Charley
Haughey, who was the minister of finance, fell from power as soon as I
bought the house, and I couldn't get the nationality." There was some
vagueness in the criterion that permitted the interpretation that one grand-
parent had to be Irish. "I had a great-great-great-great-great-grandfather,
except it also says 'significant Irish connections' in the constitution. I met the
guy who wrote the constitution, and he said the fact that you are a cousin of
Constance Gore-Booth Countess Markovich, one of the swans of Lissadel,
makes you highly significant and that makes you a citizen under our laws.
Highly significant is that there's a statue of her on St. Stephen's Green. She
looks just like my mother." Haughey "later became for many years prime
minister, by which time I sold the house and it was all moot. Everything
went wrong. It was a pretty place. But I never saw it finished and I sold it
one afternoon."

———————

Just before Thanksgiving 1968 Kit and Gene drove from the home in
Avon, Connecticut that Kit had inherited to Washington, D.C., to see Sally
and Pick, the first stop on a cross-country drive and then a trip, westward,
around the world. On a mild autumn day they lunched at a restaurant near
the National Cathedral and went by St. Albans School. Gore, of whom
Gene was immensely proud, was one of the subjects of conversation, especially since the convention fireworks were still in people's minds, partly
because the war in Vietnam, where Gene had gone as part of a military
evaluation committee, still mercilessly continued. The newly elected Nixon
administration waited to take power. Public antiwar protests intensified.
Gore had been active in the creation of the New Party, soon to be renamed
the People's Party, formed by pro–Gene McCarthy dissidents and led by
Benjamin Spock and Marcus Raskin, who refused to return to the Democratic fold and support Hubert Humphrey. Pick Vidal, a conservative Republican whose West Point class had been retired in 1963, had voted for
Nixon. Probably Gene had also. After lunch the two patriarchs, with their
wives, sat outside in the autumnal air, the Washington Monument visible in
the distance. "Gene had just had a physical," Sally recalled, "and the doctor
said he was just great. They were going to make a trip around the world. So
they came down to Washington to say good-bye. Gene had a lot of classmates there."

John F. Kennedy, Gore Vidal, and Tennessee Williams, Palm Beach, 1958.
(Courtesy of Gore Vidal)

(Right) Claire Bloom at Ravello, c. 1972.
(Courtesy of Gore Vidal)

The high-spirited Maria Britneva and Gore Vidal, c. 1960.
(Wisconsin Center for Film and Theater Research, Gore Vidal Collection)

Melvyn Douglas, Lee Tracy, Gore Vidal, Frank Lovejoy, Leora Dana, and Joe Anthony at the first reading rehearsal of *The Best Man*, New York, 1960.
(Courtesy of Lyn Austin)

President-elect Kennedy greeting the cast and author of *The Best Man* backstage, New York, 1960.
(Performing Arts Research Center, New York Public Library)

Gore Vidal welcomes John F. Kennedy, who arrives to campaign in Dutchess County, 1960.
(Wisconsin Center for Film and Theater Research, Gore Vidal Collection)

Gore Vidal campaigning in Kingston, New York, 1960. Joanne
Woodward and Paul Newman are in the audience (bottom right).
(Wisconsin Center for Film and Theater Research, Gore Vidal Collection)

Mike Pendergast (far left) and other New York State politicians with Harry Truman and Gore Vidal at a Dutchess County political event, 1960.
(Wisconsin Center for Film and Theater Research, Gore Vidal Collection)

Eugene Vidal, Gore Vidal, and Joe Hawkins on election eve, 1960, about to get the news that Gore has lost the election.
(Wisconsin Center for Film and Theater Research, Gore Vidal Collection)

Paul Newman, Joanne Woodward, Gore Vidal, and Christopher Isherwood at a performance of Vidal's *Romulus*, New York, 1962.
(Courtesy of Don Bachardy)

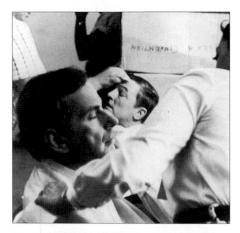

(Above) Gore Vidal at home
in Rome, c. 1964.
(Wisconsin Center for Film and Theater Research,
Gore Vidal Collection)

(Above, right) Gore Vidal and William F.
Buckley being prepared for battle,
Chicago, August 1968.
(Wisconsin Center for Film and Theater Research,
Gore Vidal Collection)

(Right) The peripatetic Gore Vidal
coming through customs on his way from
London to Monte Carlo to an international
television festival.
(Courtesy of Gore Vidal)

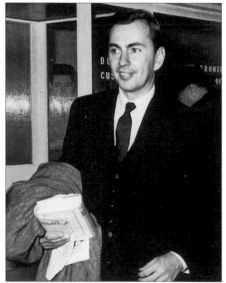

William F. Buckley and
Gore Vidal, Chicago,
August 1968.
(Wisconsin Center for Film
and Theater Research, Gore
Vidal Collection)

(Above) Jason Epstein and Gore Vidal,
Venice, 1975.

(Courtesy of Jason Epstein)

(Above, right) George Armstrong (right)
with Howard and Gore, Venice,
Christmas, 1980.

(Courtesy of George Armstrong)

(Above) George Armstrong
and Joanne Woodward on the
ferry to Torcello, Venice,
c. 1984. Gore and Paul
Newman, "the less important
figures," are visible only as
torsos in the background.

(Courtesy of George Armstrong)

(Left) The first meeting of
Gore Vidal and Italo Calvino
(left), Judith (Chichita)
Calvino (left), and Howard
Austen (center), American
Academy in Rome, 1974.

(Courtesy of Gore Vidal)

Gore Vidal at
La Rondinaia, Ravello, 1996.
(Author's photo)

Howard and Gore
at their daily chess game,
Ravello, 1996.
(Author's photo)

Howard and Gore at the
Adams Memorial at Rock
Creek Park Cemetery,
November 1994, after
arranging their own
gravesites.
(Author's photo)

At Ravello, 1996. (Author's photo)

At seventy-three, retired, white-haired, handsome, bemused by old age and relative uselessness, Gene Vidal had begun to settle into a life of recreational travel and general superfluity. He was occasionally consulted by airlines and government commissions. The heroic world of early aviation he had helped create had long passed, and whether or not he was introspective or retrospective enough to focus on his early displacement from fame and power, his son certainly had a sense of how abruptly his father's career had been diminished by his 1942 heart attack. Fortunately, his heart had repaired itself sufficiently so that he had never had another cardiac episode. For almost ten years he had been taking an anti-aging enzyme-enrichment formula, made from placentas that had nurtured fetal calves, obtained from a doctor in Florida. He believed it did him a world of good. The doctors at the Hartford Hospital were "puzzled," he wrote to Gore, "over the fact that my blood pressure has dropped from 190 to 140, my pulse has increased from 45/min to 72/min (normal), my cholesterol down from 470 to 215, etc. I must send Wolf a thank you note." From Washington, Kit and Gene drove to Jackson, Michigan, to visit Gene's favorite sister, Lurene, then to California to see his sister Margaret, who had settled with her family in Inglewood. They did not get beyond California. On New Year's Eve, Gene became ill with what appeared to be pneumonia. On New Year's Day 1969 the tests he underwent in Centinela Valley Hospital revealed lung cancer. Gore flew to Los Angeles to be with his father and stepmother. Unexpectedly, after a few weeks of treatment, the cancerous cells entirely disappeared from Gene's lungs. Delighted, he joked proudly with Kit and Gore about his recuperative powers. Still, the condition needed to be watched. For the time being, the round-the-world trip was put on hold. They soon found a small furnished apartment, and for a few weeks it looked as if he would be fine. Soon, though, his feeling of energy and general good health began to decline. By late January he was back in the hospital. Tests revealed that his left kidney had become riddled with cancerous cells. The malignancy that had not been able to sustain itself in the lungs had been a secondary colony. Suddenly, at the age of seventy-three, Gene faced the news. Kidney cancer was almost always fatal; he had at most two or three years of life.

Surgery was the best of the medical alternatives. If successful, the prognosis was still poor. Most likely the cancer had spread to other places in addition to the lungs. Gene and Kit decided to try the risky operation. Gore joined them at the hospital the night before. It seemed more than possible that Gene would not survive the surgery. When the surgeon came with release papers to be signed, Gore recalled, Gene "looked at the doctor and said, 'But I thought it was the left kidney?' The doctor got hysterical. 'Well, of course it's the left kidney!' 'But why does it say the right kidney here? You don't want to take out the only good kidney I've got!' He tortured the doctor. That was his humor." Late that night Gore returned to the Beverly Hills Hotel, bleary-eyed, exhausted. Like Kit, he feared that his father would not survive. Early the next morning, having been up most of the night, he took a walk on Beverly Drive. As he passed between Santa Monica Boulevard and Wilshire, a car pulled over. Marty Manulis, on his way to get a Sunday newspaper, astonished to see anybody walking in Beverly Hills, thought he had recognized a familiar figure. "I cruised up right past him. He was walking and I was driving. I stopped and said, 'What the hell are you doing walking in Beverly Hills and at this hour?' He mumbled something, but I noticed he was very red-eyed. I thought that he'd had a hard night or something like that. I think I made some bad joke about that, and he really kind of dismissed it in an offhand way. But he didn't have his usual ebullience. We said something about having dinner together soon, and I went on." When Gore got to the hospital, the operation had just been concluded. The kidney had been removed. Gene had survived. Later, Kit and Gore sat by Gene's bedside. "He was out of his head. But he could hear Kit and me talking. And I said, whispering, 'How is he?' And she said, 'Don't worry, he doesn't understand anything.' 'Of course I do,' he said. She said, 'He thinks he does, but this is his unconscious mind. He won't remember anything we say.' Then he said, 'Well, I do know I've got cancer!' This is a man supposedly out of his skull. I said, 'Well, maybe we should lower our voices. We're giving his limbic memories all kinds of unpleasant things to recall.'" As Gene came to his senses, he was suddenly distracted by the latest NASA space launching. "He was so fascinated, he said, 'Imagine, I've lived so long. I've lived all the way through the history of aviation. I knew the Wright brothers and I have made my contribution, and now I see men walking on the moon. I never thought I'd see that in my lifetime.'" When Gore privately asked the doctor what the prognosis was, the doctor matter-of-factly said that Gene would be dead in a few months. Angry, resentful, appalled by the doctor's tone, Gore insisted that the doctor review for him what might be done. He could not believe there was no antidote.

Always a good caretaker, Kit looked after Gene with a stoic but sinking heart. Gore visited each day at the hospital and then at the Inglewood apartment during the first week in February. The doctors had decided they could do nothing more. Since he began to recover quickly from the surgery itself, Gene was optimistic. "What should I be taking to get over this?" he asked a doctor-cousin who came by to visit. " 'What about a double martini?' 'Well,' my father said, 'I don't like martinis.' 'Well, I do,' " the doctor said, "and the doctor started drinking, and so did I. What he was saying is that it's all over and you might as well get drunk." There seemed to be a remission, or at least a pause. Surprisingly, Gene soon looked much better. His spirits rose with his coloring and his energy. He began to catch up with his correspondence. Gore hoped that the doctor's prognosis was wrong. But since even if it was right Gene would have at least a few months, perhaps as many as six, Gore said, simply, "I think I'll return to Rome." He had been away most of the summer and part of the fall and winter. From Rome he talked daily on the phone with Kit, grateful for her tireless attention to Gene. The news, though, was bad. The latest tests showed that the cancer had spread. Gene's energy disappeared. He could hardly eat. He had begun to hover somewhere between irrational and comatose, partly out of his senses when awake, often unresponsive. He sat bolt upright in bed one day and said, "If I do not get out of this motel, I shall become extinct." He got up and walked around, and then Kit put him back to bed. There appeared to be reason to believe that the enzyme supplement was keeping him alive, though it seemed not a life but a living death. The doctors saw not the remotest possibility that he would recover. On February 10 Kit rang Gore. She thought it sensible to stop the enzyme injections. Would he agree? Yes, he said. "It was going to keep him alive God knows how long, but unconscious. What was the alternative? It was a horror. He was like a vegetable. She stopped the enzyme."

The call came late in the afternoon ten days later. As soon as Gore put down the phone, he drew a cross in the margin of the manuscript on which he was working to mark the moment. In California it had been heartbreaking for him. Sometimes he had been angry, sometimes numb. Now he was mostly numb; he had not expected the inevitable to happen so quickly. He had assumed there would be time to see his father again. In Rome the news sank in, the irrevocable actuality of termination. The father he had not quarreled with once in forty-three years was gone forever. That night he went through with a dinner engagement at the Pecci-Blunts'. When he arrived with twenty or thirty other guests for dinner at the palace near the Campidoglio, the candles and chandeliers glittering, the waiters and foot-men in attendance, he told his hostess, a niece of Pope Pius XII, that his father had died earlier in the day. "I was a bit late, and she had criticized me for being late. 'My father just died.' 'Oh, dear,' she said, and the grand hostess went right on with the dinner party. And I, as the good guest, went right on too." The next day, though, she sent him a gentle note thanking him for coming under the circumstances. His own note to Kit a few days later was sincerely and gently appreciative. He had no doubt that his father had been and would continue to be "the love of her life," which she and her remarriage never gainsaid. "I'm glad it ended as swiftly as it did," he wrote to her, "and I regret I wasn't able to *do* more but my gifts as an actor are limited and much more time with him would have betrayed my distress, and done him no good. Anyway, let me say how fortunate he was to have had you with him all these years, and though you must have known ever since the first illness that your marriage to a man so much older was going to have its dreadful side, you did it all most gracefully, pleasing him and the rest of us." Kit responded that she considered herself "not only fortunate but privileged to have had nearly thirty years with your wonderful father." The "dreadful side" went on for both Kit and Gore, though there was no intimacy between them of a sort that would encourage them to do any of their grieving together or even share confidences. Years afterward Gore provided his characteristic analytic overview. "The later it comes, the loss of a father, the more unpleasant it is. If you lose a father when you're young, it's sort of, so what? You've got your own life ahead of you. You're too busy. The older you are, the more reflective it makes you. And more unpleasant than it would have been had I been twenty. We had our elective affinities or at least sympathetic affinities. Mutual respect. We never quar-reled." It was his way of admitting and remembering how painful the experience of the loss had been. In late March the person other than Kit and Gore who had loved Gene most, his sister Lurene, old, ill, recently wid-owed, about to have surgery for cataracts, wrote to Gore about her own heartache and her compassion for him. Lurene had been there when Gene was born. They had grown up together. Probably she had never loved anyone as much as she had loved her brother. "Dearest Gore—You have been in my thoughts so constantly and I feel for you so deeply because tho I am only your father's sister, I loved him so much and so long, nothing seems worth while—first without Merle and now Gene. But you are his beloved son—and I can only imagine what this loss means to you. Your relationship was so special. . . . No one ever had a more loving and devoted [father] or a prouder one. He loved *you* like our mother loved *him*. He was her very favorite of all people. Nothing ever pleased him more than a 'call' from you. He loved and *so* much appreciated all your thoughtfulness and devotion always—you kept him young because you treated him young. To me, you and he were never like father and son—but rather like two bad kids." He was "the best friend you'll ever have! So you are really hurting too and shall miss him too in spite of the fact you are still young and busy—and blessed with so much talent and deserved success."

In early May the institution to which Eugene Luther Vidal had sworn loyalty a half century before at West Point honored him at Andrews Air Force base. Pick and Sally had followed the death story with sinking hearts. Kit had called them regularly with news of Gene's changing circumstances. Soon after Kit had the body cremated in California, General Felix Vidal, retired, began to make arrangements for a gathering of Gene's classmates to bid him a ritualistic Air Force good-bye at the base outside Washington. Gore flew in from Rome to join Kit, her two children, and Pick and Sally and their daughter, accompanied by a dozen or more ancient warriors from Gene's West Point class and his long years of work and camaraderie. Among them Gore noticed "the solemn, pompous, haggard Leslie Groves," who had directed the Los Alamos project, "himself to die a few months later; and that handsome figure of the right wing General Wedemeyer." It was a doubly complicated moment for Gene Vidal's son. He had sworn his own version of the oath to "Honor, Duty, Country" that these senior military figures had sworn. On the personal level he shared their pain and bewilderment. "The generals looked dazed," he recalled, "not so much with grief as with a sense of hurt at what time does to men, and to their particular innocence." But they were the generals who in earlier incarnations had led battalions into World War II devastation and who had brought Jimmie Trimble to his brutal death on Iwo Jima. They and their surrogates were leading the ongoing carnage in Vietnam, certain there was a light at the end of the tunnel. "I could not help thinking as I walked away from them for the last time that the harm they have done to this republic and to the world elsewhere far outweighs their personal excellence, their duty, their honor." How ironic for him that through his gentle, much-loved father he had a personal connection to the warrior class. Some of that warrior blood ran within him. It gave him both insight and pause. As they stood on the runway, the airfield was totally silenced for the ceremony. No noise. No takeoffs or landings. "Pick carried the box. I wouldn't touch it," he recalled. "Thanatophobia was really working strongly." Sally recalls that both Gore and Pick "carried the ashes out toward the helicopter, and then an officer in charge . . . walked towards them and saluted and my husband saluted. Gore was holding the ashes and handed them to the officer, who saluted again and took the ashes and carried them back to the helicopter." The plane gently rose into the bright May sunshine. Everyone on the ground squinted into the sunlight to watch it disappear in the distance. "The icon of their generation, the lovely athlete of a half century before, was now entirely gone." The pilot, releasing the ashes over Virginia, saw them falling downward to the indifferent earth.

A disciplined workaholic, even during the winter of his father's death Gore kept at various writing projects, the most time-consuming a new novel, with the tentative title *Two Sisters of Ephesus*, which he worked on in Rome and Klosters. In spring 1969, not long after his father's death, Gore went alone to Amalfi, to stay in the same hotel at which he and Tennessee had stayed in 1948, in order to work, "for old times' sake," on the screenplay of *Seven Descents*. When he first saw it, he thought it "very bad," he wrote in *Two Sisters*, "but then, after some study, found parts were marvelous, and laughed aloud, hearing, as I read, the wry cadence of his voice, heard our old laughter in the courtyard of the hotel . . . and marveled to myself that so many years later I would be adapting him in a place we had once stayed before time had played its usual jokes, made him a bit mad and, for me at least, remote, made me . . . the same." *Seven Descents*, distributed eventually as *The Last of the Mobile Hot-Shots*, with Sidney Lumet directing and producing for Warner Brothers and Seven Arts, Gore undertook partly for money, mostly as a sentimental tribute to his friend. Williams hoped that Gore's association with the film would be mutually beneficial, as his adaptation of *Suddenly, Last Summer* had been. In the end the film had little success. It did, though, bring them together again, for a short time bridging a distance that Gore attributed to Tennessee's increasingly erratic behavior. For much of the sixties the playwright had struggled with failure, depression, and flight. Drugs and liquor, in semidevastating combinations and degrees, had frequently incapacitated him. Gore had seen him occasionally in New York and Key West, but the intensity of engagement, the delight in each other's company that had previously characterized their friendship was mostly gone. Maria Britneva, now always good-humoredly referred to as "The Lady St. Just," kept them in touch by her ministrations to both. When she went to Rome, as she often did, she stayed at Via Di Torre Argentina. In Key West she stayed with Tennessee. Oliver Evans, an American professor of English, tall, red-faced, loud-voiced, whom Tennessee had introduced to Gore in New Orleans in the late 1940s, provided another ongoing link. Gore, who saw him off and on in New York, liked him. "Evans was wildly funny. When he was drinking, his nose would get very red and start to bob up and down. His nose had a life of its own. And you knew as it got worse and worse that his temper was going to explode on you. Tantrums." A good friend of Paul Bowles's, Evans made the Tangiers/European circuit regularly and, with Tennessee as companion, had begun to take regular sex holidays in Bangkok. When Tennessee visited Gore in Rome in mid-July 1970, he had read Gore's comment in *Two Sisters* on his remoteness. "First of all," he wrote to Gore afterward, "it was wonderful to renew your acquaintance and I don't believe that you find me still remote, perhaps excessively *near* but not *remote*. . . . I thought the evening went delightfully. AND regardless of your crotchety attitude toward me, mine toward you is fixed as a star, not falling. When nervous you rattle like a window in a bombardment, but that isn't often and most of the time you are one of the coolest and effortlessly witty people I've known—and your writing gets sharper with the years and you are steadily more convincing in the part of a *grand seigneur*."

It was a sweet, conciliatory letter, and the next time Williams was in Rome, they spent some "lovely evenings" together. "Tenn. was in town," Gore wrote to Paul Bowles, "drinking and pill-taking and mad, sad if not dangerous to know—'Ah must leave as there is Coo dee Tah of the right and it is not safe here.' " In London in 1974 Gore delighted in Williams's comment to Claire Bloom, rehearsing for a London revival of *Streetcar,* in which she felt she gave the best performance of her life. She asked Williams what happens to Blanche afterward. "No actress has ever asked me that question." He sat "back in his chair, narrowed his eyes. . . . 'She will enjoy her time in the bin. She will seduce one or two of the more comely young doctors. Then she will be let free to open an attractive boutique in the French Quarter.' 'She wins?' 'Oh, yes,' said the Bird. 'Blanche wins.' " Williams was, though, not doing very much winning himself. Gore admired his effortlessly laconic intelligence, his intuitive humor, his funny though increasingly frustrating incoherence. But the drift soon resumed, the friendship reattenuated by distance and Williams's physical and emotional decline, their interchanges slightly exacerbated by Tennessee's awareness that the relative demand for their work as writers was in the process of being reversed. He had not had for some time and would never have again a theatrical success. By the early 1970s he could hardly find any venue for his new plays, let alone a Broadway production. Though Gore was sour about the theater since the failure of *Weekend* and his ongoing failure to get *Drawing Room Comedy* produced, it was a secondary interest. His mind and imagination were mostly on fiction and occasional essays, the next volume of which, *Homage to Daniel Shays: Collected Essays, 1952–1972,* was to establish Vidal as the premier general-audience essayist of the second half of the twentieth century on literary, social, and political topics. His three novels since returning to fiction had been bestsellers. *Julian* had been a great critical success. Though *Myra* had had a mixed reception, much of the hostility based on misunderstanding or narrow moralism, many perceptive readers, among them Richard Poirier, Fred Dupee, and Christopher Isherwood, thought it a masterpiece. At the age of forty-five, vigorous, healthy, disciplined, still immensely ambitious, Vidal had much expected of him. To most observers Williams's best work, and much of his life, seemed behind him.

The person to whom *The City and the Pillar* had been dedicated, who had always been a part of Gore's consciousness, like a friendly ghost whose real life had been lost long ago, had to have been on Gore's mind when he created in 1970 the screenplay *Jim Now,* based on the 1948 novel. Apparently a perfunctory simplification of *City*'s plot, it was not something to which he devoted either much passion or time. It had come up as something he might do, and between more passionate commitments he tried his hand at it, partly because it had been suggested that he himself might direct it. Arrangements to make a low-budget version in Rome directed by Franco Rossellini fell through. Financing was difficult to arrange, and Gore suspected that Rossellini would find a way to profit from the venture more than anyone else, perhaps by raising money for a film he had little or no intention of making.

By mid-1972 most of the Hollywood studios had declined the script, some because of the subject matter. Jimmie Trimble was becoming, though, even more of a presence than he had been, partly because, as Gore now approached his late forties, retrospective evocation and revivifying mythmaking had a greater attraction than they had had earlier. "Death, summer, youth—this triad contrives to haunt me every day of my life," he wrote in *Two Sisters,* "for it was in summer that my generation left school for war, and several dozen that one knew (but strictly did not love, except perhaps for one) were killed, and so never lived to know what I have known . . . and someone hardly remembered, a youth . . . so abruptly translated from vivid, well-loved (if briefly) flesh to a few scraps of bone and cartilage scattered among the volcanic rocks of Iwo Jima. So much was cruelly lost and one still mourns the past, particularly in darkened movie houses, weeping at bad films, or getting drunk alone while watching the Late Show on television as our summer's war is again refought and one sees sometimes what looks to be a familiar face in the battle scenes—is it Jimmie?" Always alive in his deepest consciousness, his St. Albans schoolboy friend now became more sentiently vivid. When the next year Gore had one of his rare experiences with a hallucinogenic drug, suddenly "Jimmie Trimble arrived in my bed wearing blue pajamas. . . . And I could actually feel his body." Now, with Gore more than halfway through his own life, the abrupt termination of Jimmie's seemed appositely remembered and emotionally recharged, increasingly emblematic of all that had been lost, for those who had survived the war as well as those who had not. As Gore looked into the mirror, the noticeable changes from the youthful Apollonianism he had been so long used to were a fretful reminder of the greater changes to come. Being middle-aged seemed a slightly cruel joke. Growing old had no attractions. His father's death was a wrenchingly personal dramatization of the inevitable. "Recently," he wrote in *Two Sisters,* "I dreamed of my father who died last winter. He was seated in some sort of a funicular car moving slowly opposite to me. As we came abreast of one another, I saw with dull horror that he was dead and where his eyes should have been there were bright flames. Ultimate fate of watery creatures in a fiery universe."

Though *Two Sisters, A Novel in the Form of a Memoir, A Memoir in the Form of a Novel,* had no place for Jimmie as a character, his singular evocation consorts effectively with the novel's underlying emphasis on doubling and twins. The complicated narrative has doubling, or at least dual temporalities, built into its structure just as it has a brother/sister pair of twins and two twinlike but not actual twin sisters as a central part of a screenplay within the narrative. The overall narrator who exists "NOW" is a slightly fictionalized version of the author, as is the GV of "THEN," whom we see mostly through the eyes of Eric Van Damm (who looks physically much like Jimmie Trimble), with whom GV "THEN" was in love as he was also in love with Eric's twin sister, Erica, and with whom he thinks (incorrectly, it turns out) he has fathered a child. The overall frame of the novel in the present of its beginning and end brings an Anaïs Nin–like character named Marietta Donegal to Rome to ask the fictionalized version of Gore Vidal if he will read and then help her to sell to Hollywood a screenplay that Eric wrote in 1948. Marietta, who had lived with GV in Paris for three months in 1948 and also had an affair with Eric, hopes to make a great deal of money from it. Actually, as the author and the reader soon discover, the screenplay, *Two Sisters from Ephesus*, which composes the middle third of the novel, is totally unsuitable for commercial production. Set in Greece in 356 B.C., it exists as a thematic analogue to the rest of the novel, a dramatization of the love/hate rivalry between two sisters that focuses on power, love, and art, represented by the sisters' half-brother, Herostratus, an ambitious, poetic fire-creator and -destroyer whose involvement with his sisters parallels GV's with Eric and Erica. The novel's two sisters from Ephesus purposely suggest Jacqueline Bouvier Kennedy and Lee Bouvier Radziwill, a fascination with the Kennedy-Bouvier world that Louis Auchincloss, after he read *Two Sisters*, fervently hoped Gore had finally gotten out of his system. After *Washington, D.C.* and now *Two Sisters*, as well as his essays on the Kennedys, it seemed to Louis obsessively counterproductive. The Kennedy world, though, plays only a minor role in *Two Sisters*, and probably the general reader did not catch the allusions at all, though the reviewers and the literary/social gossip chamber certainly did. The novel as a whole is not about living people, except for the author himself, whose experiment with mixing fiction and nonfiction, made fashionable by his contemporaries, Mailer and Capote, had to do with his own effort to stretch his imaginative wings by trying something different, to explore his own artistic sources, and to try working through and celebrating the mirrorlike doublings of art and life.

Two Sisters* was neither a critical nor a commercial success, the first of his novels since the success of *Julian* not to make the bestseller list. Little,

Brown was less disappointed than the author, though both had seen the handwriting on the wall from the earliest stages of the book's production. In fact, Little, Brown simply discounted its losses, so Vidal surmised, as an inevitable cost of sustaining a desirable author on its list, and looked forward to a new contract with Vidal that would keep them together for future books. It was not aware that Jason Epstein had renewed his solicitations to tempt Gore to become his author at Random House, though Gore had not yet decided what to do. *Two Sisters* had its admirers, or at least fair attention from reviewers, many of whom thought it bold, experimental, effective in parts, but not sufficiently interesting or successful overall. The difficulty of relating the full-length screenplay embedded in the partly fictional, partly autobiographical narrative to the novel as a whole baffled many.

One of the art-life doubles of *Two Sisters* soon showed up in Europe, making her appearance in both dimensions. In *Two Sisters*, Anaïs Nin, as Marietta Donegal, is Vidal's slightly parodic version of the Anaïs he had known since 1945. In the early 1960s, like Marietta, she had tried to persuade him to produce, by which she meant finance, a script she had co-authored for which she had a French director who she hoped would make movies of all her novels. Gore had declined to help. Now, in mid-1970, she had another request to make. Still searching for literary vindication, she had begun in 1966 to publish edited versions of her diaries, the materials carefully selected to be as favorable to herself as possible. The three volumes that had appeared had helped reawaken and create an interest in her work. She had begun to become a cult figure of sorts. Her enthusiasts found her romantic subjectivity and her preoccupation with feminine sexuality compelling if not liberating. For the first time she had an audience, for her diaries more than for her fiction, especially in Europe. In Rome in 1970, soon after the publication of *Two Sisters*, Gore received a telegram from Anaïs. She needed his permission to include in volume four, covering the years 1944–47 and scheduled to appear in mid-1971, what she had written about him. At the bar of the familiar Pont Royal Hôtel in Paris, after examining the text she provided, he gave his permission to include everything except a few lines that mentioned a third party. Anaïs, who seemed as beautiful as ever, gave him a "hard look." She had been told that Marietta Donegal had been based on her. Was that true? " 'I don't read that sort of book—but I was told it was a hideous caricature." She seemed to accept Gore's explanation that the character's "philosophy," not her personality or person, was loosely based on hers. No reader, though, could have mistaken the numerous ways in which Marietta Donegal resembled Gore's view of Anaïs, and many reviewers had highlighted the identification. The rest of the portrait, he told her, was fiction. "She took that well enough. She was aware that we no longer felt the same way about things. 'Anyway, you said—I was told—that I wrote well.' " If he had actually said that, he took it back in a review of volume four, "Taking a Grand Tour of Anaïs Nin's High Bohemia," that he published in the *Los Angeles Times* in September 1971, an act of distancing probably intended to break forever whatever bond remained between them. The indirect hostility that had resulted in Marietta Donegal now became explicit, though, as often the case with Gore, it was accompanied by sound judgment and some retrospective tenderness. The diaries, he wrote, had promised that one day Anaïs would be established "as a great sensibility. Now here they are, and I am not so sure. . . . Not only does she write an inflated, oracular prose, but she is never able to get outside her characters" and unable to reveal their interiors. "Anaïs is dealing with actual people. Yet I would not recognize any of them (including myself) had she not carefully labeled each specimen. . . . I do not recognize Anaïs—or myself—in these bitter pages. Yet when I think of her and the splendid times we had so many years ago, I find myself smiling, recalling with pleasure her soft voice, her French accent, and the way she always said 'yatch' instead of 'yacht.' That makes up for a lot." Furious, Anaïs felt that it ended everything, of which, anyway, there was little left. They never saw or spoke to each other again.

Another old friend, Paul Bowles, Gore had genuine affection for and no desire for distance from. He was happy to let their shared past stand. Bowles's differentness he respected, though it helped keep their meetings infrequent. At Christmas 1969 he and Howard, soon after a two-week trip to India—Gore's first to Asia or the Far East—went to Morocco, where they spent three days in Tangier and saw Bowles for dinner each night. Jane, who had been seriously ill for more than a decade and who was to have only three years more of life, was a long-term patient in a hospital in Spain. Bowles, now at work on his autobiography, had been spending part of each year in California, where Oliver Evans, teaching there himself, had arranged a position for him at California State University at Northridge. The rest of the time Bowles spent in Morocco, where his life had become a ritualized work schedule balanced by his love of North Africa and his addiction to kif.

The modest teaching salary far exceeded what he earned as a writer. "I had dinner with him," Gore recalled, "the day before he went over to Northridge for his first class. He said, 'What should I teach?' I said, 'How do I know? I've never taught.' He said, 'Well, I think I'm going to teach me. What do you think?' 'Well, at least you know the subject.' And he taught himself. That's about all they ever got out of him. Bowles, Bowles, Bowles. He was probably a lot better subject than the ones they wanted him to teach." At Paul's urging, Gore, who never smoked cigarettes and found that he could not inhale, tried the mild narcotic again and disliked it as much as ever. They still enjoyed one another's company, their differences mostly entertaining, a mutually playful respect that expressed itself, among other ways, in the nicknames they used in their correspondence by reversing the letters of their names. Gore was "Erog," Paul "Luap." Bowles, who immediately before Gore's arrival had read the Buckley–Vidal *Esquire* articles, enjoyed being brought up to date, something difficult to be in isolated Morocco. When a young American poet and Bowles admirer, Dan Halpern, came by, Vidal submitted to a lengthy interview for *Antaeus*, a magazine that Halpern, encouraged by Bowles, was about to start. The names of friends from their New York world of the 1940s and '50s came up in their dinnertime conversations. The next summer, when Gore found a blank piece of "John Treville Latouche" stationery, which gave him a start, he used it to write a note to Bowles, who thought for a moment that he was being written to by a ghost. With Howard they took a drive to Bowles's favorite point from which to view the Mediterranean, Gibraltar visible to the north. Standing there, Bowles remarked that he felt he was at the center of the world. In North Africa, Vidal felt displaced, off-center. His omphalos was at Delphi.

Another friend now became an erratic enemy. Observing Mailer in companionable conversation with Buckley at the convention in Chicago, Vidal had felt that poor recompense for the hospitality he had extended at Edgewater and his generally kind words about Mailer as a writer. He thought less of Mailer's prose of recent years: it seemed more distended, exaggerated, and Lawrencian in its celebration of male orgasmic power. Mailer of course had not gone over to the enemy ideologically, but as two miscast if not ludicrous minor-party candidates for mayor of New York, Mailer may have felt he and Buckley might talk constructively together. "At that time," Mailer recalls, he was having "a rapprochement with Buckley and the conservatives. I was trying to have some sort of better relationship with Buckley. The feud started in 1968 when Gore saw me at Chicago talking with Buckley. He must have seen that as some disloyalty or even betrayal. He seemed to me to be piqued by that, and our relationship was never the same thereafter. From that time on, Gore began to make remarks against my writings." In Vidal's view, Mailer had been "kissing Buckley's ass." In Mailer's view, Buckley had outdebated Vidal on the ABC news segments. That Buckley had called Vidal a "queer" on national television might not have disturbed Mailer, whose own homophobia was at least equal to Buckley's. Later, when Buckley hired Mailer's cousin, Charles Rembar, to represent him in his libel suit against Vidal and *Esquire,* Gore saw that as the end of what had been a competitive but still respectful relationship. It was one thing to be literary rivals, quite another for Mailer to work actively to damage him. It seemed beyond the pale for someone who represented himself as a political radical, even a socialist, to ally himself with Buckley. Mailer's antagonism, though, was not ideological; it was personal. Between the end of the 1968 convention and the Rembar recommendation in late 1971, Vidal had driven, Mailer felt, a stake into his heart. In July 1971 he had published in *The New York Review of Books* an article, "In Another Country," that covered a number of recent works on the subject of women's liberation, one of them Mailer's article in *Harper's* with the same title as his extended book version of the next year, *The Prisoner of Sex.* Vidal thought Mailer's attitude toward women reprehensible: they were breeding machines who existed to be the fruitful receptacle of the male's sacred obligation, through the mystery of sexual intercourse, to conceive children. "The Patriarchalists have been conditioned to think of women as, at best, breeders of sons," Vidal had written, "at worst, objects to be poked, humiliated, killed. . . . There has been from Henry Miller to Norman Mailer to Charles Manson a logical progression." In addition, Mailer's argument that anything that interfered with conception was evil had its blatant homophobic inferences, which Vidal made explicit in his essay. Mailer's argument "boils down to the following points. Masturbation is bad and so is contraception because the whole point to sex between man and woman is conception. . . . He links homosexuality with evil. The man who gives in to his homosexual drives is consorting with the enemy," an "exemplification of moral weakness." Like an Old Testament prophet, the supposedly freethinking and politically radical Mailer had chosen to define himself as the voice of the thundering injunction "Thou shalt not spill thy seed upon the ground." The only place to spill it was into a woman, whether she wanted to receive it or not. Henry Miller depicted women as sexual objects. Mailer claimed they were vessels for fertilization, that women's wombs belonged to men. Manson enslaved and killed female disciples and enemies, his recent semi-random murder of a movie star slashed into the national consciousness as an example of antifemale brutality. Different as Miller, Mailer, and Manson were, Vidal thought it fair to say, in a polemical essay and in response to Mailer's views, that there was a logical progression from one to the other. He did not mean that either Miller or Mailer, as individuals, would eventually become Mansons. He did mean that the attitudes of Miller and Mailer contributed to the cultural groundwork that helped Manson come into existence.

Furious, brooding, deeply hurt, Mailer waited for an opportunity to respond. The ordinary channels of communication, including a letter to *The New York Review*, did not seem sufficient. If he considered attempting to speak privately to Gore and exchange grievances, he dismissed that approach. It probably seemed insufficiently public. Mailer wanted the largest possible audience for his counterattack. To humiliate Vidal publicly seemed the next best thing to attacking him physically. From Mailer's point of view Vidal had called him, more or less, a murderer. He had put him on a level with Charles Manson. It would have been difficult for him not to think that Vidal was deliberately calling indirect attention to his having stabbed his wife over ten years before. For Vidal the distinction between a progression and an equivalence was crucial and obvious. For Mailer the distinction was impossible to see. To Vidal, his essay seemed a fair response to Mailer's essay in *Harper's*. Probably he did not anticipate that Mailer would react with blind pain and rage, and in a later revision he considerably toned down the emphasis on the connection between Mailer and Manson, implying that he had at first not realized how strongly Mailer might react and that, even after Mailer had attempted his revenge, Vidal still had some concern for his feelings. Much of this could have been ironed out privately in the fall of 1971, and Mailer might have given Vidal the opportunity to himself have written to *The New York Review* to clarify that he did not mean equivalence at all. By temperament Vidal would have found it difficult not to respond to a private request. He generally assumed that intense public debate was inherently objective. He rarely made personal attacks against his opponents, and even in the Buckley bitterness he felt he had at most only counterattacked. But Mailer, having identified himself inextricably with the aggressive pugilist, his favorite self-defining metaphor in those years, was not about to settle for anything less than some form of slugging it out before an audience. In mid-November 1971 Mailer learned that Vidal was about to appear on *The Dick Cavett Show*, to be taped on November 17 and aired on December 1. That afternoon he called Cavett, a small, slim, light-haired talk-show host with a gift for gracefully combining entertainment with serious cultural discussion and with whom Vidal had a cordial relationship. Janet Flanner, the *New Yorker* Paris correspondent, was to be the other guest. Could he also appear on the program? Cavett called Vidal just as he was leaving for the studio "to say that Mailer had rung and asked could he be on the program too." Having just had a relaxing massage, Vidal was in a good mood, happily anticipating a pleasant evening. "Cavett said, 'Do you mind?' 'No,' I said. 'No.' " Cavett, whose guest Mailer had been numbers of times previously, aware of the Mailer-Vidal hostility, assumed there would be a civilized airing of differences. But Mailer, as he later recalled, had been doing a "slow, intense burn" for four months. "By the time of the show I was explosive. I had been drinking for a few hours before the show, and I confronted Gore in the dressing room before the show. I was steamed up and very angry. I was in battle mode. I ran at him and butted him in the head in the dressing room. Being a very cool professional, Gore just went onstage and acted as if nothing had happened and told some wonderful stories, particularly the one about Eleanor Roosevelt putting flowers in her toilet bowl to keep the flowers fresh. He had the audience eating out of the palm of his hand. I mostly glowered. Soon everyone thought something dramatic was going to happen. At one point I got up and walked across the stage toward Gore. People held their breath. They thought I was going to hit him. What I did was to give him a piece of paper" that had nothing of consequence written on it. "I don't know how much of the audience response was relief and how much disappointment."

Actually the audience, the host, and his two other guests were furious at Mailer for what seemed unforgivably boorish behavior. It was also self-destructive. When Gore arrived at the television studio, Mailer already had been sitting in a chair in the green room. "Now, I had figured—I knew Norman's sensitivities and that he'd be upset about Mailer-Miller-Manson," Vidal recalled. "But I thought it was all pretty much fair comment and kind of funny and accurate. So I go into the green room and Norman is sitting watching TV. I was friendly. I came up behind him and put my hands on his shoulders. 'How are you?' He gets to his feet with great effort. Then he butted my forehead with his head and I punched his stomach. Norman wrote afterwards, 'To my surprise, he hit me back.' " Vidal came on first, then Janet Flanner. No one onstage knew what had happened in the green room. Swaggering, attempting to seem menacing, Mailer immediately let audience and participants know he had a grievance against Vidal. "This man" said that he was like Charles Manson. He demanded an apology. The dialogue veered between comic and baffling. Cavett seemed nonplussed by Mailer's truculence. The mostly unflappable Flanner, a small, elderly American with a European sense of both decorum and frankness, played the witty scold. Mailer's behavior seemed to her childish and inappropriate. Vidal declined to argue with Mailer, except for a few self-defensive comments. The audience was prepared to be entertained. Instead it was shocked, for much of what Mailer said had no context. When without any explanation Mailer challenged Gore to reveal what he had done to Jack Kerouac, the audience was baffled. "Dick Cavett, sitting there, didn't know what it was about, and no one in the audience could know," Gore recalled. "I was talking through him, raising my voice to a decibel level that would erase what he was saying. Mailer claimed that I had destroyed Kerouac. He has a great line, that I destroyed Kerouac by fucking him in the ass. To fuck him in the ass is to take the steel out of his *cojones*. Mailer was going to say that on TV." When Mailer tried to pressure Vidal to read his remarks about Mailer and Manson in his essay, a copy of which Mailer provided, Vidal simply disregarded him. Mailer's babbling about the prerogatives of genius, which seemed his justification for his behavior, reinforced the audience's alienation. When he turned directly to the studio audience and asked, "Am I crazy or are you crazy?" he was answered immediately with a unanimous chorus, "You are!" Cavett, who had been doing his best to turn the discussion to the light side, could not sustain any of his jokes or use his charm to deflect the attacks or deflate the tension. Finally, angry himself, he responded to Mailer, who had now attacked Cavett as part of a Vidal-Flanner-Cavett conspiracy against him, "Why don't you fold it five ways and put it where the moon don't shine." It was one of the only funny moments on the show. As the camera went to credits and the participants, Flanner, Vidal, and Cavett, standing, talked together, Mailer, with a slight truculence in his stride, noticeably alone, walked off, stage left, by himself.

The previous December, Howard and Gore had flown eastward from Rome on Singapore Airlines, at what seemed a bargain first-class rate, around the world. Other than the brief visit to India, it was their first experience of the Orient, highlighted by their delight in Bangkok, about whose attractions they had heard much from Oliver Evans and Tennessee Williams, among others. "So this Sunday," Gore wrote to Elaine Dundy, "we start for Teheran and head toward the rising sun, with trepidation as travel narrows the mind while distending the gut." Vidal's first visit to Persia, now Iran, brought him to a country he had visited in his reading and imagination while writing *Julian*. The visit to Iran and then to India, to which they flew from Teheran, was probably the earliest start of the writing of *Creation* at the end of the decade. The trip was gratifying, liberating. A world that he knew existed suddenly became palpable reality. An idea for a novel about modern India came to mind, and was soon dropped. In India, in Katmandu, he ran into a valued figure from his past, Rosalind Rust, whom he had not seen for almost thirty years. Rosalind, still as beautiful, was now on the far side of her difficult years of divorce and alcoholism. Except for some memories of a brief, intense romance in their adolescence, they had little to share, and the most memorable experience for Gore in Katmandu was the appearance of Jimmie Trimble in a drug-induced dream. Rossellini, who was making a film in India, and Gore met for one in a series of planning sessions about their movie. In New Delhi, just before Christmas, the American ambassador, Kenneth Keating, whom Gore had strongly supported in his senatorial race against Robert Kennedy in 1964, greeted and entertained his distinguished literary visitor.

Their eastward flight eventually flew into the realities of return, first to California, then to New York, and finally back to Rome for much of the year. Some of the inescapable realities were contentious and irritating, particularly the time spent in preparation for the Buckley libel suit, which seemed during 1971 as if it might be as costly and long-lasting as *Jarndyce* and *Jarndyce* in Dickens's *Bleak House*, and, at the end of the year, Mailer's attack on the Cavett show. Some of the response to the Bouvier-Kennedy allusions in *Two Sisters* rose almost to the level of hostility, and Gore's discussion with Louis Auchincloss about what seemed to Louis his never-ending obsession with the Kennedys went on and then expanded into an even more contentious point between the two of them, as well as between Gore and much of the world: homosexuality, heterosexuality, and bisexuality. The text at issue was Shakespeare's sonnets, which Auchincloss had reluctantly admitted probably had strong homoerotic strains. But, Vidal responded, "in a sense you contradict unwisely: you handsomely 'prove' the homoerotic (who thought up that word has saved the pride of thousands of hetero school teachers who cannot imagine a great writer not liking Miriam, the two children and a split-level ranch house) element in the sonnets then try to take it all back on the ground that S suffered a Grotonian panic at the practice. This does not take into much account the attitudes of the period— rather you color it with our own Puritan distortions, forgetting that Cromwell is not yet LP [Lord Protector] of the Realm. There is no evidence of S being a religious fundamentalist and therefore a proto-Puritan. Rather his discomfort was in the great tradition: alarm at his own lust and its unseemliness and its unlikelihood of panning out. Not only were the Elizabethans relaxed sexual opportunists but he was in the THEATRE—and that world hasn't changed from the days of Dionysus to today." In Rome, as in Bangkok, sexual opportunism was simply an ordinary way of life for innumerable people, as Gore constantly observed in regard to himself and others. On occasion it ran parallel with interests of the heart. More often it expressed physical desire and the turns of individual personality. For Vidal the subject was interesting, the practice ordinary and hardly worth, on the personal level, describing or commenting on.

There were moments of depression, of course, sometimes with work, often with the realities that the passage of time imposed on body and mind. His father's death had shaken him. The memory of Jimmie Trimble had begun to haunt him, emblematic of choices he had made in regard to conventional notions about love, sex, and relationships, notwithstanding the familial intimacy between Howard and himself. At occasional moments he was not happy with his choices, though he rarely had any sense that they could have or should have been otherwise. Sometimes his imagination and emotional engagement with the past created dislocation. "The sun has set behind St. Peter's," he wrote in *Two Sisters.* "The low-swarming birds are gone. In the west cobalt blue has become neon rose. The moon's dead face reflects the now hidden sun. I am depressed, partly at time's passage . . . and at the glum realization that I forgot to arrange to have sex today. . . . Where am I? Well, I have gone inside, turned on the lights in the living room, look for comfort to the Amalfitan stone lion which dominates the room . . . look at the marble head of Jove bought from a dealer now disappeared and wish for the hundredth time that the marble did not so much resemble those Ivory Soap Parthenons I used to carve in the third grade. The room's yellow walls usually cheer me but not now." Though by temperament he was cheerful and focused, sometimes the mirror of mind and memory dramatized change, eventual dissolution. But if it was his enemy, it was also his subject; a creative balance between elegy and celebration was his aim for both himself and his fiction. *Two Sisters* had been partly an effort at that. So too now was the new novel, of a very different sort, he had begun planning for and working out mentally.

Aaron Burr had been on his mind for a long time, and early in 1970, in Los Angeles, he bought from a rare-book dealer a small library of books about Burr and his world, including some manuscript letters that Burr had written. In 1965 Gore had considered writing a play based on Burr's life, and in November 1970, coincidentally, Roger Stevens, still eager to have Gore return to the theater and deeply involved in the creation of the Kennedy Center in Washington, urged him to write a play about the Jefferson-Burr controversy. Stevens sent him a biography of Burr he had recently read. "Whether you do or don't write a play on the subject, I think you'll find it fascinating reading." Gore, at his writing table at Via Di Torre Argentina, with his view of Rome through the high windows, had already begun preparing himself for what he now began to glimpse might be a desirable return to and reinvention of himself as a historian of American history.

Rome still seemed as good a place as any to write about America, and the choice of Rome as his residence maintained its viability, though his desire for a country home persisted. More and more he felt he needed some place to get away to, especially during the hot months, and daily living in an increasingly crowded, noisy, even dirty city had its aesthetic and practical difficulties. The terrace that extended the sky also extended the busy street. As wonderful as was the Via Di Torre Argentina apartment, Roman traffic below sometimes seemed as if it were going to drive up to and around the huge terrace. He had no desire to give up the Rome apartment. On the contrary, it had become home, handsomely decorated and furnished with books, antique furniture, and art objects, from Roman to baroque, that reflected the world he and Howard had become part of. It gave a rich cultural glow to their daily life. Outside, their local Roman streets provided a neighborhood, a variety of small shops and enduring people with whom, over the years, they became familiar and to whom they themselves were familiar, readily accepted neighbors. At favorite restaurants, in his international milieu, Gore, as Tennessee Williams had remarked, was becoming the *"grand seigneur,"* a projection of authority, accomplishment, and charm, a presence that friends enjoyed, that enemies disliked but respected. Wherever he was, he was very much *there*. The Klosters apartment seemed fine for occasional visits. The West Cork house had been a poor choice that never got off the ground. The prospect of residence and citizenship in Switzerland or Ireland soon lapsed. The bureaucratic legalisms and his own indecisiveness were too difficult to overcome. Having resided in Italy part of the year since 1963, formal Italian residency would be easy to effect, and Italian citizenship was a possibility that he had intermediaries look into in early 1972, though he went no further than inquiries, partly because by the mid-1970s the Vietnam horror ended, even if the ending itself was horrible. He was additionally content to reside in Italy for a substantial part of each year because suddenly, in late 1971, Howard found what seemed the perfect country place for them.

Earlier in the year Gore had shaken hands on the purchase of a villa in Positano, but the offer of sale had been withdrawn. Other properties came to their attention—a Venetian villa, an estate in Perugia, a villa on Elba owned by some anciently distant relative, Sir Ralph Gore. One or the other of the usual obstacles aborted each of these. The possibility of buying Mona and Eddie Bismarck's villa on Capri was discussed and dismissed as impractical. Then, in September 1971, Howard spotted a classified advertisement in Rome's *Il Messaggero* for a house called La Rondinaia, "The Swallow's Nest," in Ravello on the Amalfi coast. "I located it by pure accident . . . having known that Gore wanted a place in the country. He felt constrained in Rome. I don't know why. You move from America to go to Italy and then find that Rome is confining and you want a place in the country. But there it is." Gore recalled that in 1948 he and Tennessee had gone up from nearby Amalfi to Ravello in Williams's jeep. Ever afterward he had retained in his memory as one of the most beautiful vistas he had ever seen the view of the Tyrrhenian Sea from the belvedere of the Cimbrone, an estate that dominated the entire top of the mountain between the town of Ravello and the sharp thousand-foot descent to sea level. It had been created in the late nineteenth century by an Englishman, Lord Grimthorpe, a large, handsome house with vast ornamental gardens and decorative statuary. At his death Grimthorpe had bequeathed most of the estate to his son and a smaller piece of property of about ten acres on the lower western side in the shape of an irregular triangle to his daughter, Lucy Frost, who proceeded to have La Rondinaia built at its southwestern edge. On a nasty late-autumn day Howard, alone, went down to Ravello and saw the house for the first time. As he walked the quarter of a mile from the piazza to the house, with a vista of the sea and the distant hills to his left, a long cypress alley to his right, he intuitively felt, without even having seen the house, that Gore would want it. "When I first walked in through that gate and I saw the amount of land, I thought to myself, 'Gore's going to love it. It doesn't matter what the house looks like.' "

When Gore came down from Rome with Howard and George Armstrong and saw it, he did. But there were obstacles. The house itself—which had been completed after five years of construction in 1925, built in the Saracen style, one length of the building at the edge of the cliff with magnificent views, the other side against the cliff rising behind it, on three levels, with four bedrooms, a flowing, graceful interior design, and numbers of terraces—needed attention. During the war it had served as a convalescent home for British officers. The plumbing was dismal, the windows bad. The house could be used only in mild weather; access was difficult. The current owners, retired Italian businesspeople who lived in Rome and used it only for the summer, were eager to sell. Their aging legs made getting to the house difficult. Actually a private and level road went directly from the town square, where cars could be parked, to the house, though it was a long walk. But part of the road went across property that did not belong to La Rondinaia. The lady of La Rondinaia had had a falling-out with the lady of the private road. To get to the house, the owners of La Rondinaia had to take the only alternate route, which involved climbing steep flights of steps. Grand Italian families would not conceive of walking such a distance and over a hill. Consequently the house had been on the market for seven years. Like Edgewater, La Rondinaia came with a liability that drove down the price. The entire property, which included two agricultural terraces, was for sale for 1 billion lire. Though it was sparsely furnished, everything within came with the house. Two additional terraces, for lemon and olive groves, added another 60 million lire, in all about $272,000. Gore could pay cash. There would be no mortgage, which anyway would have been difficult for an American to get for Italian property. Early in 1972 La Rondinaia was his. He had, again and at last, what he felt was a home. In June they drove the heavily loaded old Jaguar down to Ravello. From the piazza they excitedly walked over the flights of steps until they arrived on the road level with the house. The luggage would be carried by young men from the town, happy to have employment. To the left the great sea stretched southward to Graecia Minor. To the right the cypress trees sparkled in the sun.

CHAPTER SEVENTEEN

The View
from La Rondinaia

1972–1978

ON A SPLENDID June day in 1972, as Gore Vidal looked out from his study at La Rondinaia, he saw two white eagles, catching the bright sunlight, turn characteristically golden. Soaring from their cliff habitation into the vista that opened south and westward, they framed themselves like white fire against the sky. As his gaze moved thousands of feet downward to the first point where he could see the water, there were fishing boats and ferries moving across the sea. Years later, each morning so regularly that he could anticipate its passage, an amplified voice from a tourist boat could be heard, saying in a half dozen languages, "There, in Ravello, in his villa, lives the famous American writer, Gore Vidal." To his right, a stack of yellow legal-size lined sheets covered with his nearly indecipherable scrawl represented one third of the first draft of his novel-in-progress. Conceived as his first synthesis of American history and fiction, *Burr* began Vidal's identification in the public mind with the great American revisionist narrative, a look at American history through the eyes of a knowledgeable realist with an analytical overview. Though novels like *Myra Breckinridge* would speak mainly to his literary reputation and his general notoriety, *Burr* and the other historical novels that followed made him a household name as a writer in his native country. Most Americans were not interested in literature. Many, though, were interested in their country's history, which had increasingly become the fiefdom of dry specialists. Less of it was being taught in the schools, and a certain national impoverishment, as Americans became less knowledgeable about their country's past, became evident. With *Julian*, a distant subject for modern readers, Vidal had seen the potential of historical fiction. His own mastery of the historical past could be combined with his talent for credible characterization, for vivid contextual evocation, and for driving narrative pace. With *Washington, D.C.* he had had a taste of the potential. Beginning with *Burr* he was to realize it over the next twenty years in a series of historical fictions that, like the two eagles over the Ravello cliffs, had moments in which they turned golden.

Burr had coalesced in his imagination in late 1969 or early 1970, about the time *Two Sisters* went to press. The Auchincloss connection with the Burr family was in the distant background, particularly since his relationship with his half-sister Nini was at this time as close to a friendship as it would ever be, including their shared antipathy to Nina, with whom Nini kept tenuously in touch. Having sold her Southampton house, Nina had moved to Cuernavaca, where she did little to no drinking. At her best she played bridge competitively. At her worst, her memory failing, increasingly accident-prone, addicted to sleeping pills, she could not keep track of cards, money, or people. Overall, her life still ached with chaos, occasionally almost collapsed. Once beautiful, she hated what she saw in the mirror, an increasingly isolated figure who as always blamed others for her misfortunes. She as often boasted about her successful son as complained about his alienation. With Nini, Gore's fondness had its frustrations, partly because she was taking so long to write her biography of Senator Gore—which became an unfulfilled lifelong project—mostly because of her own chaotic personal life. Her right-wing Republican politics and Washington clubbiness appalled him. Other than Howard, she was, though, the only family he had. Tommy and he had hardly any relationship. The rest were dead. Cousins and other relatives from the Gore or the Vidal side he had at most occasional contact with. That was that for blood kin, though when Nini gave birth to her third son, whose name celebrated the distant family connection to the Founding Fathers, Gore dedicated his new novel to "my nephews, Ivan, Hugh and Burr." Other than with Nini, family was essentially historical, a part of his past and America's history.

As he worked on *Burr* from late 1969 to late 1972, his sense of familial identification with America's past gave to the novel's characters a group identity and particularity, as if, in fact, each had just walked into the room. This was to be characteristic of all his historical novels, as though he had less difficulty in sustaining the metaphor of an American national family because he had virtually no immediate family in the present. Part of the compelling attraction of *Burr* was the subtextual inference that in the close-knit world of the Founding Fathers the great leaders were almost familially connected to one another. The effect came from both the vividness with which they were re-created and from the descriptive particularity of historical setting. And the creation of a totally invented narrator, whose unresolved parenthood eventually reveals to character and reader that his father is Aaron Burr himself, provides a fictionally powerful undercurrent, emphasizing the search for family. The invented personal narrative and the historical narrative become thematically inseparable, though Vidal's mastery of the fictional narrative is matched by his mastery of the historical facts. The library of about two hundred books on Burr and his contemporaries he had bought in Los Angeles and shipped to Ravello he supplemented with standard editions, especially of letters, the obvious ones identified for him by Arthur Schlesinger, whom he had asked for suggestions. That Schlesinger, now holding the Albert Schweitzer Chair in the Humanities at the City University of New York, was writing a laudatory account of Robert Kennedy's life did not diminish the cordiality between them. But time and distance, and Vidal's retrospective view that Schlesinger had been a Kennedy courtier and now was making a profession out of revisionist praise and occasional concealment, attenuated what had once been a friendship.

Another friendship, also with a professional connection to *Burr*, had grown closer. Vidal had left Little, Brown for Random House. Little, Brown had treated him handsomely. They had been successful together. *Two Sisters* had sold poorly. But the previous three novels had been bestsellers, and Gore had found the combination of Arthur Thornhill, Sr., and Ned Bradford particularly effective. His most recent volume of essays, *Reflections Upon a Sinking Ship*, had gone to two printings for a total of 9,000, a handsome sale given the genre, and the author recognized that nothing

Little, Brown could have done would have made *Two Sisters* a bestseller. In fact, its publicity and distribution people had performed well. Little, Brown had recently been purchased by Time Warner, but it still maintained its independence and reputation as a serious trade press especially effective with literary books. Though Arthur Thornhill, Sr.'s, retirement was imminent, the firm was still in good hands.

"What about our new contract?" Bradford asked Gore at the beginning of 1969. The next month Bradford had on his desk a letter from Jason Epstein: "Is there a chance that you'd let us include Gore Vidal's *Julian* in Modern Library?" The answer was yes, as it could not be otherwise, since of course Bradford knew, directly or indirectly, how eager Gore was to be in a series that specialized in canonically great writers. Little, Brown's remuneration would be small. "On the other hand," Jason responded, "we very much want Gore in the series and I know that he would like to be there too." The shrewd Bradford probably saw what was coming. By May, Jason could tell Gore that *Julian* was set for the next spring. "I must say that I'm delighted that after such coyness we're doing the book. What shall we do next?" Epstein knew that the Modern Library bait was irresistible. "I wanted Gore as an author right from when I met him. It would be silly not to. Gore said nothing at first and waited. Then I remember," Epstein recalled, "there was that quid pro quo with Modern Library. Maybe the failure of *Two Sisters* precipitated the departure from Little, Brown. We never discussed why he was leaving. One day he said he wanted to come to Random House. Something like that. I remember writing him a letter, though, about Modern Library. I would have been delighted to put *Julian* into Modern Library, but why not get him too?" Jason may have argued that Little, Brown's location in Boston made it less desirable than Random House. Or that Random House would do a better job with his books. He hardly had to do much direct persuasion. Simply to imply that Modern Library would do more of Vidal's novels was a powerful lure. In addition, they were friends, though that was never explicitly part of the discussion between 1969 and 1971 that moved Gore toward Random House. Restlessness, drift, the unwillingness to oppose gathering forces, and the latent hope that a new publisher would do more, would have fresh enthusiasm, contributed to his gradual realization that he was allowing himself to be moved. When Gore mentioned that he was contemplating a novel based on the life of Burr, Epstein, whose special interest was history and social science, encouraged him. So too did Bradford. In mid-1970 Little, Brown offered a contract for an academic to do a biographical-critical study of Vidal, an expression of their commitment to their author. "If you don't think you'll sustain any loss by such a book, why not?" Gore urged. In spring 1971 Bradford sent the contract "for the Aaron Burr novel together with a supplementary agreement making the accrued royalties," almost $300,000, "on the previous books available to you in January next year," to Gore's accountant, Michael Hecht, Bernard Reiss's protégé, who had been handling Vidal's contracts since he had left William Morris. With no word to the contrary, Bradford still proceeded as if Little, Brown were to publish *Burr*. In June, Roger Straus, having heard from Gore that he had destabilized his relationship with Little, Brown and hoping to persuade him to move to Farrar, Straus, flattered him about his "damned good essay" in *The New York Review of Books*. "I gather you worked out your LB problems before you took off. Let me know when things break loose, for obviously my interest remains."

Bradford was not surprised when finally, in September 1971, Vidal, somewhat guiltily, broke the news. "My dear Gore," he responded, "naturally I was saddened by your letter. And, yes, shocked—although, I must say, only in the way one is when told that the imminent death of a relative or friend has finally occurred. Now I hope you find some new green meadows in this country that look as fair to you in their way as those new ones of yours in [Ireland]. And let's do keep in touch," which they were to do over the next years. Once Gore made his wishes known, Bradford helped facilitate the move to Random House by cooperating in settling the complicated financial arrangements. It was an additional inducement to sign a contract with a $235,000 advance, most of it for *Burr*. Gradually his backlist was moved to Random House, though Little, Brown for some time had rights to the books it had most recently published. Bradford, who regretted Gore's departure, genuinely liked and admired him. In retrospect, Gore thought Bradford, with whom he had gotten along so well, the best editor he had ever had, with the exception of Nick Wreden, mainly because Bradford was equally enthusiastic about books as different as *Washington, D.C.*, and *Myra Breckinridge*. When in 1973 Bradford expressed interest in property in Ireland, Gore gave him the benefit of his own experience and later that year sent him an inscribed copy of the Random House edition of *Burr*. "I nearly dedicated *Burr* to you but then thought that this might be complicated all around." Bradford sent back a congratulatory note. "Clearly you're getting richer and richer. Everything considered," the stoical editor concluded, it is "a development I view for once with utter equanimity." Gore would have gotten equally rich, both he and Bradford knew, with Little, Brown, and over the next decades he faulted himself for disloyalty, or at least insufficient gratefulness, and often felt that the new publishing relationship had been a Faustian bargain in which he had lost, over the years, in a different sort of currency, more than he had gained.

For both Jason Epstein and Gore Vidal the new dimension to their relationship had its hazards, though in the long run the risk was essentially on the personal side. They had been friends since the late 1950s, from Dupee-Rovere days at Edgewater. Both ambitious, both strong-willed, during the 1960s each had pursued fame and fortune in his own way. By mid-decade Epstein had become a powerful figure in the publishing world. That Anchor Books had led the way in the creation of the paperback industry added the cachet of visionary practicality to his reputation for intellectual brilliance. Now the dominant young editor at Random House, also with high management responsibilities, he had wanted Gore to be one of his authors almost from the start of their friendship. The success of *The New York Review of Books* had provided an additional bond, though Jason, a part owner, played no editorial role. The familial connection was intensified by Gore's closeness to Barbara. An effective editor of his essays with whom he occasionally had differences of opinion, she had a talent for avoiding confrontation, a compelling need to soothe. If in the domestic and publishing bestiary Jason was the argumentative, peremptory bear, Barbara was the domesticated doe, the gracious, dark-eyed, and soft-spoken creature quietly grazing in the meadow, sensitive, easily startled, of whom Gore felt protective, fraternal. With Jason the closeness was never without some tension, partly two assertive personalities clashing, partly because from the start Gore was never sure he had done the right thing in succumbing to Jason's professional blandishments.

————————

During the year before his first summer at Ravello, as he worked on *Burr*, he alternated his interest in the political and military machinations of the Founding Fathers with his concern about America's role in the modern world, especially the seemingly unending war in Vietnam, which in his election campaign in 1968 Richard Nixon had promised to bring to a speedy conclusion, based on a plan he refused to divulge. Once elected, it was clear Nixon had no plan other than to be more brutally militaristic than even Johnson had been. For Vidal, as for many others, the Vietnam War had become a noxious trauma, its corrosive destructiveness a constant preoccupation. He talked about it, dreamed about it, argued against it. Having gradually formed the view that American history had from the beginning manifested a predilection for wealth through aggressive conquests, from Andrew Jackson's Indian Wars to the Mexican-American War, the Civil War, the Spanish-American War, and now the Vietnam War, he had begun to call America's international presence "the American Empire." It was not a phrase most Americans liked hearing. The nation on the whole maintained an unself-conscious disconnection between its view of itself as a peace-loving republic uninterested in exploiting others and the reality of its far-flung dominance. Often, under the pretense of fighting international communism, America had been expanding its own economic and political power, at great cost to domestic stability and prosperity, and in the cases of Korea and Vietnam at the expense of substantial amounts of American blood. Much as he had grown to hate Lyndon Johnson, Vidal had become even more hostile to Nixon, who, unlike Johnson, had few to no redeeming elements. As a realist, Vidal expected politicians to lie, manipulate, and maneuver. That was in the nature of their profession. But Nixon seemed excessive in these matters, and, unlike Johnson's, his domestic program seemed dedicated to maintaining and enriching his electoral base. Everything Vidal valued in public life—justice, fairness, open-mindedness, noninterference in the private life of the individual, a commitment to the Bill of Rights—the Nixon administration opposed, explicitly or covertly. The FBI, as Vidal saw in its attacks on the New Party, whose 1972 presidential candidate, Ralph Nader, he supported, had become an instrument of oppression. America seemed to be turning into a police state.

As he made progress with *Burr*, a novel partly about the politics of the eighteenth century, the idea came to him to write a satirical play about politics in the twentieth century, in which Nixon would be the main character. His dialogue would consist almost entirely of words the real Nixon had uttered in public discourse. The other main characters would be George Washington, whom he had begun to dramatize in *Burr*, Eisenhower, and John Kennedy, with two contemporary figures, called "Pro" and "Con," one loosely based on William Buckley, a Nixon supporter, the other representing his own views, who would comment on the characters. Washington would be depicted as critical of Kennedy's and Nixon's militaristic ambitions, Eisenhower as a golf-playing nonentity, Nixon as a mendacious, power-mad psychopath. Suddenly preoccupied with the idea of the play, he stopped work on *Burr*, barely under way, to write *An Evening with Richard Nixon*. Within a short time of its completion in late summer 1971, he had a publisher and a producer. Jason of course did not balk at the prospect of Random House's putting it out. "Sure, I was happy to publish *An Evening with Richard Nixon*. It was funny. It was a way of getting Gore started at Random House," and whatever minor loss there would be in printing a small edition, scheduled for March 1972, would be outweighed by having Vidal under contract for *Burr*. In mid-October, Gore sent the play to New York. "Here it is," he wrote to Jason. "I've put a red line in the margin opposite the speeches that are invented. I think there should be a different kind of type for the invented—but *not* italics. Bolder Roman, say . . . ? I'll write a one page note for the beginning, explaining what's real and what's not." That there would actually be a stage production was uncertain, in part because there had not yet been time to determine that but also because the play had limited theatrical potential. There was no plot in the conventional sense. It was a topical play about political ideas, hardly the usual stuff of Broadway box-office triumphs. Only the national preoccupation with the Vietnam War and the passion Nixon and his policies aroused made it potentially though problematically viable, especially perhaps on college campuses and in a New York theatrical situation that kept costs as low as possible. Nixon supporters would not be likely to flow in from the suburbs to see the play. The vast uncomfortable middle, uneasy with the war but unwilling to oppose it actively, would not be eager to buy tickets to be made even more uncomfortable. Spending an evening with Richard Nixon would not be much fun even in the best of circumstances. Political theater was rarely commercially successful.

That *An Evening with Richard Nixon* was to close after thirteen performances on Broadway was partly a given of the genre, mostly the result of the honorable if not idealistic misjudgments of the producer, Hillard Elkins, who was delighted to be working with Gore, hated Nixon, and hoped he might make the play a commercial success. Gore met "Hilly" through Claire Bloom, who had married him in 1970, soon after her divorce from

Rod Steiger. The marriage "obviously was over long before that," Howard recalled. "Claire had been seeing Hilly. There was a plan that he was to get in touch with her via our address. However, neither Gore nor Claire clued me into this little plot they'd hatched. So a telegram arrives for Claire Bloom care of Gore Vidal or something, and neither Claire nor Rod are in town. Rod calls and, unthinkingly, not knowing anything, I said, 'How strange, did you change agents or something?' They had changed apartments, and I thought it was probably her agent and he's got a job for Claire and doesn't know how to contact her. Steiger said, 'No.' I said, 'What do you want me to do?' He said, 'Will you do me a favor: open it and read it to me?' So I opened it and I'm reading just words. It sounds like baby talk. 'Can't wait to meet you for act 3, love and kisses,' and some name. It was from Hilly Elkins to Claire. She returned to Rome that day. Steiger confronted her with the telegram, and that was the end of the marriage. Gore, that same day, called me from New York, and I told him that this strange thing had happened. 'Why would Claire be getting telegrams here?' And he started calling me all kinds of names, 'Idiot and stupid,' and this and that! I felt, 'Oh, my God, what have I done?' The next morning at eight o'clock the doorbell rings. It's Claire. I said, 'Claire, I'm afraid I have done something so awful. I'm so mortified. I'll get on my knees.' 'You know,' she said, 'it was the best thing that could have happened to me. Otherwise I never would have found the courage to get out of this horrible marriage.' "

Elkins seemed to many as unlikely a match for Claire as had Steiger. Smart, energetic, fast-talking, domineering, with a huge wardrobe, an obsession with Napoleon, and an amusing effervescence that was both self-indulgent and charming, he had made two successful films, *Alice's Restaurant* and *A New Leaf*. He had produced a number of flashy but commercially unsuccessful Broadway plays, including *Golden Boy*, with Sammy Davis, Jr., and the musical *The Rothschilds*, as well as the economically successful *Oh! Calcutta!*, on which he worked closely with Ken Tynan. Five years younger than Vidal, a tense mix of liberal idealism and entrepreneurial commercialism, Elkins felt that there was nothing he could not do successfully, nothing that would not benefit from his salesmanship, including *An Evening with Richard Nixon*. As soon as he read the script in summer 1971, he determined to do it. Probably he raised money for the production from friends who were sympathetic to the play's message, perhaps people more interested in politics than theater. Vidal, who liked his brash high spirits, was delighted.

Soon Elkins, so dedicated to self-promotion that he had recently encouraged a book called *The Producer* that sycophantically chronicled his theater life during 1970–71, had a director, a cast, and the Shubert Theatre, "the largest musical comedy house on Broadway. I should have known then," Gore remarked, "as Claire should have known, about his acute megalomania, the phase he was going into, and I was so preoccupied I didn't notice it. I just said the theater's too big for this play. Musicals can't fill it. How can this play?" In December, Elkins tracked down the young director Ed Sherin, on holiday skiing with his sons, and soon wore down his resistance to what Sherin, with experience as a director in television, movies, and theater, most recently the Broadway success *The Great White Hope,* thought an untheatrical script. "I said, 'This is impossible. It's a political pamphlet in dialogue form.' He said, 'Don't you like it?' I said, 'Yeah, I like it.' He said, 'You mean to tell me you can't find a way to stage this?' I think Hilly wanted to do it because he wanted to do anything that would get press." An admirer of Vidal's essays and novels, Sherin shared Vidal's view of Nixon and recent American politics. When he had had a small role in *Romulus* in 1962 he had observed Gore during rehearsals looking unhappy at what seemed the play's likely failure. "I thought the play itself was miserably done," Sherin recalled. "Cyril was not fleshy enough, edgy enough, real enough for the role. You had that kind of buttery, creamy, wonderful largesse of Ritchard, but it had a vaudeville taint to it. I think that was a critical error, so that the real meaning of the play escaped the production. It was a much darker play than the one we put on." Sherin had a similar challenge with *An Evening with Richard Nixon:* how to make theatrically effective an unrealistic script grounded in a realistic contemporary political discourse consisting entirely of talk about rather than depiction of physical action or emotional tension.

Frenetically energetic, Hilly produced, Sherin directed, Claire watched nervously, filled with high expectations. Gore and Howard came from Rome in January. Sherin, who had not seen Gore for ten years, noticed that he looked older, more mature. The young man had disappeared. In February, rehearsals went into high gear in preparation for a month of tryouts. The brilliant, seriously comedic George S. Irving took on the role of Nixon. To bridge the gap between political realism and theatrical fantasy, as well as to deal with the large cast of characters, Sherin decided to make use of masks and have numbers of actors play multiple roles, including the relatively unknown Susan Sarandon. Claire thought Sherin "wonderfully creative, brilliant." Gore, looking to explain the play's failure, was less appreciative. Sherin "wasn't right for the play. But the whole thing was doomed anyway. I can't blame him for anything." During rehearsals Sherin noticed Gore's playfulness, his charm. "But I always felt that there was an agenda there. That was part of his power and also something that made me somewhat unnerved when I was around him. You always thought he was looking around the back of your head. A very bright man but very careful. Almost premeditated. It looked as if he had written the script before he'd gotten to the meeting. I'm not talking about a business meeting. I'm talking about life, about personal interactions. Very controlled, careful. The only fun that Gore ever had with me was when he would talk about my hidden desires to be a homosexual, and that was fun. He would come on a little bit about 'You don't really know what's going on inside you,' and so forth. Then he would say that pickles were very important. You had to eat a lot of dill pickles in order to keep your pecker hard, or something like that. He was charming even when he was playful, and then he said some very wonderful things to me about my work. And it bonded me to him."

As rehearsals progressed, Vidal rewrote the script, the performance version considerably different and much shorter than the Random House edition. In late March 1972 a month of previews began. Elkins had decided there would be no out-of-town openings. Gore came regularly to rehearsals. "We were perfecting it or trying to. I was giving them new stuff all the time. Hilly was hysterical. That's his nature. He was either stoned or jittery. He wasn't much help." Press releases and word of mouth let the world know that a politically inflammatory anti-Nixon play was about to open. Gore appeared on the Cavett and Susskind shows. Soon author and producer were getting anonymous hate letters, including death threats. On the one hand, they seemed preposterous. On the other, they were unnerving. "The only bomb scare that I knew of," Sherin later joked, "was that we were going to close." Apparently "a few Republicans set fire to the balcony," though it appears to have been confined to a wastepaper basket, "and there were all kinds of disruptive things," Gore recalled. Men in dark suits and white shirts, who announced that they represented the White House, came to one of the previews. As they left, one of them waved pleasantly. "When the Nixon deputy smiled and waved, we knew," Sherin recalled. " 'Enjoy your-selves,' they must have said. 'Put this on in Manhattan, the hotbed of American radicalism, it won't hurt us.' " Though the director, the producer, and the author then and later found it compelling to think they were being stalked by the FBI, the IRS, and the Watergate plumbers, a New York anti-Nixon Broadway play had no national significance. Only those involved assumed (and usually briefly) that political theater had a political impact. Elkins and Sherin were more worried that the play would not have enough theatrical impact. Sherin felt he had gone as far as he could with pratfalls. More would be counterproductive. Elkins arranged a lunch at Sardi's with Elaine May, whom he wanted to consult about adding jokes. "Elaine was rather embarrassed," Gore remembered, "but wonderfully insane. She didn't have any jokes. It wasn't her field. We had a strange meeting at Sardi's. She had just watched the play. . . . It was really kind of a seminar on comedy. How you get jokes. How you make people laugh. I knew quite as much about it as she did. But all very amiable and all pointless," because, as Sherin saw, of the gap between Vidal's belief that he had written an important political play and the producer's desire to do whatever necessary to have a commercial success. "Gore's the sweetest man in the world, but he's not the world's greatest dramatist," Sherin observed. "He's a great novelist, great essayist, and that's what *Nixon* is—a political essay in dialogue form. You want to chortle when you read it, 'Look at this. Did that asshole really say that?' 'Oh, that bastard, did he do that about Cambodia, and did he really go to the Lincoln Memorial steps and pray to Lincoln? My God!' But you don't want to see that up on the stage. That's what came out of that meeting at Sardi's. Gore said that's what it is, and it's wonderful. Elaine didn't know what to say. And Hilly was responding to the fact that he was the ringmaster at Barnum and Bailey's Circus. He just wanted to pull out any stops he could."

The play opened on May 6. Some of the reviews were respectable, though hardly glowing. The *New York Times* headlined Clive Barnes's review "Evening with Richard Nixon Is for Radical Liberals," complaining that the play had "no real drama, no real excitement." To attack Nixon this way was "no more exciting than seeing candy taken from little kids." Still, this recent British arrival conceded, "some people might like to see a mean and nasty play about our President." Very few got the opportunity. "Sorry you didn't see the play," Gore wrote to Ned Bradford. "It was one of the best evenings I've ever spent in the theatre (this quite modestly, as actors, director and Nixon et al contributed)." The play closed after two weeks. In Gore's recollection the preview audience had been ecstatic. "Then it all ended with one review in the *Times* by an Englishman who said he knew nothing about politics. He'd been a dance reviewer. A nice little fellow, but he was told to write a bad review and he did. It wasn't that bad: he kept saying how funny it was. And then he said that Gore Vidal has said mean and nasty things about *our* President. I remember that sentence." It was his third consecutive theatrical failure, "the only failure that bothered me, because I believed it was a good play." If there was ever a reasonable postmortem, it would have concluded that Sherin's analysis was sensible. It was not the subject matter, as Gore insisted, that had sunk the play but the difficulty of making it into an effective theatrical experience for a large audience. For Elkins it had been a triumph of self-assertion. "The day before the play opened, he went to bed for two weeks" in his Manhattan brownstone, which, Gore joked, "looked like Elba." His Napoleonic obsession "made everybody nervous, and it drove Hilly mad, it finally did. I don't think he even knew when the play closed. He was just lying there in bed with a great smile on his face, smoking pot. Nothing was done, not that there was anything to do." For Claire "the first night," she soon wrote Gore, "was one of the most exciting evenings in the theatre I have ever had," but "this was not just the death of a play, but a condemnation of the American people." For Gore it had been an exhausting, dispiriting experience, one that brought him to the edge of collapse, though he managed to disguise from almost everyone just how miserable he felt. For a while he worried he might be about to have a breakdown. It seemed like the misery he had experienced just after Alice Astor's and John Latouche's deaths. Soon he and Howard were back in Rome. "My blood pressure nearly took the top of my head off those last few days," he wrote to Claire. "But now it falls as my spirit soars, freed of *that* place!," by which he meant New York. In June he took possession of Ravello. The bright spring sun revived him. So too did *Burr*. By midsummer he was back at work, and almost happy.

———·———

With his forty-seventh birthday imminent, he was relieved to be in reasonably good health and at the same time fearful that the next year would bring some near-fatal misery of the sort he associated with his father and his grandfather at about the same age. Gene Vidal had had his life-shattering heart attack at the age his son was soon to turn. Senator Gore had, at the same time in his life, almost died from influenza and had never quite gotten his full strength back again. In youth his grandson had been "a hypochondriac; saw nothing but skull beneath the bone." His thanatophobia still remained strong, though over the years it had switched its focus from the undesirability of being dead to the fear of experiencing some debilitating process in which his body would waste away or, even worse, he would lose his mind without knowing it. Skittish, superstitious, there was no disaster scenario that did not occur to him while he waited for the results of ordinary medical tests. "Skin cancers fall away; but hypochondria mounts," he later wrote to Claire Bloom. "Why so many extra white cells, doctor? What— you always use cobalt for a minor sinusitis? Nothing serious of course. What an anticlimax death will be!" Fortunately, all alarms turned out to be false. Except for a tendency to high blood pressure and the 1940s hepatitis that still skewed his test results, he was in fine health, and his occasional fears alternated with an ironic self-awareness that allowed him as often to joke as to worry about death. Still, he was soon happy to have the year behind him, to be able to think, without fear of contradiction, that at least his forty-seventh year would not carry as much bad luck for him as it had for his father and grandfather.

Despite the failure of *An Evening with Richard Nixon,* much of the year had been productive. As soon as they took possession of La Rondinaia in June, Gore felt as if once again he had a home, as he had only once before felt he had, at Edgewater. Here, though, most friends had to be imported, usually for short visits, with the exception of an Englishman who lived in walking distance and who, with his dog Caligula, introduced himself soon after their arrival. A writer specializing in historical novels and books about flowers, Michael Tyler-Whittle, two years younger than Gore, had been trained in law and literature and had become an Anglican clergyman. A superb amateur botanist, he would be elected a fellow of the Linnaean Society. Deeply conservative in theology, he was an oversized, affectionate man, a lover of good food and wine, and an avid social conversationalist who thought matters of liturgy and ritual more important than considerations of personal conduct, especially sexual matters. He had faith that God would accept and forgive. Gore's sexual preferences did not distress him in the least. Recently married, he had moved in 1970 from England to the Amalfi coast, which had become the base for his ministrations to the Anglicans in the area and pastoral activities in other parts of Italy. Widely known as the "vicar of the divine coast," he and Gore immediately took to one another. Tyler-Whittle and Howard got along well. Soon he was a frequent visitor at La Rondinaia. Most other visitors had to come from a much greater distance, including Claire, probably exhausted by Hilly, with whom there was increasing tension. She came with her young daughter for two weeks in July 1972. "I think you know how much our friendship means to me," she wrote to Gore, "and that I *do* love you. I mean that completely, and see no reason to change. We are very lucky. Few people have so much between them as we do." Gore himself had communicated that sentiment to her and the world, without using her name, in *Two Sisters*. "Recently I spent an afternoon full of silences in the Protestant Cemetery," he had written, "with someone I did not have an affair with a dozen years ago—too much silence at a crucial moment on a midnight beach, and a sense she was distracted by someone else—yet we continue to see one another year after year and affection grows, unstated and undefined and all the deeper perhaps for that. . . . I think how remarkably beautiful she is, as one marriage ends and another begins, and how we are once again together, in transit, emotionally. I prepare myself for the new husband, hopefully an improvement on the old." Claire had been and continued to be a road not taken. But, as she later remarked, "it was there [that feeling with Gore]. But I was always in love with other people. I loved Gore. Very continuously. Those letters [from me to him] surprised me. No, it was never meant to come to anything. When something is there like that it will always be there. I never thought it would come to anything. I don't know why. I never really knew or thought that Gore was gay. . . . I was so dumb in those days. Awfully dumb because he didn't stop telling everybody. Certainly in Rome I did know. Those things don't matter if you want to have a life with someone, but there was never any question about that. . . . We never talked about a life together." Howard and Gore, though, did speculate then and later about what might have been. "There are many times we've spoken about what would have happened if," Howard recalled. "And I say, 'You really should have married Claire. She's wonderful company, and she would have fit right in here beautifully.' I'm not quite serious, you know. Gore sometimes says, 'Yeah, it depends.' Of all the women that we do know, she would have been the best."

Diana Phipps, who spent most of the summer on Capri, "half an hour away by boat," he also saw regularly. Her luxuriant dark hair, self-possession, and full-figured beauty he found seductive, an exception to his general inclination to be attracted to petite women like Elaine Dundy and Claire. "So it is a time of water fetes," he told Jason Epstein. The summer brilliance of the Amalfi coast quickly obliterated the dark winter he had had in New York. When Barbara came that same summer with Elizabeth Hardwick, whom he had gotten to know through Lowell and now again through the Epsteins, he rented a boat for an excursion to Capri, and he and Barbara traveled to northern Italy together. They "waddled from great meal to worse meal in the high heat of Venice." Soon he was back at work on *Burr:* "70,000 words written, about a third I should think," he wrote to Jason in late June. "Odd things are happening to my characters, but then look what happened to their republic?" He wasted little time on recriminations about *An Evening with Richard Nixon.* Anger he enjoyed, and found mostly energizing. It rarely drained him, and he could also put it aside when it suited him, especially for work, for which he lived and for which he had, so it seemed to many, great physical and emotional stamina. His hatred of political and moral evil still focused on the Vietnam War, on the self-serving exploitativeness of church and state in America, on mindless attitudes and policies about sex, drugs, environment, politics, power, and war. A ceaseless polemicist, still convinced his words might make a difference, he rarely missed an opportunity to express his views to the largest possible audience. Despite his reservations, that was why he had agreed to appear with Buckley on television and why he turned his talk-show appearances into discussions about contemporary politics rather than his own books, the newest of which, *Burr,* finished in early 1973 and published in November, was soon a critical success and a huge bestseller. For the first time since *Julian* the laudatory reviews were almost unanimous. Jason, who had visited Ravello the previous summer, was as delighted as Gore. In March, soon after Gore had finished the manuscript, he and Jason met in Nice to initiate an eating tour, which took them through the Dordogne and eventually to Madrid. Both were gastronomes and epicures. Gore loved to eat. He had no interest in cooking, even of the most rudimentary sort. At La Rondinaia there were two servants, one of whom functioned part-time as a cook. Jason loved both to consume and to prepare food. Cooking, some thought, may have been his greatest passion. As they drove from one three-star restaurant to another, they ate and drank the best France had to offer. "I remember at the end of the tour I handed him *Burr* in two plastic bags. This was in Madrid," Gore recalled. "We went to the Ritz Hotel. He left and took with him the two plastic sacks." The Random House alliance had gotten off to a brilliant start.

With the publication of *Burr*, Vidal began to refashion what had been a single historical novel set in the Washington of his childhood into a grand scheme to dramatize his view of the dominant pattern of American history. *Burr* of course takes its name from the infamous Aaron, who succeeded in killing Alexander Hamilton, his political archrival, and came as close as the vice presidency to fulfilling his highest ambition. The present of the novel, set in New York City in the 1830s, is narrated by an invented journalist, Charles Schuyler, and the past by the aged Aaron Burr himself, as past and present are woven together in a story about national and individual parentage. Schuyler's narrative of his young manhood alternates with selections from Aaron Burr's journal of the Revolutionary War period, which the elderly Burr gives him to read. As a journalist, Schuyler is assigned to learn all he can about Burr, increasingly obsessed with the disgraced Founding Father. Amid historical accident Vidal finds the material for the plot of a novel. From the textbook facts he fashions dramatic moments that are vividly given a place and a time, a dramatic and novelistic setting. The two narrative voices have strength, resonance, authenticity. Washington and Jefferson have the reality of their weaknesses as well as their strengths, and Burr is far from the villain of his own story as he takes his place as a foundered Founding Father. In the end Schuyler discovers that he is Burr's illegitimate son.

The success of *Burr* had been anticipated late the previous year with *Homage to Daniel Shays, Collected Essays 1952–1972*. Suddenly readers were aware that there was now a substantial body of formidable essays on literary and political subjects. The title essay, published in August 1972 in *The New York Review of Books*, called for more democracy, not less, as the answer to America's problems. It seemed possible for the first time that "there now exists a potential American majority willing to see its best interests served not through the restrictive Constitution of the elite but through the egalitarian vision of Daniel Shays," in which human rights were more important than property rights. It was an optimistic reading of the 1960s, partly realized, as Gore observed in the 1972 presidential election season, in the democratization of the Democratic Party's nominating process. "What do you think of the title *Homage to Daniel Shays?*" he asked Jason. "I think it works, now that the new (and the last) piece suddenly brings into focus twenty years of political uncertainty and waffling. The last sentence is a new departure." It was the Constitution itself that needed changing, Vidal had come to believe. As a document, it valued property more than human rights. It had turned both major political parties into mirror images of one another. In this crucial regard there was little to no difference between Republicans and Democrats. Unfortunately, if one wanted to be in politics, there was no alternative. The New or People's Party had failed. "I quit the People's Party," Gore wrote to a friend, "to avoid the group therapy sessions which were based on a perfect misunderstanding of human society—*any* society from Salem, Mass to Mao-Peking. Possibly the anthropologists will discover our true nature and help restore the lost Eden." To become successful in politics his grandfather had turned from Populist to Democrat. Senator Gore's grandson had now separated himself from all parties. The Senator had revered the Constitution as sacred. As a young man, he had memorized every word. His grandson now proposed that it be radically revised.

Frequent visits to America, mostly for business, helped Gore keep his finger to the pulse of American politics, which he remained eager to speak up about and contribute to, though as gadfly commentator rather than as participant. For both *Homage to Daniel Shays* and then *Burr*, he put into firm place what had already begun to be his pattern of appearances when he published a book, usually two to four weeks of radio, television, and print-journalism interviews in the major cities—particularly New York, Washington, Boston, Chicago, Los Angeles, and San Francisco—and about a week in London, usually following the American trip. In Boston, in November 1973, where he did an extensive interview for *Fag Rag*, he met John Mitzel, an activist for homosexual rights, the publisher of Glad Day Books, and later the owner of a Boston bookstore specializing in gay literature. They became friendly. Mitzel admired Gore's outspokenness, particularly on the issue of the legal mistreatment of homosexuals. As to the interview, "I sounded drunk when sober; you all the reverse! It is plain that I can never be president now," Gore wrote to him. He liked and respected Mitzel, though he told Dick Poirier, "I never do see much point to fag-mags—at least for those of us who can write elsewhere and say the same sort of thing. It is the dream of all these papers that the L.A. Chief of Police will become addicted to their style and, finally, like St. P. realize with a sudden blaze that Fags are not only GOOD but BETTER!" Whatever its ideological force, he did not want as a writer to be associated exclusively with a political or a sexual movement. In San Francisco he resumed his friendship with Joe O'Donohue, living on reduced means, whom he had not seen for almost twenty years and who solicited his help in getting his memoir-in-progress published. He found O'Donohue as amusing as ever, someone to see both for his company and for old times' sake. In autumn 1974 he spent months touring American campuses, speaking to audiences usually in the thousands, his main topics political reform and sexual civil rights. "I was only in town a few days," he told Louis Auchincloss, "after that 3 months of lecturing, whistle-stopping with splendid *large* crowds of masochists, lusting for my whip! As for such a mood in other times, look to Athens post-Syracuse, to Aristophanes, no mean lash himself and a proto-Myra-creator if ever there was one. Were our pretensions as a people and good luck (until recently) as an empire less then there would be no need for such fierce commentaries and diatribes. But we are deeply conceited . . . and so the necessary pin-pricks tend to become exercises in butchery. But to a good end, I like to think. The people-out-there, by the way, are a good deal more thoughtful than their rulers; they also know that they are being most beautifully and perfectly fucked. . . . What next?" As bitterly wounded as the nation still was by the Vietnam War, Nixon's resignation in August 1974 had taken some of the topical sting out of the subject. Clearly it was now only a matter of time before the final withdrawal. In late 1972 Vidal had remarked to Tom Driberg, "I'm sometimes in Ireland and therefore in London in my quest for *any* nationality other than this mark of Cain I bear with the rest of my unlucky countrymen." Their luck, he felt, was changing, even if slowly. Nixon's departure and the imminent end of the war made a difference.

So too, for him personally, did the success of *Homage* and *Burr*. And so did La Rondinaia, where he now extended the summers into longer stays. "The house is perfect—Italy—the gardens are beautiful," he wrote to Nini. "Ireland has sort of fizzled out for us too," Howard wrote to Ned Bradford in May 1973. "When you come and pay us a visit here you'll understand why. It's a paradise." Tom Driberg tried, to no avail, to tempt Vidal to consider buying a villa in Cyprus, with the inference that his own influence there was so great that either residence or citizenship would become available. Actually, Gore surmised, Tom's interest in getting him to Cyprus at least partly expressed his desire to spend more time there himself at little to no expense. Instead Driberg happily settled for frequent visits to La

Rondinaia, where Gore set him up for long periods in one of the guest rooms. Driberg's mission was to improve his health, which was increasingly poor, and to write a candid autobiography. In 1974, after two years of trudging over the steep steps to the entrance to the villa, Gore was able to buy access through the private road, which meant that he and his visitors could walk on a level path from the town square to the house. "We BOUGHT the right to the private road," he told Elizabeth Hardwick, "so no more climbing when next you come—soon, I hope: June, July?" As usual, Howard oversaw the redecoration at the Via Di Torre Argentina and the renovations at La Rondinaia necessary to make the house comfortable for occupancy during fall and spring as well as summer. With guests and by themselves they enjoyed boating and swimming at Amalfi, excursions to Capri, especially when Diana Phipps was there, the general sense of summertime well-being that Ravello provided. Italy never seemed more attractive to Gore. Especially at La Rondinaia, and also in Rome, he had as much privacy as he wanted for writing, more than he believed he ever could have in New York or Los Angeles. He felt in touch with the things about America he wanted to be in touch with. European television began to cover more American news. The mail brought stacks of newspapers and magazines. Knowledgeable and sophisticated visitors came through Rome regularly. His European life and American identity seemed functional and compatible.

In Rome there was now an absence that pained him. Judy Montagu, witty, tart, full of humor, alive with scowling barbs as well as warm affections, had been at the center of Anglo-Roman life, through both her own charm and her friendships with distinguished people. Whenever Princess Margaret came, Judy and Milton Gendel were her hosts. Their apartment on the Isola Tiberina served as a social and artistic center. Her friends assumed that her English and Roman life with Milton would continue for decades. Literary herself, she was at work on an edition of letters between her mother and the Liberal Prime Minister H. H. Asquith, a frequent subject of discussion with Gore. With her daughter in a British school, in the early 1970s she began to spend more time in London. Gore saw her there in the autumn of 1972. She came over to his hotel for a brief visit. To his surprise, "she had lost an enormous amount of weight. She thought she had cancer. She had a dress which buttoned down the back. She'd lost so much weight that every time she moved, rather painfully, two more buttons would open up, just fall out of the holes, and I would have to rebutton her. I would have thought there's something very wrong here." Whatever the cause of her obvious physical decline, apparently she avoided sustained medical care. In early November 1972, in London, just a little short of her fiftieth birthday, she suddenly died, perhaps an adverse reaction to an overuse of prescription drugs by a person severely weakened by illness. "She had never paused to get cured," her friend Colin Tennant wrote to the *Times of London,* quaintly stating her illness to have been consumption. "I asked Milton," Gore later recalled, " 'What killed her?' Milton for once was succinct. He said, 'Excess.' But also in her general personality. She overdid everything." Apparently some of her friends had realized she was not well. But the seriousness of her condition escaped most of them. "I feel dreadful about Judy dying," Princess Margaret told Gore in December, "as I know that if I had had her staying with me and under my not inconsiderable thumb I would have whipped her into hospital at once and tried to cure her sickness which was her downfall. Her funeral was beautiful with the tiny church packed with people bursting with love and sadness." Any excuse, including the obvious one of distance, was sufficient for Gore to avoid the service. Though far from one of the principal mourners, his strong affection and regard for her made her loss personal enough to seem principal to him. "Bad times," he wrote to Tom Driberg. "Grim about Judy." He had known her since 1948. She had been in England when he had first arrived. Then she had been in Italy as well. For him, her Roman presence had been strong, someone with whom he shared a sense of humor and a delight in chatty and catty talk, in mutual amusement. Both social creatures, they had enjoyed one another's sociability. Rome and life seemed less pleasurable without her.

The previous year Gore had helped make the case for Rome in *Fellini's Roma.* His brief scene, set in an outdoor trattoria in August during the Roman "Festival of Ourselves," had been filmed between midnight and 5 A.M. on a cold November night in 1971. Shivering, he had been asked the question, " 'Gorino, why do you live in Rome?' " "My answer varied with each take," Gore wrote two years later, "but the theme was always the same. The artist deals in illusions. Modern Rome has only three industries: the government, the Church, and the movies; each a dream-dispenser. I waffled about the world's end through over-population . . . and concluded that a city which calls itself 'eternal' is obviously the best place to watch eternity go down the drain." Watching also included an active social life with Romans, other Americans in residence, and British and American visitors. Most of his wealthy and aristocratic Roman friends, what he called his "Palace life," he began to see less of after his father's death and especially after the purchase of La Rondinaia. "One day I got tired of them and really stopped seeing them overnight. Rather rude, I must say, but I got tired of them. Romans don't care. That's why I liked them. They may or may not have taken it personally, but nothing bothers Romans." Judy Montagu's death ended the festivities at Isola Tiberina. Never having taken to one another, Gore and Milton Gendel remained uneasy if not sometimes contentious acquaintances. But with some of Judy's Anglo-Italian associates he had independent friendships, including his ongoing relationship with Princess Margaret. To be friendly with royalty was not entirely enjoyable, but during the 1970s they saw one another with enough frequency and mutual regard for the benefit to outweigh the inconvenience. "Princess Margaret is in the neighborhood," he wrote later in the decade to a new friend, Judith Halfpenny, a British-born Toronto librarian who had opened a correspondence by sending him a long letter about his work and to whom he began to send letters about twice a year. Princess Margaret is "very thin; off the booze (hepatitis); she looks like Queen Mary. I find her witty and sympathetic; every woman I know who knows her hates her. She comes to dinner tonight. Vegetables, she said wanly. Just vegetables."

Donald Stewart, an American writer with an Italian wife, alternating between Rome and Chicago, where he worked for *Playboy* magazine, entered Gore's Roman life. Stewart, a tall, handsome man whose father had been a famously successful Hollywood writer, had first met Gore at a New England winter resort in the early 1960s. A part of the *Paris Review* world, he now moved comfortably in Roman circles, which soon included, for Gore, an Italian specialist in American literature, Luigi Corsini—a Communist intellectual of sensitivity and subtlety who wrote on literature and politics—and the celebrated Italian writer Italo Calvino. Calvino turned out to be his neighbor in the nearby Piazza Campo Marzio between Via Di Torre Argentina and the Pantheon. Calvino was notoriously quiet, but he and Gore actually had conversations, the start of a friendship that included Calvino's vivacious wife, Judith, nicknamed Chichita. At his Rome apartment Gore frequently had small parties, evenings of conversation with interesting combinations of Italians and Americans, including Mickey Knox, who still lived in Rome, and of course George Armstrong. Ned Rorem, emblematic of the variety of his English and American visitors, whom he had met in New York in 1948, spent an evening in July 1970 with other guests at Via Di Torre Argentina. They had kept in touch with one another, mutually respectful, mutedly affectionate, through letters and occasional meetings. The day before, they had run into one another in the Piazza Navona. "Gore Vidal on the phone this morning," Rorem wrote in his diary, "seems not so much depressed as apologetic that I'd not recognized him. 'I've aged terribly,' he explains." When Rorem, hungry, arrived for dinner at eight-thirty, he was "ushered . . . onto a shabbily lavish roof garden. . . . 'Some day all this will be yours,' " Gore said. The romantic Rorem and the antiromantic Vidal enjoyed one another's conversation. "I'm sympathetic to virtually everything *chez lui* except the cynical stance. Those steely epigrams summing up all subjects resemble the bars of a cage through which he peers defensively. 'It's not that love's a farce—it doesn't exist.' Defensible. Yet it's just one definition, of something without definition. Rather than risk being called a softy, he affects a pose of weariness," which Rorem thought he had learned from Paul Bowles. "Still, Paul remains in Morocco and Gore in Italy. These are romantic decisions as well as practical. Vulnerability is a major factor in any artist's makeup. To disguise the fact is merely another way of making art." After hours of drinks they went as Gore's guests to La Carbonara in Campo de Fiore, dining "outdoors in the shadow of the Palazzo Farnese." A few days later, as Rorem was about to leave Rome, they had dinner again, with another group of people. After the others had gone, Gore walked Rorem halfway home in the early-morning fog. "He said: It's too bad I can't love anyone. But of course he doesn't mean it."

Longtime friends came, those from England more regularly, especially Tom Driberg and even John Bowen, who had no special Italian interest. Maria Britneva and Diana Phipps made frequent visits from London. Gore and Elaine Dundy kept in touch, mostly by mail, Elaine's funny "dear Gauze" letters part special code, mostly a delight, though her own emotional turmoil and her aspirations as a playwright kept her for the most part in the United States. The Newmans he saw mostly in America, though they eagerly did brief excursions together when the Newmans came to Italy. When they had last seen him in Los Angeles, they had given him another canine gift. The much-cherished but ill Billy, the survivor of the pair of cocker spaniels the Newmans and Howard had gotten for Gore at Edgewater, had had a dramatic final moment in Florence in 1970. Blind and deaf,

Billy was Gore's private passion and compassion, though Howard did most of the work of caring for him. They nursed and adored him. It was clear, though, that he would not survive much longer. Of the pleasures of a dog's life only his delight in eating, which he did greedily, remained. With George Armstrong they made one of their Florentine excursions, driving up from Rome in lovely mild weather. Gore, Howard, and Billy stayed at the Grand Hotel. From their terrace they had a view of the Arno. Before going to bed, they put the remnants of an expensive steak dinner out on the balcony for Billy. In the morning they were called by the hotel people: there was a dead dog on the pavement below. Billy had pushed the steak bone through the wide balustrades. Blind and deaf, he had pursued his meal beyond the edge. When George arrived in the morning, Gore came down to the lobby with Billy's corpse in a flight bag. "What's that for?" "Billy." "Billy?" "He's dead." Howard put the flight bag in the car trunk. They went on to have a scheduled lunch with Vernon Bartlett, whom Gore had not met before, a former member of Parliament now living in retirement in a villa near Lucca. "I have a little task to do," Gore said. "Do you have a shovel?" "Yes." "Lots of land?" "Of course." Gore dug a hole. Bartlett, in his seventies, insisted on helping. Then they went in and had lunch. Soon, in Los Angeles, at the Newmans', Gore was surrounded by dogs and children. The children and the other dogs disliked the newest acquisition, a small wire-haired terrier pup with one permanently bent ear. Since Billy was gone, why not take this dog off their hands? After dinner Gore drove back to the Beverly Hills Hotel with the dog in the car. That night, sleeping on his back, he was awakened by the dog's face a few inches from his. Both ears were, unexpectedly, completely up. With his ears up, his long tail, and his thin, tight-haired body, he looked a little bit like a rat, which Gore decided was now to be his name, not as disparagement but as affection. The deal and the bond were struck. Gore resolved that the dog was his forever.

Eager to see Greece again, he seized the opportunity when Claire told him she was planning to go herself and travel economically by bus throughout the country. "I thought I'd ask Gore if he'd like to go. I was going to go by myself, to get away from it all and do something I'd always wanted to do. I got a wire back from Gore saying he'd love to and he'd meet me in Athens." The marriage to Hilly had fallen apart. Gore lovingly did some hand-holding. "Through all these disastrous marriages Gore was there. He found them amusing and silly and accepted them because he loved me. He had good relationships with my husbands. When my second idiotic marriage ended, he was there to pick up the pieces." Claire stayed at the Via Di Torre Argentina apartment, though she found that the apartment itself made her uneasy in a way she later declined to talk about. It was not Gore's and Howard's sexual activities, she insisted, that had made her uncomfortable, though what Gore readily referred to as "the bunnies" may not have been part of the traffic during her visits. For Claire, Gore "turned away from women" because of his mother. "I don't think Gore is in any way gay genetically. Something happened. It seems to have turned him away from love. I don't believe that entirely. One has to accept what he says. I was aware of Gore's . . . sexual activities, but it was something I didn't . . . it was none of my business." Independent of anything else that happened, "I was always a little bit in love with Gore." Claire's mother found Gore charming and funny, but " 'why will he go on and on about the Kennedys?' " she would say. " 'Tell your friend he shouldn't go on and on.' " In March 1974 Claire met him in Athens, where they stayed at the Hotel Grande Bretagne, the start of a ten-day holiday together, first in Athens and then to all his favorite ancient sites, which he was eager to show her. Claire had never been to Greece before. He was in his element.

As they traveled together in a rented car with a driver, he helped keep her spirits up with funny references to Hilly's new lady. Hilly himself Claire had renamed "The Unmentionable." On the first day out of Athens, Claire went to the back of the car to check her suitcase. It was not there. Her favorite red-fox coat, which she had worn for years and which Gore thought ugly from the moment he saw her in it, was also gone. "I thought the coat . . . was really lovely. Gore hated it with a passion." After a moment of shock she felt relief. She would not "have to worry about toothpaste and clothes and rubbish. But he kept looking out the back window and saying, 'The red fox coat is loping down the road.' " At Nestos they climbed to the monastery. At Thermopylae, Aristodemus and *The Spartan* could not have been far from his mind. As they drove around the Peloponnese, he showed her Mycenae and Sparta. At Naphthlion one evening, as they dined, they watched the last of the rosy sunlight on the purple water. On the far side of the peninsula they headed for Olympia, where they climbed the nearby hills and looked across the breathtaking vista, then to Corinth and Delphi. At Thebes they had a wine-filled lunch and then went to the ancient theater at Epidaurus. "She was standing center on the stage, and I was way up in the top row with a camera," Gore recalled, "and I was not all that well focused myself, much less the camera. So she has a series of pictures of the top of her head only. You can see the widow's peak and the background of Epidaurus and that was it." Later "she evinced some displeasure at being removed entirely from the photograph except for her scalp," though neither of them considered the possibility that perhaps the photograph represented Gore's uncertainty about whether or not he really wanted her, in the larger sense, in the center of his picture. The trip was a great success. "Thank you for everything," she soon wrote him. "It was the dream of my life to see Mycenae, and Delphi, and I am happy I saw them with you. . . . I look back on the Greek trip as one of the great moments of my life."

For a man who had reinvented himself numbers of times as a writer, the patterns of his personal life, which had always been consistent, were now firmly in place. Daily life would alternate between Rome and Ravello and occasional travels for business or pleasure, including in December 1974 his first visit to Australia, where he publicized *Burr* and had lunch with the Prime Minister. His mainstay was work, which he did mostly at home, though he often took a manuscript with him when he traveled. By 1973 the work schedule for much of the rest of his life was set, a schedule that Howard remarked "he was born with. . . . Usually he gets up around nine-thirty. Right to his desk. Works two or three or four hours and then the rest of the day takes care of other things, though mostly he reads. That can go on till late. He's always got his nose in a book. Except when he travels, and even then. . . . The first thing he does every morning is answer his mail. . . . The little Olivetti. It's left there (by the door) and could get knocked down on the floor by anybody coming in. But I won't touch anything. I'm not allowed. . . . He writes novels in longhand but plays and essays on a typewriter. I think he was forced to do the typewriter for television plays so it would make it go faster. With novels he can be leisurely and take his time. . . . He writes a lot of notes. We have this special small stationery so that he can scribble just a line or two." More like his grandfather than either of his parents, he was almost always at work on something, a literary or political article, a television appearance, a speaking trip, a collection of essays, a historical novel, or one of what he called his inventions, the next of which, *Myron,* he began to work on in 1973, as he brought *Burr* to a conclusion. "I could not exorcise myself of Myra," he wrote to Dick Poirier in January 1974, "and so as much as I disapprove of sequels, I found myself again at her mercy. The beginning is, I gather, difficult and that will put people off, I fear. Also, unlike most novels, I have put too many things into a short space. But life is short and Myra lives!"

By early 1974 Jason and Jim Silberman, a taciturn, somewhat shy but sharp editor at Random House, essentially in agreement with Jason, had responded to *Myron*. Unenthusiastic, Jason raised questions about plot and pace, particularly that Myra makes her appearance as the other (and more interesting) half of Myron's personality later in the novel than he thought effective. "I couldn't figure out the time sequence," Gore later wrote to a friend. "My publisher thought the beginning unclear and I kept bring[ing] Myra closer and closer to page one when her original delayed entrance was, to me, gorgeous." Jason desired more narrative clarity and directness. Gore responded with some conciliatory revision. He soon saw that Jason's dissatisfaction with the novel's mechanics reflected his overall dislike of the genre, which included *Myra Breckinridge*. He wanted another *Burr*. Instead he got what he began to refer to as one of Gore's "Chinese boxes." Gore's pattern would be to alternate a historical novel with an invention. "We understood this more or less," Jason recalled. "It seemed Okay. *Myron* was the first one." But it was just barely okay. Both editor and publishing house knew that the sales for the historical novels would be much greater than for the inventions, though the issue was less sales than temperamental and aesthetic disjunction. As an editor Epstein found it almost impossible to be soothingly supportive.

> I can't pretend I like something if I don't like it, and he knew that I felt that way especially about those strange little books. All of them. I just didn't like them. . . . As an undergraduate I once went to the Chinese opera down here on Chatham Square. I wanted to see what it was. It was so disorienting. First of all, the houselights are on all through the opera. Old Chinese men are sitting around eating oranges, throwing the peels around, paying hardly any attention to what's going on on the stage. The stage is occupied by these people in fantastic costumes shrieking at the top of their lungs incomprehensibly. Men in the orchestra are dressed like the audience and playing

funny-looking violins, squeaking away. It was the strangest
experience. Then one of them would topple over on the stage,
dead. The prop man, also dressed like someone in the
audience, would come out and put a pillow under his head.
It was very confusing to me. I'm not good at being shocked.
I remember after that I was very upset for three or four
days. I couldn't pull myself together. I felt schizzy.

Clearly he could not be an enthusiastic editor for novels one of whose
purposes was to shock through aesthetic and moral transgressions. Gore
knew how Jason felt about the book. Jason knew that Gore knew. Both had
tacitly agreed to accept that as a given and proceed with their personal and
professional relationship. For the time being they were contractually bound,
though both would find it increasingly difficult to sustain personal harmony
within professional dissonance. At best, they assumed, Gore's historical
novels would keep them together as editor and author; the inventions would
not drive them apart. In March 1974, along with Silberman, a more restrained reveler than his companions, they undertook another eating tour,
partly in Gore's mind a celebration of the completion of *Myron*, scheduled
for publication late in the year. They concentrated on food, not literature.
With relentless aggressiveness, they ate and drank their way across Bordeaux. Jason apparently could consume more food, Gore more alcohol,
though both pushed their gourmet adventures into New York publishing-
world mythology. Neither accepted even the idea of restraint other than the
physical impossibility of having more. Gore dealt with the added pounds by
exercise and crash diets either at home or at spas. As to the alcohol, his daily
regimen normally, in Rome and at Ravello, included wine and drinks from
the later afternoon on. His tolerance was high. "I never saw anybody drink
as much as Gore in my life, ever," Jason later recalled. "We used to go on
these gluttonous trips around the south of France. We'd hire a car with a
driver because neither one of us could be trusted to drive. Usually just the
two of us. Must have been about a half dozen of such trips. Maybe four
times. One night we were at Rouen and we'd had a lot to drink. I could not
keep my eyes open. I didn't know which way I was walking. At the end of
dinner we walked upstairs. Gore had a bottle of Dom Perignon in his hand.
He was going to finish it." But Jason never once saw him drunk. Howard
thought "Jason and Gore were pigs. You can quote me. Pigs! And why

wasn't Barbara on the trips? There are some people who know a thing or two." Gore preferred to be called a glutton. "We were not eating everything in sight, but we were eating great meals."

To Epstein, Gore's inventions seemed drunken, chaotic, out of control. In fact, they were highly crafted, tightly structured narratives whose antirealistic imaginative flights expressed the same passions and ideas that ran through his essays and, to some extent, also the historical novels. At the beginning of *Myron* the bewildered main character finds himself suddenly in a totally strange, surreal time and place that he has entered by being pushed (by the not fully repressed Myra within him) through the screen of his television set from his San Fernando Valley home in the year 1964 onto the Hollywood set of a movie that is being filmed in 1948. Myra now attempts to reassert control over her/his body; her long-term scheme is to effect changes in the filming of *Siren of Babylon* that will help make the movie a success financially, save the movie studio and the studio system, and change the future of Hollywood by restoring the golden age of Hollywood films. The novel is structured partly as a grand psychomachy, a mental as well as physical war between Myron, eager to regain dominance, and Myra, intent on changing history and the world. In the narrative Myron's and Myra's voices alternate as they struggle for control, the conforming, brainwashed, unimaginative Myron and the creative, irrepressible, transgressive Myra. In a movie-set world, where the action occurs, a desperate but surrealistically parodic and mockingly absurd struggle occurs between Myra's effort to undo the wrong path taken in the past and Myron's effort to prevent her from succeeding. In the end mad (but mostly well-intentioned) Myra is subdued by the bland but brutally patriarchal Myron, who wants to return to his happy normalcy, to the triumphant reign of his social and political values in the age of Nixon. Like *Myra Breckinridge, Myron,* dedicated to George Armstrong, was thematically autobiographical. It too focused on issues of sexuality, gender, politics, and culture, and it especially dramatized the relationship between the divided mind of the culture and the divided psyche of the individual, an attempt by the author to create a novel that reflected his own hard-earned but still not totally secure sense of a unified and autonomous identity. He himself knew where he stood and how he felt about the critical issues. In a culture that pressured or punished nonheterosexual acts, he had established a situation that gave him great freedom to live his life as he chose. But most of those who desired sexual and political freedom had not. American society did not readily or easily provide the protections of the Bill of Rights to everyone. The pursuit of happiness was a risky venture. Great religious, political, and economic powers prospered by promoting implicit or explicit prohibitions. "Thou Shalt Nots" were written over most doors. The inventions were Vidal's attacks on the self-serving powers of repression that, in his view, unwarrantedly limited personal freedom. As long as one's freedom did not come at the expense of another's, then it seemed to him the highest value. All around him he saw coercive attempts to limit freedom, as Buckley had tried to use the libel laws to suppress his right of free speech. In *Myron,* in the first edition, the names of the conservative Supreme Court justices, whose legal decisions had supported limitations on privacy, were used mockingly, especially to refer to body parts and sexual acts. In later editions Vidal, rethinking the effectiveness of the joke, substituted normal usage. Satirical representations of Truman Capote, Norman Mailer, and even Henry James appear. The latter, the suavely mellifluous behind-the-scenes overall boss of the Hollywood studio, is black. The conventions of the realistic novel do not apply. *Myron,* which unlike *Myra* was a critical and commercial failure, takes its aesthetic cues from Swift and Sterne, its sensibility from black comedy, its agenda from Vidal's own politics, its preoccupation with television and movie-screen images and coordinates from the author's fascination with film. In the end Myron thinks his white-bread, pro-Nixon values are triumphant. He is finally totally in control of himself and "will sign off by saying that the highly articulately silent majority to which I am darned proud to belong are happy with things as they are and that we are not going to let anybody, repeat *anybody,* change things from what they are." The final chapter contains only two words, reminiscent of the reverse signatures Bowles and Vidal used when signing their letters: "!sevil aryM."

In October 1973 Vidal published in *The New York Review of Books* an essay, "West Point," that begins with his own birth and concludes with his father's death, the first of what was to be a series of essays that synthesized personal history with cultural commentary. For a personal essay "West Point" is dramatically impersonal. By personality and habit Vidal was not introspective. He preferred to turn his intellectual gaze outward, at the material world, at ideas and stories that reflected its structures and belief systems. Politics and society interested him more than psychology. He looked less into himself than at himself. At the same time, family history is central to the story, a way of positioning himself in relation to the military branch of the American empire to which his father and uncle belonged. Like many of his essays, its distinctive feature is that the intellectual exposition has a narrative, and the personal story is illustrative of larger issues and patterns in the national life. The world and its ideas exist most vividly in reference to where the viewer has been and currently stands.

By 1975, as he approached his fiftieth birthday, his views on politics and society were well known. He had been for twenty years a public man, appearing frequently in the media, print and electronic. He could be counted on to say something cogent and witty about the issues of the day. If he offended some, he entertained and stimulated others. As a visual image he had, so to speak, been aging in public, which gave an added intensity and resonance to his private response to what he saw in the full-length mirror in the apartment in Rome or at La Rondinaia or caught glimpses of reflected in storefront windows or airport passageways. The changes were unmistakable: his hairline had begun to recede, his forehead to have increased in size; black hair revealed gray flashes; olive eyes appeared darker, more prominent, as the eye wells and cheek line deepened and sharpened; the characteristic Gore-family ears seemed larger, the nose more substantial; his skin had begun to lose resilience, to show the breaks and sags of middle age. In his endless cycle of weight gain and weight loss, his posture and walk began to have an even more pronounced forward tilt, as if he were directing his center of gravity to some point slightly ahead of where he actually was; and that impression of slightly forward-propelled movement expressed emblematically the tilt of his personality toward constant engagement with what came next.

Just as he had trained himself not to look inward, except intellectually, he also preferred not to look back. He favored a disciplined ruthlessness about memories and feelings. Regret, especially remorse, he feared as disabling, though he could not suppress awareness of and regret at physical changes. That many had thought him a breathtakingly handsome young man was well and good, though he himself maintained that that had been how others had seen him, not how he had seen himself. But now to be unmistakably a middle-aged man, even if one the world thought handsome and distinguished-looking, was an entirely different order of consideration. He had been quite used to his young body; it seemed a little inconvenient and perhaps even a challenge to be asked to get used to this something else. In addition, it made unavoidable the point that there would be transformations beyond this one with which he would also have to deal and which would in turn deal with him.

Two attenuated presences from the past, who had hardly been in his mind at all, suddenly had definition again. He had not thought of Stanley Sofield or Pat Crocker in ages, neither of whom he had seen since the early 1950s. Sofield had been at the center of his St. Albans School experiences, the teacher there who had made the greatest impression on him and with whom he had kept in touch well into the 1950s. But they had not had any communication for many years. "Most sad about Sofield," he told Louis Auchincloss in late 1974, who had written him that Sofield had died of a "sudden and merciful" heart attack. "Strange how those teachers confronted during pubescence remain so vividly in the memory while the later ones blur and vanish." In April 1973 Gore learned that Pat Crocker, of whom he had been quite fond, had died of cancer in Antigua in December 1972. His mother had been with him for his last three painful months. "He is in a tomb in that beautiful little cemetery in Antigua," Penny Crocker told him in response to his consolatory letter, a genre that he took to with grace and diligence. Generally it was as close as he wanted to get to the dead. A batch of Gore's books that had been stored in Pat's house in Panajachel and twenty of his letters to Pat, which Pat had carefully saved, surfaced. Most of the books had dedications from the author to Gore, including two of Anaïs's novels, a book of poems by Louise Nicholl, a novel by Somerset Maugham, and Michael Arlen's *The Green Hat*. The list evoked much of his youth and early manhood. What, Pat's executor wanted to know, should he do with the books and letters? "Maybe you would like to file [the letters] away for some future biographer, whose task will not be any the easier from your . . . awful habit of not dating any correspondence!"

Time and distance had, long before their deaths, made Sofield and Crocker absences. But Tom Driberg's sudden exit in August 1976 removed someone who had been a vivid part of Gore's present life. They had been friends since the 1950s, and during the 1950s and early '60s had seen each other whenever visiting either America or England. They enjoyed each other's humor, talent, and capacity for entertaining outrageousness. Each lauded the other's vividness and capacity as writer and as celebrant. With Gore's move to Rome, and then the purchase of the Ravello house, they saw one another regularly. Gore was in England often enough. Tom loved Rome and Ravello even more. Whenever he could afford to get away from London (he had to appear regularly at the House of Lords in order to be eligible to collect his much-needed salary), he headed for Malta or Italy. La Rondinaia was a cost-free paradise to which he had an open invitation to come anytime. Driberg's sex life had had a sort of admirable recklessness, especially for a high-ranking Labour Party politician. Usually when he left after a visit to Ravello, where he had what was thought of as his own bedroom and where he worked on his autobiography, his thank-you letters contained entertaining accounts of his adventures with Italian boys in Florence and Venice and on the train to England. Often they were self-consciously amusing variants on Lord Bradwell, the peerage to which he had recently been elevated, as dirty old man who was at the same time a romantic idealist perfectly capable of falling in love with his latest working-class passion. Though he had little money, he was generous to those he cared for and sometimes found himself exploited or even victimized. With Gore and Howard he gradually came to be cast partly in the role of avuncular family friend. The age gap between them and Driberg's declining health elicted Gore's concern and generosity. As Driberg's health deteriorated in the early 1970s, Gore became even more solicitous, more hospitable. In August 1973, after another in a series of heart attacks, Driberg convalesced at La Rondinaia. By 1975 he had convinced himself that he could write no place else but there. Gore was happy to accept the claim. The question of how frank he could be about his sex life in his autobiography worried Driberg and became a topic of conversation among his friends. Gore advised him to write everything but reserve publication of the controversial details, such as his having given Prime Minister Bevan a blow job, for posthumous publication. It was, at the same time, both worrisomely serious and high comedy. "Can it be that our little boy is now 70!" Gore wrote to him on his birthday. "It seems like only yesterday you were, in a piping treble, commanding the honest yeomen to drop their trousers. Well, now the halcyon days begin . . . and I wait impatiently for the next chapter of The Life. Do *not* be influenced by well-wishing fools who will attempt to bowdlerize." Most lives in politics and journalism are "very like another but it is Pepys fumbling with serving girls, and Boswell's dripping cock that command our attention and common humanity. Who can really hear J. Caesar's self-advertisements? and who can resist Catullus or Horace in their private moods?" Driberg went on with the memoir. He hoped to make good progress at Ravello, where he was scheduled to spend much of August 1976, though Gore had to be away part of the time. But "you can now stay, safely, without me as Anna is a splendid dedicated maid . . . and of course the Man of God [Michael Tyler-Whittle], the Smiths and Howard are on the scene." A few days before his scheduled departure Driberg came down to London from Oxford to prepare for the trip. In a cab from Paddington Station to his Barbican apartment he had a fatal heart attack.

The year before Driberg's death Gore had brought together in London about fifty of his British friends for an elegant fiftieth-birthday party. The party had been his own idea. It seemed appropriate to celebrate and memorialize the passage of his half a century. It was almost inconceivable to him that the face he looked at in the mirror each morning when he shaved was the latest, stranger version of a face he had grown used to in a different version long ago. Recently, when he had grown a beard, it had been almost entirely white. He shaved it immediately. The fact of being fifty was ominously distinctive, unlike any other birthday, and rather than retreat into glum solitude he had decided on a celebratory event, both acknowledgment and defiance. His last big birthday bash had been twenty-five years before, at Johnny Nicholson's café in New York. This guest list would be vastly different. Of the three most prominent people in his life in 1945, one was dead. From the other two, Anaïs and Nina, he had been long estranged. Only two people who had attended the 1945 festivities, Tennessee and Howard, were there now, and practical considerations made the list mainly British. Kathleen Tynan, whom Ken had married after his divorce from Elaine, and Diana Phipps handled the party arrangements. Gore made suggestions for the guest list. He arrived in London a full week before the party, mostly to do some television appearances, including *Vidal, Profile of a Writer* for German television, part of which was to be filmed at his favorite London bookstore, Heywood Hill. The weather was foul, rainy and dark, John Saumurez Smith, the proprietor, recalled, and a fiftieth birthday was not entirely a happy occasion. The cameras inside the shop began filming him as he came to the outside front and walked through the door. As he entered, he said to the German camera crew, "What's new from Ausch-

witz?" Stunned silence. The camera crew did not know whether to laugh or
to cry. On the morning of the day of the party, as he and Howard descended
in the small mirrored elevator from their suite at the Ritz Hotel, the elevator
stopped on its way to the lobby. Jackie Kennedy stepped in, alone. It was a
complete surprise to both of them. Since they had last talked, people had
reported to him over the years that she had begun to deny she had ever even
known him. He turned his back, his face to the mirror, and semiconsciously
ran his hand through his hair. As the lift door opened, they let her exit first.
"Bye-bye," she said.

The responses to the invitations went to Diana Phipps. Princess Margaret came, smoking her usual endless chain of cigarettes. Lady Diana
Cooper, whose husband had been Churchill's ambassador to France and
who had known Gore since 1949, walked up to him, unaware he was talking
to the princess, and began talking to him. "Oh, it's *you!*" Lady Diana dryly
said when she noticed Margaret, and curtsied. Evangeline Bruce, wife of the
American ambassador to Britain, with whom Gore had become friendly,
attended, as did old London friends, including John Lehmann, now retired
from publishing; and John Bowen, mostly writing for theater and television,
and his companion David Cook; and the Tynans, he angular, tall, and
bizarrely colorful, she sharply attractive. From Gore's Hollywood world
Lee Remick, slightly reminiscent of Diana Lynn, was in town, and arrived
with her husband. Diana Phipps and Claire Bloom were in good spirits.
Marguerite Lamkin came, Speed Lamkin's sister, now a London socialite
who still occasionally worked as a drama coach and had helped Claire
perfect the American accent for her successful London performance in
Streetcar the previous year. Gore, who had known Marguerite in New York
in the 1950s, had brought them together. Antonia Fraser arrived with the
playwright Harold Pinter, whom she had recently met. Gore and Pinter
immediately discovered a shared passion for radical politics. The ubiquitous
Maria, Lady St. Just, entered on the arm of Tennessee Williams. All week
Maria spent with Gore as much free time as he had. In evening dress,
assembled in private rooms at Mark's in Mayfair, the guests had drinks, then
went in to dinner. "I looked across the room and saw Gore with Princess
Margaret on one side of him and Tennessee Williams on the other," John
Bowen recalled. Princess Margaret "was constantly needing a light. She had
a long cigarette with a holder. Tennessee Williams just giggled at her."
Claire, who thought the party stunning, "was thinking how incredible it was

that anyone could be as old as fifty." Adept at light verse, the novelist Clive James, a close friend of Diana's, read a birthday poem he had composed, "To Gore Vidal at Fifty," with lines as effervescent as "A Marvellous Boy whose golden aureola/Still scintillates as fresh as *Pepsi-Cola*." The poetic tribute was not entirely unserious:

> [Some] might cling to childhood out of self-delusion,
> But that, or any similar, confusion,
> You've always held in absolute contempt—
> The only Absolute that you exempt
> From your unwearyingly edifying
> Assault on mankind's thirst to be undying—
> A hope you've never ceased to make a mock of
> Or boldly nominate what it's a crock of.

One of the expected guests who did not show up was John Galliher, who divided his time between Paris, London, and New York. Galliher, who had been Nina's friend and lover-in-passing in the early fifties, had introduced Gore to Jackie Bouvier twenty-five years before at a party at his Georgetown flat. "Apparently your party was a dazzler," Galliher wrote to him the next week. "Diana said it was enormous fun, and Marguerite that it was the most entertaining group of people possible. Alas, I went to a dinner and afterwards after a few magic puffs and lots of vino, got involved in activities that kept me too late to go to Mark's." After the party John Bowen went with Gore to the Ritz suite where, in voices hushed so as not to awaken Howard, they talked until dawn.

———————

One party in Gore's honor that he declined to attend was his election to the National Institute of Arts and Letters. On the last day of 1975 the secretary of the institute, the poet William Meredith, had sent him the letter of notification. "Will you be kind enough to let us know by return mail (or by cable) that you accept this election?" There would be an informal dinner in New York in April, a formal induction in May. Gore cabled from Rome: "THE INSTITUTE DOES ITSELF BELATED HONOR MY CONGRATULATIONS I CANNOT OF COURSE ACCEPT MEMBERSHIP BEST WISHES TO YOU GORE VIDAL." Over the years friends had privately told him that whenever they had raised his name he had not had sufficient support. Most of his equally well-known contemporaries, and many less accomplished writers, were members. Now the better part of honor and anger seemed to dictate that he decline. Perhaps he had in mind William James's response when elected to membership in the Academy, an elite subgroup whose members were drawn from the institute, that he did not care to belong to an organization to which "his younger and shallower and vainer brother" belonged. "I note now," Gore wrote to Dick Poirier, "that every lit. prize save the Pulitzer is within the gift of the Nat'l Inst. of A and L who, impertinently, elected me a member. I was stern. Told them that I could not join them as I already belong to the Diners Club," a line which was soon stinging the ears of some, amusing many.

He was aware, of course, that his response, like his residence in Europe, might promote an already existing general disinclination among many of his peers to say kind words about his work, let alone offer him glittering prizes. Still, it seemed better to be a gadfly than a golden cow, and things were still quite golden anyway, including his appearance on the cover of *Time* in March 1976, to mark the publication of *1876* (dedicated to Claire Bloom), which he had finished the previous autumn. Dressed in nineteenth-century clothes, quill pen and manuscript in hand, framed by white clouds and blue sky, handsome face with receding hairline and white flecks in his hair, "Gore Vidals New Novel '1876': SINS OF THE FATHERS!" in bold letters against his dark coat, his half figure dominated the best possible advertisement for the novel. It had gradually dawned on him in 1973 that with *Burr* and *Washington, D.C.,* he had written the eighteenth-century beginning and the twentieth-century present of American history. By spring 1974 he decided that he would fill in some of the intervening years, and *1876*, published exactly one hundred years after its events and two hundred after the founding of the republic, would be both intellectually apposite and dramatically timely. "I am sinking into a vast novel *1876,"* he wrote to Dick Poirier in May 1974. By early 1975 he was "holed up at Ravello with *1876,"* he told Tom Driberg, "a novel about the last days of Gen. Grant's admin. and the Tilden-Hayes election. Rather pleased to be back in the past: the food is so good!" And he was soon delighted to learn, he wrote to Graham Watson, that the "Book of the Month has bought *1876* sight unseen by anyone except me and I've only written a hundred pages!" In *1876* a now elderly Schuyler and his daughter Emma sail into the port of New York in late 1875. A famous historian who feels like Rip Van Winkle, he has come to cover the election of 1876, to advance his own fortunes, and to reestablish his connection with his native country. Instantly minor celebrities in New York social life, Schuyler observes the American scene and Emma falls in love with the wealthy, married William Sanford, whose wife dies giving birth to Blaise Delacroix Sanford. Three months later Emma and William marry amid rumors that they may have had something to do with Sanford's wife's death. To escape wicked tongues the newly married couple goes to live in France. Emma's father, who suspects that his daughter has done something questionable, stays on in New York, where he dies in 1877, having experienced the Revolutionary War via Burr, the Civil War via Lincoln and Hay, and having survived until just after the republic's one-hundredth birthday. His experience is dismal and disillusioning. The small, mostly honorable world of the Founding Fathers is in the process of becoming a large, dishonorable empire. A novel written about the events of the one-hundredth anniversary of the founding of the country, it was a message for the celebrants of the two-hundredth. With his appearance on the cover of *Time*, Gore had, like his father, reached one of the apogees of American celebrity, though he appreciated the irony that not only had Henry Luce once proposed to his mother but that the owner of *Time* had very different views than Gore did of American politics past and present. That of course did not matter. In a country in which everything was commodity, *Time* and Random House were happy to be partners in the selling business. So too was Gore. *1876* quickly went to the top of the bestseller list.

The usual variant on the traditional book tour that he had worked out long ago brought him to New York in March, for television and radio appearances and for print interviews, and then to California, where under the guidance of an expert and well-known publicist, Jay Allen, who had become a friend, he did further appearances. Allen, a longtime Hollywood insider, a habitué of the Beverly Hills Hotel, courteous and amiably conversational, had become Vidal's West Coast publicist in 1968 with the publication of *Myra*. When he had Gore's schedule in hand, Jay would call Robert Dolce, Johnny Carson's talent coordinator, a great admirer of Gore's, who as "a street kid from Brooklyn" found his work and his pleasures, including a dinner with Gore in Rome, a heady thrill. "There were so few people who could bring to *The Tonight Show* statements that were so quotable the next morning as could Gore," Dolce remarked. "People who wanted to make political statements would usually go on *Face the Nation*, not *The Tonight*

Show. But Gore always was prepared enough to know who the audience was and what he could accomplish on that program. He really enjoyed it. He had a good time. I knew how courageous he was on the air and how outrageous, but I never cautioned him about anything, and he never was in questionable taste. He knew what questions were coming, and my job was to get the very best out of this person. But for most guests there was a little bit of comfort to know that you weren't going to get a curve from out of left field. You had six minutes. . . . But before he would go out—and this is fascinating— Gore would stand backstage—this remarkable man who was going to go out there and shock the audience of five hundred people and shock the nation and didn't give a fuck about what their reactions were and what they thought—he'd be behind the curtains saying, 'Oh, my God! What am I going to do!' He was as panic-stricken as anybody. And then he would go out and do it and do something remarkable."

Gore's appearances on *The Tonight Show* had become semiannual events. Carson and Vidal were alike in their combination of impromptu wit and icy discipline, which created some sparkling moments in the transient world of 1960s and '70s talk television. NBC later filmed over the tapes: none of Gore's *Tonight Show* performances survive. His most sustained performance had him in Los Angeles in late August–early September 1976 for the taping of six telecasts of Norman Lear's *Mary Hartman, Mary Hartman,* in which the comedienne Louise Lasser played a version of herself in a late-night parody of the soap-opera genre, itself a soap opera, that had attracted both a cult and a wide popular audience. Gore's new agent for American television and film, the Hollywood impresario Irving [Swifty] Lazar, known for aggressive deal-making and his elite Oscar-night parties, handled the contracts. Sue Mengers and Gore remained close. With Mengers and her husband, in the late 1970s and early '80s, Gore and Howard took brief vacations in Venice, Vienna, and Morocco. In Hollywood she hosted birthday and other parties for them, especially for Howard, who found Hollywood glamour and sociability irresistible in contrast to the comparative isolation of much of his Ravello routine. Gore's friendship with Mengers puzzled some of his friends. Jay Allen thought Mengers evil. "Gore said, 'She's so filthy-mouthed that she intrigues me.' For instance, she tells him stories about [her sexual escapades]. In her bachelor days, when she and Gore were in Morocco, she showed how adventuresome she could be. And they always appeared to be having a very humorous time together. "But I think it's her very vulgarity that intrigues him. Also, of course, they go way way back to when she was just a secretary back in New York. And he likes to say, 'We made her,' Gore and Paul Newman." Both a gentile and genteel Midwesterner, Allen did his best to understand the attraction, which had and would keep Gore a loyal friend through Mengers's rise and then fall as a premiere Hollywood power broker, though they had ended their business relationship. They were both disappointed with her disposition of the movie and television rights to *Burr*. She had optioned it to ABC for a Bicentennial miniseries special, which it soon became clear would never be made, and it now seemed too late for alternatives. Lazar eagerly promised great things.

Although Lazar had dealt with the *Mary Hartman, Mary Hartman* contracts, Gore had himself initiated the appearances directly with Lear, whose television work he admired and whom he had known for a while, though he actually hated Lear's script, which both he and Lasser rewrote as they went along. "Louise would be busy going through it adding jokes for herself," Vidal recalled, "and trying to take my jokes away from me. So we'd have little fights, and she'd say, 'I think it would be better if I said that line,' and I'd say, 'Better for you but not for me.' She industriously began to rewrite her part, which ended up, a couple of times, really screwing up the script, so I said, 'I'll rewrite mine.' We were so busy improving it that we ignored what was there and sometimes lost the laughs because of empire-building." When one of the writers, furious at changes Vidal had made in a reference to the psychiatrist R. D. Laing, said that he had changed Laing's meaning, Gore replied, " 'Well, I certainly want to be accurate, but I hate R. D. Laing.' And she said, 'Yes, but it's my script.' And I said, 'Yes, but you're putting it into Gore Vidal's mouth.' This was a real moment of surrealism. An author, using me as a fictional character to propagate something that I don't believe in, which I object to saying. It was a very strange moment. I was now totally fictional." Playing a fictionalized version of himself, Gore proposes from Rome on the telephone to Mary, who has had a nervous breakdown on the *David Susskind Show,* become famous, and been committed to an asylum in her home town of Fernwood, Ohio, that they write a book together about Mary's fascinating life. For "a book about you," he tells her, "would be a book about America, about promises unkept and also, paradoxically, about hope." When he visits her in Fernwood, she's reading *Heartland* by Mort Sahl and thinking about what should go into a time capsule to tell future generations about America in the 1970s. Vidal plays his media version of himself, forceful, authoritative, well connected, a frequent guest on the Merv Griffin and David Susskind shows. Mary wants to be released from the hospital, but the villain, a slimy hospital executive who desires publicity and fame, conspires to keep her incarcerated and himself in the spotlight. Gore obtains Mary's release by threatening to expose him on national television if he refuses to release her but to praise him if he does. Then he meets with Mary to tell her the good news but also to tell her that he is leaving that same night for Rome, where they are about to start shooting *Gore Vidal's Caligula*. "You're going to finish your book, Mary. . . . This is your story. You've got to tell it. I can't. . . . In a sense, Mary, you know, you are America." Mary responds, "I'm sure you don't care. I love you. I've never felt this way before. . . . I want you in my life. Some way always in my life." He responds, "What can I say? Thank you," a flat speech improvised to replace what he thought an even less effective line in the script. "Dearest, darling Gore," Lear soon wrote to him, "If you haven't had the opportunity to see yourself on MARY HART-MAN, let me be the 30,000th to tell you, you were sensational. If you *did* happen to see yourself, you don't have to hear from any of us. I enjoyed every moment with you."

In reality, Gore had flown to Rome immediately after the filming, though he and Howard were giving serious thought to a long stay in Los Angeles, partly for professional and mostly for personal reasons. The plug on *Mary Hartman* for *Gore Vidal's Caligula* had been done in perfect good faith. In July 1975 he had signed a contract with Franco Rossellini's Felix Cinematographica for $225,000 and 10 percent of the gross to write an original screenplay based on the life of the Roman Emperor Caligula, the point of which would be to emphasize, as he told the London *Sunday Times,* that "freedom and liberalism are aberrations in the history of the world" and that without due vigilance America and Britain were likely to get their own modern version of Roman royalty. The producer and financial sponsor of the film was Bob Guccione, the owner of *Penthouse* magazine, who was to invest $16 million in the production, which would star Malcolm McDowell, Peter O'Toole, John Gielgud, and Helen Mirren. An alliance between Guccione and Vidal struck the *Sunday Times* interviewer as "a trifle odd. . . . Vidal cocked an eyebrow. 'Bob Guccione and I were made for each other,' he declared." It turned out they were not. By mid-1976 he had become aware, indirectly, that his screen treatment had been radically changed by the director, Tinto Brass. The director—whom he soon began calling "Tinto Zinc," and who "in a properly run world would be washing windows in Venice"—and Gore had not gotten along from the beginning. Apparently Brass thought his name should be in the title, not the scriptwriter's. Also that the film should have much more sex. When Vidal complained to Guccione about the nudes and "the grotesque sex scenes," the producer urged patience. "I thought that Tinto and I were in agreement," Vidal complained to Rossellini in June 1976, "that the picture should be realistic; real uncluttered rooms, real streets, sweat, dirty clothes; above all, no fantasy, no Fellini." But Brass and his set designer were in the process of creating a baroque extravaganza that made Fellini seem a realist. Soon the revised script was being kept secret, at least from Vidal. As the film was shot in Rome over the next two years, he stayed away and was kept away. Rumors from the set, though, reached him regularly. In early 1979, when Roberto Rossellini, Franco's brother, instituted a suit claiming that the idea for the film had been his and that Vidal had plagiarized his material, Gore denied the charge but also took the legal opportunity to join him in the request that the film be "seized" in order to determine whether or not "his screenplay had been used by the director . . . and, consequently, whether or not he would accept that the name of the motion picture be *Gore Vidal's Caligula* as agreed with Felix" or that his name be associated with it in any way at all. When he finally saw the film, his strong choice was the latter. It seemed an ugly travesty, his conception of Caligula radically altered, his dialogue manipulated to reverse his meanings. "The film is a hard-core porn disaster," he wrote to Judith Halfpenny, "in which the likes of O'Toole and Gielgud flounder, under the impression that the proprietor of *Penthouse* intended to make my script." Director, producer, and author were soon trading insults. Guccione: " 'Gore's single greatest regret in life is that he wasn't born a woman. . . . As a result, he becomes bitchy and petulant.' " Brass: " 'If I ever really get mad at Gore Vidal, I'll publish his script.' " The film does have some distinction, Vidal responded. " 'It's not just another bad movie. It is a *joke* movie.' " He succeeded in getting his name removed from the title, though not from the credits, a minor price to pay for having allowed his vanity and idealism to tempt him to a partnership that had less chance to produce something intellectually serious than even the usual mass-market film venture.

That winter they returned to Los Angeles, this time not to a hotel but to a comfortable mountaintop house, rented from John Schlesinger, the award-winning director of *Billy Liar* and *Darling*, on Rising Glen Road, with a spectacular view of the city. They descended frequently for social evenings with film-industry people, mostly those Gore had come to know over the years through work. "There," he soon wrote to Judith Halfpenny, after summarizing a social evening in which the talk was primarily about movies and deals, "you have an evening in Hollywood, less the real conversation which has to do with negative costs and grosses. Celebrities, as you call them, tend to flock together largely because they have the same sort of problems. Criminals are the same." It seemed to Jay Allen that every one of the many times he stopped by, Gore was at work in his "god-damned old filthy robe. I'm sure he still has it. I'm sure he must work nineteen or twenty hours a day." On the one hand, he worked "so hard to keep his weight down so he'll look good on camera," mostly at spas, one of his favorites La Costa, near San Diego, which he now began to visit every time he was in California. On the other, Allen thought he paid insufficient attention to his wardrobe, especially for television appearances, though Jay never worked up the courage to suggest he bring a larger wardrobe and keep it fresher. "We were doing the Carson show one night and we were sitting in the dressing room before the show, and I looked over at him and his stomach was just bulging out of his [jacket] . . . and I said, 'Gore—you know the way the camera catches clearly your knees on this show—take my sleeveless sweater and put it on. I think you should wear a sleeveless sweater when you go on, and you won't be aware.' He never returned the sweater. It was midnight blue. But if you notice, now he usually wears a sweater under his jacket." Absolutely comfortable in his old robe, Gore spent much of that winter at work on *Kalki,* a new novel with an apocalyptic theme, picking up from *Messiah* in that regard but radically different, a representation of American post–Vietnam War religious and political distress, focusing on an American ex-soldier who convinces himself and much of the world that he is the latest and final incarnation of the Hindu god Vishnu, who has come to end civilization and usher in a new age. At the end, through an ironic miscalculation, he succeeds in destroying all human life. By late January 1977 Gore had sent a completed draft to Jason Epstein, who responded that *"Kalki* can and should work brilliantly" but that the flawed conception of the first-person narrator, who had no qualities of heart or mind with which the reader could identify, undermined the novel's effectiveness. Would it not work better and be more plausible in the narrative as a whole if the transexual male narrator were actually a woman? "Those who have read *[Kalki]* fear that I have lost my cunning," he confided to Judith Halfpenny. "I am trying to salvage it."

By April they had returned to Italy, where Gore began to rewrite substantially. Epstein's suggestions were helpful. "*Kalki* being re-done. Lovely idea, wrong narrator." By June 1977 he had completed the revision. Jason thought it successful, its overall effect "powerful and upsetting." Never having had and never generally needing an editor who did close editing, Gore felt ambivalent about Jason's contributions. He recognized that he had needed help in getting *Kalki* back on the right track. Still, he needed total control over the time and the conditions of intercession. He had gone to Random House, he wrote to Halfpenny, "because of my friend Jason Epstein who does like to inflict his views on me. By and large, they are ignored. Books like *Myron* distress him, and there is bickering. But nothing more. He is excellent with the historical works because he publishes the leading historians and biographers in the field and sees to it that for a small fee they vet what I've written. In the case of *1876*, the professor in question provided me with a lot of new material that I was able to use." Having just benefited from Epstein's suggestions about *Kalki*, Gore's description was ungenerous and only partly accurate. But as the title of his newest volume of essays—*Matters of Fact and of Fiction: Essays 1973–1976*, which Random House published in April—indicated, both this author-editor relationship and this author-publisher relationship had their complications. Epstein often preferred the fact to the fiction, the history to the invention. *Kalki*, published in April 1978, had a mixed reception and a modest sale. Some thought it brilliant. Others found it thin, implausible as realistic fiction. Criticism inevitably focused on the narrator. Mick Jagger, who imagined himself playing Kalki, the ex-Marine turned messianic Hindu god, optioned the film rights. The volume of essays, published in April 1977, had almost unanimously favorable reviews, and the close timing of the publication of the essays and the novel gave occasion for some reviewers to compare Vidal the essayist to Vidal the novelist. A fairer comparison would have been to *Burr* or *Myra Breckinridge*. But if *Kalki* was not Vidal at his best as novelist, in *Matters of Fact and of Fiction* he was at his best as essayist, and Stephen Spender on the front page of the *New York Times Book Review* remarked, about essays such as "The Ten Top Best-Sellers," "Calvino's Novels,"

"American Plastic: The Matter of Fiction," "Some Memories of the Glorious Bird and an Earlier Self," "President and Mrs. U. S. Grant," and "West Point," that "as a critic of manners as well as literature, Vidal is in the tradition of Matthew Arnold and Edmund Wilson."

Concerned, even worried, about Italian political and social chaos, including kidnappings, murders, and the threat that Italian residents with American citizenship would be required to pay taxes as if they were Italian citizens, Gore soon did what he had never wanted to do—he bought a handsome, substantial stucco house in the Hollywood Hills with large gardens and a swimming pool, rumored inaccurately once to have belonged to the actress Dolores Del Rio. The previous winter at Rising Glen Road had been an attempt to see whether they could live in Los Angeles. In a letter to Judith Halfpenny, Gore had described Southern California as "our Tahiti—with much the same cultural impact, and destiny." But if he were to be persuaded to return to live in the United States, the only city that seemed plausible, much as he disliked it, was Los Angeles. "We would have preferred Beverly Hills," he later remarked. "Jean Stein said that the Hollywood Hills are much more glamorous. And much cheaper because they were quite run down." "We may be back in Calif in the fall," Gore had written to Joe O'Donohue. They quickly agreed to the asking price of about $200,000, with a mortgage inherited from the seller. As always, Gore had good luck with houses. In late October 1978, taking possession, they settled in for six months or so of California life. They brought Diana Phipps, who had been thrilled at *Matters of Fact and of Fiction*'s being dedicated to her, with them. "I admire the essays more than I can say and to be somehow involved makes me inordinately proud." Now making her living as an interior decorator, she was given total charge of redoing their house on Outpost Drive. Gore settled in to continue work on the new historical novel he had started and which developed into *Creation*, about the inception of three great world religions in the fifth century B.C., as soon as he had finished the revision of *Kalki*. With various assistants, Diana began transforming the interior, mainly with billowing paisley fabrics that created a tent effect in some of the rooms. Within about six weeks she had it ready. "She's got a great sense of organization," Howard observed, "and knows how to give orders. She's also got a very short temper and she's difficult sometimes. . . . Diana's work at Outpost Drive is a bit too effeminate for me. It could go with married couples, but when two men live together, you can't live in Turkish tents. I was very uncomfortable living with it at the beginning, but once I got used to it I loved it." He also loved Hollywood social life, including a grand party they threw for Diana to celebrate the completion of what she had done. "As far as knowing how to do a place, I've had the best, from Alice Astor to Gore's mother to Diana Phipps, all of them originals and with great eyes. I wouldn't put myself in their class. But I could appreciate what they did." By the end of the winter, comfortable as the house had now become, Gore still could not envision living in Los Angeles indefinitely. Fortunately, by late 1978 Italy had reverted to its traditional low- or non-tax arrangement for resident foreigners. Early in the new year he was happy to return to Ravello.

In Washington, on a Monday morning in early April 1978, several months before leaving for Ravello, from the window of a building to which he had gone to do TV publicity for *Kalki*, Gore's eye had suddenly fixed on St. Margaret's Church. Nina, who had died that morning, was much on his mind. The beautiful eighteen-year-old debutante and her handsome Army officer had been married there over fifty-six years before. The limousine, which drove Gore from place to place through his publicity schedule on a route he had not planned, passed other familiar places, starting with the apartment building in which Senator and Mrs. Gore had died. Within a few moments he caught a glimpse of the bridge across Rock Creek Park. Soon, on the left, was the transformed version of the old Wardman Park Hotel, where he and his mother had gone to live after she had divorced Gene Vidal and where she had married Hugh Auchincloss. To the right was the road that went down to his grandfather's stone house, in which Gore had spent some of the most resonant hours of his childhood. "I was thinking about everything. And then suddenly all these places, each touching a memory." It was as if, with unplanned but uncanny appropriateness, on the morning on which he learned of his mother's death, all the places in Washington with powerful family associations were becoming part of his kaleidoscopic, surreal journey through familiar but ghostly locations.

In early March he had received a telegram: "DOCTORS AT LACKLAND AIR FORCE BASE HOSPITAL SAN ANTONIO TEXAS ADVISE THAT YOUR MOTHER IS EXPECTED TO DIE SOON—SEVERAL DAYS TO 4–5 WEEKS DEPENDING ON CIRCUMSTANCES SHE HAS LUNG CANCER AND EMPHYSEMA." In Washington, the night before, he had had dinner with his sister Nini. As much alienated from her mother as Gore, Nini had nothing good to say about her. From her early teenage years they had fought bitterly, and separated mostly, almost twins in temperament and looks. Most recently they had exchanged hard words about Nini's belief that her mother had offered to testify against her in Nini's divorce from Newton Steers. "How ridiculous," Nina wrote to Gore in one of many letters he had never answered, "as though it would ever reach such a point—or that I'd do such a thing." She had written to Nini how "shocked and amazed" she was that her daughter would believe that she "would go on the stand against" her, though, ever the combative mother, she repeated her view that Newton was more sinned against than sinning. On that Monday morning in April 1978 Nini had called Gore at his hotel with the news that Tommy had telephoned: their mother had died at Memorial Sloan-Kettering Hospital in New York, where Tommy, who had been looking after her, had brought her for treatment. Three days before, she had told Tommy that Gore had been to the hospital to visit and that she had forgiven him. As always, to those who did not know better, she was very convincing. Tommy checked the hospital records. Gore had not been there.

Nina had tried to effect a reconciliation ever since 1958. Self-justifying, she thought nothing that had happened had been her fault. Gore thought the fault entirely hers. There was no bridging the gap, and Nina had no idea of the extent to which her behavior in London seemed to him simply the last, most unacceptable aggression in a lifelong series of inconsiderate, irresponsible, and painful performances. Since she had merely been herself, why should he respond differently from all such previous occasions? They had always fought. They had always reconciled. Why not this time? Her alcoholism had both eased and increased her burdens. It had only increased his. He had unburdened himself by deciding never to see her again. To make that possible, he needed to see her as evil rather than as pathetic and ill. "I am like Turgenev and Hemingway: I detested my mother," he wrote to Judith Halfpenny in 1977, as if she were already dead. "No Oedipus there. And the detestation in each case (from what one can tell reading biographies) was not thwarted incestuous love but hatred of evil." Freud, he believed, could throw no light on his own family romance. With a less confrontational and more forgiving temperament, Tommy had increasingly taken on the burden of Nina's last years. In 1972, in Cuernavaca, she fell and hurt herself badly. With osteoporosis, her bones healed slowly. A chain-smoker, she developed severe emphysema. Addicted as she was to painkillers and sleeping pills, her mind was often addled, including her certainty that her bank account and her investments had been plundered by rapacious bankers, her valuables stolen by servants. She could no longer focus sufficiently to play bridge, which had been for so long her passion and pleasure. At her worst she confused pesos with dollars. In fact, as Tommy, who kept her financial records, knew, her resources had dwindled almost to nothing. There were no savings. When Hugh Auchincloss's financial difficulties resulted in suspending payment of her monthly stipend, the value of which inflation had reduced considerably, Tommy provided funds. In 1974, desperate, she reminded Gore that she had given him $3,000 toward the purchase of Edgewater. Sometimes her figure was $3,000, other times $6,000, as if she counted Mrs. Gore's contribution as her own. "Of course," she recognized, "at the time it was a gift not a loan. . . . I'm not an Indian giver but this last illness and broken leg has cost me $24,000. . . . This is most embarassing [sic] though it shouldn't be—parents do all they can for children then sometimes the necessity arrives for a turn about. . . . I am very proud of your hard working. Love Bommy." Could he not give her the money plus accumulated interest and then deduct it from his taxes? He authorized Hecht to send her $8,000, which Hecht did immediately and for which she thanked them both. She soon went to the Army hospital in San Antonio for treatment. Then she took an apartment in Florida. Just over seventy, she looked ravaged.

In March 1976, after reading in *Time* magazine Anaïs Nin's comment that Gore had been "abandoned" by his mother, Nina responded with a blistering, self-defensive letter to the editor, a small, comparatively innocuous portion of which *Time* published under the ambiguous but mostly ironic title "Mother Love." Instead of appealing to her son to protect her private life from becoming a public target, she launched an exculpatory attack. The full letter provided a detailed list of all the ways she had nurtured and supported him from infancy to early manhood, each ending with the rhetorical refrain, "Abandonment?" Even Henry Luce was invoked. He "was a great friend of mine" and "never would have permitted my being involved in the recent *TIME* article about Gore, in which there were such vicious quips about me." For whatever success Gene Vidal had had, she took credit. For whatever difficulty she had in raising Gore, his father was to blame. She was not at fault, she argued between the lines, for the type of man Gore had become. As usual, her claims were based on half-truths and self-serving fantasy, and the letter was in devastatingly bad taste, as if the pages of *Time* were an appropriate place for the mother of a famous son to defend herself against comments such as Anaïs's. Gore himself had said nothing critical of her in print. With her usual bad judgment, Nina destroyed whatever minuscule chance for reconciliation had existed. Hurt and furious, Gore wrote to Nini, "Nice to see your mother's rage and incomprehension continue as bones corrode with cancer and eternity opens wide! I showed the letter to Elaine Dundy who's here (and much involved with shrinks). 'The letter of an angry twelve year old' was her verdict. To have learned nothing. Ah, well, sadism is a hard and inexorable motor to some—to *her* life." Two years later there would be no deathbed reconciliation. Nina requested that her ashes be scattered over the San Francisco Mountains in New Mexico to join those of her last, most-loved husband. Tommy had the body cremated in New Jersey, the ashes shipped to his home in Vermont. They stayed in his attic for ten years. Eventually he had some of them buried next to her parents in Oklahoma City. The rest he spread on a forest road in what he thought the San Francisco Mountains. The next day he discovered he had scattered the ashes on the wrong mountains.

CHAPTER EIGHTEEN

The Same Sinking Boat

1978–1986

IN THE MID-1970s two of Vidal's literary colleagues, Truman Capote and Norman Mailer, had come back into his life, both unpleasantly, as if these well-publicized giants of American literature insisted on inscribing their names in comic headlines. Perhaps any headline was better than none. Not that he himself had forgotten or neglected either of them. In *Myron,* in 1974, Capote makes a parodic appearance as a giggling, inept gossip named Maude, a snobbish hairdresser with "a damp-looking face." Mailer appears as a drunken, semiviolent cook named Whittaker Kaiser, "a small fat old man of fifty or so with a full head of wiry gray hair," constantly threatening Myron/Myra with a meat cleaver. Kaiser proclaims that "the *real* man . . . takes one woman after another without the use of contraceptives . . . just the all-conquering sperm because contraception of any kind is as bad as masturbation and because the good burger makes the good baby." Other than *Time* magazine, which remarked on Kaiser as "a merciless lampoon" of Norman Mailer, few reviewers identified the wildly funny portrait or the eerie precision of the caricature of Capote, though many recognized Vidal's targets. Neither Mailer nor Capote responded privately to Vidal or commented in print. Probably neither had read the novel: all three had long since given up reading one another's fiction. Mailer and Vidal had not had any contact since they appeared together in 1971 on *The Dick Cavett Show*. Vidal, with his talent for moving on, had focused whatever occasional public comments he had made about Mailer since 1971 on the issues on which they differed. "Yes," he wrote to Jim Tuck, his Washington childhood playmate who had written him favorably about *Myron*, "Norman is every bit as flabby and his own conversation rather less credible than W.K.'s." The depiction of Mailer as Whittaker Kaiser expressed how much he resented Mailer's attack on him on the Cavett show and what it represented, especially Mailer's homophobia.

Vidal had last seen Capote at a party in New York, where neither said anything of consequence to the other, though later Vidal recollected that because he had not had his glasses on, he sat down "on what I thought was a stool and it was Capote." "Where was Capote sitting at the time you sat on him?" "On a smaller stool." Capote's attempt at a reconciliation in Rome in 1969, which Vidal mistrusted, did not prevent each occasionally making derogatory comments about the other for quotation, mostly witty, humorous ripostes such as Vidal's that Capote has "raised lying into an art—a minor art" and that he "belongs less to the history of literature than the history of public relations." Capote's remarks were equally hostile, particularly his on-camera comment to David Susskind, "Of course, I'm always sad about Gore. Very sad that he has to breathe every day." To Judith Halfpenny, who had queried Gore in 1976 about the rumor that he was "about to write a gossip novel," he privately expressed his disdain for both Capote and Mailer. "That is Capote's field. Most of what is written about me in the press is untrue. This is not due to malice so much as to plain incompetence. . . . I find on TV I am often supposed to talk about fashions and famous society ladies. I then remind the host that I am the one who talks about politics and Capote is the one who tells naughty stories about the rich and Mailer is the messiah."

When, in 1975, Capote told a "naughty" story about Vidal to an interviewer for *Playgirl* magazine, Vidal resorted to the law, partly a misplaced moment of admonitory moralism, partly an expression of his longstanding sensitivity to the distortions and inaccuracies widely current about the history of his relationship with the Kennedys. He felt there was ample evidence Capote had made a career out of embroidered distortions and outright lies. Capote himself readily admitted the former. Vidal told stories by stripping away ornamentation in order to reveal basic realities. The aphorism and the telling detail were his weapons. Capote embraced expansion, exaggeration, the slippery transition into self-dramatizing fantasy. Their styles clashed, their narrative strategies in literature and life differed. They had incompatible ideas about what was truth. Vidal measured claims against the world. Capote turned the world into a supporting cast for himself. Capote's performance personality, which Vidal felt gave homosexuality a bad name, revolted him. It was one thing to be a queen. It was another to be a malicious sissy whose fantasy life damaged others. In 1966 Capote's fragile career as a writer and social lion had reached its peak with the publication of *In Cold Blood* and his "Black and White" ball at the Plaza Hotel. By the early seventies he had become addicted to alcohol, drugs, and self-punishing behavior, including publishing portions of a tell-all novel-in-progress whose revelations about the easily recognized originals of its characters alienated the high-society friends on whom he depended for his social position. In September 1975 *Playgirl,* with the cover headline "Outrageous Interview with Truman Capote" and the subhead "Gore Vidal . . . 'Bobby Threw Him Out of the White House,' " quoted Capote as saying, in response to "Why did Vidal resent the Kennedys so terribly?" that he thought it went "back to when Bobby had Gore thrown out of the White House [in November 1961]. It was the only time he had ever been invited to the White House . . . he insulted Jackie's mother whom he had never met before in his *life.* . . . And Bobby and Arthur Schlesinger, I believe it was, and one of the guards just picked Gore up and carried him to the door and threw him out into Pennsylvania Avenue. That's when he began to write all those cruel pieces about the Kennedys." Capote had at first declined Richard Zoerink's request to interview him for *Playgirl.* When a mutual friend, the writer Dotson Rader, intervened, Capote consented. With a glass of vodka in hand, prompted by the interviewer, who suggested some of the sensational phrases—particularly "picked him up"—Capote felt free to repeat, expand, and refashion the core anti-Vidal rumor about Vidal's encounter with Robert Kennedy.

Over the years Vidal had attempted to correct inaccurate accounts of the incident and of his relationship with the Kennedys, most recently his letter in May 1972 to *The Atlantic Monthly* in response to an article by Gerald Clarke, who was to become Capote's biographer, quoting George

Plimpton's account of what had happened that evening at the White House. Plimpton provided his version of the angry conversation between Vidal and Kennedy, and little more. With only a general idea of what had been said, Plimpton's use of language uncharacteristic of both participants made it clear he had not actually heard the conversation. "It would seem," Vidal responded, "that my old friend George Plimpton is now trying to replace Truman Capote as the Baron Munchausen of the jet set. He's been dining out for a decade . . . on what I am supposed to have said to Bobby Kennedy and he to me. . . . The truth of the matter is that George did not hear one word of that legendary conversation, nor did Jackie. Bobby and I were out of earshot of everyone. . . . George by now believes he over-heard us, but he did not." Gore had less tolerance, though, for Capote's putting into print an equally inaccurate but more broadly sweeping account actually stating that Gore had been bodily thrown out of the White House. Plimpton's story was self-servingly good-humored, and not at all intended to harm. Capote's was an attempt to demean him, a transference of Capote's general hostility to an inaccurate, specific fabrication. It was a revenge fantasy whose only approximation to truth was that there had been some unpleasantness between Vidal and Robert Kennedy. When a copy of the interview reached Vidal at Ravello, he was shocked and angry. But he had no intention of suing. Whatever the merit of his potential case, his experience with Buckley had made him sensitive to the misuse of libel laws to discourage free speech. And it seemed reasonable to think that an interview in as meretricious a magazine as *Playgirl* would not have wide currency. A month later, in Amsterdam, he was approached at an outdoor magazine stand by an admiring stranger who had recognized him. The man pointed to a prominently displayed copy of the September issue of *Playgirl* and asked, " 'Is that true?' " At that moment Vidal decided to sue.

After consulting with Arnold Weissberger, his lawyer in New York, and then Peter Morrison, to whom he had been referred by Weissberger, he had assurance from counsel that he had a good chance of prevailing in a suit for defamation and malice. Morrison's retainer was reasonable. There seemed grounds on which to expect that Gore would recover his legal costs. The suit requested damages of $1 million. Angry, aggrieved, he thought it fair that Capote either recant or pay a price for his maliciousness. The legal process, which he knew well enough from the Buckley suit, was under way by autumn 1975, though this time he had reversed roles, convinced he might serve moral justice, put to rest once and forever inaccurate accounts of his feud with the Kennedys, and terminate conclusively the tendency of the public to associate him with Capote, as if they were birds of a feather. On the basis of a memorandum he supplied his attorney, the legal complaint that went to the Supreme Court of the State of New York in December, naming the interviewer, Capote, and *Playgirl* as defendants, initiated a series of briefs that denied the factual accuracy of Capote's statements and alleged malicious recklessness. Bewildered, angry, Capote decided to defend against the suit. He had convinced himself that his description of what had happened at the White House was accurate. In the legal procedure, Capote fantasized, Vidal would be humiliated, crushed, forever a laughingstock. Ultimately his defense rested on his claim that Lee Radziwill, whom he thought his good friend and to whom he had done good service—including creating a television opportunity for her to further her acting ambitions— was the source of his information. She had been at the White House that night. Whether she had or had not told him that Vidal had been thrown out bodily, Capote had come to believe she had. The discovery process began. Depositions were solicited. In September 1976, on his way back to Rome from Los Angeles after filming his episodes of *Mary Hartman, Mary Hartman*, Vidal spent two of his New York days being deposed. Capote had nothing to offer other than his claim that his statements were general knowledge, that he was surprised the plaintiff was challenging them, and that he expected George Plimpton, Arthur Schlesinger, and Princess Lee Bouvier Radziwill to confirm his account of the White House affair. According to his friend Donald Windham, Truman, who "was gathering affidavits for his defense," believed that "Gore didn't have a Chinaman's chance of winning." When Windham ran into Vidal in mid-September 1976, as the latter was leaving Rizzoli's and Windham was entering, Gore "had just finished two days of giving his pretrial depositions in his suit against Truman." Capote threatened to countersue. When Windham, who seemed to Vidal "a sad and bitter creature," again ran into him in New York, they talked first about Tennessee's regret that he had given the copyright of his letters to Windham for an edition. Tennessee had told Gore that Windham "had gotten him drunk and tricked him into signing away his copyright." Both Gore and Truman resented slighting remarks Tennessee had made about them in his letters to Windham. It was another example of Tennessee's "paranoia," Gore wrote to Judith Halfpenny. "But the letters are marvelous to read and do recreate that long-off time." Capote threatened to sue Williams for defamation. Vidal remarked to Windham that he supposed " 'it's all actionable. At least they show [Williams] used to be able to write. But they also show that he had a murderous streak in him as far back as the forties, to act as he did toward me and to write about me in that way.' The conversation was friendly," Windham wrote in *Lost Friendships*. "I didn't detect any hidden hostility, despite the word 'actionable.' "

Other mutual friends also attempted to persuade Vidal to drop his suit, some on the grounds of Capote's precarious health, most with the claim that it was unseemly and uncollegial for one writer to sue another. Vidal felt that the damage Capote had done him outweighed his general agreement with the collegial principle. Vidal recalls that he let Capote know he would consider dropping his suit only if Capote would agree never to speak about him in public again, though the offer never reached Capote's lawyers. Apparently the trial-balloon offer was declined. A few weeks after Windham's "encounter with Gore, Truman spent twenty-four hours at [Windham's] apartment, drinking without stopping." For a while "Gore's suit against Truman was in limbo. Truman's suit against Tennessee remained what it was, just talk."

Between 1975 and 1978 Capote's life in general moved toward incoherence and collapse, partly due to substance abuse and his increasing inability to finish his long-promised novel, *Answered Prayers*, partly because of his rejection by his socially elite former friends, whose private lives he had trashed in the excerpts *Esquire* had published. "Mr. Capote never wrote *Answered Prayers*," Gore told Judith Halfpenny in 1979. "It is [Henry James's] 'Madonna of the Future' all over again. But as this is America, if you publicize a non-existent work enough, it becomes positively palpable. It would be nice if he were to get the Nobel on the strength of *Answered Prayers* which he, indeed, never wrote. There were a few jagged pieces of what might have been a gossip-novel published in *Esquire*. The rest is silence, and litigation and . . . noise on TV." By February 1979, when Capote's request for summary judgment dismissing the complaint was denied, he was on the verge of despair and rage. Documents existed to demonstrate that Jackie Kennedy had remained warmly friendly with Gore until the publication in March 1963 of his hostile article about Bobby as the heir presumptive. It was easy to demonstrate that Vidal had known Janet Auchincloss, his half-sister Nini's stepmother, for some time before 1961 and that he had been at the White House numbers of times before, including a private dinner with the Kennedys and Alice Roosevelt. Plimpton's testimony did not support Capote's claim that Vidal had been "thrown out" of the White House. Schlesinger's diary had little help for Capote's defense, and soon, in his biography of Robert Kennedy, Schlesinger, quoting the relevant passage from his journal, remarked that "Vidal's enemies delightedly embellished the story. I can testify that he was not forcibly ejected, nor cast bodily into Pennsylvania Avenue." Worst of all, Lee Radziwill, who soon told Liz Smith, the premier gossip columnist, that this was all of no interest to her since they "were just two fags," refused to back him up. In fact, her testimony totally denied she was the source of his claims. When "quizzed by my lawyer," Gore wrote to Halfpenny, "in the company of her swain, a lawyer . . . Mrs. R denied ever having told her once bosom-friend anything about that night as she'd witnessed nothing . . . and that when he'd told her what to say to my lawyer she had been upset." *Playgirl* immediately printed a retraction. Vidal instructed his attorneys to drop his suit against the magazine, and again offered to do the same for Capote in exchange for the payment of his legal fees, now about $40,000, and a $10,000 additional payment. Capote declined.

In what he hoped was an extralegal preemptive strike, Capote now encouraged *New York* magazine to publish what he expected would be a strongly anti-Vidal version of their "feud." The front cover of the June 11, 1979, issue quoted the most pungent passage from Capote's interview in *Playgirl* and depicted Vidal flying over and out of the White House. The article itself, "The Vidal-Capote Papers," was noticeably evenhanded, and Capote's still-sharp literary intelligence managed to provide some interesting though arguable comment on both the achievement and the problem of Vidal's versatility as a writer. "Gore," he remarked, "wants to be all things to all men. I mean, he wants to be Caesar and Cleopatra at the same time, and he isn't." The article, though, did not damage Vidal and certainly had no effect on the likelihood that within a few years Capote would have to pay huge damages and double legal fees, even a small portion of which he could not afford. "We are willing to settle for an apology, one dollar damages, and my legal fees . . . happily, deductible in the land of the litigious," Gore told Halfpenny toward the end of the year. But "C.'s lawyers say that he has no money. There, for now, the matter rests." Though the judge, who in August 1979 denied Capote's request for summary dismissal, also denied

Vidal's request for summary judgment, he declared that Capote's statements were, as a matter of law, libelous per se and that Vidal's attorneys had demonstrated "actual malice." It seemed likely that unless Capote caved in, there would be a trial. His attorneys delayed and maneuvered, including a backhanded attempt to eliminate from the record Capote's self-damaging deposition. In October 1983 Capote swallowed the bitter pill. The cost of continuing was disastrous. Though only fifty-nine, he seemed aged, pale, and deathly-looking. He would apologize in writing. The question of his paying Vidal's legal fees was dropped. For some time now Vidal had been aware that at least two of his three purposes in undertaking the suit would be unrealized. "No matter what the judge determines, Mr. C. has now so muddled things as to make me seem to be his equal: a pair of publicity-mad social-climbers who make it a habit to libel and slander one another and everyone else. *Pro bono publico* is not, I suppose, possible when you have *publico* as debased as the American polity. Anyway, the expense has been formidable; the pleasure—often—intense." Capote's letter was bittersweet vindication, even if Vidal distrusted Capote's promises: "I apologize for any distress, inconvenience or expense which may have been caused you as a result of the interview with me published in the September 1975 issue of *Playgirl*. As you know, I was not present at the event about which I am quoted in the interview, and I understand from your representatives that what I am reported as saying does not accurately set forth what occurred. I can assure you that the article was not an accurate transcription of what I said, especially with regard to any remarks which might cast aspersions upon your character or behavior, and that I will avoid discussing the subject in the future."

Soon the possibility that Capote would break his word was ended, conclusively. In Rome, in April 1984, Gore wrote to Paul Bowles, whom he kept up to date on extra-Moroccan affairs with regular exchanges of letters, that a literary columnist and reviewer for *Newsweek*, Walter Clemons, who had visited him in Rome, had had a sad lunch with Capote a few weeks before. "T. seemed not to be drinking but spoke with a mouth in which the tongue (once so hummingbird-like in its dread effect) was too large and slow to shape much chat. . . . Those made mad by drink and pills like the Bird, does one judge them by what they did to themselves or by what they were before? It is a nice point." Gore's anger at Capote subsided somewhat. But not his distaste and disdain. When Capote died, in late August 1984 in

Los Angeles at the home of Joanne Carson, who had remained loyal to and endlessly solicitous of her good friend, Gore told her ex-husband, Johnny Carson, that since "I knew he would be upset by Joanne's coup . . . I promised him that I would die in *his* house. This will even things out. He was much pleased." Accounts of the funeral came from the eighty-year-old Christopher Isherwood, who spoke briefly at the ceremony and who had always found Capote amusing, and from Joan Didion and John Gregory Dunne, with whom Gore had become friendly during his recent on-again/off-again residences in Los Angeles. "As someone said when word broke that Elvis Presley was dead," he wrote to Paul Bowles, Capote's death was "a good career move. T will now be the most famous American writer of the last half of the 20th century. No one will ever read a book of his again but no one who can read will be able to avoid the thousands of books his life will inspire. Since he has told the most extraordinary lies about every famous person of our time, the hacks will have a field-day recording the sorts of lies *they* usually make up. T's affair with Camus, T's help in getting Marilyn aborted, T's blow job of Pres Kennedy. . . . Well, he is what this vulgar tinny age requires. RIP."

— · —

When, in late October 1977, on his way to California, Gore had flown into New York from Rome with Howard and his new literary agent, Owen Laster, Norman Mailer had not been particularly on his mind. But as with Capote and Vidal, they had become for one another countermeasuring rods of self-identity. Though they had not spoken since 1971, their so-called feud had the reality of each one's constantly rewriting a brief against the other, which they often inflicted on friends. And the press eagerly printed almost every offhand hostile comment each made to journalists. Mailer felt achingly unfulfilled and dissatisfied with himself about his attack on Vidal on the Cavett show. Mickey Knox, Mailer's friend, of whom Gore and Howard saw much in Rome, preferred to avoid the subject with Gore. He liked and admired Gore, and Gore, as always, was generous with invitations and attempts to further Knox's acting career. Just before Vidal published the Miller-Manson-Mailer essay in 1971 he had called Knox to the Via Di Torre Argentina apartment. "He said he wanted to show me something and he showed me the piece . . . and I read it and said, 'Gore, I wouldn't publish this.' 'Why not?' 'Why not! I don't have to tell you why not.' 'Well, you

know, it's just a progression. That's all it is.' I don't know what the hell he
ever fucking meant by that, frankly. All through the years he kept saying, 'I
don't know what all the fuss was about. It's just a progression.' But you put
Manson there in the middle. It's a problem. Let's face it." Thereafter the
subject was unavoidable. Mickey's real presence inevitably evoked the phan-
tom Norman. "I'd go to Ravello or wherever Gore was and we'd sit up till
four in the morning drinking. And only talking about Norman. There I was,
his surrogate, defending him. About everything: 'He can't write, he can't
read.' At a certain point Howard would stand up and say, 'I've heard this
before. I've had enough!' And he'd go off to bed and leave me with Gore. It
was endless. . . . It went on and on. I kept saying, 'You're crazy. You two
guys ought to make up,' and he kept saying, 'Never! Never! Never!' "

Soon after settling in at the Plaza, Gore and Howard went from a
dinner party at which Princess Margaret was the guest of honor to a large
party hosted by Lally Weymouth, a writer and journalist and the daughter
of Katharine Graham, the *Washington Post* publisher. Weymouth had invited
seventy guests to a buffet dinner in honor of Lord Weidenfeld, the British
publisher who had recently established himself in New York, and fifty
additional guests for drinks afterward. Following her flight from London,
Princess Margaret was too tired to attend. But Weidenfeld's power and
Weymouth's social connections had created a glamorous guest list: CBS's
William Paley was there; Jackie Kennedy (now Onassis); the British ambassador Peter Jay; Marella Agnelli; Katharine Graham; Jerry Brown; John
Kenneth Galbraith; Joseph Alsop; Lillian Hellman; William Styron; Susan
Sontag; Gay Talese; Jason Epstein; Clay Felker, the *Esquire* editor; Mort
Janklow, the lawyer-agent; Pete Hamill, the writer; Max Palevsky, the high-
level Democratic fund-raiser and power broker from California; and, among
others, even Sue Mengers and Sam Spiegel. When Gore and Howard arrived at about 11 P.M., the rooms of the large apartment were crowded with
guests. Aware that Jackie would be there, Howard, Gore recalled, thought
"I should make up with Jackie and this was the night when it was going to
happen." Lally Weymouth asked Gore, " 'Do you want to say hello to her?'
'No,' I said, 'I'll stay here, and if she wants to talk, she can come on in
here.' " Weymouth went to the kitchen. Mailer was talking with Onassis.
His companion, Norris Church, came to tell him that Gore had arrived.
Mailer went into the living room to find Vidal. He walked directly toward
him. Norris went with him. Sitting on a couch at one end of the room, Gore

saw him coming and rose to meet him. Accounts differ as to the dialogue. Mailer's day-after account: "I said to Vidal, 'You look like a Jewish socialist,' which is to be differentiated from a socialist Jew. The former is a way of twitting him; the latter would be anti-Semitic. You see, years ago, Vidal used to refer to me as a 'Jewish socialist.' " Mailer's account twenty years later: " 'You look like an old socialist." Vidal's account: "Mailer said, 'You look like an old Jew.' So I said in my wittiest repartee, 'Well, Norman, you look like an old Jew, too.' " All the contemporary reports from observers agree that Mailer said either "Jew" or "Jewish," though clearly it was an attempt at hostile humor, not anti-Semitism. Mailer denies the use of either word. "He said later that I said to him, 'You look like an old Jewish socialist,' which was so fucking clever of him, to turn things around, as if I were an anti-Semite."

Contemporary accounts of what then happened differ. As the ten seconds of dialogue ended, Mailer apparently threw the contents of his glass at Vidal's face, hitting him with the liquor and ice cubes. Mailer's recent comment: "Well, it's hard to hit someone cold. I was trying to work myself up to hit him. I was getting psyched up to fight. But the fact is that I was on the warpath strategically, not physically. So I couldn't hit him. But what I did was to throw my drink and ice cubes at him. He reported later that he saw a small fist coming at him. . . . But it was the drink and the ice cubes. Frustrated, I raised my arm and I threw the liquor glass down at him and hit him on the head with it. He must have been stunned and maybe blacked out for a second. It certainly would have given him a cut or at least a welt. This whole thing took about fifteen seconds." Vidal's account: "He threw the contents of the glass in my face and said to the press that it was an old street fighter's trick, to blind the other person. He then followed with what he thought would be a punch but he still had the glass in his hand. So what he does is hit my upper lip with the glass in his hand. Mind you, he's way down here. I'm much taller, and the glass goes across my lip. It doesn't do much damage, but I bite the inside and get some blood coming down from inside." As they faced one another, Mailer grabbed Vidal by the arm. Vidal grabbed Mailer's lapel and shirt front with both hands, Mailer gripping tightly, leaving bruise marks that remained for weeks, Vidal shaking Mailer, attempting to break loose his hold on his arm. For a moment they could have been perceived as being in an energetic embrace. By this time people were aware that there was a fight in progress. Those closest to the combatants had seen the scuffle. Lally Weymouth came from the kitchen to find "two guys punching each other out in my living room. . . . I didn't know who was hitting whom. Needless to say I was not thrilled to be having a fistfight at my party, and when I saw what was happening, I said, 'God, this is so awful; somebody do something,' and Clay Felker said, 'Shut up, this fight is making your party!' " Janklow, who was talking to Hamill and Felker, rushed over to try to separate the two. So did Howard. Gore shook Mailer's grip loose from his arm and shoved him away. Mailer stumbled into Palevsky, who spilled his glass of champagne over Weymouth's dress. Sam Spiegel went immediately to Mailer to try to convince him not to rush back toward Vidal, which he seemed about to do. "People almost immediately separated us," Mailer recalls. Vidal went toward the far side of the room, where, seated on the couch he'd been on when Mailer came toward him, Sue Mengers dabbed at the blood on his lip with a handkerchief. Jackie Onassis stood in the doorway watching.

From his side of the room Mailer challenged Vidal to come downstairs with him and have it out in the street. "Howard came up to me," Mailer recalls, "and said he would fight for Gore. I said, 'My fourteen-year-old son could take you.' Howard never forgave me for that remark." According to Vidal, Mailer "made several passes and said, 'Let's go outside and settle this!' Then Howard chased him out: 'Fuckin' asshole loser!' " Gore's "nothing but a mouth," Mailer insisted. Jason Epstein said, "Norman, grow up!" Mailer turned to Lally Weymouth and said, "Either he goes or I do." When she refused to ask either of them to leave, Mailer stormed out, with Norris. As he sat on the couch, stanching the blood on his lip, Gore turned and saw Jackie in the doorway watching him. He turned away. When he turned back in her direction, she was gone. The postmortems and the press war began immediately, and the funny comments. "Frankly, after speaking to both combatants," Janklow remarked, "I consider the incident to be one of the great moments of modern literature." Gore, who had already been booked for a Dick Cavett show taping the next day, used a portion of his airtime jokingly to belittle Mailer's aggression. Mailer recalls that he immediately "went to Cavett with a lawyer because of Gore's libelous remarks. We settled it by Cavett giving us each a half hour, back to back I think," which Mailer insisted on. Cavett recalls that he called Mailer and invited him to view the tape of Vidal's interview. "Poor Norman," Gore soon wrote to Ned Bradford, who was now Mailer's editor at Little, Brown, " 'wrote' all the accounts of the 28 second punch and shove (he landed on top of Max Palevsky some eight feet away from me). But the battle report was filed by yr. author with every gossip columnist in town in order to make it appear (a) there was a battle (b) he was the victor. He may yet return to fiction full-time and cut yr. losses." Soon, in California, Gore referred to the experience as "the night of the small fists." Russell Baker wrote a column in the *Times* about the literary rivals the bloodthirsty Henry James had beaten up. But "James finally retired from pugilism after Edith Wharton knocked him out for 35 minutes with her famous powder-puff uppercut during a chance meeting at Alice Roosevelt's coming-out party."

Over the next few years Mickey Knox tried, unsuccessfully, to mediate a reconciliation. From Vidal's point of view there was nothing worth reconciling. They had never really been friends, though prior to 1971 they had been amiable colleagues. Gore had not been judgmental about Mailer's violence and drunkenness in the 1960s. But he had been appalled and furious at Mailer's two assaults on him, which he saw as not in the least existential or romantic, let alone heroic. In 1984 Mailer, in the role of conciliatory elder statesman, having taken on the presidency of PEN, the international writers' organization, invited Vidal to help him bury the hatchet. Would he not join Mailer and about fifteen other writers and participate in one of a series of literary evenings in the fall of 1985 to raise money for the convocation of a PEN World Congress? And whatever his decision about participating in the public event, he wanted Gore to know that the offer of a personal reconciliation still stood, though "we won't have a full roster without you." Vidal, who feared he might find the hatchet buried in his back, could not be sure to what degree the offer of personal reconciliation was the necessary price Mailer felt he had to pay to get him to participate in the fund-raising event. "Our feud, whatever its roots for each of us, has become a luxury," Mailer wrote to Vidal in November. "It's possible in years to come that we'll both have to be manning the same sinking boat at the same time." Indeed, each independently was aware that the audience for serious literature was diminishing, the trend in the direction of decreasing sales for the literary novelists of their generation. Those who once were cultural icons had good reason to fear they were becoming peripheral. But "apart from that, I'd still like to make up," Mailer wrote. "An element in me, absolutely immune to weather and tides, runs independently fond of you." The inflated language of the personal overture seemed histrionically self-aggrandizing. And Vidal was understandably suspicious of the sincerity of the claim of fondness; after all, in their two last personal encounters Mailer had attacked him physically. "If he had so much as an atom of authenticity in his nature," Gore wrote to Paul Bowles, "one might respond to that; but all is performance and ambition, and so I shall reply amiably and with an insincerity quite equal to his: I boast, perhaps." To Bowles, privately, he characterized Mailer as "the Great Halvah Merchant" who "is now president of PEN and ricocheting around the lit. world (don't ask me where *that* is) in a mad quest for the Nobel prize (God knows he's bad enough to get it) and lit. respectability and the world's acceptance that he is really numero uno. . . . Oh, the drama of it! Imagine caring that much, at 61. Earlier, yes. But now we are such stuff as dissertations are made on and our little careers are rounded with a boredom." Mailer may have been acting sincerely in his role as peacemaker. There had been, though, too much unpleasantness between them for any reconciliation to be more than perfunctory, in this case pragmatic. Vidal agreed to participate in the fund-raising event.

In early 1985 the program took shape. Each of the eight evenings would be shared by two authors, each of whom, as a matter of preference, might take half the evening separately or join his colleague in a tandem performance. "Do you have someone you'd like to go on with?" Mailer asked Vidal in January 1985, giving him the privilege of first choice. The possibilities included the usual suspects, from Woody Allen to Tom Wolfe. With mischievous humor, Gore proposed that he and Mailer share an evening. He may have done so with the conviction that he would benefit from their juxtaposition as stage performers. "All right, fine, it'll be you and me on the date you've named," Mailer responded. "I do think, however, we've got to address ourselves to an agenda. If we have nothing to do with one another and merely give our separate hours, then everyone's going to be prodigiously disappointed. . . . The evening will be a frightful anticlimax." Mailer suggested that they might read from Shaw's *Don Juan in Hell*. He hoped that "the example of Gore Vidal and Norman Mailer having fun together on the stage will suggest that anything and everything is possible in this overweight, corrupt world of ours." Vidal proposed that on the stage together they each address the audience on whatever topic each wanted for approximately an hour and then respond to questions from a moderator.

The courtly, highly admired New York City journalist, Murray Kempton, whose columns were famous for their trenchant and iconoclastic realism and whom both writers respected, agreed to serve as moderator. As the time of the event approached, the New York literary and social rumor mill began to work up enthusiasm for what was soon being billed as a return grudge match between two sluggers who had fought it out before and who might, if the audience were lucky, once more treat everyone to a nasty performance. Would Mailer physically attack Vidal again? The betting odds were against that. Would there be at least a renewal of their war of words? Hopes were high. Subscriptions were purchased, many by well-to-do corporate PEN supporters. Celebrities arrived, including Joanne Woodward and Paul Newman, and a long list of noted New York and Los Angeles literary, movie, and social people. On the rematch night of November 17, before a $1,000-a-ticket full house at the Booth Theatre, the combatants refused to fight. As a confrontational entertainment the evening was a failure. As intellectual stimulation it had severe limits. Vidal, the classicist, had created a talk, for which he had written out the text, later to be published in *The Nation* as "The Day the American Empire Ran Out of Gas." Mailer thought it "a brilliant talk on détente between Russia and China and who was going to inherit the earth. It had nothing to do with him and with me personally. I think people were surprised. But it was one of Gore's masterstrokes to do this. It was a hell of a good essay." Mailer, the romantic, had not prepared a presentation, trusting to inspiration and spontaneity. His criticism of American "plastic" culture fell as flat as his jokes, one of which Vidal recalls as an example of Mailer's poor timing as a storyteller: "Mailer said to the audience, 'Gore says I can't tell a joke. Well, just to show him that he's wrong, I'll tell a joke right now. This wealthy self-made New York man was showing a visitor around his expensive apartment. He was showing off all the valuable things he had. "This is my expensive living-room furniture. This is a magnificent painting I bought. This is my . . ." He opened the door to a bedroom. On the bed there was a beautiful blond lady. "This is my wife," he said. In bed with the beautiful lady, fucking her, was a handsome young man. "That's me!" he said.' End of joke. Nobody laughed. It's all a matter of timing." Perhaps, though, the audience thought the joke itself not funny. "We may both be known in literary history for our feud rather than our works," Mailer admitted, and he certainly not for his jokes. To liven up his performance Mailer read a selection from his essay on the first Ali-Frazier fight. By

the time of the question-and-answer period a large part of the audience had
left. Questioners tried to arouse controversial responses or to draw Mailer
and Vidal into open conflict. Vidal declined. In Mailer's view, "he didn't
want to allow the question period to be used as vehicle for us to debate since
the evening was his already."

Whatever had been interesting about the relationship had now been
relegated to the past, footnotes to literary gossip and literary history, often
indistinguishable categories in the long-standing cultural text. Since the 1985
appearance for PEN, "we've been professionally over the feud," Mailer
feels, "and are half friendly. Gore tries not to be too nasty." When Vidal
tried to read some of Mailer's recent fiction, his judgment was mixed with
antagonism and fair praise: "every line is loaded with the agony of a man
consciously trying to be great, and I somehow think this is probably not the
way to go about it. Yet when he relaxes, he can be extraordinarily good."
Mailer found it satisfying to reserve most of his praise for Vidal as a writer
of essays. A retrospective tone began gradually, over the next decade, to
soften their respective analyses of some of their crucial divisions and differences of literary and personal temperament. The issue of manliness, though,
of early post–World War II muscle-flexing and prejudices about appropriate
male sexual roles, so important to both men, still seemed crucial to their
attempts to mediate the differences between them, personally if not intellectually. Vidal: "Norman *is* homophobic—whatever that means—but it's very
complicated. He's against masturbation. He's against condoms. Good fucks
make good babies. He's got all sorts of strange crotchets." Mailer: "No, I've
never been irked or bothered by Gore's homosexuality. Gore has always
treated his homosexuality as a rather interesting quirk caused by—whatever.
As a homosexual, he's very much a man. He insists on that and he acts that
way. In sex, he does it. . . . No one does anything to him. So he's just as
much a male as any 'convict,' so to speak, any strong male. That's never
entered into our feuding. But we have been very competitive with one
another. For me it was the same as with Jim Jones, but there was more
affection there. But I think people who love Gore's work aren't going to be
drawn to mine anyway. So there was competition, from the beginning, for
success and fame—but not for readers. Anyway, we're in the same boat.
Neither of us will have any readers if things keep going on the way they
are." As combatants they had been of interest. As amiable, cooperative
elderly writers, who still essentially did not like one another and had not

forgiven the other for wounds previously inflicted, whatever had seemed significant about their pairing seemed less so. During the next decade they were to see one another rarely, but always without visible conflict. In fact, though Vidal had not much affection to extend to Mailer, he found he quite liked Norris Church, whom Mailer had married since the encounter at Lally Weymouth's, where "Gore had the notion," Mailer recalls, "that Norris was somehow forbidding or implacable. . . . But Norris then was still working as a model and had on the company face that she always had to wear in those days. So here was this tall, rather distinguished-looking woman, whom Gore didn't know, closely observing and seemingly dispassionately looking down on the whole thing. . . . Gore and she have become quite amiable. They rather like one another." In 1993, when Mailer was raising money for the Actors Studio, Gore accepted his invitation to appear with him in a reading performance of *Don Juan in Hell* in which "Susan Sontag played Elvira, Gore played the Devil," Gay Talese played Don Juan, "and I played the statue. I also directed. Both Susan Sontag and Gore had a strong sense of how they wanted to play those roles. So as director I didn't interfere very much. I was a passive director and let them do what they wanted to do. Gore was surprisingly good. Very, very good, really. His detractors say he can be a ham. That's because as an actor his voice carries the brunt of his acting, which is true. But he's very, very good at it. This was a distinguished performance." In 1995 they both accommodated a friend of Mailer's who wanted to interview them at length for *Esquire*, though the interview had nothing especially interesting, let alone new, to add to the Mailer-Vidal saga. "I have nothing to say, only to add," had become one of Vidal's favorite comments. Both writers were becoming increasingly aware that there was less that needed saying and less time in which to add anything at all.

———————

Having signed a new two-novel contract with Random House in 1977, he had delivered *Kalki*, which had done adequately in hardcover, unexpectedly poorly in paperback. The contract, for $1.2 million—the smaller portion for *Kalki*, the larger for an unnamed novel that, it was generally agreed, would be a historical fiction—had been negotiated by Owen Laster, the senior literary agent at William Morris. Laster had been handling Vidal's backlist for the contracts Helen Strauss had negotiated before Gore himself took over handling the rights to his literary works in the United States.

Graham Watson at Curtis Brown still took care of British rights. Foreign-language contracts, except for Germany, had been managed by Little, Brown. Over the years, as Laster rose at William Morris, he had eventually, by 1976, persuaded Vidal to allow him to negotiate all his other literary contracts. A soft-spoken New Yorker, both self-effacing and clever, Laster, a great movie enthusiast in his youth who had first heard of Vidal as a famous scriptwriter, had risen through the ranks at William Morris from the mailroom in 1961, then into the television department, and finally the literary department. When Strauss left, he became the senior literary agent. In the early 1970s Gore "asked me some questions about what kind of deal I had for Michener. He might not have said Michener explicitly, but he knew that I had the big one, and I think he was fishing around. It was a very entertaining meeting: he did imitations of Truman Capote and Tennessee Williams. It was the first time I was alone with him. . . . I remember saying to him that I get paid for this kind of advice and I remember suggesting that we work together. He said, 'I bet you're going to insist on the movie situation.' I said, 'Ya.' He said, 'Well then, I don't think so.' I went back to the office and went in to see Nat Lefkowitz. 'Look,' I said, 'I think I can get Gore Vidal back as a client, but I can't get back everything. He just won't do it.' Nat said, 'Stay after him.' . . . Then he did another contract with Random House for *Myron* and *1876*. It was around the time of publication of *1876* and *Kalki* that he agreed to come to William Morris in all areas." Eager to capitalize on the success of *Burr* and *1876*, Random House had consented to part with a huge sum for the two-book contract, which helped affirm Laster's argument that not only could he relieve Vidal of tedious detail for which he had little patience and less talent but that William Morris could negotiate better contracts for him than he could for himself. When, influenced by Robert Gurland, an American lawyer practicing in London, Vidal proposed to Laster and Random House that instead of the usual arrangement for an advance against royalties the contract be structured as a loan, which the recipient, not Vidal but a newly created corporate entity, would pay back over a ten-year period, both Laster and Random House felt uneasy, partly because it was so different from the usual publishing-industry practices. As the tax advantage to Vidal would be considerable, Random House reluctantly agreed to the new configuration. "This was the summer of 1977," Laster recalls. "I was watching television, and suddenly the screen went blank. There had been a blackout in New

York, the notorious 1977 blackout. Soon afterward, during that vacation, I was talking to Gore. . . . For some reason, I think at least partly because of the blackout, Gore had become very concerned about this complicated deal." Life in the modern world, he told Laster, had become "too complicated . . . the infrastructure too fragile. Everything might collapse. He suddenly said, 'Just go to Random House and do the equivalent of an ordinary contract.' "

Jason Epstein, who probably had in mind another novel like *Burr* or *1876* as the second in the 1977 contract, discovered to his surprise that the new book Vidal was working on in Los Angeles, where he had finished *Kalki,* had nothing to do with American history. It was set in the fifth century B.C., its subject a panoramic presentation through the eyes of a fictional Persian diplomat and world traveler of the religious beliefs and cultures of Persian Zoroastrianism, Indian Buddhism, and Chinese Confucianism. Vidal's interest in religion dominated the novel, which, Epstein soon saw, combined what seemed to him an antinovelistic preoccupation with descriptive pedagogy and a fictional travel narrative in which the narrator was less important than what he observed. Epstein's notion of fiction was grounded in the realistic tradition and in the coordinates of modernism. Vidal had the eighteenth-century novel of ideas and Thomas Mann as his models, though his late-twentieth-century adaptation had its particular Vidalian obsessions, including his concern with the interaction between culture, personality, and power, as well as his general detestation of Christianity, which—with its two collegial monotheisms, Judaism and Islam—had done, he felt, great damage to the human condition. Of the three nonmonotheistic religions of *Creation,* the eventual title of the novel-in-progress, it is Confucian materialism that the novel most admires. As in *Julian,* Vidal evokes the details of the life of these disparate worlds with a specificity that makes ancient history and religions compellingly real. Retrospectively narrated in old age by Cyrus, a fictional fifth-century-B.C. Persian diplomat, his account of his adventures gives the novel its narrative unity. Having spent his life traveling to Greece, Asia Minor, India, and China as a high-level representative of his government, he finds himself, on his last mission, compelled to serve as special ambassador to the quarrelsome, uncivilized Athenians. An eager adventurer as well as diplomat, he has obtained on his various voyages pleasures, burdens, thrills, wives, and some wisdom, particularly in his lifelong effort to answer the central cosmological questions associated with the history of religion: what is the nature of existence and is there a creator of all things? As the grandson of Zoroaster and a believer in his religious philosophy, Cyrus has a passionate interest in the fundamental issues with which the dynamic emerging world religions of the first half of the fifth century B.C. are grappling. As a novelist, historian, and cultural anthropologist, Vidal puts us into Cyrus's mind: we see the Persian-Greek hostilities from the Persian viewpoint; Cyrus's Zoroastrianism, vaguely anticipating some Christian doctrine, is the touchstone against which he measures Buddhism, Tao ("The Way"), and Confucianism, the progenitors of all three of which Cyrus meets and queries. In the end it is Confucius's engagement with the ethical problems of this world (especially how to balance the interests of the individual and the community) that Cyrus finds most compelling, a novelistic striking of the characteristic Vidalian note.

What was to be both a critical and a commercial triumph did not, however, come easily. There were two problems to overcome: the size to which the manuscript quickly grew and Epstein's dissatisfaction with its execution, partly its length and his preference for a more fully novelized presentation in the realistic tradition, mostly his concern that the subject matter did not have a large enough audience to result in the sales necessary to justify the huge advance. Epstein did not believe, Vidal thought his attitude implied, that Americans cared to read about ancient religions or religious subjects at all. By late winter 1979, as Vidal's Hollywood stay drew to a close, he had done over fifteen hundred longhand pages. "I have made five visits to various health spas," he wrote to Judith Halfpenny, particularly La Costa, "and so avoided the glory and the agony of le show biz while completing the Chinese section. . . . Since I've not read the book for almost a year, I expect all sorts of surprises when it comes time to see just what pattern there is in this carpet. I suspect one large circle, which could be zero-nothing or O! Or a circle; indeed, the presiding emblem." *Voyage* was the working title. He himself preferred *O*, though Epstein disliked it. They settled on *Creation* as a compromise, though Gore was certain he would never like that title and soon grew to hate it. "It is apt, certainly. But one does not quite like the Michenerian ring." Confucius seemed to him "the only one of my Great Figures done in the round. Most likeable. I haven't got to Socrates but I suspect he'll be a minor irritant. He sets on edge the teeth of my Persian narrator. . . . The Buddha is the

Cheshire cat . . . but then he is *not.*" But doing characters in the round was not in his judgment germane to the nature and intent of *Creation*. Soon after Gore finished the manuscript in Rome and Ravello in spring and early summer, Jason registered his dissatisfaction, though he agreed with Gore that "you don't need a conventional narrative with a sustained plot and so forth; this would be impossible in any case, and would trivialize the material. Yet there are stretches where Cyrus seems to be simply a chronicler, not a participant, and the effect of this is for the reader to lose track of him as a character, and thus lose track occasionally of the story as well." Part of the problem was focus, part length: the manuscript was twelve hundred typed pages. Gore did some sustained rewriting, making substantial cuts in two sections, which he believed weakened the book. He felt he was "trudging up a mountain of work." Jason still was dissatisfied. "The first third he said he thought one of the best things he'd ever read. But the second third—he'd figured out that the American people wouldn't like it. . . . He did everything to block it, including one of the dreariest tricks in the business which was to get a copy editor to check every line I'd written. Can you prove that Tibet is actually west of China? It was nothing but dragging feet, trying not to publish it." There were other irritants, including the attempt of the Ravello municipality to hold him responsible for the damage done by mudslides to the houses a thousand feet down the mountain. "The sindaco would like me to spend a million or two dollars to shore up a very large mountain. Phrases like until hell freezes over come to my lips in dialect.

In early September, Laster, who had been vacationing in Milan, came down to Ravello for two days, his first visit to La Rondinaia, partly in the hope that he could help resolve the disagreement between Gore and Jason about *Creation*. Almost as soon as Ignazio, a Ravellese who had become Gore's regular driver (they found it easier to make an annual arrangement for regular limousine service to take them everywhere locally or to the airport at Naples than to drive themselves), had delivered Owen to La Rondinaia, Gore sat him down on the sun-filled terrace with a chapter of the manuscript. "The place is absolute paradise. It was so gorgeous," Laster recalled. "You're fifteen hundred feet up, looking down at the sea. But that was the last time I ever offered any editorial comment and certainly not in conjunction with the publisher." As Owen read, Gore walked down to Amalfi to get newspapers. When he returned, Owen remarked that maybe

Jason had a point, especially about the length of the book. Gore exploded into a tirade. "I couldn't get another word out. He was so furious with me. He was always, I think, difficult to edit. He's always wanted it his way. I recognized then that in the future I was not to take any editorial positions. Just see what Gore wanted. From that moment I backed away." As usual, Gore's situational anger affected neither his loyalty nor his hospitality. That night they went to Zacharia's in Amalfi, his favorite local restaurant, where they dined on delectable seafood, and then stayed up late drinking and talking, his usual routine with visitors, which he expanded, on Owen's next visit, to include listening to pop records, amused by some young tourists who came back to the villa with them, dancing into the morning hours. "It was totally social, nothing sexual, though Gore asked me if I wanted one of the kids, saying, 'I think that one likes you.' I wouldn't have dreamed of it, in his house." Jason's attempt to pressure Gore to make additional changes continued, particularly to make more cuts and to add touches that would increase the illusion of conventional realism. Epstein feared that the novel was still too long for its subject matter, that Americans would not make a bestseller out of a pedagogic novel about non-Western religions. By mid-fall, Gore issued an ultimatum: either publish this last version or release him from his contract. He half hoped the latter would be the case. He also regretted, even resented, that Owen's manner with Random House was conciliatory rather than confrontational. The notion of returning to Little, Brown had its attractions. Finally Epstein gave in. *Creation*, which was published in March 1981, quickly rose almost to the top of the bestseller list. When, in Vidal's view, Random House failed to capitalize on its immediate success, which he assumed came as a surprise to the publisher, and the book's sales consequently did not continue their ascent, he strongly registered his resentment to Epstein. Jason, he believed, was to blame. Though Gore could partly forgive him, the disjunction between their sensibilities, as well as what seemed to him Jason's meddling beyond his purview or his abilities, had now become even more of an ongoing consideration.

What had been a serious disjunction soon threatened to become permanently divisive. They had taken another of their eating trips through southern France, and both did their best to act as if their differences about *Creation* had not affected their personal relationship. When Gore was in New York, they had their usual social interactions, though the gradual disaffiliation between Barbara and Jason made even more pronounced the difference between the closeness of Gore and Barbara and the growing chill between Gore and Jason. "Barbara's relationship with Jason also deteriorated," Vidal recalled. "They got a divorce. Then everything improved. They still work as a team and help each other out. But they aren't in each other's way." Gore simply felt he had an insufficiently sympathetic editor who seemed to think he knew better than his author. But his editor was also his personal friend, almost a family member. After Howard and Barbara, and a less full embrace of Diana Phipps and Claire Bloom—both of whom by the early to mid-eighties Gore saw less of—Jason was one of three or four people with whom he had an intimacy familial enough to be fraternal. At Rome and Ravello there were numbers of friends at the next closest circle: Mickey Knox somewhat, but particularly George Armstrong, Luigi Corsini, and Michael Tyler-Whittle, though the last was, under pressure from his wife, to return permanently to England. In America, Christopher Isherwood and Richard Poirier had a touch of the familial. Nini had more than a touch, but differences of ideology and personality made the relationship less a friendship than a bloodline burden. Corsini, a slim, handsome man, whose fascination with America had made him one of Italy's foremost experts on American culture, visited frequently at La Rodinaia as he moved back and forth between Rome, where he lived, and Salerno, where he taught at the university. Howard was, of course, the center of Gore's personal life. Rat, whom he adored, came a bestial but important second. That Jason was also a member of the inner circle made their differences about *Creation* especially difficult, though less so for Jason, who assumed that his function as an editor and an independent personality required that he make himself bluntly clear on literary issues. If there was honor in that, there was also danger of solipsistic self-assertion. But Jason did not anticipate that such differences would undermine their friendship, as if Gore were any more capable than another author of separating his editor's lack of support for his work from the personal relationship. From the beginning Jason had felt no attraction to Gore's "Chinese boxes," though previously he had not revealed any coolness about historical works of the sort that Gore assumed *Creation* was. "Barbara liked them. I didn't hate *Myra Breckinridge,*" Epstein recalled, "but I saw the point of it too quickly. I got it right away and said, 'Okay, now what, and why bother?' He told the joke, and let's go on from here. Then he kept writing it over and over again," which was precisely his response when, after the publication of *Creation*, Gore turned to a new "invention," a surrealistic comedy as darkly wild and imaginatively satirical as *Myra Breckinridge*.

Duluth, which reached bookstores in April 1983, brought Epstein and Vidal almost to the breaking point. When Jason responded unenthusiastically to the manuscript, Gore, furious, proposed that Jason's young assistant, Gary Fisketjon, who admired *Duluth* and seemed temperamentally sympathetic to Gore's inventions, edit the new novel rather than Jason. Angry and hurt, Jason felt rejected. "I said, 'Jason, just stay away from the goddamned book. I don't want to hear your opinions. Let Gary Fisketjon handle it.' He said fine. Then he started to interfere, which was his way of destroying it. He went to the salesmen, saying this is not the Vidal book. We'll wait for the next historical. Gary was the buffer between Jason and me for *Duluth*."

Vidal himself thought more highly of his "inventions" than his historical novels, as he told Richard Poirier, who had read the new novel in manuscript and thought it brilliant. With respect and appreciation, Gore dedicated it to him. "I do value more highly the *Brecks* and *Duluths* than the historical meditations but then I like invention. Just back from a week in Moscow (where I am much read—they even study TV tapes!) and outer Mongolia (where no one is). We must hand it to our masters: the notion that USSR is a formidable opponent, ever-restless, with genocide in its heart must be, easily, the finest PR invention since Ivy Lee [Rockefeller's publicist] got J.D. Rockefeller to give away dimes." *Duluth* is, among other things, a novel that indirectly dramatizes American Cold War follies, the surreal madness of the "Russians are coming" scenario that drove American domestic and foreign-policy considerations for decades. "*Duluth* is my favorite of these books," Vidal recalled. "The same thing happened with *Duluth* as with *Myra*. 'Duluth! Love it or loathe it, *you can never leave it or lose it.*' That sentence just came thundering into my head one day as I was walking down the street in Rome. What on earth is *that*, I thought. I sat down at the desk, and there it was: the whole novel just opened itself before me." As with *Myra*, he wrote it quickly, at white heat, and he himself determined that, like *Myra*, the book would be kept as long as possible from reviewers. "*Duluth* emerges in the book stores in April" 1983, he wrote to Judith Halfpenny. "The plan is no advertising, no review copies sent out, no appearances by the author. There will be a bill-board on Sunset Blvd showing the somewhat surreal dust jacket; and another near the Queensborough Bridge, Manhattan. Then we shall see what happens. . . . The book is a tribute to the Family and, of course, to warm mature Hetero relationships; there are also tributes to Consumerism and Lying, the two American specialties."

Science fiction and the surreal as vehicles for satiric comedy dominate *Duluth*. Like *Myra*, it is a witty literary novel. Time and space are subordinated to associative changes of scene, which take their parodic tone from soap opera and from the popular novel's sentimental romance genre. Drawing on, among other things, his long exposure to popular culture, especially of the television and movie-script variety, Vidal creates a sophisticated fiction out of self-consciousness about narrative alternatives. On such topics Vidal never lacks cleverness, and *Duluth* raises cleverness to high art of the sort that Italo Calvino, who had become one of Vidal's admirers, had in mind when he cryptically commented that he considered Vidal "to be a master of that new form which is taking shape in world literature and which we may call the hyper-novel or the novel elevated to the square or to the cube." *Duluth* is beautifully bizarre. One of its subjects is, of course, itself. But that "itselfness" has a strong social conscience. It examines late-twentieth-century versions of the issues that Vidal was always interested in: justice, power, human dignity, the distribution of resources, and the human condition, particularly its social and political dimensions. In the dehumanized world of *Duluth*, all narratives have been reduced to wildly popular soap operas, and the most blatantly dramatic, comedic representations of the reduction take place not only on television and in popular fiction but in class, race, and sex wars in the streets of this new, all-purpose, cosmopolitan city ironically called Duluth, but actually a new city in a vastly rearranged American geography. It is a Duluth with palm trees, as if all American cities were inexorably slouching toward Las Vegas. It is a city of the American future made of elements of its past in which class, race warfare, and widespread public and private corruption are the main legacies. In the end it is colonized by superior beings, insectlike invaders from outer space. For Duluth substitute America, "love it or loathe it" (in the opening words of the novel), and now loved, loathed, left, lost. It is a disappointed lover's bitterly elegiac, wittily imaginative lament for what once was (at least in expectation) and now is no longer. Like many bitter elegies for past and present depredations, especially one so highly and challengingly literary, its audience was limited. It did not make the bestseller list. The critical reception was mixed to poor. The response from many was uncomprehending bewilderment. They preferred Vidal's more traditional straight narratives, preferably about American history. Some expressed angry rejection, particularly on political grounds. One reviewer said that the next time Vidal "deplores the mediocrity of American fiction on a talk show, the host should throw this book at him." A few, such as Richard Poirier, thought it a satiric masterpiece.

———

In September 1981 *Commentary* published an article, "The Boys on the Beach," by Midge Decter, the conservative writer and wife of *Commentary*'s editor, Norman Podhoretz, that Vidal felt deserved an answer. Podhoretz had made *Commentary*, whose influential readership outbalanced its modest circulation, a vehicle for neoconservative views. Vidal and Podhoretz had been amiable acquaintances in the New York literary world in the 1960s when Podhoretz, at first an outspoken liberal, had become the editor of *Commentary*, which for a time he moved to the left, especially on social issues. They had seen one another occasionally at parties. Once they had shared a taxi and chatted pleasantly. Podhoretz urged Vidal to write reviews for *Commentary*, where in 1970 he published Vidal's essay, "Literary Gangsters." With his wife, Podhoretz moved to neoconservatism in the early 1970s, as a strong supporter of the Israeli political right in particular. In Los Angeles in the late seventies, at a party at which they were both guests, he and Vidal had an argument that touched on American foreign policy. Podhoretz, whose habit was to disguise gut feelings as rational presentations relentlessly repeated as if repetition proved his point, had seemed to Vidal inappropriately and loudly argumentative, without any visible sense of humor. Now, in 1981, Barbara Epstein, horrified at Decter's article, had brought it to Gore's attention. Decter's article seemed to Vidal stereotypically homophobic, partly a response to increasing gay activism, partly an attempt to deflate the occasional claim by homosexuals that the gay lifestyle was superior to the heterosexual, and mostly a visceral loathing of alien creatures, too many of whom had turned the beaches at Fire Island, where the Podhoretzes had a summer home, into a parade ground for homosexual queens.

The 1970s indeed had been vintage years for American homophobia.

There was a backlash against the sexual and feminist liberation activity of the 1960s. Gay men, from San Francisco to Fire Island, came aggressively, and often with a sense of political cohesion, out of closets and slums. The popular culture, from rural communities to suburban enclaves to urban hard hats, continued to be pervasively homophobic either with low-keyed indifference or violent words and acts. The issue was generally "manliness." Homosexuals were not men. If Truman Capote had "not existed in his present form," Vidal wrote, "another would have been run up on the old sewing machine because that sort of *persona* must be, for a whole nation, the stereotype of what a fag is." Some American liberals identified with the gay-rights movement. It was another honorable attempt to advance civil liberties and equal rights for oppressed minorities that had begun with the Civil War. Others did not, particularly those, like Alfred Kazin and Irving Howe, who no matter how liberal their politics otherwise, felt uncomfortable with the mannerisms and, especially, the promiscuity associated with the most publicly visible and self-dramatizing gay groups. The claim that homosexuality was an illness or at least an affliction still had wide currency. In 1970 Joseph Epstein, in *Harper's* magazine, had made the case with brutal insensitivity: "If I had the power to do so, I would wish homosexuality off the face of this earth," he wrote. "I would do so because I think that it brings infinitely more pain than pleasure to those who are forced to live with it. . . . *They are different from the rest of us* . . . in a way . . . that cuts deeper than other kinds of human differences—religious, class, racial—in a way that is, somehow, more fundamental. Cursed without clear cause, afflicted without apparent cure, they are an affront to our rationality." By the end of the 1970s the conservatism that would gather triumphant force in the Reagan 1980s had begun to coalesce, a values-oriented politics that made strange bedfellows. Its narrow definition of "normalcy" made it inherently homophobic. Many intellectual liberals, some strongly and proudly identified as Jewish—such as the sociologist Irving Kristol and the historian Gertrude Himmelfarb—moved from anti-Communism to neoconservatism, strong supporters of Israel, of a large American defense budget, and of Reagan Republicanism.

In April 1978 Gore, scheduled to make appearances for *Kalki* in Boston, had been invited by John Mitzel, whom he had not seen since 1973, to speak at a fund-raising event sponsored by the Boston-Boise Committee, a civil-liberties organization dedicated to protecting homosexuals from discrimination. Mitzel, one of Vidal's most enthusiastic admirers in Boston, was an open, active proponent of civil rights for homosexuals, a writer for *Fag Rag* and *Gay Community News*, the author of a brief, idiosyncratic book, *Myra and Gore*. The Boston law-enforcement establishment, predominantly Irish-Catholic, had recently increased its enforcement of archaic anti-homosexual statutes, motivated by strong bias against what it believed perversity and by self-serving political reasons. Homosexual men were favorite targets for blackmail and exploitation. Newspapers and elected officials found it easy and profitable to whip up homophobic hysteria. A strong "anti-fag" campaign could ensure electoral victory for otherwise undistinguished district attorneys. When, in late 1977, twenty men were indicted, amid inaccurate claims by the police and banner headlines in the press, for having sex with legally underage males, the Boston-Boise Committee was formed to counter misinformantion and bias.

The authorities took up the challenge. In March 1978, in an illegal-entrapment operation, the police arrested 103 men for homosexual acts or for responding to homosexual solicitation from undercover policemen in the Boston Public Library. Paddy-wagons carted off the villains from elegant Copley Square to immediate arraignment. When Gore arrived in Boston in early April, Mitzel was delighted to introduce him to his ideological colleagues and to a packed Arlington Street Church audience, where he was the primary attraction during an evening devoted to raising money for the Boston-Boise Committee and rallying the homosexual community to fight back. His topic was "Sex and Politics in Massachusetts." With his usual combination of wit, anger, and good sense, he lambasted homophobic bigotry, puritanical Boston politics, and widespread civic corruption. The audience contained nonhomosexual civil libertarians, including Robert M. Bonin, the controversial recently appointed Superior Court chief justice, who had been selected by a liberal governor over the opposition of the entrenched legal establishment. He and his wife had purchased tickets to hear Vidal, whom they admired. A *Boston Globe* photographer had been alerted by a Bonin enemy within his office that the justice would be there. When, after Vidal's talk, Mitzel introduced them backstage, flashbulbs popped. The next day, with a photo of the two men shaking hands, the *Globe* and *Examiner* headlined "Bonin at Benefit for Sex Defendants." Sensationalistic charges and political vendettas soon overwhelmed Bonin's reasonable and spirited defenses. The charges were a combination of old, minor matters and the claim that Bonin knew he was attending a fund-raising event to help pay the legal expenses of the defendants. Apparently the event was not for that purpose, at least so far as public advertisements revealed, and Bonin claimed he had no knowledge that it was anything but a rally in favor of civil liberties at which an author he deeply admired was to speak, that he did not even know that the Boston-Boise Committee was a gay-rights group until shortly before attending. He believed he was exercising his right as a citizen to attend a public lecture by a speaker whose writings he admired. His presence did not signify agreement or disagreement with the agenda of the sponsors or the speaker. At worst his attendance was imprudent, hardly a hanging offense, but it provided a powerful pretext for his enemies to attack. Homophobia, anti-Semitism, and judicial politics—including the resentment of the former chief justice, still immensely influential in Irish-Catholic political and legal circles—soon had Bonin up on what were considered serious charges, including that he had "engaged in 'friendly conversation' with Vidal after the lecture and knew that resulting publicity 'would give the appearance' that he endorsed the criticism . . . of the administration of justice and endorsed the raising of funds for the benefit of defendants." In June, a few days short of the certainty of his being recalled by the partisan legislature, he resigned. "A fine American story with a happy ending," Gore wrote to Mitzel. "I just read the verdict. Apparently in Mass., a man of rectitude, a jurist of incorruptibility, can only prove his virtue by committing perjury. It looks like anti-fag is now the new McCarthyism."

Now, in 1981, repelled by Decter's article, Vidal immediately wrote a response, in the expectation that *The New York Review of Books* would publish it. To Vidal it seemed morally appalling and strategically mistaken for Jewish writers and intellectuals not to recognize that Jews and homosexuals were natural allies, he argued in *"Some* Jews and *The* Gays," soon renamed "Pink Triangle and Yellow Star." Barbara Epstein, who told him by phone of the editors' objections to the comparison between Jews and homosexuals, had the essay set up in type without the controversial paragraphs and brought it to him at the Plaza Hotel in the hope that he would accept her revised version. Vidal had already sent the original to Victor Navasky, the editor of *The Nation,* who was delighted to have it and published it in November 1981. It strengthened a pattern that had already been established and would grow stronger: the more radical *Nation* readily became the venue for what *The New York Review* was too timid to publish. As usual, Vidal blamed Bob Silvers, though in this case both editors were sensitive to the likely barrage of letters they might get from their readership, which included many Jewish-Americans. "The *New York Review* turned down my hard words about those Jews who attack the fags," he wrote to Judith Halfpenny. "I had said that the position of Jews and fags is the same in the USA—both equally despised by the Christian majority. *There is no analogy,* they said loftily: apparently, the Jews have absolutely won in the US and there will be no troubles ever again—even though my piece was a pretty precise sort of warning. Well . . . take a look at it. I expect a lot of turmoil, a nice row as Ld Byron would say."

It was a thorn in the side of the friendship with Barbara Epstein and reminded him of other articles of his *The New York Review* had turned down for political reasons. "Barbara was worried about the other people, the paranoid ones," Vidal later remarked. "*The New York Review* does get into enough trouble from what I call the Jewish Letterheads. The president societies. Any time they mention Israel they're going to get at least ten presidential letterheads saying, 'How can a publication with Jewish editors print such lies and so on?' Yes, the friendship has been close in spite of serious disagreements. Never being honest about their reasons." As despised or at least mistrusted minorities, Jews and homosexuals, he argued in the article, had been and would again, if Nazi-like dark forces gained the upper hand, be destroyed in the same gas chambers. Decter's depiction of homosexuals revealed ignorance, he maintained, and her strategy was to blame the victim for his victimization. On the contrary, homosexuals suffered the same sort of unprovoked persecution as that inflicted on blacks and Jews. "I would suggest that the three despised minorities join forces in order not to be destroyed. . . . After all, homosexuality is only important when made so by irrational opponents. In this as in so much else, the Jewish situation is precisely the same. . . . I would suggest a cease-fire and a common front against the common enemy, whose kindly voice is that of Ronald Reagan and whose less than kindly mind is elsewhere in the boardrooms of the Republic." Of course, some Jewish-Americans, particularly neoconservatives like Decter, Podhoretz, and Joseph Epstein, recoiled in horror. Homosexuality was a sickness. Ronald Reagan was their ally, not their enemy. The values associated with homosexuality were abhorrent. And many non-neoconservative Jews feared that making common cause with homosexuals would provoke an antagonism among Christians that would undercut the increasing acceptance of Jews as Americans. And, worse, to suggest a common gas chamber for homosexuals and Jews was to denigrate the Holocaust, a mordantly funny reference to which Vidal had used as an example of the common boat and the general disinclination of many Jews to share the Holocaust with other victims of the Nazis. "In the German concentration camps, Jews wore yellow stars while homosexualists wore pink triangles. I was present when Christopher Isherwood tried to make this point to a young Jewish movie producer. 'After all,' said Isherwood, 'Hitler killed six hundred thousand homosexuals.' The young man was not impressed. 'But Hitler killed six *million* Jews,' he said sternly. 'What are you?' asked Isherwood. 'In real estate?' " Mainstream Jewish-Americans, including liberals, mostly declined to accept Vidal's premise. Though some of their grounds varied from instance to instance, Jewish-American response in general would not and could not accept any argument that challenged the ethnocentric uniqueness of the Jewish experience, especially where the Holocaust was concerned.

Always the rationalist, usually willing if not eager to rock the boat of political correctness in both ideas and language, Vidal was treading on sacred ground. His language was refreshing to some, detestable to others. To those with a vested interest in the issue, his ideas as well as his language were unacceptable. As he recalls his conversation with Barbara Epstein about "Pink Triangle and Yellow Star," "She said, 'The Jewish situation is no way analogous to that of homosexuals.' I said, "Well, Hitler felt otherwise. After all, he was an authority, a rather negative authority, but if he thought so, I can certainly say so. If you're going to go into the scapegoating business, which American bigots love to do, each group is on the same unseaworthy boat and each will be sunk with the other.' Well, she wouldn't accept that." If the society were going to proscribe the use of words like "kike" and "fag," he would insist on purposely using them, in appropriate instances, with the self-consciousness of the raised ironic eyebrow, both to shock and to call attention to the reality and complexity of American attitudes toward minority groups. The next step after the proscription of language, he feared, would be the proscription of ideas, and unpopular ideas had a difficult, often impossible, time gaining a public forum anyway. Here was an instance in which an esteemed intellectual journal, which otherwise valued his contributions, declined to print his review-essay mainly, it would seem, because it disagreed with his ideas and feared hostile response. *The New York Review* fell far short of its implied libertarian standard. Vidal's essay made a valuable point effectively, whether or not one agreed with the central premise, which in any rational perspective was sufficiently valid to warrant publication and serious discussion. But irrational taboos and self-serving special interests made the subject difficult to handle: prior to "Pink Triangle and Yellow Star," an essay whose focus was on homophobia, there had been no particular association between Vidal and Jews other than that he shared his life with a Jewish man, that he had moved quite comfortably in the 1950s and '60s in an intellectual and media world in which he had many Jewish friends, that he had been sympathetic to and strongly supported by the Jewish community in Poughkeepsie in his 1960 congressional campaign, that he detested anti-Semitism, and that his vigorous commitment to speaking out on behalf of justice for everyone included sympathy for Jewish suffering.

Actually his mind was more on the general issues of the country than on "Pink Triangle and Yellow Star." Whatever their attitude toward homosexuals, the neoconservatives' influence on national politics was of greater importance. William Buckley now had good friends in the White House. Barry Goldwater's values were alive and well in Washington, and his son, Barry Goldwater, Jr., was the likely Republican Party candidate for senator from California in 1982. Elected in 1980, Ronald Reagan had successfully advocated an expensive defense budget and minuscule support for social welfare. As Vidal observed national politics, he began to feel the stirring of his latent desire to hold elective office. His own time would run out soon on even the possibility of fulfilling that ambition. When he toured California in the late 1970s and in 1980, speaking to audiences at college campuses, he was astounded at how much name recognition he had and how many thousands of people lined up to hear his words. In as conservative a city as Santa Barbara, five thousand people paid to listen to him. That he could be a viable candidate in 1982 in California, where he had a home, began to seem possible.

The obstacles, though, were formidable. To have a chance of being elected to the Senate he would need to have the Democratic Party nomination. His experience with the People's Party in 1968 had demonstrated the odds against a third party's having electoral success, though that had not prevented his donating $1,000 to the third-party candidacy of John Anderson in 1980. The Democratic nomination would not come cheaply. Two-term Governor Jerry Brown, the son of former governor Pat Brown, would be the candidate the party machine, weak as it was, would support. Vidal would be an outsider, with some friends within the Democratic ranks, particularly on the left; some of his Hollywood colleagues would support him; many of those who disapproved of or had fallen out with Jerry Brown would give his candidacy ballast; there would be votes for him in the gay and intellectual communities, though Brown had influence and strong supporters in both those constituencies; the generally disaffected might rally behind him, particularly those, like himself, who were disaffiliated from and found so little difference between both parties that they elevated *not* voting into a political statement. But to be competitive he would need to attract large numbers of ordinary Democrats, many of whom usually pulled the party lever automatically. That would cost money, though his estimate was that Brown's unpopularity would allow him to make a credible run at a cost that he himself could afford to pay, about $300,000. If Vidal made it a point not to accept large contributions, he could make his campaign an exemplification of his belief that elections were preposterously expensive and therefore corrupt. He could attack the huge defense budget and advocate more funds for schools, effective gun-control laws, a stronger defense of civil liberties, the decriminalization of victimless crimes, a new constitutional convention to promote more direct democracy, and a fairer tax structure that would feature a 10- to 15-percent tax on all corporations. Brown, he felt, could be beaten, and even if he himself did not in the end gain the nomination, the opportunity to have a larger platform for his views began to be difficult to resist. The expense would hardly deplete his overall resources. He did, though, have two serious concerns. If he won the nomination, where would he get the money to pay for the general campaign against a well-financed Republican opponent? That cost would be immense. He would be dependent on the Democratic Party machine and on influence-buying fat-cat contributors from the very industries and corporations he would be denouncing, though he factored in that if Barry Goldwater, Jr., were the Republican nominee he would have a weak opponent. Then $1 million of his own money, he hypothesized, would put him in the Senate. That seemed a worthwhile expenditure. But if he actually were elected, what would his life be like? "Does one want to win?" he wrote to Judith Halfpenny, who was surprised to learn of his plans. "Ah, that's a question. . . . You're right, though, that if I go to the Senate, survive the six year term (age 57–63), I'll be unable to write anything worth reading—be too old and raddled at the end to do much more than become a national *trombone* as the Italians say."

Did he actually want to give up his life as a writer? Probably not, though he would have to face that reality only if he won the election, which seemed less likely even to his friends and well-wishers than it did to him. Most thought his chances minuscule. He himself performed the enabling act of suspension of disbelief, which, combined with the attraction of having large audiences and being dramatically front and center as well as trying on, without necessarily ever having to wear, his grandfather's senatorial suit, allowed him to commit himself in his own mind to giving it a try. Six years in the Senate would provide a prominent national platform for his views. Beginning in August 1980 he more and more frequently presented his "State of the Union" talk, an elaborate form of what was to become his campaign speech, to audiences around the state and sound bites from the speech to television audiences during his usual talk-show appearances. By January 1981 newspapers were reporting that "Gore Vidal, Critic of Voting, May Seek Office," as the unfriendly *Los Angeles Times* put it. Max Palevsky, the wealthy Californian who had already made a career as a power broker, contributing large sums to Democratic candidates, and who no longer wanted to support Jerry Brown, began to push the possibility of Gore's candidacy. Palevsky, on whom Norman Mailer had fallen at Lally Weymouth's party in New York in 1977, volunteered to serve as campaign treasurer. Paul Ziffern, a prominent show-business attorney Gore had known for a long time, who had been and continued to be the most powerful behind-the-scenes Democrat in California, gave him encouragement and advice. Ziffern disliked Brown, who was his neighbor in Malibu. "Jerry had a house at that time—he was then with Linda Ronstadt—right down the beach from the Zifferns' place in Malibu," Jay Allan remembered, "and he would think nothing of coming right over the wall and into their house. So they trained their dog to attack him if he'd jump over the wall. Seriously.

They didn't like him." Ziffern gave Vidal "advice and said he'd like to see him elected but he didn't see a chance of it." Palevsky's call to the *Los Angeles Times* initiated the newspaper speculation about Vidal's running for the senate.

No, Vidal wrote to *People* magazine in February, "I have not 'thrown my hat in the ring' for the Democratic senatorial nomination in 1982. I am not a candidate. I am barely at the stage known as 'seriously considering a race,' which means, in English, where is the money going to come from?" The money, he had decided by summer 1981, would come from himself and from small contributions. "I am sauntering for the Senate," he told Judith Halfpenny. "A couple of dozen speeches about the state (I can file as late as March 16). I attack the tax structure which favors the rich (who pay little or no tax) and the corporations (who now pay almost nothing at all) and I propose doing away with the graduated income tax. One would figure the amount needed for the next year's budget and *then* raise, through taxes, the money needed with a flat 10–15% on the gross adjusted income of the corporations—more than enough to defend the free world and enrich Congress with, perhaps, the same tax for those earning more than 20,000—the rest would pay no Fed tax at all: they're broke anyway. Also, cut the Pentagon by 25%—learn to think modestly of the US as simply another country in no way special except for its megalomania and its bad management of public affairs. . . . We shall see. In the winter, in a field of three, I was 10%. I'm now down to a mere 4% but that changes with the number of appearances. The press is thrilled I'm in the race: good copy. But one is constantly warned that no issues should ever be discussed, only personalities, polls, money raised. Presently, I eschew the first, ignore the second, and do nothing about the third. People are stunned when they hear I don't want contributions yet." By Halloween his speaking schedule had intensified. Early in 1982 the interviewer for *San Diego Magazine*, who found him catching his breath and losing weight at La Costa, remarked that, unlike most candidates for statewide office, he traveled without any retinue, often by himself. It made for a distinctive but unprofessional-looking campaign. "I'm now about to be raising $ for the senate and will seldom be out of the Gilded State," he wrote to John Mitzel. On March 9, in Los Angeles, he filed for the Democratic nomination. Polls showed he was second, though a distant second, in a field of five. The Gore Vidal for U.S. Senate organization soon placed an advertisement in *The New York Review of Books*. "I don't have to explain to you who I am or what I stand for as I take this occasion, in these familiar pages, to ask for help."

For the next ninety days he energetically, methodically devoted himself to a statewide campaign in Northern and Southern California, speaking at college and university campuses, at rallies in the major and many of the minor cities. His likely supporters were in Los Angeles and San Francisco, where he attended the inevitable fund-raisers, mainly small gatherings in handsome homes in Beverly Hills and Pacific Heights. His most enthusiastic supporters were on the campuses, where much of the filming of a documentary, *Gore Vidal, The Man Who Said No*, directed by Gary Conklin, was done. Some of the shots were so arty, indirect, or irrelevant that Vidal felt they may have been purposely double-edged. Headquarters were set up at the Outpost Drive house. There was no shortage of volunteers to stuff envelopes, answer telephones, and drive him to events. Hugh Guilbeau, a young volunteer in San Francisco, accompanied him to talks and made his Northern California arrangements. At Fresno he spoke to the Democratic statewide delegates, many of whom found his wit entertaining but his politics unrealistic. Modest contributions came from friends and supporters. Elizabeth Hardwick, Christopher Isherwood, John Hallowell, and Richard Poirier, among others, sent contributions; so too did most of Gore's Hollywood friends. For the time being, money was a secondary issue. His own funds would carry him through the primary. There was a small budget for media advertisements. Saturation television exposure had not yet become a widespread campaign technique. Local radio and television covered statewide candidates, who usually scheduled appearances and press conferences in order to make the early-evening news. Questions frequently arose about whether Vidal was indeed a serious candidate, mainly because he seemed too entertaining to be a politician, too irreverent to be serious. His barbed wit encouraged some, who otherwise might have known better, to believe that he was against everything rather than for something. Jerry Brown, of course, declined to accept his challenge that they debate. The same polls that indicated Brown would lose in the general election to any of the Republican candidates showed he had a large lead over Vidal in the primary. The businessman/hairdresser Vidal Sassoon sent Gore—with a note that said, "This has to be worth 10,000 votes"—a copy of a *San Francisco Chronicle* cartoon that depicted two identical Gore Vidals, the first of whom says,

"And I have 38% name recognition," the second of whom is asked by a reporter, "How will that translate into votes, Mr. Sassoon?" Neither anti-Semitism nor homosexuality was an issue. In the Hollywood world, where Vidal had worked and played amiably with many Jews, his philo-Jewishness was taken for granted. "Norman Lear," Vidal told Armistead Maupin—the San Francisco novelist with a cult following in the gay community, who interviewed him at length for *California* magazine—had loved "Pink Triangle and Yellow Star" and "had copies sent around." It was, Vidal insisted, a political, not a sexual, document. When Maupin queried him about his sexuality, Vidal stuck to his usual line: it was a private matter; if there was any social significance to his running for the Senate, that was for others to comment on; and he and Howard were "old friends. . . . He's lived various places, I've lived various places. We travel together, we travel separately." When the actor Rock Hudson, an admirer, volunteered, with his companion, to work in his campaign, Jay Allen told Gore "that if I were you, I'd avoid that association. I'd avoid anything to do with Rock or his friend because they were such well-known homosexuals. . . . But he ignored my advice. But homosexuality never became an issue in that campaign. Let's face it. There was too much whispering going on about whether or not Jerry was homosexual."

And Brown studiously ignored him. How can I reply to one-liners? he said to reporters, attempting to avoid talking about issues and to trivialize Vidal's candidacy. A newspaper cartoon depicted Vidal behind a podium casting a fishing rod with a microphone at the end toward the mouth of Jerry Brown, represented as a sphinx decorated by signs that said, "Silence is Golden," "A Closed Mouth Catches No Flies," and "Mum's the Word." Finally, in late May, they appeared on the same program in a nondebate format, each giving a brief presentation and answering questions at the annual meeting of the American Editorial Cartoonists in San Francisco. There was a fine balance of humor and venom in the questions and answers, such as Gore's references to the secretary of state as "Alexander the Great Haig," Richard Nixon as "his satanic majesty," and Jerry Brown as "Lord of the Flies." Vidal publicly offered to give $25,000 to Brown's favorite charity if he would debate the author on election eve. Both men seemed tired. For Brown the "fatigue factor" had set in long before, partly the result of his awareness that California voters in general were tired of him on, so to speak, an existential level. Vidal, who had failed to make significant inroads on Brown's lead, had to deal with exhaustion and the reality that in the latest polls Brown had decisively pulled away from him. And both had been nervously looking over their shoulders, not so much at one another as at the Republican primary campaign. From the start the polls had shown that Brown would lose to either of the two major candidates—the initial leader, Barry Goldwater, Jr., and by a larger margin to Goldwater's competitor, Mayor Pete Wilson of San Diego. At first Wilson seemed unlikely to overtake Goldwater in the primary.

To everyone's surprise, Goldwater had begun to fade by mid-May, partly because of revelations about his private life, including drug use, mostly because he was an inept campaigner. Suddenly the well-financed Wilson seemed certain to win the nomination. That meant, as the polls showed, certain defeat for either Vidal or Brown in the general election, though Brown would undoubtedly have more financial and party support. Vidal had alienated the main sources of money as a matter of principle. As soon as Wilson seemed the likely opponent, Vidal knew that he did not have a ghost of a chance in the general election. Still, he campaigned aggressively in the waning days of the campaign, though he instructed his treasurer to spend only the minimum necessary. Most of it was his own money. On June 4, primary-election day, the *Los Angeles Times* commented that "author Gore Vidal, witty and sardonic, promised a lively campaign, but it has turned languid." *The California Eye* reported in its sophisticated election analysis that the Democratic Party exit-poll interviews made clear that Brown, "while very resourceful, suffers from a high number of negatives which led voters to vote against him rather than for Gore Vidal. . . . There is, based on these polls, a very strong belief that Brown could have been beaten in the primary with enough money, preparation and the right issues." And the right opponent. Brown received 45 percent of the vote, Vidal 15. That night, in Brown's victory speech, he featured prominently in his election platform the issues Vidal had stressed in the primary campaign. The speech sounded to Vidal as if it could have come out of his own mouth. In November, Brown was to lose decisively to Wilson. California and the American public had made a commitment to views other than Vidal's *or* Brown's. The day after the primary election Vidal was at a Westwood bookstore signing copies of his latest collection of essays, *The Second American Revolution*. The revolution itself had not and was not about to take place. Soon he was to write, in an essay called "Hollywood," that "one morning last spring, I cast a vote for myself in the Hollywood hills; then I descended to the flats of Beverly Hills for a haircut at the barber shop in the Beverly Wilshire Hotel, where I found the Wise Hack. . . . 'Why do you want to be governor of this schmattah state?' When I said that I didn't want to be *governor* (I was a candidate for the U.S. Senate) he nodded slyly. 'That's what *I* told people,' he said, cryptic as always."

--- · ---

Ironic perspective provided some relief for the loss, though there was also the balancing pleasure of returning immediately to the literary life, one expression of which was his decision to attempt to rewrite as a full-length novel a script based on the life of Lincoln that he had first conceived in 1979 as a miniseries for television, a six-hour production that Norman Lear had enthusiastically agreed to produce and had sold to Fred Silverman, the head of NBC. He also had it in mind to do it as a stage play afterward. While watching the actor Tony Perkins, his friend from Chateau Marmont days, perform in a television version of *Les Misérables,* he had suddenly had the inspiration to do a dramatization of Lincoln's life. Perkins would be perfect as the Great Emancipator. "Generally, I don't care for dictators," he wrote to Judith Halfpenny in 1979, "no matter how cute and all-American." But "ideally, with a classic subject, and the Civil War is our Trojan War, one could put the whole thing onto film. . . . After all, that is exactly what the swan of Avon was doing" in his history plays. Through much of 1979 and 1980, he renewed and increased his familiarity with Lincoln and the Civil War, acknowledging that "the best analysis of Lincoln is Wilson's in *Patriotic Gore.*" Memories of his grandparents' comments on the war from their Southern perspective gave personal depth to his reading. He detested slavery, oppression of every sort. But he wondered if it would not have been better for the North to have let the South go. Lincoln's vision of an all-powerful single nation had been realized at a heavy price. "L. is our Bismarck, and that's how I plan to show him."

When Silverman fell from power, the new regime at NBC had no interest in Vidal's script. The assumption that American history did not have a national audience still prevailed. Just before he began campaigning for the senatorial nomination, Jason Epstein, visiting at Outpost Drive and spending hours in the kitchen at his usual culinary magic, read the television script. He urged him to "make a novel out of this." But Gore had reservations, which he shared with Peter Davison, an editor at Atlantic Monthly Press who hoped to entice him away from Random House. "First, I must know what my political life will be. . . . Second, I am being made a large offer by RH for a novel about A. Lincoln, which I rather dread as I've already done it for TV (not done yet) and will do it again for the theater this spring. Third, my irritable but continuing relations with RH and Jason E." When the primary settled his political future, he was willing to consider *Lincoln*. "Both Jason and I suggested that Gore do it as a novel," Owen Laster recalled. "He wasn't enthusiastic. After Jason worked on him, he decided to do it," though it took considerable persuasion. In October 1982, at Ravello, where he arrived in a driving rain, Owen brought for signing the handsome contract that Random House had offered and Gore agreed to. Vidal insisted that a few hundred thousand dollars be returned to compensate the publisher for a portion of the unearned advance on his previous contract. "He did something very unusual," Epstein acknowledged. "Never in the history of publishing had that happened before. An expression of decency and responsibility. He thought that was the right thing to do. I was just amazed. I'll never forget that. He never wanted to be in debt to his publisher." That night at Ravello, Laster "got as drunk as I ever remember being. We went to dinner. . . . Then we came back. And Howard always disappears earlier. They had a setup then with two couches. He was lying on one couch, I on the other, facing each other. There's a bottle of wine between us. We must already have had one or two bottles at dinner and a brandy in the town square. We were drinking wine, and then Gore told me how he had wanted to be President and how he had chosen to be a writer but never stopped wanting to be President." By early November, one month after his fifty-seventh birthday, Gore was, he told Richard Poirier, "deep into *Lincoln*, an enjoyable process, all in all. For once, I start out with five years of research and two other versions behind me. He is endlessly interesting. The American Bismarck coming on like Will Rogers. . . . I trust Jason will make the fortune he and RH so richly deserve!"

Publisher and author profited greatly from *Lincoln*, a huge bestseller from its initial publication in June 1984. It was to provide the linking centerpiece of what Vidal had now reconceived as a larger, multinovel series about American history from the beginning of the republic to the twentieth century. The overall structure and pattern of the series now, as he wrote

Lincoln, became clear to him. *Burr, 1876,* and *Washington, D.C.* were already in place, *Empire* and *Hollywood* were to follow in the seven years after *Lincoln.* A final volume, *The Golden Age,* was planned as the culmination. A deep believer in history as the ultimately human subject, he desired to make history more vividly alive and intellectually credible than in textbooks, an alternative account of American history that embodies Vidal's understanding of how politics and power work, past and present. It contrasts the American republic with the American empire. In Vidal's story the Founding Fathers were a brilliant but mixed lot (George Washington the dullest of them all), who created a balance between the big-money interests of the Federalists and the small-farm, small-money, small-government civil-libertarian views of the Jeffersonians. But Jacksonian America broke the precarious balance. Land and power became the predominant concerns: the Indians east of the Mississippi were pushed westward or destroyed; slavery could not be contained, let alone abolished. Lincoln, as much villain as hero, established a nationalistic, monolithic Union, a huge, industrialized anti-Jeffersonian monster. In the next fifty years his successors, led by McKinley and Theodore Roosevelt, transformed the United States from a republic into an aggressive empire. The Monroe Doctrine had established the Caribbean and South America as an American sphere of influence. Now the Pacific was going to be an American lake. World War I, into which Woodrow Wilson elected to insert America, made the United States the dominant economic power of the world. Franklin Roosevelt's New Deal retooled American government and slightly redistributed national wealth in order to make America safe for capitalism. Immediately after World War II, Harry Truman celebrated the absolute international dominance of the United States by creating for the first time a national-security state whose underlying premise was that the Soviet Union was so great a menace that Americans must give up some of their freedoms to guard themselves permanently against the enemy. The temporary wartime OSS was converted into the permanent peacetime CIA. Its ongoing task was to balk the Soviet Union, whose strength was exaggerated by those for whom the Cold War was an economic and ideological boon. For the first time a huge peacetime Army was put in place. The defense budget became sacred. The garrison state became permanent. Those who controlled and had always controlled wealth and political power in America kept themselves rich and powerful. Inevitably, the Korean and Vietnam wars followed. As with ancient Rome, America had moved from republic to empire. Lincoln was, in Vidal's view, the pivotal figure in that movement.

A tall, dark shadow hovering over all lesser shadows, Lincoln is the only figure other than *Burr* so important in Vidal's American story that he warrants his own title. The historical character over whom he has brooded most, the Lincoln of Vidal's remythologizing is given fictional coherence by the novelist's art. Sculpting his narrative out of the years of Lincoln's presidency, Vidal created a pragmatic and manipulative politician with one overriding vision: to save the Union and by saving it to transform it into a modern, industrialized, national state so powerfully and tightly coherent that nothing can tear it apart again. Opposed to slavery, Lincoln does not believe slavery an issue worth fighting about. In favor of civil liberties, he has little hesitation in suspending them to fight the war more efficiently. Deeply sincere and incontrovertibly honest, he knows how to dissemble, to reward friends and punish enemies, to manipulate men and money, to further his cause: in sum, the consummate politician. Deeply ambivalent about Lincoln, Vidal ends up doing Lincoln the honor of deepening his complexity, humanizing his character, and making him more real by depicting him warts and all. A controversial portrait that has within it touches of Vidal's Southern inheritance—his view that just as the South should have let the slaves go, the North should have let the South go—many Lincoln enthusiasts found unsettling. Its vividness and credibility made it even the more formidable. Details of character and scene are rendered superbly. If the novel suffers from an occasional overschematism, a certain reductive sweep, the familiarity of many of the events makes that difficult to avoid. To deal with potential problems of voice and point of view, *Lincoln* is narrated in the third person. The character whose consciousness most dominates is that of Lincoln's young secretary, John Hay, later to be Theodore Roosevelt's Secretary of State and a prominent figure in *Empire*. Weaving a plot composed of facts about Lincoln and the war with fictional accounts of personal and political lives, *Lincoln* created a tapestry of conflicts that embody the issues of America's national crisis.

When *Lincoln*'s critical success, reinforced by its immense sales, was capped by its being nominated for the Pulitzer Prize, Vidal was both pleased and skeptical. He thought it unlikely that his vision of Lincoln was idealistic enough to find favor with the committee. Some Lincoln scholars, to whom

Vidal responded in two essays in 1991, "Lincoln and the Priests of Academe" in *The American Historical Review* and "Last Note on Lincoln" in *The New York Review of Books,* condemned his portrait of the sixteenth President, often with high academic condescension. Some were offended that it was not *their* Lincoln, others that it was a-less-than-*perfect* Lincoln. Soon *Newsweek*'s reviewer and literary columnist, Walter Clemons, who proposed that he become Vidal's biographer, reported to him that the three judges of the 1985 Pulitzer Prize Committee for fiction, on which he served, had selected *Lincoln,* but the general committee refused to give the award to Vidal. When Clemons persuaded Little, Brown to outbid Random House for the rights to his proposed biography and received a $350,000 advance against royalties, Jason commented to Gore, "You've led a very expensive life." Vidal's response was to search for some position between irony and self-inflation as he helped spread the news of his value. "I boasted to Bowles as well as to you," he wrote to Louis Auchincloss, "of the Clemons advance and got back one of those hard Caesarian Bowlesian letters to the effect that as he is getting so much money oughtn't he to do *all* the work? putting his usual finger on the open sore. One always does the work for them, if 'authorized.' " Gore agreed to cooperate fully with Clemons.

In January 1986 Vidal published in *The Nation* "The Day the American Empire Ran Out of Gas," the lecture he had delivered to the PEN conference the previous October. When Norman Podhoretz, in his *New York Post* column, and Midge Decter soon afterward in *Contentions,* registered their objections to Vidal's criticism of the "American Empire," he felt it desirable to answer back. In the article Vidal proposed that America's economic survival would best be served by an alliance with the Soviet Union that would allow those two countries together to compete effectively with the increasingly powerful Asian economies, which he predicted would ultimately be spearheaded by a Sino-Japanese alliance. Vidal, Decter claimed, "does not like his country." Otherwise, why would he write such a slanderously inaccurate account of America's motives and actions? America was not an "empire," let alone an evil empire. That was the Soviet Union. In his role as defender of the country's reputation, as a pro-Reagan neoconservative, as a Cold Warrior demanding a solid front against the enemy and the largest possible defense budget, as a strong supporter of the policies and values of the Israeli Likud government and its military-economic alliance with the United States, Podhoretz responded angrily to Vidal's overview of

American history and current policy. That the attack came from Vidal especially seemed a red flag to a pained patriot, though he included other of his former liberal literary friends in his indictment, especially Norman Mailer, with whom he had had a falling-out.

In March 1986, in a brief essay, Vidal characterized Podhoretz's furious response to his essay on the American empire and the desirability of an alliance between the United States and the Soviet Union as "The Empire Lovers Strike Back." Victor Navasky was delighted to publish it in *The Nation*'s anniversary issue, partly because he thought it a fine, typically Vidalian piece whose thrust was entirely political, partly because *The Nation*, which took a balanced view toward Israeli-American relations and the Palestinian issue and had strong Jewish support from the left, had little sympathy for the neoconservatives. The essay had two lines of attack. The minor one was a dissection of the issues that related to American-Israeli policy, mainly emphasizing Israel's unjust treatment of the Palestinians, comparing it to the American treatment of the Filipinos after the Spanish-American War; the other was an ad hominem attack on the Podhoretzes. Vidal argued that "in order to get military and economic support for Israel, a small number of American Jews, who should know better, have made common cause with every sort of reactionary and anti-Semitic group in the United States, from the corridors of the Pentagon to the TV studios of the evangelical Jesus-Christers. To show that their hearts are in the far-right place, they call themselves neoconservatives, and attack the likes of Mailer and me, all in the interest of supporting the likes of Sharon and Israel as opposed to the Peace Now Israelis whom they disdain." Podhoretz and Decter were "propagandists . . . for these predators." It was not a question of being pro- or anti-American or pro- or anti-Israel. It was the denunciation of certain policies advocated by particular individuals and political groups, whether American or Israeli. In the case of the Podhoretzes, it seemed to Vidal that in their support of Israel they elevated Israeli interests over American. They relentlessly exaggerated the Russian threat in order to pressure Congress into providing large sums to support the Israeli military. The solution was simple: America should not support injustice and it should not support military activities by foreign governments, not only in the case of Israel but in any instance. The obligation of American political leaders was to make rational decisions based on America's overall national interests, not in response to self-interested pressure groups. The United States, Vidal proposed, should end military aid to all Middle Eastern countries. "The Middle Easterners would then be obliged to make peace, or blow one another up, or whatever. In any case, we would be well out of it." The rhetoric and sharp ironies of the essay spotlighted the level of Vidal's contempt for the Podhoretzes and what they represented, and the politically incorrect sharpness of its language, whose ironies sensitive Jewish-American readers were not likely to take as such, was designed to shock. As a polemical piece it was witty, devastatingly dismissive of the enemy, and sublimely indifferent to the obvious fact that the Podhoretzes did not elevate Israeli interest over American. They simply saw them as *identical*. It also did not take into account that for intertwined moral, historical, and cultural reasons, there was strong American support for Israel and any Israeli government. For the Podhoretzes any effort to claim that American and Israeli interests were *not* identical was not only monstrously mistaken but monstrous. It had to rise to some higher or lower level of explanation than political differences. The Likud was *their* Israel and neoconservatism *their* America. To attack their America (or any aspect of it that they defended) was not to like America. To attack Likud's policies was to attack Israel as a whole. To criticize Likud's right-wing version of "Zionism" was to attack all Jews. The conclusion to be drawn from Vidal's attack was simple: To be strongly critical of Likud's Israel *was to be anti-Semitic*.

Vidal's "empire lovers" struck back again, this time in the form of a long essay by Podhoretz in *Commentary* in November 1986. Since "Pink Triangle and Yellow Star," Podhoretz had been certain that Vidal was a dangerous enemy. Podhoretz read as anti-Semitism Vidal's advice that blacks, Jews, and gays should effect a "cease-fire and a common front against the common enemy" because even the neoconservative Jews (whom Vidal compared to a small group of German-Jews who had embraced Nazism) might end up in "the same gas chambers with blacks and homosexuals." The title of Podhoretz's response to Vidal, "The Hate That Dare Not Speak Its Name," cleverly conflated into a single anathema homosexuality, which only the title alluded to, and anti-Semitism, a charge against Vidal that the essay was dedicated to proving. Podhoretz argued that Vidal was part of a long-standing tradition of elitist anti-Semitism, the previous epitome of which in American culture had been Henry Adams; that Vidal had indicated his anti-Jewish "animus" years before when he had associated himself with complaints by non-Jewish writers that Jewish writers dominated the American literary culture of the postwar years (it had been Capote, not Vidal, who had thus whined); that his proposal to cut off military aid to all Middle Eastern countries was tantamount to advocating the destruction of Israel; that not to support Israel was inseparable from anti-Semitism; and that the lack of outrage on the left at Vidal's essay (outrage Podhoretz had solicited by writing friends and supporters of *The Nation,* asking whether they had protested the article's appearance in the magazine) indicated the rise of a dangerous laxity on the left about this crucial issue. That compared unfavorably, Podhoretz claimed, with how William F. Buckley and the *National Review* had recently handled a similar instance within their ranks. "From Vidal's political friends on the Left, then, mainly denial, and from the editor of *The Nation,* stonewalling. From [Joseph] Sobran's political friends on the Right, mostly outrage, and from the editor of *National Review,* dissociation and repudiation of anti-Semitism." The conclusion was that "anti-Semitism had largely if not entirely been banished from its traditional home on the Right, and that today, especially in the guise of anti-Zionism, it is meeting with more and more toleration, and sometimes even approval, on the Left." Podhoretz's agenda was clear, the political uses of the charge of anti-Semitism irresistible, mostly because he, like Buckley, without the slightest doubt or vestige of intellectual nuance, believed he was absolutely right, as an a priori given, about everything to do with such issues.

During the 1980s daily life at La Rondinaia was mainly devoted to work, and the occasional pleasure of visitors, a large number of whom had assembled for a special occasion in September 1983. On an early-autumn evening Gore had waited, sitting outdoors at a café in Ravello, for the Calvinos to arrive. As the last light left the sky, his visitors, who had telephoned to tell him, without any invitation from him, that they were coming, saw him sitting "alone on the terrace. I think I'll always remember that image," Judith Calvino remarked. "He was so striking. He had on something light and something navy blue, and he wasn't much different from his younger days, the image I had seen of him in photos. . . . I'll always see Gore, no matter how he changes, like that. I had seen him before, but my private photo is that. We left our baggage at the hotel, the Palumbo. He was waiting for us there. That's my Gore Vidal. He has so much physical presence. It was not only physical. It was a man containing his biography. That's what I saw. Nothing excluded. You see what I mean? He seemed radiant. He didn't look happy. He looked as if something was eating him. But the effect was extraordinary." Whatever might have been making him unhappy had not affected his creative energy or his eagerness to engage the enemy. "Last days can be as much fun as first days," he wrote to Judith Halfpenny. "I have enjoyed this epoch enormously. But then, as they used to say when I was in the army, fire at will. One did. Does." The next day, a little after his fifty-eight birthday, Ravello had declared him an honorary citizen, a rare event, orchestrated with formal speeches, grand presentations, and celebratory decorations in the high Italian style. His friend Marella Agnelli had come from Rome. Two well-known Italian writers, Luigi Barzini and Alberto Arbasino, were there. A state dignitary from the foreign office had come to represent the Italian government. That Italy's most revered living author was also there gave even more special resonance to the occasion, and particularly to Gore, who had come to admire Italo Calvino perhaps more than any other contemporary writer and whose words of praise for him Gore found particularly gratifying. In 1974, before he knew Calvino, though he knew *of* him since 1948, he had published in *The New York Review of Books* an essay on "Calvino's Novels." "I just told Barbara that I was doing Calvino. She didn't know much about him," he recalled. "Neither did anyone else, which is why one writes pieces." Within a short time Calvino had, for the first time, an American audience, and Gore had a generous letter of thanks for his lucid, laudatory, and influential essay. That fall, "just out of the blue," Calvino and his wife, Judith, came to Gore's fund-raising lecture at the American Academy in Rome. They began to see one another socially, though never when Corsini, who had remained loyal to the Communist Party, was present. Calvino had renounced his membership. Calvino "was very cheery with me," Gore recalled. "He used to say, 'I stammer in every language.' He had uncertain English, quite good French, and I guess pretty good Spanish. . . . Whenever we gave a party that I thought would be interesting for him, they would come."

Ravello itself had reason to be proud that such a distinguished foreigner had chosen to reside there. His association with the town brought it international publicity. The tourist economy benefited. Some of the visitors were, of course, his guests, including widely recognized international celebrities from the entertainment world, from the Newmans to Mick Jagger to

Johnny Carson. Most tourist visitors to Ravello, though, did not get to see Vidal, or even his villa. They might more likely see Howard each morning at about ten-thirty, sitting outside the San Domingo bar, having his coffee and leafing through the mail. Tourists of a literary inclination would soon know which private road off the piazza led to La Rondinaia. In the formal garden of the ancient Villa Ruffolo, where the honorary-citizenship ceremony took place, the dignitaries heard Gore, at the end of the formalities, say a few graceful words he had written out celebrating "this earthly heaven, this Ravello, of blue sky and sea, gray limestone and olive," and invoking the two writers, himself and Tennessee Williams, who had come there together in March 1948, when they were young and the future unknown, riding in a jeep up from Amalfi, thinking they "had never seen such beauty before." They had walked about in the lavish gardens where the ceremony now was being held and where concerts were performed regularly during the summer season. In his speech honoring the new citizen of Ravello, Calvino, who had recently read *Duluth,* was inspired to make that novel "in which the things which happen do not conform to Vidal's principle of 'absolute uniqueness' " the controlling trope of his speech honoring the new citizen of Ravello. "I must ask myself if we are indeed in Ravello, or in a Ravello reconstructed in a Hollywood studio, with an actor playing Gore Vidal, or if we are in the TV documentary on Vidal in Ravello . . . or whether we are here on the Amalfi coast on a festive occasion, but one in 1840, when, at the end of another Vidal novel, *Burr,* the narrator learns that the most controversial of America's Founding Fathers, Aaron Burr, was his father. Or, since there is a spaceship in *Duluth,* manned by centipedes who can take on any appearance, even becoming dead ringers for U.S. political figures, perhaps we could be aboard that spaceship, which has left Duluth for Ravello, and the ETs aboard could have taken on the appearance of the American writer we are here to celebrate." But, he said, it seems that Vidal "has never left America even for one second. His passionate and polemical participation in American life is without interruption. What we see in Ravello is someone living a tranquil parallel life. Is it Vidal or his double?" That evening "there was singing (Cantore di Napoli) in the square, colored lights, the works," Gore told Judith Halfpenny good-humoredly. "I suppose now they will try to get as much mileage out of me as they do from Wagner." That night he hosted a large party. Chichita Calvino, who like her husband was passionate about American movies, remembered how "at a certain moment" she said to him, " 'I bet you have a photograph of Montgomery Clift.' It was an intuition, and he took me to a beautiful room, sort of a small library, and he immediately showed me a photograph of himself very young. He was a dangerously handsome man. And then he also had a photograph of Montgomery Clift. Gore's a great movie freak, and so am I. I didn't even ask him if he had been a friend of Clift's. The flash was, Gore must have a photo of him. I can't explain why that came to me to ask."

"Do you notice the speed with which time passes now?" Vidal, who was close to his sixtieth birthday, about to enter the seventh decade of his life, wrote to Paul Bowles in 1985. "I don't mean years, days—hours even. It is like falling into the deep end of an empty pool. . . . I race about, being public. To London for *Lincoln*. To Frankfurt to meet my foreign publishers. To Bordeaux to eat with Jason Epstein. To Naples to speak on Magna Graecia." When, with Barbara, he had visited Peggy Guggenheim in Venice and asked how she was, " 'All right for someone dying,' was her nifty retort. 'But of course that's natural,' she added. She invited me to her 80th birthday party next month. 'If I'm there, of course.' She likes being a Legend. The nose has shrunk, curiously enough, and lost its once pretty rosiness. . . . 'But you must make a speech. You won't mind?' I told her that since there was no way that she could make a habit of this sort of display, I didn't mind a one-shot." When Judith Calvino ran into Howard at the Frankfurt Book Fair in October 1986, he said, " 'Chichita, you are here. Please go and talk to Gore because he's in a terrible mood because he's sixty today.' So I went to him, and Gore was sitting down alone and fuming, and I said, 'Hello, what happened?' He said, 'I'm sixty today.' And I said, 'Well, that's no big deal.' And he said to me, 'Of course, sixty is sexy.' He had made a joke, and that helped. But he didn't believe it."

Much of the best part of life, though, was private. Less of it was spent in Rome, more and more at Ravello, writing, with undiminished energy, essays and fiction. When, in the late 1980s, Max Rabb, a consummate political operator, a lawyer with his roots in Massachusetts politics in the 1960s, was appointed ambassador to Italy by President Bush, Rabb sent regular invitations for official dinners and private social events. "Ah, if you'd only let me handle you," the Republican Rabb told Gore, "I could make you a Senator, maybe even President." Despite the embassy honors, Rome seemed less and less attractive, Ravello more comfortable, though when Michael Tyler-Whittle returned to live in England the loss was noticed. Corsini, who had visited Gore and Howard in Los Angeles, was a regular visitor, and, as the wine flowed late at night, he noticed that Gore mellowed from the coldly analytic to the sympathetically warm. On the far side of political and literary discussion was personal concern for his friends, including for George Armstrong's finances. Life as a freelance journalist had its uncertainties. George, who soon made the transition to the new computer age, helped with the preparation of manuscripts, an aspect of Gore's life that Howard left entirely to other people. He preferred his function as secretary be restricted to management of business and domestic affairs. Running La Rondinaia and Outpost Drive, arranging travel, preparing taxes, handling the flow of material to the archive at the Wisconsin State Historical Society seemed enough of a full-time job. Howard himself had become an author when, in 1970, he had co-authored a cookbook with the sculptress Beverly Pepper. With her journalist husband, she had been part of their Roman social world. One of the best moments of Gore's and Howard's day together at Ravello, as visitors often noticed, was the hour of chess and coffee after lunch on the long, overstuffed yellow couch in Gore's study. "They are a very, very solid couple," Corsini noted, "whatever is the strange nature of their relationship. Gore tells it, but you never know. . . . There was never any separation of roles. To me they were Gore and Howard. I'm influenced by the way both of them describe it, half jokingly, half seriously. What came out is this complete freedom they both had in their own private lives, corrected by their reciprocal loyalty."

Leonard Bernstein came to Ravello in 1987, on a trip to arrange to have the next year, Bernstein's seventieth, one in which by its end each of his compositions would have been performed someplace. In Rome, Max Rabb entertained Bernstein and hosted Gore and Howard with what Gore remembered as "several wild nights at the embassy. It finally came out that Max played one of the fairies in *Iolanthe,* and so Lenny sits down and does the whole piece and Max does the dance of the fairies sixty years later. Lenny and I would bad-mouth Ronald Reagan, and Max would say, 'No, you can't say that in here, you can't, you can't!' and make both of us more and more unrestrained." Bernstein proposed that Vidal rewrite the libretto of *1600 Pennsylvania Avenue,* a failed political musical Bernstein had done with Alan Jay Lerner and which he now hoped to have performed in an improved version as part of his seventieth-birthday-year celebration. " 'I'm touched that you've come to me,' I said, 'but you should have gone to

Lourdes. There's nothing that can be done with this.' " At Ravello, Gore gave Bernstein the use of his study, a rare expression of respect.

> He sat at that desk. I watched him working on two scores that he was going to conduct in Amsterdam. They're like atlases, and he had a red pencil and a blue pencil. Why? "I'm doing Mahler and I'm doing Schumann," he said. . . . "With the red one I make a track for myself through the score. With the blue one I change the instrumentation." It was fascinating to watch the way he worked. I said, "Do you hear it as you see it?" He said, "No, I see it." I said, "How does that correlate with hearing?" "What do you mean hearing? I'll hear it when the instruments play it." "Do you know what it's going to sound like?" "Well, of course I do. I see it." "But do you hear it?" "Of course I don't hear it!" I began to understand the mystique of what music is about. Closer to mathematics than language. I thought the overture was like Ives. "God, you're stupid musically," he said. "It's not Ives. It's Aaron [Copland] I'm ripping off. Can't you tell?" There was something else I liked. "Yeah, that's Aaron too. That's *Appalachian Spring*. I've already cannibalized it for something else. Can't use that one."

Most of the visitors, especially at La Rondinaia, were American, some British. Princess Margaret came for lunch whenever she was vacationing on the Amalfi coast. So too did Diana Phipps, who was soon, when the Soviet empire collapsed, to regain her family's Czech estates and castle and to separate herself from her old London life, determined to restore her family's ancient property. Though Gore much preferred to be visited than to visit, and almost never stayed anywhere but a hotel when away from home, on a blazing-hot day in July 1983 he had had lunch with Princess Margaret at Kensington Palace and then drove with her to the Royal Lodge at Windsor, where he was a houseguest. "The Q. Mother had just vacated the RL," he told Judith Halfpenny, "which is pretty much her house and gone to Sandringham and the household wanted to shut it up because no one was there but, ever forceful, *she* said, 'I *know* there are three stewards and the maid.' . . . 'But no cook, your royal highness' (it is amazing to hear those five syllables spoken naturally—my republican throat would close at the 'your'—even so, for the first time in 20 years, I addressed her as ma'am when we met at the pool and I responded to her good morning). She was standing in the unheated water rescuing bees with a large leaf while thundering at them: 'Stupid bees, get out, make honey' . . . always advising, warning, counselling." They lunched outdoors beneath an oak tree on the lawn and then dined on the terrace. The princess gave him a tour of the royal art collection. At a party nearby, hosted by Drue Heinz for her husband, with a hundred guests including the Queen, he met the "Fount of Honor . . . looking exactly as she does on the money, though darker. . . . Queen complimented Jack Heinz on his 57 varieties, 'Only I don't like the way you make your mayonnaise.' Jack's smooth response, 'That is because we do not make it for you, ma'am.' . . . It was my first meeting. 'I understand you are at the Lodge,' said the F. 'Yes,' I said. 'Which room?' 'The Blue Nursery,' I replied. *'My room,'* she thundered—the sisters have modelled themselves on the two queens in *Alice;* and then she hurtled across the lawn, scattering quick pecks of affection on cronies and dodging the deeper curtseys." Around the lodge the park at Windsor seemed almost primeval. "Huge rhododendrons. Owls hooting at night. The Blue Nursery, an ordinary blue-walled bedroom with two windows looking out over a walled rose garden with a rise of forest in the back, a little girl's room, kept the way it was when the Queen was a child with books on horses, porcelain horses, chipmunks. . . . An electric fire thing. A wash basin in the corner with running water. All out of time." In the hot weather he enjoyed the swimming pool around which they sat, drank, and gossiped for hours.

Of family visitors at La Rondinaia, there was only Nini, whose visits, like their brief times together in Washington or New York, were often at least as vexed as pleasurable. Always a gracious host, Gore had more loyalty than patience with the psychodramas and soap operas of Nini's life, which soon included divorce from Michael Straight, her second husband. Uncle Pick, Gore's closest living connection with his father, of whom he was fond and who with Sally had visited him in Italy numbers of times, had died in 1983. Only Gene's youngest sister, Margaret, who lived in Los Angeles, remained of his father's generation of Vidals. His Exeter friend, Wid Washburn, now a successful anthropologist-historian in charge of American Studies at the Smithsonian Institution, had reestablished contact in the 1970s, with a friendly letter and then some reciprocal visits in Italy and Washington. "I can't say I much cared for PEA [Phillips Exeter Academy] today," Gore wrote to him, "when I spoke there for the bicen. They struck me as dim hustlers, outside civilization. My affection for the Class of '43 is undimmed and unilluminated. If I'm alive, I'll come to the 50th." The extended family of friends still had real presence, though time and distance were attenuating some of the relationships, death ending others. Grace Stone, his novelist friend, had become elderly, infirm, the challenge of traveling from Stonington, Connecticut, to Rome, let alone Ravello, insurmountable. "Once he dragged Grace Stone there," Corsini recalled, "and she was furious. She didn't like the house because it was too far away and she was an old lady." Soon any Italian visits at all became impossible for her. Barbara Epstein was a regular visitor, usually in summers, and they always saw one another in New York. With Louis Auchincloss, whom Gore had grown even fonder of as the years passed, he continued his regular correspondence. Louis stopped by at La Rondinaia whenever he was in the area, though they saw one another usually in New York. The friendship had been additionally warmed by Gore's laudatory essay on Auchincloss's fiction, "The Great World and Louis Auchincloss," in the mid-1970s. He did an even greater service for Frederic Prokosch, whose memoir he reviewed at length in 1983, in helping him over the years get published again. He and Prokosch, who now lived with Jack Bady in the South of France, kept in friendly touch but they had not seen one another in many years. The essay was in honor of someone who had influenced him long ago.

Claire Bloom, with whom his friendship had been nothing if not intimate, visited occasionally in Rome and Ravello. She had begun a relationship with the novelist Philip Roth in the mid-1970s that was to lead to marriage in 1991 and then a well-publicized breakup in 1993. When she had asked Gore's advice about Roth, he replied, "You already have had *Portnoy's complaint*" in the form of Hilly Elkins. "Do not involve yourself with Portnoy." Elaine Dundy, her usual ebullient self, visited numbers of times, as did her successor, Kathleen Tynan, now a widow, whom Gore had become fond of. Ken's death in July 1980 was not a personal loss for Gore; they had long ago drifted apart, mostly, Gore thought, because of Ken's difficulties in sustaining friendship. He and Howard saw the Newmans on their visits to Europe and when they were all in Los Angeles. Soon after his performance in *The Verdict* in 1982, Newman had had a heart attack scare. "He lay in a hospital bed," Gore told Judith Halfpenny, "while they went up with a sort of vacuum cleaner from groin to heart, and cleaned out the valve, all visible on a TV monitor. He saw it all." As soon as Newman recovered, the four of them met in London. "Our first time there, together, since their honeymoon spent with us 26 years ago. A lot of memory land." But, as with many friends with busy professional and family lives, they saw one another less often than they once had, and the meetings were brief, the kind of drifting-away that occurs when friends live far apart and the opportunity for intimacy declines.

Maria Britneva came to visit regularly in Rome and at La Rondinaia. But there had been a devastating change for her, much less so for Gore: Tennessee Williams, in February 1983, at the age of seventy-one, had choked to death on a medicinal bottle cap. "How curious that The Bird who most feared suffocation suffocated to death: a good 7 minutes of ghostly awareness," he wrote to Paul Bowles. "There is a Bowlesian principle at work: what is most feared fearfully happens. I wish I had been less irritable with him in the last few years but the self-pity (so much vaster than my own) [was hard to tolerate]." Williams's later years had been brutally difficult—theatrical failures, drugs, alcohol. In the second of two evocatively beautiful essays on Williams, "Tennessee Williams: Someone to Laugh at the Squares With," in *The New York Review* in 1985, Vidal had focused on reminiscences of their glory years together and recalled the last time they had met. It had been on a television talk show in the early 1980s. "There were two or three other guests around a table, and the host. Abruptly, the Bird settled back in his chair and shut his eyes. The host's habitual unease became panic. After some disjointed general chat, he said, tentatively, 'Tennessee, are you asleep?' And the Bird replied, eyes still shut, 'No, I am not asleep but sometimes I shut my eyes when I am bored.' " Tennessee's death deprived Maria of the focus of her life, though as co-executor she soon perpetuated her intense involvement and manipulative control of Williams's legacy, including her refusal to give permission for his plays to be produced unless she retained control over the production. When producers refused to meet her demand, the productions usually fell through. Gore disapproved, but he still felt loyalty and love for Maria, though "[I] can't say that the Bird and I had much connection during the last 20 yrs," he wrote to Bill Gray. "Friendship with him was always a one-way street; and I tire rapidly. Also, he was not the same person I first knew—to the extent I knew him at all!"

Another of his much-admired older friends from Tennessee's generation had had his eightieth birthday in 1984. Isherwood, Gore wrote to Paul Bowles, "has decided to be Tithonus. He is amazingly healthy, preserved by alcohol, so life-like." In fact, he was without health or futurity. Later that year Gore had visited him in Malibu "as he was dying. He was small, shrunken, all beak like a new-hatched eagle. . . . I sat on the edge of the bed and kept up a stream of chatter like a radio switched on." Gore, who had just come from London, complained about the fecklessness of the English. "It's just like the grasshopper and the ant, and *they* are hopeless grasshoppers. . . . The eyes opened on that . . . and he spoke his last complete sentence to me. . . . 'So,' he demanded, 'what is wrong with grasshoppers?' " Later, in 1996, when the first volume of Isherwood's diaries was published, Gore was startled and pained to see how censorious Isherwood sometimes had been about him (and others) in his private writings, even on days on which they had been convivial together.

His relationship with Paul Bowles, now the only surviving literary friend from the Williams-Isherwood generation, was largely epistolary, though he had in mind to visit him in Morocco sometime soon. "Have you been keeping up with Tenn's posthumous-ness?" he wrote Bowles. "He is already neck and neck with Judy Garland and I suspect, in a decade, he will have gone, as they say here, *alle stelle,* passing Scott and Zelda on the way. Well, he would've liked it. Even so, there is something to be said for not being dead." Their correspondence had some of the flavor of two old veterans of lifelong literary wars exchanging notes about combat and battle fatigue. Bowles's presence as a writer had dimmed since *The Sheltering Sky,* and Gore had lent a hand to the incipient Bowles revival, at least as a writer with a cult following, by writing an introduction to the 1979 Black Sparrow Press edition of Bowles's short stories. "For the American academic," Gore wrote, as if he were also writing about himself, "Bowles is still odd man out; he writes as if *Moby-Dick* had never been written." Bowles appreciated the support, including the strong plug in Gore's essay on William Dean Howells in the twentieth-anniversary issue of *The New York Review.* "I'm happy with the preface," Bowles wrote to him. "No one else could have given me what I wanted."

Two deaths hit hard, one of a much-loved nonhuman companion, the other a man he held in warm, high esteem, a paragon of the imaginative life. By early 1983 Rat, a valued member of the family, had developed a fatal tumor. Gore and Howard grieved over his imminent departure and gave him the best medical care. Curtailing their otherwise easily indulged travel desires, they stayed at home or had a sitter for Rat when they went on short trips such as their annual New Year's visit to Venice. "The Rat continues to die at his own somewhat selfish pace but we worship him," he wrote to Judith Halfpenny at the end of 1983, "and so he has now lived exactly one year longer than the vet gave him. The tumor is huge and the smell frightful but he is lively and unaffected otherwise." Despite his condition, Gore caressed him as he always had. Some friends found the sight revolting. Gore was lovingly loyal to the end. The tumor on Rat's lower jaw had grown to "the size of a tennis ball . . . and the pus and blood grew too much—for us not for him. He continued to eat for two until the end, which occurred in Howard's arms," in January 1984. "The vet gave him a shot from the rear, he sighed, shut his eyes, and that was the end of 14 years. If there should ever be another dog, one will take some satisfaction in knowing that he will survive us." There was not to be a replacement for Rat.

On a stormy Friday morning in September 1985, Gore was driven northward from Rome to a small town on the Ligurian coast to attend a funeral neither he nor anyone else could have anticipated. Two weeks before, at the age of sixty-one, Calvino had had a cerebral hemorrhage at his vacation home, where he had been working on his Charles Eliot Norton Lectures to be delivered that fall at Harvard. "He was having more trouble than usual with the last," Gore later wrote to David Herbert Donald, the Harvard historian, "when he got up one morning, told his wife, 'It's all clear!' Sat down and wrote it straight through in a day, gave it to her that evening. She read it: to her horror, he had re-written the penultimate lecture word for word. The next morning came the stroke." Soon he was in the hospital at Siena. Then he was dead. Much of Italy went into mourning and lamentation, "as if a beloved prince had died," Vidal was to write in his essay "Calvino's Death." The President of the republic had come to the hospital to bid him good-bye. Gore, who had seen him last in May at the Via Di Torre Argentina apartment, where they had talked about Calvino's trip to America, felt the shock painfully. He and Calvino had developed a bond of mutual respect that served them both well: Vidal with validation as an international author to whose *Duluth* Calvino had given high praise, Calvino with an American audience. Vidal thought Calvino and Williams the two most talented, accomplished writers he had known. Beyond that, though, there was a current of recognition that had passed between them that allowed Gore to address Calvino as "Maestro" and that had brought the Calvinos, of their own volition, to the ceremony in Ravello bestowing Vidal's honorary citizenship. There was no jealousy, no competitiveness. For Calvino, and for Chichita, of whom he was very fond, Gore made an exception to his avoidance of funerals. Crowds gathered at the cemetery: the press, local officials, several hundred of Calvino's friends and colleagues. When Gore arrived, the hearse and the widow were not yet there. "We had to take the body from Siena to this village, which is one hour and a half away from the hospital," Chichita recalled. "I went with the hearse and I sat with the driver and the hearse was right behind me and it was nightmarish and unreal and I was horrified at the idea of going to the cemetery. I was totally horrified and completely alone. There were masses of people . . . and we got to the cemetery and I think it was my deepest feeling of horror and at the door of the cemetery looming high was Gore. And only Gore. Only he had the idea of waiting for me at the door. The other people were around the inside by the grave site. That's something I remember forever. It was a subtle thing. He gave me support." The coffin was placed four inches below the earth. Tiles were arranged over it. Masons covered the tiles with cement. The heat was oppressive. As Gore looked up from the fresh cement, he saw, staring straight at him, Calvino, "witnessing his own funeral." They stared at one another "for one brief mad moment. . . . The man I thought was Italo is his younger brother, Floriano." Later, on the drive back to Rome, under a hot sun, rain started to fall. A rainbow colored the sky in the east.

CHAPTER nINETEEN

Scenes from Later Life

1987–1996

WEBSTER COUNTY, MISSISSIPPI. May 1990. Hot weather. Air-condition-ing everywhere, the new South inscribed on the old. "White frame houses, gingerbread, front yards, splendid magnolias, mockingbirds." He had ar-rived in Webster county with a BBC television crew filming a documentary about his own life.

Gore had not heard mockingbirds since the Washington summers of his childhood, and he had never been in Mississippi before. The experience, though, had some of the feel of a return, as if his grandfather's memories, which he had heard so often as a child, were his own. He entered a green, moist, early-summer landscape heavily wooded with ancestral pines. This was where Thomas Pryor Gore had come from. The faces of the almost two hundred descendants of Thomas Tindal Gore who had congregated close to the places associated with Gore family history were eerily like his own. There were, assembled, cousins to every degree. It was one thing to joke about the two hundred similar noses and four hundred ears, another to appreciate the power of genetic inheritance. This was the family whose chromosomes he bore. Here they were in large numbers, proliferating from generation to generation, a community so formidable he had embraced its history but kept himself out of its living embrace. It was a family he wanted in principle, not in person. He had heard much about these people. He had actually, through his grandfather's recollections, seen these places: the Webster County Courthouse, the nearby Gore family house, the place at Emry where T. P. Gore was born. Suddenly he was there, in these living representations of the past, vividly evoked in his childhood by the man who had influenced him more than anyone else. And he was among legions of Gores, who welcomed their famous relative with the same combination of curiosity and apprehension with which he observed them, precisely because he had traveled a greater distance than they from the Gore family's Methodist origins, from the First and Second Great Awakenings that had left their indelible impact on this huge Southern clan. That spirit, he now discovered, was still expressively alive, especially in the younger generation of religious enthusiasts. A few days later, in Jackson, he told Eudora Welty, "sharp of eye, tongue, and full of gossip," whom he visited at her home, how alarmed he was "by the religiosity of the Gores. Admittedly the reunion was on a Sunday but *ten* hymns? two family preachers? a lot of blood of the lamb? 'Well, that's what we do on Sunday,' she said; and it was a Sunday. 'But I think they do it all week,' I said. 'They believe. They told me they do.' " That he did not didn't make him in the eyes of the family any the less a Gore; and that he was a Gore made him better than anyone who was not. Anyway, they would never accept that he was not, deep down, a Christian, ready to be awakened by their solicitations. Blood was stronger than disbelief.

A hundred years before, his grandfather, another nonbeliever, had left Mississippi with a copy of John Stuart Mill's *On Liberty* in his hand and the Constitution of the United States in his pocket. The noisy, smoke-belching train had taken the blind young man westward across the river to Texas and the Oklahoma Territory, where he found a bride and a career. His grandson had carried those Gore genes into places the Senator's world had given birth to, a culture whose frontier antecedents lived unmistakably in the configurations of the present. When his grandfather left Mississippi, not even radio had existed. When he died, the faces and voices of the Senator and his grandson had been in newsreels in a thousand movie theaters. Both had "lit out for the territory," each in his own way. Though the place names were different, the spirit was the same. T. P. Gore had never once left North

America. Going abroad was something he simply had no interest in. Foreign shores were inferior to American. His grandson carried America with him wherever he went. As for Henry James and Mark Twain, living abroad emphasized for Gore the intensity of his relationship with "home." In America he was an American who lived abroad. In Europe he was an American writer. When in his later years T. P. Gore returned to Mississippi, he was idolized by the Mississippi Gores. His grandson was shown "the fireplace from which he was given a piece of wood on a return trip." "I did have an eerie feeling," he wrote to Judith Halfpenny, "with so much kin assembled in a drab new cube of brick in the heart of Houston, Miss, where I stayed with 4th generation Dr. Gore, an amiable highly educated man, as the Gores all seem to be, mostly lawyers, doctors, preachers, one general. No entrepreneurs, I was told with mock despair. They had not gone into trade and made money, ever. T. P. Gore was their idol. The new idol is 7th cousin Albert Gore." At Yazoo City he was shown the monument to his great-great-grandfather, Thomas Tindal Gore, who, coming from Alabama to settle in Mississippi, had bought a vast tract of land from a soon-to-be-dispossessed Chickasaw Indian. At the courthouse Gore made an impromptu speech. Then he and the camera crew rolled away, down the interstate to Jackson, completing the documentary film, *Gore Vidal's Gore Vidal,* a late-twentieth-century monument to Thomas Tindal's descendant. Gore Vidal may have been aware that every turn in his own life away from a political career had been a turn away from what the Gore family reunion represented. The South is a different place from the rest of the country, he was fond of saying, and if Lincoln had been wiser, he would have let it go. It was his grandfather's South that was different, he began to realize, and as he and Eudora Welty agreed, the modern Deep South was becoming like much of the rest of the country. He had made the one visit of his lifetime.

It had been a walk down "memory lane" (a phrase he was becoming fond of), down those pathways his grandfather's stories had provided him. He had always valued highly his own and his family's past, partly because of the childhood instability his parents' temperaments and divorce had forced on him. The past provided an anchor. The Gore clan was a stable family he could both be a part of and keep at a distance. Given his strong historical temperament, it was natural that family history would interest him as history. The family sagas on both sides had resonant depth. They made his presence and his statements as an American even the more formidable. Some of his ancestors had done illustrious things. A few had been famous. The association did him credit, and as a man who lived by creating stories, by holding an audience with what he wrote and what he said, the family histories provided additional illustrative coordinates that made his tales shine more brightly, sharply, engagingly. His personal history was also a family story that preceded even his grandparents' generation, and he had become aware as early as the 1960s that he could not tell, perhaps even know, his own story fully enough if he did not know his family's origins. Much Gore family history was palpably there for him from the start. He had grown up among its latest expressions, particularly at Rock Creek Park. Vidal family history was more elusive. Family legend provided some detail. Still, little was known of what had transpired before 1848. Gene and Pick had been mostly uninterested; there was little reason to believe that the generation of Vidals after his own would have any interest at all. But it mattered to him. While Gene was alive, Gore had begun to look into Vidal family origins. His father gave what little help he could. Some of the details would always remain elusive or vague. By the late 1960s, after two visits to Feldkirch and the search for documents in Italy and Switzerland, he had begun to put together the general story, some aspects of which fascinated him, particularly that the family's likely origin was Sephardic Jewish and that Vidal had been a prominent name in Northern Italy, particularly in Venice, a city he visited regularly and for which he had great affection. "So I'm a Jew after all," he commented. "It's fascinating. I've always suspected Norman Mailer was Greek Orthodox from Russia. So we'll just change roles at the end. I'll work out the transfer."

Though he had vowed never to write his autobiography, and during the 1970s and '80s believed he would not, he was actually, in limited ways, in the process of doing precisely that. "I'm not going to write a memoir," he told Halfpenny in 1985, soon after Walter Clemons contracted to write his life, "and biographers no longer do any research. So I'd better fill in gaps for them now." He had been providing his version of some of the gaps in essays, particularly "West Point" and "On Flying," a graceful evocation of his father's career in the early days of commercial aviation. His own youth had also begun to take on quasimythic proportion in numbers of memoiristic essays, particularly those on Tennessee Williams. Vidal had been both participant and eyewitness in the making of legends. The autobiographical essays he had begun to write were both literary history and personal memoir. "Yes," he admitted, "I am getting very autobiographical, but if I don't do some of it, others will invent everything as they have already invented so much." When the BBC and Italy's RAI-TV offered him in 1985 the opportunity to write and narrate a two-hour TV documentary on Venice, he happily agreed. From the start of his Italian life, Venice had been a place he identified with, an irresistible lure for visits, especially with Barbara Epstein, and during the Christmas–New Year holiday, always with Howard, sometimes with American friends. Once, Jason Epstein recalled, "I was in Venice with Gore and an old [female] friend whom I happened to be traveling with and we were crossing the Rialto Bridge. There was a bunch of sailors. 'Seafood,' Gore said, and they both took off after them, leaving me behind." One of Gore's favorite stories about Tennessee and Maria was set in Venice. They "were sitting on the beach . . . and this very thin, elegant woman is walking along the beach. Maria, Lady St. Just, turns to Tennessee and says, 'That is Anorexia Nervosa.' Tennessee says, 'Oh, Maria, you know everyone!' " Harry's Bar, Peggy Guggenheim's palazzo, the luxurious Gritti Palace Hotel, long walks in the cold weather with touches of snow lining the canals, the pleasures of the Venetian opera house—the epicurean's Venice was also the historian's and the writer's, the setting of Mann's *Death in Venice,* the piazza that Henry James in *The Wings of the Dove* describes as the drawing room of Europe. Deepening the Venetian imprint was Gore's awareness that Vidals had come to that city when it was relatively young, as early as the fourteenth century. "Most of May–June [1985] in Venice and Crete and Naxos (we do the empire, too)," he told Halfpenny. "It is not easy among so many false notes to know which chords are least banal. I write, which I didn't want to do; and act, which I ought not to do." Among the true and revealing notes was the segment of film in which he discusses his Venetian ancestry. The camera takes him to the famous library where the records of the noble Venetian families are preserved. He is searching for evidence to tie him by lineage to Venetian fame. Alas, he tells his audience, as he runs his finger up and down the columns of the golden book, the name Vidal is not there. By the end of the year the documentary appeared on British and Italian television. George Armstrong wrote the text for the American and British print versions. Gore wanted them to be identified as co-authors. The British publisher refused, demanding Vidal's name alone, though he agreed to the formula "Edited by George Armstrong." Gore gave the entire royalty to his friend. "It is a picture book for Xmas, to go round the world with the various showings of the two films, a perfect non-book and so I have done nothing," except the preface. The project had been "a lot of work, and I grow old," he complained. "The energy isn't the same."

———·—·———

But he was soon back at his desk, "ready to be enslaved again to words," as he good-humoredly told Judith Halfpenny, with little sign of the decrease in energy he had complained of after finishing *Vidal in Venice*. In fact, the ten years from 1985 to 1995 were to be among the most productive of his life as a writer. If he complained about tiredness, it was in the context of a whirlwind of work, which included numbers of screenplays. In 1979 he had made a movie adaptation of Lucian Truscott's novel *Dress Gray*, about a West Point murder, that Frank Von Zerneck produced for Warner Brothers. Zerneck and he worked well together. It was a moderate success when it appeared as a television movie in 1986. Immediately after *Vidal in Venice* he had gone to Palermo to consult with the producer and director Michael Cimino—director of the disastrous *Heaven's Gate*, which had bankrupted United Artists—about the screenplay he had done at Cimino's request, based on Mario Puzo's novel *The Sicilian*. When Cimino came to Rome in April 1986 to enlist Vidal's services, he brought a script that he represented as entirely his own. There had been an earlier script by Steve Shagan, he told Vidal, but "he preferred that I not read it." Cimino initially described Vidal's assignment as polishing Cimino's script. Filming was to begin that summer. Setting to work immediately, doing numbers of rewrites during a three-month period, and then making further changes and additions with Cimino through the production and editing period, Vidal created almost an entirely new shooting script. "Cimino has made no major problems yet and follows, obediently, the script," Vidal told Halfpenny in August 1986, "but he is already manoeuvering to get credit for writing what I have written. Fortunately, our Guild is protective." He soon discovered he was wrong, though Cimino was not the problem. In a maneuver eerily reminiscent of what had happened with *Ben-Hur*, the Writers Guild of America, of which Shagan had been a director, awarded screenplay credit exclusively to Shagan. Furious, Vidal protested, then requested guild arbitration, this time armed with detailed records and corroborating third-party testimony to support his claim. After he had rewritten Cimino's script, he wrote to the guild, "Cimino sent me Shagan's script. There are perhaps a half dozen lines of Shagan's in the shooting script, which I, otherwise, wrote. For the record, I have every page on which I worked (from the Cimino script) to the shooting script, which is almost entirely my work." Vidal and his lawyer believed that Cimino also supported his claim. The guild soon turned down Vidal's compromise proposal that Shagan be given credit for the "screen story," Vidal for the "screenplay." Cimino also went to arbitration, where he lost, concerning not the screenplay but his agreement with the sponsoring company about the length of the film. As with *Heaven's Gate,* his "final" version was too long, though Vidal agreed with Cimino that the longer version was artistically superior to the shorter. When three anonymous arbitrators ruled Vidal should not get any credit for his contribution to the film, he sued the guild, despite rules forbidding a member's suing, on the grounds that its secret arbitration procedure was illegal. In addition, he maintained, relevant documents had purposely been withheld from the arbitrators, and the guild had not followed its own procedural rules.

Furious at what seemed an injustice, determined not to be victimized again, he was willing to spend whatever necessary to force the guild to operate in a way that was above suspicion. The California Court of Appeals ruled against the guild. The arbitrators' names had to be revealed. The guild's appeals were not upheld. But there was no movement toward a satisfactory resolution for Vidal. The guild to this day continues to keep secret the names of its arbitrators. The $250,000 he had been paid for his work on the script, almost all of which went to pay legal fees, and his victory in the California appeals court had to remain his substitute for credit for his work. "I sued over it only because I was angry at the Writer's Guild," he recalled. "I didn't want credit. I was happy not to have it." But it was enough like the *Ben-Hur* experience to impress on him, indelibly and bitterly, that making movies, as he knew all along, while usually lucrative was rarely satisfying. And he had done numbers of original scripts and adaptations that had never been made, though being made badly might have been even a worse fate. As a child of the golden films of the 1930s and '40s, never star-struck but deeply screen-struck, he was often temptable if the money were enough, if the subject appealed to him, if the circumstances seemed promising. In 1990 he was to do a screenplay at Martin Scorsese's request based on the life of Theodora and Justinian, a topic he also had in mind for a novel to be a successor to *Julian.* Scorsese liked the script, but the movie was never made. As usual, the problems were financing and timing. Though Vidal had been paid for movie options on numbers of his own novels, the options, no matter how promising at first, never produced actual films. For his work as a screenwriter he had been paid handsomely, but only *The Catered Affair*, *Suddenly*, *Last Summer*, and *The Best Man* had turned out reasonably well. It was vocation, not art. Still, if he ever had complete control over his screenplay, and if he had a director who respected it, he believed he might make a wonderful movie.

In 1989 he finally had an opportunity, though the conditions were not entirely favorable. The Turner Home Entertainment company agreed to finance a made-for-television movie that he would write based on the story of Billy the Kid, which Frank Von Zerneck would produce. Vidal had already done two versions, one for television in the 1950s, the other transformed into the unsatisfactory *The Left-Handed Gun*. Now he had the chance to do it his own way, in a film that starred Val Kilmer, a dark version of Billy as heroic innocent who finds himself trapped by the community's corruption into a highly principled but doomed criminality. Billy's temperament as rebel on behalf of justice, determined never to be a victim, Gore still identified as his own: the man who never started a fight but always fought self-defensively to a victory in the end, even if mainly a triumph of the iconoclastic spirit. Less successful as a film than he had anticipated, for reasons that had little to do with the screenplay, it still gave him satisfaction at last to do his version of *Billy*, though it demonstrated again that the collaborative nature of filmmaking made any script subject to forces beyond the author's control. Though reviews were adequate to good, the direction was relentlessly dark in color and mood, and Billy's story seemed not to appeal to Americans in the late 1980s. Also, it may have been too late in life for Gore to return to a subject he had identified with since adolescence. This last reworking lacked the freshness of the first, perhaps the inevitable difference between Vidal in his twenties and Vidal in his late sixties.

If he complained about feeling ill, it was the occasional hypochondriacal response, partly annoyance, partly fear, to the decline of his body or to environmental assaults like the nuclear-plant explosion in the Soviet Union. The irradiated clouds drifted westward on the winds. "Thanks to Chernobyl," he told Claire Bloom in June 1986, "a number of us now spit blood like 18th century poets: irritated throats from Cesium B7 in the soil. I had lungs, esophagus—the lot—checked. No cancer, just dripping sinuses, throats of fire. The govt refuses to admit just what happened." That did not prevent him, immediately after his return from a monthlong trip to Bangkok, via Laos, Burma, Tahiti, Sydney, Hong Kong, and Los Angeles, from accepting an invitation to attend a peace conference in Moscow in February 1987, with, among others, Graham Greene, Norman Mailer, and Gregory Peck, where he gave a speech on the origins of the Cold War. The invitation came "from a street in Moscow," he told Halfpenny, "no signature, just a street number, asking me to come to a Forum on a nuclear free world, Feb 14–16. This was the 11th. So I rang the Soviet consulate, the slowest most Byzantine office outside the Vatican. 'Was it too late' . . . I began. 'Come right over,' said the consul. 'But you're closed.' . . . 'We'll open,' he said. In half an hour I had my visa; another half hour I was at Aeroflot where a ticket waited."

In Moscow he saw John Kenneth Galbraith, Pierre Trudeau, Yoko Ono, and Claudia Cardinale, among other celebrities, though when he asked to see the list of writers, he was shown a dozen names, all, except Mailer and Graham Greene, unknown to him, "the usual loyal party members who are repaid, once a decade, with a slice of bread and a seat at the circus." The Mailers and he had an amiable dinner together at the flat of the editor of the Russian publishing house that published them both. "M was upset that only *Naked and D* has been published in the Soviet while five of my books have been done. He then held us riveted with an analysis of *Ancient Evenings* which he regards as his best book and must be published in Russia. Slight tension. 'The book,' said our editor, 'is just too long for us, with the paper shortage'—which is true." During the conference working sessions, the participants were divided into sections. "Alas, I was with Culture," Gore recalled, "presided over by a deputy minister, rather smooth, with Greene as figurehead. I sat next to him at a baize covered main table while several hundred lit-types made speeches at us. . . . Andrei Voisinitzen [Andrey Voznesensky] (I can never spell it) was in good form, a great charmer and considered their best poet. . . . AV knew that I knew that (Top Secret) he had fucked Mme Onassis and so every time he could get me to one side he would ask, wistfully, for news of *her*, which I gave as best I could, as learned from our sister in common. Around eleven in the morning GG would begin to wriggle beside me: he still looks about 17, a lean dirty-minded boy with a face that got, somehow, frost-bitten and worn. 'Will these French never shut up?' he moaned. Then he wriggled up some more and then he whispered, 'I've got a flask, you know. Do I dare?' 'No.' I was stern. 'Everyone will see you' (Gorbachev is harsh on the subject). 'I suppose not,' he whined. Then I took pity on him. 'Drop your notes,' I said. 'Pretend to search for them beneath the green baize, take a swig.' He sighed, 'I should never come up again, I fear.' But at lunch, he alone was supplied an entire bottle of vodka, which he drank in about an hour, no sign of drunkenness, not, indeed, at midnight either, after he and I had caroused together at the cinema club restaurant with our translators." Gorbachev impressed him considerably. "Norman was more suspicious. I turned out to be right. But he was right to be suspicious. He had followed the communist line more than I had, and he thought it was the usual bluff for Westerners. I thought something had happened there. And then Gorbachev told very funny stories about Ronald Reagan's meetings with him. Some of them were wildly funny." When they met at Vienna, Reagan had told Gorbachev "that if the earth were facing an invasion from Mars, his country and my country would become allies." Gorbachev had responded, " 'I think it's premature to worry about an invasion from Mars, but there are nuclear weapons that are here right now, and the two of us should work together and ban them.' Then Gorbachev paused, dramatically. 'The president made no reply.' " The next day, at a crowded international press session, British, French, and American journalists asked hostile, baiting questions. "I sat next to Mailer and wife on the ground that as she was the best-looking person in the hall we would not be much noticed and the press would leave Mailer and me alone. I was right. The Soviet Union fell in love with her, if not with us."

At the end of February, soon after returning from Moscow, Gore flew to Brazil, Argentina, and Spain for lectures and TV appearances in conjunction with Spanish-language editions of *Matters of Fact and of Fiction* and his new novel, *Empire*. It was the first time he had been to South America. "All sorts of changes are taking place in people's blood with AIDS as the most exciting and my own Epstein-Barr (known in LA as Epstein Bar and Grill)," which it turned out he did not have, "as one of the dullest: constant allergies, a feeling of lethargy, etc. I transcend it," he told Halfpenny, "by, in 6 months, going to Bangkok, Chiang Mai, Phuquet, Hong Kong, NYC, Moscow, Sao Paulo, Brasilia, Rio de Janeiro, Madrid, Toledo, London, Birmingham, Glasgow, Edinburgh and Moscow again." When he returned to Ravello, he was furious to discover that the gardener had murdered the two dogs living in the olive groves, two strays who had come to stay. Some

years before, the gardener had allowed Michael Tyler-Whittle's elderly
Caligula, whom they had inherited, to starve to death. He was immediately
and angrily fired. The only remaining pet was a charming homeless cat who
had wandered in the year before, "white slender with pale yellow-green
eyes, pink tipped ears, nose, paws," and had instantly become a cherished
member of the family. "She talks constantly . . . and is known as Miss
Miao to the town and the Cat from Hell around the house," he wrote to
Halfpenny. "She is incredibly clumsy but very affectionate in a most un-
catlike way but then we brought her up with two dogs and she thinks she is a
dog which means a sandpapery licking of one's nose."

At La Rondinaia through much of 1985–86 he had worked on *Manifest
Destiny*, the tentative title of the next novel in his American-history series.
When the manuscript became too long, he used much of it under the title
Empire ("*Manifest Destiny* was considered too difficult a title for our non-
reading readers"), published in June 1987, for which Random House had
paid a $1-million advance. The remainder became the core of *Empire*'s
successor, *Hollywood*, which was published in February 1990. "I knew I had
to stop at the end of *Empire* at a good point, which I found with the
showdown between Theodore Roosevelt and Hearst. But I was doing the
story really from Caroline's point of view," he recalled, "and I couldn't let
her go. Since I was going to take her up in Hollywood, that would then get
me through Woodrow Wilson. . . . So in a way these two are really one
book." The main character of *Empire* (1987), which begins precisely on the
day when the Spanish-American War is over and twenty-one years after
1876 ends, is Caroline Sanford, Emma and William's daughter, Charles
Schuyler's granddaughter, and Blaise Sanford's half-sister. The young Caroline is in England, visiting the American ambassador, John Hay, among
whose famous guests are his friends Henry Adams and Henry James and
who is about to be invited by President McKinley to become Secretary of
State. Caroline soon moves to Washington, escapes her engagement to
marry Del Hay, John Hay's son, and successfully fights her half-brother's
attempt to deprive her of her part of their inheritance. Shortly she is the
proprietor of an increasingly powerful Washington newspaper, competing
with William Randolph Hearst and her brother Blaise, Hearst's protégé, as
the marriage of image-makers and power brokers solidifies the transformation of the republic into a modern empire in which the wealthy get wealthier

and the powerful more powerful. For the restless, beautiful Caroline, the next stop is *Hollywood,* which begins in 1917 with Hearst at the White House and America about to enter World War I. Much of *Hollywood* is the story of Caroline's life in Washington and then California, her movement from the newspaper's printed page to Hollywood's silver screen within the context of American history from 1917 to 1928, Woodrow Wilson to Warren Harding, both of whom make substantial appearances. Senator Thomas P. Gore appears as himself. An important invented new character, Senator James Burden Day, a powerful up-and-coming political figure who has much in common with Senator Gore, is Caroline's married lover. A friend of Caroline's brother, Blaise, who has now become an influential Washington newspaper publisher and political operative, Day's ambition is to be President. Burden Day's history, sensibility, and political life become one of the important elements in the novel. When Caroline moves to California, soon to become a star of the silent screen, the worlds of Hollywood and of Washington are united; the country will never be the same again. Powerful California now not only makes images but determines elections. A border-state Southerner, Senator Day (his middle name indicates some of the strain) carries one of the heavy weights of American history, the North-South antagonism, still very much alive, embodied for him in his constant awareness that his father, who had fought and died for the Confederacy, would strongly disapprove of his son's politics and his Washington, D.C., world. Caroline fades from his life and then from the series.

In late November 1987 Gore was in London for *Empire*'s British publication, a new volume of essays *(Armageddon? Essays, 1983–1987),* and a single-volume reissue of *Myra/Myron* by his new British publisher, Andrew Deutsch. Its director, Tom Rosenthal, whom Gore had known since Heinemann days, was a devoted Vidal enthusiast. In general, both in America and Britain, *Empire* got superlative reviews, particularly from those sympathetic to Vidal's view of American history, but even from a reviewer as begrudging as the *New York Times*'s Christopher Lehmann-Haupt, whom Vidal disliked for what he felt was his continuation of Orville Prescott's narrow-minded moralism, though in fact Lehmann-Haupt frequently praised Vidal's historical fiction, which he reviewed glowingly. He had much less enthusiasm for *Myron* and the inventions, mainly on aesthetic grounds. Michiko Kakutani Vidal thought an even worse embodiment of the

Prescott tradition, to which she added a tendency to lecture the reader about the obvious, an exemplification of the maxim that "a little learning is a dangerous thing."

Much of the spring and summer of 1988 he spent at Ravello, working on *Hollywood* and writing essays, a volume of which, *At Home: Essays, 1982–1988*, Random House published in November 1988. For a man who had claimed he would never write an autobiography, numbers of essays in *At Home* were noticeably autobiographical, particularly the two that framed the titular theme, "At Home in Washington, D.C." and "At Home in a Roman Street" as well as "On Flying" and the essays on Prokosch, Williams, and Calvino. So too was *Hollywood*, in sly, effective ways, particularly the homage paid to Gene Vidal, who appears as Douglas Fairbanks's trainer, "tall and out of place among the stars . . . a handsome Army flier who had been an all-American football player at West Point"; and the evocation of Thomas Pryor Gore, who is an important presence in the Woodrow Wilson–Warren Harding world the novel dramatizes. Senator Burden Day "and his blind neighbor, former Senator Thomas Gore, gazed upon the moonlit woods where Gore was building a house. Defeated in 1920 after three terms in the Senate, Gore was practicing law in Washington and for the first time making money. 'The house will be just out of view, three hundred yards to the northwest of that hill.' The blind man pointed accurately with his cane. . . . Although two separate accidents had blinded him by the time he was ten, there was a legend that he had been elected Oklahoma's first senator by pretending not to be blind. Hence the pretense of reading, of seeing. . . . Some years earlier, Gore had created a sensation in the Senate by revealing that he had been offered a bribe by an oil company. No one had ever done that before and, privately, Gore's eccentricity was deplored in the cloakroom. 'I'd *starve* if it wasn't for my friends!' a Southern statesman had declaimed. . . . 'You plan to come back, don't you?' Gore looked at him. In the moonlight his single glass eye shone, while the blind one was full and reflected no light. 'When I went down in the Harding sweep, I thought it was the end of the world. Then I pulled myself together and said to myself, Here you are, fifty years old, and you've been a senator since you were thirty-seven and never had a chance to make a penny. So take time off. Build a house in Rock Creek Park. Then go back. I wrote a note and hid it in the Senate chamber, saying I'd be back one day.

Funny,' he held his cane in front of him like a dowsing rod, 'right after I hid that scrap of paper, I went into the cloakroom to collect my gear—this was the last day of the session—and suddenly I felt two arms around me and I was being given a bear-hug and I said, "Who is it?" and this voice said, "Just an old duffer going off to be hung." And it was Harding.' . . . 'He [Harding] had so much luck for so long,' Burden said. 'Now the people are ready to turn on him.' 'Sooner or later, they turn on everybody.' Gore sighed. 'I tell you, if there was any race other than the human race, I'd go join it.' "

———•———

That disenchantment was now applied to Vidal's feeling about his publisher, Random House, and his editor and friend, Jason Epstein. For years he had been complaining about the usual ineptitudes and failures that any large publisher inflicts on its books. His happy experience as a Little, Brown author in the 1960s increasingly became his benchmark against which to evaluate his dissatisfaction. Complaint was inevitable. Until the late 1980s, with the exception of the disagreement with Jason about *Creation*, it had been about minor failures of the sort authors always have with publishers. They were of less concern to Random House than its occasional discomfort at having locked itself into very expensive multiple-book contracts at a time when changing market and cultural conditions made it increasingly likely that they would not earn back the advances. As popular as Vidal was as a writer of historical novels, the audience was diminishing. Both he and Random House expected bestsellers. *Empire*, though it was critically praised, did not earn back its advance. *Hollywood* garnered neither critical nor commercial success, partly because its flaws, among its many strengths, were the kind that an increasingly less patient, less literary market for bestsellers found discouraging. Not tightly organized, partly an afterthought of *Empire*, less about Hollywood than about Washington, it was, as Epstein felt when he read the manuscript, less commercial than any of the previous historical novels. In addition, it seemed to him that Vidal's obsession with bisexuality, previously restricted to the "inventions" like *Myra* and *Myron*, was now, in *Hollywood*, becoming central to the historical novels, the result, Epstein thought, of Vidal's inability to resolve the tension between his male and female sides. He feared that conflation would turn future novels in the

series into expanded, historically based versions of the Chinese operas he
disliked and whose sales were small. Owen Laster saw the conflict moving
toward explosion.

In 1983 Gore had complained bitterly to Laster that Jason and Random
House were not behind *Duluth*. A realist, Vidal knew that *Duluth* was not
destined for mass-market success, but he felt that Random House was not
committed to giving it the support it needed to achieve success within its
limits. Whereas the book clubs rushed to embrace the historical novels, they
would not take any of the inventions. "Owen would come to me," Epstein
recalled, "and say that Gore is giving me a hard time with this. Random
House isn't supporting him, and so on. 'Well, we're doing the best we can.
But the Book-of-the-Month Club doesn't want these things.' It was *Duluth*.
And the reviews of the historical novels were not as good as they had been,
which I attributed to the intrusion of this *Myra Breckinridge* thing. . . .
Then Gore and I had lunch one day, and Gore was very angry. 'Why can't
you make the Book-of-the-Month Club take my books?' 'What am I supposed to do? Put a gun to their heads? They make their own decisions.' It
was well after *Duluth*. Maybe it was around the time of *Hollywood*. . . .
Up to that point everything was fine, except for the warnings I was getting
from Owen that Gore was unhappy." *Hollywood*, which brought them to the
edge but not over, seemed to Laster "a softer book than any of the other
historical novels. Perhaps Gore was getting tired of the historical project,"
though he had received a large advance to write the final volume in the
series, *The Golden Age*. He "was very critical of the way Random House
handled *Hollywood*, particularly publicity and promotion, though I don't
recall a lack of ads. . . . My theory—I saw it happen with other big
authors—is that Jason thought that Gore's writing was not as good as it
used to be, and I sensed that Jason somehow, not meaning to, conveyed this
to Gore. . . . I remember having lunch with Jason and going over the
declining sales from the historical novels. There was a lack of the same kind
of endorsement of his writing as before that somehow got through to Gore,
so the stage was set." Random House still had a commitment to Vidal. But it
was refracted through his editor's decreased enthusiasm about his potential
to be as good and as successful a writer of historical novels as before. A
certain mutual weariness, even disenchantment, had set in. Elements of it
had been there from the beginning. Vidal had tolerated an editor unenthusiastic about novels he valued greatly. It had been from the start a marriage

of demi-convenience, and like an old married couple they had tolerated disaffiliation because each had exercised restraint, neither had desired confrontation, and both had found reasons to assume they would go on together to the end.

When Vidal proposed in early 1990 that Random House publish a volume of his collected essays, to be called *United States* (organized on the trope that the one book united three aspects of his career—the personal, the political, and the literary), he was startled when Epstein resisted. It would be too large and expensive. In this case Epstein's reluctance was partly practical, but perhaps also cranky, a surprising response, since from the beginning Vidal's essays had attracted him "much much more than his fiction. In his own voice there was no need to pretend," Epstein observed. "He was an American version of Montaigne." For his editor, Vidal's voice as a novelist has never been fully convincing, even in the historical novels, which seemed to him best the closer they came to being essays. "I always thought about Gore that he was not really a novelist, that he had too much ego to be a writer of fiction because he couldn't subordinate himself to other people the way you have to as a novelist. You've got to become the people you impersonate, you have to have the ability to let yourself go a little bit and become the characters. He didn't seem to do that. It was always him wearing different costumes." But if Random House were to remain his publisher, it would have to bring out the essays. That Epstein allowed himself to express his reservations was self-defeating. "He sat at lunch at the Plaza," Gore recalled, "with Howard and Owen Laster and me and said, 'You can't do it, it's too large, we can't afford to make it, we can't afford to sell it,' and so on." But unless Random House drastically overpaid, it was certain not to lose money and likely to gain critical honors. "Obviously, I am not charmed that the collected essays are regarded as a drug on the market," Vidal wrote to Laster. He brooded on the possibility of changing publishers, or at least changing editors within Random House. The former was impractical though far from impossible, mainly because Random House had rights to his backlist, which he felt crucial to keep in print in as attractive a way as possible. That issue had begun to loom larger and larger, and increasing amounts of Laster's time, prodded by an anxious author, went into protecting the backlist and keeping it in print. The latter could be done, though the most likely alternative to Epstein, Gary Fisketjon, had moved to Knopf, which now belonged to the same conglomerate as Random House. General policy militated against authors moving from one house to another within the conglomerate. Also, there was a friendship, which Gore still valued, at risk. During the summer and fall of 1990 he worked at a new short novel, another in the invention mode, which he finished that winter. By the summer of 1991, when Laster, Vidal, and Epstein met in New York to determine what to do about the essays, it was now also part of the discussion. When Laster and Vidal offered to take no advance on the volume of essays, Random House agreed to publish it. Probably Epstein had already rethought his position. Since there was little to no financial risk and since he admired the essays, that issue was disposed of, though at the cost of further deterioration in the relationship by the fact of its having been an issue at all. At that lunch "Gore was tense," Epstein recalled. "I could see that he was in a strange mood, and I sensed there'd been a long series of discussions with Owen about what they're going to do about this. 'Let's wait,' I said, 'till we see the next book . . . and hope for the best.' "

Epstein hated it. *Live from Golgotha, The Gospel According to Gore Vidal,* narrated by Saint Timothy, is Vidal's culminating deconstruction of Christianity, a parodic explosion of the Gospels and Jesus into satiric and science-fiction fragments. It is also a buddy story in which the older "boy," Saint Paul, and the younger, Timothy, for a while travel together the first-century Christian religious circuit. Paul, who likes boys and Timothy especially, initiates Timothy into hilarious, exciting, and sometimes dangerous adventures as "Saint" (a.k.a. Saul/Paul) attempts to convert the heathen. Jesus' followers (or adapters) are split into two groups, those who believe that the message of the Jewish Jesus is for Jews and those who believe (as does Saint) "that Jesus had come as the messiah for everyone," that Jesus is a big, international, multicultural business not to be limited to Jews. The struggle between the warring groups is fought partly over the battleground of Timothy's attractive body, whose crucial part must be altered in order for the uncircumcised, non-Jewish Timothy to be initiated. "In the beginning was the nightmare, and the knife was with Saint Paul, and the circumcision was a Jewish notion and definitely not mine." Poor Timothy! "Little did I realize when I became a Christian and met Saint and his friends that my body—specifically my whang—was to be a battleground between two warring factions within the infant church." A marketing genius, Saint eventually wins. There is another battle in progress, so Timothy discovers, when, after Saint's death in Rome, Timothy begins to have strange extra-first-century-

A.D. visitations, which include a Sony television set, network executives from the twentieth century viciously competing to televise the crucifixion live, and a master computer hack who turns out to be the man who the world thinks was, but actually was *not,* crucified and who has time-traveled forward to the late twentieth century so that he can, electronically, reach back to the first to eliminate Christianity itself by erasing all records of its existence. In the end Lucky Timothy watches the crucifixion on TV. It is not "live" but taped. The special effects are extraordinarily beautiful. The editor wins an Emmy.

Not only did Epstein not like *Live from Golgotha,* he thought it "contemptible." The condemnation was fueled by a surprising moral outrage at Vidal's treatment of Paul's sexuality and by a literalist's sense of the necessity to be factually accurate. Epstein was, as he read it, "trying very hard to like it, and there were a few funny moments in the beginning. I actually laughed once or twice. I said that to Gore, that I'm enjoying this. I read the rest of it. I had just published a book by Elaine Pagels with a lot about St. Paul in it, which had led me to read other books on early Christianity. So I knew a certain amount about Paul and what was going on with current scholarship and so on. It was shocking. Gore didn't bother to look anything up. Paul is a revolutionary. When Paul says don't marry, he says it because if you do you'll be committed to Rome, not to us. It wasn't about sex. It was about revolution. I tried to explain that to Gore, and he was very high-and-mighty about that. . . . Then I wrote a letter, suggesting that he make some changes. . . . I didn't think the novel was funny. I thought it was forced and confusing, which I said in a polite way. I knew that that would lead to trouble. I knew that the fuse was getting short there." Vidal wondered if there had been all along some latent homophobia in Epstein that at least partly explained his dislike of *Myron,* *Duluth,* and *Live from Gologotha.* It also seemed to him possible that Epstein's hostile response to the last of these reflected visceral disapproval of Vidal's attack on right-wing Zionism that had begun with "The Empire Lovers Strike Back." Furious at what seemed to him Epstein's assumption of superior knowledge, as if the issue were whether or not Vidal's version of Saint Paul was an "accurate" one, or at least the one that Epstein thought accurate, Vidal's short fuse—which had burned low during ten years of what he thought his editor's condescension, distaste for his fiction, and pernicious neglect—detonated into an immediate explosion. In a controlled, furious letter, in response to Epstein's, he rejected both the criticism and the person from whom it had come. To Epstein, Vidal seemed to be playing, now and for much of his life, the role of Shakespeare's Coriolanus. " 'I banish thee.' He banished us and doesn't know about us anymore. He doesn't know what's going on. It's leftover socialism. It doesn't work. It has nothing to do with what's going on in this country now. And this endless sneering about America. I don't think it helps much to do that. This is an interesting country, for better or worse. You might as well figure out what's going on here and take it seriously."

Vidal believed that that was precisely what he had spent his lifetime doing. In his judgment it was Epstein who neither understood America nor him, as a political commentator and certainly not as a writer. He immediately instructed Laster to find another publisher. This was the right time to move. Random House would publish *Live from Golgotha* in 1992, *United States* in 1993. After that, a new publisher should be in place, one who would be energized by the excitement of having Vidal's name on its list. His backlist should be moved as soon as possible. Harry Evans, who had become the Random House publisher in 1990 after a career in British journalism and who was married to Tina Brown, the editor of *The New Yorker*, intervened. He was eager to keep Vidal, whom he admired as a literary star. He proposed that he himself become Vidal's editor, though the actual hands-on editing would be done by Sharon Delano, a manuscript and magazine editor in her mid-forties who had been at *The New York Review of Books* for twelve years and was happy to take on an association with a famous writer whom she admired. It was on Evans's part an attempt to flatter and conciliate, not at all a commitment to involve himself actively in publishing Vidal or to guarantee the support Vidal wanted. He was, though, persuasive; Vidal, persuadable. "As you know or do not know," Gore wrote to Richard Poirier, "I was all set to leave RH, thanks to J., but then Harry (The Consort) Evans persuaded me to stay and showed enthusiasm for my new comic invention, loathed by J. (his comments are wondrously off-the-wall: they also proved to be terminal). Anyway, all is past tense between us and Barbara makes no attempt to shift tenses so that's that. The *only* pleasure of age is shedding baggage." Jason was stunned. He had no desire to end the friendship. He did not want Gore to leave Random House either, though he would not oppose that, if Gore wanted to leave, and of course he did not oppose Evans's successful intervention. But he had assumed that the personal and professional relationships were separable. Gore believed they were not. Jason felt pained that he had been banished from any contact with someone he still cared about. Gore was too deeply hurt to continue the relationship. He felt he had been betrayed. It was a bitter end to a long friendship.

Full, active lives inevitably generate grievances, the lives of professional writers especially. Vidal's grievances were, no more and no less than for most, the residue of effort and risk. They were also sometimes energizing. Personal ruptures in lifelong relationships, though, were slow to come, no matter how long or deep the resentments. There were only two of any significance in his lifetime. The first was with his mother, the second with Jason. "I fear as fond as I am of the Epsteins," he told Halfpenny in May 1991, as he felt the rupture coming, "the statute of limitations has run out, and I can break away. Jason, all gloom in any case, should quit, cloudy trophies from his past, his glory; and I shall proceed to my end-game without Old-Man-of-the-Sea encumbrance." With Barbara, no matter what his grievances against *The New York Review of Books,* he was able to separate the personal from the professional. Still, the years had produced a long list of complaints against the *Review:* "My Barbara grows more [edgy] with time's passage," he wrote to Judith Halfpenny in May 1991. "The *Review* more irrelevant. I more irritable. She turned down one of my best pieces ["Reflections on Glory Reflected and Otherwise"], the only really memoiristic thing I've done but as it might give offense to the people amongst whom her uneasy collaborator Bob Silvers might climb socially, it will not do. For the record, they turned down 'The Holy Family' (Bob Silvers was making eyes at Bobby Kennedy then), French letters (too boring), 'Pink Star and Yellow Triangle' (can't think why—though she did say that if I removed the analogy between Jews and fags, as neither group had anything in common: I agreed that *I* saw nothing to generalize about but Hitler had, so . . .). 'Armageddon?' (Jews would be upset), 'The Day the American Empire Ran Out of Gas' (I forget why that wouldn't do), now 'Glorious Reflections' and a piece on Mencken. So I have called it quits. . . . The *NYR* grows not only duller and duller, the fate of most papers, but the writers do not question the status quo and the examined life is too dangerous for their pages. Also, they have got the *New Yorker Magazine–Encyclopedia Britannica* syndrome: every piece must contain every little fact and citation on earth for the great archive in the sky. Look how they overloaded poor Joan Didion in her piece on New York City. She is one of the few good essayists in the language, which means she is, simply, a seductive and unique voice. You can still hear her piping through the Treasurer's Report, but barely. I am forbidden politics, now the domain of the Catholic Garrulous Wills [Garry Wills], a sharp interesting writer at times, but he has never been outside the library to look at the country he generalizes so hugely about. He also believes that America is a truly Christian religious nation, quite underestimating the spontaneous hypocrisy of the lower orders when polled—so like that of their masters. But then like all our other tenured commentators, he must maintain the fiction that the US is a classless society (under God), something he probably believes and Arthur Schlesinger, say, who follows the party line in print, does not." Each time Vidal swore never to write again for the *Review*. Each time, patiently persuaded by Barbara, he relented. The stakes, of course, were not as high with the *Review* as with Random House. It was easier to publish essays in other magazines, as he increasingly did in *The Nation*, soon in *The Times Literary Supplement*, and especially in *Vanity Fair*, whose admiring publisher and editors were eager to print anything he offered them. Because of the backlist, moving to a new publisher was more formidable. And he had apparently never (or at least since the late 1960s) cared for Jason to the degree that he cared for Barbara. She had become and remained family, like his sister, even more like Howard. Disagreements, even disappointments, did not threaten the personal tie.

———————

Successful lives also generate honors, though their number is usually too small, their timeliness not timely enough. Prizes are desirable, but they come to few aspirants, or when they come, the time when they might have produced great pleasure has passed. Defenses are erected, some of them composed of irony or self-deprecation or resentment or exhaustion. Vidal, understandably, seemed hardly ever to get tired of wondering why he was not even more appreciated, and he drew on the usual range of responses to deal with it. In August 1989 he attended a day in his honor at the Edinburgh Festival. In September 1990 he presided as president at the annual Venice Film Festival, where he made a laudatory presentation for best film to Tom Stoppard, whom he admired, for *Rosencrantz and Guildenstern Are Dead*. He then himself received "a prize at Forte dei Marmi, as the most famous writer within forty miles of Vesuvius." He could always joke about fortune and misfortune. Wit burned away both pretense and ponderousness. On the subject of the Nobel Prize he quipped, "They have a short list and a long list and a non-list. I'm at the head of the non-list." His often ambivalent, sometimes antagonistic relationship with the academy mellowed slightly. Whereas Bellow, Mailer, and even Updike had begun to appear on undergraduate and graduate reading lists—the first, tentative touches of canonization—Vidal rarely if ever appeared as required reading. Occasionally an adventuresome literature course included *Myra Breckinridge*. His enthusiasts had found no way to fit his diverse oeuvre into the curriculum, and his presence as a public personality sometimes resulted in weighty academics' taking him more seriously as an entertainer than as an intellectual. Like most writers he suffered from the popularity of literary and cultural theory in English departments. At the same time he was immensely popular on campuses as a speaker, drawing huge student and public audiences even though he accepted few invitations, mostly to protect his time. That he almost always chose to speak on political rather than literary subjects expressed personal preference and his distaste for writers' contemplating themselves as writers in public. It contributed, though, to deflecting attention from his literary achievements. To some extent the rise of gay studies helped. He had become an iconic figure in the gay world, perhaps more for his wit, outspokenness, and fame than for his views on sex, which he had laid out clearly once again in "The Birds and the Bees" in *The Nation* in October 1991.

There were, though, more academic invitations than he desired, including honorary degrees, which he made a point of declining, with the exception of a degree awarded as the culmination in October 1988 of a three-day symposium at Brown University. The Brown program was in honor of John Hay, whom Gore admired. Hay had been one of the central figures in *Lincoln*. The opportunity to honor Hay made this invitation attractive. In November 1991 he lectured at East Anglia University as a favor to his friend, the critic Lorna Sage. That November he visited Dartmouth University as the centerpiece of a Vidal academic celebration. He did not in the least mind being celebrated and flattered, but he preferred even more to be read, a goal more difficult to realize. He gave during the 1990s almost annual talks to the National Press Club in Washington, which were broadcast on national television. With much to say on political topics, he had a way of saying it that commanded large audiences and that, in his white-haired seniority, made him a favorite of the Washington press corps, particularly because he was always good copy. Using selective forums to keep his name before the public made sense: a series of lectures in Germany and Scandinavia; an appearance at the Cheltenham literary festival; a lecture at the Folger Library, which had organized a series based on the movies that had influenced him; and the Lowell Lecture at Harvard, where he spoke on monotheism and its discontents, attacking the religious right as a threat to liberty, for "Jefferson's famous tree of liberty is all that we ever really had. Now, for want of nurture . . . it is dying before our eyes. Of course, the sky-god never liked it. But some of us did—and some of us do. So, perhaps through facing who and what we are, we may achieve a nation not under God but under man—or should I say our common humanity?"

With autobiography increasingly on his mind, he combined an honor that gave him great pleasure with an exploration of the impact that movies had had on him and on the United States in the 1930s and early '40s. In 1988 Alan Heimart, then the chair of Harvard's Program in the History of American Civilization, invited Gore to deliver the Massey Lectures in the History of American Civilization in spring 1991. Most likely, David Herbert Donald, the Harvard professor who had been Random House's expert reader of *Lincoln* in 1984 and with whom Gore had developed a friendship centered on their shared interest, had urged that Vidal be invited. Donald, who had written lives of Thomas Wolfe and Charles Sumner, had begun writing a biography of Lincoln. As the Vidal-Lincoln controversy had swirled in academic journals and in *The New York Review of Books*, Donald had strongly supported Vidal's depiction of Lincoln as concerned with preserving the Union, not ending slavery. He hoped that Gore's four lectures would focus on American literature, but he was delighted to have his acceptance regardless of subject, which Vidal soon told his Harvard hosts would be the films of the 1930s and '40s, under the title *Screening History* (which became a Harvard University Press book in 1993). "I know what I'd like to do," he wrote to Donald, "but I'm not sure that I can pull it off: describe the half dozen or so films that shaped me from ten to fourteen." Sharply evoking the Washington world of his grandfather and the impact of movies on his own development, *Screening History* argued that Anglophile Hollywood films had helped turn America toward involvement in World War II. Powerful vehicles of cultural, political, and psychological propaganda, films had made history. On Vidal's way to the theater for the first lecture, Stephen Thernstrom, Heimart's successor as chairman of the Program in the History of American Civilization, said to him, so he recalls,

" 'You know, don't be upset'—it was a rainy day—'if there's nobody there. We had Toni Morrison' (I had barely heard of her then) 'and we only had three hundred people.' I said, 'You'll get a lot more with me.' . . . Oh, the crowds were very enthusiastic, and a lot of kids. Usually these things draw lovers of literature, which tend not to be undergraduates but mainly graduate students or people from Cambridge, like Marian Schlesinger, who was sitting in the front row. I hadn't seen her in a long time. Justin Kaplan," the Twain and Whitman biographer, "was there. And Dan Aaron," the emeritus Harvard professor of American literature, whose books had contributed to a lively dialogue on literature and politics in America and who had been a friend of Truman Capote and Edmund Wilson. So too were other Boston and Cambridge friends. The neoconservative Thernstrom he soon disliked, sensing antagonism and sabotage. "It was a well-kept secret that I was there, but word did spread, and by the third lecture we filled the Kennedy Center. David Herbert Donald replaced Thernstrom at the podium and did a superb introduction without one note, dates and everything. A lovely gesture."

The issue of honors and prizes was given an ironic twist when *United States: Essays 1952–1992* was awarded the National Book Award for criticism. To Gore, Jason, who had not wanted to publish it, seemed all too self-congratulatory, as if he were totally responsible for its existence and success. But the award forced on Gore additional confirmation that many discriminating readers thought more highly of his essays, somewhat of an afterthought in his career, than his fiction. It was fine to be thought the Montaigne of the twentieth century. Yet to the extent that it deflected attention away from his achievements as a novelist, his reputation as an essayist was not an unmixed blessing. When he decided not to attend the award ceremony, he deputized Harold Evans, representing Random House, to read his brief acceptance speech and accept the award for him. The distance from Rome to New York was not so small that he could not use it as a justification for declining to appear, though certainly he had motives in addition to inconvenience: "Unaccustomed as I am to winning prizes in my native land," he had Evans say to the audience in November 1993, "I have not a set piece of the sort seasoned prize winners are wont to give. Who can forget Faulkner's famed 'eternal truths and verities,' that famed tautology so unlike my own bleak 'relative truth.' As you have already, I am sure, picked the wrong novelist and the wrong poet, I am not so vain as to think that you've got it right this time either. Incidentally, I did attend the first National Book Award forty years ago—that was also my last experience of book-prize-giving. My date was Dylan Thomas, dead sober for a change and terrified of everyone. The winner in fiction was my old friend James Jones, for *From Here to Eternity*. His victory was somewhat marred by Jean Stafford, one of the judges, who moved slowly if unsurely about the room, stopping before each notable to announce in a loud voice, 'The decision was *not* unanimous.' But Jimmy won, and Dylan and I retired to a tavern in the Village, and the rest was biography. In any case, I am delighted that you have encouraged Random House to continue publishing three-and-a-half-pound books by elderly writers."

Vermillion, South Dakota. June 1994. He had agreed to receive an honorary degree from the state university where his father had graduated almost three quarters of a century before. Fifty years ago, in his Army uniform, he had flown in from Colorado with his Uncle Pick, to Sioux Falls. "Fifty years later, just like clockwork," he told reporters, "I returned." In Madison, South Dakota, he saw again the house in which Gene Vidal was born, the Midwestern center of his father's generation of Vidals. Except for Aunt Margaret, they were now all dead. In his imagination, though, the Vidals and the Gores had recently been given additional life. The autobiographical impulse, pushing irrepressibly to the writerly surface, beginning with *Two Sisters* in 1970 and in the various memoiristic essays, had become insistent. Perhaps he might have declined to write a memoir if Walter Clemons had made effective use of material he had collected and the material Vidal had collected for him, including the bulging files in the archive at the Wisconsin State Historical Society, which contained boxes of Gore and Vidal family documents. But Clemons's efforts had moved from frustration to paralysis. By 1990, though he had interviewed dozens and collected additional documents, he had apparently not written a word. "Of course you're worried about the progress of the book," he wrote to Vidal in late 1990, five years since the beginning of the project, "and my ability to finish it. So am I. But I am working night and day to deliver a sizable portion in January." Little, Brown also began to express concern. "After four years of meeting every famous person I have known," Gore wrote to Louis Auchincloss, "Walter C has not written one word, nor, I fear, will he. He is diabetic, a progressive disease. My luck in these matters has always been bad. This was the moment for such a work to halt my slow fade to black but it was not to be."

Angry and impatient, he recognized that he himself was partly to blame. He had not bothered to get evaluations and recommendations, so to speak. "The only revelation is my stupidity in bypassing a half-dozen experienced biographers in favor of one who had not written anything longer than a 1500 word personality piece," he wrote to Bill Phillips, Clemons's editor at Little, Brown. Clemons was notorious in the New York literary world for his writer's block. His literary columns for *Newsweek* often provided anxious deadline jitters and delays for author and editors. Decency, charm, and intelligence, for which Clemons was beloved by many, were insufficient to the challenge. He had wanted to do it. Vidal had said yes. "Walter maintains that he is writing the book," he wrote to Halfpenny in late 1991, "and Little Brown is bearing down on him hard but the fact that after five years he has only got up to *Williwaw* indicates that though he can do research and write beautifully 1500-word cover-stories for *Newsweek*, he has no idea how to master a biography, particularly one so long and varied. I still hope but he dithers." The dithering continued. Finally, "after 7 years," Vidal wrote to Janet Caro, who had worked for him in the 1960 campaign, "Walter will present Little, Brown with a m.s.: God knows what it will be like. He's very thorough. Good critic. But, as he says sadly, the book is 'external' as I have never had a break-down, divorce, autistic child. I've seriously handicapped him but there it is." Clemons did not fulfill his promise. By late 1992 Vidal had begun to curse himself and feel cursed. "Nine years and we never saw a page. 1985 to 1994. I rang him and I said I'd wish you'd get out of this. He said no on the phone. I said, 'It's quite clear you've done nothing. You will do nothing.' He said, 'I don't think we should be having this conversation.' And I said, 'I wish we weren't having it. We're having it because you have reneged. You won't admit that you've done nothing.' Then he said, 'I'm committed to handing in three hundred pages in February.' That's after nine years, three hundred pages. 'I will hand it in then. If they like it, I will go on. If they don't, I'll withdraw.' He gave them nothing because there was nothing, and he was out." In early 1994, through an intermediary, Jay Parini, Vidal's friend and literary executor, Vidal queried this author: was he interested in becoming Vidal's biographer? I was. Two conditions: that Vidal provide full access to documents and people and that he agree in writing not to attempt to see the manuscript in any stage of its creation, that his first sight of the book in any form be on its date of publication. He agreed. Before I could approach Clemons about the availability of his files, which ostensibly contained interviews with people who had since died, Clemons, in summer 1994, at the age of sixty-four, suddenly died of a diabetic seizure. His heir refused access to any of his materials, to the puzzlement and anger of both biographer and subject. George Armstrong, also a friend of the executor, who had moved from Rome to New York in 1993, tried unsuccessfully to act as intermediary. Whatever Clemons had collected remained moldering in cartons in a Long Island City cellar.

Having taken the autobiographical route in *Screening History,* Vidal had decided by late 1991 to do his version of what Clemons was failing to do, though he would insist that it was an impressionistic memoir, not an autobiography, the latter a genre that he believed required a more formal structure and more accurate details. *"Screening History* was my trial run. It was interesting to do because I hadn't done anything like that. I hadn't really told a sustained narrative about myself, about crossing the Atlantic, about seeing Mussolini. Then I found that that was interesting to do and I had no other forum. It wasn't stuff I was going to introduce into a fiction. And then I decided, well, I would take it on myself, see what I could do with it." The chapter in *Screening History* that had focused on a 1937 film version of *The Prince and the Pauper* proved seminal. As he rewatched the film and wrote the chapter, he was suddenly more intensely preoccupied, both imaginatively and intellectually, with his relationship with Jimmie Trimble than he had been at any time since Jimmie's death in 1945. Trimble had been absorbed into his consciousness, an ongoing emotional and literary touchstone who had made his first posthumous appearance in *The City and the Pillar* in 1948, dedicated to him, and had appeared irregularly but frequently thereafter in Vidal's fiction, particularly in *Season of Comfort, Washington, D.C.,* and *Two Sisters,* and he was to appear centrally in the 1998 novel, *The Smithsonian Institution.* The memoir, to be called *Palimpsest* (referring to script written over partly erased script so that the earlier, somewhat hidden version still exists), which Vidal worked on from 1992 to 1994, presented a selective anecdotal account of Vidal's life until the age of thirty-nine. Structured as a narrative that moves between the present act of writing and the characters and incidents from the past, the Vidal of the present is as much a part of the narrative as the Vidal of the past. His parents and grandparents play prominent roles; Gore family history is central to the story. Neither euphemism nor self-analysis had any appeal to him. As Judith Calvino remarked, "I've always thought that Gore is a man without an unconscious and I do believe that. That is what allows him to be so impersonally personal. There are no bad things lurking somewhere in his body or his mind. He was born without it or he got rid of it. . . . Gore can transmit his warmth in different ways. Sometimes brutal. But he's not without warmth. Nobody else in the world would say what Gore says, 'Tell [my biographer] everything, whatever comes to your mind.' We all have our dark side that we want to hide. Maybe Gore doesn't have it. That is the most amazing feature of Gore. His absolute originality. He's a man who looks constantly at the truth with such cold eyes that very often he gets at the truth and then he's not afraid of writing about it or being written about. . . . He's courageous. He was always like that. A man of dangerous attraction."

Palimpsest is a nonintrospective memoir without a center of consciousness. Observation dominates, the eye looking outward, not inward. Emotion comes from mood, description, and intellectual analysis rather than from psychological self-investigation. Freud is not resisted but rejected, despite a narrative in which the author's mother is the primary villain: the portrait of Nina, mostly accurate, is written in unforgiving acid. "Bringing back my dreadful mother is no joy," he told Halfpenny. "So I am treating her comically. In fact, all the Auchincloss crew appear in my pages not as their actual dull rather invidious selves but as Wodehousean near-originals." The central character, though, was elusive. "I, too, explore the past nowadays only to find I never met me," he wrote to Ned Rorem. He later told his biographer, "I don't like talking about myself. And certainly not about private matters. So I don't know how you're going to do this because there isn't anything there. The fact that I was indeed infatuated for a brief period with somebody like Harold Lang, what can be made of that? There are no letters. There is no particular relationship. Just events. I did the best I could with it in *Palimpsest*. . . . Mine was a philistine family and his [Henry James's] all, more or less, dedicated to high art in one fashion or another. So if you do him, you're getting a record of intellectual life in his time. With mine, you get a political record. And an aviation one. I suppose there's enough material there. That material's got to do. There isn't anything except the books, of course, to talk about."

But there was also Jimmie Trimble. Trimble's impact on Vidal implicitly dominates the narrative: in the chapter called "The Desire and the Successful Pursuit of the Whole"; in various places throughout the narrative of Vidal's youth and Trimble's death; and in the final chapter "Section: E Lot 293½, Subdivisions 2 and 4"—the burial plots between the Clover Adams memorial and Jimmie Trimble's grave, where Gore and Howard will be buried. It is a story about love, lost love, and lovelessness, about completion and incompletion, about an only son who discovers in a boyhood friend the perfect representation of complementary otherness, of dialectical twinness. Whatever the relationship had meant to each of them while Jimmie was alive, afterward, for Gore, it took on symbolic as well as personal meaning. And Trimble's death at Iwo Jima had further transformed him, for Vidal, into a representation of America's waste of young lives, to which the Vietnam War had made him even more sensitive. "I have always hated that Rooseveltian war, and now I realize why and at so visceral—and obvious— a level. Those Marine landings were a mindless slaughter of our own." Something precious to him had been slaughtered, though he had no illusions that if Jimmie had lived, their adult relationship would have been anything other than ordinary. "Death is the mother of invention," Wallace Stevens had written, and while Vidal invented nothing about what happened between Jimmie and himself while Jimmie lived, his death had provided him with a lifelong focus for desire and for literary art. As he wrote *Palimpsest*, he began to see the pattern of his own life and of Jimmie's role in it. "It just fell into place. . . . It was the key to everything—you only see the pattern afterwards." After all, it was a memoir, he himself was the underlying subject, and it was a voyage of self-discovery as much as of self-creation. "The section on J.T. is written at last," he was soon to tell John Claiborne Davis, a new friend, "and I've solved my mysteries." Gore's own sexuality had moved in ways he doubted Jimmie's would have, if Jimmie had lived. But his days at St. Albans and his relationship with Jimmie seemed in retrospect to have been golden and sufficient unto themselves.

As he began writing *Palimpsest*, he became aware of how warm his feelings for St. Albans were. When Wid Washburn encouraged him to come to his fiftieth class reunion at Exeter, he found an excuse to decline. At the same time he began to toy with the idea of willing La Rondinaia to St. Albans as a study center. He had been eager, as he thought about *Palimpsest*, to reestablish contact with the only school at which he had been even moderately happy. In 1989, a young St. Albans Latin teacher, Wallace Ragan, had visited him in Ravello, then again in summer 1992 with John Davis, a retired English master who had known Jimmie Trimble after Gore had left for Los Alamos. He liked them both and particularly admired Davis, a fine short-story writer who intrepidly carried on despite increasing loss of vision. For a short time they were enthusiastic about possibly creating a memorial book in honor of Jimmie and other St. Albans boys who had died in World War II. Keen to learn as much as he could about Jimmie's life and death, Gore sought information and anecdotes. He was a welcome visitor at St. Albans, eagerly greeted by faculty and staff. Alfred True, the lower-form headmaster when he had been there, still had all his wits and told "Gene" Vidal stories at a dinner at which Gore Vidal was the guest of honor. With the help of an excellent researcher in Washington, Heidi Landecker, Gore collected documents and details, including eyewitness accounts of Jimmie's last days in the South Pacific and some of the brutal details of his death, though it was not yet clear whether he had been bayoneted or blown apart by a grenade or both. "Two unnerving first-hand accounts of JT's death," he wrote Davis, "one from a bitter member of his company who thinks it was all pointless and they forgotten. Jimmie wanted to know what to do if they were outnumbered. Surrender? No. They'd be tortured to death. So J stayed to the end. First a grenade then endless bayonet wounds." To Half-penny he confessed that "it has been painful bringing him back to life, but it is also exhilarating, something salvaged of that glittering youth." John Davis contributed a recollection about the Jimmie that Gore had known, the schoolboy who unself-consciously provided for others the opportunity to project their own desires and personalities onto his presence. "My own memories of Jimmy are those of unrequited libidinousness," Davis recalled. "He usually, at 17, moved through the Lane Johnston halls briskly, but when he idled along, he had a generous roll of the hips—the flexible hips of the athlete—that promised, like the Anglican definition of faith—'the substance of things hoped for, the evidence of things unseen.' But I was too much the unsure 27-year-old master to do more than cast my eyes demurely down, probably not too far down, as he passed by. Over the years since 1945, there have been a number of beautiful St. Albans boys who went the same road in Korea and Vietnam."

The memorial, which had seemed a good idea, soon ran into a major problem. When Vidal mentioned Jimmie's name to an interviewer for *Vanity Fair*, Jimmie's Washington classmates and friends became aware that Gore had made, and was going to make in greater detail in *Palimpsest*, the claim that he and Jimmie had been lovers. Worse, Jimmie's mother, Ruth Sewell, was still alive, someone well known to and of concern to Gore and Jimmie's St. Albans classmates. Friends called the ninety-year-old Washingtonian to ask whether she had seen the *Vanity Fair* article, which she had not. Naturally, they insisted on bringing it to her attention. To Mrs. Sewell and to friends of Jimmie's like Barrett Prettyman—a successful attorney, an avid collector of rare literary first editions, a trustee of St. Albans and the Folger Library, where he was to introduce Gore's talk on film in June 1993—Gore's claim seemed outrageous, offensive, and incompatible with the Jimmie they had known. If it were true, why had he not proclaimed it before? They were unaware that he had done so indirectly in *The City and the Pillar* and *The Season of Comfort*. It seemed as if Gore, exercising his imagination rather than adhering to truth, was "outing" Jimmie, and they felt protective of Mrs. Sewell. Gore pointed out to Prettyman that if he changed Jimmie's and other names, everyone in their Washington world would know who they were anyway. Prettyman "asked me, 'you mean Jimmy wasn't what he seemed to be, what he was?' I said, 'I'm not saying that he was a woman in a man's body, for God's sake. He was a man in a man's body. Men are like this. It is not an unnatural activity, except when proscribed by various religions that I'd thought we'd outgrown.' " The surviving remnants of Jimmie's Washington world wished Gore and the subject would go away. In October 1992, with Wally Ragan an uneasy facilitator, Gore had lunch with Mrs. Sewell and others, hoping to soothe troubled waters, if he could. There were Jimmie's last letters and some photographs he was eager to have copies of. It was a tense, unpleasant few hours. The circumspect Ragan was distressed to discover, when *Palimpsest* was published, that it contained an almost literal account of what had been said. "Disconcertingly, I had lunch in DC with his mother aged 90 but like 50," Gore wrote to Judith Halfpenny. "A wispy-hard Southern woman of considerable beauty. She was angry about the context the mag had given Jimmie and me. But agreed it was the busy-ness of her friends all over the world who checked in to see how shocked she was. 'Well, we both loved him,' she said at last."

March 1993. A gray, mild St. Patrick's Day in Rome. Howard greeted the half dozen movers who would work all day carrying down from the Via Di Torre Argentina apartment to the van that blocked the narrow street all their furniture and the innumerable cartons they had spent days packing. Always alert to the long arm of coincidence, Gore, waiting at La Rondinaia with Miss Miao—who after seven years with them often kept him company while he wrote, posing happily on his shoulder for photographs—noted it was the forty-fourth anniversary of his grandfather's death. To their great relief they had decided to give up the apartment they had occupied for almost thirty years. Since June 1973, when they had taken possession of La Rondinaia, it had gradually become the more comfortable of their two Italian residences. In the mid-1980s they had put in a swimming pool, a long, sleek, blue-brilliant rectangle two thirds of the way to the house from the entry gate, olive groves on the right, a vast view of high hills and the descent to the sea on the left. On the slope of the cliff, beneath the pool terrace, were rooms for changing, one decorated with original posters advertising Gore's plays and movies. "The pool is paradise at last," he wrote to Claire Bloom in 1986. "Thus, the world ends. Do come here soon." Between 1990 and 1993, in preparation for the change, they had replaced all the windows in the villa, an expensive venture essential to making it habitable during the cold months. In Rome, Howard, who had supervised the installation of the pool and the new windows, struggled with the final details of the move for which they had been preparing for some time, mostly because they found Rome less and less satisfactory.

What had seemed urbanely irresistible in the 1960s had become unlivable by the 1980s. For the last decade they had been spending on average only about three months a year in Rome anyway; the price for that was high, not only a full year's rent but the cost of attending to a deteriorating apartment at their own expense. The landlord refused to pay even for basic repairs. They were constantly interrupted by harsh banging on pipes and at their entrance door by a neighbor immediately below who expressed unintelligible, and sometimes irrational, grievances. Leaky windows and thin walls subjected them to Roman winter chill. In addition, they had become a target for burglaries, five of which had occurred in recent years, each requiring that Howard come up from La Rondinaia or fly in from wherever else he might be to attend to the details, including visits to the police station, where the authorities had no interest in being helpful. Roman street life, it seemed, had become more chaotic, less communal, their social and cultural world of less interest. Worst of all, noxious pollution became inescapable. Always a busy intersection, the corner of Via Di Torre Argentina and the Corso had become a traffic nightmare, spewing noise and dirty effluvia, suffusing the air even six stories above with what they felt in their throats and eyes to be lethal fumes. The terrace became unusable. By comparison La Rondinaia was paradise. George Armstrong, who was to leave Rome for residence in New York in July 1993, wondered if they could possibly fit into the villa all the furniture from the apartment. When the movers finally left for the drive to Ravello, Howard, in a car, carrying some of the most breakable of the precious items, was driven down quickly enough to be there before they arrived. Gore met them at the village square. One of his most precious possessions was a second-century Roman bust, after Antinous, which had been with them since Edgewater days. He had bought it decades earlier at a gallery in New York where Joe O'Donohue had worked, the only job, Gore joked, O'Donohue ever had in his life. Afraid the movers would break it, Gore carried the bust down the long path from the piazza to the house that he and Howard felt would be their last home. They had no desire to move again. They had no intention of doing so. When they left La Rondinaia, they would leave the Roman bust behind.

———————

From the terrace at La Rondinaia the view was various, permeable, breathtaking. The routine and the visual splendor coexisted, sometimes one more important than the other. The life they had led there for twenty years remained the same, other than that it went on all year, except for trips. Neither desired to go to Rome, and went only for the dentist and similar necessities. They went to Bangkok again, to Los Angeles, to La Costa, to New York and Washington for business. Gore was a guest at the White House for the presentation and celebration of a documentary about Thomas Jefferson. He found the evening boring, the documentary only slightly less so. For British television he did a three-part presentation of his own script on the history of the American presidency. When it was shown in the United States, it provoked establishment distress. Arthur Schlesinger was asked if it were not evidence that Vidal disliked his country. He replied that

Vidal didn't dislike his country: he was disappointed in it. The nation's capital seemed changed for the worse, and depleted. "I realized everybody I know in Washington is dead. There's nobody to call anymore." Even if inaccurate, it was accurate enough to express an inescapable reality. Fortunately, he had great success with younger people as diverse as Christopher Hitchens, the British-born radical journalist who had moved to America, and the actress Susan Sarandon, whom he knew from her performance in *An Evening with Richard Nixon.* Sarandon and Tim Robbins, her companion, became friends and visitors to La Rondinaia. When, in 1992, Robbins was directing and starring in a political film, *Bob Roberts,* he had induced Vidal to play the role of a United States senator. He was not hard to persuade. He got ironic satisfaction and great pleasure at suddenly becoming a sought-after cameo performer in movies as diverse as *Honor* and *Gattaca,* in his latter days finally the Mickey Rooney he had wanted to be as an adolescent. He also got to be a godfather again, this time to Sarandon and Robbins's child, as he had been before to Claire Bloom's daughter, Ken and Kathleen Tynan's daughter, and one of the Newmans' children. "Always a godfather, never a god," he liked to joke.

Gore wrote *Palimpsest,* and Miss Miao gradually died of skin cancer. Since it affected her ear and her balance, he carried her around constantly. Bad dreams sometimes brought together past and present as he worked at *Palimpsest* through 1993. "Last night I dreamed of Dah for the first time in many years. We are aboard a ship. There is no stateroom ready for him, and I have no ticket, passport. I can't find Dot. The ship pitches slightly, and I hold on to his arm as I used to do when we negotiated difficult terrain. . . . I am worried that he will fall. . . . Dah is not well; wants to lie down. I help him into a bunk. I'm afraid that the occupants will come back at any moment. Then I notice that my white cat is missing. More anxiety. I search the ship; cannot find the cat; cannot find my way back to Dah's stateroom. Wake up." Miao died in summer 1995, as *Palimpsest* made its way through publication. "For nearly two years the cancer ate away at the right ear," he wrote to Judith Halfpenny, "then began to cross her face (but never went into the system). The smell was terrible but she ate heartily. Toward the end, I would hold her six or seven hours a day as I read or wrote. One morning she could not walk—equilibrium destroyed. We sent for the vet who had rebuilt her other ear. He gave her a shot to sleep while I held her. This did not put her out. I insisted on a second. She tottered over to me on the sofa and into my arms for a nap. He said, 'She's out—it's enough to knock out a St Bernard.' I said, 'She's not out.' Finally, he lifted her off me, and the long claws came easily away from my sweater: he arranged her on her back, raised her left forepaw, inserted the needle in her heart and she gave the most horrendous scream. He said, 'O Dio!' I said, 'O shit' . . . she wriggled once, knocking the needle out. A minute later she was gone and we wrapped her in the tweed jacket I always wore when I was with her (ripped by her nails, soaked in blood and pus as was the rest of the studio). My last glimpse was the small triangular still-kitten face, eyes shut. We buried her in the garden. I am still having nightmares. As Howard says, now we have no one to talk to." They were soon given a present of two kittens.

In March 1996 I received the news from a friend in Boston that an item had appeared in the *Boston Globe* stating that Gore Vidal had been rushed at 6 A.M. the day before to the San Giovanni Hospital in Salerno because of rectal hemorrhaging. His condition was reported as stable. Tests were being done, after which a decision would be made about the length of his hospitalization. I called Barbara Epstein: "He had five polyps removed in L.A.," she said. "The doctor said don't fly for six days and no drinking. Three days later he's on his way back to Rome, an eighteen-hour flight." On an empty stomach, dehydrated, he ate a portion of eggplant covered with Tabasco sauce, drank a lot of vodka, as he later wrote to Ned Rorem, and took two aspirin, an anticoagulant. "He got home," Epstein continued, "and had some more drinks because he was exhausted." When he got up in the middle of the night to go to the bathroom, "he noticed some blood but it didn't seem very bad, so he went back to bed, woke up in a sea of blood. It all has a happy ending. When I called him, he said, 'I died!' At any rate, Howard was totally cool and did all the right things. There's a guy in the village who got a doctor. They hauled him out, and by six o'clock he was in the emergency room in the hospital in Salerno. They had first given him a coagulant, which of course made him feel immediately better. The bleeding stopped. He spent the night. He's okay. It was a terrific scare, and it was really because he didn't listen to the doctor. He's full of jokes. For a hypochondriac, he really is an iron man. The thought of four men carrying him from La Rondinaia through the gates to the town square—that must have been a sight!"

Vidal's voice on the telephone a few days later alternated between firm and fading: "I think I'm all right," he said to me. "Well, I *nearly* died. I understand now all the Romans taking to the hot bath, Seneca and so on. Bleeding to death is really perfectly pleasant. I always thought it would be painful. It's not. Curious, no sense of panic at all. 'Isn't this a fucking bore?' as I began to slide out. The thing burned its way through the duodenum into the stomach. The blood went gushing, hit my scars. They all opened up. Half of my red blood corpuscles went down the toilet. Most alarming feeling. It was rather peaceful. I wouldn't mind dying that way one bit. A hot tub, which I didn't have but which the Romans did, counteracts the only unpleasant aspect. Your head gets so cold as the blood starts to leave it. In a hot tub you can just put your head back and it warms your head and you have no sense of dying. But at exactly the right moment this doctor who roams the night among various villages—you can never find him because he's on the road—we found him and he came in no time. But one look at that emergency hospital, I knew I had better get out of there. It was a charnel house. I knew that the toilet could give you AIDS or a thousand other things! So I fled. I should probably issue a press bulletin, saying 'the account of my death has been greatly underreported.' "

Three months later I came to Ravello for a month of intense discussions. My host at the Hotel Belvedere Caruso in Ravello, after I confirmed to him that, yes, I was writing a biography of Signor Vidal, shook his head apprehensively. Perhaps he had in mind the incident of four months earlier. His concern, of course, was for the subject, not the biographer. In Italy, he told me, it was bad luck for a living man to have his biography written. He hinted that the bad luck usually took the form of an unexpected exit that would not have happened otherwise. It seemed to him a dangerous thing to write the life of a living subject. It had not been, so far, dangerous to me, and Vidal had kept his word. He had been totally cooperative, with one exception. He had not allowed me to see the diary he had kept in 1948. What, that you don't already know, he asked, would you learn from a list of the boys I had fucked and a litany of complaint about nasty reviews? "There's nothing more there." At first I was suspicious. I pressed him about it. Gradually I began to believe him. Now, for the first time, as we settled down to our discussions, he became angry with me to my face. He had just returned to Ravello from a long trip. I was tired also. Late in a long day of taping I pushed him about whether he had had sex with someone whose name had come up. "Goddamn it, I think you'll never get it through your head that these sexual things aren't what my life's about and that you'll never understand how we deal with these things in my world." If he meant it as a shot across the bow, he was also genuinely angry, and worried. I told him immediately, with equal expressiveness, that he was wrong. I had seen early on that the best way to deal with Gore's strong feelings or views when they were presented as a challenge was to state my independent response calmly but firmly, with no delay. He backed off. But he feared that his straight, comparatively bourgeois biographer would write a biography that got him and his life completely wrong. I understood the fear, and have done my best. For four years he answered every question I asked, provided access to friends and documents, spoke at length, drunk and sober, about his life and views. His honesty warranted respect. To the degree that it was preemptive, it was another expression of his superb intelligence. The inevitable happened: I grew fond of him. Had he grown fond of me? There seemed reason to think so, but about personal matters genius is never to be entirely trusted. At a minimum he seemed pleased that the job was finally getting done, and in a professional way. When Reuters cameramen set up their equipment in his study for a sound bite from him on the state of the world, I said, "Tell them something new." He said, "I'm not in the miracle business."

In October, Gore called from Ravello, just after he had returned from a brief Venetian holiday. "You nearly had an ending to the biography yesterday. You could have called it *Death in Venice*. At ten o'clock in the morning, in a driving rain, we left the Gritti Palace. There's an airport out on the Lido, which is the other end of the lagoon. Bumpy little speedboats, and we came into the wooden wharf there. Someone should have been there to help us off the boat. It's jumping up and down. Nobody. I got out and went straight into the lagoon between the wharf and the boat, scraping my foot and hand. One foot was on the wharf and one was on the boat. I was then suddenly upon neither, heading towards Neptune's cavern. All I could think of was that I was diving into cholera; hepatitis A, B, C, and D; diving into tetanus. I immediately swam to the surface, which is difficult to do wearing a raincoat filled with water. I could reach up—it's a wooden wharf with pilings. So I reached up to the wharf itself, but I was so heavy from the water in my clothes and the driving rain is falling. So I tried to pull myself up and couldn't, and then about four men came rushing down and they dragged me up onto it, where I lay, right hand and left foot bleeding. I also banged the back of my head. I'm still wondering if I have a concussion. I just thought, 'Well, *Death in Venice*. Why not? It gives Fred a lyric ending.'" Later he wrote to Ned Rorem, "Two close calls in one year. What can this mean?" Said Andreas Brown, owner of New York's Gotham Book Mart and Vidal's admirer, when he heard of the incident, "Vidal tries to walk on water—and fails."

On December 10, 1996, my wife and I were attacked on the New York City subway. I was stabbed in the chest. My clothes were drenched with blood. The bleeding was painless. As I was stretched out on the subway floor, my wife pressed her scarf tightly against the wound. When I didn't lose consciousness, I knew I was not going to die. One of my concerns, as I was rushed to Bellevue Hospital, was how much this would delay writing the book. I had hoped to begin writing on the first day of 1997. A few days later, Vidal called. Now that you too have almost bled to death, he commented, you'll be able to write more effectively about my experience. A fax soon followed: "There is no end to your thoroughness as a biographer! When I told you, after nearly bleeding to death in March, that it was a remarkably painless, even sleepy way to go, I knew that sooner or later you would check out the story and so you most dramatically have. . . . When Barbara was filling in Murray Kempton with the first details, he said wearily, 'That's enough. I'm already a Republican.'" Gore seemed very relieved not to have lost another biographer. Amid the jokes, he was unmistakably compassionate. On New Year's Day I went to the keyboard and wrote the prelude. I had told him at the start that I preferred my subjects dead. I now told him that he had become an exception to my preference, though I still hoped to be at his funeral rather than he at mine.

The fact of his own aging sustained itself, the thought of aging challenged his thanatophobia. It would be the one death he could not avoid, the funeral to which he would have to go. "I do mean to go on and on," he had written Elizabeth Hardwick in 1975. "As Geo. Sand's husband said, 'She turns on the faucet in the morning and runs smoothly until lunch.' Perhaps I should start eating a proper lunch. It's very odd, writing in middle age when youthful ambition/vanity is satiated, abandoned, and succeeded by what? The dread tap? All those words running out in the form of sentences." Sometimes his jokes helped. So too did liquor. He had gone much into adulthood before he drank alcohol at all, other than the occasional social drink. But wine had become a pleasure, a habit, a necessity in the 1960s. By the 1980s he had become by most people's standards a heavy drinker, encouraged and made tenable by his having either by inheritance or adjustment a high tolerance. Amounts that drove most others under the table found him not only sitting upright but, except for an occasional slurring, absolutely lucid. A history of heavy-drinking Gores and his mother's alcoholism forced him to give thought to his own drinking habits. No matter how much he consumed, he did not feel that drinking controlled him. He was not an alcoholic, he believed, if he restricted drinking to nonworking hours, which he actually did quite easily. Wine did not appear until late lunch, serious drinking of whiskey and vodka not till after dinner, at restaurants or in the living room or in his study, with visitors, or with Howard, whose tolerance was far less than his for both alcohol and late hours. When Gore wanted to sleep, he found alcohol a better soporific than pills. If some health problem incompatible with alcohol arose, he stopped for as long as medically necessary. When he wanted to lose weight, usually in preparation for public appearances, he went off alcohol for long periods, with no apparent difficulty. "I drank like a boy all summer," he had written to Halfpenny in October 1991, "until I looked again like Farouk. Now I have stopped forever." Unfortunately, heavy consumption contributed considerably to weight gain, and in the 1990s the cycle became increasingly telescoped. When I asked him in 1998, after he had stopped drinking for a time, whether he planned to start again, he responded, "I will immediately resume. I'm not about to give up my life." He resumed drinking and regained weight soon after he had devoted weeks or months to losing it. "What's happened in old age is that I don't go off that often to lose it, so I've been permanently heavy, where in the past only partly or impermanently heavy." Nothing about living seemed attractive enough to compete with the pleasures he still enjoyed, particularly drinking and eating whatever he liked. "One gets more done without drinking," he had told Halfpenny in August 1990, "and the memory blossoms but I shall resume once I've remembered all I want to, and sink myself into whiskey where one's sense of time is so altered that one feels in the moment immortality—a long luminous present which, not drinking, becomes a fast-moving express train named . . . Nothing."

If by the late 1990s he was too heavy to be handsome, his looks were still interesting, remnants of white hair, sharply accentuated nose and ears, piercing olive eyes, a topheaviness that had presence, a voice that riveted with depth and dramatic phrasing. He had almost persuaded himself not to care anymore about his appearance. In 1984, while losing weight, he had dyed his hair "for the first time. . . . The gray about the face had gone disagreeably white, and though I don't mind looking—or being—middle-aged, I draw the line at being aged before the frost is indeed on the pumpkin. The result is like having an old friend back in town. . . . It is not until one sees oneself on TV, over the years . . . that you feel really old and crumbling." In the 1960s he had told Halfpenny, who had just seen a videotape of *Fellini's Roma,* that he "still worked out in a gym and there was sex and motive. At 60 I said to hell with it and people now make most unkind references to my lack of beauty. I find myself peculiarly unbothered, so much for vanity which is only useful—necessary—if you're after something. No pursuit, no beauty. I am a utilitarian finally." It did not depress him. Even long interviews with his biographer about his past did not seem to darken his mood, though they were part of a consciousness of how quickly, these days, the clock seemed to be moving. "My makeup is rather cheerful. . . . Luckily, I have anger [which helps me escape depression]. But it passes very quickly." But "why would I be depressed about anything? I've never been seriously ill since 1947. Maybe I would be if I had cancer or something and was dying." But his attentive analysis and description of what it felt like to be growing old transformed the subject of dying into a life force. Still capable of great energy and motion, he hardly hesitated to travel long distances to pursue his interests, both political and literary, though even first-class air travel seemed different from what it had once been. Here the difference resulted from changes within him. On an airplane, "I used alcohol. Now I'm scared of that. I do sleep. With age, something happens with your sense of time. You get up in the morning and suddenly you're getting back to bed again. And the day is over—all old people report this, ad nauseam. But no less true for that. So a long, boring flight isn't that long. You haven't even finished the book you've brought with you because you tend to stare straight ahead. Old age is like early youth. Idyll of woolgather-ing." Yet he was capable of sharp creative focus whenever he had a task at hand, especially writing, which he kept at, mostly successfully, with extraor-dinary vigor. It was, at least for the time being, the old age of a productive writer. He still had something to say and wanted to be heard.

I HAVE COLLECTED about two thousand of Vidal's letters, most of them unpublished. These letters and oral interviews provide the evidentiary backbone of the narrative. The letters have been obtained from individuals, usually the recipients, except for those in libraries, particularly the Wisconsin State Historical Society, the University of Wisconsin, Madison (abbreviated as W); Princeton University Library (P); Columbia University Library (C); University of California at Los Angeles (UC); University of Texas Library (T); Carl Albert Congressional Research Center, University of Oklahoma (O); the Z. Smith Reynolds Library, Wake Forest University (WF); University of Delaware Library (D); the Houghton Library at Harvard University (H); Beinecke Library, Yale University (Y); Christ Church College Library, Oxford University (CC); and The American Heritage Center, University of Wyoming (WY). LB refers to the Little, Brown archives. A selection of Vidal's letters to Christopher Isherwood has been published in *The Times Literary Supplement*, 12/20/1996, 14–15, to Louis Auchincloss in *The New Yorker*, 6/9/1997, 76–77. My citations from the letters are endnoted by the names of the correspondents and the date; faxes are treated as letters; the library source of letters and other unpublished material is indicated by the appropriate abbreviation. In all instances Gore Vidal has been abbreviated as "GV." Since Vidal rarely dates his letters, I have had in most cases to establish a date (often approximate; "nd" stands for "no date") through whatever means available. Unpublished memoirs and diaries are endnoted simply as "unpublished diary of" and any other pertinent information. Published sources are documented in the conventional citation form. The direct citations for all published and unpublished materials (with the exception of oral interviews) are presented in endnotes that are grouped by chapter and keyed to the page in the book on which the quotation or paraphrase appears. Only books from which I have quoted are cited in the endnotes.

Approximately 250 interviews with the subject have produced about 2,000 pages of transcription. I have interviewed about 150 others. Oral sources for the exposition are listed chapter by chapter in a paragraph at the beginning of each chapter division that precedes the endnotes. An oral source is simply stated as "interview with" and the date of the interview provided. In all cases I am the person doing the interviewing. Since the reader cannot check my quotations and paraphrases for accuracy except against my transcriptions and tapes, it seems senseless to add pages by attaching the interview note directly (by whatever method) to the quote or paraphrase and keying it by page number. In most cases the person whose words I quote is identified by name in the exposition. I have not stated at the beginning of each chapter that material in this chapter is drawn from interviews with Gore Vidal. That would take up space with the obvious and provide a list of dates that cannot be of any use to the reader. The tapes, transcriptions, and photocopies of letters eventually will be deposited in the Gore Vidal Archive at the Wisconsin State Historical Society at the University of Wisconsin.

Chapters One through Three draw extensively on Gore-family documents held privately by Bill and Lois Gore of Natchez, Mississippi; the Gore Vidal collection of Gore family documents, Wisconsin State Historical Society, Madison; and the Eugene Luther Vidal Papers, at the American Heritage Center, University of Wyoming. The Natchez Gores provided assistance with Gore-family genealogy and expert guidance at the various Gore-family sites in Webster and Calhoun counties. The Vidal Collection in Wisconsin contains originals and copies of Gore-family and Vidal-family documents, which include genealogical narratives; letters between family members about genealogical issues; birth, baptism, marriage, and census records; documents from Spanish, Swiss, and Italian archives in regard to the Traxler and Vidal families; and newspaper clippings. The most prominent documents are: T. P. Gore, *Autobiographical Fragment*, 31 pages, nd; Mary Gore Cooper, *Gore Family*, 15 pages, nd, and *History of the Gores in Webster County*, nd, unpaginated; *Feldkircher Anzeiger*, "The Farewell to the Old Building of the Chamber of Commerce on the Schlossergasse," 16 pages, 6/19/1954. The following published material on Gore and Vidal family history has either been quoted or drawn from: Monroe Lee Billington, *Thomas Gore, The Blind Senator from Oklahoma*. Lawrence: Kansas, 1967; *Kay-Quarterly, Newsletter of the Kay Family Association*, 24 (summer 1994) and various genealogical documents provided by the Kay Family Association; Robert Cicero Latham, *The Dirt Farmers in Politics: A Study of Webster County, Mississippi, During the Rise of Democratic Factionalism, 1880–1910*. Phd. dissertation. Mitchell Memorial Library, Mississippi State University; T. T. Montgomery, *The Growth of Oklahoma*. Oklahoma City, 1933; Ken Nail, *History of Calhoun County*, Calhoun County School District, 1975; *Schweizerisches Geschlechterbuch Almanach Genealogique Suisse*, XII, Zurich, 1965; Webster County History Association, *The History of Webster County*. Curtis Media Corporation, 1985. Gore Vidal's memoir, *Palimpsest* (abbreviated *M*), New York, 1995; his *Screening History (SH)*, Cambridge, 1991; *Two Sisters, A Memoir in the Form of a Novel (TS)*, Boston, 1970; and his essays, most collected in *United States, Essays 1952–1992 (US)*, New York, 1993, are important biographical sources in Chapter's One through Three and throughout.

Chapter One

INTERVIEWS: Katharine Smith (Mrs. Katharine Vidal), 2/15/1996; Margaret (Vidal) Sutton, 3/29/1996, 3/31/1996; Sally Vidal (Mrs. Felix Vidal), 3/28/1996; Susan Milstead, 3/29/1996, 3/31/1996.

ENDNOTES

p. 3: Certificate of Holy Baptism, Washington Cathedral, 2/5/1939. W.

p. 5: "If a snake": Mary Gore Cooper, "History of the Gores in Webster County, Mississippi," unpub. typescript, 7. W.

p. 6: "The next day": Mary Gore Cooper, "History of the Gores in Webster County, Mississippi," unpub. typescript, 4. W.

p. 7: "as far as he knew": BBC Omnibus, 1995.

p. 8: "That in order": *The History of Webster County*, 23.

p. 8–9: "Somebody who loved": T. P. Gore, unpub. *Autobiographical Fragment*, nd. 2; "I dreamed I was blind": Gore, *Autobiographical Fragment*, 4. W.

p. 10: "A good many evenings": *Autobiographical Fragment*, 16. W.

p. 11: "until and unless": *Autobiographical Fragment*, 23. W.

p. 12: "I fell in love": *Autobiographical Fragment*, 31. W.

p. 15: "Jewish origin": Professor Samuel G. Armistead (Department of Spanish, University of California, Davis) concludes his detailed three-page scholarly survey of the history of the name Vidal and of Gore Vidal's Vidal-family ancestors: "There is, I believe, a very, very good chance that the Vidals were originally Jewish. With such a name and such an ancestor (Casper Vidall), in such a time and place, it would be very strange indeed if they were not."

p. 15: "sold Vidalhaus": *Feldkircher Anzeiger*, "The Farewell to the Old Building of the Chamber of Commerce on the Schlossergasse." W.

pp. 22–23: "engineer's college course": *The Coyote* [University of South Dakota yearbook], "The College of Engineering," 1917; "the best all round": unidentified newspaper clipping, 1916.

pp. 23–24: "Local boy": unidentified newspaper clipping, 1914; "vigorous plea": unidentified newspaper clipping, 1916; "demon on the gridiron": unidentified newspaper clipping, 1916; "largest crowd": unidentified newspaper clipping, 1916; "some technical school": unidentified newspaper clipping, 1916. WY.

p. 25: "attended by four": unidentified newspaper clipping, Washington, January 1922. W; "Mr. Gore and": unidentified newspaper clipping, Washington, January 1922. W; "severe bruises": *Sioux Falls Press*, 1/12/1992. W; "where Lieut. Vidal": unidentified newspaper clipping, Washington, January 1922. W.

p. 26: "She wants to be": reported by Gore Vidal as a remark made about Nina to him.

Chapter Two

INTERVIEWS: Roy Thompson, 11/28/1995, 1/8/1996, 3/26/1996; Wilson Hurley, 12/13/1995; James Tuck, 5/27/1997; Janet Bingham, 10/28/1995; Robert Taylor, 3/1/1997; Katharine Smith (Mrs. Katharine Vidal), 2/15/1996; Margaret (Vidal) Sutton, 3/29/1996, 3/31/1996; Sally Vidal (Mrs. Felix Vidal), 3/28/1996; Susan Milstead, 3/29/1996, 3/31/1996.

ENDNOTES

p. 30: "recurrent dreams": *M*, 42–43; "The child": *The Season of Comfort* (New York, 1949), 24.

p. 32: "After I nominated": *US*, 723–24.

p. 33: "alleged attack": Billington, 65–66; various Washington and Oklahoma newspaper accounts. W; "Senator Gore and his wife": *Oklahoma State Sentinel*, 2/19/1914. W.

p. 37: "in a very loud voice": *SH*, 6.

p. 37: "the lurid flames": *US*, 1061.

pp. 40–41: "in the bathroom": *TS*, 241–43; "never have": *TS*, 241–43; "central to": Robert J. Stanton and Gore Vidal, *Views from a Window: Conversations with Gore Vidal*, 1980, 60; "Milton's daughters": GV/from unpub. draft of "On Rereading the Oz books." W; "amusing tyrant": ibid.

p. 41: "I can still remember": GV/from unpub. draft of "On Rereading the Oz books." W; "Baby Gene": *Capital Capers* by George Abell, *Washington Post*, 5/5/1931. W; "passionate sightseer": *US*, 1057.

p. 42: "sick to his stomach": *Season*, 82; "as we came downstairs," GV/Fred Kaplan, 9/15/1995; "an ancient Quaker": *US*, 994–95.

p. 43: "until blood came": *Season*, 83.

p. 44: "I used to build": *M*, 43–44.

pp. 46–47: "white skylights": *Season*, 30–31; "this boy is nekkid": *US*, 1060; "a nymph": from unpub. draft of "On Rereading the Oz books." W.

p. 48: "white skeletons": *SH*, 19–21; "Before we could pass": *SH*, 19–21.

p. 50: "If he reported": unpub. interview with Gene Vidal, 9/1/1966. W.

p. 54: "We are all very grateful": Amelia Earhart/Mrs. Franklin D. Roosevelt, telegrams 9/15 and 9/17/1936. W.

p. 56: "tremendous pile": *Season*, 85.

p. 56: "the Gores": Vidal/Patrick Hurley, 9/27/1933; Vidal/Mrs. Oscar Coolican, 10/5/1933. WY; "Capital's Beauty": *Washington Post*, 11/8/1933. W.

p. 57: "We have not had": Frank Lincoln/Gene Vidal, 4/16/1934. W.

p. 59: "that all these": *Season*, 93–95.

p. 60: "He had been exceedingly": Vidal/Arthur H. Moll, 2/21/1935. WY.

p. 61: "to consider St. Albans": James Henderson/Vidal, 4/29/1934. WY; "I believe it would be": Vidal/Henderson, 5/4/1934. WY.

p. 63: "for her own use": divorce agreement, 5/16/1935. WY.

pp. 64–65: "She had been told"; "Nina was," etc.: *Season*, 98–101; "I said no": *M*, 14–15.

p. 66: "Mrs. Vidal was recently reported": Associated Press, 7/3/1935.

p. 66: "Gene politely agreed"; "theirs would be": *M*, 13–14.

p. 67: "The announcement comes"; "the bride wore": *Washington Post*, 10/16/1935. W.

Chapter Three

INTERVIEWS: Hugh [Yusha] Auchincloss, 6/6/1996; Wilson Hurley, 12/13/1995; James Tuck, 5/27/1997; Alfred True, 6/13/1995; Wallace Ragan, 6/13/1995; John C. Davis, 6/13/1995; James Birney, 11/10/1994; Barrett Prettyman, 11/2/1994; Sally Vidal (Mrs. Felix Vidal), 3/28/1996; John Hanes, 5/8/1997; Ruth Sewell, 4/15/1997; Lee Barlow, 3/25/1997.

ENDNOTES

p. 68: "to the swift": *M*, 35.

p. 72: "inventing stories," *M*, 82–83; "was of a stupidity": *SH*, 38–39; "made an insufficient offer": *SH*, p. 15.

pp. 72–75: "We want to find out" to "stardom": *US*, 1062–65.

p. 75: "relief check": *US*, 743–44; "convinced that FDR": *US*, 724.

p. 76: "the old lady," "myriad of": *SH*, 65–71.

p. 77: "drop out here": James Henderson/Gene Vidal, 4/4/1935; "as soon as he returns": Vidal/Henderson, 7/2/1935. WY.

p. 80: "the Living Statues": *SH*, 15.

p. 81: "always islands": *US*, 1075–76.

p. 84: "Miss Martin": *An Illustrated History of St. Albans School*, ed. Smith Hempstone. Washington: 1981, 61.

p. 84: "gentle grave manner": *M*, 82–83

p. 87: "We declare ourselves": "Declaration of Independence," unpub. ms., nd. W.

p. 90: "in the woods above": *M*, 32, 84.

p. 91: "kingdom of heaven": *SH*, 27.

p. 91: "the red-faced": *SH*, 40–41.

pp. 95–96: "fascist guards": *US*, 413–14; "almost as worried as": *M*, 36, *SH*, 52.

pp. 96–97: "That jaw . . . *combinazione*": Stanton, 60–61; "fascinating primitive . . . driven off": *M*, 86–87.

p. 97: "Longboats": *M*, 87.

Chapter Four

INTERVIEWS: Wilson Hurley, 12/13/1995; Oscar Steege, 10/11/1995; Alan Meyer, 11/22/1995; Sally Vidal, 3/28/1996; Katharine [Kit] Vidal, 2/15/1996; Hugh [Yusha] Auchincloss, 6/6/1996; Hamilton Bissell, 10/12/1995; Ransom Lynch, 10/12/1995; A. K. Lewis, 10/4/1995; Tish Baldrige, 7/nd/1996; Edes F. Talman, 6/nd/1996; Michael Dorn, 4/23/1996.

ENDNOTES

p. 99: "boys became men": *When Los Alamos Was a Ranch School*. Los Alamos Historical Society, 1974, 9.

p. 103: "The desert suddenly gave . . . sage-scented": GV, *The Smithsonian Institution*, 1998, 65.

p. 105: "T. recognized": *Smithsonian*, 75.

p. 106: "I am proposing": T. P. Gore/GV, 5/4/1950. O.

p. 109: "Intense blue sky": *Smithsonian*, 61; "Walking": *Harper's Bazaar*, 10/1945.

p. 113: "Aeronautic Consultant and New York Girl": *New York Herald Tribune,* 12/15/1939. WY.

p. 118: "He's the only person": GV, "H. L. Mencken The Journalist," *US,* 761–62.

p. 120: "Exeter Fair . . . there are no rules": *The "E" Book of Phillips Exeter Academy,* XLVI, 1942–43, 61.

p. 121: "looks 80 . . . get out": Otis Pease, excerpts from unpub. *Diary,* in *Exeter 1943, Fifty Years 1993.* 10/7/1940–10/13/1940, 175.

p. 123: "been elected to": Luther Hill/GV, nd/1940. W.

p. 124: "would pull": *SH,* 60.

p. 124: "Soldiers of America": John Hale Stutesman, "The Saga of the Veterans of Future Wars," *The Nassau Sovereign,* 4/1941, 9; "Communists because": ibid, 28.

p. 126: "I am crazy about . . . divine looking": Rosalind Rust, unpub. *Diary,* 1/11/1941, 1/19/1941.

p. 128: "there are, however": GV/"Communication"/editors of the *Exonian,* nd/1941. W.

p. 132: "Go on upstairs": *M,* 67–71.

Chapter Five

INTERVIEWS: Wilcomb E. Washburn, 10/10/1995; A. K. Lewis, 10/4/1995; Thomas McFarland, 12/6/1995; Nathaniel Davis, 9/22/1997; John Knowles, 7/22/1995; Tommy Auchincloss, 3/25/1997; Richard Poirier, 7/1/1996; Katharine Vidal, 2/15/1996.

ENDNOTES

p. 135: "about ten speeches": GV/T. P. Gore, 10/17/1941. O.

p. 136: "regardless of everything": GV/Gore, 10/17/1941. O.

p. 136: "Exeter commences": GV/Gore and Nina Kay Gore, 4/23/1942. O.

pp. 137–38: "denouncing that Jew": *US,* 929, 1087; "a dream showing": Wilcomb Washburn, unpub. *Diary,* 5/3/1942.

pp. 138–39: "to stop all outside . . . wonderful": GV/Gore and Nina Kay Gore, 4/23/1942. O; "These poems": Nat Davis, "Introduction" to GV, unpub. ms., *Litany for the Living and Other Poems,* 1942; "Putnam would probably": Washburn, *Diary,* 4/19/1942.

p. 139: "packed and sweltering": Pease, 182.

p. 140: "My wonder that": Washburn, *Diary,* 3/18/1942; "went over to": Washburn, *Diary,* 5/17/1942; "Instead of studying," Washburn, *Diary,* 5/31/1942.

p. 141: "Vidal stood out": Pease, *Diary,* 182; "picked up": Washburn, *Diary,* 6/5/1942.

p. 142: "busy inventing": *M,* 91.

p. 143: "The country is really": Nina Gore/GV, nd/1942. W.

pp. 143–44: "I've been doing": GV/Gene Vidal, 9/nd/1942; "That was no pose": Washburn, *Diary,* 11/4/1942; "Gave a speech": GV/T. P. Gore and Nina Kay Gore, 11/22/1942. O;

"Vidal more bombastic": Washburn, *Diary*, 1/17/1943; "Isn't it amazing": Washburn, *Diary*, 12/6/42.

pp. 144–45: "There never would be": Washburn, *Diary*, 11/19/1942; "to lead the opposition": *The Exonian*, 10/28/1942; "At heart": Washburn, *Diary*, 2/8/1943; "a congenital idiot": GV/ Gore and Nina Kay Gore, 11/22/1942. O.

p. 145: "Vidal has long talk": Washburn, *Diary*, 2/16/1943.

p. 146: "the best thing is": GV/Gene Vidal, 11/22/1942.

p. 147: "Vidal tremendously worried . . . gusto": Washburn, *Diary*, 12/9/1942.

p. 148: "We went downstairs": *M*, 32–35.

p. 149: "I cannot choose": Gore/GV, 12/10/1942. O.

pp. 150–51: "Vidal has a little X": Washburn, *Diary*, 3/1/1942; "Vidal said that either": 12/15/ 1942; "Instead of cleaning": Washburn, *Diary*, 2/3/1943; "It's funny how": Washburn, *Diary*, 4/19/1943; "I wonder if": Washburn, *Diary*, 11/29/1942.

p. 151: "What are you doing . . . happiness": Washburn, *Diary*, 12/17/1942.

p. 153: "apparently strained": Washburn, *Diary*, 2/2/1943.

p. 156: "will definitely graduate": GV/Vidal, nd/late 1942 or early 1943.

p. 159: "pitied the fact": Washburn, *Diary*, 1/6/1943; "Because he's just": Washburn, *Diary*, 4/29/1943.

p. 161: "Those attending": *The Exonian*, 3/10/1943.

p. 162: "very effectively": Otis Pease, *Diary*, 189.

pp. 163–64: "a jealous inspiration . . . why I do it": Nina Gore/GV, nd/1943. W; "onto an ancient train": *M*, 93–94; "now a goddamned engineer": GV/Vidal, 9/nd/1943.

pp. 164–65: "I compose sonnets": GV/Vidal, 9/21/1943; "having a fine time": GV/Vidal, 9/ nd/1943.

p. 165: "I always seem to catch": GV/Vidal, 9/21/1943; "very unpleasant . . . a term": GV/ Vidal, 10/nd/1943; "Maybe I should have": GV/Vidal, 10/nd/1943.

Chapter Six

INTERVIEWS: Sally Vidal, 3/28/1996; Jean Stein, 6/4/1996; John Tebbel, 11/13/1995; Wilcomb Washburn, 10/10/1995; Katharine Vidal, 2/15/1996; Betty Pollock, 3/5/1997; Carrington Tutwiler, 9/26/1996.

ENDNOTES

pp. 167–68: "Uncle Pick": GV/Gene Vidal, 11/nd/1943; "I couldn't be more upset": Nina Gore/GV, nd/1943. W.

p. 168: "human again": GV/Vidal, 11/nd/1943.

p. 169: "confident that he will like it": GV/Vidal, early/nd/1944.

p. 169: "I'm really going . . . unique": GV/Vidal, 12/nd/1943.

p. 171: "When I was CQ": *M*, 94.

p. 171: "a wonderful trip . . . in time": GV/Vidal, early/nd/1944; "after I get": early/nd/1944.

p. 173: "met everybody": GV/Vidal, early/nd/1944.

pp. 174–75: "Smokey, raw-wood": *M*, 95; "sunny Alaska": GV/Vidal, 12/28/1944.

p. 175: "a frontier town": GV/Vidal, 1/12/1945; "either (a) in command . . . coasting along": GV/Vidal, 1/12/1945; "Am getting to work": GV/Vidal, 1/12/1945.

p. 176: "which is remote": Eugene Walter, unpub. ms. nd. W; "we soldiers were briefed": *SH*, 41–42.

pp. 176–77: "a fine fellow . . . a few feet away": GV/Vidal, 1/26/1945; "it has been extremely": GV/Vidal, 2/3/1945.

pp. 177–78: "When the weather": GV/Vidal, 2/10/1945; "In fact—now . . . one hell of a game": GV/Vidal, 2/10/1945; "in for OCS": GV/Vidal, 2/3/1945; "I continue to discharge": GV/Vidal, 2/22/1945.

pp. 178–79: "it's good to hear": GV/Vidal, 2/10/1945; "Give [Kit] my best": GV/Vidal, 2/22/1945; "In another 2 months . . . on a run": GV/Gene, 3/nd/1945.

pp. 179–80: "In fact, I'm apt to be": GV/Vidal, 3/30/1945; "They've been testing": GV/Vidal, 4/3/1945.

p. 180: "It seemed impossible": *SH*, 72; "I thought your comment": T. P. Gore/GV, 5/15/1945. W.

p. 185: "I'll never forgive myself": *M*, 37.

p. 186: "who looked more like": *US*, 414–15.

p. 187: "early adolescent self": *US*, 419.

p. 188: "And so to bed": *M*, 104.

p. 189: "richer than yours": *M*, 105.

p. 190: "So Boris Karloff": *SH*, 96.

p. 192: "should be finished": GV/Kimon Friar, 10/19/1945. P.

p. 193: "I envision a collection": GV/Friar, 10/19/1945. P.

p. 196: "I sit with Dah": *M*, 60.

p. 201: "You look dramatic . . . sensual mouth": *The Diary of Anaïs Nin, Volume Four, 1944–1947*, ed. Gunther Stuhlmann, NY: 1971, 104.

Chapter Seven

INTERVIEWS: John Tebbel, 11/13/1995; Judith Jones, 12/1/1995; Carrington Tutwiler, 9/16/1996; John Macrae, 6/4/1995; Dominick Dunne, 6/19/1996; Mary Stevens, 10/20/1995.

ENDNOTES

p. 203: "Since our last": GV/Kimon Friar, nd/1945. P.

p. 203: "I think that Dutton": GV/Friar, 12/nd/1945. P; "He has great assurance": Anaïs Nin, *Diary*, 105–6.

p. 204: "I do not want": Nin, *Diary*, 106.

p. 205: "his desperate need . . . fear of women": Nin, *Diary*, 125–26.

p. 206: "What I see in the": Nin, *Diary*, 125–26; "I have been busy": GV/Carrington Tutwiler, 1/nd/1946.

pp. 206–7: "It's based on": GV/Tutwiler, 1/nd/1946; "I am very happy": GV/Tutwiler, 2/nd/1946; "Coming down the road": Nin/GV, summer/1946, "Under the Star of Writing, Letters about and to Gore Vidal, 1946–1961," *Anaïs, An International Journal*, vol. 14 (1996), 43.

pp. 207–8: "My terminal leave": GV/Tutwiler, 2/nd/1946; "in civilian clothes . . . to die": Nin, *Diary*, 121.

p. 208: "Being an editor": GV/Tutwiler, 2/nd/1946; "vivid creature": *M*, 112–13.

p. 210: "My third book": GV/Tutwiler, 2/nd/1946.

p. 211: "How does it feel?": *M*, 100–111.

pp. 212–13: "pastry-pale": *M*, 114; "You can't be": *M*, 114.

p. 214: "Gore and I decided": Nin, *Diary*, 135; "If only my grandmother": *M*, 113.

p. 216: "In the left-over": *M*, 9–10.

p. 217: "vividly engrossing": Eleanor Roosevelt, *New York World-Telegram* and Eleanor Roosevelt/GV, 5/10/1946. W; "I feel that": Nin/Gentlemen, 5/nd/1946. W.

p. 219: "My love, To say": Cornelia Claiborne/GV, 7/nd/1946, W; "Mother thinks": Claiborne/GV, 7/nd/1946. W; "Amazing what you have": Henry Miller/GV, 5/23/1946. W.

p. 219: "It is too bad": Henry Phillips/GV, 9/26/1946. W.

p. 221: "in a picturesque cottage": Nin, *Diary*, 157; "It was her idea": *M*, 125; "A group of us": Nin, *Diary*, 157.

p. 222: "New Orleans," he soon wrote her: GV/Nin, nd/1946. UC; "A Palace in an ancient city": GV/Nin, nd/1946. UC; "I was afraid to say": Nin/GV, nd/1946. W.

p. 223: "This place is growing": GV/Gene Vidal, 11/nd/1946.

pp. 223–24: "Labor is cheap": GV/Vidal, 11/nd/1946; "The family patriarch": *M*, 118–20; "There's a delightful": GV/Vidal, 11/nd/1946.

p. 227: "almost complete": GV/Nin, 11/nd/1946; "in two weeks . . . such pretensions": GV/Vidal, 11/nd/1946.

p. 227: "I can't seem to stop": GV/Vidal, 11/nd/1946; "I took my time": Nicholas Wreden/GV, 5/27/1947. W.

p. 228: "There are large": GV/Vidal, 11/nd/1946.

pp. 229–30: "with a beautiful": GV/Nin, 11/nd/1946. UC; "Everyone compliments me": GV/Vidal, 11/nd/1946; "My plans": GV/Nin, 11/nd/1946. UC.

pp. 230–31: "under a pepper tree . . . for yours": *M*, 118–20; "a small check": Nina Kay Gore/GV, 12/21/1946. W; "There are warm springs": GV/Nin, 11/nd/1946. UC.

pp. 231–32: "Just had a disturbing talk": Nin/GV, 12/nd/1946. W; "left quite a scar": Nin/GV, 11/nd/1946. W; "I've been a monk": GV/Nin, 11/nd/1946. UC.

p. 232: "there are a number": GV/Nin, 11/nd/1946. UC; "The irony of it all . . . happy and well": Nin/GV, nd/1946. W.

p. 233: "Are you coming back . . . a book enough": Nin/GV, 11/nd/1946. W; "we'll both be outcasts": GV/Nin, 11/nd/1946. UC; "He fought for me": Nin, *Diary*, 191.

p. 235: "I must construe . . . before the sun": GV/Nin, 3/nd/1947. UC.

p. 236: "remember that": *Season of Comfort*, 250.

p. 236: "My bitterness toward": GV/Nin, 6/nd/1947. UC.

pp. 237–38: "There are some intelligent": GV/Nin, 6/nd/1947. UC; "a better balance": Nin/GV, nd/1947. W.

pp. 238–39: "The Gores seemed well": Vidal/GV, nd/1947. W; "Remember," his father wrote: Vidal/GV, nd/1947.

p. 239: "we have a lousy": Vidal/GV, nd/1947.

p. 240: "how absurd to feature": Nin/GV, 6/nd/1947. W; "I should like it if you can": GV/Nin, 6/nd/1947. UC; "Maybe when I come down": Nin/GV, 6/nd/1947. W; "we will always have . . . would love you": Nin/GV, 6/nd/1947. UC.

Chapter Eight

INTERVIEWS: Joe O'Donohue, 5/25/1997; Judith Jones, 12/1/1995; Robert Giroux, 4/3/1995; Katharine Vidal, 2/15/1996; Johnny Nicholson, 7/3/1997; Graham Watson, 1/19/1996.

ENDNOTES

p. 244: "We met," Vidal wrote: "The Dancer," unpub. ms. 3. W.

p. 245: "It began then": "The Dancer," 7–8. W

p. 246: "who was quite intrigued": GV/Pat Crocker, 10/nd/1947. W; "We stayed at home . . . he'd try anything": "The Dancer," 10. W.

p. 247: "My life is completely governed . . . I guess": GV/Crocker, 10/nd/1947. W.

p. 249: "My dear Harold": GV/Harold Lang, 10/7/1947. W.

p. 249–50: "But I find the theme": GV/Lang, 10/7/1947. W; "I seem submerged": GV/Crocker, 1/nd/1948. W; "the dancer affair": GV/Crocker, 1/nd/1948. W; "on the usual sharing basis": GV/Crocker, 1/nd/1948. W.

p. 250: "I very much want you": Frederic Prokosch/GV, 2/nd/1947. W.

p. 251: "Having spent . . . yes": John Kelly/GV, 4/3/1947, 6/7/1947, 6/15/1947. W.

p. 252: "I don't need": Cornelia Claiborne/GV, nd/1947. W; "You have a Christ complex . . . a great deal": Claiborne/GV, nd/1947. W.

p. 253: "I would be glad to serve": Orville Prescott/GV, 10/28/1947. W.

p. 254: "Will you just look": *US*, 855; "for Cecil Beaton . . . photographer": GV/Pat Crocker, nd/1947. W.

pp. 254–55: "a difficult man . . . Hemingway once": *US*, 343; "*topolini*": John Horne Burns/ GV, 3/15/1948. W; "if I get a Hollywood job": GV/Anaïs Nin, 6/nd/1947. UC.

p. 255: "A short to the point story": Felix Ferry/GV, 12/16/1947. W.

pp. 256–57: "Thank you for what": Christopher Isherwood/GV, 1/6/1948. W; "with your personal": Thomas Mann/GV, 1/3/1948. W; "Already I'd heard": Nin/GV, nd/1948. W; "in the *least*": Prokosch/GV, nd/1948. W.

pp. 257–58: "The fan mail": GV/Crocker, 1/nd/1948. W; "The book sells": GV/Crocker, 2/nd/1948. W; "flatteringly violent": GV/Crocker, 1/nd/1948. W.

p. 260: "gray-faced man": *M*, 102.

p. 262: "I am writing this": Tennessee Williams/Donald Windham, 1/17/1945, *Tennessee Williams' Letters to Donald Windham, 1940–1965*, NY: 1976, 205.

p. 262: "First impressions": *US*, 476; "In Rome whenever": *TS*, 191–203.

p. 263: "I'm happy to know": Burns/GV, 3/15/1948. W; "Honey, you would love": Williams/ Windham, 2/20/1948, 207.

p. 264: "I had actually seen": *M*, 155.

pp. 264–65: "I particularly like": *US*, 1131–33; "Williams is not at all": *TS*, 271.

p. 265: "Dear Blood and Gore": Williams/GV, 3/nd/1948. W.

pp. 266–67: "That happy picture": Judith Jones/GV, 3/nd/1948. W; "Write me in care": GV/ Nin, nd/1948. UC; "Tennessee Williams and me": GV/Nina Gore, 3/nd/1948. W; "I don't think you realize . . . alike": *M*, 152.

pp. 267–68: "like some large pale fish": *US*, 1131–32; "our barbarous presence": *US*, 476; "were told the communists": *US*, 467; "This country is all wrought": T. P. Gore/GV, 2/23/1948. W; "You must be wading": Gene Vidal/GV, 4/nd/1948. W; "are not a predatory people": *TS*, 42–43.

p. 268: "the impression that": *US*, 419; "Santayana looked": *US*, 423; "He wore a dressing gown": *US*, 476–77.

p. 269: "at the old man": *US*, 1139; "He gave a sort . . . present": *M*, 157–64.

p. 270: "Like a mafia don . . . novels": *M*, 168–69.

pp. 270–71: "I am glad you did": Williams/GV, nd/1948. W; "powerful play": *M*, 169; "thrilled over the play": Nina Gore/GV, 4/16/1948; "Bright eyes": Williams/GV, nd/1948. W.

pp. 271–72: "I close now with": Williams/GV, nd/1948; "ferocious . . . we have": *TS*, 247, "as the train moved": Cameron Kay, *Thieves Fall Out*, NY: 1953, 39.

pp. 272–73: "There were a bunch . . . macabre": *M*, 176–78, *US*, 1133–34; "pronounced it the worst": *M*, 169–70.

pp. 273–74: "forever summer": *TS*, 91; "I am American literature": *M*, 185–87; "a big husky boy . . . started to wag": *Christopher Isherwood Diaries, Volume One, 1939–1960*, NY: 1996, 401.

pp. 274–75: "I do think": *Isherwood Diaries*, 401; "I don't know when": GV/John Lehmann, 5/21/1948. P; "very interesting and even": Isherwood/GV, 5/6/1948. W; "If you see Truman": GV/Lehmann, 5/nd/1948. P.

pp. 275–76: "with mischievous fantasies": *US*, 1143–44; "The instant lie": *M*, 184–85; "All the writers are": GV/John Aldridge, 5/1/1948.

p. 276: "insincere, extremely mannered": Calder Willingham/GV, 5/9/1948, W; "talked about Truman": Donald Windham, *Lost Friendships, A Memoir of Truman Capote, Tennessee Williams, and Others*, NY: 1983, 30, 44; "that you and Tennessee": Lehmann/GV, 2/25/1948. W; "I don't think I need": Lehmann/GV, 5/1/1948. W.

p. 277: "I'm very much interested": Lehmann/GV, 5/18/1948. W; "Christopher came": Lehmann/GV, 5/18/1948. W; "not very happy . . . practical": GV/Lehmann, 5/12/1948. P.

pp. 277–78: "to capture as many": Lehmann, *In My Own Time, Memoirs of a Literary Life*, Boston: 1969, 452; "short-legged": *M*, 182–84.

p. 279: "pornographic novel . . . Mind the step": *M*, 183–85.

p. 279: "down an empty street": *M*, 185; "a clever, talented": *US*, 32; "another one of those": GV/Lehmann, 10/9/1948. P.

p. 280: "nocturnal Proustian life": *Isherwood Diaries*, 400; "Marais looked . . . accent": *US*, 1143–44.

p. 281: "one of the guests . . . all of us": *TS*, 27; *M*, 169–70.

p. 282: "Why not come . . .": Isherwood/GV, 5/17/1948. W.

pp. 282–84: "V. S. Pritchett was . . . plain view": *M*, 190–92; "very excited at": Stanton, 177–78; "But we *have* to . . . disheartening": *M*, 190–91.

p. 284: "Everyone mocked . . . queen of Spain": *M*, 195–97.

p. 286: "the streets, empty . . . the walls": *M*, 178–79.

p. 287: "I used him": GV/Lehmann, 7/30/1948. P; "Now I think": Lehmann/GV, 7/14/1948. W; "A note to tell you": GV/Lehmann, 8/14/1948. P.

Chapter Nine

INTERVIEWS: John Galliher, 4/29/1996; Jason Epstein, 4/25/1995, 3/6/1997; Sam Lurie, 4/1/1996; Joe O'Donohue,. 5/24/1997; Johnny Nicholson, 7/4/1997; Graham Watson, 1/19/1996; Roy Thompson, 11/28/1995, 1/8/1996; Speed Lamkin, 2/11/1997; Ned Rorem, 12/3/1996; Romana McEwen, 1/23/1966; J. Winter Thorington, 1/14/1998; Geoffrey Moore, 5/28/1997.

ENDNOTES

pp. 289–90: "Dad will never . . . to see you": Nina Gore/GV, 6/23/1948. W; "mental health . . . Love, Bommy": Nina Gore Olds/GV, nd/1949. W.

p. 291: "considering that . . . treated": John Lehmann/GV, 9/30/1948. W; "in the midst of my": GV/Lehmann, 8/14/1948. P; "Good God": Lehmann/GV, 8/19/1948. W.

p. 291: "getting the two": GV/Lehmann, 10/2/1948. P; "Not much news": GV/Pat Crocker, 11/nd/1948. W.

p. 292: "Truman is everywhere": GV/Lehmann, 10/2/1948. P; "with much fanfare": GV/Lehmann, 11/nd/1948. P; "the way Truman would": GV/Lehmann, 12/18/1949. P.

pp. 292–93: "I think you judge": Tennessee Williams/Donald Windham, 4/8/1949, 237; "By the time we arrived": *US*, 1143–44; "uncomplimentary remarks . . . the ploy": Paul Bowles, *Without Stopping, An Autobiography*, NY: 1972, 288.

p. 294: "You're not a poet": *M*, 250; "perhaps the first": Annette Tapert and Diana Edkins, *The Power of Style*, NY: 1994, 112.

p. 295: "received, for the most": GV/Lehmann, 10/9/1948. P.

p. 295: "You'll like . . . mouth": Cecilia Sternberg, *The Journey, An Autobiography*, London: 1977, 313–14.

p. 298: "a sort of preface to Sondheim": Ned Rorem, *Knowing When to Stop*, NY: 1994, 253; "the most irresistibly quick": *The Later Diaries of Ned Rorem, 1961–1972*, San Francisco: 1983, 71.

pp. 299–300: "Serene and working": GV/Lehmann, 1/nd/1949. P; "I have such a high": Lehmann/GV, 1/17/1949. W; "break with John": Christopher Isherwood/GV, nd/1949. W.

pp. 300–01: "as to *The Season*": GV/Lehmann, 4/11/1949. P; "Did I tell you": GV/Crocker, 2/nd/1949. W; "Your disease is": Crocker/GV, 5/17/1949. W; "The mice and": GV/Lehmann, 4/11/1949. P.

p. 301: "I freely admit": GV/Lehmann 7/30/1948. P; "wept quietly": *M*, 71–72.

p. 304: "I'd like to talk": GV/John Aldridge, 5/1/1948.

pp. 304–5: "bejewelled epigrams": GV/Lehmann, 1/20/1950. P; "Thus do I": GV/Lehmann, 1/nd/1949. P; "The critics still regard": GV/Crocker, nd/1948. W.

p. 306: "I liked [your lecture]": George F. Kneller/GV, 5/2/1949. W.

p. 306: "new comets about": GV/Lehmann, 9/17/1949. P.

p. 307: "Suggest you both": Lehmann/GV, 5/18/1949. W; "BOTH ARRIVING": GV/Lehmann, 5/22/1949. P.

p. 308: "She detests London": Williams/Windham, 5/8/1949, 241.

pp. 309: "examining the literary": Bowles, *Without Stopping*, 291; "I have absolutely": Bowles/GV, 5/18/1949. W; "I must admit": Bowles/GV, 5/18/1949. W; "Morocco isn't at all": Bowles/GV, 5/18/1949. W.

p. 310: "frozen . . . nothing to worry about": Kelly/GV, 6/3/1949. W; "a lovely journey": GV/Latouche, 6/nd/1949. C.

p. 310: "unofficial . . . a sort of lighthouse": Bowles/GV, 8/13/1949. W.

pp. 311–12: "he did a little . . . waving": Bowles, *Without Stopping*, 292; "Truman gave": Bowles/GV, 8/26/1949. W.

pp. 312–13: "receiving the homage": *M*, 130–32; "I was, during": GV/Lehmann, 9/17/1949. P; "I agree, of course": GV/Lehmann, 9/17/1949. P.

p. 313: "A great deal": GV/Lehmann, 11/4/1949. P.

p. 314: "All my literary friends . . . built": GV/Crocker, 11/nd/1948. W; "Very intrigued with": Anaïs Nin/GV, 7/nd/1949. W.

p. 315: "I have to sneak": John Macrae [signed "old Uncle Jack"]/GV, nd/1959. W; "professional writers": Virginia Creed/Katherine Everard, 4/8/1950. W.

p. 319: "I spent a weekend": GV/Lehmann, 11/4/1949. P.

p. 320: "the delicately irregular line": GV/*1876*, NY: 1976, 239–44.

p. 321: "We looked and saw": GV/*1876*, 239–44.

p. 322: "I think Paul Bowles": GV/Lehmann, 9/17/1949. P.

pp. 322–23: "I still have a mad": Bowles/GV, 10/14/1949. W; "on the dock . . . before me": Bowles/GV, 12/5/1949. W; "I may also do": GV/Lehmann, 12/18/1949. P; "She even wants": *M*, 215.

pp. 323–24: "Is it true that?": Bowles/GV, 1/16/1950. W; "What nonsense": Bowles/GV, 2/22/1950. W; "You never would have done": Bowles/GV, 2/22/1950. W; "in a few days": GV/Lehmann, 11/4/1949. P; "after writing me": Williams/Windham, 1/18/1950, 252; "among the husks": GV/Lehmann, 1/20/1950. P; "I now think that": GV/Lehmann, 2/5/1950. P.

pp. 324–25: "I am working": GV/Lehmann, 1/20/1950. P; "Vidal has departed": Williams/Windham, 2/2/1950, 254; "the Endless Quest": GV/Lehmann, 2/5/1950. P.

p. 325: "Haven't seen": GV/Lehmann, 2/5/1950. P.

p. 326: "Houston is all very": GV/Lehmann, 3/14/1950. P; "a piece of total": GV/Lehmann, 3/14/1950. P.

p. 328: "I may do a short": GV/Lehmann, 3/14/1950. P; "It's one of the serious": GV/James Laughlin, nd/1950; "the monster which": GV/Lehmann, 2/10/1950. P.

p. 329: "I've had to learn": GV/Lehmann, 3/14/1950. P.

p. 329–30: "I am designing . . . prose": GV/Lehmann, 4/14/1950. P; "As a matter of fact": GV, "Pederasty and Mr. Barrett," unpub. ms., W.

p. 330: "in the throes": GV/Crocker, 6/nd/1950. W; "This city depresses": GV/Laughlin, nd/1950; "hardly think of": GV/Carl Van Vechten, 6/nd/1950. Y.

Chapter Ten

INTERVIEWS: Miles White, 3/25/1998; Howard Austen, 1/17/1996, 1/20/1996, 7/9/1996, 7/11/1996, 7/12/1996, 7/24/1996; Joseph O'Donohue, 5/24/1997; Johnny Nicholson, 7/4/1997; Tommy Auchincloss, 6/8/1995; Joe Ryle, 4/30/1996; Jason Epstein, 3/6/1997; Sam Lurie, 4/1/1996; Romana McEwen, 1/23/1996; Ted Weiss, 3/14/1998; Richard Poirier, 7/1/1996; John Aldridge, 9/16/1996; Vance Bourjaily, 9/11/1995; John Bowen, 1/22/1996; Tina Bourjaily, 10/19/1996; Louis Auchincloss, 10/21/1994; Norman Mailer, 3/15/1996, 3/16/1996, 3/17/1996; George Plimpton, 2/9/1996; Owen Laster, 2/25/1996, 3/5/1996, 3/22/1996; Theresa Baxter, 3/29/1997.

ENDNOTES

pp. 333–34: "One of those shows": GV/John Lehmann, 10/nd/1950. P; "there are no places": GV/Lehmann, 10/nd/1950. P; "I've bought an 1820": GV/Lehmann, 8/15/1950. P.

p. 334: "Meredithean comedy": GV/Lehmann, 10/nd/1950. P; "Life in the mansion": GV/Pat Crocker, 9/nd/1950. W.

p. 335: "My dear Carlo": GV/Carl Van Vechten, 9/nd/1950. Y; "I am not a naturalistic . . . pleasure": GV/Lehmann, 4/14/1950. P.

p. 336: "My place is": GV/Lehmann, 9/nd/1950. P.

p. 351: "I raced beside him": *M, 251.*

pp. 352–53: "since I plan": GV/Theodore Weiss, nd/1953; "three British poets": GV/Lehmann, nd/1951. P.

p. 353: "As for Tennessee": GV/Weiss, nd/1953.

p. 354: "My life has been": GV/Lehmann, 11/23/1951. P.

p. 355: "I am in physical": GV/Lehmann, 11/23/1951. P; "characteristically . . . dumb": Raymond Washburn/GV, 5/11/1951. W.

p. 356: "a perfect summer": GV/Anaïs Nin, 8/nd/1951. UC; "My mother, her twelve": GV/ Nin, summer/nd/1951. UC.

p. 358: "I went to Vermont": GV/Nin, 8/nd/1952. UC.

p. 359: "Material is being collected": GV/Lehmann, 11/23/1951. P.

p. 360: "I am going out . . . best writers": GV/Lehmann, 11/23/1951. P; "triumphant, in advance": GV/Lehmann, nd/1951. P.

p. 361: "I have been busy": GV/John Aldridge, 5/nd/1952.

pp. 364–65: "I am in the throes . . . New York": GV/Arabel Porter, 1/nd/1953. Y; "We made our way": *US,* 449.

p. 367: "startlingly excellent": GV/F. M. Markoe, nd/1953. Y.

p. 368: "satiric queer . . . sophomoric imitations": Jack Kerouac/Allen Ginsberg, 5/18/1952, *Selected Letters, Jack Kerouac, 1940–1956,* ed. Ann Charters, NY: 1995, 357; "recognised him from": Kerouac, *The Subterraneans,* NY: 1958, 52–53.

p. 369: "stared at me": *M,* 233.

p. 370: "You sneak": Inez Salinger/GV, 4/22/1953. W.

p. 371: "*worry* about": Henry Volkening/GV, 5/14/1948. W; "a good technician . . . generally": Audrey Wood/GV, 5/21/1948. W. "I think that rightly": Wood/GV, 2/21/1950. W.

pp. 371–72: "Mrs. Goldwyn thought": Wood/GV, 5/2/1950. W; "a happy honeymoon . . . picture": Wood/GV, 6/21/1950, 7/7/1950. W; "I am trying to buy": GV/Robert Halsband, nd/1950. W; "it is very difficult": Wood/GV, 7/18/1952. W.

Chapter Eleven

INTERVIEWS: Martin Manulis, 4/1/1996; Dominick Dunne, 6/19/1996; George Axelrod, 5/8/1997; Howard Austen, 1/17/1996, 1/20/1996, 7/9/1996, 7/11/1996, 7/12/1996, 7/24/1996; Joanne Woodward, 2/8/1996; Paul Newman, 2/8/1996; Don Bachardy, 12/28/1995, 4/3/1996; Elaine Dundy, 3/30/1996; Romana McEwen, 1/23/1996; Joe O'Donohue, 5/24/1997; Conrad Janis, 4/12/1997; Sarah Marshall, 4/16/1997; John Galliher, 4/29/1996; Sally Vidal, 3/28/1996; Oatsie Leiter [Mrs. Robert Charles], 5/14/1997; Louis Auchincloss, 10/21/1994; Nini Auchincloss, 11/28/1994, 7/19/1995.

ENDNOTES

p. 376: "You have no idea": GV/Kimon Friar, 8/nd/1954. P.

pp. 376–77: "My own days are": GV/Friar, 8/nd/1954. P; "The day after": *US*, 1157–59.

p. 377: "still smiling . . . think why": GV/Helen Harvey, 7/14/1954. W.

p. 379: "GET WRITING, PUSS": Martin Manulis/GV, 5/30/1955. W; "the role of": GV, Devil's Theater proposal, unpub. ms. nd, W.

p. 380: "Yes, I am television's . . . gold": GV/John Aldridge, 3/nd/1955.

pp. 380–81: "immense practical problem": Felix Jackson/GV, 3/2/1955. W.

pp. 381–82: "Do you realize": GV/Aldridge, 3/nd/1955; "The only sad aspect": GV/Aldridge, 3/nd/1955.

p. 382: "that he had just": *US*, 387; "if they had their way": *Isherwood Diaries*, 478.

p. 383: "I am at heart": *US*, 1157–59.

p. 383: "Too much social": Ben Gross, "Are Sponsors Lacking in Courage?" *Sunday News*, 6/23/1957. WY.

p. 385–86: "Dear Gorgeous": Cyril Ritchard/GV, 6/28/1955, 7/17/1955. W; "I have been studying": George Axelrod/GV, 7/24/1955. W.

p. 388: "a noble failure": GV/Friar, 8/nd/1954. P; "A gift for playwriting": *US*, 1157–59.

p. 389: "though by no means": GV/*Visit to a Small Planet and Other Television Plays*, Boston: 1956, 207.

p. 390: "My decision, finally": GV/*Small Planet*, 209.

p. 391: "knew what death": Stanton, 134.

p. 392: "in working out": Jerry Wald/GV, 3/23/1955. W; "he described how": *Isherwood Diaries*, 518.

p. 392: "is Christopher Isherwood": GV/John Bowen, summer/nd/1955.

p. 393: "I have finished": GV/Louis Auchincloss, 9/28/1955.

p. 396: "looked at the books . . . feeling that life . . . creative joy": *Isherwood Diaries*, 533; "I am here doing": GV/John Lehmann, 12/7/1955. P.

pp. 397–98: "I think you were": Paddy Chayevsky/GV, 2/24/1956. W.

pp. 398–99: "They definitely want": Sam Zimbalist/GV, 1/20/1956. W; "been saving for many": GV/Manulis, 3/22/1956. W; "GO AHEAD WITH": Manulis/GV, 4/10/1956. W.

p. 400: "I very much enjoyed": GV/Tom Driberg, 5/nd/1956. CC.

p. 400: "The political world . . . come down": GV/Driberg, 5/nd/1956. CC.

p. 404: "He never could": Dawn Powell, *Diaries, 1931–1965*, ed. Tim Page, NY: 1955, 361.

p. 404: "I have lost": GV/Edith Sitwell, summer/nd/1956. T.

p. 405: "uninvited return": GV/Woods S. Gray, 12/17/1956.

pp. 406–7: "He was amused": *US*, 799–800; "in a bathrobe": *M*, 10–11; "for a February debut": GV/Sitwell, summer/nd/1956. T.

p. 409: "because it costs": *US*, 1163–65.

p. 413: "In principle," Vidal agreed: GV/Fred Coe, 4/4/1957. W.

p. 413: "I shall want to pull out": GV/Harold Franklin, 5/3/1957. W.

p. 416: "I shall be happy": GV/Newton Steers, 4/17/1957. W; "raised high his": *M*, 17.

Chapter Twelve

INTERVIEWS: Joanne Woodward, 2/8/1996; Paul Newman, 2/8/1996; Claire Bloom, 2/23/ 1996; Sam Lurie, 4/1/1996; Stan Kaminsky, 4/1/1996; Miles White, 3/25/1988; Elaine Dundy, 3/30/1996; Howard Austen, 1/17/1996, 1/20/1996, 7/9/1996, 7/11/1996, 7/12/1996, 7/24/ 1996; Don Bachardy, 4/3/1996; John Bowen, 1/22/1996; Norman Mailer, 3/15/1996, 3/16/ 1996, 3/17/1996; Jason Epstein, 3/6/1997; Barbara [Andy] Dupee, 1/26/1995, 2/7/1995, 3/7/ 1995, 3/24/1997; Jack Bady, 1/7/1996; Eleanor Rovere, 5/30/1995; Barbara Epstein, 7/15/1995, 7/27/1995; Lyn Austin, 5/1/1998; Saul Bellow, 2/25/1998.

ENDNOTES

p. 418: "I am bogged down": GV/Woods S. Gray, 7/31/1957.

p. 418: "Paul, Joanne and I": GV/Gray, 7/31/1957; "extraordinarily funny": *Isherwood Diaries*, 721.

p. 419: "quite a bitch": *Isherwood Diaries*, 721; "I dread my return": GV/Ned Bradford, 6/nd/ 1957. LB.

p. 420: "probably the best T.V.": Nicholas Wreden/GV, 5/nd/1955. W; "I should have": GV/ James Oliver Brown, 2/20/1957. W.

p. 421: "I would not get": GV/Brown, 2/10/1957. W; "The Edgar Box thing": GV/Brown, 2/20/1957. W; "never been able": GV/Brown, 2/10/1957. W.

p. 424: "I have told Gore": Nina Gore/Leonard Strauss, 10/15/1957. W.

p. 424: "Gore needs to learn": Nina Gore/Strauss, 10/15/1957. W.

p. 428: "winter wonderland": *M*, 319.

p. 431: "I do agree": GV/Alec Guinness, 1/7/1958. W; "As I am interested": George Axelrod/ GV, 11/29/1957. W.

p. 432: "trying like hell": Nina Gore/GV, 12/nd/1957. W.

p. 440: "monstrous to give": Sam Zimbalist/GV, 7/3/1956. W.

p. 441: "As we drove together": *US*, 1175–77; "Roman fever": GV/Anaïs Nin, summer/nd/1958.

p. 442: "When I was finished": *US*, 1175–77.

p. 443: "I am doing a fast": GV/Paul Bowles, 5/nd/1958. D.

p. 444: "Luckily, I was on the set": *US*, 69; "This is not a going-away": Zimbalist/GV, 5/24/1958. W.

pp. 444–45: "The horses began": Morgan Hudgens/GV, 5/31/1958. W; "our first big day": Zimbalist/GV, 6/6/1958. W; "The new opening": Zimbalist/GV, 7/24/1958. W; "I rewrote the script": GV/Ann R. Stein, 3/18/1959. W.

p. 446: "I was more upset": GV/Christopher Isherwood, 11/nd/1958; "My career as a dramatist": GV/Isherwood, 11/nd/1958; "I should love a British": GV/Tom Driberg, spring/nd/1958. CC.

p. 447: "No more movies": GV/Bowles, 5/nd/1958. D; "I still have occasional": GV/Nin, summer/nd/1958. UC; "No one will believe": GV/Nin, 6/nd/1958. UC.

pp. 449–50: "Look at that": *M*, 336, Stanton, 279, *US*, 443–44; "to get a director": *Isherwood Diaries*, 777.

p. 450–51: "Gore regards me": *Isherwood Diaries*, 777; "What news of Ken": GV/Driberg, spring/nd/1958. CC; "a good deal of the Tynans": GV/Driberg, nd/1958. CC; "I gave a party": GV/Driberg, 12/nd/1958. CC.

pp. 452–53: "I can't say . . . something else": F. W. Dupee/GV, 2/17/1958. W.

Chapter Thirteen

INTERVIEWS: Patsy Walsh, 6/4/1995; William Walsh, 6/4/1995; Lyn Austin, 5/1/1998; Louis Auchincloss, 10/21/1994; Elaine Dundy, 3/30/1996; Howard Austen, 1/20/1996, 7/9/1996, 7/11/1996, 7/12/1996, 7/24/1996; Janet Caro, 5/2/1995; Joanne Woodward, 2/8/1996; Paul Newman, 2/8/1996; David Samples, 4/25/1996; Norman Mailer, 3/15/1996, 3/16/1996, 3/17/1996; Roy Thompson, 11/28/1995, 1/8/1996, 3/26/1996; George Plimpton, 2/9/1996; Arthur Schlesinger, 10/31/1996.

ENDNOTES

p. 464: "It is now your": Louis Auchincloss/GV, nd/1962. W.

p. 464: "DEAR GORE": John F. Kennedy/Gore Vidal, 9/29/1956. W.

p. 469: "I loved the way Dad": Nina Gore/GV, nd/1960 W.

p. 469: "On the morning when": GV/unpub. ms nd. W.

p. 471: "Is Gore writing": *M*, 337.

p. 471: "in a campaign": *M*, 337; "I have always felt": GV/Ray White, 9/1/1996. W.

p. 473: "Never in my lifetime": Lucien Price/GV, 5/17/1960. W.

p. 474: "The morning after": GV, "On Campaigning," unpub. essay, 1960. W.

p. 475: "Sell yourself": Ruth Davis/GV, 10/16/1960. W.

p. 478: "My husband always said . . . interested girl": GV, "On Campaigning." W; "from something you get": GV, "On Campaigning." W; "Tell your friend": *M*, 343.

p. 479: "into that vast . . . everything": GV, "On Campaigning." W; "as a reigning": GV, "On Campaigning." 1960. W; "easily the best": William Gruver/GV, 7/16/1960. W.

p. 480: "the play will be . . . Strachey": Arthur Schlesinger/GV, 3/16/1960. W.

p. 480: "Is this . . . *all*": *TS*, 73; "would tell Jack": *M*, 346; "last appeal . . . euphoric": *TS*, 73–74; "This is the ship": *M*, 346.

p. 481: "Some days I do . . . heads": GV/Christopher Isherwood, 9/nd/1960; "Jack, Jackie are doing": GV/Elaine Dundy, fall/nd/1960.

p. 482: "Needless to say . . . formidable": GV/John Kennedy, 6/12/1960. W.

pp. 486–87: "If you had not won . . . Taylor": GV/John Kennedy, 11/14/1960. W.

pp. 488–89: "Call and come": Virgil Thomson/GV, 4/1/1960. W; "But if I do it": GV/John Bowen, 10/nd/1960.

p. 489: "All my life": GV/Dundy, fall/nd/1960; "I fret about prose": GV/Isherwood, nd/1960.

pp. 493–94: "The boy taking . . . twice a week": *M*, 375, 380.

pp. 495–96: "Yes, it would be better": *M*, 369; "Just talk to Eisenhower": *M*, 361; "this was decadence": *M*, 366.

p. 499: "Don't ever do": *M*, 394.

p. 499: "the mood . . . was different": Arthur Schlesinger, diary, quoted in Anthony Haden-Guest, "The Vidal Capote Papers: A Tempest in Camelot," *New York*, 6/11/1979, 55; "and some lady . . . racket": John Kenneth Galbraith, *Ambassador's Journal, A Personal Account of the Kennedy Years*, Boston: 1969, 221–22.

p. 500: "a great deal of . . . well": Galbraith, 222; "we both behaved": GV/Louis Auchincloss, nd/1965.

p. 501: "the fight was hopeless": Roger Stevens/GV, 3/17/1962. W.

p. 504: "You do make me": GV/Isherwood, 5/nd/1962.

p. 505: "I have just come back": GV/Ambassador Matsas, 7/18/1962. W.

p. 505: "there are no facts": GV/Isherwood, 5/nd/1962.

p. 506: "Takes lots of pills": GV/Dundy, 3/nd/1962.

p. 507: "Week in Capri": GV/Dundy, 3/nd/1962; "I am here for . . . nicely written": GV/Isherwood, 5/nd/1962.

pp. 508–9: "Take, say ten . . . in the world": Jason Epstein/GV, 6/2/1961. W; "like most satirists": GV/Jason Epstein, 6/nd/1961. C.

p. 510: "Now, of course": GV/*New York Times Book Review*, 8/1962; "so bored—but then": GV/Alice Dows, 8/8/1962.

p. 510: "stood alongside": *US*, 749.

p. 512: "HEAR YOU'RE LEAVING": Nina Gore/GV, 1/2/1963. W.

Chapter Fourteen

INTERVIEWS: Theresa Baxter, 3/29/1997; Barbara Epstein, 7/15/1995, 7/26/1995; Richard Poirier, 7/1/1996; Howard Austen, 1/20/1996, 7/9/1996, 7/11/1996, 7/12/1996, 7/24/1996; Sam Lurie, 4/1/1996; Stan Kaminsky, 4/1/1996; Mickey Knox, 3/30/1996; George Armstrong, 9/5/1994; Claire Bloom, 2/23/1996; Larry Turman, 3/6/1998; Jason Epstein, 3/6/1997; Barbara Dupee, 1/26/1995, 2/7/1995, 3/7/1995; Herman Gollob, 2/18/1999; Norman Mailer, 3/15/1996, 3/16/1996, 3/17/1996; Eleanor Rovere, 5/30/1995; Alain/Marjorie Bernheim, 4/2/1996; Milton Gendel, 11/25/1997.

ENDNOTES

p. 515: "a duodenal ulcer": GV/Alice Dows, 2/nd/1963. W; "The vulture has": GV/Fred Dupee, 3/nd/1963. C; "I hope your liver": Dupee/GV, 3/6/1963. W; "Blanche nearly rode": GV/Dupee, 3/nd/1963. C.

p. 516: "Energy is": William Blake, *The Marriage of Heaven and Hell;* "I can not express": Nina Kay Gore/GV, 11/27/1962. W; "Things were rather": Thomas Gore/GV, 5/27/1963. W.

p. 517: "I know that you": Roy Thompson/GV, 5/14/1963. W; "It is a blessing": Thomas Gore/GV, 5/27/1963. W; "There's room for you": *M*, 73.

pp. 519–20: "Sorry to hear": Harold Hayes/GV, 2/18/1963. WF; "conceivably to the highest": Hayes/GV, 3/12/1963. W; "Did you read the piece": GV/Louis Auchincloss, 3/nd/1963.

p. 520: "which has stirred up": Auchincloss/GV, 3/12/1963. W; "a courier from": GV/Hayes, 3/nd/1963. WF; "came to town": GV/Richard Rovere, nd/1963. W; "The London papers": GV/Hayes. 3/nd/1963. W.

pp. 523–24: "What did you do": GV/Dupee, 3/7/1963. C; "I like [your essay": GV/Dupee, 3/nd/1963. W; "cannot be taken seriously": *US*, 342.

p. 525: "have an ulcer": GV/John Bowen, 1/nd/1963; "In a way I'm": GV/Dupee, 3/7/1963. C.

p. 526: "He has gained weight": GV/Auchincloss, 3/nd/1963; "in that euphoric state": GV/Dupee, 3/nd/1963. C.

pp. 527–28: "splendid company": GV/Tom Driberg, 7/1/1963. CC; "a hacking cough . . . hell": GV/Dupee, 4/5/1963. C; "We will arrive": Sam Lurie/GV, 4/10/1963. W; "Dear Maureen O'Hara": GV/Lurie, 4/nd/1963.

p. 531: "This was the hottest": *US*, 1215.

p. 532: "is splendid just now": GV/Dupee, 4/16/1963, C; "All in all a quiet": GV/Dows, 4/24/1963. W; "Please come": Elaine Dundy/GV, 5/nd/1963. W; "pleasantly bloating": GV/Driberg, 7/1/1963. CC.

p. 533: "I begin to think": GV/Dows, 6/20/1963. W.

p. 534: "He is quite": GV/Dows, 7/18/1963. W; "I listen to him": GV/Ned Bradford, 7/nd/ 1963. LB; "miss the country": GV/Dows, 6/20/1963. W.

p. 535: "Even at twelve . . . television": *SH*, 83–85.

pp. 536–37: "I do like": *Isherwood Diaries*, 884; "playing the role": *Isherwood Diaries*, 884.

pp. 537–38: "If your party . . . awfully wrong": GV/Driberg, 7/1/1963. CC.

p. 538: "SHOOTING COMPLETED": Larry Turman and Stuart Millar/GV, 11/11/1963. W.

p. 540: "feeling slightly bored": Howard Austen/GV, 9/22/1963. W; "I can't tell much": GV/ Bradford, 7/nd/1963. LB; "JULIAN READ BY": Bradford/GV, 10/nd/1963. W.

p. 541: "I flew back": GV/Auchincloss, 1/10/1964.

p. 542: "I have finished": GV/Auchincloss, 1/10/1964.

pp. 542–43: "the book is a *delight*": Auchincloss/GV, nd/1964. W; "B-of-M Club": GV/ Auchincloss, 3/nd/1964; "I'm so happy": GV/Dwye Evans, 1/nd/1964. Heinemann archives.

p. 545: "I have been possessed": GV/Auchincloss, 3/nd/1964. W; "So this is the year": GV/ Richard Poirier, 3/nd/1964.

p. 546: "A rather lousy": GV/Poirier, 3/nd/1964; "and in the dark days": GV/Charles W. Mixer, 7/22/1964. W; "able to read": GV/Caldwell Titcomb, 4/13/1964. W.

p. 547: "Edgewater is not": GV/Dupee, 1/18/1964. C.

p. 548: "Who present that": *US*, 980.

p. 552: "Are you, on top of": Buckley/GV, 4/16/1962. W.

p. 553–54: "was utterly unrelated": Buckley deposition, 3/27/1972, 142; "Evidently the entire": Buckley/Jayne Meadows, 3/30/1959. W.

p. 554: "Your reporter wrote": Buckley/Orvil E. Dreyfoos, *New York Times*, 10/23/1961.

p. 555: "For the record": GV/Terry, 7/nd/1964.

p. 558: "If you can come up with": GV/Jerome Kilty, 1/31/1965. W.

p. 559: "I cannot tell yet": GV/Auchincloss, 8/nd/1965.

p. 559: "It doesn't seem": GV/Gene Vidal, 4/nd/1965. W; "charming but gray": GV/Vidal, 4/nd/1965. W.

pp. 560–61: "He is now an only": GV/Rovere, 2/15/1965. W; "I am so completely": GV/ Dupee, 9/1/1965. C; "It was Guermantes": GV/Nini Auchincloss, 3/3/1965; "I don't know whether": GV/Dupee, 3/8/1965. C.

p. 561: "Paris was too much": GV/Dupee, 6/10/1965. C; "Princess Margaret arrives": GV/ Auchincloss, 8/nd/1965; "turned out to be": GV/Auchincloss, 9/nd/1965.

p. 562: "a vast undertaking": GV/Rovere, 2/16/1965. W; "is a cheery man": GV/Dupee, 2/12/ 1965. C; "Boats . . . are hideously": GV/Dupee, 2/12/1965. C; "4 films in a year": GV/ Dupee, 11/nd/1965. C.

p. 562: "Being 40 has not": GV/Dupee, 11/nd/1965. C.

Chapter Fifteen

INTERVIEWS: Herman Gollob, 2/18/1999; Richard Poirier, 7/1/1996; Howard Austen, 1/20/1996, 7/9/1996, 7/11/1996, 7/12/1996, 7/24/1996; Louis Auchincloss, 10/21/1994; Barbara Epstein, 7/15/1995, 7/26/1995; Joanne Woodward, 2/8/1996; Paul Newman, 2/8/1996; Antonia Fraser, 1/26/1996; Owen Laster, 2/29/1996, 3/5/1996, 3/22/1996; William F. Buckley [by letter in response to questions], 10/23/1996; Louis Auchincloss, 10/21/1994.

ENDNOTES

pp. 564–65: "Rome in August": GV/Louis Auchincloss, 8/nd/1965; "wreathed in friendship . . . intelligent": GV/Fred Dupee, 3/8/1965. C; "I found him positively": GV/Nini Auchincloss, 3/3/1965; "I thought you said . . . dinner": GV/Dupee, 3/14/1966. C.

pp. 565–66: "Villon music . . . performance": GV/Dupee, 7/26/1965. C; "died of a thrombosis": GV/Gene Vidal, 7/24/1965. W.

p. 568: "a fine if jumbled": *TS*, 7; "Howard is fixing": GV/Nina Auchincloss, 5/nd/1966; "The new place": GV/Vidal, 6/nd/1966. W; "We're in the new": GV/Dupee, 6/3/1966. C.

p. 569: "Not since Tolstoi . . . do it for me": GV/Ray White, 9/1/1966. W; "I have never had . . . over the wall": GV/Nina Auchincloss, nd/1966.

p. 572: "The fierceness": Barbara Epstein/GV, 10/5/1966. W; "The thought of": GV/Gene Vidal, 6/nd/1966. W.

pp. 573–74: "were written over": GV/White, 8/11/1966. W; "Just when I": GV/Nina Auchincloss, 6/nd/1965.

pp. 574–75: "Clay is *not*": GV/Auchincloss, 5/nd/1967; "My own impression": GV/Auchincloss, 5/nd/1967.

p. 576: "I struggled": GV/Dupee, spring/nd/1967. C; "very good, indeed": Epstein/GV, 4/nd/1967. W.

p. 577: "co-devising and . . . attractive": Kenneth Tynan/GV, 12/9/1966. W.

p. 580: "AM AT YOUR FEET": Joanne Woodward/GV, 6/4/1956. W; "is pretty enough": Dupee/GV, 7/6/1967. W.

p. 582: "the only real diversion": GV/Dupee, 5/28/1967.

p. 583: "Greece was depressing": GV/Vidal, 5/nd/1967. W.

p. 584: "it is really very": GV/Dupee, 7/11/1967. C; "I think the book": GV/Ned Bradford, 7/15/1967. LB; "I AM HONORED": Christopher Isherwood/GV, 8/12/1967. W.

pp. 584–85: "In my opinion it's . . . ballet": Isherwood/GV, 8/21/1967. W; "then by slow degrees": GV/Dupee, 7/11/1967. C; "Still a good deal": GV/Vidal, 8/nd/1967. W.

pp. 585–86: "I have never in my life": GV/Dupee, 5/28/1967. C; "I'm now happily": GV/Nina Auchincloss, 8/nd/1967.

pp. 586–87: "I am becoming restless": GV/Gene Vidal, 8/nd/1967. W; "a terrible place": GV/Gene Vidal, 9/nd/1967. W.

pp. 587–88: "I felt novels were finished": GV/Gene Vidal, 9/nd/1967. W; "So it goes": GV/Dupee, 9/16/1967. C; "Old Gore leading": GV/Dupee, 9/10/1967. C.

p. 588: "from one millionaire": Bradford/GV, nd/1967. W.

p. 589: "I'm trying to make up": GV/Bradford, 7/15/1967. LB; "It may well be": GV/Bradford, 7/15/1967. LB.

p. 593: "My entire life": GV/Jerry/Hazel Morrass, 3/26/1968. W; "to look muscle-bound": GV/Gene Vidal, 4/nd/1968. W.

p. 595: "I assume you are": GV/Dupee, 5/2/1968. C.

p. 598: "Vidal was achieving much": John Kenneth Galbraith, *A Life in Our Times*, Boston: 1981, 504.

p. 599: "Fuck you, you Jew": James T. Paterson, *Grand Expectations, The United States, 1945–1974*. The Oxford History of the United States. NY, 1996, 696.

p. 601: "PLEASE INFORM GORE VIDAL": Buckley/GV, 2/nd/1962, "On Experiencing Gore Vidal," *Smiling Through the Apocalypse, Esquire's History of the Sixties*, NY: 1987, 541.

Chapter Sixteen

INTERVIEWS: William F. Buckley [by letter in response to questions], 10/23/1996; Ed Weisl, 10/10/1996; Richard Poirier, 7/1/1996; Lois Wallace, 9/4/1996; Barbara Dupee, 1/26/1995, 2/2/1995; Howard Austen, 1/20/1996, 7/9/1996, 7/11/1996, 7/12/1996, 7/24/1996; Alain/Madeline Bernheim, 4/2/1996; Sally Vidal, 3/28/1996; Martin Manulis, 4/1/1996; Norman Mailer, 3/15/1996, 3/16/1996, 3/17/1996; Dick Cavett, 11/13/1996; George Armstrong, 9/5/1944.

UNPUBLISHED DOCUMENTS: Buckley/Vidal files at Simpson Thacher & Bartlett attorneys: depositions, suits, appeals, claims, counterclaims, rulings, letters, news releases, clippings; Harold Hayes Collection, University of Wake Forest: Hayes ms. account of events and letters between Hayes and Buckley and Hayes and Vidal.

ENDNOTES

p. 604: "*Mon vieux*, he began . . . my undertaking it . . . over Buckley's": Harold Hayes, unpub. ms., nd, WF, 1.

p. 605: "I told Buckley . . . what he writes": Hayes, 17. WF; "He's pretty rough": Hayes/GV, 2/26/1969. W; "How does the word 'injunction' . . . we went on": Hayes, 20. WF.

p. 607: "the man who in his essays": Buckley, "On Experiencing Gore Vidal," 571.

p. 609: "You understand, I hope": Buckley/Hayes, 4/28/1969. WF; "Dear Harold, You ask": Buckley/Hayes, 4/28/1969. WF.

p. 611: "Speaking as one publisher": Hugh Hefner/Buckley, 5/15/1969. WF.

pp. 611–12: "I am sure there is": Buckley/Hayes, 6/12/1969. WF; "Your *Esquire* piece": John Kenneth Galbraith/Buckley, 8/12/1969. WF.

p. 615: "We have won": Ed Weisl/GV, 7/11/1972. W.

p. 616: "We published that article": Hayes, *Esquire*, 11/1972.

p. 617: "which is why I now": Buckley, "On Experiencing Gore Vidal," 571.

p. 618: *"Newsweek* quite incorrectly": Arnold Gingrich/Osborn Elliot, 10/3/1972. W.

p. 619: "I do not propose . . . defamatory": Buckley/Hayes, 10/25/1972. WF.

pp. 620–21: "a brilliant *tour de force"*: Fred Dupee/GV, nd/1967; "For the last few weeks": GV/Andy Dupee, 1/20/1979.

p. 622: "shocked and furious": Howard Austen/GV, 10/9/1969. W.

p. 623 "But what else do you do": *M*, 300.

pp. 624–25: "I confess that": GV/Dear Minister [Charles Haughey], 12/19/1969. W; "fascinating trip": GV/Tom Driberg, 1/nd/1970. CC.

p. 627: "puzzled over the fact": Gene Vidal/GV, fall/nd/1968. W.

p. 630: "I'm glad it ended": GV/Katharine Vidal, 2/24/1969. WY; "not only fortunate but": Katharine Vidal/GV, 2/nd/1969. W.

pp. 630–32: "Dearest Gore—You have been": Lurene [Vidal] Jones/GV, 3/24/1969. W; "the solemn, pompous . . . entirely gone": *US*, 1093. "for old times' sake . . . the same": *TS*, 43.

p. 633: "First of all . . . *grand seigneur"*: Tennessee Williams/GV, nd/1970. W.

p. 633: "Tenn. was in town": GV/Paul Bowles, 7/15/1970. D; "No actress has ever": *M*, 155–56.

p. 635: "Death, summer, youth . . . Jimmie": *TS*, 8–9; "Jimmie Trimble arrived": *M*, 35.

p. 635: "Recently I dreamed": *TS*, 219.

p. 637: "hard look . . . caricature": *US*, 1149–50.

p. 644: "So this Sunday": GV/Elaine Dundy, 12/10/1970.

p. 645: "in a sense you contradict": GV/Louis Auchincloss, 1/nd/1971.

p. 645: "The sun has set behind": *TS*, 211.

p. 646: "Whether you do or don't": Roger Stevens, 11/20/1970. W.

Chapter Seventeen

INTERVIEWS: Jason Epstein, 4/25/1995, 3/26/1997; Michael Hecht, 6/11/1997; Howard Austen, 1/20/1996, 7/9/1996, 7/11/1996, 7/12/1996, 7/24/1996; Claire Bloom, 2/23/1996; Ed Sherin, 9/19/1996; Donald Stewart, 11/24/1997; Judith Calvino, 11/25/1997; Ned Rorem, 12/3/1996; George Armstrong, 9/5/1994; John Saumurez Smith, 1/22/1996; John Bowen, 1/22/1996; David Cook, 1/22/1996; Antonia Fraser, 1/26/1996; John Galliher, 4/29/1996; Bob Dolci, 4/3/1996; Jay Allen, 4/2/1996; Nina Auchincloss, 11/2/1994; Tommy Auchincloss, 6/8/1995.

ENDNOTES

p. 653: "What about our new": Ned Bradford/GV, 2/27/1969. W; "Is there a chance that": Jason Epstein/Bradford, 3/24/1969. LB; "On the other hand we very much": Epstein/Bradford, 5/7/1969. LB; "I must say that": Epstein/GV, 5/20/1969. W.

p. 654: If you don't think": GV/Bradford, 5/nd/1970. LB; "damned good essay": Roger Straus/ GV, 6/15/1971. W; "My dear Gore, naturally": Bradford/GV, 9/20/1971. W.

pp. 654–55: "I nearly dedicated": GV/Bradford, 8/nd/1973. LB; "Clearly you're getting": Bradford/GV, 11/30/1973. W.

p. 657: "Here it is": GV/Epstein, 10/14/1971. W.

pp. 661–62: "Sorry you didn't see": GV/Bradford, 3/nd/1972. LB; "the first night was one": Claire Bloom/GV, 5/15/1972. W.

pp. 662–63: "My blood pressure nearly": GV/Bloom, 5/23/1972; "Skin cancers fall": GV/ Bloom, 3/21/1975.

p. 664: "I think you know how much": Bloom/GV, 3/nd/1974. W.

p. 664: "Recently I spent": *TS*, 90–91; "half an hour": GV/Epstein, 6/nd/1972. W.

p. 665: "waddled from great meal": GV/Elizabeth Hardwick, summer/nd/1974. T; "70,000 words written": GV/Epstein, 6/nd/1972. W.

pp. 666–67: "What do you think of the title": GV/Epstein, 6/nd/1972. W; "I quit the People's Party": GV/John Mitzel, 2/5/1974.

pp. 667–68: "I sounded drunk": GV/Mitzel, nd/1974; "I never do see much": GV/Richard Poirier, 2/nd/1976; "I was only in town": GV/Louis Auchincloss, 12/nd/1974; "I'm sometimes in Ireland": GV/Tom Driberg, 12/nd/1972. CC.

pp. 668–69: "The house is perfect": GV/Nini Auchincloss, 1/nd/1973; "Ireland has sort of fizzled": Howard Austen/Bradford, 5/22/1973. LB; "We BOUGHT the right": GV/Hardwick, spring/nd/1974. T.

p. 670: "I feel dreadful about": Princess Margaret/GV, 12/2/1972. W; "Bad times": GV/ Driberg, 12/nd/1972. CC.

p. 670: "Gorino, why do you live?": "Epilogue by Gore Vidal" from *Roloff Beny in Italy*, NY: 1974, 408.

p. 671: "Princess Margaret is in": GV/Judith Halfpenny, 7/nd/1978.

p. 672: "Gore Vidal on the phone": Ned Rorem, *The Later Diaries of Ned Rorem, 1961–1972*. San Francisco: 1983, 333–36, 341.

p. 675: "Thank you for everything": Bloom/GV, 3/nd/1974. W.

p. 676: "I could not exorcise myself": GV/Poirier, 9/nd/1974; "I couldn't figure out": Stanton, 110–11.

p. 681: "Most sad about Sofield": GV/Auchincloss, 12/nd/1974: "He is in a tomb": Penny Crocker/GV, 2/18/1974. W.

p. 681: "Maybe you would like": John Armstrong/GV, 4/12/1973. W.

pp. 682–83: "Can it be that": GV/Driberg, 5/28/1975. CC; "you can now stay": GV/Driberg, 7/nd/1976. CC.

p. 685: "To Gore Vidal at Fifty"/Clive James, unpublished ms. W.

p. 685: "Will you be kind enough": William Meredith/GV, 12/31/1975. W; "THE INSTITUTE DOES ITSELF": GV/Meredith, 1/16/1976. W.

p. 686: "I note now": GV/Poirier, 2/nd/1976; "I am sinking into": GV/Poirier, 5/nd/1974; "holed up at Ravello": GV/Driberg, 1/28/1975. CC.

p. 686: the "Book of the Month": GV/Graham Watson, 1/nd/1975. W.

p. 690: "Dearest, darling Gore": Norman Lear/GV, 10/26/1976. W.

p. 691: "I thought that Tinto and I": GV/Franco Rossellini, 6/7/1976. W; "The film is a hard-core": GV/Halfpenny, 12/nd/1976.

p. 692: "you have an evening in Hollywood": GV/Halfpenny, 12/nd/1978.

pp. 692–93: *"Kalki* can and should": Epstein/GV, 2/15/1977. W; "Those who have read": GV/Halfpenny, 12/nd/1975; *"Kalki* being re-done": GV/Nigel Hollis, nd/1977. W; "powerful and upsetting": Epstein/GV, 2/12/1977. W; "because of my friend": GV/Halfpenny, 12/nd/1978.

p. 694: "our Tahiti": GV/Halfpenny, 12/nd/1976; "We may be back": GV/Joe O'Donohue, 7/5/1976.

p. 694: "I admire the essays": Diana Phipps/GV, nd/1977. W.

pp. 695–96: "DOCTORS AT LACKLAND": Robert Schnabel/GV, 3/4/1978. W; "How ridiculous": Nina Gore/GV, 12/6/1975. W; "shocked and amazed": Nina Gore/Nina Auchincloss, 6/3/1976. W.

p. 697: "Of course at the time it was": Nina Gore/GV, 5/19/1974. W; "mother love . . . about me": Nina Gore/*Time*, 3/8/1976. W.

p. 698: "Nice to see your mother's": GV/Nina Auchincloss, 3/nd/1976.

Chapter Eighteen

INTERVIEWS: Mickey Knox, 3/30/1996; Norman Mailer, 3/15/1996, 3/16/1996, 3/17/1996; Howard Austen, 1/17/1996, 1/20/1996, 7/9/1996, 7/11/1996, 7/12/1996, 7/24/1996; Jason Epstein, 4/25/1995, 3/26/1997; Dick Cavett, 11/13/1996; Owen Laster, 2/25/1996, 3/5/1996, 3/22/1996; Lulli Corsini, 11/23/1997; Barbara Epstein, 7/15/1995, 7/26/1995; Jay Allen, 4/2/1996; Hugh Guilbeau, 4/13/1996; Jay Allen, 4/2/1996; Norman Podhoretz, 3/26/1998; Judith Calvino, 11/25/1997; Max Rabb, 5/29/1996; Claire Bloom, 2/23/1996; Judith Halfpenny, 11/5/1994.

ENDNOTES

p. 700: "Yes . . . Norman is every bit": GV/Jim Tuck, 8/29/1975.

p. 700: "on what I thought": Anthony Haden-Guest, "The Vidal-Capote Papers, A Tempest in Camelot," *New York*, 6/11/1979, 54; "gossip . . . that is Capote's field": GV/Judith Halfpenny, 12/nd/1976.

p. 702: "It would seem": GV/*The Atlantic Monthly*, 5/nd/1972.

p. 703: "was gathering affidavits": Donald Windham, *Lost Friendships*, 119–20.

pp. 703–4: "sad and bitter": GV/Halfpenny, 7/nd/1978; "had gotten him drunk": *Lost Friendships*, 128; "but the letters are marvelous": GV/Halfpenny, 7/nd/1968; "it's all actionable . . . actionable": *Lost Friendships*, 128; "encounter with Gore . . . just talk": *Lost Friendships*, 119–20; "Mr. Capote never wrote . . . on TV": GV/Halfpenny, 9/nd/1979.

p. 705: "Vidal's enemies delightedly": Arthur Schlesinger, *Robert Kennedy and His Times,* Boston: 1978, 594; "were just two fags . . . upset": GV/Halfpenny, 9/nd/1979.

pp. 705–6: "We are willing to settle": GV/Halfpenny, 12/nd/1979; "No matter what": GV/Halfpenny, 9/nd/1979.

pp. 706–7: "I apologize for any": Truman Capote/GV, 10/31/1983. W; "T. seemed not to be drinking": GV/Paul Bowles, 4/30/1984, D; "I knew he would be": GV/Bowles, 9/nd/1984. D.

p. 707: "As someone said when": GV/Bowles, 9/nd/1994. D.

p. 710: "Poor Norman": GV/Ned Bradford, 1/nd/1977. LB.

pp. 711–12: "we won't have a full": Norman Mailer/GV, 11/20/1984. W; "Our feud, whatever . . . fond of you": Mailer/GV, 11/20/1984. W; "If he had so much as . . . boredom": GV/Bowles, 11/nd/1984. D.

p. 712: "Do you have someone": Mailer/GV, 1/17/1985. W; "All right, fine": Mailer/GV, 2/13/1985. W; "the example of": Mailer/GV, 3/14/1985. W.

p. 713: "We may both be known": Mailer quoted in Drew Featherston, "The Feud Is a Fizzle," *Newsday,* 11/20/1995.

pp. 718–19: "I have made five": GV/Halfpenny, 3/nd/1979; "It is apt, certainly . . . he is *not*": GV/Halfpenny, 3/nd/1979; "you don't need": Jason Epstein/GV, 8/21/1979. W; "trudging up": GV/Halfpenny, nd/1979.

p. 719: "The sindaco would like": GV/Halfpenny, nd/1979.

p. 722: "I do value more": GV/Richard Poirier, 8/nd/1982.

pp. 722–23: *"Duluth* emerges": GV/Halfpenny, 8/9/1984; "to be": Italo Calvino, 9/24/1983: as "Imagining Vidal" in *Gore Vidal, Writer Against the Grain,* ed. Jay Parini, NY: 1992, 31–36.

p. 725: "not existed in his": *US,* 610.

pp. 727–28: "A fine American story": GV/John Mitzel, 8/19/1978; "The *New York Review* turned down": GV/Halfpenny, 8/nd/1981.

p. 728: "I would suggest": *US,* 597, 611.

p. 729: "In the German concentration": *US,* 597–98.

p. 732: "Does one want to win": GV/Halfpenny, 8/nd/1981.

p. 733: "I am sauntering . . . contributions yet": GV/Halfpenny, 8/nd/1981.

p. 733: "I'm now about to be": GV/Mitzel, 2/16/1982.

p. 734: "This has to be worth": Vidal Sassoon/GV, 4/12/1982. W.

pp. 736–37: "one morning last spring": *US,* 1184; "Generally, I don't care for": GV/Halfpenny, 12/nd/1979.

pp. 737–38: "L. is our Bismarck": GV/Halfpenny, 1/nd/1980; "First I must know": GV/Peter Davison, 8/nd/1981. W.

p. 741: "You've led a very": GV/Halfpenny, 8/nd/1986; "I boasted to Bowles": GV/Auchincloss, 9/nd/1986.

p. 745: "Last days can be": GV/Halfpenny, 6/nd/1977.

p. 746: "I must ask myself": Italo Calvino/speech at Vidal's honorary-citizenship ceremony in Ravello, 10/3/1983. W.

p. 747: "Do you notice": GV/Bowles, 9/nd/1984. D; "all right for someone": GV/Bowles, 8/nd/1978. D.

p. 749: "the Q. Mother had just": GV/Halfpenny, 12/1/1983.

p. 751: "I can't say I much": GV/Wilcomb Washburn, 11/16/1982.

pp. 751–52: "He lay in a hospital . . . memory land": GV/Halfpenny, 5/nd/1984; "How curious that": GV/Bowles, 12/nd/1983. D.

pp. 752–53: "can't say that the bird": GV/Woods S. Gray, 7/21/1983; "has decided to be": GV/Bowles, 10/nd/1984. D; "as he was dying": GV, "Introduction," *Where Joy Resides, A Christopher Isherwood Reader*, ed. Don Bachardy and James P. White, xviii–xxiv.

pp. 753–54: "Have you been keeping up": GV/Bowles, 8/31/1983. D; "I'm happy with the preface": Bowles/GV, 4/13/1978. W; "The Rat continues to die": GV/Halfpenny, 12/1/1983; "the size of a tennis ball . . . survive us": GV/Halfpenny, 5/nd/1984.

p. 754: "He was having more trouble": GV/David Herbert Donald, 12/15/1988. W.

p. 755: "witnessing his own": *US*, 506.

Chapter Nineteen

INTERVIEWS: Jason Epstein, 4/25/1995, 3/26/1997; Tom Rosenthal, 1/21/1996; Owen Laster, 2/29/1996, 3/5/1996, 3/22/1996; Gary Fisketjon, 2/18/1997; Jay Parini, 1/14/1999; Judith Calvino, 11/25/1997; Wallace Ragan, 6/12/1995; John C. Davis, 6/13/1995; Barrett Prettyman, 11/2/1994; Ruth Sewell, 4/15/1997; Howard Austen, 1/17/1996, 1/20/1996, 7/9/1996, 7/11/1996, 7/12/1996, 7/24/1996; George Armstrong, 9/5/1994; Barbara Epstein, 7/15/1995, 7/26/1995; Andreas Brown, 10/18/1996

ENDNOTES

p. 756: "White frame houses": GV/Judith Halfpenny, 8/9/1990.

p. 757: "sharp of eye": GV/Halfpenny, 8/8/1990.

p. 758: "I did have an eerie": GV/Halfpenny, 8/8/1990.

p. 759: "I'm not going to write": GV/Halfpenny, 10/15/1985.

p. 760: "I'm getting very autobiographical": GV/Halfpenny, 5/8/1985; "Most of May–June": GV/Halfpenny, 5/nd/1984.

pp. 760–61: "It is a picture book": GV/Halfpenny, 5/8/1985; "a lot of work": GV/Halfpenny, 1/4/1984; "ready to be enslaved": GV/Halfpenny, 5/8/1985.

pp. 761–62: "Cimino has made no": GV/Halfpenny, 8/nd/1986; "Cimino sent me Shagan's": GV/Grace Reiner, Writers Guild of America, West, 10/16/1986. W.

p. 763: "Thanks to Chernobyl": GV/Claire Bloom, 6/28/1986.

p. 764: "from a street in Moscow": GV/Halfpenny, 4/nd/1987.

pp. 764–65: "the usual loyal party . . . if not with us": GV/Halfpenny, 4/nd/1987.

p. 765: "All sorts of changes": GV/Halfpenny, 4/nd/1988.

p. 766: "white slender with pale": GV/Halfpenny, 4/nd/1988.

p. 771: "Obviously, I am not charmed": GV/Owen Laster, 6/1/1990. W.

pp. 774–75: "As you know or do not": GV/Richard Poirier, 6/5/1992; "I fear as fond as I am": GV/Halfpenny, 10/nd/1991.

pp. 775–76: "My Barbara grows . . . does not": GV/Halfpenny, 5/nd/1991.

p. 776: "a prize at Forte": GV/Halfpenny, 8/9/1990.

p. 778: "I know what I'd like": GV/David Herbert Donald, 10/1/1990.

p. 779: "Unaccustomed as I am": GV/National Book Award, 11/nd/1993. W.

pp. 780–81: "Of course you're worried": Walter Clemons/GV, 12/6/1990. W; "After four years of meeting": GV/Louis Auchincloss, 12/nd/1990; "The only revelation": GV/William Phillips, 10/27/1993. W.

p. 781: "Walter maintains that he is": GV/Halfpenny, 10/nd/1991; "Walter will present Little, Brown": GV/Janet Caro, 9/nd/1993.

p. 783: "Bringing back my dreadful": GV/Halfpenny, 8/20/1993; "I, too, explore the past": GV/Ned Rorem, 9/11/1992.

p. 784: "The section on J.T.": GV/John Davis, 11/3/1993.

p. 785: "Two unnerving first-hand": GV/John Davis, 8/29/1993.

p. 786: "Disconcertingly, I had lunch": GV/Halfpenny, 8/20/1993.

p. 787: "The pool is paradise": GV/Claire Bloom, 6/18/1986.

p. 789: "Last night I dreamed": *M,* 73–74; "For nearly two years": GV/Halfpenny, 8/6/1995.

p. 793: "Two close calls": GV/Rorem, 10/10/1996; "There is no end": GV/Fred Kaplan, 12/14/1996.

pp. 793–94: "I do mean to go on": GV/Elizabeth Hardwick, 10/nd/1975. T; "I drank like a boy": GV/Halfpenny, 10/nd/1991.

pp. 794–95: "One gets more done": GV/Halfpenny, 8/9/1990; "for the first time": GV/Halfpenny, 5/nd/1984; "still worked out": GV/Halfpenny, 12/24/1992.

Additional interviews: Rhodes Allan, 9/7/1996; Owen Carle, 3/13/1997; John Dickinson, 2/10/1996; William Fitzgerald, 2/nd/1997; Miles Gore, 9/11/1996; John Hallowell, 8/9/1997; Nicholas Haslam, 1/24/1996; John Macrae, 3/19/1996; Sue Mengers, 3/29/1996; Jan Mostowski, 11/1/1996; Mike Shaw, 1/24/1996.

Acknowledgments

GORE VIDAL and Howard Austen fulfilled their initial commitment to provide total cooperation. To both of them, I am deeply grateful. With the exception of the mysterious 1948 diary, I have seen everything. I suspect the diary contains nothing that would surprise me. Having access to it withheld whetted my curiosity, which now, having completed this biography, I discharge into thin air. Neither Mr. Vidal nor Mr. Austen saw the manuscript or any portion of its publication, with the exception of my quotations from our oral interviews, which I gave Mr. Vidal the opportunity to participate in editing since they inevitably contained slips of the tongue and by-the-way comments not intended for publication; he also was allowed to see the quotations from his unpublished letters for his information but not for his response. He played no role in their selection or use. Toward the end, he expressed his desire to see the manuscript. Doubleday and I were successful in maintaining our position that it was neither in his nor our interest for him to read it before publication.

Various and many institutions have provided access and materials. They all have my appreciation and grateful acknowledgment. Foremost of these are the Wisconsin State Historical Society, Madison, and the University of Wisconsin, Madison, particularly the Wisconsin Center for Film and Theater Research, which houses the Gore Vidal Collection. Harry Miller, the librarian in charge of the manuscript reading room, and Tino Ballio, the director of the Center for Film and Theater Research, were particularly helpful, the Wisconsin staff a model of professional and generous assistance. My thanks to the Carl Albert Congressional Research Center, University of Oklahoma; the American Heritage Center, University of Wyoming; the Beinecke Collection, Yale University Library; Christ Church College Library, Oxford University; the Columbia University Rare Book and Manuscript Library; the Harry Ransom Collection, University of Texas, Austin; the Houghton Library, Harvard University; the Lilly Library, Indiana University; The John F. Kennedy Library; the Los Alamos Historical Museum; the Performing Arts Research Center, New York Public Library; Princeton University Library; the Library of the University of California at Los Angeles; the University of Delaware Library; the University of Virginia, Alderman Collection; the Museum of Television and Radio, New York; the Vanderbilt University Library television news archives; and the Z. Smith Reynolds Library, Wake Forest University. In the legal world, Simpson Thacher and Bartlett has the equivalent of institutional status. Through the good offices of Donald Oresman, the firm provided access to their numerous files on the Vidal-Buckley case. William Phillips facilitated my access to the Little, Brown files. In London, Michael Shaw of Curtis Brown made that agency's records available to me. The Guggenheim Foundation, through Thomas Tanselle, provided a copy of Vidal's fellowship application. Some of Random House's files are in the Random House Collection at the Columbia University Rare Book and Manuscript Library, where Bernard Crystal made them and the John Latouche Papers available. Unfortunately a widespread indifference in the publishing world to history of any kind has resulted in the loss or purposeful destruction of precious records from institutions as diverse as Dutton and William Morris (where Owen Laster kindly gave me access to the extant files).

Ginny Howard at Potomac School, Lisa Gornner at Landon School, and Ellis Turner at Sidwell Friends School provided Vidal's school records. Owen Carle and Robert Taylor made available their memories of and files about William Lawrence Camp. I am particularly indebted to Wallace

Ragan and John Claiborne Davis (retired) of St. Albans School for their assistance and hospitality, and to the access they provided to what remains of Vidal's St. Albans School world. Edward L. Sanderson shared with me his research into the life of Jimmie Trimble. Rachel Collinsworth, director of the Los Alamos Historical Museum, gave me access to its files relating to the Los Alamos Ranch Experimental School; numbers of Los Alamos School alumni were helpful, particularly Peter Dechert, Alan Meyer, Wilson Hurley, and Oscar Steege. Phillips Exeter staff and numbers of Vidal's classmates provided helpful cooperation, particularly Edouard L. Desrochers, Academy Archivist; Jacquelyn H. Thomas, Academy Librarian; and Philip R. Berger, Hamilton Bissell, John Spencer Dickinson, and Otis Pease.

For the Gore family in Mississippi and the world of Vidal's Gore family background I am indebted to Lois and Bill Gore's help and hospitality; I am also indebted to their son, Miles Gore; to Nini Auchincloss Straight for letters and photographs; to Tom Auchincloss for photographs and clippings; to Roy Thompson for photos and other documents. Susan Milstead in Los Angeles arranged my visits to her mother, Margaret Sutton, Gore Vidal's aunt. Katharine (Vidal) Smith in Florida and Sally Vidal (Mrs. Felix Vidal) in San Antonio cooperated graciously. Louis Auchincloss unstintingly gave me access to his large collection of letters; Barbara Epstein made available her correspondence with Vidal and access to the files of *The New York Review of Books*, Jason Epstein a photograph and two extended interviews. Barbara (Andy) Dupee trusted me with photographs, letters, and memories; Margaret Shaffer provided letters and hospitality at Bard College and arranged access to Edgewater; Elaine Dundy generously offered letters, memories, and photos; Don Bachardy provided letters, photos, and hospitality in Santa Monica; Jay Parini provided his good offices as Gore Vidal's literary executor, and contributed wise counsel.

Among those who provided documents, with permission to use them, and other forms of help, including oral testimony, and whose contributions are indicated in only some cases in the endnotes and other acknowledgments, are: John Aldridge; Rhodes Allan; Jay Allen; Roger Angell; Samuel G. Armistead; George Armstrong; R. F. Arnold; James Atlas; Hugh Auchincloss III; Lyn Austin; George Axelrod; Jack H. Bady; Tish Baldrige; Lee Barlow; Theresa Baxter; Saul Bellow; Alain Bernheim; Marjorie Bernheim; Janet Bingham; James Birney; Claire Bloom; Boaty Boatwright; Tina

Bourjaily; Vance Bourjaily; John Bowen; Paul Bowles; Andreas Brown; William F. Buckley, Jr.; Judith Calvino; Virginia Spencer Carr; Bernard Carragher; Dick Cavett; David Cook; Lulli Corsini; John Curtis; Nathaniel Davis; Sharon Delano; Michael di Capua; Robert Dolce; David Herbert Donald; Michael Dorn; Deborah Druba; Elaine Dundy; Dominick Dunne; Mark Engel; Tom Erhardt; Gary Fisketjohn; William Fitzgerald; Peggy Fox; Antonia Fraser; Jack Fricks; John Kenneth Galbraith; John Galliher; Milton Gendel; Robert Giroux; Herman Gollob; Georgina Gooding; Thomas P. Gore II; George N. Gray, Jr.; William Gruver; Hugh Guilbeau; Judith Halfpenny; John Hallowell; John Hanes; Phyliss Wreden Harholdt; Nicholas Haslam; Armis E. Hawkins; Judith Kessler Hayes; Suzette Meredith Hayes; Tom Hayes; Michael Hecht; Hugh Hefner; Clive James; Conrad Janis; Judith Jones; Stanley F. Kaminsky; Joseph Kanon; Bill Kauffman; Harry Kloman; John Knowles; Mickey Knox; Speed Lamkin; Heidi Landecker; Owen Laster; James Laughlin; Oatsie Leiter (Mrs. Robert Charles); Lyle Leverich; A. K. Lewis; Sam Lurie; Ransom Lynch; John Macrea; Romana McEwen; Thomas McFarland; Catherine McKenna; Judith McNally; Norman Mailer; Martin Manulis; Sarah Marshall; Jayne Meadows; Susan Mengers; John Mitzel; Geoffrey Moore; Jan Mostowski; Janet Caro Murphy; Anthony Neville; Paul Newman; Johnny Nicholson; Cary O'Dell; Joseph J. O'Donohue; Charles Osborne; Diana Sternbergova Phipps; George Plimpton; Norman Podhoretz; Richard Poirier; Betty Pollock; Barrett Prettyman; Max Rabb; William Riggan; Ned Rorem; Jean Rose; T. G. Rosenthal; Eleanor Rovere; Joseph Ryle; David Samples; Arthur Schlesinger; Alan U. Schwartz; Ruth Sewell; Edward Sherin; John Saumurez Smith; Sharon Snow; Jean Stein; Mary Steven; Roger Straus; Donald Stewart; Luisa Stewart; Gunther Stuhlmann; Edes F. Talman; John Tebbel; J. Winter Thorington; Alfred True; James Tuck; Lawrence Turman; Carrington Tutwiler; Frank Von Zerneck; Lois Wallace; James E. Walsh; Patsy Walsh; William Walsh; Raymond Bentley Washburne, Jr.; Wilcomb Washburn; Graham Watson; Edward Weisl; Theodore Weiss; Rene Weiss; Miles White; Leon Wieseltier; Jane B. Willingham; Bernard X. Wolff; Joanne Woodward; Merrell C. Wreden; Peter Wreden.

Susan O'Brien was of invaluable help in the latter stages of the research. At Doubleday, William Adams, Maria Carella, Debbie Cowell, Herman Gollob, Mario Pulice, Bill Thomas, and Steve Rubin were unfailingly professional and committed. Georges Borchardt and his agency staff handled their duties with exemplary competence.

Lapses of memory and organization probably have resulted in omissions from my list of helpful angels; to them I apologize. Some lesser creatures, whose names I do recall, I have not recorded here.

i NDEX